Internet & World Wide Web

HOW TO PROGRAM

FIFTH EDITION

Paul Deitel

Deitel & Associates, Inc.

Harvey Deitel

Deitel & Associates, Inc.

Abbey Deitel

Deitel & Associates, Inc.

International Edition contributions by

Soumen Mukherjee ✦ Arup Kumar Bhattacharjee

DEITEL

PEARSON

Boston Columbus Indianpolis New York San Francisco Upper Saddle River
Amsterdam Cape Town Dubai London Madrid Milan Munich Paris Montreal Toronto
Delhi Mexico City Sao Paulo Sydney Hong Kong Seoul Singapore Taipei Tokyo

Editorial Director: *Marcia J. Horton*
Editor-in-Chief: *Michael Hirsch*
Associate Editor: *Carole Snyder*
Vice President, Marketing: *Patrice Jones*
Marketing Manager: *Yezan Alayan*
Marketing Coordinator: *Kathryn Ferranti*
Vice President, Production: *Vince O'Brien*
Managing Editor: *Jeff Holcomb*
Associate Managing Editor: *Robert Engelhardt*
Publisher, International Edition: *Angshuman Chakraborty*
Acquisitions Editor, International Edition: *Somnath Basu*
Publishing Assistant, International Edition: *Shokhi Shah*
Print and Media Editor, International Edition: *Ashwitha Jayakumar*
Project Editor, International Edition: *Jayashree Arunachalam*
Operations Specialist: *Lisa McDowell*
Art Director: *Anthony Gemmellaro*
Media Editor: *Daniel Sandin*

Pearson Education Limited
Edinburgh Gate
Harlow
Essex CM20 2JE
England

and Associated Companies throughout the world

Visit us on the World Wide Web at:
www.pearsoninternationaleditions.com

ISBN 10: 0-273-76402-0
ISBN 13: 978-0-273-76402-1

British Library Cataloguing-in-Publication Data
A catalogue record for this book is available from the British Library

10 9 8 7 6 5 4 3 2
14 13 12

Typeset in AGaramond-Regular by GEX Publishing Services
Printed and bound by Courier, Westford in The United States of America

The publisher's policy is to use paper manufactured from sustainable forests.

In memory of Paul Baran,
   designer of a survivable distributed communications
   network and packet switching, which are the basis
   for the protocols used on the Internet today.

Paul, Harvey and Abbey Deitel

Trademarks

Apache is a trademark of The Apache Software Foundation.

Apple, iPhone, iPad, iOS and Safari are registered trademarks of Apple, Inc.

CSS, DOM, XHTML and XML are trademarks of the World Wide Web Consortium.

Firefox is a registered trademark of the Mozilla Foundation.

Google is a trademark of Google, Inc.

JavaScript, Java and all Java-based marks are trademarks or registered trademarks of Oracle in the United States and other countries.

Microsoft, Internet Explorer, Silverlight and the Windows logo are either registered trademarks or trademarks of Microsoft Corporation in the United States and/or other countries.

Opera is a trademark of Opera Software.

Contents

8   Contents

10 Contents

10 JavaScript: Arrays   356

11 JavaScript: Objects   392

12 Document Object Model (DOM): Objects and Collections   427

13 JavaScript Event Handling: A Deeper Look   454

18 Database: SQL, MySQL, LINQ and Java DB   649

19 PHP   696

20 Web App Development with ASP.NET in C#   740

21 Web App Development with ASP.NET in C#: A Deeper Look   790

22 Web Services in C#   821

Chapters 24–29 and Appendices E–F are PDF documents posted online at the book's Companion Website (located at www.pearsoninternationaleditions.com/deitel/).

24 Web App Development with ASP.NET in VB: A Deeper Look

Science and technology and the various forms of art,
all unite humanity in a single and interconnected system.

　　—Zhores Aleksandrovich Medvede

Welcome to Internet and web programming with *Internet & World Wide Web How to Program, Fifth Edition*! This book presents leading-edge computing technologies for students, instructors and software developers.

　　The world of computing—and Internet and web programming in particular—has changed dramatically since the last edition. This new edition focuses on HTML5 and the related technologies in its ecosystem, diving into the exciting new features of HTML5, CSS3, the latest edition of JavaScript (ECMAScript 5) and HTML5 canvas. We focus on popular key technologies that will help you build Internet- and web-based applications that interact with other applications and with databases. These form the basis of the kinds of enterprise-level, networked applications that are popular in industry today.

　　Internet & World Wide Web How to Program, 5/e is appropriate for both introductory and intermediate-level client-side and server-side programming courses. The book is also suitable for professionals who want to update their skills with the latest Internet and web programming technologies.

　　At the heart of the book is the Deitel signature "live-code approach"—concepts are presented in the context of complete working HTML5 documents, CSS3 stylesheets, JavaScript scripts, XML documents, programs and database files, rather than in code snippets. Each complete code example is accompanied by live sample executions. The source code is available at www.deitel.com/books/iw3htp5/ and at the book's Companion Website www.pearsoninternationaleditions.com/deitel/.

　　As you read the book, if you have questions, send an e-mail to deitel@deitel.com; we'll respond promptly. For updates on this book, visit www.deitel.com/books/iw3htp5/, join our communities on Facebook (www.facebook.com/deitelfan) and Twitter (@deitel), and subscribe to the *Deitel® Buzz Online* newsletter (www.deitel.com/newsletter/subscribe.html).

New and Updated Features

Here are the updates we've made for *Internet & World Wide Web How to Program, 5/e*:

- *New Chapter 1.* The new Chapter 1 engages students with intriguing facts and figures to get them excited about studying Internet and web applications development. The chapter includes a table of some of the research made possible by computers and the Internet, current technology trends and hardware discussion, the data hierarchy, a new section on social networking, a table of popular web services, a table of business and technology publications and websites that will help you stay up to date with the latest technology news and trends, and updated exercises.

- *New HTML5 features.* Chapter 3 introduces the latest features of HTML5 including the new HTML5 form input types and page structure elements (Fig. 1). *The new HTML5 features are not universally implemented in all of the web browsers.* This is changing as the browser vendors release new versions. We discuss many additional HTML5 features throughout the book.

New HTML5 features			
Form Input Types			
color	date	datetime	datetime-local
email	month	number	range
search	tel	time	url
week	input element	datalist element	autocomplete attribute
Page Structure Elements			
header	nav	figure	figcaption
article	summary	section	aside
meter	footer	text-level semantics (marking potential line breaks)	

Fig. I | New HTML5 form input types and page structure elements

- *New CSS3 features.* Chapter 5 introduces the latest features of CSS3 (Fig. 2). *The new CSS3 features are not universally implemented in all of the web browsers.* This is changing as the browser vendors release new versions.

New CSS3 features		
text shadows	rounded corners	color
box shadows	linear gradients	radial gradients
multiple background images	image borders	animations
transitions	transformations	@font-face rule
Flexible Box Layout Module	:nth-child selectors	multicolumn layouts
media queries		
Non-standard features		
text stroke	reflection	

Fig. 2 | New CSS3 features.

- *Updated treatment of JavaScript.* We've strengthened the JavaScript coverage in Chapters 6–16. JavaScript has become the *de facto* standard client-side scripting language for web-based applications due to its highly portable nature. Our treatment, which is appropriate for novices, serves two purposes—it introduces client-side scripting (Chapters 6–16), which makes web pages more dynamic and interactive, and it provides the programming foundation for the server-side scripting in PHP presented in Chapter 19. JavaScript looks similar to basic core language features in C, C++, C# and Java. Once you learn JavaScript, you've got a foothold on learning these other popular programming languages.

- *New HTML5 canvas.* Chapter 14 replaces the Flash and Silverlight chapters from the previous edition with the new HTML5 canvas element for 2D graphics (Fig. 3). canvas is built into the browser, eliminating the need for plug-ins like Flash and Silverlight, and helping you improve performance and convenience, and reduce costs. At the end of the chapter, you'll use canvas to build a fun, animated Cannon Game with audio effects, which we built in Flash in previous editions of this book.

HTML5 canvas features		
rectangles	lines	arcs and circles
shadows	quadratic curves	Bezier curves
linear gradients	radial gradients	image manipulation
images	patterns	transformations
alpha transparency	compositing	

Fig. 3 | HTML5 canvas features.

- *New and updated multimedia exercises.* Chapter 14 includes several new and updated multimedia exercises (Fig. 4).

New and updated multimedia exercises		
Cannon Game Enhancements	Random Interimage Transition	Digital Clock
Animation	Scrolling Image Marquee	Background Audio
Scrolling Marquee Sign	Automatic Jigsaw Puzzle Generator	Analog Clock
Dynamic Audio and Graphical Kaleidoscope	Horse Race	Maze Generator and Walker
One-Armed Bandit	Fireworks Designer	Shuffleboard
Game of Pool	15 Puzzle	Floor Planner
Crossword Puzzle	Coloring Black-and-White Photographs and Images	Reaction Time Tester
Rotating Images		Vacuuming Robot
		Eyesight Tester

Fig. 4 | New and updated multimedia exercises.

- *Tested on seven browsers.* For the last edition of this book, we tested all the code on two desktop browsers—Internet Explorer and Firefox. For this new edition, we tested all of the code in the most current versions of *seven* popular browsers—five for the **desktop** (**Chrome, Internet Explorer, Firefox, Opera** and **Safari**) and two for **mobile** devices (**iPhone/iPad** and **Android**). *HTML5 and CSS3 are evolving and the final standards have not been approved yet.* The browser vendors are selectively implementing features that are likely to be standardized. Some vendors have higher levels of feature compliance than others. With each new version of the browsers, the trend has been to significantly increase the amount of functionality that's been implemented. The HTML5 test site (`html5test.com`) measures how well each browser supports the pending standards and specifications. You can view test scores and see which features are supported by each browser. You can also check sites such as `http://caniuse.com/` for a list of features covered by each browser. *Not every document in this book will render properly in each browser.* Instead of choosing only capabilities that exist universally, we demonstrate exciting new features in whatever browser handles the new functionality best. As you read this book, run each example in multiple web browsers so you can view and interact with it as it was originally intended. And remember, things are changing quickly, so a browser that did not support a feature when we wrote the book could support it when you read the book.

- *Validated HTML5, CSS3 and JavaScript code.* All of the HTML5, CSS3 and JavaScript code in the book was validated using `validator.w3.org/` for HTML5, `jigsaw.w3.org/css-validator` for CSS3 and `javascriptlint.com` for JavaScript. *Not every script fully validates but most do.* Although all of the code works properly, you may receive warnings (or possibly errors) when validating code with some of the new features.

- *Smartphone and tablet apps.* You're probably familiar with the explosion of apps available for the **iPhone/iPad** and **Android** platforms. There's almost a million apps between the two. Previously, writing apps for these platforms required detailed knowledge of each, and in the case of iPhone/iPad, was strictly controlled by Apple; Android is more open. With the techniques you'll learn in this book, you'll be able to write apps that are portable between a great variety of desktop and mobile platforms, including iPhone/iPad and Android. You'll even be able to sell those apps on your own terms (or through certain app stores as well). This is an exciting possibility! It's one of the true virtues of developing with HTML5, CSS3 and JavaScript in general, and HTML5 canvas in particular. Running an HTML5 app on your smartphone or tablet is as simple as opening it in your compliant web browser. *You may still encounter some portability issues.*

- *New HTML5 web storage capabilities.* In Chapter 11, we use HTML5's new web storage capabilities to create a web application that stores a user's favorite Twitter searches on the computer for easy access at a later time. Web storage replaces the controversial cookie technology, offering lots more storage space. Chapter 11 also briefly introduces JSON, a means for creating JavaScript objects—typically for transferring data over the Internet between client-side and server-side programs.

- *Enhanced Craps game featuring HTML5 audio and video elements.* The Craps game in Chapter 9 now includes an HTML5 audio element that plays a dice-rolling sound each time the user rolls the dice. Also, we link to a page with an embedded HTML5 video element that plays a video explaining the rules of the game.

- *jQuery Ajax case study.* The previous edition of this book included a calendar application that used the Dojo libraries—which were popular at the time—to create the user interface, communicate with the server asynchronously, handle events and manipulate the DOM. Since then, jQuery has become the most popular JavaScript library. For this edition, we've updated the calendar application (Chapter 16) using jQuery and placed it online as a jQuery Ajax case study.

- *New HTML5 WebSockets and Web Workers capabilities.* We've added an online treatment of two new technologies—WebSockets, which provides a simple model for networking, and Web Workers which provides multithreading on a web page.

- *Ajax-enabled web applications.* We've updated the chapter on building Ajax-enabled web applications, with applications that demonstrate *partial-page updates* and type-ahead capabilities—each of these are key capabilities of Rich Internet Applications.

- *HTML DOM and XML DOM.* We've enhanced the treatments of HTML DOM manipulation, JavaScript events and XML DOM manipulation with JavaScript.

- *LINQ.* Since the last edition of the book, Microsoft introduced LINQ (Language-Integrated Query) to replace SQL for database access. Chapter 18 provides an introduction to LINQ basics and an introduction to LINQ to SQL (the technology that replaces SQL).

- *Updated PHP coverage.* Chapter 19 has been updated to the latest version of PHP. If you start this book as a novice and study the JavaScript in Chapters 6–13, you'll have the programming experience needed to understand server-side programming in PHP. [Our treatment of server-side programming in ASP.NET requires knowledge of C# or Visual Basic, and in JSF requires knowledge of Java.]

- *ASP.NET, ASP.NET Ajax and web services.* This updated three-chapter sequence is now provided for each of Microsoft's two key applications development languages—C# and Visual Basic. The C# chapters and the first VB chapter are in the print book and the remaining Visual Basic chapters are available online at the book's Companion Website (see the inside front cover).

- *JavaServer Faces (JSF), JSF Ajax and web services.* This updated three-chapter sequence, available online, emphasizes building Ajax-enabled JSF applications.

- *Web services.* We now provide chapters on building both SOAP-based web services *and* REST-based web services with ASP.NET in Visual Basic, ASP.NET in C# and JSF in Java.

- *Client/Server applications.* Several client-side case studies now enable students to interact with preimplemented web services that we host at test.deitel.com.

- *New and updated case studies.* The book includes rich case studies using various technologies—Deitel Cover Viewer (JavaScript/DOM), Address Book (Ajax), Cannon Game (HTML5 Canvas), Mailing List (PHP/MySQL), Guest Book and Password-Protected Books Database (ASP.NET), Address Book (JavaServer Faces) and Blackjack (JAX-WS web services).

New Pedagogic Features

- *Making a Difference exercises in Chapter 1.* We encourage you to use computers and the Internet to research and solve significant social problems. These exercises are meant to increase awareness and discussion of important issues the world is facing. We hope you'll approach them with your own values, politics and beliefs. Check out the many Making a Difference resources we provide, including our new Making a Difference Resource Center at www.deitel.com/MakingADifference for additional ideas you may want to investigate further.

- *Page numbers for key terms in chapter summaries.* For key terms that appear in the Chapters 1–19 summaries, we include the page number of the key term's defining occurrence in the text.

Dependency Chart

The chart in Fig. 5 shows the book's modular organization and the dependencies among the chapters to help instructors plan their syllabi. *Internet & World Wide Web How to Program, 5/e,* is appropriate for a variety of introductory and intermediate -level programming courses, most notably client-side programming and server-side programming. Chapters 1–23 are in the printed book; Chapters 24–29 and some appendices are online.

We recommend that you study all of a given chapter's dependencies before studying that chapter, though other orders are certainly possible. Some of the dependencies apply only to sections of chapters, so we advise instructors to browse the material before designing a course of study. This book is intended for courses that teach pure client-side web programming, courses that teach pure server-side web programming, and courses that mix and match some of each. Readers interested in studying server-side technologies should understand how to build web pages using HTML5 and CSS3, and object-based programming in JavaScript. Chapters 15 and 16 can be taught as part of a client-side unit, at the beginning of a server-side unit or split between the two.

HTML5 Accessibility Online Appendix

According to the W3C Web Accessibility Initiative, your web pages and applications should be accessible so that "people with disabilities can perceive, understand, navigate, and interact with the web, and that they can contribute to the web."[1] In an online appendix, we enumerate accessibility issues you should consider when designing web pages and web-based applications. We also provide resources that show you how to use HTML5, CSS3, JavaScript and various design techniques to create accessible web pages and applications. As appropriate, we tie the information in this appendix back to the appropriate chapters and sections so that you can see how the applications may be enhanced to improve web accessibility.

---

1. http://www.w3.org/WAI/intro/accessibility.php.

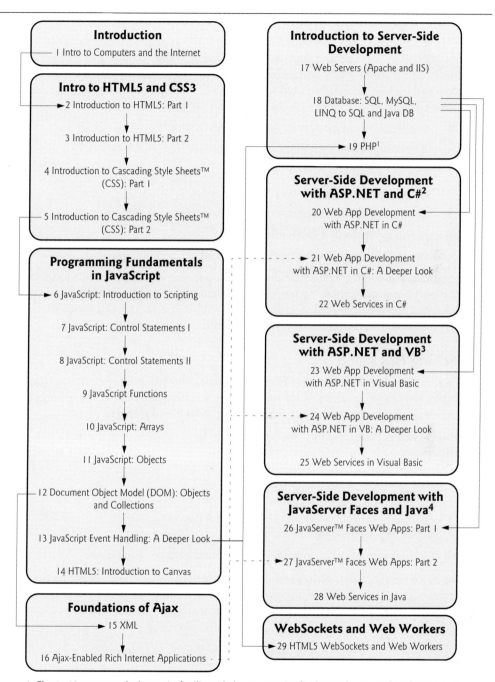

Introduction

1 Intro to Computers and the Internet

Intro to HTML5 and CSS3

2 Introduction to HTML5: Part 1

3 Introduction to HTML5: Part 2

4 Introduction to Cascading Style Sheets™ (CSS): Part 1

5 Introduction to Cascading Style Sheets™ (CSS): Part 2

Programming Fundamentals in JavaScript

6 JavaScript: Introduction to Scripting

7 JavaScript: Control Statements I

8 JavaScript: Control Statements II

9 JavaScript Functions

10 JavaScript: Arrays

11 JavaScript: Objects

12 Document Object Model (DOM): Objects and Collections

13 JavaScript Event Handling: A Deeper Look

14 HTML5: Introduction to Canvas

Foundations of Ajax

15 XML

16 Ajax-Enabled Rich Internet Applications

Introduction to Server-Side Development

17 Web Servers (Apache and IIS)

18 Database: SQL, MySQL, LINQ to SQL and Java DB

19 PHP[1]

Server-Side Development with ASP.NET and C#[2]

20 Web App Development with ASP.NET in C#

21 Web App Development with ASP.NET in C#: A Deeper Look

22 Web Services in C#

Server-Side Development with ASP.NET and VB[3]

23 Web App Development with ASP.NET in Visual Basic

24 Web App Development with ASP.NET in VB: A Deeper Look

25 Web Services in Visual Basic

Server-Side Development with JavaServer Faces and Java[4]

26 JavaServer™ Faces Web Apps: Part 1

27 JavaServer™ Faces Web Apps: Part 2

28 Web Services in Java

WebSockets and Web Workers

29 HTML5 WebSockets and Web Workers

1. Chapter 19 assumes only that you're familiar with the programming fundamentals presented in Chapters 6–13.
2. The C# chapters require knowledge of C# and the Microsoft .NET class libraries.
3. The Visual Basic chapters require knowledge of Visual Basic and the Microsoft .NET class libraries.
4. The Java chapters require knowledge of Java and the Java class libraries.

Fig. 5 | *Internet & World Wide Web How to Program, 5/e* chapter dependency chart.

HTML5 Geolocation Online Appendix

The HTML5 Geolocation API allows you to build web applications that gather location information (i.e,. latitude and longitude coordinates) using technologies like GPS, IP addresses, WiFi connections or cellular tower connections. It's supported by the seven desktop and mobile browsers we used to test the code throughout the book.

The Geolocation API specification lists several use cases,[2] including:

- finding points of interest in the user's area
- annotating content with location information
- showing the user's position on a map
- providing route navigation
- alerting the user when points of interest are nearby
- providing up-to-date local information
- tagging locations in status updates on social networking sites

For example, you could create a location-based mobile web app that uses GPS location information from a smartphone to track a runner's route on a map, calculate the distance traveled and the average speed. Similarly, you could create an app that returns a list of nearby businesses. In this online appendix, we build a mobile location-based app.

Teaching Approach

Internet & World Wide Web How to Program, 5/e, contains hundreds of complete working examples across a wide variety of markup, styling, scripting and programming languages. We stress clarity and concentrate on building well-engineered software.

Syntax Shading. For readability, we syntax shade the code, similar to the way most integrated-development environments and code editors syntax color the code. Our syntax-shading conventions are:

```
comments appear like this
keywords appear like this
constants and literal values appear like this
all other code appears in black
```

Code Highlighting. We place gray rectangles around key code segments.

Using Fonts for Emphasis. We place the key terms and the index's page reference for each defining occurrence in **bold** text for easy reference. We emphasize on-screen components in the **bold Helvetica** font (for example, the **File** menu) and program text in the Lucida font (for example, int count = 5).

Web Access. All of the source-code examples can be downloaded from:

```
www.deitel.com/books/iw3htp5
www.pearsoninternationaleditions.com/deitel
```

Objectives. The opening quotes are followed by a list of chapter objectives.

---

2. http://www.w3.org/TR/geolocation-API/#usecases_section.

Illustrations/Figures. Abundant tables, line drawings, documents, scripts, programs and program outputs are included.

Programming Tips. We include programming tips to help you focus on important aspects of software development. These tips and practices represent the best we've gleaned from a combined seven decades of programming and teaching experience.

Good Programming Practices
The Good Programming Practices *call attention to techniques that will help you produce programs that are clearer, more understandable and more maintainable.*

Common Programming Errors
Pointing out these Common Programming Errors *reduces the likelihood that you'll make them.*

Error-Prevention Tips
These tips contain suggestions for exposing and removing bugs from your programs; many of the tips describe aspects of programming that prevent bugs from getting into programs.

Performance Tips
These tips highlight opportunities for making your scripts and programs run faster or minimizing the amount of memory that they occupy.

Portability Tips
The Portability Tips *help you write code that will run on a variety of platforms.*

Software Engineering Observations
The Software Engineering Observations *highlight architectural and design issues that affect the construction of software systems, especially large-scale systems.*

Summary Bullets. We present a section-by-section bullet-list summary of the chapter for rapid review of key points. For ease of reference, we include the page number of each key term's defining occurrence in the text.

Self-Review Exercises and Answers. Extensive self-review exercises *and* answers are included for self study.

Exercises. The chapter exercises include:
- simple recall of important terminology and concepts
- What's wrong with this code?
- writing individual statements
- writing complete functions and scripts
- major projects

Index. We've included an extensive index. Defining occurrences of key terms are highlighted with a **bold** page number.

Instructor Resources

The following supplements are available to *qualified instructors only* through Pearson Education's Instructor Resource Center (www.pearsoninternationaleditions.com/deitel):

- *PowerPoint® slides* containing all the code and figures in the text, plus bulleted items that summarize key points.
- *Solutions Manual* with solutions to many of the end-of-chapter exercises. Please check the Instructor Resource Center to determine which exercises have solutions.

Please do not write to us requesting access to the Pearson Instructor's Resource Center. Access is restricted to college instructors teaching from the book. Instructors may obtain access only through their Pearson representatives. If you're not a registered faculty member, contact your Pearson representative.

Solutions are *not* provided for "project" exercises. Check out our Programming Projects Resource Center for lots of additional exercise and project possibilities (www.deitel.com/ProgrammingProjects/).

Acknowledgments

We'd like to thank Barbara Deitel for long hours devoted to this project. We're fortunate to have worked with the dedicated team of publishing professionals at Pearson. We appreciate the guidance, savvy and energy of Michael Hirsch, Editor-in-Chief of Computer Science. Carole Snyder recruited the book's reviewers and managed the review process. Bob Engelhardt managed the book's production.

Reviewers

We wish to acknowledge the efforts of our fourth and fifth edition reviewers. They scrutinized the text and the programs and provided countless suggestions for improving the presentation: Timothy Boronczyk (Consultant), Roland Bouman (MySQL AB), Chris Bowen (Microsoft), Peter Brandano (KoolConnect Technologies, Inc.), Matt Chotin (Adobe), Chris Cornutt (PHPDeveloper.org), Phil Costa (Adobe), Umachitra Damodaran (Sun Microsystems), Vadiraj Deshpande (Sun Microsystems), Justin Erenkrantz (The Apache Software Foundation), Christopher Finke (Netscape), Jesse James Garrett (Adaptive Path), Mike Harsh (Microsoft), Chris Heilmann (Mozilla), Kevin Henrikson (Zimbra.com), Tim Heuer (Microsoft), Molly E. Holtzschlag (W3C), Ralph Hooper (University of Alabama, Tuscaloosa), Chris Horton (University of Alabama), John Hrvatin (Microsoft), Johnvey Hwang (Splunk, Inc.), Joe Kromer (New Perspective and the Pittsburgh Adobe Flash Users Group), Jennifer Kyrnin (Web Design Guide at About.com), Eric Lawrence (Microsoft), Pete LePage (Microsoft), Dr. Roy Levow (Florida Atlantic University), Billy B. L. Lim (Illinois State University), Shobana Mahadevan (Sun Microsystems), Patrick Mineault (Freelance Flash Programmer), Anand Narayanaswamy (Microsoft), John Peterson (Insync and V.I.O., Inc.), Jennifer Powers (University of Albany), Ignacio Ricci (Ignacioricci.com), Jake Rutter (onerutter.com), Robin Schumacher (MySQL AB), José Antonio González Seco (Parlamento de Andalucia), Dr. George Semeczko (Royal & SunAlliance Insurance Canada), Steven Shaffer (Penn State University), Michael Smith (W3C), Karen Tegtmeyer (Model Technologies, Inc.), Paul Vencill (MITRE), Raymond Wen (Microsoft), Eric M. Wendelin (Auto-trol Technology

Corporation), Raymond F. Wisman (Indiana University), Keith Wood (Hyro, Ltd.) and Daniel Zappala (Brigham Young University).

As you read the book, we'd appreciate your comments, criticisms, corrections and suggestions for improvement. Please address all correspondence to:

```
deitel@deitel.com
```

We'll respond promptly. We hope you enjoy working with *Internet & World Wide Web How to Program, 5/e.*

Paul, Harvey and Abbey Deitel

About the Authors

Paul J. Deitel, CEO and Chief Technical Officer of Deitel & Associates, Inc., is a graduate of MIT, where he studied Information Technology. Through Deitel & Associates, Inc., he has delivered hundreds of Java, C++, C, C#, Visual Basic and Internet programming courses to industry clients, including Cisco, IBM, Siemens, Sun Microsystems, Dell, Lucent Technologies, Fidelity, NASA at the Kennedy Space Center, the National Severe Storm Laboratory, White Sands Missile Range, Rogue Wave Software, Boeing, SunGard Higher Education, Stratus, Cambridge Technology Partners, One Wave, Hyperion Software, Adra Systems, Entergy, CableData Systems, Nortel Networks, Puma, iRobot, Invensys and many more. He and his co-author, Dr. Harvey M. Deitel, are the world's best-selling programming-language textbook authors.

Dr. Harvey M. Deitel, Chairman and Chief Strategy Officer of Deitel & Associates, Inc., has 50 years of experience in the computer field. Dr. Deitel earned B.S. and M.S. degrees from MIT and a Ph.D. from Boston University. He has extensive college teaching experience, including earning tenure and serving as the Chairman of the Computer Science Department at Boston College before founding Deitel & Associates, Inc., with his son, Paul J. Deitel. He and Paul are the co-authors of dozens of books and LiveLessons video packages and they are writing many more. The Deitels' texts have earned international recognition, with translations published in Japanese, German, Russian, Chinese, Spanish, Korean, French, Polish, Italian, Portuguese, Greek, Urdu and Turkish. Dr. Deitel has delivered hundreds of professional programming seminars to major corporations, academic institutions, government organizations and the military.

Abbey Deitel, President of Deitel & Associates, Inc., is a graduate of Carnegie Mellon University's Tepper School of Management where she received a B.S. in Industrial Management. Abbey has been managing the business operations of Deitel & Associates, Inc. for 14 years. She has contributed to numerous Deitel & Associates publications and is the co-author of *iPhone for Programmers: An App-Driven Approach* and *Android for Programmers: An App-Driven Approach.*

Corporate Training from Deitel & Associates, Inc.

Deitel & Associates, Inc., is an internationally recognized corporate training and authoring organization. The company provides instructor-led courses delivered at client sites worldwide on major programming languages and platforms, such as Java™, C++, Visual C++®, C, Visual C#®, Visual Basic®, XML®, Python®, object technology, Internet and web programming,

Android™ and iPhone® app development, and a growing list of additional programming and software-development courses. The founders of Deitel & Associates, Inc., are Paul J. Deitel and Dr. Harvey M. Deitel. The company's clients include many of the world's largest companies, government agencies, branches of the military, and academic institutions. Through its 36-year publishing partnership with Prentice Hall/Pearson, Deitel & Associates publishes leading-edge programming textbooks, professional books and *LiveLessons* video courses. Deitel & Associates, Inc., and the authors can be reached via e-mail at:

```
deitel@deitel.com
```

To learn more about the company, its publications and its *Dive Into®* *Series* Corporate Training curriculum delivered at client locations worldwide, visit:

```
www.deitel.com/training/
```

subscribe to the *Deitel®* *Buzz Online* e-mail newsletter at:

```
www.deitel.com/newsletter/subscribe.html
```

and join the authors' communities on Facebook (`www.facebook.com/DeitelFan`) and Twitter (@deitel).

Individuals wishing to purchase Deitel books, and *LiveLessons* video training courses can do so through `www.deitel.com`. Bulk orders by corporations, the government, the military and academic institutions should be placed directly with Pearson. For more information, visit

```
www.pearsoninternationaleditions.com/deitel
```

Before You Begin

Please follow these instructions to download the book's examples and ensure you have a current web browser before you begin using this book.

Obtaining the Source Code

The examples for *Internet & World Wide Web How To Program, 5/e* are available for download at

```
www.deitel.com/books/iw3htp5/
```

If you're not already registered at our website, go to www.deitel.com and click the **Register** link below our logo in the upper-left corner of the page. Fill in your information. There's no charge to register, and we do not share your information with anyone. We send you only account-management e-mails unless you register separately for our free *Deitel® Buzz Online* e-mail newsletter at www.deitel.com/newsletter/subscribe.html. After registering for the site, you'll receive a confirmation e-mail with your verification code. *Click the link in the confirmation e-mail to complete your registration.* Configure your e-mail client to allow e-mails from deitel.com to ensure that the confirmation email is not filtered as junk mail.

Next, go to www.deitel.com and sign in using the **Login** link below our logo in the upper-left corner of the page. Go to www.deitel.com/books/iw3htp5/. You'll find the link to download the examples under the heading **Download Code Examples and Other Premium Content for Registered Users**. Write down the location where you choose to save the ZIP file on your computer. Extract the example files to your hard disk using a ZIP file extractor program. If you are working in a computer lab, ask your instructor where you can save the example code.

Web Browsers Used in This Book

We tested all of the code in the most current versions of *seven* popular browsers—five for the **desktop** (**Chrome, Internet Explorer, Firefox, Opera** and **Safari**) and two for **mobile** devices (**iPhone** and **Android**). HTML5 and CSS3 are evolving and the final standards have not been approved yet. The browser vendors are selectively implementing features that are likely to become a part of the standards. Some vendors have higher levels of feature compliance than others. With each new version of the browsers, the trend has been to significantly increase the amount of functionality that's been implemented. The HTML5 test site (html5test.com) measures how well each browser supports the pending standards and specifications. You can view test scores and see which features are supported by each browser. You can also check sites such as http://caniuse.com/ for a list of features covered by each browser. Not every document in this book will render properly in each browser. Instead of choosing only capabilities that exist universally, we demonstrate exciting new features in whatever browser handles the new functionality best. As you read this book, run each example in multiple web browsers so you can view and interact with it as it was originally intended. And remember, things are changing quickly, so a browser that did not support a feature when we wrote the book could support it when you read the book.

Web Browser Download Links

You can download the desktop browsers from the following locations:

- Google Chrome: `http://www.google.com/chrome`
- Mozilla Firefox: `http://www.mozilla.org/firefox/new/`
- Microsoft Internet Explorer (Windows only): `http://www.microsoft.com/ie`
- Apple Safari: `http://www.apple.com/safari/`
- Opera: `http://www.opera.com/`

We recommend that you install all the browsers that are available for your platform.

Software for the C# and Visual Basic ASP.NET Chapters

The C# (Chapters 20–22) and Visual Basic (Chapters 23–25) ASP.NET and web services chapters require Visual Web Developer 2010 Express and SQL Server 2008 Express. These tools are downloadable from `www.microsoft.com/express`. You should follow the default installation instructions for each.

Software for the JavaServer Faces and Java Web Services Chapters

The software required for the JavaServer Faces and Java Web Services chapters (Chapters 26–28) is discussed at the beginning of Chapter 26.

You're now ready to begin your web programming studies with *Internet & World Wide Web How to Program, 5/e*. We hope you enjoy the book! If you have any questions, please feel free to email us at `deitel@deitel.com`. We'll respond promptly.

Introduction to Computers and the Internet

People are using the web to build things they have not built or written or drawn or communicated anywhere else.
—Tim Berners-Lee

How wonderful it is that nobody need wait a single moment before starting to improve the world.
—Anne Frank

Man is still the most extraordinary computer of all.
—John F. Kennedy

Objectives

In this chapter you'll learn:

- Computer hardware, software and Internet basics.

- The evolution of the Internet and the World Wide Web.

- How HTML5, CSS3 and JavaScript are improving web-application development.

- The data hierarchy.

- The different types of programming languages.

- Object-technology concepts.

- And you'll see demos of interesting and fun Internet applications you can build with the technologies you'll learn in this book.

1.1 Introduction

Welcome to the exciting and rapidly evolving world of Internet and web programming! There are more than two billion Internet users worldwide—that's approximately 30% of the Earth's population.[1] In use today are more than a billion general-purpose computers, and billions more *embedded* computers are used in cell phones, smartphones, tablet computers, home appliances, automobiles and more—and many of these devices are connected to the Internet. According to a study by Cisco Internet Business Solutions Group, there were 12.5 billion Internet-enabled devices in 2010, and the number is predicted to reach 25 billion by 2015 and 50 billion by 2020.[2] The Internet and web programming technologies you'll learn in this book are designed to be *portable*, allowing you to design web pages and applications that run across an enormous range of Internet-enabled devices.

You'll begin by learning the *client-side programming* technologies used to build web pages and applications that are run on the *client* (i.e., in the browser on the user's device). You'll use HyperText Markup Language 5 (HTML5) and Cascading Style Sheets 3 (CSS3)—the recent releases of HTML and CSS technologies—to add powerful, dynamic and fun features and effects to web pages and web applications, such as audio, video, animation, drawing, image manipulation, designing pages for multiple screen sizes, access to web storage and more.

You'll learn *JavaScript*—the language of choice for implementing the client side of Internet-based applications (we discuss JavaScript in more detail in Section 1.3). Chapters 6–13 present rich coverage of JavaScript and its capabilities. You'll also learn about *jQuery*—the JavaScript library that's dramatically reshaping the world of web development. Throughout the book there's also an emphasis on *Ajax* development, which helps you create better-performing, more usable applications.

Later in the book, you'll learn *server-side programming*—the applications that respond to requests from client-side web browsers, such as searching the Internet, checking your

---

1.   www.internetworldstats.com/stats.htm.
2.   www.cisco.com/web/about/ac79/docs/innov/IoT_IBSG_0411FINAL.pdf.

bank-account balance, ordering a book from Amazon, bidding on an eBay auction and ordering concert tickets. We present condensed treatments of four popular Internet/web programming languages for building the server side of Internet- and web-based client/server applications. Chapters 19–22 and 23–28 present three popular server-side technologies, including PHP, ASP.NET (in both C# and Visual Basic) and JavaServer Faces.

Be sure to read both the Preface and the Before You Begin section to learn about the book's coverage and how to set up your computer to run the hundreds of code examples. The code is available at www.deitel.com/books/iw3htp5 and www.pearsonhighered.com/deitel. Use the source code we provide to *run every program and script* as you study it. Try each example in *multiple browsers*. If you're interested in smartphones and tablet computers, be sure to run the examples in your browsers on iPhones, iPads, Android smartphones and tablets, and others. The technologies covered in this book and browser support for them are evolving rapidly. *Not every feature of every page we build will render properly in every browser.* All seven of the browsers we use are free.

Moore's Law

Every year, you probably expect to pay at least a little more for most products and services. The opposite has been the case in the computer and communications fields, especially with regard to the costs of hardware supporting these technologies. For many decades, hardware costs have fallen rapidly. Every year or two, the capacities of computers have approximately *doubled* inexpensively. This remarkable trend often is called **Moore's Law**, named for the person who identified it, Gordon Moore, co-founder of Intel—the leading manufacturer of the processors in today's computers and embedded systems. Moore's Law and related observations apply especially to the amount of memory that computers have for programs, the amount of secondary storage (such as disk storage) they have to hold programs and data over longer periods of time, and their processor speeds—the speeds at which computers execute their programs (i.e., do their work). Similar growth has occurred in the communications field, in which costs have plummeted as enormous demand for communications bandwidth (i.e., information-carrying capacity) has attracted intense competition. We know of no other fields in which technology improves so quickly and costs fall so rapidly. Such phenomenal improvement is truly fostering the *Information Revolution.*

1.2 The Internet in Industry and Research

These are exciting times in the computer field. Many of the most influential and successful businesses of the last two decades are technology companies, including Apple, IBM, Hewlett Packard, Dell, Intel, Motorola, Cisco, Microsoft, Google, Amazon, Facebook, Twitter, Groupon, Foursquare, Yahoo!, eBay and many more. These companies are major employers of people who study computer science, information systems or related disciplines. At the time of this writing, Apple was the most valuable company in the world.

In the past, most computer applications ran on computers that were not connected to one another, whereas today's Internet applications can be written to communicate among computers throughout the world.

Figures 1.1–1.4 provide a few examples of how computers and the Internet are being used in industry and research. Figure 1.1 lists two examples of how computers and the Internet are being used to improve health care.

Name	Description
Electronic health records	These might include a patient's medical history, prescriptions, immunizations, lab results, allergies, insurance information and more. Making this information available to health care providers across a secure network improves patient care, reduces the probability of error and increases overall efficiency of the health care system.
Human Genome Project	The Human Genome Project was founded to identify and analyze the 20,000+ genes in human DNA. The project used computer programs to analyze complex genetic data, determine the sequences of the billions of chemical base pairs that make up human DNA and store the information in databases which have been made available over the Internet to researchers in many fields.

Fig. 1.1 | Computers and the Internet in health care.

Figure 1.2 provides a sample of some of the exciting ways in which computers and the Internet are being used for social good. In the exercises at the end of this chapter, you'll be asked to propose other projects that would use computers and the Internet to "make a difference."

Name	Description
AMBER™ Alert	The AMBER (America's Missing: Broadcast Emergency Response) Alert System is used to find abducted children. Law enforcement notifies TV and radio broadcasters and state transportation officials, who then broadcast alerts on TV, radio, computerized highway signs, the Internet and wireless devices. AMBER Alert recently partnered with Facebook, whose users can "Like" AMBER Alert pages by location to receive alerts in their news feeds.
World Community Grid	People worldwide can donate their unused computer processing power by installing a free secure software program that allows the World Community Grid (www.worldcommunitygrid.org) to harness unused capacity. This computing power, accessed over the Internet, is used in place of expensive supercomputers to conduct scientific research projects that are making a difference, providing clean water to third-world countries, fighting cancer, growing more nutritious rice for regions fighting hunger and more.
One Laptop Per Child (OLPC)	One Laptop Per Child (one.laptop.org) is providing low-power, inexpensive, Internet-enabled laptops to poor children worldwide—enabling learning and reducing the digital divide.

Fig. 1.2 | Projects that use computers and the Internet for social good.

We rely on computers and the Internet to communicate, navigate, collaborate and more. Figure 1.3 gives some examples of how computers and the Internet provide the infrastructure for these tasks.

Name	Description
Cloud computing	**Cloud computing** allows you to use software, hardware and information stored in the "cloud"—i.e., accessed on remote computers via the Internet and available on demand—rather than having it stored on your personal computer. Amazon is one of the leading providers of public cloud computing services. You can rent extra storage capacity using the Amazon Simple Storage Service (Amazon S3), or augment processing capabilities with Amazon's EC2 (Amazon Elastic Compute Cloud). These services, allowing you to increase or decrease resources to meet your needs at any given time, are generally more cost effective than purchasing expensive hardware to ensure that you have enough storage and processing power to meet your needs at their peak levels. Business applications (such as CRM software) are often expensive, require significant hardware to run them and knowledgeable support staff to ensure that they're running properly and securely. Using cloud computing services shifts the burden of managing these applications from the business to the service provider, saving businesses money.
GPS	Global Positioning System (GPS) devices use a network of satellites to retrieve location-based information. Multiple satellites send time-stamped signals to the GPS device, which calculates the distance to each satellite based on the time the signal left the satellite and the time the signal arrived. This information is used to determine the exact location of the device. GPS devices can provide step-by-step directions and help you easily find nearby businesses (restaurants, gas stations, etc.) and points of interest. GPS is used in numerous location-based Internet services such as check-in apps to help you find your friends (e.g., Foursquare and Facebook), exercise apps such as RunKeeper that track the time, distance and average speed of your outdoor jog, dating apps that help you find a match nearby and apps that dynamically update changing traffic conditions.
Robots	Robots can be used for day-to-day tasks (e.g., iRobot's Roomba vacuum), entertainment (e.g., robotic pets), military combat, deep sea and space exploration (e.g., NASA's Mars rover) and more. RoboEarth (www.roboearth.org) is "a World Wide Web for robots." It allows robots to learn from each other by sharing information and thus improving their abilities to perform tasks, navigate, recognize objects and more.
E-mail, Instant Messaging, Video Chat and FTP	Internet-based servers support all of your online messaging. E-mail messages go through a mail server that also stores the messages. Instant messaging (IM) and Video Chat apps, such as AIM, Skype, Yahoo! Messenger and others allow you to communicate with others in real time by sending your messages and live video through servers. FTP (file transfer protocol) allows you to exchange files between multiple computers (e.g., a client computer such as your desktop and a file server) over the Internet using the TCP/IP protocols for transferring data.

Fig. 1.3 | Examples of computers and the Internet in infrastructure.

Figure 1.4 lists a few of the exciting ways in which computers and the Internet are used in entertainment.

Name	Description
iTunes and the App Store	iTunes is Apple's media store where you can buy and download digital music, movies, television shows, e-books, ringtones and apps (for iPhone, iPod and iPad) over the Internet. Apple's iCloud service allows you to store your media purchases "in the cloud" and access them from any iOS (Apple's mobile operating system) device. In June 2011, Apple announced at their World Wide Developer Conference (WWDC) that 15 billion songs had been downloaded through iTunes, making Apple the leading music retailer. As of July 2011, 15 billion apps had been downloaded from the App Store (www.apple.com/pr/library/2011/07/07Apples-App-Store-Downloads-Top-15-Billion.html).
Internet TV	Internet TV set-top boxes (such as Apple TV and Google TV) allow you to access an enormous amount of content on demand, such as games, news, movies, television shows and more.
Game programming	Global video game revenues are expected to reach $65 billion in 2011 (uk.reuters.com/article/2011/06/06/us-videogames-factbox-idUKTRE75552I20110606). The most sophisticated games can cost as much as $100 million to develop. Activision's *Call of Duty 2: Modern Warfare*, released in 2009, earned $310 million in just one day in North America and the U.K. (news.cnet.com/8301-13772_3-10396593-52.html?tag=mncol;txt)! Online *social gaming*, which enables users worldwide to compete with one another over the Internet, is growing rapidly. Zynga—creator of popular online games such as *Farmville* and *Mafia Wars*—was founded in 2007 and already has over 265 million monthly users. To accommodate the growth in traffic, Zynga is adding nearly 1,000 servers each week (techcrunch.com/2010/09/22/zynga-moves-1-petabyte-of-data-daily-adds-1000-servers-a-week/)!

Fig. 1.4 | Examples of computers and the Internet in entertainment.

1.3 HTML5, CSS3, JavaScript, Canvas and jQuery

You'll be learning the latest versions of several key client-side, web-application development technologies in this book. This section provides a brief overview of each.

HTML5

Chapters 2–3 introduce HTML (HyperText Markup Language)—a special type of computer language called a *markup language* designed to specify the *content* and *structure* of web pages (also called documents) in a portable manner. HTML5, now under development, is the emerging version of HTML. HTML enables you to create content that will render appropriately across the extraordinary range of devices connected to the Internet—including smartphones, tablet computers, notebook computers, desktop computers, special-purpose devices such as large-screen displays at concert arenas and sports stadiums, and more.

You'll learn the basics of HTML5, then cover more sophisticated techniques such as creating tables, creating forms for collecting user input and using new features in HTML5, including page-structure elements that enable you to give meaning to the parts of a page (e.g., headers, navigation areas, footers, sections, figures, figure captions and more).

A "stricter" version of HTML called *XHTML (Extensible HyperText Markup Language)*, which is based on XML (eXtensible Markup Language, introduced in Chapter 15), is still used frequently today. Many of the server-side technologies we cover later in the book produce web pages as XHTML documents, by default, but the trend is clearly to HTML5.

Cascading Style Sheets (CSS)

Although HTML5 provides some capabilities for controlling a document's presentation, *it's better not to mix presentation with content.* HTML5 should be used only to specify a document's structure and content.

Chapters 4–5 use **Cascading Style Sheets** (**CSS**) to specify the *presentation*, or styling, of elements on a web page (e.g., fonts, spacing, sizes, colors, positioning). CSS was designed to style portable web pages *independently* of their content and structure. By separating page styling from page content and structure, you can easily change the look and feel of the pages on an *entire* website, or a portion of a website, simply by swapping out one style sheet for another. CSS3 is the current version of CSS under development. Chapter 5 introduces many new features in CSS3.

JavaScript

JavaScript is a language that helps you build *dynamic* web pages (i.e., pages that can be modified "on the fly" in response to *events*, such as user input, time changes and more) and computer applications. It enables you to do the client-side programming of web applications. In addition, there are now several projects dedicated to *server-side* JavaScript, including CommonJS (`www.commonjs.org`), Node.js (`nodejs.org`) and Jaxer (`jaxer.org`).

JavaScript was created by Netscape, the company that built the first wildly successful web browser. Both Netscape and Microsoft have been instrumental in the standardization of JavaScript by ECMA International (formerly the European Computer Manufacturers Association) as ECMAScript. ECMAScript 5, the latest version of the standard, corresponds to the version of JavaScript we use in this book.

The JavaScript chapters of the book are more than just an introduction to the language. They also present computer-programming fundamentals, including control structures, functions, arrays, recursion, strings and objects. You'll see that JavaScript is a portable scripting language and that programs written in JavaScript can run in web browsers across a wide range of devices.

Web Browsers and Web-Browser Portability

Ensuring a consistent look and feel on client-side browsers is one of the great challenges of developing web-based applications. Currently, a standard does not exist to which software vendors must adhere when creating web browsers. Although browsers share a common set of features, each browser might render pages differently. Browsers are available in many versions and on many different platforms (Microsoft Windows, Apple Macintosh, Linux, UNIX, etc.). Vendors add features to each new version that sometimes result in cross-platform incompatibility issues. It's difficult to develop web pages that render correctly on all versions of each browser.

All of the code examples in the book were tested in the five most popular desktop browsers and the two most popular mobile browsers (Fig. 1.5). Support for HTML5, CSS3 and JavaScript features varies by browser. The *HTML5 Test* website (`http://html5test.com/`) scores each browser based on its support for the latest features of these evolving standards. Figure 1.5 lists the five desktop browsers we use in reverse order of their HTML5 Test scores from most compliant to least compliant at the time of this writing. Internet Explorer 10 (IE10) is expected to have a much higher compliance rating than IE9. You can also check sites such as `http://caniuse.com/` for a list of features covered by each browser.

> **Portability Tip 1.1**
>
> *The web is populated with many different browsers, including many older, less-capable versions, which makes it difficult for authors and web-application developers to create universal solutions. The W3C is working toward the goal of a universal client-side platform (`http://www.w3.org/2006/webapi/admin/charter`).*

Browser	Approximate market share as of August 2011 (http://gs.statcounter.com)	Score out of 450 from html5test.com
Desktop browsers	*Market share*	
Google Chrome 13	17%	330
Mozilla Firefox 6	27%	298
Apple Safari 5.1	7%	293
Opera 11.5	2%	286
Internet Explorer 9	40%	141
Mobile browsers	*Mobile market share*	
iPhone	15% (of mobile browsers)	217
Android	18% (of mobile browsers)	184

Fig. 1.5 | HTML5 Test scores for the browsers used to test the examples.

jQuery

jQuery (jQuery.org) is currently the most popular of hundreds of *JavaScript libraries*.[3] jQuery simplifies JavaScript programming by making it easier to manipulate a web page's elements and interact with servers in a portable manner across various web browsers. It provides a library of custom graphical user interface (GUI) controls (beyond the basic GUI controls provided by HTML5) that can be used to enhance the look and feel of your web pages.

Validating Your HTML5, CSS3 and JavaScript Code

As you'll see, JavaScript programs typically have HTML5 and CSS3 portions as well. You must use proper HTML5, CSS3 and JavaScript syntax to ensure that browsers process your documents properly. Figure 1.6 lists the validators we used to validate the code in this book. Where possible, we eliminated validation errors.

---

3.   www.activoinc.com/blog/2008/11/03/jquery-emerges-as-most-popular-javascript-library-for-web-development/.

Technology	Validator URL
HTML5	`http://validator.w3.org/`
	`http://html5.validator.nu/`
CSS3	`http://jigsaw.w3.org/css-validator/`
JavaScript	`http://www.javascriptlint.com/`
	`http://www.jslint.com/`

Fig. 1.6 | HTML5, CSS3 and JavaScript validators.

1.4 Demos

Browse the web pages in Fig. 1.7 to get a sense of some of the things you'll be able to create using the technologies you'll learn in this book, including HTML5, CSS3, JavaScript, canvas and jQuery. Many of these sites provide links to the corresponding source code, or you can view the page's source code in your browser.

URL	Description
`https://developer.mozilla.org/en-US/demos/`	Mozilla's DemoStudio contains numerous HTML5, canvas, CSS3 and JavaScript demos that use audio, video, animation and more.
`http://js-fireworks.appspot.com/`	Enter your name or message, and this JavaScript animation then writes it using a fireworks effect over the London skyline.
`http://9elements.com/io/projects/html5/canvas/`	Uses HTML5 canvas and audio elements to create interesting effects, and ties in tweets that include the words "HTML5" and "love" (click anywhere on the screen to see the next tweet).
`http://www.zachstronaut.com/lab/text-shadow-box/text-shadow-box.html`	Animated demo of the CSS3 text-shadow effect. Use the mouse to shine a light on the text and dynamically change the direction and size of the shadow.
`http://clublime.com/lab/html5/sphere/`	Uses an HTML5 canvas to create a sphere that rotates and changes direction as you move the mouse cursor.
`http://spielzeugz.de/html5/liquid-particles.html`	The Liquid Particles demo uses an HTML5 canvas. Move the mouse around the screen and the "particles" (dots or letters) follow.
`http://www.paulbrunt.co.uk/bert/`	Bert's Breakdown is a fun video game built using an HTML5 canvas.
`http://www.openrise.com/lab/FlowerPower/`	Canvas app that allows you to draw flowers on the page, adjust their colors, change the shapes of the petals and more.

Fig. 1.7 | HTML5, CSS3, JavaScript, canvas and jQuery demos. (Part 1 of 2.)

URL	Description
`http://alteredqualia.com/canvasmol/`	Uses canvas to display a 3D molecule that can be viewed from any desired angle (0–360 degrees).
`http://pasjans-online.pl/`	The game of Solitaire built using HTML5.
`http://andrew-hoyer.com/experiments/cloth/`	Uses canvas to simulate of the movement of a piece of cloth. Click and drag the mouse to move the fabric.
`http://www.paulrhayes.com/experiments/cube-3d/`	CSS3 demo allows you to use the mouse to tilt and rotate the 3D cube. Includes a tutorial.
`http://www.effectgames.com/demos/canvascycle/`	Animated waterfall provides a nice demo of using color in HTML5 canvas.
`http://macek.github.com/google_pacman/`	The Google PAC-MAN® game (a Google Doodle) built in HTML5.
`http://www.benjoffe.com/code/games/torus/`	A 3D game similar to Tetris® built with JavaScript and canvas.
`http://code.almeros.com/code-examples/water-effect-canvas/`	Uses canvas and JavaScript to create a water rippling effect. Hover the cursor over the canvas to see the effect. The site includes a tutorial.
`http://jqueryui.com/demos/`	Numerous jQuery demos, including animations, transitions, color, interactions and more.
`http://lab.smashup.it/flip/`	Demonstrates a flip box using jQuery.
`http://tutorialzine.com/2010/09/html5-canvas-slideshow-jquery/`	Slideshow built with HTML5 canvas and jQuery (includes a tutorial).
`http://css-tricks.com/examples/Circulate/`	Learn how to create an animated circulation effect using jQuery.
`http://demo.tutorialzine.com/2010/02/photo-shoot-css-jquery/demo.html`	Uses jQuery and CSS to create a photoshoot effect, allowing you to focus on an area of the page and snap a picture (includes a tutorial).

Fig. 1.7 | HTML5, CSS3, JavaScript, canvas and jQuery demos. (Part 2 of 2.)

1.5 Evolution of the Internet and World Wide Web

The Internet—a global network of computers—was made possible by the *convergence of computing and communications technologies*. In the late 1960s, ARPA (the Advanced Research Projects Agency) rolled out blueprints for networking the main computer systems of about a dozen ARPA-funded universities and research institutions. They were to be connected with communications lines operating at a then-stunning 56 Kbps (i.e., 56,000 bits per second)—this at a time when most people (of the few who could) were connecting over telephone lines to computers at a rate of 110 bits per second. A **bit** (short for "binary digit") is the smallest data item in a computer; it can assume the value 0 or 1.

There was great excitement. Researchers at Harvard talked about communicating with the powerful Univac computer at the University of Utah to handle the intensive calculations related to their computer graphics research. Many other intriguing possibilities were raised. Academic research was about to take a giant leap forward. ARPA proceeded to implement the **ARPANET**, which eventually evolved into today's **Internet.**

Things worked out differently from what was originally planned. Rather than enabling researchers to share each other's computers, it rapidly became clear that communicating quickly and easily via electronic mail was the key early benefit of the ARPANET. This is true even today on the Internet, which facilitates communications of all kinds among the world's Internet users.

Packet Switching

One of the primary goals for ARPANET was to allow *multiple* users to send and receive information simultaneously over the *same* communications paths (e.g., phone lines). The network operated with a technique called **packet switching**, in which digital data was sent in small bundles called **packets**. The packets contained *address, error-control* and *sequencing* information. The address information allowed packets to be *routed* to their destinations. The sequencing information helped in reassembling the packets—which, because of complex routing mechanisms, could actually arrive out of order—into their original order for presentation to the recipient. Packets from different senders were intermixed on the same lines to efficiently use the available bandwidth. This packet-switching technique greatly reduced transmission costs, as compared with the cost of dedicated communications lines.

The network was designed to operate without centralized control. If a portion of the network failed, the remaining working portions would still route packets from senders to receivers over alternative paths for reliability.

TCP/IP

The protocol (i.e., set of rules) for communicating over the ARPANET became known as **TCP**—the **Transmission Control Protocol**. TCP ensured that messages were properly routed from sender to receiver and that they arrived intact.

As the Internet evolved, organizations worldwide were implementing their own networks for both intraorganization (i.e., within the organization) and interorganization (i.e., between organizations) communications. A wide variety of networking hardware and software appeared. One challenge was to get these different networks to communicate. ARPA accomplished this with the development of **IP**—the **Internet Protocol**, truly creating a **network of networks,** the current architecture of the Internet. The combined set of protocols is now commonly called **TCP/IP**. Each computer on the Internet has a unique **IP address.** The current IP standard, Internet Protocol version 4 (IPv4), has been in use since 1984 and will soon run out of possible addresses. The next-generation Internet Protocol, **IPv6**, is just starting to be deployed. It features enhanced security and a new addressing scheme, hugely expanding the number of IP addresses available so that we will not run out of IP addresses in the forseeable future.

Explosive Growth

Initially, Internet use was limited to universities and research institutions; then the military began using it intensively. Eventually, the government decided to allow access to the Internet for commercial purposes. The research and military communities were concerned that response times would become poor as the Internet became saturated with users.

In fact, the opposite has occurred. Businesses realized that they could tune their operations and offer new and better services to their clients, so they started spending vast amounts of money to develop and enhance the Internet. This generated fierce competition among communications carriers and hardware and software suppliers to meet this demand. The result is that **bandwidth** (i.e., the information-carrying capacity) on the Internet's is increasing rapidly as costs dramatically decline.

World Wide Web, HTML, HTTP

The **World Wide Web** allows computer users to execute web-based applications and to locate and view multimedia-based documents on almost any subject over the Internet. The web is a relatively recent creation. In 1989, **Tim Berners-Lee** of CERN (the European Organization for Nuclear Research) began to develop a technology for sharing information via hyperlinked text documents. Berners-Lee called his invention the **HyperText Markup Language** (**HTML**). He also wrote communication protocols to form the backbone of his new information system, which he called the World Wide Web. In particular, he wrote the **Hypertext Transfer Protocol** (**HTTP**)—a communications protocol used to send information over the web. The **URL** (**Uniform Resource Locator**) specifies the address (i.e., location) of the web page displayed in the browser window. Each web page on the Internet is associated with a unique URL. URLs usually begin with `http://`.

HTTPS

URLs of websites that handle private information, such as credit card numbers, often begin with `https://`, the abbreviation for **Hypertext Transfer Protocol Secure** (**HTTPS**). HTTPS is the standard for transferring encrypted data on the web. It combines HTTP with the Secure Sockets Layer (SSL) and the more recent Transport Layer Security (TLS) cryptographic schemes for securing communications and identification information over the web. Although there are many benefits to using HTTPS, there are a few drawbacks, most notably some performance issues because encryption and decryption consume significant computer processing resources.

Mosaic, Netscape, Emergence of Web 2.0

Web use exploded with the availability in 1993 of the Mosaic browser, which featured a user-friendly graphical interface. Marc Andreessen, whose team at the National Center for Supercomputing Applications (NCSA) developed Mosaic, went on to found Netscape, the company that many people credit with igniting the explosive Internet economy of the late 1990s. But the "dot com" economic bust brought hard times in the early 2000s. The resurgence that began in 2004 or so has been named **Web 2.0**. Google is widely regarded as the signature company of Web 2.0. Some other companies with Web 2.0 characteristics are YouTube (video sharing), Facebook (social networking), Twitter (microblogging), Groupon (social commerce), Foursquare (mobile check-in), Salesforce (business software offered as online services "in the cloud"), Craigslist (mostly free classified listings), Flickr (photo sharing), Skype (Internet telephony and video calling and conferencing, now owned by Microsoft) and Wikipedia (a free online encyclopedia).

1.6 Web Basics

In this section, we discuss the fundamentals of web-based interactions between a client web browser and a web server. In its simplest form, a *web page* is nothing more than an

HTML (HyperText Markup Language) document (with the extension `.html` or `.htm`) that describes to a web browser the document's content and structure.

Hyperlinks

HTML documents normally contain **hyperlinks**, which, when clicked, load a specified web document. Both images and text may be hyperlinked. When the mouse pointer hovers over a hyperlink, the default arrow pointer changes into a hand with the index finger pointing upward. Often hyperlinked text appears underlined and in a different color from regular text in a web page.

Originally employed as a publishing tool for scientific research, hyperlinks are widely used to reference sources, or sites that have more information on a particular topic. The paths created by hyperlinking create the effect of the "web."

When the user clicks a hyperlink, a **web server** locates the requested web page and sends it to the user's web browser. Similarly, the user can type the *address of a web page* into the browser's *address field* and press *Enter* to view the specified page.

Hyperlinks can reference other web pages, e-mail addresses, files and more. If a hyperlink's URL is in the form `mailto:`*emailAddress*, clicking the link loads your default e-mail program and opens a **message window** addressed to the specified e-mail address. If a hyperlink references a file that the browser is incapable of displaying, the browser prepares to **download** the file, and generally prompts the user for information about how the file should be stored. When a file is downloaded, it's copied onto the user's computer. Programs, documents, images, sound and video files are all examples of downloadable files.

URIs and URLs

URIs (Uniform Resource Identifiers) identify resources on the Internet. URIs that start with `http://` are called *URLs (Uniform Resource Locators)*. Common URLs refer to files, directories or server-side code that performs tasks such as database lookups, Internet searches and business-application processing. If you know the URL of a publicly available resource anywhere on the web, you can enter that URL into a web browser's address field and the browser can access that resource.

Parts of a URL

A URL contains information that directs a browser to the resource that the user wishes to access. Web servers make such resources available to web clients. Popular web servers include Apache's HTTP Server and Microsoft's Internet Information Services (IIS).

Let's examine the components of the URL

```
http://www.deitel.com/books/downloads.html
```

The text `http://` indicates that the HyperText Transfer Protocol (HTTP) should be used to obtain the resource. Next in the URL is the server's fully qualified **hostname** (for example, `www.deitel.com`)—the name of the web-server computer on which the resource resides. This computer is referred to as the **host**, because it houses and maintains resources. The hostname `www.deitel.com` is translated into an **IP (Internet Protocol) address**—a numerical value that uniquely identifies the server on the Internet. An Internet **Domain Name System (DNS) server** maintains a database of hostnames and their corresponding IP addresses and performs the translations automatically.

The remainder of the URL (/books/downloads.html) specifies the resource's location (/books) and name (downloads.html) on the web server. The location could represent an actual directory on the web server's file system. For *security* reasons, however, the location is typically a *virtual directory*. The web server translates the virtual directory into a real location on the server, thus hiding the resource's true location.

Making a Request and Receiving a Response

When given a web page URL, a web browser uses HTTP to request the web page found at that address. Figure 1.8 shows a web browser sending a request to a web server.

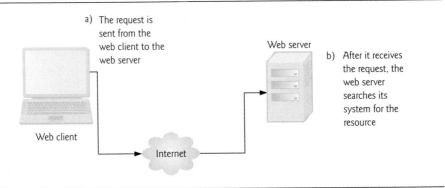

Fig. 1.8 | Client requesting a resource from a web server.

In Fig. 1.8, the web browser sends an HTTP request to the server. The request (in its simplest form) is

```
GET /books/downloads.html HTTP/1.1
```

The word **GET** is an **HTTP method** indicating that the client wishes to obtain a resource from the server. The remainder of the request provides the path name of the resource (e.g., an HTML5 document) and the protocol's name and version number (HTTP/1.1). The client's request also contains some required and optional headers.

Any server that understands HTTP (version 1.1) can translate this request and respond appropriately. Figure 1.9 shows the web server responding to a request.

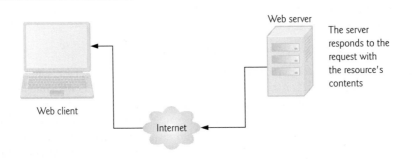

Fig. 1.9 | Client receiving a response from the web server.

The server first sends a line of text that indicates the HTTP version, followed by a numeric code and a phrase describing the status of the transaction. For example,

```
HTTP/1.1 200 OK
```

indicates success, whereas

```
HTTP/1.1 404 Not found
```

informs the client that the web server could not locate the requested resource. A complete list of numeric codes indicating the status of an HTTP transaction can be found at www.w3.org/Protocols/rfc2616/rfc2616-sec10.html.

HTTP Headers

Next, the server sends one or more **HTTP headers**, which provide additional information about the data that will be sent. In this case, the server is sending an HTML5 text document, so one HTTP header for this example would read:

```
Content-type: text/html
```

The information provided in this header specifies the **Multipurpose Internet Mail Extensions (MIME) type** of the content that the server is transmitting to the browser. The MIME standard specifies data formats, which programs can use to interpret data correctly. For example, the MIME type text/plain indicates that the sent information is text that can be displayed directly. Similarly, the MIME type image/jpeg indicates that the content is a JPEG image. When the browser receives this MIME type, it attempts to display the image.

The header or set of headers is followed by a blank line, which indicates to the client browser that the server is finished sending HTTP headers. Finally, the server sends the contents of the requested document (downloads.html). The client-side browser then renders (or displays) the document, which may involve additional HTTP requests to obtain associated CSS and images.

HTTP get and post Requests

The two most common **HTTP request types** (also known as **request methods**) are get and post. A get request typically gets (or retrieves) information from a server, such as an HTML document, an image or search results based on a user-submitted search term. A post request typically posts (or sends) data to a server. Common uses of post requests are to send form data or documents to a server.

An HTTP request often posts data to a **server-side form handler** that processes the data. For example, when a user performs a search or participates in a web-based survey, the web server receives the information specified in the HTML form as part of the request. Get requests and post requests can both be used to send data to a web server, but each request type sends the information differently.

A get request appends data to the URL, e.g., www.google.com/search?q=deitel. In this case search is the name of Google's server-side form handler, q is the name of a variable in Google's search form and deitel is the search term. The ? in the preceding URL separates the **query string** from the rest of the URL in a request. A *name/value* pair is passed to the server with the *name* and the *value* separated by an equals sign (=). If more than one *name/value* pair is submitted, each pair is separated by an ampersand (&). The server uses data passed in a query string to retrieve an appropriate resource from the server. The server then sends a response to the client. A `get` request may be initiated by submitting an HTML form whose `method` attribute is set to `"get"`, or by typing the URL (possibly containing a query string) directly into the browser's address bar. We discuss HTML forms in Chapters 2–3.

A `post` request sends form data as part of the HTTP message, not as part of the URL. A `get` request typically limits the query string (i.e., everything to the right of the ?) to a specific number of characters, so it's often necessary to send large amounts of information using the `post` method. The `post` method is also sometimes preferred because it hides the submitted data from the user by embedding it in an HTTP message. If a form submits several hidden input values along with user-submitted data, the `post` method might generate a URL like `www.searchengine.com/search`. The form data still reaches the server and is processed in a similar fashion to a `get` request, but the user does not see the exact information sent.

> **Software Engineering Observation 1.1**
>
> *The data sent in a `post` request is not part of the URL, and the user can't see the data by default. However, tools are available that expose this data, so you should not assume that the data is secure just because a `post` request is used.*

Client-Side Caching

Browsers often **cache** (save on disk) recently viewed web pages for quick reloading. If there are no changes between the version stored in the cache and the current version on the web, this speeds up your browsing experience. An HTTP response can indicate the length of time for which the content remains "fresh." If this amount of time has not been reached, the browser can avoid another request to the server. If not, the browser loads the document from the cache. Similarly, there's also the "not modified" HTTP response, indicating that the file content has not changed since it was last requested (which is information that's send in the request). Browsers typically do not cache the server's response to a `post` request, because the next `post` might not return the same result. For example, in a survey, many users could visit the same web page and answer a question. The survey results could then be displayed for the user. Each new answer would change the survey results.

1.7 Multitier Application Architecture

Web-based applications are often **multitier applications** (sometimes referred to as *n*-tier applications) that divide functionality into separate **tiers** (i.e., logical groupings of functionality). Although tiers can be located on the same computer, the tiers of web-based applications often reside on separate computers. Figure 1.10 presents the basic structure of a **three-tier web-based application**.

The **bottom tier** (also called the data tier or the information tier) maintains the application's data. This tier typically stores data in a relational database management system (RDBMS). We discuss RDBMSs in Chapter 18. For example, Amazon might have an inventory information database containing product descriptions, prices and quantities in stock. Another database might contain customer information, such as user names, billing addresses and credit card numbers. These may reside on one or more computers, which together comprise the application's data.

The **middle tier** implements business logic, controller logic and presentation logic to control interactions between the application's clients and its data. The middle tier acts as

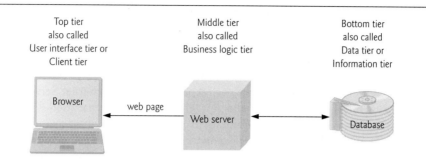

Fig. 1.10 | Three-tier architecture.

an intermediary between data in the information tier and the application's clients. The middle-tier **controller logic** processes client requests (such as requests to view a product catalog) and retrieves data from the database. The middle-tier **presentation logic** then processes data from the information tier and presents the content to the client. Web applications typically present data to clients as HTML documents.

Business logic in the middle tier enforces **business rules** and ensures that data is reliable before the application updates a database or presents data to users. Business rules dictate how clients access data and how applications process data. For example, a business rule in the middle tier of a retail store's web-based application might ensure that all product quantities remain positive. A client request to set a negative quantity in the bottom tier's product information database would be rejected by the middle tier's business logic.

The **top tier**, or client tier, is the application's user interface, which gathers input and displays output. Users interact directly with the application through the user interface, which is typically a web browser or a mobile device. In response to user actions (e.g., clicking a hyperlink), the client tier interacts with the middle tier to make requests and to retrieve data from the information tier. The client tier then displays the data retrieved for the user.

1.8 Client-Side Scripting versus Server-Side Scripting

Client-side scripting with JavaScript can be used to validate user input, to interact with the browser, to enhance web pages, and to add client/server communication between a browser and a web server.

Client-side scripting does have limitations, such as browser dependency; the browser or **scripting host** must support the scripting language and capabilities. Scripts are restricted from arbitrarily accessing the local hardware and file system for security reasons. Another issue is that client-side scripts can be viewed by the client by using the browser's source-viewing capability. Sensitive information, such as passwords or other personally identifiable data, should not be on the client. All client-side data validation should be mirrored on the server. Also, placing certain operations in JavaScript on the client can open web applications to security issues.

Programmers have more flexibility with **server-side scripts**, which often generate custom responses for clients. For example, a client might connect to an airline's web server and request a list of flights from Boston to San Francisco between April 19 and May 5. The server queries the database, dynamically generates an HTML document containing the flight list and sends the document to the client. This technology allows clients to obtain the most current flight information from the database by connecting to an airline's web server.

Server-side scripting languages have a wider range of programmatic capabilities than their client-side equivalents. Server-side scripts also have access to server-side software that extends server functionality—Microsoft web servers use **ISAPI (Internet Server Application Program Interface) extensions** and Apache HTTP Servers use **modules**. Components and modules range from programming-language support to counting the number of web-page hits. We discuss some of these components and modules in subsequent chapters.

1.9 World Wide Web Consortium (W3C)

In October 1994, Tim Berners-Lee founded an organization—the **World Wide Web Consortium (W3C)**—devoted to developing nonproprietary, interoperable technologies for the World Wide Web. One of the W3C's primary goals is to make the web universally *accessible*—regardless of disability, language or culture. The W3C home page (www.w3.org) provides extensive resources on Internet and web technologies.

The W3C is also a standards organization. Web technologies standardized by the W3C are called **Recommendations**. Current and forthcoming W3C Recommendations include the HyperText Markup Language 5 (HTML5), Cascading Style Sheets 3 (CSS3) and the Extensible Markup Language (XML). A recommendation is not an actual software product but a document that specifies a technology's role, syntax rules and so forth.

1.10 Web 2.0: Going Social

In 2003 there was a noticeable shift in how people and businesses were using the web and developing web-based applications. The term **Web 2.0** was coined by **Dale Dougherty** of O'Reilly Media[4] in 2003 to describe this trend. Generally, Web 2.0 companies use the web as a platform to create collaborative, community-based sites (e.g., social networking sites, blogs, wikis).

Web 1.0 versus Web 2.0

Web 1.0 (the state of the web through the 1990s and early 2000s) was focused on a relatively small number of companies and advertisers producing content for users to access (some people called it the "brochure web"). Web 2.0 *involves* the users—not only do they often create content, but they help organize it, share it, remix it, critique it, update it, etc. One way to look at Web 1.0 is as a *lecture*, a small number of professors informing a large audience of students. In comparison, Web 2.0 is a *conversation*, with everyone having the opportunity to speak and share views. Companies that understand Web 2.0 realize that their products and services are conversations as well.

Architecture of Participation

Web 2.0 is providing new opportunities and connecting people and content in unique ways. Web 2.0 embraces an **architecture of participation**—a design that encourages user

---

4. T. O'Reilly, "What is Web 2.0: Design Patterns and Business Models for the Next Generation of Software." September 2005 <http://www.oreillynet.com/pub/a/oreilly/tim/news/2005/09/30/what-is-web-20.html?page=1>.

interaction and community contributions. You, the user, are the most important aspect of Web 2.0—so important, in fact, that in 2006, *TIME* magazine's "Person of the Year" was "you."[5] The article recognized the social phenomenon of Web 2.0—the shift away from a *powerful few* to an *empowered many*. Several popular blogs now compete with traditional media powerhouses, and many Web 2.0 companies are built almost entirely on user-generated content. For websites like Facebook®, Twitter™, YouTube, eBay® and Wikipedia®, users create the content, while the companies provide the platforms on which to enter, manipulate and share the information. These companies *trust their users*—without such trust, users cannot make significant contributions to the sites.

The architecture of participation has influenced software development as well. Opensource software is available for anyone to use and modify with few or no restrictions (we'll say more about open source in Section 1.12). Using **collective intelligence**—the concept that a large diverse group of people will create smart ideas—communities collaborate to develop software that many people believe is better and more robust than proprietary software. Rich Internet Applications (RIAs) are being developed using technologies (such as Ajax, which we discuss throughout the book) that have the look and feel of desktop software, enhancing a user's overall experience.

Search Engines and Social Media

Search engines, including Google™, Microsoft Bing™, and many more, have become essential to sifting through the massive amount of content on the web. Social bookmarking sites such as del.icio.us allow users to share their favorite sites with others. Social media sites such as Digg™ enable the community to decide which news articles are the most significant. The way we find the information on these sites is also changing—people are **tagging** (i.e., labeling) web content by subject or keyword in a way that helps anyone locate information more effectively.

Semantic Web

In the future, computers will learn to understand the meaning of the data on the web—the beginnings of the **Semantic Web** are already appearing. Continual improvements in hardware, software and communications technologies will enable exciting new types of applications.

These topics and more are covered in our online e-book, Dive Into® Web 2.0 (available at `http://www.deitel.com/diveintoweb20/`). The e-book highlights the major characteristics and technologies of Web 2.0, providing examples of popular Web 2.0 companies and Web 2.0 Internet business and monetization models. We discuss user-generated content, blogging, content networks, social networking, location-based services and more. In the subsequent chapters of this book, you'll learn key software technologies for building web-based applications.

Google

In 1996, Stanford computer science Ph.D. candidates Larry Page and Sergey Brin began collaborating on a new search engine. In 1997, they chose the name Google—a play on the mathematical term *googol*, a quantity represented by the number "one" followed by

---

5. L. Grossman, "TIME's Person of the Year: You." *TIME*, December 2006 <http://www.time.com/time/magazine/article/0,9171,1569514,00.html>.

100 "zeros" (or 10^{100})—a staggeringly large number. Google's ability to return extremely accurate search results quickly helped it become the most widely used search engine and one of the most popular websites in the world.

Google continues to be an innovator in search technologies. For example, Google Goggles is a fascinating mobile app (available on Android and iPhone) that allows you to perform a Google search using a photo rather than entering text. You simply take a picture of a landmark, book (covers or barcodes), logo, art or wine bottle label, and Google Goggles scans the photo and returns search results. You can also take a picture of text (for example, a restaurant menu or a sign) and Google Goggles will translate it for you.

Web Services and Mashups

We include in this book a substantial treatment of web services (Chapters 22, 25 and 28) and introduce the applications-development methodology of *mashups*, in which you can rapidly develop powerful and intriguing applications by combining (often free) complementary web services and other forms of information feeds (Fig. 1.11). One of the first mashups was www.housingmaps.com, which combines the real estate listings provided by www.craigslist.org with the mapping capabilities of Google Maps to offer maps that show the locations of apartments for rent in a given area.

Web services source	How it's used
Google Maps	Mapping services
Facebook	Social networking
Foursquare	Mobile check-in
LinkedIn	Social networking for business
YouTube	Video search
Twitter	Microblogging
Groupon	Social commerce
Netflix	Movie rentals
eBay	Internet auctions
Wikipedia	Collaborative encyclopedia
PayPal	Payments
Last.fm	Internet radio
Amazon eCommerce	Shopping for books and more
Salesforce.com	Customer Relationship Management (CRM)
Skype	Internet telephony
Microsoft Bing	Search
Flickr	Photo sharing
Zillow	Real estate pricing
Yahoo Search	Search
WeatherBug	Weather

Fig. 1.11 | Some popular web services that you can use to build web applications (www.programmableweb.com/apis/directory/1?sort=mashups).

Web services, inexpensive computers, abundant high-speed Internet access, open source software and many other elements have inspired new, exciting, *lightweight business models* that people can launch with only a small investment. Some types of websites with rich and robust functionality that might have required hundreds of thousands or even millions of dollars to build in the 1990s can now be built for nominal sums.

Ajax

Ajax is one of the premier Web 2.0 software technologies (Fig. 1.12). Ajax helps Internet-based applications perform like desktop applications—a difficult task, given that such applications suffer transmission delays as data is shuttled back and forth between your computer and servers on the Internet.

Chapter	Ajax coverage
Chapter 1	This chapter introduces Ajax.
Chapters 2–14	These chapters cover several key technologies used in Ajax web applications, including HTML5, CSS3, JavaScript, JavaScript event handling, the Document Object Model (DOM) and dynamic manipulation of an HTML5 document—known as dynamic HTML.
Chapter 15	Web applications use XML extensively to represent structured data. This chapter introduces XML, XML-related technologies and key JavaScript capabilities for loading and manipulating XML documents programmatically.
Chapter 16	This chapter uses the technologies presented in Chapters 2–15 to build Ajax-enabled web applications. We use both XML and JSON (JavaScript Object Notation) to send/receive data between the client and the server. The chapter begins by building basic Ajax applications using JavaScript and the browser's XMLHttpRequest object. We then build an Ajax application using the jQuery JavaScript libraries.
Chapters 21, 24 and 27	These chapters use Ajax in Microsoft's ASP.NET with C# and in ASP.NET with Visual Basic, and in JavaServer Faces (JSF), respectively, to implement Ajax applications that use Ajax for form validation and partial-page updates.

Fig. 1.12 | Ajax coverage in *Internet & World Wide Web How to Program, 5/e.*

Social Applications

Over the last several years, there's been a tremendous increase in the number of social applications on the web. Even though the computer industry is mature, these sites were still able to become phenomenally successful in a relatively short period. Figure 1.13 discusses a few of the social applications that are making an impact.

Company	Description
Facebook	Facebook was launched in 2004 and is already worth an estimated $100 billion. By January 2011, Facebook was the most active site on the Internet with more than 750 million users who were spending 700 billion minutes on Facebook per month (www.facebook.com/press/info.php?statistics). At its current growth rate (about 5% per month), Facebook will reach one billion users in 2012, out of two billion Internet users! The activity on the site makes it extremely attractive for application developers. Each day, over 20 million applications are installed by Facebook users (www.facebook.com/press/info.php?statistics).
Twitter	Twitter (founded in 2006) has revolutionized *microblogging*. Users post tweets—messages up to 140 characters long. Approximately 140 million tweets are posted per day. You can follow the tweets of friends, celebrities, businesses, government representatives (including Barack Obama, who has 10 million followers), and so on, or you can follow tweets by subject to track news, trends and more. At the time of this writing, Lady Gaga had the most followers (over 13 million). Twitter has become the point of origin for many breaking news stories worldwide.
Groupon	Groupon, a *social commerce* site, was launched in 2008. By August 2011 the company was valued as high as $25 billion, making it the fastest growing company ever! Groupon offers daily deals in each market for restaurants, retailers, services, attractions and more. Deals are activated only after a minimum number of people sign up to buy the product or service. If you sign up for a deal and it has yet to meet the minimum, you might be inclined to tell others about the deal via e-mail, Facebook, Twitter, etc. One of the most successful national Groupon deals to date was a certificate for $50 worth of merchandise from a major retailer for $25. More than 620,000 vouchers were sold in one day (www.huffingtonpost.com/2011/06/30/the-most-successful-group_n_887711.html)!
Foursquare	Foursquare, launched in 2009, is a mobile *check-in* application that allows you to notify your friends of your whereabouts. You can download the app to your smartphone and link it to your Facebook and Twitter accounts so your friends can follow you from multiple platforms. If you do not have a smartphone, you can check in by text message. Foursquare uses GPS to determine your location. Businesses use Foursquare to send offers to users in the area. Launched in March 2009, Foursquare already has over 10 million users worldwide (foursquare.com/about).
Skype	Skype (founded in 2003) allows you to make mostly free voice and video calls over the Internet using a technology called *VoIP (Voice over IP;* IP stands for "Internet Protocol"*).* The company was recently sold to Microsoft for $8.5 billion.

Fig. 1.13 | Social applications. (Part 1 of 2.)

Company	Description
YouTube	YouTube is a video-sharing site that was founded in 2005. Within one year, the company was purchased by Google for $1.65 billion. YouTube now accounts for 8.2% of all Internet traffic (www.engadget.com/2011/05/17/study-finds-netflix-is-the-largest-source-of-internet-traffic-in/). Within one week of the release of Apple's iPhone 3GS—the first iPhone model to offer video—mobile uploads to YouTube grew 400% (www.hypebot.com/hypebot/2009/06/youtube-reports-1700-jump-in-mobile-video.html).

Fig. 1.13 | Social applications. (Part 2 of 2.)

1.11 Data Hierarchy

Data items processed by computers form a **data hierarchy** that becomes larger and more complex in structure as we progress from bits to characters to fields, and so on. Figure 1.14 illustrates a portion of the data hierarchy. Figure 1.15 summarizes the data hierarchy's levels.

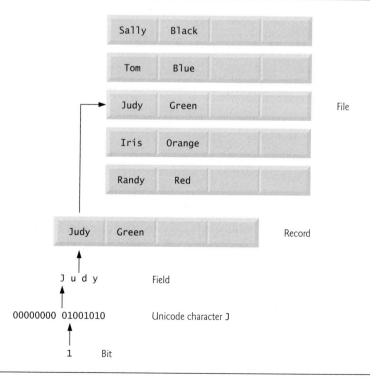

Fig. 1.14 | Data hierarchy.

Level	Description
Bits	The smallest data item in a computer can assume the value 0 or the value 1. Such a data item is called a **bit** (short for "binary digit"—a digit that can assume one of two values). It's remarkable that the impressive functions performed by computers involve only the simplest manipulations of 0s and 1s— *examining a bit's value*, *setting a bit's value* and *reversing a bit's value* (from 1 to 0 or from 0 to 1).
Characters	It's tedious for people to work with data in the low-level form of bits. Instead, they prefer to work with *decimal digits* (0–9), *letters* (A–Z and a–z), and *special symbols* (e.g., $, @, %, &, *, (,), –, +, ", :, ? and /). Digits, letters and special symbols are known as **characters**. The computer's **character set** is the set of all the characters used to write programs and represent data items. Computers process only 1s and 0s, so a computer's character set represents every character as a pattern of 1s and 0s. Java uses **Unicode**® characters that are composed of two **bytes**, each composed of eight bits. Unicode contains characters for many of the world's languages. See Appendix F for more information on Unicode. See Appendix D for more information on the **ASCII (American Standard Code for Information Interchange**) character set—the popular subset of Unicode that represents uppercase and lowercase letters, digits and some common special characters.
Fields	Just as characters are composed of bits, **fields** are composed of characters or bytes. A field is a group of characters or bytes that conveys meaning. For example, a field consisting of uppercase and lowercase letters could be used to represent a person's name, and a field consisting of decimal digits could represent a person's age.
Records	Several related fields can be used to compose a **record** (implemented as a `class` in Java). In a payroll system, for example, the record for an employee might consist of the following fields (possible types for these fields are shown in parentheses): • Employee identification number (a whole number) • Name (a string of characters) • Address (a string of characters) • Hourly pay rate (a number with a decimal point) • Year-to-date earnings (a number with a decimal point) • Amount of taxes withheld (a number with a decimal point) Thus, a record is a group of related fields. In the preceding example, all the fields belong to the same employee. A company might have many employees and a payroll record for each one.
Files	A **file** is a group of related records. [*Note:* More generally, a file contains arbitrary data in arbitrary formats. In some operating systems, a file is viewed simply as a *sequence of bytes*—any organization of the bytes in a file, such as organizing the data into records, is a view created by the application programmer.] It's not unusual for an organization to have many files, some containing billions, or even trillions, of characters of information.

Fig. 1.15 | Levels of the data hierarchy. (Part 1 of 2.)

Level	Description
Database	A **database** is an electronic collection of data that's organized for easy access and manipulation. There are various database models. In this book, we introduce relational databases in which data is stored in simple *tables*. A table includes *records* and *fields*. For example, a table of students might include first name, last name, major, year, student ID number and grade point average. The data for each student is a record, and the individual pieces of information in each record are the fields. You can search, sort and manipulate the data based on its relationship to multiple tables or databases. For example, a university might use data from the student database in combination with databases of courses, on-campus housing, meal plans, etc. We discuss databases in Chapter 18 and use them in the server-side programming chapters.

Fig. 1.15 | Levels of the data hierarchy. (Part 2 of 2.)

1.12 Operating Systems

Operating systems are software systems that make using computers more convenient for users, application developers and system administrators. Operating systems provide services that allow each application to execute safely, efficiently and *concurrently* (i.e., in parallel) with other applications. The software that contains the core components of the operating system is called the **kernel**. Popular desktop operating systems include Linux, Windows 7 and Mac OS X. Popular mobile operating systems used in smartphones and tablets include Google's Android, Apple's iOS (for iPhone, iPad and iPod Touch devices), BlackBerry OS and Windows Phone 7.

1.12.1 Desktop and Notebook Operating Systems

In this section we discuss two of the popular desktop operating systems—the proprietary Windows operating system and the open source Linux operating system.

Windows—A Proprietary Operating System
In the mid-1980s, Microsoft developed the **Windows operating system**, consisting of a graphical user interface built on top of DOS—an enormously popular personal-computer operating system of the time that users interacted with by *typing* commands. Windows borrowed from many concepts (such as icons, menus and windows) developed by Xerox PARC and popularized by early Apple Macintosh operating systems. Windows 7 is Microsoft's latest operating system—its features include enhancements to the user interface, faster startup times, further refinement of security features, touch-screen and multitouch support, and more. Windows is a *proprietary* operating system—it's controlled by Microsoft exclusively. Windows is by far the world's most widely used operating system.

Linux—An Open-Source Operating System
The Linux operating system is perhaps the greatest success of the *open-source* movement. **Open-source software** departs from the *proprietary* software development style that dominated software's early years. With open-source development, individuals and companies *contribute* their efforts in developing, maintaining and evolving software in exchange for

the right to use that software for their own purposes, typically at no charge. Open-source code is often scrutinized by a much larger audience than proprietary software, so errors often get removed faster. Open source also encourages more innovation. Enterprise systems companies, such as IBM, Oracle and many others, have made significant investments in Linux open-source development.

Some key organizations in the open-source community are the Eclipse Foundation (the Eclipse Integrated Development Environment helps programmers conveniently develop software), the Mozilla Foundation (creators of the Firefox web browser), the Apache Software Foundation (creators of the Apache web server used to develop web-based applications) and SourceForge (which provides the tools for managing open-source projects—it has over 306,000 of them under development). Rapid improvements to computing and communications, decreasing costs and open-source software have made it much easier and more economical to create a software-based business now than just a decade ago. A great example is Facebook, which was launched from a college dorm room and built with open-source software.[6]

The **Linux** kernel is the core of the most popular open-source, freely distributed, full-featured operating system. It's developed by a loosely organized team of volunteers and is popular in servers, personal computers and embedded systems. Unlike that of proprietary operating systems like Microsoft's Windows and Apple's Mac OS X, Linux source code (the program code) is available to the public for examination and modification and is free to download and install. As a result, Linux users benefit from a community of developers actively debugging and improving the kernel, an absence of licensing fees and restrictions, and the ability to completely customize the operating system to meet specific needs.

A variety of issues—such as Microsoft's market power, the small number of user-friendly Linux applications and the diversity of Linux distributions, such as Red Hat Linux, Ubuntu Linux and many others—have prevented widespread Linux use on desktop computers. But Linux has become extremely popular on servers and in embedded systems, such as Google's Android-based smartphones.

1.12.2 Mobile Operating Systems

Two of the most popular mobile operating systems are Apple's iOS and Google's Android.

iOS for iPhone®, iPad® and iPod Touch®
Apple, founded in 1976 by Steve Jobs and Steve Wozniak, quickly became a leader in personal computing. In 1979, Jobs and several Apple employees visited Xerox PARC (Palo Alto Research Center) to learn about Xerox's desktop computer that featured a graphical user interface (GUI). That GUI served as the inspiration for the Apple Lisa personal computer (designed for business customers) and, more notably, the Apple Macintosh, launched with much fanfare in a memorable Super Bowl ad in 1984. Steve Jobs left Apple in 1985 and founded NeXT Inc.

The Objective-C programming language, created by Brad Cox and Tom Love at Stepstone in the early 1980s, added capabilities for object-oriented programming (OOP) to the C programming language. In 1988, NeXT licensed Objective-C from StepStone and developed an Objective-C compiler and libraries which were used as the platform for the NeXTSTEP operating system's user interface and Interface Builder—used to con-

---

6. developers.facebook.com/opensource/.

struct graphical user interfaces. Apple's Mac OS X operating system is a descendant of NeXTSTEP. Apple's proprietary iPhone operating system, **iOS**, is derived from Apple's Mac OS X and is used in the iPhone, iPad and iPod Touch devices.

You can download apps directly onto your iPhone, iPad or iPod device through the App Store. There are over 425,000 apps in the App Store.

Google's Android

Android—the fastest growing mobile and smartphone operating system—is based on the Linux kernel and Java. Experienced Java programmers can quickly dive into Android development. One benefit of developing Android apps is the openness of the platform. The operating system is open source and free.

The Android operating system was developed by Android, Inc., which was acquired by Google in 2005. In 2007, the Open Handset Alliance™—a consortium of 34 companies initially and 84 by 2011—was formed to continue developing Android. As of June 2011, more than 500,000 Android smartphones were being activated each day![7] Android smartphones are now outselling iPhones in the United States.[8] The Android operating system is used in numerous smartphones (such as the Motorola Droid, HTC EVO™ 4G, Samsung Vibrant™ and many more), e-reader devices (such as the Barnes and Noble Nook™), tablet computers (such as the Dell Streak and the Samsung Galaxy Tab), in-store touch-screen kiosks, cars, robots, multimedia players and more.

You can download apps directly onto your Android device through Android Market and other app marketplaces. As of August 2011, there were over 250,000 apps in Google's Android Market.

1.13 Types of Programming Languages

Programmers write instructions in various programming languages, some directly understandable by computers and others requiring intermediate *translation* steps. Any computer can directly understand only its own **machine language**, defined by its hardware design. Machine languages generally consist of numbers (ultimately reduced to 1s and 0s). Such languages are cumbersome for humans.

Programming in machine language—the numbers that computers could directly understand—was simply too slow and tedious for most programmers. Instead, they began using Englishlike abbreviations to represent elementary operations. These abbreviations formed the basis of **assembly languages**. *Translator programs* called **assemblers** were developed to convert assembly-language programs to machine language. Although assembly-language code is clearer to humans, it's incomprehensible to computers until translated to machine language.

To speed the programming process even further, **high-level languages** were developed in which single statements could be written to accomplish substantial tasks. High-level languages allow you to write instructions that look almost like everyday English and contain commonly used mathematical expressions. Translator programs called **compilers** convert high-level language programs into machine language.

---

7. news.cnet.com/8301-13506_3-20074956-17/google-500000-android-devices-activated-each-day/.
8. www.pcworld.com/article/196035/android_outsells_the_iphone_no_big_surprise.html.

The process of compiling a large high-level language program into machine language can take a considerable amount of computer time. **Interpreter** programs were developed to execute high-level language programs directly, although more slowly than compiled programs. In this book we study several key programming languages, including JavaScript and PHP—each of these **scripting languages** is processed by interpreters. Figure 1.16 introduces a number of popular programming languages.

Performance Tip 1.1

Interpreters have an advantage over compilers in Internet scripting. An interpreted program can begin executing as soon as it's downloaded to the client's machine, without needing to be compiled before it can execute. On the downside, interpreted scripts generally run slower than compiled code.

Programming language	Description
C	C was implemented in 1972 by Dennis Ritchie at Bell Laboratories. It initially became widely known as the UNIX operating system's development language. Today, most of the code for general-purpose operating systems is written in C or C++.
C++	C++, an extension of C, was developed by Bjarne Stroustrup in the early 1980s at Bell Laboratories. C++ provides a number of features that "spruce up" the C language, but more important, it provides capabilities for object-oriented programming.
Objective-C	Objective-C is an object-oriented language based on C. It was developed in the early 1980s and later acquired by NeXT, which in turn was acquired by Apple. It has become the key programming language for the Mac OS X operating system and all iOS-based devices (such as iPods, iPhones and iPads).
Visual Basic	Microsoft's Visual Basic language (based on the Basic language developed at Dartmouth College in the 1960s) was introduced in the early 1990s to simplify Microsoft Windows applications development. Its latest versions support object-oriented programming.
Visual C#	Microsoft's three primary object-oriented programming languages are Visual Basic, Visual C++ (based on C++) and C# (based on C++ and Java, and developed for integrating the Internet and the web into computer applications).
Java	Sun Microsystems in 1991 funded an internal corporate research project led by James Gosling, which resulted in the C++-based object-oriented programming language called Java. A key goal of Java is to enable the writing of programs that will run on a great variety of computer systems and computer-controlled devices. This is sometimes called "write once, run anywhere." Java is used to develop large-scale enterprise applications, to enhance the functionality of web servers (the computers that provide the content we see in our web browsers), to provide applications for consumer devices (smartphones, television set-top boxes and more) and for many other purposes.

Fig. 1.16 | Popular programming languages. (Part 1 of 2.)

Programming language	Description
PHP	PHP—an object-oriented, "open-source" (see Section 1.12) "scripting" language supported by a community of users and developers—is used by numerous websites including Wikipedia and Facebook. PHP is *platform independent*—implementations exist for all major UNIX, Linux, Mac and Windows operating systems. PHP also supports many databases, including MySQL. Two other popular languages similar in concept to PHP are Perl and Python. The term "LAMP" describes four key technologies for building open-source software—Linux (operating system), Apache (web server), MySQL (database) and PHP or Perl or Python (server-side scripting languages).
Python	Python, another object-oriented scripting language, was released publicly in 1991. Developed by Guido van Rossum of the National Research Institute for Mathematics and Computer Science in Amsterdam (CWI), Python draws heavily from Modula-3—a systems-programming language. Python is "extensible"—it can be extended through classes and programming interfaces.
JavaScript	JavaScript—developed by Brendan Eich at Netscape—is the most widely used scripting language. It's primarily used to add programmability to web pages—for example, animations and interactivity with the user. It's provided with all major web browsers.
Ruby on Rails	Ruby—created in the mid-1990s by Yukihiro Matsumoto—is an open-source, object-oriented programming language with a simple syntax that's similar to Python. Ruby on Rails combines the scripting language Ruby with the Rails web-application framework developed by 37Signals. Their book, *Getting Real* (gettingreal.37signals.com/toc.php), is a must read for web developers. Many Ruby on Rails developers have reported productivity gains over other languages when developing database-intensive web applications. Ruby on Rails was used to build Twitter's user interface.
Scala	Scala (www.scala-lang.org/node/273)—short for "scalable language"—was designed by Martin Odersky, a professor at École Polytechnique Fédérale de Lausanne (EPFL) in Switzerland. Released in 2003, Scala uses both the *object-oriented* and *functional programming* paradigms and is designed to integrate with Java. Programming in Scala can significantly reduce the amount of code in your applications. Twitter and Foursquare use Scala.

Fig. 1.16 | Popular programming languages. (Part 2 of 2.)

1.14 Object Technology

Building software quickly, correctly and economically remains an elusive goal at a time when demands for new and more powerful software are soaring. *Objects*, or more precisely the *classes* objects come from, are essentially *reusable* software components. There are date objects, time objects, audio objects, video objects, automobile objects, people objects, etc. Almost any *noun* can be reasonably represented as a software object in terms of *attributes* (e.g., name, color and size) and *behaviors* (e.g., calculating, moving and communicating).

Software developers are discovering that using a modular, object-oriented design and implementation approach can make software-development groups much more productive than was possible with earlier techniques—object-oriented programs are often easier to understand, correct and modify.

The Automobile as an Object

Let's begin with a simple analogy. Suppose you want to *drive a car and make it go faster by pressing its accelerator pedal.* What must happen before you can do this? Well, before you can drive a car, someone has to *design* it. A car typically begins as engineering drawings, similar to the *blueprints* that describe the design of a house. These drawings include the design for an accelerator pedal. The pedal *hides* from the driver the complex mechanisms that actually make the car go faster, just as the brake pedal hides the mechanisms that slow the car, and the steering wheel *hides* the mechanisms that turn the car. This enables people with little or no knowledge of how engines, braking and steering mechanisms work to drive a car easily.

Before you can drive a car, it must be *built* from the engineering drawings that describe it. A completed car has an *actual* accelerator pedal to make the car go faster, but even that's not enough—the car won't accelerate on its own (hopefully!), so the driver must *press* the pedal to accelerate the car.

Methods and Classes

Let's use our car example to introduce some key object-oriented programming concepts. Performing a task in a program requires a **method**. The method houses the program statements that actually perform its tasks. It hides these statements from its user, just as a car's accelerator pedal hides from the driver the mechanisms of making the car go faster. In object-oriented programming languages, we create a program unit called a **class** to house the set of methods that perform the class's tasks. For example, a class that represents a bank account might contain one method to *deposit* money to an account, another to *withdraw* money from an account and a third to *inquire* what the account's current balance is. A class is similar in concept to a car's engineering drawings, which house the design of an accelerator pedal, steering wheel, and so on.

Instantiation

Just as someone has to *build a car* from its engineering drawings before you can actually drive a car, you must *build an object* from a class before a program can perform the tasks that the class's methods define. The process of doing this is called *instantiation.* An object is then referred to as an **instance** of its class.

Reuse

Just as a car's engineering drawings can be *reused* many times to build many cars, you can *reuse* a class many times to build many objects. Reuse of existing classes when building new classes and programs saves time and effort. Reuse also helps you build more reliable and effective systems, because existing classes and components often have gone through extensive *testing, debugging* and *performance tuning.* Just as the notion of *interchangeable parts* was crucial to the Industrial Revolution, reusable classes are crucial to the software revolution that has been spurred by object technology.

Software Engineering Observation 1.2

Use a building-block approach to creating your programs. Avoid reinventing the wheel—use existing pieces wherever possible. This software reuse is a key benefit of object-oriented programming.

Messages and Method Calls

When you drive a car, pressing its gas pedal sends a *message* to the car to perform a task—that is, to go faster. Similarly, you *send messages to an object*. Each message is implemented as a **method call** that tells a method of the object to perform its task. For example, a program might call a particular bank-account object's *deposit* method to increase the account's balance.

Attributes and Instance Variables

A car, besides having capabilities to accomplish tasks, also has *attributes*, such as its color, its number of doors, the amount of gas in its tank, its current speed and its record of total miles driven (i.e., its odometer reading). Like its capabilities, the car's attributes are represented as part of its design in its engineering diagrams (which, for example, include an odometer and a fuel gauge). As you drive an actual car, these attributes are carried along with the car. Every car maintains its *own* attributes. For example, each car knows how much gas is in its own gas tank, but *not* how much is in the tanks of *other* cars.

An object, similarly, has attributes that it carries along as it's used in a program. These attributes are specified as part of the object's class. For example, a bank-account object has a *balance attribute* that represents the amount of money in the account. Each bank-account object knows the balance in the account it represents, but *not* the balances of the *other* accounts in the bank. Attributes are specified by the class's **instance variables**.

Encapsulation

Classes **encapsulate** (i.e., wrap) attributes and methods into objects—an object's attributes and methods are intimately related. Objects may communicate with one another, but normally they're not allowed to know how other objects are implemented—implementation details are *hidden* within the objects themselves. This **information hiding** is crucial to good software engineering.

Inheritance

A new class of objects can be created quickly and conveniently by **inheritance**—the new class absorbs the characteristics of an existing class, possibly customizing them and adding unique characteristics of its own. In our car analogy, an object of class "convertible" certainly *is an* object of the more *general* class "automobile," but more *specifically*, the roof can be raised or lowered.

1.15 Keeping Up-to-Date with Information Technologies

This completes our introduction to the Internet and the web. As you work through the book, if you have a question, send an e-mail to `deitel@deitel.com` and we'll get back to you promptly. We hope you enjoy using *Internet and World Wide Web How to Program, 5/e*. Figure 1.17 lists key technical and business publications that will help you stay up-to-date with the latest news and trends in computer, Internet and web technology. Enjoy!

Publication	URL
ACM TechNews	technews.acm.org/
ACM Transactions on Accessible Computing	www.is.umbc.edu/taccess/index.html
ACM Transactions on Internet Technology	toit.acm.org/
Bloomberg BusinessWeek	www.businessweek.com
CNET	news.cnet.com
Communications of the ACM	cacm.acm.org/
Computer World	www.computerworld.com
Engadget	www.engadget.com
eWeek	www.eweek.com
Fast Company	www.fastcompany.com/
Fortune	money.cnn.com/magazines/fortune/
IEEE Computer	www.computer.org/portal/web/computer
IEEE Internet Computing	www.computer.org/portal/web/internet/home
InfoWorld	www.infoworld.com
Mashable	mashable.com
PCWorld	www.pcworld.com
SD Times	www.sdtimes.com
Slashdot	slashdot.org/
Smarter Technology	www.smartertechnology.com
Technology Review	technologyreview.com
Techcrunch	techcrunch.com
Wired	www.wired.com

Fig. 1.17 | Technical and business publications.

Self-Review Exercises

1.1 Fill in the blanks in each of the following:
   a) The company that popularized personal computing was _____.
   b) Computers process data under the control of sets of instructions called computer _____.
   c) _____ is a type of computer language that uses Englishlike abbreviations for machine-language instructions.
   d) _____ languages are most convenient to the programmer for writing programs quickly and easily.
   e) The only language a computer can directly understand is that computer's _____.
   f) The programs that translate high-level language programs into machine language are called _____.
   g) _____, or labeling content, is another key part of the collaborative theme of Web 2.0.

h) With _____ development, individuals and companies contribute their efforts in developing, maintaining and evolving software in exchange for the right to use that software for their own purposes, typically at no charge.

i) The _____ was the predecessor to the Internet.

j) The information-carrying capacity of a communications medium like the Internet is called _____.

k) The acronym TCP/IP stands for _____.

1.2 Fill in the blanks in each of the following statements.

a) The protocol for communicating over the ARPANET is known as _____ .

b) When the user clicks a hyperlink, a _____ locates the requested web page and sends it to the user's web browser.

c) The Linux operating system is perhaps the greatest success of the _____ movement.

d) Several related fields can be used to compose a _____ .

1.3 Fill in the blanks in each of the following statements (based on Section 1.14):

a) Objects, or more precisely the classes objects come from, are essentially _____ software components, which have both attributes and behaviors.

b) The _____ houses the program statements that actually perform its tasks.

c) After instantiation, an object is then referred to as a(n) _____ of its class.

d) Each message is implemented as a(n) _____ that tells a method of the object to perform its task.

e) _____ of existing classes when building new classes and programs saves time and effort.

1.4 State whether each of the following is *true* or *false*. If the statement is *false*, explain why.

a) HTML5 (HyperText Markup Language 5) is a high-level language designed to specify the content and structure of web pages in a portable manner.

b) Keeping page styling together with the page content and structure enables you to easily change the look and feel of the pages on an entire website, or a portion of a website.

c) A web server maintains a database of hostnames and their corresponding IP addresses, and performs the translations automatically.

1.5 Fill in the blanks in each of the following statements

a) ARPANET operated with a technique called _____, in which digital data was sent in small bundles called packets.

b) Each computer on the Internet has a unique _____.

c) Bit is the short form for _____.

d) Foursquare is a mobile _____ application that allows you to notify your friends of your whereabouts.

e) _____ language is called "write once, run anywhere."

f) One of the W3C's primary goals is to make the web universally _____.

Answers to Self-Review Exercises

1.1 a) Apple. b) programs. c) Assembly language. d) High-level. e) machine language. f) compilers. g) Tagging. h) open-source. i) ARPANET. j) bandwidth. k) Transmission Control Protocol/Internet Protocol.

1.2 a) Transmission Control Protocol. b) web server. c) open-source. d) record.

1.3 a) reusable. b) method. c) instance. d) method call. e) Reuse.

1.4 a) False. HTML is a markup language. b) False. By separating page styling from page content and structure, you can change the look and feel of the pages on an entire website, or a portion of a website, simply by swapping out one style sheet for another. c) False. A Domain Name System (DNS) server maintains a database of hostnames and their corresponding IP addresses, and performs the translations automatically.

1.5 a) packet switching. b) IP address. c) binary digit. d) check-in. e) Java. f) accessible.

Exercises

1.6 Fill in the blanks in each of the following statements:
  a) The process of instructing the computer to solve a problem is called _____.
  b) What type of computer language uses Englishlike abbreviations for machine-language instructions? _____.
  c) The level of computer language at which it's most convenient for you to write programs quickly and easily is _____.
  d) The only language that a computer directly understands is called that computer's _____.
  e) Web 2.0 embraces an _____—a design that encourages user interaction and community contributions.
  f) _____ is the concept that a large, diverse group of people will create smart ideas.

1.7 Fill in the blanks in each of the following statements:
  a) The _____ standard specifies data formats, which programs can use to interpret data correctly.
  b) A(n) _____ request often posts data to a server-side form handler that processes the data.
  c) Twitter (founded in 2006) has revolutionized _____.
  d) _____ in the middle tier enforces business rules and ensures that data is reliable before the application updates a database or presents data to users.

1.8 State whether each of the following is *true* or *false*. If the statement is *false*, explain why.
  a) PHP is an object-oriented, "open-source" "scripting" language supported by a community of users and developers and is used by numerous websites including Wikipedia and Facebook.
  b) Classes encapsulate (i.e., wrap) attributes and methods into objects.
  c) Apple's Mac OS X operating system is a descendant of Android.
  d) Ajax is one of the premier Web 1.0 software technologies.

1.9 Fill in the blanks in each of the following statements:
  a) _____ is the next-generation Internet Protocol that features built-in security and a new addressing scheme, significantly expanding the number of addresses available.
  b) HTML documents normally contain _____, which, when clicked, load a specified web document.
  c) A _____ contains information that directs a browser to the resource that the user wishes to access; _____ make such resources available to web clients.
  d) The two most common HTTP request types are _____ and _____.

e) Web-based applications are multitier applications. The _____ (also called the data tier or the information tier) maintains the application's data and typically stores data in a relational database management system. The _____ implements business logic, controller logic and presentation logic to control interactions between the application's clients and its data. The _____, or client tier, is the application's user interface, which gathers input and displays output.

f) _____, the fastest growing mobile and smartphone operating system. is based on the Linux kernel and Java.

1.10 What is the relationship between WWW and HTTP?

1.11 Describe the difference between HTTP *get* and *post* requests.

1.12 *(Internet in Industry and Research)* Fig. 1.5 provides some examples of desktop browsers and mobile browsers which are being used in industry and research. Find three additional examples of both browsers, and describe how each is used in the Internet and the web.

1.13 *(Programming Languages)* Describe three major types of programming languages.

1.14 *(Social Applications)* In Fig. 1.13 we listed several social applications that can be used in social interaction. Using two different social applications—either from the table or that you find online—describe a type of social application that you would like to create.

1.15 *(Internet Negatives)* There are numerous benefits of surfing the Internet and the web using mobile phones; however there are several downsides as well, such as security issues and speed. Research some of these negative aspects. List five problems and describe what could possibly be done to help solve each.

1.16 *(Web Services and Mashups)* In this chapter, we mentioned a few popular web services and mashups including Google Maps, Foursquare, LinkedIn, and YouTube. Identify another web service and mashup, and describe its application.

1.17 *(Watch as an Object)* You're probably wearing on your wrist one of the world's most common types of objects—a watch. Discuss how each of the following terms and concepts applies to the notion of a watch: object, attributes, behaviors, class, inheritance (consider, for example, an alarm clock), abstraction, modeling, messages, encapsulation, interface and information hiding.

1.18 *(Authentication)* You are receiving a lot of spam in your email account. The sources of the emails are not known. How you can minimize the spam email in your account? Discuss the issues.

1.19 *(Programmer Responsibility and Liability)* As a programmer in industry, you may develop software that could affect people's social sentiments. Suppose the help section of a software application in one of your programs contains a particular statement that could hurt the sentiments of a particular religious community. Discuss the issues.

1.20 *(Internet Addiction Disorder)* Internet addiction disorder (IAD) is a psychological disorder caused by excessive use of the Internet. Researchers have found that excessive Internet use can produce morphological changes in the structure of the human brain. Use the Internet to investigate the prevention and correction of the above problem and discuss the issues it raises.

1.21 *(Making a Difference Projects)* The following is a list of just a few worldwide organizations that are working to make a difference. Visit these sites and our Making a Difference Resource Center at www.deitel.com/makingadifference. Prepare a top 10 list of programming projects that you think could indeed "make a difference."

• www.imaginecup.com/
  The *Microsoft Image Cup* is a global competition in which students use technology to try to solve some of the world's most difficult problems, such as environmental sustainability, ending hun-

ger, emergency response, literacy and combating HIV/AIDS. Visit www.imaginecup.com/about for more information about the competition and to learn about the projects developed by previous winners. You can also find several project ideas submitted by worldwide charitable organizations at www.imaginecup.com/students/imagine-cup-solve-this. For additional ideas for programming projects that can make a difference, search the web for "making a difference" and visit the following websites:

- www.un.org/millenniumgoals
  The United Nations Millennium Project seeks solutions to major worldwide issues such as environmental sustainability, gender equality, child and maternal health, universal education and more.

- www.ibm.com/smarterplanet/
  The IBM® Smarter Planet website discusses how IBM is using technology to solve issues related to business, cloud computing, education, sustainability and more.

- www.gatesfoundation.org/Pages/home.aspx
  The Bill and Melinda Gates Foundation provides grants to organizations that work to alleviate hunger, poverty and disease in developing countries. In the United States, the foundation focusses on improving public education, particularly for people with few resources.

- www.nethope.org/
  NetHope is a collaboration of humanitarian organizations worldwide working to solve technology problems such as connectivity, emergency response and more.

- www.rainforestfoundation.org/home
  The Rainforest Foundation works to preserve rainforests and to protect the rights of the indigenous people who call the rainforests home. The site includes a list of things you can do to help.

- www.undp.org/
  The United Nations Development Programme (UNDP) seeks solutions to global challenges such as crisis prevention and recovery, energy and the environment and democratic governance.

- www.unido.org
  The United Nations Industrial Development Organization (UNIDO) seeks to reduce poverty, give developing countries the opportunity to participate in global trade, and promote energy efficiency and sustainability.

- www.usaid.gov/
  USAID promotes global democracy, health, economic growth, conflict prevention, humanitarian aid and more.

- www.toyota.com/ideas-for-good/
  Toyota's Ideas for Good website describes several Toyota technologies that are making a difference—including their Advanced Parking Guidance System, Hybrid Synergy Drive®, Solar Powered Ventilation System, T.H.U.M.S. (Total Human Model for Safety) and Touch Tracer Display. You can participate in the Ideas for Good challenge by submitting a short essay or video describing how these technologies can be used for other good purposes.

Introduction to HTML5:
Part 1

2

Objectives

In this chapter you'll:

- Understand important components of HTML5 documents.

- Use HTML5 to create web pages.

- Add images to web pages.

- Create and use hyperlinks to help users navigate web pages.

- Mark up lists of information.

- Create tables with rows and columns of data.

- Create and use forms to get user input.

2.1 Introduction

This chapter begins unlocking the power of web-based application development with HTML5. Unlike *programming languages*, such as C, C++, C#, Java and Visual Basic, HTML5 is a **markup language** that specifies the *structure* and *content* of documents that are displayed in web browsers.

We introduce some basics, then cover more sophisticated HTML5 techniques such as:

- **tables**, which are particularly useful for structuring information from **databases** (i.e., software that stores structured sets of data)

- **forms** for collecting information from web-page visitors

- **internal linking** for easier page navigation

- **meta** elements for specifying information about a document

In Chapter 3, we introduce many new features in HTML5. In Chapter 4, we discuss CSS3, a technology for specifying how web pages look.

2.2 Editing HTML5

We'll create **HTML5 documents** by typing HTML5 markup text in a *text editor* (such as Notepad, TextEdit, vi, emacs) and saving it with the .html or .htm filename extension.

Computers called *web servers* store HTML5 documents. *Clients* (such as web browsers running on your local computer or smartphone) request specific **resources** such as HTML5 documents from web servers. For example, typing www.deitel.com/books/downloads.html into a web browser's address field requests the file downloads.html from the books directory on the web server running at www.deitel.com. We discuss web servers in Chapter 17. For now, you'll simply place the HTML5 documents on your computer and *render* (i.e., display) them by opening them locally with a web browser.

2.3 First HTML5 Example

This chapter presents HTML5 markup capabilities and provides screen captures that show how a browser **renders** (that is, displays) the HTML5. You can download the examples from www.pearsonhighered.com/deitel. The HTML5 documents we show have *line numbers* for your convenience—these are *not* part of the documents. Open each HTML5 document in various web browsers so you can view and interact with it.

Figure 2.1 is an HTML5 document named main.html, which is stored in the examples/ch02 folder. This first example displays the message Welcome to HTML5! in the browser. Now let's consider each line of the document.

```
 1    <!DOCTYPE html>
 2
 3    <!-- Fig. 2.1: main.html -->
 4    <!-- First HTML5 example. -->
 5    <html>
 6       <head>
 7          <meta charset = "utf-8">
 8          <title>Welcome</title>
 9       </head>
10
11       <body>
12          <p>Welcome to HTML5!</p>
13       </body>
14    </html>
```

Tab shows contents of title element

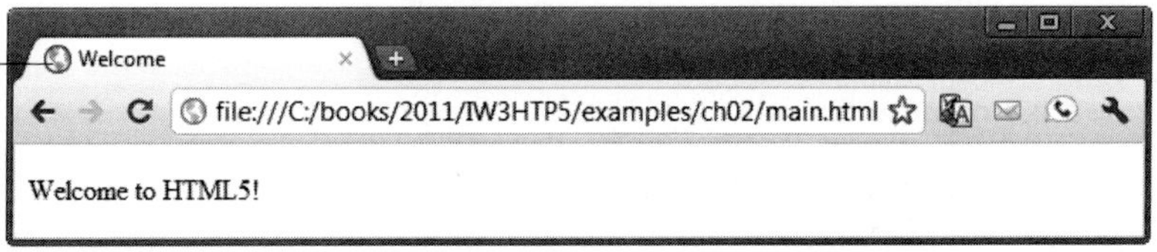

Welcome

file:///C:/books/2011/IW3HTP5/examples/ch02/main.html

Welcome to HTML5!

Fig. 2.1 | First HTML5 example.

Document Type Declaration

The **document type declaration** (**DOCTYPE**) in line 1 is *required* in HTML5 documents so that browsers render the page in **standards mode**, according to the HTML and CSS specifications. Some browsers operate in **quirks mode** to maintain backward compatibility with web pages that are not up-to-date with the latest standards. You'll include the DOCTYPE in each HTML5 document you create.

Blank Lines

We include *blank lines* (lines 2 and 10) to make our documents easier to read—the browser ignores them.

Comments

Lines 3–4 are **HTML5 comments**. You'll insert comments in your HTML5 markup to improve readability and describe the content of a document. The browser ignores comments when your document is rendered. HTML5 comments start with <!-- and end with -->. We include in our examples comments that specify the figure number and file name and state the example's purpose. We'll often include additional comments, especially to explain new features.

html, head *and* body *Elements*

HTML5 markup contains text (and images, graphics, animations, audios and videos) that represents the *content* of a document and **elements** that specify a document's *structure* and *meaning*. Some important elements are the **html** element (which starts in line 5 and ends in line 14), the **head** element (lines 6–9) and the **body** element (lines 11–13). The html element *encloses* the **head section** (represented by the head element) and the **body section** (represented by the body element). The head section contains information about the HTML5 document, such as the character set (UTF-8, the most popular character-encoding scheme for the web) that the page uses (line 7)—which helps the browser determine how to render the content—and the **title** (line 8). The head section also can contain special document-formatting instructions called **CSS3 style sheets** and client-side programs called **scripts** for creating dynamic web pages. (We introduce *CSS3 style sheets* in Chapter 4 and explain *scripting* with the JavaScript language in Chapters 6–13.) The body section contains the page's *content*, which the browser displays when the user visits the web page.

Start Tags and End Tags

HTML5 documents *delimit* most elements with a start tag and an end tag. A **start tag** consists of the element name in *angle brackets* (for example, <html> in line 5). An **end tag** consists of the element name preceded by a *forward slash* (/) in angle brackets (for example, </html> in line 14). There are several so-called "void elements" that do not have end tags.

As you'll soon see, many start tags have **attributes** that provide additional information about an element, which browsers use to determine how to process the element. Each attribute has a **name** and a **value** separated by an equals sign (=).

> **Good Programming Practice 2.1**
> *Although HTML5 element and attribute names are case insensitive (you can use uppercase and lowercase letters), it's a good practice to use only lowercase letters.*

title *Element*

Line 8 specifies a title element. This is called a **nested element**, because it's *enclosed* in the head element's start and end tags. The head element is also a nested element, because it's enclosed in the html element's start and end tags. The title element describes the web page. Titles usually appear in the **title bar** at the top of the browser window, in the browser tab on which the page is displayed, and also as the text identifying a page when users add the page to their list of **Favorites** or **Bookmarks**, enabling them to return to their favorite sites. Search engines use the title for indexing purposes and when displaying results.

> **Good Programming Practice 2.2**
> *Indenting nested elements emphasizes a document's structure and promotes readability. We use three spaces for each level of indentation.*

Line 11 begins the document's body element, which specifies the document's *content*, which may include text, images, audios and videos.

Paragraph Element (<p>...</p>)

Some elements, such as the **paragraph element** denoted with <p> and </p> in line 12, help define the structure of a document. All the text placed between the <p> and </p> tags forms one paragraph. *When a browser renders a paragraph, it places extra space above and below the paragraph text.* The key line in the program is line 12, which tells the browser to display `Welcome to HTML5!`.

End Tags
This document ends with two end tags (lines 13–14), which close the `body` and `html` elements, respectively. The `</html>` tag informs the browser that the HTML5 markup is complete.

Opening an HTML5 File in Your Default Web Browser
To open an HTML5 example from this chapter, open the folder where you saved the book's examples, browse to the Chapter 2 folder and double click the file to open it in your default web browser. At this point your browser window should appear similar to the sample screen capture shown in Fig. 2.1. We resized the browser window to save space.

2.4 W3C HTML5 Validation Service
You must use proper HTML5 syntax to ensure that browsers process your documents properly. The World Wide Web Consortium (W3C) provides a **validation service** (at `validator.w3.org`) for checking a document's syntax. Documents can be validated by

- providing the URL of an online web page
- uploading a file to the validator
- pasting code directly into a **text area** provided on the validator site

All of the HTML5 examples in this book have been validated by uploading a file to:

```
validator.w3.org/#validate-by-upload
```

To use `validator.w3.org/#validate-by-upload`, click the **Choose File** button to select a file from your computer to validate. Next, click **More Options**. In the **Document Type** drop-down list, select **HTML5 (experimental)**. Select the **Verbose Output** checkbox, then click the **Check** button to validate your document. If it contains syntax errors, the validation service displays error messages describing the errors. Since the HTML5 validator is still considered experimental, you'll receive a warning each time you validate an HTML5 document.

Error-Prevention Tip 2.1
Most browsers attempt to render HTML5 documents even if they're invalid. *This can lead to unexpected and undesirable results. Use a validation service, such as the W3C* **MarkUp Validation Service**, *to confirm that an HTML5 document is syntactically correct.*

2.5 Headings
Some text in an HTML5 document may be more important than other text. HTML5 provides six **heading elements** (`h1` through `h6`) for specifying the *relative importance* of information (Fig. 2.2). Heading element `h1` (line 12) is considered the *most significant* one and is typically rendered in a larger font than the other five (lines 13–17). Each successive heading element (`h2`, `h3`, etc.) is typically rendered in a progressively *smaller* font.

Portability Tip 2.1

The text size used to display each heading element can vary between browsers. In Chapter 4, we use CSS to control the text size and other text properties.

Look-and-Feel Observation 2.1

Placing a heading at the top of each page helps viewers understand the purpose of the page. Headers also help create an outline for a document and are indexed by search engines.

```html
1   <!DOCTYPE html>
2
3   <!-- Fig. 2.2: heading.html -->
4   <!-- Heading elements h1 through h6. -->
5   <html>
6      <head>
7         <meta charset = "utf-8">
8         <title>Headings</title>
9      </head>
10
11     <body>
12        <h1>Level 1 Heading</h1>
13        <h2>Level 2 heading</h2>
14        <h3>Level 3 heading</h3>
15        <h4>Level 4 heading</h4>
16        <h5>Level 5 heading</h5>
17        <h6>Level 6 heading</h6>
18     </body>
19  </html>
```

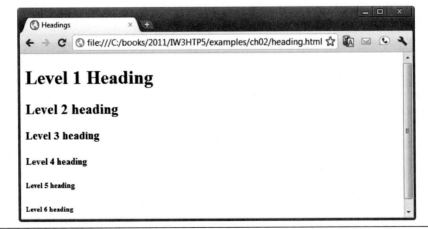

Fig. 2.2 | Heading elements h1 through h6.

2.6 Linking

One of the most important HTML5 features is the **hyperlink**, which references (or **links** to) other resources, such as HTML5 documents and images. When a user clicks a hyperlink, the browser tries to execute an action associated with it (for example, navigate to a

URL or open an e-mail client). *Any displayed element can act as a hyperlink.* Web browsers typically *underline* text hyperlinks and color their text *blue* by default so that users can distinguish hyperlinks from plain text. In Fig. 2.3, we create text hyperlinks to four websites.

```
 1   <!DOCTYPE html>
 2
 3   <!-- Fig. 2.3: links.html -->
 4   <!-- Linking to other web pages. -->
 5   <html>
 6      <head>
 7         <meta charset = "utf-8">
 8         <title>Links</title>
 9      </head>
10
11      <body>
12         <h1>Here are my favorite sites:</h1>
13         <p><strong>Click a name to visit that site.</strong></p>
14
15         <!-- create four text hyperlinks -->
16         <p><a href = "http://www.facebook.com">Facebook</a></p>
17         <p><a href = "http://www.twitter.com">Twitter</a></p>
18         <p><a href = "http://www.foursquare.com">Foursquare</a></p>
19         <p><a href = "http://www.google.com">Google</a></p>
20      </body>
21   </html>
```

Fig. 2.3 | Linking to other web pages.

Line 13 introduces the **strong element**, which indicates that its content has high importance. Browsers typically render such text in a bold font.

Links are created using the **a** (**anchor**) element. Line 16 defines a *hyperlink* to the URL assigned to attribute **href** (hypertext reference), which specifies a resource's location, such as

- a web page or location within a web page
- a file
- an e-mail address

The anchor element in line 16 links the text Facebook to a web page located at http://www.facebook.com. The browser changes the color of any text link once you've clicked the link (in this case, the links are purple rather than blue). When a URL does not indicate a specific document on the website, the web server returns a default web page. This page is often called **index.html**, but most web servers can be configured to use *any* file as the default web page for the site. If the web server cannot locate a requested document, it returns an error indication to the web browser (known as a 404 error), and the browser displays a web page containing an error message.

Software Engineering Observation 2.1

Although not required in HTML5, enclosing attribute values in either single or double quotes is recommended.

Hyperlinking to an E-Mail Address
Anchors can *link to e-mail addresses* using a **mailto:** URL. When the user clicks this type of anchored link, most browsers launch the user's default e-mail program (for example, Mozilla Thunderbird, Microsoft Outlook or Apple Mail) to enable the user to write an e-mail message to the linked address. Figure 2.4 demonstrates this type of anchor. Lines 13–14 contain an e-mail link. The form of an e-mail anchor is <a href = "mailto:*emailAddress*">...</a>. In this case, we link to the e-mail address deitel@deitel.com. Line 13 includes the e-mail address as it will appear in the message displayed on the browser.

```
 1    <!DOCTYPE html>
 2
 3    <!-- Fig. 2.4: contact.html -->
 4    <!-- Linking to an e-mail address. -->
 5    <html>
 6       <head>
 7          <meta charset = "utf-8">
 8          <title>Contact Page</title>
 9       </head>
10
11       <body>
12          <p>
13             To write to <a href = "mailto:deitel@deitel.com">
14             Deitel & Associates, Inc.</a>, click the link and your default
15             email client will open an email message and address it to us.
16          </p>
17       </body>
18    </html>
```

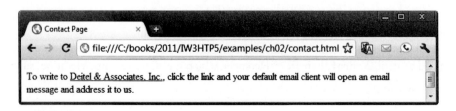

Fig. 2.4 | Linking to an e-mail address. (Part 1 of 2.)

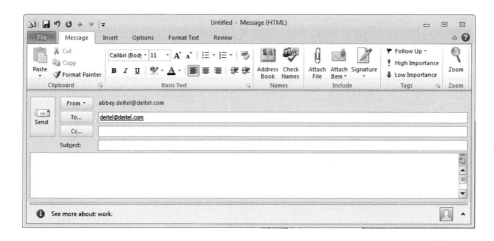

Fig. 2.4 | Linking to an e-mail address. (Part 2 of 2.)

2.7 Images

We've shown how to mark up documents that contain only text, but web pages may also contain images, animations, graphics, audios and even videos. The most popular *image formats* used by web developers today are *PNG (Portable Network Graphics)* and *JPEG (Joint Photographic Experts Group)*. Users can create images using specialized software, such as Adobe Photoshop Express (`www.photoshop.com`), G.I.M.P. (`www.gimp.org`), Inkscape (`www.inkscape.org`) and many more. Images may also be acquired from various websites, many of which offer royalty-free images (Fig. 2.5)—read each site's Terms of Service to determine if you'll need permission to use their images, especially in commercial, for-profit applications. Figure 2.6 demonstrates how to include images in web pages.

Image-sharing site	URL
Flickr®	`www.flickr.com`
Photobucket	`photobucket.com`
Fotki™	`www.fotki.com`
deviantART	`www.deviantart.com`
Picasa™	`picasa.google.com`
TinyPic®	`tinypic.com`
ImageShack	`www.imageshack.us`
FreeDigitalPhotos.net	`www.freedigitalphotos.net`
Open Stock Photography	`www.openstockphotography.org`
Open Clip Art Library	`www.openclipart.org`

Fig. 2.5 | Popular image-sharing sites.

```
 1   <!DOCTYPE html>
 2
 3   <!-- Fig. 2.6: picture.html -->
 4   <!-- Including images in HTML5 files. -->
 5   <html>
 6      <head>
 7         <meta charset = "utf-8">
 8         <title>Images</title>
 9      </head>
10
11      <body>
12         <p>
13            <img src = "cpphtp.png" width = "92" height = "120"
14               alt = "C++ How to Program book cover">
15            <img src = "jhtp.png" width = "92" height = "120"
16               alt = "Java How to Program book cover">
17         </p>
18      </body>
19   </html>
```

Internet Explorer 9 showing an image and the `alt` text for a missing image

Fig. 2.6 | Including images in HTML5 files.

Lines 13–14 use an **img element** to include an image in the document. The image file's location is specified with the **src** (source) **attribute**. This image is located in the *same* directory as the HTML5 document, so only the image's file name is required. This is known as a **relative path**—the image is stored relative to the location of the document. *Optional* attributes **width** and **height** specify the image's dimensions. You can *scale* an image by increasing or decreasing the values of the image `width` and `height` attributes. If these attributes are omitted, the browser uses the image's *actual* width and height. Images are measured in **pixels** ("picture elements"), which represent dots of color on the screen. Image-editing programs display the dimensions, in pixels, of an image. The image in Fig. 2.6 is 92 pixels wide and 120 pixels high.

Performance Tip 2.1

Always include the `width` and the `height` of an image in the `<img>` tag so that when the browser loads the HTML5 file, it will know how much screen space to provide and can lay out the page properly, even before it downloads the image. Including the `width` and `height` attributes in an `<img>` tag can help the browser load and render pages faster.

Look-and-Feel Observation 2.2

Entering new dimensions for an image that change its width-to-height ratio distorts the appearance of the image. To avoid distortion, if your image is 200 pixels wide and 100 pixels high, for example, any new dimensions should maintain the 2:1 width-to-height ratio.

2.7.1 alt Attribute

A browser may not be able to render an image for several reasons. It may not support images—as is the case with text-only browsers—or the client may have disabled image viewing to reduce download time. Every img element in an HTML5 document *must* have an **alt attribute**. If a browser cannot render an image, the browser displays the alt attribute's value. Figure 2.6 shows the Internet Explorer browser rendering a red X symbol and displaying the alt attribute's value, signifying that the image (jhtp.png) cannot be found.

The alt attribute is also important for accessibility—**speech synthesizer** software can speak the alt attribute's value so that a visually impaired user can understand what the browser is displaying. For this reason, the alt attribute should describe the image's contents.

2.7.2 Void Elements

Some HTML5 elements (called **void elements**) contain only attributes and do not mark up text (i.e., text is not placed between a start and an end tag). Although this is not required in HTML5, you can terminate void elements (such as the img element) by using the **forward slash character** (/) inside the closing right angle bracket (>) of the start tag. Foe example, lines 15–16 could be written as follows:

```
<img src = "jhtp.png" width = "92" height = "120"
    alt = "Java How to Program book cover" />
```

2.7.3 Using Images as Hyperlinks

By using images as hyperlinks, you can create graphical web pages that link to other resources. In Fig. 2.7, we create five different image hyperlinks. Clicking an image in this example takes the user to a corresponding web page—one of the other examples in this chapter.

```
1   <!DOCTYPE html>
2
3   <!-- Fig. 2.7: nav.html -->
4   <!-- Images as link anchors. -->
5   <html>
6      <head>
7         <meta charset = "utf-8">
8         <title>Navigation Bar</title>
9      </head>
10
```

Fig. 2.7 | Images as link anchors. (Part 1 of 2.)

```
11      <body>
12         <p>
13            <a href = "links.html">
14               <img src = "buttons/links.jpg" width = "65"
15                  height = "50" alt = "Links">
16            </a>
17
18            <a href = "list.html">
19               <img src = "buttons/list.jpg" width = "65"
20                  height = "50" alt = "List of Features">
21            </a>
22
23            <a href = "contact.html">
24               <img src = "buttons/contact.jpg" width = "65"
25                  height = "50" alt = "Contact Me">
26            </a>
27
28            <a href = "table1.html">
29               <img src = "buttons/table.jpg" width = "65"
30                  height = "50" alt = "Tables Page">
31            </a>
32
33            <a href = "form.html">
34               <img src = "buttons/form.jpg" width = "65"
35                  height = "50" alt = "Feedback Form">
36            </a>
37         </p>
38      </body>
39   </html>
```

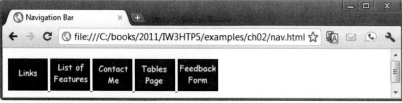

Fig. 2.7 | Images as link anchors. (Part 2 of 2.)

Lines 13–16 create an **image hyperlink** by nesting an img element in an anchor element. The img element's src attribute value specifies that this image (links.jpg) resides in a directory named buttons. The buttons directory and the HTML5 document are in the *same* directory. Images from other web documents also can be referenced by setting the src attribute to the name and location of the image. If you refer to an image on another website, the browser has to request the image resource from that site's server. [*Note:* If you're hosting a publicly available web page that uses an image from another site, you should get permission to use the image and host a copy of the image on your own website. The image's owner may require you to acknowledge their work.] Clicking an image hyperlink takes a user to the web page specified by the surrounding anchor element's href attribute. When the mouse *hovers* over a link of any kind, the URL that the link points to is displayed in the status bar at the bottom of the browser window.

2.8 Special Characters and Horizontal Rules

When marking up text, certain characters or symbols may be difficult to embed directly into an HTML5 document. Some keyboards do not provide these symbols (such as ©), or their presence in the markup may cause syntax errors (as with <). For example, the markup

```
<p>if x < 10 then increment x by 1</p>
```

results in a syntax error because it uses the less-than character (<), which is reserved for start tags and end tags such as <p> and </p>. HTML5 provides **character entity references** (in the form &*code*;) for representing special characters (Fig. 2.8). We could correct the previous line by writing

```
<p>if x &lt; 10 then increment x by 1</p>
```

which uses the character entity reference **<** for the less-than symbol (<). [*Note:* Before HTML5, the character entity reference & was required to display an & in a web page. This is no longer the case.]

Symbol	Description	Character entity reference
HTML5 character entities		
&	ampersand	&amp;
'	apostrophe	&apos;
>	greater-than	&gt;
<	less-than	&lt;
"	quote	&quot;
Other common character entities		
non-breaking space		
©	copyright	&copy;
—	em dash	&mdash;
–	en dash	&ndash;
¼	fraction 1/4	&frac14;
½	fraction 1/2	&frac12;
¾	fraction 3/4	&frac34;
…	horizontal ellipsis	&hellip;
®	registered trademark	&reg;
§	section	&sect;
TM	trademark	&trade;

Fig. 2.8 | Some common HTML character entity references.

Figure 2.9 demonstrates how to use special characters in an HTML5 document. For an extensive list of character entities, see

www.w3.org/TR/REC-html40/sgml/entities.html

```
 1   <!DOCTYPE html>
 2
 3   <!-- Fig. 2.9: contact2.html -->
 4   <!-- Inserting special characters. -->
 5   <html>
 6      <head>
 7         <meta charset = "utf-8">
 8         <title>Contact Page</title>
 9      </head>
10
11      <body>
12         <p>
13            <a href = "mailto:deitel@deitel.com">Send an email to
14            Deitel &amp; Associates, Inc.</a>.
15         </p>
16
17         <hr> <!-- inserts a horizontal rule -->
18
19         <!-- special characters are entered -->
20         <!-- using the form &code; -->
21         <p>All information on this site is <strong>&copy;
22            Deitel & Associates, Inc. 2012.</strong> </p>
23
24         <!-- to strike through text use <del> element -->
25         <!-- to subscript text use <sub> element -->
26         <!-- to superscript text use <sup> element -->
27         <!-- these elements are nested inside other elements -->
28         <p><del>You may download 3.14 x 10<sup>2</sup>
29            characters worth of information from this site.</del>
30            The first item in the series is x<sub>1</sub>.</p>
31         <p>Note: &lt; &frac14; of the information
32            presented here is updated daily.</p>
33      </body>
34   </html>
```

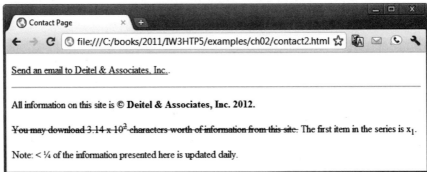

Fig. 2.9 | Inserting special characters.

The paragraph in lines 12–15 allows the user to click the link to send an e-mail to Deitel & Associates, Inc. In this case, we represented the & with the character entity reference & to show that it still works even though it's not required in HTML5.

In addition to special characters, this document introduces a **horizontal rule**, indicated by the **<hr>** tag in line 17. Most browsers render a horizontal rule as a horizontal line with extra space above and below it. As a professional, you'll see lots of older code—known as *legacy code*. The horizontal rule element should be considered a legacy element and you should avoid using it. As you'll learn, CSS can be used to add horizontal rules and other formatting to documents.

Lines 21–22 contain other special characters, which can be expressed as either character entity references (coded using word abbreviations such as © for copyright) or **numeric character references**—decimal or **hexadecimal** (**hex**) values representing special characters. For example, the & character is represented in decimal and hexadecimal notation as & and &, respectively. Hexadecimal numbers are base 16 numbers—digits in a hexadecimal number have values from 0 to 15 (a total of 16 different values). The letters A–F represent the hexadecimal digits corresponding to decimal values 10–15. Thus in hexadecimal notation we can have numbers like 876 consisting solely of decimal-like digits, numbers like DA19F consisting of digits and letters, and numbers like DCB consisting solely of letters. We discuss hexadecimal numbers in detail in Appendix E, Number Systems, which is available online at www.deitel.com/books/iw3htp5/.

In lines 28–30, we introduce four new elements. Most browsers render the **del** element as *strike-through text*. With this format users can indicate document revisions. To **superscript** text (i.e., raise text above the baseline and in a decreased font size) or **subscript** text (i.e., lower text below the baseline and in a decreased font size), use the **sup** or **sub** element, respectively. We also use character entity reference < for a less-than sign and ¼ for the fraction 1/4 (line 31).

2.9 Lists

Now we show how to use *lists* in a web page to organize content that similar in nature. Figure 2.10 displays text in an **unordered list** (i.e., a simple bullet-style list that does not order its items by letter or number). The unordered-list element **ul** (lines 16–22) creates a list in which each item begins with a bullet symbol (typically a *disc*). Each entry in an unordered list is an **li** (**list item**) element (lines 18–21). Most web browsers render each li element on a new line with a bullet symbol indented from the beginning of the line.

```
1   <!DOCTYPE html>
2
3   <!-- Fig. 2.10: links2.html -->
4   <!-- Unordered list containing hyperlinks. -->
5   <html>
6      <head>
7         <meta charset = "utf-8">
8         <title>Links</title>
9      </head>
10
11     <body>
12        <h1>Here are my favorite sites</h1>
13        <p><strong>Click on a name to go to that page</strong></p>
```

Fig. 2.10 | Unordered list containing hyperlinks. (Part 1 of 2.)

```
14
15          <!-- create an unordered list -->
16          <ul>
17              <!-- the list contains four list items -->
18              <li><a href = "http://www.youtube.com">YouTube</a></li>
19              <li><a href = "http://www.wikipedia.org">Wikipedia</a></li>
20              <li><a href = "http://www.amazon.com">Amazon</a></li>
21              <li><a href = "http://www.linkedin.com">LinkedIn</a></li>
22          </ul>
23      </body>
24  </html>
```

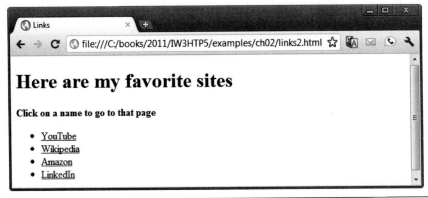

Fig. 2.10 | Unordered list containing hyperlinks. (Part 2 of 2.)

Nested Lists

Lists may be *nested* to represent *hierarchical* relationships, as in a multilevel outline. Figure 2.11 demonstrates **nested lists** and **ordered lists**. The ordered-list element **ol** creates a list in which each item begins with a number.

In many browsers, the items in the outermost unordered list (lines 15–55) are preceded by *discs*. List items nested inside the unordered list of line 15 are preceded in many browsers by *hollow circular bullets*. A web browser indents each nested list to indicate a hierarchical relationship. The first ordered list (lines 29–33) includes two items. Items in an ordered list are enumerated 1., 2., 3. and so on. Nested ordered lists are enumerated in the same manner. Although not demonstrated in this example, subsequent nested unordered list items are often preceded by *square bullets*. The bullet styles used may vary by browser.

```
1   <!DOCTYPE html>
2
3   <!-- Fig. 2.11: list html    >
4   <!-- Nested lists and ordered lists. -->
5   <html>
6       <head>
```

Fig. 2.11 | Nested lists and ordered lists. (Part 1 of 3.)

```
7            <meta charset = "utf-8">
8            <title>Lists</title>
9        </head>
10
11       <body>
12           <h1>The Best Features of the Internet</h1>
13
14           <!-- create an unordered list -->
15           <ul>
16               <li>You can meet new people from countries around
17                   the world.</li>
18               <li>
19                   You have access to new media as it becomes public:
20
21                   <!-- this starts a nested unordered list, which uses a -->
22                   <!-- different bullet. The list ends when you -->
23                   <!-- close the <ul> tag. -->
24                   <ul>
25                       <li>New games</li>
26                       <li>New applications
27
28                           <!-- nested ordered list -->
29                           <ol>
30                               <li>For business</li>
31                               <li>For pleasure</li>
32                           </ol>
33                       </li> <!-- ends line 27 new applications li-->
34
35                       <li>Around the clock news</li>
36                       <li>Search engines</li>
37                       <li>Shopping</li>
38                       <li>Programming
39
40                           <!-- another nested ordered list -->
41                           <ol>
42                               <li>XML</li>
43                               <li>Java</li>
44                               <li>HTML5</li>
45                               <li>JavaScript</li>
46                               <li>New languages</li>
47                           </ol>
48                       </li> <!-- ends programming li of line 38 -->
49                   </ul> <!-- ends the nested list of line 24 -->
50               </li>
51
52               <li>Links</li>
53               <li>Keeping in touch with old friends</li>
54               <li>It's the technology of the future!</li>
55           </ul> <!-- ends the unordered list of line 15 -->
56       </body>
57   </html>
```

Fig. 2.11 | Nested lists and ordered lists. (Part 2 of 3.)

Fig. 2.11 | Nested lists and ordered lists. (Part 3 of 3.)

2.10 Tables

Tables are frequently used to organize data into *rows* and *columns*. Our first example (Fig. 2.12) creates a table with six rows and two columns to display price information for various fruits. Tables are defined with the **table** element (lines 13–58). Line 13 specifies the **table** element's start tag. The **border** attribute with the value "1" specifies that the browser should place borders around the table and the table's cells. The border attribute is a legacy attribute that you should avoid. When we introduce CSS3 (Chapter 4), we'll use CSS's **border** property, which is the preferred way to format a **table**'s borders.

The **caption** element (lines 17–18) specifies a table's title. Text in this element is typically rendered above the table. In addition, it's good practice to include a general description of a table's information in the table element's **summary attribute**—one of the many HTML5 features that make web pages more accessible to users with disabilities. Speech devices use this attribute to make the table more *accessible* to users with visual impairments.

```
 1   <!DOCTYPE html>
 2
 3   <!-- Fig. 2.12: table1.html -->
 4   <!-- Creating a basic table. -->
 5   <html>
 6      <head>
 7         <meta charset = "utf-8">
```

Fig. 2.12 | Creating a basic table. (Part 1 of 3.)

```
 8          <title>A simple HTML5 table</title>
 9       </head>
10
11       <body>
12          <!-- the <table> tag opens a table -->
13          <table border = "1">
14
15             <!-- the <caption> tag summarizes the table's -->
16             <!-- contents (this helps visually impaired people) -->
17             <caption><strong>Table of Fruits (1st column) and
18                Their Prices (2nd column)</strong></caption>
19
20             <!-- the <thead> section appears first in the table -->
21             <!-- it formats the table header area -->
22             <thead>
23                <tr> <!-- <tr> inserts a table row -->
24                   <th>Fruit</th> <!-- insert a heading cell -->
25                   <th>Price</th>
26                </tr>
27             </thead>
28
29             <!-- the <tfoot> section appears last in the table -->
30             <!-- it formats the table footer -->
31             <tfoot>
32                <tr>
33                   <th>Total</th>
34                   <th>$3.75</th>
35                </tr>
36             </tfoot>
37
38             <!-- all table content is enclosed -->
39             <!-- within the <tbody> -->
40             <tbody>
41                <tr>
42                   <td>Apple</td> <!-- insert a data cell -->
43                   <td>$0.25</td>
44                </tr>
45                <tr>
46                   <td>Orange</td>
47                   <td>$0.50</td>
48                </tr>
49                <tr>
50                   <td>Banana</td>
51                   <td>$1.00</td>
52                </tr>
53                <tr>
54                   <td>Pineapple</td>
55                   <td>$2.00</td>
56                </tr>
57             </tbody>
58          </table>
59       </body>
60    </html>
```

Fig. 2.12 | Creating a basic table. (Part 2 of 3.)

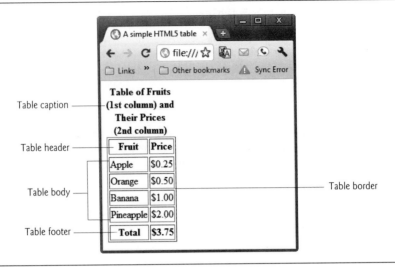

Table caption — Table of Fruits (1st column) and Their Prices (2nd column)

Table header —

Table body —

Table footer —

Table border —

Fruit	Price
Apple	$0.25
Orange	$0.50
Banana	$1.00
Pineapple	$2.00
Total	**$3.75**

Fig. 2.12 | Creating a basic table. (Part 3 of 3.)

A table has three distinct sections—**head**, **body** and **foot**. The head section (or header cell) is defined with a **thead** element (lines 22–27), which contains header information such as column names. Each **tr** element (lines 23–26) defines an individual **table row**. The *columns* in the thead section are defined with **th** elements. Most browsers *center* text formatted by th (table header column) elements and display them in *bold*. Table header elements (lines 24–25) are *nested* inside table row elements.

The body section, or **table body**, contains the table's *primary data*. The table body (lines 40–57) is defined in a **tbody** element. In the table body, each **tr** element specifies one row. **Data cells** contain individual pieces of data and are defined with **td** (table data) elements in each row.

The **tfoot** section (lines 31–36) is defined with a **tfoot** (table foot) element. The text placed in the footer commonly includes *calculation results* and *footnotes*. Here, we manually entered the calculation total. In later chapters, we'll show how to perform such calculations dynamically. Like other sections, the tfoot section can contain table rows, and each row can contain cells. As in the thead section, cells in the foot section are created using th elements, instead of the td elements used in the table body. Before HTML5, the tfoot section was required to appear above the tbody section of the table. As of HTML5, the tfoot section can be *above* or *below* the tbody section in the code.

In this example, we specified only the table's data, *not* its formatting. As you can see, in the browser's default formatting each column is only as wide as its largest element, and the table itself is not visually appealing. In Chapter 4, we'll use CSS to specify HTML5 elements' formats.

Using **rowspan** *and* **colspan** *with Tables*

Figure 2.12 explored a basic table's structure. Figure 2.13 presents another table example and introduces new attributes that allow you to build more complex tables.

The table begins in line 14. *Table cells are sized to fit the data they contain*, but you can control a table's formatting using CSS3. You can create cells that apply to more than one row or column using the attributes **rowspan** and **colspan**. The values assigned to these attributes specify the number of rows or columns occupied by a cell. The th element at lines 22–25 uses the attribute rowspan = "2" to allow the cell containing the picture of the camel to use two vertically adjacent cells (thus the cell *spans* two rows). The th element in lines 28–31 uses the attribute colspan = "4" to widen the header cell (containing Camelid comparison and Approximate as of 10/2011) to span four cells.

Line 29 introduces the **br** element, which most browsers render as a **line break**. Any markup or text following a br element is rendered on the next line, which in this case appears within the same four-column span. Like the img element, br is an example of a *void element*. Like the hr element, br is considered a legacy formatting element that you should avoid using—in general, formatting should be specified using CSS.

```
 1    <!DOCTYPE html>
 2
 3    <!-- Fig. 2.13: table2.html -->
 4    <!-- Complex HTML5 table. -->
 5    <html>
 6       <head>
 7          <meta charset = "utf-8">
 8          <title>Tables</title>
 9       </head>
10
11       <body>
12          <h1>Table Example: Spanning Rows and Columns</h1>
13
14          <table border = "1">
15             <caption>A more complex sample table</caption>
16
17             <thead>
18                <!-- rowspans and colspans merge the specified -->
19                <!-- number of cells vertically or horizontally -->
20                <tr>
21                   <!-- merge two rows -->
22                   <th rowspan = "2">
23                      <img src = "camel.png" width = "205"
24                         height = "167" alt = "Picture of a camel">
25                   </th>
26
27                   <!-- merge four columns -->
28                   <th colspan = "4">
29                      <strong>Camelid comparison</strong><br>
30                      Approximate as of 10/2011
31                   </th>
32                </tr>
33                <tr>
34                   <th># of humps</th>
35                   <th>Indigenous region</th>
36                   <th>Spits?</th>
37                   <th>Produces wool?</th>
38                </tr>
39             </thead>
```

Fig. 2.13 | Complex HTML5 table. (Part 1 of 2.)

```
40          <tbody>
41            <tr>
42              <th>Camels (bactrian)</th>
43              <td>2</td>
44              <td>Africa/Asia</td>
45              <td>Yes</td>
46              <td>Yes</td>
47            </tr>
48            <tr>
49              <th>Llamas</th>
50              <td>1</td>
51              <td>Andes Mountains</td>
52              <td>Yes</td>
53              <td>Yes</td>
54            </tr>
55          </tbody>
56        </table>
57      </body>
58  </html>
```

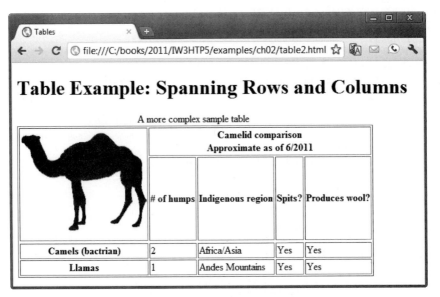

Fig. 2.13 | Complex HTML5 table. (Part 2 of 2.)

2.11 Forms

When browsing websites, users often need to provide information such as search queries, e-mail addresses and zip codes. HTML5 provides a mechanism, called a **form**, for collecting data from a user.

Data that users enter on a web page is normally sent to a *web server* that provides access to a site's resources (for example, HTML5 documents, images, animations, videos). These resources are located either on the same machine as the web server or on a machine that the web server can access through the Internet. When a browser requests a publicly available web page or file that's located on a server, the server processes the request and returns the requested resource. A request contains the *name* and *path* of the desired resource and the *protocol* (method of communication). HTML5 documents are requested and transferred via the Hypertext Transfer Protocol (HTTP).

Figure 2.14 is a simple form that sends data to the web server for processing. The web server typically returns a web page back to the web browser—this page often indicates whether or not the form's data was processed correctly. [*Note:* This example demonstrates only client-side functionality. If you submit this form (by clicking **Submit**), the browser will simply display www.deitel.com (the site specified in the form's action), because we haven't yet specified how to process the form data on the server. In later chapters, we present the *server-side programming* (for example, in PHP, ASP.NET and JavaServer Faces) necessary to process information entered into a form.]

```html
 1   <!DOCTYPE html>
 2
 3   <!-- Fig. 2.14: form.html -->
 4   <!-- Form with a text field and hidden fields. -->
 5   <html>
 6      <head>
 7         <meta charset = "utf-8">
 8         <title>Forms</title>
 9      </head>
10
11      <body>
12         <h1>Feedback Form</h1>
13
14         <p>Please fill out this form to help
15            us improve our site.</p>
16
17         <!-- this tag starts the the form, gives the -->
18         <!-- method of sending information and the -->
19         <!-- location of the form-processing script -->
20         <form method = "post" action = "http://www.deitel.com">
21            <!-- hidden inputs contain non-visual -->
22            <!-- information that will also be submitted -->
23            <input type = "hidden" name = "recipient"
24               value = "deitel@deitel.com">
25            <input type = "hidden" name = "subject"
26               value = "Feedback Form">
27            <input type = "hidden" name = "redirect"
28               value = "main.html">
29
30            <!-- <input type = "text"> inserts a text field -->
31            <p><label>Name:
32               <input name = "name" type = "text" size = "25"
33                  maxlength = "30">
34            </label></p>
35
```

Fig. 2.14 | Form with a text field and hidden fields. (Part I of 2.)

```
36                    <p>
37                       <!-- input types "submit" and "reset" insert -->
38                       <!-- buttons for submitting and clearing the -->
39                       <!-- form's contents, respectively -->
40                       <input type = "submit" value = "Submit">
41                       <input type = "reset" value = "Clear">
42                    </p>
43                 </form>
44              </body>
45           </html>
```

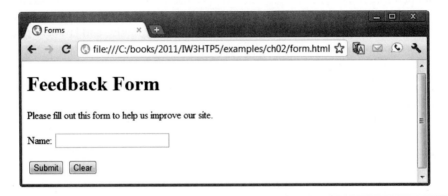

Fig. 2.14 | Form with a text field and hidden fields. (Part 2 of 2.)

method *Attribute of the* form *Element*
The form is defined in lines 20–43 by a **form** element. Attribute **method** (line 20) specifies how the form's data is sent to the web server. Using method = **"post"** appends form data to the browser request, which contains the protocol (HTTP) and the requested resource's URL. This method of passing data to the server is *transparent*—the user doesn't see the data after the form is submitted. The other possible value, method = **"get"**, appends form data directly to the end of the URL of the script, where it's visible in the browser's **Address** field. The *post* and *get* methods for sending form data are discussed in detail in Chapter 17.

action *Attribute of the* form *Element*
The **action** attribute in the form element in line 20 specifies the URL of a *script on the web server* that will be invoked to process the form's data. Since we haven't introduced server-side programming yet, we set this attribute to http://www.deitel.com for now.

Lines 24–43 define **input** elements that specify data to provide to the script that processes the form (also called the **form handler**). There are several types of input elements. An input's type is determined by its **type attribute**. This form uses a text input, a submit input, a reset input and three hidden inputs.

Hidden Inputs
Forms can contain visual and nonvisual components. *Visual components* include clickable buttons and other graphical user interface components with which users interact. *Nonvi-*

sual components, called **hidden inputs** (lines 23–28), store any data that you specify, such as e-mail addresses and HTML5 document file names that act as links.

The three hidden input elements in lines 23–28 have the type attribute hidden, which allows you to *send form data that's not input by a user.* The hidden inputs are an e-mail address to which the data will be sent, the e-mail's subject line and a URL for the browser to open after submission of the form. Two other input attributes are **name**, which identifies the input element, and **value**, which provides the value that will be sent (or posted) to the web server. The server uses the name attribute to get the corresponding value from the form.

text input *Element*

The **text** input in lines 32–33 inserts a **text field** in the form. Users can type data in text fields. The label element (lines 31–34) provides users with information about the input element's purpose. The input element's **size** attribute specifies the number of characters visible in the text field. Optional attribute **maxlength** limits the number of characters input into the text field—in this case, the user is not permitted to type more than 30 characters.

submit *and* reset input *Elements*

Two input elements in lines 40–41 create two buttons. The **submit** input element is a button. When the submit button is pressed, the form's data is sent to the location specified in the form's action attribute. The **value** attribute sets the text displayed on the button. The **reset** input element allows a user to reset all form elements to their default values. The value attribute of the reset input element sets the text displayed on the button (the default value is **Reset** if you omit the value attribute).

Additional Form Elements

In the previous example, you saw basic elements of HTML5 forms. Now we introduce elements and attributes for creating more complex forms. Figure 2.15 contains a form that solicits user feedback about a website.

The **textarea** element (lines 31–32) inserts a *multiline text area* into the form. The number of rows is specified with the **rows** attribute, and the number of columns (i.e., characters per line) with the **cols** attribute. In this example, the textarea is four rows high and 36 characters wide. To display *default text* in the textarea, place the text between the <textarea> and </textarea> tags. Default text can be specified in other input types, such as text fields, by using the value attribute.

```
1   <!DOCTYPE html>
2
3   <!-- Fig. 2.15: form2.html -->
4   <!-- Form using a variety of components. -->
5   <html>
6      <head>
7         <meta charset = "utf-8">
8         <title>More Forms</title>
9      </head>
10
```

Fig. 2.15 | Form using a variety of components. (Part 1 of 4.)

```
11    <body>
12       <h1>Feedback Form</h1>
13       <p>Please fill out this form to help
14          us improve our site.</p>
15
16       <form method = "post" action = "http://www.deitel.com">
17
18          <input type = "hidden" name = "recipient"
19             value = "deitel@deitel.com">
20          <input type = "hidden" name = "subject"
21             value = "Feedback Form">
22          <input type = "hidden" name = "redirect"
23             value = "main.html">
24
25          <p><label>Name:
26                <input name = "name" type = "text" size = "25">
27             </label></p>
28
29          <!-- <textarea> creates a multiline textbox -->
30          <p><label>Comments:<br>
31             <textarea name = "comments"
32                rows = "4" cols = "36">Enter comments here.</textarea>
33          </label></p>
34
35          <!-- <input type = "password"> inserts a -->
36          <!-- textbox whose display is masked with -->
37          <!-- asterisk characters -->
38          <p><label>E-mail Address:
39             <input name = "email" type = "password"  size = "25">
40          </label></p>
41
42          <p>
43             <strong>Things you liked:</strong><br>
44
45             <label>Site design
46                <input name = "thingsliked" type = "checkbox"
47                   value = "Design"></label>
48             <label>Links
49                <input name = "thingsliked" type = "checkbox"
50                   value = "Links"></label>
51             <label>Ease of use
52                <input name = "thingsliked" type = "checkbox"
53                   value = "Ease"></label>
54             <label>Images
55                <input name = "thingsliked" type = "checkbox"
56                   value = "Images"></label>
57             <label>Source code
58                <input name = "thingsliked" type = "checkbox"
59                   value = "Code"></label>
60          </p>
61
62          <!-- <input type = "radio"> creates a radio -->
63          <!-- button. The difference between radio buttons -->
```

Fig. 2.15 | Form using a variety of components. (Part 2 of 4.)

```
64              <!-- and checkboxes is that only one radio button -->
65              <!-- in a group can be selected. -->
66              <p>
67                  <strong>How did you get to our site?:</strong><br>
68
69                  <label>Search engine
70                      <input name = "howtosite" type = "radio"
71                          value = "search engine" checked></label>
72                  <label>Links from another site
73                      <input name = "howtosite" type = "radio"
74                          value = "link"></label>
75                  <label>Deitel.com Web site
76                      <input name = "howtosite" type = "radio"
77                          value = "deitel.com"></label>
78                  <label>Reference in a book
79                      <input name = "howtosite" type = "radio"
80                          value = "book"></label>
81                  <label>Other
82                      <input name = "howtosite" type = "radio"
83                          value = "other"></label>
84              </p>
85
86              <p>
87                  <label>Rate our site:
88
89                      <!-- the <select> tag presents a drop-down -->
90                      <!-- list with choices indicated by the -->
91                      <!-- <option> tags -->
92                      <select name = "rating">
93                          <option selected>Amazing</option>
94                          <option>10</option>
95                          <option>9</option>
96                          <option>8</option>
97                          <option>7</option>
98                          <option>6</option>
99                          <option>5</option>
100                         <option>4</option>
101                         <option>3</option>
102                         <option>2</option>
103                         <option>1</option>
104                         <option>Awful</option>
105                     </select>
106                 </label>
107             </p>
108
109             <p>
110                 <input type = "submit" value = "Submit">
111                 <input type = "reset" value = "Clear">
112             </p>
113         </form>
114     </body>
115 </html>
```

Fig. 2.15 | Form using a variety of components. (Part 3 of 4.)

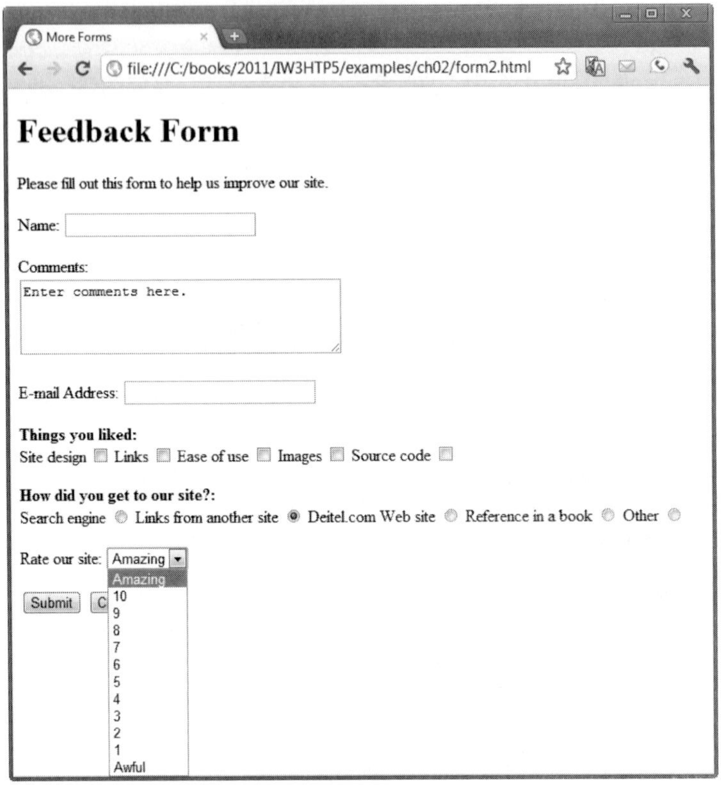

Fig. 2.15 | Form using a variety of components. (Part 4 of 4.)

The **password** input in line 39 inserts a password box with the specified size (maximum number of displayed characters). A password box allows users to enter sensitive information, such as credit card numbers and passwords, by "masking" the information input with asterisks (*). The actual value input is sent to the web server, not the masking characters.

Lines 45–59 introduce the **checkbox** input element. checkboxes enable users to select an option. When a user selects a checkbox, a *check mark* appears in the checkbox. Otherwise, the checkbox remains empty. Each checkbox input creates a new checkbox. checkboxes can be used individually or in groups. checkboxes that belong to a group are assigned the same name (in this case, `"thingsliked"`).

> **Common Programming Error 2.1**
>
> *When your* form *has several* checkboxes *with the same* name, *make sure that they have different* values, *or the web server scripts will not be able to distinguish them.*

After the checkboxes, we present two more ways to allow the user to make choices. In this example, we introduce two new input types. The first is the **radio button** (lines 69–83) specified with type **radio**. radio buttons are similar to checkboxes, except that only one radio button in a group of radio buttons may be selected at any time. The radio buttons in a group all have the same name attributes and are distinguished by their different value attributes. The attribute checked (line 71) indicates which radio button, if any, is selected initially. The checked attribute also applies to checkboxes.

Common Programming Error 2.2

Not setting the name *attributes of the* radio *buttons in a group to the same name is a logic error because it lets the user select all of the* radio *buttons at the same time.*

The **select** element (lines 92–105) provides a *drop-down list* from which the user can select an item. The name attribute identifies the drop-down list. The **option** elements (lines 93–104) add items to the drop-down list. The option element's **selected** attribute specifies which item *initially* is displayed as the selected item in the select element. If no option element is marked as selected, the browser selects the *first* option by default.

2.12 Internal Linking

Earlier in the chapter, we discussed how to hyperlink one web page to another. Figure 2.16 introduces **internal linking**—a mechanism that enables the user to jump between locations in the same document. Internal linking is useful for long documents that contain many sections. Clicking an internal link enables the user to find a section *without scrolling* through the entire document.

```
1   <!DOCTYPE html>
2
3   <!-- Fig. 2.16: internal.html -->
4   <!-- Internal Linking -->
5   <html>
6      <head>
7         <meta charset = "utf-8">
8         <title>Internal Links</title>
9      </head>
10
11     <body>
12        <!-- id attribute creates an internal hyperlink destination -->
13        <h1 id = "features">The Best Features of the Internet</h1>
14
15        <!-- an internal link's address is "#id" -->
16        <p><a href = "#bugs">Go to <em>Favorite Bugs</em></a></p>
17
18        <ul>
19           <li>You can meet people from countries
20              around the world.</li>
21           <li>You have access to new media as it becomes public:
22              <ul>
23                 <li>New games</li>
24                 <li>New applications
25                    <ul>
26                       <li>For Business</li>
27                       <li>For Pleasure</li>
28                    </ul>
29                 </li>
```

Fig. 2.16 | Internal hyperlinks to make pages more navigable. (Part 1 of 3.)

```
30
31                    <li>Around the clock news</li>
32                    <li>Search Engines</li>
33                    <li>Shopping</li>
34                    <li>Programming
35                       <ul>
36                          <li>HTML5</li>
37                          <li>Java</li>
38                          <li>Dynamic HTML</li>
39                          <li>Scripts</li>
40                          <li>New languages</li>
41                       </ul>
42                    </li>
43                 </ul>
44              </li>
45
46              <li>Links</li>
47              <li>Keeping in touch with old friends</li>
48              <li>It is the technology of the future!</li>
49           </ul>
50
51           <!-- id attribute creates an internal hyperlink destination -->
52           <h1 id = "bugs">My 3 Favorite Bugs</h1>
53           <p>
54              <!-- internal hyperlink to features -->
55              <a href = "#features">Go to <em>Favorite Features</em></a>
56           </p>
57           <ol>
58              <li>Fire Fly</li>
59              <li>Gal Ant</li>
60              <li>Roman Tic</li>
61           </ol>
62        </body>
63     </html>
```

a) Browser before the user clicks the internal link

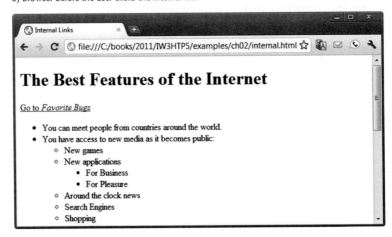

Fig. 2.16 | Internal hyperlinks to make pages more navigable. (Part 2 of 3.)

b) Browser after the user clicks the internal link

Fig. 2.16 | Internal hyperlinks to make pages more navigable. (Part 3 of 3.)

Line 13 contains a tag with the `id` attribute (set to `"features"`) for an **internal hyperlink**. To link to a tag with this attribute inside the same web page, the `href` attribute of an anchor element includes the `id` attribute value, preceded by a pound sign (as in `#features`). Line 55 contains a hyperlink with the `id features` as its target. Clicking this hyperlink in a web browser scrolls the browser window to the `h1` tag in line 13. You may have to resize your browser to a small window and scroll down before clicking the link to see the browser scroll to the `h1` element.

A hyperlink can also reference an internal link in *another* document by specifying the document name followed by a pound sign and the `id` value, as in:

```
href = "filename.html#id"
```

For example, to link to a tag with the `id` attribute `booklist` in `books.html`, `href` is assigned `"books.html#booklist"`. You can send the browser to an internal link on another website by appending the pound sign and id value of an element to any URL, as in:

```
href = "URL/filename.html#id"
```

2.13 meta Elements

Search engines catalog sites by following links from page to page (often known as *spidering* or *crawling* the site) and saving identification and classification information for each page. One way that search engines catalog pages is by reading the content in each page's **meta** elements, which specify information about a document. Using the `meta` element is one of many methods of **search engine optimization (SEO)**—the process of designing and tuning your website to maximize your *findability* and improve your rankings in organic (nonpaid) search engine results.

Two important attributes of the `meta` element are **name**, which identifies the type of `meta` element, and **content**, which provides the information search engines use to catalog pages. Figure 2.17 introduces the `meta` element.

```
 1    <!DOCTYPE html>
 2
 3    <!-- Fig. 2.17: meta.html -->
 4    <!-- meta elements provide keywords and a description of a page. -->
 5    <html>
 6       <head>
 7          <meta charset = "utf-8">
 8          <title>Welcome</title>
 9
10          <!-- <meta> tags provide search engines with -->
11          <!-- information used to catalog a site      -->
12          <meta name = "keywords" content = "web page, design,
13             HTML5, tutorial, personal, help, index, form,
14             contact, feedback, list, links, deitel">
15          <meta name = "description" content = "This website will
16             help you learn the basics of HTML5 and web page design
17             through the use of interactive examples and
18             instruction.">
19       </head>
20       <body>
21          <h1>Welcome to Our Website!</h1>
22
23          <p>We have designed this site to teach about the wonders
24          of <strong><em>HTML5</em></strong>. <em>HTML5</em> is
25          better equipped than <em>HTML</em> to represent complex
26          data on the Internet. <em>HTML5</em> takes advantage of
27          XML's strict syntax to ensure well-formedness. Soon you
28          will know about many of the great features of
29          <em>HTML5.</em></p>
30
31          <p>Have Fun With the Site!</p>
32       </body>
33    </html>
```

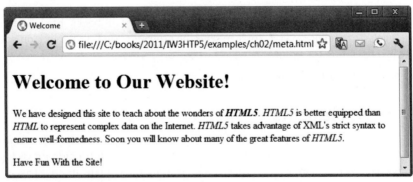

Fig. 2.17 | meta elements provide keywords and a description of a page.

Lines 12–14 demonstrate a "keywords" meta element. The content attribute of such a meta element provides search engines with a list of words that describe the page. These words are compared with words in search requests. Thus, including meta elements and their content information can draw more viewers to your site.

Lines 15–18 demonstrate a "description" meta element. The content attribute of such a meta element provides a three- to four-line description of a site, written in sentence form. Search engines also use this description to catalog your site and sometimes display this information as part of the search results.

Software Engineering Observation 2.2

meta *elements are not visible to users. They must be placed inside the* head *section of your HTML5 document; otherwise they will not be read by search engines.*

2.14 Web Resources

www.deitel.com/html5

Visit our online HTML5 Resource Center to find categorized links to mostly free HTML5 introductions, tutorials, demos, videos, documentation, books, blogs, forums, sample chapters and more.

Summary

Section 2.1 Introduction
- HTML5 is a markup language that specifies the structure and content of documents that are displayed in web browsers.

Section 2.2 Editing HTML5
- Computers called web servers store HTML5 documents.
- Clients (for example, web browsers running on your local computer or smartphone) request specific resources (p. 70) such as HTML5 documents from web servers.

Section 2.3 First HTML5 Example
- The document type declaration (DOCTYPE; p. 71) is *required* in HTML5 documents so that browsers render the page in standards mode (p. 71).
- HTML5 comments (p. 71) always start with <!-- (p. 71) and end with --> (p. 71). The browser ignores all text inside a comment.
- The html element (p. 72) encloses the head section (represented by the head element; p. 72) and the body section (represented by the body element; p. 72).
- The head section contains information about the HTML5 document, such as its title (p. 72). It also can contain special document-formatting instructions called style sheets (p. 72) and client-side programs called scripts (p. 72) for creating dynamic web pages.
- The body section contains the page's content, which the browser displays when the user visits the web page.
- HTML5 documents delimit an element with start and end tags. A start tag (p. 72) consists of the element name in angle brackets (for example, <html>). An end tag (p. 72) consists of the element name preceded by a forward slash (/) in angle brackets (for example, </html>).
- The title element names a web page. The title usually appears in the colored bar (called the title bar; p. 72) at the top of the browser window and also appears as the text identifying a page when users add your page to their list of **Favorites** or **Bookmarks**.
- The paragraph element (p. 72), denoted with <p> and </p>, helps define the structure of a document. All the text placed between the <p> and </p> tags forms one paragraph.

Section 2.4 W3C HTML5 Validation Service
• You must use proper HTML5 syntax to ensure that browsers process your documents properly.
• The World Wide Web Consortium (W3C) provides a validation service (validator.w3.org; p. 73) for checking a document's syntax.

Section 2.5 Headings
• HTML5 provides six heading elements (h1 through h6; p. 73) for specifying the relative importance of information. Heading element h1 is considered the most significant and is rendered in a larger font than the other five. Each successive heading element (h2, h3, etc.) is rendered in a progressively smaller font.

Section 2.6 Linking
• Hyperlinks (p. 74) reference (or link to) other resources, such as HTML5 documents and images.
• The strong element (p. 75) typically causes the browser to render text in a bold font.
• Links are created using the a (anchor) element (p. 75). The href ("hypertext reference") attribute (p. 75) specifies the location of a linked resource, such as a web page, a file or an e-mail address.
• Anchors can link to an e-mail address using a mailto: URL (p. 76). When someone clicks this type of anchored link, most browsers launch the default e-mail program to initiate an e-mail message addressed to the linked address.

Section 2.7 Images
• The img element's (p. 78) src attribute (p. 78) specifies an image's location.
• Every img element in an HTML5 document must have an alt attribute (p. 79). If a browser cannot render an image, the browser displays the alt attribute's value.
• The alt attribute helps you create accessible web pages (p. 79) for users with disabilities, especially those with vision impairments who use text-only browsers.
• Void HTML5 elements (such as img; p. 79) contain only attributes, do not mark up text and do not have a closing tag.

Section 2.8 Special Characters and Horizontal Rules
• HTML5 provides character entity references in the form &*code*; (p. 81) for representing characters.
• Most browsers render a horizontal rule (p. 83), indicated by the <hr> tag (a void element), as a horizontal line with a blank line above and below it.
• Special characters can also be expressed as numeric character references (p. 83)—decimal or hexadecimal (hex; p. 83) values.
• Most browsers render the del element (p. 83) as strike-through text. With this format users can indicate document revisions.

Section 2.9 Lists
• The unordered-list element ul (p. 83) creates a list in which each item begins with a bullet symbol (called a disc). Each entry in an unordered list is an li (list item) element (p. 83). Most web browsers render these elements on a new line with a bullet symbol indented from the beginning of the line.
• Lists may be nested to represent hierarchical data relationships.
• The ordered-list element ol (p. 84) creates a list in which each item begins with a number.

Section 2.10 Tables

- Tables are frequently used to organize data into rows and columns. Tables are defined with the table element (p. 86).

- The caption element (p. 86) specifies a table's title. The text inside the <caption> tag is rendered above the table by most browsers. It's good practice to include a general description of a table's information in the table element's summary attribute—one of the many HTML5 features that make web pages more accessible to users with disabilities. Speech devices use this attribute to make the table more accessible to users with visual impairments.

- A table has three distinct sections: head, body and foot (p. 88). The head section (or header cell) is defined with a thead element (p. 88), which contains header information such as column names.

- Each tr element (p. 88) defines an individual table row (p. 88). The columns in the head section are defined with th elements (p. 88).

- The table body, defined in a tbody element (p. 88), contains the table's primary data.

- The foot section is defined with a tfoot element (p. 88). The text placed in the footer commonly includes calculation results and footnotes.

- You can create larger data cells using the attributes rowspan (p. 89) and colspan (p. 89). The values assigned to these attributes specify the number of rows or columns occupied by a cell.

- The br element (p. 89) causes most browsers to render a line break (p. 89). Any markup or text following a br element is rendered on the next line.

Section 2.11 Forms

- HTML5 provides forms (p. 90) for collecting information from a user.

- Forms can contain visual and nonvisual components. Visual components include clickable buttons and other graphical user-interface components with which users interact. Nonvisual components, called hidden inputs (p. 93), store any data that you specify, such as e-mail addresses and HTML5 document file names that act as links.

- A form is defined by a form element (p. 92).

- Nonvisual components, called hidden inputs (p. 93), store any data that you specify.

- Attribute method (p. 92) specifies how the form's data is sent to the web server.

- The action attribute (p. 92) in the form element specifies the URL of the script on the web server that will be invoked to process the form's data.

- The text input (p. 93) inserts a text field into the form. Users can type data into text fields.

- The input element's size attribute (p. 93) specifies the number of characters visible in the text field. Optional attribute maxlength (p. 93) limits the number of characters input into the text field.

- The submit input (p. 93) is a button that, when pressed, sends the user to the location specified in the form's attribute. The reset input element sets the text displayed on the button (the default value is **Reset** if you omit the value attribute).

- The textarea element (p. 93) inserts a multiline text area into a form. The number of rows is specified with the rows attribute (p. 93) and the number of columns (i.e., characters per line) with the cols attribute (p. 93).

- The password input (p. 96) inserts a password box with the specified size (maximum number of characters allowed).

- A password box allows users to enter sensitive information, such as credit card numbers and passwords, by "masking" the information input with asterisks (*). Asterisks are usually the masking character used for password boxes. The actual value input is sent to the web server, not the characters that mask the input.

- checkboxes (p. 96) enable users to select from a set of options. When a user selects a checkbox, a check mark appears in the checkbox. Otherwise, the checkbox remains empty. checkboxes can be used individually or in groups. checkboxes that are part of the same group have the same name.

- radio buttons (p. 96) are similar to checkboxes, except that only one radio button in a group can be selected at any time. The radio buttons in a group all have the same name attribute and are distinguished by their different value attributes.

- The select element (p. 97) provides a drop-down list from which the user can select an item. The name attribute identifies the drop-down list. The option element adds items to the drop-down list.

Section 2.12 *Internal Linking*
- Internal linking (p. 99) is a mechanism that enables the user to jump between locations in the same document.

- To link to a tag with its attribute inside the same web page, the href attribute of an anchor element includes the id attribute value preceded by a pound sign (as in #features).

Section 2.13 meta *Elements*
- Search engines catalog sites by following links from page to page (often known as spidering or crawling) and saving identification and classification information for each page.

- One way that search engines catalog pages is by reading the content in each page's meta elements (p. 99), which specify information about a document.

- Two important attributes of the meta element are name (p. 99), which identifies the type of meta element, and content (p. 99), which provides information search engines use to catalog pages.

- The content attribute of a keywords meta element provides search engines with a list of words that describe the page. These words are compared with words in search requests.

- The content attribute of a description meta element provides a three- to four-line description of a site, written in sentence form. Search engines also use this description to catalog your site and sometimes display this information as part of the search results.

Self-Review Exercises

2.1   State whether each of the following is *true* or *false*. If *false*, explain why.
  a) All the text placed between the <a> and </a> tags forms one paragraph.
  b) A form is defined by a form element.
  c) Anchors can link to an e-mail address using a href attribute
  d) HTML5 provides five heading elements.
  e) Each th element defines an individual table row.

2.2   Fill in the blanks in each of the following:
  a) A form is defined by a(n) _____ element.
  b) In HTML5, one can specify the width of any column, either in _____ or as a(n) _____ of the table width.
  c) The heading element _____ has the largest font and the heading element _____ has the progressively smallest font.
  d) HTML5 _____ always start with <! -- and end with -->.
  e) Tables are defined with the _____ element
  f) The _____ attribute in the form element specifies the URL of the script on the web server that will be invoked to process the form's data.
  g) The table body, defined in a _____ element, contains the table's primary data.
  h) The img element's _____ attribute specifies an image's location.

Answers to Self-Review Exercises

2.1   a) False. All the text placed between the `<p>` and `</p>` tags forms one paragraph. b) True. c) False. Anchors can link to an e-mail address using a `mailto:` URL. d) False. HTML5 provides six heading elements (`h1` through `h6`). e) False. Each `tr` element defines an individual table row.

2.2   a) `form`. b) pixels, percentage. c) `h1`, `h6`. d) comments. e) `table`. f) `action`. g) `tbody`. h) `src`.

Exercises

2.3   Use HTML5 to create a document that contains the following text:

```
Internet and World Wide Web How to Program: Fifth Edition
Welcome to the world of Internet programming. We have provided coverage for
many Internet-related topics.
```

Write the first line in `title`. Use `h2` and `h4` for text (the second and third lines of text). Insert a horizontal rule between the `h2` element and the `h4` element. Open your new document in a web browser to view the marked-up document.

2.4   An image named `deitel.png` is 400 pixels wide and 300 pixels high. Write an HTML5 statement using the `width` and `height` attributes of the `img` element to perform each of the following transformations:
    a) Increase the size of the image by 10 percent.
    b) Increase the size of the image by 20 percent.
    c) Change the width-to-height ratio to 3:1, keeping the `width` attained in part (a). [This will distort the image.]

2.5   Create a link to each of the following:
    a) The file `home.html`, located in the `students` directory.
    b) The file `home.html`, located in the `web` subdirectory of the `students` directory.
    c) The file `home.html`, located in the `internet` directory in your parent directory. [*Hint:* .. signifies parent directory.]
    d) The Vice President's e-mail address (`vicepresident@whitehouse.gov`).
    e) The file named `Demo` in the `install` directory of `ftp.dvdrom.com`. [*Hint:* Use `ftp://`.]

2.6   Create an HTML5 document containing an ordered list of two items— soft drinks and fast food. Each ordered list should contain a nested, unordered list of your favorite variety. Provide three varieties in each unordered list.

2.7   Create an HTML5 document that uses an *image* as an *e-mail link*. Use attribute `alt` to provide a description of the image and link.

2.8   Create an HTML5 document that contains links to your four favorite news web sites. Your page should contain the heading "My Favorite News Web Sites." Click on each of these links to test your page.

2.9   Create an HTML5 document that contains an ordered list with links to any five examples presented in this chapter. [*Hint:* Place any five examples from this chapter in an `examples` directory then link to the files in that directory.]

2.10   Identify each of the following HTML5 items as either an *element* or an *attribute*:
    a) `head`
    b) `height`
    c) `rowspan`
    d) `body`
    e) `title`

      f) `ol`
      g) `id`

2.11 State which of the following statements are *true* and which are *false*. If *false*, explain why.
    a) The input element's `maxlength` attribute specifies the number of characters visible in the text field.
    b) Forms can contain visual and nonvisual components.
    c) A table has three distinct sections: `head`, `body` and `foot`.
    d) Most browsers render the `<br>` element as strike-through text.

2.12 Fill in the blanks in each of the following:
    a) The browser _____ all text inside a comment.
    b) The _____ section contains information about the HTML5 document.
    c) All the text placed between the _____ and _____ tags forms one paragraph.
    d) The table body, defined in a(n) _____ element, contains the table's primary data.

2.13 Categorize each of the following as an element or an attribute:
    a) `method`
    b) `meta`
    c) `form`
    d) `rows`
    e) `thead`
    f) `cols`

2.14 Create the HTML5 markup that produces the table shown in Fig. 2.18. Use `<em>` and `<strong>` tags as necessary. The image (`camel.png`) is included in the Chapter 2 examples directory.

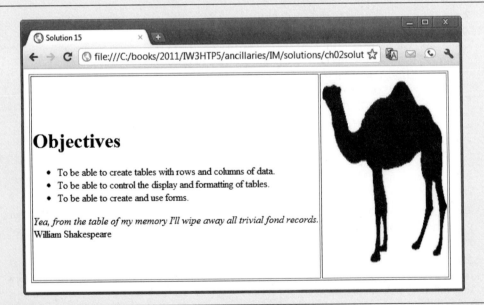

Fig. 2.18 | HTML5 table for Exercise 2.14.

2.15 Write an HTML5 document that produces the table shown in Fig. 2.19.

2.16 A local university has asked you to create an HTML5 document that allows prospective college students to provide feedback about their campus visit. Your HTML5 document should contain a form with text fields for a name and e-mail. Provide checkboxes that allow prospective students to

Fig. 2.19 | HTML5 table for Exercise 2.15.

indicate what they liked most about the campus. The checkboxes should include: campus, students, location, atmosphere, dorm rooms and sports. Also, provide radio buttons that ask the prospective students how they became interested in the college. Options should include: friends, television, Internet and other. In addition, provide a text area for additional comments, a submit button and a reset button. Use post to sent the information in the form to `http://www.deitel.com`.

2.17   Create an HTML5 document titled "Internet and World Wide Web: How to Program." Use <meta> tags to include a series of keywords that describe your document.

2.18   Why is the following markup *invalid*?

```
<h1> Internet and World Wide Web
<hr />
<h2>And some more text...</h2>
```

3

Introduction to HTML5: Part 2

Form ever follows function.
—Louis Sullivan

I listen and give input only if somebody asks.
—Barbara Bush

Objectives

In this chapter you'll:

- Build a form using the new HTML5 **input** types.

- Specify an **input** element in a form as the one that should receive the focus by default.

- Use self-validating **input** elements.

- Specify temporary **placeholder** text in various **input** elements

- Use **autocomplete input** elements that help users re-enter text that they've previously entered in a form.

- Use a **datalist** to specify a list of values that can be entered in an **input** element and to autocomplete entries as the user types.

- Use HTML5's new page-structure elements to delineate parts of a page, including headers, sections, figures, articles, footers and more.

3.1 Introduction

We now continue our presentation of HTML5 by discussing various new features, including:

- new `input` element types for colors, dates, times, e-mail addresses, numbers, ranges of integer values, telephone numbers, URLs, search queries, months and weeks—browsers that don't support these `input` types simply render them as standard text `input` elements

- autocompletion capabilities that help users quickly re-enter text that they've previously entered in a form

- `datalist`s for providing lists of allowed values that a user can enter in an `input` element and for autocompleting those values as the user types

- page-structure elements that enable you to delineate and give meaning to the parts of a page, such as headers, navigation areas, footers, sections, articles, asides, summaries/details, figures, figure captions and more

Support for the features presented in this chapter varies among browsers, so for our sample outputs we've used several browsers. We'll discuss many more new HTML5 features throughout the remaining chapters.

3.2 New HTML5 Form `input` Types

Figure 3.1 demonstrates HTML5's new form `input` types. These are not yet universally supported by all browsers. In this example, we provide sample outputs from a variety of browsers so that you can see how the `input` types behave in each.

```
1   <!DOCTYPE html>
2
3   <!-- Fig. 3.1: newforminputtypes.html -->
4   <!-- New HTML5 form input types and attributes. -->
5   <html>
6      <head>
7         <meta charset="utf-8">
8         <title>New HTML5 Input Types</title>
9      </head>
10
11     <body>
12        <h1>New HTML5 Input Types Demo</h1>
13        <p>This form demonstrates the new HTML5 input types
14           and the placeholder, required and autofocus attributes.
15        </p>
16
17        <form method = "post" action = "http://www.deitel.com">
18           <p>
19              <label>Color:
20                 <input type = "color" autofocus />
21                 (Hexadecimal code such as #ADD8E6)
22              </label>
23           </p>
24           <p>
25              <label>Date:
26                 <input type = "date" />
27                 (yyyy-mm-dd)
28              </label>
29           </p>
30           <p>
31              <label>Datetime:
32                 <input type = "datetime" />
33                 (yyyy-mm-ddThh:mm+ff:gg, such as 2012-01-27T03:15)
34              </label>
35           </p>
36           <p>
37              <label>Datetime-local:
38                 <input type = "datetime-local" />
39                 (yyyy-mm-ddThh:mm, such as 2012-01-27T03:15)
40              </label>
41           </p>
42           <p>
43              <label>Email:
44                 <input type = "email" placeholder = "name@domain.com"
45                 required /> (name@domain.com)
46              </label>
47           </p>
48           <p>
49              <label>Month:
50                 <input type = "month" /> (yyyy-mm)
51              </label>
52           </p>
53           <p>
```

Fig. 3.1 | New HTML5 form input types and attributes. (Part 1 of 2.)

```
54              <label>Number:
55                  <input type = "number"
56                      min = "0"
57                      max = "7"
58                      step = "1"
59                      value = "4" />
60              </label> (Enter a number between 0 and 7)
61          </p>
62          <p>
63              <label>Range:
64                  0 <input type = "range"
65                      min = "0"
66                      max = "20"
67                      value = "10" /> 20
68              </label>
69          </p>
70          <p>
71              <label>Search:
72                  <input type = "search" placeholder = "search query" />
73              </label> (Enter your search query here.)
74          </p>
75          <p>
76              <label>Tel:
77                  <input type = "tel" placeholder = "(###) ###-####"
78                      pattern = "\(\d{3}\) +\d{3}-\d{4}" required />
79                      (###) ###-####
80              </label>
81          </p>
82          <p>
83              <label>Time:
84                  <input type = "time" /> (hh:mm:ss.ff)
85              </label>
86          </p>
87          <p>
88              <label>URL:
89                  <input type = "url"
90                      placeholder = "http://www.domainname.com" />
91                      (http://www.domainname.com)
92              </label>
93          </p>
94          <p>
95              <label>Week:
96                  <input type = "week" />
97                      (yyyy-Wnn, such as 2012-W01)
98              </label>
99          </p>
100         <p>
101             <input type = "submit" value = "Submit" />
102             <input type = "reset" value = "Clear" />
103         </p>
104     </form>
105   </body>
106 </html>
```

Fig. 3.1 | New HTML5 form input types and attributes. (Part 2 of 2.)

3.2.1 input Type color

The **color input type** (Fig. 3.1, lines 20–21) enables the user to enter a color. At the time of this writing, most browsers render the color input type as a text field in which the user can enter a hexadecamal code or a color name. In the future, when you click a color input, browsers will likely display a *color picker* similar to the Microsoft Windows color dialog shown in Fig. 3.2.

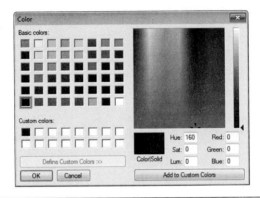

Fig. 3.2 | A dialog for choosing colors.

autofocus Attribute

The **autofocus attribute** (Fig. 3.1, line 20)—an optional attribute that can be used in only one input element on a form—automatically gives the focus to the input element, allowing the user to begin typing in that element immediately. Figure 3.3 shows auto-focus on the color element—the first input element in our form—as rendered in Chrome. You do not need to include autofocus in your forms.

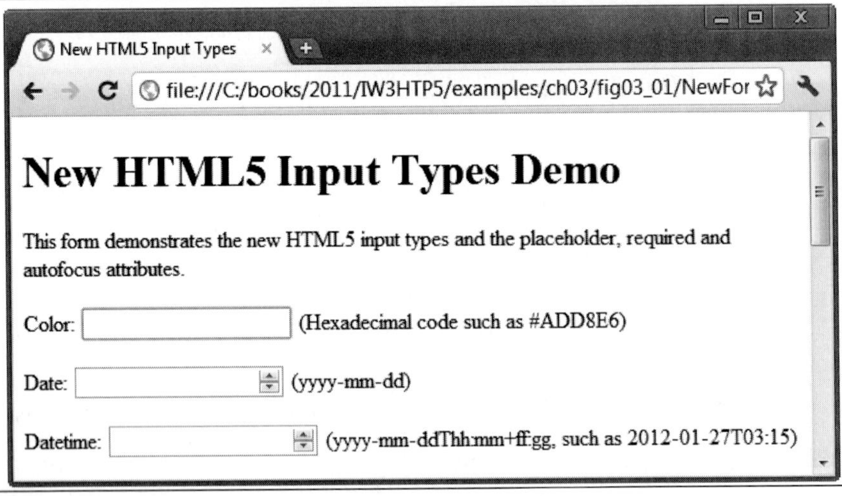

![New HTML5 Input Types Demo browser window]

New HTML5 Input Types Demo

This form demonstrates the new HTML5 input types and the placeholder, required and autofocus attributes.

Color: [   ] (Hexadecimal code such as #ADD8E6)

Date: [   ] (yyyy-mm-dd)

Datetime: [   ] (yyyy-mm-ddThh:mm+ff.gg, such as 2012-01-27T03:15)

Fig. 3.3 | Autofocus in the color input element using Chrome.

Validation

Traditionally it's been difficult to validate user input, such as ensuring that an e-mail address, URL, date or time is entered in the proper format. The new HTML 5 input types are *self validating* on the client side, eliminating the need to add complicated JavaScript code to your web pages to validate user input, reducing the amount of invalid data submitted and consequently reducing Internet traffic between the server and the client to correct invalid input. *The server should still validate all user input.*

When a user enters data into a form then submits the form (in this example, by clicking the **Submit** button), the browser immediately checks the self-validating elements to ensure that the data is correct. For example, if a user enters an incorrect hexadecimal color value when using a browser that renders the color elements as a text field (e.g., Chrome), a callout pointing to the element will appear, indicating that an invalid value was entered (Fig. 3.4). Figure 3.5 lists each of the new HTML5 input types and provides examples of the proper formats required for each type of data to be valid.

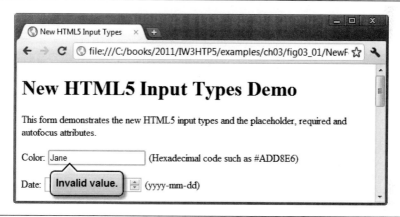

Fig. 3.4 | Validating a color input in Chrome.

input type	Format
color	Hexadecimal code
date	yyyy-mm-dd
datetime	yyyy-mm-dd
datetime-local	yyyy-mm-ddThh:mm
month	yyyy-mm
number	Any numerical value
email	name@domain.com
url	http://www.domainname.com
time	hh:mm
week	yyyy-Wnn

Fig. 3.5 | Self-validating input types.

If you want to bypass validation, you can add the **formnovalidate attribute** to input type submit in line 101:

```
<input type = "submit" value = "Submit" formnovalidate />
```

3.2.2 input Type date

The **date input type** (lines 26–27) enables the user to enter a date in the form yyyy-mm-dd. Firefox and Internet Explorer display a text field in which a user can enter a date such as 2012-01-27. Chrome and Safari display a **spinner control**—a text field with an up-down arrow (🔼) on the right side—allowing the user to select a date by clicking the up or down arrow. The start date is the *current date*. Opera displays a calendar from which you can choose a date. In the future, when the user clicks a date input, browsers are likely to display a date control similar to the Microsoft Windows one shown in Fig. 3.6.

Fig. 3.6 | A date chooser control.

3.2.3 input Type datetime

The **datetime input type** (lines 32–33) enables the user to enter a date (year, month, day), time (hour, minute, second, fraction of a second) and the time zone set to UTC (Coordinated Universal Time or Universal Time, Coordinated). Currently, most of the browsers render datetime as a text field; Chrome renders an up-down control and Opera renders a date and time control. For more information on the datetime input type, visit:

```
www.w3.org/TR/html5/states-of-the-type-attribute.html#
    date-and-time-state
```

3.2.4 input Type datetime-local

The **datetime-local input type** (lines 38–39) enables the user to enter the date and time in a *single* control. The data is entered as year, month, day, hour, minute, second and fraction of a second. Internet Explorer, Firefox and Safari all display a text field. Opera displays a date and time control. For more information on the datetime-local input type, visit:

```
www.w3.org/TR/html5/states-of-the-type-attribute.html#
    local-date-and-time-state
```

3.2.5 `input` Type `email`

The **email input type** (lines 44–45) enables the user to enter an e-mail address or a list of e-mail addresses separated by commas (if the `multiple` attribute is specified). Currently, all of the browsers display a text field. If the user enters an *invalid* e-mail address (i.e., the text entered is *not* in the proper format) and clicks the **Submit** button, a callout asking the user to enter an e-mail address is rendered pointing to the `input` element (Fig. 3.7). HTML5 does not check whether an e-mail address entered by the user actually exists—rather it just validates that the e-mail address is in the *proper format*.

Fig. 3.7 | Validating an e-mail address in Chrome.

placeholder Attribute

The **placeholder** attribute (lines 44, 72 and 77) allows you to place temporary text in a text field. Generally, `placeholder` text is *light gray* and provides an example of the text and/or text format the user should enter (Fig. 3.8). When the *focus* is placed in the text field (i.e., the cursor is in the text field), the `placeholder` text disappears—it's not "submitted" when the user clicks the **Submit** button (unless the user types the same text).

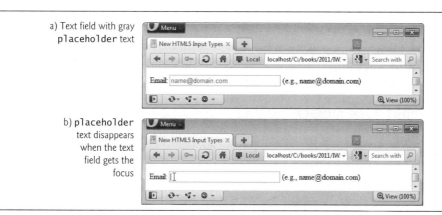

a) Text field with gray placeholder text

b) placeholder text disappears when the text field gets the focus

Fig. 3.8 | `placeholder` text disappears when the `input` element gets the focus.

HTML5 supports `placeholder` text for only six `input` types—`text`, `search`, `url`, `tel`, `email` and `password`. Because the user's browser might not support `placeholder` text, we've added descriptive text to the right of each `input` element.

required Attribute

The **required attribute** (lines 45 and 78) forces the user to enter a value before submitting the form. You can add required to any of the input types. In this example, the user *must* enter an e-mail address and a telephone number before being able to submit the form. For example, if the user fails to enter an e-mail address and clicks the **Submit** button, a callout pointing to the empty element appears, asking the user to enter the information (Fig. 3.9).

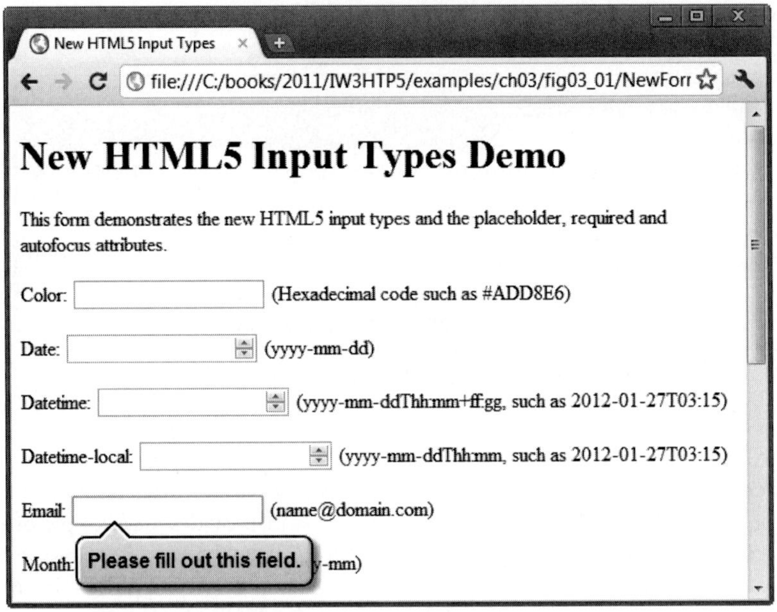

Fig. 3.9 | Demonstrating the required attribute in Chrome.

3.2.6 input Type month

The **month input type** (line 50) enables the user to enter a year and month in the format yyyy-mm, such as 2012-01. If the user enters the data in an improper format (e.g., January 2012) and submits the form, a callout stating that an invalid value was entered appears.

3.2.7 input Type number

The **number input type** (lines 55–59) enables the user to enter a numerical value—mobile browsers typically display a numeric keypad for this input type. Internet Explorer, Firefox and Safari display a text field in which the user can enter a number. Chrome and Opera render a spinner control for adjusting the number. The min attribute sets the minimum valid number, in this case "0". The max attribute sets the maximum valid number, which we set to "7". The step attribute determines the increment in which the numbers increase. For example, we set the step to "1", so the number in the spinner control increases or decreases by one each time the up or down arrow, respectively, in the spinner control is clicked. If you change the step attribute to "2", the number in the spinner control will increase or decrease by two each time the up or down arrow, respectively, is clicked. The value attribute sets the initial value displayed in the form (Fig. 3.10). The spinner control includes only the valid numbers. If the user attempts to enter an invalid value by typing in the text field, a callout pointing to the number input element will instruct the user to enter a valid value.

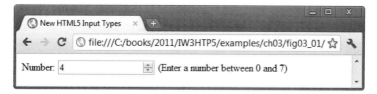

Fig. 3.10 | input type number with a value attribute of 4 as rendered in Chrome.

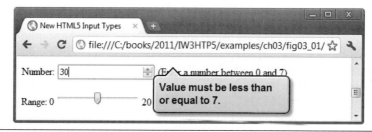

Fig. 3.11 | Chrome checking for a valid number.

3.2.8 input Type range

The **range input type** (lines 64–67) appears as a *slider* control in Chrome, Safari and Opera (Fig. 3.12). You can set the minimum and maximum and specify a value. In our example, the min attribute is "0", the max attribute is "20" and the value attribute is "10", so the slider appears near the center of the range when the document is rendered. The range input type is *inherently self-validating* when it is rendered by the browser as a slider control, because *the user is unable to move the slider outside the bounds of the minimum or maximum value*. A range input is more useful if the user can see the current value changing while dragging the thumb—this can be accomplished with JavaScript, as you'll learn later in the book.

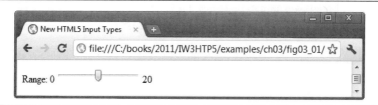

Fig. 3.12 | range slider with a value attribute of 10 as rendered in Chrome.

3.2.9 input Type search

The **search input type** (line 72) provides a search field for entering a query. This input element is functionally equivalent to an input of type text. When the user begins to type in the search field, Chrome and Safari display an **X** that can be clicked to clear the field (Fig. 3.13).

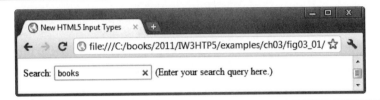

Fig. 3.13 | Entering a search query in Chrome.

3.2.10 input Type tel

The **tel input type** (lines 77–79) enables the user to enter a telephone number—mobile browsers typically display a keypad specific to entering phone numbers for this input type. At the time of this writing, the tel input type is rendered as a text field in all of the browsers. The length and format of telephone numbers varies greatly based on location, making validation quite complex. HTML5 does *not* self validate the tel input type. To ensure that the user enters a phone number in a proper format, we've added a pattern attribute (line 79) that uses a *regular expression* to determine whether the number is in the format:

    (555) 555-5555

When the user enters a phone number in the wrong format, a callout appears requesting the proper format, pointing to the tel input element (Fig. 3.14). Visit www.regexlib.com for a search engine that helps you find already implemented regular expressions that you can use to validate inputs.

Fig. 3.14 | Validating a phone number using the pattern attribute in the tel input type.

3.2.11 input Type time

The **time input type** (line 84) enables the user to enter an hour, minute, seconds and fraction of second (Fig. 3.15). The HTML5 specification indicates that a time must have two digits representing the hour, followed by a colon (:) and two digits representing the minute. Optionally, you can also include a colon followed by two digits representing the seconds and a period followed by one or more digits representing a fraction of a second (shown as ff in our sample text to the right of the time input element in Fig. 3.15.

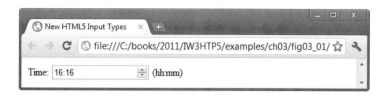

Fig. 3.15 | `time` input as rendered in Chrome.

3.2.12 input Type url

The **url input type** (lines 89–91) enables the user to enter a URL. The element is rendered as a text field, and the proper format is `http://www.deitel.com`. If the user enters an improperly formatted URL (e.g., `www.deitel.com` or `www.deitelcom`), the URL will *not* validate (Fig. 3.16). HTML5 does not check whether the URL entered is valid; rather it validates that the URL entered is in the proper format.

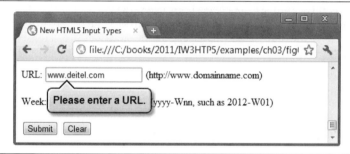

Fig. 3.16 | Validating a URL in Chrome.

3.2.13 input Type week

The **week input type** enables the user to select a year and week number in the format yyyy-Wnn, where nn is 01–53—for example, 2012-W01 represents the first week of 2012. Internet Explorer, Firefox and Safari render a text field. Chrome renders an up-down control. Opera renders *week control* with a down arrow that, when clicked, brings up a calendar for the current month with the corresponding week numbers listed down the left side.

3.3 input and datalist Elements and autocomplete Attribute

Figure 3.17 shows how to use the new autocomplete attribute and datalist element.

3.3.1 input Element autocomplete Attribute

The **autocomplete attribute** (line 18) can be used on input types to automatically fill in the user's information based on previous input—such as name, address or e-mail. You can enable autocomplete for an entire form or just for specific elements. For example, an online order form might set automcomplete = "on" for the name and address inputs and set autocomplete = "off" for the credit card and password inputs for security purposes.

Error-Prevention Tip 3.1

The autocomplete attribute works only if you specify a name or id attribute for the input element.

```
 1   <!DOCTYPE html>
 2
 3   <!-- Fig. 3.17: autocomplete.html -->
 4   <!-- New HTML5 form autocomplete attribute and datalist element. -->
 5   <html>
 6      <head>
 7         <meta charset="utf-8">
 8         <title>New HTML5 autocomplete Attribute and datalist Element</title>
 9      </head>
10
11      <body>
12         <h1>Autocomplete and Datalist Demo</h1>
13         <p>This form demonstrates the new HTML5 autocomplete attribute
14            and the datalist element.
15         </p>
16
17         <!-- turn autocomplete on -->
18         <form method = "post" autocomplete = "on">
19            <p><label>First Name:
20               <input type = "text" id = "firstName"
21                  placeholder = "First name" /> (First name)
22               </label></p>
23            <p><label>Last Name:
24               <input type = "text" id = "lastName"
25                  placeholder = "Last name" /> (Last name)
26               </label></p>
27            <p><label>Email:
28               <input type = "email" id = "email"
29                  placeholder = "name@domain.com" /> (name@domain.com)
30               </label></p>
31            <p><label for = "txtList">Birth Month:
32               <input type = "text" id = "txtList"
33                  placeholder = "Select a month" list = "months" />
34               <datalist id = "months">
35                  <option value = "January">
36                  <option value = "February">
37                  <option value = "March">
38                  <option value = "April">
39                  <option value = "May">
40                  <option value = "June">
41                  <option value = "July">
42                  <option value = "August">
43                  <option value = "September">
44                  <option value = "October">
```

Fig. 3.17 | New HTML5 form autocomplete attribute and datalist element. (Part 1 of 3.)

```
45                    <option value = "November">
46                    <option value = "December">
47                </datalist>
48            </label></p>
49        <p><input type = "submit" value = "Submit" />
50            <input type = "reset" value = "Clear" /></p>
51        </form>
52    </body>
53  </html>
```

a) Form rendered in Firefox before the user interacts with it

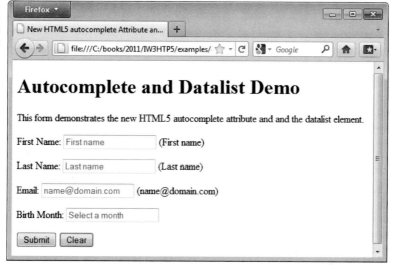

b) autocomplete automatically fills in the data when the user returns to a form submitted previously and begins typing in the **First Name** input element; clicking Jane inserts that value in the input

Fig. 3.17 | New HTML5 form autocomplete attribute and datalist element. (Part 2 of 3.)

c) autocomplete with a datalist showing the previously entered value (June) followed by all items that match what the user has typed so far; clicking an item in the autocomplete list inserts that value in the input

datalist values filtered by what's been typed so far

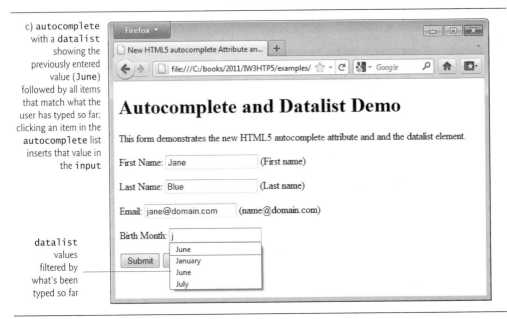

Fig. 3.17 | New HTML5 form autocomplete attribute and datalist element. (Part 3 of 3.)

3.3.2 datalist Element

The **datalist element** (lines 32–47) provides input options for a text input element. At the time of this writing, datalist support varies by browser. In this example, we use a datalist element to obtain the user's birth month. Using Opera, when the user clicks in the text field, a drop-down list of the months of the year appears. If the user types "M" in the text field, the list on months is narrowed to March and May. When using Firefox, the drop-down list of months appears only after the user begins typing in the text field. If the user types "M", all months containing the letter "M" or "m" appear in the drop-down list—March, May, September, November and December.

3.4 Page-Structure Elements

HTML5 introduces several new page-structure elements (Fig. 3.18) that meaningfully identify areas of the page as headers, footers, articles, navigation areas, asides, figures and more.

```
 1   <!DOCTYPE html>
 2
 3   <!-- Fig. 3.18: sectionelements.html -->
 4   <!-- New HTML5 section elements. -->
 5   <html>
 6      <head>
 7         <meta charset="utf-8">
 8         <title>New HTML5 Section Elements</title>
 9      </head>
```

Fig. 3.18 | New HTML5 section elements. (Part 1 of 6.)

```
10
11    <body>
12       <header> <!-- header element creates a header for the page -->
13          <img src = "deitellogo.png" alt = "Deitel logo" />
14          <h1>Welcome to the Deitel Buzz Online<h1>
15
16          <!-- time element inserts a date and/or time -->
17          <time>2012-01-17</time>
18
19       </header>
20
21       <section id = "1"> <!-- Begin section 1 -->
22          <nav> <!-- nav element groups navigation links  -->
23             <h2> Recent Publications</h2>
24             <ul>
25                <li><a href = "http://www.deitel.com/books/iw3htp5">
26                   Internet & World Wide Web How to Program, 5/e</a></li>
27                <li><a href = "http://www.deitel.com/books/androidfp/">
28                   Android for Programmers: An App-Driven Approach</a>
29                </li>
30                <li><a href = "http://www.deitel.com/books/iphonefp">
31                   iPhone for Programmers: An App-Driven Approach</a></li>
32                <li><a href = "http://www.deitel.com/books/jhtp9/">
33                   Java How to Program, 9/e</a></li>
34                <li><a href = "http://www.deitel.com/books/cpphtp8/">
35                   C++ How to Program, 8/e</a></li>
36                <li>
37                   <a href = "http://www.deitel.com/books/vcsharp2010htp">
38                      Visual C# 2010 How to Program, 4/e</a></li>
39                <li><a href = "http://www.deitel.com/books/vb2010htp">
40                   Visual Basic 2010 How to Program</a></li>
41             </ul>
42          </nav>
43       </section>
44
45       <section id = "2"> <!-- Begin section 2 -->
46          <h2>How to Program Series Books</h2>
47          <h3><em>Java How to Program, 9/e</em></h3>
48
49          <figure> <!-- figure element describes the image -->
50             <img src = "jhtp.jpg" alt = "Java How to Program, 9/e" />
51
52             <!-- figurecaption element inserts a figure caption -->
53             <figcaption><em>Java How to Program, 9/e</em>
54                cover.</figcaption>
55          </figure>
56
57          <!--article element represents content from another source -->
58          <article>
59             <header>
60                <h5>From
61                   <em>
62                      <a href = "http://www.deitel.com/books/jhtp9/">
```

Fig. 3.18 | New HTML5 section elements. (Part 2 of 6.)

```
63              Java How to program, 9/e: </a>
64            </em>
65          </h5>
66        </header>
67
68        <p>Features include:
69          <ul>
70            <li>Rich coverage of fundamentals, including
71              <!-- mark element highlights text -->
72              <mark>two chapters on control statements.</mark></li>
73            <li>Focus on <mark>real-world examples.</mark></li>
74            <li><mark>Making a Difference exercises set.</mark></li>
75            <li>Early introduction to classes, objects,
76              methods and strings.</li>
77            <li>Integrated exception handling.</li>
78            <li>Files, streams and object serialization.</li>
79            <li>Optional modular sections on language and
80              library features of the new Java SE 7.</li>
81            <li>Other topics include: Recursion, searching,
82              sorting, generic collections, generics, data
83              structures, applets, multimedia,
84              multithreading, databases/JDBC&trade;, web-app
85              development, web services and an optional
86              ATM Object-Oriented Design case study.</li>
87          </ul>
88
89        <!-- summary element represents a summary for the -->
90        <!-- content of the details element -->
91        <details>
92          <summary>Recent Edition Testimonials</summary>
93          <ul>
94            <li>"Updated to reflect the state of the
95              art in Java technologies; its deep and
96              crystal clear explanations make it
97              indispensable. The social-consciousness
98              [Making a Difference] exercises are
99              something really new and refreshing."
100             <strong>&mdash;Jos&eacute; Antonio
101             Gonz&aacute;lez Seco, Parliament of
102             Andalusia</strong></li>
103           <li>"Gives new programmers the benefit of the
104             wisdom derived from many years of software
105             development experience."<strong>
106             &mdash;Edward F. Gehringer, North Carolina
107             State University</strong></li>
108           <li>"Introduces good design practices and
109             methodologies right from the beginning.
110             An excellent starting point for developing
111             high-quality robust Java applications."
112             <strong>&mdash;Simon Ritter,
113             Oracle Corporation</strong></li>
114           <li>"An easy-to-read conversational style.
115             Clear code examples propel readers to
```

Fig. 3.18 | New HTML5 section elements. (Part 3 of 6.)

```
116                        become proficient in Java."
117                     <strong>&mdash;Patty Kraft, San Diego State
118                     University</strong></li>
119                  <li>"A great textbook with a myriad of examples
120                     from various application domains&mdash;
121                     excellent for a typical CS1 or CS2 course."
122                     <strong>&mdash;William E. Duncan, Louisiana
123                     State University</strong></li>
124               </ul>
125            </details>
126         </p>
127      </article>
128
129      <!-- aside element represents content in a sidebar that's -->
130      <!-- related to the content around the element -->
131      <aside>
132         The aside element is not formatted by the browsers.
133      </aside>
134
135      <h2>Deitel Developer Series Books</h2>
136      <h3><em>Android for Programmers: An App-Driven Approach
137         </em></h3>
138         Click <a href = "http://www.deitel.com/books/androidfp/">
139         here</a> for more information or to order this book.
140
141      <h2>LiveLessons Videos</h2>
142      <h3><em>C# 2010 Fundamentals LiveLessons</em></h3>
143      Click <a href = "http://www.deitel.com/Books/LiveLessons/">
144      here</a> for more information about our LiveLessons videos.
145   </section>
146
147   <section id = "3"> <!-- Begin section 3 -->
148      <h2>Results from our Facebook Survey</h2>
149      <p>If you were a nonprogrammer about to learn Java for the first
150         time, would you prefer a course that taught Java in the
151         context of Android app development? Here are the results from
152         our survey:</p>
153
154         <!-- meter element represents a scale within a range -->
155         0 <meter min = "0"
156         max = "54"
157         value = "14"></meter> 54
158      <p>Of the 54 responders, 14 (green) would prefer to
159      learn Java in the context of Android app development.</p>
160   </section>
161
162   <!-- footer element represents a footer to a section or page, -->
163   <!-- usually containing information such as author name, -->
164   <!-- copyright, etc. -->
165   <footer>
166      <!-- wbr element indicates the appropriate place to break a -->
167      <!-- word when the text wraps -->
168      <h6>&copy; 1992-2012 by Deitel &amp; Associ<wbr>ates, Inc.
```

Fig. 3.18 | New HTML5 section elements. (Part 4 of 6.)

```
169            All Rights Reserved.<h6>
170         <!-- address element represents contact information for a -->
171         <!-- document or the nearest body element or article -->
172         <address>
173            Contact us at <a href = "mailto:deitel@deitel.com">
174            deitel@deitel.com</a>
175         </address>
176      </footer>
177   </body>
178 </html>
```

a) Chrome browser showing the **header** element and a **nav** element that contains an unordered list of links

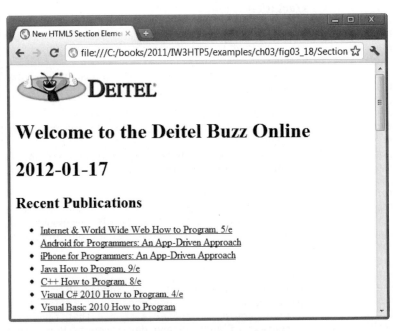

b) Chrome browser showing the beginning of a **section** containing a **figure** and a **figurecaption**

Fig. 3.18 | New HTML5 section elements. (Part 5 of 6.)

c) Chrome browser showing an `article` containing a `header`, some content and a collapsed `details` element, followed by an `aside` element

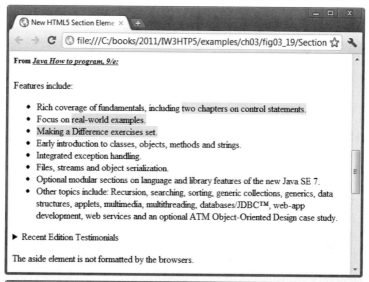

d) Chrome browser showing the end of the `section` that started in part (b)

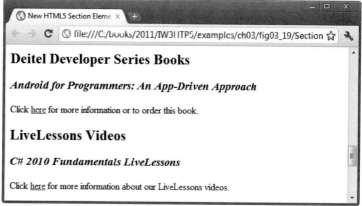

e) Chrome browser showing the last `section` containing a `meter` element, followed by a `footer` element

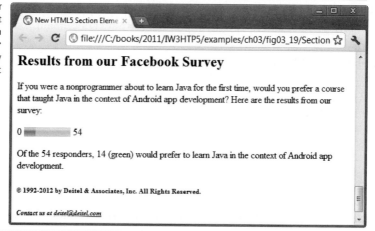

Fig. 3.18 | New HTML5 section elements. (Part 6 of 6.)

3.4.1 header Element

The **header element** (lines 12–19) creates a header for this page that contains both text and graphics. The header element can be used multiple times on a page and can include HTML headings (<h1> through <h6>), navigation, images and logos and more. For an example, see the top of the front page of your favorite newspaper.

t*ime Element*
The **time element** (line 17), which does not need to be enclosed in a header, enables you to identify a date (as we do here), a time or both.

3.4.2 nav Element

The **nav element** (lines 22–42) groups navigation links. In this example, we used the heading **Recent Publications** and created a **ul** element with seven **li** elements that link to the corresponding web pages for each book.

3.4.3 figure Element and figcaption Element

The **figure element** (lines 49–55) describes a figure (such as an image, chart or table) in the document so that it could be moved to the side of the page or to another page. The figure element does not include any styling, but you can style the element using CSS. The **figcaption element** (lines 53–54) provides a caption for the image in the figure element.

3.4.4 article Element

The **article** element (lines 58–127) describes standalone content that could potentially be used or distributed elsewhere, such as a news article, forum post or blog entry. You can nest article elements. For example, you might have reader comments about a magazine nested as an article within the magazine article.

3.4.5 summary Element and details Element

The **summary element** (line 92) displays a right-pointing arrow next to a summary or caption when the document is rendered in a browser (Fig. 3.19). When clicked, the arrow points downward and reveals the content in the **details element** (lines 91–125).

3.4.6 section Element

The **section element** describes a section of a document, usually with a heading for each section—these elements can be nested. For example, you could have a section element for a book, then nested sections for each chapter name in the book. In this example, we broke the document into three sections—the first is **Recent Publications** (lines 21–43). The section element may also be nested in an article.

3.4.7 aside Element

The **aside element** (lines 131–133) describes content that's related to the surrounding content (such as an article) but is somewhat separate from the flow of the text. For example, an aside in a news story might include some background history. A print advertisement might include an aside with product testimonials from users.

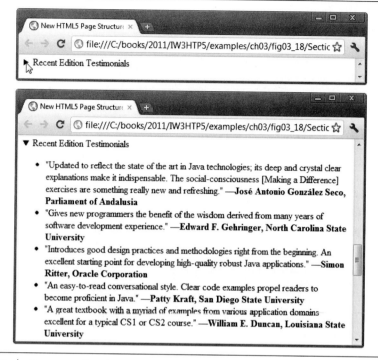

Fig. 3.19 | Demonstrating the `summary` and `detail` elements.

3.4.8 `meter` Element

The **meter element** (lines 155–157) renders a visual representation of a measure within a range (Fig. 3.20). In this example, we show the results of a recent web survey we did. The `min` attribute is "0" and a `max` attribute is "54" —indicating the total number of responses to our survey. The `value` attribute is "14", representing the total number of people who responded "yes" to our survey question.

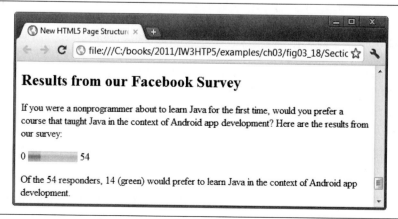

Fig. 3.20 | Chrome rendering the `meter` element.

3.4.9 footer Element

The **footer element** (lines 165–176) describes a *footer*—content that usually appears at the bottom of the content or section element. In this example, we use the footer to describe the copyright notice and contact information. You can use CSS3 to style the footer and position it on the page.

3.4.10 Text-Level Semantics: mark Element and wbr Element

The **mark element** (lines 72–74) highlights the text that's enclosed in the element. The **wbr** element (line 168) indicates the appropriate place to break a word when the text wraps to multiple lines. You might use wbr to prevent a word from breaking in an awkward place.

Summary

Section 3.2 New HTML5 Form **input** *Types*

- HTML5 introduces several new form input types and attributes. These are not yet universally supported by all browsers.
- The Opera browser offers robust support of the new input types.
- We provide sample outputs from a variety of browsers so that you can see how the input types behave differently in each.

Section 3.2.1 **input** *Type* **color**

- The color input type (p. 112) enables the user to enter a color.
- Most browsers render the color input type as a text field in which the user can enter a hexadecimal code.
- In the future, when the user clicks a color input, browsers will likely display a dialog from which the the user can select a color.
- The autofocus attribute (p. 112)—which can be used in only one input element on a form—places the cursor in the text field after the browser loads and renders the page. You do not need to include autofocus in your forms.
- The new HTML 5 input types self validate on the client side, eliminating the need to add JavaScript code to validate user input and reducing the amount of invalid data submitted.
- When a user enters data into a form then submits the form, the browser immediately checks that the data is correct.
- If you want to bypass validation, you can add the formnovalidate attribute (p. 114) to input type submit.
- Using JavaScript, we can customize the validation process.

Section 3.2.2 **input** *Type* **date**

- The date input type (p. 114) enables the user to enter a date in the format yyyy-mm-dd.
- Firefox and Internet Explorer all display a text field in which a user can enter a date such as 2012-01-27.
- Chrome and Safari display a spinner control (p. 114)—a text field with an up-down arrow (⬍) on the right side—allowing the user to select a date by clicking the up or down arrows.
- Opera displays a calendar.

Section 3.2.3 input Type datetime

- The datetime input type (p. 114) enables the user to enter a date (year, month, day), time (hour, minute, second, fraction of a second) and the time zone set to UTC (Coordinated Universal Time or Universal Time, Coordinated).

Section 3.2.4 input Type datetime-local

- The datetime-local input type (p. 114) enables the user to enter the date and time in a *single* control.
- The date is entered as year, month, day, hour, minute, second and fraction of a second.

Section 3.2.5 input Type email

- The email input type (p. 115) enables the user to enter an e-mail address or list of e-mail addresses separated by commas.
- If the user enters an invalid e-mail address (i.e., the text entered is not in the proper format) and clicks the **Submit** button, a callout asking the user to enter an e-mail address is rendered pointing to the input element.
- HTML5 does not validate whether an e-mail address entered by the user actually exists—rather it just validates that the information is in the *proper format*.
- The placeholder attribute (p. 115) allows you to place temporary text in a text field. Generally, placeholder text is light gray and provides an example of the text and text format the user should enter. When the focus is placed in the text field (i.e., the cursor is in the text field), the placeholder text disappears—it's not "submitted" when the user clicks the **Submit** button (unless the user types the same text).
- Add descriptive text to the right of each input element in case the user's browser does not support placeholder text.
- The required attribute (p. 116) forces the user to enter a value before submitting the form.
- You can add required to any of the input types. If the user fails to fill enter a required item, a callout pointing to the empty element appears, asking the user to enter the information.

Section 3.2.6 input Type month

- The month input type (p. 116) enables the user to enter a year and month in the format yyyy-mm, such as 2012-01.
- If the user enters a month in an improper format and clicks the **Submit** button, a callout stating that an invalid value was entered appears.

Section 3.2.7 input Type number

- The number input type (p. 116) enables the user to enter a numerical value.
- The min attribute sets the minimum valid number, in this case "0".
- The max attribute sets the maximum valid number, which we set to "7".
- The step attribute determines the increment in which the numbers increase. For example, if we set the step to "2", the number in the spinner control will increase or decrease by two each time the up or down arrow, respectively, in the spinner control is clicked.
- The value attribute sets the initial value displayed in the form.
- The spinner control includes only the valid numbers. If the user attempts to enter an invalid value by typing in the text field, a callout pointing to the number input element will instruct the user to enter a valid value.

Section 3.2.8 input *Type* range

- The range input type (p. 117) appears as a *slider* control in Chrome, Safari and Opera.
- You can set the minimum and maximum and specify a value.
- The slider appears at the value in the range when the HTML5 document is rendered.
- The range input type is inherently self-validating when it's rendered by the browser as a slider control, because the user is unable to move the slider outside the bounds of the minimum or maximum value.

Section 3.2.9 input *Type* search

- The search input type (p. 117) provides a search field for entering a query and is functionally equivalent to an input of type text.
- When the user begins to type in the search field, Chrome and Safari display an **X** that can be clicked to clear the field.

Section 3.2.10 input *Type* tel

- The tel input type (p. 118) enables the user to enter a telephone number.
- At the time of this writing, the tel input type is rendered as a text field in all of the browsers.
- The length and format of telephone numbers varies greatly based on location, making validation quite complex. HTML5 does not self validate the tel input type. To ensure that the user enters a phone number in a proper format, you can use the pattern attribute.
- When the user enters a phone number in the wrong format, a callout requesting the proper format appears, pointing to the tel input element.

Section 3.2.11 input *Type* time

- The time input type (p. 118) enables the user to enter an hour, minute, second and fraction of a second.

Section 3.2.12 input *Type* url

- The url input type (p. 119) enables the user to enter a URL. The element is rendered as a text field. If the user enters an improperly formatted URL, it will not validate. HTML5 does not ensure that the URL entered actually exists.

Section 3.2.13 input *Type* week

- The week input type (p. 119) enables the user to select a year and week number in the format yyyy-Wnn.
- Opera renders week control with a down arrow that, when clicked, brings up a calendar control.

Section 3.3.1 input *Element* autocomplete *Attribute*

- The autocomplete attribute (p. 119) can be used on input types to automatically fill in the user's information based on previous input.
- You can enable autocomplete for an entire form or just for specific elements.

Section 3.3.2 datalist *Element*

- The datalist element (p. 122) provides input options for a text input element. The browser can use these options to display autocomplete options to the user.

Section 3.4 Page-Structure Elements

- HTML5 introduces several new page structure elements.

Section 3.4.1 `header` Element
- The `header` element (p. 128) creates a header for the page that contains text, graphics or both.
- The `header` element may be used multiple times on a page and often includes HTML headings.
- The `time` element (p. 128) enables you to identify a date, a time or both.

Section 3.4.2 `nav` Element
- The `nav` element (p. 128) groups navigation links.

Section 3.4.3 `figure` Element and `figcaption` Element
- The `figure` element (p. 128) describes an image in the document so that it could be moved to the side of the page or to another page.
- The `figcaption` element (p. 128) provides a caption for the image in the `figure` element.

Section 3.4.4 `article` Element
- The `article` element (p. 128) describes content that's separate from the main content of the page and might be used or distributed elsewhere, such as a news article, forum post or blog entry.
- `article` elements can be nested.

Section 3.4.5 `summary` Element and `details` Element
- The `summary` element (p. 128) displays a right-pointing arrow next to a summary or caption when the document is rendered in a browser. When clicked, the arrow points downward and reveals the content in the `details` element (p. 128).

Section 3.4.6 `section` Element
- The `section` element (p. 128) describes a section of a document, usually with a heading for each section.
- `section` elements can be nested.

Section 3.4.7 `aside` Element
- The `aside` element (p. 128) describes content that's related to the surrounding content (such as an `article`) but that's somewhat separate from the flow of the text.
- `nav` elements can be nested in an `aside` element.

Section 3.4.8 `meter` Element
- The `meter` element (p. 129) renders a visual representation of a measure within a range.
- Useful meter attributes are `min`, `max` and `value`.

Section 3.4.9 `footer` Element
- The `footer` element (p. 130) describes a *footer*—content that usually appears at the bottom of the content or `section` element.
- You can use CSS3 to style the footer and position it on the page.

Section 3.4.10 Text-Level Semantics: `mark` Element and `wbr` Element
- The `mark` element (p. 130) enables you to highlight text.
- The `wbr` element (p. 130) indicates the appropriate place to break a word when the text wraps to multiple lines. You might use `wbr` to prevent a word from breaking in an awkward place.

Self-Review Exercises

3.1 Fill in the blanks in each of the following:

a) HTML5 has _____ for providing lists of allowed values that a user can enter in an input element, and for autocompleting those values as the user types.

b) The _____ attribute determines the increment in which the numbers increase.

c) You can use _____ to style the footer and position it on the page.

d) The _____ element enables you to highlight text.

e) The _____ attribute forces the user to enter a value before submitting the form.

f) For input type search, Chrome and Safari display a(n) _____ that can be clicked to clear the field.

g) The _____ attribute allows you to place temporary text in a text field.

h) Opera renders _____ with a down arrow that, when clicked, brings up a calendar for the current month with the corresponding week numbers listed.

i) The _____ element provides a caption for the image in the figure element.

j) A print advertisement might include a(n) _____ with product testimonials from users.

3.2 State whether each of the following is *true* or *false*. If *false*, explain why.

a) Any particular HTML5 form input types must render identically in every HTML5-compliant browser.

b) When the focus is placed in the text field (i.e., the cursor is in the text field), the placeholder text is submitted to the server.

c) You do not need to include autofocus in your forms.

d) The new HTML 5 input types are self validating on the client side, eliminating the need to add complicated scripts to your forms to validate user input and reducing the amount of invalid data submitted.

e) The range input type is inherently self-validating when it's rendered by the browser as a slider control, because the user is unable to move the slider outside the bounds of the minimum or maximum value.

f) HTML5 self validates the tel input type.

g) If the user enters an improperly formatted URL in a url input type, it will not validate. HTML5 does not validate that the URL entered actually exists.

h) The nav element displays a drop-down menu of hyperlinks.

i) The header element may be used only one time on a page.

j) nav elements can be nested in an aside element.

k) You might use the brk to prevent awkward word breaks.

Answers to Self-Review Exercises

3.1 a) datalists. b) step. c) CSS3. d) mark. e) required. f) X. g) placeholder. h) week control. i) figcaption. j) aside.

3.2 a) False. The rendering of input types can vary among browsers. b) False. When the focus is placed in the text field, the placeholder text disappears. It's not "submitted" when the user clicks the **Submit** button (unless the user types the same text). c) True. d) True. e) True. f) False. The length and format of telephone numbers varies greatly based on location, making validation quite complex, so HTML5 does not self validate the tel input type. To ensure that the user enters a phone number in a proper format, we use the pattern attribute. g) True. h) False. The nav element groups navigation links. i) False. The header element may be used multiple times on a page and often includes HTML headings (<h1> through <h6>) j) True. k) False. You might use the wbr to prevent awkward word breaks.

Exercises

3.3 Fill in the blanks in each of the following:

a) Opera displays a color _____ control that shows the default color (black) with a down arrow that, when clicked, shows a drop-down with 20 basic colors.

b) If you want to bypass validation, you can add the _____ attribute to input type.

c) Chrome displays a(n) _____, a text field with an updown arrow on the right side—allowing the user to select a date by clicking the up or down arrows.

d) The _____ enables the user to enter an e-mail address or a list of e-mail addresses separated by commas.

e) The week input type enables the user to select a year and week number in the format _____.

f) The _____ attribute is used to place a string in a text field.

g) The _____ element describes a section of a document, usually with a heading for each section.

h) The _____ input type enables the user to enter a telephone number.

3.4 State whether each of the following is *true* or *false*. If *false*, explain why.

a) Using HTML, we can customize the validation process.

b) The autofocus attribute—which can be used in only one input element on a form—places the cursor in the text field after the browser loads and renders the page.

c) The autocomplete attribute allows you to place temporary text in a text field.

d) The nav element groups navigation links.

e) The imgcaption element provides a caption for the image in the figure element.

f) The time element enables you to identify a date, a time, or both.

g) The choice input type appears as a *slider* control in Chrome, Safari and Opera.

h) The editorial element describes content that's separate from the main content of the page and might be used or distributed elsewhere, such as a news article, forum post or blog entry.

i) The header element may be used multiple times on a page and often includes HTML headings.

j) section elements cannot be nested.

3.5 Write an HTML5 element (or elements) to accomplish each of the following tasks:

a) Teachers were asked to evaluate students in an examination on a scale of 1 to 100. Use a meter element with text to its left and right to indicate that the average rating was 65 out of 100.

b) Create a details element that displays the summary text "Student Results" for Part (a). When the user clicks the arrow next to the summary text, an explanatory paragraph about the survey should be displayed.

c) Create a text input element for a telephone number. The element should automatically receive the focus when the form is rendered in a browser.

d) How to bypass validation procedure.

e) Use a datalist to provide an autocomplete list for five fruits.

f) Create a range input element that allows the user to select a number from 5 to 50.

g) Specify how autocomplete should always be allowed for a form. Show only the form's opening tag.

h) Use a mark element to highlight the first sentence in the following paragraph.

```
<p> Teachers were asked to evaluate students in an examination
on a scale of 1 to 100. The average result was 65. </p>
```

3.6 *(College Registration Form with Optional Survey)* Create a college registration form to obtain a user's first name, last name, telephone number, and e-mail address. In addition, include an optional survey question that asks the user's qualification. Place the optional survey question in a details element so that the user can expand the details element to see the question.

3.7 *(Creating an Autocomplete Form)* Create a simple number entry form using an number input element in which the user can enter a number. Using the Firefox web browser, test the form by entering 345 and submitting the form. Then enter a 3 in the input element to see previous entries that started with 3–345 should be displayed below the input element. Enter 367 and submit the form again. Now enter a 3 in the input element to see previous entries that started with 3–345 and 367 should be displayed below the input element. Try this with your own search queries as well.

3.8 (Creating an Autocomplete Form with a datalist) Create an autocomplete input element with an associated datalist that contains the months of the year.

3.9 *(Laying Out Book Pages in HTML5: Creating the Sections)* Mark up the paragraph text from Section 3.2.1 of this chapter as a web page using page-structure elements. The text is provided in the exerciseTextAndImages folder with this chapter's examples. Do not include the figures in this exercise.

3.10 *(Laying Out Book Pages in HTML5: Adding Figures)* Modify your solution to Exercise 3.9 to add the section's graphics as figures. The images are provided in the exerciseTextAndImages folder with this chapter's examples.

3.11 *(Laying Out Book Pages in HTML5: Adding a details Element)* Modify your solution to Exercise 3.10 to add the table in Fig. 3.5. Use the figure caption as the summary and format the table as an HTML table element inside the details element.

Introduction to Cascading Style Sheets™ (CSS): Part 1

Fashions fade, style is eternal.
—Yves Saint Laurent

How liberating to work in the margins, outside a central perception.
—Don DeLillo

Objectives

In this chapter you'll:

- Control a website's appearance with style sheets.

- Use a style sheet to give all the pages of a website the same look and feel.

- Use the `class` attribute to apply styles.

- Specify the precise font, size, color and other properties of displayed text.

- Specify element backgrounds and colors.

- Understand the box model and how to control margins, borders and padding.

- Use style sheets to separate presentation from content.

4.1 Introduction

In Chapters 2–3, we introduced HTML5 for marking up information to be rendered in a browser. In this chapter and Chapter 5, we shift our focus to formatting and presenting information. To do this, we use a W3C technology called **Cascading Style Sheets 3** (**CSS3**) that allows you to specify the *presentation* of elements on a web page (e.g., fonts, spacing, sizes, colors, positioning) *separately* from the document's *structure and content* (section headers, body text, links, etc.). This **separation of structure from presentation** simplifies maintaining and modifying web pages, especially on large-scale websites. In Chapter 5, we introduce many new features in CSS3.

HTML5 was designed to specify the content and structure of a document. Though HTML5 has some attributes that control presentation, *it's better not to mix presentation with content*. If a website's presentation is determined entirely by a style sheet, you can simply swap in a new style sheet to completely change the site's appearance.

The W3C provides a CSS3 code validator at `jigsaw.w3.org/css-validator/`. This tool can help you make sure that your code is correct and will work on CSS3-compliant browsers. We've run this validator on every CSS3/HTML5 document in this book. For more CSS3 information, check out our CSS3 Resource Center at `www.deitel.com/css3`.

4.2 Inline Styles

You can declare document styles inline in the HTML5 markup, in embedded style sheets or in separate CSS files. This section presents **inline styles** that declare an individual element's format using the HTML5 attribute **style**. Inline styles *override* any other styles applied using the techniques we discuss later in the chapter. Figure 4.1 applies inline styles to p elements to *alter* their font size and color.

Software Engineering Observation 4.1

Inline styles do not truly separate presentation from content. To apply similar styles to multiple elements, use embedded style sheets or external style sheets, introduced later in this chapter.

```
 1   <!DOCTYPE html>
 2
 3   <!-- Fig. 4.1: inline.html -->
 4   <!-- Using inline styles -->
 5   <html>
 6      <head>
 7         <meta charset = "utf-8">
 8         <title>Inline Styles</title>
 9      </head>
10      <body>
11         <p>This text does not have any style applied to it.</p>
12
13         <!-- The style attribute allows you to declare -->
14         <!-- inline styles. Separate multiple -->
15         <!-- style properties with a semicolon. -->
16         <p style = "font-size: 20pt;">This text has the
17            <em>font-size</em> style applied to it, making it 20pt.
18         </p>
19
20         <p style = "font-size: 20pt; color: deepskyblue;">
21            This text has the <em>font-size</em> and
22            <em>color</em> styles applied to it, making it
23            20pt and deep sky blue.</p>
24      </body>
25   </html>
```

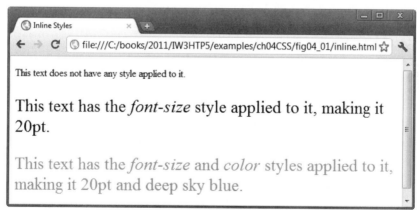

Fig. 4.1 | Using inline styles.

The first inline style declaration appears in line 16. Attribute `style` specifies an element's style. Each **CSS property** (**font-size** in this case) is followed by a colon and a value. In line 16, we declare this particular p element to use a 20-point font size.

Line 20 specifies the two properties, `font-size` and **color**, separated by a semicolon. In this line, we set the given paragraph's `color` to deepskyblue. Hexadecimal codes may be used in place of color names. Figure 4.2 contains the HTML standard color set. We provide a list of extended hexadecimal color codes and color names in Appendix B. You can also find a complete list of HTML standard and extended colors at www.w3.org/TR/css3-color/.

Color name	Value	Color name	Value
aqua	#00FFFF	navy	#000080
black	#000000	olive	#808000
blue	#0000FF	purple	#800080
fuchsia	#FF00FF	red	#FF0000
gray	#808080	silver	#C0C0C0
green	#008000	teal	#008080
lime	#00FF00	yellow	#FFFF00
maroon	#800000	white	#FFFFFF

Fig. 4.2 | HTML standard colors and hexadecimal RGB values.

4.3 Embedded Style Sheets

A second technique for using style sheets is **embedded style sheets**, which enable you to *embed* a CSS3 document in an HTML5 document's head section. Figure 4.3 creates an embedded style sheet containing four styles.

```
1   <!DOCTYPE html>
2
3   <!-- Fig. 4.3: embedded.html -->
4   <!-- Embedded style sheet. -->
5   <html>
6      <head>
7         <meta charset = "utf-8">
8         <title>Embedded Style Sheet</title>
9
10        <!-- this begins the style sheet section -->
11        <style type = "text/css">
12           em       { font-weight: bold;
13                      color: black; }
14           h1       { font-family: tahoma, helvetica, sans-serif; }
15           p        { font-size: 12pt;
16                      font-family: arial, sans-serif; }
17           .special { color: purple; }
18        </style>
19     </head>
20     <body>
21        <!-- this attribute applies the .special style class -->
22        <h1 class = "special">Deitel & Associates, Inc.</h1>
23
24        <p>Deitel & Associates, Inc. is an authoring and
25           corporate training organization specializing in
26           programming languages, Internet and web technology,
27           iPhone and Android app development, and object
28           technology education.</p>
29
```

Fig. 4.3 | Embedded style sheet. (Part 1 of 2.)

```
30        <h1>Clients</h1>
31        <p class = "special"> The company's clients include many
32            <em>Fortune 1000 companies</em>, government agencies,
33            branches of the military and business organizations.</p>
34      </body>
35    </html>
```

Fig. 4.3 | Embedded style sheet. (Part 2 of 2.)

The style *Element and MIME Types*

The style element (lines 11–18) defines the *embedded style sheet*. Styles placed in the head apply to matching elements wherever they appear in the body. The style element's type attribute specifies the **MIME (Multipurpose Internet Mail Extensions) type** that describes the style element's content. CSS documents use the MIME type text/css. As of HTML5, the default type for a style element is "text/css", so this attribute is no longer needed—we kept it here because you'll see this used in legacy HTML code. Figure 4.4 lists common MIME types used in this book. For a complete list of MIME types, visit:

www.w3schools.com/media/media_mimeref.asp

MIME type	Description
text/css	CSS documents
image/png	PNG images
text/javascript	JavaScript markup
text/plain	Plain text
image/jpeg	JPEG image
text/html	HTML markup

Fig. 4.4 | A few common MIME types.

The style sheet's body (lines 12–17) declares the **CSS rules** for the style sheet. To achieve the separation between the CSS3 code and the HTML5 that it styles, we'll use a **CSS selector** to specify the elements that will be styled according to a rule. Our first rule (line 12) begins with the selector em, which selects all **em elements** in the document. An **em element** indicates that its contents should be *emphasized*. Browsers usually render em elements in an *italic* font. Each rule's body is enclosed in *curly braces* ({ and }). CSS rules in embedded style sheets use the same syntax as inline styles; the property name is followed by a colon (:) and the property value. Multiple properties are separated by semicolons (;). The **font-weight** property in line 12 specifies the "boldness" of text. Possible values are bold, normal (the default), bolder (bolder than bold text) and lighter (lighter than normal text). Boldness also can be specified with multiples of 100, from 100 to 900. Text specified as normal is equivalent to 400, and bold text is equivalent to 700. However, many systems do not have fonts that can scale with this level of precision, so using these numeric values might not display the desired effect.

In this example, all em elements will be displayed in a bold black font. We also apply styles to all h1 and p elements (lines 14–16).

Style Classes

Line 17 declares a selector for a **style class** named special. Style-class declarations are preceded by a period (.). They define styles that can be applied to *any* element. In this example, class special sets color to purple. We'll show how to apply a style class momentarily. You can also declare id selectors. If an element in your page has an id, you can declare a selector of the form *#elementId* to specify that element's style.

font-family *Property*

The **font-family** property (line 14) specifies the name of the font to use. Not all users have the same fonts installed on their computers, so CSS allows you to specify a comma-separated list of fonts to use for a particular style. The browser attempts to use the fonts in the order in which they appear in the list. It's advisable to end a font list with a **generic font family** name in case the other fonts are not installed on the user's computer (Fig. 4.5). In this example, if the tahoma font is not found on the system, the browser will look for the helvetica font. If neither is found, the browser will display its default sans-serif font.

Generic font families	Examples
serif	times new roman, georgia
sans-serif	arial, verdana, futura
cursive	script
fantasy	critter
monospace	courier, fixedsys

Fig. 4.5 | Generic font families.

font-size *Property*

Property **font-size** (line 15) specifies a 12-point font. Other possible measurements in addition to pt (point) are introduced in Section 4.4. Relative values—xx-small, x-small, small, smaller, medium, large, larger, x-large and xx-large—also can be used. Generally, *relative font-size values are preferred over points, because an author does not know the specific measurements of each client's display.* Relative values permit more flexible viewing of web pages. For example, users can change font sizes the browser displays for readability.

A user may view a web page on a handheld device with a small screen. Specifying a fixed font size (such as 18pt) prevents the browser from scaling fonts. A relative font size, such as large or larger, allows the browser to determine the *actual size* of the text displayed. Using relative sizes also makes pages more accessible to users with disabilities. Users with impaired vision, for example, may configure their browser to use a larger default font, upon which all relative sizes are based. Text that the author specifies to be smaller than the main text still displays in a smaller size font. Accessibility is an important consideration—in 1998, Congress passed the Section 508 Amendment to the Rehabilitation Act of 1973, mandating that websites of federal government agencies be accessible to disabled users. For more information, visit www.access-board.gov/508.htm.

Applying a Style Class
Line 22 uses the HTML5 attribute **class** in an h1 element to apply a style class—in this case, the class named special (declared with the .special selector in the style sheet on line 17). When the browser renders the h1 element, the text appears on screen with the properties of both an h1 element (tahoma, helvetica or sans-serif font defined in line 14) and the .special style class applied (the color purple defined in line 17). The browser also still applies its own default style to the h1 element—the header is displayed in a large font size. Similarly, all em elements will still be italicized by the browser, but they will also be bold as a result of lines 12–13.

The formatting rules for both the p element and the .special class are applied to the text in lines 31–33. In many cases, the styles applied to an element (the **parent** or **ancestor element**) also apply to the element's *nested elements* (**child** or **descendant elements**). The em element nested in the p element in line 32 **inherits** the style from the p element (namely, the 12-point font size in line 15) but retains its italic style. So styles defined for the paragraph and *not* defined for the em element are still applied to this em element that's nested in the p element. Multiple values of one property can be set or inherited on the same element, so the browser must reduce them to one value for that property per element before they're rendered. We discuss the rules for resolving these conflicts in the next section.

4.4 Conflicting Styles

Styles may be defined by a **user**, an **author** or a **user agent**. A user is a person viewing your web page, you're the author—the person who writes the document—and the user agent is the program used to render and display the document (e.g., a web browser).

- Styles **cascade** (and hence the term "Cascading Style Sheets"), or flow together, such that the ultimate appearance of elements on a page results from combining styles defined in several ways.

- Styles defined by the user take precedence over styles defined by the user agent.

- Styles defined by authors take precedence over styles defined by the user.

Most styles defined for parent elements are also **inherited** by child (nested) elements. This makes sense for most styles, such as font properties, but there are certain properties that you don't want to be inherited. For example, the background-image property allows you to set an image as the background of an element. If the body element is assigned a background image, we don't want the same image to be in the background of every element in the body of our page. Instead, the background-image property of all child elements retains its default value of none. In this section, we discuss the rules for *resolving conflicts* between *styles defined for elements* and styles inherited from parent and ancestor elements.

Figure 4.3 contains an example of inheritance in which a child em element inherits the font-size property from its parent p element. However, in Fig. 4.3, the child em element has a color property that *conflicts with* (i.e., has a different value than) the color property of its parent p element. Properties defined for child and descendant elements have a higher **specificity** than properties defined for parent and ancestor elements. Conflicts are resolved in favor of properties with a *higher* specificity, so the child's styles take precedence. Figure 4.6 illustrates examples of inheritance and specificity.

```
1   <!DOCTYPE html>
2
3   <!-- Fig. 4.6: advanced.html -->
4   <!-- Inheritance in style sheets. -->
5   <html>
6      <head>
7         <meta charset = "utf-8">
8         <title>More Styles</title>
9         <style type = "text/css">
10           body     { font-family: arial, helvetica, sans-serif; }
11           a.nodec  { text-decoration: none; }
12           a:hover  { text-decoration: underline; }
13           li em    { font-weight: bold; }
14           h1, em   { text-decoration: underline; }
15           ul       { margin-left: 20px; }
16           ul ul    { font-size: .8em; }
17        </style>
18     </head>
19     <body>
20        <h1>Shopping list for Monday:</h1>
21
22        <ul>
23           <li>Milk</li>
24           <li>Bread
25              <ul>
26                 <li>white bread</li>
27                 <li>Rye bread</li>
28                 <li>Whole wheat bread</li>
29              </ul>
30           </li>
31           <li>Carrots</li>
32           <li>Yogurt</li>
33           <li>Pizza <em>with mushrooms</em></li>
34        </ul>
35
36        <p><em>Go to the</em>
37           <a class = "nodec" href = "http://www.deitel.com">
38              Grocery store</a>
39        </p>
40     </body>
41  </html>
```

Fig. 4.6 | Inheritance in style sheets. (Part 1 of 2.)

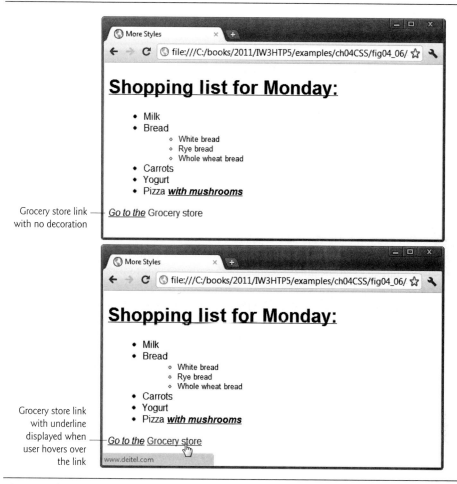

Grocery store link with no decoration

Grocery store link with underline displayed when user hovers over the link

Fig. 4.6 | Inheritance in style sheets. (Part 2 of 2.)

Line 11 applies property text-decoration to all a elements whose class attribute is set to nodec (line 37). The text-decoration property applies **decorations** to text in an element. By default, browsers underline the text of an a (anchor) element. Here, we set the text-decoration property to none to indicate that the browser should *not* underline hyperlinks. Other possible values for text-decoration include overline, line-through and underline. The .nodec appended to a is a *more specific* class selector; this style in line 11 applies only to a (anchor) elements that specify the nodec in their class attribute.

Portability Tip 4.1

To ensure that your style sheets work in various web browsers, test them on many client web browsers, and use the W3C CSS Validator.

Line 12 specifies a style for hover, which is a **pseudo-class**. Pseudo-classes give you access to information that's not declared in the document, such as whether the mouse is hovering over an element or whether the user has previously clicked (visited) a particular hyperlink. The **hover pseudo-class** is activated dynamically when the user moves the mouse cursor over (that is, hovers over) an element. Pseudo-classes are separated by a *colon* (with no surrounding spaces) from the name of the element to which they're applied.

Common Programming Error 4.1

Including a space before or after the colon separating a pseudo-class from the name of the element to which it's applied prevents the pseudo-class from being applied properly.

Line 13 causes all em elements that are children of li elements to be bold. In the screen output of Fig. 4.6, Go to the (contained in an em element in line 36) does not appear bold, because the em element is *not* nested in an li element. However, the em element containing with mushrooms (line 33) *is* nested in an li element, so it's formatted in bold. The syntax for applying rules to multiple elements is similar. In line 14, we separate the selectors with a *comma* to apply an *underline* style rule to all h1 *and* all em elements.

Line 15 assigns a 20-pixel left margin to all ul elements. We'll discuss the margin properties in detail in Section 4.10. A pixel is a **relative-length measurement**—it varies in size, based on screen resolution. Other relative lengths include **em** (which, as a measurement, means the font's uppercase *M* height—the most frequently used font measurement), **ex** (the font's *x*-height—usually set to a lowercase *x*'s height) and percentages (e.g., font-size: 50%). To set an element to display text at 150 percent of its default text size, you could use

```
font-size: 1.5em
```

or

```
font-size: 150%
```

Other units of measurement available in CSS are **absolute-length measurements**—i.e., units that do *not* vary in size based on the system. These units are **in** (inches), **cm** (centimeters), **mm** (millimeters), **pt** (points; 1 pt = 1/72 in) and **pc** (picas; 1 pc = 12 pt). Line 16 specifies that all nested unordered lists (ul elements that are descendants of ul elements) are to have font size .8em. [*Note:* When setting a style property that takes a measurement (e.g. font-size, margin-left), no units are necessary if the value is zero.]

Good Programming Practice 4.1

Whenever possible, use relative-length measurements. If you use absolute-length measurements, your document may not scale well on some client browsers (e.g., smartphones).

4.5 Linking External Style Sheets

Style sheets are a convenient way to create a document with a uniform theme. With **external style sheets** (i.e., *separate* documents that contain only CSS rules), you can provide a *uniform look and feel* to an entire website (or to a portion of one). You can also *reuse* the same external style sheet across multiple websites. Different pages on a site can all use the same style sheet. When changes to the styles are required, you need to modify only a single CSS file to make style changes across *all* the pages that use those styles. This concept is sometimes known as **skinning**. While embedded style sheets separate content from presentation, both are still contained in a *single* file, preventing a web designer and a content author from conveniently working in parallel. External style sheets solve this problem by separating the content and style into separate files.

Figure 4.7 presents an external style sheet. Lines 1–2 are **CSS comments**. These may be placed in any type of CSS code (i.e., inline styles, embedded style sheets and external style sheets) and always start with /* and end with */. Text between these delimiters is ignored by the browser. The rules in this external style sheet are the same as those in the embedded style sheet in Fig. 4.6, lines 10–16.

```
1   /* Fig. 4.7: styles.css */
2   /* External style sheet */
3   body     { font-family: arial, helvetica, sans-serif; }
4   a.nodec  { text-decoration: none; }
5   a:hover  { text-decoration: underline; }
6   li em    { font-weight: bold; }
7   h1, em   { text-decoration: underline; }
8   ul       { margin-left: 20px; }
9   ul ul    { font-size: .8em; }
```

Fig. 4.7 | External style sheet.

Figure 4.8 contains an HTML5 document that references the external style sheet. Lines 9–10 show a **link** element that uses the **rel** attribute to specify a **relationship** between the current document and another document. Here, we declare the linked document to be a **stylesheet** for this document. The type attribute specifies the related document's MIME type as text/css. The href attribute provides the style sheet document's URL. Using just the file name styles.css, as we do here, indicates that styles.css is in the same directory as external.html. The rendering results are the same as in Fig. 4.6.

```
1   <!DOCTYPE html>
2
3   <!-- Fig. 4.8: external.html -->
4   <!-- Linking an external style sheet. -->
5   <html>
6     <head>
7       <meta charset = "utf-8">
8       <title>Linking External Style Sheets</title>
9       <link rel = "stylesheet" type = "text/css"
10         href = "styles.css">
11    </head>
12    <body>
13      <h1>Shopping list for <em>Monday</em>:</h1>
14
15      <ul>
16        <li>Milk</li>
17        <li>Bread
18          <ul>
19            <li>white bread</li>
20            <li>Rye bread</li>
21            <li>Whole wheat bread</li>
22          </ul>
23        </li>
```

Fig. 4.8 | Linking an external style sheet. (Part 1 of 2.)

```
24          <li>Carrots</li>
25          <li>Yogurt</li>
26          <li>Pizza <em>with mushrooms</em></li>
27       </ul>
28
29       <p><em>Go to the</em>
30          <a class = "nodec" href = "http://www.deitel.com">
31             Grocery store</a>
32       </p>
33    </body>
34 </html>
```

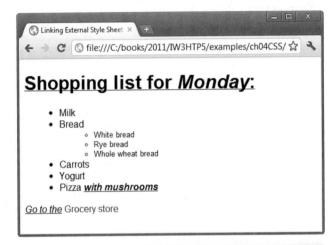

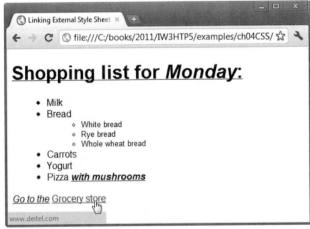

Fig. 4.8 | Linking an external style sheet. (Part 2 of 2.)

4.6 Positioning Elements: Absolute Positioning, z-index

Before CSS, controlling element positioning in HTML documents was difficult—the browser determined positioning. CSS introduced the **position** property and a capability called **absolute positioning**, which gives you greater control over how document elements are displayed. Figure 4.9 demonstrates absolute positioning.

```
1   <!DOCTYPE html>
2
3   <!-- Fig. 4.9: positioning.html -->
4   <!-- Absolute positioning of elements. -->
5   <html>
6      <head>
7         <meta charset = "utf-8">
8         <title>Absolute Positioning</title>
9         <style type = "text/css">
10           .background_image { position: absolute;
11                               top: 0px;
12                               left: 0px;
13                               z-index: 1; }
14           .foreground_image { position: absolute;
15                               top: 25px;
16                               left: 100px;
17                               z-index: 2; }
18           .text             { position: absolute;
19                               top: 25px;
20                               left: 100px;
21                               z-index: 3;
22                               font-size: 20pt;
23                               font-family: tahoma, geneva, sans-serif; }
24        </style>
25     </head>
26     <body>
27        <p><img src = "background_image.png" class = "background_image"
28           alt = "First positioned image" /></p>
29
30        <p><img src = "foreground_image.png" class = "foreground_image"
31           alt = "Second positioned image" /></p>
32
33        <p class = "text">Positioned Text</p>
34     </body>
35   </html>
```

Fig. 4.9 | Absolute positioning of elements. (Part 1 of 2.)

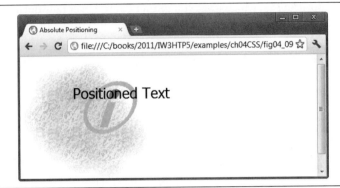

Fig. 4.9 | Absolute positioning of elements. (Part 2 of 2.)

Normally, elements are positioned on the page in the order in which they appear in the HTML5 document. Lines 10–13 define a style called background_image for the first img element (background_image.png) on the page. Specifying an element's position as absolute removes the element from the normal flow of elements on the page, instead positioning it according to the distance from the top, left, right or bottom margins of its **containing block-level element**. This means that it's displayed on its own line and has a **virtual box** around it. Some examples of block-level elements include section, div, p and heading elements (h1 through h6). Here, we position the element to be 0 pixels away from both the top and left margins of its containing element. In line 27, this style is applied to the image, which is contained in a p element.

The **z-index** property allows you to *layer overlapping elements*. Elements that have *higher* z-index values are displayed in *front* of elements with *lower* z-index values. In this example, .background_image has the lowest z-index (1), so it displays in the background. The .foreground_image CSS rule (lines 14–17) gives the circle image (foreground_image.png, in lines 30–31) a z-index of 2, so it displays in front of background_image.png. The p element in line 33 is given a z-index of 3 in line 21, so its content (Positioned Text) displays in front of the other two. If you do not specify a z-index or if elements have the same z-index value, the elements are placed from background to foreground in the order in which they're encountered in the document. The default z-index value is 0.

4.7 Positioning Elements: Relative Positioning, span

Absolute positioning is not the only way to specify page layout. Figure 4.10 demonstrates relative positioning, in which elements are positioned *relative to other elements*.

Setting the position property to relative, as in class super (lines 15–16), lays out the element on the page and *offsets* it by the specified top, bottom, left or right value. Unlike absolute positioning, relative positioning keeps elements in the general flow of elements on the page, so positioning is relative to other elements in the flow. Recall that ex (line 16) is the *x*-height of a font, a relative-length measurement typically equal to the height of a lowercase *x*. Class super (lines 15–16) lays out the text at the end of the sentence as superscript, and class sub (lines 17–18) lays out the text as subscript relative to the other text. Class shiftleft (lines 19–20) shifts the text at the end of the sentence left and class shiftright (lines 21–22) shifts the text right.

```
 1   <!DOCTYPE html>
 2
 3   <!-- Fig. 4.10: positioning2.html -->
 4   <!-- Relative positioning of elements. -->
 5   <html>
 6      <head>
 7         <meta charset = "utf-8">
 8         <title>Relative Positioning</title>
 9         <style type = "text/css">
10            p           { font-size: 1.3em;
11                          font-family: verdana, arial, sans-serif; }
12            span        { color: red;
13                          font-size: .6em;
14                          height: 1em; }
15            .super      { position: relative;
16                          top: -1ex; }
17            .sub        { position: relative;
18                          bottom: -1ex; }
19            .shiftleft  { position: relative;
20                          left: -1ex; }
21            .shiftright { position: relative;
22                          right: -1ex; }
23         </style>
24      </head>
25      <body>
26         <p>The text at the end of this sentence
27            <span class = "super">is in superscript</span>.</p>
28
29         <p>The text at the end of this sentence
30            <span class = "sub">is in subscript</span>.</p>
31
32         <p>The text at the end of this sentence
33            <span class = "shiftleft">is shifted left</span>.</p>
34
35         <p>The text at the end of this sentence
36            <span class = "shiftright">is shifted right</span>.</p>
37      </body>
38   </html>
```

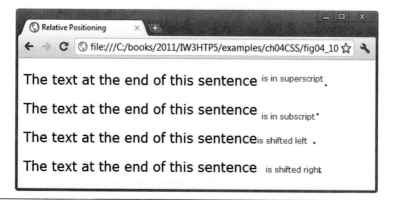

Fig. 4.10 | Relative positioning of elements.

Inline and Block-Level Elements

We introduce the **span** element in line 27. Lines 12–14 define the CSS rule for all span elements in this example. The span's height determines how much vertical space it will occupy. The font-size determines the size of the text inside the span.

Element span is a **grouping element**—by default, it does not apply any formatting to its contents. Its primary purpose is to apply CSS rules or id attributes to a section of text. Element span is an **inline-level element**—it does not change the flow of elements in the document. Examples of inline elements include span, img, a, em and strong. The **div** element is also a grouping element, but it's a block-level element. We'll discuss inline and block-level elements in more detail in Section 4.10.

4.8 Backgrounds

CSS provides control over the backgrounds of block-level elements. CSS can set a background color or add background images to HTML5 elements. Figure 4.11 adds a corporate logo to the bottom-right corner of the document. This logo stays *fixed* in the corner even when the user scrolls up or down the screen.

background-image Property

The **background-image** property (line 10) specifies the image URL for the image logo.png in the format url(*fileLocation*). You can also set the **background-color** property (line 14) in case the image is not found (and to fill in areas the image does not cover).

```
1   <!DOCTYPE html>
2
3   <!-- Fig. 4.11: background.html -->
4   <!-- Adding background images and indentation -->
5   <html>
6      <head>
7         <meta charset = "utf-8">
8         <title>Background Images</title>
9         <style type = "text/css">
10           body   { background-image: url(logo.png);
11                    background-position: bottom right;
12                    background-repeat: no-repeat;
13                    background-attachment: fixed;
14                    background-color: lightgrey; }
15           p      { font-size: 18pt;
16                    color: Darkblue;
17                    text-indent: 1em;
18                    font-family: arial, sans-serif; }
19           .dark  { font-weight: bold; }
20        </style>
21     </head>
22     <body>
23        <p>
24           This example uses the background-image,
25           background-position and background-attachment
26           styles to place the <span class = "dark">Deitel
```

Fig. 4.11 | Adding background images and indentation. (Part 1 of 2.)

```
27            & Associates, Inc.</span> logo in the
28            bottom-right corner of the page. Notice how the logo
29            stays in the proper position when you resize the
30            browser window. The background-color fills in where
31            there is no image.
32       </p>
33    </body>
34  </html>
```

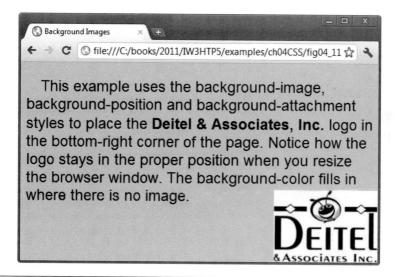

Fig. 4.11 | Adding background images and indentation. (Part 2 of 2.)

background-position *Property*

The **background-position** property (line 11) places the image on the page. The keywords top, bottom, center, left and right are used individually or in combination for vertical and horizontal positioning. You can position an image using lengths by specifying the horizontal length followed by the vertical length. For example, to position the image as *horizontally centered* (positioned at 50 percent of the distance across the screen) and 30 pixels from the top, use

```
background-position: 50% 30px;
```

background-repeat *Property*

The **background-repeat** property (line 12) controls background image **tiling**, which places *multiple copies* of the image next to each other to fill the background. Here, we set the tiling to no-repeat to display only one copy of the background image. Other values include repeat (the default) to tile the image *vertically and horizontally*, repeat-x to tile the image only *horizontally* or repeat-y to tile the image only *vertically*.

background-attachment: fixed *Property*

The next property setting, **background-attachment: fixed** (line 13), fixes the image in the position specified by **background-position**. Scrolling the browser window will *not* move the image from its position. The default value, scroll, moves the image as the user scrolls through the document.

text-indent property

Line 17 uses the **text-indent** property to indent the first line of text in the element by a specified amount, in this case 1em. You might use this property to create a web page that reads more like a novel, in which the first line of every paragraph is indented.

font-style property

Another CSS property that formats text is the **font-style** property, which allows you to set text to none, italic or oblique (oblique is simply more slanted than italic—the browser will default to italic if the system or font does not support oblique text).

4.9 Element Dimensions

In addition to positioning elements, CSS rules can specify the actual *dimensions* of each page element. Figure 4.12 demonstrates how to set the dimensions of elements.

```
 1  <!DOCTYPE html>
 2
 3  <!-- Fig. 4.12: width.html -->
 4  <!-- Element dimensions and text alignment. -->
 5  <html>
 6     <head>
 7        <meta charset = "utf-8">
 8        <title>Box Dimensions</title>
 9        <style type = "text/css">
10           p { background-color: lightskyblue;
11               margin-bottom: .5em;
12               font-family: arial, helvetica, sans-serif; }
13        </style>
14     </head>
15     <body>
16        <p style = "width: 20%">Here is some
17           text that goes in a box which is
18           set to stretch across twenty percent
19           of the width of the screen.</p>
20
21        <p style = "width: 80%; text-align: center">
22           Here is some CENTERED text that goes in a box
23           which is set to stretch across eighty percent of
24           the width of the screen.</section>
25
26        <p style = "width: 20%; height: 150px; overflow: scroll">
27           This box is only twenty percent of
28           the width and has a fixed height.
29           What do we do if it overflows? Set the
30           overflow property to scroll!</p>
31     </body>
32  </html>
```

Fig. 4.12 | Element dimensions and text alignment. (Part 1 of 2.)

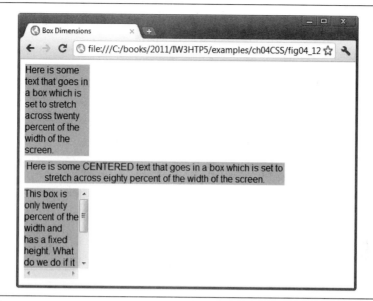

Fig. 4.12 | Element dimensions and text alignment. (Part 2 of 2.)

Specifying the `width` and `height` of an Element

The inline style in line 16 illustrates how to set the **width** of an element on screen; here, we indicate that the p element should occupy 20 percent of the screen width. If not specified, the width will fit the size of the browser window. The height of an element can be set similarly, using the **height** property. The width and height values also can be specified as relative or absolute lengths. For example,

```
width: 10em
```

sets the element's width to 10 times the font size. This works only for block-level elements.

`text-align` Property

Most elements are left-aligned by default, but this alignment can be altered. Line 21 sets text in the element to be center aligned; other values for the **text-align** property include left and right.

`overflow` Property and Scroll Bars

In the third p element, we specify a percentage width and a pixel height. One problem with setting *both* dimensions of an element is that the content inside the element can exceed the set boundaries, in which case the element is simply made large enough for all the content to fit. However, in line 26, we set the **overflow** property to scroll, a setting that adds scroll bars if the text overflows the boundaries.

4.10 Box Model and Text Flow

All *block-level* HTML5 elements have a *virtual box* drawn around them, based on what is known as the **box model**. When the browser renders an element using the box model, the content is surrounded by **padding**, a **border** and a **margin** (Fig. 4.13).

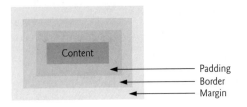

Fig. 4.13 | Box model for block-level elements.

CSS controls the border using three properties: **border-width**, **border-color** and **border-style**. We illustrate these properties in Fig. 4.14.

```
1    <!DOCTYPE html>
2
3    <!-- Fig. 4.14: borders.html -->
4    <!-- Borders of block-level elements. -->
5    <html>
6       <head>
7          <meta charset = "utf-8">
8          <title>Borders</title>
9          <style type = "text/css">
10            div     { text-align: center;
11                      width: 50%;
12                      position: relative;
13                      left: 25%;
14                      border-width: 6px; }
15            .thick  { border-width: thick; }
16            .medium { border-width: medium; }
17            .thin   { border-width: thin; }
18            .solid  { border-style: solid; }
19            .double { border-style: double; }
20            .groove { border-style: groove; }
21            .ridge  { border-style: ridge; }
22            .dotted { border-style: dotted; }
23            .inset  { border-style: inset; }
24            .outset { border-style: outset; }
25            .dashed { border-style: dashed; }
26            .red    { border-color: red; }
27            .blue   { border-color: blue; }
28         </style>
29      </head>
30      <body>
31         <div class = "solid">Solid border</div><hr>
32         <div class = "double">Double border</div><hr>
33         <div class = "groove">Groove border</div><hr>
34         <div class = "ridge">Ridge border</div><hr>
35         <div class = "dotted">Dotted border</div><hr>
36         <div class = "inset">Inset border</div><hr>
37         <div class = "thick dashed">Thick dashed border</div><hr>
38         <div class = "thin red solid">Thin red solid border</div><hr>
```

Fig. 4.14 | Borders of block-level elements. (Part 1 of 2.)

```
39          <div class = "medium blue outset">Medium blue outset border</div>
40      </body>
41  </html>
```

Fig. 4.14 | Borders of block-level elements. (Part 2 of 2.)

The border-width property may be set to any valid CSS length (e.g., em, ex, px) or to the predefined value of thin, medium or thick. The **border-color property** sets the color. [*Note:* This property has different meanings for different border styles—e.g., some display the border color in multiple shades.] The border-style options are none, hidden, dotted, dashed, solid, double, groove, ridge, inset and outset. Borders groove and ridge have opposite effects, as do inset and outset. When border-style is set to none, no border is rendered. Each border property may be set for an individual side of the box (e.g., border-top-style or border-left-color).

Floating Elements
We've seen with absolute positioning that it's possible to remove elements from the normal flow of text. Floating allows you to move an element to one side of the screen; other content in the document then *flows around* the floated element. Figure 4.15 demonstrates how floating elements and the box model can be used to control the layout of an entire page.

Looking at the HTML5 code, we can see that the general structure of this document consists of a header and two main sections. Each section contains an h1 subheading and a paragraph of text.

Block-level elements (such as sections) render with a *line break* before and after their content, so the header and two sections will render vertically one on top of another. In the absence of our styles, the h1s that represent our subheadings would also stack vertically on top of the text in the p tags. However, in line 24 we set the float property to right in the class floated, which is applied to the h1 headings. This causes each h1 to float to the right edge of its containing element, while the paragraph of text will flow around it.

```
 1  <!DOCTYPE html>
 2
 3  <!-- Fig. 4.15: floating.html -->
 4  <!-- Floating elements. -->
 5  <html>
 6    <head>
 7      <meta charset = "utf-8">
 8      <title>Flowing Text Around Floating Elements</title>
 9      <style type = "text/css">
10        header    { background-color: skyblue;
11                    text-align: center;
12                    font-family: arial, helvetica, sans-serif;
13                    padding: .2em; }
14        p         { text-align: justify;
15                    font-family: verdana, geneva, sans-serif;
16                    margin: .5em; }
17        h1        { margin-top: 0px; }
18        .floated  { background-color: lightgrey;
19                    font-size: 1.5em;
20                    font-family: arial, helvetica, sans-serif;
21                    padding: .2em;
22                    margin-left: .5em;
23                    margin-bottom: .5em;
24                    float: right;
25                    text-align: right;
26                    width: 50%; }
27        section   { border: 1px solid skyblue; }
28      </style>
29    </head>
30    <body>
31      <header><img src = "deitel.png" alt = "Deitel" /></header>
32      <section>
33        <h1 class = "floated">Corporate Training and Authoring</h1>
34        <p>Deitel & Associates, Inc. is an internationally
35           recognized corporate training and authoring organization
36           specializing in programming languages, Internet/web
37           technology, iPhone and Android app development and
38           object technology education. The company provides courses
39           on Java, C++, C#, Visual Basic, C, Internet and web
40           programming, Object Technology and iPhone and Android
41           app development.</p>
42      </section>
43      <section>
44        <h1 class = "floated">Programming Books and Videos</h1>
45        <p>Through its publishing
46           partnership with Pearson, Deitel & Associates,
47           Inc. publishes leading-edge programming textbooks,
48           professional books and interactive web-based and DVD
49           LiveLessons video courses.</p>
50      </section>
51    </body>
52  </html>
```

Fig. 4.15 | Floating elements. (Part 1 of 2.)

Fig. 4.15 | Floating elements. (Part 2 of 2.)

margin and **padding** *Properties*

Line 16 assigns a margin of .5em to all paragraph elements. The **margin property** sets the space between the outside of an element's border and all other content on the page. Line 21 assigns .2em of padding to the floated h1s. The **padding property** determines the distance between the content inside an element and the inside of the element's border. Margins for individual sides of an element can be specified (lines 17, 22 and 23) by using the properties **margin-top**, **margin-right**, **margin-left** and **margin-bottom**. Padding can be specified in the same way, using **padding-top**, **padding-right**, **padding-left** and **padding-bottom**. To see the effects of margins and padding, try putting the margin and padding properties inside comments and observing the difference.

In line 27, we assign a border to the section boxes using a shorthand declaration of the border properties, which allow you to define all three border properties in one line. The syntax for this shorthand is

```
border: width style color
```

Our border is one pixel thick, solid, and the same color as the background-color property of the header (line 10). This allows the border to blend with the header and makes the page appear as one box with a line dividing its sections.

4.11 Media Types and Media Queries

CSS **media types** allow you to decide what a page should look like, depending on the kind of media being used to display the page. The most common media type for a web page is the **screen media type**, which is a standard computer screen. Other media types in CSS include **handheld**, **braille**, **speech** and **print**. The handheld medium is designed for mobile Internet devices such as smartphones, while braille is for machines that can read or print web pages in braille. speech styles allow you to give a speech-synthesizing web browser more information about the content of a page. The `print` media type affects a web page's appearance when it's printed. For a complete list of CSS media types, see

```
http://www.w3.org/TR/REC-CSS2/media.html#media-types
```

Media types allow you to decide how a page should be presented on any one of these media without affecting the others. Figure 4.16 gives a simple classic example that applies one set of styles when the document is *viewed on all media (including screens) other than a printer*, and another when the document is *printed*. To see the difference, look at the screen captures below the paragraph or use the **Print Preview** feature in your browser if it has one.

```
 1   <!DOCTYPE html>
 2
 3   <!-- Fig. 4.16: mediatypes.html -->
 4   <!-- CSS media types. -->
 5   <html>
 6      <head>
 7         <meta charset = "utf-8">
 8         <title>Media Types</title>
 9         <style type = "text/css">
10            @media all
11            {
12               body  { background-color: steelblue; }
13               h1    { font-family: verdana, helvetica, sans-serif;
14                       color: palegreen; }
15               p     { font-size: 12pt;
16                       color: white;
17                       font-family: arial, sans-serif; }
18            } /* End @media all declaration. */
19            @media print
20            {
21               body  { background-color: white; }
22               h1    { color: seagreen; }
23               p     { font-size: 14pt;
24                       color: steelblue;
25                       font-family: "times new roman", times, serif; }
26            } /* End @media print declaration. */
27         </style>
28      </head>
29      <body>
30         <h1>CSS Media Types Example</h1>
31
32         <p>
33            This example uses CSS media types to vary how the page
34            appears in print and how it appears on any other media.
35            This text will appear in one font on the screen and a
36            different font on paper or in a print preview. To see
37            the difference in Internet Explorer, go to the Print
38            menu and select Print Preview. In Firefox, select Print
39            Preview from the File menu.
40         </p>
41      </body>
42   </html>
```

Fig. 4.16 | CSS media types. (Part 1 of 2.)

a) Background color appears on the screen.

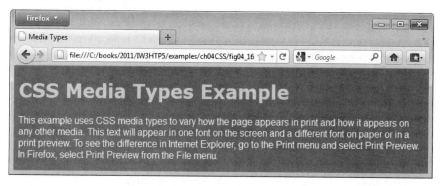

b) Background color is set to white for the `print` media type.

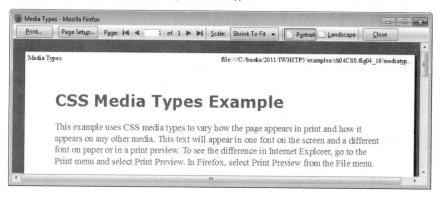

Fig. 4.16 | CSS media types. (Part 2 of 2.)

In line 10, we begin a block of styles that applies to all media types, declared by `@media all` and enclosed in curly braces (`{` and `}`). In lines 10–18, we define some styles for *all* media types. Lines 19–26 set styles to be applied only when the page is printed.

The styles we applied for all media types look nice on a screen but would *not* look good on a printed page. A colored background would use a lot of ink, and a black-and-white printer may print a page that's hard to read because there isn't enough contrast between the colors.

 Look-and-Feel Observation 4.1

Pages with dark background colors and light text use a lot of ink and may be difficult to read when printed, especially on a black-and white-printer. Use the `print` *media type to avoid this.*

 Look-and-Feel Observation 4.2

In general, sans-serif fonts look better on a screen, while serif fonts look better on paper. The print *media type allows your web page to display a sans-serif font on a screen and change to a serif font when it's printed.*

To solve these problems, we apply specific styles for the print media type. We change the body's background-color, the color of the h1 tag, and the font-size, color, and font-family of the p tag to be more suited for printing *and* viewing on paper. Notice that most of these styles conflict with the declarations in the section for all media types. Since the print media type has *higher specificity* than the all media type, the print styles override the all media type's styles when the page is printed. The h1's font-family property is *not* overridden in the print section, so it retains its old value when the page is printed.

Media Queries

Media queries (covered in detail in Section 5.17) allow you to format your content to specific output devices. Media queries include a media type and expressions that check the **media features** of the output device. Some of the common media features include:

- **width**—the width of the part of the screen on which the document is rendered, including any scrollbars
- **height**—the height of the part of the screen on which the document is rendered, including any scrollbars
- **device-width**—the width of the screen of the output device
- **device-height**—the height of the screen of the output device
- **orientation**—if the height is greater than the width, orientation is portrait, and if the width is greater than the height, orientation is landscape
- **aspect-ratio**—the ratio of width to height
- **device-aspect-ratio**—the ratio of device-width to device-height

For a complete list of media features and for more information on media queries, see

```
http://www.w3.org/TR/css3-mediaqueries/
```

4.12 Drop-Down Menus

Drop-down menus are a good way to provide navigation links without using a lot of screen space. In this section, we take a second look at the :hover pseudo-class and introduce the display property to create a simple drop-down menu using CSS3 and HTML5.

We've already seen the :hover pseudo-class used to change a link's style when the mouse hovers over it. We'll use this feature in a more advanced way to cause a menu to appear when the mouse hovers over a menu button. Another important property is **display**, which allows you to decide whether an element is rendered on the page or not. Possible values include block, inline and none. The block and inline values display the element as a block element or an inline element, while none stops the element from being rendered. The code for the drop-down menu is shown in Fig. 4.17.

```
1    <!DOCTYPE html>
2
3    <!-- Fig. 4.17: dropdown.html -->
4    <!-- CSS drop-down menu. -->
```

Fig. 4.17 | CSS drop-down menu. (Part 1 of 3.)

```
5    <html>
6       <head>
7          <meta charset = "utf-8">
8          <title>
9             Drop-Down Menu
10         </title>
11         <style type = "text/css">
12            body            { font-family: arial, sans-serif }
13            nav             { font-weight: bold;
14                              color: white;
15                              border: 2px solid royalblue;
16                              text-align: center;
17                              width: 10em;
18                              background-color: royalblue; }
19            nav ul          { display: none;
20                              list-style: none;
21                              margin: 0;
22                              padding: 0; }
23            nav:hover ul    { display: block }
24            nav ul li       { border-top: 2px solid royalblue;
25                              background-color: white;
26                              width: 10em;
27                              color: black; }
28            nav ul li:hover { background-color: powderblue; }
29            a               { text-decoration: none; }
30         </style>
31      </head>
32      <body>
33         <nav>Menu
34            <ul>
35               <li><a href = "#">Home</a></li>
36               <li><a href = "#">News</a></li>
37               <li><a href = "#">Articles</a></li>
38               <li><a href = "#">Blog</a></li>
39               <li><a href = "#">Contact</a></li>
40            </ul>
41         </nav>
42      </body>
43   </html>
```

a) A collapsed menu

Fig. 4.17 | CSS drop-down menu. (Part 2 of 3.)

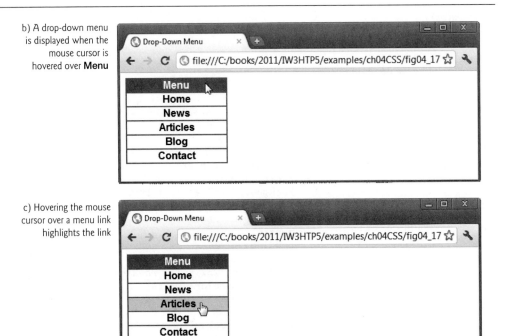

b) A drop-down menu is displayed when the mouse cursor is hovered over **Menu**

c) Hovering the mouse cursor over a menu link highlights the link

Fig. 4.17 | CSS drop-down menu. (Part 3 of 3.)

Lines 33–41 create a nav element containing the the text Menu and an unordered list (ul) of five links that should appear in the drop-down menu—Home, News, Articles, Blog and Contact. Initially, Menu is the only text visible on the page. When the mouse cursor hovers over the nav element, the five links appear below the menu.

The drop-down menu functionality is located in the CSS3 code. Two lines define the drop-down functionality. Line 19 sets display to none for any unordered list (ul) that's nested in a nav. This instructs the browser not to render the ul's contents. Line 23, which is similar to line 19, selects only ul elements nested in a nav element that currently has the mouse hovering over it. Setting display to block specifies that when the mouse is over the nav, the ul will be displayed as a block-level element.

The style in line 28 is applied only to a li element that's a child of a ul element in a nav element, and only when that li has the mouse cursor over it. This style changes the background-color of the currently highlighted menu option. The rest of the CSS simply adds style to the menu's components.

This drop-down menu is just one example of more advanced CSS formatting. Many additional resources are available online for CSS navigation menus and lists.

4.13 (Optional) User Style Sheets

Users can define their own **user style sheets** to format pages based on their preferences. For example, people with *visual impairments* may want to increase the page's text size. You need to *be careful not to inadvertently override user preferences with defined styles.* This section discusses possible conflicts between **author styles** and **user styles**. For the purpose of this section, we demonstrate the concepts in Internet Explorer 9.

Figure 4.18 contains an author style. The font-size is set to 9pt for all <p> tags that have class note applied to them.

```
 1   <!DOCTYPE html>
 2
 3   <!-- Fig. 4.18: user_absolute.html -->
 4   <!-- pt measurement for text size. -->
 5   <html>
 6      <head>
 7         <meta charset = "utf-8">
 8         <title>User Styles</title>
 9         <style type = "text/css">
10            .note { font-size: 9pt; }
11         </style>
12      </head>
13      <body>
14         <p>Thanks for visiting my website. I hope you enjoy it.
15         </p><p class = "note">Please Note: This site will be
16         moving soon. Please check periodically for updates.</p>
17      </body>
18   </html>
```

Fig. 4.18 | pt measurement for text size.

User style sheets are *external style sheets.* Figure 4.19 shows a user style sheet that sets the body's font-size to 20pt, color to yellow and background-color to navy. The font-size value specified in the user style sheet conflicts with the one in line 10 of Fig. 4.18.

```
 1   /* Fig. 4.19: userstyles.css */
 2   /* A user style sheet */
 3   body      { font-size: 20pt;
 4               color: yellow;
 5               background-color: navy; }
```

Fig. 4.19 | A user style sheet.

Adding a User Style Sheet
User style sheets are *not* linked to a document; rather, they're set in the browser's options. To add a user style sheet in IE9, select **Internet Options...**, located in the **Tools** menu. In

the **Internet Options** dialog (Fig. 4.20) that appears, click **Accessibility...**, check the **Format documents using my style sheet** checkbox, and type the location of the user style sheet. IE9 applies the user style sheet to any document it loads. To add a user style sheet in Firefox, find your Firefox profile using the instructions at www.mozilla.org/support/firefox/profile#locate and place a style sheet called userContent.css in the chrome subdirectory. For information on adding a user style sheet in Chrome, see www.google.com/support/forum/p/Chrome/thread?tid=1fa0dd079dbdc2ff&hl=en.

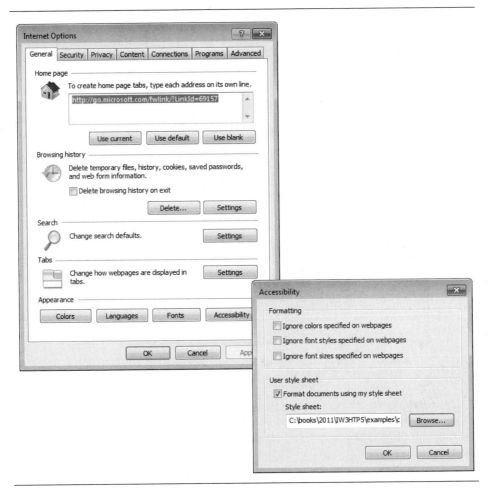

Fig. 4.20 | User style sheet in Internet Explorer 9.

The web page from Fig. 4.18 is displayed in Fig. 4.21, with the user style sheet from Fig. 4.19 applied.

Defining font-size *in a User Style Sheet*
In the preceding example, if the user defines font-size in a user style sheet, the author style has a higher precedence and *overrides* the user style. The 9pt font specified in the author style sheet overrides the 20pt font specified in the user style sheet. This small font may

Fig. 4.21 | User style sheet applied with `pt` measurement.

make pages difficult to read, especially for individuals with *visual impairments*. You can avoid this problem by using relative measurements (e.g., em or ex) instead of absolute measurements, such as pt. Figure 4.22 changes the `font-size` property to use a relative measurement (line 10) that does *not* override the user style set in Fig. 4.19. Instead, the font size displayed is relative to the one specified in the user style sheet. In this case, text enclosed in the <p> tag displays as 20pt, and <p> tags that have the class `note` applied to them are displayed in 15pt (.75 times 20pt).

```
 1   <!DOCTYPE html>
 2
 3   <!-- Fig. 4.22: user_relative.html -->
 4   <!-- em measurement for text size. -->
 5   <html>
 6      <head>
 7         <meta charset = "utf-8">
 8         <title>User Styles</title>
 9         <style type = "text/css">
10            .note { font-size: .75em; }
11         </style>
12      </head>
13      <body>
14         <p>Thanks for visiting my website. I hope you enjoy it.
15         </p><p class = "note">Please Note: This site will be
16         moving soon. Please check periodically for updates.</p>
17      </body>
18   </html>
```

Fig. 4.22 | em measurement for text size.

Figure 4.23 displays the web page from Fig. 4.22 in Internet Explorer with the user style sheet from Fig. 4.19 applied. Note that the second line of text displayed is larger than the same line of text in Fig. 4.21.

Fig. 4.23 | User style sheet applied with em measurement.

4.14 Web Resources

http://www.deitel.com/css3

The Deitel CSS3 Resource Center contains links to some of the best CSS3 information on the web. There you'll find categorized links to tutorials, references, code examples, demos, videos, and more. Check out the demos section for more advanced examples of layouts, menus and other web-page components.

Summary

Section 4.1 Introduction
- Cascading Style Sheets™ 3 (CSS3; p. 138) allows you to specify the presentation of elements on a web page (e.g., fonts, spacing, sizes, colors, positioning) separately from the structure and content of the document (section headers, body text, links, etc.).
- This separation of structure from presentation (p. 138) simplifies maintaining and modifying web pages, especially on large-scale websites.

Section 4.2 Inline Styles
- An inline style (p. 138) allows you to declare a style for an individual element by using the style attribute (p. 138) in the element's start tag.
- Each CSS property (such as font-size, p. 139) is followed by a colon and the value of the attribute. Multiple property declarations are separated by a semicolon.
- The color property (p. 139) sets text color. Hexadecimal codes or color names may be used.

Section 4.3 Embedded Style Sheets
- Embedded style sheets (p. 140) enable you to embed an entire CSS3 document in an HTML5 document's head section.
- Styles that are placed in a style element use selectors (p. 141) to apply style elements throughout the entire document body.
- An em element indicates that its contents should be emphasized. Browsers usually render em elements in an italic font.

- `style` element attribute `type` specifies the MIME type (the specific encoding format, p. 141) of the style sheet. Style sheets use `text/css`.
- Each rule body (p. 141) in a style sheet begins and ends with a curly brace ({ and }).
- The `font-weight` property (p. 142) specifies the "boldness" of text. Possible values are `bold`, `normal` (the default), `bolder` (bolder than bold text) and `lighter` (lighter than `normal` text).
- Boldness also can be specified with multiples of 100, from 100 to 900. Text specified as `normal` is equivalent to 400, and `bold` text is equivalent to 700.
- Style-class declarations are preceded by a period and are applied to elements of the specific class. The `class` attribute (p. 143) applies a style class to an element.
- The CSS rules in a style sheet use the same format as inline styles.
- The `background-color` attribute specifies the background color of the element.
- The `font-family` property (p. 142) names a specific font that should be displayed. Generic font families allow authors to specify a type of font instead of a specific one, in case a browser does not support a specific font.
- The `font-size` property (p. 142) specifies the size used to render the font.
- You should end a font list with a generic font family (p. 142) name in case the other fonts are not installed on the user's computer.
- In many cases, the styles applied to an element (the parent or ancestor element, p. 143) also apply to the element's nested elements (child or descendant elements, p. 143).

Section 4.4 Conflicting Styles

- Styles may be defined by a user, an author or a user agent. A user (p. 143) is a person viewing your web page, you're the author (p. 143)—the person who writes the document—and the user agent (p. 143) is the program used to render and display the document (e.g., a web browser).
- Styles cascade (hence the term "Cascading Style Sheets," p. 143), or flow together, such that the ultimate appearance of elements on a page results from combining styles defined in several ways.
- Most styles are inherited from parent elements (p. 143). Styles defined for children (p. 143) have higher specificity (p. 144) and take precedence over the parent's styles.
- Pseudo-classes (p. 145) give the author access to information that's not declared in the document, such as whether the mouse is hovering over an element or whether the user has previously clicked (visited) a particular hyperlink. The `hover` pseudo-class (p. 146) is activated when the user moves the mouse cursor over an element.
- The `text-decoration` property (p. 145) applies decorations to text in an element, such as `underline`, `overline` and `line-through`.
- To apply rules to multiple elements, separate the elements with commas in the style sheet.
- To apply rules only to a certain type of element that's a child of another type, separate the element names with spaces.
- A pixel is a relative-length measurement (p. 146): It varies in size based on screen resolution. Other relative lengths are `em` (p. 146), `ex` (p. 146) and percentages.
- The other units of measurement available in CSS are absolute-length measurements (p. 146)— that is, units that do not vary in size. These units can be `in` (inches), `cm` (centimeters, p. 146), `mm` (millimeters, p. 146), `pt` (points; 1 `pt` = 1/72 `in`, p. 146) or `pc` (picas; 1 `pc` = 12 `pt`).

Section 4.5 Linking External Style Sheets

- With external style sheets (i.e., separate documents that contain only CSS rules; p. 146), you can provide a uniform look and feel to an entire website (or to a portion of one).

- When you need to change styles, you need to modify only a single CSS file to make style changes across all the pages that use those styles. This is sometimes known as skinning (p. 146).
- CSS comments (p. 147) may be placed in any type of CSS code (i.e., inline styles, embedded style sheets and external style sheets) and always start with /* and end with */.
- link's rel attribute (p. 147) specifies a relationship between two documents (p. 147). For style sheets, the rel attribute declares the linked document to be a stylesheet (p. 147) for the document. The type attribute specifies the MIME type of the related document as text/css. The href attribute provides the URL for the document containing the style sheet.

Section 4.6 Positioning Elements: Absolute Positioning, z-index
- The CSS position property (p. 148) allows absolute positioning (p. 149), which provides greater control over where on a page elements reside. Specifying an element's position as absolute removes it from the normal flow of elements on the page and positions it according to distance from the top, left, right or bottom margin of its parent element.
- The z-index property (p. 150) allows a developer to layer overlapping elements. Elements that have higher z-index values are displayed in front of elements with lower z-index values.

Section 4.7 Positioning Elements: Relative Positioning, span
- Unlike absolute positioning, relative positioning keeps elements in the general flow on the page and offsets them by the specified top, left, right or bottom value.
- Element span (p. 152) is a grouping element (p. 152)—it does not apply any inherent formatting to its contents. Its primary purpose is to apply CSS rules or id attributes to a section of text.
- span is an inline-level element (p. 152)—it applies formatting to text without changing the flow of the document. Examples of inline elements include span, img, a, em and strong.
- The div element is also a grouping element, but it's a block-level element. This means it's displayed on its own line and has a virtual box around it. Examples of block-level elements (p. 152) include div (p. 152), p and heading elements (h1 through h6).

Section 4.8 Backgrounds
- Property background-image specifies the URL of the image, in the format url(*fileLocation*). The property background-position (p. 153) places the image on the page using the values top, bottom, center, left and right individually or in combination for vertical and horizontal positioning. You can also position by using lengths.
- The background-repeat property (p. 153) controls the tiling of the background image (p. 153). Setting the tiling to no-repeat displays one copy of the background image on screen. The background-repeat property can be set to repeat (the default) to tile the image vertically and horizontally, to repeat-x to tile the image only horizontally or to repeat-y to tile the image only vertically.
- The background-attachment (p. 153) setting fixed fixes the image in the position specified by background-position. Scrolling the browser window will not move the image from its set position. The default value, scroll, moves the image as the user scrolls the window.
- The text-indent property (p. 154) indents the first line of text in the element by the specified amount.
- The font-style property (p. 154) allows you to set text to none, italic or oblique.

Section 4.9 Element Dimensions
- An element's dimensions can be set with CSS by using properties height and width (p. 155).
- Text in an element can be centered using text-align (p. 155); other values for the text-align property are left and right.

- A problem with setting both vertical and horizontal dimensions of an element is that the content inside the element might sometimes exceed the set boundaries, in which case the element grows to fit the content. You can set the overflow property (p. 155) to scroll; this setting adds scroll bars if the text overflows the boundaries set for it.

Section 4.10 Box Model and Text Flow
- All block-level HTML5 elements have a virtual box drawn around them, based on what is known as the box model (p. 155).
- When the browser renders elements using the box model, the content of each element is surrounded by padding (p. 155), a border (p. 155) and a margin (p. 155).
- The border-width property (p. 156) may be set to any of the CSS lengths or to the predefined value of thin, medium or thick.
- The border-styles (p. 156) available are none, hidden, dotted, dashed, solid, double, groove, ridge, inset and outset.
- The border-color property (p. 156) sets the color used for the border.
- The class attribute allows more than one class to be assigned to an element by separating each class name from the next with a space.
- Browsers normally place text and elements on screen in the order in which they appear in the document. Elements can be removed from the normal flow of text. Floating allows you to move an element to one side of the screen; other content in the document will then flow around the floated element.
- CSS uses a box model to render elements on screen. The content of each element is surrounded by padding, a border and margins. The properties of this box are easily adjusted.
- The margin property (p. 159) determines the distance between the outside edge of the element's border and any adjacent element.
- Margins for individual sides of an element can be specified by using margin-top, margin-right, margin-left and margin-bottom.
- The padding property (p. 159) determines the distance between the content inside an element and the inside edge of the border. Padding also can be set for each side of the box by using padding-top, padding-right, padding-left and padding-bottom.

Section 4.11 Media Types and Media Queries
- CSS media types (p. 159) allow you to decide what a page should look like depending on the kind of media being used to display the page. The most commonly used for a web page is the screen media type (p. 159), which is a standard computer screen.
- A block of styles that applies to all media types is declared by @media all and enclosed in curly braces. To create a block of styles that apply to a single media type such as print, use @media print and enclose the style rules in curly braces.
- Other media types in CSS 2 include handheld, braille, aural and print. The handheld medium (p. 159) is designed for mobile Internet devices, while braille (p. 159) is for machines that can read or print web pages in braille. aural styles (p. 159) allow the programmer to give a speech-synthesizing web browser more information about the content of the web page. The print media type (p. 159) affects a web page's appearance when it's printed.
- Media queries (p. 162) allow you to format your content to specific output devices. Media queries include a media type and expressions that check the devices' media features (p. 162).

Section 4.12 Drop-Down Menus
- The :hover pseudo-class is used to apply styles to an element when the mouse cursor is over it.

- The display property (p. 162) allows you to decide whether an element is displayed as a block element or inline element or not rendered at all (none).

Section 4.13 (Optional) User Style Sheets

- Users can define their own user style sheets (p. 164) to format pages based on their preferences.
- Absolute font-size measurements override user style sheets, while relative font sizes will yield to a user-defined style.
- If the user defines font size in a user style sheet, the author style (p. 165) has a higher precedence and overrides the user style.

Self-Review Exercises

4.1 Assume that the size of the base font on a system is 12 points.
  a) How big is a 24-point font in ems?
  b) How big is a 6-point font in ems?
  c) How big is a 48-point font in picas?
  d) How big is a 6-point font in inches?
  e) How big is a 2-inch font in picas?

4.2 Fill in the blanks in the following statements:
  a) The _____ property sets text color.
  b) Each CSS property is followed by a(n) _____ and the value of the attribute. Multiple property declarations are separated by a(n) _____.
  c) A(n) _____ element indicates that its contents should be emphasized.
  d) Embedded style sheets enable you to embed an entire CSS3 document in an HTML5 document's _____ section.
  e) The text-decoration property applies decorations to text in an element, such as _____, _____ and _____.
  f) The _____ property may be set to any of the CSS lengths or to the predefined value of thin, medium or thick.
  g) If the user defines font-size in a user style sheet, the author style has a(n) _____ precedence and overrides the user style.
  h) The _____ property allows you to decide if an element is displayed as a block element, inline element, or is not rendered at all.
  i) Each rule body in a style sheet begins and ends with a(n) _____ brace.
  j) 1 picas is equal to _____ points.

Answers to Self-Review Exercises

4.1 a) 2 ems. b) 0.50 ems. c) 4 picas. d) 1/2 inch. e) 12 picas.

4.2 a) color. b) colon, semicolon. c) em. d) head. e) underline, overline, line-through. f) border-width. g) higher. h) display. i) curly. j) 12.

Exercises

4.3 Write a CSS rule that makes all text 3 times larger than the base font of the system and colors the text green.

4.4 Write a CSS rule that places a background image at the bottom right of the page with no repeat option. The image should remain in place when the user scrolls up or down.

4.5   Write a CSS rule that gives all h2 and h3 elements a padding of 0.7 ems, a solid border style and a margin of 0.7 ems.

4.6   Write a CSS rule that changes the color of all elements containing attribute class = "red-Move" to red and shifts them down 30 pixels and right 25 pixels.

4.7   Make a layout template that contains two paragraphs. Use float to line up the two paragraphs as columns side by side. Give both paragraphs a border and a background color of light blue so you can see where they are.

4.8   Add an *embedded style sheet* to the HTML5 document in Fig. 2.3. The style sheet should contain a rule that displays h1 elements in green. In addition, create a rule that displays all links in red without underlining them. When the mouse hovers over a link, change the link's background color to yellow with an underline.

4.9   Make a navigation button using a div with a link inside it. Give it a border, background, and text color, and make them change when the user hovers the mouse over the button. Use an external style sheet. Make sure your style sheet validates at http://jigsaw.w3.org/css-validator/. Note that some warnings may be unavoidable, but your CSS should have no errors.

5

Introduction to Cascading Style Sheets™ (CSS): Part 2

Art is when things appear rounded.
—Maurice Denis

In matters of style, swim with the current; in matters of principle, stand like a rock.
—Thomas Jefferson

Everything that we see is a shadow cast by that which we do not see.
—Martin Luther King, Jr.

Objectives

In this chapter you'll:

- Add text shadows and text-stroke effects.
- Create rounded corners.
- Add shadows to elements.
- Create linear and radial gradients, and reflections.
- Create animations, transitions and transformations.
- Use multiple background images and image borders.
- Create a multicolumn layout.
- Use flexible box model layout and :nth-child selectors.
- Use the @font-face rule to specify fonts for a web page.
- Use RGBA and HSLA colors.
- Use vendor prefixes.
- Use media queries to customize content to fit various screen sizes.

5.1 Introduction

In the preceding chapter we presented "traditional" CSS capabilities. In this chapter, we introduce many features new to CSS3 (see the Objectives).

These capabilities are being built into the browsers, resulting in faster and more economical web development and better client-side performance. This reduces the need for JavaScript libraries and sophisticated graphics software packages such as Adobe Photoshop, Adobe Illustrator, Corel PaintShop Pro and Gimp to create interesting effects.

CSS3 is still under development. We demonstrate many key CSS3 capabilities that are in the draft standard, as well as a few nonstandard capabilities that may eventually be added.

5.2 Text Shadows

The CSS3 **text-shadow property** makes it easy to add a **text shadow** effect to *any* text (Fig. 5.1). First we add a `text-shadow` property to our styles (line 12). The property has four values: `-4px`, `4px`, `6px` and `DimGrey`, which represent:

- Horizontal offset of the shadow—the number of pixels that the `text-shadow` will appear to the *left* or the *right* of the text. In this example, the horizontal offset of the shadow is `-4px`. A *negative* value moves the `text-shadow` to the *left*; a *positive* value moves it to the *right*.

- Vertical offset of the shadow—the number of pixels that the `text-shadow` will be shifted *up* or *down* from the text. In this example, the vertical offset of the shadow is `4px`. A *negative* value moves the shadow *up*, whereas a *positive* value moves it *down*.

- **blur radius**—the blur (in pixels) of the shadow. A blur-radius of `0px` would result in a shadow with a sharp edge (no blur). The greater the value, the greater the blurring of the edges. We used a blur radius of `6px`.

- `color`—determines the color of the `text-shadow`. We used `dimgrey`.

```
 1   <!DOCTYPE html>
 2
 3   <!-- Fig. 5.1: textshadow.html -->
 4   <!-- Text shadow in CSS3. -->
 5   <html>
 6      <head>
 7         <meta charset = "utf-8">
 8         <title>Text Shadow</title>
 9         <style type = "text/css">
10            h1
11            {
12               text-shadow: -4px 4px 6px dimgrey; /* add shadow */
13               font-size: 400%; /* increasing the font size */
14            }
15         </style>
16      </head>
17      <body>
18         <h1>Text Shadow</h1>
19      </body>
20   </html>
```

DimGrey text-
shadow

Fig. 5.1 | Text shadow in CSS3.

5.3 Rounded Corners

The **border-radius property** allows you to add **rounded corners** to an element (Fig. 5.2). In this example, we create two rectangles with solid Navy borders. For the first rectangle, we set the border-radius to 15px (line 17). This adds slightly rounded corners to the rectangle. For the second rectangle, we increase the border-radius to 50px (line 27), making the left and right sides completely round. Any border-radius value greater than half of the shortest side length produces a completely round end. You can also specify the radius for each corner with border-top-left-radius, border-top-right-radius, border-bottom-left-radius and border-bottom-right-radius.

```
 1   <!DOCTYPE html>
 2
 3   <!-- Fig. 5.2: roundedcorners.html -->
 4   <!-- Using border-radius to add rounded corners to two elements. -->
 5   <html>
 6      <head>
 7         <meta charset = "utf-8">
```

Fig. 5.2 | Using border-radius to add rounded corners to two elements. (Part 1 of 2.)

```
 8        <title>Rounded Corners</title>
 9        <style type = "text/css">
10           div
11           {
12              border: 3px solid navy;
13              padding: 5px 20px;
14              background: lightcyan;
15              width: 200px;
16              text-align: center;
17              border-radius: 15px; /* adding rounded corners */
18              margin-bottom: 20px;
19           }
20           #round2
21           {
22              border: 3px solid navy;
23              padding: 5px 20px;
24              background: lightcyan;
25              width: 200px;
26              text-align: center;
27              border-radius: 50px; /* increasing border-radius */
28           }
29        </style>
30     </head>
31     <body>
32        <div>The border-radius property adds rounded corners
33           to an element.</div>
34        <div id = "round2">Increasing the border-radius rounds the corners
35           of the element more.</div>
36     </body>
37  </html>
```

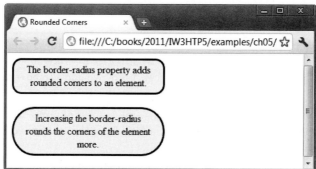

Fig. 5.2 | Using `border-radius` to add rounded corners to two elements. (Part 2 of 2.)

5.4 Color

CSS3 allows you to express color in several ways in addition to standard color names (such as Aqua) or hexadecimal RGB values (such as #00FFFF for Aqua). **RGB** (Red, Green, Blue) or **RGBA** (Red, Green, Blue, Alpha) gives you greater control over the exact colors in your web pages. The value for each color—red, green and blue—can range from 0 to 255. The *alpha* value—which represents *opacity*—can be any value in the range 0.0 (fully transparent) through 1.0 (fully opaque). For example, if you were to set the background color as follows:

```
background: rgba(255, 0, 0, 0.5);
```

the resulting color would be a half-opaque red. Using RGBA colors gives you far more options than using only the existing HTML color names—there are over 140 HTML color names, whereas there are 16,777,216 different RGB colors (256 x 256 x 256) and varying opacities of each.

CSS3 also allows you to express color using **HSL (hue, saturation, lightness)** or **HSLA (hue, saturation, lightness, alpha)** values. The *hue* is a color or shade expressed as a value from 0 to 359 representing the degrees on a color wheel (a wheel is 360 degrees). The colors on the wheel progress in the order of the colors of the rainbow—red, orange, yellow, green, blue, indigo and violet. The value for red, which is at the beginning of the wheel, is 0. Green hues have values around 120 and blue hues have values around 240. A hue value of 359, which is just left of 0 on the wheel, would result in a red hue. The *saturation*—the intensity of the hue—is expressed as a percentage, where 100% is fully saturated (the full color) and 0% is gray. *Lightness*—the intensity of light or luminance of the hue— is also expressed as a percentage. A lightness of 50% is the actual hue. If you *decrease* the amount of light to 0%, the color appears completely dark (black). If you *increase* the amount of light to 100%, the color appears completely light (white). For example, if you wanted to use an `hsla` value to get the same color red as in our example of an `rgba` value, you would set the `background` property as follows:

```
background: hsla(0, 100%, 50%, 0.5);
```

The resulting color would be a half-opaque red. An excellent tool that allows you to pick colors from a color wheel to find the corresponding RGB and HSL values is available at:

```
http://www.workwithcolor.com/hsl-color-schemer-01.htm
```

5.5 Box Shadows

You can shadow *any* block-level element in CSS3. Figure 5.3 shows you how to create a **box shadow**. The `div` style in lines 10–19 indicates that `div`s are 200px-by-200px boxes with a `Plum`-colored background (lines 12–14). Next, we add the **box-shadow property** with four values (line 15):

- Horizontal offset of the shadow (25px)—the number of pixels that the `box-shadow` will appear to the left or the right of the box. A *positive* value moves the `box-shadow` to the *right*

- Vertical offset of the shadow (25px)—the number of pixels the `box-shadow` will be shifted up or down from the box. A *positive* value moves the `box-shadow` *down*.

- Blur radius—A blur-radius of 0px would result in a shadow with a sharp edge (no blur). The greater the value, the more the edges of the shadow are blurred. We used a blur radius of 10px.

- Color—the `box-shadow`'s color (in this case, `dimgrey`).

In lines 20–26, we create a style that's applied only to the second `div`, which changes the `box-shadow`'s horizontal offset to -25px and vertical offset to -25px (line 25) to show the effects of using negative values. A *negative* horizontal offset value moves the `box-shadow` to the *left*. A *negative* vertical offset value moves the shadow *up*.

```
 1   <!DOCTYPE html>
 2
 3   <!-- Fig. 5.3: boxshadow.html -->
 4   <!-- Creating box-shadow effects. -->
 5   <html>
 6      <head>
 7         <meta charset = "utf-8">
 8         <title>Box Shadow</title>
 9         <style type = "text/css">
10            div
11            {
12               width: 200px;
13               height: 200px;
14               background-color: plum;
15               box-shadow: 25px 25px 50px dimgrey;
16               float: left;
17               margin-right: 120px;
18               margin-top: 40px;
19            }
20            #box2
21            {
22               width: 200px;
23               height: 200px;
24               background-color: plum;
25               box-shadow: -25px -25px 50px dimgrey;
26            }
27            h2
28            {
29               text-align: center;
30            }
31         </style>
32      </head>
33      <body>
34         <div><h2>Box Shadow Bottom and Right</h2></div>
35         <div id = "box2"><h2>Box Shadow Top and Left</h2></div>
36      </body>
37   </html>
```

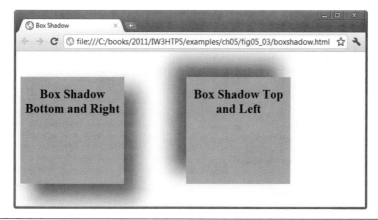

Fig. 5.3 | Creating box-shadow effects.

5.6 Linear Gradients; Introducing Vendor Prefixes

Linear gradients are a type of image that gradually transitions from one color to the next horizontally, vertically or diagonally. You can transition between as many colors as you like and specify the points at which to change colors, called **color-stops**, represented in pixels or percentages along the *gradient line*—the angle at which the gradient extends. *You can use gradients in any property that accepts an image.*

Creating Linear Gradients

In Fig. 5.4, we create three linear gradients—*vertical, horizontal* and *diagonal*—in separate rectangles. As you study this example, you'll notice that the background property for each of the three linear gradient styles (vertical, horizontal and diagonal) is defined multiple times in each style—once for WebKit-based browsers, once for Mozilla Firefox and once using the standard CSS3 syntax for linear gradients. This occurs frequently when working with CSS3, because many of its features are not yet finalized. In the meantime, many of the browsers have gone ahead and begun implementing these features so you can use them now. Later in this section, we'll discuss the *vendor prefixes* that allow us to use many of CSS3's evolving features.

```
 1   <!DOCTYPE html>
 2
 3   <!-- Fig. 5.4: lineargradient.html -->
 4   <!-- Linear gradients in CSS3. -->
 5   <html>
 6      <head>
 7         <meta charset = "utf-8">
 8         <title>Linear Gradient</title>
 9         <style type = "text/css">
10         div
11         {
12            width: 200px;
13            height: 200px;
14            border: 3px solid navy;
15            padding: 5px 20px;
16            text-align: center;
17            background: -webkit-gradient(
18               linear, center top, center bottom,
19               color-stop(15%, white), color-stop(50%, lightsteelblue),
20               color-stop(75%, navy) );
21            background: -moz-linear-gradient(
22               top center, white 15%, lightsteelblue 50%, navy 75% );
23            background: linear-gradient(
24               to bottom, white 15%, lightsteelblue 50%, navy 75% );
25            float: left;
26            margin-right: 15px;
27         }
28         #horizontal
29         {
30            width: 200px;
31            height: 200px;
```

Fig. 5.4 | Linear gradients in CSS3. (Part 1 of 2.)

```
32              border: 3px solid orange;
33              padding: 5px 20px;
34              text-align: center;
35              background: -webkit-gradient(
36                 linear, left top, right top,
37                 color-stop(15%, white), color-stop(50%, yellow),
38                 color-stop(75%, orange) );
39              background: -moz-linear-gradient(
40                 left, white 15%, yellow 50%, orange 75% );
41              background: linear-gradient(
42                 90deg, white 15%, yellow 50%, orange 75% );
43                 margin-right: 15px;
44           }
45        #angle
46        {
47              width: 200px;
48              height: 200px;
49              border: 3px solid Purple;
50              padding: 5px 20px;
51              text-align: center;
52              background: -webkit-gradient(
53                 linear, left top, right bottom,
54                 color-stop(15%, white), color-stop(50%, plum),
55                 color-stop(75%, purple) );
56              background: -moz-linear-gradient(
57                 top left, white 15%, plum 50%, purple 75% );
58              background: linear-gradient(
59                 45deg, white 15%, plum 50%, purple 75% );
60           }
61        </style>
62     </head>
63     <body>
64        <div><h2>Vertical Linear Gradient</h2></div>
65        <div id = "horizontal"><h2>Horizontal Linear Gradient</h2></div>
66        <div id = "angle"><h2>Diagonal Linear Gradient</h2></div>
67     </body>
68  </html>
```

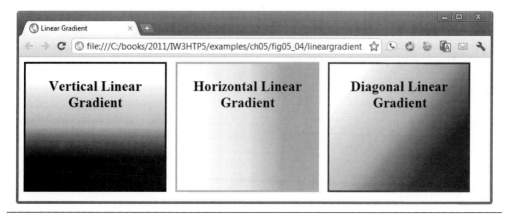

Fig. 5.4 | Linear gradients in CSS3. (Part 2 of 2.)

WebKit Vertical Linear Gradient

The example's body contains three div elements. The first has a vertical linear gradient from top to bottom. We're creating a background gradient, so we begin with the background property. The linear gradient syntax for WebKit (lines 17–20) differs slightly from that for Firefox (lines 21–22). For WebKit browsers, we use -webkit-gradient. We then specify the type of gradient (linear) and the *direction* of the linear gradient, from center top to center bottom (line 18). This creates a gradient that gradually changes colors from the top to the bottom. Next, we specify the **color-stops** for the linear gradient (lines 19–20). Within each color-stop are two values—the first is the *location* of the stop (e.g., 15%, which is 15% down from the top of the box) and the second is the *color* (e.g., white). We transition from white at the top to lightsteelblue in the center to navy at the bottom. You can use as many color-stops as you like.

Mozilla Vertical Linear Gradient

For Mozilla browsers, we use -moz-linear-gradient (line 21). In line 22, we specify the gradient-line (top center), which is the direction of the gradient. After the gradient-line we specify each color and color-stop (line 22).

Standard Vertical Linear Gradient

The standard CSS3 syntax for linear gradients is also slightly different. First, we specify the linear-gradient (line 23). In line 24, we include the values for the gradient. We begin with the direction of the gradient (top), followed by each color and color-stop (line 22).

Horizontal Linear Gradient

In lines 28–44 we create a rectangle with a *horizontal* (left-to-right) gradient that gradually changes from white to yellow to orange. For WebKit, the direction of the gradient is left top to right top (line 36), followed by the colors and color-stops (lines 37–38). For Mozilla, we specify the gradient-line (left), followed by the colors and color-stops (line 40). The standard CSS3 syntax begins with the direction (left), indicating that the gradient changes from left to right, followed by the colors and color-stops (lines 42–43). The direction can also be specified in degrees, with 0 degrees straight up and positive degrees progressing clockwise. For a left-to-right gradient, you'd specify 90deg. For top-to-bottom, you'd specify 0deg.

Diagonal Linear Gradient

In the third rectangle we create a *diagonal* linear gradient that gradually changes from white to plum to purple (lines 45–60). For WebKit, the direction of the gradient is left top to right bottom (line 53), followed by the colors and color-stops (lines 54–55). For Mozilla, we specify the gradient-line (top left), followed by the colors and color-stops (line 57). The standard CSS3 syntax begins with the direction (135deg), indicating that the gradient changes at a 45-degree angle, followed by the colors and color-stops (line 59).

Vendor Prefixes

In this example (Fig. 5.4), lines 17–24, 35–42 and 52–59 each define three versions of the background style for defining the linear gradients. The versions in lines 17, 35, and 52 and lines 21, 39 and 56 contain the prefixes -webkit- and -moz-, respectively. These are **vendor prefixes** (Fig. 5.5) and are used for properties that are still being finalized in the CSS specification but have already been implemented in various browsers.

Vendor prefix	Browsers
-ms-	Internet Explorer
-moz-	Mozilla-based browsers, including Firefox
-o-	Opera and Opera Mobile
-webkit-	WebKit-based browsers, including Google Chrome, Safari (and Safari on the iPhone) and Android

Fig. 5.5 | Vendor prefixes.

Prefixes are *not* available for every browser or for every property. For example, at the time of this writing, linear gradients were implemented only in WebKit-based browsers and Mozilla Firefox. If we remove the prefixed versions of the linear gradient styles in this example, the gradients will *not* appear when the page is rendered in a WebKit-based browser or Firefox. If you run this program in browsers that don't support gradients yet, the gradients will *not* appear. It's good practice to include the multiple prefixes when they're available so that your pages render properly in the various browsers. As the CSS3 features are finalized and incorporated fully into the browsers, the prefixes will become unnecessary. For example, we did not use any prefixes for the box-shadow example (Fig. 5.3) because it's fully implemented in WebKit-based, Firefox, Opera and Internet Explorer browsers. Many of the new CSS3 features have not yet been implemented in Internet Explorer—we expect this to change with IE 10.

When using vendor prefixes in styles, always place them *before* the nonprefixed version (as in lines 17–22 of Fig. 5.4). The last version of the style that a given browser supports takes precedence and the browser will use it. So, by listing the standard non-prefixed version last, the browser will use the standard version over the prefixed version when the standard version is supported. To save space in the remainder of this chapter, we *do not* include all vendor prefixes for every example. Some online tools that can help you add the appropriate vendor prefixes to your code are:

```
http://prefixmycss.com/
http://cssprefixer.appspot.com/
```

There are also several sites that list the CSS3 and HTML5 features supported in each of the major browsers, including:

```
http://caniuse.com/
http://findmebyip.com/litmus/
```

5.7 Radial Gradients

Radial gradients are similar to linear gradients, but the color changes gradually from an inner point (the *start*) to an outer circle (the *end*) (Fig. 5.6). In this example, the **radial-**

gradient property (lines 16–18) has three values. The first is the position of the start of the radial gradient—in this case, the center of the rectangle. Other possible values for the position include top, bottom, left and right. The second value is the *start color* (yellow), and the third is the *end color* (red). The resulting effect is a box with a yellow center that gradually changes to red in a circle around the starting position. In this case, notice that other than the vendor prefixes, the syntax of the gradient is identical for WebKit browsers, Mozilla and the standard CSS3 radial-gradient.

```
 1   <!DOCTYPE html>
 2
 3   <!-- Fig. 5.6: radialgradient.html -->
 4   <!-- Radial gradients in CSS3. -->
 5   <html>
 6      <head>
 7         <meta charset = "utf-8">
 8         <title>Radial Gradient</title>
 9         <style type = "text/css">
10         div
11         {
12            width: 200px;
13            height: 200px;
14            padding: 5px;
15            text-align: center;
16            background: -webkit-radial-gradient(center, yellow, red);
17            background: -moz-radial-gradient(center, yellow, red);
18            background: radial-gradient(center, yellow, red);
19         }
20         </style>
21      </head>
22      <body>
23         <div><h2>Radial Gradient</h2></div>
24      </body>
25   </html>
```

Radial gradient begins with yellow in the center, then changes to red in a circle as it moves toward the edges of the box

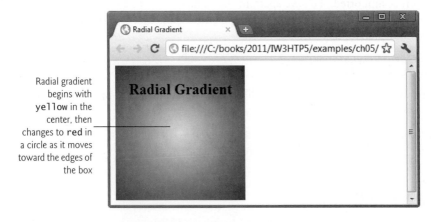

Fig. 5.6 | Radial gradients in CSS3.

5.8 (Optional: WebKit Only) Text Stroke

The -webkit-text-stroke property is a nonstandard property for WebKit-based browsers that allows you to add an outline (text stroke) around text. Four of the seven browsers we use in this book are WebKit based—Safari and Chrome on the desktop and the mobile browsers in iOS and Android. Currently, the CSS3 specification is evolving and this property is not likely to appear as part of the standard in the short term. However, WebKit tends to be leading edge, so it's possible that this feature could be added later.

Line 12 in Fig. 5.7 sets the color of the h1 text to LightCyan. We add a -webkit-text-stroke with two values (line 13)—the outline *thickness* (2px) and the *color* of the text stroke (black). We used the font-size 500% here so you could see the outline better. This nonstandard effect can be implemented for a one pixel stroke—with a bit more effort—using pure CSS3 as shown at http://css-tricks.com/7405-adding-stroke-to-web-text/.

```html
 1   <!DOCTYPE html>
 2
 3   <!-- Fig. 5.7: textstroke.html -->
 4   <!-- Text stroke in CSS3. -->
 5   <html>
 6      <head>
 7         <meta charset = "utf-8">
 8         <title>Text Stroke</title>
 9         <style type = "text/css">
10            h1
11            {
12               color: lightcyan;
13               -webkit-text-stroke: 2px black; /* vendor prefix */
14               font-size: 500%; /* increasing the font size */
15            }
16         </style>
17      </head>
18   <body>
19      <h1>Text Stroke</h1>
20   </body>
21   </html>
```

Fig. 5.7 | A text-stroke rendered in Chrome.

5.9 Multiple Background Images

CSS3 allows you to add **multiple background images** to an element (Fig. 5.8). The style at lines 10–16 begins by adding two background-images—logo.png and ocean.png (line

12). Next, we specify each image's placement using property background-position (line 13). The comma-separated list of values matches the order of the comma-separated list of images in the background-image property. The first value—bottom right—places the first image, logo.png, in the bottom-right corner of the background in the border-box. The last value—100% center—centers the entire second image, ocean.png, in the content-box so that it appears behind the content and stretches to fill the content-box. The **background-origin** (line 14) determines where each image is placed using the box model we discussed in Fig. 4.13. The first image (logo.png) is in the outermost border-box, and the second image (ocean.png) is in the innermost content-box.

```
 1   <!DOCTYPE html>
 2
 3   <!-- Fig. 5.8: multiplebackgrounds.html -->
 4   <!-- Multiple background images in CSS3. -->
 5   <html>
 6      <head>
 7         <meta charset = "utf-8">
 8         <title>Multiple Backgrounds</title>
 9         <style type = "text/css">
10            div.background
11            {
12               background-image: url(logo.png), url(ocean.png);
13               background-position: bottom right, 100% center;
14               background-origin: border-box, content-box;
15               background-repeat: no-repeat, repeat;
16            }
17            div.content
18            {
19               padding: 10px 15px;
20               color: white;
21               font-size: 150%;
22            }
23         </style>
24      </head>
25      <body>
26         <div class = "background">
27         <div class = "content">
28            <p>Deitel & Associates, Inc., is an internationally recognized
29               authoring and corporate training organization. The company
30               offers instructor-led courses delivered at client sites
31               worldwide on programming languages and other software topics
32               such as C++, Visual C++<sup>&reg;</sup>, C, Java&trade;,
33               C#<sup>&reg;</sup>, Visual Basic<sup>&reg;</sup>,
34               Objective-C<sup>&reg;</sup>, XML<sup>&reg;</sup>,
35               Python<sup>&reg;</sup>, JavaScript, object technology,
36               Internet and web programming, and Android and iPhone app
37               development.</p>
38         </div></div>
39      </body>
40   </html>
```

Fig. 5.8 | Multiple background images in CSS3. (Part 1 of 2.)

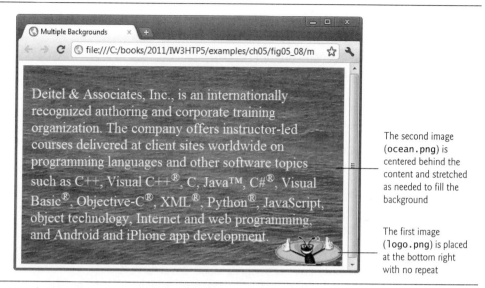

The second image
(`ocean.png`) is
centered behind the
content and stretched
as needed to fill the
background

The first image
(`logo.png`) is placed
at the bottom right
with no repeat

Fig. 5.8 | Multiple background images in CSS3. (Part 2 of 2.)

5.10 (Optional: WebKit Only) Reflections

Figure 5.9 shows how to add a simple **reflection** of an image using the **-webkit-box-re-flect property** (lines 13–17 and 20–23). Like -webkit-text-stroke, this is a nonstandard property that's available only in WebKit-based browsers for now, but it's an elegant effect that we wanted to show.

The -webkit-box-reflect property's first value is the *direction* of the reflection—in this case, below (line 13) or right (line 20). The direction value may be above, below, left, or right. The second value is the offset, which determines the space between the image and its reflection. In this example, the offset is 5px, so there's a small space between the image and its reflection. Optionally, you can specify a gradient to apply to the reflection. The gradient in lines 14–16 causes the bottom reflection to fade away from top to bottom. The gradient in lines 21–23 causes the right reflection to fade away from left to right. The reflection effects shown here can be accomplished using pure CSS3—with a lot more code. For one example of this, see http://www.xhtml-lab.com/css/create-reflection-effect-using-css3.

```
1    <!DOCTYPE html>
2
3    <!-- Fig. 5.9: reflection.html -->
4    <!-- Reflections in CSS3. -->
5    <html>
6       <head>
7          <meta charset = "utf-8">
8          <title>Reflection</title>
9          <style type = "text/css">
```

Fig. 5.9 | Reflections in CSS3. (Part 1 of 2.)

```
10          img { margin: 10px; }
11          img.below
12          {
13             -webkit-box-reflect: below 5px
14                -webkit-gradient(
15                   linear, left top, left bottom,
16                   from(transparent), to(white));
17          }
18          img.right
19          {
20             -webkit-box-reflect: right 5px
21                -webkit-gradient(
22                   linear, right top, left top,
23                   from(transparent), to(white));
24          }
25       </style>
26    </head>
27    <body>
28       <img class = "below" src = "jhtp.png" width = "138" height = "180"
29          alt = "Java How to Program book cover">
30       <img class = "right" src = "jhtp.png" width = "138" height = "180"
31          alt = "Java How to Program book cover">
32    </body>
33 </html>
```

Fig. 5.9 | Reflections in CSS3. (Part 2 of 2.)

5.11 Image Borders

The CSS3 **border-image property** uses images to place a border around *any* block-level element (Fig. 5.10). In line 12, we set a div's border-width to 30px, which is the thickness of the border we're placing around the element. Next, we specify a `width` of 234px, which is the width of the entire rectangular border (line 13).

Stretching an Image Border

In this example, we create two image border styles. In the first (lines 16–22), we stretch (and thus distort) the sides of the image to fit around the element while leaving the corners of the border image unchanged (not stretched). The `border-image` property has six values (lines 18–21):

- `border-image-source`—the URL of the image to use in the border (in this case, `url(border.png)`).

```
 1   <!DOCTYPE html>
 2
 3   <!-- Fig. 5.10: imageborder.html -->
 4   <!-- Stretching and repeating an image to create a border. -->
 5   <html>
 6      <head>
 7         <meta charset = "utf-8">
 8         <title>Image Border</title>
 9         <style type = "text/css">
10            div
11            {
12               border-width: 30px;
13               width: 234px;
14               padding: 20px 20px;
15            }
16            #stretch
17            {
18               -webkit-border-image: url(border.png) 80 80 80 80 stretch;
19               -moz-border-image: url(border.png) 80 80 80 80 stretch;
20               -o-border-image: url(border.png) 80 80 80 80 stretch;
21               border-image: url(border.png) 80 80 80 80 stretch;
22            }
23            #repeat
24            {
25               -webkit-border-image:url(border.png) 34% 34% repeat;
26               -moz-border-image:url(border.png) 34% 34% repeat;
27               -o-border-image:url(border.png) 34% 34% repeat;
28               border-image:url(border.png) 34% 34% repeat;
29            }
30         </style>
31      </head>
32      <body>
33         <h2>Image Borders</h2>
34         <img src = "border.png" alt = "image used to demonstrate borders">
35         <p><div id="stretch">Stretching the image border</div></p>
36         <p><div id="repeat">Repeating the image border</div></p>
37      </body>
38   </html>
```

Fig. 5.10 | Stretching and repeating an image to create a border. (Part 1 of 2.)

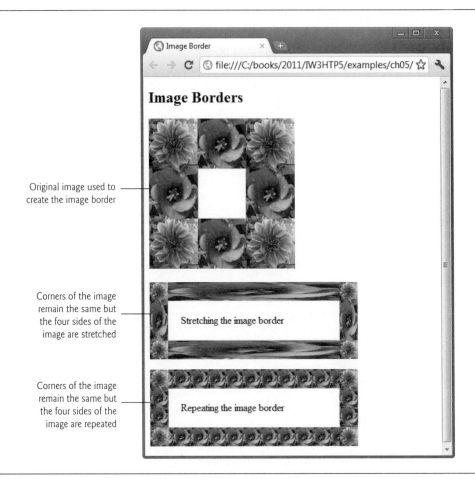

Original image used to create the image border

Corners of the image remain the same but the four sides of the image are stretched

Corners of the image remain the same but the four sides of the image are repeated

Fig. 5.10 | Stretching and repeating an image to create a border. (Part 2 of 2.)

- **border-image-slice**—expressed with four space-separated values in pixels (in this case, 80 80 80 80). These values are the *inward offsets* from the top, right, bottom and left sides of the image. Since our original image is square, we used the same value for each. The border-image-slice divides the image into nine *regions*: four corners, four sides and a middle, which is transparent unless otherwise specified. These regions may overlap. If you use values that are larger than the actual image size, the border-image-slice values will be interpreted as 100%. *You may not use negative values.* We could express the border-image-slice in *two* values—80 80—in which case the first value would represent the top and bottom, and the second value the left and right. The border-image-slice may also be expressed in percentages, which we demonstrate in the second part of this example.

- **border-image-repeat**—specifies how the regions of the border image are scaled and *tiled* (repeated). By indicating stretch just *once*, we create a border that will stretch the top, right, bottom and left regions to fit the area. You may specify *two* values for the border-image-repeat property. For example, if we specified stretch repeat, the top and bottom regions of the image border would be *stretched*, and the right and left regions of the border would be repeated (i.e., *tiled*) to fit the area. Other possible values for the `border-image-repeat` property include round and `space`. If you specify round, the regions are repeated using only whole tiles, and the border image is scaled to fit the area. If you specify `space`, the regions are repeated to fill the area using only whole tiles, and any excess space is distributed evenly around the tiles.

Repeating an Image Border

In lines 23–29 we create an image border by repeating the regions to fit the space. The border-image property includes four values:

- `border-image-source`—the URL of the image to use in the border (once again, `url(border.png)`).

- `border-image-slice`—in this case, we provided *two* values expressed in percentages (34% 34%) for the top/bottom and left/right, respectively.

- `border-image-repeat`—the value repeat specifies that the tiles are repeated to fit the area, using partial tiles to fill the excess space.

For additional information about the `border-image` property, see

```
http://www.w3.org/TR/2002/WD-css3-border-20021107/
    #the-border-image-uri
```

5.12 Animation; Selectors

In Fig. 5.11, we create a simple *animation* of an image that moves in a diamond pattern as it changes opacity.

```
1   <!DOCTYPE html>
2
3   <!-- Fig. 5.11: animation.html -->
4   <!-- Animation in CSS3. -->
5   <html>
6      <head>
7         <meta charset = "utf-8">
8         <title>Animation</title>
9         <style type = "text/css">
10           img
11           {
12              position: relative;
13              -webkit-animation: movingImage linear 10s 1s 2 alternate;
14              -moz-animation: movingImage linear 10s 1s 2 alternate;
15              animation: movingImage linear 10s 2 1s alternate;
16           }
17           @-webkit-keyframes movingImage
18           {
19              0%    {opacity: 0; left: 50px; top: 0px;}
```

Fig. 5.11 | Animation in CSS3. The dotted lines show the diamond path that the image takes. (Part 1 of 2.)

```
20          25%  {opacity: 1; left: 0px; top:5 0px;}
21          50%  {opacity: 0; left: 50px; top: 100px;}
22          75%  {opacity: 1; left: 100px; top: 50px;}
23          100% {opacity: 0; left: 50px; top: 0px;}
24      }
25      @-moz-keyframes movingImage
26      {
27          0%   {opacity: 0; left: 50px; top: 0px;}
28          25%  {opacity: 1; left: 0px; top:5 0px;}
29          50%  {opacity: 0; left: 50px; top: 100px;}
30          75%  {opacity: 1; left: 100px; top: 50px;}
31          100% {opacity: 0; left: 50px; top: 0px;}
32      }
33      @keyframes movingImage
34      {
35          0%   {opacity: 0; left: 50px; top: 0px;}
36          25%  {opacity: 1; left: 0px; top: 50px;}
37          50%  {opacity: 0; left: 50px; top: 100px;}
38          75%  {opacity: 1; left: 100px; top: 50px;}
39          100% {opacity: 0; left: 50px; top: 0px;}
40      }
41      </style>
42   </head>
43   <body>
44      <img src = "jhtp.png" width = "138" height = "180"
45         alt = "Java How to Program book cover">
46      <div></div>
47   </body>
48 </html>
```

The animation starts and ends at the top of the diamond, moving the image in the counterclockwise direction initially. When the animation reaches the top of the diamond, the animation reverses, continuing in the clockwise direction. The animation terminates when the image reaches the top of the diamond for a second time.

Fig. 5.11 | Animation in CSS3. The dotted lines show the diamond path that the image takes, (Part 2 of 2.)

animation Property

The **animation property** (lines 13–15) allows you to represent several animation properties in a *shorthand* notation, rather than specifying each separately, as in:

```
animation-name: movingImage;
animation-timing-function: linear;
animation-duration: 10s;
animation-delay: 1s;
animation-iteration-count: 2;
animation-direction: alternate;
```

In the shorthand notation, the values are listed in the following order:

- **animation-name**—represents the name of the animation (movingImage). This name associates the animation with the keyframes that define various properties of the element being animated at different stages of the animation. We'll discuss keyframes shortly.

- **animation-timing-function** (lines 13–15)—determines how the animation progresses in one cycle of its duration. Possible values include linear, ease, ease-in, ease-out, ease-in-out, cubic-bezier. The value linear, which we use in this example, specifies that the animation will move at the same speed from start to finish. The default value, ease, starts slowly, increases speed, then ends slowly. The ease-in value starts slowly, then speeds up, whereas the ease-out value starts faster, then slows down. The ease-in-out starts and ends slowly. Finally, the cubic-bezier value allows you to customize the timing function with four values between 0 and 1, such as cubic-bezier(1,0,0,1).

- **animation-duration**—specifies the time in seconds (s) or milliseconds (ms) that the animation takes to complete one iteration (10s in this case). The default duration is 0.

- **animation-delay**—specifies the number of seconds (1s in this case) or milliseconds after the page loads before the animation begins. The default value is 0. If the animation-delay is negative, such as -3s, the animation will begin three seconds into its cycle.

- **animation-iteration-count**—specifies the number of times the animation will run. The default is 1. You may use the value infinite to repeat the animation continuously.

- **animation-direction**—specifies the direction in which the animation will run. The value alternate used here specifies that the animation will run in alternating directions—in this case, counterclockwise (as we define with our keyframes), then clockwise. The default value, normal, would run the animation in the same direction for each cycle.

The shorthand animation property cannot be used with the **animation-play-state property**—it must be specified separately. If you do not include the animation-play-state, which specifies whether the animation is paused or running, it defaults to running.

@keyframes Rule and Selectors

For the element being animated, the **@keyframes rule** (lines 17, 25 and 33) defines the element's properties that will change during the animation, the values to which those properties will change, and when they'll change. The **@keyframes rule** is followed by the name of the animation (movingImage) to which the keyframes are applied. CSS **rules** consist of one or more **selectors** followed by a **declaration block** in curly braces ({}). Selectors enable you to apply styles to elements of a particular type or attribute. A declaration block consists of one or more declarations, each of which includes the property name followed by a colon (:), a value and a semicolon (;). You may include multiple declarations in a declaration block. For example, consider line 19:

```
0% {opacity: 0; left: 50px; top 0px;}
```

The selector, 0%, is followed by a declaration block with three declarations—opacity, left and right.

In this example, the @keyframes rule includes five selectors to represent the points-in-time for our animation. Recall that our animation will take 10 seconds (10s in lines 13–15) to complete. In that context, 0% indicates the beginning of a single animation cycle, 25% represents 2.5 seconds into the animation, 50% represents 5 seconds into the animation, 75% represents 7.5 seconds into the animation and 100% represents the end of a single animation cycle. You can break down the animation into as many points as you like. At each point, we specify the opacity of the image and the image position in pixels from the left and from the top. We begin and end the animation at the same point—left: 50px; top: 0px;—creating a diamond pattern along which the image moves.

5.13 Transitions and Transformations

With CSS3 **transitions**, you can change an element's style over a specified duration—for example, you can vary an element's opacity from opaque to transparent over a duration of one second. CSS3 **transformations** allow you to *move, rotate, scale* and *skew* elements. And you can make transitions and transformations occur simultaneously, doing things like having objects grow and change their color at once. Note that transitions are similar in concept to the animations (Section 5.12), but transitions allow you to specify only the starting and ending values of the CSS properties being changed. An animation's keyframes enable you to control intermediate states throughout the animation's duration.

5.13.1 transition and transform Properties

Figure 5.12 uses the **transition** and **transform properties** to scale and rotate an image 360 degrees when the cursor *hovers* over it. We begin by defining the transition (line 16). For each property that will change, the transition property specifies the duration of that change. In this case, we indicate that a transform (discussed shortly) will take four seconds, but we could specify a comma-separated list of property names that will change and the individual durations over which each property will change. For example:

```
transition: transform 4s, opacity 2s;
```

indicates that a transform takes four seconds to apply and the opacity changes over two seconds—thus, the transform will continue for another two seconds after the opacity change completes. In this example, we define the transform only when the user *hovers* the mouse over the image.

```
 1   <!DOCTYPE html>
 2
 3   <!-- Fig. 5.12: transitions.html -->
 4   <!-- Transitions in CSS3. -->
 5   <html>
 6      <head>
 7         <meta charset = "utf-8">
 8         <title>Transitions</title>
 9         <style type = "text/css">
10            img
11            {
12               margin: 80px;
13               -webkit-transition: -webkit-transform 4s;
14               -moz-transition: -moz-transform 4s;
15               -o-transition: -o-transform 4s;
16               transition: transform 4s;
17            }
18            img:hover
19            {
20               -webkit-transform: rotate(360deg) scale(2, 2);
21               -moz-transform: rotate(360deg) scale(2, 2);
22               -o-transform: rotate(360deg) scale(2, 2);
23               transform: rotate(360deg) scale(2, 2);
24            }
25         </style>
26      </head>
27      <body>
28         <img src = "cpphtp.png" width = "76" height = "100"
29            alt = "C++ How to Program book cover">
30      </body>
31   </html>
```

a)   b)   c)   d)

Fig. 5.12 | Transitioning an image over a four-second duration and applying `rotate` and `scale` transforms.

The `:hover` pseudo-class (lines 18–24) formerly worked only for anchor elements but now works with *any* element. In this example, we use `:hover` to begin the rotation and scaling of the image. The `transform` property (line 23) specifies that the image will rotate 360deg and will scale to twice its original width and height when the mouse hovers over the image. The `transform` property uses **transformation functions**, such as **rotate** and

scale, to perform the transformations. The rotate transformation function receives the number of degrees. Negative values cause the element to rotate left. A value of 720deg would cause the element to rotate clockwise twice. The scale transformation function specifies how to scale the width and height. The value 1 represents the original width or original height, so values greater than 1 increase the size and values less than 1 decrease the size. A complete list of CSS3 transformation functions can be found at:

> www.w3.org/TR/css3-2d-transforms/#transform-functions

5.13.2 Skew

CSS3 transformations also allow you to **skew** block-level elements, slanting them at an angle either horizontally (skewX) or vertically (skewY). In the following example, we use the animation and transform properties to skew an element (a rectangle and text) horizontally by 45 degrees (Fig. 5.13). First we create a rectangle with a LightGreen background, a solid DarkGreen border and rounded corners. The animation property (lines 21–23) specifies that the element will skew in a three-second (3s) interval for an infinite duration. The fourth value, linear, is the animation-timing-function.

```
1   <!DOCTYPE html>
2
3   <!-- Fig. 5.13: skew.html -->
4   <!-- Skewing and transforming elements in CSS3. -->
5   <html>
6      <head>
7         <meta charset = "utf-8">
8         <title>Skew</title>
9         <style type = "text/css">
10           .skew .textbox
11           {
12              margin-left: 75px;
13              background: lightgreen;
14              height: 100px;
15              width: 200px;
16              padding: 25px 0;
17              text-align: center;
18              font-size: 250%;
19              border: 3px solid DarkGreen;
20              border-radius: 15px;
21              -webkit-animation: skew 3s infinite linear;
22              -moz-animation: skew 3s infinite linear;
23              animation: skew 3s infinite linear;
24           }
25           @-webkit-keyframes skew
26           {
27              from { -webkit-transform: skewX(0deg); }
28              25% { -webkit-transform: skewX(45deg); }
29              50% { -webkit-transform: skewX(0); }
30              75% { -webkit-transform: skewX(-45deg); }
31              to { -webkit-transform: skewX(0); }
32           }
```

Fig. 5.13 | Skewing and transforming elements in CSS3. (Part 1 of 2.)

```
33          @-moz-keyframes skew
34          {
35             from { -webkit-transform: skewX(0deg); }
36             25% { -webkit-transform: skewX(45deg); }
37             50% { -webkit-transform: skewX(0); }
38             75% { -webkit-transform: skewX(-45deg); }
39             to { -webkit-transform: skewX(0); }
40          }
41          @-keyframes skew
42          {
43             from { -webkit-transform: skewX(0deg); }
44             25% { -webkit-transform: skewX(45deg); }
45             50% { -webkit-transform: skewX(0); }
46             75% { -webkit-transform: skewX(-45deg); }
47             to { -webkit-transform: skewX(0); }
48          }
49       </style>
50    </head>
51    <body>
52       <div class = "box skew">
53       <div class = "textbox">Skewing Text</div>
54       </div>
55    </body>
56 </html>
```

a) Bordered div at skewed left position   b) Bordered div at centered position   c) Bordered div at skewed right position

Fig. 5.13 | Skewing and transforming elements in CSS3. (Part 2 of 2.)

Next, we use the @keyframes rule and selectors to specify the angle of the skew transformation at different intervals (lines 25–48). When the page is rendered, the element is not skewed (0deg; lines 27, 35 and 43). The transformation then skews the element 45 degrees (45deg) to the right (lines 28, 36 and 44), back to 0deg (lines 29, 37 and 45) and then left by 45deg (lines 30, 38 and 46) and back to 0deg (lines 31, 39 and 47).

5.13.3 Transitioning Between Images

We can also use the transition property to create the visually beautiful effect of *melting* one image into another (Fig. 5.14). The transition property includes three values. First, we specify that the transition will occur on the opacity of the image. The second value, 4s, is the transition-duration. The third value, ease-in-out, is the transition-timing-function. Next, we define :hover with an opacity of 0, so when the cursor hovers over the top image, its opacity becomes fully transparent, revealing the bottom image directly behind it (lines 22–23). In lines 28–29 we add the bottom and top images, placing one directly behind the other.

```
 1   <!DOCTYPE html>
 2
 3   <!-- Fig. 5.14: meltingimages.html -->
 4   <!-- Melting one image into another using CSS3. -->
 5   <html>
 6      <head>
 7         <meta charset = "utf-8">
 8         <title>Melting Images</title>
 9         <style type = "text/css">
10            #cover
11            {
12               position: relative;
13               margin: 0 auto;
14            }
15            #cover img
16            {
17               position: absolute;
18               left: 0;
19               -webkit-transition: opacity 4s ease-in-out;
20               transition: opacity 4s ease-in-out;
21            }
22            #cover img.top:hover
23               { opacity:0; }
24         </style>
25      </head>
26      <body>
27         <div id = "cover">
28            <img class = "bottom" src = "jhtp.png" alt = "Java 9e cover">
29            <img class = "top" src = "jhtp8.png" alt = "Java 8e cover">
30         </div>
31      </body>
32   </html>
```

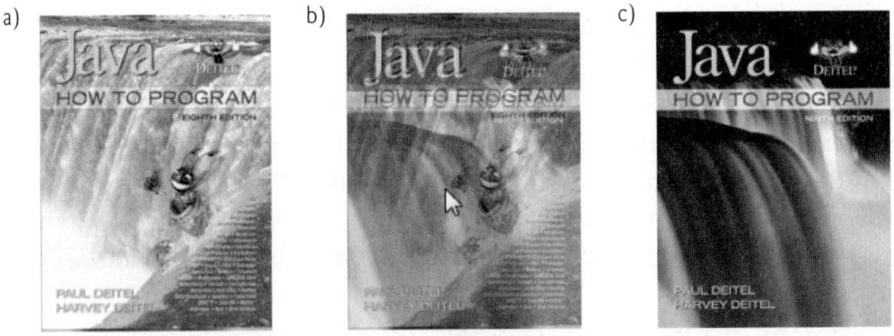

Fig. 5.14 | Melting one image into another using CSS3.

5.14 Downloading Web Fonts and the @font-face Rule

Using the **@font-face rule**, you can specify fonts for a web page, even if they're not installed on the user's system. You can use *downloadable fonts* to help ensure a uniform look across client sites. In Fig. 5.15, we use the Google web font named "Calligraffitti." You can find numerous free, open-source web fonts at `http://www.google.com/webfonts`. *Make sure the fonts you get from other sources have no legal encumbrances.*

```
 1   <!DOCTYPE html>
 2
 3   <!-- Fig. 5.15: embeddedfonts.html -->
 4   <!-- Embedding fonts for use in your web page. -->
 5   <html>
 6      <head>
 7         <meta charset = "utf-8">
 8         <title>Embedded Fonts</title>
 9         <link href = 'http://fonts.googleapis.com/css?family=Calligraffitti'
10            rel = 'stylesheet' type = 'text/css'>
11         <style type = "text/css">
12            body
13            {
14               font-family: "Calligraffitti";
15               font-size: 48px;
16               text-shadow: 3px 3px 3px DimGrey;
17            }
18         </style>
19      </head>
20      <body>
21         <div>
22            <b>Embedding the Google web font "Calligraffitti"</b>
23         </div>
24      </body>
25   </html>
```

Fig. 5.15 | Embedding fonts for use in your web page.

To get Google's Calligraffitti font, go to `http://www.google.com/webfonts` and use the search box on the site to find the font "Calligraffitti." You can find this by using the search box on the site. Next, click **Quick-use** to get the `link` to the style sheet that contains the @font-face rule. Paste that `link` element into the head section of your document (lines 9–10). The referenced CSS style sheet contains the following CSS rules:

```
@media screen {
@font-face {
  font-family: 'Calligraffitti';
  font-style: normal;
  font-weight: normal;
  src: local('Calligraffiti'),
    url('http://themes.googleusercontent.com/static/fonts/
      calligraffitti/v1/vLVN2Y-z65rVu1R71WdvyKIZAuDcNtpCWuPSaIR0Ie8
      .woff') format('woff');
}
}
```

The @media screen rule specifies that the font will be used when the document is rendered on a computer screen (as discussed in Section 4.11). The @font-face rule includes the font-family (Calligraffitti), font-style (normal) and font-weight (normal). You may include multiple fonts with varying styles and weights. The @font-face rule also includes the *location* of the font.

5.15 Flexible Box Layout Module and :nth-child Selectors

Flexible Box Layout Module (FBLM) makes it easy to align the contents of boxes, change their size, change their order dynamically, and lay out the contents in any direction. In the example of Fig. 5.16, we create flexible divs for four of our programming tips. When the mouse hovers over one of the divs, the div expands, the text changes from black to white, the background color changes and the layout of the text changes.

Lines 48–66 define a div to which we apply the flexbox CSS class. That div contains four other divs. The flexbox class's display property is set to the new CSS3 value box (lines 16–17). The **box-orient property** specifies the orientation of the box layout (lines 18–19). The default value is horizontal (which we specified anyway). You can also use vertical. For the nested divs, we specify a one-second ease-out transition (lines 23–24). This will take effect when these the :hover pseudo-class style (lines 38–39) is applied to one of these divs to expand it.

```
1  <!DOCTYPE html>
2
3  <!-- Fig. 5.16: fblm.html -->
4  <!-- Flexible Box Layout Module. -->
5  <html>
6    <head>
7      <meta charset = "utf-8">
8      <title>Flexible Box Layout Model</title>
9      <link href = 'http://fonts.googleapis.com/css?family=Rosario'
10        rel = 'stylesheet' type = 'text/css'>
11      <style type = "text/css">
12      .flexbox
13      {
14        width: 600px;
15        height: 420px;
```

Fig. 5.16 | Flexible Box Layout Module. (Part 1 of 3.)

```
16              display: -webkit-box;
17              display: box;
18              -webkit-box-orient: horizontal;
19              box-orient: horizontal;
20           }
21           .flexbox > div
22           {
23              -webkit-transition: 1s ease-out;
24              transition: 1s ease-out;
25              -webkit-border-radius: 10px;
26              border-radius: 10px;
27              border: 2px solid black;
28              width: 120px;
29              margin: 10px -10px 10px 0px;
30              padding: 20px 20px 20px 20px;
31              box-shadow: 10px 10px 10px dimgrey;
32           }
33           .flexbox > div:nth-child(1){ background-color: lightgrey; }
34           .flexbox > div:nth-child(2){ background-color: lightgrey; }
35           .flexbox > div:nth-child(3){ background-color: lightgrey; }
36           .flexbox > div:nth-child(4){ background-color: lightgrey; }
37
38           .flexbox > div:hover {
39              width: 200px; color: white; font-weight: bold; }
40           .flexbox > div:nth-child(1):hover { background-color: royalblue; }
41           .flexbox > div:nth-child(2):hover { background-color: crimson; }
42           .flexbox > div:nth-child(3):hover { background-color: crimson; }
43           .flexbox > div:nth-child(4):hover { background-color: darkgreen; }
44           p { height: 250px; overflow: hidden; font-family: "Rosario" }
45        </style>
46     </head>
47     <body>
48        <div class = "flexbox">
49        <div><img src = "GPP.png" alt = "Good programming practice icon">
50           <p>Good Programming Practices call attention to techniques that
51           will help you produce programs that are clearer, more
52           understandable and more maintainable.</p></div>
53        <div><img src = "EPT.png" alt = "Error prevention tip icon">
54           <p>Error-Prevention Tips contain suggestions for exposing bugs
55           and removing them from your programs; many describe aspects of
56           programming that prevent bugs from getting into programs in
57           the first place.</p></div>
58        <div><img src = "CPE.png" alt = "Common programming error icon">
59           <p>Common Programming Errors point out the errors that students
60           tend to make frequently. These Common Programming Errors reduce
61           the likelihood that you'll make the same mistakes.</p></div>
62        <div><img src = "SEO.png"><p>Software Engineering Observations
63           highlight architectural and design issues that affect the
64           construction of software systems, especially large-scale
65           systems.</p></div>
66        </div>
67     </body>
68  </html>
```

Fig. 5.16 | Flexible Box Layout Module. (Part 2 of 3.)

a) Each nested `div` has a light background color and black text to start. Some of the text is hidden.

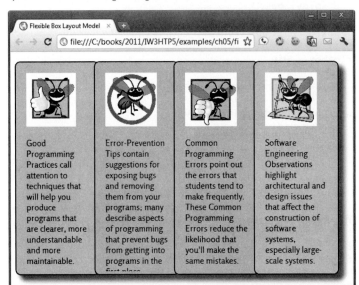

b) When the mouse hovers over `:nth-child(2)`, the flexbox expands, the `background-color` changes to `Crimson`, the overflow text is revealed and the text changes to a bold `white` font

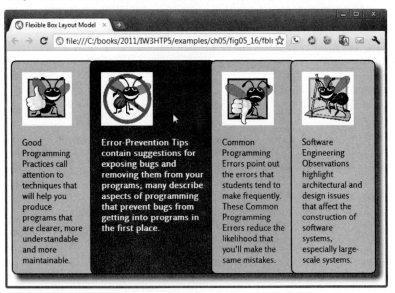

Fig. 5.16 | Flexible Box Layout Module. (Part 3 of 3.)

`:nth-child` *Selectors*
In CSS3, you can use selectors to easily select elements to style based on their *attributes*. For example, you could select every other row in a table and change the background color

to blue, making the table easier to read. You can also use selectors to enable or disable input elements. In lines 33–36 we use **:nth-child selectors** to select each of the four div elements in the flexbox div to style. The style in line 33 uses div:nth-child(1) to select the div element that's the *first* child of its parent and applies the background-color LightBlue. Similarly, div:nth-child(2) selects the div element that's the *second* child of its parent, div:nth-child(3) selects the *third* child of its parent, and div:nth-child(4) selects the *fourth* child of its parent—each applies a specified background-color.

Next, lines 38–43 define styles that are applied to the nested div elements when the mouse hovers over them. The style at lines 38–39 sets the width (200px), color (white) and font-weight (bold). Next, we use :nth-child selectors to specify a new background color for each nested div (line 40–43).

Finally, we style the p element—the text within each div (line 44). We specify a paragraph height of 250px and the overflow as hidden, which hides any text that does not fit in the specified paragraph height. In the output, notice that the text in the *second* child element (the Error-Prevention Tips), the overflow text is hidden. When the mouse hovers over the element, all of the text is revealed. We also specify the Google font "Rosario", which we embedded in our style sheet (lines 9–10).

Selectors are a large topic. In later chapters, we'll demonstrate additional CSS3 selector capabilities. To learn more about their powerful capabilities, visit:

```
http://www.w3.org/TR/css3-selectors/
```

5.16 Multicolumn Layout

CSS3 allows you to easily create **multicolumn layouts**. In Figure 5.17, we create a three-column layout by setting the **column-count property** to 3 (lines 15–18) and the **column-gap property** (the spacing between columns) to 30px (lines 20–23). We then add a thin black line between each column using the **column-rule property** (lines 25–28). When you run this example, try resizing your browser window. You'll notice that the width of the columns changes to fit the three-column layout in the browser. In Section 5.17, we'll show you how to use media queries to modify this example so the number of columns varies dynamically based on the size of the device screen or browser window, allowing you to customize the layout for devices such as smartphones, tablets, notebooks, desktops and more.

```
1   <!DOCTYPE html>
2
3   <!-- Fig. 5.17: multicolumns.html -->
4   <!-- Multicolumn text in CSS3. -->
5   <html>
6      <head>
7         <meta charset = "utf-8">
8         <title>Multicolumns</title>
9         <style type = "text/css">
10            p
11            { margin:0.9em 0em; }
12            .multicolumns
13            {
```

Fig. 5.17 | Multicolumn text in CSS3. (Part 1 of 3.)

```
14              /* setting the number of columns to 3 */
15              -webkit-column-count: 3;
16              -moz-column-count: 3;
17              -o-column-count: 3;
18              column-count: 3;
19              /* setting the space between columns to 30px */
20              -webkit-column-gap: 30px;
21              -moz-column-gap: 30px;
22              -o-column-gap: 30px;
23              column-gap: 30px;
24              /* adding a 1px black line between each column */
25              -webkit-column-rule: 1px outset black;
26              -moz-column-rule: 1px outset black;
27              -o-column-rule: 1px outset black;
28              column-rule: 1px outset black;
29           }
30        </style>
31     </head>
32     <body>
33        <header>
34           <h1>Computers, Hardware and Software<h1/>
35        </header>
36        <div class = "multicolumns">
37           <p>A computer is a device that can perform computations and make
38              logical decisions phenomenally faster than human beings can.
39              Many of today's personal computers can perform billions of
40              calculations in one second&mdash;more than a human can perform
41              in a lifetime. Supercomputers are already performing thousands
42              of trillions (quadrillions) of instructions per second! To put
43              that in perspective, a quadrillion-instruction-per-second
44              computer can perform in one second more than 100,000
45              calculations for every person on the planet! And&mdash;these
46              "upper limits" are growing quickly!</p>
47           <p>Computers process data under the control of sets of
48              instructions called computer programs. These programs guide
49              the computer through orderly sets of actions specified by
50              people called computer programmers. The programs that run on a
51              computer are referred to as software. In this book, you'll
52              learn today's key programming methodology that's enhancing
53              programmer productivity, thereby reducing software-development
54              costs&mdash;object-oriented programming.</p>
55           <p>A computer consists of various devices referred to as hardware
56              (e.g., the keyboard, screen, mouse, hard disks, memory, DVDs
57              and processing units). Computing costs are dropping
58              dramatically, owing to rapid developments in hardware and
59              software technologies. Computers that might have filled large
60              rooms and cost millions of dollars decades ago are now
61              inscribed on silicon chips smaller than a fingernail, costing
62              perhaps a few dollars each. Ironically, silicon is one of the
63              most abundant materials&mdash;it's an ingredient in common
64              sand. Silicon-chip technology has made computing so economical
65              that more than a billion general-purpose computers are in use
66              worldwide, and this is expected to double in the next few
```

Fig. 5.17 | Multicolumn text in CSS3. (Part 2 of 3.)

```
67              years.</p>
68          <p>Computer chips (microprocessors) control countless devices.
69              These embedded systems include anti-lock brakes in cars,
70              navigation systems, smart home appliances, home security
71              systems, cell phones and smartphones, robots, intelligent
72              traffic intersections, collision avoidance systems, video game
73              controllers and more. The vast majority of the microprocessors
74              produced each year are embedded in devices other than general-
75              purpose computers.</p>
76          <footer>
77              <em>&copy; 2012 by Pearson Education, Inc.
78                  All Rights Reserved.</em>
79          </footer>
80      </div>
81  </body>
82 </html>
```

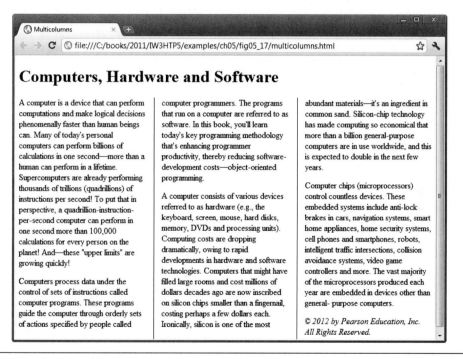

Fig. 5.17 | Multicolumn text in CSS3. (Part 3 of 3.)

5.17 Media Queries

With CSS *media types* (Section 4.11), you can vary your styling based on the type of device on which your page is being presented. The classic examples are varying font styles and sizes, based on whether a page is printed or displayed on a screen. Users generally prefer sans-serif fonts on screens and serif fonts on paper. With CSS3 *media queries* you can determine the finer attributes of the media on which the user is viewing the page, such as the *length* and *width* of the viewing area on the screen, to better customize your presentation.

In Section 5.16 we created a page with a multicolumn layout that included three columns of text and a thin black rule between each column. No matter how you resized your browser window, the text was *still* rendered in three columns, even if the columns had to be extremely narrow. In Fig. 5.18, we modify that multicolumn example to alter the numbers of columns and the rules between columns based on the screen size of the device on which the page is viewed.

@media-Rule

The **@media rule** is used to determine the type *and size* of device on which the page is rendered. When the browser looks at the rule, the result is either *true* or *false*. The rule's styles are applied only if the result is true. First, we use the @media rule to determine whether the page is being rendered on a handheld device (e.g., a smartphone) with a max-width of 480px, or a device with a screen that has a max-device-width of 480px, or on a screen having max-width of 480px (lines 13–15). If this is *true*, we set the column-count to 1—the page will be rendered in a single column on handheld devices such as an iPhone or in browser windows that have been resized to 480px or less (lines 17–19).

```
 1   <!DOCTYPE html>
 2
 3   <!-- Fig. 5.18: mediaqueries.html -->
 4   <!-- Using media queries to reformat a page based on the device width. -->
 5   <html>
 6      <head>
 7         <meta charset = "utf-8">
 8         <title>Media Queries</title>
 9         <style type = "text/css">
10            p
11            { margin: 0.9em 0em; }
12            /* styles for smartphones with screen widths 480px or smaller */
13            @media handheld and (max-width: 480px),
14               screen and (max-device-width: 480px),
15               screen and (max-width: 480px)
16            {
17               div {
18                  -webkit-column-count: 1;
19                  column-count: 1; }
20            }
21            /* styles for devices with screen widths of 481px to 1024px */
22            @media only screen and (min-width: 481px) and
23               (max-width: 1024px)
24            {
25               div {
26                  -webkit-column-count: 2;
27                  column-count: 2;
28                  -webkit-column-gap: 30px;
29                  column-gap: 30px;
30                  -webkit-column-rule: 1px outset black;
31                  column-rule: 1px outset black; }
32            }
```

Fig. 5.18 | Using media queries to reformat a page based on the device width. (Part 1 of 4.)

```
33          /* styles for devices with screen widths of 1025px or greater */
34          @media only screen and (min-width: 1025px)
35          {
36              div {
37                  -webkit-column-count: 3;
38                  column-count: 3;
39                  -webkit-column-gap: 30px;
40                  column-gap: 30px;
41                  -webkit-column-rule: 1px outset black;
42                  column-rule: 1px outset black; }
43          }
44      </style>
45   </head>
46   <body>
47      <header>
48          <h1>Computers, Hardware and Software</h1>
49      </header>
50      <div>
51          <p>A computer is a device that can perform computations and make
52              logical decisions phenomenally faster than human beings can.
53              Many of today's personal computers can perform billions of
54              calculations in one second&mdash;more than a human can perform
55              in a lifetime. Supercomputers are already performing thousands
56              of trillions (quadrillions) of instructions per second! To put
57              that in perspective, a quadrillion-instruction-per-second
58              computer can perform in one second more than 100,000
59              calculations for every person on the planet! And&mdash;these
60              "upper limits" are growing quickly!</p>
61          <p>Computers process data under the control of sets of
62              instructions called computer programs. These programs guide
63              the computer through orderly sets of actions specified by
64              people called computer programmers. The programs that run on a
65              computer are referred to as software. In this book, you'll
66              learn today's key programming methodology that's enhancing
67              programmer productivity, thereby reducing software-development
68              costs&mdash;object-oriented programming.</p>
69          <p>A computer consists of various devices referred to as hardware
70              (e.g., the keyboard, screen, mouse, hard disks, memory, DVDs
71              and processing units). Computing costs are dropping
72              dramatically, owing to rapid developments in hardware and
73              software technologies. Computers that might have filled large
74              rooms and cost millions of dollars decades ago are now
75              inscribed on silicon chips smaller than a fingernail, costing
76              perhaps a few dollars each. Ironically, silicon is one of the
77              most abundant materials&mdash;it's an ingredient in common
78              sand. Silicon-chip technology has made computing so economical
79              that more than a billion general-purpose computers are in use
80              worldwide, and this is expected to double in the next few
81              years.</p>
82          <p>Computer chips (microprocessors) control countless devices.
83              These embedded systems include anti-lock brakes in cars,
84              navigation systems, smart home appliances, home security
85              systems, cell phones and smartphones, robots, intelligent
```

Fig. 5.18 | Using media queries to reformat a page based on the device width. (Part 2 of 4.)

```
86              traffic intersections, collision avoidance systems, video game
87              controllers and more. The vast majority of the microprocessors
88              produced each year are embedded in devices other than general-
89              purpose computers.</p>
90          <footer>
91              <em>&copy; 2012 by Pearson Education, Inc.
92                  All Rights Reserved.</em>
93          </footer>
94      </div>
95    </body>
96  </html>
```

a) Styles for smartphones with screen widths 480px or smaller

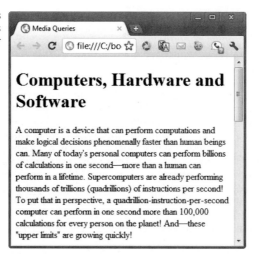

b) Styles for devices with screen widths of **481px** to **1024px**

Fig. 5.18 | Using media queries to reformat a page based on the device width. (Part 3 of 4.)

c) Styles for devices with screen widths of **1024px** or greater

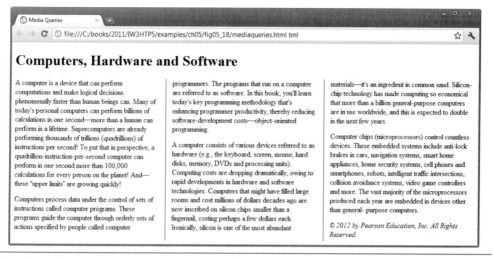

Fig. 5.18 | Using media queries to reformat a page based on the device width. (Part 4 of 4.)

If the condition in lines 13–15 is *false*, a second @media rule determines whether the page is being rendered on devices with a min-width of 481px and a max-width of 1024px (lines 22–23). If this condition is *true*, we set the column-count to 2 (lines 26–27), the column-gap (the space between columns) to 30px (lines 28–29) and the column-rule (the vertical line between the columns) to 1px outset black (lines 30–31).

If the conditions in the first two @media rules are *false*, we use a third @media rule to determine whether the page is being rendered on devices with a min-width of 1025px (line 34). If the condition of this rule is *true*, we set the column-count to 3 (lines 37–38), the column-gap to 30px (lines 39–40) and the column-rule to 1px outset black (lines 41–42).

5.18 Web Resources

http://www.w3.org/Style/CSS/
W3C home page for CSS3.

http://www.deitel.com/css3/
The Deitel CSS3 Resource Center includes links to tutorials, examples, the W3C standards documentation and more.

http://layerstyles.org
http://www.colorzilla.com/gradient-editor/
http://css3generator.com/
http://css3please.com/
Sites that help you generate cross-browser CSS3 code.

http://findmebyip.com/litmus/
Find the CSS3 features that are supported by each of the major browsers.

http://cssprefixer.appspot.com/
The CSSPrefixer tool helps you add vendor prefixes to your CSS3 code.

http://css-tricks.com/examples/HSLaExplorer/
A CSS demo that allows you to play with HSLA colors.

Summary

Section 5.2 Text Shadows

- The CSS3 `text-shadow` property (p. 175) makes it easy to add a text-shadow effect to any text. The shadow's horizontal offset is the number of pixels that the `text-shadow` will appear to the left or the right of the text. A negative value moves the `text-shadow` to the left; a positive value moves it to the right. The vertical offset is the number of pixels that the `text-shadow` will be shifted up or down from the text. A negative value moves the shadow up, whereas a positive value moves it down.

- The blur radius (p. 175) has a value of 0 (no shadow) or greater.

Section 5.3 Rounded Corners

- The `border-radius` property (p. 176) adds rounded corners (p. 176) to any element.

Section 5.4 Color

- RGBA (Red, Green, Blue, Alpha, p. 177) gives you greater control over the exact colors in your web pages. The value for each color—red, green and blue—can range from 0 to 255. The alpha value—which represents opacity—can be any value in the range 0.0 (fully transparent) through 1.0 (fully opaque).

- CSS3 also allows you to express color using HSLA (hue, saturation, lightness, alpha) values (p. 178).

- The hue is a color or shade expressed as a value from 0 to 359 representing the degrees on a color wheel (a wheel is 360 degrees). The colors on the wheel progress in the order of the colors of the rainbow—red, orange, yellow, green, blue, indigo and violet.

- The saturation (p. 178)—the intensity of the hue—is expressed as a percentage, where 100% is fully saturated (the full color) and 0% is gray.

- Lightness (p. 178)—the intensity of light or luminance of the hue—is also expressed as a percentage. A lightness of 50% is the actual hue. If you decrease the amount of light to 0%, the color appears completely dark (black). If you increase the amount of light to 100%, the color appears completely light (white).

Section 5.5 Box Shadows

- The `box-shadow` property (p. 178) adds a shadow to an element.

- The horizontal offset of the shadow defines the number of pixels that the `box-shadow` will appear to the left or the right of the box. The vertical offset of the shadow defines the number of pixels the `box-shadow` will be shifted up or down from the box.

- The blur radius of the shadow can have a value of 0 (no shadow) or greater.

Section 5.6 Linear Gradients; Introducing Vendor Prefixes

- Linear gradients (p. 180) are a type of image that gradually transitions from one color to the next horizontally, vertically or diagonally.

- You can transition between as many colors as you like and specify the points at which to change colors, called `color-stops` (p. 180), represented in pixels or percentages along the so-called gradient line.

- You can use gradients in any property that accepts an image.

- Browsers currently implement gradients differently, so you'll need vendor prefixes and different syntax for each browser.

- Vendor prefixes (e.g., -webkit- and -moz-, p. 183) are used for properties that are still being finalized in the CSS specification but have already been implemented in various browsers.
- Prefixes are not available for every browser or for every property.
- It's good practice to include the multiple prefixes when they're available so that your pages render properly in the various browsers.
- Always place vendor-prefixed styles before the nonprefixed version. The last version of the style that a given browser supports takes precedence and will be used by the browser.

Section 5.7 Radial Gradients
- Radial gradients (p. 183) are similar to linear gradients, but the color changes gradually from an inner circle (the start) to an outer circle (the end).
- The radial-gradient property (p. 183) has three values. The first is the position of the start of the radial gradient (center). Other possible values for the position include top, bottom, left and right. The second value is the start color, and the third is the end color.
- Other than the vendor prefixes, the syntax of the gradient is identical for WebKit browsers, Mozilla Firefox and the standard CSS3 radial-gradient.

Section 5.8 (Optional: WebKit Only) Text Stroke
- The -webkit-text-stroke property (p. 185) is a nonstandard property for WebKit-based browsers that allows you to add an outline (text stroke) around text. The -webkit-text-stroke property has two values—the thickness of the outline and the color of the text stroke.

Section 5.9 Multiple Background Images
- CSS3 allows you to add multiple background images (p. 185) to an element.
- We specify each image's placement using property background-position. The comma-separated list of values matches the order of the comma-separated list of images in the background-image property.
- The background-origin (p. 154) determines where each image is placed using the box model.

Section 5.10 (Optional: WebKit Only) Reflections
- The -webkit-box-reflect property (p. 187) allows you to add a simple reflection (p. 187) of an image. Like -webkit-text-stroke, this is a nonstandard property that's available only in WebKit-based browsers for now.
- The property's first value is the *direction* of the reflection. The direction value may be above, below, left, or right.
- The second value is the offset, which determines the space between the image and its reflection.
- Optionally, you can specify a gradient to apply to the reflection.

Section 5.11 Image Borders
- The CSS3 border-image property (p. 188) uses images to place a border around any element.
- The border-width is the thickness of the border being placed around the element. The width is the width of the entire rectangular border.
- The border-image-source (p. 189) is the URL of the image to use in the border.
- The border-image-slice (p. 190) specifies the inward offsets from the top, right, bottom and left sides of the image.
- The border-image-slice divides the image into nine regions: four corners, four sides and a middle, which is transparent unless otherwise specified. You may not use negative values.

- We can express the `border-image-slice` in just two values, in which case the first value represents the top and bottom, and the second value the left and right.

- The `border-image-slice` may be expressed in pixels or percentages.

- `border-image-repeat` (p. 190) specifies how the regions of the border image are scaled and tiled (repeated). By indicating `stretch` just once, we create a border that will stretch the top, right, bottom and left regions to fit the area.

- You may specify two values for the `border-image-repeat` property. For example, if we specified `stretch repeat`, the top and bottom regions of the image border would be stretched, and the right and left regions of the border would be repeated (i.e., tiled) to fit the space, using partial tiles to fill the excess space.

- Other possible values for the `border-image-repeat` property include `round` and `space`. If you specify `round`, the regions are repeated using only whole tiles, and the border image is scaled to fit the area. If you specify `space`, the regions are repeated to fill the area using only whole tiles, and any excess space is distributed evenly around the tiles.

Section 5.12 Animation; Selectors

- The `animation` property (p. 193) allows you to represent several animation properties in a shorthand notation, rather than specifying each animation property separately.

- The `animation-name` (p. 193) represents the name of the animation. This name associates the animation with the keyframes that define various properties of the element being animated at different stages of the animation.

- The `animation-timing-function` (p. 193) determines how the animation progresses in one cycle of its duration. Possible values include `linear`, `ease`, `ease-in`, `ease-out`, `ease-in-out`, `cubic-bezier`. The value `linear` specifies that the animation will move at the same speed from start to finish. The default value, `ease`, starts slowly, increases speed, then ends slowly. The `ease-in` value starts slowly, then speeds up, whereas the `ease-out` value starts faster, then slows down. The `ease-in-out` starts and ends slowly. Finally, the `cubic-bezier` value allows you to customize the timing function with four values between 0 and 1, such as `cubic-bezier(1,0,0,1)`.

- The `animation-duration` (p. 193) specifies the time in seconds (s) or milliseconds (ms) that the animation takes to complete one iteration. The default duration is 0.

- The `animation-delay` (p. 193) specifies the number of seconds or milliseconds after the page loads before the animation begins. The default value is 0. If the `animation-delay` is negative, such as `-3s`, the animation begins three seconds into its cycle.

- The `animation-iteration-count` (p. 193) specifies the number of times the animation will run. The default is 1. You may use the value `infinite` to repeat the animation continuously.

- The `animation-direction` (p. 193) specifies the direction in which the animation will run. The value `alternate` used here specifies that the animation will run in alternating directions. The default value, `normal`, would run the animation in the same direction for each cycle.

- The shorthand `animation` property cannot be used with the `animation-play-state` property (p. 193)—it must be specified separately. If you do not include the `animation-play-state`, which specifies whether the animation is paused or running, it defaults to running.

- For the element being animated, the `@keyframes rule` (p. 193) defines the element's properties that will change during the animation, the values to which those properties will change, and when they'll change.

- The `@keyframes` rule is followed by the name of the animation to which the keyframes are applied. Rules (p. 194) consist of one or more selectors (p. 194) followed by a declaration block (p. 194) in curly braces (`{}`).

- Selectors enable you to apply styles to elements of a particular type or attribute.
- A declaration block consists of one or more declarations, each of which includes the property name followed by a colon (:), a value and a semicolon (;). You may include multiple declarations in a declaration block.

Section 5.13 Transitions and Transformations
- With CSS3 transitions (p. 194), you can change an element's style over a specified duration.
- CSS3 transformations (p. 194) allow you to move, rotate, scale and skew elements.
- Transitions are similar in concept to animations, but transitions allow you to specify only the starting and ending values of the CSS properties being changed. An animation's keyframes enable you to control intermediate states throughout the animation's duration.
- For each property that will change, the transition property (p. 194) specifies the duration of that change.
- As of CSS3, the :hover pseudo-class now works with any element.
- The transform property (p. 194) uses transformation functions (p. 195), such as rotate (p. 195) and scale (p. 196), to perform the transformations.
- The rotate transformation function receives number of degrees. Negative values cause the element to rotate left. A value of 720deg would cause the element to rotate clockwise twice.
- The scale transformation function specifies how to scale the width and height. The value 1 represents the original width or original height, so values greater than 1 increase the size and values less than 1 decrease the size.
- CSS3 transformations also allow you to skew (p. 196) block-level elements, slanting them at an angle either horizontally (skewX) or vertically (skewY).
- The transition-duration is the amount of time it takes to complete the transition.
- The transition-timing-function determines how the transition progresses in one cycle of its duration.

Section 5.14 Downloading Web Fonts and the @font-face Rule
- Using the @font-face rule (p. 198), you can specify fonts for a web page, even if they're not installed on the user's system. Downloadable fonts help ensure a uniform look across client sites.
- You can find numerous free, open-source web fonts at http://www.google.com/webfonts. Make sure the fonts you get from other sources have no legal encumbrances.
- The @media screen rule specifies that the font will be used when the document is rendered on a computer screen.
- The @font-face rule includes the font-family, font-style and font-weight. Multiple fonts can be specified with varying styles and weights. The @font-face rule also includes the font's location.

Section 5.15 Flexible Box Layout Module and :nth-child Selectors
- Flexible Box Layout Module (FBLM, p. 200) makes it easy to align the contents of boxes, change their size, change their order dynamically, and lay out the contents in any direction.
- The box-orient property (p. 200) specifies the orientation of the box layout. The default value is horizontal. You can also use vertical.
- In CSS3, you can use selectors to easily style attributes. For example, you can select every other row in a table and change the background color to blue, making the table easier to read. You can also use selectors to enable or disable input elements.

- We use :nth-child selectors (p. 203) to select each of the for the four div elements in the flex-box div to style.
- div:nth-child(1) selects the div element that's the first child of its parent and applies the specified style. Similarly, div:nth-child(2) selects the div element that's the second child of its parent, div:nth-child(3) selects the third child of its parent, and div:nth-child(4) selects the fourth child of its parent.
- Setting the overflow to hidden hides any text that does not fit in the specified paragraph height.

Section 5.16 Multicolumn Layout
- CSS3 allows you to easily create multicolumn layouts (p. 203) using the column-count property (p. 203).
- The column-gap property (p. 203) specifies the spacing between columns.
- Add lines between columns using the column-rule property (p. 203).
- Resizing your browser window changes the width of the columns to fit the three-column layout in the browser.

Section 5.17 Media Queries
- With CSS3 media queries you can determine the finer attributes of the media on which the user is viewing the page, such as the length and width of the viewing area on the screen, to customize your presentation.
- The @media rule (p. 206) is used to determine the type and size of device on which the page is rendered. When the browser looks at the rule, the result is either true or false. The rule's styles are applied only if the result is true.

Self-Review Exercises

5.1 Fill in the blanks in the following statements:
   a) The _____ property makes it easy to add a text shadow effect to any text.
   b) The _____ property allows you to add rounded corners to any element.
   c) CSS3 includes two new ways to express color—_____ and_____.
   d) The _____ defines the number of pixels that the box-shadow will appear to the left or the right of the box.
   e) _____ are similar to linear gradients, but the color changes gradually from an inner circle (the start) to an outer circle (the end).
   f) The _____ divides the image into nine regions: four corners, four sides and a middle, which is transparent unless otherwise specified.
   g) The animation-timing-function determines how the animation progresses in one cycle of its duration. Possible values include _____, _____, _____, _____, _____ and _____.
   h) For the element being animated, the _____ defines the element's properties that will change during the animation, the values to which those properties will change, and when they'll change.
   i) _____ are similar in concept to animations, but they allow you to specify only the starting and ending values of the CSS properties being changed. An animation's keyframes enable you to control intermediate states throughout the animation's duration.
   j) CSS3 _____ allow you to move, rotate, scale and skew elements.
   k) _____ consist of one or more selectors followed by a declaration block in curly braces ({}).
   l) In CSS3, you can use _____ to easily style attributes.

5.2   State whether each of the following is *true* or *false*. If *false*, explain why.

    a) The @font-face rule specifies that an embedded font will be used when the document is rendered on a computer screen.

    b) You can use gradients in any property that accepts an image.

    c) A horizontal gradient gradually changes from top to bottom.

    d) You can add lines between columns using the column-gap property.

    e) The @media rule determines the type and size of device on which the page is rendered. When the browser looks at the rule, the result is either true or false. The rule's styles are applied only if the result is false.

    f) To add multiple background images to an element, use the background-position to specify where each image is placed using the box model.

Answers to Self-Review Exercises

5.1   a) text-shadow. b) border-radius. c) RGBA and HSLA. d) horizontal offset. e) Radial gradients. f) border-image-slice. g) linear, ease, ease-in, ease-out, ease-in-out, cubic-bezier. h) @keyframes rule. i) Transitions. j) transformations. k) Rules. l) selectors.

5.2   a) False. The @media screen rule specifies that an embedded font will be used when the document is rendered on a computer screen. b) True. c) False. A horizontal gradient gradually changes from left to right. d) False. You can add lines between columns using the column-rule property. e) The @media rule's styles are applied only if the result is true. f) False. The background-origin specifies where each image is placed using the box model.

Exercises

For each of the following, build and render a web page that makes the indicated effect(s) appear. Validate your page with the following validators:

    1. For CSS3: http://jigsaw.w3.org/css-validator/ (under **More Options > Profile**, select CSS level 3) [*Note:* Many CSS3 properties will not validate because they're not yet standardized.]

    2. For HTML5: http://validator.w3.org/#validate_by_upload

Also, test your page with as many as possible of the seven browsers we're using in this book.

5.3   *(Text Shadow)* Create a text shadow on the phrase "New features in CSS3" with an offset-x of 4px, an offset-y of 10px, a blur radius of 12px and a text-shadow color red.

5.4   *(Text Stroke)* Create a text stroke on the phrase "New WebKit features". Make the color of the text green. Use a 5px Navy text-stroke and set the font-size to 600%.

5.5   *(Rounded Corners)* Create three div elements, each with a width and height of 200px. On the first element, create slightly rounded corners using a border of 6px black and border-radius of 20px. On the second element, use a border of 6px black and increase the border-radius to 100px. On the third, use a border of 6px black and increase the border-radius to 200px. Make the background-color of each element red. Inside of each element, display the value of the border-radius in normal text.

5.6   *(Box Shadow)* Create three div elements of varying colors, each with a width and height of 400px. On the first box, add a DimGrey box-shadow with an offset-x of 30px and offset-y of 30px a blur radius of 30px. On the second box, add a DimGrey box-shadow with an offset-x of -30px and offset-y of -30px a blur radius of 60px. On the third box, add a DimGrey box-shadow with an offset-x of 30px and offset-y of 30px a blur radius of 20px.

5.7   *(Linear Gradient)* Create a div element with a width and height of 400px. Create a diagonal linear gradient using five colors.

5.8   *(Radial Gradient)* Create a div element with a width and height of 400px. Create a radial gradient with four colors. Start the gradient in the bottom-left corner with the colors changing as they move along the gradient line to the right.

5.9   *(Animation)* Create an infinite animation of an element moving in a square pattern.

5.10   *(Skew)* Modify the skew example in Fig. 5.13 to skew the element top to bottom 15 deg, then left to right 15 deg, alternating infinitely.

5.11   *(Melting Images)* Modify the example in Fig. 5.14 using five pictures. It might be interesting to try pictures of you or a family member at different ages or a landscape at various times. Set the transition-duration to 3s and a transition-timing-function to linear.

5.12   *(Multicolumn Text)* Change the format of the example in Fig. 5.17 to four columns, add an author name and increase the space between columns to 40px color and thickness of the column-rule.

5.13   *(FBLM)* Modify the example in Fig. 5.16 to use a vertical flexbox.

5.14   *(Transformation with :hover)* Create a transformation program that includes four images. When the user hovers over an image, the size of the image increases by 30%.

5.15   *(Reflection)* Create a reflection of an image 5px to the right of the original image.

5.16   *(Media Queries)* Create your own multicolumn web page and use media queries to adjust the formatting to use one column for mobile devices that have a maximum width of 480px.

JavaScript: Introduction to Scripting

6

Comment is free, but facts are sacred.
—C. P. Scott

The creditor hath a better memory than the debtor.
—James Howell

When faced with a decision, I always ask, "What would be the most fun?"
—Peggy Walker

Objectives

In this chapter you will:

- Write simple JavaScript programs.

- Use input and output statements.

- Learn basic memory concepts.

- Use arithmetic operators.

- Learn the precedence of arithmetic operators.

- Write decision-making statements to choose among alternative courses of action.

- Use relational and equality operators to compare data items.

6.1 Introduction

In this chapter, we begin our introduction to the **JavaScript**[1] **scripting language**, which is used to enhance the functionality and appearance of web pages.[2]

In Chapters 6–11, we present a detailed discussion of JavaScript—the *de facto* standard client-side scripting language for web-based applications due to its highly portable nature. Our treatment of JavaScript serves two purposes—it introduces client-side scripting (used in Chapters 6–18), which makes web pages more dynamic and interactive, and it provides the programming foundation for the server-side scripting presented later in the book.

Before you can run code examples with JavaScript on your computer, you may need to change your browser's security settings. By default, Internet Explorer 9 *prevents* scripts on your local computer from running, and displays a warning message. To allow scripts to run in files on your computer, select **Internet Options** from the **Tools** menu. Click the **Advanced** tab and scroll down to the **Security** section of the **Settings** list. Check the box labeled **Allow active content to run in files on My Computer**. Click **OK** and restart Internet Explorer. HTML5 documents on your own computer that contain JavaScript code will now run properly. Firefox, Chrome, Opera, Safari (including on the iPhone) and the Android browser have JavaScript enabled by default.

6.2 Your First Script: Displaying a Line of Text with JavaScript in a Web Page

We begin with a simple **script** (or **program**) that displays the text `"Welcome to JavaScript Programming!"` in the HTML5 document. All major web browsers contain **JavaScript interpreters**, which process the commands written in JavaScript. The JavaScript code and its result are shown in Fig. 6.1.

---

1. Many people confuse the scripting language JavaScript with the programming language Java. Java is a full-fledged object-oriented programming language. Java is popular for developing large-scale distributed enterprise applications and web applications. JavaScript is a browser-based scripting language developed by Netscape and implemented in all major browsers.

2. JavaScript was originally created by Netscape. Both Netscape and Microsoft have been instrumental in the standardization of JavaScript by ECMA International—formerly the European Computer Manufacturers' Association—as ECMAScript (`www.ecma-international.org/publications/standards/ECMA-262.htm`). The latest version of JavaScript is based on ECMAScript 5.

```
 I   <!DOCTYPE html>
 2
 3   <!-- Fig. 6.1: welcome.html -->
 4   <!-- Displaying a line of text. -->
 5   <html>
 6      <head>
 7         <meta charset = "utf-8">
 8         <title>A First Program in JavaScript</title>
 9         <script type = "text/javascript">
10
11            document.writeln(
12               "<h1>Welcome to JavaScript Programming!</h1>" );
13
14         </script>
15      </head><body></body>
16   </html>
```

Script result

Welcome to JavaScript Programming!

Fig. 6.1 | Displaying a line of text.

Lines 11–12 do the "real work" of the script, namely, displaying the phrase Welcome to JavaScript Programming! as an h1 heading in the web page.

Line 6 starts the <head> section of the document. For the moment, the JavaScript code we write will appear in the <head> section. The browser interprets the contents of the <head> section first, so the JavaScript programs we write there execute *before* the <body> of the HTML5 document displays. In later chapters on JavaScript, we illustrate **inline scripting**, in which JavaScript code is written in the <body> of an HTML5 document.

The **script** Element and Commenting Your Scripts
Line 9 uses the **<script>** tag to indicate to the browser that the text which follows is part of a script. The **type** attribute specifies the MIME type of the script as well as the **scripting language** used in the script—in this case, a text file written in javascript. In HTML5, the default MIME type for a <script> is "text/html", so you can omit the type attribute from your <script> tags. We've introduced this here, because you'll see it in legacy HTML documents with embedded JavaScripts.

Strings
Lines 11–12 instruct the browser's JavaScript interpreter to perform an **action**, namely, to display in the web page the **string** of characters contained between the **double quotation** (") **marks** (also called a **string literal**). Individual white-space characters between words in a string are *not* ignored by the browser. However, if consecutive spaces appear in a string,

browsers condense them to a single space. Also, browsers ignore *leading white-space characters* (i.e., white space at the beginning of a string).

Software Engineering Observation 6.1

Strings in JavaScript can be enclosed in either double quotation marks (") or single quotation marks (').

Using the document Object

Lines 11–12 use the browser's **document object**, which represents the HTML5 document the browser is currently displaying. This object allows you to specify text to display in the HTML5 document. The browser creates a set of objects that allow you to access and manipulate *every* element of an HTML5 document. In the next several chapters, we overview some of these objects as we discuss the Document Object Model (DOM).

An object resides in the computer's memory and contains information used by the script. The term **object** normally implies that **attributes** (**data**) and **behaviors** (**methods**) are associated with the object. The object's methods use the attributes to perform useful actions for the **client of the object** (i.e., the script that calls the methods). A method may require additional information (**arguments**) to perform its actions; this information is enclosed in parentheses after the name of the method in the script. In lines 11–12, we call the document object's **writeln method** to write a line of HTML5 markup in the HTML5 document. The parentheses following the method name writeln contain the one argument that method writeln requires (in this case, the string of HTML5 that the browser is to display). Method writeln instructs the browser to write the argument string into the web page for rendering. If the string contains HTML5 elements, the browser interprets these elements and renders them on the screen. In this example, the browser displays the phrase Welcome to JavaScript Programming! as an h1-level HTML5 heading, because the phrase is enclosed in an h1 element.

Statements

The code elements in lines 11–12, including document.writeln, its argument in the parentheses (the string) and the **semicolon** (;), together are called a **statement**. Every statement ends with a semicolon (also known as the **statement terminator**)—although this practice is *not* required by JavaScript, it's recommended as a way of avoiding subtle problems. Line 14 indicates the end of the script. In line 15, the tags <body> and </body> specify that this HTML5 document has an empty body.

Good Programming Practice 6.1

Terminate every statement with a semicolon. This notation clarifies where one statement ends and the next statement begins.

Common Programming Error 6.1

Forgetting the ending </script> tag for a script may prevent the browser from interpreting the script properly and may prevent the HTML5 document from loading properly.

Open the HTML5 document in your browser. If the script contains no syntax errors, it should produce the output shown in Fig. 6.1.

Common Programming Error 6.2

JavaScript is case sensitive. *Not using the proper uppercase and lowercase letters is a syntax error. A syntax error occurs when the script interpreter cannot recognize a statement. The interpreter normally issues an error message to help you locate and fix the incorrect statement. Syntax errors are violations of the rules of the programming language. The interpreter notifies you of a syntax error when it attempts to execute the statement containing the error. Each browser has its own way to display JavaScript Errors. For example, Firefox has the Error Console (in its Web Developer menu) and Chrome has the JavaScript console (in its Tools menu). To view script errors in IE9, select* **Internet Options...** *from the* **Tools** *menu. In the dialog that appears, select the* **Advanced** *tab and click the checkbox labeled* **Display a notification about every script error** *under the* **Browsing** *category.*

Error-Prevention Tip 6.1

When the interpreter reports a syntax error, sometimes the error is not in the line indicated by the error message. First, check the line for which the error was reported. If that line does not contain errors, check the preceding several lines in the script.

A Note About `document.writeln`

In this example, we displayed an `h1` HTML5 element in the web browser by using `document.writeln` to write the element into the web page. For simplicity in Chapters 6–9, we'll continue to do this as we focus on presenting fundamental JavaScript programming concepts. Typically, you'll display content by modifying an existing element in a web page—a technique we'll begin using in Chapter 10.

A Note About Embedding JavaScript Code into HTML5 Documents

In Section 4.5, we discussed the benefits of placing CSS3 code in external style sheets and linking them to your HTML5 documents. For similar reasons, JavaScript code is typically placed in a separate file, then included in the HTML5 document that uses the script. This makes the code more reusable, because it can be included into any HTML5 document—as is the case with the many JavaScript libraries used in professional web development today. We'll begin separating both CSS3 and JavaScript into separate files starting in Chapter 10.

6.3 Modifying Your First Script

This section continues our introduction to JavaScript programming with two examples that modify the example in Fig. 6.1.

Displaying a Line of Colored Text

A script can display `Welcome to JavaScript Programming!` in many ways. Figure 6.2 displays the text in magenta, using the CSS `color` property. Most of this example is identical to Fig. 6.1, so we concentrate only on lines 11–13 of Fig. 6.2, which display one line of text in the document. The first statement uses `document` method **`write`** to display a string. Unlike `writeln`, `write` does not position the output cursor in the HTML5 document at the beginning of the next line after writing its argument. [*Note:* The output cursor keeps track of where the next character appears in the document's markup, not where the next character appears in the web page as rendered by the browser.] The next character written in the document appears immediately after the last character written with `write`. Thus, when lines 12–13 execute, the first character written, "W," appears immediately after the last character displayed

```
1   <!DOCTYPE html>
2
3   <!-- Fig. 6.2: welcome2.html -->
4   <!-- Printing one line with multiple statements. -->
5   <html>
6      <head>
7         <meta charset = "utf-8">
8         <title>Printing a Line with Multiple Statements</title>
9         <script type = "text/javascript">
10           <!--
11           document.write( "<h1 style = 'color: magenta'>" );
12           document.write( "Welcome to JavaScript " +
13              "Programming!</h1>" );
14           // -->
15        </script>
16     </head><body></body>
17  </html>
```

Magenta text ——— **Welcome to JavaScript Programming!**

Fig. 6.2 | Printing one line with separate statements.

with `write` (the > character inside the right double quote in line 11). Each `write` or `writeln` statement resumes writing characters where the last `write` or `writeln` statement stopped writing characters. So, after a `writeln` statement, the next output appears on the beginning of the next line. Thus, the two statements in lines 11–13 result in one line of HTML5 text. Remember that statements in JavaScript are separated by semicolons (;). Therefore, lines 12–13 represent only one complete statement. JavaScript allows large statements to be split over many lines. The + operator (called the "concatenation operator" when used in this manner) in line 12 joins two strings together—it's explained in more detail later in this chapter.

Common Programming Error 6.3
Splitting a JavaScript statement in the middle of a string is a syntax error.

The preceding discussion has nothing to do with the actual *rendering* of the HTML5 text. Remember that the browser does *not* create a new line of text unless the browser window is too narrow for the text being rendered or the browser encounters an HTML5 element that explicitly starts a new line—for example, <p> to start a new paragraph.

Common Programming Error 6.4
Many people confuse the writing of HTML5 text with the rendering of HTML5 text. Writing HTML5 text creates the HTML5 that will be rendered by the browser for presentation to the user.

Nesting Quotation Marks

Recall that a string can be delimited by single (') or double (") quote characters. Within a string, you can't nest quotes of the same type, but you can nest quotes of the other type. A string that's delimited by double quotes, can contain single quotes. Similarly. a string that's delimited by single quotes, can contain nest double quotes. Line 11 nests single quotes inside a double-quoted string to quote the style attribute's value in the h1 element.

Displaying Text in an Alert Dialog

The first two scripts in this chapter display text in the HTML5 document. Sometimes it's useful to display information in windows called **dialogs** (or **dialog boxes**) that "pop up" on the screen to grab the user's attention. Dialogs typically display important messages to users browsing the web page. JavaScript allows you easily to display a dialog box containing a message. The script in Fig. 6.3 displays Welcome to JavaScript Programming! as three lines in a predefined dialog called an **alert dialog**.

```
1   <!DOCTYPE html>
2
3   <!-- Fig. 6.3: welcome3.html -->
4   <!-- Alert dialog displaying multiple lines. -->
5   <html>
6      <head>
7         <meta charset = "utf-8">
8         <title>Printing Multiple Lines in a Dialog Box</title>
9         <script type = "text/javascript">
10            <!--
11            window.alert( "Welcome to\nJavaScript\nProgramming!" );
12            // -->
13         </script>
14      </head>
15      <body>
16         <p>Click Refresh (or Reload) to run this script again.</p>
17      </body>
18   </html>
```

Title bar ————

Welcome to
JavaScript
Programming!

Clicking the **OK** button dismisses the dialog.

OK — Mouse cursor

Fig. 6.3 | Alert dialog displaying multiple lines.

The window Object

Line 11 in the script uses the browser's **window** object to display an alert dialog. The argument to the window object's **alert** method is the string to display. Executing the preceding statement displays the dialog shown in Fig. 6.3. The **title bar** of this Chrome dialog contains the string **JavaScript Alert** to indicate that the browser is presenting a message to the user. The dialog provides an **OK** button that allows the user to **dismiss** (i.e., **close**) the dialog by clicking the button. To dismiss the dialog, position the **mouse cursor** (also called the **mouse pointer**) over the **OK** button and click the mouse, or simply press the *Enter* key. The contents of the dialog vary by browser. You can refresh the page to run the script again.

Escape Sequences

The alert dialog in this example contains three lines of plain text. Normally, a dialog displays a string's characters exactly as they appear. However, the dialog does not display the characters \n (line 11). The **backslash** (\) in a string is an **escape character**. It indicates that a "special" character is to be used in the string. When a backslash is encountered in a string, the next character is combined with the backslash to form an **escape sequence**. The escape sequence \n is the **newline character**, which causes the **cursor** (i.e., the current screen position indicator) to move to the beginning of the *next* line in the dialog. Some other common JavaScript escape sequences are listed in Fig. 6.4. The \n and \t escape sequences in the table do not affect HTML5 rendering unless they're in a **pre element** (this element displays the text between its tags in a fixed-width font exactly as it's formatted between the tags, including leading white-space characters and consecutive white-space characters).

Escape sequence	Description
\n	*New line*—position the screen cursor at the beginning of the next line.
\t	*Horizontal tab*—move the screen cursor to the next tab stop.
\\	*Backslash*—used to represent a backslash character in a string.
\"	*Double quote*—used to represent a double-quote character in a string contained in double quotes. For example, `window.alert( "\"in double quotes\"" );` displays "in double quotes" in an alert dialog.
\'	*Single quote*—used to represent a single-quote character in a string. For example, `window.alert( '\'in single quotes\'' );` displays 'in single quotes' in an alert dialog.

Fig. 6.4 | Some common escape sequences.

6.4 Obtaining User Input with prompt Dialogs

Scripting gives you the ability to generate part or all of a web page's content at the time it's shown to the user. A script can adapt the content based on input from the user or other variables, such as the time of day or the type of browser used by the client. Such web pages are said to be *dynamic*, as opposed to *static*, since their content has the ability to change. The next two subsections use scripts to demonstrate dynamic web pages.

6.4.1 Dynamic Welcome Page

Our next script creates a dynamic welcome page that obtains the user's name, then displays it on the page. The script uses another *predefined* dialog box from the window object—a **prompt** dialog—which allows the user to enter a value that the script can use. The script asks the user to enter a name, then displays the name in the HTML5 document. Figure 6.5 presents the script and sample output. In later chapters, we'll obtain inputs via GUI components in HTML5 forms, as introduced in Chapters 2–3.]

```
1   <!DOCTYPE html>
2
3   <!-- Fig. 6.5: welcome4.html -->
4   <!-- Prompt box used on a welcome screen -->
5   <html>
6      <head>
7         <meta charset = "utf-8">
8         <title>Using Prompt and Alert Boxes</title>
9         <script type = "text/javascript">
10           <!--
11           var name; // string entered by the user
12
13           // read the name from the prompt box as a string
14           name = window.prompt( "Please enter your name" );
15
16           document.writeln( "<h1>Hello " + name +
17              ", welcome to JavaScript programming!</h1>" );
18           // -->
19        </script>
20     </head><body></body>
21   </html>
```

Fig. 6.5 | Prompt box used on a welcome screen.

Declarations, Keywords and Variables

Line 11 is a **declaration** that contains the JavaScript **keyword** var. Keywords are words that have special meaning in JavaScript. The keyword **var** at the beginning of the statement indicates that the word name is a **variable**. A variable is a location in the computer's memory where a value can be stored for use by a script. All variables have a *name* and *value*, and should be declared with a var statement before they're used in a script.

Identifiers and Case Sensitivity

The name of a variable can be any valid **identifier**. An identifier is a series of characters consisting of letters, digits, underscores (_) and dollar signs ($) that does *not* begin with a digit and is *not* a reserved JavaScript keyword. [*Note:* A complete list of reserved keywords can be found in Fig. 7.2.] Identifiers may *not* contain spaces. Some valid identifiers are Welcome, $value, _value, m_inputField1 and button7. The name 7button is not a valid identifier, because it begins with a digit, and the name input field is not valid, because it contains a space. Remember that JavaScript is **case sensitive**—uppercase and lowercase letters are considered to be different characters, so name, Name and NAME are different identifiers.

Good Programming Practice 6.2

Choosing meaningful variable names helps a script to be "self-documenting" (i.e., easy to understand by simply reading the script).

Good Programming Practice 6.3

By convention, variable-name identifiers begin with a lowercase first letter. Each subsequent word should begin with a capital first letter. For example, identifier itemPrice *has a capital* P *in its second word,* Price.

Common Programming Error 6.5

Splitting a statement in the middle of an identifier is a syntax error.

Declarations end with a *semicolon* and can be split over several lines with each variable in the declaration separated by a *comma*—known as a **comma-separated list** of variable names. Several variables may be declared either in one or in multiple declarations.

JavaScript Comments

It's helpful to indicate the purpose of each variable in the script by placing a JavaScript comment at the end of each line in the declaration. In line 11, a **single-line comment** that begins with the characters // states the purpose of the variable in the script. This form of comment is called a single-line comment because it terminates at the end of the line in which it appears. A // comment can begin at any position in a line of JavaScript code and continues until the end of the line. Comments do not cause the browser to perform any action when the script is interpreted; rather, comments are *ignored* by the JavaScript interpreter.

Good Programming Practice 6.4

Although it's not required, declare each variable on a separate line. This allows for easy insertion of a comment next to each declaration. This is a widely followed professional coding standard.

Multiline Comments

You can also write **multiline comments**. For example,

```
/* This is a multiline
   comment. It can be
   split over many lines. */
```

is a multiline comment spread over several lines. Such comments begin with the delimiter /* and end with the delimiter */. All text between the delimiters of the comment is *ignored* by the interpreter.

JavaScript adopted comments delimited with /* and */ from the C programming language and single-line comments delimited with // from the C++ programming language. JavaScript programmers generally prefer C++-style single-line comments over C-style comments. Throughout this book, we use C++-style single-line comments.

`window` *Object's* `prompt` *Method*

Line 13 is a comment indicating the purpose of the statement in the next line. Line 14 calls the `window` object's `prompt` method, which displays the dialog in Fig. 6.6. The dialog allows the user to enter a string representing the user's name.

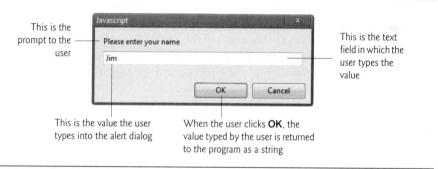

Fig. 6.6 | Prompt dialog displayed by the `window` object's `prompt` method.

The argument to `prompt` specifies a message telling the user what to type in the text field. This message is called a *prompt* because it directs the user to take a specific action. An optional second argument, separated from the first by a comma, may specify the default string displayed in the text field; our code does not supply a second argument. In this case, most browsers leave the text field empty, and Internet Explorer displays the default value `undefined`. The user types characters in the text field, then clicks the **OK** button to submit the string to the script. We normally receive input from a user through a GUI component such as the `prompt` dialog, as in this script, or through an HTML5 form GUI component, as we'll see in later chapters.

The user can type anything in the text field of the `prompt` dialog. For this script, whatever the user enters is considered the name. If the user clicks the **Cancel** button, no string value is sent to the script. Instead, the `prompt` dialog submits the value **null**, a JavaScript keyword signifying that a variable has no value. Note that `null` is not a string literal, but rather a predefined term indicating the absence of value. Writing a `null` value to the document, however, displays the word `null` in the web page.

Assignment Operator

The statement in line 14 *assigns* the value returned by the `window` object's `prompt` method (a string containing the characters typed by the user—or the default value or `null` if the **Cancel** button is clicked) to variable name by using the **assignment operator**, =. The statement is read as, "name gets the value returned by `window.prompt("Please enter your name")`." The =

operator is called a **binary operator** because it has *two* **operands**—name and the result of the expression window.prompt("Please enter your name"). This entire statement is called an **assignment** because it assigns a value to a variable. The expression to the right of the assignment operator is always evaluated *first*.

> **Good Programming Practice 6.5**
> *Place a space on each side of a binary operator. This format makes the operator stand out and makes the script more readable.*

String Concatenation

Lines 16–17 use document.writeln to display the new welcome message. The expression inside the parentheses uses the operator + to "add" a string (the literal "<h1>Hello, "), the variable name (the string that the user entered in line 14) and another string (the literal ", welcome to JavaScript programming!</h1>"). JavaScript has a version of the + operator for **string concatenation** that enables a string and a value of another data type (including another string) to be combined. The result of this operation is a new (and normally longer) string. If we assume that name contains the string literal "Jim", the expression evaluates as follows: JavaScript determines that the two operands of the first + operator (the string "<h1>Hello, " and the value of variable name) are both strings, then concatenates the two into one string. Next, JavaScript determines that the two operands of the second + operator (the result of the first concatenation operation, the string "<h1>Hello, Jim", and the string ", welcome to JavaScript programming!</h1>") are both strings and concatenates the two. This results in the string "<h1>Hello, Jim, welcome to JavaScript programming!</h1>". The browser renders this string as part of the HTML5 document. Note that the space between Hello, and Jim is part of the string "<h1>Hello, ".

As you'll see later, the + operator used for string concatenation can convert other variable types to strings if necessary. Because string concatenation occurs between two strings, JavaScript must convert other variable types to strings before it can proceed with the operation. For example, if a variable age has an integer value equal to 21, then the expression "my age is " + age evaluates to the string "my age is 21". JavaScript converts the value of age to a string and concatenates it with the existing string literal "my age is ".

After the browser interprets the <head> section of the HTML5 document (which contains the JavaScript), it then interprets the <body> of the HTML5 document (which is empty; line 20) and renders the HTML5. The HTML5 page is *not* rendered until the prompt is dismissed because the prompt pauses execution in the head, before the body is processed. If you reload the page after entering a name, the browser will execute the script again and so you can change the name.

6.4.2 Adding Integers

Our next script illustrates another use of prompt dialogs to obtain input from the user. Figure 6.7 inputs two *integers* (whole numbers, such as 7, –11, 0 and 31914) typed by a user at the keyboard, computes the sum of the values and displays the result.

Lines 11–15 declare the variables firstNumber, secondNumber, number1, number2 and sum. Single-line comments state the purpose of each of these variables. Line 18 employs a prompt dialog to allow the user to enter a string representing the first of the two integers that will be added. The script assigns the first value entered by the user to the variable `firstNumber`. Line 21 displays a prompt dialog to obtain the second number to add and assigns this value to the variable `secondNumber`.

```
1   <!DOCTYPE html>
2
3   <!-- Fig. 6.7: addition.html -->
4   <!-- Addition script. -->
5   <html>
6      <head>
7         <meta charset = "utf-8">
8         <title>An Addition Program</title>
9         <script type = "text/javascript">
10           <!--
11           var firstNumber; // first string entered by user
12           var secondNumber; // second string entered by user
13           var number1; // first number to add
14           var number2; // second number to add
15           var sum; // sum of number1 and number2
16
17           // read in first number from user as a string
18           firstNumber = window.prompt( "Enter first integer" );
19
20           // read in second number from user as a string
21           secondNumber = window.prompt( "Enter second integer" );
22
23           // convert numbers from strings to integers
24           number1 = parseInt( firstNumber );
25           number2 = parseInt( secondNumber );
26
27           sum = number1 + number2; // add the numbers
28
29           // display the results
30           document.writeln( "<h1>The sum is " + sum + "</h1>" );
31           // -->
32        </script>
33     </head><body></body>
34   </html>
```

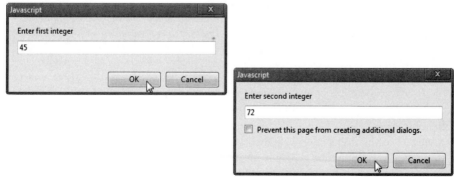

Fig. 6.7 | Addition script. (Part 1 of 2.)

Fig. 6.7 | Addition script. (Part 2 of 2.)

As in the preceding example, the user can type anything in the prompt dialog. For this script, if the user either types a non-integer value or clicks the **Cancel** button, a logic error will occur, and the sum of the two values will appear in the HTML5 document as **NaN** (meaning **not a number**). A logic error is caused by syntactically correct code that produces an incorrect result. In Chapter 11, we discuss the Number object and its methods that can determine whether a value is a number.

Recall that a prompt dialog returns to the script as a string the value typed by the user. Lines 24–25 convert the two strings input by the user to integer values that can be used in a calculation. Function **parseInt** converts its string argument to an integer. Line 24 assigns to the variable number1 the integer that function parseInt returns. Similarly, line 25 assigns an integer value to variable number2. Any subsequent references to number1 and number2 in the script use these integer values. We refer to parseInt as a **function** rather than a method because we do not precede the function call with an object name (such as document or window) and a dot (.). The term method means that the function belongs to a particular object. For example, method writeln belongs to the document object and method prompt belongs to the window object.

Line 27 calculates the sum of the variables number1 and number2 using the **addition operator**, +, and assigns the result to variable sum by using the assignment operator, =. Notice that the + operator can perform both addition and string concatenation. In this case, the + operator performs addition, because *both* operands contain integers. After line 27 performs this calculation, line 30 uses document.writeln to display the result of the addition on the web page.

Common Programming Error 6.6

Confusing the + operator used for string concatenation with the + operator used for addition often leads to undesired results. For example, if integer variable y has the value 5, the expression "y + 2 = " + y + 2 results in "y + 2 = 52", not "y + 2 = 7", because first the value of y (i.e., 5) is concatenated with the string "y + 2 = ", then the value 2 is concatenated with the new, larger string "y + 2 = 5". The expression "y + 2 = " + (y + 2) produces the string "y + 2 = 7" because the parentheses ensure that y + 2 is calculated.

Validating JavaScript
As discussed in the Preface, we validated our code using HTML5, CSS3 and JavaScript validation tools. Browsers are generally forgiving and don't typically display error messages to the user. As a programmer, you should thoroughly test your web pages and validate them. Validation tools report two types of messages—*errors* and *warnings*. Typically, you must resolve errors; otherwise, your web pages probably won't render or execute correctly.

Pages with warnings normally render and execute correctly; however, some organizations have strict protocols indicating that all pages must be free of both warnings and errors before they can be posted on a live website.

When you validate this example at www.javascriptlint.com, lines 24–25 produce the warning message:

```
parseInt missing radix parameter
```

Function parseInt has an optional second parameter, known as the *radix*, that specifies the base number system that's used to parse the number (e.g., 8 for octal, 10 for decimal and 16 for hexadecimal). The default is base 10, but you can specify any base from 2 to 32. For example, the following statement indicates that firstNumber should be treated as a decimal (base 10) integer:

```
number1 = parseInt( firstNumber, 10 );
```

This prevents numbers in other formats like octal (base 8) from being converted to incorrect values.

6.5 Memory Concepts

Variable names such as number1, number2 and sum actually correspond to **locations** in the computer's memory. Every variable has a **name**, a **type** and a **value**.

In the addition script in Fig. 6.7, when line 24 executes, the string firstNumber (previously entered by the user in a prompt dialog) is converted to an integer and placed into a memory location to which the name number1 has been assigned by the interpreter. Suppose the user entered the string 45 as the value for firstNumber. The script converts firstNumber to an integer, and the computer places the integer value 45 into location number1, as shown in Fig. 6.8. Whenever a value is placed in a memory location, the value *replaces* the previous value in that location. The previous value is lost.

number1	45

Fig. 6.8 | Memory location showing the name and value of variable number1.

Suppose that the user enters 72 as the second integer. When line 25 executes, the script converts secondNumber to an integer and places that integer value, 72, into location number2; then the memory appears as shown in Fig. 6.9.

number1	45
number2	72

Fig. 6.9 | Memory locations after inputting values for variables number1 and number2.

Once the script has obtained values for number1 and number2, it adds the values and places the sum into variable sum. The statement

```
sum = number1 + number2;
```

performs the addition and also replaces sum's previous value. After sum is calculated, the memory appears as shown in Fig. 6.10. Note that the values of number1 and number2 appear exactly as they did before they were used in the calculation of sum. These values were used, but not destroyed, when the computer performed the calculation—when a value is read from a memory location, the process is *nondestructive*.

number1	45
number2	72
sum	117

Fig. 6.10 | Memory locations after calculating the sum of number1 and number2.

Data Types in JavaScript

Unlike its predecessor languages C, C++ and Java, *JavaScript does not require variables to have a declared type before they can be used in a script*. A variable in JavaScript can contain a value of *any* data type, and in many situations JavaScript automatically converts between values of different types for you. For this reason, JavaScript is referred to as a **loosely typed language**. When a variable is declared in JavaScript, but is not given a value, the variable has an **undefined** value. Attempting to use the value of such a variable is normally a logic error.

When variables are declared, they're not assigned values unless you specify them. Assigning the value null to a variable indicates that it does *not* contain a value.

6.6 Arithmetic

Many scripts perform arithmetic calculations. Figure 6.11 summarizes the **arithmetic operators**. Note the use of various special symbols not used in algebra. The **asterisk** (*) indicates multiplication; the **percent sign** (%) is the **remainder operator**, which will be discussed shortly. The arithmetic operators in Fig. 6.11 are *binary* operators, because each operates on *two* operands. For example, the expression sum + value contains the binary operator + and the two operands sum and value.

JavaScript operation	Arithmetic operator	Algebraic expression	JavaScript expression
Addition	+	$f + 7$	f + 7
Subtraction	–	$p - c$	p – c
Multiplication	*	bm	b * m
Division	/	$x/y \ or \ \frac{x}{y} \ or \ x \div y$	x / y
Remainder	%	$r \bmod s$	r % s

Fig. 6.11 | Arithmetic operators.

Remainder Operator, %

JavaScript provides the remainder operator, %, which yields the remainder after division. The expression x % y yields the remainder after x is divided by y. Thus, 17 % 5 yields 2 (i.e., 17 divided by 5 is 3, with a remainder of 2), and 7.4 % 3.1 yields 1.2. In later chapters, we consider applications of the remainder operator, such as determining whether one number is a *multiple* of another. *There's no arithmetic operator for exponentiation in JavaScript.* (Chapter 8 shows how to perform exponentiation in JavaScript using the Math object's pow method.)

Arithmetic expressions in JavaScript must be written in straight-line form to facilitate entering scripts into the computer. Thus, expressions such as "a divided by b" must be written as a / b, so that all constants, variables and operators appear in a *straight line*. The following algebraic notation is generally *not* acceptable to computers:

$$\frac{a}{b}$$

Parentheses are used to *group* expressions in the same manner as in algebraic expressions. For example, to multiply a times the quantity b + c we write:

```
a * ( b + c )
```

Operator Precedence

JavaScript applies the operators in arithmetic expressions in a precise sequence determined by the following **rules of operator precedence**, which are generally the same as those followed in algebra:

1. Multiplication, division and remainder operations are applied *first*. If an expression contains several multiplication, division and remainder operations, operators are applied from *left to right*. Multiplication, division and remainder operations are said to have the *same level of precedence*.

2. Addition and subtraction operations are applied next. If an expression contains several addition and subtraction operations, operators are applied from *left to right*. Addition and subtraction operations have the *same level of precedence*.

The rules of operator precedence enable JavaScript to apply operators in the correct order. When we say that operators are applied from *left to right*, we're referring to the **associativity** of the operators—the *order* in which operators of equal priority are evaluated. We'll see that some operators associate from *right to left*. Figure 6.12 summarizes the rules of operator precedence. The table in Fig. 6.12 will be expanded as additional JavaScript operators are introduced. A complete precedence chart is included in Appendix C.

Operator(s)	Operation(s)	Order of evaluation (precedence)
*, / or %	Multiplication Division Remainder	Evaluated first. If there are several such operations, they're evaluated from left to right.
+ or -	Addition Subtraction	Evaluated last. If there are several such operations, they're evaluated from left to right.

Fig. 6.12 | Precedence of arithmetic operators.

Let's consider several algebraic expressions. Each example lists an algebraic expression and the equivalent JavaScript expression.

The following is an example of an arithmetic mean (average) of five terms:

Algebra: $m = \dfrac{a + b + c + d + e}{5}$

JavaScript: m = (a + b + c + d + e) / 5;

Parentheses are required to group the addition operators, because division has higher precedence than addition. The *entire quantity* (a + b + c + d + e) is to be divided by 5. If the parentheses are erroneously omitted, we obtain a + b + c + d + e / 5, which evaluates as

$$a + b + c + d + \dfrac{e}{5}$$

and would not lead to the correct answer.

The following is an example of the equation of a straight line:

Algebra: $y = mx + b$

JavaScript: y = m * x + b;

No parentheses are required. The multiplication operator is applied first, because multiplication has a higher precedence than addition. The assignment occurs last, because it has a lower precedence than multiplication and addition.

As in algebra, it's acceptable to use *unnecessary parentheses* in an expression to make the expression clearer. These are also called **redundant parentheses**. For example, the preceding second-degree polynomial might be parenthesized as follows:

y = (a * x * x) + (b * x) + c;

6.7 Decision Making: Equality and Relational Operators

This section introduces a version of JavaScript's **if statement** that allows a script to make a decision based on the truth or falsity of a **condition**. If the condition is met (i.e., the condition is *true*), the statement in the body of the if statement is executed. If the condition is *not* met (i.e., the condition is *false*), the statement in the body of the if statement is *not* executed. We'll see an example shortly.

Conditions in if statements can be formed by using the **equality operators** and **relational operators** summarized in Fig. 6.13. The relational operators all have the *same* level of precedence and associate from left to right. The equality operators both have the same level of precedence, which is lower than the precedence of the relational operators. The equality operators also associate from left to right. Each comparison results in a value of true or false.

Common Programming Error 6.7

Confusing the equality operator, ==, with the assignment operator, =, is a logic error. The equality operator should be read as "is equal to," and the assignment operator should be read as "gets" or "gets the value of." Some people prefer to read the equality operator as "double equals" or "equals equals."

Standard algebraic equality operator or relational operator	JavaScript equality or relational operator	Sample JavaScript condition	Meaning of JavaScript condition
Equality operators			
=	==	x == y	x is equal to y
≠	!=	x != y	x is not equal to y
Relational operators			
>	>	x > y	x is greater than y
<	<	x < y	x is less than y
≥	>=	x >= y	x is greater than or equal to y
≤	<=	x <= y	x is less than or equal to y

Fig. 6.13 | Equality and relational operators.

The script in Fig. 6.14 uses four if statements to display a time-sensitive greeting on a welcome page. The script obtains the local time from the user's computer and converts it from 24-hour clock format (0–23) to a 12-hour clock format (0–11). Using this value, the script displays an appropriate greeting for the current time of day. The script and sample output are shown in Fig. 6.14. Lines 11–13 declare the variables used in the script. Also note that JavaScript allows you to assign a value to a variable when it's declared.

Creating and Using a New **Date** Object

Line 12 sets the variable now to a new **Date object**, which contains information about the current local time. In Section 6.2, we introduced the document object, which encapsulates data pertaining to the current web page. Here, we use JavaScript's built-in Date object to acquire the current local time. We create a new object by using the **new** operator followed by the type of the object, in this case Date, and a pair of parentheses. Some objects require that arguments be placed in the parentheses to specify details about the object to be created. In

```
1   <!DOCTYPE html>
2
3   <!-- Fig. 6.14: welcome5.html -->
4   <!-- Using equality and relational operators. -->
5   <html>
6      <head>
7         <meta charset = "utf-8">
8         <title>Using Relational Operators</title>
9         <script type = "text/javascript">
10            <!--
11            var name; // string entered by the user
12            var now = new Date();      // current date and time
13            var hour = now.getHours(); // current hour (0-23)
14
15            // read the name from the prompt box as a string
16            name = window.prompt( "Please enter your name" );
```

Fig. 6.14 | Using equality and relational operators. (Part 1 of 2.)

```
17
18          // determine whether it's morning
19          if ( hour < 12 )
20              document.write( "<h1>Good Morning, " );
21
22          // determine whether the time is PM
23          if ( hour >= 12 )
24          {
25              // convert to a 12-hour clock
26              hour = hour - 12;
27
28              // determine whether it is before 6 PM
29              if ( hour < 6 )
30                  document.write( "<h1>Good Afternoon, " );
31
32              // determine whether it is after 6 PM
33              if ( hour >= 6 )
34                  document.write( "<h1>Good Evening, " );
35          } // end if
36
37          document.writeln( name +
38              ", welcome to JavaScript programming!</h1>" );
39          // -->
40      </script>
41  </head><body></body>
42  </html>
```

Fig. 6.14 | Using equality and relational operators. (Part 2 of 2.)

this case, we leave the parentheses empty to create a *default* Date object containing information about the current date and time. After line 12 executes, the variable now refers to the new Date object. We did not need to use the new operator when we used the document and window objects because these objects always are created by the browser. Line 13 sets the variable hour to an integer equal to the current hour (in a 24-hour clock format) returned by the Date object's getHours method. Chapter 11 presents a more detailed discussion of the Date object's attributes and methods, and of objects in general. The script uses window.prompt to allow the user to enter a name to display as part of the greeting (line 16).

Decision-Making with the if Statement
To display the correct time-sensitive greeting, the script must determine whether the user is visiting the page during the morning, afternoon or evening. The first if statement (lines

19–20) compares the value of variable hour with 12. If hour is less than 12, then the user is visiting the page during the morning, and the statement at line 20 outputs the string "Good morning". If this condition is not met, line 20 is not executed. Line 23 determines whether hour is greater than or equal to 12. If hour is greater than or equal to 12, then the user is visiting the page in either the afternoon or the evening. Lines 24–35 execute to determine the appropriate greeting. If hour is less than 12, then the JavaScript interpreter does not execute these lines and continues to line 37.

Blocks and Decision-Making with Nested **if** Statements

The brace { in line 24 begins a **block** of statements (lines 24–35) that are executed together if hour is greater than or equal to 12. Line 26 subtracts 12 from hour, converting the current hour from a 24-hour clock format (0–23) to a 12-hour clock format (0–11). The if statement (line 29) determines whether hour is now less than 6. If it is, then the time is between noon and 6 PM, and line 30 outputs the beginning of an HTML5 h1 element ("<h1>Good Afternoon, "). If hour is greater than or equal to 6, the time is between 6 PM and midnight, and the script outputs the greeting "Good Evening" (lines 33–34). The brace } in line 35 ends the block of statements associated with the if statement in line 23. Note that if statements can be **nested**—one if statement can be placed *inside* another. The if statements that determine whether the user is visiting the page in the afternoon or the evening (lines 29–30 and lines 33–34) execute only if the script has already established that hour is greater than or equal to 12 (line 23). If the script has already determined the current time of day to be morning, these additional comparisons are not performed. Chapter 7 discusses blocks and nested if statements. Finally, lines 37–38 output the rest of the HTML5 h1 element (the remaining part of the greeting), which does not depend on the time of day.

Good Programming Practice 6.6

Include comments after the closing curly brace of control statements (such as if statements) to indicate where the statements end, as in line 35 of Fig. 6.14.

Note the *indentation* of the if statements throughout the script. Such indentation enhances script readability.

Good Programming Practice 6.7

Indent the statement in the body of an if statement to make the body of the statement stand out and to enhance script readability.

The Empty Statement

Note that there's *no* semicolon (;) at the end of the first line of each if statement. Including such a semicolon would result in a *logic error* at execution time. For example,

```
if ( hour < 12 ) ;
    document.write( "<h1>Good Morning, " );
```

would actually be interpreted by JavaScript erroneously as

```
if ( hour < 12 )
    ;
document.write( "<h1>Good Morning, " );
```

where the semicolon on the line by itself—called the **empty statement**—is the statement to execute if the condition in the `if` statement is true. When the empty statement executes, no task is performed in the script. The script then continues with the next statement, which executes regardless of whether the condition is true or false. In this example, `"<h1>Good Morning, "` would be printed *regardless* of the time of day.

Error-Prevention Tip 6.2

A lengthy statement may be spread over several lines. If a single statement must be split across lines, choose breaking points that make sense, such as after a comma in a comma-separated list or after an operator in a lengthy expression. If a statement is split across two or more lines, indent all subsequent lines.

Validating This Example's Script

When you validate this example with `www.javascriptlint.com`, the following warning message is displayed for the `if` statements in lines 19, 29 and 33:

```
block statement without curly braces
```

You saw that an `if` statement's body may contain multiple statements in a block that's delimited by curly braces (lines 23–35). The curly braces are not required for an `if` statement that has a one-statement body, such as the ones in lines 19, 29 and 33. Many programmers consider it a good practice to enclose *every* `if` statement's body in curly braces—in fact, many organizations require this. For this reason, the validator issues the preceding warning message. You can eliminate this example's warning messages by enclosing the `if` statement bodies in curly braces. For example, the `if` at lines 19–20 can be written as:

```
if ( hour < 12 )
{
    document.write( "<h1>Good Morning, " );
}
```

The Strict Equals (===) and Strict Does Not Equal (!==) Operators

As we mentioned in Section 6.5, JavaScript can convert between types for you. This includes cases in which you're comparing values. For example, the comparison `"75" == 75` yields the value `true` because JavaScript converts the string `"75"` to the number 75 before performing the equality (`==`) comparison. To prevent implicit conversions in comparisons, which can lead to unexpected results, JavaScript provides the **strict equals (===)** and **strict does not equal (!==)** operators. The comparison `"75" === 75` yields the value `false` because one operand is a string and the other is a number. Similarly, `75" !== 75` yields `true` because the operand's types are not equal, therefore the values are not equal. If you do not use these operators when comparing values to `null`, `0`, `true`, `false` or the empty string (`""`), `javascriptlint.com`'s JavaScript validator displays warnings of potential implicit conversions.

Operator Precedence Chart

The chart in Fig. 6.15 shows the precedence of the operators introduced in this chapter. The operators are shown from top to bottom in decreasing order of precedence. Note that all of these operators, with the exception of the assignment operator, =, associate from left to right. Addition is left associative, so an expression like x + y + z is evaluated as if it had been written as (x + y) + z. The assignment operator, =, associates from right to left, so an expression like x = y = 0 is evaluated as if it had been written as x = (y = 0), which first assigns the value 0 to variable y, then assigns the result of that assignment, 0, to x.

> **Good Programming Practice 6.8**
> *Refer to the operator precedence chart when writing expressions containing many opera-*
> *tors. Confirm that the operations are performed in the order in which you expect them to*
> *be performed. If you're uncertain about the order of evaluation, use parentheses to force*
> *the order, exactly as you would do in algebraic expressions. Be sure to observe that some*
> *operators, such as assignment (=), associate from right to left rather than from left to right.*

Operators	Associativity	Type
* / %	left to right	multiplicative
+ -	left to right	additive
< <= > >=	left to right	relational
== != === !===	left to right	equality
=	right to left	assignment

Fig. 6.15 | Precedence and associativity of the operators discussed so far.

6.8 Web Resources

www.deitel.com/javascript

The Deitel JavaScript Resource Center contains links to some of the best JavaScript resources on the web. There you'll find categorized links to JavaScript tools, code generators, forums, books, libraries, frameworks and more. Also check out the tutorials for all skill levels, from introductory to advanced.

Summary

Section 6.1 Introduction
- JavaScript (p. 218) is used to enhance the functionality and appearance of web pages.

Section 6.2 Your First Script: Displaying a Line of Text with JavaScript in a Web Page
- Often, JavaScripts appear in the <head> section of the HTML5 document.
- The browser interprets the contents of the <head> section first.
- The <script> tag indicates to the browser that the text that follows is part of a script (p. 218). Attribute type (p. 219) specifies the MIME type of the scripting language used in the script— such as text/javascript.
- A string of characters (p. 219) can be contained between double (") quotation marks (p. 219).
- A string (p. 219) is sometimes called a character string, a message or a string literal.
- The browser's document object (p. 220) represents the HTML5 document the browser is currently displaying. The document object allows a you to specify HTML5 text to display in the document.
- The browser creates a complete set of objects that allow you to access and manipulate every element of an HTML5 document.

- An object (p. 220) resides in the computer's memory and contains information used by the script. The term object normally implies that attributes (data) (p. 220) and behaviors (methods) (p. 220) are associated with the object. The object's methods use the attributes' data to perform useful actions for the client of the object (i.e., the script that calls the methods).

- The document object's `writeln` method (p. 220) writes a line of HTML5 text in a document.

- Every statement ends with a semicolon (also known as the statement terminator; p. 220), although this practice is not required by JavaScript.

- JavaScript is case sensitive. Not using the proper uppercase and lowercase letters is a syntax error.

Section 6.3 Modifying Your First Script
- Sometimes it's useful to display information in windows called dialogs (or dialog boxes; p. 223) that "pop up" on the screen to grab the user's attention. Dialogs typically display important messages to the user browsing the web page.

- The browser's `window` object (p. 223) uses method `alert` (p. 223) to display an alert dialog.

- The escape sequence \n is the newline character (p. 224). It causes the cursor in the HTML5 document to move to the beginning of the next line.

Section 7.4 Obtaining User Input with *prompt* Dialogs
- Keywords (p. 225) are words with special meaning in JavaScript.

- The keyword `var` (p. 225) at the beginning of the statement indicates that the word name is a variable. A variable (p. 225) is a location in the computer's memory where a value can be stored for use by a script. All variables have a name and value, and should be declared with a var statement before they're used in a script.

- The name of a variable can be any valid identifier consisting of letters, digits, underscores (_) and dollar signs ($) that does not begin with a digit and is not a reserved JavaScript keyword.

- Declarations end with a semicolon and can be split over several lines with each variable in the declaration separated by a comma—known as a comma-separated list of variable names. Several variables may be declared in one declaration or in multiple declarations.

- It's helpful to indicate the purpose of a variable in the script by placing a JavaScript comment at the end of the variable's declaration. A single-line comment (p. 226) begins with the characters // and terminates at the end of the line. Comments do not cause the browser to perform any action when the script is interpreted; rather, comments are ignored by the JavaScript interpreter.

- Multiline comments begin with the delimiter /* and end with the delimiter */. All text between the delimiters of the comment is ignored by the interpreter.

- The `window` object's `prompt` method displays a dialog into which the user can type a value. The first argument is a message (called a prompt) that directs the user to take a specific action. An optional second argument, separated from the first by a comma, may specify the default string to be displayed in the text field.

- A variable is assigned a value with an assignment (p. 228), using the assignment operator, =. The = operator is called a binary operator (p. 228), because it has two operands (p. 228).

- JavaScript has a version of the + operator for string concatenation (p. 228) that enables a string and a value of another data type (including another string) to be concatenated.

Section 6.5 Memory Concepts
- Every variable has a name, a type and a value.

- When a value is placed in a memory location, the value replaces the previous value in that location. When a value is read out of a memory location, the process is nondestructive.

- JavaScript does not require variables to have a declared type before they can be used in a script. A variable in JavaScript can contain a value of any data type, and in many situations, JavaScript automatically converts between values of different types for you. For this reason, JavaScript is referred to as a loosely typed language (p. 232).

- When a variable is declared in JavaScript, but is not given a value, it has an undefined value (p. 232). Attempting to use the value of such a variable is normally a logic error.

- When variables are declared, they're not assigned default values, unless you specify them. To indicate that a variable does not contain a value, you can assign the value null to it.

Section 6.6 Arithmetic
- The basic arithmetic operators (+, -, *, /, and %; p. 232) are binary operators, because each operates on two operands.

- Parentheses can be used to group expressions in the same manner as in algebraic expressions.

- JavaScript applies the operators in arithmetic expressions in a precise sequence determined by the following rules of operator precedence (p. 233).

- When we say that operators are applied from left to right, we're referring to the associativity of the operators (p. 233). Some operators associate from right to left.

Section 6.7 Decision Making: Equality and Relational Operators
- JavaScript's if statement (p. 234) allows a script to make a decision based on the truth or falsity of a condition. If the condition is met (i.e., the condition is true; p. 234), the statement in the body of the if statement is executed. If the condition is not met (i.e., the condition is false), the statement in the body of the if statement is not executed.

- Conditions in if statements can be formed by using the equality operators (p. 234) and relational operators (p. 234).

Self-Review Exercises

6.1   Fill in the blanks in each of the following statements:
  a) _____ begins a single-quote character in a string.
  b) Every JavaScript comment should start with a(n) _____.
  c) Multiline comments begin with delimiter _____.
  d) The _____ document uses writeln method.
  e) The name of a variable can be any valid _____.
  f) In JavaScript the operator for remainder, not equal to and equal to are _____, _____ and _____ respectively.

6.2   State whether each of the following is *true* or *false*. If *false*, explain why.
  a) Comments cause the computer to print the text after the // on the screen when the script is executed.
  b) JavaScript considers the variables number and NuMbEr to be identical.
  c) The remainder operator (%) can be used only with numeric operands.
  d) The arithmetic operators *, /, %, + and - all have the same level of precedence.
  e) Method parseInt converts an integer to a string.

6.3   Write JavaScript statements to accomplish each of the following tasks:
  a) Declare variables a, itIsAVariable, p79356 and number3.
  b) Display a dialog asking the user to enter a number. Show a default value of 5 in the text field.
  c) Convert a string to an integer, and store the converted value in variable newValue. Assume that the string is stored in oldValue.

d) If the variable number is greater than 17, display "The variable number is greater than 17" in a message dialog.

e) Output a line of HTML5 text using a `document.write` statement that will display the message "This is a JavaScript program" in the HTML5 document.

6.4 Identify and correct the errors in each of the following statements:

a) `if ( c !< 17 );`
   `window.alert( "c is not less than 17" );`

b) `if ( c =< 17 )`
   `window.alert( "c is equal to or less than 17" );`

6.5 Write a statement (or comment) to accomplish each of the following tasks:

a) Give a comment that a script will calculate the sum of three integers. [Hint: Use text that helps to document a script.]

b) Declare the variables i, j, k and sum.

c) Declare the variables iVal, jVal and kVal.

d) Prompt the user to enter the first integer value, read the value from the user and store it in the variable iVal, with default value 0.

e) Prompt the user to enter the second value, read the value from the user and store it in the variable jVal, with default value 5.

f) Prompt the user to enter the third value, read the value from the user and store it in the variable kVal, with default value 10.

g) Convert iVal to an integer, and store the result in the variable i.

h) Convert jVal to an integer, and store the result in the variable j.

i) Convert kVal to an integer, and store the result in the variable k.

j) Compute the sum of the three integers contained in variables i, j and k, and assign the sum to the variable result.

k) Write a line of HTML5 text containing the string "The sum is" followed by the value of the variable sum.

6.6 Using the statements you wrote in Exercise 6.5, write a complete script that calculates and prints the sum of three integers.

Answers to Self-Review Exercises

6.1 a) \'. b) <!--. c) /*. d) object. e) identifier. f) %, !=, ==.

6.2 a) False. Comments do not cause any action to be performed when the script is executed. They're used to document scripts and improve their readability. b) False. JavaScript is case sensitive, so these variables are distinct. c) True. d) False. The operators *, / and % are on the same level of precedence, and the operators + and - are on a lower level of precedence. e) False. Function parseInt converts a string to an integer value.

6.3
a) `var a, itIsAVariable, p79356, number3;`
b) `value = window.prompt( "Enter a number", "5" );`
c) `var newValue = parseInt( oldValue );`
d) `if ( number > 17 )`
e) `document.write( "This is a JavaScript program" );`

6.4 a) Error: There should not be an exclamation sign in the condition of the if statement.
   Correction: Remove the exclamation sign in the condition of the if statement.

[*Note:* This is a syntax error. There is no logical operator of "not less than". We only have the logical operator of "not equal to", i.e. !=.]

b) Error: The relational operator =< is incorrect.
   Correction: Change =< to <=.

6.5   a) `// Calculate the sum of three integers`
        b) `var i, j, k, sum;`
        c) `var iVal, jVal, kVal;`
        d) `iVal = window.prompt( "Enter first integer:", "0" );`
        e) `jVal = window.prompt( "Enter second integer:", "5" );`
        f) `kVal = window.prompt( "Enter third integer:", "10" );`
        g) `i = parseInt( iVal );`
        h) `j = parseInt( jVal );`
        i) `k = parseInt( kVal );`
        j) `sum = i * j * k;`
        k) `document.writeln( "<h1>The sum is " + sum + "</h1>" );`

6.6   The script is as follows:

```
1   <!DOCTYPE html>
2
3   <!-- Exercise 7.6: sum.html -->
4   <html>
5      <head>
6         <meta charset = "utf-8">
7         <title> Sum of Three Integers</title>
8         <script type = "text/javascript">
9            <!--
10           // Calculate the sum of three integers
11           var i, j, k, sum;
12           var iVal, jVal, kVal;
13
14           iVal = window.prompt( "Enter first integer:", "0" );
15           jVal = window.prompt( "Enter second integer:", "5" );
16           kVal = window.prompt( "Enter third integer:", "10" );
17
18           i = parseInt( iVal );
19           j = parseInt( jVal );
20           k = parseInt( kVal );
21
22           sum = i + j + k;
23           document.writeln( "<h1>The sum is " + sum + "<h1>" );
24           // -->
25        </script>
26     </head><body></body>
27  </html>
```

Exercises

6.7   Fill in the blanks in each of the following statements:
a) _____ are words with special meaning in JavaScript.
b) Conditions in if statements can be formed by using the _____ operators and _____ operators.
c) When a value is read out of a memory location, the process is _____.
d) Function _____ converts its string argument to an integer.
e) Every variable has a _____, a _____ and a value.

6.8   Write JavaScript statements that accomplish each of the following tasks:
a) Display the message **"Enter three numbers"** using the document object.
b) Assign the sum of variables x and y to variable z.
c) State that a program performs a simple result calculation.

6.9   State whether each of the following is *true* or *false*. If *false*, explain why.
a) JavaScript is case insensitive.
b) The following are all valid variable names: a_under_bal_, k998034_m, t85, jk897, his_sales$9, her_$account_total_bal, x, y$, z, ij, z_0.
c) The keyword variable at the beginning of the statement indicates that the word name is a variable.
d) The following are all invalid variable names: 5u, 96, 75k7, p45, 8c.

6.10   Fill in the blanks in each of the following statements:
a) If an expression contains several multiplication, division and remainder operations, operators are applied from _____.
b) The window object's _____ method displays a dialog into which the user can type a value.
c) The browser interprets the contents of the _____ section first.

6.11   What displays in the message dialog when each of the given JavaScript statements is performed? Assume that x = 5 and y = 7.
a) `window.alert( "x = " + x + "Y = " + y );`
b) `window.alert( "The value of Y + Y is " + ( y + y ) + ", double of Y" );`
c) `window.alert( "x =" + "5" );`
d) `window.alert( ( y - x ) + " = " + ( y - x ) );`

6.12   Which of the following JavaScript statements contain variables whose values are changed?
a) `a = a + b + c + 17;`
b) `window.alert( "x = " + x );`
c) `document.write( "a = 5" );`
d) `stringText = window.prompt( "Enter a text:" );`

6.13   Given $y = ax^2 + 9x$, which of the following are correct JavaScript statements for this equation?
a) `y = a * x * x  + 9 * x;`
b) `y = a * x * x * (x + 9);`
c) `y = (a * x) * x * (x + 9);`
d) `y = (a * x) * x + x * 9;`

e) y = a * (x * x) + 9 * x;
f) y = a * x * (x * x + 9 * x);

6.14   State the order of evaluation of the operators in each of the following JavaScript statements, and show the value of x after each statement is performed.

a) x = 8 + 2 * 3 / 2 - 3;
b) x = 3 % 3 + 3 * 3 - 3 / 3;
c) x = (2 * 4 * (2 + (4 * 2 / (2))));

6.15   Write a script that displays the letters A to D on the same line, with each pair of adjacent letters separated by two spaces. Write the script using the following methods:

a)   Using one document.write statement.
b)   Using two document.write statements.

6.16   Write a script that asks the user to enter two numbers, obtains the two numbers from the user and outputs text that displays the sum, product, difference and quotient of the two numbers. Use the techniques shown in Fig. 6.7.

6.17   Write a script that asks the user to enter two integers, obtains the numbers from the user and outputs text that displays the smaller number followed by the words "is smaller" in an alert dialog. If the numbers are equal, output HTML5 text that displays the message "These numbers are equal." Use the techniques shown in Fig. 6.14.

6.18   Write a script that takes four integers from the user and displays the sum, average, product, smallest and largest of the numbers in an alert dialog.

6.19   Write a script that gets from the user the radius of a circle and outputs HTML5 text that displays the circle's diameter, circumference and area. Use the constant value 3.14159 for π. Use the GUI techniques shown in Fig. 6.7. [*Note:* You may also use the predefined constant Math.PI for the value of π. This constant is more precise than the value 3.14159. The Math object is defined by Java-Script and provides many common mathematical capabilities.] Use the following formulas (*r* is the radius): *diameter = 2r, circumference = 2\pi r, area = \pi r^2*.

6.20   Write a script that reads four integers and determines and outputs HTML5 text that displays the multiplication of the largest and smallest integers in the group. Use only the scripting techniques you learned in this chapter.

6.21   Write a script that reads an integer and determines and outputs HTML5 text that displays whether it can be divided by 5 or 7. [*Hint:* Use the remainder operator.]

6.22   Write a script that reads in two integers and determines and outputs HTML5 text that displays whether the first is a square of the second. [*Hint:* Use the division operator.]

6.23   Write a script that inputs three numbers and determines and outputs HTML5 text that displays the count of how many numbers are greater than 10, how many numbers are less than 10, and how many numbers are equal to of 10.

6.24   Write a script that calculates the squares and cubes of the numbers from 6 to 11 and outputs HTML5 text that displays the resulting values in an HTML5 table format, as show below in Fig.6.16. [*Note:* This script does not require any input from the user.]

Number	square	cube
6	36	216
7	49	343
8	64	512
9	81	729
10	100	1000
11	121	1331

7

JavaScript: Control Statements I

Objectives

In this chapter you will:

- Learn basic problem-solving techniques.

- Develop algorithms through the process of top-down, stepwise refinement.

- Use the `if` and `if...else` selection statements to choose among alternative actions.

- Use the `while` repetition statement to execute statements in a script repeatedly.

- Implement counter-controlled repetition and sentinel-controlled repetition.

- Use the increment, decrement and assignment operators.

7.1 Introduction

Before writing a script to solve a problem, we must have a thorough understanding of the problem and a carefully planned approach to solving it. When writing a script, it's equally essential to understand the types of building blocks that are available and to employ proven program-construction principles. In this chapter and Chapter 8, we discuss these issues as we present the theory and principles of *structured programming*.

7.2 Algorithms

Any computable problem can be solved by executing a series of actions in a specific order. A **procedure** for solving a problem in terms of

1. the **actions** to be executed, and

2. the **order** in which the actions are to be executed

is called an **algorithm**. Correctly specifying the order in which the actions are to execute is important—this is called **program control**. In this chapter and Chapter 8, we investigate the program-control capabilities of JavaScript.

7.3 Pseudocode

Pseudocode is an informal language that helps you develop algorithms. The pseudocode we present here is useful for developing algorithms that will be converted to structured portions of JavaScript programs. Pseudocode is similar to everyday English; it's convenient and user friendly, although it's not an actual computer programming language.

> **Software Engineering Observation 7.1**
>
> *Pseudocode is often used to "think out" a script during the script-design process. Carefully prepared pseudocode can easily be converted to JavaScript.*

7.4 Control Statements

Normally, statements in a script execute one after the other in the order in which they're written. This process is called **sequential execution**. Various JavaScript statements we'll soon discuss enable you to specify that the next statement to execute may not necessarily be the next one in sequence. This is known as **transfer of control**.

During the 1960s, it became clear that the indiscriminate use of transfers of control was the root of much difficulty experienced by software development groups. The finger of blame was pointed at the **goto statement**, which allowed the programmer to specify a transfer of control to one of a wide range of possible destinations in a program. Research demonstrated that programs could be written without goto statements. The notion of so-called **structured programming** became almost synonymous with "goto elimination." JavaScript does not have a goto statement. Structured programs are clearer, easier to debug and modify and more likely to be bug free in the first place.

Research determined that all programs could be written in terms of only three **control structures**, namely the **sequence structure**, the **selection structure** and the **repetition structure**. The sequence structure is built into JavaScript—unless directed otherwise, the computer executes JavaScript statements one after the other in the order in which they're written (i.e., in sequence). The flowchart segment of Fig. 7.1 illustrates a typical sequence structure in which two calculations are performed in order.

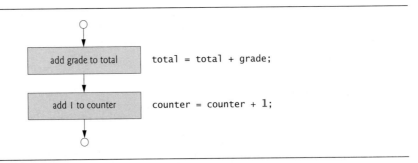

Fig. 7.1 | Flowcharting JavaScript's sequence structure.

A **flowchart** is a graphical representation of an algorithm or of a portion of an algorithm. Flowcharts are drawn using certain special-purpose symbols, such as rectangles, diamonds, ovals and small circles; these symbols are connected by arrows called **flowlines**, which indicate the order in which the actions of the algorithm execute.

Like pseudocode, flowcharts often are useful for developing and representing algorithms, although many programmers prefer pseudocode. Flowcharts show clearly how control structures operate; that's all we use them for in this text.

Consider the flowchart segment for the sequence structure in Fig. 7.1. For simplicity, we use the **rectangle symbol** (or **action symbol**) to indicate *any* type of action, including a *calculation* or an *input/output* operation. The flowlines in the figure indicate the *order* in which the actions are performed—the first action adds grade to total, then the second action adds 1 to counter. JavaScript allows us to have as many actions as we want in a sequence structure. Anywhere a single action may be placed, as we'll soon see, we may place several actions in sequence.

In a flowchart that represents a *complete* algorithm, **oval symbols** containing the words "Begin" and "End" represent the start and end of the algorithm, respectively. In a flowchart that shows only a portion of an algorithm, as in Fig. 7.1, the oval symbols are omitted in favor of using **small circle symbols**, also called **connector symbols**.

Perhaps the most important flowcharting symbol is the **diamond symbol**, also called the **decision symbol**, which indicates that a decision is to be made. We discuss the diamond symbol in the next section.

JavaScript provides three types of selection structures; we discuss each in this chapter and in Chapter 8. The `if` selection statement performs (selects) an action if a condition is *true* or skips the action if the condition is *false*. The `if...else` selection statement performs an action if a condition is *true* and performs a *different* action if the condition is *false*. The `switch` selection statement (Chapter 8) performs one of many different actions, depending on the value of an expression.

The `if` statement is called a **single-selection statement** because it *selects* or *ignores* a single action (or, as we'll soon see, a single group of actions). The `if...else` statement is a **double-selection statement** because it *selects* between two *different* actions (or *groups* of actions). The `switch` statement is a **multiple-selection statement** because it selects among many different actions (or *groups* of actions).

JavaScript provides four repetition statements—`while`, `do...while`, `for` and `for...in`. (`do...while` and `for` are covered in Chapter 8; `for...in` is covered in Chapter 10.) Each of the words `if`, `else`, `switch`, `while`, `do`, `for` and `in` is a JavaScript **keyword**. These words are reserved by the language to implement various features, such as JavaScript's control structures. In addition to keywords, JavaScript has other words that are reserved for use by the language, such as the values `null`, `true` and `false`, and words that are reserved for possible future use. A complete list of JavaScript reserved words is shown in Fig. 7.2.

Common Programming Error 7.1

Using a keyword as an identifier (e.g., for variable names) is a syntax error.

JavaScript reserved keywords				
break	case	catch	continue	default
delete	do	else	false	finally
for	function	if	in	instanceof
new	null	return	switch	this
throw	true	try	typeof	var
void	while	with		
Keywords that are reserved but not used by JavaScript				
class	const	enum	export	extends
implements	import	interface	let	package
private	protected	public	static	super
yield				

Fig. 7.2 | JavaScript reserved keywords.

As we've shown, JavaScript has only eight control statements: sequence, three types of selection and four types of repetition. A script is formed by combining control statements as necessary to implement the script's algorithm. Each control statement is flowcharted with two small circle symbols, one at the *entry point* to the control statement and one at the *exit point*.

Single-entry/single-exit control statements make it easy to build scripts; the control statements are attached to one another by connecting the exit point of one to the entry point of the next. This process is similar to the way in which a child stacks building blocks, so we call it **control-statement stacking**. We'll learn that there's only one other way in which control statements may be connected—**control-statement nesting**. Thus, algorithms in JavaScript are constructed from only eight different types of control statements combined in only two ways.

7.5 `if` Selection Statement

A selection statement is used to choose among alternative courses of action in a script. For example, suppose that the passing grade on an examination is 60 (out of 100). Then the pseudocode statement

> *If student's grade is greater than or equal to 60*
>   *Print "Passed"*

determines whether the condition "student's grade is greater than or equal to 60" is true or false. If the condition is *true*, then "Passed" is printed, and the next pseudocode statement in order is "performed" (remember that pseudocode is *not* a *real* programming language). If the condition is *false*, the print statement is *ignored*, and the next pseudocode statement in order is performed.

Note that the second line of this selection statement is *indented*. Such indentation is optional but is highly recommended, because it emphasizes the inherent structure of structured programs. The JavaScript interpreter ignores *white-space characters*—blanks, tabs and newlines used for indentation and vertical spacing.

Good Programming Practice 7.1

Consistently applying reasonable indentation conventions improves script readability. We use three spaces per indent.

The preceding pseudocode *If* statement can be written in JavaScript as

```
if ( studentGrade >= 60 )
   document.writeln( "<p>Passed</p>" );
```

The JavaScript code corresponds closely to the pseudocode. This similarity is the reason that pseudocode is a useful script-development tool. The statement in the body of the `if` statement outputs the character string `"Passed"` in the HTML5 document.

The flowchart in Fig. 7.3 illustrates the single-selection `if` statement. This flowchart contains what is perhaps the most important flowcharting symbol—the *diamond symbol* (or *decision symbol*), which indicates that a *decision* is to be made. The decision symbol contains an expression, such as a condition, that can be either **true** or **false**. The decision symbol has two flowlines emerging from it. One indicates the path to follow in the script when the expression in the symbol is *true*; the other indicates the path to follow in the script when the expression is *false*. A decision can be made on any expression that evaluates to a value of JavaScript's boolean type (i.e., any expression that evaluates to `true` or `false`—also known as a **boolean expression**).

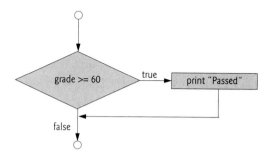

Fig. 7.3 | Flowcharting the single-selection if statement.

Software Engineering Observation 7.2

In JavaScript, any nonzero numeric value in a condition evaluates to true, *and 0 evaluates to* false. *For strings, any string containing one or more characters evaluates to* true, *and the empty string (the string containing no characters, represented as* ""*) evaluates to* false. *Also, a variable that's been declared with* var *but has not been assigned a value evaluates to* false.

Note that the if statement is a single-entry/single-exit control statement. We'll soon learn that the flowcharts for the remaining control statements also contain (besides small circle symbols and flowlines) only rectangle symbols, to indicate the *actions* to be performed, and diamond symbols, to indicate *decisions* to be made. This type of flowchart emphasizes the **action/decision model of programming**. We'll discuss the variety of ways in which actions and decisions may be written.

7.6 if...else Selection Statement

The if selection statement performs an indicated action only when the condition evaluates to true; otherwise, the action is skipped. The **if...else selection** statement allows you to specify that *a different* action is to be performed when the condition is true than when the condition is false. For example, the pseudocode statement

> *If student's grade is greater than or equal to 60*
> *Print "Passed"*
> *Else*
> *Print "Failed"*

prints Passed if the student's grade is greater than or equal to 60 and prints Failed if the student's grade is less than 60. In either case, after printing occurs, the next pseudocode statement in sequence (i.e., the next statement after the whole if...else statement) is performed. Note that the body of the *Else* part of the statement is also indented.

Good Programming Practice 7.2

Indent both body statements of an if...else *statement.*

The preceding pseudocode *If…Else* statement may be written in JavaScript as

```
if ( studentGrade >= 60 )
   document.writeln( "<p>Passed</p>" );
else
   document.writeln( "<p>Failed</p>" );
```

The flowchart in Fig. 7.4 illustrates the `if...else` selection statement's flow of control. Once again, note that the only symbols in the flowchart besides small circles and arrows are rectangles for actions and a diamond for a decision.

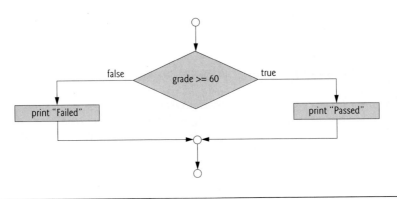

Fig. 7.4 | Flowcharting the double-selection `if...else` statement.

Conditional Operator (?:)

JavaScript provides an operator, called the **conditional operator (?:)**, that's closely related to the `if...else` statement. The operator `?:` is JavaScript's only **ternary operator**—it takes *three* operands. The operands together with the `?:` form a **conditional expression**. The first operand is a boolean expression, the second is the value for the conditional expression if the expression evaluates to `true` and the third is the value for the conditional expression if the expression evaluates to `false`. For example, the following statement

```
document.writeln( studentGrade >= 60 ? "Passed" : "Failed" );
```

contains a conditional expression that evaluates to the string `"Passed"` if the condition `studentGrade >= 60` is true and evaluates to the string `"Failed"` if the condition is false. Thus, this statement with the conditional operator performs essentially the same operation as the preceding `if...else` statement.

Nested `if...else` Statements

Nested `if...else` statements test for multiple cases by placing `if...else` statements *inside* `if...else` statements. For example, the following pseudocode statement indicates that the script should print A for exam grades greater than or equal to 90, B for grades in the range 80 to 89, C for grades in the range 70 to 79, D for grades in the range 60 to 69 and F for all other grades:

> *If student's grade is greater than or equal to 90*
> *Print "A"*
> *Else*
> *If student's grade is greater than or equal to 80*
>   *Print "B"*
> *Else*
>   *If student's grade is greater than or equal to 70*
>   *Print "C"*
>   *Else*
>   *If student's grade is greater than or equal to 60*
>   *Print "D"*
>   *Else*
>   *Print "F"*

This pseudocode may be written in JavaScript as

```
if ( studentGrade >= 90 )
   document.writeln( "A" );
else
   if ( studentGrade >= 80 )
      document.writeln( "B" );
   else
      if ( studentGrade >= 70 )
         document.writeln( "C" );
      else
         if ( studentGrade >= 60 )
            document.writeln( "D" );
         else
            document.writeln( "F" );
```

If studentGrade is greater than or equal to 90, all four conditions will be true, but only the document.writeln statement after the *first* test will execute. After that particular document.writeln executes, the else part of the outer if...else statement is skipped.

Good Programming Practice 7.3

If there are several levels of indentation, each level should be indented the same additional amount of space.

Most programmers prefer to write the preceding if statement in the equivalent form:

```
if ( grade >= 90 )
   document.writeln( "A" );
else if ( grade >= 80 )
   document.writeln( "B" );
else if ( grade >= 70 )
   document.writeln( "C" );
else if ( grade >= 60 )
   document.writeln( "D" );
else
   document.writeln( "F" );
```

The latter form is popular because it avoids the deep indentation of the code to the right. Such deep indentation can force lines to be split and decrease script readability.

*Dangling-**else** Problem*

It's important to note that the JavaScript interpreter always associates an else with the previous if, unless told to do otherwise by the placement of braces ({}). The following code illustrates the **dangling-else problem**. For example,

```
if ( x > 5 )
    if ( y > 5 )
        document.writeln( "<p>x and y are > 5</p>" );
else
    document.writeln( "<p>x is <= 5</p>" );
```

appears to indicate with its indentation that if x is greater than 5, the if structure in its body determines whether y is also greater than 5. If so, the body of the nested if structure outputs the string "x and y are > 5". Otherwise, it *appears* that if x is *not* greater than 5, the else part of the if...else structure outputs the string "x is <= 5".

Beware! The preceding nested if statement does *not* execute as it appears. The interpreter actually interprets the preceding statement as

```
if ( x > 5 )
    if ( y > 5 )
        document.writeln( "<p>x and y are > 5</p>" );
    else
        document.writeln( "<p>x is <= 5</p>" );
```

in which the body of the first if statement is a nested if...else statement. This statement tests whether x is greater than 5. If so, execution continues by testing whether y is also greater than 5. If the second condition is true, the proper string—"x and y are > 5"—is displayed. However, if the second condition is false, the string "x is <= 5" is displayed, even though we know that x is greater than 5.

To force the *first* nested if statement to execute as it was intended originally, we must write it as follows:

```
if ( x > 5 )
{
    if ( y > 5 )
        document.writeln( "<p>x and y are > 5</p>" );
}
else
    document.writeln( "<p>x is <= 5</p>" );
```

The braces ({}) indicate to the JavaScript interpreter that the second if statement is in the *body* of the first if statement and that the else is matched with the *first* if statement.

Blocks

The if selection statement expects only *one* statement in its body. To include *several* statements in an if statement's body, enclose the statements in braces ({ and }). This also can be done in the else section of an if...else statement. A set of statements contained within a pair of braces is called a **block**.

Software Engineering Observation 7.3

A block can be placed anywhere in a script that a single statement can be placed.

Software Engineering Observation 7.4

Unlike individual statements, a block does not end with a semicolon. However, each statement within the braces of a block should end with a semicolon.

The following example includes a block in the else part of an if...else statement:

```
if ( grade >= 60 )
    document.writeln( "<p>Passed</p>" );
else
{
    document.writeln( "<p>Failed</p>" );
    document.writeln( "<p>You must take this course again.</p>" );
}
```

In this case, if grade is less than 60, the script executes *both* statements in the body of the else and prints

```
Failed
You must take this course again.
```

Note the braces surrounding the two statements in the else clause. These braces are important. Without them, the statement

```
document.writeln( "<p>You must take this course again.</p>" );
```

would be *outside* the body of the else part of the if and would execute *regardless* of whether the grade is less than 60.

Syntax errors (e.g., when one brace in a block is left out of the script) are caught by the interpreter when it attempts to interpret the code containing the syntax error. They prevent the browser from executing the code. While many browsers notify users of errors, that information is of little use to them. That's why it's important to validate your JavaScripts and thoroughly test them. A **logic error** (e.g., the one caused when both braces around a block are left out of the script) also has its effect at execution time. A **fatal logic error** causes a script to fail and terminate prematurely. A **nonfatal logic error** allows a script to continue executing, but it produces incorrect results.

Software Engineering Observation 7.5

Just as a block can be placed anywhere a single statement can be placed, it's also possible to have no statement at all (the empty statement) in such places. We represent the empty statement by placing a semicolon (;) where a statement would normally be.

7.7 while Repetition Statement

A *repetition structure* (also known as a **loop**) allows you to specify that a script is to repeat an action while some condition remains *true*. The pseudocode statement

> *While there are more items on my shopping list*
> *Purchase next item and cross it off my list*

describes the repetition that occurs during a shopping trip. The condition "there are more items on my shopping list" may be true or false. If it's true, then the action "Purchase next item and cross it off my list" is performed. This action is performed *repeatedly* while the condition remains true. The statement(s) contained in the *While* repetition structure constitute its body. The body of a loop such as the *While* structure may be a single statement or a block. Eventually, the condition becomes false—when the last item on the shopping list has been purchased and crossed off the list. At this point, the repetition terminates, and the first pseudocode statement after the repetition structure "executes."

Common Programming Error 7.2

If the body of a while *statement never causes the while statement's condition to become true, a logic error occurs. Normally, such a repetition structure will never terminate—an error called an* **infinite loop***. Many browsers show a dialog allowing the user to terminate a script that contains an infinite loop.*

As an example of a while statement, consider a script segment designed to find the first power of 2 larger than 1000. Variable product begins with the value 2. The statement is as follows:

```
var product = 2;

while ( product <= 1000 )
    product = 2 * product;
```

When the while statement finishes executing, product contains the result 1024. The flowchart in Fig. 7.5 illustrates the flow of control of the preceding while repetition statement. Once again, note that (besides small circles and arrows) the flowchart contains *only* a rectangle symbol and a diamond symbol.

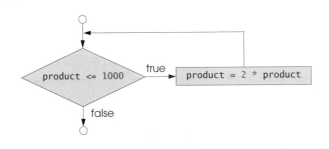

Fig. 7.5 | Flowcharting the while repetition statement.

When the script enters the while statement, product is 2. The script repeatedly multiplies variable product by 2, so product takes on the values 4, 8, 16, 32, 64, 128, 256, 512 and 1024 successively. When product becomes 1024, the condition product <= 1000 in the while statement becomes false. This terminates the repetition, with 1024 as product's final value. Execution continues with the next statement after the while statement. [*Note:* If a while statement's condition is initially false, the body statement(s) will *never* execute.]

The flowchart clearly shows the repetition. The flowline emerging from the rectangle wraps back to the decision, which the script tests each time through the loop until the decision eventually becomes false. At this point, the while statement exits, and control passes to the next statement in the script.

7.8 Formulating Algorithms: Counter-Controlled Repetition

To illustrate how to develop algorithms, we solve several variations of a class-average problem. Consider the following problem statement:

> *A class of ten students took a quiz. The grades (integers in the range 0 to 100) for this quiz are available to you. Determine the class average on the quiz.*

The class average is equal to the sum of the grades divided by the number of students (10 in this case). The algorithm for solving this problem on a computer must input each of the grades, perform the averaging calculation and display the result.

Let's use pseudocode to list the actions to execute and specify the order in which they should execute. We use **counter-controlled repetition** to input the grades one at a time. This technique uses a variable called a **counter** to control the number of times a set of statements executes. In this example, repetition terminates when the counter exceeds 10. In this section, we present a pseudocode algorithm (Fig. 7.6) and the corresponding script (Fig. 7.7). In the next section, we show how to develop pseudocode algorithms. Counter-controlled repetition often is called **definite repetition**, because the number of repetitions is known before the loop begins executing.

```
 1   Set total to zero
 2   Set grade counter to one
 3
 4   While grade counter is less than or equal to ten
 5       Input the next grade
 6       Add the grade into the total
 7       Add one to the grade counter
 8
 9   Set the class average to the total divided by ten
10   Print the class average
```

Fig. 7.6 | Pseudocode algorithm that uses counter-controlled repetition to solve the class-average problem.

```
 1   <!DOCTYPE html>
 2
 3   <!-- Fig. 7.7: average.html -->
 4   <!-- Counter-controlled repetition to calculate a class average. -->
 5   <html>
 6      <head>
 7         <meta charset = "utf-8">
 8         <title>Class Average Program</title>
 9         <script>
10
11            var total; // sum of grades
12            var gradeCounter; // number of grades entered
13            var grade; // grade typed by user (as a string)
14            var gradeValue; // grade value (converted to integer)
```

Fig. 7.7 | Counter-controlled repetition to calculate a class average. (Part 1 of 2.)

```
15          var average; // average of all grades
16
17          // initialization phase
18          total = 0; // clear total
19          gradeCounter = 1; // prepare to loop
20
21          // processing phase
22          while ( gradeCounter <= 10 ) // loop 10 times
23          {
24
25             // prompt for input and read grade from user
26             grade = window.prompt( "Enter integer grade:", "0" );
27
28             // convert grade from a string to an integer
29             gradeValue = parseInt( grade );
30
31             // add gradeValue to total
32             total = total + gradeValue;
33
34             // add 1 to gradeCounter
35             gradeCounter = gradeCounter + 1;
36          } // end while
37
38          // termination phase
39          average = total / 10;    // calculate the average
40
41          // display average of exam grades
42          document.writeln(
43             "<h1>Class average is " + average + "</h1>" );
44
45       </script>
46    </head><body></body>
47 </html>
```

a) This dialog is displayed 10 times. User input is 100, 88, 93, 55, 68, 77, 83, 95, 73 and 62. User enters each grade and presses **OK**.

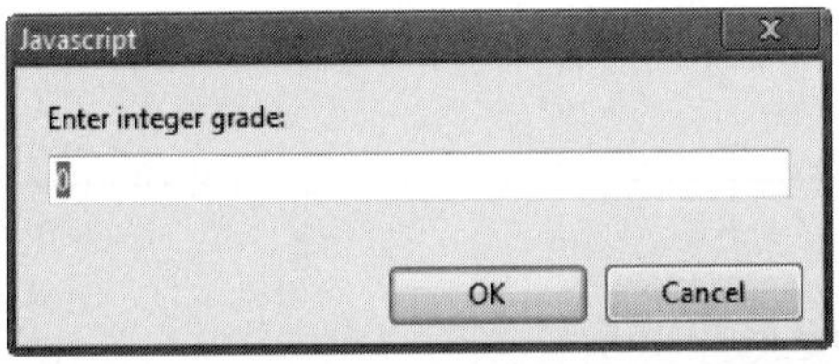

Javascript   x

Enter integer grade:

0

                                OK   Cancel

b) The class average is displayed in a web page

Class Average Program   x   +

← → C   file:///C:/books/2011/IW ☆ 🅰 ✉ 🔧

📁 Links 📁 Publishing   »   📁 Other bookmarks ⚠ Sync Error

Class average is 79.4

Fig. 7.7 | Counter-controlled repetition to calculate a class average. (Part 2 of 2.)

Variables Used in the Algorithm

Note the references in the algorithm to a total and a counter. A **total** is a variable in which a script accumulates the sum of a series of values. A counter is a variable a script uses to count—in this case, to count the number of grades entered. Variables that store totals should normally be initialized to zero before they're used in a script.

Lines 11–15 declare variables `total`, `gradeCounter`, `grade`, `gradeValue`, `average`. The variable `grade` will store the *string* the user types into the `prompt` dialog. The variable `gradeValue` will store the integer value of the `grade` the user enters into the `prompt` dialog.

Initializing Variables

Lines 18–19 are assignments that initialize `total` to 0 and `gradeCounter` to 1. Note that variables `total` and `gradeCounter` are initialized before they're used in a calculation.

Common Programming Error 7.3

Not initializing a variable that will be used in a calculation results in a logic error that produces the value NaN ("Not a Number").

The `while` Repetition Statement

Line 22 indicates that the `while` statement continues iterating while the value of `grade-Counter` is less than or equal to 10. Line 26 corresponds to the pseudocode statement "*Input the next grade.*" The statement displays a `prompt` dialog with the prompt "Enter integer grade:" on the screen.

After the user enters the `grade`, line 29 converts it from a string to an integer. We *must* convert the string to an integer in this example; otherwise, the addition operation in line 32 will be a *string-concatenation*.

Next, the script updates the `total` with the new `gradeValue` entered by the user. Line 32 adds `gradeValue` to the previous value of `total` and assigns the result to `total`. This statement seems a bit strange, because it does not follow the rules of algebra. Keep in mind that JavaScript operator precedence evaluates the addition (+) operation before the assignment (=) operation. The value of the expression on the *right* side of the assignment operator always *replaces* the value of the variable on the *left* side.

The script now is ready to increment the variable `gradeCounter` to indicate that a grade has been processed and to read the next grade from the user. Line 35 adds 1 to `gradeCounter`, so the condition in the `while` statement will eventually become `false` and terminate the loop. After this statement executes, the script continues by testing the condition in the `while` statement in line 22. If the condition is still `true`, the statements in lines 26–35 repeat. Otherwise the script continues execution with the first statement in sequence after the body of the loop (i.e., line 39).

Calculating and Displaying the Results

Line 39 assigns the results of the average calculation to variable `average`. Lines 42–43 write a line of HTML5 text in the document that displays the string "Class average is " followed by the value of variable `average` as an `<h1>` element.

Testing the Program

Open the HTML5 document in a web browser to execute the script. This script parses any user input as an integer. In the sample execution in Fig. 7.7, the sum of the values entered

(100, 88, 93, 55, 68, 77, 83, 95, 73 and 62) is 794. Although the script treats all input as integers, the averaging calculation in the script does not produce an integer. Rather, the calculation produces a **floating-point number** (i.e., a number containing a decimal point). The average of the 10 integers input by the user in this example is 79.4. If your script requires the user to enter floating-point numbers, you can convert the user input from strings to numbers using the JavaScript function parseFloat, which we introduce in Section 9.2.

Software Engineering Observation 7.6

If the string passed to parseInt contains a floating-point numeric value, parseInt simply truncates the floating-point part. For example, the string "27.95" results in the integer 27, and the string "-123.45" results in the integer -123. If the string passed to parseInt does begin with a numeric value, parseInt returns NaN (not a number). If you need to know whether parseInt returned NaN, JavaScript provides the function isNaN, which determines whether its argument has the value NaN and, if so, returns true; otherwise, it returns false.

Floating-Point Numbers

JavaScript actually represents all numbers as floating-point numbers in memory. Floating-point numbers often develop through division, as shown in this example. When we divide 10 by 3, the result is 3.3333333..., with the sequence of 3s repeating *infinitely*. The computer allocates only a *fixed* amount of space to hold such a value, so the stored floating-point value can be only an approximation. Although floating-point numbers are not always 100 percent precise, they have numerous applications. For example, when we speak of a "normal" body temperature of 98.6, we do not need to be precise to a large number of digits. When we view the temperature on a thermometer and read it as 98.6, it may actually be 98.5999473210643. The point here is that few applications require such high-precision floating-point values, so calling this number simply 98.6 is fine for many applications.

A Note About Input Via prompt Dialogs

In this example, we used prompt dialogs to obtain user input. Typically, such input would be accomplished via form elements in an HTML5 document, but this requires additional scripting techniques that are introduced starting in Chapter 9. For now, we'll continue to use prompt dialogs.

7.9 Formulating Algorithms: Sentinel-Controlled Repetition

Let's generalize the class-average problem. Consider the following problem:

> *Develop a class-averaging script that will process an arbitrary number of grades each time the script is run.*

In the first class-average example, the number of grades (10) was known in advance. In this example, no indication is given of how many grades the user will enter. The script must process an *arbitrary* number of grades. How can the script determine when to stop the input of grades? How will it know when to calculate and display the class average?

One way to solve this problem is to use a special value called a **sentinel value** (also called a **signal value**, a **dummy value** or a **flag value**) to indicate the end of data entry. The user types in grades until all legitimate grades have been entered. Then the user types the sentinel value to indicate that the last grade has been entered. Sentinel-controlled repetition is often called **indefinite repetition**, because the number of repetitions is not known before the loop begins executing.

Clearly, you must choose a sentinel value that *cannot* be confused with an acceptable input value. −1 is an acceptable sentinel value for this problem, because grades on a quiz are normally nonnegative integers from 0 to 100. Thus, an execution of the class-average script might process a stream of inputs such as 95, 96, 75, 74, 89 and −1. The script would compute and print the class average for the grades 95, 96, 75, 74 and 89 (−1 is the sentinel value, so it should *not* enter into the average calculation).

Developing the Pseudocode Algorithm with Top-Down, Stepwise Refinement: The Top and First Refinement

We approach the class-average script with a technique called **top-down, stepwise refinement**, a technique that's essential to the development of well-structured algorithms. We begin with a pseudocode representation of the **top**:

> *Determine the class average for the quiz*

The top is a single statement that conveys the script's overall purpose. As such, the top is, in effect, a *complete* representation of a script. Unfortunately, the top rarely conveys sufficient detail from which to write the JavaScript algorithm. Therefore we must begin a refinement process. First, we divide the top into a series of smaller tasks and list them in the order in which they need to be performed, creating the following **first refinement**:

> *Initialize variables*
> *Input, sum up and count the quiz grades*
> *Calculate and print the class average*

Here, only the sequence structure is used; the steps listed are to be executed in order, one after the other.

Software Engineering Observation 7.7

Each refinement, as well as the top itself, is a complete *specification of the algorithm; only the level of detail varies.*

Proceeding to the Second Refinement

To proceed to the next level of refinement (the **second refinement**), we commit to specific variables. We need a running total of the numbers, a count of how many numbers have been processed, a variable to receive the string representation of each grade as it's input, a variable to store the value of the grade after it's converted to an integer and a variable to hold the calculated average. The pseudocode statement

> *Initialize variables*

may be refined as follows:

> *Initialize total to zero*
> *Initialize gradeCounter to zero*

Only the variables *total* and *gradeCounter* are initialized before they're used; the variables *average*, *grade* and *gradeValue* (for the calculated average, the user input and the integer representation of the *grade*, respectively) need not be initialized, because their values are determined as they're calculated or input.

The pseudocode statement

Input, sum up and count the quiz grades

requires a repetition statement that successively inputs each grade. We do not know in advance how many grades are to be processed, so we'll use *sentinel-controlled repetition*. The user will enter legitimate grades, one at a time. After entering the last legitimate grade, the user will enter the sentinel value. The script will test for the sentinel value after the user enters each grade and will terminate the loop when the sentinel value is encountered. The second refinement of the preceding pseudocode statement is then

> *Input the first grade (possibly the sentinel)*
> *While the user has not as yet entered the sentinel*
>   *Add this grade into the running total*
>   *Add one to the grade counter*
>   *Input the next grade (possibly the sentinel)*

In pseudocode, we do *not* use braces around the pseudocode that forms the body of the *While* structure. We simply indent the pseudocode under the *While* to show that it belongs to the body of the *While*. Remember, pseudocode is only an *informal* development aid.

The pseudocode statement

Calculate and print the class average

may be refined as follows:

> *If the counter is not equal to zero*
>   *Set the average to the total divided by the counter*
>   *Print the average*
> *Else*
>   *Print "No grades were entered"*

We test for the possibility of **division by zero**—a logic error that, if undetected, would cause the script to produce invalid output. The complete second refinement of the pseudocode algorithm for the class-average problem is shown in Fig. 7.8.

Error-Prevention Tip 7.1
When performing division by an expression whose value could be zero, explicitly test for this case, and handle it appropriately in your script (e.g., by displaying an error message) rather than allowing the division by zero to occur.

Software Engineering Observation 7.8
Many algorithms can be divided logically into three phases: an initialization phase *that initializes the script variables, a* processing phase *that inputs data values and adjusts variables accordingly, and a* termination phase *that calculates and prints the results.*

The Complete Second Refinement

The pseudocode algorithm in Fig. 7.8 solves the more general class-average problem. This algorithm was developed after only two refinements. Sometimes more refinements are necessary.

1	*Initialize total to zero*
2	*Initialize gradeCounter to zero*
3	
4	*Input the first grade (possibly the sentinel)*
5	
6	*While the user has not as yet entered the sentinel*
7	*Add this grade into the running total*
8	*Add one to the grade counter*
9	*Input the next grade (possibly the sentinel)*
10	
11	*If the counter is not equal to zero*
12	*Set the average to the total divided by the counter*
13	*Print the average*
14	*Else*
15	*Print "No grades were entered"*

Fig. 7.8 | Sentinel-controlled repetition to solve the class-average problem.

Software Engineering Observation 7.9

You terminate the top-down, stepwise refinement process after specifying the pseudocode algorithm in sufficient detail for you to convert the pseudocode to JavaScript. Then, implementing the JavaScript is normally straightforward.

Software Engineering Observation 7.10

Experience has shown that the most difficult part of solving a problem on a computer is developing the algorithm for the solution.

Software Engineering Observation 7.11

Many experienced programmers write scripts without ever using script-development tools like pseudocode. As they see it, their ultimate goal is to solve the problem on a computer, and writing pseudocode merely delays the production of final outputs. Although this approach may work for simple and familiar problems, it can lead to serious errors in large, complex projects.

Implementing Sentinel-Controlled Repetition to Calculate a Class Average

Figure 7.9 shows the JavaScript and a sample execution. Although each grade is an integer, the averaging calculation is likely to produce a number with a decimal point (a real number).

In this example, we see that control structures may be *stacked* on top of one another (in sequence) just as a child stacks building blocks. The `while` statement (lines 29–43) is followed immediately by an `if...else` statement (lines 46–55) in sequence. Much of the code in this script is identical to the code in Fig. 7.7, so we concentrate in this example on the new features.

```
1   <!DOCTYPE html>
2
3   <!-- Fig. 7.9: average2.html -->
4   <!-- Sentinel-controlled repetition to calculate a class average. -->
5   <html>
6      <head>
7         <meta charset = "utf-8">
8         <title>Class Average Program: Sentinel-controlled Repetition</title>
9         <script>
10
11            var total; // sum of grades
12            var gradeCounter; // number of grades entered
13            var grade; // grade typed by user (as a string)
14            var gradeValue; // grade value (converted to integer)
15            var average; // average of all grades
16
17            // initialization phase
18            total = 0; // clear total
19            gradeCounter = 0; // prepare to loop
20
21            // processing phase
22            // prompt for input and read grade from user
23            grade = window.prompt(
24               "Enter Integer Grade, -1 to Quit:", "0" );
25
26            // convert grade from a string to an integer
27            gradeValue = parseInt( grade );
28
29            while ( gradeValue != -1 )
30            {
31               // add gradeValue to total
32               total = total + gradeValue;
33
34               // add 1 to gradeCounter
35               gradeCounter = gradeCounter + 1;
36
37               // prompt for input and read grade from user
38               grade = window.prompt(
39                  "Enter Integer Grade, -1 to Quit:", "0" );
40
41               // convert grade from a string to an integer
42               gradeValue = parseInt( grade );
43            } // end while
44
45            // termination phase
46            if ( gradeCounter != 0 )
47            {
48               average = total / gradeCounter;
49
50               // display average of exam grades
51               document.writeln(
52                  "<h1>Class average is " + average + "</h1>" );
53            } // end if
```

Fig. 7.9 | Sentinel-controlled repetition to calculate a class average. (Part I of 2.)

```
54              else
55                  document.writeln( "<p>No grades were entered</p>" );
56
57          </script>
58      </head><body></body>
59  </html>
```

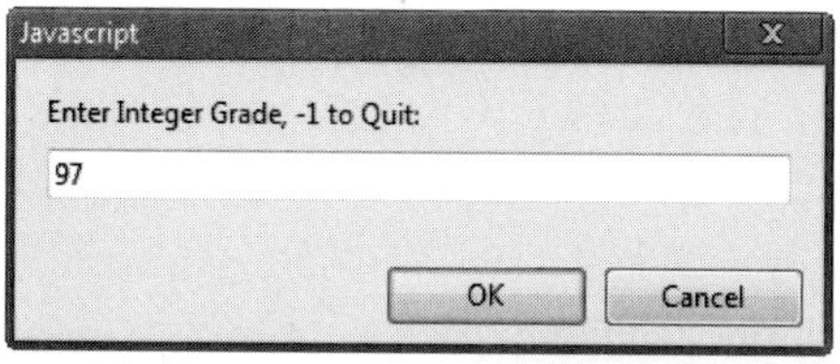

Javascript   X

Enter Integer Grade, -1 to Quit:

97

OK   Cancel

This dialog is displayed four times. User input is 97, 88, 72 and −1.

Class Average Program: Ser × +

C   file:///C:/books/2011/IW3HTP5/examp ☆ 🗛 ✉ 🔧

☐ Links ☐ Publishing ☐ Social   » ☐ Other bookmarks ⚠ Sync Error

Class average is 85.66666666666667

Fig. 7.9 | Sentinel-controlled repetition to calculate a class average. (Part 2 of 2.)

Line 19 initializes gradeCounter to 0, because no grades have been entered yet. Remember that the script uses *sentinel-controlled repetition*. To keep an accurate record of the number of grades entered, the script increments gradeCounter only after processing a valid grade value.

Script Logic for Sentinel-Controlled Repetition vs. Counter-Controlled Repetition

Note the difference in logic for sentinel-controlled repetition as compared with the counter-controlled repetition in Fig. 7.7. In counter-controlled repetition, we read a value from the user during each iteration of the while statement's body for the specified number of iterations. In sentinel-controlled repetition, we read one value (lines 23–24) and convert it to an integer (line 27) before the script reaches the while statement. The script uses this value to determine whether the script's flow of control should enter the body of the while statement. If the while statement's condition is false (i.e., the user typed the sentinel as the first grade), the script ignores the body of the while statement (i.e., no grades were entered). If the condition is true, the body begins execution and processes the value entered by the user (i.e., adds the value to the total in line 32). After processing the value, the script increments gradeCounter by 1 (line 35), inputs the next grade from the user (lines 38–39) and converts the grade to an integer (line 42), before the end of the while statement's body. When the script reaches the closing right brace (}) of the body in line 43, execution continues with the next test of the condition of the while statement (line 29), using the new value just entered by the user to determine whether the while statement's body should execute again. Note that the next value always is input from the user immediately before the script evaluates the condition of the while statement. This order allows us to determine whether the value just entered by the user is the sentinel value *before* processing it (i.e., adding it to the `total`). If the value entered *is* the sentinel value, the `while` statement terminates and the script does not add the value to the `total`.

Note the block in the `while` loop in Fig. 7.9 (lines 30–43). Without the braces, the last three statements in the body of the loop would fall *outside* the loop, causing the code to be interpreted incorrectly, as follows:

```
while ( gradeValue != -1 )
   // add gradeValue to total
   total = total + gradeValue;

// add 1 to gradeCounter
gradeCounter = gradeCounter + 1;

// prompt for input and read grade from user
grade = window.prompt(
   "Enter Integer Grade, -1 to Quit:", "0" );

// convert grade from a string to an integer
gradeValue = parseInt( grade );
```

This interpretation would cause an *infinite loop* in the script if the user did not input the sentinel -1 as the first input value in lines 23–24 (i.e., before the `while` statement).

7.10 Formulating Algorithms: Nested Control Statements

Let's work through another complete problem. We once again formulate the algorithm using pseudocode and top-down, stepwise refinement, and write a corresponding script.

Consider the following problem statement:

> *A college offers a course that prepares students for the state licensing exam for real estate brokers. Last year, 10 of the students who completed this course took the licensing exam. Naturally, the college wants to know how well its students performed. You've been asked to write a script to summarize the results. You've been given a list of these 10 students. Next to each name is written a 1 if the student passed the exam and a 2 if the student failed.*
>
> *Your script should analyze the results of the exam as follows:*
>
> 1. *Input each test result (i.e., a 1 or a 2). Display the message "Enter result" on the screen each time the script requests another test result.*
>
> 2. *Count the number of test results of each type.*
>
> 3. *Display a summary of the test results indicating the number of students who passed and the number of students who failed.*
>
> 4. *If more than eight students passed the exam, print the message "Bonus to instructor!"*

After reading the problem statement carefully, we make the following observations:

1. The script must process test results for 10 students. A counter-controlled loop will be used.

2. Each test result is a number—either a 1 or a 2. Each time the script reads a test result, the script must determine whether the number is a 1 or a 2. We test for a 1 in our algorithm. If the number is not a 1, we assume that it's a 2.

3. Two counters are used to keep track of the exam results—one to count the number of students who passed the exam and one to count the number of students who failed the exam.

After the script processes all the results, it must decide whether more than eight students passed the exam. Let's proceed with top-down, stepwise refinement. We begin with a pseudocode representation of the top:

Analyze exam results and decide whether a bonus should be paid

Once again, it's important to emphasize that the top is a complete representation of the script, but that several refinements are necessary before the pseudocode can be evolved naturally into JavaScript. Our first refinement is as follows:

Initialize variables
Input the 10 exam grades and count passes and failures
Print a summary of the exam results and decide whether a bonus should be paid

Here, too, even though we have a complete representation of the entire script, further refinement is necessary. We now commit to specific variables. Counters are needed to record the passes and failures; a counter will be used to control the looping process, and a variable is needed to store the user input. The pseudocode statement

Initialize variables

may be refined as follows:

Initialize passes to zero
Initialize failures to zero
Initialize student to one

Note that only the counters for the number of passes, the number of failures and the number of students are initialized. The pseudocode statement

Input the 10 exam grades and count passes and failures

requires a loop that successively inputs the result of each exam. Here, it's known in advance that there are precisely 10 exam results, so counter-controlled repetition is appropriate. Inside the loop (i.e., *nested* within the loop), a double-selection structure will determine whether each exam result is a pass or a failure and will increment the appropriate counter accordingly. The refinement of the preceding pseudocode statement is then

While student counter is less than or equal to ten
    Input the next exam result
    If the student passed
        Add one to passes
    Else
        Add one to failures
    Add one to student counter

Blank lines can be used to set off the *If...Else* control structure to improve script readability. The pseudocode statement

Print a summary of the exam results and decide whether a bonus should be paid

may be refined as follows:

> *Print the number of passes*
> *Print the number of failures*
> *If more than eight students passed*
> *Print "Bonus to instructor!"*

Complete Second Refinement of Pseudocode and Conversion to JavaScript

The complete second refinement appears in Fig. 7.10. Note that blank lines are also used to set off the *While* statement for script readability.

1	*Initialize passes to zero*
2	*Initialize failures to zero*
3	*Initialize student to one*
4	
5	*While student counter is less than or equal to ten*
6	*Input the next exam result*
7	
8	*If the student passed*
9	*Add one to passes*
10	*Else*
11	*Add one to failures*
12	*Add one to student counter*
13	
14	*Print the number of passes*
15	*Print the number of failures*
16	
17	*If more than eight students passed*
18	*Print "Bonus to Instructor!"*

Fig. 7.10 | Examination-results problem pseudocode.

This pseudocode is now refined sufficiently for conversion to JavaScript. The JavaScript and two sample executions are shown in Fig. 7.11.

```html
1   <!DOCTYPE html>
2
3   <!-- Fig. 7.11: analysis.html -->
4   <!-- Examination-results calculation. -->
5   <html>
6      <head>
7         <meta charset = "utf-8">
8         <title>Analysis of Examination Results</title>
9         <script>
10
11            // initializing variables in declarations
12            var passes = 0; // number of passes
13            var failures = 0; // number of failures
14            var student = 1; // student counter
15            var result; // an exam result
```

Fig. 7.11 | Examination-results calculation. (Part 1 of 3.)

```
16
17            // process 10 students; counter-controlled loop
18            while ( student <= 10 )
19            {
20               result = window.prompt( "Enter result (1=pass,2=fail)", "0" );
21
22               if ( result == "1" )
23                  passes = passes + 1;
24               else
25                  failures = failures + 1;
26
27               student = student + 1;
28            } // end while
29
30            // termination phase
31            document.writeln( "<h1>Examination Results</h1>" );
32            document.writeln( "<p>Passed: " + passes +
33               "; Failed: " + failures + "</p>" );
34
35            if ( passes > 8 )
36               document.writeln( "<p>Bonus to instructor!</p>" );
37
38         </script>
39      </head><body></body>
40   </html>
```

a) This dialog is displayed 10 times. User input is 1, 2, 1, 1, 1, 1, 1, 1, 1 and 1.

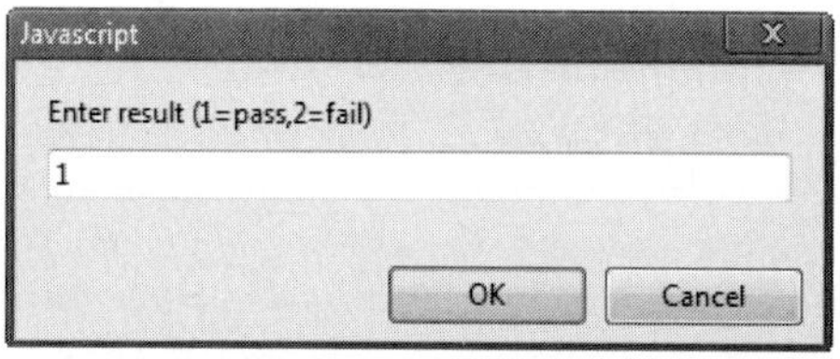

b) Nine students passed and one failed, therefore "Bonus to instructor!" is printed.

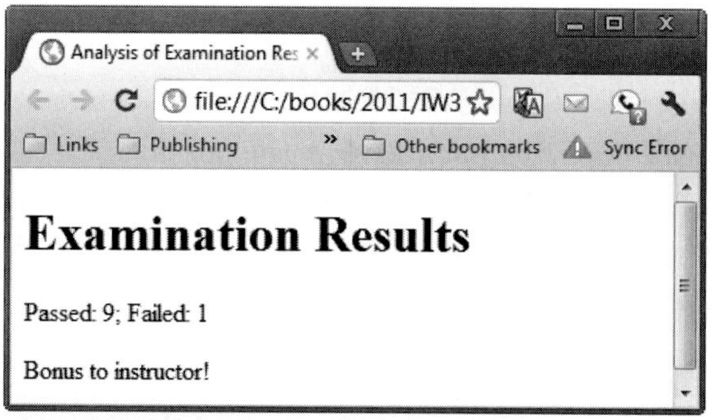

c) This dialog is displayed 10 times. User input is 1, 2, 1, 2, 2, 1, 2, 2, 1 and 1.

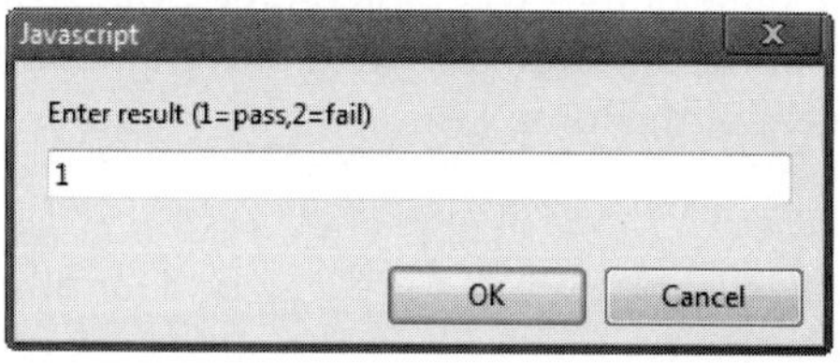

Fig. 7.11 | Examination-results calculation. (Part 2 of 3.)

d) Five students passed and
five failed, so no bonus is paid
to the instructor.

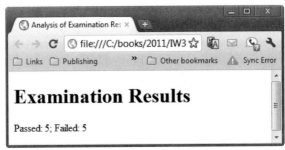

Examination Results

Passed: 5; Failed: 5

Fig. 7.11 | Examination-results calculation. (Part 3 of 3.)

Lines 12–15 declare the variables used to process the examination results. Note that JavaScript allows *variable initialization* to be incorporated into declarations (passes is assigned 0, failures is assigned 0 and student is assigned 1). Some scripts may require reinitialization at the beginning of each repetition; such reinitialization would normally occur in assignment statements.

The processing of the exam results occurs in the while statement in lines 18–28. Note that the if...else statement in lines 22–25 in the loop tests only whether the exam result was 1; it assumes that all other exam results are 2. Normally, you should validate the values input by the user (i.e., determine whether the values are correct).

Good Programming Practice 7.4

When inputting values from the user, validate the input to ensure that it's correct. If an input value is incorrect, prompt the user to input the value again. The HTML5 self-validating controls can help you check the formatting of your data, but you may need additional tests to check that properly formatted values make sense in the context of your application.

7.11 Assignment Operators

JavaScript provides several additional assignment operators (called **compound assignment operators**) for abbreviating assignment expressions. For example, the statement

```
c = c + 3;
```

can be abbreviated with the **addition assignment operator, +=,** as

```
c += 3;
```

The += operator adds the value of the expression on the *right* of the operator to the value of the variable on the *left* of the operator and stores the result in the variable on the *left* of the operator. Any statement of the form

variable = *variable operator expression*;

where *operator* is one of the binary operators +, -, *, / or % (or others we'll discuss later in the text), can be written in the form

variable operator = *expression*;

Thus, the assignment c += 3 adds 3 to c. Figure 7.12 shows the arithmetic assignment operators, sample expressions using these operators and explanations of the meaning of the operators.

Assignment operator	Initial value of variable	Sample expression	Explanation	Assigns
+=	c = 3	c += 7	c = c + 7	10 to c
-=	d = 5	d -= 4	d = d - 4	1 to d
*=	e = 4	e *= 5	e = e * 5	20 to e
/=	f = 6	f /= 3	f = f / 3	2 to f
%=	g = 12	g %= 9	g = g % 9	3 to g

Fig. 7.12 | Arithmetic assignment operators.

7.12 Increment and Decrement Operators

JavaScript provides the unary **increment operator** (++) and **decrement operator** (--) (summarized in Fig. 7.13). If a variable c is incremented by 1, the increment operator, ++, can be used rather than the expression c = c + 1 or c += 1. If an increment or decrement operator is placed *before* a variable, it's referred to as the **preincrement** or **predecrement operator**, respectively. If an increment or decrement operator is placed *after* a variable, it's referred to as the **postincrement** or **postdecrement operator**, respectively.

Operator	Example	Called	Explanation
++	++a	preincrement	Increment a by 1, then use the new value of a in the expression in which a resides.
++	a++	postincrement	Use the current value of a in the expression in which a resides, then increment a by 1.
--	--b	predecrement	Decrement b by 1, then use the new value of b in the expression in which b resides.
--	b--	postdecrement	Use the current value of b in the expression in which b resides, then decrement b by 1.

Fig. 7.13 | Increment and decrement operators.

Preincrementing (or predecrementing) a variable causes the script to increment (decrement) the variable by 1, then use the new value of the variable in the expression in which it appears. Postincrementing (postdecrementing) the variable causes the script to use the current value of the variable in the expression in which it appears, then increment (decrement) the variable by 1.

The script in Fig. 7.14 demonstrates the difference between the preincrementing and postincrementing versions of the ++ increment operator. Postincrementing the variable c

```
1    <!DOCTYPE html>
2
3    <!-- Fig. 7.14: increment.html -->
4    <!-- Preincrementing and Postincrementing. -->
5    <html>
6       <head>
7          <meta charset = "utf-8">
8          <title>Preincrementing and Postincrementing</title>
9          <script>
10
11            var c;
12
13            c = 5;
14            document.writeln( "<h3>Postincrementing</h3>" );
15            document.writeln( "<p>" + c ); // prints 5
16            // prints 5 then increments
17            document.writeln( " " + c++ );
18            document.writeln( " " + c + "</p>" ); // prints 6
19
20            c = 5;
21            document.writeln( "<h3>Preincrementing</h3>" );
22            document.writeln( "<p>" + c ); // prints 5
23            // increments then prints 6
24            document.writeln( " " + ++c );
25            document.writeln( " " + c + "</p>" ); // prints 6
26
27         </script>
28      </head><body></body>
29   </html>
```

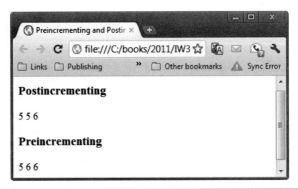

Fig. 7.14 | Preincrementing and postincrementing.

causes it to be incremented *after* it's used in the document.writeln method call (line 17). Preincrementing the variable c causes it to be incremented *before* it's used in the document.writeln method call (line 24). The script displays the value of c before and after the ++ operator is used. The decrement operator (--) works similarly.

Good Programming Practice 7.5

For readability, unary operators should be placed next to their operands, with no intervening spaces.

The three assignment statements in Fig. 7.11 (lines 23, 25 and 27, respectively),

```
passes = passes + 1;
failures = failures + 1;
student = student + 1;
```

can be written more concisely with assignment operators as

```
passes += 1;
failures += 1;
student += 1;
```

with preincrement operators as

```
++passes;
++failures;
++student;
```

or with postincrement operators as

```
passes++;
failures++;
student++;
```

When incrementing or decrementing a variable in a statement by itself, the preincrement and postincrement forms have the *same* effect, and the predecrement and postdecrement forms have the same effect. It's only when a variable appears in the context of a larger expression that preincrementing the variable and post-incrementing the variable have different effects. Predecrementing and postdecrementing behave similarly.

Common Programming Error 7.4

*Attempting to use the increment or decrement operator on an expression other than a **left-hand-side expression**—commonly called an **lvalue**—is a syntax error. A left-hand-side expression is a variable or expression that can appear on the left side of an assignment operation. For example, writing ++(x + 1) is a syntax error, because (x + 1) is not a left-hand-side expression.*

Figure 7.15 lists the precedence and associativity of the operators introduced to this point. The operators are shown top-to-bottom in decreasing order of precedence. The second column describes the associativity of the operators at each level of precedence. The conditional operator (?:), the unary operators increment (++) and decrement (--) and the assignment operators =, +=, -=, *=, /= and %= associate from *right to left*. All other operators shown here associate from *left to right*. The third column names the groups of operators.

Operator	Associativity	Type
++ --	right to left	unary
* / %	left to right	multiplicative
+ -	left to right	additive
< <= > >=	left to right	relational

Fig. 7.15 | Precedence and associativity of the operators discussed so far. (Part 1 of 2.)

Operator	Associativity	Type
`==` `!=` `===` `!===`	left to right	equality
`?:`	right to left	conditional
`=` `+=` `-=` `*=` `/=` `%=`	right to left	assignment

Fig. 7.15 | Precedence and associativity of the operators discussed so far. (Part 2 of 2.)

7.13 Web Resources

`www.deitel.com/javascript/`

The Deitel JavaScript Resource Center contains links to some of the best JavaScript resources on the web. There you'll find categorized links to JavaScript tools, code generators, forums, books, libraries, frameworks and more. Also check out the tutorials for all skill levels, from introductory to advanced. Be sure to visit the related Resource Centers on HTML5 (`www.deitel.com/html5/`) and CSS3 (`www.deitel.com/css3/`).

Summary

Section 7.2 Algorithms
- Any computable problem can be solved by executing a series of actions in a specific order.
- A procedure (p. 247) for solving a problem in terms of the actions (p. 247) to execute and the order in which the actions are to execute (p. 247) is called an algorithm (p. 247).
- Specifying the order in which the actions are to be executed in a computer program is called program control (p. 247).

Section 7.3 Pseudocode
- Pseudocode (p. 247) is an informal language that helps you develop algorithms.
- Carefully prepared pseudocode may be converted easily to a corresponding script.

Section 7.4 Control Statements
- Normally, statements in a script execute one after the other, in the order in which they're written. This process is called sequential execution (p. 247).
- Various JavaScript statements enable you to specify that the next statement to be executed may not necessarily be the next one in sequence. This is known as transfer of control (p. 248).
- All scripts could be written in terms of only three control structures—namely, the sequence structure, (p. 248) the selection structure (p. 248) and the repetition structure (p. 248).
- A flowchart (p. 248) is a graphical representation of an algorithm or of a portion of an algorithm. Flowcharts are drawn using certain special-purpose symbols, such as rectangles (p. 248), diamonds (p. 249), ovals (p. 248) and small circles (p. 248); these symbols are connected by arrows called flowlines (p. 248), which indicate the order in which the actions of the algorithm execute.
- JavaScript provides three selection structures. The `if` selection statement (p. 249) performs an action only if a condition is true. The `if...else` selection statement performs an action if a condition is true and a different action if the condition is false. The `switch` selection statement performs one of many different actions, depending on the value of an expression.
- JavaScript provides four repetition statements—`while` (p. 249), `do...while`, `for` and `for...in`.

- Keywords (p. 249) cannot be used as identifiers (e.g., for variable names).
- Single-entry/single-exit control structures (p. 250) make it easy to build scripts. Control statements are attached to one another by connecting the exit point of one control statement to the entry point of the next. This procedure is called control-statement stacking (p. 250). There's only one other way control statements may be connected: control-statement nesting (p. 250).

Section 7.5 *if Selection Statement*
- The JavaScript interpreter ignores white-space characters: blanks, tabs and newlines used for indentation and vertical spacing. Programmers insert white-space characters to enhance script clarity.
- A decision can be made on any expression that evaluates to true or false (p. 250).
- The indentation convention you choose should be carefully applied throughout your scripts. It's difficult to read scripts that do not use uniform spacing conventions.

Section 7.6 *if...else Selection Statement*
- The conditional operator (?:; p. 252) is closely related to the if...else statement. Operator ?: is JavaScript's only ternary operator—it takes three operands. The operands together with the ?: operator form a conditional expression (p. 252). The first operand is a boolean expression, the second is the value for the conditional expression if the boolean expression evaluates to true and the third is the value for the conditional expression if the boolean expression evaluates to false.
- Nested if...else statements (p. 252) test for multiple cases by placing if...else statements inside other if...else structures.
- The JavaScript interpreter always associates an else with the previous if, unless told to do otherwise by the placement of braces ({}).
- The if selection statement expects only one statement in its body. To include several statements in the body, enclose the statements in a block (p. 254) delimited by braces ({ and }).
- A logic error (p. 255) has its effect at execution time. A fatal logic error (p. 255) causes a script to fail and terminate prematurely. A nonfatal logic error (p. 255) allows a script to continue executing, but the script produces incorrect results.

Section 7.7 *while Repetition Statement*
- The while repetition statement allows the you to specify that an action is to be repeated while some condition remains true.

Section 7.8 *Formulating Algorithms: Counter-Controlled Repetition*
- Counter-controlled repetition (p. 257) is often called definite repetition, because the number of repetitions is known before the loop begins executing.
- Uninitialized variables used in mathematical calculations result in logic errors and produce the value NaN (not a number).
- JavaScript represents all numbers as floating-point numbers in memory. Floating-point numbers (p. 260) often develop through division. The computer allocates only a fixed amount of space to hold such a value, so the stored floating-point value can only be an approximation.

Section 7.9 *Formulating Algorithms: Sentinel-Controlled Repetition*
- In sentinel-controlled repetition, a special value called a sentinel value (also called a signal value, a dummy value or a flag value, p. 260) indicates the end of data entry. Sentinel-controlled repetition is often called indefinite repetition (p. 261), because the number of repetitions is not known in advance.
- It's necessary to choose a sentinel value that cannot be confused with an acceptable input value.

- Top-down, stepwise refinement (p. 261) is a technique essential to the development of well-structured algorithms. The top (p. 261) is a single statement that conveys the overall purpose of the script. As such, the top is, in effect, a complete representation of a script. The stepwise refinement process divides the top into a series of smaller tasks. Terminate the top-down, stepwise refinement process when the pseudocode algorithm is specified in sufficient detail for you to be able to convert the pseudocode to JavaScript.

Section 7.10 Formulating Algorithms: Nested Control Statements
- Control statements can be nested to perform more complex tasks.

Section 7.11 Assignment Operators
- JavaScript provides the arithmetic assignment operators +=, -=, *=, /= and %= (p. 270), which abbreviate certain common types of expressions.

Section 7.12 Increment and Decrement Operators
- The increment operator, ++ (p. 271), and the decrement operator, -- (p. 271), increment or decrement a variable by 1, respectively. If the operator is prefixed to the variable, the variable is incremented or decremented by 1, then used in its expression. If the operator is postfixed to the variable, the variable is used in its expression, then incremented or decremented by 1.

Self-Review Exercises

7.1 Fill in the blanks in each of the following statements:
  a) JavaScript provides four repetition statements— _____, _____, _____and _____.
  b) JavaScript represents all numbers as _____ numbers in memory.
  c) _____ is an informal language that helps you to develop algorithms.
  d) A(n) _____ has its effect at execution time. A(n) _____ causes a script to fail and terminate prematurely. A(n) _____ allows a script to continue executing, but the script produces incorrect results.

7.2 Write four JavaScript statements that each subtract 1 from variable x, which contains a number.

7.3 Write JavaScript statements to accomplish each of the following tasks:
  a) Assign the product of x and y to z, and decrement the value of x by 1 after the calculation. Use only one statement.
  b) Test whether the value of the variable count is less than 15. If it is, print "Count is less than 15".
  c) Increment the variable x by 1, then add it to the variable total. Use only one statement.
  d) Calculate the product after p is multiplied by variable product, and assign the result to p. Write this statement in two different ways.

7.4 Write a JavaScript statement to accomplish each of the following tasks:
  a) Declare variables product and y.
  b) Assign 5 to variable y.
  c) Assign 1 to variable product.
  d) Multiply variable y with variable product, and assign the result to variable product.
  e) Print "The product is: ", followed by the value of variable product.

7.5 Write a script including statements for variable declaration and assignment that will calculate and print the sum of the integers from 1 to 10. Use the while statement to loop through the calculation and increment statements. The loop should terminate when the value of x becomes 11.

7.6 Determine the value of each variable after the calculation is performed. Assume that, when each statement begins executing, all variables have the integer value 3.

a) `product *= x--;`
b) `quotient /= --x;`

7.7 Identify and correct the *errors* in each of the following segments of code:

a)
```
while ( c <= 5 ) {
    product *= c;
    ++c;
```

b)
```
if ( gender == 1 )
    document.writeln( "Woman" );
else;
    document.writeln( "Man" );
```

7.8 What is wrong with the following `while` repetition statement?
```
while ( z >= 0 )
    sum += z;
```

Answers to Self-Review Exercises

7.1 a) `while, do…while, for, for....in`. b) floating-point. c) Pseudocode. d) logic error, fatal logic error, nonfatal logic error.

7.2
```
x = x -1;
x -= 1;
--x;
x--;
```

7.3
a) `z = x++ + y;`
b)
```
if ( count < 15 )
    document.writeln( "Count is lesser than 15" );
```
c) `total += ++x;`
d)
```
p *= product;
p = p * product;
```

7.4
a) `var product, y;`
b) `y = 5;`
c) `product = 1;`
d) `product *= y; or product = product * 1;`
e) `document.writeln( "The product is: " + product );`

7.5 The solution is as follows:

```
1   <!DOCTYPE html>
2
3   <!-- Exercise 7.5: ex08_05.html -->
4   <html>
5     <head>
6       <meta charset = "utf-8">
7       <title>Sum the Integers from 1 to 10</title>
8       <script>
9         var sum; // stores the total
10        var x; //counter control variable
11
12        x = 1;
13        sum = 0;
14
```

```
15          while ( x <= 10 )
16          {
17             sum += x;
18             ++x;
19          } // end while
20          document.writeln( "The sum is: " + sum );
21       </script>
22    </head><body></body>
23 </html>
```

7.6 a) product = 9, x = 2;
b) quotient = 1.5, x = 2;

7.7 a) Error: Missing the closing right brace of the while body.
Correction: Add closing right brace after the statement ++c;.
b) Error: The ; after else causes a logic error. The second output statement always executes.
Correction: Remove the semicolon after else.

7.8 The value of the variable z is never changed in the body of the while statement. Therefore, if the loop-continuation condition (z >= 0) is true, an *infinite loop* is created. To prevent the creation of the infinite loop, z must be decremented so that it eventually becomes less than 0.

Exercises

7.9 Identify and correct the *errors* in each of the following segments of code. [*Note:* There may be more than one error in each piece of code; unless declarations are present, assume all variables are properly declared and initialized.]

a)
```
if ( age >= 65 );
   document.writeln( "Age greater than or equal to 65" );
else
   document.writeln( "Age is less than 65" );
```

b)
```
var x = 1, total;
while ( x <= 10 )
{
   total += x;
   ++x;
}
```

c)
```
var x = 1;
var total = 0;
While ( x <= 100 )
   total += x;
   ++x;
```

d)
```
var y = 5;
while ( y > 0 )
{
   document.writeln( y );
   ++y;
```

7.10   Without running it, determine what the following script prints:

```
 1    <!DOCTYPE html>
 2
 3    <!-- Exercise 7.10: ex08_10.html -->
 4    <html>
 5       <head>
 6          <meta charset = "utf-8">
 7          <title>Mystery Script</title>
 8          <script type = "text/javascript">
 9          <!--
10             var y;
11             var x = 1;
12             var total = 0;
13
14             while ( x <= 15 )
15             {
16                y = x * x * x;
17                document.writeln( "<p>" + y + "</p>" );
18                total += y;
19                ++x;
20             } // end while
21
22             document.writeln( "<p>Total is " + total + "</p>" );
23             //-->
24          </script>
25       </head><body></body>
26    </html>
```

For Exercises 7.11–7.14, perform each of the following steps:
    a) Read the problem statement.
    b) Formulate the algorithm using pseudocode and top-down, stepwise refinement.
    c) Define the algorithm in JavaScript.
    d) Test, debug and execute the JavaScript.
    e) Process three complete sets of data.

7.11   Drivers are concerned with the mileage obtained by their automobiles. One driver has kept track of several tankfuls of gasoline by recording the number of miles driven and the number of gallons used for each tankful. Develop a script that will take as input the miles driven and gallons used (both as integers) for each tankful. The script should calculate and output HTML5 text that displays the number of miles per gallon obtained for each tankful and prints the combined number of miles per gallon obtained for all tankfuls up to this point. Use prompt dialogs to obtain the data from the user.

7.12   Develop a script that will determine whether a department-store customer has exceeded the credit limit on a charge account. For each customer, the following facts are available:
    a) Account number
    b) Balance at the beginning of the month
    c) Total of all items charged by this customer this month
    d) Total of all credits applied to this customer's account this month
    e) Allowed credit limit
    The script should input each of these facts from a prompt dialog as an integer, calculate the new balance (= *beginning balance* + *charges* − *credits*), display the new balance and determine whether the new balance exceeds the customer's credit limit. For customers whose credit limit is exceeded, the script should output HTML5 text that displays the message "Credit limit exceeded."

7.13   A large company pays its salespeople on a commission basis. The salespeople receive $200 per week, plus 9 percent of their gross sales for that week. For example, a salesperson who sells $5000 worth of merchandise in a week receives $200 plus 9 percent of $5000, or a total of $650. You have been supplied with a list of the items sold by each salesperson. The values of these items are as follows:

```
Item    Value
1       239.99
2       129.75
3       99.95
4       350.89
```

Develop a script that inputs one salesperson's items sold for last week, calculates the salesperson's earnings and outputs HTML5 text that displays the salesperson's earnings.

7.14 Develop a script that will determine the gross pay for each of three employees. The company pays "straight time" for the first 40 hours worked by each employee and pays "time and a half" for all hours worked in excess of 40 hours. You're given a list of the employees of the company, the number of hours each employee worked last week and the hourly rate of each employee. Your script should input this information for each employee, determine the employee's gross pay and output HTML5 text that displays the employee's gross pay. Use prompt dialogs to input the data.

7.15 The process of finding the *largest* value (i.e., the maximum of a group of values) is used frequently in computer applications. For example, a script that determines the winner of a sales contest would input the number of units sold by each salesperson. The salesperson who sells the most units wins the contest. Write a pseudocode algorithm and then a script that inputs a series of 10 single-digit numbers as characters, determines the largest of the numbers and outputs a message that displays the largest number. Your script should use three variables as follows:

a) `counter`: A counter to count to 10 (i.e., to keep track of how many numbers have been input and to determine when all 10 numbers have been processed);

b) `number`: The current digit input to the script;

c) `largest`: The largest number found so far.

7.16 Write a script that uses looping to print the following table of values. Output the results in an HTML5 table. Use CSS to center the data in each column.

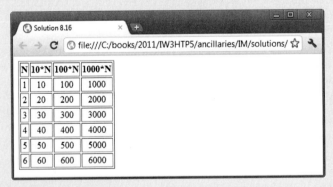

7.17 Using an approach similar to that in Exercise 7.15, find the *two* largest values among the 10 digits entered. [*Note*: You may input each number only once.]

7.18 Without running it, determine what the following script prints:

```
1    <!DOCTYPE html>
2
3    <!-- Exercise 7.18: ex08_18.html -->
4    <html>
5       <head>
```

```
6            <meta charset = "utf-8">
7            <title>Mystery Script</title>
8            <script>
9
10              var row = 10;
11              var column;
12
13              while ( row >= 1 )
14              {
15                 column = 1;
16                 document.writeln( "<p>" );
17
18                 while ( column <= 10 )
19                 {
20                    document.write( row % 2 == 1 ? "<" : ">" );
21                    ++column;
22                 } // end while
23
24                 --row;
25                 document.writeln( "</p>" );
26              } // end while
27
28           </script>
29        </head><body></body>
30     </html>
```

7.19 *(Dangling-Else Problem)* Determine the output for each of the given segments of code when x is 9 and y is 11, and when x is 11 and y is 9. Note that the interpreter ignores the indentation in a script. Also, the JavaScript interpreter always associates an else with the previous if, unless told to do otherwise by the placement of braces ({}). You may not be sure at first glance which if an else matches. This situation is referred to as the "dangling-else" problem. We've eliminated the indentation from the given code to make the problem more challenging. [*Hint:* Apply the indentation conventions you have learned.]

a)
```
if ( x < 10 )
if ( y > 10 )
document.writeln( "<p>*****</p>" );
else
document.writeln( "<p>#####</p>" );
document.writeln( "<p>$$$$$</p>" );
```

b)
```
if ( x < 10 )
{
if ( y > 10 )
document.writeln( "<p>*****</p>" );
}
else
{
document.writeln( "<p>#####</p>" );
document.writeln( "<p>$$$$$</p>" );
}
```

7.20 A palindrome is a number or a text phrase that reads the same backward and forward. For example, each of the following five-digit integers is a palindrome: 12321, 55555, 45554 and 11611. Write a script that reads in a five-digit integer and determines whether it's a palindrome. If the number is not five digits long, display an alert dialog indicating the problem to the user. Allow the user to enter a new value after dismissing the alert dialog. [*Hint:* It's possible to do this exercise with the techniques learned in this chapter. You'll need to use both division and remainder operations to "pick off" each digit.]

7.21   Write a script that outputs HTML5 text that keeps displaying in the browser window the multiples of the integer 2—namely, 2, 4, 8, 16, 32, 64, etc. Your loop should *not terminate* (i.e., you should create an *infinite loop*). What happens when you run this script?

7.22   A company wants to transmit data over the telephone, but it's concerned that its phones may be tapped. All of its data is transmitted as four-digit integers. It has asked you to write a script that will *encrypt* its data so that the data may be transmitted more securely. Your script should read a four-digit integer entered by the user in a prompt dialog and encrypt it as follows: Replace each digit by *(the sum of that digit plus 7) modulus 10*. Then swap the first digit with the third, and swap the second digit with the fourth. Then output HTML5 text that displays the encrypted integer.

7.23   Write a script that inputs an encrypted four-digit integer (from Exercise 7.22) and *decrypts* it to form the original number.

JavaScript: Control Statements II

8

Objectives

In this chapter you'll:

- Learn the essentials of counter-controlled repetition

- Use the for and do...while repetition statements to execute statements in a program repeatedly.

- Perform multiple selection using the switch selection statement.

- Use the break and continue program-control statements

- Use the logical operators to make decisions.

8.1 Introduction

In this chapter, we introduce JavaScript's remaining control statements (with the exception of for...in, which is presented in Chapter 10). In later chapters, you'll see that control statements also are helpful in manipulating objects.

8.2 Essentials of Counter-Controlled Repetition

Counter-controlled repetition requires:

1. The *name* of a control variable (or loop counter).

2. The *initial value* of the control variable.

3. The *increment* (or *decrement*) by which the control variable is modified each time through the loop (also known as *each iteration of the loop*).

4. The condition that tests for the *final value* of the control variable to determine whether looping should continue.

To see the four elements of counter-controlled repetition, consider the simple script shown in Fig. 8.1, which displays lines of HTML5 text that illustrate the seven different font sizes supported by HTML5. The declaration in line 11 *names* the control variable (counter), *reserves* space for it in memory and sets it to an *initial value* of 1. The declaration and initialization of counter could also have been accomplished by these statements:

```
var counter; // declare counter
counter = 1; // initialize counter to 1
```

Lines 15–16 in the while statement write a paragraph element consisting of the string "HTML5 font size" concatenated with the control variable counter's value, which represents the font size. An inline CSS style attribute sets the font-size property to the value of counter concatenated with ex.

Line 17 in the while statement *increments* the control variable by 1 for each iteration of the loop (i.e., each time the body of the loop is performed). The loop-continuation condition (line 13) in the while statement tests whether the value of the control variable is less than or equal to 7 (the *final value* for which the condition is true). Note that the body of this while statement executes even when the control variable is 7. The loop terminates when the control variable exceeds 7 (i.e., counter becomes 8).

```
 I  <!DOCTYPE html>
 2
 3  <!-- Fig. 8.1: WhileCounter.html -->
 4  <!-- Counter-controlled repetition. -->
 5  <html>
 6     <head>
 7        <meta charset = "utf-8">
 8        <title>Counter-Controlled Repetition</title>
 9        <script>
10
11           var counter = 1; // initialization
12
13           while ( counter <= 7 ) // repetition condition
14           {
15              document.writeln( "<p style = 'font-size: " +
16                 counter + "ex'>HTML5 font size " + counter + "ex</p>" );
17              ++counter; // increment
18           } //end while
19
20        </script>
21     </head><body></body>
22  </html>
```

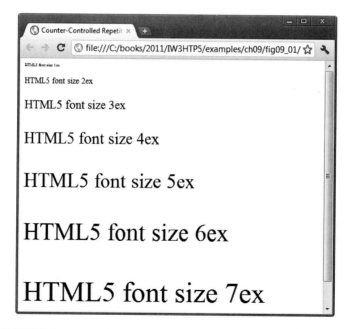

Fig. 8.1 | Counter-controlled repetition.

8.3 for Repetition Statement

The **for repetition statement** conveniently handles all the details of counter-controlled repetition. Figure 8.2 illustrates the power of the for statement by reimplementing the script of Fig. 8.1. The outputs of these scripts are identical.

```
1   <!DOCTYPE html>
2
3   <!-- Fig. 8.2: ForCounter.html -->
4   <!-- Counter-controlled repetition with the for statement. -->
5   <html>
6      <head>
7         <meta charset="utf-8">
8         <title>Counter-Controlled Repetition</title>
9         <script>
10
11            // Initialization, repetition condition and
12            // incrementing are all included in the for
13            // statement header.
14            for ( var counter = 1; counter <= 7; ++counter )
15               document.writeln( "<p style = 'font-size: " +
16                  counter + "ex'>HTML5 font size " + counter + "ex</p>" );
17
18         </script>
19      </head><body></body>
20   </html>
```

Fig. 8.2 | Counter-controlled repetition with the for statement.

When the for statement begins executing (line 14), the control variable counter is declared *and* initialized to 1. Next, the loop-continuation condition, counter <= 7, is checked. The condition contains the *final value* (7) of the control variable. The initial value of counter is 1. Therefore, the condition is satisfied (i.e., true), so the body statement (lines 15–16) writes a paragraph element in the body of the HTML5 document. Then, variable counter is incremented in the expression ++counter and the loop continues execution with the loop-continuation test. The control variable is now equal to 2, so the final value is not exceeded and the program performs the body statement again (i.e., performs the next iteration of the loop). This process continues until the control variable counter becomes 8, at which point the loop-continuation test fails and the repetition terminates.

The program continues by performing the first statement after the for statement. (In this case, the script terminates, because the interpreter reaches the end of the script.)

Figure 8.3 takes a closer look at the for statement at line 14 of Fig. 8.2. The for statement's first line (including the keyword for and everything in parentheses after it) is often called the **for statement header**. Note that the for statement "does it all"—it specifies each of the items needed for counter-controlled repetition with a control variable. Remember that a block is a group of statements enclosed in curly braces that can be placed anywhere that a single statement can be placed, so you can use a block to put multiple statements into the body of a for statement, if necessary.

A Closer Look at the **for** *Statement's Header*
Figure 8.3 uses the loop-continuation condition counter <= 7. If you incorrectly write counter < 7, the loop will execute only *six* times. This is an example of the common logic error called an **off-by-one error**.

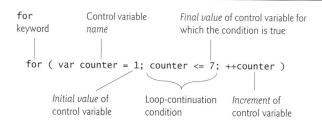

Fig. 8.3 | for statement header components.

*General Format of a **for** Statement*
The general format of the for statement is

> **for** (*initialization*; *loopContinuationTest*; *increment*)
> *statements*

where the *initialization* expression names the loop's control variable and provides its initial value, *loopContinuationTest* is the expression that tests the loop-continuation condition (containing the final value of the control variable for which the condition is true), and *increment* is an expression that increments the control variable.

*Optional Expressions in a **for** Statement Header*
The three expressions in the for statement's header are optional. If *loopContinuationTest* is omitted, the loop-continuation condition is true, thus creating an *infinite loop*. One might omit the *initialization* expression if the control variable is initialized before the loop. One might omit the *increment* expression if the increment is calculated by statements in the loop's body or if no increment is needed. The two semicolons in the header are required.

*Arithmetic Expressions in the **for** Statement's Header*
The initialization, loop-continuation condition and increment portions of a for statement can contain arithmetic expressions. For example, assume that x = 2 and y = 10. If x and y are not modified in the body of the loop, then the statement

```
for ( var j = x; j <= 4 * x * y; j += y / x )
```

is equivalent to the statement

```
for ( var j = 2; j <= 80; j += 5 )
```

Negative Increments
The "increment" of a for statement may be negative, in which case it's really a *decrement* and the loop actually counts *downward*.

Loop-Continuation Condition Initially false
If the loop-continuation condition initially is false, the for statement's body is not performed. Instead, execution proceeds with the statement following the for statement.

Error-Prevention Tip 8.1
Although the value of the control variable can be changed in the body of a for statement, avoid changing it, because doing so can lead to subtle errors.

Flowcharting a **for** *Statement*

The for statement is flowcharted much like the while statement. For example, Fig. 8.4 shows the flowchart of the for statement in lines 14–17 of Fig. 8.2. This flowchart makes it clear that the initialization occurs only once and that incrementing occurs *after* each execution of the body statement. Note that, besides *small circles* and *arrows*, the flowchart contains only *rectangle symbols* and a *diamond symbol*.

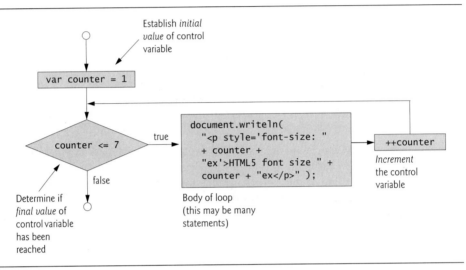

Fig. 8.4 | for repetition statement flowchart.

8.4 Examples Using the for Statement

The examples in this section show methods of varying the control variable in a for statement. In each case, we write the appropriate for header. Note the change in the relational operator for loops that *decrement* the control variable.

a) Vary the control variable from 1 to 100 in increments of 1.

```
for ( var i = 1; i <= 100; ++i )
```

b) Vary the control variable from 100 to 1 in increments of -1 (i.e., *decrements* of 1).

```
for ( var i = 100; i >= 1; --i )
```

c) Vary the control variable from 7 to 77 in steps of 7.

```
for ( var i = 7; i <= 77; i += 7 )
```

d) Vary the control variable from 20 to 2 in steps of -2.

```
for ( var i = 20; i >= 2; i -= 2 )
```

 Common Programming Error 8.1

Not using the proper relational operator in the loop-continuation condition of a loop that counts downward (e.g., using i <= 1 instead of i >= 1 in a loop that counts down to 1) is a logic error.

*Summing Integers with a **for** Statement*
Figure 8.5 uses the for statement to sum the even integers from 2 to 100. Note that the increment expression (line 13) adds 2 to the control variable number *after* the body executes during each iteration of the loop. The loop terminates when number has the value 102 (which is *not* added to the sum), and the script continues executing at line 16.

```
1   <!DOCTYPE html>
2
3   <!-- Fig. 8.5: Sum.html -->
4   <!-- Summation with the for repetition structure. -->
5   <html>
6      <head>
7         <meta charset = "utf-8">
8         <title>Sum the Even Integers from 2 to 100</title>
9         <script>
10
11            var sum = 0;
12
13            for ( var number = 2; number <= 100; number += 2 )
14               sum += number;
15
16            document.writeln( "The sum of the even integers " +
17               "from 2 to 100 is " + sum );
18
19         </script>
20      </head><body></body>
21   </html>
```

Fig. 8.5 | Summation with the for repetition structure.

The body of the for statement in Fig. 8.5 actually could be merged into the rightmost (increment) portion of the for header by using a comma, as follows:

```
for ( var number = 2; number <= 100; sum += number, number += 2)
   ;
```

In this case, the comma represents the **comma operator**, which guarantees that the expression to its left is evaluated before the expression to its right. Similarly, the initialization sum= 0 could be merged into the initialization section of the for statement.

Good Programming Practice 8.1

Although statements preceding a for statement and in the body of a for statement can often be merged into the for header, avoid doing so, because it makes the program more difficult to read.

*Calculating Compound Interest with the **for** Statement*

The next example computes compound interest (compounded yearly) using the for statement. Consider the following problem statement:

> *A person invests $1000.00 in a savings account yielding 5 percent interest. Assuming that all the interest is left on deposit, calculate and print the amount of money in the account at the end of each year for 10 years. Use the following formula to determine the amounts:*
>
> $$a = p\,(1 + r)^{\,n}$$
>
> *where*
>
> > p is the original amount invested (i.e., the principal)
> > r is the annual interest rate
> > n is the number of years
> > a is the amount on deposit at the end of the nth year.

This problem involves a loop that performs the indicated calculation for each of the 10 years the money remains on deposit. Figure 8.6 presents the solution to this problem, displaying the results in a table. Lines 9–18 define an embedded CSS style sheet that formats various aspects of the table. The CSS property **border-collapse** (line 11) with the value collapse indicates that the table's borders should be merged so that there is no extra space between adjacent cells or between cells and the table's border. Lines 13–14 specify the formatting for the table, td and th elements, indicating that they should all have a 1px solid black border and padding of 4px around their contents.

```
1    <!DOCTYPE html>
2
3    <!-- Fig. 8.6: Interest.html -->
4    <!-- Compound interest calculation with a for loop. -->
5    <html>
6       <head>
7          <meta charset = "utf-8">
8          <title>Calculating Compound Interest</title>
9          <style type = "text/css">
10            table        { width: 300px;
11                            border-collapse: collapse;
12                            background-color: lightblue; }
13            table, td, th { border: 1px solid black;
14                            padding: 4px; }
15            th           { text-align: left;
16                            color: white;
17                            background-color: darkblue; }
18            tr.oddrow    { background-color: white; }
19         </style>
20         <script>
21
22            var amount; // current amount of money
23            var principal = 1000.00; // principal amount
24            var rate = 0.05; // interest rate
25
```

Fig. 8.6 | Compound interest calculation with a for loop. (Part 1 of 2.)

```
26       document.writeln("<table>" ); // begin the table
27       document.writeln(
28          "<caption>Calculating Compound Interest</caption>" );
29       document.writeln(
30          "<thead><tr><th>Year</th>" ); // year column heading
31       document.writeln(
32          "<th>Amount on deposit</th>" ); // amount column heading
33       document.writeln( "</tr></thead><tbody>" );
34
35       // output a table row for each year
36       for ( var year = 1; year <= 10; ++year )
37       {
38          amount = principal * Math.pow( 1.0 + rate, year );
39
40          if ( year % 2 !== 0 )
41             document.writeln( "<tr class='oddrow'><td>" + year +
42                "</td><td>" + amount.toFixed(2) + "</td></tr>" );
43          else
44             document.writeln( "<tr><td>" + year +
45                "</td><td>" + amount.toFixed(2) + "</td></tr>" );
46       } //end for
47
48       document.writeln( "</tbody></table>" );
49
50    </script>
51    </head><body></body>
52 </html>
```

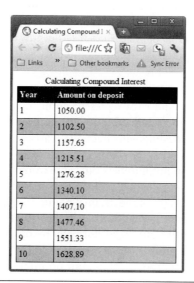

Fig. 8.6 | Compound interest calculation with a `for` loop. (Part 2 of 2.)

Outputting the Beginning of an HTML5 `table`
Lines 22–24 declare three variables and initialize principal to 1000.0 and rate to .05.
Line 26 writes an HTML5 <table> tag, and lines 27–28 write the caption that summa-
rizes the table's content. Lines 29–30 create the table's header section (<thead>), a row

(`<tr>`) and a column heading (`<th>`) containing "Year." Lines 31–32 create a table heading for "`Amount on deposit`", write the closing `</tr>` and `</thead>` tags, and write the opening tag for the body of the table (`<body>`).

Performing the Interest Calculations

The `for` statement (lines 36–46) executes its body 10 times, incrementing control variable year from 1 to 10 (note that year represents *n* in the problem statement). JavaScript does *not* include an exponentiation operator—instead, we use the `Math` object's pow method. `Math.pow(x, y)` calculates the value of x raised to the yth power. Method `Math.pow` takes two numbers as arguments and returns the result. Line 38 performs the calculation using the formula given in the problem statement.

Formatting the `table` Rows

Lines 40–45 write a line of HTML5 markup that creates the next row in the table. If it's an odd-numbered row, line 41 indicates that the row should be formatted with the CSS style class oddrow (defined on line 18)—this allows us to format the background color differently for odd- and even-numbered rows to make the table more readable. The first column is the current year value. The second column displays the value of amount. Line 48 writes the closing `</tbody>` and `</table>` tags after the loop terminates.

Number Method `toFixed`

Lines 42 and 45 introduce the **Number object** and its **toFixed method**. The variable amount contains a numerical value, so JavaScript represents it as a `Number` object. The toFixed method of a `Number` object formats the value by rounding it to the specified number of decimal places. On line 34, `amount.toFixed(2)` outputs the value of amount with *two* decimal places, which is appropriate for dollar amounts.

A Warning about Displaying Rounded Values

Variables `amount`, `principal` and `rate` represent numbers in this script. Remember that JavaScript represents all numbers as floating-point numbers. This feature is convenient in this example, because we're dealing with fractional parts of dollars and need a type that allows decimal points in its values.

Unfortunately, floating-point numbers can cause trouble. Here's a simple example of what can go wrong when using floating-point numbers to represent dollar amounts displayed with two digits to the right of the decimal point: Two dollar amounts stored in the machine could be 14.234 (which would normally be rounded to 14.23 for display as a dollar amount) and 18.673 (which would normally be rounded to 18.67). When these amounts are added, they produce the *internal* sum 32.907, which would normally be rounded to 32.91 for display purposes. Thus your printout could appear as:

```
   14.23
 + 18.67
 -------
   32.91
```

but a person adding the individual numbers as printed would expect the sum to be 32.90. You've been warned!

8.5 switch Multiple-Selection Statement

Previously, we discussed the if single-selection statement and the if...else double-selection statement. Occasionally, an algorithm will contain a series of decisions in which a variable or expression is tested separately for each of the values it may assume, and different actions are taken for each value. JavaScript provides the switch multiple-selection statement to handle such decision making. The script in Fig. 8.7 demonstrates three different CSS list formats determined by the value the user enters.

```
1   <!DOCTYPE html>
2
3   <!-- Fig. 8.7: SwitchTest.html -->
4   <!-- Using the switch multiple-selection statement. -->
5   <html>
6      <head>
7         <meta charset = "utf-8">
8         <title>Switching between HTML5 List Formats</title>
9         <script>
10
11            var choice; // user's choice
12            var startTag; // starting list item tag
13            var endTag; // ending list item tag
14            var validInput = true; // true if input valid else false
15            var listType; // type of list as a string
16
17            choice = window.prompt( "Select a list style:\n" +
18               "1 (numbered), 2 (lettered), 3 (roman numbered)", "1" );
19
20            switch ( choice )
21            {
22               case "1":
23                  startTag = "<ol>";
24                  endTag = "</ol>";
25                  listType = "<h1>Numbered List</h1>";
26                  break;
27               case "2":
28                  startTag = "<ol style = 'list-style-type: upper-alpha'>";
29                  endTag = "</ol>";
30                  listType = "<h1>Lettered List</h1>";
31                  break;
32               case "3":
33                  startTag = "<ol style = 'list-style-type: upper-roman'>";
34                  endTag = "</ol>";
35                  listType = "<h1>Roman Numbered List</h1>";
36                  break;
37               default:
38                  validInput = false;
39                  break;
40            } //end switch
41
42            if ( validInput === true )
43            {
```

Fig. 8.7 | Using the switch multiple-selection statement. (Part 1 of 3.)

```
44               document.writeln( listType + startTag );
45
46               for ( var i = 1; i <= 3; ++i )
47                  document.writeln( "<li>List item " + i + "</li>" );
48
49               document.writeln( endTag );
50            } //end if
51            else
52               document.writeln( "Invalid choice: " + choice );
53
54         </script>
55      </head><body></body>
56   </html>
```

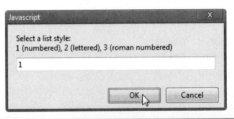

Fig. 8.7 | Using the switch multiple-selection statement. (Part 2 of 3.)

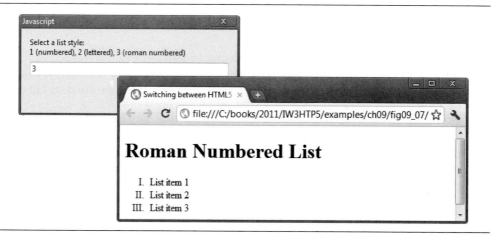

Fig. 8.7 | Using the switch multiple-selection statement. (Part 3 of 3.)

Line 11 declares the variable choice. This variable stores the user's choice, which determines what type of HTML5 ordered list to display. Lines 12–13 declare variables startTag and endTag, which will store the HTML5 tags that will be used to create the list element. Line 14 declares variable validInput and initializes it to true. The script uses this variable to determine whether the user made a valid choice (indicated by the value of true). If a choice is invalid, the script sets validInput to false. Line 15 declares variable listType, which will store an h1 element indicating the list type. This heading appears before the list in the HTML5 document.

Lines 17–18 prompt the user to enter a 1 to display a numbered list, a 2 to display a lettered list and a 3 to display a list with roman numerals. Lines 20–40 define a **switch statement** that assigns to the variables startTag, endTag and listType values based on the value input by the user in the prompt dialog. We create these different lists using the CSS property **list-style-type**, which allows us to set the numbering system for the list. Possible values include decimal (numbers—the *default*), lower-roman (lowercase Roman numerals), upper-roman (uppercase Roman numerals), lower-alpha (lowercase letters), upper-alpha (uppercase letters), and more.

The switch statement consists of a series of **case labels** and an optional **default case** (which is normally placed last). When the flow of control reaches the switch statement, the script evaluates the **controlling expression** (choice in this example) in the parentheses following keyword switch. The value of this expression is compared with the value in each of the case labels, starting with the first case label. Assume that the user entered 2. Remember that the value typed by the user in a prompt dialog is returned as a string. So, the string 2 is compared to the string in each case in the switch statement. If a match occurs (case "2":), the statements for that case execute. For the string 2 (lines 28–31), we set startTag to an opening ol tag with the style property list-style-type set to upper-alpha, set endTag to "</ol>" to indicate the end of an ordered list and set listType to "<h1>Lettered List</h1>". If no match occurs between the controlling expression's value and a case label, the default case executes and sets variable validInput to false.

The **break** statement in line 31 causes program control to proceed with the first statement after the switch statement. The break statement is used because the cases in a switch statement would otherwise run together. If break is not used anywhere in a switch statement, then each time a match occurs in the statement, the statements for that case *and* all the remaining cases execute.

Next, the flow of control continues with the if statement in line 42, which tests whether the variable validInput is true. If so, lines 44–49 write the listType, the startTag, three list items (<li>) and the endTag. Otherwise, the script writes text in the HTML5 document indicating that an invalid choice was made (line 52).

Flowcharting the switch Statement

Each case can have multiple actions (statements). The switch statement is different from others in that braces are *not* required around multiple actions in a case of a switch. The general switch statement (i.e., using a break in each case) is flowcharted in Fig. 8.8.

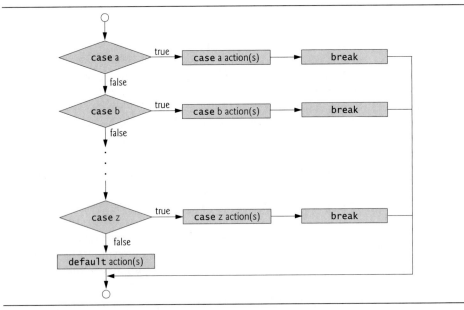

Fig. 8.8 | switch multiple-selection statement.

The flowchart makes it clear that each break statement at the end of a case causes control to exit from the switch statement immediately. The break statement is *not* required for the last case in the switch statement (or the default case, when it appears last), because program control simply continues with the next statement after the switch statement. Having several case labels listed together (e.g., case 1: case 2: with no statements between the cases) simply means that the *same* set of actions is to occur for each of these cases.

8.6 do...while Repetition Statement

The **do...while repetition statement** is similar to the while statement. In the while statement, the loop-continuation test occurs at the *beginning* of the loop, *before* the body of the loop executes. The do...while statement tests the loop-continuation condition *after* the loop body executes—therefore, *the loop body always executes at least once.* When a do...while terminates, execution continues with the statement after the while clause. It's not necessary to use braces in a do...while statement if there's only one statement in the body.

The script in Fig. 8.9 uses a do...while statement to display each of the six different HTML5 heading types (h1 through h6). Line 11 declares control variable counter and initializes it to 1. Upon entering the do...while statement, lines 14–16 write a line of HTML5 text in the document. The value of control variable counter is used to create the starting and ending header tags (e.g., <h1> and </h1>) and to create the line of text to display (e.g., This is an h1 level head). Line 17 increments the counter before the loop-continuation test occurs at the bottom of the loop.

```
1   <!DOCTYPE html>
2
3   <!-- Fig. 8.9: DoWhileTest.html -->
4   <!-- Using the do...while repetition statement. -->
5   <html>
6      <head>
7         <meta charset = "utf-8">
8         <title>Using the do...while Repetition Statement</title>
9         <script>
10
11            var counter = 1;
12
13            do {
14               document.writeln( "<h" + counter + ">This is " +
15                  "an h" + counter + " level head" + "</h" +
16                  counter + ">" );
17               ++counter;
18            } while ( counter <= 6 );
19
20         </script>
21
22      </head><body></body>
23   </html>
```

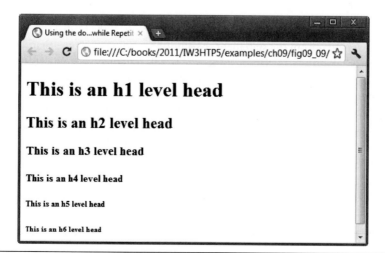

Fig. 8.9 | Using the do...while repetition statement.

Flowcharting the do...while Statement
The do...while flowchart in Fig. 8.10 makes it clear that the loop-continuation test does
not occur until the action executes at least *once*.

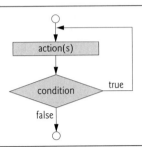

Fig. 8.10 | do...while repetition statement flowchart.

Common Programming Error 8.2
*Infinite loops are caused when the loop-continuation condition never becomes false in a
while, for or do...while statement. To prevent this, make sure that there's not a semicolon immediately after the header of a while or for statement. In a counter-controlled
loop, make sure that the control variable is incremented (or decremented) in the body of
the loop. In a sentinel-controlled loop, the sentinel value should eventually be input.*

8.7 break and continue Statements

In addition to the selection and repetition statements, JavaScript provides the statements
break and **continue** to alter the flow of control. Section 8.5 demonstrated how break can
be used to terminate a switch statement's execution. This section shows how to use break
in repetition statements.

break Statement
The break statement, when executed in a while, for, do...while or switch statement,
causes *immediate exit* from the statement. Execution continues with the first statement after the structure. Figure 8.11 demonstrates the break statement in a for repetition statement. During each iteration of the for statement in lines 13–19, the script writes the value
of count in the HTML5 document. When the if statement in line 15 detects that count
is 5, the break in line 16 executes. This statement terminates the for statement, and the
program proceeds to line 21 (the next statement in sequence immediately after the for
statement), where the script writes the value of count when the loop terminated (i.e., 5).
The loop executes line 18 only *four* times.

```
 I   <!DOCTYPE html>
 2
 3   <!-- Fig. 8.11: BreakTest.html -->
 4   <!-- Using the break statement in a for statement. -->
```

Fig. 8.11 | Using the break statement in a for statement. (Part I of 2.)

```
 5   <html>
 6      <head>
 7         <meta charset = "utf-8">
 8         <title>
 9            Using the break Statement in a for Statement
10         </title>
11         <script>
12
13            for ( var count = 1; count <= 10; ++count )
14            {
15               if ( count == 5 )
16                  break; // break loop only if count == 5
17
18               document.writeln( count + " " );
19            } //end for
20
21            document.writeln(
22               "<p>Broke out of loop at count = " + count + "</p>" );
23
24         </script>
25      </head><body></body>
26   </html>
```

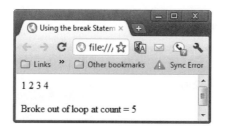

Fig. 8.11 | Using the break statement in a for statement. (Part 2 of 2.)

continue *Statement*

The continue statement, when executed in a while, for or do...while statement, skips the remaining statements in the body of the statement and proceeds with the next iteration of the loop. In while and do...while statements, the loop-continuation test evaluates immediately after the continue statement executes. In for statements, the increment expression executes, then the loop-continuation test evaluates. Improper placement of continue before the increment in a while may result in an *infinite loop*.

Figure 8.12 uses continue in a for statement to skip line 19 if line 16 determines that the value of count is 5. When the continue statement executes, the script skips the remainder of the for statement's body (line 19). Program control continues with the increment of the for statement's control variable (line 14), followed by the loop-continuation test to determine whether the loop should continue executing. Although break and continue execute quickly, you can accomplish what they do with the other control statements, which many programmers feel results in better engineered software.

```
1    <!DOCTYPE html>
2
3    <!-- Fig. 8.12: ContinueTest.html -->
4    <!-- Using the continue statement in a for statement. -->
5    <html>
6       <head>
7          <meta charset = "utf-8">
8          <title>
9             Using the continue Statement in a for Statement
10         </title>
11
12         <script>
13
14            for ( var count = 1; count <= 10; ++count )
15            {
16               if ( count == 5 )
17                  continue; // skip remaining loop code only if count == 5
18
19               document.writeln( count + " " );
20            } //end for
21
22            document.writeln( "<p>Used continue to skip printing 5</p>" );
23
24         </script>
25
26      </head><body></body>
27   </html>
```

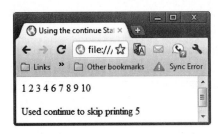

Fig. 8.12 | Using the `continue` statement in a `for` statement.

8.8 Logical Operators

So far, we've studied only **simple conditions** such as count <= 10, total > 1000 and number != sentinelValue. These conditions were expressed in terms of the relational operators >, <, >= and <=, and the equality operators == and !=. Each decision tested *one* condition. To make a decision based on multiple conditions, we performed these tests in separate statements or in nested if or if...else statements.

JavaScript provides **logical operators** that can be used to form more complex conditions by *combining* simple conditions. The logical operators are && **(logical AND)**, || **(logical OR)** and ! **(logical NOT, also called logical negation)**.

&& (Logical AND) Operator

Suppose that, at some point in a program, we wish to ensure that two conditions are *both* true before we choose a certain path of execution. In this case, we can use the logical && operator, as follows:

```
if ( gender == 1 && age >= 65 )
    ++seniorFemales;
```

This if statement contains two simple conditions. The condition gender == 1 might be evaluated to determine, for example, whether a person is a female. The condition age >= 65 is evaluated to determine whether a person is a senior citizen. The if statement then considers the combined condition

```
gender == 1 && age >= 65
```

This condition is true if and only if *both* of the simple conditions are true. If this combined condition is indeed true, the count of seniorFemales is incremented by 1. If either or both of the simple conditions are false, the program skips the incrementing and proceeds to the statement following the if statement. The preceding combined condition can be made more readable by adding redundant parentheses:

```
( gender == 1 ) && ( age >= 65 )
```

The table in Fig. 8.13 summarizes the && operator. The table shows all four possible combinations of false and true values for *expression1* and *expression2*. Such tables are often called **truth tables**. JavaScript evaluates to false or true all expressions that include relational operators, equality operators and/or logical operators.

expression1	expression2	expression1 && expression2
false	false	false
false	true	false
true	false	false
true	true	true

Fig. 8.13 | Truth table for the && (logical AND) operator.

|| (Logical OR) Operator

Now let's consider the || (logical OR) operator. Suppose we wish to ensure that *either or both* of two conditions are true before we choose a certain path of execution. In this case, we use the || operator, as in the following program segment:

```
if ( semesterAverage >= 90 || finalExam >= 90 )
    document.writeln( "Student grade is A" );
```

This statement also contains two simple conditions. The condition semesterAverage >= 90 is evaluated to determine whether the student deserves an "A" in the course because of a solid performance throughout the semester. The condition finalExam >= 90 is evaluated to determine whether the student deserves an "A" in the course because of an outstanding performance on the final exam. The if statement then considers the combined condition

```
semesterAverage >= 90 || finalExam >= 90
```

and awards the student an "A" if either or both of the simple conditions are true. Note that the message "Student grade is A" is *not* printed *only* when *both* of the simple conditions are false. Figure 8.14 is a truth table for the logical OR operator (||).

expression1	expression2	expression1 || expression2
false	false	false
false	true	true
true	false	true
true	true	true

Fig. 8.14 | Truth table for the || (logical OR) operator.

The && operator has a higher precedence than the || operator. Both operators associate from left to right. An expression containing && or || operators is evaluated only until truth or falsity is known. Thus, evaluation of the expression

```
gender == 1 && age >= 65
```

stops immediately if gender is not equal to 1 (i.e., the entire expression is false) and continues if gender is equal to 1 (i.e., the entire expression could still be true if the condition age >= 65 is true). Similarly, the || operator immediately returns true if the first operand is true. This performance feature for evaluation of logical AND and logical OR expressions is called **short-circuit evaluation**.

! (Logical Negation) Operator

JavaScript provides the ! (logical negation) operator to enable you to "reverse" the meaning of a condition (i.e., a true value becomes false, and a false value becomes true). Unlike the logical operators && and ||, which combine two conditions (i.e., they're *binary* operators), the logical negation operator has only a single condition as an operand (i.e., it's a *unary* operator). The logical negation operator is placed before a condition to choose a path of execution if the original condition (without the logical negation operator) is false, as in the following program segment:

```
if ( ! ( grade == sentinelValue ) )
    document.writeln( "The next grade is " + grade );
```

The parentheses around the condition grade == sentinelValue are needed because the logical negation operator has a higher precedence than the equality operator. Figure 8.15 is a truth table for the logical negation operator.

In most cases, you can avoid using logical negation by expressing the condition differently with an appropriate relational or equality operator. For example, the preceding statement may also be written as follows:

```
if ( grade != sentinelValue )
    document.writeln( "The next grade is " + grade );
```

expression	!expression
false	true
true	false

Fig. 8.15 | Truth table for operator ! (logical negation).

Boolean Equivalents of Nonboolean Values

An interesting feature of JavaScript is that most nonboolean values can be converted to a boolean true or false value (if they're being used in a context in which a boolean value is needed). Nonzero numeric values are considered to be true. The numeric value zero is considered to be false. Any string that contains characters is considered to be true. The empty string (i.e., the string containing no characters) is considered to be false. The value null and variables that have been declared but not initialized are considered to be false. All objects (such as the browser's document and window objects and JavaScript's Math object) are considered to be true.

Operator Precedence and Associativity

Figure 8.16 shows the precedence and associativity of the JavaScript operators introduced up to this point. The operators are shown top to bottom in decreasing order of precedence.

Operator						Associativity	Type
++	--	!				right to left	unary
*	/	%				left to right	multiplicative
+	-					left to right	additive
<	<=	>	>=			left to right	relational
==	!=	===	!==			left to right	equality
&&						left to right	logical AND
||						left to right	logical OR
?:						right to left	conditional
=	+=	-=	*=	/=	%=	right to left	assignment

Fig. 8.16 | Precedence and associativity of the operators discussed so far.

8.9 Web Resources

www.deitel.com/javascript/

The Deitel JavaScript Resource Center contains links to some of the best JavaScript resources on the web. There you'll find categorized links to JavaScript tools, code generators, forums, books, libraries, frameworks and more. Also check out the tutorials for all skill levels, from introductory to advanced. Be sure to visit the related Resource Centers on HTML5 (www.deitel.com/HTML5/) and CSS3 (www.deitel.com/css3/).

Summary

Section 8.2 Essentials of Counter-Controlled Repetition
- Counter-controlled repetition requires: the name of a control variable, the initial value of the control variable, the increment (or decrement) by which the control variable is modified each time through the loop, and the condition that tests for the final value of the control variable to determine whether looping should continue.

Section 8.3 **for** Repetition Statement
- The for statement (p. 285) conveniently handles all the details of counter-controlled repetition with a control variable.
- The for statement's first line (including the keyword for and everything in parentheses after it) is often called the for statement header (p. 286).
- You can use a block to put multiple statements into the body of a for statement.
- The for statement takes three expressions: an initialization, a condition and an expression.
- The three expressions in the for statement are optional. The two semicolons in the for statement are required.
- The initialization, loop-continuation condition and increment portions of a for statement can contain arithmetic expressions.
- The "increment" of a for statement may be negative, in which case it's called a decrement and the loop actually counts downward.
- If the loop-continuation condition initially is false, the body of the for statement is not performed. Instead, execution proceeds with the statement following the for statement.

Section 8.4 Examples Using the **for** Statement
- JavaScript does not include an exponentiation operator. Instead, we use the Math object's pow method for this purpose. Math.pow(x, y) calculates the value of x raised to the yth power.
- Floating-point numbers can cause trouble as a result of rounding errors.
- To prevent implicit conversions in comparisons, which can lead to unexpected results, JavaScript provides the strict equals (===) and strict does not equal (!==) operators.

Section 8.5 **switch** Multiple-Selection Statement
- JavaScript provides the switch multiple-selection statement (p. 295), in which a variable or expression is tested separately for each of the values it may assume. Different actions are taken for each value.
- The CSS property list-style-type (p. 295) allows you to set the numbering system for the list. Possible values include decimal (numbers—the default), lower-roman (lowercase roman numerals), upper-roman (uppercase roman numerals), lower-alpha (lowercase letters), upper-alpha (uppercase letters), and more.
- The switch statement consists of a series of case labels and an optional default case (which is normally placed last, p. 295). When the flow of control reaches the switch statement, the script evaluates the controlling expression in the parentheses following keyword switch. The value of this expression is compared with the value in each of the case labels, starting with the first case label (p. 295). If the comparison evaluates to true, the statements after the case label are executed in order until a break statement is reached.
- The break statement is used as the last statement in each case to exit the switch statement immediately.

- Each case can have multiple actions (statements). The switch statement is different from other statements in that braces are not required around multiple actions in a case of a switch.

- The break statement is not required for the last case in the switch statement, because program control automatically continues with the next statement after the switch statement.

- Having several case labels listed together (e.g., case 1: case 2: with no statements between the cases) simply means that the same set of actions is to occur for each case.

Section 8.6 do...while *Repetition Statement*
- The do...while statement (p. 296) tests the loop-continuation condition *after* the loop body executes—therefore, *the loop body always executes at least once.*

Section 8.7 break *and* continue *Statements*
- The break statement, when executed in a repetition statement, causes immediate exit from the statement. Execution continues with the first statement after the repetition statement.

- The continue statement, when executed in a repetition statement, skips the remaining statements in the loop body and proceeds with the next loop iteration. In while and do...while statements, the loop-continuation test evaluates immediately after the continue statement executes. In for statements, the increment expression executes, then the loop-continuation test evaluates.

Section 8.8 *Logical Operators*
- JavaScript provides logical operators that can be used to form more complex conditions by combining simple conditions. The logical operators are && (logical AND; p. 300), || (logical OR; p. 300) and ! (logical NOT, also called logical negation; p. 300).

- The && operator is used to ensure that two conditions are both true before choosing a certain path of execution.

- JavaScript evaluates to false or true all expressions that include relational operators, equality operators and/or logical operators.

- The || (logical OR) operator is used to ensure that either or both of two conditions are true before choosing choose a certain path of execution.

- The && operator has a higher precedence than the || operator. Both operators associate from left to right.

- An expression containing && or || operators is evaluated only until truth or falsity is known. This is called short-circuit evaluation (p. 302).

- JavaScript provides the ! (logical negation) operator to enable you to "reverse" the meaning of a condition (i.e., a true value becomes false, and a false value becomes true).

- The logical negation operator has only a single condition as an operand (i.e., it's a unary operator). The logical negation operator is placed before a condition to evaluate to true if the original condition (without the logical negation operator) is false.

- The logical negation operator has a higher precedence than the equality operator.

- Most nonboolean values can be converted to a boolean true or false value. Nonzero numeric values are considered to be true. The numeric value zero is considered to be false. Any string that contains characters is considered to be true. The empty string (i.e., the string containing no characters) is considered to be false. The value null and variables that have been declared but not initialized are considered to be false. All objects (e.g., the browser's document and window objects and JavaScript's Math object) are considered to be true.

Self-Review Exercises

8.1 State whether each of the following is *true* or *false*. If *false*, explain why.
  a) The `default` case is required in the `switch` selection statement.
  b) The break statement is required in the last case of a `switch` selection statement.
  c) The expression (x > y && a < b) is true if either x > y is true or a < b is true.
  d) An expression containing the | | operator is true if either or both of its operands is true.

8.2 Write a JavaScript statement or a set of statements to accomplish each of the following tasks:
  a) Find the sum of the even integers between 2 and 100. Use a `for` structure. Assume that the variables `sum` and `count` have been declared.
  b) Calculate the value of 4.5 raised to the power of 4. Use the `pow` method.
  c) Print the integers from 5 to 30 by using a `while` loop and the counter variable `i`. Assume that the variable `i` has been declared, but not initialized. Print only five integers per line. [*Hint*: Use the calculation `i % 5`. When the value of this expression is 0, start a new paragraph in the HTML5 document.]
  d) Repeat Exercise 8.2 (c), but using a `for` statement.

8.3 Find the error in each of the following code segments, and explain how to correct it:
  a)
```
x = 5;
while ( x <= 100 );
    ++x;
}
```
  b)
```
switch ( i )
{
    case 10:
        document.writeln( "The number is 10" );
    case 20:
        document.writeln( "The number is 20" );
        default;
        document.writeln( "The number is not 10 or 20" );
        break;
}
```
  c) The following code should print the values from 10 to 20:
```
n = 10;
while ( n < 20 )
    document.writeln( n++ );
```

Answers to Self-Review Exercises

8.1 a) False. The `default` case is optional. If no default action is needed, then there's no need for a `default` case. b) False. The break statement is used to exit the `switch` statement. The break statement is not required for the last case in a `switch` statement. c) False. Both of the relational expressions must be true for the entire expression to be true when using the && operator. d) True.

8.2
  a)
```
sum = 0;
for ( count = 2; count <= 100; count += 2 )
    sum += count;
```
  b) `Math.pow( 4.5, 4 )`
  c)
```
i = 5;
document.writeln( "<p>" );
while ( i <= 30 ) {
```

```
        document.write( i + " " );
        if ( i % 5 == 0 )
            document.write( "</p><p>" );
        i++;
    }
    document.writeln( "<p>" );
d)  document.writeln( "<p>" );
    for ( i = 5; i <= 30; i++ ) {
        document.write( i + " " );
        if ( i % 5 == 0 )
            document.write( "</p><p>" );
    }
    document.writeln( "</p>" );
```

8.3   a) Error: The semicolon inside the `while` condition, and there's a missing left brace.
Correction: Remove the semicolon, and remove the }.

      b) Error: Missing `break` statement in the statements for the second case. Missing end braces.
Correction: Add a `break` statement at the end of the statements for the second `case` and
end braces. Note that this missing statement is not necessarily an error if you want the
statement of `default`: to execute every time the `case 20`: statement executes.

      c) Error: Improper relational operator used in the `while` repetition-continuation condition.
Correction: Use <= rather than =.

Exercises

8.4   Find the error in each of the following segments of code [*Note*: There may be more than
one error]:

      a)
```
While ( x < 100 )
    document.writeln( x );
```

      b) The following code should print whether the integer value is odd or even:
```
switch ( value % 2 ) {
    case 3:
        document.writeln( "Even integer" );
    case 4:
        document.writeln( "Odd integer" );
}
```

      c) The following code should output the even integers from 24 to 2:
```
for ( x = 24; x >= 2; x += 2 )
    document.writeln( x );
```

      d) The following code should output the odd integers from 1 to 99:
```
counter = 1;
do {
    document.writeln( counter );
    counter += 2;
} While ( counter < 99 );
```

8.5   What does the following script do?

```
1   <!DOCTYPE html>
2
3   <!-- Exercise 8.5: ex08_05.html -->
4   <html>
```

```
5      <head>
6        <meta charset = "utf-8">
7        <title>Mystery</title>
8        <script>
9
10         document.writeln( "<table>" );
11
12         for ( var i = 1; i <= 7; i++ )
13         {
14            document.writeln( "<tr>" );
15
16            for ( var j = 1; j <= 5; j++ )
17               document.writeln( "<td>(" + i + ", " + j + ")</td>" );
18
19            document.writeln( "</tr>" );
20         } // end for
21
22         document.writeln( "</table>" );
23
24      </script>
25    </head><body />
26 </html>
```

8.6   Write a script that finds the smallest of several nonnegative integers. Assume that the first value read specifies the number of values to be input from the user.

8.7   Write a script that calculates the product of the odd integers from 1 to 15, then outputs HTML5 text that displays the results.

8.8   Modify the compound interest program in Fig. 8.6 to repeat its steps for interest rates of 5, 6, 7, 8, 9 and 10 percent. Use a for statement to vary the interest rate. Use a separate table for each rate.

8.9   One interesting application of computers is drawing graphs and bar charts (sometimes called histograms). Write a script that reads five numbers between 1 and 30. For each number read, output HTML5 text that displays a line containing the same number of adjacent asterisks. For example, if your program reads the number 7, it should output HTML5 text that displays *******.

8.10   *("The Twelve Days of Christmas" Song)* Write a script that uses repetition and a switch structures to print the song "The Twelve Days of Christmas." You can find the words at the site

    www.santas.net/twelvedaysofchristmas.htm

8.11   A mail-order house sells five different products whose retail prices are as follows: product 1, $2.98; product 2, $4.50; product 3, $9.98; product 4, $4.49; and product 5, $6.87. Write a script that reads a series of pairs of numbers as follows:
    a) Product number
    b) Quantity sold for one day

Your program should use a switch statement to determine each product's retail price and should calculate and output HTML5 that displays the total retail value of all the products sold last week. Use a prompt dialog to obtain the product number and quantity from the user. Use a sentinel-controlled loop to determine when the program should stop looping and display the final results.

8.12   Assume x=1, y=2, z=3 and t=2. What does each of the following statements print? Are the parentheses necessary in each case?
    a) document.writeln(x != 1);
    b) document.writeln(y >= 3);
    c) document.writeln(x == 1 && y < 4);

d) document.writeln(t != 9 & z <= t);

e) document.writeln(y > x || z != t);

f) document.writeln(z - t < y || 2 - y >= z);

g) document.writeln(!(z == t));

8.13 Given the following switch statement:

```
1   switch ( k )
2   {
3     case 1:
4     --k;
5       break;
6     case 2:
7       break;
8     case 3:
9       k++;
10      break;
11    case 4:
12      --k;
13      break;
14    default:
15      k *= 2;
16  }
17
18  x = k++;
```

What values are assigned to x when k has values of 1, 2, 3, 4 and 10?

9

JavaScript: Functions

E pluribus unum.
(One composed of many.)
—Virgil

Call me Ishmael.
—Herman Melville

When you call me that, smile.
—Owen Wister

O! call back yesterday, bid time return.
—William Shakespeare

Objectives

In this chapter you will:

- Construct programs modularly from small pieces called functions.

- Define new functions.

- Pass information between functions.

- Use simulation techniques based on random number generation.

- Use the new HTML5 `audio` and `video` elements

- Use additional global methods.

- See how the visibility of identifiers is limited to specific regions of programs.

9.1 Introduction

Most computer programs that solve real-world problems are much larger than those presented in the first few chapters of this book. Experience has shown that the best way to develop and maintain a large program is to construct it from small, simple pieces, or **modules**. This technique is called **divide and conquer**. This chapter describes many key features of JavaScript that facilitate the design, implementation, operation and maintenance of large scripts.

You'll start using JavaScript to interact programatically with elements in a web page so you can obtain values from elements (such as those in HTML5 `forms`) and place content into web-page elements. We'll also take a brief excursion into simulation techniques with random number generation and develop a version of the casino dice game called craps that uses most of the programming techniques you've used to this point in the book. In the game, we'll also introduce HTML5's new `audio` and `video` elements that enable you to embed audio and video in your web pages. We'll also programmatically interact with the `audio` element to play the audio in response to a user interaction with the game.

9.2 Program Modules in JavaScript

Scripts that you write in JavaScript typically contain of one or more pieces called **functions**. You'll combine new functions that you write with prepackaged functions and objects available in JavaScript. The prepackaged functions that belong to JavaScript objects (such as `Math.pow`, introduced previously) are called **methods**.

JavaScript provides several objects that have a rich collection of methods for performing common mathematical calculations, string manipulations, date and time manipulations, and manipulations of collections of data called arrays. These objects (discussed in Chapters 10–11) make your job easier, because they provide many of the capabilities you'll frequently need.

You can write functions to define tasks that may be used at many points in a script. These are referred to as **programmer-defined functions**. The actual statements defining the function are written only once and are hidden from other functions.

A function is **invoked** (that is, made to perform its designated task) by a **function call**. The function call specifies the function name and provides information (as **arguments**) that the called function needs to perform its task. A common analogy for this structure is the hierarchical form of management. A boss (the **calling function**, or **caller**) asks a worker (the **called function**) to perform a task and **return** (i.e., report back) the results when the task is done. *The boss function does not know how the worker function performs its designated tasks.* The worker may call other worker functions—the boss will be unaware of this. We'll soon see how this *hiding of implementation details* promotes good software engineering. Figure 9.1 shows the boss function communicating with several worker functions in a hierarchical manner. Note that worker1 also acts as a "boss" function to worker4 and worker5, and worker4 and worker5 report back to worker1.

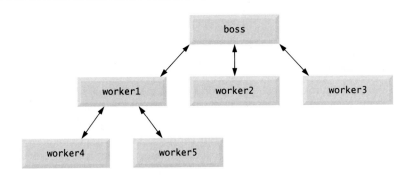

Fig. 9.1 | Hierarchical boss-function/worker-function relationship.

Functions are invoked by writing the name of the function, followed by a left parenthesis, followed by a comma-separated list of zero or more arguments, followed by a right parenthesis. For example, a programmer desiring to convert a string stored in variable inputValue to a floating-point number and add it to variable total might write

```
total += parseFloat( inputValue );
```

When this statement executes, the JavaScript function **parseFloat** converts the string in the inputValue variable to a floating-point value and adds that value to total. Variable inputValue is function parseFloat's argument. Function parseFloat takes a string representation of a floating-point number as an argument and returns the corresponding floating-point numeric value. Function arguments may be constants, variables or expressions.

Methods are called in the same way but require the name of the object to which the method belongs and a dot preceding the method name. For example, we've already seen the syntax document.writeln("Hi there.");. This statement calls the document object's writeln method to output the text.

9.3 Function Definitions

We now consider how you can write your own customized functions and call them in a script.

9.3.1 Programmer-Defined Function square

Consider a script (Fig. 9.2) that uses a function square to calculate the squares of the integers from 1 to 10. [*Note:* We continue to show many examples in which the body element of the HTML5 document is empty and the document is created directly by JavaScript. In this chapter and later ones, we also show examples in which scripts interact with the elements in the body of a document.]

Invoking Function square

The for statement in lines 17–19 outputs HTML5 that displays the results of squaring the integers from 1 to 10. Each iteration of the loop calculates the square of the current value of control variable x and outputs the result by writing a line in the HTML5 document. Function square is invoked, or called, in line 19 with the expression square(x). When program control reaches this expression, the program calls function square (defined in lines 23–26). The parentheses () in line 19 represent the **function-call operator**, which has high precedence. At this point, the program makes a copy of the value of x (the argument) and program control transfers to the first line of the function square's definition (line 23). Function square receives the copy of the value of x and stores it in the *parameter* y. Then

```
 1   <!DOCTYPE html>
 2
 3   <!-- Fig. 9.2: SquareInt.html -->
 4   <!-- Programmer-defined function square. -->
 5   <html>
 6      <head>
 7         <meta charset = "utf-8">
 8         <title>A Programmer-Defined square Function</title>
 9         <style type = "text/css">
10            p { margin: 0; }
11         </style>
12         <script>
13
14            document.writeln( "<h1>Square the numbers from 1 to 10</h1>" );
15
16            // square the numbers from 1 to 10
17            for ( var x = 1; x <= 10; ++x )
18               document.writeln( "<p>The square of " + x + " is " +
19                  square( x ) + "</p>" );
20
21            // The following square function definition's body is executed
22            // only when the function is called explicitly as in line 19
23            function square( y )
24            {
25               return y * y;
26            } // end function square
27
28         </script>
29      </head><body></body> <!-- empty body element -->
30   </html>
```

Fig. 9.2 | Programmer-defined function square. (Part 1 of 2.)

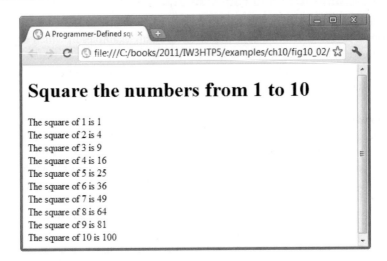

Fig. 9.2 | Programmer-defined function `square`. (Part 2 of 2.)

square calculates y * y. The result is returned (passed back) to the point in line 19 where square was invoked. Lines 18–19 concatenate the string "<p>The square of ", the value of x, the string " is ", the value returned by function square and the string "</p>", and write that line of text into the HTML5 document to create a new paragraph in the page. This process is repeated 10 times.

square Function Definition
The definition of function square (lines 23–26) shows that square expects a single parameter y. Function square uses this name in its body to manipulate the value passed to square from the function call in line 19. The **return statement** in square passes the result of the calculation y * y back to the calling function. JavaScript keyword var is *not* used to declare function parameters (line 25).

Flow of Control in a Script That Contains Functions
In this example, function square follows the rest of the script. When the for statement terminates, program control does *not* flow sequentially into function square. A function must be called *explicitly* for the code in its body to execute. Thus, when the for statement in this example terminates, the script terminates.

General Format of a Function Definition
The general format of a function definition is

```
function function-name( parameter-list )
{
    declarations and statements
}
```

The *function-name* is any valid identifier. The *parameter-list* is a comma-separated list containing the names of the parameters received by the function when it's called (remember that the arguments in the function call are assigned to the corresponding parameters in the function definition). There should be one argument in the function call for each parameter in the function definition. If a function does *not* receive any values, the *parameter-list* is *empty* (i.e., the function name is followed by an empty set of parentheses). The *declarations* and *statements* between the braces form the **function body**.

> ### Common Programming Error 9.1
> *Forgetting to return a value from a function that's supposed to return a value is a logic error.*

Returning Program Control from a Function Definition

There are three ways to return control to the point at which a function was invoked. If the function does *not* return a result, control returns when the program reaches the function-ending right brace (}) or executes the statement

```
return;
```

If the function *does* return a result, the statement

```
return expression;
```

returns the value of *expression* to the caller. When a `return` statement executes, control returns immediately to the point at which the function was invoked.

9.3.2 Programmer-Defined Function `maximum`

The script in our next example (Fig. 9.3) uses a programmer-defined function called `maximum` to determine and return the largest of three floating-point values.]

```
 1   <!DOCTYPE html>
 2
 3   <!-- Fig. 9.3: maximum.html -->
 4   <!-- Programmer-Defined maximum function. -->
 5   <html>
 6      <head>
 7         <meta charset = "utf-8">
 8         <title>Maximum of Three Values</title>
 9         <style type = "text/css">
10            p { margin: 0; }
11         </style>
12         <script>
13
14            var input1 = window.prompt( "Enter first number", "0" );
15            var input2 = window.prompt( "Enter second number", "0" );
16            var input3 = window.prompt( "Enter third number", "0" );
17
18            var value1 = parseFloat( input1 );
19            var value2 = parseFloat( input2 );
20            var value3 = parseFloat( input3 );
```

Fig. 9.3 | Programmer-defined `maximum` function. (Part I of 2.)

```
21
22          var maxValue = maximum( value1, value2, value3 );
23
24          document.writeln( "<p>First number: " + value1 + "</p>" +
25              "<p>Second number: " + value2 + "</p>" +
26              "<p>Third number: " + value3 + "</p>" +
27              "<p>Maximum is: " + maxValue + "</p>" );
28
29          // maximum function definition (called from line 22)
30          function maximum( x, y, z )
31          {
32              return Math.max( x, Math.max( y, z ) );
33          } // end function maximum
34
35      </script>
36   </head><body></body>
37 </html>
```

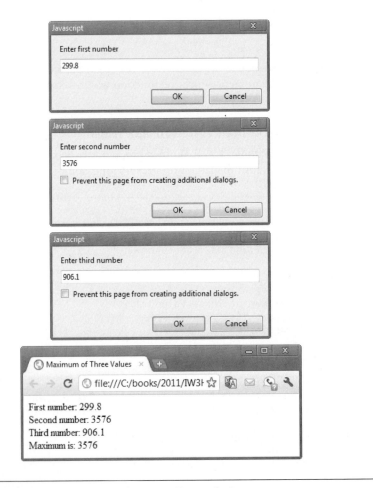

Fig. 9.3 | Programmer-defined `maximum` function. (Part 2 of 2.)

The three floating-point values are input by the user via prompt dialogs (lines 14–16). Lines 18–20 use function parseFloat to convert the strings entered by the user to floating-point values. The statement in line 22 passes the three floating-point values to function maximum (defined in lines 30–33). The function then determines the largest value and returns that value to line 22 by using the return statement (line 32). The returned value is assigned to variable maxValue. Lines 24–27 display the three floating-point values entered by the user and the calculated maxValue.

The first line of the function definition indicates that the function is named maximum and takes parameters x, y and z. Also, the body of the function contains the statement which returns the largest of the three floating-point values, using two calls to the Math object's max method. First, method Math.max is invoked with the values of variables y and z to determine the larger of the two values. Next, the value of variable x and the result of the first call to Math.max are passed to method Math.max. Finally, the result of the second call to Math.max is returned to the point at which maximum was invoked (line 22).

9.4 Notes on Programmer-Defined Functions

All variables declared with the keyword var in function definitions are **local variables**— this means that they can be accessed *only* in the function in which they're defined. A function's parameters are also considered to be local variables.

There are several reasons for modularizing a program with functions. The divide-and-conquer approach makes program development more manageable. Another reason is **software reusability** (i.e., using existing functions as building blocks to create new programs). With good function naming and definition, significant portions of programs can be created from standardized functions rather than built by using customized code. For example, we did not have to define how to convert strings to integers and floating-point numbers— JavaScript already provides function parseInt to convert a string to an integer and function parseFloat to convert a string to a floating-point number. A third reason is to avoid repeating code in a program.

Software Engineering Observation 9.1
If a function's task cannot be expressed concisely, perhaps the function is performing too many different tasks. It's usually best to break such a function into several smaller functions.

Common Programming Error 9.2
Redefining a function parameter as a local variable in the function is a logic error.

Good Programming Practice 9.1
Do not use the same name for an argument passed to a function and the corresponding parameter in the function definition. Using different names avoids ambiguity.

Software Engineering Observation 9.2
To promote software reusability, every function should be limited to performing a single, well-defined task, and the name of the function should describe that task effectively. Such functions make programs easier to write, debug, maintain and modify.

9.5 Random Number Generation

We now take a brief and hopefully entertaining excursion into a popular programming application, namely simulation and game playing. In this section and the next, we develop a carefully structured game-playing program that includes multiple functions. The program uses most of the control statements we've studied.

There's something in the air of a gambling casino that invigorates people, from the high rollers at the plush mahogany-and-felt craps tables to the quarter poppers at the one-armed bandits. It's the **element of chance**, the possibility that luck will convert a pocketful of money into a mountain of wealth. The element of chance can be introduced through the Math object's **random method**.

Consider the following statement:

```
var randomValue = Math.random();
```

Method random generates a floating-point value from 0.0 up to, but *not* including, 1.0. If random truly produces values at random, then every value in that range has an equal **chance** (or **probability**) of being chosen each time random is called.

9.5.1 Scaling and Shifting Random Numbers

The range of values produced directly by random is often different than what is needed in a specific application. For example, a program that simulates coin tossing might require only 0 for heads and 1 for tails. A program that simulates rolling a six-sided die would require random integers in the range 1–6. A program that randomly predicts the next type of spaceship, out of four possibilities, that will fly across the horizon in a video game might require random integers in the range 0–3 or 1–4.

To demonstrate method random, let's develop a program that simulates 30 rolls of a six-sided die and displays the value of each roll (Fig. 9.4). We use the multiplication operator (*) with random as follows (line 21):

```
Math.floor( 1 + Math.random() * 6 )
```

The preceding expression multiplies the result of a call to Math.random() by 6 to produce a value from 0.0 up to, but *not* including, 6.0. This is called *scaling* the range of the random numbers. Next, we add 1 to the result to *shift* the range of numbers to produce a number in the range 1.0 up to, but not including, 7.0. Finally, we use method **Math.floor** to determine the closest integer *not greater than* the argument's value—for example, Math.floor(1.75) is 1 and Math.floor(6.75) is 6. Figure 9.4 confirms that the results are in the range 1 to 6. To add space between the values being displayed, we output each value as an li element in an ordered list. The CSS style in line 11 places a margin of 10 pixels to the right of each li and indicates that they should display inline rather than vertically on the page.

```
1   <!DOCTYPE html>
2
3   <!-- Fig. 9.4: RandomInt.html -->
4   <!-- Random integers, shifting and scaling. -->
5   <html>
6      <head>
```

Fig. 9.4 | Random integers, shifting and scaling. (Part 1 of 2.)

```
7           <meta charset = "utf-8">
8           <title>Shifted and Scaled Random Integers</title>
9           <style type = "text/css">
10             p, ol { margin: 0; }
11             li    { display: inline; margin-right: 10px; }
12          </style>
13          <script>
14
15             var value;
16
17             document.writeln( "<p>Random Numbers</p><ol>" );
18
19             for ( var i = 1; i <= 30; ++i )
20             {
21                value = Math.floor( 1 + Math.random() * 6 );
22                document.writeln( "<li>" + value + "</li>" );
23             } // end for
24
25             document.writeln( "</ol>" );
26
27          </script>
28       </head><body></body>
29    </html>
```

Fig. 9.4 | Random integers, shifting and scaling. (Part 2 of 2.)

9.5.2 Displaying Random Images

Web content that varies randomly can add dynamic, interesting effects to a page. In the next example, we build a **random image generator**—a script that displays four randomly selected die images every time the user clicks a **Roll Dice** button on the page. For the script in Fig. 9.5 to function properly, the directory containing the file RollDice.html must also contain the six die images with the filenames die1.png, die2.png, die3.png, die4.png, die5.png and die6.png—these are included with this chapter's examples.

```
1   <!DOCTYPE html>
2
3   <!-- Fig. 9.5: RollDice.html -->
4   <!-- Random dice image generation using Math.random. -->
5   <html>
6      <head>
7         <meta charset = "utf-8">
```

Fig. 9.5 | Random dice image generation using Math.random. (Part 1 of 3.)

```
8    <title>Random Dice Images</title>
9    <style type = "text/css">
10       li { display: inline; margin-right: 10px; }
11       ul { margin: 0; }
12    </style>
13    <script>
14       // variables used to interact with the i mg elements
15       var die1Image;
16       var die2Image;
17       var die3Image;
18       var die4Image;
19
20       // register button listener and get the img elements
21       function start()
22       {
23          var button = document.getElementById( "rollButton" );
24          button.addEventListener( "click", rollDice, false );
25          die1Image = document.getElementById( "die1" );
26          die2Image = document.getElementById( "die2" );
27          die3Image = document.getElementById( "die3" );
28          die4Image = document.getElementById( "die4" );
29       } // end function rollDice
30
31       // roll the dice
32       function rollDice()
33       {
34          setImage( die1Image );
35          setImage( die2Image );
36          setImage( die3Image );
37          setImage( die4Image );
38       } // end function rollDice
39
40       // set image source for a die
41       function setImage( dieImg )
42       {
43          var dieValue = Math.floor( 1 + Math.random() * 6 );
44          dieImg.setAttribute( "src", "die" + dieValue + ".png" );
45          dieImg.setAttribute( "alt",
46             "die image with " + dieValue + " spot(s)" );
47       } // end function setImage
48
49       window.addEventListener( "load", start, false );
50    </script>
51  </head>
52  <body>
53     <form action = "#">
54        <input id = "rollButton" type = "button" value = "Roll Dice">
55     </form>
56     <ol>
57        <li><img id = "die1" src = "blank.png" alt = "die 1 image"></li>
58        <li><img id = "die2" src = "blank.png" alt = "die 2 image"></li>
59        <li><img id = "die3" src = "blank.png" alt = "die 3 image"></li>
```

Fig. 9.5 | Random dice image generation using `Math.random`. (Part 2 of 3.)

```
60                <li><img id = "die4" src = "blank.png" alt = "die 4 image"></li>
61            </ol>
62        </body>
63    </html>
```

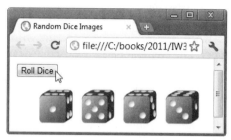

Fig. 9.5 | Random dice image generation using `Math.random`. (Part 3 of 3.)

User Interactions Via Event Handling

Until now, all user interactions with scripts have been through either a `prompt` dialog (in which the user types an input value for the program) or an `alert` dialog (in which a message is displayed to the user, and the user can click **OK** to dismiss the dialog). Although these dialogs are valid ways to receive input from a user and to display messages, they're fairly limited in their capabilities. A `prompt` dialog can obtain only one value at a time from the user, and a message dialog can display only one message.

Inputs are typically received from the user via an HTML5 `form` (such as one in which the user enters name and address information). Outputs are typically displayed to the user in the web page (e.g., the die images in this example). To begin our introduction to more elaborate user interfaces, this program uses an HTML5 `form` (discussed in Chapters 2–3) and a new graphical user interface concept—GUI **event handling**. This is our first example in which the JavaScript executes in response to the user's interaction with an element in a `form`. This interaction causes an *event*. Scripts are often used to respond to user initiated events.

The **body** Element

Before we discuss the script code, consider the body element (lines 52–62) of this document. The elements in the body are used extensively in the script.

The **form** Element

Line 53 begins the definition of an HTML5 `form` element. The HTML5 standard requires that every `form` contain an `action` attribute, but because this form does not post its information to a web server, the string `"#"` is used simply to allow this document to validate. The `#` symbol by itself represents the current page.

The **button input** Element and Event-Driven Programming

Line 54 defines a **button** input element with the `id` `"rollButton"` and containing the value **Roll Dice** which is displayed on the button. As you'll see, this example's script will handle the button's **click event**, which occurs when the user clicks the button. In this example, clicking the button will call function `rollDice`, which we'll discuss shortly.

This style of programming is known as **event-driven programming**—the user *interacts* with an element in the web page, the script is notified of the *event* and the script processes the event. The user's interaction with the GUI "drives" the program. The button click is known as the **event**. The function that's called when an event occurs is known as an **event handler**. When a GUI event occurs in a form, the browser calls the specified event-handling function. Before any event can be processed, each element must know which event-handling function will be called when a particular event occurs. Most HTML5 elements have several different event types. The event model is discussed in detail in Chapter 13.

The img Elements

The four img elements (lines 57–60) will display the four randomly selected dice. Their id attributes (die1, die2, die3 and die4, respectively) can be used to apply CSS styles and to enable script code to refer to these element in the HTML5 document. Because the id attribute, if specified, must have a unique value among all id attributes in the page, JavaScript can reliably refer to any single element via its id attribute. In a moment we'll see how this is done. Each img element displays the image blank.png (an empty white image) when the page first renders.

Specifying a Function to Call When the Browser Finishes Loading a Document

From this point forward, many of our examples will execute a JavaScript function when the document finishes loading in the web browser window. This is accomplished by handling the window object's **load event**. To specify the function to call when an event occurs, you **registering an event handler** for that event. We register the window's load event handler at line 49. Method **addEventListener** is available for every DOM node. The method takes three arguments:

- the first is the name of the event for which we're registering a handler
- the second is the function that will be called to handle the event
- the last argument is typically false—the true value is beyond this book's scope

Line 49 indicates that function start (lines 21–29) should execute as soon as the page finishes loading.

Function start

When the window's load event occurs, function start registers the **Roll Dice** button's click event handler (lines 23–24), which instructs the browser to **listen for events** (click events in particular). If no event handler is specified for the **Roll Dice** button, the script will not respond when the user presses the button. Line 23 uses the document object's **getElementById method**, which, given an HTML5 element's id as an argument, finds the element with the matching id attribute and returns a JavaScript object representing the element. This object allows the script to programmatically interact with the corresponding element in the web page. For example, line 24 uses the object representing the button to call function addEventListener—in this case, to indicate that function rollDice should be called when the button's click event occurs. Lines 25–28 get the objects representing the four img elements in lines 57–60 and assign them to the script variables in declared in lines 15–18.

Function `rollDice`

The user clicks the **Roll Dice** button to roll the dice. This event invokes function `rollDice` (lines 32–38) in the script. Function `rollDice` takes no arguments, so it has an empty parameter list. Lines 34–37 call function `setImage` (lines 41–47) to randomly select and set the image for a specified `img` element.

Function `setImage`

Function `setImage` (lines 41–47) receives one parameter (`dieImg`) that represents the specific `img` element in which to display a randomly selected image. Line 43 picks a random integer from 1 to 6. Line 44 demonstrates how to access an `img` element's `src` attribute programmatically in JavaScript. Each JavaScript object that represents an element of the HTML5 document has a **setAttribute** method that allows you to change the values of most of the HTML5 element's attributes. In this case, we change the `src` attribute of the `img` element referred to by `dieImg`. The `src` attribute specifies the location of the image to display. We set the `src` to a concatenated string containing the word `"die"`, a randomly generated integer from 1 to 6 and the file extension `".png"` to complete the image file name. Thus, the script dynamically sets the `img` element's `src` attribute to the name of one of the image files in the current directory.

Continuing to Roll the Dice

The program then waits for the user to click the **Roll Dice** button again. Each time the user does so, the program calls `rollDice`, which repeatedly calls `setImage` to display new die images.

9.5.3 Rolling Dice Repeatedly and Displaying Statistics

To show that the random values representing the dice occur with approximately equal likelihood, let's allow the user to roll 12 dice at a time and keep statistics showing the number of times each face occurs and the percentage of the time each face is rolled (Fig. 9.6). This example is similar to the one in Fig. 9.5, so we'll focus only on the new features.

Script Variables

Lines 22–28 declare and initialize counter variables to keep track of the number of times each of the six die values appears and the total number of dice rolled. Because these variables are declared outside the script's functions, they're accessible to all the functions in the script.

```
1    <!DOCTYPE html>
2
3    <!-- Fig. 9.6: RollDice.html -->
4    <!-- Rolling 12 dice and displaying frequencies. -->
5    <html>
6       <head>
7          <meta charset = "utf-8">
8          <title>Die Rolling Frequencies</title>
9          <style type = "text/css">
10            img              { margin-right: 10px; }
```

Fig. 9.6 | Rolling 12 dice and displaying frequencies. (Part 1 of 4.)

```
11              table           { width: 200px;
12                                  border-collapse: collapse;
13                                  background-color: lightblue; }
14              table, td, th { border: 1px solid black;
15                                  padding: 4px;
16                                  margin-top: 20px; }
17              th               { text-align: left;
18                                  color: white;
19                                  background-color: darkblue; }
20        </style>
21        <script>
22            var frequency1 = 0;
23            var frequency2 = 0;
24            var frequency3 = 0;
25            var frequency4 = 0;
26            var frequency5 = 0;
27            var frequency6 = 0;
28            var totalDice = 0;
29
30            // register button event handler
31            function start()
32            {
33                var button = document.getElementById( "rollButton" );
34                button.addEventListener( "click", rollDice, false );
35            } // end function start
36
37            // roll the dice
38            function rollDice()
39            {
40                var face;  // face rolled
41
42                // loop to roll die 12 times
43                for ( var i = 1; i <= 12; ++i )
44                {
45                    face = Math.floor( 1 + Math.random() * 6 );
46                    tallyRolls( face ); // increment a frequency counter
47                    setImage( i, face ); // display appropriate die image
48                    ++totalDice; // increment total
49                } // end die rolling loop
50
51                updateFrequencyTable();
52            } // end function rollDice
53
54            // increment appropriate frequency counter
55            function tallyRolls( face )
56            {
57                switch ( face )
58                {
59                    case 1:
60                        ++frequency1;
61                        break;
```

Fig. 9.6 | Rolling 12 dice and displaying frequencies. (Part 2 of 4.)

```
 62                case 2:
 63                    ++frequency2;
 64                    break;
 65                case 3:
 66                    ++frequency3;
 67                    break;
 68                case 4:
 69                    ++frequency4;
 70                    break;
 71                case 5:
 72                    ++frequency5;
 73                    break;
 74                case 6:
 75                    ++frequency6;
 76                    break;
 77             } // end switch
 78          } // end function tallyRolls
 79
 80          // set image source for a die
 81          function setImage( dieNumber, face )
 82          {
 83             var dieImg = document.getElementById( "die" + dieNumber );
 84             dieImg.setAttribute( "src", "die" + face + ".png" );
 85             dieImg.setAttribute( "alt", "die with " + face + " spot(s)" );
 86          } // end function setImage
 87
 88          // update frequency table in the page
 89          function updateFrequencyTable()
 90          {
 91             var tableDiv = document.getElementById( "frequencyTableDiv" );
 92
 93             tableDiv.innerHTML = "<table>" +
 94                "<caption>Die Rolling Frequencies</caption>" +
 95                "<thead><th>Face</th><th>Frequency</th>" +
 96                "<th>Percent</th></thead>" +
 97                "<tbody><tr><td>1</td><td>" + frequency1 + "</td><td>" +
 98                formatPercent(frequency1 / totalDice) + "</td></tr>" +
 99                "<tr><td>2</td><td>" + frequency2 + "</td><td>" +
100                formatPercent(frequency2 / totalDice)+ "</td></tr>" +
101                "<tr><td>3</td><td>" + frequency3 + "</td><td>" +
102                formatPercent(frequency3 / totalDice) + "</td></tr>" +
103                "<tr><td>4</td><td>" + frequency4 + "</td><td>" +
104                formatPercent(frequency4 / totalDice) + "</td></tr>" +
105                "<tr><td>5</td><td>" + frequency5 + "</td><td>" +
106                formatPercent(frequency5 / totalDice) + "</td></tr>" +
107                "<tr><td>6</td><td>" + frequency6 + "</td><td>" +
108                formatPercent(frequency6 / totalDice) + "</td></tr>" +
109                "</tbody></table>";
110          } // end function updateFrequencyTable
111
112          // format percentage
113          function formatPercent( value )
114          {
```

Fig. 9.6 | Rolling 12 dice and displaying frequencies. (Part 3 of 4.)

```
115                 value *= 100;
116                 return value.toFixed(2);
117             } // end function formatPercent
118
119             window.addEventListener( "load", start, false );
120         </script>
121     </head>
122     <body>
123         <p><img id = "die1" src = "blank.png" alt = "die 1 image">
124             <img id = "die2" src = "blank.png" alt = "die 2 image">
125             <img id = "die3" src = "blank.png" alt = "die 3 image">
126             <img id = "die4" src = "blank.png" alt = "die 4 image">
127             <img id = "die5" src = "blank.png" alt = "die 5 image">
128             <img id = "die6" src = "blank.png" alt = "die 6 image"></p>
129         <p><img id = "die7" src = "blank.png" alt = "die 7 image">
130             <img id = "die8" src = "blank.png" alt = "die 8 image">
131             <img id = "die9" src = "blank.png" alt = "die 9 image">
132             <img id = "die10" src = "blank.png" alt = "die 10 image">
133             <img id = "die11" src = "blank.png" alt = "die 11 image">
134             <img id = "die12" src = "blank.png" alt = "die 12 image"></p>
135         <form action = "#">
136             <input id = "rollButton" type = "button" value = "Roll Dice">
137         </form>
138         <div id = "frequencyTableDiv"></div>
139     </body>
140 </html>
```

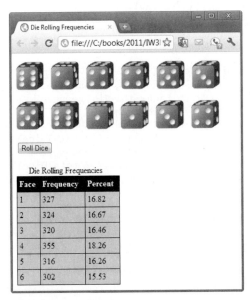

Fig. 9.6 | Rolling 12 dice and displaying frequencies. (Part 4 of 4.)

Function rollDice

As in Fig. 9.5, when the user presses the **Roll Dice** button, function rollDice (lines 38–52) is called. This function calls functions tallyRolls and setImage for each of the twelve img elements in the document (lines 123–134), then calls function updateFrequen-cyTable to display the number of times each die face appeared and the percentage of total dice rolled.

Function *tallyRolls*
Function tallyRolls (lines 55–78) contains a switch statement that uses the randomly chosen face value as its controlling expression. Based on the value of face, the program increments one of the six counter variables during each iteration of the loop. No default case is provided in this switch statement, because the statement in line 45 produces only the values 1, 2, 3, 4, 5 and 6. In this example, the default case would never execute. After we study arrays in Chapter 10, we discuss an elegant way to replace the entire switch statement in this program with a *single* line of code.

Function *setImage*
Function setImage (lines 81–86) sets the image source and alt text for the specified img element.

Function *updateFrequencyTable*
Function updateFrequencyTable (lines 89–110) creates a table and places it in the div element at line 131 in the document's body. Line 91 gets the object representing that div and assigns it to the local variable tableDiv. Lines 93–109 build a string representing the table and assign it to the tableDiv object's **innerHTML property**, which places HTML5 code into the element that tableDiv represents and allows the browser to render that HTML5 in the element. Each time we assign HTML markup to an element's innerHTML property, the tableDiv's content is completely replaced with the content of the string.

Function *formatPercent*
Function updateFrequencyTable calls function formatPercent (lines 113–117) to format values as percentages with two digits to the right of the decimal point. The function simply multiplies the value it receives by 100, then returns the value after calling its to-Fixed method with the argument 2, so that the number has two digits of precision to the right of the decimal point.

Generalized Scaling and Shifting of Random Values
The values returned by random are always in the range

```
0.0 ≤ Math.random() < 1.0
```

Previously, we demonstrated the statement

```
face = Math.floor( 1 + Math.random() * 6 );
```

which simulates the rolling of a six-sided die. This statement always assigns an integer (at random) to variable face, in the range $1 \leq$ face ≤ 6. Note that the width of this range (i.e., the number of consecutive integers in the range) is 6, and the starting number in the range is 1. Referring to the preceding statement, we see that the width of the range is determined by the number used to scale random with the multiplication operator (6 in the preceding statement) and that the starting number of the range is equal to the number (1 in the preceding statement) added to Math.random() * 6. We can generalize this result as

```
face = Math.floor( a + Math.random() * b );
```

where a is the **shifting value** (which is equal to the first number in the desired range of consecutive integers) and b is the **scaling factor** (which is equal to the width of the desired range of consecutive integers).

9.6 Example: Game of Chance; Introducing the HTML5 audio and video Elements

One of the most popular games of chance is a dice game known as craps, which is played in casinos and back alleys throughout the world. The rules of the game are straightforward:

> *A player rolls two dice. Each die has six faces. These faces contain one, two, three, four, five and six spots, respectively. After the dice have come to rest, the sum of the spots on the two upward faces is calculated. If the sum is 7 or 11 on the first throw, the player wins. If the sum is 2, 3 or 12 on the first throw (called "craps"), the player loses (i.e., the "house" wins). If the sum is 4, 5, 6, 8, 9 or 10 on the first throw, that sum becomes the player's "point." To win, you must continue rolling the dice until you "make your point" (i.e., roll your point value). You lose by rolling a 7 before making the point.*

The script in Fig. 9.7 simulates the game of craps. Note that the player must roll *two* dice on the first and all subsequent rolls. When you load this document, you can click the link at the top of the page to browse a separate document (Fig. 9.8) containing a video that explains the basic rules of the game. To start a game, click the **Play** button. A message below the button displays the game's status after each roll. If you don't win or lose on the first roll, click the **Roll** button to roll again. [*Note:* This example uses some features that, at the time of this writing, worked only in Chrome, Safari and Internet Explorer 9.]

The body Element
Before we discuss the script code, we discuss the body element (lines 150–177) of this document. The elements in the body are used extensively in the script.

```
1   <!DOCTYPE html>
2
3   <!-- Fig. 9.7: Craps.html -->
4   <!-- Craps game simulation. -->
5   <html>
6      <head>
7         <meta charset = "utf-8">
8         <title>Craps Game Simulation</title>
9         <style type = "text/css">
10           p.red   { color: red }
11           img     { width: 54px; height: 54px; }
12           div     { border: 5px ridge royalblue;
13                     padding: 10px; width: 120px;
14                     margin-bottom: 10px; }
15           .point { margin: 0px; }
16        </style>
17        <script>
```

Fig. 9.7 | Craps game simulation. (Part 1 of 6.)

```
18          // variables used to refer to page elements
19          var pointDie1Img; // refers to first die point img
20          var pointDie2Img; // refers to second die point img
21          var rollDie1Img; // refers to first die roll img
22          var rollDie2Img; // refers to second die roll img
23          var messages; // refers to "messages" paragraph
24          var playButton; // refers to Play button
25          var rollButton; // refers to Roll button
26          var dicerolling; // refers to audio clip for dice
27
28          // other variables used in program
29          var myPoint; // point if no win/loss on first roll
30          var die1Value; // value of first die in current roll
31          var die2Value; // value of second die in current roll
32
33          // starts a new game
34          function startGame()
35          {
36             // get the page elements that we'll interact with
37             dicerolling = document.getElementById( "dicerolling" );
38             pointDie1Img = document.getElementById( "pointDie1" );
39             pointDie2Img = document.getElementById( "pointDie2" );
40             rollDie1Img = document.getElementById( "rollDie1" );
41             rollDie2Img = document.getElementById( "rollDie2" );
42             messages = document.getElementById( "messages" );
43             playButton = document.getElementById( "play" );
44             rollButton = document.getElementById( "roll" );
45
46             // prepare the GUI
47             rollButton.disabled = true; // disable rollButton
48             setImage( pointDie1Img ); // reset image for new game
49             setImage( pointDie2Img ); // reset image for new game
50             setImage( rollDie1Img ); // reset image for new game
51             setImage( rollDie2Img ); // reset image for new game
52
53             myPoint = 0; // there is currently no point
54             firstRoll(); // roll the dice to start the game
55          } // end function startGame
56
57          // perform first roll of the game
58          function firstRoll()
59          {
60             var sumOfDice = rollDice(); // first roll of the dice
61
62             // determine if the user won, lost or must continue rolling
63             switch (sumOfDice)
64             {
65                case 7: case 11: // win on first roll
66                   messages.innerHTML =
67                      "You Win!!! Click Play to play again.";
68                   break;
```

Fig. 9.7 | Craps game simulation. (Part 2 of 6.)

```
69              case 2: case 3: case 12: // lose on first roll
70                  messages.innerHTML =
71                      "Sorry. You Lose. Click Play to play again.";
72                  break;
73              default: // remember point
74                  myPoint = sumOfDice;
75                  setImage( pointDie1Img, die1Value );
76                  setImage( pointDie2Img, die2Value );
77                  messages.innerHTML = "Roll Again!";
78                  rollButton.disabled = false; // enable rollButton
79                  playButton.disabled = true; // disable playButton
80                  break;
81          } // end switch
82      } // end function firstRoll
83
84      // called for subsequent rolls of the dice
85      function rollAgain()
86      {
87          var sumOfDice = rollDice(); // subsequent roll of the dice
88
89          if (sumOfDice == myPoint)
90          {
91              messages.innerHTML =
92                  "You Win!!! Click Play to play again.";
93              rollButton.disabled = true; // disable rollButton
94              playButton.disabled = false; // enable playButton
95          } // end if
96          else if (sumOfDice == 7) // craps
97          {
98              messages.innerHTML =
99                  "Sorry. You Lose. Click Play to play again.";
100             rollButton.disabled = true; // disable rollButton
101             playButton.disabled = false; // enable playButton
102         } // end else if
103     } // end function rollAgain
104
105     // roll the dice
106     function rollDice()
107     {
108         dicerolling.play(); // play dice rolling sound
109
110         // clear old die images while rolling sound plays
111         die1Value = NaN;
112         die2Value = NaN;
113         showDice();
114
115         die1Value = Math.floor(1 + Math.random() * 6);
116         die2Value = Math.floor(1 + Math.random() * 6);
117         return die1Value + die2Value;
118     } // end function rollDice
119
```

Fig. 9.7 | Craps game simulation. (Part 3 of 6.)

```
120        // display rolled dice
121        function showDice()
122        {
123           setImage( rollDie1Img, die1Value );
124           setImage( rollDie2Img, die2Value );
125        } // end function showDice
126
127        // set image source for a die
128        function setImage( dieImg, dieValue )
129        {
130           if ( isFinite( dieValue ) )
131              dieImg.src = "die" + dieValue + ".png";
132           else
133              dieImg.src = "blank.png";
134        } // end function setImage
135
136        // register event liseners
137        function start()
138        {
139           var playButton = document.getElementById( "play" );
140           playButton.addEventListener( "click", startGame, false );
141           var rollButton = document.getElementById( "roll" );
142           rollButton.addEventListener( "click", rollAgain, false );
143           var diceSound = document.getElementById( "dicerolling" );
144           diceSound.addEventListener( "ended", showDice, false );
145        } // end function start
146
147        window.addEventListener( "load", start, false );
148     </script>
149  </head>
150  <body>
151     <audio id = "dicerolling" preload = "auto">
152        <source src = "http://test.deitel.com/dicerolling.mp3"
153           type = "audio/mpeg">
154        <source src = "http://test.deitel.com/dicerolling.ogg"
155           type = "audio/ogg">
156        Browser does not support audio tag</audio>
157     <p><a href = "CrapsRules.html">Click here for a short video
158        explaining the basic Craps rules</a></p>
159     <div id = "pointDiv">
160        <p class = "point">Point is:</p>
161        <img id = "pointDie1" src = "blank.png"
162           alt = "Die 1 of Point Value">
163        <img id = "pointDie2" src = "blank.png"
164           alt = "Die 2 of Point Value">
165     </div>
166     <div class = "rollDiv">
167        <img id = "rollDie1" src = "blank.png"
168           alt = "Die 1 of Roll Value">
169        <img id = "rollDie2" src = "blank.png"
170           alt = "Die 2 of Roll Value">
171     </div>
```

Fig. 9.7 | Craps game simulation. (Part 4 of 6.)

```
172          <form action = "#">
173             <input id = "play" type = "button" value = "Play">
174             <input id = "roll" type = "button" value = "Roll">
175          </form>
176          <p id = "messages" class = "red">Click Play to start the game</p>
177       </body>
178    </html>
```

a) Win on the first roll. In this case, the `pointDiv` does not show any dice and the **Roll** button remains disabled.

b) Loss on the first roll. In this case, the `pointDiv` does not show any dice and the **Roll** button remains disabled.

c) First roll is a 5, so the user's point is 5. The **Play** button is disabled and the **Roll** button is enabled.

d) User won on a subsequent roll. The **Play** button is enabled and the **Roll** button is disabled.

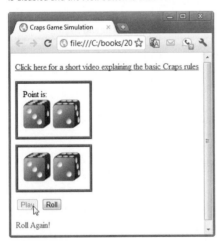

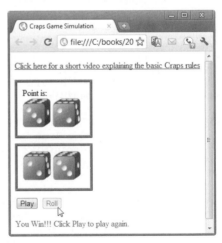

Fig. 9.7 | Craps game simulation. (Part 5 of 6.)

e) First roll is a 6, so the user's point is 6. The **Play** button is disabled and the **Roll** button is enabled.

f) User lost on a subsequent roll. The **Play** button is enabled and the **Roll** button is disabled.

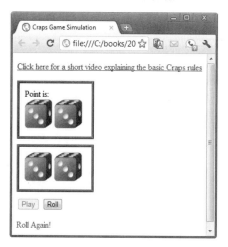

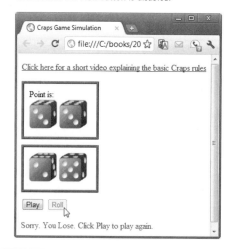

Fig. 9.7 | Craps game simulation. (Part 6 of 6.)

The HTML5 *audio* Element

Line 151–156 define an HTML5 **audio element**, which is used to embed audio into a web page. We specify an id for the element, so that we can *programmatically* control when the audio clip plays, based on the user's interactions with the game. Setting the **preload** attribute to "auto" indicates to the browser that it should consider downloading the audio clip so that it's ready to be played when the game needs it. Under certain conditions the browser can ignore this attribute—for example, if the user is on a low-bandwidth Internet connection.

Not all browsers support the same audio file formats, but most support MP3, OGG and/or WAV format. All of the browsers we tested in this book support MP3, OGG or both. For this reason, nested in the audio element are *two* **source** elements specifying the locations of the audio clip in MP3 and OGG formats, respectively. Each source element specifies a src and a type attribute. The src attribute specifies the location of the audio clip. The type attribute specifies the clip's MIME type—audio/mpeg for the MP3 clip and audio/ogg for the OGG clip (WAV would be audio/x-wav; MIME types for these and other formats can be found online). When a web browser that supports the audio element encounters the source elements, it will chose the first audio source that represents one of the browser's supported formats. If the browser does not support the audio element, the text in line 156 will be displayed.

We used the online audio-file converter at

```
media.io
```

to convert our audio clip to other formats. Many other online and downloadable file converters are available on the web.

The Link to the `CrapsRules.html` Page
Lines 157–158 display a link to a separate web page in which we use an HTML5 `video` element to display a short video that explains the basic rules for the game of Craps. We discuss this web page at the end of this section.

`pointDiv` and `rollDiv`
The `div` elements at lines 159–171 contain the `img` elements in which we display die images representing the user's point and the current roll of the dice, respectively. Each `img` element has an `id` attribute so that we can interact with it programmatically. Because the `id` attribute, if specified, must have a unique value, JavaScript can reliably refer to any single element via its `id` attribute.

The `form` Element
Lines 172–175 define an HTML5 `form` element containing two `button` `input` elements. Each `button`'s `click` event handler indicates the action to take when the user clicks the corresponding button. In this example, clicking the **Play** button causes a call to function `startGame` and clicking the **Roll** button causes a call to function `rollAgain`. Initially, the **Roll** button is disabled, which prevents the user from initiating an event with this button.

The `p` Element
Line 176 defines a p element in which the game displays status messages to the user.

The Script Variables
Lines 19–31 create variables that are used throughout the script. Recall that because these are declared outside the script's functions, they're accessible to all the functions in the script. The variables in lines 19–26 are used to interact with various page elements in the script. Variable `myPoint` (line 29) stores the point if the player does not win or lose on the first roll. Variables `die1Value` and `die2Value` keep track of the die values for the current roll.

Function `startGame`
The user clicks the **Play** button to start the game and perform the first roll of the dice. This event invokes function `startGame` (lines 34–55), which takes no arguments. Line 37–44 use the `document` object's `getElementById` method to get the page elements that the script interacts with programmatically.

The **Roll** button should be enabled *only* if the user does not win or lose on the first roll. For this reason, line 47 disables the **Roll** button by setting its **disabled property** to `true`. Each `input` element has a `disabled` property.

Lines 48–51 call function `setImage` (defined in lines 128–134) to display the image `blank.png` for the `img` elements in the `pointDiv` and `rollDiv`. We'll replace `blank.png` with die images throughout the game as necessary.

Finally, line 53 sets `myPoint` to 0, because there can be a point value only *after* the first roll of the dice, and line 54 calls method `firstRoll` (defined in lines 58–82) to perform the first roll of the dice.

Function `firstRoll`
Function `firstRoll` (lines 58–82) calls function `rollDice` (defined in lines 106–118) to roll the dice and get their sum, which is stored in the local variable `sumOfDice`. Because

this variable is defined *inside* the firstRoll function, it's accessible only inside that function. Next, the switch statement (lines 63–81) determines whether the game is won or lost, or whether it should continue with another roll. If the user won or lost, lines 66–67 or 70–71 display an appropriate message in the messages paragraph (p) element with the object's innerHTML property. After the first roll, if the game is not over, the value of local variable sumOfDice is saved in myPoint (line 74), the images for the rolled die values are displayed (lines 75–76) in the pointDiv and the message "Roll Again!" is displayed in the displayed in the messages paragraph (p) element. Also, lines 78–79 enable the **Roll** button and disable the **Play** button, respectively. Function firstRoll takes no arguments, so it has an empty parameter list.

Software Engineering Observation 9.3

Variables declared inside the body of a function are known only in that function. If the same variable names are used elsewhere in the program, they'll be entirely separate variables in memory.

Error-Prevention Tip 9.1

Initializing variables when they're declared in functions helps avoid incorrect results and interpreter messages warning of uninitialized data.

Function rollAgain

The user clicks the **Roll** button to continue rolling if the game was not won or lost on the first roll. Clicking this button calls the rollAgain function (lines 85–103), which takes no arguments. Line 87 calls function rollDice and stores the sum locally in sumOfDice, then lines 89–102 determine whether the user won or lost on the current roll, display an appropriate message in the messages paragraph (p) element, disable the **Roll** and enable the **Play** button. In either case, the user can now click **Play** to play another game. If the user did not win or lose, the program waits for the user to click the **Roll** button again. Each time the user clicks **Roll**, function rollAgain executes and, in turn, calls the rollDice function to produce a new value for sumOfDice.

Function rollDice

We define a function rollDice (lines 106–118), which takes no arguments, to roll the dice and compute their sum. Function rollDice is defined once but is called from lines 60 and 87 in the program. The function returns the sum of the two dice (line 117). Line 108 *plays* the audio clip declared at lines 151–165 by calling its **play method**, which plays the clip once. As you'll soon see, we use the audio element's **ended event**, which occurs when the clip finishes playing, to indicate when to display the new die images. Lines 111–112 set variables die1Value and die2Value to NaN so that the call to showDice (line 113) can display the blank.png image while the dice sound is playing. Lines 115–116 pick two random values in the range 1 to 6 and assign them to the script variables die1Value and die2Value, respectively.

Function showDice

Function showDice (lines 121–125) is called when the dice rolling sound finishes playing. At this point, lines 123–124 display the die images representing the die values that were rolled in function rollDice.

Function `setImage`

Function `setImage` (lines 128–134) takes two arguments—the `img` element that will display an image and the value of a die to specify which die image to display. You might have noticed that we called this function with *one* argument in lines 48–51 and with *two* arguments in lines 75–76 and 123–124. If you call `setImage` with only one argument, the second parameter's value will be *undefined*. In this case, we display the image `blank.png` (line 133). Line 130 uses global JavaScript function **`isFinite`** to determine whether the parameter `dieValue` contains a number—if it does, we'll display the die image that corresponds to that number (line 131). Function `isFinite` returns `true` only if its argument is a valid number in the range supported by JavaScript. You can learn more about JavaScript's valid numeric range in Section 8.5 of the JavaScript standard:

```
www.ecma-international.org/publications/files/ECMA-ST/Ecma-262.pdf
```

Function `start`

Function `start` (lines 137–145) is called when the window's `load` event occurs to register `click` event handlers for this examples two `button`s (lines 139–142) and for the `ended` event of the `audio` element (lines 143–144).

Program-Control Mechanisms

Note the use of the various program-control mechanisms. The craps program uses five functions—`startGame`, `firstRoll`, `rollAgain`, `rollDice` and `setImage`—and the `switch` and nested `if...else` statements. Also, note the use of multiple `case` labels in the `switch` statement to execute the same statements (lines 65 and 69). In the exercises at the end of this chapter, we investigate additional characteristics of the game of craps.

`CrapsRules.html` *and the HMTL5* `video` *Element*

When the user clicks the hyperlink in `Craps.html` (Fig. 9.7, lines 157–158), the `CrapsRules.html` is displayed in the browser. This page consists of a link back to `Craps.html` (Fig. 9.8, line 11) and an HTML5 **`video` element** (lines 12–25) that displays a video explaining the basic rules for the game of Craps.

```
 1    <!DOCTYPE html>
 2
 3    <!-- Fig. 9.8: CrapsRules.html -->
 4    <!-- Web page with a video of the basic rules for the dice game Craps. -->
 5    <html>
 6       <head>
 7          <meta charset = "utf-8">
 8          <title>Craps Rules</title>
 9       </head>
10       <body>
11          <p><a href = "Craps.html">Back to Craps Game</a></p>
12          <video controls>
13             <source src = "CrapsRules.mp4" type = "video/mp4">
14             <source src = "CrapsRules.webm" type = "video/webm">
15             A player rolls two dice. Each die has six faces that contain
16             one, two, three, four, five and six spots, respectively. The
```

Fig. 9.8 | Web page that displays a video of the basic rules for the dice game Craps. (Part 1 of 2.)

```
17          sum of the spots on the two upward faces is calculated. If the
18          sum is 7 or 11 on the first throw, the player wins. If the sum
19          is 2, 3 or 12 on the first throw (called "craps"), the player
20          loses (i.e., the "house" wins). If the sum is 4, 5, 6, 8, 9 or
21          10 on the first throw, that sum becomes the player's "point."
22          To win, you must continue rolling the dice until you "make your
23          point" (i.e., roll your point value). You lose by rolling a 7
24          before making the point.
25      </video>
26    </body>
27  </html>
```

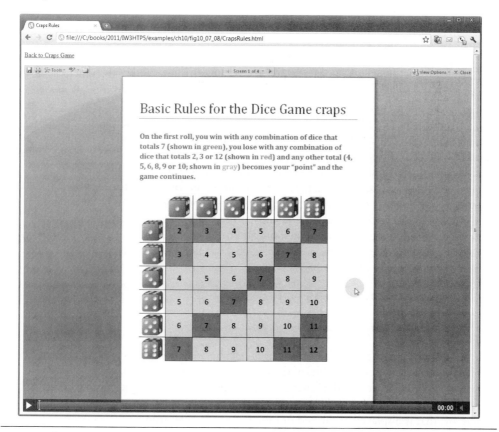

Fig. 9.8 | Web page that displays a video of the basic rules for the dice game Craps. (Part 2 of 2.)

The video element's **controls attribute** indicates that we'd like the video player in the browser to display controls that allow the user to control video playback (e.g., play and pause). As with audio, not all browsers support the same video file formats, but most support MP4, OGG and/or WebM formats. For this reason, nested in the video element are two source elements specifying the locations of this example's video clip in MP4 and WebM formats. The src attribute of each specifies the location of the video. The type attribute specifies the video's MIME type—video/mp4 for the MP4 video and video/webm for the WebM video (MIME types for these and other formats can be found online). When a web browser that supports the video element encounters the source elements, it will choose the first video source that represents one of the browser's supported formats. If the browser does not support the video element, the text in lines 15–24 will be displayed.

We used the downloadable video converter at

> www.mirovideoconverter.com

to convert our video from MP4 to WebM format. For more information on the HTML5 audio and video elements, visit:

> dev.opera.com/articles/view/everything-you-need-to-know-about-
>   html5-video-and-audio/

9.7 Scope Rules

Chapters 6–8 used identifiers for variable names. The attributes of variables include *name*, *value* and *data type* (e.g., string, number or boolean). We also use identifiers as names for user-defined functions. Each identifier in a program also has a scope.

The **scope** of an identifier for a variable or function is the portion of the program in which the identifier can be referenced. **Global variables** or **script-level variables** that are declared in the head element are accessible in *any* part of a script and are said to have **global scope**. Thus every function in the page's script(s) can potentially use the variables.

Identifiers declared inside a function have **function** (or **local**) **scope** and can be used only in that function. Function scope begins with the opening left brace ({) of the function in which the identifier is declared and ends at the function's terminating right brace (}). Local variables of a function and function parameters have function scope. If a local variable in a function has the same name as a global variable, the global variable is "hidden" from the body of the function.

Good Programming Practice 9.2

Avoid local-variable names that hide global-variable names. This can be accomplished by simply avoiding the use of duplicate identifiers in a script.

The script in Fig. 9.9 demonstrates the **scope rules** that resolve conflicts between global variables and local variables of the same name. Once again, we use the window's load event (line 53), which calls the function start when the HTML5 document is completely loaded into the browser window. In this example, we build an output string (declared at line 14) that is displayed at the end of function start's execution.

```
1    <!DOCTYPE html>
2
3    <!-- Fig. 9.9: scoping.html -->
4    <!-- Scoping example. -->
5    <html>
6       <head>
7          <meta charset = "utf-8">
```

Fig. 9.9 | Scoping example. (Part 1 of 3.)

```
 8        <title>Scoping Example</title>
 9        <style type = "text/css">
10           p       { margin: 0px; }
11           p.space { margin-top: 10px; }
12        </style>
13        <script>
14           var output; // stores the string to display
15           var x = 1; // global variable
16
17           function start()
18           {
19              var x = 5; // variable local to function start
20
21              output = "<p>local x in start is " + x + "</p>";
22
23              functionA(); // functionA has local x
24              functionB(); // functionB uses global variable x
25              functionA(); // functionA reinitializes local x
26              functionB(); // global variable x retains its value
27
28              output += "<p class='space'>local x in start is " + x +
29                 "</p>";
30              document.getElementById( "results" ).innerHTML = output;
31           } // end function start
32
33           function functionA()
34           {
35              var x = 25; // initialized each time functionA is called
36
37              output += "<p class='space'>local x in functionA is " + x +
38                 " after entering functionA</p>";
39              ++x;
40              output += "<p>local x in functionA is " + x +
41                 " before exiting functionA</p>";
42           } // end functionA
43
44           function functionB()
45           {
46              output += "<p class='space'>global variable x is " + x +
47                 " on entering functionB";
48              x *= 10;
49              output += "<p>global variable x is " + x +
50                 " on exiting functionB</p>";
51           } // end functionB
52
53           window.addEventListener( "load", start, false );
54        </script>
55     </head>
56     <body>
57        <div id = "results"></div>
58     </body>
59  </html>
```

Fig. 9.9 | Scoping example. (Part 2 of 3.)

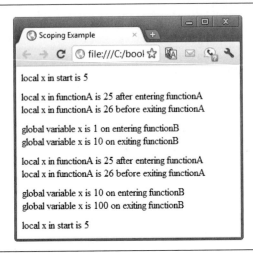

Fig. 9.9 | Scoping example. (Part 3 of 3.)

Global variable x (line 15) is declared and initialized to 1. This global variable is *hidden* in any block (or function) that declares a variable named x. Function start (lines 17–31) declares a local variable x (line 19) and initializes it to 5. Line 21 creates a paragraph element containing x's value as a string and assigns the string to the global variable output (which is displayed later). In the sample output, this shows that the global variable x is *hidden* in start.

The script defines two other functions—functionA and functionB—each taking no arguments and returning nothing. Each function is called twice from function start (lines 23–26). Function functionA defines local variable x (line 35) and initializes it to 25. When functionA is called, the variable's value is placed in a paragraph element and appended to variable output to show that the global variable x is *hidden* in functionA; then the variable is incremented and appended to output again before the function exits. Each time this function is called, local variable x is re-created and initialized to 25.

Function functionB does not declare any variables. Therefore, when it refers to variable x, the global variable x is used. When functionB is called, the global variable's value is placed in a paragraph element and appended to variable output, then it's multiplied by 10 and appended to variable output again before the function exits. The next time function functionB is called, the global variable has its modified value, 10, which again gets multiplied by 10, and 100 is output. Finally, lines 28–29 append the value of local variable x in start to variable output, to show that none of the function calls modified the value of x in start, because the functions all referred to variables in other scopes. Line 30 uses the document object's getElementById method to get the results div element (line 57), then assigns variable output's value to the element's innerHTML property, which renders the HTML in variable output on the page.

9.8 JavaScript Global Functions

JavaScript provides nine standard global functions. We've already used parseInt, parseFloat and isFinite. Some of the global functions are summarized in Fig. 9.10.

Global function	Description
isFinite	Takes a numeric argument and returns true if the value of the argument is not NaN, Number.POSITIVE_INFINITY or Number.NEGATIVE_INFINITY (values that are not numbers or numbers outside the range that JavaScript supports)—otherwise, the function returns false.
isNaN	Takes a numeric argument and returns true if the value of the argument is not a number; otherwise, it returns false. The function is commonly used with the return value of parseInt or parseFloat to determine whether the result is a proper numeric value.
parseFloat	Takes a string argument and attempts to convert the *beginning* of the string into a floating-point value. If the conversion is unsuccessful, the function returns NaN; otherwise, it returns the converted value (e.g., parseFloat("abc123.45") returns NaN, and parseFloat("123.45abc") returns the value 123.45).
parseInt	Takes a string argument and attempts to convert the beginning of the string into an integer value. If the conversion is unsuccessful, the function returns NaN; otherwise, it returns the converted value (for example, parseInt("abc123") returns NaN, and parseInt("123abc") returns the integer value 123). This function takes an optional second argument, from 2 to 36, specifying the **radix** (or **base**) of the number. Base 2 indicates that the first argument string is in **binary** format, base 8 that it's in **octal** format and base 16 that it's in **hexadecimal** format. See Appendix E, for more information on binary, octal and hexadecimal numbers.

Fig. 9.10 | JavaScript global functions.

The global functions in Fig. 9.10 are all part of JavaScript's **Global object**. The Global object contains all the global variables in the script, all the user-defined functions in the script and all the functions listed in Fig. 9.10. Because global functions and user-defined functions are part of the Global object, some JavaScript programmers refer to these functions as methods. You do not need to use the Global object directly—JavaScript references it for you. For information on JavaScript's other global functions, see Section 15.1.2 of the ECMAScript Specification:

www.ecma-international.org/publications/files/ECMA-ST/Ecma-262.pdf

9.9 Recursion

The programs we've discussed thus far are generally structured as functions that call one another in a disciplined, hierarchical manner. A **recursive function** is a function that calls *itself*, either directly, or indirectly through another function. **Recursion** is an important computer science topic. In this section, we present a simple example of recursion.

We consider recursion conceptually first; then we examine several programs containing recursive functions. Recursive problem-solving approaches have a number of elements in common. A recursive function is called to solve a problem. The function actually knows how to solve only the simplest case(s), or **base case(s)**. If the function is called with a base case, the function returns a result. If the function is called with a more complex problem, it divides the problem into two conceptual pieces—a piece that the function knows how to process (the base case) and a piece that the function does not know how to process. To make recursion feasible, the latter piece must resemble the original problem but be a simpler or smaller version of it. Because this new problem looks like the original problem, the function invokes (calls) a fresh copy of *itself* to go to work on the smaller problem; this invocation is referred to as a **recursive call**, or the **recursion step**. The recursion step also normally includes the keyword `return`, because its result will be combined with the portion of the problem the function knew how to solve to form a result that will be passed back to the original caller.

The recursion step executes while the original call to the function is still open (i.e., it has not finished executing). The recursion step can result in many more recursive calls as the function divides each new subproblem into two conceptual pieces. For the recursion eventually to terminate, each time the function calls itself with a simpler version of the original problem, *the sequence of smaller and smaller problems must converge on the base case.* At that point, the function recognizes the base case, returns a result to the previous copy of the function, and a sequence of returns ensues up the line until the original function call eventually returns the final result to the caller. This process sounds exotic when compared with the conventional problem solving we've performed to this point.

As an example of these concepts at work, let's write a recursive program to perform a popular mathematical calculation. The *factorial* of a nonnegative integer n, written $n!$ (and pronounced "n factorial"), is the product

$$n \cdot (n-1) \cdot (n-2) \cdot \ldots \cdot 1$$

where 1! is equal to 1 and 0! is defined as 1. For example, 5! is the product $5 \cdot 4 \cdot 3 \cdot 2 \cdot 1$, which is equal to 120.

The factorial of an integer (`number` in the following example) greater than or equal to zero can be calculated **iteratively** (non-recursively) using a `for` statement, as follows:

```
var factorial = 1;

for ( var counter = number; counter >= 1; --counter )
   factorial *= counter;
```

A *recursive* definition of the factorial function is arrived at by observing the following relationship:

$$n! = n \cdot (n-1)!$$

For example, 5! is clearly equal to 5 * 4!, as is shown by the following equations:

```
5! = 5 · 4 · 3 · 2 · 1
5! = 5 · (4 · 3 · 2 · 1)
5! = 5 · (4!)
```

The evaluation of 5! would proceed as shown in Fig. 9.11. Figure 9.11(a) shows how the succession of recursive calls proceeds until 1! is evaluated to be 1, which terminates the recursion. Figure 9.11(b) shows the values returned from each recursive call to its caller until the final value is calculated and returned.

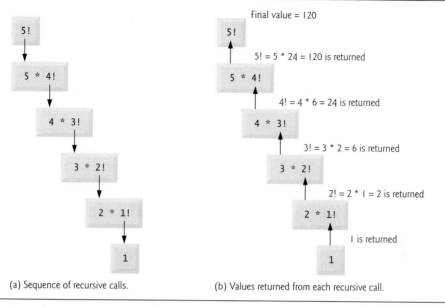

(a) Sequence of recursive calls.   (b) Values returned from each recursive call.

Fig. 9.11 | Recursive evaluation of 5!.

Figure 9.12 uses recursion to calculate and print the factorials of the integers 0 to 10. The recursive function factorial first tests (line 27) whether a terminating condition is true, i.e., whether number is less than or equal to 1. If so, factorial returns 1, no further recursion is necessary and the function returns. If number is greater than 1, line 30 expresses the problem as the product of number and the value returned by a recursive call to factorial evaluating the factorial of number - 1. Note that factorial(number - 1) is a simpler problem than the original calculation, factorial(number).

```
1   <!DOCTYPE html>
2
3   <!-- Fig. 9.12: FactorialTest.html -->
4   <!-- Factorial calculation with a recursive function. -->
5   <html>
6      <head>
7         <meta charset = "utf-8">
8         <title>Recursive Factorial Function</title>
9         <style type = "text/css">
10           p        { margin: 0px; }
11        </style>
12        <script>
13           var output = ""; // stores the output
14
15           // calculates factorials of 0 - 10
16           function calculateFactorials()
17           {
```

Fig. 9.12 | Factorial calculation with a recursive function. (Part 1 of 2.)

```
18        for ( var i = 0; i <= 10; ++i )
19            output += "<p>" + i + "! = " + factorial( i ) + "</p>";
20
21        document.getElementById( "results" ).innerHTML = output;
22    } // end function calculateFactorials
23
24    // Recursive definition of function factorial
25    function factorial( number )
26    {
27        if ( number <= 1 )  // base case
28            return 1;
29        else
30            return number * factorial( number - 1 );
31    } // end function factorial
32
33    window.addEventListener( "load", calculateFactorials, false );
34  </script>
35  </head>
36  <body>
37    <h1>Factorials of 0 to 10</h1>
38    <div id = "results"></div>
39  </body>
40 </html>
```

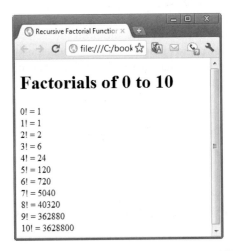

Fig. 9.12 | Factorial calculation with a recursive function. (Part 2 of 2.)

Function factorial (lines 25–31) receives as its argument the value for which to calculate the factorial. As can be seen in the screen capture in Fig. 9.12, factorial values become large quickly.

Common Programming Error 9.3

Omitting the base case and writing the recursion step incorrectly so that it does not converge on the base case are both errors that cause infinite recursion, eventually exhausting memory. This situation is analogous to the problem of an infinite loop in an iterative (non-recursive) solution.

Error-Prevention Tip 9.2

Internet Explorer displays an error message when a script seems to be going into infinite recursion. Firefox simply terminates the script after detecting the problem. This allows the user of the web page to recover from a script that contains an infinite loop or infinite recursion.

9.10 Recursion vs. Iteration

In the preceding section, we studied a function that can easily be implemented either recursively or iteratively. In this section, we compare the two approaches and discuss why you might choose one approach over the other in a particular situation.

Both iteration and recursion are based on a control statement: Iteration uses a *repetition* statement (e.g., for, while or do...while); recursion uses a *selection* statement (e.g., if, if...else or switch).

Both iteration and recursion involve repetition: Iteration explicitly uses a repetition statement; recursion achieves repetition through repeated function calls.

Iteration and recursion each involve a termination test: Iteration terminates when the loop-continuation condition fails; recursion terminates when a base case is recognized.

Iteration both with counter-controlled repetition and with recursion gradually approaches termination: Iteration keeps modifying a counter until the counter assumes a value that makes the loop-continuation condition fail; recursion keeps producing simpler versions of the original problem until the base case is reached.

Both iteration and recursion can occur infinitely: An infinite loop occurs with iteration if the loop-continuation test never becomes false; infinite recursion occurs if the recursion step does not reduce the problem each time via a sequence that converges on the base case or if the base case is incorrect.

One *negative* aspect of recursion is that function calls require a certain amount of time and memory space not directly spent on executing program instructions. This is known as *function-call overhead*. Because recursion uses repeated function calls, this overhead greatly affects the performance of the operation. In many cases, using repetition statements in place of recursion is more efficient. However, some problems can be solved more elegantly (and more easily) with recursion.

Software Engineering Observation 9.4

Any problem that can be solved recursively can also be solved iteratively (non-recursively). A recursive approach is normally chosen in preference to an iterative approach when the recursive approach more naturally mirrors the problem and results in a program that's easier to understand and debug. Another reason to choose a recursive solution is that an iterative solution may not be apparent.

Performance Tip 9.1

Avoid using recursion in performance-critical situations. Recursive calls take time and consume additional memory.

In addition to the factorial function example (Fig. 9.12), we also provide recursion exercises—raising an integer to an integer power (Exercise 9.29) and "What does the following function do?" (Exercise 9.30). Also, Fig. 15.25 uses recursion to traverse an XML document tree.

Summary

Section 9.1 Introduction
- The best way to develop and maintain a large program is to construct it from small, simple pieces, or modules (p. 311). This technique is called divide and conquer (p. 311).

Section 9.2 Program Modules in JavaScript
- JavaScript programs are written by combining new functions (p. 311) that the programmer writes with "prepackaged" functions and objects available in JavaScript.
- The term method (p. 311) implies that the function belongs to a particular object. We refer to functions that belong to a particular JavaScript object as methods; all others are referred to as functions.
- JavaScript provides several objects that have a rich collection of methods for performing common mathematical calculations, string manipulations, date and time manipulations, and manipulations of collections of data called arrays. These objects make your job easier, because they provide many of the capabilities programmers frequently need.
- You can define functions that perform specific tasks and use them at many points in a script. These functions are referred to as programmer-defined functions (p. 311). The actual statements defining the function are written only once and are hidden from other functions.
- Functions are invoked (p. 312) by writing the name of the function, followed by a left parenthesis, followed by a comma-separated list of zero or more arguments, followed by a right parenthesis.
- Methods are called in the same way as functions (p. 312) but require the name of the object to which the method belongs and a dot preceding the method name.
- Function arguments (p. 312) may be constants, variables or expressions.

Section 9.3 Function Definitions
- The return statement passes information from inside a function back to the point in the program where it was called.
- A function must be called explicitly for the code in its body to execute.
- The format of a function definition is

      function *function-name*(*parameter-list*)
      {
          declarations and statements
      }

- Each function should perform a single, well-defined task, and the name of the function should express that task effectively. This promotes software reusability (p. 317).
- There are three ways to return control to the point at which a function was invoked. If the function does not return a result, control returns when the program reaches the function-ending right brace or when the statement return; is executed. If the function does return a result, the statement return *expression*; returns the value of *expression* to the caller.

Section 9.4 Notes on Programmer-Defined Functions
- All variables declared with the keyword var in function definitions are local variables (p. 317)—this means that they can be accessed only in the function in which they're defined.
- A function's parameters (p. 317) are considered to be local variables. When a function is called, the arguments in the call are assigned to the corresponding parameters in the function definition.
- Code that's packaged as a function can be executed from several locations in a program by calling the function.

Section 9.5 Random Number Generation

- Method random generates a floating-point value from 0.0 up to, but not including, 1.0.

- JavaScript can execute actions in response to the user's interaction with an element in an HTML5 form. This is referred to as GUI event handling (p. 322).

- An HTML5 element's click event handler (p. 321) indicates the action to take when the user of the HTML5 document clicks on the element.

- In event-driven programming (p. 322), the user interacts with an element, the script is notified of the event (p. 322) and the script processes the event. The user's interaction with the GUI "drives" the program. The function that's called when an event occurs is known as an event-handling function or event handler.

- The getElementById method (p. 322), given an id as an argument, finds the HTML5 element with a matching id attribute and returns a JavaScript object representing the element.

- The scaling factor (p. 328) determines the size of the range. The shifting value (p. 328) is added to the result to determine where the range begins.

Section 9.6 Example: Game of Chance; Introducing the HTML5 audio and video Elements

- An HTML5 audio element (p. 333) embeds audio into a web page. Setting the preload attribute (p. 333) to "auto" indicates to the browser that it should consider downloading the audio clip so that it's ready to be played.

- Not all browsers support the same audio file formats, but most support MP3, OGG and/or WAV format. For this reason, you can use source elements (p. 333) nested in the audio element to specify the locations of an audio clip in different formats. Each source element specifies a src and a type attribute. The src attribute specifies the location of the audio clip. The type attribute specifies the clip's MIME type.

- When a web browser that supports the audio element encounters the source elements, it chooses the first audio source that represents one of the browser's supported formats.

- When interacting with an audio element from JavaScript, you can use the play method (p. 335) to play the clip once.

- Global JavaScript function isFinite (p. 336) returns true only if its argument is a valid number in the range supported by JavaScript.

- The HTML5 video element (p. 336) embeds a video in a web page.

- The video element's controls attribute (p. 337) indicates that the video player in the browser should display controls that allow the user to control video playback.

- As with audio, not all browsers support the same video file formats, but most support MP4, OGG and/or WebM formats. For this reason, you can use source elements nested in the video element to specify the locations of a video clip's multiple formats.

Section 9.7 Scope Rules

- Each identifier in a program has a scope (p. 338). The scope of an identifier for a variable or function is the portion of the program in which the identifier can be referenced.

- Global variables or script-level variables (i.e., variables declared in the head element of the HTML5 document, p. 338) are accessible in any part of a script and are said to have global scope (p. 338). Thus every function in the script can potentially use the variables.

- Identifiers declared inside a function have function (or local) scope (p. 338) and can be used only in that function. Function scope begins with the opening left brace ({) of the function in which the identifier is declared and ends at the terminating right brace (}) of the function. Local variables of a function and function parameters have function scope.

- If a local variable in a function has the same name as a global variable, the global variable is "hidden" from the body of the function.

Section 9.8 JavaScript Global Functions

- JavaScript provides several global functions as part of a Global object (p. 341). This object contains all the global variables in the script, all the user-defined functions in the script and all the built-in global functions listed in Fig. 9.10.
- You do not need to use the Global object directly; JavaScript uses it for you.

Section 9.9 Recursion

- A recursive function (p. 341) calls itself, either directly, or indirectly through another function.
- A recursive function knows how to solve only the simplest case, or base case. If the function is called with a base case, it returns a result. If the function is called with a more complex problem, it knows how to divide the problem into two conceptual pieces—a piece that the function knows how to process (the base case, p. 342) and a simpler or smaller version of the original problem.
- The function invokes (calls) a fresh copy of itself to go to work on the smaller problem; this invocation is referred to as a recursive call or the recursion step (p. 342).
- The recursion step executes while the original call to the function is still open (i.e., it has not finished executing).
- For recursion eventually to terminate, each time the function calls itself with a simpler version of the original problem, the sequence of smaller and smaller problems must converge on the base case. At that point, the function recognizes the base case, returns a result to the previous copy of the function, and a sequence of returns ensues up the line until the original function call eventually returns the final result to the caller.

Section 9.10 Recursion vs. Iteration

- Both iteration and recursion involve repetition: Iteration explicitly uses a repetition statement; recursion achieves repetition through repeated function calls.
- Iteration and recursion each involve a termination test: Iteration terminates when the loop-continuation condition fails; recursion terminates when a base case is recognized.
- Iteration both with counter-controlled repetition and with recursion gradually approaches termination: Iteration keeps modifying a counter until the counter assumes a value that makes the loop-continuation condition fail; recursion keeps producing simpler versions of the original problem until the base case is reached.

Self-Review Exercises

9.1   Fill in the blanks in each of the following statements:
   a) The term _____ implies that the function belongs to a particular object.
   b) Function arguments may be _____ or _____.
   c) All variables declared in function definitions are _____ variables.
   d) An HTML5 element's _____ attribute indicates the action to take when the user of the HTML5 document clicks on the element.
   e) JavaScript provides several global functions as part of a(n) _____ object

9.2   For the program in Fig. 9.13, state the scope (either global scope or function scope) of each of the following elements:

a) The variable x.
b) The variable y.
c) The function cube.
d) The function output.

```
1    <!DOCTYPE html>
2
3    <!-- Exercise 9.2: cube.html -->
4    <html>
5       <head>
6          <meta charset = "utf-8">
7          <title>Scoping</title>
8          <script>
9             var x;
10
11            function output()
12            {
13               for ( x = 1; x <= 10; x++ )
14                  document.writeln( "<p>" + cube( x ) + "</p>" );
15            } // end function output
16
17            function cube( y )
18            {
19               return y * y * y;
20            } // end function cube
21
22            window.addEventListener( "load", output, false );
23         </script>
24      </head><body></body>
25   </html>
```

Fig. 9.13 | Scope exercise.

9.3 Fill in the blanks in each of the following statements:
 a) Programmer-defined functions, global variables and JavaScript's global functions are all part of the _____ object.
 b) Function _____ determines whether its argument is or is not a number.
 c) Function _____ takes a string argument and returns a string in which all spaces, punctuation, accent characters and any other character that's not in the ASCII character set are encoded in a hexadecimal format.
 d) Function _____ takes a string argument representing JavaScript code to execute.
 e) Function _____ takes a string as its argument and returns a string in which all characters that were previously encoded with escape are decoded.

9.4 Fill in the blanks in each of the following statements:
 a) The _____ method is given an id as an argument.
 b) The _____ factor determines the size of the range. The _____ number is added to the result to determine where the range begins.
 c) Method random generates a floating-point value from _____ up to, but not including, 1.0.
 d) The HTML5 _____ element embeds a video in a web page.

9.5 Locate the error in each of the following program segments and explain how to correct it:
 a) fn()
   {
      document.writeln("Inside method fn");
   }

b) `// This function should return the difference of its arguments`
```
function differ( x, y )
{
    var result;
    result = x - y;
}
```

c)
```
function f( a );
{
    document.writeln( a );
}
```

9.6 Write a complete JavaScript program to prompt the user for the radius of a sphere, then call function `sphereVolume` to calculate and display the volume of the sphere. Use the statement

```
volume = ( 4.0 / 3.0 ) * Math.PI * Math.pow( radius, 3 );
```

to calculate the volume. The user should enter the radius in an HTML5 input element of type "number" in a form. Give the input element the `id` value "inputField". You can use this `id` with the document object's `getElementById` method to get the element for use in the script. To access the string in the `inputField`, use its `value` property as in `inputField.value`, then convert the string to a number using `parseFloat`. Use an input element of type "button" in the form to allow the user to initiate the calculation. [*Note:* In HTML5, input elements of type "number" have a property named `valueAsNumber` that enables a script to get the floating-point number in the input element without having to convert it from a string to a number using `parseFloat`. At the time of this writing, `valueAsNumber` was not supported in all browsers.]

Answers to Self-Review Exercises

9.1 a) method. b) constants, variables. c) local. d) `onclick`. e) `Global`.

9.2 a) global scope. b) function scope. c) global scope. d) global scope.

9.3 a) `Global`. b) `isNaN`. c) `escape`. d) `eval`. e) `unescape`.

9.4 a) `getElementById`. b) scaling, shift. c) 0.0. d) video.

9.5 a) Error: Every function definition should start with the keyword function.
Correction: Add function before `fn( )`.
b) Error: The function is supposed to return a value, but does not.
Correction: Either delete variable `result` and place the statement
```
return x - y;
```
in the function or add the following statement at the end of the function body:
```
return result;
```
c) Error: No semicolon after the statement: `document.writeln( a )`.
Correction: Add a semicolon after the statement: `document.writeln( a )`.

9.6 The solution below calculates the volume of a sphere using the radius entered by the user.

```
1   <!DOCTYPE html>
2
3   <!-- Exercise 9.6: volume.html -->
4   <html>
5     <head>
6       <meta charset = "utf-8">
7       <title>Calculating Sphere Volume</title>
8       <script>
```

```
 9          function start()
10          {
11             var button = document.getElementById( "calculateButton" );
12             button.addEventListener( "click", displayVolume, false );
13          } // end function start
14
15          function displayVolume()
16          {
17             var inputField = document.getElementById( "radiusField" );
18             var radius = parseFloat( inputField.value );
19             var result = document.getElementById( "result" );
20             result.innerHTML = "Sphere volume is: " + sphereVolume( radius );
21          } // end function displayVolume
22
23          function sphereVolume( radius )
24          {
25             return ( 4.0 / 3.0 ) * Math.PI * Math.pow( radius, 3 );
26          } // end function sphereVolume
27
28          window.addEventListener( "load", start, false );
29       </script>
30    </head>
31    <body>
32       <form action = "#">
33          <p><label>Radius:
34             <input id = "radiusField" type = "number"></label>
35             <input id = "calculateButton" type = "button" value = "Calculate"></p>
36       </form>
37       <p id = "result"></p>
38    </body>
39 </html>
```

Exercises

9.7   Write a script that uses a form to get the radius of a circle from the user, then calls the function circlePerimeter to calculate the perimeter of the circle and display the result in a paragraph on the page. To get the number from the form, use the techniques shown in Self-Review Exercise 9.6.

9.8   A parking garage charges a $4.00 minimum fee to park for up to two hours. The garage charges an additional $0.50 per hour for each hour *or part thereof* in excess of two hours. The maximum charge for any given 24-hour period is $12.00. Assume that no car parks for longer than 24 hours at a time. Write a script that calculates and displays the parking charges for each customer who parked a car in this garage yesterday. You should use a form to input from the user the hours parked for each customer. The program should display the charge for the current customer and should calculate and display the running total of yesterday's receipts. The program should use the function calculateCharges to determine the charge for each customer. To get the number from the form, use the techniques shown in Self-Review Exercise 9.6.

9.9 Write a function distance that calculates the slope between two points $(x1, y1)$ and $(x2, y2)$. All numbers and return values should be floating-point values. Incorporate this function into a script that enables the user to enter the coordinates of the points through an HTML5 form. To get the numbers from the form, use the techniques shown in Self-Review Exercise 9.6.

9.10 Answer each of the following questions:
a) What is the scope of an identifier?
b) What is function scope?
c) What is the scope of a script-level variable?
d) What happens if a local variable in a function has the same name as a global variable?

9.11 Write statements that assign random integers to the variable n in the following ranges:
a) $1 \leq n \leq 5$
b) $1 \leq n \leq 1000$
c) $0 \leq n \leq 99$
d) $1000 \leq n \leq 1100$
e) $-2 \leq n \leq 2$
f) $-1 \leq n \leq 11$

9.12 For each of the following sets of integers, write a single statement that will print a number at random from the set:
a) 2, 4, 8, 10, 12, 14.
b) 5, 7, 9, 11, 13.
c) 2, 6, 10, 14, 18, 22.

9.13 Write a function SumN(m, n) that returns the value of

```
m + m+ ... + n times.
```

For example, SumN(3, 4) = 3 + 3 + 3 + 3. Assume that m and n are integers. Function SumN should use a for or while statement to control the calculation. Do not use any math library functions. Incorporate this function into a script that reads integer values from an HTML5 form for m and n and performs the calculation with the SumN function. The HTML5 form should consist of two text fields and a button to initiate the calculation. The user should interact with the program by typing numbers in both text fields then clicking the button.

9.14 Write a function maximum that finds, for a pair of integers, the maximum value between the two numbers. The function should take two integer arguments and return the maximum value. Incorporate this function into a script that inputs a series of pairs of integers (one pair at a time). The HTML5 form should consist of two text fields and a button to initiate the calculation. The user should interact with the program by typing numbers in both text fields, then clicking the button.

9.15 Write a script that inputs integers (one at a time) and passes them one at a time to a function isPositive, which finds whether a number is positive or negative. The function should take an integer argument and return true if the integer is positive and false otherwise. Use sentinel- controlled looping and a prompt dialog.

9.16 Write program segments that accomplish each of the following tasks:
a) Calculate the integer part of the quotient when integer a is divided by integer b.
b) Calculate the integer remainder when integer a is divided by integer b.
c) Use the program pieces developed in parts (a) and (b) to write a function displayDigits that receives an integer between 1 and 99999 and prints it as a series of digits, each pair of which is separated by two spaces. For example, the integer 4562 should be printed as

4 5 6 2

d) Incorporate the function developed in part (c) into a script that inputs an integer from a `prompt` dialog and invokes `displayDigits` by passing to the function the integer entered.

9.17 Implement the following functions:

a) Function `celsius` returns the Celsius equivalent of a Fahrenheit temperature, using the calculation

```
C = 5.0 / 9.0 * ( F - 32 );
```

b) Function `fahrenheit` returns the Fahrenheit equivalent of a Celsius temperature, using the calculation

```
F = 9.0 / 5.0 * C + 32;
```

c) Use these functions to write a script that enables the user to enter either a Fahrenheit or a Celsius temperature and displays the Celsius or Fahrenheit equivalent.

Your HTML5 document should contain two buttons—one to initiate the conversion from Fahrenheit to Celsius and one to initiate the conversion from Celsius to Fahrenheit.

9.18 Write a function `maximum3` that returns the largest of three floating-point numbers. Use the `Math.max` function to implement `maximum3`. Incorporate the function into a script that reads three values from the user and determines the largest value.

9.19 The factorial of a number n is `n * (n - 1) * (n - 2)* … *2 * 1`. For example, the factorial of 4 is 24, of 5 is 120, etc.

a) Write a function that determines the factorial of a number.

b) Use this function in a script that determines and prints the factorial of all numbers between 1 and 10. Display the results in a `<textarea>`.

9.20 Write a function `averageGrade` that inputs a student's marks and returns the grade E (Excellent) if the student's average is 90–100, G (Good) if the average is 80–89, A (Average) if the average is 70–79, B (Bad) if the average is 60–69, and F (Fail) if the average is lower than 60. Incorporate the function into a script that reads a value from the user.

9.21 Write a script that simulates coin tossing. Let the program toss the coin each time the user clicks the **Toss** button. Count the number of times each side of the coin appears. Display the results. The program should call a separate function `flip` that takes no arguments and returns `false` for tails and `true` for heads. [*Note:* If the program realistically simulates the coin tossing, each side of the coin should appear approximately half the time.]

9.22 Computers are playing an increasing role in education. Write a program that will help an elementary-school student learn multiplication. Use `Math.random` to produce two positive one-digit integers. It should then display a question such as

```
How much is 6 times 7?
```

The student then types the answer into a text field. Your program checks the student's answer. If it's correct, display the string `"Very good!"` and generate a new question. If the answer is wrong, display the string `"No. Please try again."` and let the student try the same question again repeatedly until he or she finally gets it right. A separate function should be used to generate each new question. This function should be called once when the script begins execution and each time the user answers the question correctly.

9.23 The use of computers in education is referred to as **computer-assisted instruction** (CAI). One problem that develops in CAI environments is student fatigue. This problem can be eliminated by varying the computer's dialogue to hold the student's attention. Modify the program in Exercise 9.22 to print one of a variety of comments for each correct answer and each incorrect answer. The set of responses for correct answers is as follows:

```
Very good!
Excellent!
Nice work!
Keep up the good work!
```

The set of responses for incorrect answers is as follows:

```
No. Please try again.
Wrong. Try once more.
Don't give up!
No. Keep trying.
```

Use random number generation to choose a number from 1 to 4 that will be used to select an appropriate response to each answer. Use a switch statement to issue the responses.

9.24 More sophisticated computer-assisted instruction systems monitor the student's performance over a period of time. The decision to begin a new topic is often based on the student's success with previous topics. Modify the program in Exercise 9.23 to count the number of correct and incorrect responses typed by the student. After the student answers 10 questions, your program should calculate the percentage of correct responses. If the percentage is lower than 75 percent, display Please ask your instructor for extra help, and reset the quiz so another student can try it.

9.25 Write a script that plays a "guess the number" game as follows: Your program chooses the number to be guessed by selecting a random integer in the range 1 to 1000. The script displays the prompt Guess a number between 1 and 1000 next to a text field. The player types a first guess into the text field and clicks a button to submit the guess to the script. If the player's guess is incorrect, your program should display Too high. Try again. or Too low. Try again. to help the player "zero in" on the correct answer and should clear the text field so the user can enter the next guess. When the user enters the correct answer, display Congratulations. You guessed the number! and clear the text field so the user can play again. [*Note:* The guessing technique employed in this problem is similar to a **binary search**, which we discuss in Chapter 10, JavaScript: Arrays.]

9.26 Modify the program of Exercise 9.25 to count the number of guesses the player makes. If the number is 10 or fewer, display Either you know the secret or you got lucky! If the player guesses the number in 10 tries, display Ahah! You know the secret! If the player makes more than 10 guesses, display You should be able to do better! Why should it take no more than 10 guesses? Well, with each good guess, the player should be able to eliminate half of the numbers. Now show why any number 1 to 1000 can be guessed in 10 or fewer tries.

9.27 *(Project)* Exercises 9.22 through 9.24 developed a computer-assisted instruction program to teach an elementary-school student multiplication. This exercise suggests enhancements to that program.

    a) Modify the program to allow the user to enter a grade-level capability. A grade level of 1 means to use only single-digit numbers in the problems, a grade level of 2 means to use numbers as large as two digits, and so on.

    b) Modify the program to allow the user to pick the type of arithmetic problems he or she wishes to study. An option of 1 means addition problems only, 2 means subtraction problems only, 3 means multiplication problems only, 4 means division problems only and 5 means to intermix randomly problems of all these types.

9.28   Modify the craps program in Fig. 9.7 to allow wagering. Initialize variable bankBalance to 1000 dollars. Prompt the player to enter a wager. Check whether   the wager is less than or equal to bankBalance and, if not, have the user reenter wager until a valid wager is entered. After a valid wager is entered, run one game of craps. If the player wins, increase bankBalance by wager, and print the new bankBalance. If the player loses, decrease bankBalance by wager, print the new bankBalance, check whether bankBalance has become zero and, if so, print the message Sorry. You busted! As the game progresses, print various messages to create some chatter, such as Oh, you're going for broke, huh? or Aw c'mon, take a chance! or You're up big. Now's the time to cash in your chips!. Implement the chatter as a separate function that randomly chooses the string to display.

9.29   Write a recursive function power(*base*, *exponent*) that, when invoked, returns

$base^{exponent}$

for example, power(3, 4) = 3 * 3 * 3 * 3. Assume that *exponent* is an integer greater than or equal to 1. The recursion step would use the relationship

$base^{exponent} = base \cdot base^{exponent-1}$

and the terminating condition occurs when *exponent* is equal to 1, because

$base^1 = base$

Incorporate this function into a script that enables the user to enter the *base* and *exponent*.

9.30   What does the following function do?

```
// Parameter n must be a positive
// integer to prevent infinite recursion
function too( n )
{
   if ( n == 1 )
      return 1;
   else
      return n * too( n - 1 );
}
```

10

JavaScript: Arrays

Yea, from the table of my memory I'll wipe away all trivial fond records.
—William Shakespeare

Praise invariably implies a reference to a higher standard.
—Aristotle

With sobs and tears he sorted out Those of the largest size...
—Lewis Carroll

Attempt the end, and never stand to doubt; Nothing's so hard, but search will find it out.
—Robert Herrick

Objectives

In this chapter you'll:

- Declare arrays, initialize arrays and refer to individual elements of arrays.

- Store lists and tables of values in arrays.

- Pass arrays to functions.

- Search and sort arrays.

- Declare and manipulate multidimensional arrays.

10.1 Introduction

Arrays are data structures consisting of related data items. JavaScript arrays are "dynamic" entities in that they can change size after they're created. Many techniques demonstrated in this chapter are used frequently in Chapters 12–13 when we introduce the collections that allow you to dynamically manipulate all of an HTML5 document's elements.

10.2 Arrays

An array is a group of memory locations that all have the same name and normally are of the same type (although this attribute is *not required* in JavaScript). To refer to a particular location or element in the array, we specify the name of the array and the **position number** of the particular element in the array.

Figure 10.1 shows an array of integer values named c. This array contains 12 **elements**. We may refer to any one of these elements by giving the array's name followed by the *position number* of the element in square brackets ([]). The first element in every array is the **zeroth element**. Thus, the first element of array c is referred to as c[0], the second element as c[1], the seventh element as c[6] and, in general, the ith element of array c is referred to as c[i-1]. Array names follow the same conventions as other identifiers.

The position number in square brackets is called an **index** and must be an integer or an integer expression. If a program uses an expression as an index, then the expression is evaluated to determine the value of the index. For example, if the variable a is equal to 5 and b is equal to 6, then the statement

```
c[ a + b ] += 2;
```

adds 2 to the value of array element c[11]. An indexed array name can be used on the left side of an assignment to place a new value into an array element. It can also be used on the right side of an assignment to assign its value to another variable.

Let's examine array c in Fig. 10.1 more closely. The array's **name** is c. The array's **length** is 12 and can be found by using the array's **length property**, as in:

```
c.length
```

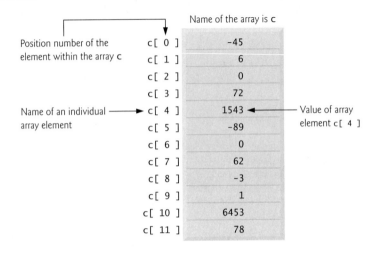

Fig. 10.1 | Array with 12 elements.

The array's 12 elements are referred to as c[0], c[1], c[2], ..., c[11]. The **value** of c[0] is -45, the value of c[1] is 6, the value of c[2] is 0, the value of c[7] is 62 and the value of c[11] is 78. The following statement calculates the sum of the values contained in the first three elements of array c and stores the result in variable sum:

```
sum = c[ 0 ] + c[ 1 ] + c[ 2 ];
```

The brackets that enclose an array index are a JavaScript operator. Brackets have the same level of precedence as parentheses. Figure 10.2 shows the precedence and associativity of the operators introduced so far in the text. They're shown from top to bottom in decreasing order of precedence.

Operators					Associativity	Type
()	[]	.			left to right	highest
++	--	!			right to left	unary
*	/	%			left to right	multiplicative
+	-				left to right	additive
<	<=	>	>=		left to right	relational
==	!=				left to right	equality
&&					left to right	logical AND
||					left to right	logical OR
?:					right to left	conditional
=	+=	-=	*=	/= %=	right to left	assignment

Fig. 10.2 | Precedence and associativity of the operators discussed so far.

10.3 Declaring and Allocating Arrays

Arrays occupy space in memory. Actually, an array in JavaScript is an **Array object**. You use the **new operator** to create an array and to specify the number of elements in an array. The new operator creates an object as the script executes by obtaining enough memory to store an object of the type specified to the right of new. To allocate 12 elements for integer array c, use a new expression like:

```
var c = new Array( 12 );
```

The preceding statement can also be performed in two steps, as follows:

```
var c; // declares a variable that will hold the array
c = new Array( 12 ); // allocates the array
```

When arrays are created, the elements are *not* initialized—they have the value undefined.

10.4 Examples Using Arrays

This section presents several examples of creating and manipulating arrays.

10.4.1 Creating, Initializing and Growing Arrays

Our next example (Figs. 10.3–10.4) uses operator new to allocate an array of five elements and an empty array. The script demonstrates initializing an array of existing elements and also shows that an array can grow dynamically to accommodate new elements. The array's values are displayed in HTML5 tables.

HTML5 Document for Displaying Results
Figure 10.3 shows the HTML5 document in which we display the results. You'll notice that we've placed the CSS styles and JavaScript code into separate files. Line 9 links the CSS file tablestyle.css to this document as shown in Chapter 4. (There are no new concepts in the CSS file used in this chapter, so we don't show them in the text.) Line 10 demonstrates how to link a script that's stored in a separate file to this document. To do so, use the script element's **src attribute** to specify the location of the JavaScript file (named with the **.js filename extension**). This document's body contains two divs in which we'll display the contents of two arrays. When the document finishes loading, the JavaScript function start (Fig. 10.4) is called.

> **Software Engineering Observation 10.1**
> *It's considered good practice to separate your JavaScript scripts into separate files so that they can be reused in multiple web pages.*

```
1  <!DOCTYPE html>
2
3  <!-- Fig. 10.3: InitArray.html -->
4  <!-- Web page for showing the results of initializing arrays. -->
5  <html>
6     <head>
```

Fig. 10.3 | Web page for showing the results of initializing arrays. (Part 1 of 2.)

```
7          <meta charset = "utf-8">
8          <title>Initializing an Array</title>
9          <link rel = "stylesheet" type = "text/css" href = "tablestyle.css">
10         <script src = "InitArray.js"></script>
11     </head>
12     <body>
13         <div id = "output1"></div>
14         <div id = "output2"></div>
15     </body>
16  </html>
```

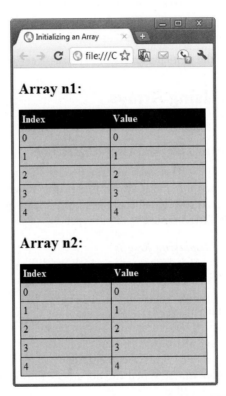

Fig. 10.3 | Web page for showing the results of initializing arrays. (Part 2 of 2.)

Script that Creates, Initializes and Displays the Contents of Arrays
Figure 10.4 presents the script used by the document in Fig. 10.3. Function start (lines 3–24) is called when the window's load event occurs.

```
1   // Fig. 10.4: InitArray.js
2   // Create two arrays, initialize their elements and display them
3   function start()
4   {
```

Fig. 10.4 | Create two arrays, initialize their elements and display them. (Part 1 of 2.)

```
5       var n1 = new Array( 5 ); // allocate five-element array
6       var n2 = new Array(); // allocate empty array
7
8       // assign values to each element of array n1
9       var length = n1.length; // get array's length once before the loop
10
11      for ( var i = 0; i < length; ++i )
12      {
13          n1[ i ] = i;
14      } // end for
15
16      // create and initialize five elements in array n2
17      for ( i = 0; i < 5; ++i )
18      {
19          n2[ i ] = i;
20      } // end for
21
22      outputArray( "Array n1:", n1, document.getElementById( "output1" ) );
23      outputArray( "Array n2:", n2, document.getElementById( "output2" ) );
24  } // end function start
25
26  // output the heading followed by a two-column table
27  // containing indices and elements of "theArray"
28  function outputArray( heading, theArray, output )
29  {
30      var content = "<h2>" + heading + "</h2><table>" +
31          "<thead><th>Index</th><th>Value</th></thead><tbody>";
32
33      // output the index and value of each array element
34      var length = theArray.length; // get array's length once before loop
35
36      for ( var i = 0; i < length; ++i )
37      {
38          content += "<tr><td>" + i + "</td><td>" + theArray[ i ] +
39              "</td></tr>";
40      } // end for
41
42      content += "</tbody></table>";
43      output.innerHTML = content; // place the table in the output element
44  } // end function outputArray
45
46  window.addEventListener( "load", start, false );
```

Fig. 10.4 | Create two arrays, initialize their elements and display them. (Part 2 of 2.)

Line 5 creates array n1 with five elements. Line 6 creates array n2 as an *empty* array. Lines 9–14 use a for statement to initialize the elements of n1 to their index values (0 to 4). With arrays, we use zero-based counting so that the loop can access *every* array element. Line 9 uses the expression n1.length to determine the array's length. JavaScript's arrays are dynamically resizable, so it's important to get an array's length once before a loop that processes the array—in case the script changes the array's length. In this example, the array's length is 5, so the loop continues executing as long as the value of control variable i is less than 5. This process is known as **iterating through the array's elements**. For a five-element array, the index values are 0 through 4, so using the less-than operator, <, guarantees that the loop does not attempt to access an element beyond the end of the array. Zero-based counting is usually used to iterate through arrays.

Growing an Array Dynamically

Lines 17–20 use a for statement to add five elements to the array n2 and initialize each element to its index value (0 to 4). The array grows dynamically to accommodate each value as it's assigned to each element of the array.

Software Engineering Observation 10.2

JavaScript automatically reallocates an array when a value is assigned to an element that's outside the bounds of the array. Elements between the last element of the original array and the new element are undefined.

Lines 22–23 invoke function outputArray (defined in lines 28–44) to display the contents of each array in an HTML5 table in a corresponding div. Function outputArray receives three arguments—a string to be output as an h2 element before the HTML5 table that displays the contents of the array, the array to output and the div in which to place the table. Lines 36–40 use a for statement to define each row of the table.

Error-Prevention Tip 10.1

When accessing array elements, the index values should never go below 0 and should be less than the number of elements in the array (i.e., one less than the array's size), unless it's your explicit intent to grow the array by assigning a value to a nonexistent element.

Using an Initializer List

If an array's element values are known in advance, the elements can be allocated and initialized in the declaration of the array. There are two ways in which the initial values can be specified. The statement

```
var n = [ 10, 20, 30, 40, 50 ];
```

uses a comma-separated **initializer list** enclosed in square brackets ([and]) to create a five-element array with indices of 0, 1, 2, 3 and 4. The array size is determined by the number of values in the initializer list. The preceding declaration does *not* require the new operator to create the Array object—this functionality is provided by the JavaScript interpreter when it encounters an array declaration that includes an initializer list. The statement

```
var n = new Array( 10, 20, 30, 40, 50 );
```

also creates a five-element array with indices of 0, 1, 2, 3 and 4. In this case, the initial values of the array elements are specified as arguments in the parentheses following new Array. The size of the array is determined by the number of values in parentheses. It's also possible to reserve a space in an array for a value to be specified later by using a comma as a **place holder** in the initializer list. For example, the statement

```
var n = [ 10, 20, , 40, 50 ];
```

creates a five-element array in which the third element (n[2]) has the value undefined.

10.4.2 Initializing Arrays with Initializer Lists

The example in Figs. 10.5–10.6 creates three Array objects to demonstrate initializing arrays with initializer lists. Figure 10.5 is nearly identical to Fig. 10.3 but provides three divs in its body element for displaying this example's arrays.

```
 1   <!DOCTYPE html>
 2
 3   <!-- Fig. 10.5: InitArray2.html -->
 4   <!-- Web page for showing the results of initializing arrays. -->
 5   <html>
 6      <head>
 7         <meta charset = "utf-8">
 8         <title>Initializing an Array</title>
 9         <link rel = "stylesheet" type = "text/css" href = "tablestyle.css">
10         <script src = "InitArray2.js"></script>
11      </head>
12      <body>
13         <div id = "output1"></div>
14         <div id = "output2"></div>
15         <div id = "output3"></div>
16      </body>
17   </html>
```

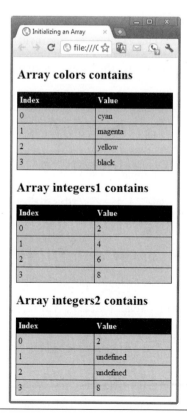

Fig. 10.5 | Web page for showing the results of initializing arrays.

The start function in Fig. 10.6 demonstrates array initializer lists (lines 7–9) and displays each array in an HTML5 table using the same function outputArray as Fig. 10.4. Note that when array integers2 is displayed in the web page, the elements with indices 1 and 2 (the second and third elements of the array) appear in the web page as undefined. These are the two elements for which we did not supply values in line 9.

```
 1   // Fig. 10.6: InitArray2.js
 2   // Initializing arrays with initializer lists.
 3   function start()
 4   {
 5      // Initializer list specifies the number of elements and
 6      // a value for each element.
 7      var colors = new Array( "cyan", "magenta","yellow", "black" );
 8      var integers1 = [ 2, 4, 6, 8 ];
 9      var integers2 = [ 2, , , 8 ];
10
11      outputArray( "Array colors contains", colors,
12         document.getElementById( "output1" ) );
13      outputArray( "Array integers1 contains", integers1,
14         document.getElementById( "output2" ) );
15      outputArray( "Array integers2 contains", integers2,
16         document.getElementById( "output3" ) );
17   } // end function start
18
19   // output the heading followed by a two-column table
20   // containing indices and elements of "theArray"
21   function outputArray( heading, theArray, output )
22   {
23      var content = "<h2>" + heading + "</h2><table>" +
24         "<thead><th>Index</th><th>Value</th></thead><tbody>";
25
26      // output the index and value of each array element
27      var length = theArray.length; // get array's length once before loop
28
29      for ( var i = 0; i < length; ++i )
30      {
31         content += "<tr><td>" + i + "</td><td>" + theArray[ i ] +
32            "</td></tr>";
33      } // end for
34
35      content += "</tbody></table>";
36      output.innerHTML = content; // place the table in the output element
37   } // end function outputArray
38
39   window.addEventListener( "load", start, false );
```

Fig. 10.6 | Initializing arrays with initializer lists.

10.4.3 Summing the Elements of an Array with for and for...in

The example in Figs. 10.7–10.8 sums an array's elements and displays the results. The document in Fig. 10.7 shows the results of the script in Fig. 10.8.

```
 1   <!DOCTYPE html>
 2
 3   <!-- Fig. 10.7: SumArray.html -->
 4   <!-- HTML5 document that displays the sum of an array's elements. -->
 5   <html>
 6      <head>
 7         <meta charset = "utf-8">
 8         <title>Sum Array Elements</title>
 9         <script src = "SumArray.js"></script>
10      </head>
11      <body>
12         <div id = "output"></div>
13      </body>
14   </html>
```

Fig. 10.7 | HTML5 document that displays the sum of an array's elements.

The script in Fig. 10.8 sums the values contained in theArray, the 10-element integer array declared, allocated and initialized in line 5. The statement in line 14 in the body of the first for statement does the totaling.

```
 1   // Fig. 10.8: SumArray.js
 2   // Summing the elements of an array with for and for...in
 3   function start()
 4   {
 5      var theArray = [ 1, 2, 3, 4, 5, 6, 7, 8, 9, 10 ];
 6      var total1 = 0, total2 = 0;
 7
 8      // iterates through the elements of the array in order and adds
 9      // each element's value to total1
10      var length = theArray.length; // get array's length once before loop
11
12      for ( var i = 0; i < length; ++i )
13      {
14         total1 += theArray[ i ];
15      } // end for
16
17      var results = "<p>Total using indices: " + total1 + "</p>";
18
19      // iterates through the elements of the array using a for... in
20      // statement to add each element's value to total2
21      for ( var element in theArray )
22      {
23         total2 += theArray[ element ];
24      } // end for
25
26      results += "<p>Total using for...in: " + total2 + "</p>";
27      document.getElementById( "output" ).innerHTML = results;
28   } // end function start
29
30   window.addEventListener( "load", start, false );
```

Fig. 10.8 | Summing the elements of an array with for and for...in. (Part 1 of 2.)

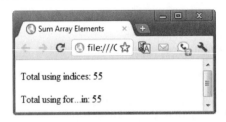

Fig. 10.8 | Summing the elements of an array with for and for...in. (Part 2 of 2.)

The for...in Repetition Statement

In this example, we introduce JavaScript's **for...in statement**, which enables a script to perform a task for each element in an array (or, as we'll see in Chapters 12–13, for each element in a *collection*). Lines 21–24 show the syntax of a for...in statement. Inside the parentheses, we declare the element variable used to select each element in the object to the right of keyword in (theArray in this case). When you use for...in, JavaScript automatically determines the number of elements in the array. As the JavaScript interpreter iterates over theArray's elements, variable element is assigned a value that can be used as an index for theArray. In the case of an array, the value assigned is an index in the range from 0 up to, but not including, theArray.length. Each value is added to total2 to produce the sum of the elements in the array.

> **Error-Prevention Tip 10.2**
>
> *When iterating over all the elements of an array, use a for...in statement to ensure that you manipulate only the existing elements. The for...in statement skips any undefined elements in the array.*

10.4.4 Using the Elements of an Array as Counters

In Section 9.5.3, we indicated that there's a more elegant way to implement the dice-rolling example presented in that section. The example allowed the user to roll 12 dice at a time and kept statistics showing the number of times and the percentage of the time each face occurred. An array version of this example is shown in Figs. 10.9–10.10. We divided the example into three files—style.css contains the styles (not shown here), Roll-Dice.html (Fig. 10.9) contains the HTML5 document and RollDice.js (Fig. 10.10) contains the JavaScript.

```
 1   <!DOCTYPE html>
 2
 3   <!-- Fig. 10.9: RollDice.html -->
 4   <!-- HTML5 document for the dice-rolling example. -->
 5   <html>
 6      <head>
 7         <meta charset = "utf-8">
 8         <title>Roll a Six-Sided Die 6000000 Times</title>
 9         <link rel = "stylesheet" type = "text/css" href = "style.css">
```

Fig. 10.9 | HTML5 document for the dice-rolling example. (Part 1 of 2.)

```
10          <script src = "RollDice.js"></script>
11      </head>
12      <body>
13          <p><img id = "die1" src = "blank.png" alt = "die 1 image">
14              <img id = "die2" src = "blank.png" alt = "die 2 image">
15              <img id = "die3" src = "blank.png" alt = "die 3 image">
16              <img id = "die4" src = "blank.png" alt = "die 4 image">
17              <img id = "die5" src = "blank.png" alt = "die 5 image">
18              <img id = "die6" src = "blank.png" alt = "die 6 image"></p>
19          <p><img id = "die7" src = "blank.png" alt = "die 7 image">
20              <img id = "die8" src = "blank.png" alt = "die 8 image">
21              <img id = "die9" src = "blank.png" alt = "die 9 image">
22              <img id = "die10" src = "blank.png" alt = "die 10 image">
23              <img id = "die11" src = "blank.png" alt = "die 11 image">
24              <img id = "die12" src = "blank.png" alt = "die 12 image"></p>
25          <form action = "#">
26              <input id = "rollButton" type = "button" value = "Roll Dice">
27          </form>
28          <div id = "frequencyTableDiv"></div>
29      </body>
30  </html>
```

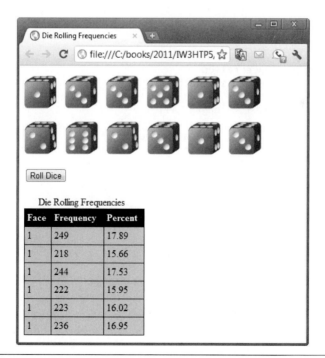

Fig. 10.9 | HTML5 document for the dice-rolling example. (Part 2 of 2.)

In Fig. 10.10, lines 3–5 declare the scripts global variables. The frequency array (line 3) contains seven elements representing the counters we use in this script. We ignore element 0 of the array and use only the elements that correspond to values on the sides of a die (the elements with indices 1–6). Variable totalDice tracks the total number of dice rolled. The dieImages array contains 12 elements that will refer to the 12 img elements in the HTML document (Fig. 10.9).

```
1   // Fig. 10.10: RollDice.js
2   // Summarizing die-rolling frequencies with an array instead of a switch
3   var frequency = [ , 0, 0, 0, 0, 0, 0 ]; // frequency[0] uninitialized
4   var totalDice = 0;
5   var dieImages = new Array(12); // array to store img elements
6
7   // get die img elements
8   function start()
9   {
10      var button = document.getElementById( "rollButton" );
11      button.addEventListener( "click", rollDice, false );
12      var length = dieImages.length; // get array's length once before loop
13
14      for ( var i = 0; i < length; ++i )
15      {
16         dieImages[ i ] = document.getElementById( "die" + (i + 1) );
17      } // end for
18   } // end function start
19
20   // roll the dice
21   function rollDice()
22   {
23      var face;  // face rolled
24      var length = dieImages.length;
25
26      for ( var i = 0; i < length; ++i )
27      {
28         face = Math.floor( 1 + Math.random() * 6 );
29         tallyRolls( face ); // increment a frequency counter
30         setImage( i, face ); // display appropriate die image
31         ++totalDice; // increment total
32      } // end for
33
34      updateFrequencyTable();
35   } // end function rollDice
36
37   // increment appropriate frequency counter
38   function tallyRolls( face )
39   {
40      ++frequency[ face ]; // increment appropriate counte
41   } // end function tallyRolls
42
43   // set image source for a die
44   function setImage( dieImg )
45   {
46      dieImages[ dieNumber ].setAttribute( "src", "die" + face + ".png" );
47      dieImages[ dieNumber ].setAttribute( "alt",
48         "die with " + face + " spot(s)" );
49   } // end function setImage
```

Fig. 10.10 | Summarizing die-rolling frequencies with an array instead of a switch. (Part 1 of 2.)

```
50
51    // update frequency table in the page
52    function updateFrequencyTable()
53    {
54       var results = "<table><caption>Die Rolling Frequencies</caption>" +
55          "<thead><th>Face</th><th>Frequency</th>" +
56          "<th>Percent</th></thead><tbody>";
57       var length = frequency.length;
58
59       // create table rows for frequencies
60       for ( var i = 1; i < length; ++i )
61       {
62          results += "<tr><td>1</td><td>" + i + "</td><td>" +
63             formatPercent(frequency[ i ] / totalDice) + "</td></tr>";
64       } // end for
65
66       results += "</tbody></table>";
67       document.getElementById( "frequencyTableDiv" ).innerHTML = results;
68    } // end function updateFrequencyTable
69
70    // format percentage
71    function formatPercent( value )
72    {
73       value *= 100;
74       return value.toFixed(2);
75    } // end function formatPercent
76
77    window.addEventListener( "load", start, false );
```

Fig. 10.10 | Summarizing die-rolling frequencies with an array instead of a `switch`. (Part 2 of 2.)

When the document finishes loading, the script's `start` function (lines 8–18) is called to register the button's event handler and to get the `img` elements and store them in the global array `dieImages` for use in the rest of the script. Each time the user clicks the **Roll Dice** button, function `rollDice` (lines 21–35) is called to roll 12 dice and update the results on the page.

The `switch` statement in Fig. 9.6 is replaced by line 40 in function `tallyRolls`. This line uses the random `face` value (calculated at line 28) as the index for the array `frequency` to determine which element to increment during each iteration of the loop. Because the random number calculation in line 28 produces numbers from 1 to 6 (the values for a six-sided die), the `frequency` array must have seven elements (index values 0 to 6). Also, lines 60–64 of this program generate the table rows that were written one line at a time in Fig. 9.6. We can loop through array `frequency` to help produce the output, so we do not have to enumerate each HTML5 table row as we did in Fig. 9.6.

10.5 Random Image Generator Using Arrays

In Chapter 9, we created a random image generator that required image files to be named with the word `die` followed by a number from 1 to 6 and the file extension `.png` (e.g, `die1.png`). In this example (Figs. 10.11–10.12), we create a more elegant random image generator that does not require the image filenames to contain integers in sequence. This version uses an array `pictures` to store the names of the image files as strings. Each time you click the image in the document (Fig. 10.11), the script generates a random integer and uses it as an index into the `pictures` array. The script updates the `img` element's `src` attribute with the image filename at the randomly selected position in the `pictures` array. In addition, we update the `alt` attribute with an appropriate description of the image from the `descriptions` array.

```
1   <!DOCTYPE html>
2
3   <!-- Fig. 10.11: RandomPicture.html -->
4   <!-- HTML5 document that displays randomly selected images. -->
5   <html>
6      <head>
7         <meta charset = "utf-8">
8         <title>Random Image Generator</title>
9         <script src = "RandomPicture.js"></script>
10     </head>
11     <body>
12        <img id = "image" src = "CPE.png" alt = "Common Programming Error">
13     </body>
14  </html>
```

Fig. 10.11 | HTML5 document that displays randomly selected images.

The script (Fig. 10.12) declares the array `pictures` in line 4 and initializes it with the names of seven image files—the files contain our bug icons that we associate with our programming tips. Lines 5–8 create a separate array `descriptions` that contains the `alt` text for the corresponding images in the `pictures` array. When the user clicks the `img` element in the document, function `pickImage` (lines 12–17) is called to pick a random integer `index` from 0 to 6 and display the associated image. Line 15 uses that `index` to get a value from the `pictures` array, appends `".png"` to it, then sets the `img` element's `src` attribute to the new image file name. Similarly, line 16 uses the `index` to get the corresponding text from the `descriptions` array and assigns that text to the `img` element's `alt` attribute.

```
1   // Fig. 10.12: RandomPicture2.js
2   // Random image selection using arrays
3   var iconImg;
4   var pictures = [ "CPE", "EPT", "GPP", "GUI", "PERF", "PORT", "SEO" ];
```

Fig. 10.12 | Random image selection using arrays. (Part 1 of 2.)

```
 5    var descriptions = [ "Common Programming Error",
 6       "Error-Prevention Tip", "Good Programming Practice",
 7       "Look-and-Feel Observation", "Performance Tip", "Portability Tip",
 8       "Software Engineering Observation" ];
 9
10    // pick a random image and corresponding description, then modify
11    // the img element in the document's body
12    function pickImage()
13    {
14       var index = Math.floor( Math.random() * 7 );
15       iconImg.setAttribute( "src", pictures[ index ] + ".png" );
16       iconImg.setAttribute( "alt", descriptions[ index ] );
17    } // end function pickImage
18
19    // registers iconImg's click event handler
20    function start()
21    {
22       iconImg = document.getElementById( "iconImg" );
23       iconImg.addEventListener( "click", pickImage, false );
24    } // end function start
25
26    window.addEventListener( "load", start, false );
```

Fig. 10.12 | Random image selection using arrays. (Part 2 of 2.)

10.6 References and Reference Parameters

Two ways to pass arguments to functions (or methods) in many programming languages are **pass-by-value** and **pass-by-reference**. When an argument is passed to a function by value, a *copy* of the argument's value is made and is passed to the called function. In JavaScript, numbers, boolean values and strings are passed to functions by value.

With pass-by-reference, the caller gives the called function access to the caller's data and allows the called function to *modify* the data if it so chooses. This procedure is accomplished by passing to the called function the **address in memory** where the data resides. Pass-by-reference can *improve performance* because it can eliminate the overhead of copying large amounts of data, but it can *weaken security* because the called function can access the caller's data. In JavaScript, all objects (and thus all arrays) are passed to functions by reference.

Error-Prevention Tip 10.3
With pass-by-value, changes to the copy of the value received by the called function do not affect the original variable's value in the calling function. This prevents the accidental side effects that hinder the development of correct and reliable software systems.

Software Engineering Observation 10.3
When information is returned from a function via a return statement, numbers and boolean values are returned by value (i.e., a copy is returned), and objects are returned by reference (i.e., a reference to the object is returned). When an object is passed-by-reference, it's not necessary to return the object, because the function operates on the original object in memory.

The name of an array actually is a *reference* to an object that contains the array elements and the length variable. To pass a reference to an object into a function, simply specify the reference name in the function call. The reference name is the identifier that the program uses to manipulate the object. Mentioning the reference by its parameter name in the body of the called function actually refers to the original object in memory, and the original object is accessed directly by the called function.

10.7 Passing Arrays to Functions

To pass an array argument to a function, specify the array's name (a reference to the array) without brackets. For example, if array hourlyTemperatures has been declared as

```
var hourlyTemperatures = new Array( 24 );
```

then the function call

```
modifyArray( hourlyTemperatures );
```

passes array hourlyTemperatures to function modifyArray. As stated in Section 10.2, every array object in JavaScript knows its own size (via the length attribute). Thus, when we pass an array object into a function, we do not pass the array's size separately as an argument. Figure 10.4 demonstrated this concept.

Although entire arrays are passed by reference, *individual numeric and boolean array elements* are passed *by value* exactly as simple numeric and boolean variables are passed. Such simple single pieces of data are called **scalars**, or **scalar quantities**. Objects referred to by individual array elements are still passed by reference. To pass an array element to a function, use the indexed name of the element as an argument in the function call.

For a function to receive an array through a function call, the function's parameter list must specify a parameter that will refer to the array in the body of the function. JavaScript does not provide a special syntax for this purpose—it simply requires that the identifier for the array be specified in the parameter list. For example, the function header for function modifyArray might be written as

```
function modifyArray( b )
```

indicating that modifyArray expects to receive a parameter named b. Arrays are passed by reference, and therefore when the called function uses the array name b, it refers to the actual array in the caller (array hourlyTemperatures in the preceding call). The script in Figures 10.13–10.14 demonstrates the difference between passing an entire array and passing an array element. The body of the document in Fig. 10.13 contains the p elements that the script in Fig. 10.14 uses to display the results.

```
1   <!DOCTYPE html>
2
3   <!-- Fig. 10.13: PassArray.html -->
4   <!-- HTML document that demonstrates passing arrays and -->
5   <!-- individual array elements to functions. -->
6   <html>
```

Fig. 10.13 | HTML document that demonstrates passing arrays and individual array elements to functions. (Part 1 of 2.)

```
7       <head>
8          <meta charset = "utf-8">
9          <title>Arrays as Arguments</title>
10         <link rel = "stylesheet" type = "text/css" href = "style.css">
11         <script src = "PassArray.js"></script>
12      </head>
13      <body>
14         <h2>Effects of passing entire array by reference</h2>
15         <p id = "originalArray"></p>
16         <p id = "modifiedArray"></p>
17         <h2>Effects of passing array element by value</h2>
18         <p id = "originalElement"></p>
19         <p id = "inModifyElement"></p>
20         <p id = "modifiedElement"></p>
21      </body>
22   </html>
```

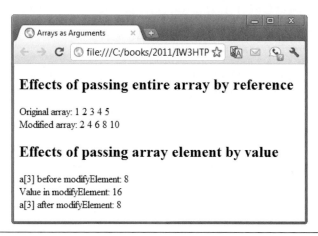

Fig. 10.13 | HTML document that demonstrates passing arrays and individual array elements to functions. (Part 2 of 2.)

 Software Engineering Observation 10.4

JavaScript does not check the number of arguments or types of arguments that are passed to a function. It's possible to pass any number of values to a function.

When the document of Fig. 10.13 loads, function start (Fig. 10.14, lines 3–20) is called. Lines 8–9 invoke outputArray to display the array a's contents before it's modified. Function outputArray (lines 23–26) receives a string to display, the array to display and the element in which to place the content. Line 25 uses Array method **join** to create a string containing all the elements in theArray. Method join takes as its argument a string containing the **separator** that should be used to separate the array elements in the string that's returned. If the argument is not specified, the empty string is used as the separator.

Line 10 invokes modifyArray (lines 29–35) and passes it array a. The function multiplies each element by 2. To illustrate that array a's elements were modified, lines 11–12 invoke outputArray again to display the array a's contents after it's modified. As the screen capture in Fig. 10.13 shows, the elements of a are indeed modified by modifyArray.

```
 1    // Fig. 10.14: PassArray.js
 2    // Passing arrays and individual array elements to functions.
 3    function start()
 4    {
 5       var a = [ 1, 2, 3, 4, 5 ];
 6
 7       // passing entire array
 8       outputArray( "Original array: ", a,
 9          document.getElementById( "originalArray" ) );
10       modifyArray( a );   // array a passed by reference
11       outputArray( "Modified array: ", a,
12          document.getElementById( "modifiedArray" ) );
13
14       // passing individual array element
15       document.getElementById( "originalElement" ).innerHTML =
16          "a[3] before modifyElement: " + a[ 3 ];
17       modifyElement( a[ 3 ] ); // array element a[3] passed by value
18       document.getElementById( "modifiedElement" ).innerHTML =
19          "a[3] after modifyElement: " + a[ 3 ];
20    } // end function start()
21
22    // outputs heading followed by the contents of "theArray"
23    function outputArray( heading, theArray, output )
24    {
25       output.innerHTML = heading + theArray.join( " " );
26    } // end function outputArray
27
28    // function that modifies the elements of an array
29    function modifyArray( theArray )
30    {
31       for ( var j in theArray )
32       {
33          theArray[ j ] *= 2;
34       } // end for
35    } // end function modifyArray
36
37    // function that modifies the value passed
38    function modifyElement( e )
39    {
40       e *= 2; // scales element e only for the duration of the function
41       document.getElementById( "inModifyElement" ).innerHTML =
42          "Value in modifyElement: " + e;
43    } // end function modifyElement
44
45    window.addEventListener( "load", start, false );
```

Fig. 10.14 | Passing arrays and individual array elements to functions.

Lines 15–16 display the value of a[3] before the call to modifyElement. Line 17 invokes modifyElement (lines 38–43), passing a[3] as the argument. Remember that a[3] actually is one integer value in the array, and that numeric values and boolean values are always passed to functions by value. Therefore, a *copy* of a[3] is passed. Function modify-Element multiplies its argument by 2, stores the result in its parameter e, then displays e's value. A parameter is a local variable in a function, so when the function terminates, the local variable is no longer accessible. Thus, when control is returned to start, the unmodified original value of a[3] is displayed by the statement in lines 18–19.

10.8 Sorting Arrays with Array Method sort

Sorting data (putting data in a particular order, such as ascending or descending) is one of the most important computing functions. The Array object in JavaScript has a built-in method **sort** for sorting arrays. The example in Figs. 10.15–10.16 demonstrates the Array object's sort method. The unsorted and sorted values are displayed in Figs. 10.15's paragraph elements (lines 14–15).

```
 1   <!DOCTYPE html>
 2
 3   <!-- Fig. 10.15: Sort.html -->
 4   <!-- HTML5 document that displays the results of sorting an array. -->
 5   <html>
 6      <head>
 7         <meta charset = "utf-8">
 8         <title>Array Method sort</title>
 9         <link rel = "stylesheet" type = "text/css" href = "style.css">
10         <script src = "Sort.js"></script>
11      </head>
12      <body>
13         <h1>Sorting an Array</h1>
14         <p id = "originalArray"></p>
15         <p id = "sortedArray"></p>
16      </body>
17   </html>
```

Fig. 10.15 | HTML5 document that displays the results of sorting an array.

By default, Array method sort (with no arguments) uses *string* comparisons to determine the sorting order of the array elements. The strings are compared by the ASCII values of their characters. [*Note:* String comparison is discussed in more detail in Chapter 11.] In this script (Fig. 10.16), we'd like to sort an array of *integers*.

Method sort (line 9) takes as its argument the name of a **comparator function** that compares its two arguments and returns one of the following:

- a negative value if the first argument is *less than* the second argument,

```
 1    // Fig. 10.16: Sort.js
 2    // Sorting an array with sort.
 3    function start()
 4    {
 5       var a = [ 10, 1, 9, 2, 8, 3, 7, 4, 6, 5 ];
 6
 7       outputArray( "Data items in original order: ", a,
 8          document.getElementById( "originalArray" ) );
 9       a.sort( compareIntegers );  // sort the array
10       outputArray( "Data items in ascending order: ", a,
11          document.getElementById( "sortedArray" ) );
12    } // end function start
13
14    // output the heading followed by the contents of theArray
15    function outputArray( heading, theArray, output )
16    {
17       output.innerHTML = heading + theArray.join( " " );
18    } // end function outputArray
19
20    // comparison function for use with sort
21    function compareIntegers( value1, value2 )
22    {
23       return parseInt( value1 ) - parseInt( value2 );
24    } // end function compareIntegers
25
26    window.addEventListener( "load", start, false );
```

Fig. 10.16 | Sorting an array with sort.

- zero if the arguments are *equal,* or
- a positive value if the first argument is *greater than* the second argument.

This example uses the comparator function compareIntegers (defined in lines 21–24). It calculates the difference between the integer values of its two arguments (function parse-Int ensures that the arguments are handled properly as integers).

Line 9 invokes Array object a's sort method and passes function compareIntegers as an argument. Method sort then uses function compareIntegers to compare elements of the array a to determine their sorting order.

Software Engineering Observation 10.5

Functions in JavaScript are considered to be data. Therefore, functions can be assigned to variables, stored in arrays and passed to functions just like other data types.

10.9 Searching Arrays with Array Method indexOf

When working with data stored in arrays, it's often necessary to determine whether an array contains a value that matches a certain *key value*. The process of locating a particular element value in an array is called *searching*. The Array object in JavaScript has built-in methods **indexOf** and **lastIndexOf** for searching arrays. Method indexOf searches for the first occurrence of the specified key value, and method lastIndexOf searches for the last occurrence of the specified key value. If the key value is found in the array, each method returns the index of that value; otherwise, -1 is returned. The example in Figs. 10.17–10.18 demonstrates method `indexOf`. You enter the integer search key in the form's number input element (Fig. 10.17, line 14) then press the `button` (lines 15–16) to invoke the script's `buttonPressed` function, which performs the search and displays the results in the paragraph at line 17.

```
1    <!DOCTYPE html>
2
3    <!-- Fig. 10.17: search.html -->
4    <!-- HTML5 document for searching an array with indexOf. -->
5    <html>
6       <head>
7          <meta charset = "utf-8">
8          <title>Search an Array</title>
9          <script src = "search.js"></script>
10      </head>
11      <body>
12         <form action   = "#">
13            <p><label>Enter integer search key:
14               <input id = "inputVal" type = "number"></label>
15               <input id = "searchButton" type = "button" value = "Search">
16            </p>
17            <p id = "result"></p>
18         </form>
19      </body>
20   </html>
```

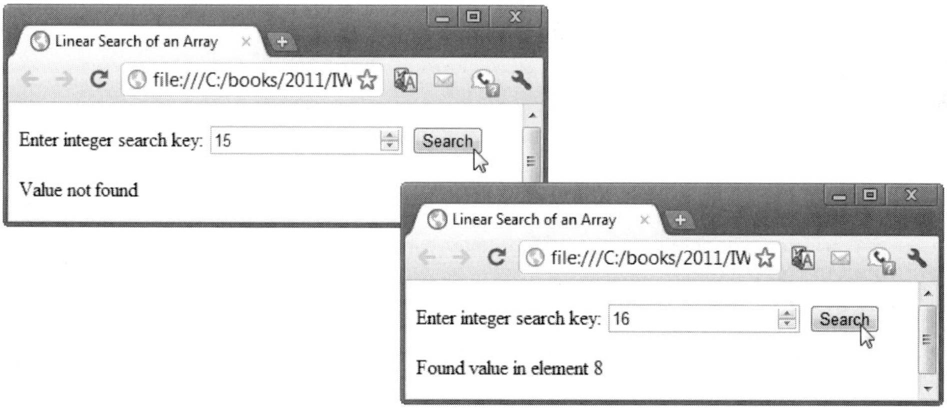

Fig. 10.17 | HTML5 document for searching an array with `indexOf`.

The script in Fig. 10.18 creates an array containing 100 elements (line 3), then initializes the array's elements with the even integers from 0 to 198 (lines 6–9). When the user presses the `button` in Fig. 10.17, function `buttonPressed` (lines 12–32) performs the search and displays the results. Line 15 gets the `inputVal` number input element, which contains the key value specified by the user, and line 18 gets the paragraph where the script displays the results. Next, we get the integer value entered by the user (line 21). Every input element has a **value property** that can be used to get or set the element's value.

Finally, line 22 performs the search by calling method indexOf on the array a, and lines 24–31 display the results.

```
1    // Fig. 10.18: search.js
2    // Search an array with indexOf.
3    var a = new Array( 100 );  // create an array
4
5    // fill array with even integer values from 0 to 198
6    for ( var i = 0; i < a.length; ++i )
7    {
8       a[ i ] = 2 * i;
9    } // end for
10
11   // function called when "Search" button is pressed
12   function buttonPressed()
13   {
14      // get the input text field
15      var inputVal = document.getElementById( "inputVal" );
16
17      // get the result paragraph
18      var result = document.getElementById( "result" );
19
20      // get the search key from the input text field then perform the search
21      var searchKey = parseInt( inputVal.value );
22      var element = a.indexOf( searchKey );
23
24      if ( element != -1 )
25      {
26         result.innerHTML = "Found value in element " + element;
27      } // end if
28      else
29      {
30         result.innerHTML = "Value not found";
31      } // end else
32   } // end function buttonPressed
33
34   // register searchButton's click event handler
35   function start()
36   {
37      var searchButton = document.getElementById( "searchButton" );
38      searchButton.addEventListener( "click", buttonPressed, false );
39   } // end function start
40
41   window.addEventListener( "load", start, false );
```

Fig. 10.18 | Search an array with indexOf.

Optional Second Argument to indexOf and lastIndexOf
You can pass an optional second argument to methods indexOf and lastIndexOf that represents the index from which to start the search. By default, this argument's value is 0 and the methods search the entire array. If the argument is greater than or equal to the array's length, the methods simply return -1. If the argument's value is negative, it's used as an offset from the end of the array. For example, the 100-element array in Fig. 10.18 has in-

dices from 0 to 99. If we pass -10 as the second argument, the search will begin from index 89. If a negative second argument results in an index value less than 0 as the start point, the entire array will be searched.

10.10 Multidimensional Arrays

Multidimensional arrays with two indices are often used to represent *tables* of values consisting of information arranged in **rows** and **columns**. To identify a particular table element, we must specify the two indices; by convention, the first identifies the element's row and the second the element's column. Arrays that require two indices to identify a particular element are called **two-dimensional arrays**.

Multidimensional arrays can have *more* than two dimensions. JavaScript does not support multidimensional arrays directly, but it does allow you to specify arrays whose elements are also arrays, thus achieving the same effect. When an array contains one-dimensional arrays as its elements, we can imagine these one-dimensional arrays as rows of a table, and the positions in these arrays as columns. Figure 10.19 illustrates a two-dimensional array named a that contains three rows and four columns (i.e., a three-by-four array—three one-dimensional arrays, each with four elements). In general, an array with *m* rows and *n* columns is called an *m-by-n* **array**.

Every element in array a is identified in Fig. 10.19 by an element name of the form a[row][column]—a is the name of the array, and row and column are the indices that uniquely identify the row and column, respectively, of each element in a. The element names in row 0 all have a first index of 0; the element names in column 3 all have a second index of 3.

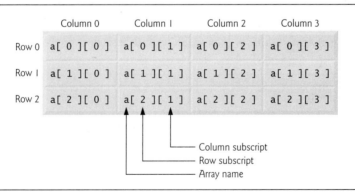

Fig. 10.19 | Two-dimensional array with three rows and four columns.

Arrays of One-Dimensional Arrays
Multidimensional arrays can be initialized in declarations like a one-dimensional array. Array b with two rows and two columns could be declared and initialized with the statement

```
var b = [ [ 1, 2 ], [ 3, 4 ] ];
```

The values are grouped by row in square brackets. The array [1, 2] initializes element b[0], and the array [3, 4] initializes element b[1]. So 1 and 2 initialize b[0][0] and b[0][1], respectively. Similarly, 3 and 4 initialize b[1][0] and b[1][1], respectively. The interpreter determines the number of rows by counting the number of subinitializer lists—arrays nested within the outermost array. The interpreter determines the number of columns in each row by counting the number of values in the subarray that initializes the row.

Two-Dimensional Arrays with Rows of Different Lengths

The rows of a two-dimensional array can vary in length. The declaration

```
var b = [ [ 1, 2 ], [ 3, 4, 5 ] ];
```

creates array b with row 0 containing two elements (1 and 2) and row 1 containing three elements (3, 4 and 5).

Creating Two-Dimensional Arrays with *new*

A multidimensional array in which each row has a *different* number of columns can be allocated dynamically, as follows:

```
var b;
b = new Array( 2 );       // allocate two rows
b[ 0 ] = new Array( 5 ); // allocate columns for row 0
b[ 1 ] = new Array( 3 ); // allocate columns for row 1
```

The preceding code creates a two-dimensional array with two rows. Row 0 has five columns, and row 1 has three columns.

Two-Dimensional Array Example: Displaying Element Values

The example in Figs. 10.20–10.21 initializes two-dimensional arrays in declarations and uses nested for…in loops to **traverse the arrays** (i.e., manipulate every element of the array). When the document in Fig. 10.20 loads, the script's start function displays the results of initializing the arrays.

The script's start function declares and initializes two arrays (Fig. 10.21, lines 5–9). The declaration of array1 (lines 5–6) provides six initializers in two sublists. The first sublist

```
1   <!DOCTYPE html>
2
3   <!-- Fig. 10.20: InitArray3.html -->
4   <!-- HTML5 document showing multidimensional array initialization. -->
5   <html>
6     <head>
7       <meta charset = "utf-8">
8       <title>Multidimensional Arrays</title>
9       <link rel = "stylesheet" type = "text/css" href = "style.css">
10      <script src = "InitArray3.js"></script>
11    </head>
12    <body>
13      <h2>Values in array1 by row</h2>
14      <div id = "output1"></div>
15      <h2>Values in array2 by row</h2>
16      <div id = "output2"></div>
17    </body>
18  </html>
```

Fig. 10.20 | HTML5 document showing multidimensional array initialization. (Part 1 of 2.)

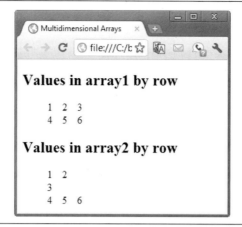

Fig. 10.20 | HTML5 document showing multidimensional array initialization. (Part 2 of 2.)

initializes row 0 of the array to the values 1, 2 and 3; the second sublist initializes row 1 of the array to the values 4, 5 and 6. The declaration of array2 (lines 7–9) provides six initializers in three sublists. The sublist for row 0 explicitly initializes the row to have two elements, with values 1 and 2, respectively. The sublist for row 1 initializes the row to have one element, with value 3. The sublist for row 2 initializes the third row to the values 4, 5 and 6.

```
1   // Fig. 10.21: InitArray3.js
2   // Initializing multidimensional arrays.
3   function start()
4   {
5      var array1 = [ [ 1, 2, 3 ], // row 0
6                     [ 4, 5, 6 ] ]; // row 1
7      var array2 = [ [ 1, 2 ], // row 0
8                     [ 3 ], // row 1
9                     [ 4, 5, 6 ] ]; // row 2
10
11     outputArray( "Values in array1 by row", array1,
12        document.getElementById( "output1" ) );
13     outputArray( "Values in array2 by row", array2,
14        document.getElementById( "output2" ) );
15  } // end function start
16
17  // display array contents
18  function outputArray( heading, theArray, output )
19  {
20     var results = "";
21
22     // iterates through the set of one-dimensional arrays
23     for ( var row in theArray )
24     {
25        results += "<ol>"; // start ordered list
26
```

Fig. 10.21 | Initializing multidimensional arrays. (Part 1 of 2.)

```
27         // iterates through the elements of each one-dimensional array
28         for ( var column in theArray[ row ] )
29         {
30             results += "<li>" + theArray[ row ][ column ] + "</li>";
31         } // end inner for
32
33         results += "</ol>"; // end ordered list
34      } // end outer for
35
36      output.innerHTML = results;
37   } // end function outputArray
38
39   window.addEventListener( "load", start, false );
```

Fig. 10.21 | Initializing multidimensional arrays. (Part 2 of 2.)

Function start calls function outputArray twice (lines 11–14) to display each array's elements in the web page. Function outputArray (lines 18–37) receives a string heading to output before the array, the array to output (called theArray) and the element in which to display the array. The function uses a nested for...in statement (lines 23–34) to output each row of a two-dimensional array as an ordered list. Using CSS, we set each list item's display property to inline so that the list items appear unnumbered from left to right on the page, rather than numbered and listed vertically (the default). The outer for...in statement iterates over the rows of the array. The inner for...in statement iterates over the columns of the current row being processed. The nested for...in statement in this example could have been written with for statements, as follows:

```
var numberOfRows = theArray.length;

for ( var row = 0; row < numberOfRows; ++row )
{
    results += "<ol>"; // start ordered list
    var numberOfcolumns = theArray[ row ].length;

    for ( var column = 0; j < numberOfcolumns; ++j )
    {
        results += "<li>" + theArray[ row ][ column ] + "</li>";
    } // end inner for

    results += "</ol>"; // end ordered list
} // end outer for
```

Just before the outer for statement, the expression theArray.length determines the number of rows in the array. Just before the inner for statement, the expression theArray[row].length determines the number of columns in the current row of the array. This enables the loop to determine, for each row, the exact number of columns.

Common Multidimensional-Array Manipulations with for and for...in Statements
Many common array manipulations use for or for...in repetition statements. For example, the following for statement sets all the elements in row 2 of array a in Fig. 10.19 to zero:

```
var columns = a[ 2 ].length;

for ( var col = 0; col < columns; ++col )
{
   a[ 2 ][ col ] = 0;
}
```

We specified row 2; therefore, we know that the first index is always 2. The for loop varies only the second index (i.e., the column index). The preceding for statement is equivalent to the assignment statements

```
a[ 2 ][ 0 ] = 0;
a[ 2 ][ 1 ] = 0;
a[ 2 ][ 2 ] = 0;
a[ 2 ][ 3 ] = 0;
```

The following for...in statement is also equivalent to the preceding for statement:

```
for ( var col in a[ 2 ] )
{
   a[ 2 ][ col ] = 0;
}
```

The following nested for statement determines the total of all the elements in array a:

```
var total = 0;
var rows = a.length;

for ( var row = 0; row < rows; ++row )
{
   var columns = a[ row ].length;

   for ( var col = 0; col < columns; ++col )
   {
      total += a[ row ][ col ];
   }
}
```

The for statement totals the elements of the array, one row at a time. The outer for statement begins by setting the row index to 0, so that the elements of row 0 may be totaled by the inner for statement. The outer for statement then increments row to 1, so that the elements of row 1 can be totaled. Then the outer for statement increments row to 2, so that the elements of row 2 can be totaled. The result can be displayed when the nested for statement terminates. The preceding for statement is equivalent to the following for...in statement:

```
var total = 0;

for ( var row in a )
{
   for ( var col in a[ row ] )
   {
      total += a[ row ][ col ];
   }
}
```

Summary

Section 10.1 Introduction
- Arrays (p. 357) are data structures consisting of related data items (sometimes called collections of data items.
- JavaScript arrays are "dynamic" entities in that they can change size after they're created.

Section 10.2 Arrays
- An array is a group of memory locations that all have the same name and normally are of the same type (although this attribute is not required in JavaScript).
- Each individual location is called an element (p. 357). Any one of these elements may be referred to by giving the name of the array followed by the position number (an integer normally referred to as the index, p. 357) of the element in square brackets ([]).
- The first element in every array is the zeroth element (p. 357). In general, the ith element of array c is referred to as c[i-1]. Array names (p. 357) follow the same conventions as other identifiers.
- An indexed array name can be used on the left side of an assignment to place a new value (p. 358) into an array element. It can also be used on the right side of an assignment operation to assign its value to another variable.
- Every array in JavaScript knows its own length (p. 357), which it stores in its length attribute.

Section 10.3 Declaring and Allocating Arrays
- JavaScript arrays are represented by Array objects (p. 359).
- Arrays are created with operator new (p. 359).

Section 10.4 Examples Using Arrays
- To link a JavaScript file to an HTML document, use the script element's src attribute (p. 359) to specify the location of the JavaScript file.
- Zero-based counting is usually used to iterate through arrays.
- JavaScript automatically reallocates an array when a value is assigned to an element that's outside the bounds of the original array. Elements between the last element of the original array and the new element have undefined values.
- Arrays can be created using a comma-separated initializer list (p. 362) enclosed in square brackets ([and]). The array's size is determined by the number of values in the initializer list.
- The initial values of an array can also be specified as arguments in the parentheses following new Array. The size of the array is determined by the number of values in parentheses.
- JavaScript's for...in statement (p. 366) enables a script to perform a task for each element in an array. This process is known as iterating over the elements of an array.

Section 10.5 Random Image Generator Using Arrays
- We create a more elegant random image generator than the one in Chapter 9 that does not require the image filenames to be integers by using a pictures array to store the names of the image files as strings and accessing the array using a randomized index.

Section 10.6 References and Reference Parameters
- Two ways to pass arguments to functions (or methods) in many programming languages are pass-by-value and pass-by-reference (p. 371).

- When an argument is passed to a function by value, a *copy* of the argument's value is made and is passed to the called function.
- In JavaScript, numbers, boolean values and strings are passed to functions by value.
- With pass-by-reference, the caller gives the called function access to the caller's data and allows it to modify the data if it so chooses. Pass-by-reference can improve performance because it can eliminate the overhead of copying large amounts of data, but it can weaken security because the called function can access the caller's data.
- In JavaScript, all objects (and thus all arrays) are passed to functions by reference.
- The name of an array is actually a reference to an object that contains the array elements and the length variable, which indicates the number of elements in the array.

Section 10.7 Passing Arrays to Functions
- To pass an array argument to a function, specify the name of the array (a reference to the array) without brackets.
- Although entire arrays are passed by reference, individual numeric and boolean array elements are passed by value exactly as simple numeric and boolean variables are passed. Such simple single pieces of data are called scalars, or scalar quantities (p. 372). To pass an array element to a function, use the indexed name of the element as an argument in the function call.
- Method join (p. 373) takes as its argument a string containing the separator (p. 373) that should be used to separate the elements of the array in the string that's returned. If the argument is not specified, the empty string is used as the separator.

Section 10.8 Sorting Arrays with **Array** Method **sort**
- Sorting data (putting data in a particular order, such as ascending or descending, p. 375) is one of the most important computing functions.
- The Array object in JavaScript has a built-in method sort (p. 375) for sorting arrays.
- By default, Array method sort (with no arguments) uses string comparisons to determine the sorting order of the array elements.
- Method sort takes as its optional argument the name of a function (called the comparator function, p. 375) that compares its two arguments and returns a negative value, zero, or a positive value, if the first argument is less than, equal to, or greater than the second, respectively.
- Functions in JavaScript are considered to be data. Therefore, functions can be assigned to variables, stored in arrays and passed to functions just like other data types.

Section 10.9 Searching Arrays with **Array** Method **indexOf**
- Array method indexOf (p. 376) searches for the first occurrence of a value and, if found, returns the value's array index; otherwise, it returns -1. Method lastIndexOf searches for the last occurrence.

Section 10.10 Multidimensional Arrays
- To identify a particular two-dimensional multidimensional array element, we must specify the two indices; by convention, the first identifies the element's row (p. 379) and the second the element's column (p. 379).
- In general, an array with *m* rows and *n* columns is called an *m*-by-*n* array (p. 379).
- Every element in a two-dimensional array (p. 379) is accessed using an element name of the form a[row][column]; a is the name of the array, and row and column are the indices that uniquely identify the row and column, respectively, of each element in a.
- Multidimensional arrays are maintained as arrays of arrays.

Self-Review Exercises

10.1 Fill in the blanks in each of the following statements:
a) Every array in JavaScript knows its own length by _____ attribute.
b) To link a JavaScript file to an HTML document, we use the _____ attribute.
c) Zero-based counting is usually used to iterate through _____.
d) An array with *p* rows and *q* columns is called a(n) _____.
e) The _____ property contains an array of all the form's controls.

10.2 State whether each of the following is *true* or *false*. If *false*, explain why.
a) An array can store many different types of values.
b) An array index should normally be a floating-point value.
c) An individual array element that's passed to a function and modified in it will contain the modified value when the called function completes execution.

10.3 Write JavaScript statements (regarding array `fractions`) to accomplish each of the following tasks:
a) Declare an array with 15 elements, and initialize the elements of the array to 1.
b) Refer to element 5 of the array.
c) Refer to array element 7.
d) Assign the value 3.14 to array element 6.
e) Assign the value 4.444 to the lowest-numbered element of the array.
f) Multiply all the elements of the array, using a `for…in` statement. Define variable y as a control variable for the loop.

10.4 Write JavaScript statements (regarding array `table`) to accomplish each of the following tasks:
a) Declare and create the array with four rows and four columns.
b) Display the number of elements present in the second row.
c) Use a `for…in` statement to initialize each element of the array to the multiplication of its row and column indices. Assume that the variables i and j are declared as control variables.

10.5 Find the error(s) in each of the following program segments, and correct them.
a)
```
var a = new Array( 20 );
for ( var j = 0; j = 30, ++i )
{
    a[ j ] = 0;
}
```
b)
```
var b = [ [ 2, 2, 3 ], [ 3, 4, 7 ] ];
b[ 0, 0 ] = 8;
```

Answers to Self-Review Exercises

10.1 a) `length`. b) `src`. c) arrays. d) p-by-q array. e) `elements`.

10.2 a) True. b). False. An array index must be an integer or an integer expression. c) False. Individual primitive-data-type elements are passed by value. If a reference to an array is passed, then modifications to the elements of the array are reflected in the original element of the array. Also, an individual element of an object type passed to a function is passed by reference, and changes to the object will be reflected in the original array element.

10.3 a) `var fractions = [ 1, 1, 1, 1, 1, 1, 1, 1, 1, 1, 1, 1, 1, 1, 1 ];`
b) `fractions[ 5 ]`

```
c)  fractions[ 7 ]
d)  fractions[ 6 ] = 3.14;
e)  fractions[ 0 ] = 4.444;
f)  var total = 1;
    for ( var y in fractions )
    {
       total *= fractions[ y ];
    }
```

10.4 a) `var table = new Array( new Array( 4 ), new Array( 4 ),`
`new Array( 4 ), new Array( 4 ) );`
b) `document.write( "total: " + (table[ 1 ].length ) );`
c)
```
for ( var i in table )
{
   for ( var j in table[ i ] )
   {
      table[ i ][ j ] = i * j;
   }
}
```

10.5 a) Error: Referencing an array element outside the bounds of the array (`a[20]`). [*Note*: This error is actually a logic error, not a syntax error.] Correction: Change the `j < 30` to `j < 20`. b) Error: The array indexing is done incorrectly. Correction: Change the statement to `b[0][0] = 8;`.

Exercises

10.6 Fill in the blanks in each of the following statements:
a) JavaScript arrays are _____ entities.
b) Arrays are created with operator _____.
c) Two ways to pass arguments to functions (or methods) in many programming languages are _____ and _____.
d) In JavaScript, _____, _____ and _____ are passed to functions by value.
e) Multidimensional arrays are maintained as _____.

10.7 State whether each of the following is *true* or *false*. If *false*, explain why.
a) Arrays are data structures consisting of related data items, sometimes called collections of data items.
b) The first element in every array is the first element.
c) Pass-by-reference can improve performance but can weaken security.
d) Method concatenate takes as its argument a string containing the separator that should be used to separate the elements of the array in the string that's returned.
e) The binary search algorithm is more efficient than the linear search algorithm.

10.8 Write JavaScript statements to accomplish each of the following tasks:
a) Allocate 25 elements in an integer array.
b) Create and initialize a five-element array with indices of 0, 1, 2, 3 and 4.
c) Write statements to pass an array argument to a function.
d) Create an array b with two rows and two columns and initialize it.
e) Create a multidimensional array in which each row has a different number of columns which can be allocated dynamically.

10.9   Consider a three-by-four array a that will store integer number.
 a) Write a statement that declares and creates array a.
 b) How many rows does a have?
 c) How many columns does a have?
 d) How many elements does a have?
 e) Write the names of all the elements in row 2 of a.
 f) Write the names of all the elements in the second column of a.
 g) Write a single statement that sets the element of a in row 2 and column 3 to zero.
 h) Write a series of statements that initializes each element of a to one. Do not use a repetition statement.
 i) Write a nested for statement that initializes each element of a to one.
 j) Write a series of statements that determines and prints the largest value in array a.
 k) Write a non-repetition statement that displays the elements of the second row of a.
 l) Write a series of statements that prints the array a in neat, tabular format. List the column indices as headings across the top, and list the row indices at the left of each row.

10.10 Use a one-dimensional array to solve the following problem: A company pays its salespeople on a commission basis. The salespeople receive $200 per week plus 9 percent of their gross sales for that week. For example, a salesperson who grosses $5000 in sales in a week receives $200 plus 9 percent of $5000, or a total of $650. Write a script (using an array of counters) that obtains the gross sales for each employee through an HTML5 form and determines how many of the salespeople earned salaries in each of the following ranges (assume that each salesperson's salary is truncated to an integer amount):
 a) $200–299
 b) $300–399
 c) $400–499
 d) $500–599
 e) $600–699
 f) $700–799
 g) $800–899
 h) $900–999
 i) $1000 and over

10.11 Write statements that perform the following operations for a one-dimensional array:
 a) Set the 15 elements of array counts to zeros.
 b) Add 2 to each of the 20 elements of array bonus.
 c) Display the seven values of array bestScores, separated by spaces.

10.12 Write JavaScript statements to sum the values contained in an array named theArray. The 20-element integer array must first be declared, allocated and initialized. The summation of the elements of the array must to be done with for and for...in statements.

10.13 Label the elements of two-by-four two-dimensional array table to indicate the order in which they're set to five by the following program segment:

```
for ( var row in table )
{
   for ( var col in table[ row ] )
   {
      table[ row ][ col ] = 5;
   }
}
```

10.14 Write a script to simulate the rolling of two dice. The script should use `Math.random` to roll the first die and again to roll the second die. The sum of the two values should then be calculated. [*Note:* Since each die can show an integer value from 1 to 6, the sum of the values will vary from 2 to 12, with 7 being the most frequent sum, and 2 and 12 the least frequent sums. Figure 10.22 shows the 36 possible combinations of the two dice. Your program should roll the dice 36,000 times. Use a one-dimensional array to tally the number of times each possible sum appears. Display the results in an HTML5 table. Also determine whether the totals are reasonable (e.g., there are six ways to roll a 7, so approximately 1/6 of all the rolls should be 7).]

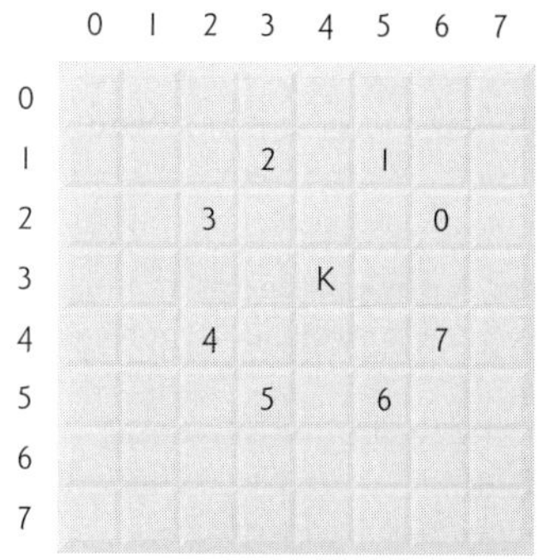

Fig. 10.22 | The 36 possible combinations of the two dice.

10.15 *(Turtle Graphics)* The Logo language, which is popular among young computer users, made the concept of *turtle graphics* famous. Imagine a mechanical turtle that walks around the room under the control of a JavaScript program. The turtle holds a pen in one of two positions, up or down. When the pen is down, the turtle traces out shapes as it moves; when the pen is up, the turtle moves about freely without writing anything. In this problem, you'll simulate the operation of the turtle and create a computerized sketchpad as well.

Use a 20-by-20 array `floor` that's initialized to zeros. Read commands from an array that contains them. Keep track of the current position of the turtle at all times and of whether the pen is currently up or down. Assume that the turtle always starts at position (0, 0) of the floor, with its pen up. The set of turtle commands your script must process are as in Fig. 10.23.

Suppose that the turtle is somewhere near the center of the floor. The following "program" would draw and print a 12-by-12 square, then leave the pen in the up position:

Command	Meaning
1	Pen up
2	Pen down
3	Turn right
4	Turn left
5,10	Move forward 10 spaces (or a number other than 10)
6	Print the 20-by-20 array
9	End of data (sentinel)

Fig. 10.23 | Turtle-graphics commands.

```
2
5,12
3
5,12
3
5,12
3
5,12
1
6
9
```

As the turtle moves with the pen down, set the appropriate elements of array floor to 1s. When the 6 command (print) is given, display an asterisk or some other character of your choosing wherever there's a 1 in the array. Wherever there's a zero, display a blank. Write a script to implement the turtle-graphics capabilities discussed here. Write several turtle-graphics programs to draw interesting shapes. Add other commands to increase the power of your turtle-graphics language.

10.16   *(The Sieve of Eratosthenes)* A prime integer is an integer greater than 1 that's evenly divisible only by itself and 1. The Sieve of Eratosthenes is an algorithm for finding prime numbers. It operates as follows:

    a) Create an array with all elements initialized to 1 (true). Array elements with prime indices will remain as 1. All other array elements will eventually be set to zero.

    b) Set the first two elements to zero, since 0 and 1 are not prime. Starting with array index 2, every time an array element is found whose value is 1, loop through the remainder of the array and set to zero every element whose index is a multiple of the index for the element with value 1. For array index 2, all elements beyond 2 in the array that are multiples of 2 will be set to zero (indices 4, 6, 8, 10, etc.); for array index 3, all elements beyond 3 in the array that are multiples of 3 will be set to zero (indices 6, 9, 12, 15, etc.); and so on.

When this process is complete, the array elements that are still set to 1 indicate that the index is a prime number. These indices can then be printed. Write a script that uses an array of 1000 elements to determine and print the prime numbers between 1 and 999. Ignore element 0 of the array.

10.17   *(Simulation: The Tortoise and the Hare)* In this problem, you'll re-create one of the truly great moments in history, namely the classic race of the tortoise and the hare. You'll use random number generation to develop a simulation of this memorable event.

    Our contenders begin the race at square 1 of 70 squares. Each square represents a possible position along the race course. The finish line is at square 70. The first contender to reach or pass square 70 is rewarded with a pail of fresh carrots and lettuce. The course weaves its way up the side of a slippery mountain, so occasionally the contenders lose ground.

    There's a clock that ticks once per second. With each tick of the clock, your script should adjust the position of the animals according to the rules in Fig. 10.24.

Animal	Move type	Percentage of the time	Actual move
Tortoise	Fast plod	50%	3 squares to the right
	Slip	20%	6 squares to the left
	Slow plod	30%	1 square to the right

Fig. 10.24 | Rules for adjusting the position of the tortoise and the hare. (Part 1 of 2.)

Animal	Move type	Percentage of the time	Actual move
Hare	Sleep	20%	No move at all
	Big hop	20%	9 squares to the right
	Big slip	10%	12 squares to the left
	Small hop	30%	1 square to the right
	Small slip	20%	2 squares to the left

Fig. 10.24 | Rules for adjusting the position of the tortoise and the hare. (Part 2 of 2.)

Use variables to keep track of the positions of the animals (i.e., position numbers are 1–70). Start each animal at position 1 (i.e., the "starting gate"). If an animal slips left before square 1, move the animal back to square 1.

Generate the percentages in Fig. 10.24 by producing a random integer i in the range $1 \leq i \leq 10$. For the tortoise, perform a "fast plod" when $1 \leq i \leq 5$, a "slip" when $6 \leq i \leq 7$ and a "slow plod" when $8 \leq i \leq 10$. Use a similar technique to move the hare.

Begin the race by printing

```
BANG !!!!!
AND THEY'RE OFF !!!!!
```

Then, for each tick of the clock (i.e., each repetition of a loop), print a 70-position line showing the letter T in the position of the tortoise and the letter H in the position of the hare. Occasionally, the contenders will land on the same square. In this case, the tortoise bites the hare, and your script should print OUCH!!! beginning at that position. All print positions other than the T, the H or the OUCH!!! (in case of a tie) should be blank.

After each line is printed, test whether either animal has reached or passed square 70. If so, print the winner, and terminate the simulation. If the tortoise wins, print TORTOISE WINS!!! YAY!!! If the hare wins, print Hare wins. Yuck! If both animals win on the same tick of the clock, you may want to favor the turtle (the "underdog"), or you may want to print It's a tie. If neither animal wins, perform the loop again to simulate the next tick of the clock. When you're ready to run your script, assemble a group of fans to watch the race. You'll be amazed at how involved your audience gets!

Later in the book, we introduce a number of Dynamic HTML capabilities, such as graphics, images, animation and sound. As you study those features, you might enjoy enhancing your tortoise-and-hare contest simulation.

11

JavaScript: Objects

My object all sublime
I shall achieve in time.
—W. S. Gilbert

Is it a world to hide virtues in?
—William Shakespeare

Objectives

In this chapter you'll:

- Learn object-based programming terminology and concepts.

- Learn the concepts of encapsulation and data hiding.

- Learn the value of object orientation.

- Use the methods of the JavaScript objects `Math`, `String`, `Date`, `Boolean` and `Number`.

- Use HTML5 web storage to create a web application that stores user data locally.

- Represent objects simply using JSON.

11.1 Introduction

This chapter presents a more formal treatment of **objects**. We presented a brief introduction to object-oriented programming concepts in Chapter 1. This chapter overviews—and serves as a reference for—several of JavaScript's built-in objects and demonstrates many of their capabilities. We use HTML5's new web storage capabilities to create a web application that stores a user's favorite Twitter searches on the computer for easy access at a later time. We also provide a brief introduction to JSON, a means for creating JavaScript objects—typically for transferring data over the Internet between client-side and server-side programs (a technique we discuss in Chapter 16). In subsequent chapters on the Document Object Model and JavaScript Events, you'll work with many objects provided by the browser that enable scripts to manipulate the elements of an HTML5 document.

11.2 Math Object

The `Math` object's methods enable you to conveniently perform many common mathematical calculations. As shown previously, an object's methods are called by writing the name of the object followed by a dot (`.`) and the name of the method. In parentheses following the method name are arguments to the method. For example, to calculate the square root of 900 you might write

```
var result = Math.sqrt( 900 );
```

which first calls method `Math.sqrt` to calculate the square root of the number contained in the parentheses (900), then assigns the result to a variable. The number 900 is the argument of the `Math.sqrt` method. The above statement would return 30. Some `Math`-object methods are summarized in Fig. 11.1.

Software Engineering Observation 11.1

The difference between invoking a stand-alone function and invoking a method of an object is that an object name and a dot are not required to call a stand-alone function.

The `Math` object defines several properties that represent commonly used mathematical constants. These are summarized in Fig. 11.2. [*Note:* By convention, the names of constants are written in all uppercase letters so that they stand out in a program.]

Method	Description	Examples
abs(x)	Absolute value of x.	abs(7.2) is 7.2 abs(0) is 0 abs(-5.6) is 5.6
ceil(x)	Rounds x to the smallest integer not less than x.	ceil(9.2) is 10 ceil(-9.8) is -9.0
cos(x)	Trigonometric cosine of x (x in radians).	cos(0) is 1
exp(x)	Exponential method e^x.	exp(1) is 2.71828 exp(2) is 7.38906
floor(x)	Rounds x to the largest integer not greater than x.	floor(9.2) is 9 floor(-9.8) is -10.0
log(x)	Natural logarithm of x (base e).	log(2.718282) is 1 log(7.389056) is 2
max(x, y)	Larger value of x and y.	max(2.3, 12.7) is 12.7 max(-2.3, -12.7) is -2.3
min(x, y)	Smaller value of x and y.	min(2.3, 12.7) is 2.3 min(-2.3, -12.7) is -12.7
pow(x, y)	x raised to power y (x^y).	pow(2, 7) is 128 pow(9, .5) is 3.0
round(x)	Rounds x to the closest integer.	round(9.75) is 10 round(9.25) is 9
sin(x)	Trigonometric sine of x (x in radians).	sin(0) is 0
sqrt(x)	Square root of x.	sqrt(900) is 30 sqrt(9) is 3
tan(x)	Trigonometric tangent of x (x in radians).	tan(0) is 0

Fig. 11.1 | Math object methods.

Constant	Description	Value
Math.E	Base of a natural logarithm (e).	Approximately 2.718
Math.LN2	Natural logarithm of 2.	Approximately 0.693
Math.LN10	Natural logarithm of 10.	Approximately 2.302
Math.LOG2E	Base 2 logarithm of e.	Approximately 1.442
Math.LOG10E	Base 10 logarithm of e.	Approximately 0.434
Math.PI	π—the ratio of a circle's circumference to its diameter.	Approximately 3.141592653589793
Math.SQRT1_2	Square root of 0.5.	Approximately 0.707
Math.SQRT2	Square root of 2.0.	Approximately 1.414

Fig. 11.2 | Properties of the Math object.

11.3 String Object

In this section, we introduce JavaScript's string- and character-processing capabilities. The techniques discussed here are appropriate for processing names, addresses, telephone numbers and other text-based data.

11.3.1 Fundamentals of Characters and Strings

Characters are the building blocks of JavaScript programs. Every program is composed of a sequence of characters grouped together meaningfully that's interpreted by the computer as a series of instructions used to accomplish a task.

A string is a series of characters treated as a single unit. A string may include letters, digits and various **special characters**, such as +, -, *, /, and $. JavaScript supports the set of characters called **Unicode®**, which represents a large portion of the world's languages. (We discuss Unicode in detail in Appendix F.) A string is an object of type **String**. **String literals** or **string constants** are written as a sequence of characters in double or single quotation marks, as follows:

```
"John Q. Doe"              (a name)
'9999 Main Street'         (a street address)
"Waltham, Massachusetts"   (a city and state)
'(201) 555-1212'           (a telephone number)
```

A `String` may be assigned to a variable in a declaration. The declaration

```
var color = "blue";
```

initializes variable `color` with the `String` object containing the string "blue". `Strings` can be compared via the relational (<, <=, > and >=) and equality operators (==, ===, != and !==). The comparisons are based on the Unicode values of the corresponding characters. For example, the expression "h" < "H" evaluates to false because lowercase letters have higher Unicode values.

11.3.2 Methods of the String Object

The `String` object encapsulates the attributes and behaviors of a string of characters. It provides many methods (behaviors) that accomplish useful tasks such as selecting characters from a string, combining strings (called **concatenation**), obtaining *substrings* (portions) of a string, searching for substrings within a string, *tokenizing strings* (i.e., splitting strings into individual words) and converting strings to all uppercase or lowercase letters. The `String` object also provides several methods that generate HTML5 tags. Figure 11.3 summarizes many `String` methods. Figures 11.4–11.9 demonstrate some of these methods.

Method	Description
charAt(*index*)	Returns a string containing the character at the specified *index*. If there's no character at the *index*, charAt returns an empty string. The first character is located at *index* 0.

Fig. 11.3 | Some String-object methods. (Part 1 of 2.)

Method	Description
charCodeAt(*index*)	Returns the Unicode value of the character at the specified *index*, or NaN (not a number) if there's no character at that *index*.
concat(*string*)	Concatenates its argument to the end of the string on which the method is invoked. The original string is not modified; instead a new String is returned. This method is the same as adding two strings with the string-concatenation operator + (e.g., s1.con-cat(s2) is the same as s1 + s2).
fromCharCode(*value1*, *value2*, ...)	Converts a list of Unicode values into a string containing the corresponding characters.
indexOf(*substring*, *index*)	Searches for the *first* occurrence of *substring* starting from position *index* in the string that invokes the method. The method returns the starting index of *substring* in the source string or −1 if *substring* is not found. If the *index* argument is not provided, the method begins searching from index 0 in the source string.
lastIndexOf(*substring*, *index*)	Searches for the *last* occurrence of *substring* starting from position *index* and searching toward the beginning of the string that invokes the method. The method returns the starting index of *substring* in the source string or −1 if *substring* is not found. If the *index* argument is not provided, the method begins searching from the *end* of the source string.
replace(*searchString*, *replaceString*)	Searches for the substring *searchString*, replaces the first occurrence with *replaceString* and returns the modified string, or returns the original string if no replacement was made.
slice(*start*, *end*)	Returns a string containing the portion of the string from index *start* through index *end*. If the *end* index is not specified, the method returns a string from the *start* index to the end of the source string. A negative *end* index specifies an offset from the end of the string, starting from a position one past the end of the last character (so −1 indicates the last character position in the string).
split(*string*)	Splits the source string into an array of strings (tokens), where its *string* argument specifies the delimiter (i.e., the characters that indicate the end of each token in the source string).
substr(*start*, *length*)	Returns a string containing *length* characters starting from index *start* in the source string. If *length* is not specified, a string containing characters from *start* to the end of the source string is returned.
substring(*start*, *end*)	Returns a string containing the characters from index *start* up to but not including index *end* in the source string.
toLowerCase()	Returns a string in which all uppercase letters are converted to lowercase letters. Non-letter characters are not changed.
toUpperCase()	Returns a string in which all lowercase letters are converted to uppercase letters. Non-letter characters are not changed.

Fig. 11.3 | Some String-object methods. (Part 2 of 2.)

11.3.3 Character-Processing Methods

The example in Figs. 11.4–11.5 demonstrates some of the String object's character-processing methods, including:

- **charAt**—returns the character at a specific position
- **charCodeAt**—returns the Unicode value of the character at a specific position
- **fromCharCode**—returns a string created from a series of Unicode values
- **toLowerCase**—returns the lowercase version of a string
- **toUpperCase**—returns the uppercase version of a string

The HTML document (Fig. 11.4) calls the script's start function to display the results in the results div. [*Note:* Throughout this chapter, we show the CSS style sheets only if there are new features to discuss. You can view each example's style-sheet contents by opening the style sheet in a text editor.]

```
 1   <!DOCTYPE html>
 2
 3   <!-- Fig. 11.4: CharacterProcessing.html -->
 4   <!-- HTML5 document to demonstrate String methods charAt, charCodeAt,
 5      fromCharCode, toLowercase and toUpperCase. -->
 6   <html>
 7      <head>
 8         <meta charset = "utf-8">
 9         <title>Character Processing</title>
10         <link rel = "stylesheet" type = "text/css" href = "style.css">
11         <script src = "CharacterProcessing.js"></script>
12      </head>
13      <body>
14         <div id = "results"></div>
15      </body>
16   </html>
```

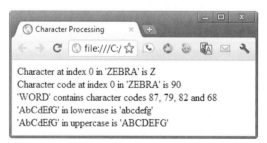

Fig. 11.4 | HTML5 document to demonstrate methods charAt, charCodeAt, fromCharCode, toLowercase and toUpperCase.

In the script (Fig. 11.5), lines 10–11 get the first character in String s ("ZEBRA") using String method charAt and append it to the result string. Method **charAt** returns a string containing the character at the specified index (0 in this example). Indices for the characters in a string start at 0 (the first character) and go up to (but do not include) the string's length (e.g., if the string contains five characters, the indices are 0 through 4). If the index is outside the bounds of the string, the method returns an empty string.

```
1   // Fig. 11.5: CharacterProcessing.js
2   // String methods charAt, charCodeAt, fromCharCode,
3   // toLowercase and toUpperCase.
4   function start()
5   {
6      var s = "ZEBRA";
7      var s2 = "AbCdEfG";
8      var result = "";
9
10     result = "<p>Character at index 0 in '" + s + "' is " +
11        s.charAt( 0 ) + "</p>";
12     result += "<p>Character code at index 0 in '" + s + "' is " +
13        s.charCodeAt( 0 ) + "</p>";
14
15     result += "<p>'" + String.fromCharCode( 87, 79, 82, 68 ) +
16        "' contains character codes 87, 79, 82 and 68</p>";
17
18     result += "<p>'" + s2 + "' in lowercase is '" +
19        s2.toLowerCase() + "'</p>";
20     result += "<p>'" + s2 + "' in uppercase is '" +
21        s2.toUpperCase() + "'</p>";
22
23     document.getElementById( "results" ).innerHTML = result;
24  } // end function start
25
26  window.addEventListener( "load", start, false );
```

Fig. 11.5 | String methods charAt, charCodeAt, fromCharCode, toLowercase and toUpperCase.

Lines 12–13 get the character code for the first character in String s ("ZEBRA") by calling String method charCodeAt. Method charCodeAt returns the Unicode value of the character at the specified index (0 in this example). If the index is outside the bounds of the string, the method returns NaN.

String method fromCharCode receives as its argument a comma-separated list of Unicode values and builds a string containing the character representations of those Unicode values. Lines 15–16 create the string "WORD", which consists of the character codes 87, 79, 82 and 68. Note that we use the String object to call method fromCharCode, rather than a specific String variable. Appendix D, ASCII Character Set, contains the character codes for the ASCII character set—a subset of the Unicode character set (Appendix F) that contains only Western characters.

Lines 18–21 use String methods **toLowerCase** and **toUpperCase** to get versions of String s2 ("AbCdEfG") in all lowercase letters and all uppercase letters, respectively.

11.3.4 Searching Methods

The example in Figs. 11.6–11.7 demonstrates the String-object methods **indexOf** and **lastIndexOf** that *search* for a specified substring in a string. All the searches in this example are performed on a global string named letters in the script (Fig. 11.7, line 3). The user types a substring in the HTML5 form searchForm's inputField and presses the **Search** button to search for the substring in letters. Clicking the **Search** button calls function buttonPressed (lines 5–18) to respond to the click event and perform the searches. The results of each search are displayed in the div named results.

In the script (Fig. 11.7), lines 10–11 use String method indexOf to determine the location of the *first* occurrence in string letters of the string inputField.value (i.e., the string the user typed in the inputField text field). If the substring is found, the index at which the first occurrence of the substring begins is returned; otherwise, –1 is returned.

```
 1   <!DOCTYPE html>
 2
 3   <!-- Fig. 11.6: SearchingStrings.html -->
 4   <!-- HTML document to demonstrate methods indexOf and lastIndexOf. -->
 5   <html>
 6      <head>
 7         <meta charset = "utf-8">
 8         <title>Searching Strings</title>
 9         <link rel = "stylesheet" type = "text/css" href = "style.css">
10      <script src = "SearchingStrings.js"></script>
11      </head>
12      <body>
13         <form id = "searchForm" action = "#">
14            <h1>The string to search is:
15               abcdefghijklmnopqrstuvwxyzabcdefghijklm</h1>
16            <p>Enter the substring to search for
17            <input id = "inputField" type = "search">
18            <input id = "searchButton" type = "button" value = "Search"></p>
19            <div id = "results"></div>
20         </form>
21      </body>
22   </html>
```

Fig. 11.6 | HTML document to demonstrate methods indexOf and lastIndexOf. (Part 1 of 2.)

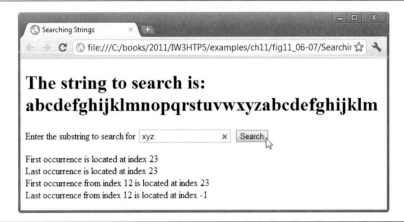

Fig. 11.6 | HTML document to demonstrate methods `indexOf` and `lastIndexOf`. (Part 2 of 2.)

Lines 12–13 use `String` method `lastIndexOf` to determine the location of the *last* occurrence in `letters` of the string in `inputField`. If the substring is found, the index at which the last occurrence of the substring begins is returned; otherwise, −1 is returned.

Lines 14–15 use `String` method `indexOf` to determine the location of the *first* occurrence in string `letters` of the string in the `inputField` text field, starting from index 12 in `letters`. If the substring is found, the index at which the first occurrence of the substring (starting from index 12) begins is returned; otherwise, −1 is returned.

Lines 16–17 use `String` method `lastIndexOf` to determine the location of the *last* occurrence in `letters` of the string in the `inputField` text field, starting from index 12 in `letters` and moving toward the beginning of the input. If the substring is found, the index at which the first occurrence of the substring (if one appears before index 12) begins is returned; otherwise, −1 is returned.

```
1   // Fig. 11.7: SearchingStrings.js
2   // Searching strings with indexOf and lastIndexOf.
3   var letters = "abcdefghijklmnopqrstuvwxyzabcdefghijklm";
4
5   function buttonPressed()
6   {
7      var inputField = document.getElementById( "inputField" );
8
9      document.getElementById( "results" ).innerHTML =
10        "<p>First occurrence is located at index " +
11           letters.indexOf( inputField.value ) + "</p>" +
12        "<p>Last occurrence is located at index " +
13           letters.lastIndexOf( inputField.value ) + "</p>" +
14        "<p>First occurrence from index 12 is located at index " +
15           letters.indexOf( inputField.value, 12 ) + "</p>" +
16        "<p>Last occurrence from index 12 is located at index " +
17           letters.lastIndexOf( inputField.value, 12 ) + "</p>";
18   } // end function buttonPressed
```

Fig. 11.7 | Searching strings with `indexOf` and `lastIndexOf`. (Part 1 of 2.)

```
19
20   // register click event handler for searchButton
21   function start()
22   {
23      var searchButton = document.getElementById( "searchButton" );
24      searchButton.addEventListener( "click", buttonPressed, false );
25   } // end function start
26
27   window.addEventListener( "load", start, false );
```

Fig. 11.7 | Searching strings with `indexOf` and `lastIndexOf`. (Part 2 of 2.)

11.3.5 Splitting Strings and Obtaining Substrings

When you read a sentence, your mind breaks it into individual words, or **tokens**, each of which conveys meaning to you. The process of breaking a string into tokens is called **tokenization**. Interpreters also perform tokenization. They break up statements into such individual pieces as keywords, identifiers, operators and other elements of a programming language. The example in Figs. 11.8–11.9 demonstrates `String` method **split**, which breaks a string into its component tokens. Tokens are separated from one another by **delimiters**, typically white-space characters such as blanks, tabs, newlines and carriage returns. Other characters may also be used as delimiters to separate tokens. The HTML5 document displays a form containing a text field where the user types a sentence to tokenize. The results of the tokenization process are displayed in a `div`. The script also demonstrates `String` method **substring**, which returns a portion of a string.

The user types a sentence into the text field with `id` `inputField` and presses the **Split** button to tokenize the string. Function `splitButtonPressed` (Fig. 11.9) is called in respons to the button's `click` event.

```
 1   <!DOCTYPE html>
 2
 3   <!-- Fig. 11.8: SplitAndSubString.html -->
 4   <!-- HTML document demonstrating String methods split and substring. -->
 5   <html>
 6      <head>
 7         <meta charset = "utf-8">
 8         <title>split and substring</title>
 9         <link rel = "stylesheet" type = "text/css" href = "style.css">
10         <script src = "SplitAndSubString.js"></script>
11      </head>
12      <body>
13         <form action = "#">
14            <p>Enter a sentence to split into words:</p>
15            <p><input id = "inputField" type = "text">
16               <input id = "splitButton" type = "button" value = "Split"></p>
17            <div id = "results"></p>
18         </form>
19      </body>
20   </html>
```

Fig. 11.8 | HTML document demonstrating `String` methods `split` and `substring`. (Part 1 of 2.)

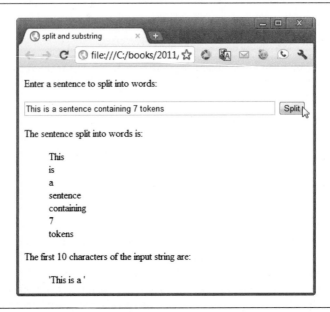

Fig. 11.8 | HTML document demonstrating `String` methods `split` and `substring`. (Part 2 of 2.)

In the script (Fig. 11.9), line 5 gets the value of the input field and stores it in variable `inputString`. Line 6 calls `String` method `split` to tokenize `inputString`. The argument to method `split` is the **delimiter string**—the string that determines the end of each token in the original string. In this example, the space character delimits the tokens. The delimiter string can contain multiple characters to be used as delimiters. Method `split` returns an array of strings containing the tokens. Line 11 uses `Array` method `join` to combine the tokens in array `tokens` and separate each token with `</p><p class = 'indent'>` to end one paragraph element and start a new one. Line 13 uses `String` method `substring` to obtain a string containing the first 10 characters of the string the user entered (still stored in `inputString`). The method returns the substring from the **starting index** (0 in this example) up to but not including the **ending index** (10 in this example). If the ending index is greater than the length of the string, the substring returned includes the characters from the starting index to the end of the original string. The result of the string concatenations in lines 9–13 is displayed in the document's `results` div.

```
1   // Fig. 11.9: SplitAndSubString.js
2   // String object methods split and substring.
3   function splitButtonPressed()
4   {
5      var inputString = document.getElementById( "inputField" ).value;
6      var tokens = inputString.split( " " );
7
8      var results = document.getElementById( "results" );
```

Fig. 11.9 | String-object methods `split` and `substring`. (Part 1 of 2.)

```
9      results.innerHTML = "<p>The sentence split into words is: </p>" +
10         "<p class = 'indent'>" +
11         tokens.join( "</p><p class = 'indent'>" ) + "</p>" +
12         "<p>The first 10 characters of the input string are: </p>" +
13         "<p class = 'indent'>'" + inputString.substring( 0, 10 ) + "'</p>";
14   } // end function splitButtonPressed
15
16   // register click event handler for searchButton
17   function start()
18   {
19      var splitButton = document.getElementById( "splitButton" );
20      splitButton.addEventListener( "click", splitButtonPressed, false );
21   } // end function start
22
23   window.addEventListener( "load", start, false );
```

Fig. 11.9 | String-object methods `split` and `substring`. (Part 2 of 2.)

11.4 Date Object

JavaScript's **Date** object provides methods for date and time manipulations. These can be performed based on the computer's **local time zone** or based on World Time Standard's **Coordinated Universal Time** (abbreviated UTC)—formerly called **Greenwich Mean Time (GMT)**. Most methods of the Date object have a local time zone and a UTC version. Date-object methods are summarized in Fig. 11.10.

Method	Description
getDate() getUTCDate()	Returns a number from 1 to 31 representing the day of the month in local time or UTC.
getDay() getUTCDay()	Returns a number from 0 (Sunday) to 6 (Saturday) representing the day of the week in local time or UTC.
getFullYear() getUTCFullYear()	Returns the year as a four-digit number in local time or UTC.
getHours() getUTCHours()	Returns a number from 0 to 23 representing hours since midnight in local time or UTC.
getMilliseconds() getUTCMilliSeconds()	Returns a number from 0 to 999 representing the number of milliseconds in local time or UTC, respectively. The time is stored in hours, minutes, seconds and milliseconds.
getMinutes() getUTCMinutes()	Returns a number from 0 to 59 representing the minutes for the time in local time or UTC.
getMonth() getUTCMonth()	Returns a number from 0 (January) to 11 (December) representing the month in local time or UTC.
getSeconds() getUTCSeconds()	Returns a number from 0 to 59 representing the seconds for the time in local time or UTC.

Fig. 11.10 | Date-object methods. (Part 1 of 2.)

Method	Description
getTime()	Returns the number of milliseconds between January 1, 1970, and the time in the Date object.
getTimezoneOffset()	Returns the difference in minutes between the current time on the local computer and UTC (Coordinated Universal Time).
setDate(*val*) setUTCDate(*val*)	Sets the day of the month (1 to 31) in local time or UTC.
setFullYear(*y*, *m*, *d*) setUTCFullYear(*y*, *m*, *d*)	Sets the year in local time or UTC. The second and third arguments representing the month and the date are optional. If an optional argument is not specified, the current value in the Date object is used.
setHours(*h*, *m*, *s*, *ms*) setUTCHours(*h*, *m*, *s*, *ms*)	Sets the hour in local time or UTC. The second, third and fourth arguments, representing the minutes, seconds and milliseconds, are optional. If an optional argument is not specified, the current value in the Date object is used.
setMilliSeconds(*ms*) setUTCMilliseconds(*ms*)	Sets the number of milliseconds in local time or UTC.
setMinutes(*m*, *s*, *ms*) setUTCMinutes(*m*, *s*, *ms*)	Sets the minute in local time or UTC. The second and third arguments, representing the seconds and milliseconds, are optional. If an optional argument is not specified, the current value in the Date object is used.
setMonth(*m*, *d*) setUTCMonth(*m*, *d*)	Sets the month in local time or UTC. The second argument, representing the date, is optional. If the optional argument is not specified, the current date value in the Date object is used.
setSeconds(*s*, *ms*) setUTCSeconds(*s*, *ms*)	Sets the seconds in local time or UTC. The second argument, representing the milliseconds, is optional. If this argument is not specified, the current milliseconds value in the Date object is used.
setTime(*ms*)	Sets the time based on its argument—the number of elapsed milliseconds since January 1, 1970.
toLocaleString()	Returns a string representation of the date and time in a form specific to the computer's locale. For example, September 13, 2007, at 3:42:22 PM is represented as *09/13/07 15:47:22* in the United States and *13/09/07 15:47:22* in Europe.
toUTCString()	Returns a string representation of the date and time in the form: *15 Sep 2007 15:47:22 UTC*.
toString()	Returns a string representation of the date and time in a form specific to the locale of the computer (*Mon Sep 17 15:47:22 EDT 2007* in the United States).
valueOf()	The time in number of milliseconds since midnight, January 1, 1970. (Same as getTime.)

Fig. 11.10 | Date-object methods. (Part 2 of 2.)

The example in Figs. 11.11–11.12 demonstrates many of the local-time-zone methods in Fig. 11.10. The HTML document (Fig. 11.11) provides several `sections` in which the results are displayed.

Date-Object Constructor with No Arguments

In the script (Fig. 11.12), line 5 creates a new `Date` object. The `new` operator creates the `Date` object. The empty parentheses indicate a call to the `Date` object's **constructor** with no arguments. A constructor is an *initializer* method for an object. *Constructors are called automatically when an object is allocated with new.* The `Date` constructor with no arguments initializes the `Date` object with the local computer's current date and time.

Methods *toString, toLocaleString, toUTCString and valueOf*

Lines 9–12 demonstrate the methods `toString`, `toLocaleString`, `toUTCString` and `valueOf`. Method `valueOf` returns a large integer value representing the total number of milliseconds between midnight, January 1, 1970, and the date and time stored in `Date` object `current`.

Date-Object get *Methods*

Lines 16–25 demonstrate the `Date` object's *get* methods for the local time zone. The method `getFullYear` returns the year as a four-digit number. The method `getTimeZoneOffset` returns the difference in minutes between the local time zone and UTC time (i.e., a difference of four hours in our time zone when this example was executed).

```
 1   <!DOCTYPE html>
 2
 3   <!-- Fig. 11.11: DateTime.html -->
 4   <!-- HTML document to demonstrate Date-object methods. -->
 5   <html>
 6      <head>
 7         <meta charset = "utf-8">
 8         <title>Date and Time Methods</title>
 9         <link rel = "stylesheet" type = "text/css" href = "style.css">
10         <script src = "DateTime.js"></script>
11      </head>
12      <body>
13         <h1>String representations and valueOf</h1>
14         <section id = "strings"></section>
15         <h1>Get methods for local time zone</h1>
16         <section id = "getMethods"></section>
17         <h1>Specifying arguments for a new Date</h1>
18         <section id = "newArguments"></section>
19         <h1>Set methods for local time zone</h1>
20         <section id = "setMethods"></section>
21      </body>
22   </html>
```

Fig. 11.11 | HTML document to demonstrate `Date`-object methods. (Part 1 of 2.)

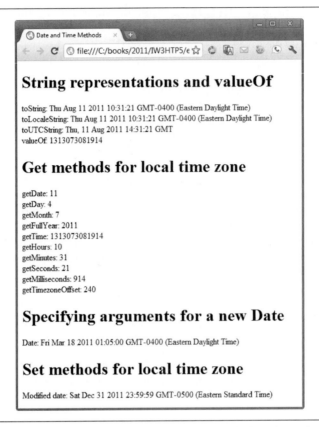

Fig. 11.11 | HTML document to demonstrate Date-object methods. (Part 2 of 2.)

```
1   // Fig. 11.12: DateTime.js
2   // Date and time methods of the Date object.
3   function start()
4   {
5      var current = new Date();
6
7      // string-formatting methods and valueOf
8      document.getElementById( "strings" ).innerHTML =
9         "<p>toString: " + current.toString() + "</p>" +
10        "<p>toLocaleString: " + current.toLocaleString() + "</p>" +
11        "<p>toUTCString: " + current.toUTCString() + "</p>" +
12        "<p>valueOf: " + current.valueOf() + "</p>";
13
14     // get methods
15     document.getElementById( "getMethods" ).innerHTML =
16        "<p>getDate: " + current.getDate() + "</p>" +
17        "<p>getDay: " + current.getDay() + "</p>" +
18        "<p>getMonth: " + current.getMonth() + "</p>" +
19        "<p>getFullYear: " + current.getFullYear() + "</p>" +
```

Fig. 11.12 | Date and time methods of the Date object. (Part 1 of 2.)

```
20          "<p>getTime: " + current.getTime() + "</p>" +
21          "<p>getHours: " + current.getHours() + "</p>" +
22          "<p>getMinutes: " + current.getMinutes() + "</p>" +
23          "<p>getSeconds: " + current.getSeconds() + "</p>" +
24          "<p>getMilliseconds: " + current.getMilliseconds() + "</p>" +
25          "<p>getTimezoneOffset: " + current.getTimezoneOffset() + "</p>";
26
27       // creating a Date
28       var anotherDate = new Date( 2011, 2, 18, 1, 5, 0, 0 );
29       document.getElementById( "newArguments" ).innerHTML =
30          "<p>Date: " + anotherDate + "</p>";
31
32       // set methods
33       anotherDate.setDate( 31 );
34       anotherDate.setMonth( 11 );
35       anotherDate.setFullYear( 2011 );
36       anotherDate.setHours( 23 );
37       anotherDate.setMinutes( 59 );
38       anotherDate.setSeconds( 59 );
39       document.getElementById( "setMethods" ).innerHTML =
40          "<p>Modified date: " + anotherDate + "</p>";
41    } // end function start
42
43    window.addEventListener( "load", start, false );
```

Fig. 11.12 | Date and time methods of the Date object. (Part 2 of 2.)

Date-*Object Constructor with Arguments*

Line 28 creates a new Date object and supplies arguments to the Date constructor for *year*, *month, date, hours, minutes, seconds* and *milliseconds*. The *hours, minutes, seconds* and *milliseconds* arguments are all optional. If an argument is not specified, 0 is supplied in its place. For *hours, minutes* and *seconds*, if the argument to the right of any of these is specified, it too must be specified (e.g., if the *minutes* argument is specified, the *hours* argument must be specified; if the *milliseconds* argument is specified, all the arguments must be specified).

Date-*Object* set *Methods*

Lines 33–38 demonstrate the Date-object *set* methods for the local time zone. Date objects represent the month internally as an integer from 0 to 11. These values are off by one from what you might expect (i.e., 1 for January, 2 for February, …, and 12 for December). When creating a Date object, you must specify 0 to indicate January, 1 to indicate February, …, and 11 to indicate December.

Common Programming Error 11.1

Assuming that months are represented as numbers from 1 to 12 leads to off-by-one errors when you're processing Dates.

Date-*Object* **parse** *and* **UTC** *Methods*

The Date object provides methods **Date.parse** and **Date.UTC** *that can be called without creating a new Date object.* Date.parse receives as its argument a string representing a date and time, and returns the number of milliseconds between midnight, January 1, 1970, and the specified date and time. This value can be converted to a Date object with the statement

```
var theDate = new Date( numberOfMilliseconds );
```

Method parse converts the string using the following rules:

- Short dates can be specified in the form MM-DD-YY, MM-DD-YYYY, MM/DD/YY or MM/DD/YYYY. The month and day are not required to be two digits.

- Long dates that specify the complete month name (e.g., "January"), date and year can specify the month, date and year in any order.

- Text in parentheses within the string is treated as a comment and ignored. Commas and white-space characters are treated as delimiters.

- All month and day names must have at least two characters. The names are not required to be unique. If the names are identical, the name is resolved as the last match (e.g., "Ju" represents "July" rather than "June").

- If the name of the day of the week is supplied, it's ignored.

- All standard time zones (e.g., EST for Eastern Standard Time), Coordinated Universal Time (UTC) and Greenwich Mean Time (GMT) are recognized.

- When specifying hours, minutes and seconds, separate them with colons.

- In 24-hour-clock format, "PM" should not be used for times after 12 noon.

Date method UTC returns the number of milliseconds between midnight, January 1, 1970, and the date and time specified as its arguments. The arguments to the UTC method include the required *year*, *month* and *date*, and the optional *hours*, *minutes*, *seconds* and *milliseconds*. If any of the *hours*, *minutes*, *seconds* or *milliseconds* arguments is not specified, a zero is supplied in its place. For the *hours*, *minutes* and *seconds* arguments, if the argument to the right of any of these arguments in the argument list is specified, that argument must also be specified (e.g., if the *minutes* argument is specified, the *hours* argument must be specified; if the *milliseconds* argument is specified, all the arguments must be specified). As with the result of Date.parse, the result of Date.UTC can be converted to a Date object by creating a new Date object with the result of Date.UTC as its argument.

11.5 Boolean and Number Objects

JavaScript provides the **Boolean** and **Number** objects as **object wrappers** for boolean true/false values and numbers, respectively. These wrappers define methods and properties useful in manipulating boolean values and numbers.

When a JavaScript program requires a boolean value, JavaScript automatically creates a Boolean object to store the value. JavaScript programmers can create Boolean objects explicitly with the statement

```
var b = new Boolean( booleanValue );
```

The *booleanValue* specifies whether the Boolean object should contain true or false. If *booleanValue* is false, 0, null, Number.NaN or an empty string (""), or if no argument is supplied, the new Boolean object contains false. Otherwise, the new Boolean object contains true. Figure 11.13 summarizes the methods of the Boolean object.

Method	Description
toString()	Returns the string "true" if the value of the Boolean object is true; otherwise, returns the string "false".
valueOf()	Returns the value true if the Boolean object is true; otherwise, returns false.

Fig. 11.13 | Boolean-object methods.

JavaScript automatically creates Number objects to store numeric values in a script. You can create a Number object with the statement

```
var n = new Number( numericValue );
```

The constructor argument *numericValue* is the number to store in the object. Although you can explicitly create Number objects, normally the JavaScript interpreter creates them as needed. Figure 11.14 summarizes the methods and properties of the Number object.

Method or property	Description
toString(*radix*)	Returns the string representation of the number. The optional *radix* argument (a number from 2 to 36) specifies the number's base. Radix 2 results in the *binary* representation, 8 in the *octal* representation, 10 in the *decimal* representation and 16 in the *hexadecimal* representation. See Appendix E, Number Systems, for an explanation of the binary, octal, decimal and hexadecimal number systems.
valueOf()	Returns the numeric value.
Number.MAX_VALUE	The largest value that can be stored in a JavaScript program.
Number.MIN_VALUE	The smallest value that can be stored in a JavaScript program.
Number.NaN	*Not a number*—a value returned from an arithmetic expression that doesn't result in a number (e.g., parseInt("hello") cannot convert the string "hello" to a number, so parseInt would return Number.NaN.) To determine whether a value is NaN, test the result with function isNaN, which returns true if the value is NaN; otherwise, it returns false.
Number.NEGATIVE_INFINITY	A value less than -Number.MAX_VALUE.
Number.POSITIVE_INFINITY	A value greater than Number.MAX_VALUE.

Fig. 11.14 | Number-object methods and properties.

11.6 document Object

The **document** object, which we've used extensively, is provided by the browser and allows JavaScript code to manipulate the current document in the browser. The document object has several properties and methods, such as method document.getElementByID, which has been used in many examples. Figure 11.15 shows the methods of the document object that are used in this chapter. We'll cover several more in Chapter 12.

Method	Description
getElementById(*id*)	Returns the HTML5 element whose id attribute matches *id*.
getElementByTagName(*tagName*)	Returns an array of the HTML5 elements with the specified *tagName*.

Fig. 11.15 | document-object methods.

11.7 Favorite Twitter Searches: HTML5 Web Storage

Before HTML5, websites could store only small amounts of text-based information on a *user's* computer using cookies. A **cookie** is a *key/value pair* in which each *key* has a corresponding *value*. The key and value are both strings. Cookies are stored by the browser on the *user's* computer to maintain client-specific information during and between browser sessions. A website might use a cookie to record user preferences or other information that it can retrieve during the client's subsequent visits. For example, a website can retrieve the user's name from a cookie and use it to display a personalized greeting. Similarly, many websites used cookies during a browsing session to track user-specific information, such as the contents of an online shopping cart.

When a user visits a website, the browser locates any cookies written by that website and sends them to the server. *Cookies may be accessed only by the web server and scripts of the website from which the cookies originated* (i.e., a cookie set by a script on amazon.com can be read only by amazon.com servers and scripts). The browser sends these cookies with *every* request to the server.

Problems with Cookies
There are several problems with cookies. One is that they're extremely limited in size. Today's web apps often allow users to manipulate large amounts of data, such as documents or thousands of emails. Some web applications allow so-called *offline access*—for example, a word-processing web application might allow a user to access documents locally, even when the computer is not connected to the Internet. Cookies cannot store entire documents.

Another problem is that a user often opens many tabs in the same browser window. If the user browses the same site from multiple tabs, all of the site's cookies are shared by the pages in each tab. This could be problematic in web applications that allow the user to purchase items. For example, if the user is purchasing different items in each tab, with cookies it's possible that the user could accidentally purchase the same item twice.

Introducing localStorage and sessionStorage
As of HTML5, there are two new mechanisms for storing key/value pairs that help eliminate some of the problems with cookies. Web applications can use the window object's **localStorage property** to store up to several megabytes of key/value-pair string data on the user's computer and can access that data across browsing sessions and browser tabs. Unlike cookies, data in the localStorage object is not sent to the web server with each request. Each website domain (such as deitel.com or google.com) has a separate local-

Storage object—all the pages from a given domain share one localStorage object. Typically, 5MB are reserved for each localStorage object, but a web browser can ask the user if more space should be allocated when the space is full.

Web applications that need access to data for *only* a browsing session and that must keep that data *separate* among multiple tabs can use the window object's **sessionStorage property**. There's a separate sessionStorage object for every browsing session, including separate tabs that are accessing the same website.

Favorite Twitter Searches *App Using* localStorage *and* sessionStorage

To demonstrate these new HTML5 storage capabilities, we'll implement a **Favorite Twitter Searches** app. Twitter's search feature is a great way to follow trends and see what people are saying about specific topics. The app we present here allows users to save their favorite (possibly lengthy) Twitter search strings with easy-to-remember, user-chosen, short tag names. Users can then conveniently follow the tweets on their favorite topics by visiting this web page and clicking the link for a saved search. Twitter search queries can be finely tuned using Twitter's search operators (dev.twitter.com/docs/using-search)—but more complex queries are lengthy, time consuming and error prone to type. The user's favorite searches are saved using localStorage, so they're immediately available each time the user browses the app's web page.

Figure 11.16(a) shows the app when it's loaded for the first time. The app uses sessionStorage to determine whether the user has visited the page previously during the current browsing session. If not, the app displays a welcome message. The user can save many searches and view them in alphabetical order. Search queries and their corresponding tags are entered in the text inputs at the top of the page. Clicking the **Save** button adds the new search to the favorites list. Clicking a the link for a saved search requests the search page from Twitter's website, passing the user's saved search as an argument, and displays the search results in the web browser.

a) **Favorite Twitter Searches** app when it's loaded for the first time in this browsing session and there are no tagged searches

Welcome message appears only on the first visit to the page during this browsing session

Enter Twitter search query here

Tag your search

Fig. 11.16 | Sample outputs from the **Favorite Twitter Searches** web application. (Part 1 of 2.)

b) App with several saved searches and the user saving a new search

Saved searches

c) App after new search is saved—the user is about to click the Deitel search

d) Results of touching the **Deitel** link

Fig. 11.16 | Sample outputs from the **Favorite Twitter Searches** web application. (Part 2 of 2.)

Figure 11.16(b) shows the app with several previously saved searches. Figure 11.16(c) shows the user entering a new search. Figure 11.16(d) shows the result of touching the **Deitel** link, which searches for tweets from Deitel—specified in Fig. 11.16(c) with the Twitter search from:Deitel. You can edit the searches using the **Edit** buttons to the right of each search link. This enables you to tweak your searches for better results after you save them as favorites. Touching the **Clear All Saved Searches** button removes all the searches from the favorites list. Some browsers support localStorage and sessionStorage only for web pages that are downloaded from a web server, not for web pages that are loaded directly from the local file system. So, we've posted the app online for testing at:

```
http://test.deitel.com/iw3htp5/ch11/fig11_20-22/
    FavoriteTwitterSearches.html
```

Favorite Twitter Searches HTML5 Document

The **Favorite Twitter Searches** application contains three files—FavoriteTwitterSearches.html (Fig. 11.17), styles.css (Fig. 11.18) and FavoriteTwitterSearches.js (Fig. 11.18). The HTML5 document provides a form (lines 14–24) that allows the user to enter new searches. Previously tagged searches are displayed in the div named searches (line 26).

```html
1   <!DOCTYPE html>
2
3   <!-- Fig. 11.17: FavoriteTwitterSearchs.html -->
4   <!-- Favorite Twitter Searches web application. -->
5   <html>
6   <head>
7      <title>Twitter Searches</title>
8      <link rel = "stylesheet" type = "text/css" href = "style.css">
9      <script src = "FavoriteTwitterSearches.js"></script>
10  </head>
11  <body>
12     <h1>Favorite Twitter Searches</h1>
13     <p id = "welcomeMessage"></p>
14     <form action = "#">
15        <p><input id = "query" type = "text"
16           placeholder = "Entery Twitter search query">
17           <a href = "https://dev.twitter.com/docs/using-search">
18              Twitter search operators</a></p>
19        <p><input id = "tag" type = "text" placeholder = "Tag your query">
20           <input type = "button" value = "Save"
21              id = "saveButton">
22           <input type = "button" value = "Clear All Saved Searches"
23              id = "clearButton"></p>
24     </form>
25     <h1>Previously Tagged Searches</h1>
26     <div id = "searches"></div>
27  </body>
28  </html>
```

Fig. 11.17 | Favorite Twitter Searches web application.

CSS for Favorite Twitter Searches

Figure 11.18 contains the CSS styles for this app. Line 3 uses a CSS3 attribute selector to select all input elements that have the type "text" and sets their width to 250px. Each link that represents a saved search is displayed in a span that has a fixed width (line 6). To specify the width, we set the display property of the spans to inline-block. Line 8 specifies a **:first-child selector** that's used to select the first list item in the unordered list of saved searches that's displayed at the bottom of the web page. Lines 9–10 and 11–12 use **:nth-child selectors** to specify the styles of the odd (first, third, fifth, etc.) and even (second, fourth, sixth, etc.) list items, respectively. We use these selectors or alternate the background colors of the saved searches.

```
 1   p { margin: 0px; }
 2   #welcomeMessage { margin-bottom: 10px; font-weight: bold; }
 3   input[type = "text"] { width: 250px; }
 4
 5   /* list item styles */
 6   span { margin-left: 10px; display: inline-block; width: 100px; }
 7   li { list-style-type: none; width: 220px;}
 8   li:first-child { border-top: 1px solid grey; }
 9   li:nth-child(even) { background-color: lightyellow;
10      border-bottom: 1px solid grey; }
11   li:nth-child(odd) { background-color: lightblue;
12      border-bottom: 1px solid grey; }
```

Fig. 11.18 | Styles used in the **Favorite Twitter Searches** app.

Script for Favorite Twitter Searches

Figure 11.19 presents the JavaScript for the **Favorite Twitter Searches** app. When the HTML5 document in Fig. 11.17 loads, function start (lines 80–87) is called to register event handlers and call function loadSearches (lines 7–44). Line 9 uses the sessionStorage object to determine whether the user has already visited the page during this browsing session. The **getItem method** receives a name of a key as an argument. If the key exists, the method returns the corresponding string value; otherwise, it returns null. If this is the user's first visit to the page during this browsing session, line 11 uses the **setItem method** to set the key "herePreviously" to the string "true", then lines 12–13 display a welcome message in the welcomeMessage paragraph element. Next, line 16 gets the localStorage object's **length**, which represents the number of key/value pairs stored. Line 17 creates an array and assigns it to the script variable tags, then lines 20–23 get the keys from the localStorage object and store them in the tags array. Method **key** (line 22) receives an index as an argument and returns the corresponding key. Line 25 sorts the tags array, so that we can display the searches in alphabetical order by tag name (i.e., key). Lines 27–42 build the unordered list of links representing the saved searches. Line 33 calls the localStorage object's getItem method to obtain the search string for a given tag and appends the search string to the Twitter search URL (line 28). Notice that, for simplicity, lines 37 and 38 use the onclick attributes of the dynamically generated **Edit** and **Delete** buttons to set the buttons' event handlers—this is an older mechanism for registering event handlers. To register these with the elements' addEventListener method, we'd have to dynamically locate the buttons in the page after we've created them, then register the event handlers, which would require significant additional code. Separately, notice that each event handler is receiving the button input element's id as an argument—this enables the event handler to use the id value when handling the event. [*Note:* The localStorage and sessionStorage properties and methods we discuss throughout this section apply to both objects.]

```
1   // Fig. 11.19: FavoriteTwitterSearchs.js
2   // Storing and retrieving key/value pairs using
3   // HTML5 localStorage and sessionStorage
4   var tags; // array of tags for queries
5
6   // loads previously saved searches and displays them in the page
7   function loadSearches()
8   {
9      if ( !sessionStorage.getItem( "herePreviously" ) )
10     {
11        sessionStorage.setItem( "herePreviously", "true" );
12        document.getElementById( "welcomeMessage" ).innerHTML =
13           "Welcome to the Favorite Twitter Searches App";
14     } // end if
15
16     var length = localStorage.length; // number of key/value pairs
17     tags = []; // create empty array
18
19     // load all keys
20     for (var i = 0; i < length; ++i)
21     {
22        tags[i] = localStorage.key(i);
23     } // end for
24
25     tags.sort(); // sort the keys
26
27     var markup = "<ul>"; // used to store search link markup
28     var url = "http://search.twitter.com/search?q=";
29
30     // build list of links
31     for (var tag in tags)
32     {
33        var query = url + localStorage.getItem(tags[tag]);
34        markup += "<li><span><a href = '" + query + "'>" + tags[tag] +
35           "</a></span>" +
36           "<input id = '" + tags[tag] + "' type = 'button' " +
37              "value = 'Edit' onclick = 'editTag(id)'>" +
38           "<input id = '" + tags[tag] + "' type = 'button' " +
39              "value = 'Delete' onclick = 'deleteTag(id)'>";
40     } // end for
41
42     markup += "</ul>";
43     document.getElementById("searches").innerHTML = markup;
44  } // end function loadSearches
45
```

Fig. 11.19 | Storing and retrieving key/value pairs using HTML5 localStorage and sessionStorage. (Part 1 of 2.)

```
46    // deletes all key/value pairs from localStorage
47    function clearAllSearches()
48    {
49       localStorage.clear();
50       loadSearches(); // reload searches
51    } // end function clearAllSearches
52
53    // saves a newly tagged search into localStorage
54    function saveSearch()
55    {
56       var query = document.getElementById("query");
57       var tag = document.getElementById("tag");
58       localStorage.setItem(tag.value, query.value);
59       tag.value = ""; // clear tag input
60       query.value = ""; // clear query input
61       loadSearches(); // reload searches
62    } // end function saveSearch
63
64    // deletes a specific key/value pair from localStorage
65    function deleteTag( tag )
66    {
67       localStorage.removeItem( tag );
68       loadSearches(); // reload searches
69    } // end function deleteTag
70
71    // display existing tagged query for editing
72    function editTag( tag )
73    {
74       document.getElementById("query").value = localStorage[ tag ];
75       document.getElementById("tag").value = tag;
76       loadSearches(); // reload searches
77    } // end function editTag
78
79    // register event handlers then load searches
80    function start()
81    {
82       var saveButton = document.getElementById( "saveButton" );
83       saveButton.addEventListener( "click", saveSearch, false );
84       var clearButton = document.getElementById( "clearButton" );
85       clearButton.addEventListener( "click", clearAllSearches, false );
86       loadSearches(); // load the previously saved searches
87    } // end function start
88
89    window.addEventListener( "load", start, false );
```

Fig. 11.19 | Storing and retrieving key/value pairs using HTML5 `localStorage` and `sessionStorage`. (Part 2 of 2.)

Function `clearAllSearches` (lines 47–51) is called when the user clicks the **Clear All Saved Searches** button. The **clear method** of the `localStorage` object (line 49) removes all key/value pairs from the object. We then call `loadSearches` to refresh the list of saved searches in the web page.

Function `saveSearch` (lines 54–62) is called when the user clicks **Save** to save a search. Line 58 uses the `setItem` method to store a key/value pair in the `localStorage` object. If the key already exits, `setItem` replaces the corresponding value; otherwise, it creates a new key/value pair. We then call `loadSearches` to refresh the list of saved searches in the web page.

Function `deleteTag` (lines 65–69) is called when the user clicks the **Delete** button next to a particular search. The function receives the tag representing the key/value pair to delete, which we set in line 38 as the button's `id`. Line 67 uses the `removeItem` **method** to remove a key/value pair from the `localStorage` object. We then call `loadSearches` to refresh the list of saved searches in the web page.

Function `editTag` (lines 72–77) is called when the user clicks the **Edit** button next to a particular search. The function receives the tag representing the key/value pair to edit, which we set in line 36 as the button's `id`. In this case, we display the corresponding key/value pair's contents in the `input` elements with the `ids` `"tag"` and `"query"`, respectively, so the user can edit them. Line 74 uses the `[]` operator to access the value for a specified key (`tag`)—this performs the same task as calling `getItem` on the `localStorage` object. We then call `loadSearches` to refresh the list of saved searches in the web page.

11.8 Using JSON to Represent Objects

In 1999, **JSON (JavaScript Object Notation)**—a simple way to represent JavaScript objects as strings—was introduced as an alternative to XML as a data-exchange technique. JSON has gained acclaim due to its simple format, making objects easy to read, create and parse. Each JSON object is represented as a list of property names and values contained in curly braces, in the following format:

```
{ propertyName1 : value1, propertyName2 : value2 }
```

Arrays are represented in JSON with square brackets in the following format:

```
[ value0, value1, value2 ]
```

Each value can be a string, a number, a JSON object, `true`, `false` or `null`. To appreciate the simplicity of JSON data, examine this representation of an array of address-book entries that we'll use in Chapter 16:

```
[ { first: 'Cheryl', last: 'Black' },
  { first: 'James', last: 'Blue' },
  { first: 'Mike', last: 'Brown' },
  { first: 'Meg', last: 'Gold' } ]
```

JSON provides a straightforward way to manipulate objects in JavaScript, and many other programming languages now support this format. In addition to simplifying object creation, JSON allows programs to easily extract data and efficiently transmit it across the Internet. JSON integrates especially well with Ajax applications, discussed in Chapter 16. See Section 16.6 for a more detailed discussion of JSON, as well as an Ajax-specific example. For more information on JSON, visit our JSON Resource Center at `www.deitel.com/json`.

Summary

Section 11.2 *Math Object*

- `Math`-object methods (p. 393) enable you to perform many common mathematical calculations.
- An object's methods are called by writing the name of the object followed by a dot (.) and the name of the method. In parentheses following the method name are arguments to the method.

Section 11.3 *String Object*

- Characters are the building blocks of JavaScript programs. Every program is composed of a sequence of characters grouped together meaningfully that's interpreted by the computer as a series of instructions used to accomplish a task.
- A string is a series of characters treated as a single unit.
- A string may include letters, digits and various special characters, such as +, -, *, /, and $.
- JavaScript supports Unicode (p. 395), which represents a large portion of the world's languages.
- String literals or string constants (p. 395) are written as a sequence of characters in double or single quotation marks.
- Combining strings is called concatenation (p. 395).
- String method `charAt` (p. 397) returns the character at a specific index in a string. Indices for the characters in a string start at 0 (the first character) and go up to (but do not include) the string's `length` (i.e., if the string contains five characters, the indices are 0 through 4). If the index is outside the bounds of the string, the method returns an empty string.
- String method `charCodeAt` (p. 397) returns the Unicode value of the character at a specific index in a string. If the index is outside the bounds of the string, the method returns `NaN`. String method `fromCharCode` (p. 397) creates a string from a list of Unicode values.
- String method `toLowerCase` (p. 397) returns the lowercase version of a string. String method `toUpperCase` (p. 397) returns the uppercase version of a string.
- String method `indexOf` (p. 398) determines the location of the first occurrence of its argument in the string used to call the method. If the substring is found, the index at which the first occurrence of the substring begins is returned; otherwise, -1 is returned. This method receives an optional second argument specifying the index from which to begin the search.
- String method `lastIndexOf` (p. 398) determines the location of the last occurrence of its argument in the string used to call the method. If the substring is found, the index at which the last occurrence of the substring begins is returned; otherwise, -1 is returned. This method receives an optional second argument specifying the index from which to begin the search.
- The process of breaking a string into tokens (p. 401) is called tokenization (p. 401). Tokens are separated from one another by delimiters, typically white-space characters such as blank, tab, newline and carriage return. Other characters may also be used as delimiters to separate tokens.
- String method `split` (p. 401) breaks a string into its component tokens. The argument to method `split` is the delimiter string (p. 402)—the string that determines the end of each token in the original string. Method `split` returns an array of strings containing the tokens.
- String method `substring` returns the substring from the starting index (its first argument, p. 402) up to but not including the ending index (its second argument, p. 402). If the ending index is greater than the length of the string, the substring returned includes the characters from the starting index to the end of the original string.

Section 11.4 *Date Object*

- JavaScript's `Date` object (p. 403) provides methods for date and time manipulations.

- Date and time processing can be performed based either on the computer's local time zone (p. 403) or on World Time Standard's Coordinated Universal Time (abbreviated UTC, p. 403)—formerly called Greenwich Mean Time (GMT, p. 403).

- Most methods of the Date object have a local time zone and a UTC version.

- Date method parse receives as its argument a string representing a date and time and returns the number of milliseconds between midnight, January 1, 1970, and the specified date and time.

- Date method UTC (p. 407) returns the number of milliseconds between midnight, January 1, 1970, and the date and time specified as its arguments. The arguments to the UTC method include the required year, month and date, and the optional hours, minutes, seconds and milliseconds. If any of the hours, minutes, seconds or milliseconds arguments is not specified, a zero is supplied in its place. For the hours, minutes and seconds arguments, if the argument to the right of any of these arguments is specified, that argument must also be specified (e.g., if the minutes argument is specified, the hours argument must be specified; if the milliseconds argument is specified, all the arguments must be specified).

Section 11.5 *Boolean and Number Objects*

- JavaScript provides the Boolean (p. 408) and Number (p. 408) objects as object wrappers for boolean true/false values and numbers, respectively.

- When a boolean value is required in a JavaScript program, JavaScript automatically creates a Boolean object to store the value.

- JavaScript programmers can create Boolean objects explicitly with the statement

        var b = **new** Boolean(*booleanValue*);

  The argument *booleanValue* specifies the value of the Boolean object (true or false). If *boolean-Value* is false, 0, null, Number.NaN or the empty string (""), or if no argument is supplied, the new Boolean object contains false. Otherwise, the new Boolean object contains true.

- JavaScript automatically creates Number objects to store numeric values in a JavaScript program.

- JavaScript programmers can create a Number object with the statement

        var n = **new** Number(*numericValue*);

  The argument *numericValue* is the number to store in the object. Although you can explicitly create Number objects, normally they're created when needed by the JavaScript interpreter.

Section 11.6 *document Object*

- JavaScript provides the document object (p. 409) for manipulating the document that's currently visible in the browser window.

Section 11.7 *Favorite Twitter Searches: HTML5 Web Storage*

- Before HTML5, websites could store only small amounts of text-based information on a user's computer using cookies. A cookie (p. 410) is a key/value pair in which each key has a corresponding value. The key and value are both strings.

- Cookies are stored by the browser on the user's computer to maintain client-specific information during and between browser sessions.

- When a user visits a website, the browser locates any cookies written by that website and sends them to the server. Cookies may be accessed only by the web server and scripts of the website from which the cookies originated.

- Web applications can use the window object's localStorage property (p. 410) to store up to several megabytes of key/value-pair string data on the user's computer and can access that data across browsing sessions and browser tabs.

- Unlike cookies, data in the localStorage object is not sent to the web server with each request.
- Each website domain has a separate localStorage object—all the pages from a given domain share it. Typically, 5MB are reserved for each localStorage object, but a web browser can ask the user whether more space should be allocated when the space is full.
- Web applications that need access to key/value pair data for only a browsing session and that must keep that data separate among multiple tabs can use the window object's sessionStorage property (p. 411). There's a separate sessionStorage object for every browsing session, including separate tabs that are accessing the same website.
- A CSS3 :first-child selector (p. 414) selects the first child of an element.
- A CSS3 :nth-child selector (p. 414) with the argument "odd" selects the odd child elements, and one with the argument "even" selects the even child elements.
- The localStorage and sessionStorage method getItem (p. 414) receives a name of a key as an argument. If the key exists, the method returns the corresponding string value; otherwise, it returns null. Method setItem (p. 414) sets a key/value pair. If the key already exits, setItem replaces the value for the specified key; otherwise, it creates a new key/value pair.
- The localStorage and sessionStorage length property (p. 414) returns the number of key/value pairs stored in the corresponding object.
- The localStorage and sessionStorage method key (p. 414) receives an index as an argument and returns the corresponding key.
- The localStorage and sessionStorage method clear (p. 416) removes all key/value pairs from the corresponding object.
- The localStorage and sessionStorage method removeItem (p. 417) removes a key/value pair from the corresponding object.
- In addition to getItem, you can use the [] operator to access the value for a specified key in a localStorage or sessionStorage object.

Section 11.8 Using JSON to Represent Objects
- JSON (JavaScript Object Notation, p. 417) is a simple way to represent JavaScript objects as strings.
- JSON was introduced in 1999 as an alternative to XML for data exchange.
- Each JSON object is represented as a list of property names and values contained in curly braces, in the following format:

    { *propertyName1* : *value1*, *propertyName2* : *value2* }

- Arrays are represented in JSON with square brackets in the following format:

    [*value0*, *value1*, *value2*]

- Values in JSON can be strings, numbers, JSON objects, true, false or null.

Self-Review Exercise

11.1 Fill in the blanks in each of the following statements:
   a) Because JavaScript uses objects to perform many tasks, JavaScript is commonly referred to as a(n) _____.
   b) All objects have _____ and exhibit _____.
   c) The methods of the _____ object allow you to perform many common mathematical calculations.
   d) Invoking (or calling) a method of an object is referred to as _____.

e) String literals or string constants are written as a sequence of characters in _____ or _____.

f) Indices for the characters in a string start at _____.

g) `String` methods _____ and _____ search for the first and last occurrences of a substring in a `String`, respectively.

h) The process of breaking a string into tokens is called _____.

i) Date and time processing can be performed based on the _____ or on World Time Standard's _____.

j) `Date` method _____ receives as its argument a string representing a date and time and returns the number of milliseconds between midnight, January 1, 1970, and the specified date and time.

k) Web applications can use the `window` object's _____ property to store up to several megabytes of key/value-pair string data on the user's computer and can access that data across browsing sessions and browser tabs.

l) Web applications that need access to key/value pair data for only a browsing session and that must keep that data separate among multiple tabs can use the window object's _____ property.

m) A CSS3 _____ selector selects the first child of an element.

n) A CSS3 _____ selector with the argument `"odd"` selects the odd child elements, and one with the argument `"even"` selects the even child elements.

Answers to Self-Review Exercise

11.1 a) object-based programming language. b) attributes, behaviors. c) `Math`. d) sending a message to the object. e) double quotation marks, single quotation marks. f) 0. g) `indexOf`, `lastIndexOf`. h) tokenization. i) computer's local time zone, Coordinated Universal Time (UTC). j) parse. k) `localStorage`. l) `sessionStorage`. m) `:first-child`. n) `:nth-child`.

Exercises

11.2 Create a web page that contains four buttons. Each button, when clicked, should cause an alert dialog to display a different time or date in relation to the current time. Create a `Now` button that alerts the current time and date and a `Yesterday` button that alerts the time and date 24 hours ago. The other two buttons should alert the time and date ten years ago and one week from today.

11.3 Write a script that tests as many of the `Math` library functions in Fig. 11.1 as you can. Exercise each of these functions by having your program display tables of return values for several argument values in an HTML5 `textarea`.

11.4 `Math` method `floor` may be used to round a number to a specific decimal place. For example, the statement

```
y = Math.floor( x * 10 + .5 ) / 10;
```

rounds x to the tenths position (the first position to the right of the decimal point). The statement

```
y = Math.floor( x * 100 + .5 ) / 100;
```

rounds x to the hundredths position (i.e., the second position to the right of the decimal point). Write a script that defines four functions to round a number x in various ways:

a) `roundToInteger( number )`

b) `roundToTenths( number )`

c) `roundToHundredths( number )`

d) `roundToThousandths( number )`

For each value read, your program should display the original value, the number rounded to the nearest integer, the number rounded to the nearest tenth, the number rounded to the nearest hundredth and the number rounded to the nearest thousandth.

11.5 Modify the solution to Exercise 11.4 to use Math method round instead of method floor.

11.6 Write a script that uses relational and equality operators to compare two Strings input by the user through an HTML5 form. Display whether the first string is less than, equal to or greater than the second.

11.7 Write a script that uses random number generation to create sentences. Use four arrays of strings called article, noun, verb and preposition. Create a sentence by selecting a word at random from each array in the following order: article, noun, verb, preposition, article and noun. As each word is picked, concatenate it to the previous words in the sentence. The words should be separated by spaces. When the final sentence is output, it should start with a capital letter and end with a period.

The arrays should be filled as follows: the article array should contain the articles "the", "a", "one", "some" and "any"; the noun array should contain the nouns "boy", "girl", "dog", "town" and "car"; the verb array should contain the verbs "drove", "jumped", "ran", "walked" and "skipped"; the preposition array should contain the prepositions "to", "from", "over", "under" and "on".

The program should generate 20 sentences to form a short story and output the result to an HTML5 textarea. The story should begin with a line reading "Once upon a time..." and end with a line reading "THE END".

11.8 *(Limericks)* A limerick is a humorous five-line verse in which the first and second lines rhyme with the fifth, and the third line rhymes with the fourth. Using techniques similar to those developed in Exercise 11.7, write a script that produces random limericks. Polishing this program to produce good limericks is a challenging problem, but the result will be worth the effort!

11.9 *(Pig Latin)* Write a script that encodes English-language phrases in pig Latin. Pig Latin is a form of coded language often used for amusement. Many variations exist in the methods used to form pig Latin phrases. For simplicity, use the following algorithm:

To form a pig Latin phrase from an English-language phrase, tokenize the phrase into an array of words using String method split. To translate each English word into a pig Latin word, place the first letter of the English word at the end of the word and add the letters "ay." Thus the word "jump" becomes "umpjay," the word "the" becomes "hetay" and the word "computer" becomes "omputercay." Blanks between words remain as blanks. Assume the following: The English phrase consists of words separated by blanks, there are no punctuation marks and all words have two or more letters. Function printLatinWord should display each word. Each token (i.e., word in the sentence) is passed to method printLatinWord to print the pig Latin word. Enable the user to input the sentence through an HTML5 form. Keep a running display of all the converted sentences in an HTML5 textarea.

11.10 Write a script that inputs a telephone number as a string in the form (555) 555-5555. The script should use String method split to extract the area code as a token, the first three digits of the phone number as a token and the last four digits of the phone number as a token. Display the area code in one text field and the seven-digit phone number in another text field.

11.11 Write a script that inputs a line of text, tokenizes it with String method split and outputs the tokens in reverse order.

11.12 Write a script that inputs text from an HTML5 form and outputs it in uppercase and lowercase letters.

11.13 Write a script that inputs several lines of text and a search character and uses String method indexOf to determine the number of occurrences of the character in the text.

11.14   Write a script based on the program in Exercise 11.13 that inputs several lines of text and uses `String` method `indexOf` to determine the total number of occurrences of each letter of the alphabet in the text. Uppercase and lowercase letters should be counted together. Store the totals for each letter in an array, and print the values in tabular format in an HTML5 `textarea` after the totals have been determined.

11.15   Write a script that reads a series of strings and outputs in an HTML5 `textarea` only those strings beginning with the character "b."

11.16   Write a script that reads a series of strings and outputs in an HTML5 `textarea` only those strings ending with the characters "ed."

11.17   Write a script that inputs an integer code for a character and displays the corresponding character.

11.18   Modify your solution to Exercise 11.17 so that it generates all possible three-digit codes in the range 000 to 255 and attempts to display the corresponding characters. Display the results in an HTML5 `textarea`.

11.19   Write your own version of the `String` method `indexOf` and use it in a script.

11.20   Write your own version of the `String` method `lastIndexOf` and use it in a script.

11.21   Write a program that reads a five-letter word from the user and produces all possible three-letter words that can be derived from the letters of the five-letter word. For example, the three-letter words produced from the word "bathe" include the commonly used words "ate," "bat," "bet," "tab," "hat," "the" and "tea." Output the results in an HTML5 `textarea`.

11.22   *(Printing Dates in Various Formats)* Dates are printed in several common formats. Write a script that reads a date from an HTML5 form and creates a `Date` object in which to store it. Then use the various methods of the `Date` object that convert `Dates` into strings to display the date in several formats.

Special Section: Challenging String-Manipulation Projects

The preceding exercises are keyed to the text and designed to test the reader's understanding of fundamental string-manipulation concepts. This section includes a collection of intermediate and advanced string-manipulation exercises. The reader should find these problems challenging, yet entertaining. The problems vary considerably in difficulty. Some require an hour or two of program writing and implementation. Others are useful for lab assignments that might require two or three weeks of study and implementation. Some are challenging term projects.

11.23   *(Text Analysis)* The availability of computers with string-manipulation capabilities has resulted in some rather interesting approaches to analyzing the writings of great authors. Much attention has been focused on whether William Shakespeare really wrote the works attributed to him. Some scholars believe there's substantial evidence indicating that Christopher Marlowe actually penned these masterpieces. Researchers have used computers to find similarities in the writings of these two authors. This exercise examines three methods for analyzing texts with a computer.

   a)   Write a script that reads several lines of text from the keyboard and prints a table indicating the number of occurrences of each letter of the alphabet in the text. For example, the phrase

```
To be, or not to be: that is the question:
```

contains one "a," two "b's," no "c's," etc.

b) Write a script that reads several lines of text and prints a table indicating the number of one-letter words, two-letter words, three-letter words, etc., appearing in the text. For example, the phrase

```
Whether 'tis nobler in the mind to suffer
```

contains

Word length	Occurrences
1	0
2	2
3	1
4	2 (including 'tis)
5	0
6	2
7	1

c) Write a script that reads several lines of text and prints a table indicating the number of occurrences of each different word in the text. The first version of your program should include the words in the table in the same order in which they appear in the text. For example, the lines

```
To be, or not to be: that is the question:
Whether 'tis nobler in the mind to suffer
```

contain the word "to" three times, the word "be" twice, and the word "or" once. A more interesting (and useful) printout should then be attempted in which the words are sorted alphabetically.

11.24 *(Check Protection)* Computers are frequently employed in check-writing systems such as payroll and accounts payable applications. Many strange stories circulate regarding weekly paychecks being printed (by mistake) for amounts in excess of $1 million. Incorrect amounts are printed by computerized check-writing systems because of human error and/or machine failure. Systems designers build controls into their systems to prevent erroneous checks from being issued.

Another serious problem is the intentional alteration of a check amount by someone who intends to cash a check fraudulently. To prevent a dollar amount from being altered, most computerized check-writing systems employ a technique called *check protection.*

Checks designed for imprinting by computer contain a fixed number of spaces in which the computer may print an amount. Suppose a paycheck contains eight blank spaces in which the computer is supposed to print the amount of a weekly paycheck. If the amount is large, then all eight of those spaces will be filled, for example:

```
1,230.60 (check amount)
--------
12345678 (position numbers)
```

On the other hand, if the amount is less than $1000, then several of the spaces will ordinarily be left blank. For example,

```
  99.87
--------
12345678
```

contains three blank spaces. If a check is printed with blank spaces, it's easier for someone to alter the amount of the check. To prevent a check from being altered, many check-writing systems insert *leading asterisks* to protect the amount as follows:

```
***99.87
--------
12345678
```

Write a script that inputs a dollar amount to be printed on a check, then prints the amount in check-protected format with leading asterisks if necessary. Assume that nine spaces are available for printing the amount.

11.25 *(Writing the Word Equivalent of a Check Amount)* Continuing the discussion in the preceding exercise, we reiterate the importance of designing check-writing systems to prevent alteration of check amounts. One common security method requires that the check amount be both written in numbers and spelled out in words. Even if someone is able to alter the numerical amount of the check, it's extremely difficult to change the amount in words.

Many computerized check-writing systems do not print the amount of the check in words. Perhaps the main reason for this omission is that most high-level languages used in commercial applications do not contain adequate string-manipulation features. Another reason is that the logic for writing word equivalents of check amounts is somewhat involved.

Write a script that inputs a numeric check amount and writes the word equivalent of the amount. For example, the amount 112.43 should be written as

```
ONE HUNDRED TWELVE and 43/100
```

11.26 *(Metric Conversion Program)* Write a script that will assist the user with metric conversions. Your program should allow the user to specify the names of the units as strings (e.g., centimeters, liters, grams, for the metric system and inches, quarts, pounds, for the English system) and should respond to simple questions such as

```
"How many inches are in 2 meters?"
"How many liters are in 10 quarts?"
```

Your program should recognize invalid conversions. For example, the question

```
"How many feet are in 5 kilograms?"
```

is not a meaningful question because "feet" is a unit of length whereas "kilograms" is a unit of mass.

11.27 *(Project: A Spell Checker)* Many popular word-processing software packages have built-in spell checkers.

In this project, you're asked to develop your own spell-checker utility. We make suggestions to help get you started. You should then consider adding more capabilities. Use a computerized dictionary (if you have access to one) as a source of words.

Why do we type so many words with incorrect spellings? In some cases, it's because we simply do not know the correct spelling, so we make a best guess. In some cases, it's because we transpose two letters (e.g., "defualt" instead of "default"). Sometimes we double-type a letter accidentally (e.g., "hanndy" instead of "handy"). Sometimes we type a nearby key instead of the one we intended (e.g., "biryhday" instead of "birthday"). And so on.

Design and implement a spell-checker application in JavaScript. Your program should maintain an array wordList of strings. Enable the user to enter these strings.

Your program should ask a user to enter a word. The program should then look up the word in the wordList array. If the word is present in the array, your program should print "Word is spelled correctly."

If the word is not present in the array, your program should print "word is not spelled correctly." Then your program should try to locate other words in wordList that might be the word the user intended to type. For example, you can try all possible single transpositions of adjacent letters to discover that the word "default" is a direct match to a word in wordList. Of course, this implies that your program will check all other single transpositions, such as "edfault," "dfeault," "deafult," "defalut" and "defautl." When you find a new word that matches one in wordList, print that word in a message, such as "Did you mean "default?""

Implement any other tests you can develop, such as replacing each double letter with a single letter, to improve the value of your spell checker.

11.28 *(Project: Crossword Puzzle Generator)* Most people have worked a crossword puzzle, but few have ever attempted to generate one. Generating a crossword puzzle is suggested here as a string-manipulation project requiring substantial sophistication and effort.

You must resolve many issues to get even the simplest crossword puzzle generator program working. For example, how does one represent the grid of a crossword puzzle in the computer? Should one use a series of strings, or use double-subscripted arrays?

You need a source of words (i.e., a computerized dictionary) that can be directly referenced by the program. In what form should these words be stored to facilitate the complex manipulations required by the program?

The really ambitious reader will want to generate the clues portion of the puzzle, in which the brief hints for each across word and each down word are printed for the puzzle worker. Merely printing a version of the blank puzzle itself is not a simple problem.

Document Object Model (DOM): Objects and Collections

12

Objectives

In this chapter you will:

- Use JavaScript and the W3C Document Object Model to create dynamic web pages.

- Learn the concept of DOM nodes and DOM trees.

- Traverse, edit and modify elements in an HTML5 document.

- Change CSS styles dynamically.

- Create JavaScript animations.

12.1 Introduction

In this chapter we introduce the **Document Object Model** (DOM). The DOM gives you scripting access to *all* the elements on a web page. Inside the browser, the whole web page—paragraphs, forms, tables, etc.—is represented in an **object hierarchy**. Using JavaScript, you can dynamically create, modify and remove elements in the page.

We introduce the concepts of DOM nodes and DOM trees. We discuss properties and methods of DOM nodes and cover additional methods of the document object. We show how to dynamically change style properties, which enables you to create effects, such as user-defined background colors and animations.

Software Engineering Observation 12.1

With the DOM, HTML5 elements can be treated as objects, and many attributes of HTML5 elements can be treated as properties of those objects. Then objects can be scripted with JavaScript to achieve dynamic effects.

12.2 Modeling a Document: DOM Nodes and Trees

As we saw in previous chapters, the document's getElementById method is the simplest way to access a specific element in a page. The method returns objects called **DOM nodes**. *Every* piece of an HTML5 page (elements, attributes, text, etc.) is modeled in the web browser by a DOM node. All the nodes in a document make up the page's **DOM tree**, which describes the relationships among elements. Nodes are related to each other through child-parent relationships. An HTML5 element *inside* another element is said to be its **child**—the containing element is known as the **parent**. A node can have multiple children but only one parent. Nodes with the same parent node are referred to as **siblings**.

Today's desktop browsers provide developer tools that can display a visual representation of a document's DOM tree. Figure 12.1 shows how to access the developer tools for each of the desktop browsers we use for testing web apps in this book. For the most part, the developer tools are similar across the browsers. [*Note:* For Firefox, you must first install the DOM Inspector add-on from https://addons.mozilla.org/en-US/firefox/addon/dom-inspector-6622/. Other developer tools are available in the Firefox menu's **Web Developer** menu item, and more Firefox web-developer add-ons are available from https://addons.mozilla.org/en-US/firefox/collections/mozilla/webdeveloper/.]

Browser	Command to display developer tools
Chrome	Windows/Linux: *Control + Shift + i* Mac OS X: *Command + Option + i*
Firefox	Windows/Linux: *Control + Shift + i* Mac OS X: *Command + Shift + i*
Internet Explorer	*F12*
Opera	Windows/Linux: *Control + Shift + i* Mac OS X: *Command + Option + i*
Safari	Windows/Linux: *Control + Shift + i* Mac OS X: *Command + Option + i*

Fig. 12.1 | Commands for displaying developer tools in desktop browsers.

Viewing a Document's DOM

Figure 12.2 shows an HTML5 document in the Chrome web browser. At the bottom of the window, the document's DOM tree is displayed in the **Elements** tab of the Chrome developer tools. The HTML5 document contains a few simple elements. A node can be expanded and collapsed using the ▸ and ▾ arrows next to a given node. Figure 12.2 shows all the nodes in the document fully expanded. The **html** node at the top of the tree is called the **root node**, because it has no parent. Below the **html** node, the **head** node is indented to signify that the **head** node is a child of the **html** node. The **html** node represents the html element (lines 5–21).

```
 1   <!DOCTYPE html>
 2
 3   <!-- Fig. 12.2: domtree.html -->
 4   <!-- Demonstration of a document's DOM tree. -->
 5   <html>
 6      <head>
 7         <meta charset = "utf-8">
 8         <title>DOM Tree Demonstration</title>
 9      </head>
10      <body>
11         <h1>An HTML5 Page</h1>
12         <p>This page contains some basic HTML5 elements. The DOM tree
13            for the document contains a DOM node for every element</p>
14         <p>Here's an unordered list:</p>
15         <ul>
16            <li>One</li>
17            <li>Two</li>
18            <li>Three</li>
19         </ul>
20      </body>
21   </html>
```

Fig. 12.2 | Demonstration of a document's DOM tree. (Part 1 of 2.)

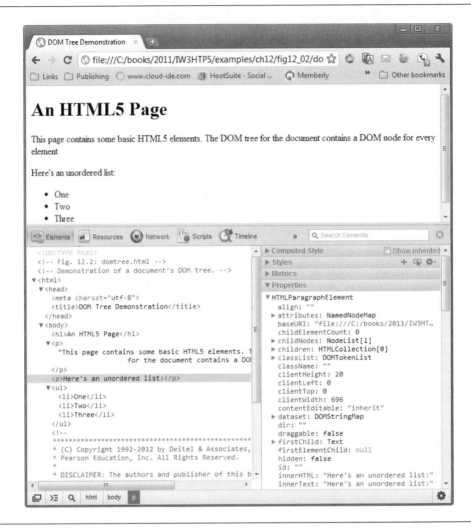

Fig. 12.2 | Demonstration of a document's DOM tree. (Part 2 of 2.)

The **head** and **body** nodes are siblings, since they're both children of the **html** node. The **head** contains the **meta** and **title** nodes. The **body** node contains nodes representing each of the elements in the document's body element. The **li** nodes are children of the **ul** node, since they're nested inside it.

When you select a node in the left side of the developer tools **Elements** tab, the node's details are displayed in the right side. In Fig. 12.2, we selected the **p** node just before the unordered list. In the **Properties** section, you can see values for that node's many properties, including the innerHTML property that we've used in many examples.

In addition to viewing a document's DOM structure, the developer tools in each browser typically enable you to view and modify styles, view and debug JavaScripts used in the document, view the resources (such as images) used by the document, and more. See each browser's developer tools documentation online for more detailed information.

12.3 Traversing and Modifying a DOM Tree

The DOM enables you to programmatically access a document's elements, allowing you to modify its contents dynamically using JavaScript. This section introduces some of the DOM-node properties and methods for traversing the DOM tree, modifying nodes and creating or deleting content dynamically.

The example in Figs. 12.3–12.5 demonstrates several DOM node features and two additional document-object methods. It allows you to highlight, modify, insert and remove elements.

CSS

Figure 12.3 contains the CSS for the example. The CSS class highlighted (line 14) is applied dynamically to elements in the document as we add, remove and select elements using the form in Fig. 12.4.

```
 1   /* Fig. 12.3: style.css */
 2   /* CSS for dom.html. */
 3   h1, h3        { text-align: center;
 4                   font-family: tahoma, geneva, sans-serif; }
 5   p             { margin-left: 5%;
 6                   margin-right: 5%;
 7                   font-family: arial, helvetica, sans-serif; }
 8   ul            { margin-left: 10%; }
 9   a             { text-decoration: none; }
10   a:hover       { text-decoration: underline; }
11   .nav          { width: 100%;
12                   border-top: 3px dashed blue;
13                   padding-top: 10px; }
14   .highlighted  { background-color: yellow; }
15   input         { width: 150px; }
16   form > p      { margin: 0px; }
```

Fig. 12.3 | CSS for basic DOM functionality example.

HTML5 Document

Figure 12.4 contains the HTML5 document that we'll manipulate dynamically by modifying its DOM. Each element in this example has an id attribute, which we also display at the beginning of the element in square brackets. For example, the id of the h1 element in lines 13–14 is set to bigheading, and the heading text begins with [bigheading]. This allows you to see the id of each element in the page. The body also contains an h3 heading, several p elements, and an unordered list. A div element (lines 29–48) contains the remainder of the document. Line 30 begins a form. Lines 32–46 contain the controls for modifying and manipulating the elements on the page. The click event handlers (registered in Fig. 12.5) for the six buttons call corresponding functions to perform the actions described by the buttons' values.

JavaScript

The JavaScript code (Fig. 12.5) begins by declaring two variables. Variable currentNode (line 3) keeps track of the currently highlighted node—the functionality of each button

```
 1    <!DOCTYPE html>
 2
 3    <!-- Fig. 12.4: dom.html -->
 4    <!-- Basic DOM functionality. -->
 5    <html>
 6       <head>
 7          <meta charset = "utf-8">
 8          <title>Basic DOM Functionality</title>
 9          <link rel = "stylesheet" type = "text/css" href = "style.css">
10          <script src = "dom.js"></script>
11       </head>
12       <body>
13          <h1 id = "bigheading" class = "highlighted">
14             [bigheading] DHTML Object Model</h1>
15          <h3 id = "smallheading">[smallheading] Element Functionality</h3>
16          <p id = "para1">[para1] The Document Object Model (DOM) allows for
17             quick, dynamic access to all elements in an HTML5 document for
18             manipulation with JavaScript.</p>
19          <p id = "para2">[para2] For more information, check out the
20             "JavaScript and the DOM" section of Deitel's
21             <a id = "link" href = "http://www.deitel.com/javascript">
22                [link] JavaScript Resource Center.</a></p>
23          <p id = "para3">[para3] The buttons below demonstrate:(list)</p>
24          <ul id = "list">
25             <li id = "item1">[item1] getElementById and parentNode</li>
26             <li id = "item2">[item2] insertBefore and appendChild</li>
27             <li id = "item3">[item3] replaceChild and removeChild</li>
28          </ul>
29          <div id = "nav" class = "nav">
30             <form onsubmit = "return false" action = "#">
31                <p><input type = "text" id = "gbi" value = "bigheading">
32                   <input type = "button" value = "Get By id"
33                      id = "byIdButton"></p>
34                <p><input type = "text" id = "ins">
35                   <input type = "button" value = "Insert Before"
36                      id = "insertButton"></p>
37                <p><input type = "text" id = "append">
38                   <input type = "button" value = "Append Child"
39                      id = "appendButton"></p>
40                <p><input type = "text" id = "replace">
41                   <input type = "button" value = "Replace Current"
42                      id = "replaceButton()"></p>
43                <p><input type = "button" value = "Remove Current"
44                      id = "removeButton"></p>
45                <p><input type = "button" value = "Get Parent"
46                      id = "parentButton"></p>
47             </form>
48          </div>
49       </body>
50    </html>
```

Fig. 12.4 | HTML5 document that's used to demonstrate DOM functionality for dynamically adding, removing and selecting elements. (Part 1 of 2.)

The document when it first loads. It begins with the large heading highlighted.

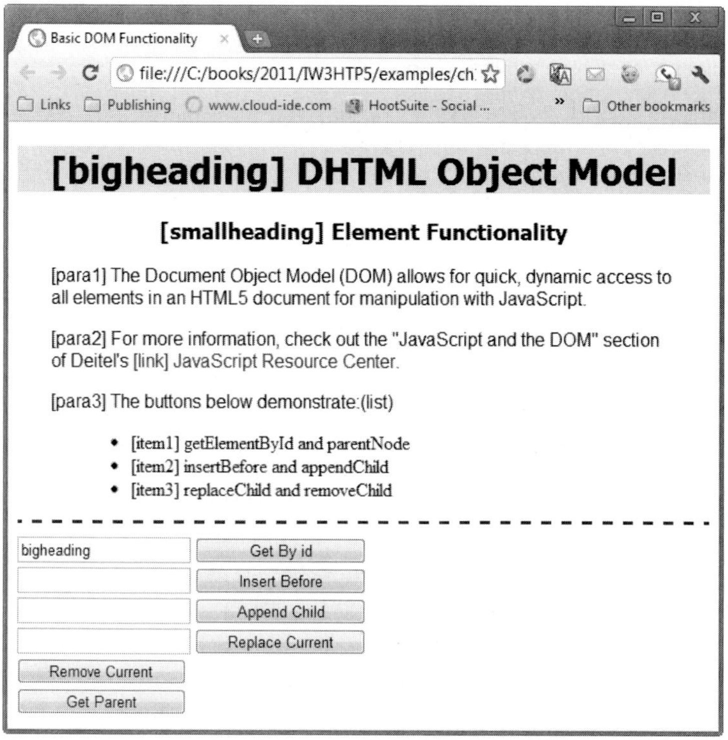

Fig. 12.4 | HTML5 document that's used to demonstrate DOM functionality for dynamically adding, removing and selecting elements. (Part 2 of 2.)

depends on which node is currently selected. Function `start` (lines 7–24) registers the event handlers for the document's `buttons`, then initializes `currentNode` to the `h1` element with `id` `bigheading`. This function is set up to be called when the `window`'s `load` event (line 27) occurs. Variable `idcount` (line 4) is used to assign a unique `id` to any new elements that are created. The remainder of the JavaScript code contains event-handling functions for the `buttons` and two helper functions that are called by the event handlers. We now discuss each `button` and its corresponding event handler in detail.

```
1   // Fig. 12.5: dom.js
2   // Script to demonstrate basic DOM functionality.
3   var currentNode; // stores the currently highlighted node
4   var idcount = 0; // used to assign a unique id to new elements
5
6   // register event handlers and initialize currentNode
7   function start()
8   {
```

Fig. 12.5 | Script to demonstrate basic DOM functionality. (Part 1 of 3.)

```
 9        document.getElementById( "byIdButton" ).addEventListener(
10           "click", byId, false );
11        document.getElementById( "insertButton" ).addEventListener(
12           "click", insert, false );
13        document.getElementById( "appendButton" ).addEventListener(
14           "click", appendNode, false );
15        document.getElementById( "replaceButton" ).addEventListener(
16           "click", replaceCurrent, false );
17        document.getElementById( "removeButton" ).addEventListener(
18           "click", remove, false );
19        document.getElementById( "parentButton" ).addEventListener(
20           "click", parent, false );
21
22        // initialize currentNode
23        currentNode = document.getElementById( "bigheading" );
24     } // end function start
25
26     // call start after the window loads
27     window.addEventListener( "load", start, false );
28
29     // get and highlight an element by its id attribute
30     function byId()
31     {
32        var id = document.getElementById( "gbi" ).value;
33        var target = document.getElementById( id );
34
35        if ( target )
36           switchTo( target );
37     } // end function byId
38
39     // insert a paragraph element before the current element
40     // using the insertBefore method
41     function insert()
42     {
43        var newNode = createNewNode(
44           document.getElementById( "ins" ).value );
45        currentNode.parentNode.insertBefore( newNode, currentNode );
46        switchTo( newNode );
47     } // end function insert
48
49     // append a paragraph node as the child of the current node
50     function appendNode()
51     {
52        var newNode = createNewNode(
53           document.getElementById( "append" ).value );
54        currentNode.appendChild( newNode );
55        switchTo( newNode );
56     } // end function appendNode
57
58     // replace the currently selected node with a paragraph node
59     function replaceCurrent()
60     {
```

Fig. 12.5 | Script to demonstrate basic DOM functionality. (Part 2 of 3.)

```
61      var newNode = createNewNode(
62         document.getElementById( "replace" ).value );
63      currentNode.parentNode.replaceChild( newNode, currentNode );
64      switchTo( newNode );
65   } // end function replaceCurrent
66
67   // remove the current node
68   function remove()
69   {
70      if ( currentNode.parentNode == document.body )
71         alert( "Can't remove a top-level element." );
72      else
73      {
74         var oldNode = currentNode;
75         switchTo( oldNode.parentNode );
76         currentNode.removeChild( oldNode );
77      }
78   } // end function remove
79
80   // get and highlight the parent of the current node
81   function parent()
82   {
83      var target = currentNode.parentNode;
84
85      if ( target != document.body )
86         switchTo( target );
87      else
88         alert( "No parent." );
89   } // end function parent
90
91   // helper function that returns a new paragraph node containing
92   // a unique id and the given text
93   function createNewNode( text )
94   {
95      var newNode = document.createElement( "p" );
96      nodeId = "new" + idcount;
97      ++idcount;
98      newNode.setAttribute( "id", nodeId ); // set newNode's id
99      text = "[" + nodeId + "] " + text;
100     newNode.appendChild( document.createTextNode( text ) );
101     return newNode;
102  } // end function createNewNode
103
104  // helper function that switches to a new currentNode
105  function switchTo( newNode )
106  {
107     currentNode.setAttribute( "class", "" ); // remove old highlighting
108     currentNode = newNode;
109     currentNode.setAttribute( "class", "highlighted" ); // highlight
110     document.getElementById( "gbi" ).value =
111        currentNode.getAttribute( "id" );
112  } // end function switchTo
```

Fig. 12.5 | Script to demonstrate basic DOM functionality. (Part 3 of 3.)

Finding and Highlighting an Element Using **getElementById, setAttribute** *and* **getAttribute**

The first row of the form (Fig. 12.4, lines 31–33) allows the user to enter the id of an element into the text field and click the **Get By Id** button to find and highlight the element, as shown in Fig. 12.6. The button's click event calls function byId.

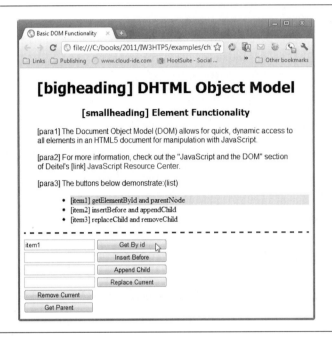

Fig. 12.6 | The document of Figure 12.4 after using the **Get By id** button to select item1.

The byId function (Fig. 12.5, lines 30–37) uses getElementById to assign the contents of the text field to variable id. Line 33 uses getElementById to find the element whose id attribute matches variable id and assign it to variable target. If an element is found with the given id, an object is returned; otherwise, null is returned. Line 35 checks whether target is an object—any object used as a boolean expression is true, while null is false. If target evaluates to true, line 36 calls the switchTo function with target as its argument.

The switchTo function (lines 105–112) is used throughout the script to highlight an element in the page. The current element is given a yellow background using the style class highlighted, defined in the CSS styles. This function introduces the DOM element methods **setAttribute** and **getAttribute**, which allow you to modify an attribute value and get an attribute value, respectively. Line 107 uses setAttribute to set the current node's class attribute to the empty string. This clears the class attribute to remove the highlighted class from the currentNode before we highlight the new one.

Line 108 assigns the newNode object (passed into the function as a parameter) to variable currentNode. Line 109 uses setAttribute to set the new node's class attribute to the CSS class highlighted.

Finally, lines 110–111 use getAttribute to get the currentNode's id and assign it to the input field's value property. While this isn't necessary when switchTo is called by byId, we'll see shortly that other functions call switchTo. This line ensures that the text field's value contains the currently selected node's id. Notice that we did not use setAttribute to change the value of the input field. Methods setAttribute and getAttribute do not work for user-modifiable content, such as the value displayed in an input field.

*Creating and Inserting Elements Using **insertBefore** and **appendChild***
The second and third rows in the form (Fig. 12.4, lines 34–39) allow the user to create a new element and insert it before or as a child of the current node, respectively. If the user enters text in the second text field and clicks **Insert Before**, the text is placed in a new paragraph element, which is inserted into the document before the currently selected element, as in Fig. 12.7. The button's click event calls function insert (Fig. 12.5, lines 41–47).

Lines 43–44 call the function createNewNode, passing it the value of the "ins" input field as an argument. Function createNewNode, defined in lines 93–102, creates a paragraph node containing the text passed to it. Line 95 creates a p element using the document object's **createElement method**, which creates a new DOM node, taking the tag name as an argument. Though createElement *creates* an element, it does not *insert* the element on the page.

Line 96 creates a unique id for the new element by concatenating "new" and the value of idcount before incrementing idcount. Line 98 uses setAttribute to set the id of the new element. Line 99 concatenates the element's id in square brackets to the beginning of text (the parameter containing the paragraph's text).

Line 100 introduces two new methods. The document's **createTextNode method** creates a node that contains only text. Given a string argument, createTextNode inserts the

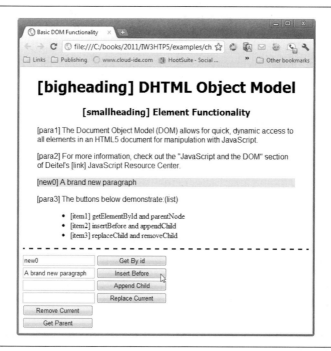

Fig. 12.7 | The document of Figure 12.4 after selecting para3 with the **Get By id** button, then using the **Insert Before** button to insert a new paragraph before para3.

string into the text node. We create a new text node containing the contents of variable text. This new node is then used as the argument to the **appendChild method**, which is called on the new paragraph's node. Method appendChild inserts a child node (passed as an argument) after any existing children of the node on which it's called.

After the p element is created, line 101 returns the node to the calling function insert, where it's assigned to newNode (line 43). Line 45 inserts the new node before the currently selected one. Property **parentNode** contains the node's parent. In line 45, we use this property to get currentNode's parent. Then we call the **insertBefore method** (line 45) on the parent with newNode and currentNode as its arguments. This inserts newNode as a child of the parent directly before currentNode. Line 46 uses our switchTo function to update the currentNode to the newly inserted node and highlight it in the document.

The input field and button in the third table row allow the user to append a new paragraph node as a child of the current element (Fig. 12.8). This feature uses a procedure similar to the insert function. Lines 52–53 in function appendNode create a new node, line 54 inserts it as a child of the current node, and line 55 uses switchTo to update current-Node and highlight the new node.

Fig. 12.8 | The document of Figure 12.4 after using the **Append Child** button to append a child to the new paragraph in Figure 12.7.

Replacing and Removing Elements Using replaceChild and removeChild
The next two table rows (Fig. 12.4, lines 40–44) allow the user to replace the current element with a new p element or simply remove the current element. When the user clicks **Replace Current** (Fig. 12.9), function replaceCurrent (Fig. 12.5, lines 59–65) is called.

Fig. 12.9 | The document of Figure 12.4 after using the **Replace Current** button to replace the paragraph created in Figure 12.8.

In function `replaceCurrent`, lines 61–62 call `createNewNode`, in the same way as in `insert` and `appendNode`, getting the text from the correct input field. Line 63 gets the parent of `currentNode`, then calls the `replaceChild` method on the parent. The **replaceChild method** receives as its first argument the new node to insert and as its second argument the node to replace.

Clicking the **Remove Current** button (Fig. 12.10) calls the `remove` function (Fig. 12.5, lines 68–77) to remove the current element entirely and highlights the parent. If the node's parent is the body element, line 71 displays an error message—the program does not allow the entire body element to be selected. Otherwise, lines 74–76 remove the current element. Line 74 stores the old `currentNode` in variable `oldNode`. We do this to maintain a reference to the node to be removed after we've changed the value of `currentNode`. Line 75 calls `switchTo` to highlight the parent node. Line 76 uses the **removeChild method** to remove the `oldNode` (a child of the new `currentNode`) from its place in the HTML5 document. In general,

```
parent.removeChild( child );
```

looks in *parent*'s list of children for *child* and removes it.

The `form`'s **Get Parent** button selects and highlights the parent element of the currently highlighted element (Fig. 12.11) by calling the `parent` function (Fig. 12.5, lines 81–89). The function simply gets the parent node (line 83), makes sure it's not the body element and calls `switchTo` to highlight the parent; otherwise, we display an error if the parent node is the body element.

Fig. 12.10 | The document of Figure 12.4 after using the **Remove Current** button to remove the paragraph highlighted in Figure 12.9.

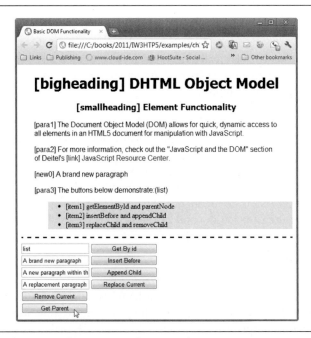

Fig. 12.11 | The document of Figure 12.4 after using the **Get By id** button to item2, then using the **Get Parent** button to select item2's parent—the unordered list.

12.4 DOM Collections

The Document Object Model contains several **collections**, which are groups of related objects on a page. DOM collections are accessed as properties of DOM objects such as the document object or a DOM node. The document object has properties containing the

- **images** collection
- **links** collection
- **forms** collection
- **anchors** collection

These collections contain all the elements of the corresponding type on the page. The example of Figs. 12.12–12.14 uses the **links** collection to extract all the links on a page and display them at the bottom of the page.

CSS

Figure 12.12 contains the CSS for the example.

```
 1   /* Fig. 12.12: style.css */
 2   /* CSS for collections.html. */
 3   body          { font-family: arial, helvetica, sans-serif }
 4   h1            { font-family: tahoma, geneva, sans-serif;
 5                   text-align: center }
 6   p a           { color: DarkRed }
 7   ul            { font-size: .9em; }
 8   li            { display: inline;
 9                   list-style-type: none;
10                   border-right: 1px solid gray;
11                   padding-left: 5px; padding-right: 5px; }
12   li:first-child { padding-left: 0px; }
13   li:last-child  { border-right: none; }
14   a             { text-decoration: none; }
15   a:hover       { text-decoration: underline; }
```

Fig. 12.12 | CSS for `collections.html`.

HTML5 Document

Figure 12.13 presents the example's HTML5 document. The body contains two paragraphs (lines 14–28) with links at various places in the text and an empty div (line 29) with the id "links".

```
1   <!DOCTYPE html>
2
3   <!-- Fig. 12.13: collections.html -->
4   <!-- Using the links collection. -->
5   <html>
6      <head>
```

Fig. 12.13 | Using the `links` collection. (Part 1 of 2.)

```
7          <meta charset="utf-8">
8          <title>Using Links Collection</title>
9          <link rel = "stylesheet" type = "text/css" href = "style.css">
10         <script src = "collections.js"></script>
11      </head>
12      <body>
13         <h1>Deitel Resource Centers</h1>
14         <p><a href = "http://www.deitel.com/">Deitel's website</a>
15            contains a growing
16            <a href = "http://www.deitel.com/ResourceCenters.html">list
17            of Resource Centers</a> on a wide range of topics. Many
18            Resource centers related to topics covered in this book,
19            <a href = "http://www.deitel.com/books/iw3htp5">Internet &
20            World Wide Web How to Program, 5th Edition</a>. We have
21            Resource Centers on
22            <a href = "http://www.deitel.com/Web2.0">Web 2.0</a>,
23            <a href = "http://www.deitel.com/Firefox">Firefox</a> and
24            <a href = "http://www.deitel.com/IE9">Internet Explorer 9</a>,
25            <a href = "http://www.deitel.com/HTML5">HTML5</a>, and
26            <a href = "http://www.deitel.com/JavaScript">JavaScript</a>.
27            Watch for related new Resource Centers.</p>
28         <p>Links in this page:</p>
29         <div id = "links"></div>
30      </body>
31   </html>
```

Fig. 12.13 | Using the links collection. (Part 2 of 2.)

JavaScript
Function processlinks (Fig. 12.14) is called when the window's load event occurs (as specified in line 20). The function declares variable linksList (line 5) to store the document's links collection, which is accessed with the links property of the document object. Line 6 creates the string (contents) that will contain all the document's links as an unordered list, to be inserted into the "links" div later. Lines 9–14 iterate through the links collection. The collection's **length property** specifies the number of items in the collection.

Line 11 stores the current link. You access the elements of the collection using indices in square brackets, just as we did with arrays. DOM collection objects have one property

```
1   // Fig. 12.14: collections.js
2   // Script to demonstrate using the links collection.
3   function processLinks()
4   {
5      var linksList = document.links; // get the document's links
6      var contents = "<ul>";
7
8      // concatenate each link to contents
9      for ( var i = 0; i < linksList.length; ++i )
10     {
11        var currentLink = linksList[ i ];
12        contents += "<li><a href='" + currentLink.href + "'>" +
13           currentLink.innerHTML + "</li>";
14     } // end for
15
16     contents += "</ul>";
17     document.getElementById( "links" ).innerHTML = contents;
18  } // end function processLinks
19
20  window.addEventListener( "load", processLinks, false );
```

Fig. 12.14 | Script to demonstrate using the links collection.

and two methods—the `length` property, the **`item` method** and the **`namedItem` method**. The `item` method—an alternative to the square bracketed indices—receives an an integer argument and returns the corresponding item in the collection. The `namedItem` method receives an element `id` as an argument and finds the element with that `id` in the collection.

Lines 12–13 add to the `contents` string an `li` element containing the current link. Variable `currentLink` (a DOM node representing an a element) has an **`href` property** representing the link's `href` attribute. Line 17 inserts the contents into the empty `div` with id `"links"` to show all the links on the page in one location.

Collections allow easy access to all elements of a single type in a page. This is useful for gathering elements into one place and for applying changes to those elements across an entire page. For example, the `forms` collection could be used to disable all form inputs after a `submit` button has been pressed to avoid multiple submissions while the next page loads.

12.5 Dynamic Styles

An element's style can be changed dynamically. Often such a change is made in response to user events, which we discuss in Chapter 13. Style changes can create mouse-hover effects, interactive menus and animations. The example in Figs. 12.15–12.16 changes the document body's `background-color` style property in response to user input. The document (Fig. 12.15) contains just a paragraph of text.

```
1   <!DOCTYPE html>
2
3   <!-- Fig. 12.15: dynamicstyle.html -->
4   <!-- Dynamic styles. -->
```

Fig. 12.15 | Dynamic styles. (Part 1 of 2.)

```
5    <html>
6       <head>
7          <meta charset="utf-8">
8          <title>Dynamic Styles</title>
9          <script src = "dynamicstyle.js"></script>
10      </head>
11      <body>
12         <p>Welcome to our website!</p>
13      </body>
14   </html>
```

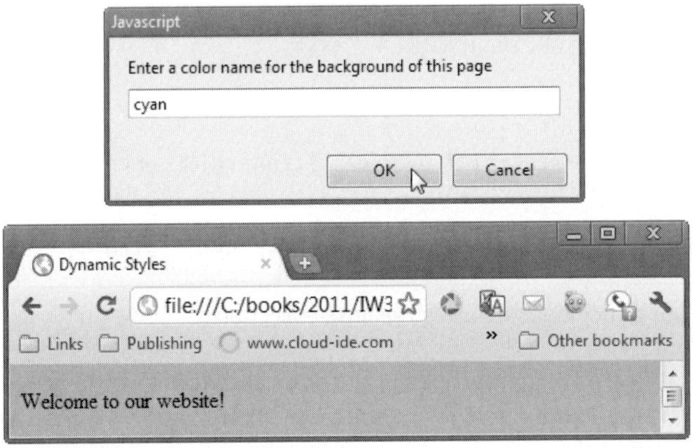

Fig. 12.15 | Dynamic styles. (Part 2 of 2.)

Function start (Fig. 12.16) is called when the window's load event occurs (as specified in line 11). The function prompts the user to enter a color name, then sets the body element's background color to that value. [*Note:* An error occurs if the value entered is not a valid color. See Appendix B, HTML Colors, for a list of color names.] The document object's **body property** refers to the body element. We then use the setAttribute method to set the style attribute with the user-specified color for the background-color CSS property. If you have predefined CSS style classes defined for your document, you can also use the setAttribute method to set the class attribute. So, if you had a class named .red you could set the class attribute's value to "red" to apply the style class.

```
1    // Fig. 12.16: dynamicstyle.js
2    // Script to demonstrate dynamic styles.
3    function start()
4    {
5       var inputColor = prompt( "Enter a color name for the " +
6          "background of this page", "" );
7       document.body.setAttribute( "style",
8          "background-color: " + inputColor );
9    } // end function start
10
11   window.addEventListener( "load", start, false );
```

Fig. 12.16 | Script to demonstrate dynamic styles.

12.6 Using a Timer and Dynamic Styles to Create Animated Effects

The example of Figs. 12.17–12.19 introduces the window object's setInterval and clearInterval methods, combining them with dynamic styles to create animated effects. This example is a basic image viewer that allows you to select a book cover and view it in a larger size. When the user clicks a thumbnail image, the larger version grows from the top-left corner of the main image area.

CSS
Figure 12.17 contains the CSS styles used in the example.

```
 1   /* Fig. 12.17: style.css */
 2   /* CSS for coverviewer.html. */
 3   #thumbs    { width: 192px;
 4                height: 370px;
 5                padding: 5px;
 6                float: left }
 7   #mainimg   { width: 289px;
 8                padding: 5px;
 9                float: left }
10   #imgCover  { height: 373px }
11   img        { border: 1px solid black }
```

Fig. 12.17 | CSS for coverviewer.html.

HTML5 Document
The HTML5 document (Fig. 12.18) contains two div elements, both floated left using styles defined in Fig. 12.17 to present them side by side. The left div contains the full-size image jhtp.jpg, which appears when the page loads. The right div contains six thumbnail images. Each responds to its click event by calling the display function (as registered in Fig. 12.19) and passing it the filename of the corresponding full-size image.

```
 1   <!DOCTYPE html>
 2
 3   <!-- Fig. 12.18: coverviewer.html -->
 4   <!-- Dynamic styles used for animation. -->
 5   <html>
 6      <head>
 7         <meta charset = "utf-8">
 8         <title>Deitel Book Cover Viewer</title>
 9         <link rel = "stylesheet" type = "text/css" href = "style.css">
10         <script src = "coverviewer.js"></script>
11      </head>
```

Fig. 12.18 | Dynamic styles used for animation. (Part 1 of 4.)

```
12    <body>
13       <div id = "mainimg">
14          <img id = "imgCover" src = "fullsize/jhtp.jpg"
15             alt = "Full cover image">
16       </div>
17       <div id = "thumbs" >
18          <img src = "thumbs/jhtp.jpg" id = "jhtp"
19             alt = "Java How to Program cover">
20          <img src = "thumbs/iw3htp.jpg" id = "iw3htp"
21             alt = "Internet & World Wide Web How to Program cover">
22          <img src = "thumbs/cpphtp.jpg" id = "cpphtp"
23             alt = "C++ How to Program cover">
24          <img src = "thumbs/jhtplov.jpg" id = "jhtplov"
25             alt = "Java How to Program LOV cover">
26          <img src = "thumbs/cpphtplov.jpg" id = "cpphtplov"
27             alt = "C++ How to Program LOV cover">
28          <img src = "thumbs/vcsharphtp.jpg" id = "vcsharphtp"
29             alt = "Visual C# How to Program cover">
30       </div>
31    </body>
32 </html>
```

a) The cover viewer page loads with the cover of *Java How to Program, 9/e*

Fig. 12.18 | Dynamic styles used for animation. (Part 2 of 4.)

b) When the user clicks the thumbnail of *Internet & World Wide Web How to Program, 5/e*, the full-size image begins growing from the top-left corner of the window

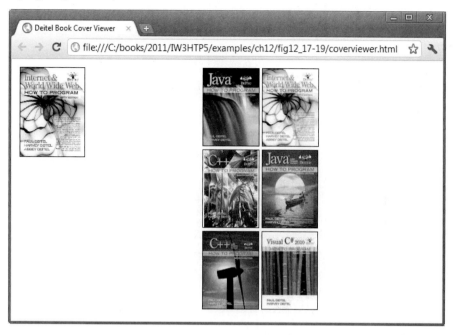

c) The cover continues to grow

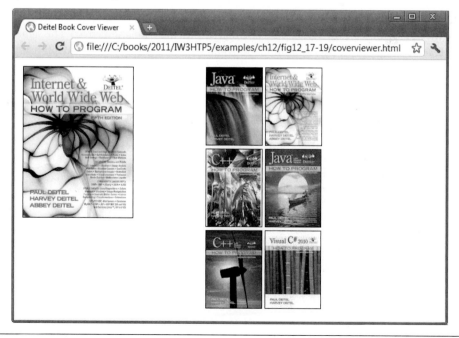

Fig. 12.18 | Dynamic styles used for animation. (Part 3 of 4.)

d) The animation finishes when the cover reaches its full size

Fig. 12.18 | Dynamic styles used for animation. (Part 4 of 4.)

JavaScript
Figure 12.19 contains the JavaScript code that creates the animation effect. The same effects can be achieved by declaring animations and transitions in CSS3, as we demonstrated in Sections 5.12–5.13.

```
 1  // Fig. 12.19: coverviewer.js
 2  // Script to demonstrate dynamic styles used for animation.
 3  var interval = null; // keeps track of the interval
 4  var speed = 6; // determines the speed of the animation
 5  var count = 0; // size of the image during the animation
 6
 7  // called repeatedly to animate the book cover
 8  function run()
 9  {
10     count += speed;
11
12     // stop the animation when the image is large enough
13     if ( count >= 375 )
14     {
15        window.clearInterval( interval );
16        interval = null;
17     } // end if
```

Fig. 12.19 | Script to demonstrate dynamic styles used for animation. (Part 1 of 2.)

```
18
19      var bigImage = document.getElementById( "imgCover" );
20      bigImage.setAttribute( "style", "width: " + (0.7656 * count + "px;") +
21         "height: " + (count + "px;") );
22   } // end function run
23
24   // inserts the proper image into the main image area and
25   // begins the animation
26   function display( imgfile )
27   {
28      if ( interval )
29         return;
30
31      var bigImage = document.getElementById( "imgCover" );
32      bigImage.setAttribute( "style", "width: 0px; height: 0px;" );
33      bigImage.setAttribute( "src", "fullsize/" + imgfile );
34      bigImage.setAttribute( "alt", "Large version of " + imgfile );
35      count = 0; // start the image at size 0
36      interval = window.setInterval( "run()", 10 ); // animate
37   } // end function display
38
39   // register event handlers
40   function start()
41   {
42      document.getElementById( "jhtp" ).addEventListener(
43         "click", function() { display( "jhtp.jpg" ); }, false );
44      document.getElementById( "iw3htp" ).addEventListener(
45         "click", function() { display( "iw3htp.jpg" ); }, false );
46      document.getElementById( "cpphtp" ).addEventListener(
47         "click", function() { display( "cpphtp.jpg" ); }, false );
48      document.getElementById( "jhtplov" ).addEventListener(
49         "click", function() { display( "jhtplov.jpg" ); }, false );
50      document.getElementById( "cpphtplov" ).addEventListener(
51         "click", function() { display( "cpphtplov.jpg" ); }, false );
52      document.getElementById( "vcsharphtp" ).addEventListener(
53         "click", function() { display( "vcsharphtp.jpg" ); }, false );
54   } // end function start
55
56   window.addEventListener( "load", start, false );
```

Fig. 12.19 | Script to demonstrate dynamic styles used for animation. (Part 2 of 2.)

The display function (lines 26–36) dynamically updates the image in the left div to the one the user clicked. Lines 28–29 prevent the rest of the function from executing if interval is defined (i.e., an animation is in progress.) Line 31 gets the left div by its id, imgCover. Line 32 sets the image's style attribute, using 0px for the width and height—the initial size of the image before the animation begins. Next, line 33 sets the image's src attribute to the specified image file in the fullsize directory, and line 34 sets its required alt attribute. Line 35 sets count, the variable that controls the animation, to 0.

Line 36 introduces the window object's **setInterval method**, which creates a timer that controls our animation. This method takes two parameters—a statement to execute repeatedly, and an integer specifying how often to execute it, in milliseconds. We use setInterval to call function run (lines 8–22) every 10 milliseconds. The setInterval method returns a unique identifier to keep track of that particular interval timer—we assign this identifier to the variable interval. This identifier can be used later to stop the timer (and thus, the animation) when the image has finished growing.

The run function increases the height of the image by the value of speed and updates its width accordingly to keep the aspect ratio consistent. The run function is called every 10 milliseconds, so the image grows dynamically. Line 10 adds the value of speed (declared and initialized to 6 in line 4) to count, which keeps track of the animation's progress and determines the current size of the image. If the image has grown to its full height (375), line 15 uses the window's **clearInterval method** to terminate the timer, which prevents function run from being called again until the user clicks another thumbnail image. We pass to clearInterval the interval-timer identifier (stored in interval) that setInterval created in line 36. Since each interval timer has its own unique identifier, scripts can keep track of multiple interval timers and choose which one to stop when calling clearInterval.

Line 19 gets the imgCover element, and lines 20–21 set its width and height CSS properties. Note that line 20 multiplies count by a scaling factor of 0.7656—this is the aspect ratio of the width to the height for the images used in this example. Run the code example and click on a thumbnail image to see the full animation effect.

Function start—Using Anonymous functions

Function start (lines 40–54) registers the click event handlers for the img elements in the HTML5 document. In each case, we define an **anonymous function** to handle the event. An anonymous function is defined with no name—it's created in nearly the same way as any other function, but with no identifier after the keyword function. This notation is useful when creating a function for the sole purpose of assigning it to an event handler. It's also useful when you must provide arguments to the function, since you cannot provide a function call as the second argument to addEventListener—if you did, the JavaScript interpreter would call the function, then pass the result of the function call to addEventListener. In line 43, the code

```
function() { display( "jhtp.jpg" ); }
```

defines an anonymous function that calls function display with the name of the image file to display.

Summary

Section 12.1 Introduction
- The Document Object Model (p. 428) gives you access to all the elements on a web page. Using JavaScript, you can dynamically create, modify and remove elements in the page.

Section 12.2 Modeling a Document: DOM Nodes and Trees
- The getElementById method returns objects called DOM nodes (p. 428). Every element in an HTML5 page is modeled in the web browser by a DOM node.
- All the nodes in a document make up the page's DOM tree (p. 428), which describes the relationships among elements.

- Nodes are related to each other through child-parent relationships. An HTML5 element inside another element is said to be its child (p. 428)—the containing element is known as the parent (p. 428). A node can have multiple children but only one parent. Nodes with the same parent node are referred to as siblings (p. 428).

- The document node in a DOM tree is called the root node (p. 429), because it has no parent.

Section 12.3 Traversing and Modifying a DOM Tree

- DOM element methods setAttribute and getAttribute (p. 436) allow you to modify an attribute value and get an attribute value of an element, respectively.

- The document object's createElement method (p. 437) creates a new DOM node, taking the tag name as an argument. Note that while createElement *creates* an element, it does not *insert* the element on the page.

- The document's createTextNode method (p. 437) creates a DOM node that can contain only text. Given a string argument, createTextNode inserts the string into the text node.

- Method appendChild (p. 438) is called on a parent node to insert a child node (passed as an argument) after any existing children.

- The parentNode property (p. 438) of any DOM node contains the node's parent.

- The insertBefore method (p. 438) is called on a parent having a new child and an existing child as arguments. The new child is inserted as a child of the parent directly before the existing child.

- The replaceChild method (p. 439) is called on a parent, taking a new child and an existing child as arguments. The method inserts the new child into its list of children in place of the existing child.

- The removeChild method (p. 439) is called on a parent with a child to be removed as an argument.

Section 12.4 DOM Collections

- The DOM contains several collections (p. 441), which are groups of related objects on a page. DOM collections are accessed as properties of DOM objects such as the document object (p. 441) or a DOM node.

- The document object has properties containing the images collection (p. 441), links collection (p. 441), forms collection and anchors collection (p. 441). These collections contain all the elements of the corresponding type on the page.

- To find the number of elements in the collection, use the collection's length property (p. 442).

- To access items in a collection, use square brackets just as you would with an array, or use the item method. The item method (p. 443) of a DOM collection is used to access specific elements in a collection, taking an index as an argument. The namedItem method (p. 443) takes a name as a parameter and finds the element in the collection, if any, whose id attribute or name attribute matches it.

- The href property of a DOM link node refers to the link's href attribute (p. 443).

Section 12.5 Dynamic Styles

- An element's style can be changed dynamically. Often such a change is made in response to user events. Such style changes can create many effects, including mouse-hover effects, interactive menus, and animations.

- A document object's body property refers to the body element (p. 444) in the HTML5 page.

- The setInterval method (p. 449) of the window object repeatedly executes a statement on a certain interval. It takes two parameters—a statement to execute repeatedly, and an integer specifying how often to execute it, in milliseconds. The setInterval method returns a unique identifier to keep track of that particular interval.

• The window object's clearInterval method (p. 450) stops the repetitive calls of object's set-Interval method. We pass to clearInterval the interval identifier that setInterval returned.

Self-Review Exercises

12.1 State whether each of the following is *true* or *false*. If *false*, explain why.
a) The Document Object Model does not give access to all the elements on a web page.
b) The getElementById method returns objects called DOM nodes
c) The document node in a DOM tree is called the child node
d) Nodes are related to each other through peer-to-peer relationships.
e) The removeChild method is called on the root with a child to be removed as an argument.
f) The parentNode property of any DOM node contains the node's parent.
g) All the nodes in a document make up the page's DOM tree, which does not describe relationships among elements.
h) The document object's createElement method inserts an element on the page.
i) To find the number of elements in the collection, use the collection's width property.

12.2 Fill in the blanks for each of the following statements.
a) We pass to clearInterval the interval identifier that _____ returned.
b) The document object's createElement method creates a new DOM node, taking the _____ as an argument.
c) Method _____ is called on a parent node to insert a child node
d) Using JavaScript, you can _____ create, modify and remove elements in the page.
e) Nodes are related to each other through _____ relationships.

Answers to Self-Review Exercises

12.1 a) False. The Document Object Model gives you access to all the elements on a web page. b) True. c) False. The document node in a DOM tree is called the root node. d) False. Nodes are related to each other through child-parent relationships. e) False. The removeChild method is called on a parent with a child to be removed as an argument. f) True. g) False. All the nodes in a document make up the page's DOM tree, which describes the relationships among elements. h) False. createElement *creates* an element, it does not *insert* the element on the page. i) False. To find the number of elements in the collection, use the collection's length property.

12.2 a) setInterval. b) tagname. c) appendChild. d) dynamically. e) child-parent.

Exercises

12.3 Modify Fig. 12.3 to use red as a background color to highlight all the links. Use yellow for the text in the links, instead of displaying them in a box at the bottom.

12.4 Use a browser's developer tools to view the DOM tree of the document in Fig. 12.4. Look at the document tree of your favorite website. Explore the information these tools give you in the right panel(s) about an element when you click it.

12.5 Write a script that contains a button and a counter in a div. The button should decrement the counter each time it's clicked with a default initial value of 100.

12.6 Create a web page in which the user is allowed to select the page's background color and whether the page uses serif or sans serif fonts. Then change the body element's style attribute accordingly.

12.7 *(15 Puzzle)* Write a web page that enables the user to play the game of 15. There's a 4-by-4 board (implemented as an HTML5 table) for a total of 16 slots. One of the slots is empty. The other slots are occupied by 15 tiles, randomly numbered from 1 through 15. Any tile next to the currently empty slot can be moved into the currently empty slot by clicking on the tile. Your program should create the board with the tiles out of order. The user's goal is to arrange the tiles in sequential order row by row. Using the DOM and the click event, write a script that allows the user to swap the positions of the open position and an adjacent tile. [*Hint:* The click event should be specified for each table cell.]

12.8   Modify your solution to Exercise 12.7 to determine when the game is over, then prompt the user to determine whether to play again. If so, scramble the numbers using the Math.random method.

12.9   Modify your solution to Exercise 12.8 to use an image that's split into 16 pieces of equal size. Discard one of the pieces and randomly place the other 15 pieces in the HTML5 table.

13

JavaScript Event Handling: A Deeper Look

The wisest prophets make sure of the event first.
—Horace Walpole

Do you think I can listen all day to such stuff?
—Lewis Carroll

The user should feel in control of the computer; not the other way around. This is achieved in applications that embody three qualities: responsiveness, permissiveness, and consistency.
—*Inside Macintosh, Volume 1*
Apple Computer, Inc., 1985

We are responsible for actions performed in response to circumstances for which we are not responsible.
—Allan Massie

Objectives

In this chapter you'll:

- Learn the concepts of events, event handlers and event bubbling.

- Create and register event handlers that respond to mouse and keyboard events.

- Use the **event** object to get information about an event.

- Recognize and respond to many common events.

13.1 Introduction

We've seen that HTML5 pages can be controlled via scripting, and we've already used several events—load, submit and click—to trigger calls to JavaScript functions. This chapter takes a deeper look into **JavaScript events**, which allow scripts to respond to user interactions and modify the page accordingly. Events allow scripts to respond to a user who is moving the mouse, entering form data, pressing keys and much more. Events and event handling help make web applications more dynamic and interactive. We give examples of event handling several common events and list other useful events.

13.2 Reviewing the `load` Event

In several earlier examples, we used the `window` object's `load` event to begin executing scripts. This event fires when the `window` finishes loading successfully (i.e., all its children are loaded and all external files referenced by the page are loaded). Actually, *every* DOM element has a `load` event, but it's most commonly used on the *window* object. The example of Figs. 13.1–13.2 reviews the `load` event. The `load` event's handler creates an interval timer that updates a span with the number of seconds that have elapsed since the document was loaded. The document's (Fig. 13.1) paragraph contains the span (line 14).

```
 1   <!DOCTYPE html>
 2
 3   <!-- Fig. 13.1: onload.html -->
 4   <!-- Demonstrating the load event. -->
 5   <html>
 6      <head>
 7         <meta charset = "utf-8">
 8         <title>load Event</title>
 9         <link rel = "stylesheet" type = "text/css" href = "style.css">
10         <script src = "load.js"></script>
11      </head>
12      <body>
13         <p>Seconds you have spent viewing this page so far:
14         <span id = "soFar">0</span></p>
15      </body>
16   </html>
```

Fig. 13.1 | Demonstrating the `window`'s `load` event. (Part 1 of 2.)

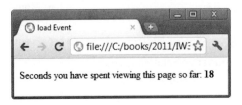

Seconds you have spent viewing this page so far: 18

Fig. 13.1 | Demonstrating the window's load event. (Part 2 of 2.)

Registering an Event Handler

An **event handler** is a function that responds to an event. Assigning an event handler to an event for a DOM node is called **registering an event handler**. The script (Fig. 13.2) registers the window's load event handler at line 18. Method addEventListener is available for every DOM node. The method takes three arguments:

- The first is the name of the event for which we're registering a handler.

- The second is the function that will be called to handle the event.

- The last argument is typically false—the true value is beyond this book's scope.

Line 19 indicates that when the load event occurs, function startTimer (lines 6–9) should execute. This function uses method window.setInterval to specify that function updateTime (lines 12–16) should be called every 1000 milliseconds. The updateTime function increments variable seconds and updates the counter in the span named "soFar".

```
1   // Fig. 13.2: load.js
2   // Script to demonstrate the load event.
3   var seconds = 0;
4
5   // called when the page loads to begin the timer
6   function startTimer()
7   {
8      window.setInterval( "updateTime()", 1000 );
9   } // end function startTimer
10
11  // called every 1000 ms to update the timer
12  function updateTime()
13  {
14     ++seconds;
15     document.getElementById( "soFar" ).innerHTML = seconds;
16  } // end function updateTime
17
18  window.addEventListener( "load", startTimer, false );
```

Fig. 13.2 | Script that registers window's load event handler and handles the event.

Note that the load event enables us to access the elements in the HTML5 page *after* they're fully loaded. If a script loaded in the document's head section contains statements that appear outside any script functions, those statements execute when the script loads—that is, *before* the body has loaded. If such a statement attempted to use getElementById to get a DOM node for an HTML5 element in the body, getElementById would return null. Another solution to this problem is to place the script as the last item in the document's body element—in that case, before the script executes, the body's nested elements will have already been created.

Registering Multiple Event Handlers
Method addEventListener can be called multiple times on a DOM node to register more than one event-handling method for an event. For example, if you wanted to perform a visual effect when the mouse is over a button and perform a task when that button is pressed, you could register mouseover and click event handlers.

Removing Event Listeners
It's also possible to remove an event listener by calling **removeEventListener** with the same arguments that you passed to addEventListener to register the event handler.

A Note About Older Event-Registration Models
We use the W3C standard event-registration model, which is supported by all of the browsers we use in this book. In legacy HTML and JavaScript code, you'll frequently encounter two other event-registration models—the inline model and the traditional model.

The inline model places calls to JavaScript functions directly in HTML code. For example, the following code indicates that JavaScript function start should be called when the body element loads:

```
<body onload = "start()">
```

The onload attribute corresponds to the body element's load event. By current web development standards, it's generally considered poor practice to intermix HTML and JavaScript code in this manner.

The traditional model uses a property of an object to specify an event handler. For example, the following JavaScript code indicates that function start should be called when document loads:

```
document.onload = "start()";
```

The onload property corresponds to the document object's load event. Though this property is specified in JavaScript and not in the HTML5 document, there are various problems with using it. In particular, if another statement assigns a different value to document.onload, the original value is replaced, which may not be the intended result.

For more information about these older event-registration models, visit these sites:

```
www.onlinetools.org/articles/unobtrusivejavascript/chapter4.html
www.quirksmode.org/js/introevents.html
```

13.3 Event mousemove and the event Object

This section introduces the **mousemove event**, which occurs whenever the user moves the mouse over the web page. We also discuss the event object, which contains information about the event that occurred. The example in Figs. 13.3–13.5 creates a simple drawing program that allows the user to draw inside a table element in red or blue by holding down the *Shift* key or *Ctrl* key and moving the mouse over the box. (In the next chapter, we'll introduce HTML5's new canvas element for creating graphics.) We do not show the example's `style.css` file, because the styles it contains have all been demonstrated previously.

HTML5 Document

The document's body (Fig. 13.3, lines 12–18) has a `table` with a `caption` that provides instructions on how to use the program and an empty `tbody`. The document's `load` event will call a function named `createCanvas` (Fig. 13.4) to fill the `table` with rows and columns.

```
1   <!DOCTYPE html>
2
3   <!-- Fig. 13.3: draw.html -->
4   <!-- A simple drawing program. -->
5   <html>
6      <head>
7         <meta charset="utf-8">
8         <title>Simple Drawing Program</title>
9         <link rel = "stylesheet" type = "text/css" href = "style.css">
10        <script src = "draw.js"></script>
11     </head>
12     <body>
13        <table id = "canvas">
14           <caption>Hold <em>Ctrl</em> (or <em>Control</em>) to draw blue.
15              Hold <em>Shift</em> to draw red.</caption>
16           <tbody id = "tablebody"></tbody>
17        </table>
18     </body>
19  </html>
```

a) User holds the *Shift* key and moves the mouse to draw in red.

Fig. 13.3 | Simple drawing program. (Part 1 of 2.)

b) User holds the
Ctrl key and moves
the mouse to draw
in blue.

Fig. 13.3 | Simple drawing program. (Part 2 of 2.)

Function createCanvas in draw.js
The createCanvas function (Fig. 13.4, lines 4–25) fills in the table with a grid of cells. The
style.css file used in this example contains a CSS rule that sets the width and height of
every td element to 4px. Another CSS rule in the file sets the table to 400px wide and uses
the border-collapse CSS property to eliminate space between the table cells.

```
1   // Fig. 13.4: draw.js
2   // A simple drawing program.
3   // initialization function to insert cells into the table
4   function createCanvas()
5   {
6      var side = 100;
7      var tbody = document.getElementById( "tablebody" );
8
9      for ( var i = 0; i < side; ++i )
10     {
11        var row = document.createElement( "tr" );
12
13        for ( var j = 0; j < side; ++j )
14        {
15           var cell = document.createElement( "td" );
16           row.appendChild( cell );
17        } // end for
18
19        tbody.appendChild( row );
20     } // end for
```

Fig. 13.4 | JavaScript code for the simple drawing program. (Part 1 of 2.)

```
21
22      // register mousemove listener for the table
23      document.getElementById( "canvas" ).addEventListener(
24         "mousemove", processMouseMove, false );
25   } // end function createCanvas
26
27   // processes the onmousemove event
28   function processMouseMove( e )
29   {
30      if ( e.target.tagName.toLowerCase() == "td" )
31      {
32         // turn the cell blue if the Ctrl key is pressed
33         if ( e.ctrlKey )
34         {
35            e.target.setAttribute( "class", "blue" );
36         } // end if
37
38         // turn the cell red if the Shift key is pressed
39         if ( e.shiftKey )
40         {
41            e.target.setAttribute( "class", "red" );
42         } // end if
43      } // end if
44   } // end function processMouseMove
45
46   window.addEventListener( "load", createCanvas, false );
```

Fig. 13.4 | JavaScript code for the simple drawing program. (Part 2 of 2.)

Line 6 defines variable side and sets it to 100—we use this as the number of rows and the number of columns in each row for a total of 10,000 table cells. Line 7 stores the tbody element so that we can append rows to it as they're generated. The outer loop creates each table row and the inner loop creates each cell. The inner loop uses DOM method createElement to create a td elemen and appends the cell as a child of the row.

Lines 23–24 set function processMouseMove as the table's mousemove event handler, which effectively specifies that function as the mousmove event handler for the table and all of its nested elements. An element's mousemove event fires whenever the user moves the mouse over that element.

Function *processMouseMove in draw.js*

At this point, the table is set up and function processMouseMove (lines 28–44) is called whenever the mouse moves over the table. When the browser calls an event-handling function, it passes an **event object** to the function. That object contains information about the event that caused the event-handling function to be called. Figure 13.5 shows several properties of the event object.

If an event-handling function is defined with a parameter (as in line 28), the function can use the event object. The function parameter is commonly named e. Function processMouseMove colors the cell the mouse moves over, depending on the key that's pressed when the event occurs. When the mouse moves over the table, the td element that the mouse moved over receives the event first. If that element does not have an event handler

Property	Description
altKey	This value is true if the *Alt* key was pressed when the event fired.
cancelBubble	Set to true to prevent the event from bubbling. Defaults to false. (See Section 13.7, Event Bubbling.)
clientX and clientY	The coordinates of the mouse cursor inside the client area (i.e., the active area where the web page is displayed, excluding scrollbars, navigation buttons, etc.).
ctrlKey	This value is true if the *Ctrl* key was pressed when the event fired.
keyCode	The ASCII code of the key pressed in a keyboard event. See Appendix D for more information on the ASCII character set.
screenX and screenY	The coordinates of the mouse cursor on the screen coordinate system.
shiftKey	This value is true if the *Shift* key was pressed when the event fired.
target	The DOM object that received the event.
type	The name of the event that fired.

Fig. 13.5 | Some event-object properties.

for the mouseover event, the event is sent to the td element's parent element, and so on— this is known as **event bubbling** (which we discuss in more detail in Section 13.7). This process continues until a mouseover event handler is found—in this case, the one for the table element. The event object, however, always contains the specific element that original received the event. This is stored in the object's **target property**. Line 30 uses this property to get the element's tag name. If the tag name is "td", then lines 33–42 do the actual drawing. The event object's **ctrlKey property** (line 33) contains a boolean which reflects whether the *Ctrl* key was pressed during the event. If ctrlKey is true, line 35 changes the color of the target table cell by setting its class attribute to the CSS class blue (defined in style.css). Similarly, if the **shiftKey property** of the event object is true, the *Shift* key is pressed and line 41 changes the color of the cell to red by setting its class attribute to the CSS class blue. This simple function allows the user to draw inside the table on the page in red and blue. You'll add more functionality to this example in the exercises at the end of this chapter.

13.4 Rollovers with mouseover and mouseout

Two more events fired by mouse movements are mouseover and mouseout. When the mouse cursor moves into an element, a **mouseover event** occurs for that element. When the cursor leaves the element, a **mouseout event** occurs. The example in Figs. 13.6–13.7 uses these events to achieve a **rollover effect** that updates text when the mouse cursor moves over it. We also introduce a technique for creating rollover images—though you've already seen that image rollover effects can be accomplished with CSS3 as well. We do not show the example's style.css file, because the styles it contains have all been demonstrated previously.

HTML5 Document

The HTML5 document (Fig. 13.6) contains an h1 with a nested img, a paragraph and a div with a nested unordered list. The unordered list contains the hexadecimal color codes for 16 basic HTML colors. Each list item's id is set to the color name for the hexadecimal color value that's displayed. The style.css file provides CSS rules that set the div's width and border and that display the unordered list's elements in inline-block format. The div's width allows only four list items per line.

```
1   <!DOCTYPE html>
2
3   <!-- Fig 13.6: mouseoverout.html -->
4   <!-- Events mouseover and mouseout. -->
5   <html>
6      <head>
7         <meta charset = "utf-8">
8         <title>Events mouseover and mouseout</title>
9         <link rel = "stylesheet" type = "text/css" href = "style.css">
10        <script src = "mouseoverout.js"></script>
11     </head>
12     <body>
13        <h1><img src = "heading1.png" id = "heading"
14           alt = "Heading Image"></h1>
15        <p>Can you tell a color from its hexadecimal RGB code
16        value? Look at the hex code, guess its color. To see
17        what color it corresponds to, move the mouse over the
18        hex code. Moving the mouse out of the hex code's table
19        cell will display the color name.</p>
20        <div>
21           <ul>
22              <li id = "Black">#000000</li>
23              <li id = "Blue">#0000FF</li>
24              <li id = "Magenta">#FF00FF</li>
25              <li id = "Gray">#808080</li>
26              <li id = "Green">#008000</li>
27              <li id = "Lime">#00FF00</li>
28              <li id = "Maroon">#800000</li>
29              <li id = "Navy">#000080</li>
30              <li id = "Olive">#808000</li>
31              <li id = "Purple">#800080</li>
32              <li id = "Red">#FF0000</li>
33              <li id = "Silver">#C0C0C0</li>
34              <li id = "Cyan">#00FFFF</li>
35              <li id = "Teal">#008080</li>
36              <li id = "Yellow">#FFFF00</li>
37              <li id = "White">#FFFFFF</li>
38           </ul>
39        </div>
40     </body>
41  </html>
```

Fig. 13.6 | HTML5 document to demonstrate mouseover and mouseout. (Part 1 of 3.)

a) The page loads with the blue heading image and all the hex codes in black.

Blue image —

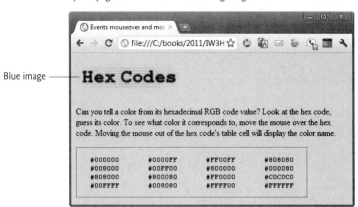

b) The heading image switches to an image with green text when the mouse rolls over it.

Green image —

c) When mouse rolls over a hex code, the text color changes to the color represented by the hex code. Notice that the heading image has become blue again because the mouse is no longer over it.

Text now displayed in blue

Fig. 13.6 | HTML5 document to demonstrate mouseover and mouseout. (Part 2 of 3.)

d) When the mouse leaves the hex code's table cell, the text changes to the name of the color.

![Browser window titled "Events mouseover and mou" showing a page with a heading "Hex Codes". Text reads: "Can you tell a color from its hexadecimal RGB code value? Look at the hex code, guess its color. To see what color it corresponds to, move the mouse over the hex code. Moving the mouse out of the hex code's table cell will display the color name." Below is a table of hex codes.]

#000000	Blue	#FF00FF	#808080
#008000	#00FF00	#800000	#000080
#808000	#800080	#FF0000	#C0C0C0
#00FFFF	#008080	#FFFF00	#FFFFFF

Fig. 13.6 | HTML5 document to demonstrate `mouseover` and `mouseout`. (Part 3 of 3.)

Script-Level Variables in *mouseoverout.js*

Figure 13.7 presents the JavaScript code for this example. To create a *rollover effect* for the image in the heading, lines 3–6 create two new JavaScript `Image` objects—`image1` and `image2`. Image `image2` displays when the mouse *hovers* over the image. Image `image1` displays when the mouse is *outside* the image. The script sets the `src` properties of each `Image` in lines 4 and 6, respectively. Creating `Image` objects preloads the images, so the browser does *not* need to download the rollover image the first time the script displays the image. If the image is large or the connection is slow, downloading would cause a noticeable delay in the image update.

 Performance Tip 13.1

Preloading images used in rollover effects prevents a delay the first time an image is displayed.

```
 1   // Fig 13.7: mouseoverout.js
 2   // Events mouseover and mouseout.
 3   image1 = new Image();
 4   image1.src = "heading1.png";
 5   image2 = new Image();
 6   image2.src = "heading2.png";
 7
 8   function mouseOver( e )
 9   {
10      // swap the image when the mouse moves over it
11      if ( e.target.getAttribute( "id" ) == "heading" )
12      {
13         e.target.setAttribute( "src", image2.getAttribute( "src" ) );
14      } // end if
15
```

Fig. 13.7 | Processing the `mouseover` and `mouseout` events. (Part 1 of 2.)

```
16        // if the element is an li, assign its id to its color
17        // to change the hex code's text to the corresponding color
18        if ( e.target.tagName.toLowerCase() == "li"  )
19        {
20           e.target.setAttribute( "style",
21              "color: " + e.target.getAttribute( "id" ) );
22        } // end if
23     } // end function mouseOver
24
25     function mouseOut( e )
26     {
27        // put the original image back when the mouse moves away
28        if ( e.target.getAttribute( "id" ) == "heading" )
29        {
30           e.target.setAttribute( "src", image1.getAttribute( "src" ) );
31        } // end if
32
33        // if the element is an li, assign its id to innerHTML
34        // to display the color name
35        if ( e.target.tagName.toLowerCase() == "li"  )
36        {
37           e.target.innerHTML = e.target.getAttribute( "id" );
38        } // end if
39     } // end function mouseOut
40
41     document.addEventListener( "mouseover", mouseOver, false );
42     document.addEventListener( "mouseout", mouseOut, false );
```

Fig. 13.7 | Processing the mouseover and mouseout events. (Part 2 of 2.)

Function mouseOver and mouseOut
Lines 41–42 register functions mouseOver and mouseOut to handle the mouseover and mouseout events, respectively.

Lines 11–14 in the mouseOver function handle the mouseover event for the heading image. We use the event object's target property (line 11) to get the id of the DOM object that received the event. If the event target's id attribute is the string "heading", line 13 sets the img element's src attribute to the src attribute of the appropriate Image object (image2). The same task occurs with image1 in the mouseOut function (lines 28–31).

The script handles the mouseover event for the list items in lines 18–22. This code tests whether the event's target is an li element. If so, the code sets the element's style attribute, using the color name stored in the id as the value of the style's color property. Lines 35–38 handle the mouseout event by changing the innerHTML in the list item (i.e., the target) to the color name specified in the target's id.

13.5 Form Processing with focus and blur

The **focus** and **blur** events can be useful when dealing with form elements that allow user input. The focus event fires when an element gains the focus (i.e., when the user clicks a form field or uses the *Tab* key to move between form elements), and blur fires when an element loses the focus, which occurs when another control gains the focus. The example in Figs. 13.8–13.9 demonstrates these events.

HTML5 Document

The HTML5 document in Fig. 13.8 contains a form followed by a paragraph in which we'll display help text for the input element that currently has the focus.

```
1   <!DOCTYPE html>
2
3   <!-- Fig. 13.8: focusblur.html -->
4   <!-- Demonstrating the focus and blur events. -->
5   <html>
6      <head>
7         <meta charset = "utf-8">
8         <title>A Form Using focus and blur</title>
9         <link rel = "stylesheet" type = "text/css" href = "style.css">
10        <script src = "focusblur.js"></script>
11     </head>
12     <body>
13        <form id = "myForm" action = "">
14           <p><label class = "fixed" for = "name">Name:</label>
15              <input type = "text" id =  "name"
16                 placeholder = "Enter name"></p>
17           <p><label class = "fixed" for = "email">E-mail:</label>
18              <input type = "email" id = "email"
19                 placeholder = "Enter e-mail address"></p>
20           <p><label>Click here if you like this site
21              <input type = "checkbox" id =  "like"></label></p>
22           <p><label for = "comments">Any comments?</label></p>
23           <textarea id =  "comments"
24              placeholder = "Enter comments here"></textarea>
25           <p><input id = "submit" type = "submit">
26              <input id = "reset" type = "reset"></p>
27        </form>
28        <p id = "helpText"></p>
29     </body>
30  </html>
```

a) The blue message at the bottom of the page instructs the user to enter a name when the **Name:** field has the focus.

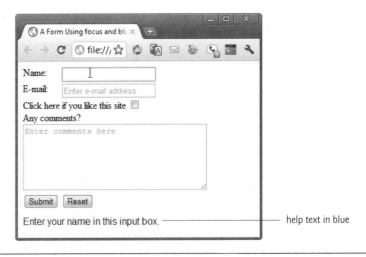

Fig. 13.8 | Demonstrating the focus and blur events. (Part I of 2.)

b) The message changes depending on which field has focus—this window shows the help text for the comments textarea.

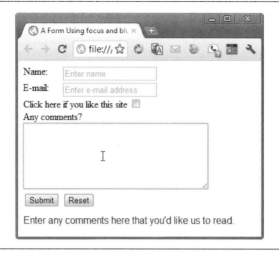

Fig. 13.8 | Demonstrating the focus and blur events. (Part 2 of 2.)

*JavaScript for the **focus** and **blur** Events*
The script in Fig. 13.9 registers the event handlers for the window's load event (line 35) and for the form elements' focus and blur events.

```
 1   // Fig. 13.9: focusblur.js
 2   // Demonstrating the focus and blur events.
 3   var helpArray = [ "Enter your name in this input box.",
 4     "Enter your e-mail address in the format user@domain.",
 5     "Check this box if you liked our site.",
 6     "Enter any comments here that you'd like us to read.",
 7     "This button submits the form to the server-side script.",
 8     "This button clears the form.", "" ];
 9   var helpText;
10
11   // initialize helpTextDiv and register event handlers
12   function init()
13   {
14      helpText = document.getElementById( "helpText" );
15
16      // register listeners
17      registerListeners( document.getElementById( "name" ), 0 );
18      registerListeners( document.getElementById( "email" ), 1 );
19      registerListeners( document.getElementById( "like" ), 2 );
20      registerListeners( document.getElementById( "comments" ), 3 );
21      registerListeners( document.getElementById( "submit" ), 4 );
22      registerListeners( document.getElementById( "reset" ), 5 );
23   } // end function init
24
25   // utility function to help register events
26   function registerListeners( object, messageNumber )
27   {
```

Fig. 13.9 | Demonstrating the focus and blur events. (Part 1 of 2.)

```
28    object.addEventListener( "focus",
29       function() { helpText.innerHTML = helpArray[ messageNumber ]; },
30       false );
31    object.addEventListener( "blur",
32       function() { helpText.innerHTML = helpArray[ 6 ]; }, false );
33 } // end function registerListener
34
35 window.addEventListener( "load", init, false );
```

Fig. 13.9 | Demonstrating the focus and blur events. (Part 2 of 2.)

Script-Level Variables
The helpArray (lines 3–8) contains the messages that are displayed when each input element receives the focus. Variable helpText (line 9) will refer to the paragraph in which the help text will be displayed.

Function init
When the window's load event occurs, function init (lines 12–23) executes. Line 14 gets the helpText paragraph element from the document. Then, lines 17–22 call the function registerListeners (lines 26–33) once for each element in the form. The first argument in each call is the element for which we'll register the focus and blur events, and the second argument a helpArray index that indicates which message to display for the element.

Function registerListeners—Using Anonymous functions
Function registerListeners registers the focus and blur events for the object it receives as its first argument. In each case, we define an **anonymous function** to handle the event. An anonymous function is defined with no name—it's created in nearly the same way as any other function, but with no identifier after the keyword function. This notation is useful when creating a function for the sole purpose of assigning it to an event handler. We never call the function ourselves, so we don't need to give it a name, and it's more concise to create the function and register it as an event handler at the same time. For example, line 29

```
function() { helpText.innerHTML = helpArray[ messageNumber ]; }
```

defines an anonymous function that sets the helpText paragraph's innerHTML property to the string in helpArray at index messageNumber. For the blur event handler, line 32 defines an anonymous function that sets the helpText paragraph's innerHTML property to the empty string in helpArray[6].

13.6 More Form Processing with submit and reset

Two more events for processing forms are submit (which you've seen in earlier chapters) and **reset**. These events fire when a form is submitted or reset, respectively (Fig. 13.10). This example enhances the one in Fig. 13.8. The HTML5 document is identical, so we don't show it here. The new JavaScript code for this example is in lines 24–36, which register event handlers for the form's submit and reset events.

Line 24 gets the form element ("myForm"), then lines 25–30 register an anonymous function for its submit event. The anonymous function executes in response to the user's submitting the form by clicking the **Submit** button or pressing the *Enter* key. Line 28 introduces the window object's **confirm method**. As with alert and prompt, we do *not* need to prefix the call with window and a dot (.). The confirm dialog asks the users a question, presenting them with an **OK** button and a **Cancel** button. If the user clicks **OK**, confirm returns true; otherwise, confirm returns false.

```
1   // Fig. 13.8: focusblur.js
2   // Demonstrating the focus and blur events.
3   var helpArray = [ "Enter your name in this input box.",
4     "Enter your e-mail address in the format user@domain.",
5     "Check this box if you liked our site.",
6     "Enter any comments here that you'd like us to read.",
7     "This button submits the form to the server-side script.",
8     "This button clears the form.", "" ];
9   var helpText;
10
11  // initialize helpTextDiv and register event handlers
12  function init()
13  {
14     helpText = document.getElementById( "helpText" );
15
16     // register listeners
17     registerListeners( document.getElementById( "name" ), 0 );
18     registerListeners( document.getElementById( "email" ), 1 );
19     registerListeners( document.getElementById( "like" ), 2 );
20     registerListeners( document.getElementById( "comments" ), 3 );
21     registerListeners( document.getElementById( "submit" ), 4 );
22     registerListeners( document.getElementById( "reset" ), 5 );
23
24     var myForm = document.getElementById( "myForm" );
25     myForm.addEventListener( "submit",
26        function()
27        {
28           return confirm( "Are you sure you want to submit?" );
29        }, // end anonymous function
30        false );
31     myForm.addEventListener( "reset",
32        function()
33        {
34           return confirm( "Are you sure you want to reset?" );
35        }, // end anonymous function
36        false );
37  } // end function init
38
39  // utility function to help register events
40  function registerListeners( object, messageNumber )
41  {
42     object.addEventListener( "focus",
43        function() { helpText.innerHTML = helpArray[ messageNumber ]; },
44        false );
```

Fig. 13.10 | Demonstrating the focus and blur events. (Part 1 of 2.)

```
45      object.addEventListener( "blur",
46          function() { helpText.innerHTML = helpArray[ 6 ]; }, false );
47   } // end function registerListener
48
49   window.addEventListener( "load", init, false );
```

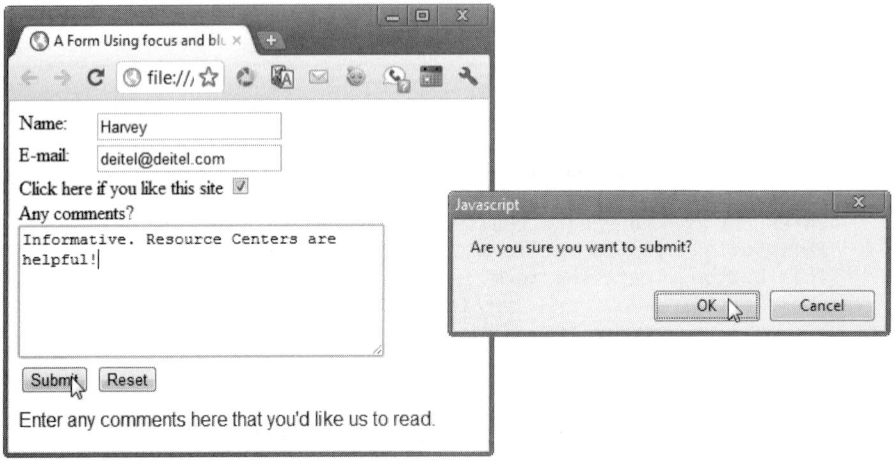

Fig. 13.10 | Demonstrating the focus and blur events. (Part 2 of 2.)

Our event handlers for the form's submit and reset events simply return the value of the confirm dialog, which asks the users if they're sure they want to submit or reset (lines 28 and 34, respectively). By returning either true or false, the event handlers dictate whether the default action for the event—in this case *submitting* or *resetting* the form—is taken. Other default actions, such as following a hyperlink, can be prevented by returning false from a click event handler on the link. If an event handler returns true or does not return a value, the default action is taken once the event handler finishes executing.

13.7 Event Bubbling

Event bubbling is the process by which events fired on *child* elements "bubble" up to their *parent* elements. When an event is fired on an element, it's first delivered to the element's event handler (if any), then to the parent element's event handler (if any). This might result in event handling that was *not* intended. *If you intend to handle an event in a child element alone, you should cancel the bubbling of the event in the child element's event-handling code by using the **cancelBubble** property of the event object*, as shown in Figs. 13.11–13.12.

```
1    <!DOCTYPE html>
2
3    <!-- Fig. 13.11: bubbling.html -->
4    <!-- Canceling event bubbling. -->
5    <html>
```

Fig. 13.11 | Canceling event bubbling. (Part 1 of 2.)

```
 6        <head>
 7          <meta charset="utf-8">
 8          <title>Event Bubbling</title>
 9          <script src = "bubbling.js">
10        </head>
11        <body>
12          <p id = "bubble">Bubbling enabled.</p>
13          <p id = "noBubble">Bubbling disabled.</p>
14        </body>
15   </html>
```

a) User clicks the first paragraph, for which bubbling is enabled.

b) Paragraph's event handler causes an alert.

c) Document's event handler causes another alert, because the event bubbles up to the document.

d) User clicks the second paragraph, for which bubbling is disabled.

e) Paragraph's event handler causes an alert. The document's event handler is not called.

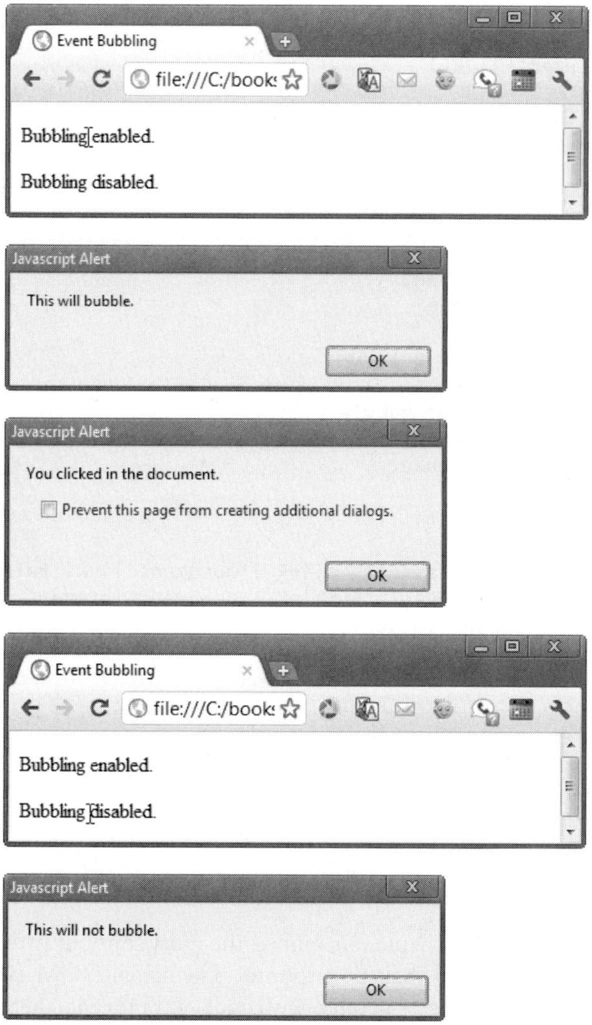

Fig. 13.11 | Canceling event bubbling. (Part 2 of 2.)

Clicking the first p element triggers a call to bubble (Fig. 13.12, lines 8–12). Then, because line 22 registers the document's click event, documentClick is also called. This occurs because the click event bubbles up to the document. This is probably not the desired result. Clicking the second p element calls noBubble (lines 14–18), which disables the event bubbling for this event by setting the cancelBubble property of the event object to true. The default value of cancelBubble is false, so the statement in line 11 is unnecessary.

> **Common Programming Error 13.1**
>
> *Forgetting to cancel event bubbling when necessary may cause unexpected results in your scripts.*

```
1   // Fig. 13.12: bubbling.js
2   // Canceling event bubbling.
3   function documentClick()
4   {
5      alert( "You clicked in the document." );
6   } // end function documentClick
7
8   function bubble( e )
9   {
10     alert( "This will bubble." );
11     e.cancelBubble = false;
12  } // end function bubble
13
14  function noBubble( e )
15  {
16     alert( "This will not bubble." );
17     e.cancelBubble = true;
18  } // end function noBubble
19
20  function registerEvents()
21  {
22     document.addEventListener( "click", documentClick, false );
23     document.getElementById( "bubble" ).addEventListener(
24        "click", bubble, false );
25     document.getElementById( "noBubble" ).addEventListener(
26        "click", noBubble, false );
27  } // end function registerEvents
28
29  window.addEventListener( "load", registerEvents, false );
```

Fig. 13.12 | Canceling event bubbling.

13.8 More Events

The events we covered in this chapter are among the most commonly used. Figure 13.13 lists some common events and their descriptions. The actual DOM event names begin with "on", but we show the names you use with addEventListener here.

13.9 Web Resource

www.quirksmode.org/js/introevents.html
An introduction and reference site for JavaScript events. Includes comprehensive information on history of events, the different event models, and making events work across multiple browsers.

Event	Description
abort	Fires when image transfer has been interrupted by user.
change	Fires when a new choice is made in a select element, or when a text input is changed and the element loses focus.
click	Fires when the user clicks the mouse.
dblclick	Fires when the user double clicks the mouse.
focus	Fires when a form element gets the focus.
keydown	Fires when the user pushes down a key.
keypress	Fires when the user presses then releases a key.
keyup	Fires when the user releases a key.
load	Fires when an element and all its children have loaded.
mousedown	Fires when a mouse button is pressed.
mousemove	Fires when the mouse moves.
mouseout	Fires when the mouse leaves an element.
mouseover	Fires when the mouse enters an element.
mouseup	Fires when a mouse button is released.
reset	Fires when a form resets (i.e., the user clicks a reset button).
resize	Fires when the size of an object changes (i.e., the user resizes a window or frame).
select	Fires when a text selection begins (applies to input or textarea).
submit	Fires when a form is submitted.
unload	Fires when a page is about to unload.

Fig. 13.13 | Common events.

Summary

Section 13.1 Introduction
- JavaScript events (p. 455) allow scripts to respond to user interactions and modify the page accordingly.
- Events and event handling help make web applications more responsive, dynamic and interactive.

Section 13.2 Reviewing the load Event
- Functions that handle events are called event handlers (p. 456). Assigning an event handler to an event on a DOM node is called registering an event handler (p. 456).
- The load event fires whenever an element finishes loading successfully.
- If a script in the head attempts to get a DOM node for an HTML5 element in the body, getElementById returns null because the body has not yet loaded.
- Method addEventListener can be called multiple times on a DOM node to register more than one event-handling method for an event.

- You can remove an event listener by calling removeEventListener (p. 457) with the same arguments that you passed to addEventListener to register the event handler.
- The inline model of event registration places calls to JavaScript functions directly in HTML code.
- The traditional model of event registration uses a property of an object to specify an event handler.

Section 13.3 Event mousemove and the event Object
- The mousemove event (p. 457) fires whenever the user moves the mouse.
- The event object (p. 460) stores information about the event that called the event-handling function.
- The event object's ctrlKey property (p. 461) contains a boolean which reflects whether the *Ctrl* key was pressed during the event.
- The event object's shiftKey property (p. 461) reflects whether the *Shift* key was pressed during the event.
- In an event-handling function, this refers to the DOM object on which the event occurred.
- The event object stores in its target property the node on which the action occurred.

Section 13.4 Rollovers with mouseover and mouseout
- When the mouse cursor enters an element, a mouseover event (p. 461) occurs for that element. When the mouse cursor leaves the element, a mouseout event (p. 461) occurs for that element.
- Creating an Image object and setting its src property preloads the image.

Section 13.5 Form Processing with focus and blur
- The focus event (p. 465) fires when an element gains focus (i.e., when the user clicks a form field or uses the *Tab* key to move between form elements).
- blur (p. 465) fires when an element loses focus, which occurs when another control gains the focus.

Section 13.6 More Form Processing with submit and reset
- The submit and reset events (p. 468) fire when a form is submitted or reset, respectively.
- An anonymous function (p. 468) is a function that's defined with no name—it's created in nearly the same way as any other function, but with no identifier after the keyword function.
- Anonymous functions are useful when creating a function for the sole purpose of assigning it to an event handler.
- The confirm method (p. 469) asks the users a question, presenting them with an **OK** button and a **Cancel** button. If the user clicks **OK**, confirm returns true; otherwise, confirm returns false.
- By returning either true or false, event handlers dictate whether the default action for the event is taken.
- If an event handler returns true or does not return a value, the default action is taken once the event handler finishes executing.

Section 13.7 Event Bubbling
- Event bubbling (p. 470) is the process whereby events fired in child elements "bubble" up to their parent elements. When an event is fired on an element, it's first delivered to the element's event handler (if any), then to the parent element's event handler (if any).
- If you intend to handle an event in a child element alone, you should cancel the bubbling of the event in the child element's event-handling code by using the cancelBubble property (p. 470) of the event object.

Self-Review Exercises

13.1 Fill in the blanks in each of the following statements:

a) If a script in the head attempts to get a DOM node for an HTML5 element in the body, _____ returns _____ because the body has not yet loaded.

b) Method _____ can be called multiple times on a DOM node to register more than one event-handling method for an event.

c) The _____ keyword allows us to use one event handler to apply a change to one of many DOM elements, depending on which one received the event.

d) The confirm method asks the users a question, presenting them with an OK button and a(n) _____ button. If the user clicks OK, confirm returns _____.

e) When an event is fired on an element, it's first delivered to the _____ event handler, then to the _____ element's event handler.

13.2 State whether each of the following is *true* or *false*. If the statement is *false*, explain why.

a) An anonymous function has a special identifier after the keyword function.

b) In an event-handling function, this refers to the DOM object on which the event occurred.

c) The focus event fires when an element gains focus.

d) If an event handler returns true or does not return a value, the default action is taken once the event handler finishes executing.

e) The event object stores in its source property the node on which the action occurred.

Answers to Self-Review Exercises

13.1 a) getElementById, null. b) addEventListener. c) this. d) Cancel, true. e) element's, parent.

13.2 a) False. An anonymous function has no identifier after the keyword function. b) True. c) True. d) True. e) False. The event object stores in its target property the node on which the action occurred.

Exercises

13.3 Add an erase feature to the drawing program in Fig. 13.3. Try setting the background color of the table cell over which the mouse moved to white when the *Alt* key is pressed.

13.4 Add a button to your program from Exercise 13.3 to erase the entire drawing window.

13.5 You have a server-side script that cannot handle any ampersands (&) in the form data. Write a function that converts all ampersands in a form field to " and " when the field loses focus (blur).

13.6 Write a function that responds to a click anywhere on the page by displaying an alert dialog. Display the event name if the user held *Shift* during the mouse click. Display the element name that triggered the event if the user held *Ctrl* during the mouse click.

13.7 Use CSS absolute positioning, mousedown, mousemove, mouseup and the clientX/clientY properties of the event object to create a program that allows you to drag and drop an image. When the user clicks the image, it should follow the cursor until the mouse button is released.

13.8 Modify Exercise 13.7 to allow multiple images to be dragged and dropped in the same page.

14

HTML5: Introduction to canvas

Objectives

In this chapter you'll:

- Draw lines, rectangles, arcs, circles, ellipses and text.

- Draw gradients and shadows.

- Draw images, create patterns and convert a color image to black and white.

- Draw Bezier and quadratic curves.

- Rotate, scale and transform.

- Dynamically resize a **canvas** to fill the window.

- Use alpha transparency and compositing techniques.

- Create an HTML5 **canvas**-based game app with sound and collision detection that's easy to code and fun to play.

14.1 Introduction[1]

It's taken us a while to get here, working hard to present many of the great new features of HTML5 and CSS3, and scripting in JavaScript. Now it's time to exercise your creativity and have some fun.

Most people enjoy drawing. The **canvas element**, which you'll learn to use in this chapter, provides a JavaScript application programming interface (API) with methods for drawing two-dimensional bitmapped graphics and animations, manipulating fonts and images, and inserting images and videos.

The canvas element is supported by all of the browsers we've used to test the book's examples. To get a sense of the wide range of its capabilities, review the chapter objectives and outline. A key benefit of canvas is that it's built into the browser, eliminating the need for plug-ins like Flash and Silverlight, thereby improving performance and convenience and reducing costs. At the end of the chapter we'll build a fun **Cannon Game**, which in previous editions of this book was built in Flash.

14.2 canvas Coordinate System

To begin drawing, we first must understand canvas's **coordinate system** (Fig. 14.1), a scheme for identifying every point on a canvas. By default, the upper-left corner of a can-

---

1. Due to the large number of examples in this chapter, most of the examples use embedded JavaScripts.

vas has the coordinates (0, 0). A coordinate pair has both an *x*-**coordinate** (the **horizontal coordinate**) and a *y*-**coordinate** (the **vertical coordinate**). The *x*-coordinate is the horizontal distance to the right from the left border of a canvas. The *y*-coordinate is the vertical distance downward from the top border of a canvas. The *x*-**axis** defines every horizontal coordinate, and the *y*-**axis** defines every vertical coordinate. You position text and shapes on a canvas by specifying their *x* and *y*-coordinates. Coordinate space units are measured in pixels ("picture elements"), which are the smallest units of resolution on a screen.

> **Portability Tip 14.1**
> *Different screens vary in resolution and thus in density of pixels so graphics may vary in appearance on different screens.*

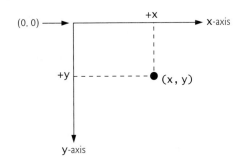

Fig. 14.1 | canvas coordinate system. Units are measured in pixels.

14.3 Rectangles

Now we're ready to create a canvas and start drawing. Figure 14.2 demonstrates how to draw a rectangle with a border on a canvas.

```
 1   <!DOCTYPE html>
 2
 3   <!-- Fig. 14.2: drawrectangle.html -->
 4   <!-- Drawing a rectangle on a canvas. -->
 5   <html>
 6      <head>
 7         <meta charset = "utf-8">
 8         <title>Drawing a Rectangle</title>
 9      </head>
10      <body>
11         <canvas id = "drawRectangle" width = "300" height = "100"
12            style = "border: 1px solid black;">
13            Your browser does not support Canvas.
14         </canvas>
15         <script type>
16            var canvas = document.getElementById("drawRectangle");
17            var context = canvas.getContext("2d")
```

Fig. 14.2 | Drawing a rectangle with a border on a canvas. (Part 1 of 2.)

```
18              context.fillStyle = "yellow";
19              context.fillRect(5, 10, 200, 75);
20              context.strokeStyle = "royalblue";
21              context.lineWidth = 6;
22              context.strokeRect(4, 9, 201, 76);
23          </script>
24      </body>
25  </html>
```

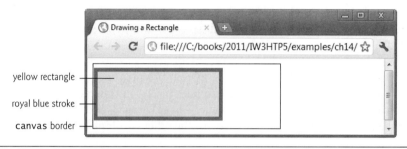

Fig. 14.2 | Drawing a rectangle with a border on a canvas. (Part 2 of 2.)

Creating a Canvas
The canvas element has two attributes—width and height. The default width is 300 and the default height 150. In lines 11–12, we create a canvas starting with a **canvasID**—in this case, "drawRectangle". Many people use "myCanvas" or something similar. Assigning a unique ID to a canvas allows you to access it like any other element, and to use more than one canvas on a page. Next, we specify the canvas's width (300) and height (100), and a border of 1px solid black. You do not need to include a visible border. In line 13 we include the *fallback text* Your browser does not support canvas. This will appear if the user runs the application in a browser that does not support canvas. To save space, we have not included it in the subsequent examples.

Graphics Contexts and Graphics Objects
Now we're ready to write our JavaScript (lines 15–23). First, we use the **getElementById method** to get the canvas element using the ID (line 16). Next we get the **context** object. A context represents a 2D rendering surface that provides methods for drawing on a canvas. The context contains attributes and methods for drawing, font manipulation, color manipulation and other graphics-related actions.

Drawing the Rectangle
To draw the rectangle, we specify its color by setting the **fillStyle attribute** to yellow (line 18). The **fillRect method** then draws the rectangle using the arguments *x*, *y*, *width* and *height*, where *x* and *y* are the coordinates for the top-left corner of the rectangle (line 19). In this example, we used the values 5, 10, 200 and 75, respectively.
    Next, we add a border, or *stroke*, to the rectangle. The **strokeStyle attribute** (line 20) specifies the stroke color or style (in this case, royalblue). The **lineWidth attribute** specifies the stroke width in coordinate space units (line 21). Finally, the **strokeRect method** specifies the coordinates of the stroke using the arguments *x*, *y*, *width* and *height*. We used values that are one coordinate off in each direction from the outer edges of the

rectangle—4, 9, 201 and 76. If the width *and* height are 0, no stroke will appear. If only one of the width *or* height values is 0, the result will be a line, not a rectangle.

14.4 Using Paths to Draw Lines

To draw lines and complex shapes in canvas, we use **paths**. A path can have zero or more **subpaths**, each having one or more points connected by lines or curves. If a subpath has fewer than two points, no path is drawn.

Figure 14.3 uses paths to draw lines on a canvas. The **beginPath method** starts the line's path (line 19). The **moveTo method** sets the *x*- and *y*-coordinates of the path's origin (line 20). From the point of origin, we use the **lineTo method** to specify the destinations for the path (lines 21–23). The **lineWidth attribute** is used to change the thickness of the line (line 24). The default lineWidth is 1 pixel. We then use the **lineJoin attribute** to specify the style of the corners where two lines meet—in this case, bevel (line 25). The lineJoin attribute has three possible values—bevel, round, and miter. The value bevel gives the path sloping corners. We'll discuss the other two lineJoin values shortly.

```
 1   <!DOCTYPE html>
 2
 3   <!-- Fig. 14.3: lines.html -->
 4   <!-- Drawing lines on a canvas. -->
 5   <html>
 6      <head>
 7         <meta charset = "utf-8">
 8         <title>Drawing Lines</title>
 9      </head>
10      <body>
11         <canvas id = "drawLines" width = "400" height = "200"
12            style = "border: 1px solid black;">
13         </canvas>
14         <script>
15            var canvas = document.getElementById("drawLines");
16            var context = canvas.getContext("2d")
17
18            // red lines without a closed path
19            context.beginPath(); // begin a new path
20            context.moveTo(10, 10); // path origin
21            context.lineTo(390, 10);
22            context.lineTo(390, 30);
23            context.lineTo(10, 30);
24            context.lineWidth = 10; // line width
25            context.lineJoin = "bevel" // line join style
26            context.lineCap = "butt"; // line cap style
27            context.strokeStyle = "red" // line color
28            context.stroke(); //draw path
29
30            // orange lines without a closed path
31            context.beginPath(); //begin a new path
32            context.moveTo(40, 75); // path origin
33            context.lineTo(40, 55);
```

Fig. 14.3 | Drawing lines on a canvas. (Part 1 of 2.)

```
34        context.lineTo(360, 55);
35        context.lineTo(360, 75);
36        context.lineWidth = 20; // line width
37        context.lineJoin = "round" // line join style
38        context.lineCap = "round"; // line cap style
39        context.strokeStyle = "orange" //line color
40        context.stroke(); // draw path
41
42        // green lines with a closed path
43        context.beginPath(); // begin a new path
44        context.moveTo(10, 100); // path origin
45        context.lineTo(390, 100);
46        context.lineTo(390, 130);
47        context.closePath() // close path
48        context.lineWidth = 10; // line width
49        context.lineJoin = "miter" // line join style
50        context.strokeStyle = "green" // line color
51        context.stroke(); // draw path
52
53        // blue lines without a closed path
54        context.beginPath(); // begin a new path
55        context.moveTo(40, 140); // path origin
56        context.lineTo(360, 190);
57        context.lineTo(360, 140);
58        context.lineTo(40, 190);
59        context.lineWidth = 5; // line width
60        context.lineCap = "butt"; // line cap style
61        context.strokeStyle = "blue" // line color
62        context.stroke(); // draw path
63     </script>
64   </body>
65 </html>
```

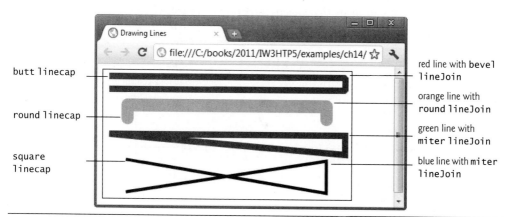

Fig. 14.3 | Drawing lines on a canvas. (Part 2 of 2.)

The **lineCap attribute** specifies the style of the end of the lines. There are three possible values—butt, round, and square. A butt lineCap (line 26) specifies that the line ends have edges perpendicular to the direction of the line and *no additional cap*. We'll demonstrate the other lineCap styles shortly.

Next, the **strokeStyle attribute** specifies the line color—in this case, red (line 27). Finally, the **stroke method** draws the line on the canvas (line 28). The default stroke color is black.

To demonstrate the different lineJoin and lineCap styles, we draw additional lines. First we draw orange lines (lines 31–40) with a lineWidth of 20 (line 36). The round lineJoin creates rounded corners (line 37). Then, the round lineCap adds a *semicircular* cap to the ends of the path (line 38)—the cap's diameter is equal to the width of the line.

Next, we draw green lines (lines 43–51) with a lineWidth of 10 (line 48). After we specify the destinations of the path, we use the **closePath method** (line 47) which closes the path by drawing a straight line from the last specified destination (line 46) back to the point of the path's origin (line 44). The miter lineJoin (line 49) *bevels* the lines at an angle where they meet. For example, the lines that meet at a 90-degree angle have edges beveled at 45-degree angles where they meet. Since the path is closed, we do not specify a lineCap style for the green line. If we did not close the path (line 47), the *previous* lineCap style that we specified for the orange line above in line 36 would be applied to the green line. Such settings are said to be *sticky*—they continue to apply until they're changed.

Finally, we draw blue lines (lines 54–62) with a lineWidth of 5. The butt lineCap adds a rectangular cap to the line ends (line 60). The length of the cap is equal to the line width, and the width of the cap is equal to half the line width. The edge of the square lineCap is perpendicular to the direction of the line.

14.5 Drawing Arcs and Circles

Arcs are portions of the circumference of a circle. To draw an arc, you specify the arc's **starting angle** and **ending angle** measured in *radians*—the ratio of the arc's length to its radius. The arc is said to sweep from its starting angle to its ending angle. Figure 14.4 depicts two arcs. The arc at the left of the figure sweeps *counterclockwise* from zero radians to $\pi/2$ radians, resulting in an arc that sweeps three quarters of the circumference a circle. The arc at the right of the figure sweeps *clockwise* from zero radians to $\pi/2$ radians.

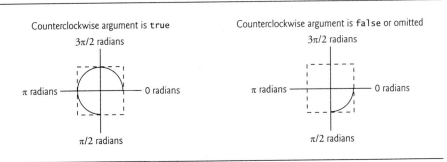

Fig. 14.4 | Positive and negative arc angles.

Figure 14.5 shows how to draw arcs and circles using the **arc method**. We start by drawing a filled mediumslateblue circle (lines 18–21). The beginPath method starts the path (line 18). Next, the arc method draws the circle using five arguments (line 20). The first two arguments represent the *x*- and *y*-coordinates of the center of the circle—in this case, 35, 50. The third argument is the radius of the circle. The fourth and fifth arguments are the arc's starting and ending angles in radians. In this case, the ending angle is Math.PI*2. The constant Math.PI is the JavaScript representation of the mathematical constant π, the ratio of a circle's circumference to its diameter. 2π radians represents a 360-degree arc, π radians is 180 degrees and π/2 radians is 90 degrees. There's an optional sixth argument of the arc method which we'll discuss shortly. To draw the circle to the canvas, we specify a fillStyle of mediumslateblue (line 20), then draw the circle using the fill method.

```
 1   <!DOCTYPE html>
 2
 3   <!-- Fig. 14.5: drawingarcs.html -->
 4   <!-- Drawing arcs and a circle on a canvas. -->
 5   <html>
 6      <head>
 7         <meta charset = "utf-8">
 8         <title>Arcs and Circles</title>
 9      </head>
10      <body>
11         <canvas id = "drawArcs" width = "225" height = "100">
12         </canvas>
13         <script>
14            var canvas = document.getElementById("drawArcs");
15            var context = canvas.getContext("2d")
16
17            // draw a circle
18            context.beginPath();
19            context.arc(35, 50, 30, 0, Math.PI * 2);
20            context.fillStyle = "mediumslateblue";
21            context.fill();
22
23            // draw an arc counterclockwise
24            context.beginPath();
25            context.arc(110, 50, 30, 0, Math.PI, false);
26            context.stroke();
27
28            // draw a half-circle clockwise
29            context.beginPath();
30            context.arc(185, 50, 30, 0, Math.PI, true);
31            context.fillStyle = "red";
32            context.fill();
33
34            // draw an arc counterclockwise
35            context.beginPath();
36            context.arc(260, 50, 30, 0, 3 * Math.PI / 2);
37            context.strokeStyle = "darkorange";
38            context.stroke();
39         </script>
40      </body>
41   </html>
```

Fig. 14.5 | Drawing arcs and circles on a canvas. (Part 1 of 2.)

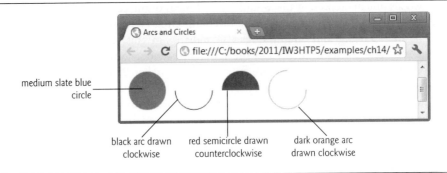

medium slate blue circle

black arc drawn clockwise

red semicircle drawn counterclockwise

dark orange arc drawn clockwise

Fig. 14.5 | Drawing arcs and circles on a canvas. (Part 2 of 2.)

In lines 24–26 we draw a black arc that sweeps *clockwise*. Using the arc method, we draw an arc with a center at 110, 50, a radius of 30, a starting angle of 0 and an ending angle of Math.PI (180 degrees). The sixth argument is *optional* and specifies the direction in which the arc's path is drawn. By default, the sixth argument is false, indicating that the arc is drawn *clockwise*. If the argument is true, the arc is drawn *counterclockwise* (or *anticlockwise*). We draw the arc using the stroke method (line 26).

Next, we draw a filled red semicircle counterclockwise so that it sweeps upward (lines 29–32). In this case, arguments of the arc method include a center of 185, 50, a radius of 30, a starting angle of 0 and an ending angle of Math.PI (180 degrees). To draw the arc counterclockwise, we use the sixth argument, true. We specify a fillStyle of red (line 31), then draw the semicircle using the fill method (line 32).

Finally, we draw a darkorange 270-degree clockwise arc (lines 35–38). Using the arc method (line 36), we draw an arc with a center at 260, 50, a radius of 30, a starting angle of 0 and an ending angle of 3*Math.PI/2 (270 degrees). Since we do not include the optional sixth argument, it defaults to false, drawing the arc *clockwise*. Then we specify a strokeStyle of darkorange (line 37) and draw the arc using the stroke method (line 38).

14.6 Shadows

In the next example, we add shadows to two filled rectangles (Fig. 14.6). We create a shadow that drops *below* and to the *right* of the first rectangle (lines 19–22). We start by specifying the **shadowBlur attribute**, setting its value to 10 (line 19). By default, the blur is 0 (no blur). The *higher* the value, the *more blurred* the edges of the shadow will appear. Next, we set the **shadowOffsetX attribute** to 15, which moves the shadow to the *right* of the rectangle (line 20). We then set the **shadowOffsetY attribute** to 15, which moves the shadow *down* from the rectangle (line 21). Finally, we specify the **shadowColor attribute** as blue (line 22).

```
1    <!DOCTYPE html>
2
3    <!-- Fig. 14.6: shadows.html -->
4    <!-- Creating shadows on a canvas. -->
5    <html>
```

Fig. 14.6 | Creating shadows on a canvas. (Part 1 of 2.)

```
6      <head>
7         <meta charset = "utf-8">
8         <title>Shadows</title>
9      </head>
10     <body>
11        <canvas id = "shadow" width = "525" height = "250"
12           style = "border: 1px solid black;">
13        </canvas>
14        <script>
15
16           // shadow effect with positive offsets
17           var canvas = document.getElementById("shadow");
18           var context = canvas.getContext("2d")
19           context.shadowBlur = 10;
20           context.shadowOffsetX = 15;
21           context.shadowOffsetY = 15;
22           context.shadowColor = "blue";
23           context.fillStyle = "cyan";
24           context.fillRect(25, 25, 200, 200);
25
26           // shadow effect with negative offsets
27           context.shadowBlur = 20;
28           context.shadowOffsetX = -20;
29           context.shadowOffsetY = -20;
30           context.shadowColor = "gray";
31           context.fillStyle = "magenta";
32           context.fillRect(300, 25, 200, 200);
33        </script>
34     </body>
35  </html>
```

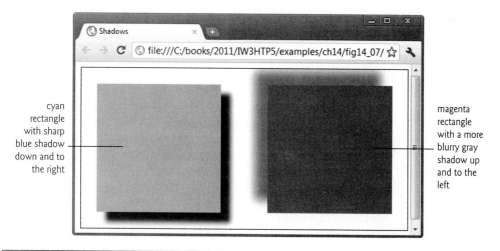

cyan rectangle with sharp blue shadow down and to the right

magenta rectangle with a more blurry gray shadow up and to the left

Fig. 14.6 | Creating shadows on a canvas. (Part 2 of 2.)

For the second rectangle, we create a shadow that shifts *above* and to the *left* of the rectangle (lines 28–29). Notice that the shadowBlur is 20 (line 27). The effect is a shadow on which the edges appear more blurred than on the shadow of the first rectangle. Next, we specify the `shadowOffsetX`, setting its value to -20. Using a *negative* `shadowOffsetX` moves the shadow to the *left* of the rectangle (line 28). We then specify the `shadowOffsetY` attribute, setting its value to -20 (line 29). Using a *negative* `shadowOffsetY` moves the shadow *up* from the rectangle. Finally, we specify the `shadowColor` as gray (line 30). The default values for the `shadowOffsetX` and `shadowOffsetY` are 0 (no shadow).

14.7 Quadratic Curves

Figure 14.7 demonstrates how to draw a rounded rectangle using lines to draw the straight sides and **quadratic curves** to draw the rounded corners. Quadratic curves have a starting point, an ending point and a *single* point of inflection.

The **quadraticCurveTo method** uses four arguments. The first two, *cpx* and *cpy*, are the coordinates of the *control point*—the point of the curve's inflection. The third and fourth arguments, *x* and *y*, are the coordinates of the *ending point*. The *starting point* is the last subpath destination, specified using the `moveTo` or `lineTo` methods. For example, if we write

```
context.moveTo(5, 100);
context.quadraticCurveTo(25, 5, 95, 50);
```

the curve starts at (5, 100), curves at (25, 5) and ends at (95, 50).

Unlike in CSS3, rounded rectangles are *not* built into canvas. To create a rounded rectangle, we use the `lineTo` method to draw the straight sides of the rectangle and the `quadraticCurveTo` to draw the rounded corners.

```
 1   <!DOCTYPE html>
 2
 3   <!-- Fig. 14.7: roundedrectangle.html -->
 4   <!-- Drawing a rounded rectangle on a canvas. -->
 5   <html>
 6      <head>
 7         <meta charset = "utf-8">
 8         <title>Quadratic Curves</title>
 9      </head>
10      <body>
11         <canvas id = "drawRoundedRect" width = "130" height = "130"
12            style = "border: 1px solid black;">
13         </canvas>
14         <script>
15            var canvas = document.getElementById("drawRoundedRect");
16            var context = canvas.getContext("2d")
17            context.beginPath();
18            context.moveTo(15, 5);
19            context.lineTo(95, 5);
20            context.quadraticCurveTo(105, 5, 105, 15);
21            context.lineTo(105, 95);
22            context.quadraticCurveTo(105, 105, 95, 105);
23            context.lineTo(15, 105);
24            context.quadraticCurveTo(5, 105, 5, 95);
25            context.lineTo(5, 15);
```

Fig. 14.7 | Drawing a rounded rectangle on a `canvas`. (Part 1 of 2.)

```
26              context.quadraticCurveTo(5, 5, 15, 5);
27              context.closePath();
28              context.fillStyle = "yellow";
29              context.fill(); //fill with the fillStyle color
30              context.strokeStyle = "royalblue";
31              context.lineWidth = 6;
32              context.stroke(); //draw 6-pixel royalblue border
33          </script>
34      </body>
35  </html>
```

Each corner is a quadratic curve with a radius of 10

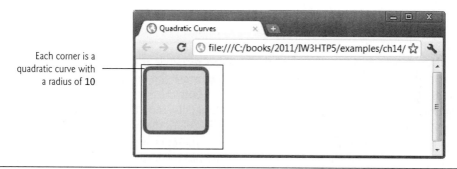

Fig. 14.7 | Drawing a rounded rectangle on a `canvas`. (Part 2 of 2.)

The rounded rectangle in this example has a `width` of 100, a `height` of 100 and a `radius` of 10 with which we calculate the points in the quadratic curves used to draw the rounded corners. The x- and y-coordinates for the rounded rectangle are both 5. We'll use these values to calculate the coordinates for each of the points in the path of our drawing.

As in the previous example, we start the path with the `beginPath` method (line 17). We start the drawing in the *top left*, then move *clockwise* using the `moveTo` method (line 18). We use the formula *x + radius* to calculate the first argument (15) and use our original y-coordinate (5) as the second argument.

We then use the `lineTo` method to draw a line from the starting point to the *top-right* side of the drawing (line 19). For the first argument, we use the formula *x + width − radius* to calculate the x-coordinate (in this case, 95). The second argument is simply the original y-coordinate (5).

To draw the *top-right rounded corner*, we use the `quadraticCurveTo` method with the arguments *cpx, cpy, x, y* (line 20). We calculate the value of the first argument, *cpx*, using the formula *x + width*, which is 105. The second argument, *cpy*, is the same as our original y-coordinate (5). We calculate the value of the third argument using the formula *x + width*, which is 105. To calculate the value of the fourth argument, we use the formula *y + radius*, which is 15.

We use the `lineTo` method to draw the *right side* of the rounded rectangle (line 21). The first argument is equal to *x + width*, in this case, 105. To calculate the second argument, we use the formula *y + height - radius*, which is 95.

Next, we draw the *bottom-right corner* using the `quadraticCurveTo` method (line 22). We use the formula *x + width* to calculate the first argument (105), and the formula *y + height* to calculate the second argument (105). We use the formula *x + width − radius* to determine the third argument (95). Then we use the formula *y + height* to determine the fourth argument (105).

We then draw the *bottom edge* of the rectangle with the `lineTo` method (line 23). The formula *x + radius* is used to calculate the first argument (15) and the formula *y + height* to calculate the second argument (105).

Next, we draw the *bottom-left corner* using the `quadraticCurveTo` method (line 24). The first argument is simply our original *x*-coordinate (5). We use the formula *y + height* to calculate the second argument (105). The third argument is the same as our original *x*-coordinate (5). The formula *y + height – radius* is then used to calculate the fourth argument (95).

We draw the *left side* of the rounded rectangle using the `lineTo` method (line 25). Again, the first argument is the original *x*-coordinate (5). The formula *y + radius* is then used to calculate the second argument (15).

We draw the *top-left corner* of the rounded rectangle using the `quadraticCurveTo` method (line 26). The first and second arguments are the original *x*- and *y*-coordinates (both 5). To calculate the third argument (15), we use the formula *x + radius*. The fourth argument is simply the original *y*-coordinate (5). Finally, the `closePath` method closes the path for the rounded rectangle by drawing a line back to the path's origin (line 27).

We specify a `fillStyle` of `yellow`, then use the `fill` method to draw the rounded rectangle to the `canvas` (lines 28–29). Finally, we place a border around the rounded rectangle by specifying a `strokeStyle` of `royalblue` (line 30) and a `lineWidth` of 6 (line 31), and then use the `stroke` method to draw the border (line 32).

14.8 Bezier Curves

Bezier curves have a starting point, an ending point and *two* control points through which the curve passes. These can be used to draw curves with one or two points of inflection, depending on the coordinates of the four points. For example, you might use a Bezier curve to draw complex shapes with *s*-shaped curves. The **bezierCurveTo method** uses six arguments. The first two arguments, *cp1x* and *cp1y*, are the coordinates of the first control point. The third and fourth arguments, *cp2x* and *cp2y*, are the coordinates for the second control point. Finally, the fifth and sixth arguments, *x* and *y*, are the coordinates of the ending point. The starting point is the last subpath destination, specified using either the `moveTo` or `lineTo` method. Figure 14.8 demonstrates how to draw an *s*-shaped Bezier curve using the `bezierCurveTo` method.

```
 1   <!DOCTYPE html>
 2
 3   <!-- Fig. 14.8: beziercurves.html -->
 4   <!-- Drawing a Bezier curve on a canvas. -->
 5   <html>
 6      <head>
 7         <meta charset = "utf-8">
 8         <title>Bezier Curves</title>
 9      </head>
10      <body>
```

Fig. 14.8 | Drawing a Bezier curve on a `canvas`. (Part 1 of 2.)

```
11          <canvas id = "drawBezier" width = "150" height = "150"
12            style = "border: 1px solid black;">
13          </canvas>
14          <script>
15            var canvas = document.getElementById("drawBezier");
16            var context = canvas.getContext("2d")
17            context.beginPath();
18            context.moveTo(115, 20);
19            context.bezierCurveTo(12, 37, 176, 77, 32, 133);
20            context.lineWidth = 10;
21            context.strokeStyle = "red";
22            context.stroke();
23          </script>
24        </body>
25      </html>
```

Fig. 14.8 | Drawing a Bezier curve on a `canvas`. (Part 2 of 2.)

The `beginPath` method starts the path of the Bezier curve (line 17), then the `moveTo` method specifies the path's starting point (line 18). Next, the `bezierCurveTo` method specifies the three points in the Bezier curve (line 19). The first and second arguments (12 and 37) are the first control point. The third and fourth arguments (176 and 77) are the second control point. The fifth and sixth arguments (32 and 133) are the ending point.

The `lineWidth` attribute specifies the thickness of the line (line 20). The `strokeStyle` attribute specifies a stroke color of red. Finally, the `stroke` method draws the Bezier curve.

14.9 Linear Gradients

Figure 14.9 fills three separate canvases with linear gradients—vertical, horizontal and diagonal. On the first canvas (lines 13–25), we draw a *vertical* gradient. In line 19, we use the **createLinearGradient method**—the first two arguments are the *x*- and *y*-coordinates of the gradient's start, and the last two are the *x*- and *y*-coordinates of the end. In this example, we use (0, 0) for the start of the gradient and (0, 200) for the end. The start and end have the *same x*-coordinates but *different y*-coordinates, so the start of the gradient is a point at the top of the canvas directly above the point at the end of the gradient at the bottom. This creates a vertical linear gradient that starts at the top and changes as the gradient moves to the bottom of the canvas. We'll show how to create horizontal and diagonal gradients by altering these values.

```
 1   <!DOCTYPE html>
 2
 3   <!-- Fig. 14.9: lineargradient.html -->
 4   <!-- Drawing linear gradients on a canvas. -->
 5   <html>
 6      <head>
 7         <meta charset = "utf-8">
 8         <title>Linear Gradients</title>
 9      </head>
10      <body>
11
12         <!-- vertical linear gradient -->
13         <canvas id = "linearGradient" width = "200" height = "200"
14            style = "border: 1px solid black;">
15         </canvas>
16         <script>
17            var canvas = document.getElementById("linearGradient");
18            var context = canvas.getContext("2d");
19            var gradient = context.createLinearGradient(0, 0, 0, 200);
20            gradient.addColorStop(0, "white");
21            gradient.addColorStop(0.5, "lightsteelblue");
22            gradient.addColorStop(1, "navy");
23            context.fillStyle = gradient;
24            context.fillRect(0, 0, 200, 200);
25         </script>
26
27         <!-- horizontal linear gradient -->
28         <canvas id = "linearGradient2" width = "200" height = "200"
29            style = "border: 2px solid orange;">
30         </canvas>
31         <script>
32            var canvas = document.getElementById("linearGradient2");
33            var context = canvas.getContext("2d");
34            var gradient = context.createLinearGradient(0, 0, 200, 0);
35            gradient.addColorStop(0, "white");
36            gradient.addColorStop(0.5, "yellow");
37            gradient.addColorStop(1, "orange");
38            context.fillStyle = gradient;
39            context.fillRect(0, 0, 200, 200);
40         </script>
41
42         <!-- diagonal linear gradient -->
43         <canvas id = "linearGradient3" width = "200" height = "200"
44            style = "border: 2px solid purple;">
45         </canvas>
46         <script>
47            var canvas = document.getElementById("linearGradient3");
48            var context = canvas.getContext("2d");
49            var gradient = context.createLinearGradient(0, 0, 45, 200);
50            gradient.addColorStop(0, "white");
51            gradient.addColorStop(0.5, "plum");
52            gradient.addColorStop(1, "purple");
53            context.fillStyle = gradient;
```

Fig. 14.9 | Drawing linear gradients on a canvas. (Part 1 of 2.)

```
54          context.fillRect(0, 0, 200, 200);
55        </script>
56      </body>
57    </html>
```

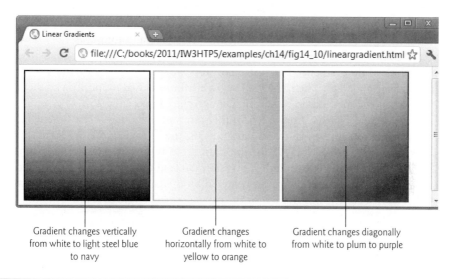

Gradient changes vertically
from white to light steel blue
to navy

Gradient changes
horizontally from white to
yellow to orange

Gradient changes diagonally
from white to plum to purple

Fig. 14.9 | Drawing linear gradients on a canvas. (Part 2 of 2.)

Next, we use the **addColorStop** method to add three *color stops* (lines 20–22). (For a definition of color stops, see Section 5.6.) Each color stop has a positive value between 0 (the start of the gradient) and 1 (the end of the gradient). For each color stop, we specify a color (white, lightsteelblue and navy). The fillStyle method specifies a gradient (line 23) and then the fillRect method draws the gradient on the canvas (line 24).

On the second canvas (lines 28–40), we draw a *horizontal* gradient. In line 34, we use the createLinearGradient method where the first two arguments are (0, 0) for the start of the gradient and (200, 0) for the end. Note that in this case, the start and end have *different* x-coordinates but the *same* y-coordinates, horizontally aligning the start and end. This creates a horizontal linear gradient that starts at the left and changes as the gradient moves to the right edge of the canvas.

On the third canvas (lines 43–55), we draw a *diagonal* gradient. In line 49, we use the createLinearGradient method again. The first two arguments are (0, 0)—the coordinates of the starting position of the gradient in the top left of the canvas. The last two arguments are (135, 200)—the ending position of the gradient. This creates a diagonal linear gradient that starts at the top left and changes at an angle as the gradient moves to the right edge of the canvas.

14.10 Radial Gradients

Next, we show how to create two different *radial* gradients on a canvas (Fig. 14.10). A radial gradient is comprised of two circles—an *inner circle* where the gradient starts and an *outer circle* where it ends. In lines 18–19, we use the **createRadialGradient** method whose first three arguments are the *x*- and *y*-coordinates and the radius of the gradient's start circle, respectively, and whose last three arguments are the *x*- and *y*-coordinates and the radius of the end circle. In this example, we use (100, 100, 10) for the start circle and (100, 100, 125) for the end circle. Note that these are *concentric* circles—they have the *same x*- and *y*-coordinates but each has a *different* radius. This creates a radial gradient that starts in a common center and changes as it moves outward to the end circle.

Next, the gradient.addColorStop method is used to add four *color stops* (lines 20–23). Each color stop has a positive value between 0 (the start circle of the gradient) and 1 (the end circle of the gradient). For each color stop, we specify a color (in this case, white, yellow, orange and red). Then, the fillStyle attribute is used to specify a gradient (line 24). The fillRect method draws the gradient on the canvas (line 25).

On the second canvas (lines 29–43), the start and end circles have *different x*- and *y*-coordinates, altering the effect. In lines 35–36, the createRadialGradient method uses the arguments (20, 150, 10) for the start circle and (100, 100, 125) for the end circle. These are *not* concentric circles. The start circle of the gradient is near the bottom left of the canvas and the end circle is centered on the canvas. This creates a radial gradient that starts near the bottom left of the canvas and changes as it moves to the right.

```
1    <!DOCTYPE html>
2
3    <!-- Fig. 14.10: radialgradient.html -->
4    <!-- Drawing radial gradients on a canvas. -->
5    <html>
6       <head>
7          <meta charset = "utf-8">
8          <title>Radial Gradients</title>
9       </head>
10      <body>
11         <!-- radial gradient with concentric circles -->
12         <canvas id = "radialGradient" width = "200" height = "200"
13            style = "border: 1px solid black;">
14         </canvas>
15         <script>
16            var canvas = document.getElementById("radialGradient");
17            var context = canvas.getContext("2d")
18            var gradient = context.createRadialGradient(
19               100, 100, 10, 100, 100, 125);
20            gradient.addColorStop(0, "white");
21            gradient.addColorStop(0.5, "yellow");
22            gradient.addColorStop(0.75, "orange");
23            gradient.addColorStop(1, "red");
24            context.fillStyle = gradient;
25            context.fillRect(0, 0, 200, 200);
26         </script>
27
28         <!-- radial gradient with nonconcentric circles -->
29         <canvas id = "radialGradient2" width = "200" height = "200"
30            style = "border: 1px solid black;">
31         </canvas>
```

Fig. 14.10 | Drawing radial gradients on a canvas. (Part 1 of 2.)

```
32          <script>
33             var canvas = document.getElementById("radialGradient2");
34             var context = canvas.getContext("2d")
35             var gradient = context.createRadialGradient(
36                20, 150, 10, 100, 100, 125);
37             gradient.addColorStop(0, "red");
38             gradient.addColorStop(0.5, "orange");
39             gradient.addColorStop(0.75, "yellow");
40             gradient.addColorStop(1, "white");
41             context.fillStyle = gradient;
42             context.fillRect(0, 0, 200, 200);
43          </script>
44       </body>
45    </html>
```

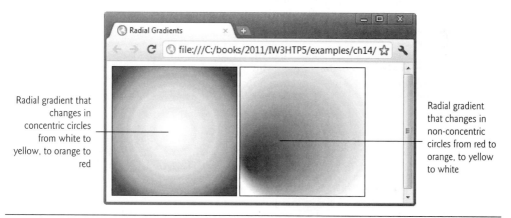

Radial gradient that changes in concentric circles from white to yellow, to orange to red

Radial gradient that changes in non-concentric circles from red to orange, to yellow to white

Fig. 14.10 | Drawing radial gradients on a canvas. (Part 2 of 2.)

14.11 Images

Figure 14.11 uses the **drawImage method** to draw an image to a canvas. In line 10, we create a new Image object and store it in the variable image. Line 11 locates the image source, "yellowflowers.png". Our function draw (lines 13–18) is called to draw the image after the document and all of its resources load. The drawImage method (line 17) draws the image to the canvas using five arguments. The first argument can be an image, canvas or video element. The second and third arguments are the destination x- and destination y-coordinates—these indicate the position of the top-left corner of the image on the canvas. The fourth and fifth arguments are the *destination width* and *destination height*. If the values do not match the size of the image, it will be *stretched* to fit.

```
1    <!DOCTYPE html>
2
3    <!-- Fig. 14.11: image.html -->
4    <!-- Drawing an image to a canvas. -->
5    <html>
```

Fig. 14.11 | Drawing an image to a canvas. (Part 1 of 2.)

```
 6     <head>
 7        <meta charset = "utf-8">
 8        <title>Images</title>
 9        <script>
10           var image = new Image();
11           image.src = "yellowflowers.png";
12
13           function draw()
14           {
15              var canvas = document.getElementById("myimage");
16              var context = canvas.getContext("2d")
17              context.drawImage(image, 0, 0, 175, 175);
18           } // end function draw
19
20           window.addEventListener( "load", draw, false );
21        </script>
22     </head>
23     <body>
24        <canvas id = "myimage" width = "200" height = "200"
25           style = "border: 1px solid Black;">
26        </canvas>
27     </body>
28  </html>
```

Fig. 14.11 | Drawing an image to a canvas. (Part 2 of 2.)

Note that you can call drawImage in three ways. In its simplest form, you can use

```
context.drawImage(image, dx, dy)
```

where *dx* and *dy* represent the position of the top-left corner of the image on the destination canvas. The default width and height are the source image's width and height. Or, as we did in this example, you can use

```
context.drawImage(image, dx, dy, dw, dh)
```

where *dw* is the specified width of the image on the destination canvas and *dh* is the specified height of the image on the destination canvas. Finally, you can use

```
context.drawImage(image, sx, sy, sw, sh, dx, dy, dw, dh)
```

where *sx* and *sy* are the coordinates of the top-left corner of the source image, *sw* is the source image's width and *sh* its height.

14.12 Image Manipulation: Processing the Individual Pixels of a canvas

Figure 14.12 shows how to obtain a canvas's pixels and manipulate their red, green, blue and alpha (RGBA) values. For security reasons, some browsers allow a script to get an image's pixels only if the document is requested from a web server, not if the file is loaded from the local computer's file system. For this reason, you can test this example at

```
http://test.deitel.com/iw3htp5/ch14/fig14_12/imagemanipulation.html
```

The HTML5 document's body (lines 123–135) defines a 750-by-250 pixel canvas element on which we'll draw an original image, a version of the image showing any changes you make to the RGBA values, and a version of the image converted to grayscale. You can change the RGBA values with the input elements of type range defined in the body. You can adjust the amount of red, green or blue from 0 to 500% of its original value—on a pixel-by-pixel basis, we calculate the new amount of red, green or blue accordingly. For the alpha, you can adjust the value from 0 (completely transparent) to 255 (completely opaque). The script begins when the window's load event (registered in line 120) calls function start.

```
 1   <!DOCTYPE html>
 2
 3   <!-- Fig. 14.12: imagemanipulation.html -->
 4   <!-- Manipulating an image's pixels to change colors and transparency. -->
 5   <html>
 6      <head>
 7         <meta charset = "utf-8">
 8         <title>Manipulating an Image</title>
 9         <style>
10            label { display: inline-block; width: 3em; }
11            canvas { border: 1px solid black; }
12            input[type="range"] { width: 600px; }
13         </style>
14         <script>
15            var context; // context for drawing on canvas
16            var redRange; // % of original red pixel value
17            var greenRange; // % of original green pixel value
18            var blueRange; // % of original blue pixel value
19            var alphaRange; // alpha amount value
20
21            var image = new Image(); // image object to store loaded image
22            image.src = "redflowers.png"; // set the image source
23
24            function start()
25            {
26               var canvas = document.getElementById( "thecanvas" );
```

Fig. 14.12 | Manipulating an image's pixels to change colors and transparency. (Part 1 of 4.)

```
27              context = canvas.getContext("2d")
28              context.drawImage(image, 0, 0); // original image
29              context.drawImage(image, 250, 0); // image for user change
30              processGrayscale(); // display grayscale of original image
31
32              // configure GUI events
33              redRange = document.getElementById( "redRange" );
34              redRange.addEventListener( "change",
35                 function() { processImage( this.value, greenRange.value,
36                    blueRange.value ); }, false );
37              greenRange = document.getElementById( "greenRange" );
38              greenRange.addEventListener( "change",
39                 function() { processImage( redRange.value, this.value,
40                    blueRange.value ); }, false )
41              blueRange = document.getElementById( "blueRange" );
42              blueRange.addEventListener( "change",
43                 function() { processImage( redRange.value,
44                    greenRange.value, this.value ); }, false )
45              alphaRange = document.getElementById( "alphaRange" );
46              alphaRange.addEventListener( "change",
47                 function() { processAlpha( this.value ); }, false )
48              document.getElementById( "resetButton" ).addEventListener(
49                 "click", resetImage, false );
50           } // end function start
51
52           // sets the alpha value for every pixel
53           function processAlpha( newValue )
54           {
55              // get the ImageData object representing canvas's content
56              var imageData = context.getImageData(0, 0, 250, 250);
57              var pixels = imageData.data; // pixel info from ImageData
58
59              // convert every pixel to grayscale
60              for ( var i = 3; i < pixels.length; i += 4 )
61              {
62                 pixels[ i ] = newValue;
63              } // end for
64
65              context.putImageData( imageData, 250, 0 ); // show grayscale
66           } // end function processImage
67
68           // sets the RGB values for every pixel
69           function processImage( redPercent, greenPercent, bluePercent )
70           {
71              // get the ImageData object representing canvas's content
72              context.drawImage(image, 250, 0);
73              var imageData = context.getImageData(0, 0, 250, 250);
74              var pixels = imageData.data; // pixel info from ImageData
75
76              //set percentages of red, green and blue in each pixel
77              for ( var i = 0; i < pixels.length; i += 4 )
78              {
79                 pixels[ i ] *= redPercent / 100;
```

Fig. 14.12 | Manipulating an image's pixels to change colors and transparency. (Part 2 of 4.)

```
80                  pixels[ i + 1 ] *= greenPercent / 100;
81                  pixels[ i + 2 ] *= bluePercent / 100;
82              } // end for
83
84              context.putImageData( imageData, 250, 0 ); // show grayscale
85          } // end function processImage
86
87          // creates grayscale version of original image
88          function processGrayscale()
89          {
90              // get the ImageData object representing canvas's content
91              context.drawImage(image, 500, 0);
92              var imageData = context.getImageData(0, 0, 250, 250);
93              var pixels = imageData.data; // pixel info from ImageData
94
95              // convert every pixel to grayscale
96              for ( var i = 0; i < pixels.length; i += 4 )
97              {
98                  var average =
99                      (pixels[ i ] * 0.30 + pixels[ i + 1 ] * 0.59 +
100                     pixels[ i + 2 ] * 0.11).toFixed(0);
101
102                 pixels[ i ] = average;
103                 pixels[ i + 1 ] = average;
104                 pixels[ i + 2 ] = average;
105             } // end for
106
107             context.putImageData( imageData, 500, 0 ); // show grayscale
108         } // end function processGrayscale
109
110         // resets the user manipulated image and the sliders
111         function resetImage()
112         {
113             context.drawImage(image, 250, 0);
114             redRange.value = 100;
115             greenRange.value = 100;
116             blueRange.value = 100;
117             alphaRange.value = 255;
118         } // end function resetImage
119
120         window.addEventListener( "load", start, false );
121     </script>
122 </head>
123 <body>
124    <canvas id = "thecanvas" width = "750" height = "250" ></canvas>
125    <p><label>Red:</label> 0 <input id = "redRange"
126       type = "range" max = "500" value = "100"> 500%</p>
127    <p><label>Green:</label> 0 <input id = "greenRange"
128       type = "range" max = "500" value = "100"> 500%</p>
129    <p><label>Blue:</label> 0 <input id = "blueRange"
130       type = "range" max = "500" value = "100"> 500%</p>
131    <p><label>Alpha:</label> 0 <input id = "alphaRange"
132       type = "range" max = "255" value = "255"> 255</p>
```

Fig. 14.12 | Manipulating an image's pixels to change colors and transparency. (Part 3 of 4.)

```
133          <p><input id = "resetButton" type = "button"
134             value = "Reset Image">
135      </body>
136  </html>
```

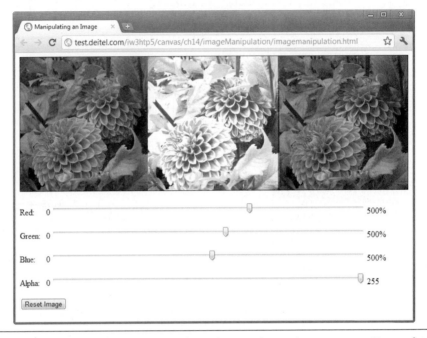

Fig. 14.12 | Manipulating an image's pixels to change colors and transparency. (Part 4 of 4.)

Script-Level Variables and Loading the Original Image
Lines 15–21 declare the script-level variables. Variables redRange, greenRange, blueRange and alphaRange will refer to the four range inputs so that we can easily access their values in the script's other functions. Variable image represents the original image to draw. Line 21 creates an Image object and line 22 uses it to load the image redflower.png, which is provided with the example.

Function start
Lines 28–29 draw the original image twice—once in the upper-left corner of the canvas and once 250 pixels to the right. Line 30 calls function processGrayscale to create the grayscale version of the image which will appear at *x*-coordinate 500. Lines 33–49 get the range input elements and register their event handlers. For the redRange, greenRange and blueRange elements, we register for the change event and call processImage with the values of these three range inputs. For the alphRange elements we register for the change event and call processAlpha with the value of that range input.

Function processAlpha
Function processAlpha (lines 53–66) applies the new alpha value to every pixel in the image. Line 56 calls canvas method **getImageData** to obtain an object that contains the pixels we wish to manipulate. The method receives a bounding rectangle representing the

portion of the canvas to get—in this case, a 250-pixel square from the upper-left corner. The returned object contains an array named data (line 57) which stores every pixel in the selected rectangular area as four elements in the array. Each pixel's data is stored in the order red value, green value, blue value, alpha value. So, the first four elements in the array represent the RGBA values of the pixel in row 0 and column 0, the next four elements represent the pixel in row 0 and column 1, etc.

Lines 60–63 iterate through the array processing every fourth element, which represents the alpha value in each pixel, and assigning it the new alpha value. Line 65 uses canvas method **putImageData** to place the updated pixels on the canvas with the upper-left corner of the processed image at location 250, 0.

Function *processImage*
Function processImage (lines 69–85) is similar to function processAlpha except that its loop (lines 77–82) processes the first three of every four elements—that is, the ones that represent a pixel's RGB values.

Function *processGrayscale*
Function processGrayscale (lines 88–108) is similar to function processImage except that its loop (lines 96–105) performs a weighted-average calculation to determine the new value assigned to the red, green and blue components of a given pixel. We used the formula for converting from RGB to grayscale provided at http://en.wikipedia.org/wiki/Grayscale.

Function *resetImage*
Function resetImage (lines 111–118) resets the on-screen images and the range input elements to their original values.

14.13 Patterns

Figure 14.13 demonstrates how to draw a *pattern* on a canvas. Lines 10–11 create and load the image we'll use for our pattern. Function start (lines 13–21) is called in response to the window's load event. Line 17 uses the **createPattern method** to create the pattern. This method takes two arguments. The first is the image we're using for the pattern, which can be an image element, a canvas element or a video element. The second specifies how the image will repeat to create the pattern and can be one of four values—repeat (repeats horizontally and vertically), repeat-x (repeats horizontally), repeat-y (repeats vertically) or no-repeat. In line 18, we specify the coordinates for the pattern on the canvas. The first image in the pattern is drawn so that its top left is at the origin of the coordinate space. We then specify the fillStyle attribute (pattern) and use the fill method to draw the pattern to the canvas.

```
1   <!DOCTYPE html>
2
3   <!-- Fig. 14.13: pattern.html -->
4   <!-- Creating a pattern using an image on a canvas. -->
5   <html>
```

Fig. 14.13 | Creating a pattern using an image on a canvas. (Part 1 of 2.)

```
 6      <head>
 7         <meta charset = "utf-8">
 8         <title>Patterns</title>
 9         <script>
10            var image = new Image();
11            image.src = "yellowflowers.png";
12
13            function start()
14            {
15               var canvas = document.getElementById("pattern");
16               var context = canvas.getContext("2d");
17               var pattern = context.createPattern(image, "repeat");
18               context.rect(5, 5, 385, 200);
19               context.fillStyle = pattern;
20               context.fill();
21            } // end function start
22
23            window.addEventListener( "load", start, false );
24         </script>
25      </head>
26      <body>
27         <canvas id = "pattern" width = "400" height = "200"
28            style = "border: 1px solid black;">
29         </canvas>
30      </body>
31   </html>
```

Fig. 14.13 | Creating a pattern using an image on a canvas. (Part 2 of 2.)

14.14 Transformations

The next several examples show you how to use canvas transformation methods including translate, scale, rotate and transform.

14.14.1 scale and translate Methods: Drawing Ellipses

Figure 14.14 demonstrates how to draw ellipses. In line 18, we change the *transformation matrix* (the coordinates) on the canvas using the **translate method** so that the *center of* the canvas becomes the origin (0, 0). To do this, we use half the canvas width as the *x*-coordinate and half the canvas height as the *y*-coordinate (line 18). This will enable us to center the ellipse on the canvas. We then use the **scale method** to *stretch* a circle to create an ellipse (line 19). The *x* value represents the *horizontal scale factor*; the *y* value represents the *vertical scale factor*—in this case, our scale factor indicates that the ratio of the width to the height is 1:3, which will create a tall, thin ellipse. Next, we draw the circle that we want to stretch using the beginPath method to start the path, then the arc method to draw the circle (lines 20–21). Notice that the *x*- and *y*-coordinates for the center of the circle are (0, 0), which is now the *center* of the canvas (*not* the top-left corner). We then specify a fillStyle of orange (line 22) and draw the ellipse to the canvas using the fill method (line 23).

Next, we create a horizontal purple ellipse on a separate canvas (lines 26–39). We use a scale of 3, 2 (line 34), indicating that the ratio of the width to the height is 3:2. This results in an ellipse that is shorter and wider.

```
 1   <!DOCTYPE html>
 2
 3   <!-- Fig. 14.14: ellipse.html -->
 4   <!-- Drawing an ellipse on a canvas. -->
 5   <html>
 6      <head>
 7         <meta charset = "utf-8">
 8         <title>Ellipse</title>
 9      </head>
10      <body>
11         <!-- vertical ellipse -->
12         <canvas id = "drawEllipse" width = "200" height = "200"
13            style = "border: 1px solid black;">
14         </canvas>
15         <script>
16            var canvas = document.getElementById("drawEllipse");
17            var context = canvas.getContext("2d")
18            context.translate(canvas.width / 2, canvas.height / 2);
19            context.scale(1, 3);
20            context.beginPath();
21            context.arc(0, 0, 30, 0, 2 * Math.PI, true);
22            context.fillStyle = "orange";
23            context.fill();
24         </script>
25
26         <!-- horizontal ellipse -->
27         <canvas id = "drawEllipse2" width = "200" height = "200"
28            style = "border: 1px solid black;">
29         </canvas>
30         <script>
31            var canvas = document.getElementById("drawEllipse2");
32            var context = canvas.getContext("2d")
33            context.translate(canvas.width / 2, canvas.height / 2);
34            context.scale(3, 2);
35            context.beginPath();
```

Fig. 14.14 | Drawing an ellipse on a canvas. (Part 1 of 2.)

```
36          context.arc(0, 0, 30, 0, 2 * Math.PI, true);
37          context.fillStyle = "indigo";
38          context.fill();
39       </script>
40    </body>
41 </html>
```

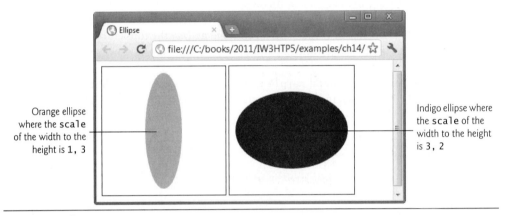

Orange ellipse where the scale of the width to the height is 1, 3

Indigo ellipse where the scale of the width to the height is 3, 2

Fig. 14.14 | Drawing an ellipse on a canvas. (Part 2 of 2.)

14.14.2 rotate Method: Creating an Animation

Figure 14.15 uses the **rotate method** to create an animation of a rotating rectangle on a canvas. First, we create the JavaScript function startRotating (lines 18–22). Just as we did in the previous example, we change the transformation matrix on the canvas using the translate method, making the center of the canvas the origin with the *x*, *y* values (0, 0) (line 20). This allows us to rotate the rectangle (which is centered on the canvas) around its center.

```
1  <!DOCTYPE html>
2
3  <!-- Fig. 14.15: rotate.html -->
4  <!-- Using the rotate method to rotate a rectangle on a canvas. -->
5  <html>
6     <head>
7        <meta charset = "utf-8">
8        <title>Rotate</title>
9     </head>
10    <body>
11       <canvas id = "rotateRectangle" width = "200" height = "200"
12          style = "border: 1px solid black;">
13       </canvas>
14       <script>
15          var canvas = document.getElementById("rotateRectangle");
16          var context = canvas.getContext("2d")
17
```

Fig. 14.15 | Using the rotate method to rotate a rectangle on a canvas. (Part 1 of 2.)

```
18      function startRotating()
19      {
20          context.translate(canvas.width / 2, canvas.height / 2);
21          setInterval(rotate, 10);
22      }
23
24      function rotate()
25      {
26          context.clearRect(-100, -100, 200, 200);
27          context.rotate(Math.PI / 360);
28          context.fillStyle = "lime";
29          context.fillRect(-50, -50, 100, 100);
30      }
31
32      window.addEventListener( "load", startRotating, false );
33   </script>
34   </body>
35 </html>
```

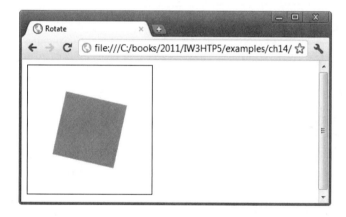

Fig. 14.15 | Using the `rotate` method to rotate a rectangle on a `canvas`. (Part 2 of 2.)

In line 21, we use the `setInterval` method of the `window` object. The first argument is the name of the function to call (`rotate`) and the second is the number of milliseconds between calls.

Next, we create the JavaScript function `rotate` (lines 24–30). We use the **clearRect method** to clear the rectangle's pixels from the `canvas`, converting them back to transparent as the rectangle rotates (line 26). This method takes four arguments—*x*, *y*, *width* and *height*. Since the center of the canvas has the *x*- and *y*-coordinates (0, 0), the top-left corner of the canvas is now (-100, -100). The width and height of the canvas remain the same (200, 200). If you were to remove the `clearRect` method, the pixels would remain on the canvas, and after one full rotation of the rectangle, you would see a circle.

Next, the `rotate` method takes one argument—the angle of the clockwise rotation, expressed in radians (line 27). We then specify the rectangle's `fillStyle` (`lime`) and draw the rectangle using the `fillRect` method. Notice that its *x*- and *y*-coordinates are the translated coordinates, (-50, -50) (line 29).

14.14.3 transform Method: Drawing Skewed Rectangles

The **transform method** allows you to skew, scale, rotate and translate elements without using the separate transformation methods discussed earlier in this section. The transform method takes six arguments in the format (*a*, *b*, *c*, *d*, *e*, *f*). The first argument, *a*, is the *x*-scale—the factor by which to scale the element horizontally. For example, a value of 2 would double the element's width. The second argument, *b*, is the *y*-skew. The third argument, *c*, is the *x*-skew. The greater the value of the *x*- and *y*-skew, the more the element will be skewed horizontally and vertically, respectively. The fourth argument, *d*, is the *y*-scale—the factor by which to scale the element vertically. The fifth argument, *e*, is the *x*-translation and the sixth argument, *f*, is the *y*-translation. The default *x*- and *y*-scale values are 1. The default values of the *x*- and *y*-skew and the *x*- and *y*-translation are 0, meaning there is no skew or translation.

Figure 14.16 uses the transform method to *skew*, *scale* and *translate* two rectangles. On the first canvas (lines 12–32), we declare the variable rectangleWidth and assign it the value 120, and declare the variable rectangleHeight and assign it the value 60 (lines 18–19).

```
 1   <!DOCTYPE html>
 2
 3   <!-- Fig. 14.16: skew.html -->
 4   <!-- Using the translate and transform methods to skew rectangles. -->
 5   <html>
 6      <head>
 7         <meta charset = "utf-8">
 8         <title>Skew</title>
 9      </head>
10      <body>
11         <!-- skew left -->
12         <canvas id = "transform" width = "320" height = "150"
13            style = "border: 1px solid Black;">
14         </canvas>
15         <script>
16            var canvas = document.getElementById("transform");
17            var context = canvas.getContext("2d");
18            var rectangleWidth = 120;
19            var rectangleHeight = 60;
20            var scaleX = 2;
21            var skewY = 0;
22            var skewX = 1;
23            var scaleY = 1;
24            var translationX = -10;
25            var translationY = 30;
26            context.translate(canvas.width / 2, canvas.height / 2);
27            context.transform(scaleX, skewY, skewX, scaleY,
28               translationX, translationY);
29            context.fillStyle = "red";
30            context.fillRect(-rectangleWidth / 2, -rectangleHeight / 2,
31               rectangleWidth, rectangleHeight);
32         </script>
```

Fig. 14.16 | Using the translate and transform methods to skew rectangles. (Part 1 of 2.)

```
33
34           <!-- skew right -->
35           <canvas id = "transform2" width = "220" height = "150"
36              style = "border: 1px solid Black;">
37           <script>
38              var canvas = document.getElementById("transform2");
39              var context = canvas.getContext("2d");
40              var rectangleWidth = 120;
41              var rectangleHeight = 60;
42              var scaleX = 1;
43              var skewY = 0;
44              var skewX = -1.5;
45              var scaleY = 2;
46              var translationX = 0;
47              var translationY = 0;
48              context.translate(canvas.width / 2, canvas.height / 2);
49              context.transform(scaleX, skewY, skewX, scaleY,
50                 translationX, translationY);
51              context.fillStyle = "blue";
52              context.fillRect(-rectangleWidth / 2, -rectangleHeight / 2,
53                 rectangleWidth, rectangleHeight);
54           </script>
55        </body>
56     </html>
```

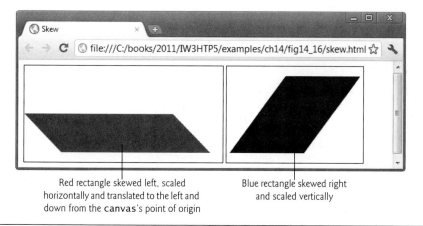

Red rectangle skewed left, scaled
horizontally and translated to the left and
down from the **canvas**'s point of origin

Blue rectangle skewed right
and scaled vertically

Fig. 14.16 | Using the translate and transform methods to skew rectangles. (Part 2 of 2.)

In lines 20–25, we declare variables for each of the arguments that will be used in the transform method and assign each a value. scaleX is assigned the value 2 to double the width of the rectangle. skewY is assigned the value 0 (the default value) so there's no vertical skew. skewX is assigned the value 1 to skew the rectangle horizontally to the left. Increasing this value would increase the angle of the skew. scaleY is assigned the value 1 (the default value) so the rectangle is *not* scaled vertically (line 20). translationX is assigned the value -10 to shift the position of the rectangle left of the point of origin. Finally, translationY is assigned the value 30 to shift the rectangle down from the point of origin.

In line 26, the `translate` method centers the point of origin (0, 0) on the canvas. Next, the `transform` method scales and skews the rectangle horizontally, then shifts its center left and down from the point of origin.

In lines 35–54 we create a second canvas to demonstrate how different values can be used to transform a rectangle. In this case, the value of `scaleX` is 1 (the default), so there is no horizontal scale. The value of `skewY` is 0. In line 44, `skewX` is assigned `-1.5`. The *negative* value causes the rectangle to skew *right*. Next, the variable `scaleY` is assigned 2 to double the height of the rectangle. Finally, the variables `translationX` and `translationY` are each assigned 0 (the default) so that the rectangle remains centered on the canvas's point of origin.

14.15 Text

Figure 14.17 shows you how to draw text on a canvas. We draw two lines of text. For the first line, we color the text using a `fillStyle` of red (line 19). We use the **font attribute** to specify the style, size and font of the text—in this case, `italic 24px serif` (line 20).

```
1   <!DOCTYPE html>
2
3   <!-- Fig. 14.17: text.html -->
4   <!-- Drawing text on a canvas. -->
5   <html>
6      <head>
7         <meta charset = "utf-8">
8         <title>Text</title>
9      </head>
10     <body>
11        <canvas id = "text" width = "230" height = "100"
12           style = "border: 1px solid black;">
13        </canvas>
14        <script>
15           var canvas = document.getElementById("text");
16           var context = canvas.getContext("2d")
17
18           // draw the first line of text
19           context.fillStyle = "red";
20           context.font = "italic 24px serif";
21           context.textBaseline = "top";
22           context.fillText ("HTML5 Canvas", 0, 0);
23
24           // draw the second line of text
25           context.font = "bold 30px sans-serif";
26           context.textAlign = "center";
27           context.lineWidth = 2;
28           context.strokeStyle = "navy";
29           context.strokeText("HTML5 Canvas", 115, 50);
30        </script>
31     </body>
32  </html>
```

Fig. 14.17 | Drawing text on a canvas. (Part 1 of 2.)

Italic, serif, red text with a `textBaseline` attribute of `top`

Bold, serif text with a `textAlign` attribute of `center`

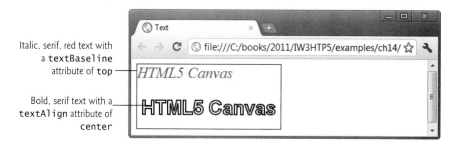

Fig. 14.17 | Drawing text on a `canvas`. (Part 2 of 2.)

Next, we use **`textBaseline` attribute** to specify the alignment points of the text (line 21). There are six different `textBaseline` attribute values (Fig. 14.18). To see how each value aligns the font, see the graphic in the HTML5 canvas specification at

```
http://www.whatwg.org/specs/web-apps/current-work/multipage/the-
canvas-element.html#text-0
```

Value	Description
top	Top of the em square
hanging	Hanging baseline
middle	Middle of the em square
alphabetic	Alphabetic baseline (the default value)
ideographic	Ideographic baseline
bottom	Bottom of the em square

Fig. 14.18 | `textBaseline` values.

Now we use the **`fillText` method** to draw the text to the canvas (line 22). This method takes three arguments. The first is the text being drawn to the `canvas`. The second and third arguments are the *x*- and *y*-coordinates. You may include the optional fourth argument, `maxWidth`, to limit the width of the text.

Lines 25–29 draw the second line of text to the canvas. In this case, the `font` attribute specifies a `bold`, `30px`, `sans-serif` font (line 25). We center the text on the canvas using the **`textAlign` attribute** which specifies the horizontal alignment of the text relative to the *x*-coordinate of the text (line 26). Figure 14.19 describes the five `textAlign` attribute values.

Value	Description
left	Text is left aligned.
right	Text is right aligned.

Fig. 14.19 | `textAlign` attribute values. (Part 1 of 2.)

Value	Description
center	Text is centered.
start (the default value)	Text is left aligned if the start of the line is left-to-right; text is right aligned if the start of the text is right-to-left.
end	Text is right aligned if the end of the line is left-to-right; text is left aligned if the end of the text is right-to-left.

Fig. 14.19 | textAlign attribute values. (Part 2 of 2.)

We use the lineWidth attribute to specify the thickness of the stroke used to draw the text—in this case, 2 (line 27). Next, we specify the strokeStyle to specify the color of the text (line 28). Finally, we use strokeText to specify the text being drawn to the canvas and its *x*- and *y*-coordinates (line 29). By using strokeText instead of fillText, we draw outlined text instead of filled text. Keep in mind that once text is on a canvas it's just bits—it can no longer be manipulated as text.

14.16 Resizing the canvas to Fill the Browser Window

Figure 14.20 demonstrates how to dynamically resize a canvas to fill the window. To do this, we draw a yellow rectangle so you can see how it fills the canvas.

```
1   <!DOCTYPE html>
2
3   <!-- Fig. 14.20: fillingwindow.html -->
4   <!-- Resizing a canvas to fill the window. -->
5   <html>
6      <head>
7         <meta charset = "utf-8">
8         <title>Filling the Window</title>
9         <style type = "text/css">
10           canvas { position: absolute; left: 0px; top: 0px;
11              width: 100%; height: 100%; }
12        </style>
13     </head>
14     <body>
15        <canvas id = "resize"></canvas>
16        <script>
17           function draw()
18           {
19              var canvas = document.getElementById( "resize" );
20              var context = canvas.getContext( "2d" );
21              context.fillStyle = "yellow";
22              context.fillRect(
23                 0, 0, context.canvas.width, context.canvas.height );
24           } // end function draw
```

Fig. 14.20 | Dynamically resizing a canvas to fill the window. (Part 1 of 2.)

```
25
26                window.addEventListener( "load", draw, false );
27         </script>
28      </body>
29   </html>
```

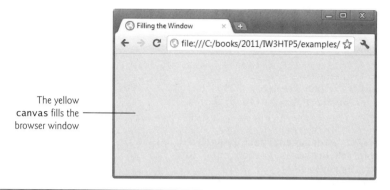

The yellow canvas fills the browser window

Fig. 14.20 | Dynamically resizing a canvas to fill the window. (Part 2 of 2.)

First we use a CSS style sheet to set the position of the canvas to absolute and set both its width and height to 100%, rather than using fixed coordinates (lines 10–11). This places the canvas at the top left of the screen and allows the canvas width and height to be resized to 100% of those of the window. Do not include a border on the canvas.

We use JavaScript function draw to draw the canvas when the application is rendered (lines 17 and 26). Line 21 specifies the color of the rectangle by setting the fillStyle to yellow. We use fillRect to draw the color to the canvas. Recall that in previous examples, the four coordinates we used for method fillRect were x, y, x1, y1, where x1 and y1 represent the coordinates of the bottom-right corner of the rectangle. In this example, the x- and y-coordinates are (0, 0)—the top left of the canvas The the x1 value is context.canvas.width and the y1 value is context.value.height, so no matter the size of the window, the x1 value will always be the width of the canvas and the y1 value will always be the height of the canvas.

14.17 Alpha Transparency

In Figure 14.21, we use the **globalAlpha attribute** to demonstrate three different alpha transparencies. To do this, we create three canvases, each with a fully opaque rectangle and an overlapping circle and varying transparencies. The globalAlpha value can be any number between 0 (fully transparent) and 1 (the default value, which is fully opaque).

On the first canvas we specify a globalAlpha attribute value of 0.9 to create a circle that's *mostly opaque* (line 23). On the second canvas we specify a globalAlpha attribute value of 0.5 to create a circle that's *semitransparent* (line 41). Notice in the output that in the area where the circle overlaps the rectangle, the rectangle is visible. On the third canvas we specify a globalAlpha attribute value of 0.15 to create a circle that's *almost entirely transparent* (line 59). In the area where the circle overlaps the rectangle, the rectangle is even more visible.

```
 1   <!DOCTYPE html>
 2
 3   <!-- Fig. 14.21: alpha.html -->
 4   <!-- Using the globalAlpha attribute on a canvas. -->
 5   <html>
 6      <head>
 7         <meta charset = "utf-8">
 8         <title>Alpha Transparency</title>
 9      </head>
10      <body>
11
12         <!-- 0.75 alpha value -->
13         <canvas id = "alpha" width = "200" height = "200"
14            style = "border: 1px solid black;">
15         </canvas>
16         <script>
17            var canvas = document.getElementById("alpha");
18            var context = canvas.getContext("2d")
19            context.beginPath();
20            context.rect(10, 10, 120, 120);
21            context.fillStyle = "purple";
22            context.fill();
23            context.globalAlpha = 0.9;
24            context.beginPath();
25            context.arc(120, 120, 65, 0, 2 * Math.PI, false);
26            context.fillStyle = "lime";
27            context.fill();
28         </script>
29
30         <!-- 0.5 alpha value -->
31         <canvas id = "alpha2" width = "200" height = "200"
32            style = "border: 1px solid black;">
33         </canvas>
34         <script>
35            var canvas = document.getElementById("alpha2");
36            var context = canvas.getContext("2d")
37            context.beginPath();
38            context.rect(10, 10, 120, 120);
39            context.fillStyle = "purple";
40            context.fill();
41            context.globalAlpha = 0.5;
42            context.beginPath();
43            context.arc(120, 120, 65, 0, 2 * Math.PI, false);
44            context.fillStyle = "lime";
45            context.fill();
46         </script>
47
48         <!-- 0.15 alpha value -->
49         <canvas id = "alpha3" width = "200" height = "200"
50            style = "border: 1px solid black;">
51         </canvas>
52         <script>
53            var canvas = document.getElementById("alpha3");
```

Fig. 14.21 | Using the globalAlpha attribute on a canvas. (Part 1 of 2.)

```
54              var context = canvas.getContext("2d")
55              context.beginPath();
56              context.rect(10, 10, 120, 120);
57              context.fillStyle = "purple";
58              context.fill();
59              context.globalAlpha = 0.15;
60              context.beginPath();
61              context.arc(120, 120, 65, 0, 2 * Math.PI, false);
62              context.fillStyle = "lime";
63              context.fill();
64          </script>
65      </body>
66  </html>
```

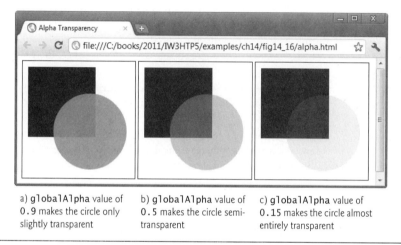

a) globalAlpha value of 0.9 makes the circle only slightly transparent

b) globalAlpha value of 0.5 makes the circle semi-transparent

c) globalAlpha value of 0.15 makes the circle almost entirely transparent

Fig. 14.21 | Using the globalAlpha attribute on a canvas. (Part 2 of 2.)

14.18 Compositing

Compositing allows you to control the layering of shapes and images on a canvas using two attributes—the globalAlpha attribute described in the previous example, and the **globalCompositeOperation attribute**. There are 11 globalCompositeOperation attribute values (Fig. 14.22). The *source* is the image being drawn to a canvas. The *destination* is the current bitmap on a canvas.

Value	Description
source-atop	The source is placed on top of the destination image. If both images are opaque, the source is displayed where the images overlap. If the source is transparent but the destination image is opaque, the destination image is displayed where the images overlap. The destination image is transparent where there is no overlap.

Fig. 14.22 | globalCompositeOperation values. (Part 1 of 2.)

Value	Description
source-in	The source image is displayed where the images overlap and both are opaque. Both images are transparent where there is no overlap.
source-out	If the source image is opaque and the destination image is transparent, the source image is displayed where the images overlap. Both images are transparent where there is no overlap.
source-over (default)	The source image is placed over the destination image. The source image is displayed where it's opaque and the images overlap. The destination image is displayed where there is no overlap.
destination-atop	The destination image is placed on top of the source image. If both images are opaque, the destination image is displayed where the images overlap. If the destination image is transparent but the source image is opaque, the source image is displayed where the images overlap. The source image is transparent where there is no overlap.
destination-in	The destination image is displayed where the images overlap and both are opaque. Both images are transparent where there is no overlap.
destination-out	If the destination image is opaque and the source image is transparent, the destination image is displayed where the images overlap. Both images are transparent where there is no overlap.
destination-over	The destination image is placed over the source image. The destination image is displayed where it's opaque and the images overlap. The source image is displayed where there is no overlap.
lighter	Displays the sum of the source-image color and destination-image color—up to the maximum RGB color value (255)—where the images overlap. Both images are normal elsewhere.
copy	If the images overlap, only the source image is displayed (the destination is ignored).
xor	Source-image xor (exclusive-or) destination. The images are transparent where they overlap and normal elsewhere.

Fig. 14.22 | `globalCompositeOperation` values. (Part 2 of 2.)

In Fig. 14.23, we demonstrate six of the compositing effects (lines 21–49). In this example, the destination image is a large `red` rectangle (lines 18–19) and the source images are six `lime` rectangles.

```
1   <!DOCTYPE html>
2
3   <!-- Fig. 14.23: image.html -->
4   <!-- Compositing on a canvas. -->
```

Fig. 14.23 | Demonstrating compositing on a `canvas`. (Part 1 of 3.)

```html
5    <html>
6       <head>
7          <meta charset = "utf-8">
8          <title>Compositing</title>
9       </head>
10      <body>
11         <canvas id = "composite" width = "220" height = "200">
12         </canvas>
13         <script>
14            function draw()
15            {
16               var canvas = document.getElementById("composite");
17               var context = canvas.getContext("2d")
18               context.fillStyle = "red";
19               context.fillRect(5, 50, 210, 100);
20
21               // source-atop
22               context.globalCompositeOperation = "source-atop";
23               context.fillStyle = "lime";
24               context.fillRect(10, 20, 60, 60);
25
26               // source-over
27               context.globalCompositeOperation = "source-over";
28               context.fillStyle = "lime";
29               context.fillRect(10, 120, 60, 60);
30
31               // destination-over
32               context.globalCompositeOperation = "destination-over";
33               context.fillStyle = "lime";
34               context.fillRect(80, 20, 60, 60);
35
36               // destination-out
37               context.globalCompositeOperation = "destination-out";
38               context.fillStyle = "lime";
39               context.fillRect(80, 120, 60, 60);
40
41               // lighter
42               context.globalCompositeOperation = "lighter";
43               context.fillStyle = "lime";
44               context.fillRect(150, 20, 60, 60);
45
46               // xor
47               context.globalCompositeOperation = "xor";
48               context.fillStyle = "lime";
49               context.fillRect(150, 120, 60, 60);
50            } // end function draw
51
52            window.addEventListener( "load", draw, false );
53         </script>
54      </body>
55   </html>
```

Fig. 14.23 | Demonstrating compositing on a canvas. (Part 2 of 3.)

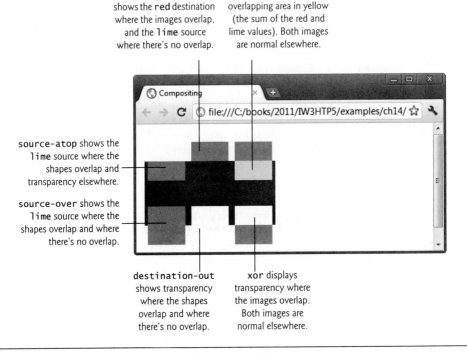

destination-over shows the red destination where the images overlap, and the lime source where there's no overlap.

lighter displays the overlapping area in yellow (the sum of the red and lime values). Both images are normal elsewhere.

source-atop shows the lime source where the shapes overlap and transparency elsewhere.

source-over shows the lime source where the shapes overlap and where there's no overlap.

destination-out shows transparency where the shapes overlap and where there's no overlap.

xor displays transparency where the images overlap. Both images are normal elsewhere.

Fig. 14.23 | Demonstrating compositing on a canvas. (Part 3 of 3.)

14.19 Cannon Game

Now let's have some fun! The **Cannon Game** app challenges you to destroy a seven-piece moving target before a ten-second time limit expires (Fig. 14.24).[2] The game consists of four visual components—a *cannon* that you control, a *cannonball* fired by the cannon, the *seven-piece target* and a moving *blocker* that defends the target to make the game more challenging. You aim the cannon by clicking the screen—the cannon then aims where you clicked and fires a cannonball. You can fire a cannonball only if there is *not* another one on the screen.

The game begins with a *10-second time limit*. Each time you hit a target section, you are *rewarded* with three seconds being *added* to the time limit; each time you hit the blocker, you are *penalized* with two seconds being *subtracted* from the time limit. You win by destroying all seven target sections before time runs out. If the timer reaches zero, you lose. When the game ends, it displays an alert dialog indicating whether you won or lost, and shows the number of shots fired and the elapsed time (Fig. 14.25).

When the cannon fires, the game plays a *firing sound*. The target consists of seven pieces. When a cannonball hits a piece of the target, a *glass-breaking sound* plays and that piece disappears from the screen. When the cannonball hits the blocker, a *hit sound* plays

---

2. The **Cannon Game** currently works in Chrome, Internet Explorer 9 and Safari. It does not work properly in Opera, Firefox, iPhone and Android.

and the cannonball bounces back. The blocker cannot be destroyed. The target and blocker move *vertically* at different speeds, changing direction when they hit the top or bottom of the screen. At any time, the blocker and the target can be moving in the same or different directions.

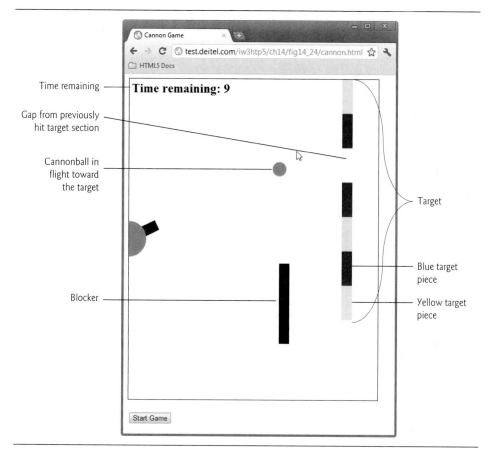

Fig. 14.24 | Completed **Cannon Game** app.

a) alert dialog displayed after user destroys all seven target sections

b) alert dialog displayed when game ends before user destroys all seven targets

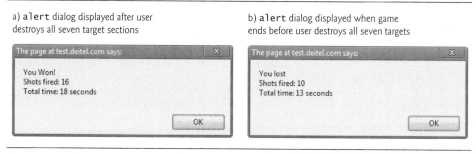

Fig. 14.25 | **Cannon Game** app alerts showing a win and a loss.

14.19.1 HTML5 Document

Figure 14.26 shows the HTML5 document for the **Cannon Game**. Lines 15–20 use HTML5 audio elements to load the game's sounds, which are located in the same folder as the HTML5 document. Recall from Chapter 9 that the HTML5 audio element may contain multiple source elements for the audio file in several formats, so that you can support cross-browser playback of the sounds. For this app, we've included only MP3 files. We set the audio element's preload attribute to auto to indicate that the sounds should be loaded *immediately* when the page loads. Line 22 creates a **Start Game** button which the user will click to launch the game. After a game is over, this button remains on the screen so that the user can click it to play again.

```html
 1   <!DOCTYPE html>
 2
 3   <!-- Fig. 14.26: cannon.html -->
 4   <!-- Cannon Game HTML5 document. -->
 5   <html>
 6      <head>
 7         <meta charset = "utf-8">
 8         <title>Cannon Game</title>
 9         <style type = "text/css">
10            canvas { border: 1px solid black; }
11         </style>
12         <script src = "cannon.js"></script>
13      </head>
14      <body>
15         <audio id = "blockerSound" preload = "auto">
16            <source src = "blocker_hit.mp3" type = "audio/mpeg"></audio>
17         <audio id = "targetSound" preload = "auto">
18            <source src = "target_hit.mp3" type = "audio/mpeg"></audio>
19         <audio id = "cannonSound" preload = "auto">
20            <source src = "cannon_fire.mp3" type = "audio/mpeg"></audio>
21         <canvas id = "theCanvas" width = "480" height = "600"></canvas>
22         <p><input id = "startButton" type = "button" value = "Start Game">
23         </p>
24      </body>
25   </html>
```

Fig. 14.26 | Cannon Game HTML5 document.

14.19.2 Instance Variables and Constants

Figure 14.27 lists the **Cannon Game**'s numerous constants and instance variables. Most are self-explanatory, but we'll explain each as we encounter it in the discussion.

```javascript
 1   // Fig. 14.27 cannon.js
 2   // Logic of the Cannon Game
 3   var canvas; // the canvas
 4   var context; // used for drawing on the canvas
```

Fig. 14.27 | Cannon Game variable declarations. (Part 1 of 2.)

```
 5
 6   // constants for game play
 7   var TARGET_PIECES = 7; // sections in the target
 8   var MISS_PENALTY = 2; // seconds deducted on a miss
 9   var HIT_REWARD = 3; // seconds added on a hit
10   var TIME_INTERVAL = 25; // screen refresh interval in milliseconds
11
12   // variables for the game loop and tracking statistics
13   var intervalTimer; // holds interval timer
14   var timerCount; // times the timer fired since the last second
15   var timeLeft; // the amount of time left in seconds
16   var shotsFired; // the number of shots the user has fired
17   var timeElapsed; // the number of seconds elapsed
18
19   // variables for the blocker and target
20   var blocker; // start and end points of the blocker
21   var blockerDistance; // blocker distance from left
22   var blockerBeginning; // blocker distance from top
23   var blockerEnd; // blocker bottom edge distance from top
24   var initialBlockerVelocity; // initial blocker speed multiplier
25   var blockerVelocity; // blocker speed multiplier during game
26
27   var target; // start and end points of the target
28   var targetDistance; // target distance from left
29   var targetBeginning; // target distance from top
30   var targetEnd; // target bottom's distance from top
31   var pieceLength; // length of a target piece
32   var initialTargetVelocity; // initial target speed multiplier
33   var targetVelocity; // target speed multiplier during game
34
35   var lineWidth; // width of the target and blocker
36   var hitStates; // is each target piece hit?
37   var targetPiecesHit; // number of target pieces hit (out of 7)
38
39   // variables for the cannon and cannonball
40   var cannonball; // cannonball image's upper-left corner
41   var cannonballVelocity; // cannonball's velocity
42   var cannonballOnScreen; // is the cannonball on the screen
43   var cannonballRadius; // cannonball radius
44   var cannonballSpeed; // cannonball speed
45   var cannonBaseRadius; // cannon base radius
46   var cannonLength; // cannon barrel length
47   var barrelEnd; // the end point of the cannon's barrel
48   var canvasWidth; // width of the canvas
49   var canvasHeight; // height of the canvas
50
51   // variables for sounds
52   var targetSound;
53   var cannonSound;
54   var blockerSound;
55
```

Fig. 14.27 | Cannon Game variable declarations. (Part 2 of 2.)

14.19.3 Function setupGame

Figure 14.28 shows function setupGame. Later in the script, line 408 registers the window object's load event handler so that function setupGame is called when the cannon.html page loads.

Lines 71–78 create the blocker, target, cannonball and barrelEnd as JavaScript Objects. You can create your own properties on such Objects simply by assigning a value to a property name. For example, lines 72–73 create start and end properties to represent the start and end points, respectively, of the blocker. Each is initialized as an Object so that it, in turn, can contain x and y properties representing the coordinates of the point. Function resetElements (Fig. 14.30) sets the initial values of the x and y properties for the start and end of the blocker and target.

We create boolean array hitStates (line 81) to keep track of which of the target's seven pieces have been hit (and thus should not be drawn). Lines 84–86 get references to the audio elements that represent the game's sounds—we use these to call play on each audio at the appropriate time.

```
56   // called when the app first launches
57   function setupGame()
58   {
59      // stop timer if document unload event occurs
60      document.addEventListener( "unload", stopTimer, false );
61
62      // get the canvas, its context and setup its click event handler
63      canvas = document.getElementById( "theCanvas" );
64      context = canvas.getContext("2d");
65
66      // start a new game when user clicks Start Game button
67      document.getElementById( "startButton" ).addEventListener(
68         "click", newGame, false );
69
70      // JavaScript Object representing game items
71      blocker = new Object(); // object representing blocker line
72      blocker.start = new Object(); // will hold x-y coords of line start
73      blocker.end = new Object(); // will hold x-y coords of line end
74      target = new Object(); // object representing target line
75      target.start = new Object(); // will hold x-y coords of line start
76      target.end = new Object(); // will hold x-y coords of line end
77      cannonball = new Object(); // object representing cannonball point
78      barrelEnd = new Object(); // object representing end of cannon barrel
79
80      // initialize hitStates as an array
81      hitStates = new Array(TARGET_PIECES);
82
83      // get sounds
84      targetSound = document.getElementById( "targetSound" );
85      cannonSound = document.getElementById( "cannonSound" );
86      blockerSound = document.getElementById( "blockerSound" );
87   } // end function setupGame
88
```

Fig. 14.28 | Cannon Game function setupGame.

14.19.4 Functions startTimer and stopTimer

Figure 14.29 presents functions startTimer and stopTimer which manage the click event handler and the interval timer. As you know, users interact with this app by clicking the mouse on the device's screen. A click aligns the cannon to face the point of the click and fires the cannon. Line 92 in function startTimer *registers* function fireCannonball as the canvas's click event handler. Once the game is over, we don't want the user to be able to click the canvas anymore, so line 99 in function stopTimer *removes* the canvas's click event handler.

Line 93 in function startTimer creates an interval timer that calls updatePositions to update the game every TIME_INTERVAL (Fig. 14.27, line 10) milliseconds. TIME_INTERVAL can be adjusted to increase or decrease the CannonView's refresh rate. Based on the value of the TIME_INTERVAL constant (25), updatePositions is called approximately 40 times per second. When the game is over, stopTimer is called and line 100 terminates the interval timer so that updatePositions is not called again until the user starts a new game.

```
89   // set up interval timer to update game
90   function startTimer()
91   {
92      canvas.addEventListener( "click", fireCannonball, false );
93      intervalTimer = window.setInterval( updatePositions, TIME_INTERVAL );
94   } // end function startTimer
95
96   // terminate interval timer
97   function stopTimer()
98   {
99      canvas.removeEventListener( "click", fireCannonball, false );
100     window.clearInterval( intervalTimer );
101  } // end function stopTimer
102
```

Fig. 14.29 | Cannon Game functions startTimer and stopTimer.

14.19.5 Function resetElements

Function resetElements (Fig. 14.30) is called by function newGame to position and scale the size of the game elements relative to the size of the canvas. The calculations performed here *scale* the game's on-screen elements based on the canvas's pixel width and height—we arrived at our scaling factors via trial and error until the game surface looked good. Lines 141–142 set the end point of the cannon's barrel to point horizontally and to the right from the midpoint of the left border of the canvas.

```
103  // called by function newGame to scale the size of the game elements
104  // relative to the size of the canvas before the game begins
105  function resetElements()
106  {
```

Fig. 14.30 | Cannon Game function resetElements. (Part 1 of 2.)

```
107     var w = canvas.width;
108     var h = canvas.height;
109     canvasWidth = w; // store the width
110     canvasHeight = h; // store the height
111     cannonBaseRadius = h / 18; // cannon base radius 1/18 canvas height
112     cannonLength = w / 8; // cannon length 1/8 canvas width
113
114     cannonballRadius = w / 36; // cannonball radius 1/36 canvas width
115     cannonballSpeed = w * 3 / 2; // cannonball speed multiplier
116
117     lineWidth = w / 24; // target and blocker 1/24 canvas width
118
119     // configure instance variables related to the blocker
120     blockerDistance = w * 5 / 8; // blocker 5/8 canvas width from left
121     blockerBeginning = h / 8; // distance from top 1/8 canvas height
122     blockerEnd = h * 3 / 8; // distance from top 3/8 canvas height
123     initialBlockerVelocity = h / 2; // initial blocker speed multiplier
124     blocker.start.x = blockerDistance;
125     blocker.start.y = blockerBeginning;
126     blocker.end.x = blockerDistance;
127     blocker.end.y = blockerEnd;
128
129     // configure instance variables related to the target
130     targetDistance = w * 7 / 8; // target 7/8 canvas width from left
131     targetBeginning = h / 8; // distance from top 1/8 canvas height
132     targetEnd = h * 7 / 8; // distance from top 7/8 canvas height
133     pieceLength = (targetEnd - targetBeginning) / TARGET_PIECES;
134     initialTargetVelocity = -h / 4; // initial target speed multiplier
135     target.start.x = targetDistance;
136     target.start.y = targetBeginning;
137     target.end.x = targetDistance;
138     target.end.y = targetEnd;
139
140     // end point of the cannon's barrel initially points horizontally
141     barrelEnd.x = cannonLength;
142     barrelEnd.y = h / 2;
143  } // end function resetElements
144
```

Fig. 14.30 | Cannon Game function resetElements. (Part 2 of 2.)

14.19.6 Function newGame

Function newGame (Fig. 14.31) is called when the user clicks the **Start Game** button; the function initializes the game's instance variables. Lines 152–153 initialize all the elements of the hitStates array to false to indicate that none of the targets have been destroyed. Lines 155–162 initialize key variables in preparation for launching a fresh game. In particular, line 160 indicates that no cannonball is on the screen—this enables the cannon to fire a cannonball when the user next clicks the screen. Line 164 invokes function startTimer to start the game loop for the new game.

```
145    // reset all the screen elements and start a new game
146    function newGame()
147    {
148        resetElements(); // reinitialize all the game elements
149        stopTimer(); // terminate previous interval timer
150
151        // set every element of hitStates to false--restores target pieces
152        for (var i = 0; i < TARGET_PIECES; ++i)
153            hitStates[i] = false; // target piece not destroyed
154
155        targetPiecesHit = 0; // no target pieces have been hit
156        blockerVelocity = initialBlockerVelocity; // set initial velocity
157        targetVelocity = initialTargetVelocity; // set initial velocity
158        timeLeft = 10; // start the countdown at 10 seconds
159        timerCount = 0; // the timer has fired 0 times so far
160        cannonballOnScreen = false; // the cannonball is not on the screen
161        shotsFired = 0; // set the initial number of shots fired
162        timeElapsed = 0; // set the time elapsed to zero
163
164        startTimer(); // starts the game loop
165    } // end function newGame
166
```

Fig. 14.31 | Cannon Game function newGame.

14.19.7 Function updatePositions: Manual Frame-by-Frame Animation and Simple Collision Detection

This app performs its animations *manually* by updating the positions of all the game elements at fixed time intervals. Line 93 (Fig. 14.29) in function startTimer created an interval timer that calls function updatePositions (Fig. 14.32) to update the game every 25 milliseconds (i.e., 40 times per second). This function also performs simple *collision detection* to determine whether the cannonball has collided with any of the canvas's edges, with the blocker or with a section of the target. Game-development frameworks generally provide more sophisticated, built-in collision-detection capabilities.

```
167    // called every TIME_INTERVAL milliseconds
168    function updatePositions()
169    {
170        // update the blocker's position
171        var blockerUpdate = TIME_INTERVAL / 1000.0 * blockerVelocity;
172        blocker.start.y += blockerUpdate;
173        blocker.end.y += blockerUpdate;
174
175        // update the target's position
176        var targetUpdate = TIME_INTERVAL / 1000.0 * targetVelocity;
177        target.start.y += targetUpdate;
178        target.end.y += targetUpdate;
179
```

Fig. 14.32 | Cannon Game function updatePositions. (Part 1 of 3.)

```
180     // if the blocker hit the top or bottom, reverse direction
181     if (blocker.start.y < 0 || blocker.end.y > canvasHeight)
182        blockerVelocity *= -1;
183
184     // if the target hit the top or bottom, reverse direction
185     if (target.start.y < 0 || target.end.y > canvasHeight)
186        targetVelocity *= -1;
187
188     if (cannonballOnScreen) // if there is currently a shot fired
189     {
190        // update cannonball position
191        var interval = TIME_INTERVAL / 1000.0;
192
193        cannonball.x += interval * cannonballVelocityX;
194        cannonball.y += interval * cannonballVelocityY;
195
196        // check for collision with blocker
197        if ( cannonballVelocityX > 0 &&
198           cannonball.x + cannonballRadius >= blockerDistance &&
199           cannonball.x + cannonballRadius <= blockerDistance + lineWidth &&
200           cannonball.y - cannonballRadius > blocker.start.y &&
201           cannonball.y + cannonballRadius < blocker.end.y)
202        {
203           blockerSound.play(); // play blocker hit sound
204           cannonballVelocityX *= -1; // reverse cannonball's direction
205           timeLeft -= MISS_PENALTY; // penalize the user
206        } // end if
207
208        // check for collisions with left and right walls
209        else if (cannonball.x + cannonballRadius > canvasWidth ||
210           cannonball.x - cannonballRadius < 0)
211        {
212           cannonballOnScreen = false; // remove cannonball from screen
213        } // end else if
214
215        // check for collisions with top and bottom walls
216        else if (cannonball.y + cannonballRadius > canvasHeight ||
217           cannonball.y - cannonballRadius < 0)
218        {
219           cannonballOnScreen = false; // make the cannonball disappear
220        } // end else if
221
222        // check for cannonball collision with target
223        else if (cannonballVelocityX > 0 &&
224           cannonball.x + cannonballRadius >= targetDistance &&
225           cannonball.x + cannonballRadius <= targetDistance + lineWidth &&
226           cannonball.y - cannonballRadius > target.start.y &&
227           cannonball.y + cannonballRadius < target.end.y)
228        {
229           // determine target section number (0 is the top)
230           var section =
231              Math.floor((cannonball.y - target.start.y) / pieceLength);
232
```

Fig. 14.32 | **Cannon Game** function updatePositions. (Part 2 of 3.)

```
233                // check whether the piece hasn't been hit yet
234                if ((section >= 0 && section < TARGET_PIECES) &&
235                    !hitStates[section])
236                {
237                    targetSound.play(); // play target hit sound
238                    hitStates[section] = true; // section was hit
239                    cannonballOnScreen = false; // remove cannonball
240                    timeLeft += HIT_REWARD; // add reward to remaining time
241
242                    // if all pieces have been hit
243                    if (++targetPiecesHit == TARGET_PIECES)
244                    {
245                        stopTimer(); // game over so stop the interval timer
246                        draw(); // draw the game pieces one final time
247                        showGameOverDialog("You won!"); // show winning dialog
248                    } // end if
249                } // end if
250            } // end else if
251        } // end if
252
253        ++timerCount; // increment the timer event counter
254
255        // if one second has passed
256        if (TIME_INTERVAL * timerCount >= 1000)
257        {
258            --timeLeft; // decrement the timer
259            ++timeElapsed; // increment the time elapsed
260            timerCount = 0; // reset the count
261        } // end if
262
263        draw(); // draw all elements at updated positions
264
265        // if the timer reached zero
266        if (timeLeft <= 0)
267        {
268            stopTimer();
269            showGameOverDialog("You lost"); // show the losing dialog
270        } // end if
271    } // end function updatePositions
272
```

Fig. 14.32 | Cannon Game function `updatePositions`. (Part 3 of 3.)

The function begins by updating the positions of the `blocker` and the `target`. Lines 171–173 change the `blocker`'s position by multiplying `blockerVelocity` by the amount of time that has passed since the last update and adding that value to the current *x*- and *y*-coordinates. Lines 176–178 do the same for the `target`. If the `blocker` has collided with the top or bottom wall, its direction is *reversed* by multiplying its velocity by -1 (lines 181–182). Lines 185–186 perform the same check and adjustment for the full length of the `target`, including any sections that have already been hit.

Line 188 checks whether the cannonball is on the screen. If it is, we update its position by adding the distance it should have traveled since the last timer event. This is calculated by multiplying its velocity by the amount of time that passed (lines 193–194).

Lines 198–201 check whether the cannonball has collided with the blocker. We perform simple *collision detection*, based on the rectangular boundary of the cannonball. Four conditions must be met if the cannonball is in contact with the blocker:

- The cannonball has reached the blocker's distance from the left edge of the screen.

- The cannonball has not yet passed the blocker.

- Part of the cannonball must be lower than the top of the blocker.

- Part of the cannonball must be higher than the bottom of the blocker.

If all these conditions are met, we play blocker hit sound (line 203), *reverse* the cannonball's direction on the screen (line 204) and *penalize* the user by *subtracting* MISS_PENALTY from timeLeft.

We remove the cannonball if it reaches any of the screen's edges. Lines 209–212 test whether the cannonball has *collided* with the left or right wall and, if it has, remove the cannonball from the screen. Lines 216–219 remove the cannonball if it collides with the top or bottom of the screen.

We then check whether the cannonball has hit the target (lines 223–227). These conditions are similar to those used to determine whether the cannonball collided with the blocker. If the cannonball hit the target, we determine which *section* of the target was hit. Lines 230–231 accomplish this—dividing the distance between the cannonball and the bottom of the target by the length of a piece. This expression evaluates to 0 for the topmost section and 6 for the bottommost. We check whether that section was previously hit, using the hitStates array (lines 234–235). If it wasn't, we play the target hit sound, set the corresponding hitStates element to true and remove the cannonball from the screen. We then add HIT_REWARD to timeLeft, increasing the game's time remaining. We increment targetPiecesHit, then determine whether it's equal to TARGET_PIECES (line 243). If so, the game is over, so we call function stopTimer to stop the interval timer and function draw to perform the final update of the game elements on the screen. Then we call showGameOverDialog with the string "You won!".

We increment the timerCount, keeping track of the number of times we've updated the on-screen elements' positions (line 253). If the product of TIME_INTERVAL and timerCount is >= 1000 (i.e., one second has passed since timeLeft was last updated), we decrement timeLeft, increment timeElapsed and reset timerCount to zero (lines 256–260). Then we draw all the elements at their updated positions (line 263). If the timer has reached zero, the game is over—we call function stopTimer and call function showGameOverDialog with the string "You Lost" (lines 266–269).

14.19.8 Function fireCannonball

When the user clicks the mouse on the canvas, the click event handler calls function fireCannonball (Fig. 14.33) to fire a cannonball. If there's already a cannonball on the screen, another cannot be fired, so the function returns immediately; otherwise, it fires the cannon. Line 279 calls alignCannon to aim the cannon at the click point and get the cannon's angle. Lines 282–283 "load" the cannon (that is, position the cannonball inside the cannon). Then, lines 286 and 289 calculate the horizontal and vertical components of the cannonball's velocity. Next, we set cannonballOnScreen to true so that the cannonball will be drawn by function draw (Fig. 14.35) and increment shotsFired. Finally, we play the cannon's firing sound (cannonSound).

```
273  // fires a cannonball
274  function fireCannonball(event)
275  {
276     if (cannonballOnScreen) // if a cannonball is already on the screen
277        return; // do nothing
278
279     var angle = alignCannon(event); // get the cannon barrel's angle
280
281     // move the cannonball to be inside the cannon
282     cannonball.x = cannonballRadius; // align x-coordinate with cannon
283     cannonball.y = canvasHeight / 2; // centers ball vertically
284
285     // get the x component of the total velocity
286     cannonballVelocityX = (cannonballSpeed * Math.sin(angle)).toFixed(0);
287
288     // get the y component of the total velocity
289     cannonballVelocityY = (-cannonballSpeed * Math.cos(angle)).toFixed(0);
290     cannonballOnScreen = true; // the cannonball is on the screen
291     ++shotsFired; // increment shotsFired
292
293     // play cannon fired sound
294     cannonSound.play();
295  } // end function fireCannonball
296
```

Fig. 14.33 | Cannon Game function fireCannonball.

14.19.9 Function alignCannon

Function alignCannon (Fig. 14.34) aims the cannon at the point where the user clicked the mouse on the screen. Lines 302–303 get the *x*- and *y*-coordinates of the click from the event argument. We compute the vertical distance of the mouse click from the center of the screen. If this is not zero, we calculate the cannon barrel's angle from the horizontal (line 313). If the click is on the lower half of the screen we adjust the angle by Math.PI (line 317). We then use the cannonLength and the angle to determine the *x*- and *y*-coordinates for the end point of the cannon's barrel (lines 320–322)—this is used in function draw (Fig. 14.35) to draw a line from the cannon base's center at the left edge of the screen to the cannon barrel's end point.

```
297  // aligns the cannon in response to a mouse click
298  function alignCannon(event)
299  {
300     // get the location of the click
301     var clickPoint = new Object();
302     clickPoint.x = event.x;
303     clickPoint.y = event.y;
```

Fig. 14.34 | Cannon Game function alignCannon. (Part 1 of 2.)

```
304
305    // compute the click's distance from center of the screen
306    // on the y-axis
307    var centerMinusY = (canvasHeight / 2 - clickPoint.y);
308
309    var angle = 0; // initialize angle to 0
310
311    // calculate the angle the barrel makes with the horizontal
312    if (centerMinusY !== 0) // prevent division by 0
313       angle = Math.atan(clickPoint.x / centerMinusY);
314
315    // if the click is on the lower half of the screen
316    if (clickPoint.y > canvasHeight / 2)
317       angle += Math.PI; // adjust the angle
318
319    // calculate the end point of the cannon's barrel
320    barrelEnd.x = (cannonLength * Math.sin(angle)).toFixed(0);
321    barrelEnd.y =
322       (-cannonLength * Math.cos(angle) + canvasHeight / 2).toFixed(0);
323
324    return angle; // return the computed angle
325 } // end function alignCannon
326
```

Fig. 14.34 | Cannon Game function alignCannon. (Part 2 of 2.)

14.19.10 Function draw

When the screen needs to be *redrawn*, the draw function (Fig. 14.35) renders the game's on-screen elements—the cannon, the cannonball, the blocker and the seven-piece target. We use various canvas properties to specify drawing characteristics, including color, line thickness, font size and more, and various canvas functions to draw text, lines and circles.

Lines 333–336 display the time remaining in the game. If the cannonball is on the screen, lines 341–346 draw the cannonball in its current position.

We display the cannon barrel (lines 350–355), the cannon base (lines 358–362), the blocker (lines 365–369) and the target pieces (lines 372–398).

Lines 377–398 iterate through the target's sections, drawing each in the correct color—blue for the odd-numbered pieces and yellow for the others. Only those sections that haven't been hit are displayed.

```
327 // draws the game elements to the given Canvas
328 function draw()
329 {
330    canvas.width = canvas.width; // clears the canvas (from W3C docs)
331
332    // display time remaining
333    context.fillStyle = "black";
334    context.font = "bold 24px serif";
335    context.textBaseline = "top";
336    context.fillText("Time remaining: " + timeLeft, 5, 5);
```

Fig. 14.35 | Cannon Game function draw. (Part 1 of 3.)

```
337
338      // if a cannonball is currently on the screen, draw it
339      if (cannonballOnScreen)
340      {
341         context.fillStyle = "gray";
342         context.beginPath();
343         context.arc(cannonball.x, cannonball.y, cannonballRadius,
344            0, Math.PI * 2);
345         context.closePath();
346         context.fill();
347      } // end if
348
349      // draw the cannon barrel
350      context.beginPath(); // begin a new path
351      context.strokeStyle = "black";
352      context.moveTo(0, canvasHeight / 2); // path origin
353      context.lineTo(barrelEnd.x, barrelEnd.y);
354      context.lineWidth = lineWidth; // line width
355      context.stroke(); // draw path
356
357      // draw the cannon base
358      context.beginPath();
359      context.fillStyle = "gray";
360      context.arc(0, canvasHeight / 2, cannonBaseRadius, 0, Math.PI*2);
361      context.closePath();
362      context.fill();
363
364      // draw the blocker
365      context.beginPath(); // begin a new path
366      context.moveTo(blocker.start.x, blocker.start.y); // path origin
367      context.lineTo(blocker.end.x, blocker.end.y);
368      context.lineWidth = lineWidth; // line width
369      context.stroke(); //draw path
370
371      // initialize currentPoint to the starting point of the target
372      var currentPoint = new Object();
373      currentPoint.x = target.start.x;
374      currentPoint.y = target.start.y;
375
376      // draw the target
377      for (var i = 0; i < TARGET_PIECES; ++i)
378      {
379         // if this target piece is not hit, draw it
380         if (!hitStates[i])
381         {
382            context.beginPath(); // begin a new path for target
383
384            // alternate coloring the pieces yellow and blue
385            if (i % 2 === 0)
386               context.strokeStyle = "yellow";
387            else
388               context.strokeStyle = "blue";
389
```

Fig. 14.35 | Cannon Game function draw. (Part 2 of 3.)

```
390        context.moveTo(currentPoint.x, currentPoint.y); // path origin
391        context.lineTo(currentPoint.x, currentPoint.y + pieceLength);
392        context.lineWidth = lineWidth; // line width
393        context.stroke(); // draw path
394     } // end if
395
396     // move currentPoint to the start of the next piece
397     currentPoint.y += pieceLength;
398   } // end for
399 } // end function draw
400
```

Fig. 14.35 | Cannon Game function draw. (Part 3 of 3.)

14.19.11 Function showGameOverDialog

When the game ends, the showGameOverDialog function (Fig. 14.36) displays an alert indicating whether the player won or lost, the number of shots fired and the total time elapsed. Line 408 registers the window object's load event handler so that function setupGame is called when the cannon.html page loads.

```
401 // display an alert when the game ends
402 function showGameOverDialog(message)
403 {
404    alert(message + "\nShots fired: " + shotsFired +
405       "\nTotal time: " + timeElapsed + " seconds ");
406 } // end function showGameOverDialog
407
408 window.addEventListener("load", setupGame, false);
```

Fig. 14.36 | Cannon Game function showGameOverDialog.

14.20 save and restore Methods

The canvas's **state** includes its current style and transformations, which are maintained in a stack. The **save method** is used to save the context's current state. The **restore method** restores the context to its previous state. Figure 14.37 demonstrates using the save method to change a rectangle's fillStyle and the restore method to restore the fillStyle to the previous settings in the stack.

```
1  <!DOCTYPE html>
2
3  <!-- Fig. 14.37: saveandrestore.html -->
4  <!-- Saving the current state and restoring the previous state. -->
5  <html>
6     <head>
7        <meta charset = "utf-8">
8        <title>Save and Restore</title>
9     </head>
```

Fig. 14.37 | Saving the current state and restoring the previous state. (Part 1 of 2.)

```
10      <body>
11         <canvas id = "save" width = "400" height = "200">
12         </canvas>
13         <script>
14            function draw()
15            {
16               var canvas = document.getElementById("save");
17               var context = canvas.getContext("2d")
18
19               // draw rectangle and save the settings
20               context.fillStyle = "red"
21               context.fillRect(0, 0, 400, 200);
22               context.save();
23
24               // change the settings and save again
25               context.fillStyle = "orange"
26               context.fillRect(0, 40, 400, 160);
27               context.save();
28
29               // change the settings again
30               context.fillStyle = "yellow"
31               context.fillRect(0, 80, 400, 120);
32
33               // restore to previous settings and draw new rectangle
34               context.restore();
35               context.fillRect(0, 120, 400, 80);
36
37               // restore to original settings and draw new rectangle
38               context.restore();
39               context.fillRect(0, 160, 400, 40);
40            }
41            window.addEventListener( "load", draw, false );
42         </script>
43      </body>
44   </html>
```

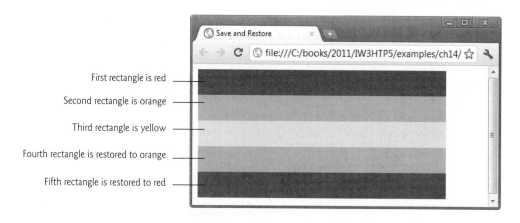

Fig. 14.37 | Saving the current state and restoring the previous state. (Part 2 of 2.)

We begin by drawing a red rectangle (lines 20–21), then using the **save** method to save its style (line 22). Next, we draw an orange rectangle and save its style (lines 25–27). Then we draw a yellow rectangle (lines 30–31) without saving its style.

Now we draw two rectangles, restoring the previous styles in reverse order of the stack—last in, first out. Line 34 uses the **restore** method to revert to the last-saved style in the stack. Then we draw a new rectangle (line 35). The result is an orange rectangle.

We use the `restore` method again to revert back to the first-saved style (line 38), then draw a fifth rectangle (line 39). The result is a red rectangle.

14.21 A Note on SVG

We've devoted this chapter to the new HTML5 `canvas`. Most current browsers also support **SVG (Scalable Vector Graphics)**, which offers a different approach to developing 2D graphics. Although we do not present SVG, we'll compare it briefly to HTML5 `canvas` so you can determine which might be more appropriate for particular applications.

SVG has been around since the early 2000s and is a mature technology with well-established standards. `canvas` is part of the HTML5 initiative and is an emerging technology with evolving standards.

`canvas` graphics are bitmapped—they're made of pixels. *Vector graphics* are made of scalable geometric primitives such as line segments and arcs.

Drawing is convenient in each of these technologies, but the mechanisms are different. SVG is XML-based, so it uses a *declarative* approach—you say *what* you want and SVG builds it for you. HTML5 `canvas` is JavaScript-based, so it uses an *imperative* approach—you say *how* to build your graphics by programming in JavaScript.

Anything you draw on a `canvas` ultimately becomes nothing more than bits. With SVG, each separate part of your graphic becomes an *object* that can be manipulated through the DOM. So, for example, it's easy to attach event handlers to items in SVG graphics. This makes SVG graphics more appropriate for interactive applications.

`canvas` is a low-level capability that offers *higher performance* than SVG; this makes `canvas` more appropriate for applications with intense performance demands, such as game programming. The DOM manipulation in SVG can degrade performance, particularly for more complex graphics.

SVG graphics easily and accurately scale to larger or smaller drawing surfaces. `canvas` graphics can be scaled, but the results may not be as eye pleasing.

SVG is more appropriate for accessibility applications for people with disabilities. It's easier, for example, for people with low vision or vision impairments to work with the XML text in an SVG document than with the pixels in a `canvas`.

`canvas` is more appropriate for pixel-manipulation applications (such as color-to-black-and-white image conversion; Section 14.12) and game-playing applications (such as the Cannon Game in Section 14.19). SVG has better animation capabilities, so game developers often use a *mix* of both the `canvas` and SVG approaches.

SVG has better text-rendering capabilities. And the text is still an object after it's on the screen, so you can easily edit it and change its attributes. Text on a `canvas` is "lost" in the bits, so it's difficult to modify.

SVG is more convenient for cross-platform graphics, which is becoming especially important with the proliferation of "form factors," such as desktops, notebooks, smartphones, tablets and various special-purpose devices such as car navigation systems.

An additional problem for canvas-based applications is that some web users disable JavaScript in their browsers. You should consider mastering both technologies.

14.22 A Note on canvas 3D

At the time of this writing, 3D functionality was not yet supported in canvas, though various tools and plug-ins enable you to create 3D effects. It's widely expected that a future version of the HTML5 canvas specification will support 3D capabilities. Figure 14.38 lists several websites with fun and interesting 3D examples.

URL	Description
http://www.kevs3d.co.uk/dev/html5logo/	Spinning 3D HTML5 logo.
http://sebleedelisle.com/demos/ GravityParticles/ParticlesForces3D2.html	A basic 3D particle distribution system.
http://www.kevs3d.co.uk/dev/canvask3d/ k3d_test.html	Includes several 3D shapes that rotate when clicked.
http://alteredqualia.com/canvasmol/#DNA	Spinning 3D molecules.
http://deanm.github.com/pre3d/monster.html	A cube that morphs into other 3D shapes.
http://html5canvastutorials.com/demos/ webgl/html5_canvas_webgl_3d_world/	Click and drag the mouse to smoothly change perspective in a 3D room.
http://onepixelahead.com/2010/09/24/10- awesome-html5-canvas-3d-examples/	Ten HTML5 canvas 3D examples including games and animations.
http://sixrevisions.com/web-development/ how-to-create-an-html5-3d-engine/	The tutorial, "How to Create an HTML5 3D Engine."
http://sebleedelisle.com/2011/02/html5- canvas-3d-particles-uniform-distribution/	The short tutorial, "HTML5 Canvas 3D Particles Uniform Distribution."
http://www.script-tutorials.com/ how-to-create-3d-canvas-object-in-html5/	The tutorial, "How to Create Animated 3D Canvas Objects in HTML5."
http://blogs.msdn.com/b/davrous/archive/ 2011/05/27/how-to-add-the-3d-animated- html5-logo-into-your-webpages-thanks-to- lt-canvas-gt.aspx	The tutorial, "How to Add the 3D Animated HTML5 Logo to Your Webpages."
http://www.bitstorm.it/blog/en/2011/05/ 3d-sphere-html5-canvas/	The tutorial, "Draw Old School 3D Sphere with HTML5."

Fig. 14.38 | HTML5 canvas 3D demos and tutorials.

Summary

Section 14.2 canvas Coordinate System
- The canvas coordinate system (p. 477) is a scheme for identifying every point on a canvas.
- By default, the upper-left corner of a canvas has the coordinates (0, 0).

- A coordinate pair has both an *x*-coordinate (the horizontal coordinate; p. 478) and a *y*-coordinate (the vertical coordinate; p. 478).

- The *x*-coordinate (p. 478) is the horizontal distance to the right from the left border of a canvas. The *y*-coordinate (p. 478) is the vertical distance downward from the top border of a canvas.

- The *x*-axis (p. 478) defines every horizontal coordinate, and the *y*-axis (p. 478) defines every vertical coordinate.

- You position text and shapes on a canvas by specifying their *x*- *y*-coordinates.

- Coordinate space units are measured in pixels ("picture elements"), which are the smallest units of resolution on a screen.

Section 14.3 Rectangles
- A canvas is a rectangular area in which you can draw.

- The canvas element (p. 479) has two attributes—width and height. The default width is 300, and the default height is 150.

- The fillStyle (p. 479) specifies the color of the rectangle.

- To specify the coordinates of the rectangle, we use fillRect (p. 479) in the format (x, y, w, h), where x and y are the coordinates for the top-left corner of the rectangle, w is the width of the rectangle and h is the height.

- The strokeStyle (p. 479) specifies the stroke color and lineWidth (p. 479) specifies the line width.

- The strokeRect method (p. 479) specifies the path of the stroke in the format (x, y, w, h).

- If the width and height are 0, no stroke will appear. If either the width or the height is 0, the result will be a line, not a rectangle.

Section 14.4 Using Paths to Draw Lines
- The beginPath method (p. 480) starts the path.

- The moveTo method (p. 480) sets the *x*- and *y*-coordinates of the path's origin.

- From the point of origin, we use the lineTo method (p. 480) specify the destinations for the path.

- The lineWidth attribute (p. 480) is used to change the thickness of the line. The default lineWidth is 1.0.

- The lineJoin attribute (p. 480) specifies the style of the corners where two lines meet. It has three possible values—bevel, round, and miter.

- The bevel lineJoin gives the path sloping corners.

- The lineCap attribute (p. 481) defines the style of the line ends. There are three possible values—butt, round, and square.

- A butt lineCap specifies that the line ends have edges perpendicular to the direction of the line and *no additional cap*.

- The strokeStyle attribute (p. 482) specifies the line color.

- The stroke method (p. 482) draws lines on a canvas. The default stroke color is black.

- The round lineJoin creates rounded corners. Then, the round lineCap adds a semicircular cap to the ends of the path. The diameter of the added cap is equal to the width of the line.

- The closePath method (p. 482) closes the path by drawing a line from the last specified destination back to the point of the path's origin.

- The miter lineJoin bevels the lines at an angle where they meet. For example, the lines that meet at a 90-degree angle have edges bevelled at 45-degree angles where they meet.

- A `square` `lineCap` adds a rectangular cap to the line ends. The length of the cap is equal to the line width, and the width of the cap is equal to half of the line width. The edge of the `square` `lineCap` is perpendicular to the direction of the line.

Section 14.5 Drawing Arcs and Circles

- Arcs are portions of the circumference of a circle. To draw an arc, you specify the arc's starting angle and ending angle (p. 482) measured in *radians*—the ratio of the arc's length to its radius.

- The `arc` method (p. 482) draws the circle using five arguments. The first two arguments represent the *x*- and *y*-coordinates of the center of the circle. The third argument is the radius of the circle. The fourth and fifth arguments are the arc's starting and ending angles in radians.

- The sixth argument is optional and specifies the direction in which the arc's path is drawn. By default, the sixth argument is `false`, indicating that the arc is drawn clockwise. If the argument is `true`, the arc is drawn counterclockwise (or anticlockwise).

- The constant `Math.PI` is the JavaScript representation of the mathematical constant π, the ratio of a circle's circumference to its diameter. 2π radians represents a 360-degree arc, π radians is 180 degrees and $\pi/2$ radians is 90 degrees.

Section 14.6 Shadows

- The `shadowBlur` attribute (p. 484) specifies the blur and color or a shadow. By default, the blur is 0 (no blur). The higher the value, the more blurred the edges of the shadow will appear.

- A positive `shadowOffsetX` attribute (p. 484) moves the shadow to the right of the rectangle.

- A positive `shadowOffsetY` attribute (p. 484) moves the shadow down from the rectangle

- The `shadowColor` attribute (p. 484) specifies the color of the shadow.

- Using a negative `shadowOffsetX` moves the shadow to the left of the rectangle.

- Using a negative `shadowOffsetY` moves the shadow up from the rectangle.

- The default value for the `shadowOffsetX` and `shadowOffsetY` is 0 (no shadow).

Section 14.7 Quadratic Curves

- Quadratic curves (p. 486) have a starting point, an ending point and a single point of inflection.

- The `quadraticCurveTo` method (p. 486) uses four arguments. The first two, *cpx* and *cpy*, are the are the coordinates of the control point—the point of the curve's inflection. The third and fourth arguments, *x* and *y*, are the coordinates of the ending point. The starting point is the last subpath destination, specified using the `moveTo` or `lineTo` methods.

Section 14.8 Bezier Curves

- Bezier curves (p. 488) have a starting point, an ending point and two control points through which the curve passes. These can be used to draw curves with one or two points of inflection, depending on the coordinates of the four points.

- The `bezierCurveTo` method (p. 488) uses six arguments. The first two arguments, *cp1x* and *cp1y*, are the coordinates of the first control point. The third and fourth arguments, *cp2x* and *cp2y*, are the coordinates for the second control point. Finally, the fifth and sixth arguments, *x* and *y*, are the coordinates of the ending point. The starting point is the last subpath destination, specified using either the `moveTo` or `lineTo` method.

Section 14.9 Linear Gradients

- The `createLinearGradient` method (p. 489) has four arguments that represent `x0`, `y0`, `x1`, `y1`, where the first two arguments are the *x*- and *y*-coordinates of the gradient's start and the last two are the *x*- and *y*-coordinates of the end.

- The start and end have the same *x*-coordinates but different *y*-coordinates, so the start of the gradient is a point at the top of the canvas directly above the point at the end of the gradient at the bottom. This creates a vertical linear gradient that starts at the top and changes as it moves to the bottom of the canvas.

- The addColorStop method (p. 491) adds color stops to the gradient. Note that each color stop has a positive value between 0 (the start of the gradient) and 1 (the end of the gradient). For each color stop, specify a color.

- The fillStyle method specifies a gradient, then the fillRect method draws the gradient on the canvas.

- To draw a horizontal gradient, use the createLinearGradient method where the start and end have different *x*-coordinates but the same *y*-coordinates.

Section 14.10 Radial Gradients

- A radial gradient is comprised of two circles—an inner circle where the gradient starts and an outer circle where the gradient ends.

- The createRadialGradient method (p. 491) has six arguments that represent x0, y0, r0, x1, y1, r1, where the first three arguments are the *x*- and *y*-coordinates and the radius of the gradient's start circle, and the last three arguments are the *x*- and *y*-coordinates and the radius of the end circle.

- Drawing concentric circles with the same *x*- and *y*-coordinates but different radiuses creates a radial gradient that starts in a common center and changes as it moves outward to the end circle.

- If the start and end circles are not concentric circles, the effect is altered.

Section 14.11 Images

- The drawImage method (p. 493) draws an image to a canvas using five arguments. The first argument can be an image, canvas or video element. The second and third arguments are the destination *x*- and destination *y*-coordinates—these indicate the position of the top-left corner of the image on the canvas. The fourth and fifth arguments are the destination width and destination height.

Section 14.12 Image Manipulation: Processing the Individual Pixels of a canvas

- You can obtain a canvas's pixels and manipulate their red, green, blue and alpha (RGBA) values.

- You can change the RGBA values with the input elements of type range defined in the body.

- The method getImageData (p. 498) obtains an object that contains the pixels to manipulate. The method receives a bounding rectangle representing the portion of the canvas to get.

- The returned object contains an array named data which stores every pixel in the selected rectangular area as four elements in the array. Each pixel's data is stored in the order red, green, blue, alpha. So, the first four elements in the array represent the RGBA values of the pixel in row 0 and column 0, the next four elements represent the pixel in row 0 and column 1, etc.

Section 14.13 Patterns

- The createPattern method (p. 499) takes two arguments. The first argument is the image for the pattern, which can be an image element, a canvas element or a video element. The second argument specifies how the image will be repeated to create the pattern and can be one of four values—repeat (repeats horizontally and vertically), repeat-x (repeats horizontally), repeat-y (repeats vertically) or no-repeat.

- Use the fillStyle attribute pattern and use the fill method to draw the pattern to the canvas.

Section 14.14 Transformations

- You can change the transformation matrix (the coordinates) on the canvas using method translate (p. 500) so that the center of the canvas becomes the point of origin with the *x*, *y* values 0, 0.

- The scale method (p. 501) can stretch a circle to create an ellipse. The *x* value represents the horizontal scale factor, the *y* value the vertical scale factor.

- The rotate method (p. 502) allows you to create animated rotations on a canvas.

- To rotate an image around its center, change the transformation matrix on the canvas using the translate method. The rotate method takes one argument—the angle of the clockwise rotation, expressed in radians.

- The setInterval method (p. 503) of the window object takes two arguments. The first is the name of the function to call (rotate) and the second is the number of milliseconds between calls.

- The clearRect method (p. 503) clears the rectangle's pixels from the canvas, converting them back to transparent. This method takes four arguments—*x*, *y*, *width* and *height*.

- The transform method (p. 504) allows you to skew, scale, rotate and translate elements without using separate transformation methods.

- The transform method takes six arguments in the format (*a*, *b*, *c*, *d*, *e*, *f*) based on a transformation matrix. The first argument, *a*, is the *x*-scale—the factor by which to scale an element horizontally. The second argument, *b*, is the *y*-skew. The third argument, *c*, is the *x*-skew. The fourth argument, *d*, is the *y*-scale—the factor by which to scale an element vertically. The fifth argument, *e*, is the *x*-translation and the sixth argument, *f*, is the *y*-translation.

Section 14.15 Text

- The font attribute (p. 506) specifies the style, size and font of the text.

- The textBaseline attribute (p. 507) specifies the alignment points of the text. There are six different attribute values—top, hanging, middle, alphabetic, ideographic and bottom.

- Method fillText (p. 507) draws the text to the canvas. This method takes three arguments. The first is the text being drawn to the canvas. The second and third arguments are the *x*- and *y*-coordinates. You may include the optional fourth argument, maxWidth, to limit the width of the text.

- The textAlign attribute (p. 507) specifies the horizontal alignment of the text relative to the *x*-coordinate of the text. There are five possible textAlign attribute values—left, right, center, start (the default value) and end.

- The lineWidth attribute specifies the thickness of the stroke used to draw the text.

- The strokeStyle specifies the color of the text.

- Using strokeText instead of fillText draws outlined text instead of filled text.

Section 14.16 Resizing the **canvas** to Fill the Browser Window

- Use a CSS style sheet to set the position of the canvas to absolute and set both its width and height to 100%, rather than using fixed coordinates.

- Use JavaScript function draw to draw the canvas when the application is rendered.

- Use the fillRect method to draw the color to the canvas. The *x*- and *y*-coordinates are 0, 0—the top left of the canvas. The the x1 value is context.canvas.width and the y1 value is context.value.height, so no matter the size of the window, the x1 value will always be the width of the canvas and the y1 value the height of the canvas.

Section 14.17 Alpha Transparency

- The globalAlpha attribute (p. 509) value can be any number between 0 (fully transparent) and 1 (the default value, which is fully opaque).

Section 14.18 Compositing

- Compositing (p. 511) allows you to control the layering of shapes and images on a canvas using two attributes—the globalAlpha attribute and the globalCompositeOperation attribute (p. 511).

- There are 11 globalCompositeOperation attribute values. The source is the image being drawn to the canvas. The destination is the current bitmap on the canvas.

- If you use source-in, the source image is displayed where the images overlap and both are opaque. Both images are transparent where there is no overlap.

- Using source-out, if the source image is opaque and the destination is transparent, the source image is displayed where the images overlap. Both images are transparent where there is no overlap.

- source-over (the default value) places the source image over the destination. The source image is displayed where it's opaque and the images overlap. The destination is displayed where there is no overlap.

- destination-atop places the destination on top of the source image. If both images are opaque, the destination is displayed where the images overlap. If the destination is transparent but the source image is opaque, the source image is displayed where the images overlap. The source image is transparent where there is no overlap.

- destination-in displays the destination image where the images overlap and both are opaque. Both images are transparent where there is no overlap.

- Using destination-out, if the destination image is opaque and the source image is transparent, the destination is displayed where the images overlap. Both images are transparent where there is no overlap.

- destination-over places the destination image over the source image. The destination image is displayed where it's opaque and the images overlap. The source image is displayed where there's no overlap.

- lighter displays the sum of the source-image color and destination-image color—up to the maximum RGB color value (255)—where the images overlap. Both images are normal elsewhere.

- Using copy, if the images overlap, only the source image is displayed (the destination is ignored).

- With xor, the images are transparent where they overlap and normal elsewhere.

Section 14.19 Cannon Game

- The HTML5 audio element may contain multiple source elements for the audio file in several formats, so that you can support cross-browser playback of the sounds.

- You can create your own properties on JavaScript Objects simply by assigning a value to a property name.

- Collision detection determines whether the cannonball has collided with any of the canvas's edges, with the blocker or with a section of the target. Game-development frameworks generally provide more sophisticated, built-in collision-detection capabilities.

Section 14.20 save and restore Methods

- The canvas's state (p. 528) includes its current style and transformations, which are maintained in a stack.

- The save method (p. 528) is used to save the context's current state.

- The restore method (p. 528) restores the context to its previous state.

Section 14.21 A Note on SVG

- Vector graphics are made of scalable geometric primitives such as line segments and arcs.

- SVG (Scalable Vector Graphics, p. 498) is XML-based, so it uses a declarative approach—you say what you want and SVG builds it for you. HTML5 canvas is JavaScript-based, so it uses an imperative approach–you say how to build your graphics by programming in JavaScript.

- With SVG, each separate part of your graphic becomes an object that can be manipulated through the DOM.

- SVG is more convenient for cross-platform graphics, which is becoming especially important with the proliferation of "form factors," such as desktops, notebooks, smartphones, tablets and various special-purpose devices such as car navigation systems.

Self-Review Exercises

14.1 State whether each of the following is *true* or *false*. If *false*, explain why.
   a) The strokeStyle attribute specifies the line width.
   b) The bevel lineJoin gives the path square corners.
   c) canvas's roundedRect method is used to build rounded rectangles.
   d) The fillRect method is used to specify a color or gradient.
   e) By default, the origin (0, 0) is located at the exact center of the monitor.
   f) The restore method restores the context to its initial state.
   g) The canvas's state includes its current style and transformations, which are maintained in a stack.

14.2 Fill in the blanks in each of the following:
   a) The canvas element has two attributes—_____ and _____.
   b) When drawing a rectangle, the _____ method specifies the path of the stroke in the format (*x*, *y*, *w*, *h*).
   c) The lineCap attribute has the possible values _____, _____, and _____.
   d) The _____ method draws a line from the last specified destination back to the point of the path's origin.
   e) The _____ method specifies the three points in the Bezier curve.
   f) The _____ attribute specifies the color of the shadow.
   g) _____ are portions of the circumference of a circle and are measured in _____.
   h) The _____ method is used to save the context's current state.

Answers to Self-Review Exercises

14.1 a) False. The strokeStyle attribute specifies the stroke color. b) False. The bevel lineJoin gives the path sloping corners. c) False. Unlike CSS3, there's no roundedRect method in canvas. d) False. The fillStyle method specifies a color gradient, then the fillRect method draws the color or gradient on the canvas. e) False. The origin (0, 0) corresponds to the upper-left corner of the canvas by default. f) False. The restore method restores the context to its previous state. g) True.

14.2 a) width, height. b) strokeRect. c) butt, round, square. d) closePath. e) bezierCurveTo. f) shadowColor. g) Arcs, radians. h) save.

Exercises

14.3 State whether each of the following is *true* or *false*. If *false*, explain why.
   a) The moveTo method sets the *x*- and *y*-coordinates of the path's destination.
   b) A square lineCap specifies that the line ends have edges perpendicular to the direction of the line and no additional cap.
   c) A vertical gradient has different *x*-coordinates but the same *y*-coordinates.
   d) In the canvas coordinate system, *x* values increase from left to right.

e) Bezier curves have a starting point, an ending point and a single point of inflection.

14.4 Fill in the blanks in each of the following:
a) The _____ method starts the path.
b) The lineJoin attribute has three possible values—_____, _____, and _____.
c) The _____ attribute specifies the line color.
d) The _____ lineJoin bevels the lines at an angle where they meet.
e) Each color stop in a gradient has a value between _____ (the start of the gradient) and _____ (the end of the gradient).
f) The _____ attribute specifies the horizontal alignment of text relative to the *x*-coordinate of the text.
g) The constant _____ is the JavaScript representation of the mathematical constant π.

14.5 *(Text Shadow)* Create a shadow on the phrase "HTML5 Canvas" with an offset-x of 4px, an offset-y of 10px, a blur radius of 3px and a text-shadow color red.

14.6 *(Rounded Rectangle)* Generalize the example in Fig. 14.7 into a roundedRect function and call it thrice with different arguments to place three different rounded rectangles on the canvas.

14.7 *(Diagonal Linear Gradient)* Create a canvas with a width and height of 250px. Create a diagonal linear gradient using the following colors —Red, Yellow, Green, Blue, Gray.

14.8 *(Horizontal Linear Gradient)* Draw a non-rectangular shape using lines, then add a horizontal linear gradient to the shape with three color stops.

14.9 *(Radial Gradient)* Create a canvas with a width and height of 250px. Create a radial gradient with three colors. Start the gradient in the bottom-left corner with the colors changing as they move to the right.

14.10 *(Shadows)* Create two canvases. On the first, draw a rectangle. Add a shadow that's offset up and to the left of the rectangle and that has a shadowBlur of 30. On the second canvas, draw a triangle. Add a shadow that's offset down and to the right of the triangle and has a shadowBlur of 15.

14.11 *(Concentric Circles)* Write a script that draws ten concentric circles. The circles should be separated from one another by 8 pixels. Vary the colors and thicknesses of each.

14.12 *(Changing the Font)* Enable a user to dynamically change the font style and size as required.

14.13 *(Live Canvas Coordinate System)* Draw the canvas coordinate system. As you move the mouse around, dynamically display its *x*- and *y*- coordinates at the extreme left corner.

14.14 *(Moving Circle)* Crate a square canvas with a width and height of 500. Write a script that continuously moves a circle counterclockwise in a diamond pattern so that the circle touches the center of each edge of the canvas.

14.15 *(Draw Street Signs)* Go to http://mutcd.fhwa.dot.gov/ser-shs_millennium_eng.htm and find three different street signs of your choosing. Draw each on a canvas.

14.16 *(Printing in a Larger Font)* Write a script that enables a (visually impaired) user to dynamically scale the font size of text on a canvas to a comfortable size. Use a slider to control the font size.

14.17 *(Painting)* Create a painting application that allows the you to create art by clicking and dragging the mouse across the canvas. Include options for changing the drawing color and line thickness. Provide red, green and blue sliders that allow you to select the RGB color. Include a color swatch below the three sliders so that as you move each slider, the color swatch shows you the current drawing color. Provide a line-width dialog with a single slider that controls the thickness of the line that you'll draw. Also include options that allow you to turn the cursor into an eraser, to clear the screen and to save the current drawing. At any point, you should be able to clear the entire drawing from the canvas.

14.18 *(Fireworks Text Skywriter)* The website http://js-fireworks.appspot.com/ is a fun HTML5 application that uses canvas. You can enter a message, which is then written in the sky over the London skyline using a fireworks effect. The author provides the open-source code. Modify the example to create your own skywriting effect over an image of your choosing.

14.19 *(Live canvas Coordinate System)* Draw the canvas coordinate system. As you move the mouse around, dynamically display its *x*- and *y*-coordinates.

14.20 *(Kaleidoscope)* Create an animated kaleidoscope effect.

14.21 *(Random Lines Art)* Write a script that draws 50 lines with random lengths, locations, widths, orientations, colors, and transparencies.

14.22 *(Creating Random 2D Art)* Create random art using at least two circles, rectangles and triangles.

14.23 *(Flashing Image)* Write a script that repeatedly flashes an image on the screen. Do this by alternating the image with a plain background-color image.

14.24 *(Cannon Game Enhancements)* In Section 14.19 we showed you how to write a Cannon Game using JavaScript and HTML5 canvas. Add the following enhancements and others of your choosing:

1. Add an "explosion animation" each time the cannonball hits one of the sections of the target. Match the animation with the "explosion sound" that plays when a piece of the target is hit.

2. Play a sound when the blocker hits the top or the bottom of the screen.

3. Play a sound when the target hits the top ot the bottom of the screen.

4. Add a trail to the cannonball; erase it when the cannonball hits the target.

5. Modify the click events so that a single tap aims the cannon, and the second single tap fires it.

6. Add a scoring mechanism and keep track of the all-time best score.

7. Using CSS3 Media Queries, determine the size of the display area and scale the cannon game elements accordingly.

14.25 *(Randomly Erasing an Image)* Suppose an image is displayed in a canvas. One way to erase the image is simply to set every pixel to the same background color immediately, but the visual effect is dull. Write a JavaScript program that displays an image, then erases it by using random-number generation to select individual pixels to erase. After most of the image is erased, erase all the remaining pixels at once. You might try several variants of this problem. For example, you might display lines, circles or shapes randomly to erase regions of the screen.

14.26 *(Text Flasher)* Create a script that repeatedly flashes text on the screen. Do this by alternating the text with a plain background-color image. Allow the user to control the "blink speed" and the background color or pattern.

14.27 *(Digital Clock)* Implement a script that displays a digital clock on the screen. Include alarm-clock functionality.

14.28 *(Analog Clock)* Create a script that displays an analog clock with hour, minute and second hands that move appropriately as the time changes.

14.29 *(Calling Attention to an Image)* If you want to emphasize an image, you might place a row of simulated light bulbs around it. You can let the light bulbs flash in unison or fire on and off in sequence one after the other.

14.30 *(Animation)* Create a general-purpose JavaScript animation. It should allow the user to specify the sequence of frames to be displayed, the speed at which the images are displayed, audios and videos to be played while the animation is running and so on.

14.31 *(Random Interimage Transition)* In Fig. 5.14, we used CSS3 to *"melt"* one image into another. This provides a nice visual effect. If you're displaying one image in a given area on the screen and you'd like to transition to another image in the same area, store the new screen image in an off-screen "buffer" and *randomly* copy pixels from it to the display area, overlaying the pixels already at those locations. When the vast majority of the pixels have been copied, copy the entire new image to the display area to be sure you're displaying the complete new image. You might try several variants of this problem. For example, select all the pixels in a randomly chosen straight line or shape in the new image and overlay them above the corresponding positions of the old image.

14.32 *(Background Audio)* Add background audio to one of your favorite applications.

14.33 *(Scrolling Marquee Sign)* Create a script that scrolls dotted characters from right to left (or from left to right if that's appropriate for your language) across a marquee-like display sign. As an option, display the text in a continuous loop, so that after the text disappears at one end, it reappears at the other.

14.34 *(Scrolling-Image Marquee)* Create a script that scrolls a series of images across a marquee screen.

14.35 *(Dynamic Audio and Graphical Kaleidoscope)* Write a kaleidoscope script that displays reflected graphics to simulate the popular children's toy. Incorporate audio effects that "mirror" your script's dynamically changing graphics.

14.36 *(Automatic Jigsaw Puzzle Generator)* Create a jigsaw puzzle generator and manipulator. The user specifies an image. Your script loads and displays the image, then breaks it into randomly selected shapes and shuffles them. The user then uses the mouse to move the pieces around to solve the puzzle. Add appropriate audio sounds as the pieces are moved around and snapped back into place. You might keep tabs on each piece and where it really belongs—then use audio effects to help the user get the pieces into the correct positions.

14.37 *(Maze Generator and Walker)* Develop a multimedia-based maze generator and traverser script. Let the user customize the maze by specifying the number of rows and columns and by indicating the level of difficulty. Have an animated mouse walk the maze. Use audio to dramatize the movement of your mouse character.

14.38 *(Maze Traversal Using Recursive Backtracking)* The grid of #s and dots (.) in Fig. 14.39 is a two-dimensional array representation of a maze. The #s represent the walls of the maze, and the dots represent locations in the possible paths through the maze. A move can be made only to a location in the array that contains a dot.

Write a *recursive* method (`mazeTraversal`) to walk through mazes like the one in Fig. 14.39. The method should receive as arguments a 12-by-12 character array representing the maze and the current location in the maze (the first time this method is called, the current location should be the entry point of the maze). As `mazeTraversal` attempts to locate the exit, it should place the character x in each square in the path. There's a simple algorithm for walking through a maze that guarantees finding the exit (assuming there's an exit—if there's no exit, you'll arrive at the starting location again). For details, visit: `http://en.wikipedia.org/wiki/Maze_solving_algorithm#Wall_follower`.

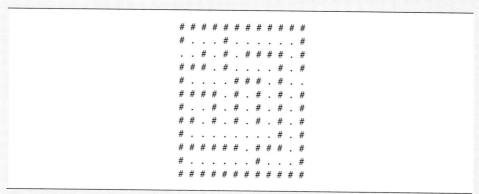

Fig. 14.39 | Two-dimensional array representation of a maze.

14.39 *(Generating Mazes Randomly)* Write a method mazeGenerator that takes as an argument a two-dimensional 12-by-12 character array and randomly produces a maze. The method should also provide the starting and ending locations of the maze. Test your method mazeTraversal from Exercise 14.38, using several randomly generated mazes.

14.40 *(Mazes of Any Size)* Generalize methods mazeTraversal and mazeGenerator of Exercise 14.38 and Exercise 14.39 to process mazes of any width and height.

14.41 *(One-Armed Bandit)* Develop a multimedia simulation of a "one-armed bandit." Have three spinning wheels. Place symbols and images of various fruits on each wheel. Use random-number generation to simulate the spinning of each wheel and the stopping of each wheel on a symbol.

14.42 *(Horse Race)* Create a simulation of a horse race. Have multiple contenders. Use audios for a race announcer. Play the appropriate audios to indicate the correct status of each contender throughout the race. Use audios to announce the final results. You might try to simulate the kinds of horse-racing games that are often played at carnivals. The players take turns at the mouse and have to perform some skill-oriented manipulation with it to advance their horses.

14.43 *(Shuffleboard)* Develop a multimedia-based simulation of the game of shuffleboard. Use appropriate audio and visual effects.

14.44 *(Game of Pool)* Create a multimedia-based simulation of the game of pool. Each player takes turns using the mouse to position a pool cue and hit it against the ball at the appropriate angle to try to make other balls fall into the pockets. Your script should keep score.

14.45 *(Fireworks Designer)* Create a script that enables the user to create a customized fireworks display. Create a variety of fireworks demonstrations. Then orchestrate the firing of the fireworks for maximum effect. You might synchronize your fireworks with audios or videos.

14.46 *(Floor Planner)* Develop a script that will help someone arrange furniture in a room.

14.47 *(Crossword Puzzle)* Crossword puzzles are among the most popular pastimes. Develop a multimedia-based crossword-puzzle script. Your script should enable the player to place and erase words easily. Tie your script to a large computerized dictionary. Your script also should be able to suggest completion of words on which letters have already been filled in. Provide other features that will make the crossword-puzzle enthusiast's job easier.

14.48 *(15 Puzzle)* Write a multimedia-based script that enables the user to play the game of 15. The game is played on a 4-by-4 board having a total of 16 slots. One slot is empty; the others are occupied by 15 tiles numbered 1 through 15. The user can move any tile next to the currently empty slot into that slot by clicking on the tile. Your script should create the board with the tiles in random order. The goal is to arrange the tiles into sequential order, row by row.

14.49 *(Reaction Time/Reaction Precision Tester)* Create a script that moves a randomly created shape around the screen. The user moves the mouse to catch and click on the shape. The shape's speed and size can be varied. Keep statistics on how long the user typically takes to catch a shape of a given size and speed. The user will have more difficulty catching faster-moving, smaller shapes.

14.50 *(Rotating Images)* Create a script that lets you rotate an image through some number of degrees (out of a maximum of 360 degrees). The script should let you specify that you want to spin the image continuously. It should let you adjust the spin speed dynamically.

14.51 *(Coloring Black-and-White Photographs and Images)* Create a script that lets you paint a black-and-white photograph with color. Provide a color palette for selecting colors. Your script should let you apply different colors to different regions of the image.

14.52 *(Vacuuming Robot)* Start with a blank canvas that represents the floor of the room. Add obstacles such as a chair, couch, table legs, floor-standing vase, etc. Add your vacuum-cleaning robot. Start it moving in a random direction. It must avoid obstacles and must eventually vacuum the entire room. It has a known width and height. Keep track of which pixels have been "vacuumed." Keep track of the percentage of the canvas that has been vacuumed and how much time it has taken.

14.53 *(Eyesight Tester)* You've probably had your eyesight tested several times—to qualify for a driver's license, etc. In these exams, you're asked to cover one eye, then read out loud the letters from an eyesight chart called a Snellen chart. The letters are arranged in 11 rows and include only the letters C, D, E, F, L, N, O, P, T, Z. The first row has one letter in a very large font. As you move down the page, the number of letters in each row increases by one and the font size of the letters decreases, ending with a row of 11 letters in a very small font. Your ability to read the letters accurately measures your visual acuity. Create an eyesight testing chart similar to the Snellen chart used by medical professionals. To learn more about the Snellen chart and to see an example, visit `http:/ /en.wikipedia.org/wiki/Snellen_chart`.

XML

15

*Like everything metaphysical,
the harmony between thought
and reality is to be found in the
grammar of the language.*
—Ludwig Wittgenstein

*I played with an idea, and grew
willful; tossed it into the air;
transformed it; let it escape and
recaptured it; made it iridescent
with fancy, and winged it with
paradox.*
—Oscar Wilde

Objectives

In this chapter you'll:

- Mark up data using XML.

- Learn how XML namespaces help provide unique XML element and attribute names.

- Create DTDs and schemas for specifying and validating the structure of an XML document.

- Create and use simple XSL style sheets to render XML document data.

- Retrieve and manipulate XML data programmatically using JavaScript.

15.1 Introduction

The **Extensible Markup Language** (XML) was developed in 1996 by the **World Wide Web Consortium's (W3C's)** XML Working Group. XML is a widely supported **open technology** (i.e., nonproprietary technology) for describing data that has become the standard format for data exchanged between applications over the Internet.

Web applications use XML extensively, and web browsers provide many XML-related capabilities. Sections 15.2–15.7 introduce XML and XML-related technologies—XML namespaces for providing unique XML element and attribute names, and Document Type Definitions (DTDs) and XML Schemas for validating XML documents. These sections support the use of XML in many subsequent chapters. Sections 15.8–15.9 present additional XML technologies and key JavaScript capabilities for loading and manipulating XML documents programmatically—this material is optional but is recommended if you plan to use XML in your own applications.

15.2 XML Basics

XML permits document authors to create **markup** (i.e., a text-based notation for describing data) for virtually any type of information, enabling them to create entirely new markup languages for describing any type of data, such as mathematical formulas, software-configuration instructions, chemical molecular structures, music, news, recipes and financial reports. XML describes data in a way that human beings can understand and computers can process.

Figure 15.1 is a simple XML document that describes information for a baseball player. We focus on lines 5–9 to introduce basic XML syntax. You'll learn about the other elements of this document in Section 15.3.

```
1   <?xml version = "1.0"?>
2
3   <!-- Fig. 15.1: player.xml -->
4   <!-- Baseball player structured with XML -->
5   <player>
6      <firstName>John</firstName>
7      <lastName>Doe</lastName>
8      <battingAverage>0.375</battingAverage>
9   </player>
```

Fig. 15.1 | XML that describes a baseball player's information.

XML Elements

XML documents contain text that represents content (i.e., data), such as John (line 6 of Fig. 15.1), and **elements** that specify the document's structure, such as firstName (line 6 of Fig. 15.1). XML documents delimit elements with **start tags** and **end tags**. A start tag consists of the element name in **angle brackets** (e.g., <player> and <firstName> in lines 5 and 6, respectively). An end tag consists of the element name preceded by a **forward slash** (/) in angle brackets (e.g., </firstName> and </player> in lines 6 and 9, respectively). An element's start and end tags enclose text that represents a piece of data (e.g., the player's firstName—John—in line 6, which is enclosed by the <firstName> start tag and </firstName> end tag). Every XML document must have exactly one **root element** that contains all the other elements. In Fig. 15.1, the root element is player (lines 5–9).

XML Vocabularies

XML-based markup languages—called XML **vocabularies**—provide a means for describing particular types of data in standardized, structured ways. Some XML vocabularies include XHTML (Extensible HyperText Markup Language), MathML™ (for mathematics), VoiceXML™ (for speech), CML (Chemical Markup Language—for chemistry), XBRL (Extensible Business Reporting Language—for financial data exchange) and others that we discuss in Section 15.7.

Massive amounts of data are currently stored on the Internet in many formats (e.g., databases, web pages, text files). Much of this data, especially that which is passed between systems, will soon take the form of XML. Organizations see XML as the future of data encoding. Information-technology groups are planning ways to integrate XML into their systems. Industry groups are developing custom XML vocabularies for most major industries that will allow business applications to communicate in common languages. For example, many web services allow web-based applications to exchange data seamlessly through standard protocols based on XML.

The next generation of the web is being built on an XML foundation, enabling you to develop more sophisticated web-based applications. XML allows you to assign meaning to what would otherwise be random pieces of data. As a result, programs can "understand" the data they manipulate. For example, a web browser might view a street address in a simple web page as a string of characters without any real meaning. In an XML document, however, this data can be clearly identified (i.e., marked up) as an address. A program that uses the document can recognize this data as an address and provide links to a map of that location, driving directions from that location or other location-specific information. Likewise, an application can recognize names of people, dates, ISBN numbers and any other type of XML-encoded data. The application can then present users with other related information, providing a richer, more meaningful user experience.

Viewing and Modifying XML Documents

XML documents are highly portable. Viewing or modifying an XML document—which is a text file that usually ends with the .xml filename extension—does not require special software, although many software tools exist, and new ones are frequently released that make it more convenient to develop XML-based applications. Any text editor that supports ASCII/Unicode characters can open XML documents for viewing and editing. Also, most web browsers can display XML documents in a formatted manner that shows the

XML's structure (as we show in Section 15.3). An important characteristic of XML is that it's both human and machine readable.

Processing XML Documents

Processing an XML document requires software called an **XML parser** (or **XML processor**). A parser makes the document's data available to applications. While reading an XML document's contents, a parser checks that the document follows the syntax rules specified by the W3C's XML Recommendation (www.w3.org/XML). XML syntax requires a single root element, a start tag and end tag for each element, and properly nested tags (i.e., the end tag for a nested element must appear before the end tag of the enclosing element). Furthermore, XML is case sensitive, so the proper capitalization must be used in elements. A document that conforms to this syntax is a **well-formed XML document** and is syntactically correct. We present fundamental XML syntax in Section 15.3. If an XML parser can process an XML document successfully, that XML document is well-formed. Parsers can provide access to XML-encoded data in well-formed documents only. XML parsers are often built into browsers and other software.

Validating XML Documents

An XML document can reference a **Document Type Definition (DTD)** or a **schema** that defines the document's proper structure. When an XML document references a DTD or a schema, some parsers (called **validating parsers**) can read it and check that the XML document follows the structure it defines. If the XML document conforms to the DTD/schema (i.e., has the appropriate structure), the document is **valid**. For example, if in Fig. 15.1 we were referencing a DTD that specified that a player element must have firstName, lastName and battingAverage elements, then omitting the lastName element (line 7 in Fig. 15.1) would invalidate the XML document player.xml. However, it would still be well-formed, because it follows proper XML syntax (i.e., it has one root element, each element has a start tag and an end tag, and the elements are nested properly). By definition, a valid XML document is well-formed. Parsers that cannot check for document conformity against DTDs/schemas are **non-validating parsers**—they determine only whether an XML document is well-formed, not whether it's valid.

We discuss validation, DTDs and schemas, as well as the key differences between these two types of structural specifications, in Sections 15.5–15.6. For now, note that schemas are XML documents themselves, whereas DTDs are not. As you'll learn in Section 15.6, this difference presents several advantages in using schemas over DTDs.

Software Engineering Observation 15.1

DTDs and schemas are essential for business-to-business (B2B) transactions and mission-critical systems. Validating XML documents ensures that disparate systems can manipulate data structured in standardized ways and prevents errors caused by missing or malformed data.

Formatting and Manipulating XML Documents

Most XML documents contain only data, so applications that process XML documents must decide how to manipulate or display the data. For example, a PDA (personal digital assistant) may render an XML document differently than a wireless phone or a desktop computer. You can use **Extensible Stylesheet Language (XSL)** to specify rendering instructions for different platforms. We discuss XSL in Section 15.8.

XML-processing programs can also search, sort and manipulate XML data using XSL. Some other XML-related technologies are XPath (XML Path Language—a language for accessing parts of an XML document), XSL-FO (XSL Formatting Objects—an XML vocabulary used to describe document formatting) and XSLT (XSL Transformations—a language for transforming XML documents into other documents). We present XSLT and XPath in Section 15.8.

15.3 Structuring Data

In this section and throughout this chapter, we create our own XML markup. XML allows you to describe data precisely in a well-structured format.

XML Markup for an Article
In Fig. 15.2, we present an XML document that marks up a simple article using XML. The line numbers shown are for reference only and are not part of the XML document.

```
 1   <?xml version = "1.0"?>
 2
 3   <!-- Fig. 15.2: article.xml -->
 4   <!-- Article structured with XML -->
 5   <article>
 6      <title>Simple XML</title>
 7      <date>July 4, 2007</date>
 8      <author>
 9         <firstName>John</firstName>
10         <lastName>Doe</lastName>
11      </author>
12      <summary>XML is pretty easy.</summary>
13      <content>This chapter presents examples that use XML.</content>
14   </article>
```

Fig. 15.2 | XML used to mark up an article.

XML Declaration
This document begins with an **XML declaration** (line 1), which identifies the document as an XML document. The **version attribute** specifies the XML version to which the document conforms. The current XML standard is version 1.0. Though the W3C released a version 1.1 specification in February 2004, this newer version is not yet widely supported. The W3C may continue to release new versions as XML evolves to meet the requirements of different fields.

Portability Tip 15.1

Documents should include the XML declaration to identify the version of XML used. A document that lacks an XML declaration might be assumed to conform to the latest version of XML—when it does not, errors could result.

Blank Space and Comments

As in most markup languages, blank lines (line 2), white spaces and indentation help improve readability. Blank lines are normally ignored by XML parsers. XML comments (lines 3–4), which begin with <!-- and end with -->, can be placed almost anywhere in an XML document and can span multiple lines. There must be one end marker (-->) for each begin marker (<!--).

Common Programming Error 15.1

Placing any characters, including white space, before the XML declaration is an error.

Common Programming Error 15.2

In an XML document, each start tag must have a matching end tag; omitting either tag is an error. Soon, you'll learn how such errors are detected.

Common Programming Error 15.3

XML is case sensitive. Using different cases for the start-tag and end-tag names for the same element is a syntax error.

Root Node and XML Prolog

In Fig. 15.2, article (lines 5–14) is the root element. The lines that precede the root element (lines 1–4) are the XML **prolog**. In an XML prolog, the XML declaration must appear before the comments and any other markup.

XML Element Names

The elements we use in the example do not come from any specific markup language. Instead, we chose the element names and markup structure that best describe our particular data. You can invent elements to mark up your data. For example, element title (line 6) contains text that describes the article's title (e.g., Simple XML). Similarly, date (line 7), author (lines 8–11), firstName (line 9), lastName (line 10), summary (line 12) and content (line 13) contain text that describes the date, author, the author's first name, the author's last name, a summary and the content of the document, respectively. XML element names can be of any length and may contain letters, digits, underscores, hyphens and periods. However, they must begin with either a letter or an underscore, and they should not begin with "xml" in any combination of uppercase and lowercase letters (e.g., XML, Xml, xMl), as this is reserved for use in the XML standards.

Common Programming Error 15.4

Using a white-space character in an XML element name is an error.

Good Programming Practice 15.1

XML element names should be meaningful to humans and should not use abbreviations.

Nesting XML Elements

XML elements are **nested** to form hierarchies—with the root element at the top of the hierarchy. This allows document authors to create parent/child relationships between data items. For example, elements `title`, `date`, `author`, `summary` and `content` are children of `article`. Elements `firstName` and `lastName` are children of `author`. We discuss the hierarchy of Fig. 15.2 later in this chapter (Fig. 15.23).

>
> ### Common Programming Error 15.5
> *Nesting XML tags improperly is a syntax error. For example, `<x><y>hello</x></y>` is an error, because the `</y>` tag must precede the `</x>` tag.*

Any element that contains other elements (e.g., `article` or `author`) is a **container element**. Container elements also are called **parent elements**. Elements nested inside a container element are **child elements** (or children) of that container element. If those child elements are at the same nesting level, they're **siblings** of one another.

Viewing an XML Document in a Web Browser
The XML document in Fig. 15.2 is simply a text file named `article.xml`. It does not contain formatting information for the article. This is because XML is a technology for describing the structure of data. The formatting and displaying of data from an XML document are application-specific issues. For example, when the user loads `article.xml` in a web browser, the browser parses and displays the document's data. Each browser has a built-in **style sheet** to format the data. The resulting format of the data (Fig. 15.3) is similar to the format of the listing in Fig. 15.2. In Section 15.8, we show how you can create your own style sheets to transform XML data into formats suitable for display.

The down arrow (▼) and right arrow (▶) in the screen shots of Fig. 15.3 are not part of the XML document. Google Chrome places them next to every container element. A down arrow indicates that the browser is displaying the container element's child elements. Clicking the down arrow next to an element collapses that element (i.e., causes the browser to hide the container element's children and replace the down arrow with a right arrow). Conversely, clicking the right arrow next to an element expands that element (i.e.,

a) `article.xml` with all elements expanded

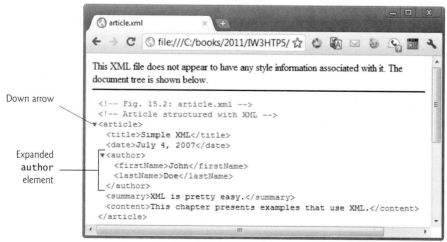

Fig. 15.3 | `article.xml` displayed in the Google Chrome browser. (Part 1 of 2.)

b) `article.xml` with the `author` element collapsed

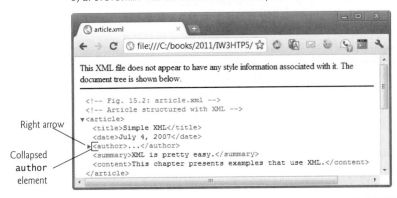

Right arrow

Collapsed
author
element

Fig. 15.3 | `article.xml` displayed in the Google Chrome browser. (Part 2 of 2.)

causes the browser to display the container element's children and replace the right arrow with a down arrow). This behavior is similar to viewing the directory structure in a file-manager window (like Windows Explorer on Windows or Finder on Mac OS X) or another similar directory viewer. In fact, a directory structure often is modeled as a series of tree structures, in which the **root** of a tree represents a disk drive (e.g., `C:`), and **nodes** in the tree represent directories. Parsers often store XML data as tree structures to facilitate efficient manipulation, as discussed in Section 15.9. [*Note:* Some browsers display minus and plus signs, rather than down and right arrows.]

XML Markup for a Business Letter

Now that you've seen a simple XML document, let's examine a more complex one that marks up a business letter (Fig. 15.4). Again, we begin the document with the XML declaration (line 1) that states the XML version to which the document conforms.

```
1   <?xml version = "1.0"?>
2
3   <!-- Fig. 15.4: letter.xml -->
4   <!-- Business letter marked up with XML -->
5   <!DOCTYPE letter SYSTEM "letter.dtd">
6
7   <letter>
8      <contact type = "sender">
9         <name>Jane Doe</name>
10        <address1>Box 12345</address1>
11        <address2>15 Any Ave.</address2>
12        <city>Othertown</city>
13        <state>Otherstate</state>
14        <zip>67890</zip>
15        <phone>555-4321</phone>
16        <flag gender = "F" />
17     </contact>
```

Fig. 15.4 | Business letter marked up with XML. (Part 1 of 2.)

```
18
19      <contact type = "receiver">
20         <name>John Doe</name>
21         <address1>123 Main St.</address1>
22         <address2></address2>
23         <city>Anytown</city>
24         <state>Anystate</state>
25         <zip>12345</zip>
26         <phone>555-1234</phone>
27         <flag gender = "M" />
28      </contact>
29
30      <salutation>Dear Sir:</salutation>
31
32      <paragraph>It is our privilege to inform you about our new database
33         managed with XML. This new system allows you to reduce the
34         load on your inventory list server by having the client machine
35         perform the work of sorting and filtering the data.
36      </paragraph>
37
38      <paragraph>Please visit our website for availability and pricing.
39      </paragraph>
40
41      <closing>Sincerely,</closing>
42      <signature>Ms. Jane Doe</signature>
43   </letter>
```

Fig. 15.4 | Business letter marked up with XML. (Part 2 of 2.)

Line 5 specifies that this XML document references a DTD. Recall from Section 15.2 that DTDs define the structure of the data for an XML document. For example, a DTD specifies the elements and parent/child relationships between elements permitted in an XML document.

Error-Prevention Tip 15.1
An XML document is not required to reference a DTD, but validating XML parsers can use a DTD to ensure that the document has the proper structure.

Portability Tip 15.2
Validating an XML document helps guarantee that independent developers will exchange data in a standardized form that conforms to the DTD.

DOCTYPE

The DOCTYPE reference (line 5) contains three items: the name of the root element that the DTD specifies (letter); the keyword **SYSTEM** (which denotes an **external DTD**—a DTD declared in a separate file, as opposed to a DTD declared locally in the same file); and the DTD's name and location (i.e., letter.dtd in the current directory; this could also be a fully qualified URL). DTD document filenames typically end with the **.dtd** extension. We discuss DTDs and letter.dtd in detail in Section 15.5.

Validating an XML Document Against a DTD
Many online tools can validate your XML documents against DTDs (Section 15.5) or schemas (Section 15.6). The validator at

```
http://www.xmlvalidation.com/
```

can validate XML documents against either DTDs or schemas. To use it, you can either paste your XML document's code into a text area on the page or upload the file. If the XML document references a DTD, the site asks you to paste in the DTD or upload the DTD file. You can also select a checkbox for validating against a schema instead. You can then click a button to validate your XML document.

The XML Document's Contents
Root element `letter` (lines 7–43 of Fig. 15.4) contains the child elements `contact`, `contact`, `salutation`, `paragraph`, `paragraph`, `closing` and `signature`. Data can be placed between an element's tags or as **attributes**—name/value pairs that appear within the angle brackets of an element's start tag. Elements can have any number of attributes (separated by spaces) in their start tags. The first `contact` element (lines 8–17) has an attribute named `type` with **attribute value** `"sender"`, which indicates that this `contact` element identifies the letter's sender. The second `contact` element (lines 19–28) has attribute `type` with value `"receiver"`, which indicates that this `contact` element identifies the recipient of the letter. Like element names, attribute names are case sensitive, can be any length, may contain letters, digits, underscores, hyphens and periods, and must begin with either a letter or an underscore character. A `contact` element stores various items of information about a contact, such as the contact's name (represented by element `name`), address (represented by elements `address1`, `address2`, `city`, `state` and `zip`), phone number (represented by element `phone`) and gender (represented by attribute `gender` of element `flag`). Element `salutation` (line 30) marks up the letter's salutation. Lines 32–39 mark up the letter's body using two `paragraph` elements. Elements `closing` (line 41) and `signature` (line 42) mark up the closing sentence and the author's "signature," respectively.

> **Common Programming Error 15.6**
> *Failure to enclose attribute values in double ("") or single (' ') quotes is a syntax error.*

Line 16 introduces the **empty element** `flag`. An empty element is one that does not have any content. Instead, it sometimes places data in attributes. Empty element `flag` has one attribute that indicates the gender of the contact (represented by the parent `contact` element). Document authors can close an empty element either by placing a slash immediately preceding the right angle bracket, as shown in line 16, or by explicitly writing an end tag, as in line 22:

```
<address2></address2>
```

The `address2` element in line 22 is empty because there's no second part to this contact's address. However, we must include this element to conform to the structural rules specified in the XML document's DTD—`letter.dtd` (which we present in Section 15.5). This DTD specifies that each `contact` element must have an `address2` child element (even if it's empty). In Section 15.5, you'll learn how DTDs indicate required and optional elements.

15.4 XML Namespaces

XML allows document authors to create custom elements. This extensibility can result in **naming collisions** among elements in an XML document that have the same name. For example, we may use the element book to mark up data about a Deitel publication. A stamp collector may use the element book to mark up data about a book of stamps. Using both of these elements in the same document could create a naming collision, making it difficult to determine which kind of data each element contains.

An XML **namespace** is a collection of element and attribute names. XML namespaces provide a means for document authors to unambiguously refer to elements with the same name (i.e., prevent collisions). For example,

```
<subject>Geometry</subject>
```

and

```
<subject>Cardiology</subject>
```

use element subject to mark up data. In the first case, the subject is something one studies in school, whereas in the second case, the subject is a field of medicine. Namespaces can differentiate these two subject elements—for example:

```
<highschool:subject>Geometry</highschool:subject>
```

and

```
<medicalschool:subject>Cardiology</medicalschool:subject>
```

Both highschool and medicalschool are **namespace prefixes**. A document author places a namespace prefix and colon (:) before an element name to specify the namespace to which that element belongs. Document authors can create their own namespace prefixes using virtually any name except the reserved namespace prefix xml. In the subsections that follow, we demonstrate how document authors ensure that namespaces are unique.

Common Programming Error 15.7

Attempting to create a namespace prefix named xml in any mixture of uppercase and lowercase letters is a syntax error—the xml namespace prefix is reserved for internal use by XML itself.

Differentiating Elements with Namespaces

Figure 15.5 demonstrates namespaces. In this document, namespaces differentiate two distinct elements—the file element related to a text file and the file document related to an image file.

```
1   <?xml version = "1.0"?>
2
3   <!-- Fig. 15.5: namespace.xml -->
4   <!-- Demonstrating namespaces -->
5   <text:directory
6      xmlns:text = "urn:deitel:textInfo"
7      xmlns:image = "urn:deitel:imageInfo">
```

Fig. 15.5 | XML namespaces demonstration. (Part 1 of 2.)

```
 8
 9        <text:file filename = "book.xml">
10           <text:description>A book list</text:description>
11        </text:file>
12
13        <image:file filename = "funny.jpg">
14           <image:description>A funny picture</image:description>
15           <image:size width = "200" height = "100" />
16        </image:file>
17     </text:directory>
```

Fig. 15.5 | XML namespaces demonstration. (Part 2 of 2.)

The xmlns Attribute

Lines 6–7 use the XML-namespace reserved attribute **xmlns** to create two namespace prefixes—text and image. Each namespace prefix is bound to a series of characters called a **Uniform Resource Identifier (URI)** that uniquely identifies the namespace. Document authors create their own namespace prefixes and URIs. A URI is a way to identifying a resource, typically on the Internet. Two popular types of URI are **Uniform Resource Name (URN)** and **Uniform Resource Locator (URL)**.

Unique URIs

To ensure that namespaces are unique, document authors must provide unique URIs. In this example, we use urn:deitel:textInfo and urn:deitel:imageInfo as URIs. These URIs employ the URN scheme that is often used to identify namespaces. Under this naming scheme, a URI begins with "urn:", followed by a unique series of additional names separated by colons.

Another common practice is to use URLs, which specify the location of a file or a resource on the Internet. For example, www.deitel.com is the URL that identifies the home page of the Deitel & Associates website. Using URLs guarantees that the namespaces are unique because the domain names (e.g., www.deitel.com) are guaranteed to be unique. For example, lines 5–7 could be rewritten as

```
<text:directory
    xmlns:text = "http://www.deitel.com/xmlns-text"
    xmlns:image = "http://www.deitel.com/xmlns-image">
```

where URLs related to the deitel.com domain name serve as URIs to identify the text and image namespaces. The parser does not visit these URLs, nor do these URLs need to refer to actual web pages. They each simply represent a unique series of characters used to differentiate URI names. In fact, any string can represent a namespace. For example, our image namespace URI could be hgjfkdlsa4556, in which case our prefix assignment would be

```
xmlns:image = "hgjfkdlsa4556"
```

Namespace Prefix

Lines 9–11 use the text namespace prefix for elements file and description. The end tags must also specify the namespace prefix text. Lines 13–16 apply namespace prefix image to the elements file, description and size. Attributes do not require namespace prefixes (although they can have them), because each attribute is already part of an element that specifies the namespace prefix. For example, attribute `filename` (line 9) is implicitly part of namespace `text` because its element (i.e., `file`) specifies the `text` namespace prefix.

Specifying a Default Namespace

To eliminate the need to place namespace prefixes in each element, document authors may specify a **default namespace** for an element and its children. Figure 15.6 demonstrates using a default namespace (`urn:deitel:textInfo`) for element `directory`.

```
 1   <?xml version = "1.0"?>
 2
 3   <!-- Fig. 15.6: defaultnamespace.xml -->
 4   <!-- Using default namespaces -->
 5   <directory xmlns = "urn:deitel:textInfo"
 6      xmlns:image = "urn:deitel:imageInfo">
 7
 8      <file filename = "book.xml">
 9         <description>A book list</description>
10      </file>
11
12      <image:file filename = "funny.jpg">
13         <image:description>A funny picture</image:description>
14         <image:size width = "200" height = "100" />
15      </image:file>
16   </directory>
```

Fig. 15.6 | Default namespace demonstration.

Line 5 defines a default namespace using attribute `xmlns` with no prefix specified but with a URI as its value. Once we define this, child elements belonging to the namespace need not be qualified by a namespace prefix. Thus, element `file` (lines 8–10) is in the default namespace `urn:deitel:textInfo`. Compare this to lines 9–10 of Fig. 15.5, where we had to prefix the `file` and `description` element names with the namespace prefix `text`.

The default namespace applies to the `directory` element and all elements that are not qualified with a namespace prefix. However, we can use a namespace prefix to specify a different namespace for a particular element. For example, the `file` element in lines 12–15 of Fig. 15.16 includes the `image` namespace prefix, indicating that this element is in the `urn:deitel:imageInfo` namespace, not the default namespace.

Namespaces in XML Vocabularies

XML-based languages, such as XML Schema (Section 15.6) and Extensible Stylesheet Language (XSL) (Section 15.8), often use namespaces to identify their elements. Each vocabulary defines special-purpose elements that are grouped in namespaces. These namespaces help prevent naming collisions between predefined elements and user-defined elements.

15.5 Document Type Definitions (DTDs)

Document Type Definitions (DTDs) are one of two main types of documents you can use to specify XML document structure. Section 15.6 presents W3C XML Schema documents, which provide an improved method of specifying XML document structure.

Software Engineering Observation 15.2

XML documents can have many different structures, and for this reason an application cannot be certain whether a particular document it receives is complete, ordered properly, and not missing data. DTDs and schemas (Section 15.6) solve this problem by providing an extensible way to describe XML document structure. Applications should use DTDs or schemas to confirm whether XML documents are valid.

Software Engineering Observation 15.3

Many organizations and individuals are creating DTDs and schemas for a broad range of applications. These collections—called **repositories**—*are available free for download from the web (e.g.,* www.xml.org, www.oasis-open.org).

Creating a Document Type Definition
Figure 15.4 presented a simple business letter marked up with XML. Recall that line 5 of letter.xml references a DTD—letter.dtd (Fig. 15.7). This DTD specifies the business letter's element types and attributes and their relationships to one another.

```
 1   <!-- Fig. 15.7: letter.dtd      -->
 2   <!-- DTD document for letter.xml -->
 3
 4   <!ELEMENT letter ( contact+, salutation, paragraph+,
 5      closing, signature )>
 6
 7   <!ELEMENT contact ( name, address1, address2, city, state,
 8      zip, phone, flag )>
 9   <!ATTLIST contact type CDATA #IMPLIED>
10
11   <!ELEMENT name ( #PCDATA )>
12   <!ELEMENT address1 ( #PCDATA )>
13   <!ELEMENT address2 ( #PCDATA )>
14   <!ELEMENT city ( #PCDATA )>
15   <!ELEMENT state ( #PCDATA )>
16   <!ELEMENT zip ( #PCDATA )>
17   <!ELEMENT phone ( #PCDATA )>
18   <!ELEMENT flag EMPTY>
19   <!ATTLIST flag gender (M | F) "M">
20
21   <!ELEMENT salutation ( #PCDATA )>
22   <!ELEMENT closing ( #PCDATA )>
23   <!ELEMENT paragraph ( #PCDATA )>
24   <!ELEMENT signature ( #PCDATA )>
```

Fig. 15.7 | Document Type Definition (DTD) for a business letter.

A DTD describes the structure of an XML document and enables an XML parser to verify whether an XML document is valid (i.e., whether its elements contain the proper attributes and appear in the proper sequence). DTDs allow users to check document structure and to exchange data in a standardized format. A DTD expresses the set of rules for document structure using an EBNF (Extended Backus-Naur Form) grammar. DTDs are not themselves XML documents. [*Note:* EBNF grammars are commonly used to define programming languages. To learn more about EBNF grammars, visit en.wikipedia.org/wiki/EBNF or www.garshol.priv.no/download/text/bnf.html.]

Common Programming Error 15.8

For documents validated with DTDs, any document that uses elements, attributes or nesting relationships not explicitly defined by a DTD is an invalid document.

Defining Elements in a DTD

The **ELEMENT element type declaration** in lines 4–5 defines the rules for element letter. In this case, letter contains one or more contact elements, one salutation element, one or more paragraph elements, one closing element and one signature element, in that sequence. The **plus sign (+) occurrence indicator** specifies that the DTD requires one or more occurrences of an element. Other occurrence indicators include the **asterisk (*)**, which indicates an optional element that can occur zero or more times, and the **question mark (?)**, which indicates an optional element that can occur at most once (i.e., zero or one occurrence). If an element does not have an occurrence indicator, the DTD requires exactly one occurrence.

The contact element type declaration (lines 7–8) specifies that a contact element contains child elements name, address1, address2, city, state, zip, phone and flag—in that order. The DTD requires exactly one occurrence of each of these elements.

Defining Attributes in a DTD

Line 9 uses the **ATTLIST attribute-list declaration** to define an attribute named type for the contact element. Keyword **#IMPLIED** specifies that if the parser finds a contact element without a type attribute, the parser can choose an arbitrary value for the attribute or can ignore the attribute. Either way the document will still be valid (if the rest of the document is valid)—a missing type attribute will not invalidate the document. Other keywords that can be used in place of #IMPLIED in an ATTLIST declaration include **#REQUIRED** and **#FIXED**. Keyword **#REQUIRED** specifies that the attribute must be present in the element, and keyword **#FIXED** specifies that the attribute (if present) must have the given fixed value. For example,

```
<!ATTLIST address zip CDATA #FIXED "01757">
```

indicates that attribute zip (if present in element address) must have the value 01757 for the document to be valid. If the attribute is not present, then the parser, by default, uses the fixed value that the ATTLIST declaration specifies.

Character Data vs. Parsed Character Data

Keyword **CDATA** (line 9) specifies that attribute type contains **character data** (i.e., a string). A parser will pass such data to an application without modification.

Software Engineering Observation 15.4

DTD syntax cannot describe an element's or attribute's data type. For example, a DTD cannot specify that a particular element or attribute can contain only integer data.

Keyword **#PCDATA** (line 11) specifies that an element (e.g., name) may contain **parsed character data** (i.e., data that's processed by an XML parser). Elements with parsed character data cannot contain markup characters, such as less than (<), greater than (>) or ampersand (&). The document author should replace any markup character in a #PCDATA element with the character's corresponding **character entity reference**. For example, the character entity reference < should be used in place of the less-than symbol (<), and the character entity reference > should be used in place of the greater-than symbol (>). A document author who wishes to use a literal ampersand should use the entity reference & instead—parsed character data can contain ampersands (&) only for inserting entities. See Appendix A, HTML Special Characters, for a list of other character entity references.

> **Common Programming Error 15.9**
>
> *Using markup characters (e.g., <, > and &) in parsed character data is an error. Use character entity references (e.g., <, > and &) instead.*

Defining Empty Elements in a DTD

Line 18 defines an empty element named flag. Keyword **EMPTY** specifies that the element does not contain any data between its start and end tags. Empty elements commonly describe data via attributes. For example, flag's data appears in its gender attribute (line 19). Line 19 specifies that the gender attribute's value must be one of the enumerated values (M or F) enclosed in parentheses and delimited by a vertical bar (|) meaning "or." Note that line 19 also indicates that gender has a default value of M.

Well-Formed Documents vs. Valid Documents

In Section 15.3, we demonstrated how to use the Microsoft XML Validator to validate an XML document against its specified DTD. The validation revealed that the XML document letter.xml (Fig. 15.4) is well-formed and valid—it conforms to letter.dtd (Fig. 15.7). Recall that a well-formed document is syntactically correct (i.e., each start tag has a corresponding end tag, the document contains only one root element, etc.), and a valid document contains the proper elements with the proper attributes in the proper sequence. An XML document cannot be valid unless it's well-formed.

When a document fails to conform to a DTD or a schema, an XML validator displays an error message. For example, the DTD in Fig. 15.7 indicates that a contact element must contain the child element name. A document that omits this child element is still well-formed but is not valid. Figure 15.8 shows the error message displayed by the validator at www.xmlvalidation.com for a version of the letter.xml file that's missing the first contact element's name element.

15.6 W3C XML Schema Documents

In this section, we introduce schemas for specifying XML document structure and validating XML documents. Many developers in the XML community believe that DTDs are not flexible enough to meet today's programming needs. For example, DTDs lack a way of indicating what specific type of data (e.g., numeric, text) an element can contain, and DTDs are not themselves XML documents, forcing developers to learn multiple grammars and developers to create multiple types of parsers. These and other limitations have led to the development of schemas.

Fig. 15.8 | Error message when validating `letter.xml` with a missing contact name.

Unlike DTDs, schemas do not use EBNF grammar. Instead, they use XML syntax and are actually XML documents that programs can manipulate. Like DTDs, schemas are used by validating parsers to validate documents.

In this section, we focus on the W3C's **XML Schema** vocabulary (note the capital "S" in "Schema"). To refer to it, we use the term XML Schema in the rest of the chapter. For the latest information on XML Schema, visit www.w3.org/XML/Schema. For tutorials on XML Schema concepts beyond what we present here, visit www.w3schools.com/schema/default.asp.

Recall that a DTD describes an XML document's structure, not the content of its elements. For example,

```
<quantity>5</quantity>
```

contains character data. If the document that contains element `quantity` references a DTD, an XML parser can validate the document to confirm that this element indeed does contain PCDATA content. However, the parser cannot validate that the content is numeric; DTDs do not provide this capability. So, unfortunately, the parser also considers

```
<quantity>hello</quantity>
```

to be valid. An application that uses the XML document containing this markup should test that the data in element `quantity` is numeric and take appropriate action if it's not.

XML Schema enables schema authors to specify that element `quantity`'s data must be numeric or, even more specifically, an integer. A parser validating the XML document against this schema can determine that 5 conforms and hello does not. An XML document that conforms to a schema document is **schema valid**, and one that does not conform is **schema invalid**. Schemas are XML documents and therefore must themselves be valid.

Validating Against an XML Schema Document

Figure 15.9 shows a schema-valid XML document named book.xml, and Fig. 15.10 shows the pertinent XML Schema document (book.xsd) that defines the structure for book.xml. By convention, schemas use the **.xsd** extension. We used an online XSD schema validator provided at

> www.xmlforasp.net/SchemaValidator.aspx

to ensure that the XML document in Fig. 15.9 conforms to the schema in Fig. 15.10. To validate the schema document itself (i.e., book.xsd) and produce the output shown in Fig. 15.10, we used an online XSV (XML Schema Validator) provided by the W3C at

> www.w3.org/2001/03/webdata/xsv

These tools are free and enforce the W3C's specifications regarding XML Schemas and schema validation.

```
1   <?xml version = "1.0"?>
2
3   <!-- Fig. 15.9: book.xml -->
4   <!-- Book list marked up as XML -->
5   <deitel:books xmlns:deitel = "http://www.deitel.com/booklist">
6      <book>
7         <title>Visual Basic 2010 How to Program</title>
8      </book>
9      <book>
10        <title>Visual C# 2010 How to Program, 4/e</title>
11     </book>
12     <book>
13        <title>Java How to Program, 9/e</title>
14     </book>
15     <book>
16        <title>C++ How to Program, 8/e</title>
17     </book>
18     <book>
19        <title>Internet and World Wide Web How to Program, 5/e</title>
20     </book>
21  </deitel:books>
```

Fig. 15.9 | Schema-valid XML document describing a list of books.

```
1   <?xml version = "1.0"?>
2
3   <!-- Fig. 15.10: book.xsd         -->
4   <!-- Simple W3C XML Schema document -->
```

Fig. 15.10 | XML Schema document for book.xml. (Part 1 of 2.)

```
5    <schema xmlns = "http://www.w3.org/2001/XMLSchema"
6       xmlns:deitel = "http://www.deitel.com/booklist"
7       targetNamespace = "http://www.deitel.com/booklist">
8
9       <element name = "books" type = "deitel:BooksType"/>
10
11      <complexType name = "BooksType">
12         <sequence>
13            <element name = "book" type = "deitel:SingleBookType"
14               minOccurs = "1" maxOccurs = "unbounded"/>
15         </sequence>
16      </complexType>
17
18      <complexType name = "SingleBookType">
19         <sequence>
20            <element name = "title" type = "string"/>
21         </sequence>
22      </complexType>
23   </schema>
```

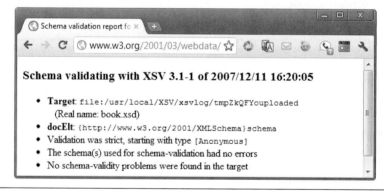

Fig. 15.10 | XML Schema document for `book.xml`. (Part 2 of 2.)

Figure 15.9 contains markup describing several Deitel books. The `books` element (line 5) has the namespace prefix `deitel`, indicating that the `books` element is a part of the `http://www.deitel.com/booklist` namespace.

Creating an XML Schema Document
Figure 15.10 presents the XML Schema document that specifies the structure of `book.xml` (Fig. 15.9). This document defines an XML-based language (i.e., a vocabulary) for writing XML documents about collections of books. The schema defines the elements, attributes and parent/child relationships that such a document can (or must) include. The schema also specifies the type of data that these elements and attributes may contain.

Root element **schema** (Fig. 15.10, lines 5–23) contains elements that define the structure of an XML document such as `book.xml`. Line 5 specifies as the default namespace the standard W3C XML Schema namespace URI—**http://www.w3.org/2001/XMLSchema**. This namespace contains predefined elements (e.g., root-element `schema`) that comprise the XML Schema vocabulary—the language used to write an XML Schema document.

Portability Tip 15.3

W3C XML Schema authors specify URI http://www.w3.org/2001/XMLSchema *when referring to the XML Schema namespace. This namespace contains predefined elements that comprise the XML Schema vocabulary. Specifying this URI ensures that validation tools correctly identify XML Schema elements and do not confuse them with those defined by document authors.*

Line 6 binds the URI http://www.deitel.com/booklist to namespace prefix deitel. As we discuss momentarily, the schema uses this namespace to differentiate names created by us from names that are part of the XML Schema namespace. Line 7 also specifies http://www.deitel.com/booklist as the **targetNamespace** of the schema. This attribute identifies the namespace of the XML vocabulary that this schema defines. Note that the targetNamespace of book.xsd is the same as the namespace referenced in line 5 of book.xml (Fig. 15.9). This is what "connects" the XML document with the schema that defines its structure. When a schema validator examines book.xml and book.xsd, it will recognize that book.xml uses elements and attributes from the http://www.deitel.com/booklist namespace. The validator also will recognize that this namespace is the namespace defined in book.xsd (i.e., the schema's targetNamespace). Thus the validator knows where to look for the structural rules for the elements and attributes used in book.xml.

Defining an Element in XML Schema

In XML Schema, the **element** tag (line 9 of Fig. 15.10) defines an element to be included in an XML document that conforms to the schema. In other words, element specifies the actual *elements* that can be used to mark up data. Line 9 defines the books element, which we use as the root element in book.xml (Fig. 15.9). Attributes **name** and **type** specify the element's name and type, respectively. An element's type indicates the data that the element may contain. Possible types include XML Schema-defined types (e.g., string, double) and user-defined types (e.g., BooksType, which is defined in lines 11–16 of Fig. 15.10). Figure 15.11 lists several of XML Schema's many built-in types. For a complete list of built-in types, see Section 3 of the specification found at www.w3.org/TR/xmlschema-2.

Type	Description	Range or structure	Examples
string	A character string		"hello"
boolean	True or false	true, false	true
decimal	A decimal numeral	$i * (10^n)$, where i is an integer and n is an integer that's less than or equal to zero.	5, -12, -45.78
float	A floating-point number	$m * (2^e)$, where m is an integer whose absolute value is less than 2^{24} and e is an integer in the range -149 to 104. Plus three additional numbers: positive infinity, negative infinity and not-a-number (NaN).	0, 12, -109.375, NaN

Fig. 15.11 | Some XML Schema types. (Part 1 of 2.)

Type	Description	Range or structure	Examples
double	A floating-point number	$m * (2^e)$, where m is an integer whose absolute value is less than 2^{53} and e is an integer in the range -1075 to 970. Plus three additional numbers: positive infinity, negative infinity and not-a-number (NaN).	0, 12, -109.375, NaN
long	A whole number	-9223372036854775808 to 9223372036854775807, inclusive.	1234567890, -1234567890
int	A whole number	-2147483648 to 2147483647, inclusive.	1234567890, -1234567890
short	A whole number	-32768 to 32767, inclusive.	12, -345
date	A date consisting of a year, month and day	yyyy-mm with an optional dd and an optional time zone, where yyyy is four digits long and mm and dd are two digits long.	2005-05-10
time	A time consisting of hours, minutes and seconds	hh:mm:ss with an optional time zone, where hh, mm and ss are two digits long.	16:30:25-05:00

Fig. 15.11 | Some XML Schema types. (Part 2 of 2.)

In this example, books is defined as an element of type deitel:BooksType (line 9). BooksType is a user-defined type (lines 11–16 of Fig. 15.10) in the namespace http://www.deitel.com/booklist and therefore must have the namespace prefix deitel. It's not an existing XML Schema type.

Two categories of type exist in XML Schema—**simple types** and **complex types**. They differ only in that simple types cannot contain attributes or child elements and complex types can.

A user-defined type that contains attributes or child elements must be defined as a complex type. Lines 11–16 use element **complexType** to define BooksType as a complex type that has a child element named book. The sequence element (lines 12–15) allows you to specify the sequential order in which child elements must appear. The element (lines 13–14) nested within the complexType element indicates that a BooksType element (e.g., books) can contain child elements named book of type deitel:SingleBookType (defined in lines 18–22). Attribute **minOccurs** (line 14), with value 1, specifies that elements of type BooksType must contain a minimum of one book element. Attribute **maxOccurs** (line 14), with value **unbounded**, specifies that elements of type BooksType may have any number of book child elements.

Lines 18–22 define the complex type SingleBookType. An element of this type contains a child element named title. Line 20 defines element title to be of simple type string. Recall that elements of a simple type cannot contain attributes or child elements. The schema end tag (</schema>, line 23) declares the end of the XML Schema document.

A Closer Look at Types in XML Schema

Every element in XML Schema has a type. Types include the built-in types provided by XML Schema (Fig. 15.11) or user-defined types (e.g., SingleBookType in Fig. 15.10).

Every simple type defines a **restriction** on an XML Schema-defined type or a restriction on a user-defined type. Restrictions limit the possible values that an element can hold.

Complex types are divided into two groups—those with **simple content** and those with **complex content**. Both can contain attributes, but only complex content can contain child elements. Complex types with simple content must extend or restrict some other existing type. Complex types with complex content do not have this limitation. We demonstrate complex types with each kind of content in the next example.

The schema document in Fig. 15.12 creates both simple types and complex types. The XML document in Fig. 15.13 (laptop.xml) follows the structure defined in Fig. 15.12 to describe parts of a laptop computer. A document such as laptop.xml that conforms to a schema is known as an **XML instance document**—the document is an instance (i.e., example) of the schema.

```
1    <?xml version = "1.0"?>
2    <!-- Fig. 15.12: computer.xsd -->
3    <!-- W3C XML Schema document   -->
4
5    <schema xmlns = "http://www.w3.org/2001/XMLSchema"
6       xmlns:computer = "http://www.deitel.com/computer"
7       targetNamespace = "http://www.deitel.com/computer">
8
9       <simpleType name = "gigahertz">
10         <restriction base = "decimal">
11            <minInclusive value = "2.1"/>
12         </restriction>
13      </simpleType>
14
15      <complexType name = "CPU">
16         <simpleContent>
17            <extension base = "string">
18               <attribute name = "model" type = "string"/>
19            </extension>
20         </simpleContent>
21      </complexType>
22
23      <complexType name = "portable">
24         <all>
25            <element name = "processor" type = "computer:CPU"/>
26            <element name = "monitor" type = "int"/>
27            <element name = "CPUSpeed" type = "computer:gigahertz"/>
28            <element name = "RAM" type = "int"/>
29         </all>
30         <attribute name = "manufacturer" type = "string"/>
31      </complexType>
32
33      <element name = "laptop" type = "computer:portable"/>
34   </schema>
```

Fig. 15.12 | XML Schema document defining simple and complex types.

```
 1   <?xml version = "1.0"?>
 2
 3   <!-- Fig. 15.13: laptop.xml            -->
 4   <!-- Laptop components marked up as XML -->
 5   <computer:laptop xmlns:computer = "http://www.deitel.com/computer"
 6      manufacturer = "IBM">
 7
 8      <processor model = "Centrino">Intel</processor>
 9      <monitor>17</monitor>
10      <CPUSpeed>2.4</CPUSpeed>
11      <RAM>256</RAM>
12   </computer:laptop>
```

Fig. 15.13 | XML document using the `laptop` element defined in `computer.xsd`.

Line 5 of Fig. 15.12 declares the default namespace to be the standard XML Schema namespace—any elements without a prefix are assumed to be in that namespace. Line 6 binds the namespace prefix `computer` to the namespace `http://www.deitel.com/computer`. Line 7 identifies this namespace as the `targetNamespace`—the namespace being defined by the current XML Schema document.

To design the XML elements for describing laptop computers, we first create a simple type in lines 9–13 using the **simpleType** element. We name this `simpleType` `gigahertz` because it will be used to describe the clock speed of the processor in gigahertz. Simple types are restrictions of a type typically called a **base type**. For this `simpleType`, line 10 declares the base type as `decimal`, and we restrict the value to be at least `2.1` by using the **minInclusive** element in line 11.

Next, we declare a `complexType` named `CPU` that has **simpleContent** (lines 16–20). Remember that a complex type with simple content can have attributes but not child elements. Also recall that complex types with simple content must extend or restrict some XML Schema type or user-defined type. The **extension** element with attribute **base** (line 17) sets the base type to `string`. In this `complexType`, we extend the base type `string` with an attribute. The **attribute** element (line 18) gives the `complexType` an attribute of type `string` named `model`. Thus an element of type `CPU` must contain `string` text (because the base type is `string`) and may contain a `model` attribute that's also of type `string`.

Last, we define type `portable`, which is a `complexType` with complex content (lines 23–31). Such types are allowed to have child elements and attributes. The element **all** (lines 24–29) encloses elements that must each be included once in the corresponding XML instance document. These elements can be included in any order. This complex type holds four elements—`processor`, `monitor`, `CPUSpeed` and `RAM`. They're given types `CPU`, `int`, `gigahertz` and `int`, respectively. When using types `CPU` and `gigahertz`, we must include the namespace prefix `computer`, because these user-defined types are part of the `computer` namespace (`http://www.deitel.com/computer`)—the namespace defined in the current document (line 7). Also, `portable` contains an attribute defined in line 30. The `attribute` element indicates that elements of type `portable` contain an attribute of type `string` named `manufacturer`.

Line 33 declares the actual element that uses the three types defined in the schema. The element is called `laptop` and is of type `portable`. We must use the namespace prefix `computer` in front of `portable`.

We've now created an element named `laptop` that contains child elements `pro-cessor`, `monitor`, `CPUSpeed` and `RAM`, and an attribute `manufacturer`. Figure 15.13 uses the `laptop` element defined in the `computer.xsd` schema. Once again, we used an online XSD schema validator (`www.xmlforasp.net/SchemaValidator.aspx`) to ensure that this XML instance document adheres to the schema's structural rules.

Line 5 declares namespace prefix `computer`. The `laptop` element requires this prefix because it's part of the `http://www.deitel.com/computer` namespace. Line 6 sets the laptop's `manufacturer` attribute, and lines 8–11 use the elements defined in the schema to describe the laptop's characteristics.

This section introduced W3C XML Schema documents for defining the structure of XML documents, and we validated XML instance documents against schemas using an online XSD schema validator. Section 15.7 discusses several XML vocabularies and demonstrates the MathML vocabulary.

15.7 XML Vocabularies

XML allows authors to create their own tags to describe data precisely. People and organizations in various fields of study have created many different kinds of XML for structuring data. Some of these markup languages are: **MathML (Mathematical Markup Language)**, **Scalable Vector Graphics (SVG)**, **Wireless Markup Language (WML)**, **Extensible Business Reporting Language (XBRL)**, **Extensible User Interface Language (XUL)** and **Product Data Markup Language (PDML)**. Two other examples of XML vocabularies are W3C XML Schema and the Extensible Stylesheet Language (XSL), which we discuss in Section 15.6 and Section 15.8, respectively. The following subsections describe MathML and other custom markup languages.

15.7.1 MathML™

Until recently, computers typically required specialized software packages such as TeX and LaTeX for displaying complex mathematical expressions. This section introduces MathML, which the W3C developed for describing mathematical notations and expressions. The Firefox and Opera browsers can render MathML. There are also plug-ins or extensions available that enable you to render MathML in other browsers.

MathML markup describes mathematical expressions for display. MathML is divided into two types of markup—**content** markup and **presentation** markup. Content markup provides tags that embody mathematical concepts. Content MathML allows programmers to write mathematical notation specific to different areas of mathematics. For instance, the multiplication symbol has one meaning in set theory and another in linear algebra. Content MathML distinguishes between different uses of the same symbol. Programmers can take content MathML markup, discern mathematical context and evaluate the marked-up mathematical operations. Presentation MathML is directed toward formatting and displaying mathematical notation. We focus on Presentation MathML in the MathML examples.

Simple Equation in MathML

Figure 15.14 uses MathML to mark up a simple expression. For this example, we show the expression rendered in Firefox.

```
 1   <?xml version="1.0" encoding="iso-8859-1"?>
 2   <!DOCTYPE math PUBLIC "-//W3C//DTD MathML 2.0//EN"
 3      "http://www.w3.org/TR/MathML2/dtd/mathml2.dtd">
 4
 5   <!-- Fig. 15.14: mathml1.mml -->
 6   <!-- MathML equation. -->
 7   <math xmlns="http://www.w3.org/1998/Math/MathML">
 8      <mn>2</mn>
 9      <mo>+</mo>
10      <mn>3</mn>
11      <mo>=</mo>
12      <mn>5</mn>
13   </math>
```

Fig. 15.14 | Expression marked up with MathML and displayed in the Firefox browser.

By convention, MathML files end with the `.mml` filename extension. A MathML document's root node is the `math` element, and its default namespace is `http://www.w3.org/1998/Math/MathML` (line 7). The **mn element** (line 8) marks up a number. The **mo element** (line 9) marks up an operator (e.g., +). Using this markup, we define the expression 2 + 3 = 5, which any MathML capable browser can display.

Algebraic Equation in MathML
Let's consider using MathML to mark up an algebraic equation containing exponents and arithmetic operators (Fig. 15.15). For this example, we again show the expression rendered in Firefox.

```
 1   <?xml version="1.0" encoding="iso-8859-1"?>
 2   <!DOCTYPE math PUBLIC "-//W3C//DTD MathML 2.0//EN"
 3      "http://www.w3.org/TR/MathML2/dtd/mathml2.dtd">
 4
 5   <!-- Fig. 15.15: mathml2.html -->
 6   <!-- MathML algebraic equation. -->
 7   <math xmlns="http://www.w3.org/1998/Math/MathML">
 8      <mn>3</mn>
 9      <mo>&InvisibleTimes;</mo>
10      <msup>
11         <mi>x</mi>
12         <mn>2</mn>
13      </msup>
14      <mo>+</mo>
```

Fig. 15.15 | Algebraic equation marked up with MathML and displayed in the Firefox browser. (Part 1 of 2.)

```
15        <mn>x</mn>
16        <mo>&minus;</mo>
17        <mfrac>
18            <mn>2</mn>
19            <mi>x</mi>
20        </mfrac>
21        <mo>=</mo>
22        <mn>0</mn>
23    </math>
```

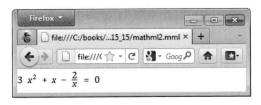

Fig. 15.15 | Algebraic equation marked up with MathML and displayed in the Firefox browser. (Part 2 of 2.)

Line 9 uses **entity reference ⁢** to indicate a multiplication operation without explicit **symbolic representation** (i.e., the multiplication symbol does not appear between the 3 and x). For exponentiation, lines 10–13 use the **msup element**, which represents a superscript. This msup element has two children—the expression to be superscripted (i.e., the base) and the superscript (i.e., the exponent). Correspondingly, the msub element represents a subscript. To display variables such as x, line 11 uses **identifier element mi**.

To display a fraction, lines 17–20 use the **mfrac element**. Lines 18–19 specify the numerator and the denominator for the fraction. If either the numerator or the denominator contains more than one element, it must appear in an mrow element.

Calculus Expression in MathML
Figure 15.16 marks up a calculus expression that contains an integral symbol and a square-root symbol.

```
1    <?xml version="1.0" encoding="iso-8859-1"?>
2    <!DOCTYPE math PUBLIC "-//W3C//DTD MathML 2.0//EN"
3        "http://www.w3.org/TR/MathML2/dtd/mathml2.dtd">
4
5    <!-- Fig. 15.16 mathml3.html -->
6    <!-- Calculus example using MathML -->
7    <math xmlns="http://www.w3.org/1998/Math/MathML">
8        <mrow>
9            <msubsup>
10               <mo>&int;</mo>
11               <mn>0</mn>
12               <mrow>
13                   <mn>1</mn>
```

Fig. 15.16 | Calculus expression marked up with MathML and displayed in the Firefox browser. (Part 1 of 2.)

```
14          <mo>&minus;</mo>
15          <mi>y</mi>
16       </mrow>
17     </msubsup>
18     <msqrt>
19       <mn>4</mn>
20       <mo>&InvisibleTimes;</mo>
21       <msup>
22          <mi>x</mi>
23          <mn>2</mn>
24       </msup>
25       <mo>+</mo>
26       <mi>y</mi>
27     </msqrt>
28     <mo>&delta;</mo>
29     <mi>x</mi>
30   </mrow>
31 </math>
```

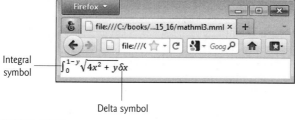

Fig. 15.16 | Calculus expression marked up with MathML and displayed in the Firefox browser. (Part 2 of 2.)

Lines 8–30 group the entire expression in an **mrow element**, which is used to group elements that are positioned horizontally in an expression. The entity reference **∫** (line 10) represents the integral symbol, while the **msubsup element** (lines 9–17) specifies the subscript and superscript for a base expression (e.g., the integral symbol). Element mo marks up the integral operator. The msubsup element requires three child elements—an operator (e.g., the integral entity, line 10), the subscript expression (line 11) and the superscript expression (lines 12–16). Element mn (line 11) marks up the number (i.e., 0) that represents the subscript. Element mrow (lines 12–16) marks up the superscript expression (i.e., 1-y).

Element **msqrt** (lines 18–27) represents a square-root expression. Line 28 introduces entity reference δ for representing a lowercase delta symbol. Delta is an operator, so line 28 places this entity in element mo. To see other operations and symbols in MathML, visit www.w3.org/Math.

15.7.2 Other Markup Languages

Literally hundreds of markup languages derive from XML. Every day developers find new uses for XML. Figure 15.18 summarizes a few of these markup languages. The website

www.service-architecture.com/xml/articles/index.html

provides a nice list of common XML vocabularies and descriptions.

Markup language	Description
Chemical Markup Language (CML)	Chemical Markup Language (CML) is an XML vocabulary for representing molecular and chemical information. Many previous methods for storing this type of information (e.g., special file types) inhibited document reuse. CML takes advantage of XML's portability to enable document authors to use and reuse molecular information without corrupting important data in the process.
VoiceXML™	The VoiceXML Forum founded by AT&T, IBM, Lucent and Motorola developed VoiceXML. It provides interactive voice communication between humans and computers through a telephone, PDA (personal digital assistant) or desktop computer. IBM's VoiceXML SDK can process VoiceXML documents. Visit www.voicexml.org for more information on VoiceXML.
Synchronous Multimedia Integration Language (SMIL™)	SMIL is an XML vocabulary for multimedia presentations. The W3C was the primary developer of SMIL, with contributions from some companies. Visit www.w3.org/AudioVideo for more on SMIL.
Research Information Exchange Markup Language (RIXML)	RIXML, developed by a consortium of brokerage firms, marks up investment data. Visit www.rixml.org for more information on RIXML.
Geography Markup Language (GML)	OpenGIS developed the Geography Markup Language to describe geographic information. Visit www.opengis.org for more information on GML.
Extensible User Interface Language (XUL)	The Mozilla Project created the Extensible User Interface Language for describing graphical user interfaces in a platform-independent way.

Fig. 15.17 | Various markup languages derived from XML.

15.8 Extensible Stylesheet Language and XSL Transformations

Extensible Stylesheet Language (XSL) documents specify how programs are to render XML document data. XSL is a group of three technologies—**XSL-FO (XSL Formatting Objects)**, **XPath (XML Path Language)** and **XSLT (XSL Transformations)**. XSL-FO is a vocabulary for specifying formatting, and XPath is a string-based language of expressions used by XML and many of its related technologies for effectively and efficiently locating structures and data (such as specific elements and attributes) in XML documents.

The third portion of XSL—XSL Transformations (XSLT)—is a technology for transforming XML documents into other documents—i.e., transforming the structure of the XML document data to another structure. XSLT provides elements that define rules for transforming one XML document to produce a different XML document. This is useful when you want to use data in multiple applications or on multiple platforms, each of which may be designed to work with documents written in a particular vocabulary. For example, XSLT allows you to convert a simple XML document to an HTML5 document that presents the XML document's data (or a subset of the data) formatted for display in a web browser.

Transforming an XML document using XSLT involves two tree structures—the **source tree** (i.e., the XML document to transform) and the **result tree** (i.e., the XML document to create). XPath locates parts of the source-tree document that match **templates** defined in an **XSL style sheet**. When a match occurs, the matching template executes and adds its result to the result tree. When there are no more matches, XSLT has transformed the source tree into the result tree. The XSLT does not analyze every node of the source tree; it selectively navigates the source tree using XPath's `select` and `match` attributes. For XSLT to function, the source tree must be properly structured. Schemas, DTDs and validating parsers can validate document structure before using XPath and XSLTs.

A Simple XSL Example

Figure 15.18 lists an XML document that describes various sports. The output shows the result of the transformation (specified in the XSLT template of Fig. 15.19). Some web browsers will perform transformations on XML files only if they are accessed from a web server. For this reason, we've posted the example online at

```
http://test.deitel.com/iw3htp5/ch15/Fig15_18-19/sports.xml
```

Also, to save space, we do not show the contents of the example's CSS file here.

```
 1   <?xml version = "1.0"?>
 2   <?xml-stylesheet type = "text/xsl" href = "sports.xsl"?>
 3
 4   <!-- Fig. 15.18: sports.xml -->
 5   <!-- Sports Database -->
 6
 7   <sports>
 8      <game id = "783">
 9         <name>Cricket</name>
10
11         <paragraph>
12            More popular among commonwealth nations.
13         </paragraph>
14      </game>
15
16      <game id = "239">
17         <name>Baseball</name>
18
19         <paragraph>
20            More popular in America.
21         </paragraph>
22      </game>
23
24      <game id = "418">
25         <name>Soccer (Futbol)</name>
26
27         <paragraph>
28            Most popular sport in the world.
29         </paragraph>
30      </game>
31   </sports>
```

Fig. 15.18 | XML document that describes various sports. (Part 1 of 2.)

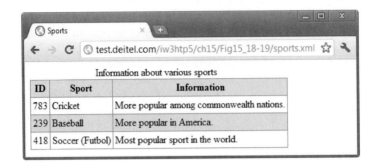

Fig. 15.18 | XML document that describes various sports. (Part 2 of 2.)

To perform transformations, an XSLT processor is required. Popular XSLT processors include Microsoft's MSXML and the Apache Software Foundation's **Xalan 2** (xml.apache.org). The XML document in Fig. 15.18 is transformed into an XHTML document when it's loaded into the web browser.

Line 2 (Fig. 15.18) is a **processing instruction (PI)** that references the XSL style sheet sports.xsl (Fig. 15.19). A processing instruction is embedded in an XML document and provides application-specific information to whichever XML processor the application uses. In this particular case, the processing instruction specifies the location of an XSLT document with which to transform the XML document. The **<?** and **?>** (line 2, Fig. 15.18) delimit a processing instruction, which consists of a **PI target** (e.g., xml-stylesheet) and a **PI value** (e.g., type = "text/xsl" href = "sports.xsl"). The PI value's type attribute specifies that sports.xsl is a text/xsl file (i.e., a text file containing XSL content). The href attribute specifies the name and location of the style sheet to apply—in this case, sports.xsl in the current directory.

Software Engineering Observation 15.5

XSL enables document authors to separate data presentation (specified in XSL documents) from data description (specified in XML documents).

Common Programming Error 15.10

You'll sometimes see the XML processing instruction <?xml-stylesheet?> written as <?xml:stylesheet?> with a colon rather than a dash. The version with a colon results in an XML parsing error in Firefox.

Figure 15.19 shows the XSL document for transforming the structured data of the XML document of Fig. 15.18 into an XHTML document for presentation. By convention, XSL documents have the filename extension **.xsl**.

```
1   <?xml version = "1.0"?>
2   <!-- Fig. 15.19: sports.xsl -->
3   <!-- A simple XSLT transformation -->
4
```

Fig. 15.19 | XSLT that creates elements and attributes in an HTML5 document. (Part 1 of 2.)

```
 5   <!-- reference XSL style sheet URI -->
 6   <xsl-stylesheet version = "1.0"
 7      xmlns:xsl = "http://www.w3.org/1999/XSL/Transform">
 8
 9      <xsl:output method = "html" doctype-system = "about:legacy-compat" />
10      <xsl:template match = "/"> <!-- match root element -->
11
12      <html xmlns = "http://www.w3.org/1999/xhtml">
13         <head>
14            <meta charset = "utf-8"/>
15            <link rel = "stylesheet" type = "text/css" href = "style.css"/>
16            <title>Sports</title>
17         </head>
18
19         <body>
20            <table>
21            <caption>Information about various sports</caption>
22               <thead>
23                  <tr>
24                     <th>ID</th>
25                     <th>Sport</th>
26                     <th>Information</th>
27                  </tr>
28               </thead>
29
30               <!-- insert each name and paragraph element value -->
31               <!-- into a table row. -->
32               <xsl:for-each select = "/sports/game">
33                  <tr>
34                     <td><xsl:value-of select = "@id"/></td>
35                     <td><xsl:value-of select = "name"/></td>
36                     <td><xsl:value-of select = "paragraph"/></td>
37                  </tr>
38               </xsl:for-each>
39            </table>
40         </body>
41      </html>
42
43      </xsl:template>
44   </xsl:stylesheet>
```

Fig. 15.19 | XSLT that creates elements and attributes in an HTML5 document. (Part 2 of 2.)

Lines 6–7 begin the XSL style sheet with the **stylesheet** start tag. Attribute **version** specifies the XSLT version to which this document conforms. Line 7 binds namespace prefix **xsl** to the W3C's XSLT URI (i.e., http://www.w3.org/1999/XSL/Transform).

Outputting the DOCTYPE
Line 9 uses element **xsl:output** to write an HTML5 document type declaration (DOC-TYPE) to the result tree (i.e., the XML document to be created). At the time of this writing, the W3C has not yet updated the XSLT recommendation (standard) to support the HTML5 DOCTYPE—in the meantime, they recommend setting the attribute doctype-

system to the value about:legacy-compat to produce an HTML5 compatible DOCTYPE using XSLT.

Templates

XSLT uses **templates** (i.e., **xsl:template** elements) to describe how to transform particular nodes from the source tree to the result tree. A template is applied to nodes that are specified in the required match attribute. Line 10 uses the **match** attribute to select the **document root** (i.e., the conceptual part of the document that contains the root element and everything below it) of the XML source document (i.e., sports.xml). The XPath character / (a forward slash) always selects the document root. Recall that XPath is a string-based language used to locate parts of an XML document easily. In XPath, a leading forward slash specifies that we're using **absolute addressing** (i.e., we're starting from the root and defining paths down the source tree). In the XML document of Fig. 15.18, the child nodes of the document root are the two processing-instruction nodes (lines 1–2), the two comment nodes (lines 4–5) and the sports-element node (lines 7–31). The template in Fig. 15.19, line 14, matches a node (i.e., the root node), so the contents of the template are now added to the result tree.

Repetition in XSL

The browser's XML processor writes the HTML5 in lines 13–28 (Fig. 15.19) to the result tree exactly as it appears in the XSL document. Now the result tree consists of the DOCTYPE definition and the HTML5 code from lines 13–28. Lines 32–38 use element **xsl:for-each** to iterate through the source XML document, searching for game elements. Attribute **select** is an XPath expression that specifies the nodes (called the **node set**) on which the xsl:for-each operates. Again, the first forward slash means that we're using absolute addressing. The forward slash between sports and game indicates that game is a child node of sports. Thus, the xsl:for-each finds game nodes that are children of the sports node. The XML document sports.xml contains only one sports node, which is also the document root node. After finding the elements that match the selection criteria, the xsl:for-each processes each element with the code in lines 33–37 (these lines produce one row in a table each time they execute) and places the result in the result tree.

Line 34 uses element **value-of** to retrieve attribute id's value and place it in a td element in the result tree. The XPath symbol @ specifies that id is an attribute node of the context node game. Lines 35–36 place the name and paragraph element values in td elements and insert them in the result tree. When an XPath expression has no beginning forward slash, the expression uses **relative addressing**. Omitting the beginning forward slash tells the xsl:value-of select statements to search for name and paragraph elements that are children of the context node, not the root node. Owing to the last XPath expression selection, the current context node is game, which indeed has an id attribute, a name child element and a paragraph child element.

Using XSLT to Sort and Format Data

Figure 15.20 presents an XML document (sorting.xml) that marks up information about a book. Note that several elements of the markup describing the book appear out of order (e.g., the element describing Chapter 3 appears before the element describing Chapter 2). We arranged them this way purposely to demonstrate that the XSL style sheet referenced in line 2 (sorting.xsl) can sort the XML file's data for presentation purposes.

```
 1   <?xml version = "1.0"?>
 2   <?xml-stylesheet type = "text/xsl" href = "sorting.xsl"?>
 3
 4   <!-- Fig. 15.20: sorting.xml -->
 5   <!-- XML document containing book information -->
 6   <book isbn = "999-99999-9-X">
 7      <title>Deitel&apos;s XML Primer</title>
 8
 9      <author>
10         <firstName>Jane</firstName>
11         <lastName>Blue</lastName>
12      </author>
13
14      <chapters>
15         <frontMatter>
16            <preface pages = "2" />
17            <contents pages = "5" />
18            <illustrations pages = "4" />
19         </frontMatter>
20
21         <chapter number = "3" pages = "44">Advanced XML</chapter>
22         <chapter number = "2" pages = "35">Intermediate XML</chapter>
23         <appendix number = "B" pages = "26">Parsers and Tools</appendix>
24         <appendix number = "A" pages = "7">Entities</appendix>
25         <chapter number = "1" pages = "28">XML Fundamentals</chapter>
26      </chapters>
27
28      <media type = "CD" />
29   </book>
```

Fig. 15.20 | XML document containing book information.

Figure 15.21 presents an XSL document (sorting.xsl) for transforming the XML document sorting.xml (Fig. 15.20) to HTML5. (To save space, we do not show the contents of the example's CSS file here.) Recall that an XSL document navigates a source tree and builds a result tree. In this example, the source tree is XML, and the output tree is HTML5. Line 12 of Fig. 15.21 matches the root element of the document in Fig. 15.20. Line 13 outputs an html start tag to the result tree. In line 14, the <xsl:apply-templates/> element specifies that the XSLT processor is to apply the xsl:templates defined in this XSL document to the current node's (i.e., the document root's) children. The content from the applied templates is output in the html element that ends at line 15. You can view the results of the transformation at:

```
http://test.deitel.com/iw3htp5/ch15/Fig15_20-21/sorting.xml
```

```
 1   <?xml version = "1.0"?>
 2
 3   <!-- Fig. 15.21: sorting.xsl -->
 4   <!-- Transformation of book information into HTML5 -->
```

Fig. 15.21 | XSL document that transforms sorting.xml into HTML5. (Part 1 of 3.)

```
5   <xsl:stylesheet version = "1.0"
6      xmlns:xsl = "http://www.w3.org/1999/XSL/Transform">
7
8      <!-- write XML declaration and DOCTYPE DTD information -->
9      <xsl:output method = "html" doctype-system = "about:legacy-compat" />
10
11     <!-- match document root -->
12     <xsl:template match = "/">
13        <html>
14           <xsl:apply-templates/>
15        </html>
16     </xsl:template>
17
18     <!-- match book -->
19     <xsl:template match = "book">
20        <head>
21           <meta charset = "utf-8"/>
22           <link rel = "stylesheet" type = "text/css" href = "style.css"/>
23           <title>ISBN <xsl:value-of select = "@isbn"/> -
24              <xsl:value-of select = "title"/></title>
25        </head>
26
27        <body>
28           <h1><xsl:value-of select = "title"/></h1>
29           <h2>by
30              <xsl:value-of select = "author/lastName"/>,
31              <xsl:value-of select = "author/firstName"/></h2>
32
33           <table>
34
35              <xsl:for-each select = "chapters/frontMatter/*">
36                 <tr>
37                    <td>
38                       <xsl:value-of select = "name()"/>
39                    </td>
40
41                    <td>
42                       ( <xsl:value-of select = "@pages"/> pages )
43                    </td>
44                 </tr>
45              </xsl:for-each>
46
47              <xsl:for-each select = "chapters/chapter">
48                 <xsl:sort select = "@number" data-type = "number"
49                    order = "ascending"/>
50                 <tr>
51                    <td>
52                       Chapter <xsl:value-of select = "@number"/>
53                    </td>
54
55                    <td>
56                       <xsl:value-of select = "text()"/>
```

Fig. 15.21 | XSL document that transforms sorting.xml into HTML5. (Part 2 of 3.)

```
57                         ( <xsl:value-of select = "@pages"/> pages )
58                     </td>
59                 </tr>
60             </xsl:for-each>
61
62             <xsl:for-each select = "chapters/appendix">
63                 <xsl:sort select = "@number" data-type = "text"
64                     order = "ascending"/>
65                 <tr>
66                     <td>
67                         Appendix <xsl:value-of select = "@number"/>
68                     </td>
69
70                     <td>
71                         <xsl:value-of select = "text()"/>
72                         ( <xsl:value-of select = "@pages"/> pages )
73                     </td>
74                 </tr>
75             </xsl:for-each>
76         </table>
77
78         <p>Pages:
79             <xsl:variable name = "pagecount"
80                 select = "sum(chapters//*/@pages)"/>
81             <xsl:value-of select = "$pagecount"/>
82         <p>Media Type: <xsl:value-of select = "media/@type"/></p>
83     </body>
84     </xsl:template>
85 </xsl:stylesheet>
```

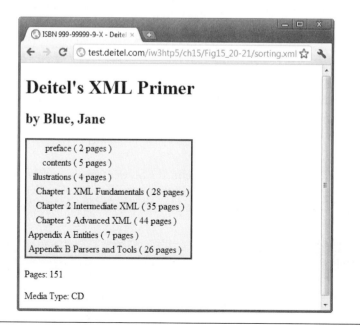

Fig. 15.21 | XSL document that transforms `sorting.xml` into HTML5. (Part 3 of 3.)

Lines 19–84 specify a template that matches element book. The template indicates how to format the information contained in book elements of sorting.xml (Fig. 15.20) as HTML5.

Lines 23–24 create the title for the HTML5 document. We use the book's ISBN (from attribute isbn) and the contents of element title to create the string that appears in the browser window's title bar (**ISBN 999-99999-9-X - Deitel's XML Primer**).

Line 28 creates a header element that contains the book's title. Lines 29–31 create a header element that contains the book's author. Because the context node (i.e., the current node being processed) is book, the XPath expression author/lastName selects the author's last name, and the expression author/firstName selects the author's first name.

Line 35 selects each element (indicated by an asterisk) that's a child of element front-Matter. Line 38 calls **node-set function name** to retrieve the current node's element name (e.g., preface). The current node is the context node specified in the xsl:for-each (line 35). Line 42 retrieves the value of the pages attribute of the current node.

Line 47 selects each chapter element. Lines 48–49 use element **xsl:sort** to sort chapters by number in ascending order. Attribute **select** selects the value of attribute number in context node chapter. Attribute **data-type**, with value "number", specifies a numeric sort, and attribute **order**, with value "ascending", specifies ascending order. Attribute data-type also accepts the value "text" (line 63), and attribute order also accepts the value "descending". Line 56 uses **node-set function text** to obtain the text between the chapter start and end tags (i.e., the name of the chapter). Line 57 retrieves the value of the pages attribute of the current node. Lines 62–75 perform similar tasks for each appendix.

Lines 79–80 use an **XSL variable** to store the value of the book's total page count and output the page count to the result tree. Attribute **name** specifies the variable's name (i.e., pagecount), and attribute select assigns a value to the variable. Function **sum** (line 80) totals the values for all page attribute values. The two slashes between chapters and * indicate a **recursive descent**—the MSXML processor will search for elements that contain an attribute named pages in all descendant nodes of chapters. The XPath expression

```
//*
```

selects all the nodes in an XML document. Line 81 retrieves the value of the newly created XSL variable pagecount by placing a dollar sign in front of its name.

Summary of XSL Stylesheet Elements
This section's examples used several predefined XSL elements to perform various operations. Figure 15.22 lists these and several other commonly used XSL elements. For more information on these elements and XSL in general, see www.w3.org/Style/XSL.

Element	Description
<xsl:apply-templates>	Applies the templates of the XSL document to the children of the current node.

Fig. 15.22 | XSL style-sheet elements. (Part 1 of 2.)

Element	Description
`<xsl:apply-templates match = "expression">`	Applies the templates of the XSL document to the children of *expression*. The value of the attribute match (i.e., *expression*) must be an XPath expression that specifies elements.
`<xsl:template>`	Contains rules to apply when a specified node is matched.
`<xsl:value-of select = "expression">`	Selects the value of an XML element and adds it to the output tree of the transformation. The required `select` attribute contains an XPath expression.
`<xsl:for-each select = "expression">`	Applies a template to every node selected by the XPath specified by the `select` attribute.
`<xsl:sort select = "expression">`	Used as a child element of an `<xsl:apply-templates>` or `<xsl:for-each>` element. Sorts the nodes selected by the `<xsl:apply-template>` or `<xsl:for-each>` element so that the nodes are processed in sorted order.
`<xsl:output>`	Has various attributes to define the format (e.g., XML), version (e.g., 1.0, 2.0), document type and media type of the output document. This tag is a top-level element—it can be used only as a child element of an `xml:stylesheet`.
`<xsl:copy>`	Adds the current node to the output tree.

Fig. 15.22 | XSL style-sheet elements. (Part 2 of 2.)

15.9 Document Object Model (DOM)

Although an XML document is a text file, retrieving data from the document using traditional sequential file-processing techniques is neither practical nor efficient, especially for adding and removing elements dynamically.

Upon successfully parsing a document, some XML parsers store document data as tree structures in memory. Figure 15.23 illustrates the tree structure for the root element of the document `article.xml` (Fig. 15.2). This hierarchical tree structure is called a **Document Object Model (DOM) tree**, and an XML parser that creates this type of structure is known as a **DOM parser**. Each element name (e.g., `article`, `date`, `firstName`) is represented by a node. A node that contains other nodes (called **child nodes** or children) is called a **parent node** (e.g., `author`). A parent node can have many children, but a child node can have only one parent node. Nodes that are peers (e.g., `firstName` and `lastName`) are called **sibling nodes**. A node's **descendant nodes** include its children, its children's children and so on. A node's **ancestor nodes** include its parent, its parent's parent and so on. Many of the XML DOM capabilities you'll see in this section are similar or identical to those of the HTML5 DOM you learned in Chapter 12.

The DOM tree has a single **root node**, which contains all the other nodes in the document. For example, the root node of the DOM tree that represents `article.xml` (Fig. 15.23) contains a node for the XML declaration (line 1), two nodes for the comments (lines 3–4) and a node for the XML document's root element `article` (line 5).

To introduce document manipulation with the XML Document Object Model, we provide a scripting example (Figs. 15.24–15.25) that uses JavaScript and XML. This

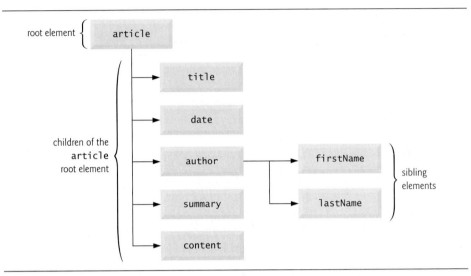

Fig. 15.23 | Tree structure for the document `article.xml` of Fig. 15.2.

example loads the XML document `article.xml` (Fig. 15.2) and uses the XML DOM API to display the document's element names and values. The example also provides buttons that enable you to navigate the DOM structure. As you click each button, an appropriate part of the document is highlighted.

HTML5 Document

Figure 15.24 contains the HTML5 document. When this document loads, the `load` event calls our JavaScript function `start` (Fig. 15.25) to register event handlers for the buttons in the document and to load and display the contents of `article.xml` in the `div` at line 21 (`outputDiv`). Lines 13–20 define a form consisting of five buttons. When each button is pressed, it invokes one of our JavaScript functions to navigate `article.xml`'s DOM structure. (To save space, we do not show the contents of the example's CSS file here.) Some browsers allow you to load XML documents dynamically only when accessing the files from a web server. For this reason, you can test this example at:

```
http://test.deitel.com/iw3htp5/ch15/Fig15_24-25/XMLDOMTraversal.xml
```

```
 1   <!DOCTYPE html>
 2
 3   <!-- Fig. 15.24: XMLDOMTraversal.html -->
 4   <!-- Traversing an XML document using the XML DOM. -->
 5   <html>
 6   <head>
 7      <meta charset = "utf-8">
 8      <link rel = "stylesheet" type = "text/css" href = "style.css">
 9      <script src = "XMLDOMTraversal.js"></script>
10      <title>Traversing an XML document using the XML DOM</title>
11   </head>
```

Fig. 15.24 | Traversing an XML document using the XML DOM. (Part 1 of 5.)

```
12   <body id = "body">
13      <form action = "#">
14         <input id = "firstChild" type = "button" value = "firstChild">
15         <input id = "nextSibling" type = "button" value = "nextSibling">
16         <input id = "previousSibling" type = "button"
17            value = "previousSibling">
18         <input id = "lastChild" type = "button" value = "lastChild">
19         <input id = "parentNode" type = "button" value = "parentNode">
20      </form>
21      <div id = "outputDiv"></div>
22   </body>
23   </html>
```

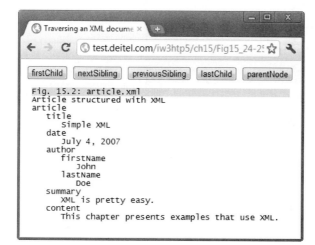

a) Comment node at the beginning of `article.xml` is highlighted when the XML document first loads

b) User clicked the **nextSibling** button to highlight the second comment node

Fig. 15.24 | Traversing an XML document using the XML DOM. (Part 2 of 5.)

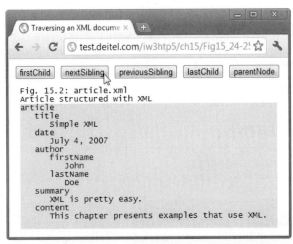

c) User clicked the **nextSibling** button again to highlight the `article` node

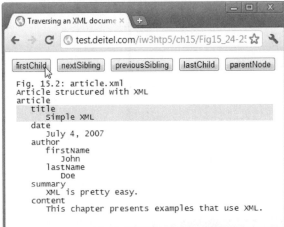

d) User clicked the **firstChild** button to highlight the `article` node's `title` child node

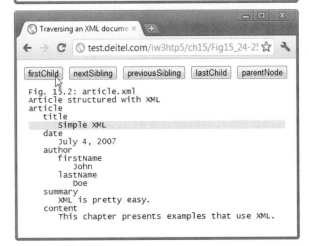

e) User clicked the **firstChild** button again to highlight the `title` node's text child node

Fig. 15.24 | Traversing an XML document using the XML DOM. (Part 3 of 5.)

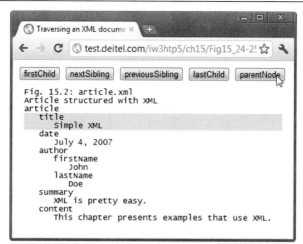

f) User clicked the **parentNode** button to highlight the text node's parent `title` node

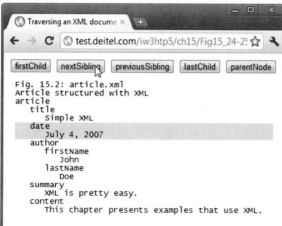

g) User clicked the **nextSibling** button to highlight the `title` node's `date` sibling node

h) User clicked the **nextSibling** button to highlight the `date` node's `author` sibling node

Fig. 15.24 | Traversing an XML document using the XML DOM. (Part 4 of 5.)

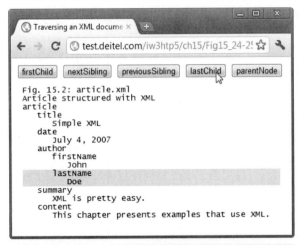

i) User clicked the **lastChild** button to highlight the author node's last child node (lastName)

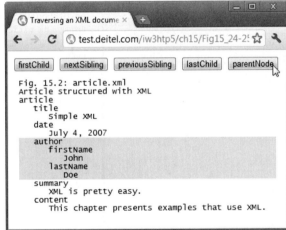

j) User clicked the **parentNode** button to highlight the lastName node's author parent node

Fig. 15.24 | Traversing an XML document using the XML DOM. (Part 5 of 5.)

JavaScript Code

Figure 15.24 lists the JavaScript code that manipulates this XML document and displays its content in an HTML5 page. Line 187 indicates that the document's load event handler should call the script's start function.

```
1   <!-- Fig. 15.25: XMLDOMTraversal.html -->
2   <!-- JavaScript for traversing an XML document using the XML DOM. -->
3   var outputHTML = ""; // stores text to output in outputDiv
4   var idCounter = 1; // used to create div IDs
5   var depth = -1; // tree depth is -1 to start
6   var current = null; // represents the current node for traversals
7   var previous = null; // represents prior node in traversals
```

Fig. 15.25 | JavaScript for traversing an XML document using the XML DOM. (Part 1 of 5.)

```
 8
 9    // register event handlers for buttons and load XML document
10    function start()
11    {
12       document.getElementById( "firstChild" ).addEventListener(
13          "click", processFirstChild, false );
14       document.getElementById( "nextSibling" ).addEventListener(
15          "click", processNextSibling, false );
16       document.getElementById( "previousSibling" ).addEventListener(
17          "click", processPreviousSibling, false );
18       document.getElementById( "lastChild" ).addEventListener(
19          "click", processLastChild, false );
20       document.getElementById( "parentNode" ).addEventListener(
21          "click", processParentNode, false );
22       loadXMLDocument( 'article.xml' )
23    } // end function start
24
25    // load XML document based on whether the browser is IE7 or Firefox 2
26    function loadXMLDocument( url )
27    {
28       var xmlHttpRequest = new XMLHttpRequest();
29       xmlHttpRequest.open( "get", url, false );
30       xmlHttpRequest.send( null );
31       var doc = xmlHttpRequest.responseXML;
32       buildHTML( doc.childNodes ); // display the nodes
33       displayDoc(); // display the document and highlight current node
34    } // end function loadXMLDocument
35
36    // traverse xmlDocument and build HTML5 representation of its content
37    function buildHTML( childList )
38    {
39       ++depth; // increase tab depth
40
41       // display each node's content
42       for ( var i = 0; i < childList.length; i++ )
43       {
44          switch ( childList[ i ].nodeType )
45          {
46             case 1: // Node.ELEMENT_NODE; value used for portability
47                outputHTML += "<div id=\"id" + idCounter + "\">";
48                spaceOutput( depth ); // insert spaces
49                outputHTML += childList[ i ].nodeName; // show node's name
50                ++idCounter; // increment the id counter
51
52                // if current node has children, call buildHTML recursively
53                if ( childList[ i ].childNodes.length != 0 )
54                   buildHTML( childList[ i ].childNodes );
55
56                outputHTML += "</div>";
57                break;
58             case 3: // Node.TEXT_NODE; value used for portability
59             case 8: // Node.COMMENT_NODE; value used for portability
```

Fig. 15.25 | JavaScript for traversing an XML document using the XML DOM. (Part 2 of 5.)

```
60            // if nodeValue is not 3 or 6 spaces (Firefox issue),
61            // include nodeValue in HTML
62            if ( childList[ i ].nodeValue.indexOf( "   " ) == -1 &&
63               childList[ i ].nodeValue.indexOf( "      " ) == -1 )
64            {
65               outputHTML += "<div id=\"id" + idCounter + "\">";
66               spaceOutput( depth ); // insert spaces
67               outputHTML += childList[ i ].nodeValue + "</div>";
68               ++idCounter; // increment the id counter
69            } // end if
70         } // end switch
71      } // end for
72
73      --depth; // decrease tab depth
74   } // end function buildHTML
75
76   // display the XML document and highlight the first child
77   function displayDoc()
78   {
79      document.getElementById( "outputDiv" ).innerHTML = outputHTML;
80      current = document.getElementById( 'id1' );
81      setCurrentNodeStyle( current.getAttribute( "id" ), true );
82   } // end function displayDoc
83
84   // insert nonbreaking spaces for indentation
85   function spaceOutput( number )
86   {
87      for ( var i = 0; i < number; i++ )
88      {
89         outputHTML += "   ";
90      } // end for
91   } // end function spaceOutput
92
93   // highlight first child of current node
94   function processFirstChild()
95   {
96      if ( current.childNodes.length == 1 && // only one child
97         current.firstChild.nodeType == 3 )  // and it's a text node
98      {
99         alert( "There is no child node" );
100     } // end if
101     else if ( current.childNodes.length > 1 )
102     {
103        previous = current; // save currently highlighted node
104
105        if ( current.firstChild.nodeType != 3 ) // if not text node
106           current = current.firstChild; // get new current node
107        else // if text node, use firstChild's nextSibling instead
108           current = current.firstChild.nextSibling; // get first sibling
109
110        setCurrentNodeStyle( previous.getAttribute( "id" ), false );
111        setCurrentNodeStyle( current.getAttribute( "id" ), true );
112     } // end if
```

Fig. 15.25 | JavaScript for traversing an XML document using the XML DOM. (Part 3 of 5.)

```
113      else
114         alert( "There is no child node" );
115   } // end function processFirstChild
116
117   // highlight next sibling of current node
118   function processNextSibling()
119   {
120      if ( current.getAttribute( "id" ) != "outputDiv" &&
121         current.nextSibling )
122      {
123         previous = current; // save currently highlighted node
124         current = current.nextSibling; // get new current node
125         setCurrentNodeStyle( previous.getAttribute( "id" ), false );
126         setCurrentNodeStyle( current.getAttribute( "id" ), true );
127      } // end if
128      else
129         alert( "There is no next sibling" );
130   } // end function processNextSibling
131
132   // highlight previous sibling of current node if it is not a text node
133   function processPreviousSibling()
134   {
135      if ( current.getAttribute( "id" ) != "outputDiv" &&
136         current.previousSibling && current.previousSibling.nodeType != 3 )
137      {
138         previous = current; // save currently highlighted node
139         current = current.previousSibling; // get new current node
140         setCurrentNodeStyle( previous.getAttribute( "id" ), false );
141         setCurrentNodeStyle( current.getAttribute( "id" ), true );
142      } // end if
143      else
144         alert( "There is no previous sibling" );
145   } // end function processPreviousSibling
146
147   // highlight last child of current node
148   function processLastChild()
149   {
150      if ( current.childNodes.length == 1 &&
151         current.lastChild.nodeType == 3 )
152      {
153         alert( "There is no child node" );
154      } // end if
155      else if ( current.childNodes.length != 0 )
156      {
157         previous = current; // save currently highlighted node
158         current = current.lastChild; // get new current node
159         setCurrentNodeStyle( previous.getAttribute( "id" ), false );
160         setCurrentNodeStyle( current.getAttribute( "id" ), true );
161      } // end if
162      else
163         alert( "There is no child node" );
164   } // end function processLastChild
165
```

Fig. 15.25 | JavaScript for traversing an XML document using the XML DOM. (Part 4 of 5.)

```
166  // highlight parent of current node
167  function processParentNode()
168  {
169     if ( current.parentNode.getAttribute( "id" ) != "body" )
170     {
171        previous = current; // save currently highlighted node
172        current = current.parentNode; // get new current node
173        setCurrentNodeStyle( previous.getAttribute( "id" ), false );
174        setCurrentNodeStyle( current.getAttribute( "id" ), true );
175     } // end if
176     else
177        alert( "There is no parent node" );
178  } // end function processParentNode
179
180  // set style of node with specified id
181  function setCurrentNodeStyle( id, highlight )
182  {
183     document.getElementById( id ).className =
184        ( highlight ? "highlighted" : "" );
185  } // end function setCurrentNodeStyle
186
187  window.addEventListener( "load", start, false );
```

Fig. 15.25 | JavaScript for traversing an XML document using the XML DOM. (Part 5 of 5.)

Global Script Variables

Lines 3–7 declare several variables used throughout the script. Variable outputHTML stores the markup that will be placed in outputDiv. Variable idCounter is used to track the unique id attributes that we assign to each element in the outputHTML markup. These ids will be used to dynamically highlight parts of the document when the user clicks the buttons in the form. Variable depth determines the indentation level for the content in article.xml. We use this to structure the output using the nesting of the elements in article.xml. Variables current and previous track the current and previous nodes in article.xml's DOM structure as the user navigates it.

Function start

Function start (lines 10–23) registers event handlers for each of the buttons in Fig. 15.24, then calls function loadXMLDocument.

Function loadXMLDocument

Function loadXMLDocument (lines 26–35) loads the XML document at the specified URL. Line 28 creates an **XMLHttpRequest object**, which can be used to load an XML document. Typically, such an object is used with Ajax to make asynchronous requests to a server—the topic of the next chapter. Here, we need to load an XML document immediately for use in this example. Line 29 uses the XMLHttpRequest object's **open method** to create a get request for an XML document at a specified URL. When the last argument's value is false, the request will be made synchronously—that is, the script will not continue until the document is received. Next, line 30 executes the XMLHttpRequest, which actually loads the XML document. The argument null to the **send method** indicates that no data is being sent to the server as part of this request. When the request completes, the resulting XML document is stored in the XMLHttpRequest object's responseXML property, which we assign to local variable doc. When this completes, we call our buildHTML method (defined in lines 37–74) to construct an HTML5 representation of the XML document. The expression doc.child-Nodes is a list of the XML document's top-level nodes. Line 33 calls our displayDoc function (lines 77–82) to display the contents of article.xml in outputDiv.

Function *buildHTML*
Function buildHTML (lines 37–74) is a recursive function that receives a list of nodes as an argument. Line 39 increments the depth for indentation purposes. Lines 42–71 iterate through the nodes in the list. The switch statement (lines 44–70) uses the current node's **nodeType property** to determine whether the current node is an element (line 46), a text node (i.e., the text content of an element; line 58) or a comment node (line 59). If it's an element, then we begin a new div element in our HTML5 (line 47) and give it a unique id. Then function spaceOutput (defined in lines 85–91) appends **nonbreaking spaces (&nb-sp;)**—i.e., spaces that the browser is not allowed to collapse or that can be used to keep words together—to indent the current element to the correct level. Line 49 appends the name of the current element using the node's **nodeName property**. If the current element has children, the length of the current node's childNodes list is nonzero and line 54 recursively calls buildHTML to append the current element's child nodes to the markup. When that recursive call completes, line 56 completes the div element that we started at line 47.

If the current element is a text node, lines 62–63 obtain the node's value with the **nodeValue property** and use the string method indexOf to determine whether the node's value starts with three or six spaces. Some XML parsers do not ignore the white space used for indentation in XML documents. Instead they create text nodes containing just the space characters. The condition in lines 62–63 enables us to ignore these nodes in such browsers. If the node contains text, lines 65–67 append a new div to the markup and use the node's nodeValue property to insert that text in the div. Line 73 in buildHTML decrements the depth counter.

> **Portability Tip 15.4**
> *Firefox's XML parser does not ignore white space used for indentation in XML documents. Instead, it creates text nodes containing the white-space characters.*

Function *displayDoc*
In function displayDoc (lines 77–82), line 79 uses the DOM's getElementById method to obtain the outputDiv element and set its innerHTML property to the new markup generated by buildHTML. Then, line 80 sets variable current to refer to the div with id 'id1' in the new markup, and line 81 uses our setCurrentNodeStyle method (defined at lines 181–185) to highlight that div.

Functions *processFirstChild* and *processLastChild*
Function processFirstChild (lines 94–115) is invoked by the onclick event of the firstChild button. If the current node has only one child and it's a text node (lines 96–97), line 99 displays an alert dialog indicating that there's no child node—we navigate only to nested XML elements in this example. If there are two or more children, line 103 stores the value of current in previous, and lines 105–108 set current to refer to its **firstChild** (if this child is not a text node) or its firstChild's **nextSibling** (if the

firstChild is a text node)—again, this is to ensure that we navigate only to nodes that represent XML elements. Then lines 110–111 unhighlight the previous node and highlight the new current node. Function processLastChild (lines 148–164) works similarly, using the current node's **lastChild** property.

Functions *processNextSibling and processPreviousSibling*

Function processNextSibling (lines 118–130) first ensures that the current node is not the outputDiv and that nextSibling exists. If so, lines 123–124 adjust the previous and current nodes accordingly and update their highlighting. Function processPreviousSibling (lines 133–145) works similarly, ensuring first that the current node is not the outputDiv, that previousSibling exists and that previousSibling is not a text node.

Function *processParentNode*

Function processParentNode (lines 167–178) first checks whether the current node's **parentNode** is the HTML5 page's body. If not, lines 171–174 adjust the previous and current nodes accordingly and update their highlighting.

Common DOM Properties

The tables in Figs. 15.26–15.31 describe many common DOM properties and methods. Some of the key DOM objects are **Node** (a node in the tree), **NodeList** (an ordered set of Nodes), **Document** (the document), **Element** (an element node), **Attr** (an attribute node) and **Text** (a text node). There are many more objects, properties and methods than we can possibly list here. Our XML Resource Center (www.deitel.com/XML/) includes links to various DOM reference websites.

Property/Method	Description
nodeType	An integer representing the node type.
nodeName	The name of the node.
nodeValue	A string or null depending on the node type.
parentNode	The parent node.
childNodes	A NodeList (Fig. 15.27) with all the children of the node.
firstChild	The first child in the Node's NodeList.
lastChild	The last child in the Node's NodeList.
previousSibling	The node preceding this node; null if there's no such node.
nextSibling	The node following this node; null if there's no such node.
attributes	A collection of Attr objects (Fig. 15.30) containing the attributes for this node.
insertBefore	Inserts the node (passed as the first argument) before the existing node (passed as the second argument). If the new node is already in the tree, it's removed before insertion. The same behavior is true for other methods that add nodes.

Fig. 15.26 | Common Node properties and methods. (Part 1 of 2.)

Property/Method	Description
replaceChild	Replaces the second argument node with the first argument node.
removeChild	Removes the child node passed to it.
appendChild	Appends the node it receives to the list of child nodes.

Fig. 15.26 | Common Node properties and methods. (Part 2 of 2.)

Property/Method	Description
item	Method that receives an index number and returns the element node at that index. Indices range from 0 to *length* – 1. You can also access the nodes in a NodeList via array indexing.
length	The total number of nodes in the list.

Fig. 15.27 | NodeList property and method.

Property/Method	Description
documentElement	The root node of the document.
createElement	Creates and returns an element node with the specified tag name.
createAttribute	Creates and returns an Attr node (Fig. 15.30) with the specified name and value.
createTextNode	Creates and returns a text node that contains the specified text.
getElementsByTagName	Returns a NodeList of all the nodes in the subtree with the name specified as the first argument, ordered as they would be encountered in a preorder traversal. An optional second argument specifies either the direct child nodes (0) or any descendant (1).

Fig. 15.28 | Document property and methods.

Property/Method	Description
tagName	The name of the element.
getAttribute	Returns the value of the specified attribute.
setAttribute	Changes the value of the attribute passed as the first argument to the value passed as the second argument.
removeAttribute	Removes the specified attribute.
getAttributeNode	Returns the specified attribute node.
setAttributeNode	Adds a new attribute node with the specified name.

Fig. 15.29 | Element property and methods.

Property	Description
value	The specified attribute's value.
name	The name of the attribute.

Fig. 15.30 | Attr properties.

Property	Description
data	The text contained in the node.
length	The number of characters contained in the node.

Fig. 15.31 | Text properties.

Locating Data in XML Documents with XPath

Although you can use XML DOM capabilities to navigate through and manipulate nodes, this is not the most efficient means of locating data in an XML document's DOM tree. A simpler way to locate nodes is to search for lists of nodes matching search criteria that are written as XPath expressions. Recall that XPath (XML Path Language) provides a syntax for locating specific nodes in XML documents effectively and efficiently. XPath is a string-based language of expressions used by XML and many of its related technologies (such as XSLT, discussed in Section 15.8).

The example of Figs. 15.32–15.34 enables the user to enter XPath expressions in an HTML5 form. (To save space, we do not show the contents of the example's CSS file here.) When the user clicks the **Get Matches** button, the script applies the XPath expression to the XML DOM and displays the matching nodes.

HTML5 Document

When the HTML5 document (Fig. 15.32) loads, its load event calls loadDocument (as specified in Fig. 15.33, line 61) to load the sports.xml file (Fig. 15.34). The user specifies the XPath expression in the input element at line 14 (of Fig. 15.32). When the user clicks the **Get Matches** button (line 15), its click event handler invokes our processXPathExpression function (Fig. 15.33) to locate any matches and display the results in outputDiv (Fig. 15.32, line 17). Some browsers allow you to load XML documents dynamically only when accessing the files from a web server. For this reason, you can test this example at:

```
http://test.deitel.com/iw3htp5/ch15/Fig15_24-25/XMLDOMTraversal.xml
```

```
 1  <!DOCTYPE html>
 2
 3  <!-- Fig. 15.32: xpath.html -->
 4  <!-- Using XPath to locate nodes in an XML document. -->
 5  <html>
 6  <head>
```

Fig. 15.32 | Using XPath to locate nodes in an XML document. (Part 1 of 2.)

```
 7        <meta charset = "utf-8">
 8        <link rel = "stylesheet" type = "text/css" href = "style.css">
 9        <script src = "xpath.js"></script>
10        <title>Using XPath</title>
11    </head>
12    <body id = "body">
13        <form id = "myForm" action = "#">
14            <input id = "inputField" type = "text">
15            <input id = "matchesButton" type = "button" value = "Get Matches">
16        </form>
17        <div id = "outputDiv"></div>
18    </body>
19    </html>
```

a) Selecting the `sports` node

b) Selecting the `game` nodes from the `sports` node

c) Selecting the `name` node from each `game` node

d) Selecting the `paragraph` node from each `game` node

e) Selecting the `game` with the `id` attribute value 239

f) Selecting the `game` with `name` element value `Cricket`

Fig. 15.32 | Using XPath to locate nodes in an XML document. (Part 2 of 2.)

JavaScript
The script of Fig. 15.33 loads the XML document `sports.xml` (Fig. 15.34) using the same techniques we presented in Fig. 15.25, so we focus on only the new features in this example.

```
1   // Fig. 15.33: xpath.html
2   // JavaScript that uses XPath to locate nodes in an XML document.
3   var doc; // variable to reference the XML document
4   var outputHTML = ""; // stores text to output in outputDiv
5
6   // register event handler for button and load XML document
7   function start()
8   {
9      document.getElementById( "matchesButton" ).addEventListener(
10         "click", processXPathExpression, false );
11     loadXMLDocument( "sports.xml" );
12  } // end function start
13
14  // load XML document programmatically
15  function loadXMLDocument( url )
16  {
17     var xmlHttpRequest = new XMLHttpRequest();
18     xmlHttpRequest.open( "get", url, false );
19     xmlHttpRequest.send( null );
20     doc = xmlHttpRequest.responseXML;
21  } // end function loadXMLDocument
22
23  // display the XML document
24  function displayHTML()
25  {
26     document.getElementById( "outputDiv" ).innerHTML = outputHTML;
27  } // end function displayDoc
28
29  // obtain and apply XPath expression
30  function processXPathExpression()
31  {
32     var xpathExpression = document.getElementById( "inputField" ).value;
33     var result;
34     outputHTML = "";
35
36     if ( !doc.evaluate ) // Internet Explorer
37     {
38        result = doc.selectNodes( xpathExpression );
39
40        for ( var i = 0; i < result.length; i++ )
41        {
42           outputHTML += "<p>" + result.item( i ).text + "</p>";
43        } // end for
44     } // end if
45     else // other browsers
46     {
47        result = doc.evaluate( xpathExpression, doc, null,
48           XPathResult.ORDERED_NODE_ITERATOR_TYPE, null );
49        var current = result.iterateNext();
50
51        while ( current )
52        {
```

Fig. 15.33 | Using XPath to locate nodes in an XML document. (Part I of 2.)

```
53                outputHTML += "<p>" + current.textContent + "</p>";
54                current = result.iterateNext();
55            } // end while
56        } // end else
57
58        displayHTML();
59    } // end function processXPathExpression
60
61    window.addEventListener( "load", start, false );
```

Fig. 15.33 | Using XPath to locate nodes in an XML document. (Part 2 of 2.)

Function *processXPathExpression*

Function processXPathExpression (Fig. 15.33, lines 30–59) obtains the XPath expression (line 32) from the inputField. Internet Explorer and other browsers handle XPath processing differently, so this function contains an if...else statement to handle the differences.

Lines 36–44 apply the XPath expression in Internet Explorer (or any other browser that does not support to evaluate method on an XML document object), and lines 45–56 apply the XPath expression in all other browsers. In IE, the XML document object's **selectNodes method** (line 38) receives an XPath expression as an argument and returns a collection of elements that match the expression. Lines 40–43 iterate through the results and mark up each one in a separate p element. After this loop completes, line 58 displays the generated markup in outputDiv.

For other browsers, lines 47–48 invoke the XML document object's **evaluate method**, which receives five arguments—the XPath expression, the document to apply the expression to, a namespace resolver, a result type and an XPathResult object into which to place the results. The result type XPathResult.ORDERED_NODE_ITERATOR_TYPE indicates that the method should return an object that can be used to iterate through the results in the order they appeared in the XML document. If the last argument is null, the function simply returns a new **XPathResult object** containing the matches. The namespace resolver argument can be null if you're not using XML namespace prefixes in the XPath processing. Lines 47–55 iterate through the XPathResult and mark up the results. Line 49 invokes the XPathResult's iterateNext method to position to the first result. If there's a result, the condition in line 51 will be true, and line 53 creates a p element for that result. Line 54 then positions to the next result. After this loop completes, line 58 displays the generated markup in outputDiv.

sports.xml

Figure 15.34 shows the XML document sports.xml that we use in this example. [*Note:* The versions of sports.xml presented in Fig. 15.34 and Fig. 15.18 are nearly identical. In the current example, we do not want to apply an XSLT, so we omit the processing instruction found in line 2 of Fig. 15.18. We also removed extra blank lines to save space.]

```
1    <?xml version = "1.0"?>
2
3    <!-- Fig. 15.34: sports.xml -->
```

Fig. 15.34 | XML document that describes various sports. (Part 1 of 2.)

```
4   <!-- Sports Database        -->
5   <sports>
6     <game id = "783">
7         <name>Cricket</name>
8         <paragraph>
9            More popular among commonwealth nations.
10        </paragraph>
11    </game>
12    <game id = "239">
13        <name>Baseball</name>
14        <paragraph>
15           More popular in America.
16        </paragraph>
17    </game>
18    <game id = "418">
19        <name>Soccer (Futbol)</name>
20        <paragraph>
21           Most popular sport in the world.
22        </paragraph>
23    </game>
24  </sports>
```

Fig. 15.34 | XML document that describes various sports. (Part 2 of 2.)

Function *processXPathExpression*

Figure 15.35 summarizes the XPath expressions that we demonstrated in Fig. 15.32's sample outputs.

Expression	Description
/sports	Matches all sports nodes that are child nodes of the document root node.
/sports/game	Matches all game nodes that are child nodes of sports, which is a child of the document root.
/sports/game/name	Matches all name nodes that are child nodes of game. The game is a child of sports, which is a child of the document root.
/sports/game/paragraph	Matches all paragraph nodes that are child nodes of game. The game is a child of sports, which is a child of the document root.
/sports/game [@id='239']	Matches the game node with the id number 239. The game is a child of sports, which is a child of the document root.
/sports/game [name='Cricket']	Matches all game nodes that contain a child element whose name is Cricket. The game is a child of sports, which is a child of the document root.

Fig. 15.35 | XPath expressions and descriptions.

15.10 Web Resources

www.deitel.com/XML/

The Deitel XML Resource Center focuses on the vast amount of free XML content available online, plus some for-sale items. Start your search here for tools, downloads, tutorials, podcasts, wikis, documentation, conferences, FAQs, books, e-books, sample chapters, articles, newsgroups, forums, downloads from CNET's download.com, jobs and contract opportunities, and more that will help you develop XML applications.

Summary

Section 15.1 Introduction

- The eXtensible Markup Language (XML; p. 544) is a portable, widely supported, open (i.e., nonproprietary) technology for data storage and exchange.

Section 15.2 XML Basics

- XML documents are readable by both humans and machines.
- XML permits document authors to create custom markup for any type of information. This enables document authors to create entirely new markup languages (p. 544) that describe specific types of data, including mathematical formulas, chemical molecular structures, music and recipes.
- An XML parser (p. 546) is responsible for identifying components of XML documents (typically files with the .xml extension) and then storing those components in a data structure for manipulation.
- An XML document can optionally reference a Document Type Definition (DTD, p. 546) or schema that defines the XML document's structure.
- An XML document that conforms to a DTD/schema (i.e., has the appropriate structure) is valid.
- If an XML parser (validating or non-validating; p. 546) can process an XML document successfully, that XML document is well-formed (p. 546).

Section 15.3 Structuring Data

- An XML document begins with an XML declaration (p. 547), which identifies the document as an XML document. The version attribute (p. 547) specifies the version of XML syntax used in the document.
- XML comments begin with <!-- and end with -->.
- An XML document contains text that represents its content (i.e., data) and elements that specify its structure. XML documents delimit an element with start and end tags.
- The root element (p. 550) of an XML document encompasses all its other elements.
- XML element names can be of any length and can contain letters, digits, underscores, hyphens and periods. However, they must begin with either a letter or an underscore, and they should not begin with "xml" in any combination of uppercase and lowercase letters, as this is reserved for use in the XML standards.
- When a user loads an XML document in a browser, a parser parses the document, and the browser uses a style sheet to format the data for display.
- Data can be placed between tags or in attributes (name/value pairs that appear within the angle brackets of start tags, p. 552). Elements can have any number of attributes.

Section 15.4 XML Namespaces

- XML allows document authors to create their own markup, and as a result, naming collisions (i.e., two different elements that have the same name, p. 553) can occur. XML namespaces (p. 553) provide a means for document authors to prevent collisions.

- Each namespace prefix (p. 553) is bound to a Uniform Resource Identifier (URI, p. 554) that uniquely identifies the namespace. A URI is a series of characters that differentiate names. Document authors create their own namespace prefixes. Any name can be used as a namespace prefix, but the namespace prefix xml is reserved for use in XML standards.

- To eliminate the need to place a namespace prefix in each element, authors can specify a default namespace for an element and its children. We declare a default namespace using keyword xmlns (p. 554) with a URI as its value.

- Document authors commonly use URLs (Uniform Resource Locators, p. 554) for URIs, because domain names (e.g., deitel.com) in URLs must be unique.

Section 15.5 Document Type Definitions (DTDs)

- DTDs and schemas specify documents' element types and attributes and their relationships to one another.

- DTDs and schemas enable an XML parser to verify whether an XML document is valid (i.e., its elements contain the proper attributes and appear in the proper sequence).

- A DTD expresses the set of rules for document structure using an EBNF (Extended Backus-Naur Form) grammar.

- In a DTD, an ELEMENT element type declaration (p. 557) defines the rules for an element. An ATTLIST attribute-list declaration (p. 557) defines attributes for a particular element.

Section 15.6 W3C XML Schema Documents

- XML schemas use XML syntax and are themselves XML documents.

- Unlike DTDs, XML Schema (p. 559) documents can specify what type of data (e.g., numeric, text) an element can contain.

- An XML document that conforms to a schema document is schema valid (p. 560).

- Two categories of types exist in XML Schema: simple types and complex types (p. 563). Simple types cannot contain attributes or child elements; complex types can.

- Every simple type defines a restriction on an XML Schema-defined schema type or on a user-defined type.

- Complex types can have either simple content or complex content. Both can contain attributes, but only complex content can contain child elements.

- Whereas complex types with simple content must extend or restrict some other existing type, complex types with complex content do not have this limitation.

Section 15.7 XML Vocabularies

- XML allows authors to create their own tags to describe data precisely.

- Some of these XML vocabularies include MathML (Mathematical Markup Language, p. 566), Scalable Vector Graphics (SVG, p. 566), Wireless Markup Language (WML, p. 566), Extensible Business Reporting Language (XBRL, p. 566), Extensible User Interface Language (XUL, p. 566), Product Data Markup Language (PDML, p. 566), W3C XML Schema and Extensible Stylesheet Language (XSL).

- MathML markup describes mathematical expressions for display. MathML is divided into two types of markup—content markup (p. 566) and presentation markup (p. 566).

- Content markup provides tags that embody mathematical concepts. Content MathML allows programmers to write mathematical notation specific to different areas of mathematics.

- Presentation MathML is directed toward formatting and displaying mathematical notation.

- By convention, MathML files end with the .mml filename extension.

- A MathML document's root node is the math element and its default namespace is http://www.w3.org/1998/Math/MathML.

- The mn element (p. 567) marks up a number. The mo element (p. 567) marks up an operator.

- Entity reference ⁢ (p. 568) indicates a multiplication operation without explicit symbolic representation (p. 568).

- The msup element (p. 568) represents a superscript. It has two children—the expression to be superscripted (i.e., the base) and the superscript (i.e., the exponent). Correspondingly, the msub element (p. 568) represents a subscript.

- To display variables, use identifier element mi (p. 568).

- The mfrac element (p. 568) displays a fraction. If either the numerator or the denominator contains more than one element, it must appear in an mrow element (p. 569).

- An mrow element is used to group elements that are positioned horizontally in an expression.

- The entity reference ∫ (p. 569) represents the integral symbol.

- The msubsup element (p. 569) specifies the subscript and superscript of a symbol. It requires three child elements—an operator, the subscript expression and the superscript expression.

- Element msqrt (p. 569) represents a square-root expression.

- Entity reference δ represents a lowercase delta symbol.

Section 15.8 Extensible Stylesheet Language and XSL Transformations

- eXtensible Stylesheet Language (XSL; p. 570) can convert XML into any text-based document. XSL documents have the extension .xsl.

- XPath (p. 570) is a string-based language of expressions used by XML and many of its related technologies for effectively and efficiently locating structures and data (such as specific elements and attributes) in XML documents.

- XPath is used to locate parts of the source-tree document that match templates defined in an XSL style sheet. When a match occurs (i.e., a node matches a template), the matching template executes and adds its result to the result tree (p. 571). When there are no more matches, XSLT has transformed the source tree (p. 571) into the result tree.

- The XSLT does not analyze every node of the source tree; it selectively navigates the source tree using XPath's select and match attributes.

- For XSLT to function, the source tree must be properly structured. Schemas, DTDs and validating parsers can validate document structure before using XPath and XSLTs.

- XSL style sheets (p. 571) can be connected directly to an XML document by adding an xml:stylesheet processing instruction to the XML document.

- Two tree structures are involved in transforming an XML document using XSLT—the source tree (the document being transformed) and the result tree (the result of the transformation).

- The XPath character / (a forward slash) always selects the document root. In XPath, a leading forward slash specifies that we're using absolute addressing.

- An XPath expression with no beginning forward slash uses relative addressing (p. 574).

- XSL element value-of retrieves an attribute's value. The @ symbol specifies an attribute node.

- XSL node-set function name (p. 578) retrieves the current node's element name.
- XSL node-set function text (p. 578) retrieves the text between an element's start and end tags.
- The XPath expression //* selects all the nodes in an XML document.

Section 15.9 Document Object Model (DOM)

- Although an XML document is a text file, retrieving data from the document using traditional sequential file-processing techniques is neither practical nor efficient, especially for adding and removing elements dynamically.
- Upon successfully parsing a document, some XML parsers store document data as tree structures in memory. This hierarchical tree structure is called a Document Object Model (DOM) tree (p. 579), and an XML parser that creates this type of structure is known as a DOM parser (p. 579).
- Each element name is represented by a node. A node that contains other nodes is called a parent node. A parent node (p. 579) can have many children, but a child node (p. 579) can have only one parent node.
- Nodes that are peers are called sibling nodes (p. 579).
- A node's descendant nodes (p. 579) include its children, its children's children and so on. A node's ancestor nodes (p. 579) include its parent, its parent's parent and so on.
- Many of the XML DOM capabilities are similar or identical to those of the HTML5 DOM.
- The DOM tree has a single root node (p. 579), which contains all the other nodes in the document.
- An XMLHttpRequest object can be used to load an XML document.
- The XMLHttpRequest object's open method (p. 588) can be used to create a get request for an XML document at a specified URL. When the last argument's value is false, the request will be made synchronously.
- XMLHttpRequest method send (p. 588) executes the request to load the XML document. When the request completes, the resulting XML document is stored in the XMLHttpRequest object's responseXML property.
- A document's childNodes property contains a list of the XML document's top-level nodes.
- A node's nodeType property (p. 589) contains the type of the node.
- Nonbreaking spaces (, p. 589) are spaces that the browser is not allowed to collapse or that can be used to keep words together.
- The name of an element can be obtained by the node's nodeName property (p. 589).
- If the currrent node has children, the length of the node's childNodes list is nonzero.
- The nodeValue property (p. 589) returns the value of an element.
- Node property firstChild (p. 589) refers to the first child of a given node. Similarly, lastChild (p. 590) refers to the last child of a given node.
- Node property nextSibling (p. 589) refers to the next sibling in a list of children of a particular node. Similarly, previousSibling refers to the current node's previous sibling.
- Property parentNode (p. 590) refers to the current node's parent node.
- A simpler way to locate nodes is to search for lists of node-matching search criteria that are written as XPath expressions.
- In IE, the XML document object's selectNodes method (p. 595) receives an XPath expression as an argument and returns a collection of elements that match the expression.
- Other browsers search for XPath matches using the XML document object's evaluate method (p. 595), which receives five arguments—the XPath expression, the document to apply the ex-

pression to, a namespace resolver, a result type and an XPathResult object (p. 595) into which to place the results. If the last argument is null, the function simply returns a new XPathResult object containing the matches. The namespace resolver argument can be null if you're not using XML namespace prefixes in the XPath processing.

Self-Review Exercises

15.1 Which of the following are valid XML element names? (Select all that apply.)
- a) `yourQualification`
- b) `your Qualification`
- c) `your.Qualification`
- d) `your_Qualification`
- e) `your-Qualification1`
- f) `5_yourQualification`

15.2 State which of the following statements are *true* and which are *false*. If *false*, explain why.
- a) XML is a technology for creating markup languages.
- b) XML markup is delimited by forward and backward slashes (/ and \).
- c) All XML start tags must have corresponding end tags.
- d) Parsers check an XML document's syntax.
- e) XML does not support namespaces.
- f) When creating XML elements, document authors must use the set of XML tags provided by the W3C.
- g) The pound character (#), dollar sign ($), ampersand (&) and angle brackets (< and >) are examples of XML reserved characters.
- h) XML is not case sensitive.
- i) XML Schemas are better than DTDs, because DTDs lack a way of indicating what specific type of data (e.g., numeric, text) an element can contain, and DTDs are not themselves XML documents.
- j) DTDs are written using an XML vocabulary.
- k) Schema is a technology for locating information in an XML document.

15.3 Fill in the blanks for each of the following:
- a) XML comments begin with <! -- and end with _____.
- b) A(n) _____ object can be used to load an XML document.
- c) Nodes that are peers are called _____.
- d) _____ markup describes mathematical expressions for display.
- e) Entity reference _____ represents a lowercase delta symbol in XML.
- f) A document's _____ property contains a list of the XML document's top-level nodes.
- g) The XPath expression _____ selects all the nodes in an XML document.
- h) In XPath, a leading forward slash specifies that we're using _____.
- i) XSL element _____ retrieves an attribute's value.

15.4 In Fig. 15.2, we subdivided the author element into more detailed pieces. How might you subdivide the address element? Use the address Baker Street, London, 6789, as an example.

15.5 Write a processing instruction that includes style sheet book.xsl.

15.6 Write an XPath expression that locates salutation nodes in letter.xml (Fig. 15.4).

Answers to Self-Review Exercises

15.1 a, c, d, e. [Choice b is incorrect because it contains a space. Choice f is incorrect because the first character is a number.]

15.2 a) True. b) False. In an XML document, markup text is delimited by tags enclosed in angle brackets (< and >) with a forward slash just after the < in the end tag. c) True. d) True. e) False. XML does support namespaces. f) False. When creating tags, document authors can use any valid name but should avoid ones that begin with the reserved word xml (also XML, Xml, etc.). g) False. XML reserved characters include the ampersand (&), the left angle bracket (<) and the right angle bracket (>), but not # and $. h) False. XML is case sensitive. i) True. j) False. DTDs use EBNF grammar, which is not XML syntax. k) False. XPath is a technology for locating information in an XML document. XML Schema provides a means for type checking XML documents and verifying their validity.

15.3 a) --> . b) XMLHttpRequest. c) sibling nodes. d) MathML. e) δ. f) childNodes. g) //*. h) absolute addressing . i) value-of.

15.4
```
<address>
    <street>Baker Street</street>
    <city>London</city>
    <pin>6789</pin>
</address>
```

15.5 `<?xsl:stylesheet type = "text/xsl" href = "book.xsl"?>`

15.6 `/salutation /contact.`

Exercises

15.7 *(Nutrition Information XML Document)* Create an XML document that marks up the nutrition facts for a package of Grandma White's cookies. A package of cookies has a serving size of 1 package and the following nutritional value per serving: 260 calories, 100 fat calories, 11 grams of fat, 2 grams of saturated fat, 5 milligrams of cholesterol, 210 milligrams of sodium, 36 grams of total carbohydrates, 2 grams of fiber, 15 grams of sugars and 5 grams of protein. Name this document nutrition.xml. Load the XML document into your web browser. [*Hint:* Your markup should contain elements describing the product name, serving size/amount, calories, sodium, cholesterol, proteins, etc. Mark up each nutrition fact/ingredient listed above.]

15.8 *(Nutrition Information XML Schema)* Write an XML Schema document (nutrition.xsd) specifying the structure of the XML document created in Exercise 15.7.

15.9 *(Nutrition Information XSL Style Sheet)* Write an XSL style sheet for your solution to Exercise 15.7 that displays the nutritional facts in an HTML5 table.

15.10 *(Sorting XSLT Modification)* Modify Fig. 15.21 (sorting.xsl) to sort by the number of pages rather than by chapter number. Save the modified document as sorting_byPage.xsl.

Ajax-Enabled Rich Internet Applications with XML and JSON

16

Objectives

In this chapter you will:

- Learn what Ajax is and why it's important for building Rich Internet Applications.

- Use asynchronous requests to give web applications the feel of desktop applications.

- Use the `XMLHttpRequest` object to manage asynchronous requests to servers and to receive asynchronous responses.

- Use XML with the DOM.

- Create a full-scale Ajax-enabled application.

16.1 Introduction

Despite the tremendous technological growth of the Internet over the past decade, the usability of web applications has lagged behind that of desktop applications. **Rich Internet Applications (RIAs)** are web applications that approximate the look, feel and usability of desktop applications. Two key attributes of RIAs are performance and a rich GUI.

RIA performance comes from **Ajax (Asynchronous JavaScript and XML)**, which uses client-side scripting to make web applications more responsive. Ajax applications separate client-side user interaction and server communication and run them *in parallel*, reducing the delays of server-side processing normally experienced by the user.

There are many ways to implement Ajax functionality. **"Raw" Ajax** uses JavaScript to send asynchronous requests to the server, then updates the page using the DOM. "Raw" Ajax is best suited for creating small Ajax components that asynchronously update a section of the page. However, when writing "raw" Ajax you need to deal directly with cross-browser portability issues, making it impractical for developing large-scale applications. These portability issues are hidden by **Ajax toolkits**, such as jQuery, ASP.NET Ajax and JSF's Ajax capabilities, which provide powerful ready-to-use controls and functions that enrich web applications and simplify JavaScript coding by making it cross-browser compatible.

Traditional web applications use HTML5 forms to build GUIs that are simple by comparison with those of Windows, Macintosh and desktop systems in general. You can achieve rich GUIs in RIAs with JavaScript toolkits providing powerful ready-to-use controls and functions that enrich web applications.

Previous chapters discussed HTML5, CSS3, JavaScript, the DOM and XML. This chapter uses these technologies to build Ajax-enabled web applications. The client side of Ajax applications is written in HTML5 and CSS3 and uses JavaScript to add functionality to the user interface. XML is used to structure the data passed between server and client. We'll also use JSON (JavaScript Object Notation) for this purpose. The Ajax component that manages interaction with the server is usually implemented with JavaScript's **XMLHttpRequest object**—commonly abbreviated as **XHR**. The server processing can be implemented using any server-side technology, such as PHP, ASP.NET and JavaServer Faces, each of which we cover in later chapters.

We begin with several examples that build basic Ajax applications using JavaScript and the XMLHttpRequest object. In subsequent chapters, we use tools such as ASP.NET Ajax and JavaServer Faces to build Ajax-enabled RIAs. We also include an online introduction to jQuery.

16.1.1 Traditional Web Applications vs. Ajax Applications

In this section, we consider the key differences between traditional web applications and Ajax-based web applications.

16.1.2 Traditional Web Applications

Figure 16.1 presents the typical interactions between the client and the server in a traditional web application, such as one that employs a user registration form. The user first fills in the form's fields, then submits the form (Fig. 16.1, *Step 1*). The browser generates a request to the server, which receives the request and processes it (*Step 2*). The server generates and sends a response containing the exact page that the browser will render (*Step 3*), which causes the browser to load the new page (*Step 4*) and temporarily makes the browser window blank. Note that the client *waits* for the server to respond and *reloads the entire page* with the data from the response (*Step 4*). While such a **synchronous request** is being processed on the server, the user *cannot* interact with the client web page. Frequent long periods of waiting, due perhaps to Internet congestion, have led some users to refer to the World Wide Web as the "World Wide Wait;" this situation has improved greatly in recent years. If the user interacts with and submits another form, the process begins again (*Steps 5–8*).

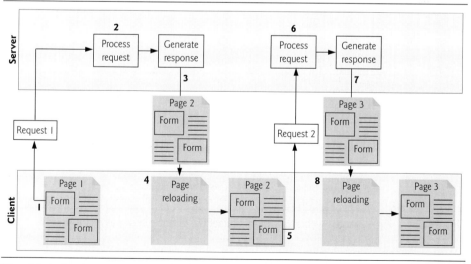

Fig. 16.1 | Classic web application reloading the page for every user interaction.

This model was originally designed for a web of hypertext documents—what some people call the "brochure web." As the web evolved into a full-scale *applications platform*, the model shown in Fig. 16.1 yielded erratic application performance. Every *full-page refresh* required users to re-establish their understanding of the full-page contents. Users sought a model that would yield the responsive feel of desktop applications.

16.1.3 Ajax Web Applications

Ajax applications add a layer between the client and the server to manage communication between the two (Fig. 16.2). When the user interacts with the page, the client creates an XMLHttpRequest object to manage a request (*Step 1*). The XMLHttpRequest object sends the request to the server (*Step 2*) and awaits the response. The requests are **asynchronous**, so the user can continue interacting with the application on the client side while the server processes the earlier request *concurrently*. Other user interactions could result in additional requests to the server (*Steps 3* and *4*). Once the server responds to the original request (*Step 5*), the XMLHttpRequest object that issued the request calls a client-side function to process the data returned by the server. This function—known as a **callback function**—uses **partial page updates** (*Step 6*) to display the data in the existing web page *without reloading the entire page*. At the same time, the server may be responding to the second request (*Step 7*) and the client side may be starting to do another partial page update (*Step 8*). The callback function updates *only* a designated part of the page. Such partial page updates help make web applications more responsive, making them feel more like desktop applications. The web application does *not* load a new page while the user interacts with it.

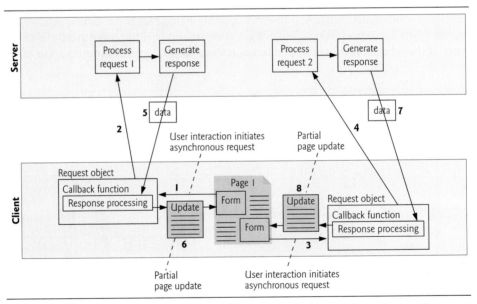

Fig. 16.2 | Ajax-enabled web application interacting with the server asynchronously.

16.2 Rich Internet Applications (RIAs) with Ajax

Ajax improves the user experience by making interactive web applications more responsive. Consider a registration form with a number of fields (e.g., first name, last name e-mail address, telephone number, etc.) and a **Register** (or **Submit**) button that sends the entered data to the server. Usually each field has rules that the user's entries have to follow (e.g., valid e-mail address, valid telephone number, etc.).

When the user clicks **Register**, an HTML5 form sends the server *all* of the data to be validated (Fig. 16.3). While the server is validating the data, the user *cannot* interact with the page. The server finds invalid data, generates a new page identifying the errors in the form and sends it back to the client—which renders the page in the browser. Once the user fixes the errors and clicks the **Register** button, the cycle repeats until no errors are found, then the data is stored on the server. The *entire* page reloads every time the user submits invalid data.

Ajax-enabled forms are more interactive. Rather than the *entire* form being sent to be validated, entries can be validated individually, dynamically, as the user enters data into the fields. For example, consider a website registration form that requires a valid e-mail address. When the user enters an e-mail address into the appropriate field, then moves to the next form field to continue entering data, an *asynchronous* request is sent to the server to validate the e-mail address. If it's not valid, the server sends an error message that's displayed on the page informing the user of the problem (Fig. 16.4). By sending each entry *asynchronously*, the user can address each invalid entry quickly, versus making edits and resubmitting the entire form repeatedly until all entries are valid. Simple validation like this for e-mails and phone numbers can also be accomplished with HTML5's new input elements that you learned in Chapter 3, rather than using Ajax. Asynchronous requests could also be used to fill some fields based on previous fields (e.g., automatically filling in the "city" and "state" fields based on the ZIP code entered by the user).

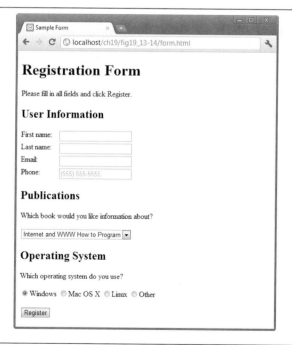

a) A sample registration form in which the user has not filled in the required fields, but attempts to submit the form anyway by clicking **Register**.

Fig. 16.3 | Classic HTML5 form: The user submits the form to the server, which validates the data (if any). Server responds indicating any fields with invalid or missing data. (Part 1 of 2.)

b) The server responds by indicating all the form fields with missing or invalid data. The user must correct the problems and resubmit the *entire* form repeatedly until *all* errors are corrected.

Error message in red

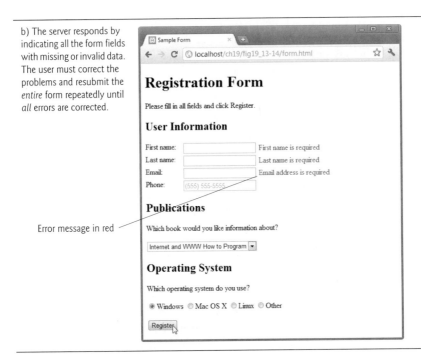

Fig. 16.3 | Classic HTML5 form: The user submits the form to the server, which validates the data (if any). Server responds indicating any fields with invalid or missing data. (Part 2 of 2.)

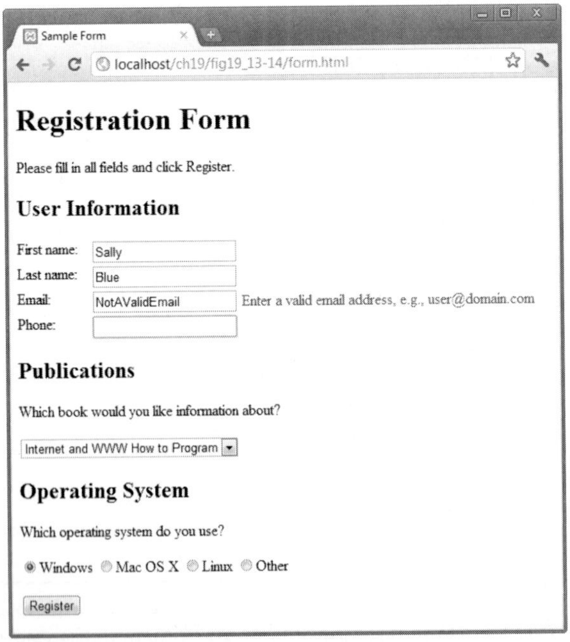

Fig. 16.4 | Ajax-enabled form shows errors asynchronously when user moves to another field.

16.3 History of Ajax

The term Ajax was coined by Jesse James Garrett of Adaptive Path in February 2005, when he was presenting the previously unnamed technology to a client. The technologies of Ajax (HTML, JavaScript, CSS, the DOM and XML) had all existed for many years prior to 2005.

Asynchronous page updates can be traced back to earlier browsers. In the 1990s, Netscape's LiveScript language made it possible to include scripts in web pages (e.g., web forms) that could run on the client. LiveScript evolved into JavaScript. In 1998, Microsoft introduced the XMLHttpRequest object to create and manage asynchronous requests and responses. Popular applications like Flickr and Google's Gmail use the XMLHttpRequest object to update pages dynamically. For example, Flickr uses the technology for its text editing, tagging and organizational features; Gmail continuously checks the server for new e-mail; and Google Maps allows you to drag a map in any direction, downloading the new areas on the map without reloading the entire page.

The name Ajax immediately caught on and brought attention to its component technologies. Ajax has enabled "webtop" applications to challenge the dominance of established desktop applications. This has become increasingly significant as more and more computing moves to "the cloud."

16.4 "Raw" Ajax Example Using the XMLHttpRequest Object

In this section, we use the XMLHttpRequest object to create and manage asynchronous requests. This object, which resides on the client, is the layer between the client and the server that manages asynchronous requests in Ajax applications. It's supported on most browsers, though they may implement it differently—a common issue with browsers. To initiate an asynchronous request (shown in Fig. 16.5), you create an instance of the XMLHttpRequest object, then use its open method to set up the request and its send method to initiate the request. We summarize the XMLHttpRequest properties and methods in Figs. 16.6–16.7.

Figure 16.5 presents an Ajax application in which the user interacts with the page by moving the mouse over book-cover images; a detailed code walkthrough follows the figure. We use the mouseover and mouseout events to trigger events when the user moves the mouse over and out of an image, respectively. The mouseover event calls function getContent with the URL of the document containing the book's description. The function makes this request asynchronously using an XMLHttpRequest object. When the XMLHttpRequest object receives the response, the book description is displayed below the book images. When the user moves the mouse out of the image, the mouseout event calls function clearContent to clear the display box. These tasks are accomplished without reloading the page on the client. You can test-drive this example at http://test.deitel.com/iw3htp5/ch16/fig16_05/SwitchContent.html.

Performance Tip 16.1

When an Ajax application requests a file from a server, such as an HTML5 document or an image, the browser typically caches that file. Subsequent requests for the same file can load it from the browser's cache rather than making the round trip to the server again.

Software Engineering Observation 16.1

For security purposes, the XMLHttpRequest *object doesn't allow a web application to request resources from domains other than the one that served the application. For this reason, the web application and its resources must reside on the same web server (this could be a web server on your local computer). This is commonly known as the* **same origin policy (SOP)**. *SOP aims to close a vulnerability called* **cross-site scripting**, *also known as XSS, which allows an attacker to compromise a website's security by injecting a malicious script onto the page from another domain. To get content from another domain securely, you can implement a* **server-side proxy**—*an application on the web application's web server—that can make requests to other servers on the web application's behalf.*

16.4.1 Asynchronous Requests

The function getContent (lines 46–63) sends the asynchronous request. Line 51 creates the XMLHttpRequest object, which manages the asynchronous request. We store the object in the global variable asyncRequest (declared at line 13) so that it can be accessed anywhere in the script. You can test this web page at test.deitel.com/iw3htp5/ch16/fig16_05/SwitchContent.html.

Line 56 calls the XMLHttpRequest open method to prepare an asynchronous GET request. In this example, the url parameter specifies the address of an HTML document containing the description of a particular book. When the third argument is true, the request is *asynchronous*. The URL is passed to function getContent in response to the onmouseover event for each image. Line 57 sends the asynchronous request to the server by calling the XMLHttpRequest send method. The argument null indicates that this request is not submitting data in the body of the request.

```
1    <!DOCTYPE html>
2
3    <!-- Fig. 16.5: SwitchContent.html -->
4    <!-- Asynchronously display content without reloading the page. -->
5    <html>
6    <head>
7       <meta charset = "utf-8">
8       <style type = "text/css">
9          .box { border: 1px solid black; padding: 10px }
10      </style>
11      <title>Switch Content Asynchronously</title>
12      <script>
13         var asyncRequest; // variable to hold XMLHttpRequest object
14
15         // set up event handlers
16         function registerListeners()
17         {
18            var img;
19            img = document.getElementById( "cpphtp" );
20            img.addEventListener( "mouseover",
21               function() { getContent( "cpphtp8.html" ); }, false );
22            img.addEventListener( "mouseout", clearContent, false );
23            img = document.getElementById( "iw3htp" );
```

Fig. 16.5 | Asynchronously display content without reloading the page. (Part 1 of 4.)

```
24            img.addEventListener( "mouseover",
25               function() { getContent( "iw3htp.html" ); }, false );
26            img.addEventListener( "mouseout", clearContent, false );
27            img = document.getElementById( "jhtp" );
28            img.addEventListener( "mouseover",
29               function() { getContent( "jhtp.html" ); }, false );
30            img.addEventListener( "mouseout", clearContent, false );
31            img = document.getElementById( "vbhtp" );
32            img.addEventListener( "mouseover",
33               function() { getContent( "vbhtp.html" ); }, false );
34            img.addEventListener( "mouseout", clearContent, false );
35            img = document.getElementById( "vcshtp" );
36            img.addEventListener( "mouseover",
37               function() { getContent( "vcshtp.html" ); }, false );
38            img.addEventListener( "mouseout", clearContent, false );
39            img = document.getElementById( "javafp" );
40            img.addEventListener( "mouseover",
41               function() { getContent( "javafp.html" ); }, false );
42            img.addEventListener( "mouseout", clearContent, false );
43         } // end function registerListeners
44
45         // set up and send the asynchronous request.
46         function getContent( url )
47         {
48            // attempt to create XMLHttpRequest object and make the request
49            try
50            {
51               asyncRequest = new XMLHttpRequest(); // create request object
52
53               // register event handler
54               asyncRequest.addEventListener(
55                  "readystatechange", stateChange, false);
56               asyncRequest.open( "GET", url, true ); // prepare the request
57               asyncRequest.send( null ); // send the request
58            } // end try
59            catch ( exception )
60            {
61               alert( "Request failed." );
62            } // end catch
63         } // end function getContent
64
65         // displays the response data on the page
66         function stateChange()
67         {
68            if ( asyncRequest.readyState == 4 && asyncRequest.status == 200 )
69            {
70               document.getElementById( "contentArea" ).innerHTML =
71                  asyncRequest.responseText; // places text in contentArea
72            } // end if
73         } // end function stateChange
74
```

Fig. 16.5 | Asynchronously display content without reloading the page. (Part 2 of 4.)

```
75        // clear the content of the box
76        function clearContent()
77        {
78            document.getElementById( "contentArea" ).innerHTML = "";
79        } // end function clearContent
80
81        window.addEventListener( "load", registerListeners, false );
82     </script>
83  </head>
84  <body>
85     <h1>Mouse over a book for more information.</h1>
86     <img id = "cpphtp" alt = "C++ How to Program book cover"
87        src = "http://test.deitel.com/images/thumbs/cpphtp8.jpg">
88     <img id = "iw3htp" alt = "Internet & WWW How to Program book cover"
89        src = "http://test.deitel.com/images/thumbs/iw3htp5.jpg">
90     <img id = "jhtp" alt = "Java How to Program book cover"
91        src = "http://test.deitel.com/images/thumbs/jhtp9.jpg">
92     <img id = "vbhtp" alt = "Visual Basic 2010 How to Program book cover"
93        src = "http://test.deitel.com/images/thumbs/vb2010htp.jpg">
94     <img id = "vcshtp" alt = "Visual C# 2010 How to Program book cover"
95        src = "http://test.deitel.com/images/thumbs/vcsharp2010htp.jpg">
96     <img id = "javafp" alt = "Java for Programmers book cover"
97        src = "http://test.deitel.com/images/thumbs/javafp.jpg">
98     <div class = "box" id = "contentArea"></div>
99  </body>
100 </html>
```

a) User hovers over C++ *How to Program* book-cover image, causing an asynchronous request to the server to obtain the book's description. When the response is received, the application performs a *partial page update* to display the description.

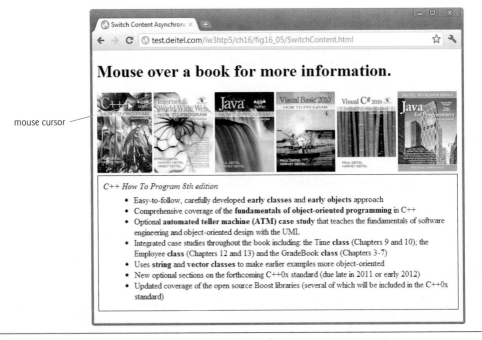

Fig. 16.5 | Asynchronously display content without reloading the page. (Part 3 of 4.)

b) User hovers over *Internet & World Wide Web How to Program* book-cover image, causing the process to repeat.

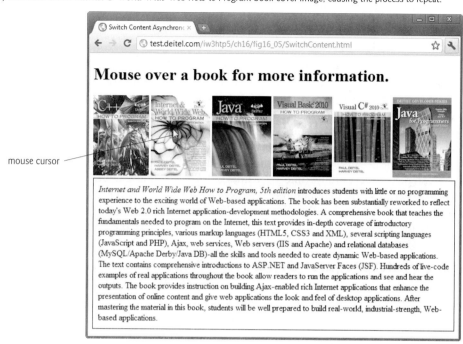

Fig. 16.5 | Asynchronously display content without reloading the page. (Part 4 of 4.)

16.4.2 Exception Handling

Lines 59–62 introduce **exception handling**. An **exception** is an indication of a problem that occurs during a program's execution. The name "exception" implies that the problem occurs infrequently. Exception handling enables you to create applications that can *handle* (i.e., resolve) exceptions—often allowing a program to continue executing as if no problem had been encountered.

Lines 49–58 contain a **try block**, which encloses the code that might cause an exception and the code that should not execute if an exception occurs (i.e., if an exception occurs in a statement of the try block, the remaining code in the try block is skipped). A try block consists of the keyword try followed by a block of code enclosed in curly braces ({}). If there's a problem sending the request—e.g., if a user tries to access the page using an older browser that does not support XMLHttpRequest—the try block terminates immediately and a **catch block** (also called a **catch clause** or **exception handler**) catches (i.e., receives) and *handles* the exception. The catch block (lines 59–62) begins with the keyword catch and is followed by a parameter in parentheses—called the exception parameter—and a block of code enclosed in curly braces. The exception parameter's name (exception in this example) enables the catch block to interact with a caught exception object (for example, to obtain the *name* of the exception or an *exception-specific error message* via the exception object's name and message properties, respectively). In this case, we simply display our own error message "Request Failed" and terminate the getContent function. The request can fail because a user accesses the web page with an older browser or the content that's being requested is located on a different domain.

16.4.3 Callback Functions

The stateChange function (lines 66–73) is the callback function that's called when the client receives the response data. Lines 54–55 *register* function stateChange as the event handler for the XMLHttpRequest object's **readystatechange** event. Whenever the request makes progress, the XMLHttpRequest object calls the readystatechange event handler. This progress is monitored by the readyState property, which has a value from 0 to 4. The value 0 indicates that the request is *not initialized* and the value 4 indicates that the request is *complete*—all the values for this property are summarized in Fig. 16.6. If the request completes successfully (line 68), lines 70–71 use the XMLHttpRequest object's responseText property to obtain the *response data* and place it in the div element named contentArea (defined at line 98). We use the DOM's getElementById method to get this div element, and use the element's innerHTML property to place the content in the div.

16.4.4 XMLHttpRequest Object Event, Properties and Methods

Figures 16.6 and 16.7 summarize some of the XMLHttpRequest object's properties and methods, respectively. The properties are crucial to interacting with asynchronous requests. The methods initialize, configure and send asynchronous requests.

Event or Property	Description
readystatechange	Register a listener for this event to specify the *callback* function—the event handler that gets called when the server responds.
readyState	Keeps track of the request's progress. It's usually used in the callback function to determine when the code that processes the response should be launched. The readyState value 0 signifies that the request is uninitialized; 1 that the request is loading; 2 that the request has been loaded; 3 that data is actively being sent from the server; and 4 that the request has been completed.
responseText	Text that's returned to the client by the server.
responseXML	If the server's response is in XML format, this property contains the XML document; otherwise, it's empty. It can be used like a document object in JavaScript, which makes it useful for receiving complex data (e.g., populating a table).
status	HTTP status code of the request. A status of 200 means that request was *successful*. A status of 404 means that the requested resource was *not found*. A status of 500 denotes that there was an *error* while the server was processing the request. For a complete status reference, visit www.w3.org/Protocols/rfc2616/rfc2616-sec10.html.
statusText	Additional information on the request's status. It's often used to display the error to the user when the request fails.

Fig. 16.6 | XMLHttpRequest object event and properties.

Method	Description
open	Initializes the request and has two *mandatory* parameters—method and URL. The method parameter specifies the purpose of the request—typically GET or POST. The URL parameter specifies the address of the file on the server that will generate the response. A third optional Boolean parameter specifies whether the request is *asynchronous*—it's set to true by default.
send	Sends the request to the server. It has one optional parameter, data, which specifies the *data to be POSTed to the server*—it's set to null by default.
setRequestHeader	Alters the request header. The two parameters specify the header and its new value. It's often used to set the content-type field.
getResponseHeader	Returns the header data that precedes the response body. It takes one parameter, the name of the header to retrieve. This call is often used to *determine the response's type*, to parse the response correctly.
getAllResponseHeaders	Returns an array that contains all the headers that precede the response body.
abort	Cancels the current request.

Fig. 16.7 | XMLHttpRequest object methods.

16.5 Using XML and the DOM

When passing structured data between the server and the client, Ajax applications often use XML because it's easy to generate and parse. When the XMLHttpRequest object receives XML data, it parses and stores the data as an XML DOM object in the responseXML property. The example in Fig. 16.8 asynchronously requests from a server XML documents containing URLs of book-cover images, then displays the images in the page. The code that configures the asynchronous request is the same as in Fig. 16.5. You can test-drive this application at

http://test.deitel.com/iw3htp5/ch16/fig16_08/PullImagesOntoPage.html

```
1   <!DOCTYPE html>
2
3   <!-- Fig. 16.8: PullImagesOntoPage.html -->
4   <!-- Image catalog that uses 1Ajax to request XML data asynchronously. -->
5   <html>
6   <head>
7   <meta charset="utf-8">
8   <title> Pulling Images onto the Page </title>
9   <style type = "text/css">
10     li { display: inline-block; padding: 4px; width: 120px; }
11     img { border: 1px solid black }
12  </style>
```

Fig. 16.8 | Image catalog that uses Ajax to request XML data asynchronously. (Part 1 of 4.)

```
13   <script>
14      var asyncRequest; // variable to hold XMLHttpRequest object
15
16      // set up and send the asynchronous request to get the XML file
17      function getImages( url )
18      {
19         // attempt to create XMLHttpRequest object and make the request
20         try
21         {
22            asyncRequest = new XMLHttpRequest(); // create request object
23
24            // register event handler
25            asyncRequest.addEventListener(
26               "readystatechange", processResponse, false);
27            asyncRequest.open( "GET", url, true ); // prepare the request
28            asyncRequest.send( null ); // send the request
29         } // end try
30         catch ( exception )
31         {
32            alert( 'Request Failed' );
33         } // end catch
34      } // end function getImages
35
36      // parses the XML response; dynamically creates an undordered list and
37      // populates it with the response data; displays the list on the page
38      function processResponse()
39      {
40         // if request completed successfully and responseXML is non-null
41         if ( asyncRequest.readyState == 4 && asyncRequest.status == 200 &&
42            asyncRequest.responseXML )
43         {
44            clearImages(); // prepare to display a new set of images
45
46            // get the covers from the responseXML
47            var covers = asyncRequest.responseXML.getElementsByTagName(
48               "cover" )
49
50            // get base URL for the images
51            var baseUrl = asyncRequest.responseXML.getElementsByTagName(
52               "baseurl" ).item( 0 ).firstChild.nodeValue;
53
54            // get the placeholder div element named covers
55            var output = document.getElementById( "covers" );
56
57            // create an unordered list to display the images
58            var imagesUL = document.createElement( "ul" );
59
60            // place images in unordered list
61            for ( var i = 0; i < covers.length; ++i )
62            {
63               var cover = covers.item( i ); // get a cover from covers array
64
```

Fig. 16.8 | Image catalog that uses Ajax to request XML data asynchronously. (Part 2 of 4.)

```
65                      // get the image filename
66                      var image = cover.getElementsByTagName( "image" ).
67                         item( 0 ).firstChild.nodeValue;
68
69                      // create li and img element to display the image
70                      var imageLI = document.createElement( "li" );
71                      var imageTag = document.createElement( "img" );
72
73                      // set img element's src attribute
74                      imageTag.setAttribute( "src", baseUrl + escape( image ) );
75                      imageLI.appendChild( imageTag ); // place img in li
76                      imagesUL.appendChild( imageLI ); // place li in ul
77                   } // end for statement
78
79                   output.appendChild( imagesUL ); // append ul to covers div
80                } // end if
81             } // end function processResponse
82
83             // clears the covers div
84             function clearImages()
85             {
86                document.getElementById( "covers" ).innerHTML = "";
87             } // end function clearImages
88
89             // register event listeners
90             function registerListeners()
91             {
92                document.getElementById( "all" ).addEventListener(
93                   "click", function() { getImages( "all.xml" ); }, false );
94                document.getElementById( "simply" ).addEventListener(
95                   "click", function() { getImages( "simply.xml" ); }, false );
96                document.getElementById( "howto" ).addEventListener(
97                   "click", function() { getImages( "howto.xml" ); }, false );
98                document.getElementById( "dotnet" ).addEventListener(
99                   "click", function() { getImages( "dotnet.xml" ); }, false );
100               document.getElementById( "javaccpp" ).addEventListener(
101                  "click", function() { getImages( "javaccpp.xml" ); }, false );
102               document.getElementById( "none" ).addEventListener(
103                  "click", clearImages, false );
104            } // end function registerListeners
105
106            window.addEventListener( "load", registerListeners, false );
107         </script>
108      </head>
109      <body>
110         <input type = "radio" name ="Books" value = "all"
111            id = "all"> All Books
112         <input type = "radio" name = "Books" value = "simply"
113            id = "simply"> Simply Books
114         <input type = "radio" name = "Books" value = "howto"
115            id = "howto"> How to Program Books
116         <input type = "radio" name = "Books" value = "dotnet"
117            id = "dotnet"> .NET Books
```

Fig. 16.8 | Image catalog that uses Ajax to request XML data asynchronously. (Part 3 of 4.)

```
118    <input type = "radio" name = "Books" value = "javaccpp"
119       id = "javaccpp"> Java/C/C++ Books
120    <input type = "radio" checked name = "Books" value = "none"
121       id = "none"> None
122    <div id = "covers"></div>
123 </body>
124 </html>
```

a) User clicks the **All Books** radio button to display all the book covers. The application sends an *asynchronous* request to the server to obtain an XML document containing the list of book-cover filenames. When the response is received, the application performs a *partial page update* to display the set of book covers.

b) User clicks the **How to Program Books** radio button to select a subset of book covers to display. Application sends an *asynchronous* request to the server to obtain an XML document containing the appropriate subset of book-cover filenames. When the response is received, the application performs a *partial page update* to display the subset of book covers.

Fig. 16.8 | Image catalog that uses Ajax to request XML data asynchronously. (Part 4 of 4.)

When the XMLHttpRequest object receives the response, it invokes the callback function processResponse (lines 38–81). We use XMLHttpRequest object's responseXML property to access the XML returned by the server. Lines 41–42 check that the request was successful and that the responseXML property is not empty. The XML file that we requested includes a baseURL node that contains the address of the image directory and a collection of cover nodes that contain image filenames. responseXML is a document object, so we can extract data from it using the XML DOM functions. Lines 47–52 use the DOM's method **getElementsByTagName** to extract all the image filenames from cover nodes and the URL of the directory from the baseURL node. Since the baseURL has no child nodes, we use item(0).firstChild.nodeValue to obtain the directory's address and store it in variable baseURL. The image filenames are stored in the covers array.

As in Fig. 16.5 we have a placeholder div element (line 122) to specify where the image table will be displayed on the page. Line 55 stores the div in variable output, so we can fill it with content later in the program.

Lines 58–77 generate an HTML5 unordered list dynamically, using the createElement, setAttribute and appendChild HTML5 DOM methods. Method createElement creates an HTML5 element of the specified type. Method appendChild inserts one HTML5 element into another. Line 58 creates the ul element. Each iteration of the for statement obtains the filename of the image to be inserted (lines 63–67), creates an li element to hold the image (line 70) and creates an <img> element (line 71). Line 74 sets the image's src attribute to the image's URL, which we build by concatenating the filename to the base URL of the HTML5 document. Lines 75–76 insert the <img> element into the li element and the li element into the ul element. Once all the images have been inserted into the unordered list, the list is inserted into the placeholder element covers that's referenced by variable output (line 79). This element is located on the bottom of the web page.

Function clearImages (lines 84–87) is called to clear images when the user clicks the **None** radio button. The text is cleared by setting the innerHTML property of the placeholder element to an empty string.

16.6 Creating a Full-Scale Ajax-Enabled Application

Our next example demonstrates additional Ajax capabilities. The web application interacts with a web service to obtain data and to modify data in a server-side database. The web application and server communicate with a data format called JSON (JavaScript Object Notation). In addition, the application demonstrates *server-side validation* that occurs in parallel with the user interacting with the web application. You can test-drive the application at http://test.deitel.com/iw3htp5/ch16/fig16_09-10/AddressBook.html.

16.6.1 Using JSON

JSON (JavaScript Object Notation)—a simple way to represent JavaScript objects as strings—is a simpler alternative to XML for passing data between the client and the server. Each object in JSON is represented as a list of property names and values contained in curly braces, in the following format:

> { *"propertyName1"* : *value1*, *"propertyName2"*: *value2* }

Arrays are represented in JSON with square brackets in the following format:

> [*value1*, *value2*, *value3*]

Each value can be a string, a number, a JSON representation of an object, `true`, `false` or `null`. You can convert JSON strings into JavaScript objects with JavaScript's `JSON.parse` function. JSON strings are easier to create and parse than XML and require fewer bytes. For these reasons, JSON is commonly used to communicate in client/server interaction.

16.6.2 Rich Functionality

The previous examples in this chapter requested data from files on the server. The example in Figs. 16.9–16.10 is an address-book application that communicates with a server-side web service. The application uses server-side processing to give the page the functionality and usability of a desktop application. We use JSON to encode server-side responses and to create objects on the fly. Figure 16.9 presents the HTML5 document. Figure 16.10 presents the JavaScript.

Initially the address book loads a list of entries, each containing a first and last name (Fig. 16.9(a)). Each time the user clicks a name, the address book uses Ajax functionality to load the person's address from the server and expand the entry *without reloading the page* (Fig. 16.9(b))—and it does this *in parallel* with allowing the user to click other names.

The application allows the user to search the address book by typing a last name. As the user enters each keystroke, the application *asynchronously* calls the server to obtain the list of names in which the last name starts with the characters the user has entered so far (Fig. 16.9(c), (d) and (e))—a popular feature called **type-ahead**.

The application also enables the user to add another entry to the address book by clicking the **Add an Entry** button (Fig. 16.9(f)). The application displays a form that enables live field validation.

As the user fills out the form, the ZIP code is eventually entered, and when the user tabs to the next field, the `blur` event handler for the ZIP-code field makes an Ajax call to the server. The server then validates the ZIP code, uses the valid zip code to obtain the corresponding city and state from a ZIP-code web service and returns this information to the client (Fig. 16.9(g). [If the ZIP code were invalid, the web service would return an error to the server, which would then send an error message back to the client.]

When the user enters the telephone number and moves the cursor out of the **Telephone:** field, the `blur` event handler for that field uses an Ajax call to the server to validate the telephone number—if it were invalid, the server would return an error message to the client.

When the **Submit** button is clicked, the button's event handler determines that some required data is missing and displays the message "**First Name and Last Name must have a value.**" at the bottom of the screen (Fig. 16.9(h)). The user enters the missing data and clicks **Submit** again (Fig. 16.9(i)). The client-side code revalidates the data, determines that it's correct and sends it to the server. The server performs its own validation, then returns the updated address book, which is displayed on the client, with the new name added in (Fig. 16.9(j)).

```
1   <!DOCTYPE html>
2
3   <!-- Fig. 16.9 addressbook.html -->
4   <!-- Ajax enabled address book application. -->
```

Fig. 16.9 | Ajax-enabled address-book application. (Part 1 of 4.)

```
5   <html>
6   <head>
7      <meta charset="utf-8">
8      <title>Address Book</title>
9      <link rel = "stylesheet" type = "text/css" href = "style.css">
10     <script src = "AddressBook.js"></script>
11  </head>
12  <body>
13     <div>
14        <input id = "addressBookButton" type = "button"
15           value = "Address Book">
16        <input id = "addEntryButton" type = "button"
17           value = "Add an Entry">
18     </div>
19     <div id = "addressBook"">
20        <p>Search By Last Name: <input id = "searchInput"></p>
21        <div id = "Names"></div>
22     </div>
23     <div id = "addEntry" style = "display : none">
24        <p><label>First Name:</label> <input id = "first"></p>
25        <p><label>Last Name:</label> <input id = "last"></p>
26        <p class = "head">Address:</p>
27        <p><label>Street:</label> <input id = "street"></p>
28        <p><label>City:</label> <span id = "city" class = "validator">
29           </span></p>
30        <p><label>State:</label> <span id = "state" class = "validator">
31           </span></p>
32        <p><label>Zip:</label> <input id = "zip">
33           <span id = "validateZip" class = "validator"></span></p>
34        <p><label>Telephone:</label> <input id = "phone">
35           <span id = "validatePhone" class = "validator"></span></p>
36        <p><input id = "submitButton" type = "button" value = "Submit"></p>
37        <div id = "success" class = "validator"></div>
38     </div>
39  </body>
40  </html>
```

a) Page is loaded. All the entries are displayed.

b) User clicks on an entry. The entry expands, showing the address and the telephone.

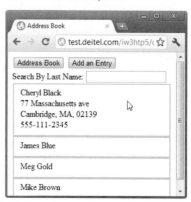

Fig. 16.9 | Ajax-enabled address-book application. (Part 2 of 4.)

c) User types "B" in the search field. Application loads the entries whose last names start with "B".

d) User types "Bl" in the search field. Application loads the entries whose last names start with "Bl".

e) User types "Bla" in the search field. Application loads the entries whose last names start with "Bla".

f) User clicks **Add an Entry** button. The form allowing user to add an entry is displayed.

g) User enters a valid ZIP code, then tabs to the next field. The server finds the city and state associated with the ZIP code entered and displays them on the page.

h) The user enters a telephone number and tries to submit the data. The application does not allow this, because the First Name and Last Name are empty.

Fig. 16.9 | Ajax-enabled address-book application. (Part 3 of 4.)

i) The user enters the last name and the first name and clicks the **Submit** button.

j) The address book is redisplayed with the new name added in.

Fig. 16.9 | Ajax-enabled address-book application. (Part 4 of 4.)

```
1    // Fig. 16.10 addressbook.js
2    // Ajax-enabled address-book JavaScript code
3    // URL of the web service
4    var webServiceUrl = "/AddressBookWebService/Service.svc";
5
6    var phoneValid = false; // indicates if the telephone is valid
7    var zipValid = false; //indicates if the ZIP code is valid
8
9    // get a list of names from the server and display them
10   function showAddressBook()
11   {
12      // hide the "addEntry" form and show the address book
13      document.getElementById( "addEntry" ).style.display = "none";
14      document.getElementById( "addressBook" ).style.display = "block";
15
16      callWebService( "/getAllNames", parseData );
17   } // end function showAddressBook
18
19   // send the asynchronous request to the web service
20   function callWebService( methodAndArguments, callBack )
21   {
22      // build request URL string
23      var requestUrl = webServiceUrl + methodAndArguments;
24
25      // attempt to send the asynchronous request
26      try
27      {
28         var asyncRequest = new XMLHttpRequest(); // create request
29
30         // set up callback function and store it
31         asyncRequest.addEventListener("readystatechange",
32            function() { callBack( asyncRequest ); }, false);
```

Fig. 16.10 | JavaScript code for the address-book application. (Part 1 of 6.)

```
33
34        // send the asynchronous request
35        asyncRequest.open( "GET", requestUrl, true );
36        asyncRequest.setRequestHeader("Accept",
37           "application/json; charset=utf-8" );
38        asyncRequest.send(); // send request
39     } // end try
40     catch ( exception )
41     {
42        alert ( "Request Failed" );
43     } // end catch
44  } // end function callWebService
45
46  // parse JSON data and display it on the page
47  function parseData( asyncRequest )
48  {
49     // if request has completed successfully, process the response
50     if ( asyncRequest.readyState == 4 && asyncRequest.status == 200 )
51     {
52        // convert the JSON string to an Object
53        var data = JSON.parse(asyncRequest.responseText);
54        displayNames( data ); // display data on the page
55     } // end if
56  } // end function parseData
57
58  // use the DOM to display the retrieved address-book entries
59  function displayNames( data )
60  {
61     // get the placeholder element from the page
62     var listBox = document.getElementById( "Names" );
63     listBox.innerHTML = ""; // clear the names on the page
64
65     // iterate over retrieved entries and display them on the page
66     for ( var i = 0; i < data.length; ++i )
67     {
68        // dynamically create a div element for each entry
69        // and a fieldset element to place it in
70        var entry = document.createElement( "div" );
71        var field = document.createElement( "fieldset" );
72        entry.onclick = function() { getAddress( this, this.innerHTML ); };
73        entry.id = i; // set the id
74        entry.innerHTML = data[ i ].First + " " + data[ i ].Last;
75        field.appendChild( entry ); // insert entry into the field
76        listBox.appendChild( field ); // display the field
77     } // end for
78  } // end function displayAll
79
80  // search the address book for input
81  // and display the results on the page
82  function search( input )
83  {
84     // get the placeholder element and delete its content
85     var listBox = document.getElementById( "Names" );
```

Fig. 16.10 | JavaScript code for the address-book application. (Part 2 of 6.)

```
86      listBox.innerHTML = ""; // clear the display box
87
88      // if no search string is specified, all the names are displayed
89      if ( input == "" ) // if no search value specified
90      {
91         showAddressBook(); // Load the entire address book
92      } // end if
93      else
94      {
95         callWebService( "/search/" + input, parseData );
96      } // end else
97   } // end function search
98
99   // Get address data for a specific entry
100  function getAddress( entry, name )
101  {
102     // find the address in the JSON data using the element's id
103     // and display it on the page
104     var firstLast = name.split(" "); // convert string to array
105     var requestUrl = webServiceUrl + "/getAddress/"
106        + firstLast[ 0 ] + "/" + firstLast[ 1 ];
107
108     // attempt to send an asynchronous request
109     try
110     {
111        // create request object
112        var asyncRequest = new XMLHttpRequest();
113
114        // create a callback function with 2 parameters
115        asyncRequest.addEventListener("readystatechange",
116           function() { displayAddress( entry, asyncRequest ); }, false);
117
118        asyncRequest.open( "GET", requestUrl, true );
119        asyncRequest.setRequestHeader("Accept",
120           "application/json; charset=utf-8"); // set response datatype
121        asyncRequest.send(); // send request
122     } // end try
123     catch ( exception )
124     {
125        alert ( "Request Failed." );
126     } // end catch
127  } // end function getAddress
128
129  // clear the entry's data
130  function displayAddress( entry, asyncRequest )
131  {
132     // if request has completed successfully, process the response
133     if ( asyncRequest.readyState == 4 && asyncRequest.status == 200 )
134     {
135        // convert the JSON string to an object
136        var data = JSON.parse(asyncRequest.responseText);
137        var name = entry.innerHTML // save the name string
138        entry.innerHTML = name + "<br>" + data.Street +
```

Fig. 16.10 | JavaScript code for the address-book application. (Part 3 of 6.)

```
139            "<br>" + data.City + ", " + data.State
140            + ", " + data.Zip + "<br>" + data.Telephone;
141
142         // change event listener
143         entry.onclick = function() { clearField( entry, name ); };
144      } // end if
145   } // end function displayAddress
146
147   // clear the entry's data
148   function clearField( entry, name )
149   {
150      entry.innerHTML = name; // set the entry to display only the name
151      entry.onclick = function() { getAddress( entry, name ); };
152   } // end function clearField
153
154   // display the form that allows the user to enter more data
155   function addEntry()
156   {
157      document.getElementById( "addressBook" ).style.display = "none";
158      document.getElementById( "addEntry" ).style.display = "block";
159   } // end function addEntry
160
161   // send the ZIP code to be validated and to generate city and state
162   function validateZip( zip )
163   {
164      callWebService ( "/validateZip/" + zip, showCityState );
165   } // end function validateZip
166
167   // get city and state that were generated using the zip code
168   // and display them on the page
169   function showCityState( asyncRequest )
170   {
171      // display message while request is being processed
172      document.getElementById( "validateZip" ).
173         innerHTML = "Checking zip...";
174
175      // if request has completed successfully, process the response
176      if ( asyncRequest.readyState == 4 )
177      {
178         if ( asyncRequest.status == 200 )
179         {
180            // convert the JSON string to an object
181            var data = JSON.parse(asyncRequest.responseText);
182
183            // update ZIP-code validity tracker and show city and state
184            if ( data.Validity == "Valid" )
185            {
186               zipValid = true; // update validity tracker
187
188               // display city and state
189               document.getElementById( "validateZip" ).innerHTML = "";
190               document.getElementById( "city" ).innerHTML = data.City;
191               document.getElementById( "state" ).
```

Fig. 16.10 | JavaScript code for the address-book application. (Part 4 of 6.)

```
192                      innerHTML = data.State;
193              } // end if
194              else
195              {
196                 zipValid = false; // update validity tracker
197                 document.getElementById( "validateZip" ).
198                    innerHTML = data.ErrorText; // display the error
199
200                 // clear city and state values if they exist
201                 document.getElementById( "city" ).innerHTML = "";
202                 document.getElementById( "state" ).innerHTML = "";
203              } // end else
204           } // end if
205           else if ( asyncRequest.status == 500 )
206           {
207              document.getElementById( "validateZip" ).
208                 innerHTML = "Zip validation service not avaliable";
209           } // end else if
210        } // end if
211  } // end function showCityState
212
213  // send the telephone number to the server to validate format
214  function validatePhone( phone )
215  {
216     callWebService( "/validateTel/" + phone, showPhoneError );
217  } // end function validatePhone
218
219  // show whether the telephone number has correct format
220  function showPhoneError( asyncRequest )
221  {
222     // if request has completed successfully, process the response
223     if ( asyncRequest.readyState == 4 && asyncRequest.status == 200 )
224     {
225        // convert the JSON string to an object
226        var data = JSON.parse(asyncRequest.responseText);
227
228        if ( data.ErrorText != "Valid Telephone Format" )
229        {
230           phoneValid = false; // update validity tracker
231           document.getElementById( "validatePhone" ).innerHTML =
232              data.ErrorText; // display the error
233        } // end if
234        else
235        {
236           phoneValid = true; // update validity tracker
237        } // end else
238     } // end if
239  } // end function showPhoneError
240
241  // enter the user's data into the database
242  function saveForm()
243  {
244     // retrieve the data from the form
```

Fig. 16.10 | JavaScript code for the address-book application. (Part 5 of 6.)

```
245      var first = document.getElementById( "first" ).value;
246      var last = document.getElementById( "last" ).value;
247      var street = document.getElementById( "street" ).value;
248      var city = document.getElementById( "city" ).innerHTML;
249      var state = document.getElementById( "state" ).innerHTML;
250      var zip = document.getElementById( "zip" ).value;
251      var phone = document.getElementById( "phone" ).value;
252
253      // check if data is valid
254      if ( !zipValid || !phoneValid  )
255      {
256         // display error message
257         document.getElementById( "success" ).innerHTML =
258            "Invalid data entered. Check form for more information";
259      } // end if
260      else if ( ( first == "" ) || ( last == "" ) )
261      {
262         // display error message
263         document.getElementById("success").innerHTML =
264            "First Name and Last Name must have a value.";
265      } // end if
266      else
267      {
268         // hide the form and show the address book
269         document.getElementById( "addEntry" ).style.display = "none";
270         document.getElementById( "addressBook" ).style.display = "block";
271
272         // call the web service to insert data into the database
273         callWebService( "/addEntry/" + first + "/" + last + "/" + street +
274            "/" + city + "/" + state + "/" + zip + "/" + phone, parseData );
275      } // end else
276   } // end function saveForm
277
278   // register event listeners
279   function start()
280   {
281      document.getElementById( "addressBookButton" ).addEventListener(
282         "click", showAddressBook, false );
283      document.getElementById( "addEntryButton" ).addEventListener(
284         "click", addEntry, false );
285      document.getElementById( "searchInput" ).addEventListener(
286         "keyup", function() { search( this.value ); } , false );
287      document.getElementById( "zip" ).addEventListener(
288         "blur", function() { validateZip( this.value ); } , false );
289      document.getElementById( "phone" ).addEventListener(
290         "blur", function() { validatePhone( this.value ); } , false );
291      document.getElementById( "submitButton" ).addEventListener(
292         "click", saveForm , false );
293
294      showAddressBook();
295   } // end function start
296
297   window.addEventListener( "load", start, false );
```

Fig. 16.10 | JavaScript code for the address-book application. (Part 6 of 6.)

16.6.3 Interacting with a Web Service on the Server

When the page loads, the load event (Fig. 16.10, line 297) calls the start function (lines 279–295) to register various event listeners and to call showAddressBook, which loads the address book onto the page. Function showAddressBook (lines 10–17) shows the address-Book element and hides the addEntry element (lines 13–14). Then it calls function call-WebService to make an *asynchronous* request to the server (line 16). Our program uses an ASP.NET REST web service that we created for this example to do the server-side processing. The web service contains a collection of methods, including getAllNames, that can be called from a web application. To invoke a method you specify the web service URL followed by a forward slash (/), the name of the method to call, a forward slash and the arguments separated by forward slashes. Function callWebService requires a string containing the method to call on the server and the arguments to the method in the format described above. In this case, the function we're invoking on the server requires no arguments, so line 16 passes the string "/getAllNames" as the first argument to callWebService.

Function callWebService (lines 20–44) contains the code to call our web service, given a string containing the web-service method to call and the arguments to that method (if any), and the name of a callback function. The web-service method to call and its arguments are appended to the request URL (line 23). In this first call, we do not pass any parameters because the web method that returns all the entries requires none. However, future web method calls will include arguments in the methodAndArguments parameter. Lines 28–38 prepare and send the request, using functionality similar to that in the previous two examples. There are many types of user interactions in this application, each requiring a separate asynchronous request. For this reason, we pass the appropriate asyncRequest object as an argument to the function specified by the callBack parameter. However, event handlers cannot receive arguments, so lines 31–32 register an anonymous function for asyncRequest's readystatechange event. When this anonymous function gets called, it calls function callBack and passes the asyncRequest object as an argument. Lines 36–37 set an Accept request header to receive JSON-formatted data.

16.6.4 Parsing JSON Data

Each of our web service's methods in this example returns a JSON representation of an object or array of objects. For example, when the web application requests the list of names in the address book, the list is returned as a JSON array, as shown in Fig. 16.11. Each object in Fig. 16.11 has the attributes first and last.

```
1   [ { "first": "Cheryl", "last": "Black" },
2     { "first": "James", "last": "Blue" },
3     { "first": "Mike", "last": "Brown" },
4     { "first": "Meg", "last": "Gold" } ]
```

Fig. 16.11 | Address-book data formatted in JSON.

When the XMLHttpRequest object receives the response, it calls function parseData (Fig. 16.10, lines 47–56). Line 53 calls the JSON.parse function, which converts the JSON string into a JavaScript object. Then line 54 calls function displayNames (lines 59–78), which displays the first and last name of each address-book entry passed to it. Lines

62–63 use the HTML5 DOM to store the placeholder div element Names in the variable listbox and clear its content. Once parsed, the JSON string of address-book entries becomes an array, which this function traverses (lines 66–77).

16.6.5 Creating HTML5 Elements and Setting Event Handlers on the Fly

Line 71 uses an HTML5 fieldset element to create a box in which the entry will be placed. Line 72 registers an anonymous function that calls getAddress as the onclick event handler for the div created in line 70. This enables the user to expand each address-book entry by clicking it. The arguments to getAddress are generated dynamically and not evaluated until the getAddress function is called. This enables each function to receive arguments that are specific to the entry the user clicked. Line 74 displays the names on the page by accessing the first (first name) and last (last name) fields of each element of the data array. To determine which address the user clicked, we introduce the **this keyword**. The meaning of this depends on its context. In an event-handling function, this refers to the DOM object on which the event occurred. Our function uses this to refer to the clicked entry. The this keyword allows us to use one event handler to apply a change to one of many DOM elements, depending on which one received the event.

Function getAddress (lines 100–127) is called when the user clicks an entry. This request must keep track of the entry where the address is to be displayed on the page. Lines 115–116 set as the callback function an anonymous function that calls displayAddress with the entry element as an argument. Once the request completes successfully, lines 136–140 parse the response and display the addresses. Line 143 updates the div's onclick event handler to hide the address data when that div is clicked again by the user. When the user clicks an expanded entry, function clearField (lines 148–152) is called. Lines 150–151 reset the entry's content and its onclick event handler to the values they had before the entry was expanded.

You'll notice that we registered **click**-event handlers for the items in the fieldset by using the onclick property of each item, rather than the addEventListener method. We did this for simplicity in this example because we want to modify the event handler for each item's **click** event based on whether the item is currently displaying just the contact's name or its complete address. Each call to addEventListener adds another event listener to the object on which it's called—for this example, that could result in many event listeners being called for one entry that the user clicks repeatedly. Using the onclick property allows you to set *only one* listener at a time for a paticular event, which makes it easy for us to switch event listeners as the user clicks each item in the contact list.

16.6.6 Implementing Type-Ahead

The input element declared in line 20 of Fig. 16.9 enables the user to search the address book by last name. As soon as the user starts typing in the input box, the keyup event handler (registered at lines 285–286 in Fig. 16.10) calls the search function (lines 82–97), passing the input element's value as an argument. The search function performs an asynchronous request to locate entries with last names that start with its argument value. When the response is received, the application displays the matching list of names. Each time the user changes the text in the input box, function search is called again to make another asynchronous request.

The search function first clears the address-book entries from the page (lines 85–86). If the input argument is the empty string, line 91 displays the entire address book by calling function showAddressBook. Otherwise line 95 sends a request to the server to search the data. Line 95 creates a string to represent the method and argument that callWebService will append to the request URL. When the server responds, callback function parseData is invoked, which calls function displayNames to display the results on the page.

16.6.7 Implementing a Form with Asynchronous Validation

When the **Add an Entry** button in the HTML5 document is clicked, the addEntry function (lines 155–159) is called, which hides the addressBook div and shows the addEntry div that allows the user to add a person to the address book. The addEntry div in the HTML5 document contains a set of entry fields, some of which have event handlers (registered in the JavaScript start function) that enable validation that occurs *asynchronously* as the user continues to interact with the page. When a user enters a ZIP code, then moves the cursor to another field, the validateZip function (lines 162–165) is called. This function calls an external web service to validate the ZIP code. If it's valid, that external web service returns the corresponding city and state. Line 164 calls the callWebService function with the appropriate method and argument, and specifies showCityState (lines 169–211) as the callback function.

ZIP-code validation can take significant time due to network delays. The function showCityState is called every time the request object's readyState property changes. Until the request completes, lines 172–173 display "Checking zip..." on the page. After the request completes, line 181 converts the JSON response text to an object. The response object has four properties—Validity, ErrorText, City and State. If the request is valid, line 186 updates the zipValid script variable that keeps track of ZIP-code validity, and lines 189–192 show the city and state that the server generated using the ZIP code. Otherwise lines 196–198 update the zipValid variable and show the error code. Lines 201–202 clear the city and state elements. If our web service fails to connect to the ZIP-code validator web service, lines 207–208 display an appropriate error message.

Similarly, when the user enters the telephone number, the function validatePhone (lines 214–217) sends the phone number to the server. Once the server responds, the showPhoneError function (lines 220–239) updates the validatePhone script variable and shows the error message, if the web service returned one.

When the **Submit** button is clicked, the saveForm function is called (lines 242–276). Lines 245–251 retrieve the data from the form. Lines 254–259 check if the ZIP code and telephone number are valid, and display the appropriate error message in the Success element on the bottom of the page. Before the data can be entered into a database on the server, both the first-name and last-name fields must have a value. Lines 260–265 check that these fields are not empty and, if they're empty, display the appropriate error message. Once all the data entered is valid, lines 266–275 hide the entry form and show the address book. Lines 273–274 call function callWebService to invoke the addEntry function of our web service with the data for the new contact. Once the server saves the data, it queries the database for an updated list of entries and returns them; then function parseData displays the entries on the page.

Summary

Section 16.1 Introduction

- Despite the tremendous technological growth of the Internet over the past decade, the usability of web applications has lagged behind that of desktop applications.
- Rich Internet Applications (RIAs, p. 604) are web applications that approximate the look, feel and usability of desktop applications. RIAs have two key attributes—performance and rich GUI.
- RIA performance comes from Ajax (Asynchronous JavaScript and XML, p. 604), which uses client-side scripting to make web applications more responsive.
- Ajax applications separate client-side user interaction and server communication and run them in parallel, making the delays of server-side processing more transparent to the user.
- "Raw" Ajax (p. 604) uses JavaScript to send asynchronous requests to the server, then updates the page using the DOM.
- When writing "raw" Ajax you need to deal directly with cross-browser portability issues, making it impractical for developing large-scale applications.
- Portability issues are hidden by Ajax toolkits (p. 604), which provide powerful ready-to-use controls and functions that enrich web applications and simplify JavaScript coding by making it cross-browser compatible.
- We achieve rich GUI in RIAs with Ajax toolkits and with RIA environments such as Adobe's Flex, Microsoft's Silverlight and JavaServer Faces. Such toolkits and environments provide powerful ready-to-use controls and functions that enrich web applications.
- The client-side of Ajax applications is written in HTML5 and CSS3 and uses JavaScript to add functionality to the user interface.
- XML and JSON are used to structure the data passed between the server and the client.
- The Ajax component that manages interaction with the server is usually implemented with JavaScript's `XMLHttpRequest` object (p. 604)—commonly abbreviated as XHR.
- In traditional web applications, the user fills in the form's fields, then submits the form. The browser generates a request to the server, which receives the request and processes it. The server generates and sends a response containing the exact page that the browser will render, which causes the browser to load the new page and temporarily makes the browser window blank. The client *waits* for the server to respond and *reloads the entire page* with the data from the response.
- While a synchronous request (p. 605) is being processed on the server, the user cannot interact with the client web browser.
- The synchronous model was originally designed for a web of hypertext documents—what some people call the "brochure web." This model yielded "choppy" application performance.
- In an Ajax application, when the user interacts with a page, the client creates an `XMLHttpRequest` object to manage a request. The `XMLHttpRequest` object sends the request to and awaits the response from the server. The requests are asynchronous (p. 606), allowing the user to continue interacting with the application while the server processes the request concurrently. When the server responds, the `XMLHttpRequest` object that issued the request invokes a callback function (p. 606), which typically uses partial page updates (p. 606) to display the returned data in the existing web page without reloading the entire page.
- The callback function updates only a designated part of the page. Such partial page updates help make web applications more responsive, making them feel more like desktop applications.

Section 16.2 Rich Internet Applications (RIAs) with Ajax

- A classic HTML5 registration form sends all of the data to be validated to the server when the user clicks the **Register** button. While the server is validating the data, the user cannot interact with the page. The server finds invalid data, generates a new page identifying the errors in the form and sends it back to the client—which renders the page in the browser. Once the user fixes the errors and clicks the **Register** button, the cycle repeats until no errors are found; then the data is stored on the server. The entire page reloads every time the user submits invalid data.

- Ajax-enabled forms are more interactive. Entries are validated dynamically as the user enters data into the fields. If a problem is found, the server sends an error message that's asynchronously displayed to inform the user of the problem. Sending each entry asynchronously allows the user to address invalid entries quickly, rather than making edits and resubmitting the entire form repeatedly until all entries are valid. Asynchronous requests could also be used to fill some fields based on previous fields' values.

Section 16.3 History of Ajax
- The term Ajax was coined by Jesse James Garrett of Adaptive Path in February 2005, when he was presenting the previously unnamed technology to a client.
- All of the technologies involved in Ajax (HTML5, JavaScript, CSS, dynamic HTML, the DOM and XML) had existed for many years before the term "Ajax" was coined.
- In 1998, Microsoft introduced the XMLHttpRequest object to create and manage asynchronous requests and responses.
- Popular applications like Flickr, Google's Gmail and Google Maps use the XMLHttpRequest object to update pages dynamically.
- The name Ajax immediately caught on and brought attention to its component technologies. Ajax has quickly become one of the hottest technologies in web development, as it enables web-top applications to challenge the dominance of established desktop applications.

Section 16.4 "Raw" Ajax Example Using the XMLHttpRequest Object
- The XMLHttpRequest object (which resides on the client) is the layer between the client and the server that manages asynchronous requests in Ajax applications. This object is supported on most browsers, though they may implement it differently.
- To initiate an asynchronous request, you create an instance of the XMLHttpRequest object, then use its open method to set up the request and its send method to initiate the request.
- When an Ajax application requests a file from a server, the browser typically caches that file. Subsequent requests for the same file can load it from the browser's cache.
- For security purposes, the XMLHttpRequest object does not allow a web application to request resources from servers other than the one that served the web application.
- Making a request to a different server is known as cross-site scripting (also known as XSS, p. 610). You can implement a server-side proxy—an application on the web application's web server—that can make requests to other servers on the web application's behalf.
- When the third argument to XMLHttpRequest method open is true, the request is asynchronous.
- An exception (p. 613) is an indication of a problem that occurs during a program's execution.
- Exception handling (p. 613) enables you to create applications that can resolve (or handle) exceptions—in some cases allowing a program to continue executing as if no problem had been encountered.
- A try block (p. 613) encloses code that might cause an exception and code that should not execute if an exception occurs. A try block consists of the keyword try followed by a block of code enclosed in curly braces ({}).
- When an exception occurs, a try block terminates immediately and a catch block (also called a catch clause or exception handler, p. 613) catches (i.e., receives) and handles the exception.

- The catch block begins with the keyword catch (p. 613) and is followed by an exception parameter in parentheses and a block of code enclosed in curly braces.

- The exception parameter's name enables the catch block to interact with a caught exception object, which contains name and message properties.

- A callback function is registered as the event handler for the XMLHttpRequest object's readystatechange event (p. 614). Whenever the request makes progress, the XMLHttpRequest calls the readystatechange event handler.

- Progress is monitored by the readyState property, which has a value from 0 to 4. The value 0 indicates that the request is not initialized and the value 4 indicates that the request is complete.

Section 16.5 Using XML and the DOM
- When passing structured data between the server and the client, Ajax applications often use XML because it consumes little bandwidth and is easy to parse.

- When the XMLHttpRequest object receives XML data, the XMLHttpRequest object parses and stores the data as a DOM object in the responseXML property.

- The XMLHttpRequest object's responseXML property contains the XML returned by the server.

- DOM method createElement creates an HTML5 element of the specified type.

- DOM method setAttribute adds or changes an attribute of an HTML5 element.

- DOM method appendChild inserts one HTML5 element into another.

- The innerHTML property of a DOM element can be used to obtain or change the HTML5 that's displayed in a particular element.

Section 16.6 Creating a Full-Scale Ajax-Enabled Application
- JSON (JavaScript Object Notation, p. 619)—a simple way to represent JavaScript objects as strings—is an alternative way (to XML) for passing data between the client and the server.

- Each JSON object is represented as a list of property names and values contained in curly braces.

- An array is represented in JSON with square brackets containing a comma-separated list of values.

- Each value in a JSON array can be a string, a number, a JSON representation of an object, true, false or null.

- JavaScript's JSON.parse function can convert JSON strings into JavaScript objects.

- JSON strings are easier to create and parse than XML and require fewer bytes. For these reasons, JSON is commonly used to communicate in client/server interaction.

- To implement type-ahead (p. 620), you can use an element's keyup-event handler to make asynchronous requests.

Self-Review Exercises

16.1 Fill in the blanks in each of the following statements:
   a) Ajax applications use _____ requests to create Rich Internet Applications.
   b) In Ajax applications, the _____ object manages asynchronous interaction with the server.
   c) The event handler called when the server responds is known as a(n) _____ function.
   d) The _____ attribute can be accessed through the DOM to update an HTML5 element's content without reloading the page.
   e) JavaScript's XMLHttpRequest object is commonly abbreviated as _____.
   f) _____ is a simple way to represent JavaScript objects as strings.
   g) Making a request to a different server is known as _____.

h) JavaScript's _____ function can convert JSON strings into JavaScript objects.

i) A(n) _____ encloses code that might cause an exception and code that should not execute if an exception occurs.

j) The XMLHttpRequest object's _____ contains the XML returned by the server.

16.2 State whether each of the following is *true* or *false*. If *false*, explain why.

a) Ajax applications must use XML for server responses.

b) The technologies that are used to develop Ajax applications have existed since the 1990s.

c) To handle an Ajax response, register for the XMLHttpRequest object's readystatechanged event.

d) An Ajax application can be implemented so that it never needs to reload the page on which it runs.

e) The responseXML property of the XMLHttpRequest object stores the server's response as a raw XML string.

f) An exception indicates successful completion of a program's execution.

g) When the third argument to XMLHttpRequest method open is false, the request is asynchronous.

h) For security purposes, the XMLHttpRequest object does not allow a web application to request resources from servers other than the one that served the web application.

i) The innerHTML property of a DOM element can be used to obtain or change the HTML5 that's displayed in a particular element.

Answers to Self-Review Exercises

16.1 a) asynchronous. b) XMLHttpRequest. c) callback. d) innerHTML. e) XHR. f) JSON. g) cross-site scripting (or XSS). h) JSON.parse. i) try block. j) responseXML property.

16.2 a) False. Ajax applications can use any type of textual data as a response. For example, we used JSON in this chapter.

b) True.

c) True.

d) True.

e) False. If the response data has XML format, the XMLHttpRequest object parses it and stores it in a document object.

f) False. An exception is an indication of a problem that occurs during a program's execution.

g) False. The third argument to XMLHttpRequest method open must be true to make an asynchronous request.

h) True.

i) True.

Exercises

16.3 Describe the differences between client/server interactions in traditional web applications and client/server interactions in Ajax web applications.

16.4 Consider the AddressBook application in Fig. 16.9. Describe how you could reimplement the type-ahead capability so that it could perform the search using data previously downloaded rather than making an asynchronous request to the server after every keystroke.

16.5 Describe each of the following terms in the context of Ajax:

a) type-ahead

b) edit-in-place

      c) partial page update
      d) asynchronous request
      e) `XMLHttpRequest`
      f) "raw" Ajax
      g) callback function
      h) same origin policy
      i) Ajax libraries
      j) RIA

[*Note to Instructors and Students:* Owing to security restrictions on using `XMLHttpRequest`, Ajax applications must be placed on a web server (even one on your local computer) to enable them to work correctly, and when they need to access other resources, those must reside on the same web server. *Students:* You'll need to work closely with your instructors in order to understand your lab setup, so that you can run your solutions to the exercises (the examples are already posted on our web server), and in order to run many of the other server-side applications that you'll learn later in the book.]

16.6 The XML files used in the book-cover catalog example (Fig. 16.8) also store the titles of the books in a `title` attribute of each cover node. Modify the example so that every time the mouse hovers over an image, the book's title is displayed below the image.

16.7 Create an Ajax-enabled version of the feedback form from Fig. 2.15. As the user moves between form fields, ensure that each field is nonempty. For the e-mail field, ensure that the e-mail address has a valid format. In addition, create an XML file that contains a list of e-mail addresses that are not allowed to post feedback. Each time the user enters an e-mail address, check whether it's on that list; if so, display an appropriate message.

16.8 Create an Ajax-based product catalog that obtains its data from JSON files located on the server. The data should be separated into four JSON files. The first should be a summary file, containing a list of products. Each product should have a title, an image filename for a thumbnail image and a price. The second file should contain a list of descriptions for each product. The third file should contain a list of filenames for the full-size product images. The last file should contain a list of the thumbnail-image file names. Each item in a catalogue should have a unique ID that should be included with the entries for that product in every file. Next, create an Ajax-enabled web page that displays the product information in a table. The catalog should initially display a list of product names with their associated thumbnail images and prices. When the mouse hovers over a thumbnail image, the larger product image should be displayed. When the user moves the mouse away from that image, the original thumbnail should be redisplayed. You should provide a button that the user can click to display the product description.

Web Servers
(Apache and IIS)

Objectives

In this chapter you'll:

- Learn about a web server's functionality.

- Install Apache HTTP Server and Microsoft IIS Express.

- Test the book's examples using Apache and IIS Express.

17.1 Introduction

In this chapter, we discuss the specialized software—called a **web server**—that responds to client requests (typically from a web browser) by providing resources such as XHTML documents. For example, when users enter a Uniform Resource Locator (URL) address, such as www.deitel.com, into a web browser, they're requesting a specific document from a web server. The web server maps the URL to a resource on the server (or to a file on the server's network) and returns the requested resource to the client. During this interaction, the web server and the client communicate using the platform-independent Hypertext Transfer Protocol (HTTP), a protocol for transferring requests and files over the Internet or a local intranet.

We also discuss two web servers—the open source **Apache HTTP Server** and **Microsoft's Internet Information Services Express (IIS Express)**—that you can install on your own computer for testing your web pages and web applications.

Because this chapter is essentially a concise series of installation instructions to prepare you for the server-side chapters of the book, it does not include a summary or exercises.

17.2 HTTP Transactions

In this section, we discuss the fundamentals of web-based interactions between a client web browser and a web server. In its simplest form, a *web page* is nothing more than an HTML (HyperText Markup Language) document (with the extension .html or .htm) that describes to a web browser the document's content and structure.

HTML documents normally contain hyperlinks that link to different pages or to other parts of the same page. When the user clicks a hyperlink, the requested web page loads into the user's web browser. Similarly, the user can type the address of a page into the browser's address field.

URIs and URLs
URIs (Uniform Resource Identifiers) identify resources on the Internet. URIs that start with http:// are called *URLs (Uniform Resource Locators)*. Common URLs refer to files, directories or server-side code that performs tasks such as database lookups, Internet searches and business-application processing. If you know the URL of a publicly available resource

anywhere on the web, you can enter that URL into a web browser's address field and the browser can access that resource.

Parts of a URL

A URL contains information that directs a browser to the resource that the user wishes to access. Web servers make such resources available to web clients.

Let's examine the components of the URL

```
http://www.deitel.com/books/downloads.html
```

The text `http://` indicates that the HyperText Transfer Protocol (HTTP) should be used to obtain the resource. Next in the URL is the server's fully qualified **hostname** (for example, `www.deitel.com`)—the name of the web-server computer on which the resource resides. This computer is referred to as the **host**, because it houses and maintains resources. The hostname `www.deitel.com` is translated into an **IP (Internet Protocol) address**—a numerical value that uniquely identifies the server on the Internet. An Internet **Domain Name System (DNS) server** maintains a database of hostnames and their corresponding IP addresses and performs the translations automatically.

The remainder of the URL (`/books/downloads.html`) specifies the resource's location (`/books`) and name (`downloads.html`) on the web server. The location could represent an actual directory on the web server's file system. For *security* reasons, however, the location is typically a *virtual directory*. The web server translates the virtual directory into a real location on the server, thus hiding the resource's true location.

Making a Request and Receiving a Response

When given a web page URL, a web browser uses HTTP to request the web page found at that address. Figure 17.1 shows a web browser sending a request to a web server.

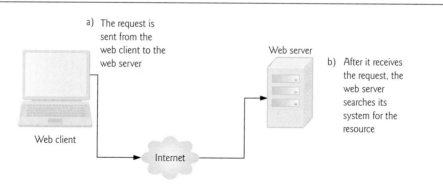

a) The request is sent from the web client to the web server

Web client

Internet

Web server

b) After it receives the request, the web server searches its system for the resource

Fig. 17.1 | Client interacting with web server. *Step 1:* The GET request.

In Fig. 17.1, the web browser sends an HTTP request to the server. The request (in its simplest form) is

```
GET /books/downloads.html HTTP/1.1
```

The word **GET** is an **HTTP method** indicating that the client wishes to obtain a resource from the server. The remainder of the request provides the path name of the resource (e.g., an HTML5 document) and the protocol's name and version number (HTTP/1.1). The client's request also contains some required and optional headers.

Any server that understands HTTP (version 1.1) can translate this request and respond appropriately. Figure 17.2 shows the web server responding to a request.

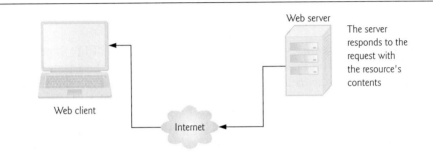

Fig. 17.2 | Client interacting with web server. *Step 2:* The HTTP response.

The server first sends a line of text that indicates the HTTP version, followed by a numeric code and a phrase describing the status of the transaction. For example,

```
HTTP/1.1 200 OK
```

indicates success, whereas

```
HTTP/1.1 404 Not found
```

informs the client that the web server could not locate the requested resource. A complete list of numeric codes indicating the status of an HTTP transaction can be found at www.w3.org/Protocols/rfc2616/rfc2616-sec10.html.

HTTP Headers

Next, the server sends one or more **HTTP headers**, which provide additional information about the data that will be sent. In this case, the server is sending an HTML5 text document, so one HTTP header for this example would read:

```
Content-type: text/html
```

The information provided in this header specifies the **Multipurpose Internet Mail Extensions (MIME) type** of the content that the server is transmitting to the browser. The MIME standard specifies data formats, which programs can use to interpret data correctly. For example, the MIME type text/plain indicates that the sent information is text that can be displayed directly. Similarly, the MIME type image/jpeg indicates that the content is a JPEG image. When the browser receives this MIME type, it attempts to display the image.

The header or set of headers is followed by a blank line, which indicates to the client browser that the server is finished sending HTTP headers. Finally, the server sends the contents of the requested document (downloads.html). The client-side browser then renders (or displays) the document, which may involve additional HTTP requests to obtain associated CSS and images.

HTTP **get** *and* **post** *Requests*

The two most common **HTTP request types** (also known as **request methods**) are get and post. A get request typically gets (or retrieves) information from a server, such as an HTML document, an image or search results based on a user-submitted search term. A post request typically posts (or sends) data to a server. Common uses of post requests are to send form data or documents to a server.

An HTTP request often posts data to a **server-side form handler** that processes the data. For example, when a user performs a search or participates in a web-based survey, the web server receives the information specified in the HTML form as part of the request. Get requests and post requests can both be used to send data to a web server, but each request type sends the information differently.

A get request appends data to the URL, e.g., www.google.com/search?q=deitel. In this case search is the name of Google's server-side form handler, q is the name of a variable in Google's search form and deitel is the search term. The ? in the preceding URL separates the **query string** from the rest of the URL in a request. A *name/value* pair is passed to the server with the *name* and the *value* separated by an equals sign (=). If more than one *name/value* pair is submitted, each pair is separated by an ampersand (&). The server uses data passed in a query string to retrieve an appropriate resource from the server. The server then sends a response to the client. A get request may be initiated by submitting an HTML form whose method attribute is set to "get", or by typing the URL (possibly containing a query string) directly into the browser's address bar. We discuss HTML forms in Chapters 2–3.

A post request sends form data as part of the HTTP message, not as part of the URL. A get request typically limits the query string (i.e., everything to the right of the ?) to a specific number of characters, so it's often necessary to send large amounts of information using the post method. The post method is also sometimes preferred because it hides the submitted data from the user by embedding it in an HTTP message. If a form submits several hidden input values along with user-submitted data, the post method might generate a URL like www.searchengine.com/search. The form data still reaches the server and is processed in a similar fashion to a get request, but the user does not see the exact information sent.

Software Engineering Observation 17.1

The data sent in a post request is not part of the URL, and the user can't see the data by default. However, tools are available that expose this data, so you should not assume that the data is secure just because a post request is used.

Client-Side Caching

Browsers often **cache** (save on disk) recently viewed web pages for quick reloading. If there are no changes between the version stored in the cache and the current version on the web, this speeds up your browsing experience. An HTTP response can indicate the length of time for which the content remains "fresh." If this amount of time has not been reached, the browser can avoid another request to the server. If not, the browser loads the document from the cache. Similarly, there's also the "not modified" HTTP response, indicating that the file content has not changed since it was last requested (which is information that's send in the request). Browsers typically do not cache the server's response to a post request, because the next post might not return the same result. For example, in a survey, many users could visit the same web page and answer a question. The survey results could then be displayed for the user. Each new answer would change the survey results.

17.3 Multitier Application Architecture

Web-based applications are often **multitier applications** (sometimes referred to as *n*-**tier applications**) that divide functionality into separate **tiers** (i.e., logical groupings of functionality). Although tiers can be located on the same computer, the tiers of web-based applications often reside on separate computers. Figure 17.3 presents the basic structure of a **three-tier web-based application**.

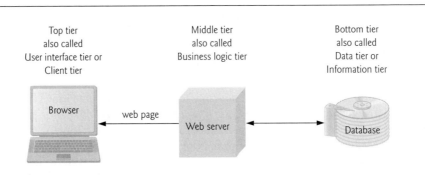

Top tier
also called
User interface tier or
Client tier

Middle tier
also called
Business logic tier

Bottom tier
also called
Data tier or
Information tier

Browser

web page

Web server

Database

Fig. 17.3 | Three-tier architecture.

The **bottom tier** (also called the data tier or the information tier) maintains the application's data. This tier typically stores data in a relational database management system (RDBMS). We discuss RDBMSs in Chapter 18. For example, Amazon might have an inventory information database containing product descriptions, prices and quantities in stock. Another database might contain customer information, such as user names, billing addresses and credit card numbers. These may reside on one or more computers, which together comprise the application's data.

The **middle tier** implements business logic, controller logic and presentation logic to control interactions between the application's clients and its data. The middle tier acts as an intermediary between data in the information tier and the application's clients. The middle-tier **controller logic** processes client requests (such as requests to view a product catalog) and retrieves data from the database. The middle-tier **presentation logic** then processes data from the information tier and presents the content to the client. Web applications typically present data to clients as HTML documents.

Business logic in the middle tier enforces **business rules** and ensures that data is reliable before the application updates a database or presents data to users. Business rules dictate how clients access data and how applications process data. For example, a business rule in the middle tier of a retail store's web-based application might ensure that all product quantities remain positive. A client request to set a negative quantity in the bottom tier's product information database would be rejected by the middle tier's business logic.

The **top tier**, or client tier, is the application's user interface, which gathers input and displays output. Users interact directly with the application through the user interface, which is typically a web browser or a mobile device. In response to user actions (e.g., clicking a hyperlink), the client tier interacts with the middle tier to make requests and to retrieve data from the information tier. The client tier then displays the data retrieved for the user.

17.4 Client-Side Scripting versus Server-Side Scripting

Client-side scripting with JavaScript can be used to validate user input, to interact with the browser, to enhance web pages, and to add client/server communication between a browser and a web server.

Client-side scripting does have limitations, such as browser dependency; the browser or **scripting host** must support the scripting language and capabilities. Scripts are restricted from arbitrarily accessing the local hardware and file system for security reasons. Another issue is that client-side scripts can be viewed by the client using the browser's source-viewing capability. Sensitive information, such as passwords or other personally identifiable data, should not be on the client. All client-side data validation should be mirrored on the server. Also, placing certain operations in JavaScript on the client can open web applications to security issues.

Programmers have more flexibility with **server-side scripts**, which often generate custom responses for clients. For example, a client might connect to an airline's web server and request a list of flights from Boston to San Francisco between April 19 and May 5. The server queries the database, dynamically generates an HTML document containing the flight list and sends the document to the client. This technology allows clients to obtain the most current flight information from the database by connecting to an airline's web server.

Server-side scripting languages have a wider range of programmatic capabilities than their client-side equivalents. Server-side scripts also have access to server-side software that extends server functionality—Microsoft web servers use **ISAPI (Internet Server Application Program Interface) extensions** and Apache HTTP Servers use **modules**. Components and modules range from programming-language support to counting the number of web-page hits. We discuss some of these components and modules in subsequent chapters.

17.5 Accessing Web Servers

To request documents from web servers, users must know the hostnames on which the web server software resides. Users can request documents from **local web servers** (i.e., ones residing on users' machines) or **remote web servers** (i.e., ones residing on different machines).

Local web servers can be accessed through your computer's name or through the name `localhost`—a hostname that references the local machine and normally translates to the IP address 127.0.0.1 (known as the **loopback address**). We sometimes use `localhost` in this book for demonstration purposes. To display the machine name in Windows, Mac OS X or Linux, run the `hostname` command in a command prompt or terminal window.

A remote web server referenced by a fully qualified hostname or an IP address can also serve documents. In the URL `http://www.deitel.com/books/downloads.html`, the middle portion, `www.deitel.com`, is the server's fully qualified hostname.

17.6 Apache, MySQL and PHP Installation

This section shows how to install the software you need for running web apps using PHP. The Apache HTTP Server, maintained by the Apache Software Foundation, is the most popular web server in use today because of its stability, efficiency, portability, security and small size. It's open source software that runs on Linux, Mac OS X, Windows and numerous other platforms. MySQL (discussed in more detail in Section 18.5) is the most popular open-source database management system. It, too, runs on Linux, Mac OS X and Windows. PHP (Chapter 19) is the most popular server-side scripting language for creating dynamic, data-driven web applications.

The Apache HTTP Server, MySQL database server and PHP can each be downloaded and installed separately, but this also requires additional configuration on your part. There are many integrated installers that install and configure the Apache HTTP Server, MySQL database server and PHP for you on various operating-system platforms. For simplicity, we'll use the XAMPP integrated installer provided by the Apache Friends website (www.apachefriends.org).

17.6.1 XAMPP Installation

The XAMPP integrated installer for Apache, MySQL and PHP is available for Windows, Mac OS X and Linux. Chapters 18 and 19 assume that you've used the XAMPP installer to set up the software. Go to

```
http://www.apachefriends.org/en/xampp.html
```

then choose the installer for your platform. Carefully follow the provided installation instructions and *be sure to read the entire installation page for your platform!* We assume in Chapters 18 and 19 that you used the default installation options here.

Microsoft Web Platform Installer

If you'd prefer to use PHP with Microsoft's IIS Express and SQL Server Express, you can use their Web Platform Installer to set up and configure PHP:

```
http://www.microsoft.com/web/platform/phponwindows.aspx
```

Please note, however, that Chapter 19 assumes you're using PHP with MySQL and the Apache HTTP Server.

17.6.2 Running XAMPP

Once you've installed XAMPP, you can start the Apache and MySQL servers for each platform as described below.

Windows

Go to your c:\xampp folder (or the folder in which you installed XAMPP) and double click xampp_start.exe. If you need to stop the servers (e.g., so you can shut down your computer), use xampp_stop.exe in the same folder.

Mac OS X

Go to your Applications folder (or the folder in which you installed XAMPP), then open the XAMPP folder and run XAMP Control.app. Click the **Start** buttons in the control panel to start the servers. If you need to stop the servers (e.g., so you can shut down your computer), you can stop them by clicking the **Stop** buttons.

Linux

Open a shell and enter the command

```
/opt/lampp/lampp start
```

If you need to stop the servers (e.g., so you can shut down your computer), open a shell and enter the command

```
/opt/lampp/lampp stop
```

17.6.3 Testing Your Setup

Once you've started the servers, you can open any web browser on your computer and enter the address

```
http://localhost/
```

to confirm that the web server is up and running. If it is, you'll see a web page similar to the one in Fig. 17.4. You're now ready to go!

Fig. 17.4 | default XAMPP webpage displayed on Windows.

17.6.4 Running the Examples Using Apache HTTP Server

Now that the Apache HTTP Server is running on your computer, you can copy the book's examples into XAMPP's htdocs folder. Assuming you copy the entire examples folder into the htdocs folder, you can run the examples in Chapters 2–16 and 19 with URLs of the form

```
http://localhost/examples/chapter/figure/filename
```

where *chapter* is one of the chapter folders (e.g., ch03), *figure* is a folder for a particular example (e.g., fig03_01) and *filename* is the page to load (e.g., NewFormInputTypes.html). So, you can run the first example in Chapter 3 with

```
http://localhost/examples/ch03/fig03_01/NewFormInputTypes.html
```

[*Note:* The ch02 examples folder does not contain any subfolders.]

17.7 Microsoft IIS Express and WebMatrix

Microsoft Internet Information Services Express (IIS Express) is a web server that can be installed on computers running Microsoft Windows. Once it's running, you can use it to test web pages and web applications on your local computer. A key benefit of IIS Express is that it can be installed *without* administrator privileges on all versions of Windows XP, Windows Vista, Windows 7 and Windows Server 2008. IIS Express can be downloaded and installed by itself, or you can install it in a bundle with Microsoft's **WebMatrix**—a free development tool for building PHP and ASP.NET web apps. We provide links for each below. When you use IIS Express without administrator privileges, it can serve documents only to web browsers installed on your local computer.

17.7.1 Installing and Running IIS Express

If you simply want to test your web pages on IIS Express, you can install it from:

```
www.microsoft.com/web/gallery/install.aspx?appid=IISExpress
```

We recommend using the default installation options. Once you've installed IIS Express you can learn more about using it at:

```
learn.iis.net/page.aspx/860/iis-express/
```

17.7.2 Installing and Running WebMatrix

You can install the WebMatrix and IIS Express bundle from:

```
www.microsoft.com/web/gallery/install.aspx?appid=IISExpress
```

Again, we recommend using the default installation options. You can run WebMatrix by opening the **Start** menu and selecting **All Programs > Microsoft WebMatrix > Microsoft Web-Matrix**. This will also start IIS Express. Microsoft provides tutorials on how to use Web-Matrix at:

```
www.microsoft.com/web/post/web-development-101-using-webmatrix
```

17.7.3 Running the Client-Side Examples Using IIS Express

Once you have IIS Express installed, you can use it to test the examples in Chapters 2–16. When you start IIS Express, you can specify the folder on your computer that contains the documents you'd like to serve. To execute IIS Express, open a Command Prompt window and change directories to the IIS Express folder. On 32-bit Windows versions, use the command

```
cd "c:\Program Files\IIS Express"
```

On 64-bit Windows versions, use the command

```
cd "c:\Program Files (x86)\IIS Express"
```

Launching IIS Express
If the book's examples are in a folder named c:\examples, you can use the command

```
iisexpress /path:c:\examples
```

to start IIS. You can stop the server simply by typing Q in the Command Prompt window.

Testing a Client-Side Example
You can now run your examples with URLs of the form

> http://localhost:8080/*chapter*/*figure*/*filename*

where *chapter* is one of the chapter folders (e.g., ch03), *figure* is a folder for a particular example (e.g., fig03_01) and *filename* is the page to load (e.g., NewFormInputTypes.html). So, you can run the first example in Chapter 3 with

> http://localhost:8080/ch03/fig03_01/NewFormInputTypes.html

[*Note:* The ch02 examples folder does not contain any subfolders.]

17.7.4 Running the PHP Examples Using IIS Express

The easiest way to test Chapter 19's PHP examples is to use WebMatrix to enable PHP for the ch19 folder in the book's examples. To do so, perform the following steps.

1. Run WebMatrix by opening the **Start** menu and selecting **All Programs > Microsoft WebMatrix > Microsoft WebMatrix**.

2. In the **Quick Start - Microsoft WebMatrix** window, select **Site From Folder**.

3. Locate and select the ch19 folder in the **Select Folder** window, then click the **Select Folder** button.

This opens the ch19 folder as a website in WebMatrix (Fig. 17.5).

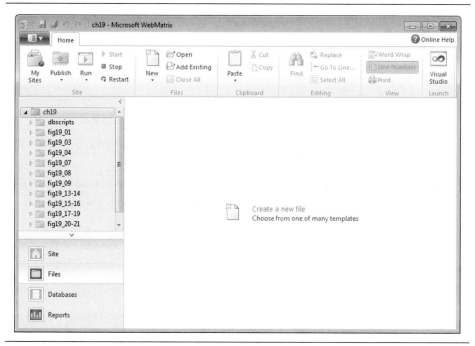

Fig. 17.5 | The ch19 examples folder in WebMatrix.

Enabling PHP

To enable PHP, perform the following steps:

1. Click the **Site** option in the bottom-left corner of the window.

2. Click Settings and ensure that **Enable PHP** is checked (Fig. 17.6). [*Note:* The first time you do this, WebMatrix will ask you for permission to install PHP. You *must* do this to test the PHP examples.]

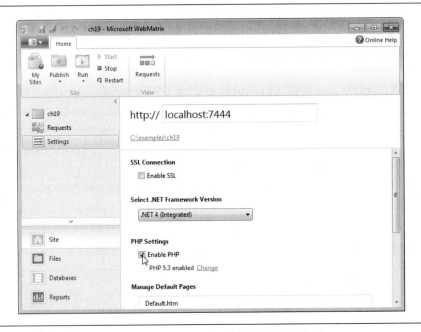

Fig. 17.6 | Enabling PHP for the `ch19` examples folder in WebMatrix.

Running a PHP Example

You can now run the PHP examples directly from WebMatrix. To do so:

1. Click the **Files** option in the bottom-left corner of the window.

2. Open the folder for the example you wish to test.

3. Right-click the example's PHP script file and select **Launch in browser**.

This opens your default browser and requests the selected PHP script file.

Database: SQL, MySQL, LINQ and Java DB

18

Objectives

In this chapter, you'll:

- Learn fundamental relational database concepts.

- Learn Structured Query Language (SQL) capabilities for retrieving data from and manipulating data in a database.

- Configure a MySQL user account.

- Create MySQL databases.

- Learn fundamental concepts of Microsoft's Language Integrated Query (LINQ)

18.1 Introduction

A **database** is an organized collection of data. There are many different strategies for organizing data to facilitate easy access and manipulation. A **database management system** (**DBMS**) provides mechanisms for storing, organizing, retrieving and modifying data for many users. Database management systems allow for the access and storage of data without concern for the internal representation of data.

Today's most popular database systems are *relational databases*. A language called **SQL**—pronounced "sequel," or as its individual letters—is the international standard language used almost universally with relational databases to perform **queries** (i.e., to request information that satisfies given criteria) and to manipulate data. [*Note:* As you learn about SQL, you'll see some authors writing "a SQL statement" (which assumes the pronunciation "sequel") and others writing "an SQL statement" (which assumes that the individual letters are pronounced). In this book we pronounce SQL as "sequel."]

Programs connect to, and interact with, a relational database via an **interface**—software that facilitates communication between a database management system and a program. For example, Java developers can use the JDBC interface to interact with databases. Similarly, ASP.NET programmers communicate with databases and manipulate their data through interfaces provided by .NET.

18.2 Relational Databases

A **relational database** is a logical representation of data that allows the data to be accessed without consideration of its physical structure. A relational database stores data in **tables**.

Figure 18.1 illustrates a sample table that might be used in a personnel system. The table name is Employee, and its primary purpose is to store the attributes of employees. Tables are composed of **rows**, and rows are composed of **columns** in which values are stored. This table consists of six rows. The Number column of each row is the table's **primary key**—a column (or group of columns) with a *unique* value that cannot be duplicated in other rows. This guarantees that each row can be identified by its primary key. Good examples of primary-key columns are a social security number, an employee ID number and a part number in an inventory system, as values in each of these columns are guaranteed to be unique. The rows in Fig. 18.1 are displayed in order by primary key. In this case, the rows are listed in increasing order, but we could also use decreasing order.

Number	Name	Department	Salary	Location
23603	Jones	413	1100	New Jersey
24568	Kerwin	413	2000	New Jersey
34589	Larson	642	1800	Los Angeles
35761	Myers	611	1400	Orlando
47132	Neumann	413	9000	New Jersey
78321	Stephens	611	8500	Orlando

Row { } — Primary key — Column

Fig. 18.1 | Employee table sample data.

Rows in tables are not guaranteed to be stored in any particular order. As we'll demonstrate in an upcoming example, programs can specify ordering criteria when requesting data from a database.

Each column represents a different data attribute. Rows are normally unique (by primary key) within a table, but particular column values may be duplicated between rows. For example, three different rows in the Employee table's Department column contain number 413.

Different users of a database are often interested in different data and different relationships among the data. Most users require only subsets of the rows and columns. Queries specify which subsets of the data to select from a table. You use SQL to define queries. For example, you might select data from the Employee table to create a result that shows where each department is located, presenting the data sorted in increasing order by department number. This result is shown in Fig. 18.2. SQL is discussed in Section 18.4.

Department	Location
413	New Jersey
611	Orlando
642	Los Angeles

Fig. 18.2 | Result of selecting distinct Department and Location data from table Employee.

18.3 Relational Database Overview: A books Database

We now overview relational databases in the context of a sample books database we created for this chapter. Before we discuss SQL, we discuss the *tables* of the books database. We use this database to introduce various database concepts, including how to use SQL to obtain information from the database and to manipulate the data. We provide a script to create the database. You can find the script in the examples directory for this chapter. Section 18.5.2 explains how to use this script. The database consists of three tables: Authors, AuthorISBN and Titles.

Authors Table
The Authors table (described in Fig. 18.3) consists of three columns that maintain each author's unique ID number, first name and last name. Figure 18.4 contains sample data from the Authors table of the books database.

Column	Description
AuthorID	Author's ID number in the database. In the books database, this integer column is defined as **autoincremented**—for each row inserted in this table, the AuthorID value is increased by 1 automatically to ensure that each row has a unique AuthorID. This column represents the table's primary key.
FirstName	Author's first name (a string).
LastName	Author's last name (a string).

Fig. 18.3 | Authors table from the books database.

AuthorID	FirstName	LastName
1	Paul	Deitel
2	Harvey	Deitel
3	Abbey	Deitel
4	Michael	Morgano
5	Eric	Kern

Fig. 18.4 | Sample data from the Authors table.

AuthorISBN Table
The AuthorISBN table (described in Fig. 18.5) consists of two columns that maintain each ISBN and the corresponding author's ID number. This table associates authors with their books. Both columns are foreign keys that represent the relationship between the tables Authors and Titles—one row in table Authors may be associated with many rows in table Titles, and vice versa. The combined columns of the AuthorISBN table represent the table's *primary key*—thus, each row in this table must be a *unique* combination of an AuthorID and an ISBN. Figure 18.6 contains sample data from the AuthorISBN table of the books database. [*Note:* To save space, we have split the contents of this table into two col-

umns, each containing the AuthorID and ISBN columns.] The AuthorID column is a **foreign key**—a column in this table that matches the primary-key column in another table (i.e., AuthorID in the Authors table). Foreign keys are specified when creating a table. The foreign key helps maintain the **Rule of Referential Integrity**—every foreign-key value must appear as another table's primary-key value. This enables the DBMS to determine whether the AuthorID value for a particular book is *valid*. Foreign keys also allow related data in multiple tables to be selected from those tables for analytic purposes—this is known as **joining** the data.

Column	Description
AuthorID	The author's ID number, a foreign key to the Authors table.
ISBN	The ISBN for a book, a foreign key to the Titles table.

Fig. 18.5 | AuthorISBN table from the books database.

AuthorID	ISBN	AuthorID	ISBN
1	0132152134	2	0132575663
2	0132152134	1	0132662361
1	0132151421	2	0132662361
2	0132151421	1	0132404168
1	0132575663	2	0132404168
1	013705842X	1	0132121360
2	013705842X	2	0132121360
3	013705842X	3	0132121360
4	013705842X	4	0132121360
5	013705842X		

Fig. 18.6 | Sample data from the AuthorISBN table of books.

Titles *Table*
The Titles table described in Fig. 18.7 consists of four columns that stand for the ISBN, the title, the edition number and the copyright year. The table is in Fig. 18.8.

Column	Description
ISBN	ISBN of the book (a string). The table's primary key. ISBN is an abbreviation for "International Standard Book Number"—a numbering scheme that publishers use to give every book a unique identification number.
Title	Title of the book (a string).

Fig. 18.7 | Titles table from the books database. (Part 1 of 2.)

Column	Description
EditionNumber	Edition number of the book (an integer).
Copyright	Copyright year of the book (a string).

Fig. 18.7 | Titles table from the books database. (Part 2 of 2.)

ISBN	Title	EditionNumber	Copyright
0132152134	Visual Basic 2010 How to Program	5	2011
0132151421	Visual C# 2010 How to Program	4	2011
0132575663	Java How to Program	9	2012
0132662361	C++ How to Program	8	2012
0132404168	C How to Program	6	2010
013705842X	iPhone for Programmers: An App-Driven Approach	1	2010
0132121360	Android for Programmers: An App-Driven Approach	1	2012

Fig. 18.8 | Sample data from the Titles table of the books database .

Entity-Relationship (ER) Diagram

There's a one-to-many relationship between a primary key and a corresponding foreign key (e.g., one author can write many books). A foreign key can appear many times in its own table, but only once (as the primary key) in another table. Figure 18.9 is an **entity-relationship (ER) diagram** for the books database. This diagram shows the *database tables* and the *relationships* among them. The first compartment in each box contains the table's name and the remaining compartments contain the table's columns. The names in italic are primary keys. *A table's primary key uniquely identifies each row in the table.* Every row must have a primary-key value, and that value must be unique in the table. This is known as the **Rule of Entity Integrity**. Again, for the AuthorISBN table, the primary key is the combination of both columns.

Fig. 18.9 | Table relationships in the books database.

Common Programming Error 18.1
Not providing a value for every column in a primary key breaks the Rule of Entity Integrity and causes the DBMS to report an error.

Common Programming Error 18.2
Providing the same primary-key value in multiple rows causes the DBMS to report an error.

The lines connecting the tables (Fig. 18.9) represent the relationships between the tables. Consider the line between the AuthorISBN and Authors tables. On the Authors end of the line is a 1, and on the AuthorISBN end is an infinity symbol (∞), indicating a **one-to-many relationship** in which every author in the Authors table can have an arbitrary number of books in the AuthorISBN table. The relationship line links the AuthorID column in Authors (i.e., its primary key) to the AuthorID column in AuthorISBN (i.e., its foreign key). The AuthorID column in the AuthorISBN table is a foreign key.

Common Programming Error 18.3
Providing a foreign-key value that does not appear as a primary-key value in another table breaks the Rule of Referential Integrity and causes the DBMS to report an error.

The line between Titles and AuthorISBN illustrates another *one-to-many relationship*; a title can be written by any number of authors. In fact, the sole purpose of the AuthorISBN table is to provide a *many-to-many relationship* between Authors and Titles—an author can write many books and a book can have many authors.

18.4 SQL

We now overview SQL in the context of our books database. The next several subsections discuss the SQL keywords listed in Fig. 18.10 in the context of SQL queries and statements. Other SQL keywords are beyond this text's scope. To learn other keywords, refer to the SQL reference guide supplied by the vendor of the DBMS you're using.

SQL keyword	Description
SELECT	Retrieves data from one or more tables.
FROM	Tables involved in the query. Required in every SELECT.
WHERE	Criteria for selection that determine the rows to be retrieved, deleted or updated. Optional in a SQL query or a SQL statement.
GROUP BY	Criteria for grouping rows. Optional in a SELECT query.
ORDER BY	Criteria for ordering rows. Optional in a SELECT query.
INNER JOIN	Merge rows from multiple tables.
INSERT	Insert rows into a specified table.
UPDATE	Update rows in a specified table.
DELETE	Delete rows from a specified table.

Fig. 18.10 | SQL query keywords.

18.4.1 Basic SELECT Query

Let us consider several SQL queries that extract information from database books. A SQL query "selects" rows and columns from one or more tables in a database. Such selections are performed by queries with the **SELECT** keyword. The basic form of a SELECT query is

> SELECT * FROM *tableName*

in which the **asterisk** (*) *wildcard character* indicates that all columns from the *tableName* table should be retrieved. For example, to retrieve all the data in the Authors table, use

> SELECT * FROM Authors

Most programs do not require all the data in a table. To retrieve only specific columns, replace the * with a comma-separated list of column names. For example, to retrieve only the columns AuthorID and LastName for all rows in the Authors table, use the query

> SELECT AuthorID, LastName FROM Authors

This query returns the data listed in Fig. 18.11.

AuthorID	LastName
1	Deitel
2	Deitel
3	Deitel
4	Morgano
5	Kern

Fig. 18.11 | Sample AuthorID and LastName data from the Authors table.

Software Engineering Observation 18.1

In general, you process results by knowing in advance the order of the columns in the result—for example, selecting AuthorID and LastName from table Authors ensures that the columns will appear in the result with AuthorID as the first column and LastName as the second. Programs typically process result columns by specifying the column number in the result (starting from 1 for the first column). Selecting columns by name avoids returning unneeded columns and protects against changes to the order of the columns in the table(s) by returning the columns in the exact order specified.

Common Programming Error 18.4

If you assume that the columns are always returned in the same order from a query that uses the asterisk (*), the program may process the results incorrectly.

18.4.2 WHERE Clause

In most cases, it's necessary to locate rows in a database that satisfy certain **selection criteria**. Only rows that satisfy the selection criteria (formally called **predicates**) are selected. SQL uses the optional **WHERE clause** in a query to specify the selection criteria for the query. The basic form of a query with selection criteria is

SELECT *columnName1*, *columnName2*, ... **FROM** *tableName* **WHERE** *criteria*

For example, to select the `Title`, `EditionNumber` and `Copyright` columns from table `Titles` for which the `Copyright` date is greater than 2010, use the query

```
SELECT Title, EditionNumber, Copyright
    FROM Titles
    WHERE Copyright > '2010'
```

Strings in SQL are delimited by single (') rather than double (") quotes. Figure 18.12 shows the result of the preceding query.

Title	EditionNumber	Copyright
Visual Basic 2010 How to Program	5	2011
Visual C# 2010 How to Program	4	2011
Java How to Program	9	2012
C++ How to Program	8	2012
Android for Programmers: An App-Driven Approach	1	2012

Fig. 18.12 | Sampling of titles with copyrights after 2005 from table `Titles`.

Pattern Matching: Zero or More Characters

The `WHERE` clause criteria can contain the operators <, >, <=, >=, =, <> and `LIKE`. Operator **LIKE** is used for **pattern matching** with wildcard characters **percent (%)** and **underscore (_)**. Pattern matching allows SQL to search for strings that match a given pattern.

A pattern that contains a percent character (%) searches for strings that have zero or more characters at the percent character's position in the pattern. For example, the next query locates the rows of all the authors whose last name starts with the letter D:

```
SELECT AuthorID, FirstName, LastName
    FROM Authors
    WHERE LastName LIKE 'D%'
```

This query selects the two rows shown in Fig. 18.13—three of the five authors have a last name starting with the letter D (followed by zero or more characters). The % symbol in the `WHERE` clause's `LIKE` pattern indicates that any number of characters can appear after the letter D in the `LastName`. The pattern string is surrounded by single-quote characters.

AuthorID	FirstName	LastName
1	Paul	Deitel
2	Harvey	Deitel
3	Abbey	Deitel

Fig. 18.13 | Authors whose last name starts with D from the `Authors` table.

Portability Tip 18.1

See the documentation for your database system to determine whether SQL is case sensitive on your system and to determine the syntax for SQL keywords.

Portability Tip 18.2

Read your database system's documentation carefully to determine whether it supports the LIKE *operator as discussed here.*

Pattern Matching: Any Character

An underscore (_) in the pattern string indicates a single wildcard character at that position in the pattern. For example, the following query locates the rows of all the authors whose last names start with any character (specified by _), followed by the letter o, followed by any number of additional characters (specified by %):

```
SELECT AuthorID, FirstName, LastName
   FROM Authors
   WHERE LastName LIKE '_o%'
```

The preceding query produces the row shown in Fig. 18.14, because only one author in our database has a last name that contains the letter o as its second letter.

AuthorID	FirstName	LastName
4	Michael	Morgano

Fig. 18.14 | The only author from the Authors table whose last name contains o as the second letter.

18.4.3 ORDER BY Clause

The rows in the result of a query can be sorted into ascending or descending order by using the optional **ORDER BY clause**. The basic form of a query with an ORDER BY clause is

```
SELECT columnName1, columnName2, ... FROM tableName ORDER BY column ASC
SELECT columnName1, columnName2, ... FROM tableName ORDER BY column DESC
```

where ASC specifies ascending order (lowest to highest), DESC specifies descending order (highest to lowest) and *column* specifies the column on which the sort is based. For example, to obtain the list of authors in ascending order by last name (Fig. 18.15), use the query

```
SELECT AuthorID, FirstName, LastName
   FROM Authors
   ORDER BY LastName ASC
```

AuthorID	FirstName	LastName
1	Paul	Deitel

Fig. 18.15 | Sample data from table Authors in ascending order by LastName. (Part 1 of 2.)

AuthorID	FirstName	LastName
2	Harvey	Deitel
3	Abbey	Deitel
5	Eric	Kern
4	Michael	Morgano

Fig. 18.15 | Sample data from table `Authors` in ascending order by `LastName`. (Part 2 of 2.)

Sorting in Descending Order

The default sorting order is ascending, so ASC is optional. To obtain the same list of authors in descending order by last name (Fig. 18.16), use the query

```
SELECT AuthorID, FirstName, LastName
    FROM Authors
    ORDER BY LastName DESC
```

AuthorID	FirstName	LastName
4	Michael	Morgano
5	Eric	Kern
1	Paul	Deitel
2	Harvey	Deitel
3	Abbey	Deitel

Fig. 18.16 | Sample data from table `Authors` in descending order by `LastName`.

Sorting By Multiple Columns

Multiple columns can be used for sorting with an ORDER BY clause of the form

```
ORDER BY column1 sortingOrder, column2 sortingOrder, ...
```

where *sortingOrder* is either ASC or DESC. The *sortingOrder* does not have to be identical for each column. The query

```
SELECT AuthorID, FirstName, LastName
    FROM Authors
    ORDER BY LastName, FirstName
```

sorts all the rows in ascending order by last name, then by first name. If any rows have the same last-name value, they're returned sorted by first name (Fig. 18.17).

Combining the *WHERE* and *ORDER BY* Clauses

The WHERE and ORDER BY clauses can be combined in one query, as in

```
SELECT ISBN, Title, EditionNumber, Copyright
    FROM Titles
    WHERE Title LIKE '%How to Program'
    ORDER BY Title ASC
```

AuthorID	FirstName	LastName
3	Abbey	Deitel
2	Harvey	Deitel
1	Paul	Deitel
5	Eric	Kern
4	Michael	Morgano

Fig. 18.17 | Sample data from `Authors` in ascending order by `LastName` and `FirstName`.

which returns the `ISBN`, `Title`, `EditionNumber` and `Copyright` of each book in the `Titles` table that has a `Title` ending with `"How to Program"` and sorts them in ascending order by `Title`. The query results are shown in Fig. 18.18.

ISBN	Title	Edition-Number	Copy-right
0132404168	C How to Program	6	2010
0132662361	C++ How to Program	8	2012
0132575663	Java How to Program	9	2012
0132152134	Visual Basic 2005 How to Program	5	2011
0132151421	Visual C# 2005 How to Program	4	2011

Fig. 18.18 | Sampling of books from table `Titles` whose titles end with `How to Program` in ascending order by `Title`.

18.4.4 Merging Data from Multiple Tables: INNER JOIN

Database designers often split related data into separate tables to ensure that a database does not store data redundantly. For example, in the `books` database, we use an `AuthorISBN` table to store the relationship data between authors and their corresponding titles. If we did not separate this information into individual tables, we'd need to include author information with each entry in the `Titles` table. This would result in the database's storing *duplicate* author information for authors who wrote multiple books. Often, it's necessary to merge data from multiple tables into a single result. Referred to as joining the tables, this is specified by an **INNER JOIN** operator, which merges rows from two tables by matching values in columns that are common to the tables. The basic form of an `INNER JOIN` is:

```
SELECT columnName1, columnName2, ...
FROM table1
INNER JOIN table2
    ON table1.columnName = table2.columnName
```

The **ON clause** of the `INNER JOIN` specifies the columns from each table that are compared to determine which rows are merged. For example, the following query produces a list of authors accompanied by the ISBNs for books written by each author:

```
SELECT FirstName, LastName, ISBN
FROM Authors
INNER JOIN AuthorISBN
   ON Authors.AuthorID = AuthorISBN.AuthorID
ORDER BY LastName, FirstName
```

The query merges the FirstName and LastName columns from table Authors with the ISBN column from table AuthorISBN, sorting the result in ascending order by LastName and FirstName. Note the use of the syntax *tableName.columnName* in the ON clause. This syntax, called a **qualified name**, specifies the columns from each table that should be compared to join the tables. The "*tableName.*" syntax is required if the columns have the same name in both tables. The same syntax can be used in any SQL statement to distinguish columns in different tables that have the same name. In some systems, table names qualified with the database name can be used to perform cross-database queries. As always, the query can contain an ORDER BY clause. Figure 18.19 shows the results of the preceding query, ordered by LastName and FirstName. [*Note:* To save space, we split the result of the query into two parts, each containing the FirstName, LastName and ISBN columns.]

FirstName	LastName	ISBN	FirstName	LastName	ISBN
Abbey	Deitel	013705842X	Paul	Deitel	0132151421
Abbey	Deitel	0132121360	Paul	Deitel	0132575663
Harvey	Deitel	0132152134	Paul	Deitel	0132662361
Harvey	Deitel	0132151421	Paul	Deitel	0132404168
Harvey	Deitel	0132575663	Paul	Deitel	013705842X
Harvey	Deitel	0132662361	Paul	Deitel	0132121360
Harvey	Deitel	0132404168	Eric	Kern	013705842X
Harvey	Deitel	013705842X	Michael	Morgano	013705842X
Harvey	Deitel	0132121360	Michael	Morgano	0132121360
Paul	Deitel	0132152134			

Fig. 18.19 | Sampling of authors and ISBNs for the books they have written in ascending order by LastName and FirstName.

Software Engineering Observation 18.2
If a SQL statement includes columns with the same name from multiple tables, the statement must precede those column names with their table names and a dot (e.g., Authors.AuthorID).

Common Programming Error 18.5
Failure to qualify names for columns that have the same name in two or more tables is an error.

18.4.5 INSERT Statement

The **INSERT** statement inserts a row into a table. The basic form of this statement is

> **INSERT INTO** *tableName* (*columnName1*, *columnName2*, ..., *columnNameN*)
>   **VALUES** (*value1*, *value2*, ..., *valueN*)

where *tableName* is the table in which to insert the row. The *tableName* is followed by a comma-separated list of column names in parentheses (this list is not required if the IN-SERT operation specifies a value for every column of the table in the correct order). The list of column names is followed by the SQL keyword **VALUES** and a comma-separated list of values in parentheses. The values specified here must match the columns specified after the table name in both order and type (e.g., if *columnName1* is supposed to be the FirstName column, then *value1* should be a string in single quotes representing the first name). Always explicitly list the columns when inserting rows. If the table's column order changes or a new column is added, using only VALUES may cause an error. The INSERT statement

> **INSERT INTO** Authors (FirstName, LastName)
>   **VALUES** ('Sue', 'Red')

inserts a row into the Authors table. The statement indicates that values are provided for the FirstName and LastName columns. The corresponding values are 'Sue' and 'Smith'. We do not specify an AuthorID in this example because AuthorID is an autoincremented column in the Authors table. For every row added to this table, the DBMS assigns a unique AuthorID value that is the next value in the autoincremented sequence (i.e., 1, 2, 3 and so on). In this case, Sue Red would be assigned AuthorID number 6. Figure 18.20 shows the Authors table after the INSERT operation. [*Note:* Not every database management system supports autoincremented columns. Check the documentation for your DBMS for alternatives to autoincremented columns.]

AuthorID	FirstName	LastName
1	Paul	Deitel
2	Harvey	Deitel
3	Abbey	Deitel
4	Michael	Morgano
5	Eric	Kern
6	Sue	Red

Fig. 18.20 | Sample data from table Authors after an INSERT operation.

Common Programming Error 18.6

It's normally an error to specify a value for an autoincrement column.

Common Programming Error 18.7

SQL delimits strings with single quotes ('). A string containing a single quote (e.g., O'Malley) must have two single quotes in the position where the single quote appears (e.g., 'O''Malley'). The first acts as an escape character for the second. Not escaping single-quote characters in a string that's part of a SQL statement is a SQL syntax error.

18.4.6 UPDATE Statement

An **UPDATE** statement modifies data in a table. Its basic form is

```
UPDATE tableName
    SET columnName1 = value1, columnName2 = value2, ..., columnNameN = valueN
    WHERE criteria
```

where *tableName* is the table to update. The *tableName* is followed by keyword **SET** and a comma-separated list of column name/value pairs in the format *columnName = value*. The optional WHERE clause provides criteria that determine which rows to update. Though not required, the WHERE clause is typically used, unless a change is to be made to every row. The UPDATE statement

```
UPDATE Authors
    SET LastName = 'Black'
    WHERE LastName = 'Red' AND FirstName = 'Sue'
```

updates a row in the Authors table. The statement indicates that LastName will be assigned the value Black for the row in which LastName is equal to Red and FirstName is equal to Sue. [*Note:* If there are multiple rows with the first name "Sue" and the last name "Red," this statement will modify all such rows to have the last name "Black."] If we know the AuthorID in advance of the UPDATE operation (possibly because we searched for it previously), the WHERE clause can be simplified as follows:

```
WHERE AuthorID = 6
```

Figure 18.21 shows the Authors table after the UPDATE operation has taken place.

AuthorID	FirstName	LastName
1	Paul	Deitel
2	Harvey	Deitel
3	Abbey	Deitel
4	Michael	Morgano
5	Eric	Kern
6	Sue	Black

Fig. 18.21 | Sample data from table Authors after an UPDATE operation.

18.4.7 DELETE Statement

A SQL **DELETE** statement removes rows from a table. Its basic form is

```
DELETE FROM tableName WHERE criteria
```

where *tableName* is the table from which to delete. The optional WHERE clause specifies the criteria used to determine which rows to delete. If this clause is omitted, all the table's rows are deleted. The DELETE statement

```
DELETE FROM Authors
    WHERE LastName = 'Black' AND FirstName = 'Sue'
```

deletes the row for Sue Black in the `Authors` table. If we know the `AuthorID` in advance of the `DELETE` operation, the `WHERE` clause can be simplified as follows:

```
WHERE AuthorID = 5
```

Figure 18.22 shows the `Authors` table after the `DELETE` operation has taken place.

AuthorID	FirstName	LastName
1	Paul	Deitel
2	Harvey	Deitel
3	Abbey	Deitel
4	Michael	Morgano
5	Eric	Kern

Fig. 18.22 | Sample data from table `Authors` after a `DELETE` operation.

18.5 MySQL

In 1994, TcX, a Swedish consulting firm, needed a fast and flexible way to access its tables. Unable to find a database server that could accomplish the required task adequately, Michael Widenius, the principal developer at TcX, decided to create his own database server. The resulting product was called *MySQL* (pronounced "my sequel"), a robust and scalable relational database management system (RDBMS).

MySQL, now owned by Oracle, is a multiuser, multithreaded (i.e., allows multiple simultaneous connections) RDBMS server that uses SQL to interact with and manipulate data. The MySQL Manual (`www.mysql.com/why-mysql/topreasons.html`) lists numerous benefits of MySQL. A few important benefits include:

1. Scalability. You can embed it in an application or use it in massive data warehousing environments.

2. Performance. You can optimize performance based on the purpose of the database in your application.

3. Support for many programming languages. Later chapters demonstrate how to access a MySQL database from PHP (Chapter 19) .

4. Implementations of MySQL for Windows, Mac OS X, Linux and UNIX.

5. Handling large databases (e.g., tens of thousands of tables with millions of rows).

For these reasons and more, MySQL is the database of choice for many businesses, universities and individuals. MySQL is an open source software product. [*Note:* Under certain situations, a commercial license is required for MySQL. See `www.mysql.com/about/legal` for details]

MySQL Community Edition
MySQL Community Edition is an open-source database management system that executes on many platforms, including Windows, Linux, and Mac OS X. Complete information about MySQL is available from `www.mysql.com`. The data-driven web applications in

Chapter 19 manipulate MySQL databases using the version of MySQL that you installed with XAMPP in Chapter 17.

18.5.1 Instructions for Setting Up a MySQL User Account

For the MySQL examples to execute correctly, you need to set up a user account so you can create, delete and modify databases. Open the XAMPP control panel and start the MySQL server, then follow the steps below to set up a user account:

1. Next, you'll start the MySQL monitor so you can set up a user account. (The following commands assume that you followed the default installation instructions for XAMPP as discussed in Chapter 17.) In Windows, open a Command Prompt and execute the command

    ```
    mysql -h localhost -u root
    ```

    In Mac OS X, open a Terminal window and execute the command

    ```
    /Applications/XAMPP/xamppfiles/bin/mysql -h localhost -u root
    ```

    In Linux, open a shell and execute the command

    ```
    /opt/lamp/bin/mysql -h localhost -u root
    ```

    The -h option indicates the host (i.e., computer) on which the MySQL server is running—in this case your local computer (localhost). The -u option indicates the user account that will be used to log in to the server—root is the default user account that is created during installation to allow you to configure the server. Once you've logged in, you'll see a mysql> prompt at which you can type commands to interact with the MySQL server.

2. At the mysql> prompt, type

    ```
    USE mysql;
    ```

    and press *Enter* to select the built-in database named mysql, which stores server information, such as user accounts and their privileges for interacting with the server. Each command must end with a semicolon. To confirm the command, MySQL issues the message "Database changed."

3. Next, you'll add the iw3htp user account to the mysql built-in database. The mysql database contains a table called user with columns that represent the user's name, password and various privileges. To create the iw3htp user account with the password password, execute the following commands from the mysql> prompt:

    ```
    create user 'iw3htp'@'localhost' identified by 'password';
    grant select, insert, update, delete, create, drop, references,
        execute on *.* to 'deitel'@'localhost';
    ```

    This creates the *user account* iw3htp with the *password* password with and privileges needed to create the databases used in Chapter 19 and manipulate them.

4. Type the command

    ```
    exit;
    ```

    to terminate the MySQL monitor.

18.5.2 Creating Databases in MySQL

For each MySQL database we use in Chapter 19, we provide a SQL script in a `.sql` file that sets up the database and its tables. You can execute these scripts in the MySQL monitor. In this chapter's examples directory, you'll find the following scripts:

- `books.sql`—creates the `books` database discussed in Section 18.3
- `products.sql`—creates the `Products` database used in Section 19.9
- `mailinglist.sql`—creates the `MailingList` database used in Section 19.11
- `URLs.sql`—creates the `URL` database used in Exercise 19.9.

Executing a SQL Script
To execute a SQL script:

1. Start the MySQL monitor using the username and password you created in Section 18.5.1. In Windows, open a Command Prompt and execute the command

   ```
   mysql -h localhost -u iw3htp -p
   ```

   In Mac OS X, open a Terminal window and execute the command

   ```
   /Applications/XAMPP/xampp files/bin/mysql -h localhost -u iw3htp -p
   ```

   In Linux, open a shell and execute the command

   ```
   /opt/lamp/bin/mysql -h localhost -u iw3htp -p
   ```

   The `-p` option prompts you for the password for the `iw3htp` user account. When prompted, enter the password `password`.

2. Execute the script with the `source` command. For example:

   ```
   source books.sql;
   ```

   creates the books database.

3. Repeat *Step 2* for each SQL script now, so the databases are ready for use in Chapter 19.

4. Type the command

   ```
   exit;
   ```

   to terminate the MySQL monitor.

18.6 (Optional) Microsoft Language Integrate Query (LINQ)

[*Note:* Sections 18.6–18.9 support the database-driven C# ASP.NET examples in Chapters 20–22, which assume that you already know C#. Chapters 23–25 also use LINQ to access databases from Visual Basic ASP.NET examples. Those chapters assume that you already know Visual Basic. For more information on LINQ in VB, visit the site `msdn.microsoft.com/en-us/library/bb397910.aspx`.]

The next several sections introduce C#'s **LINQ (Language Integrated Query)** capabilities. LINQ allows you to write **query expressions**, similar to SQL queries, that retrieve information from a wide variety of data sources, not just databases. We use **LINQ to Objects** in this section to query arrays and Lists, selecting elements that satisfy a set of conditions—this is known as **filtering**.

18.6.1 Querying an Array of int Values Using LINQ

First, we demonstrate querying an array of integers using LINQ. Repetition statements that filter arrays focus on the process of getting the results—iterating through the elements and checking whether they satisfy the desired criteria. LINQ specifies the conditions that selected elements must satisfy. This is known as **declarative programming**—as opposed to **imperative programming** (which we've been doing so far) in which you specify the actual steps to perform a task. The next several statements assume that the integer array

```
int[] values = { 2, 9, 5, 0, 3, 7, 1, 4, 8, 5 };
```

is declared. The query

```
var filtered =
    from value in values
    where value > 4
    select value;
```

specifies that the results should consist of all the ints in the values array that are greater than 4 (i.e., 9, 5, 7, 8 and 5). It *does not* specify *how* those results are obtained—the C# compiler generates all the necessary code automatically, which is one of the great strengths of LINQ. To use LINQ to Objects, you must import the System.Linq namespace (line 4).

The from Clause and Implicitly Typed Local Variables

A LINQ query begins with a **from clause**, which specifies a **range variable** (value) and the data source to query (values). The range variable represents each item in the data source (one at a time), much like the control variable in a foreach statement. We do not specify the range variable's type. Since it is assigned one element at a time from the array values, which is an int array, the compiler determines that the range variable value should be of type int. This is a C# feature called **implicitly typed local variables**, which enables the compiler to *infer* a local variable's type based on the context in which it's used.

Introducing the range variable in the from clause at the beginning of the query allows the IDE to provide *IntelliSense* while you write the rest of the query. The IDE knows the range variable's type, so when you enter the range variable's name followed by a dot (.) in the code editor, the IDE can display the range variable's methods and properties.

The var Keyword and Implicitly Typed Local Variables

You can also declare a local variable and let the compiler infer the variable's type based on the variable's initializer. To do so, the **var keyword** is used in place of the variable's type when declaring the variable. Consider the declaration

```
var x = 7;
```

Here, the compiler *infers* that the variable x should be of type int, because the compiler assumes that whole-number values, like 7, are of type int. Similarly, in the declaration

```
var y = -123.45;
```

the compiler infers that y should be of type double, because the compiler assumes that floating-point number values, like -123.45, are of type double. Typically, implicitly typed local variables are used for more complex types, such as the collections of data returned by LINQ queries.

The where Clause

If the condition in the **where** clause evaluates to true, the element is *selected*—i.e., it's included in the results. Here, the ints in the array are included only if they're greater than 4. An expression that takes an element of a collection and returns true or false by testing a condition on that element is known as a **predicate**.

The select Clause

For each item in the data source, the **select** clause determines what value appears in the results. In this case, it's the int that the range variable currently represents. A LINQ query typically ends with a select clause.

Iterating Through the Results of the LINQ Query

The foreach statement

```
foreach ( var element in filtered )
    Console.Write( " {0}", element );
```

displays the query results. A foreach statement can iterate through the contents of an array, collection or the results of a LINQ query, allowing you to process each element in the array, collection or query. The preceding foreach statement iterates over the query result filtered, displaying each of its items.

LINQ vs. Repetition Statements

It would be simple to display the integers greater than 4 using a repetition statement that tests each value before displaying it. However, this would intertwine the code that selects elements and the code that displays them. With LINQ, these are kept separate, making the code easier to understand and maintain.

The orderby Clause

The **orderby** clause sorts the query results in ascending order. The query

```
var sorted =
    from value in values
    orderby value
    select value;
```

sorts the integers in array values into ascending order and assigns the results to variable sorted. To sort in descending order, use **descending** in the orderby clause, as in

```
orderby value descending
```

An **ascending** modifier also exists but isn't normally used, because it's the default. Any value that can be compared with other values of the same type may be used with the orderby clause. A value of a simple type (e.g., int) can always be compared to another value of the same type.

The following two queries

```
var sortFilteredResults =
    from value in filtered
    orderby value descending
    select value;
var sortAndFilter =
    from value in values
    where value > 4
    orderby value descending
    select value;
```

generate the same results, but in different ways. The first query uses LINQ to sort the results of the filtered query presented earlier in this section. The second query uses both the where and orderby clauses. Because queries can operate on the results of other queries, it's possible to build a query one step at a time, and pass the results of queries between methods for further processing.

More on Implicitly Typed Local Variables

Implicitly typed local variables can also be used to initialize arrays without explicitly giving their type. For example, the following statement creates an array of int values:

```
var array = new[] { 32, 27, 64, 18, 95, 14, 90, 70, 60, 37 };
```

Note that there are no square brackets on the left side of the assignment operator, and that new[] is used to specify that the variable is an array.

An Aside: Interface IEnumerable<T>

As we mentioned, the foreach statement can iterate through the contents of arrays, collections and LINQ query results. Actually, foreach iterates over any so-called IEnumerable<T> object, which just happens to be what a LINQ query returns. **IEnumerable<T>** is an interface that describes the functionality of any object that can be iterated over and thus offers methods to access each element.

C# arrays are IEnumerable<T> objects, so a foreach statement can iterate over an array's elements. Similarly, each LINQ query returns an IEnumerable<T> object. Therefore, you can use a foreach statement to iterate over the results of any LINQ query. The notation <T> indicates that the interface is a generic interface that can be used with any type of data (for example, ints, strings or Employees).

18.6.2 Querying an Array of Employee Objects Using LINQ

LINQ is not limited to querying arrays of primitive types such as ints. It can be used with most data types, including strings and user-defined classes. It cannot be used when a query does not have a defined meaning—for example, you cannot use orderby on objects that are not comparable. Comparable types in .NET are those that implement the IComparable interface. All built-in types, such as string, int and double implement IComparable. Figure 18.23 presents the Employee class we use in this section. Figure 18.24 uses LINQ to query an array of Employee objects.

```csharp
1   // Fig. 18.23: Employee.cs
2   // Employee class with FirstName, LastName and MonthlySalary properties.
3   public class Employee
4   {
5      private decimal monthlySalaryValue; // monthly salary of employee
6
7      // auto-implemented property FirstName
8      public string FirstName { get; set; }
9
10     // auto-implemented property LastName
11     public string LastName { get; set; }
12
13     // constructor initializes first name, last name and monthly salary
14     public Employee( string first, string last, decimal salary )
15     {
16        FirstName = first;
17        LastName = last;
18        MonthlySalary = salary;
19     } // end constructor
20
21     // property that gets and sets the employee's monthly salary
22     public decimal MonthlySalary
23     {
24        get
25        {
26           return monthlySalaryValue;
27        } // end get
28        set
29        {
30           if ( value >= 0M ) // if salary is nonnegative
31           {
32              monthlySalaryValue = value;
33           } // end if
34        } // end set
35     } // end property MonthlySalary
36
37     // return a string containing the employee's information
38     public override string ToString()
39     {
40        return string.Format( "{0,-10} {1,-10} {2,10:C}",
41           FirstName, LastName, MonthlySalary );
42     } // end method ToString
43  } // end class Employee
```

Fig. 18.23 | Employee class.

```csharp
1   // Fig. 18.24: LINQWithArrayOfObjects.cs
2   // LINQ to Objects using an array of Employee objects.
3   using System;
4   using System.Linq;
5
```

Fig. 18.24 | LINQ to Objects using an array of Employee objects. (Part 1 of 3.)

```
6   public class LINQWithArrayOfObjects
7   {
8      public static void Main( string[] args )
9      {
10        // initialize array of employees
11        Employee[] employees = {
12           new Employee( "Jason", "Red", 5000M ),
13           new Employee( "Ashley", "Green", 7600M ),
14           new Employee( "Matthew", "Indigo", 3587.5M ),
15           new Employee( "James", "Indigo", 4700.77M ),
16           new Employee( "Luke", "Indigo", 6200M ),
17           new Employee( "Jason", "Blue", 3200M ),
18           new Employee( "Wendy", "Brown", 4236.4M ) }; // end init list
19
20        // display all employees
21        Console.WriteLine( "Original array:" );
22        foreach ( var element in employees )
23           Console.WriteLine( element );
24
25        // filter a range of salaries using && in a LINQ query
26        var between4K6K =
27           from e in employees
28           where e.MonthlySalary >= 4000M && e.MonthlySalary <= 6000M
29           select e;
30
31        // display employees making between 4000 and 6000 per month
32        Console.WriteLine( string.Format(
33           "\nEmployees earning in the range {0:C}-{1:C} per month:",
34           4000, 6000 ) );
35        foreach ( var element in between4K6K )
36           Console.WriteLine( element );
37
38        // order the employees by last name, then first name with LINQ
39        var nameSorted =
40           from e in employees
41           orderby e.LastName, e.FirstName
42           select e;
43
44        // header
45        Console.WriteLine( "\nFirst employee when sorted by name:" );
46
47        // attempt to display the first result of the above LINQ query
48        if ( nameSorted.Any() )
49           Console.WriteLine( nameSorted.First() );
50        else
51           Console.WriteLine( "not found" );
52
53        // use LINQ to select employee last names
54        var lastNames =
55           from e in employees
56           select e.LastName;
57
```

Fig. 18.24 | LINQ to Objects using an array of Employee objects. (Part 2 of 3.)

```
58          // use method Distinct to select unique last names
59          Console.WriteLine( "\nUnique employee last names:" );
60          foreach ( var element in lastNames.Distinct() )
61             Console.WriteLine( element );
62
63          // use LINQ to select first and last names
64          var names =
65             from e in employees
66             select new { e.FirstName, Last = e.LastName };
67
68          // display full names
69          Console.WriteLine( "\nNames only:" );
70          foreach ( var element in names )
71             Console.WriteLine( element );
72
73          Console.WriteLine();
74       } // end Main
75    } // end class LINQWithArrayOfObjects
```

```
Original array:
Jason      Red          $5,000.00
Ashley     Green        $7,600.00
Matthew    Indigo       $3,587.50
James      Indigo       $4,700.77
Luke       Indigo       $6,200.00
Jason      Blue         $3,200.00
Wendy      Brown        $4,236.40

Employees earning in the range $4,000.00-$6,000.00 per month:
Jason      Red          $5,000.00
James      Indigo       $4,700.77
Wendy      Brown        $4,236.40

First employee when sorted by name:
Jason      Blue         $3,200.00

Unique employee last names:
Red
Green
Indigo
Blue
Brown

Names only:
{ FirstName = Jason, Last = Red }
{ FirstName = Ashley, Last = Green }
{ FirstName = Matthew, Last = Indigo }
{ FirstName = James, Last = Indigo }
{ FirstName = Luke, Last = Indigo }
{ FirstName = Jason, Last = Blue }
{ FirstName = Wendy, Last = Brown }
```

Fig. 18.24 | LINQ to Objects using an array of Employee objects. (Part 3 of 3.)

Accessing the Properties of a LINQ Query's Range Variable

Line 28 of Fig. 18.24 shows a where clause that accesses the properties of the range variable. In this example, the compiler infers that the range variable is of type Employee based on its knowledge that employees was defined as an array of Employee objects (lines 11–18). Any bool expression can be used in a where clause. Line 28 uses the conditional AND (&&) operator to combine conditions. Here, only employees that have a salary between $4,000 and $6,000 per month, inclusive, are included in the query result, which is displayed in lines 35–36.

Sorting a LINQ Query's Results By Multiple Properties

Line 41 uses an orderby clause to sort the results according to multiple properties—specified in a comma-separated list. In this query, the employees are sorted alphabetically by last name. Each group of Employees that have the same last name is then sorted within the group by first name.

Any, *First* and *Count* Extension Methods

Line 48 introduces the query result's **Any** method, which returns true if there's at least one element, and false if there are no elements. The query result's **First** method (line 49) returns the first element in the result. You should check that the query result is not empty (line 48) before calling First.

We've not specified the class that defines methods First and Any. Your intuition probably tells you they're methods declared in the IEnumerable<T> interface, but they aren't. They're actually extension methods, but they can be used as if they were methods of IEnumerable<T>.

LINQ defines many more extension methods, such as **Count**, which returns the number of elements in the results. Rather than using Any, we could have checked that Count was nonzero, but it's more efficient to determine whether there's at least one element than to count all the elements. The LINQ query syntax is actually transformed by the compiler into extension method calls, with the results of one method call used in the next. It's this design that allows queries to be run on the results of previous queries, as it simply involves passing the result of a method call to another method.

Selecting a Portion of an Object

Line 56 uses the select clause to select the range variable's LastName property rather than the range variable itself. This causes the results of the query to consist of only the last names (as strings), instead of complete Employee objects. Lines 60–61 display the unique last names. The **Distinct extension method** (line 60) removes duplicate elements, causing all elements in the result to be unique.

Creating New Types in the *select* Clause of a LINQ Query

The last LINQ query in the example (lines 65–66) selects the properties FirstName and LastName. The syntax

```
new { e.FirstName, Last = e.LastName }
```

creates a new object of an **anonymous type** (a type with no name), which the compiler generates for you based on the properties listed in the curly braces ({}). In this case, the anonymous type consists of properties for the first and last names of the selected Employee. The LastName property is assigned to the property Last in the select clause. This shows how you can specify a new name for the selected property. If you don't specify a new name, the property's original name is used—this is the case for FirstName in this example. The preceding query is an example of a **projection**—it performs a transformation on the data. In this case, the transformation creates new objects containing only the FirstName and Last properties. Transformations can also manipulate the data. For example, you could give all employees a 10% raise by multiplying their MonthlySalary properties by 1.1.

When creating a new anonymous type, you can select any number of properties by specifying them in a comma-separated list within the curly braces ({}) that delineate the anonymous type definition. In this example, the compiler automatically creates a new class having properties FirstName and Last, and the values are copied from the Employee objects. These selected properties can then be accessed when iterating over the results. Implicitly typed local variables allow you to use anonymous types because you do not have to explicitly state the type when declaring such variables.

When the compiler creates an anonymous type, it automatically generates a ToString method that returns a string representation of the object. You can see this in the program's output—it consists of the property names and their values, enclosed in braces.

18.6.3 Querying a Generic Collection Using LINQ

You can use LINQ to Objects to query Lists just as arrays. In Fig. 18.25, a List of strings is converted to uppercase and searched for those that begin with "R".

```
1   // Fig. 18.25: LINQWithListCollection.cs
2   // LINQ to Objects using a List< string >.
3   using System;
4   using System.Linq;
5   using System.Collections.Generic;
6
7   public class LINQWithListCollection
8   {
9      public static void Main( string[] args )
10     {
11        // populate a List of strings
12        List< string > items = new List< string >();
13        items.Add( "aQua" ); // add "aQua" to the end of the List
14        items.Add( "RusT" ); // add "RusT" to the end of the List
15        items.Add( "yElLow" ); // add "yElLow" to the end of the List
16        items.Add( "rEd" ); // add "rEd" to the end of the List
17
18        // convert all strings to uppercase; select those starting with "R"
19        var startsWithR =
20           from item in items
21           let uppercaseString = item.ToUpper()
22           where uppercaseString.StartsWith( "R" )
23           orderby uppercaseString
24           select uppercaseString;
25
26        // display query results
27        foreach ( var item in startsWithR )
28           Console.Write( "{0} ", item );
```

Fig. 18.25 | LINQ to Objects using a List<string>. (Part 1 of 2.)

```
29
30       Console.WriteLine(); // output end of line
31
32       items.Add( "rUbY" ); // add "rUbY" to the end of the List
33       items.Add( "SaFfRon" ); // add "SaFfRon" to the end of the List
34
35       // display updated query results
36       foreach ( var item in startsWithR )
37          Console.Write( "{0} ", item );
38
39       Console.WriteLine(); // output end of line
40    } // end Main
41 } // end class LINQWithListCollection
```

```
RED RUST
RED RUBY RUST
```

Fig. 18.25 | LINQ to Objects using a List<string>. (Part 2 of 2.)

Line 21 uses LINQ's **let clause** to create a new range variable. This is useful if you need to store a temporary result for use later in the LINQ query. Typically, let declares a new range variable to which you assign the result of an expression that operates on the query's original range variable. In this case, we use string method **ToUpper** to convert each item to uppercase, then store the result in the new range variable uppercaseString. We then use the new range variable uppercaseString in the where, orderby and select clauses. The where clause (line 22) uses string method **StartsWith** to determine whether uppercaseString starts with the character "R". Method StartsWith performs a case-sensitive comparison to determine whether a string starts with the string received as an argument. If uppercaseString starts with "R", method StartsWith returns true, and the element is included in the query results. More powerful string matching can be done using .NET's regular-expression capabilities.

The query is created only once (lines 20–24), yet iterating over the results (lines 27–28 and 36–37) gives two different lists of colors. This demonstrates LINQ's **deferred execution**—the query executes only when you access the results—such as iterating over them or using the Count method—not when you define the query. This allows you to create a query once and execute it many times. Any changes to the data source are reflected in the results each time the query executes.

There may be times when you do not want this behavior, and want to retrieve a collection of the results immediately. LINQ provides extension methods ToArray and ToList for this purpose. These methods execute the query on which they're called and give you the results as an array or List<T>, respectively. These methods can also improve efficiency if you'll be iterating over the results multiple times, as you execute the query only once.

C# has a feature called **collection initializers**, which provide a convenient syntax (similar to array initializers) for initializing a collection. For example, lines 12–16 of Fig. 18.25 could be replaced with the following statement:

```
List< string > items =
   new List< string > { "aQua", "RusT", "yElLow", "rEd" };
```

18.7 (Optional) LINQ to SQL

[*Note:* This section supports Chapters 20–22.] LINQ to SQL enables you to access data in *SQL Server databases* using the same LINQ syntax introduced in Section 18.6. You interact with the database via classes that are automatically generated from the database schema by the IDE's **LINQ to SQL Designer**. For each table in the database, the IDE creates two classes:

- A class that represents a row of the table: This class contains properties for each column in the table. LINQ to SQL creates objects of this class—called **row objects**—to store the data from individual rows of the table.

- A class that represents the table: LINQ to SQL creates an object of this class to store a collection of row objects that correspond to all of the rows in the table.

Relationships between tables are also taken into account in the generated classes:

- In a row object's class, an additional property is created for each foreign key. This property returns the row object of the corresponding primary key in another table. For example, the class that represents the rows of the Books database's AuthorISBN table also contains an Author property and a Title property—from any AuthorISBN row object, you can access the full author and title information.

- In the class for a row object, an additional property is created for the collection of row objects with foreign-keys that reference the row object's primary key. For example, the LINQ to SQL class that represents the rows of the Books database's Authors table contains an AuthorISBNs property that you can use to get all of the books written by that author. The IDE automatically adds the "s" to "AuthorISBN" to indicate that this property represents a collection of AuthorISBN objects. Similarly, the LINQ to SQL class that represents the rows of the Titles table also contains an AuthorISBNs property that you can use to get all of the co-authors of a particular title.

Once generated, the LINQ to SQL classes have full *IntelliSense* support in the IDE.

IQueryable Interface
LINQ to SQL works through the **IQueryable interface**, which inherits from the IEnumerable interface introduced in Section 18.6. When a LINQ to SQL query on an IQueryable object executes against the database, the results are loaded into objects of the corresponding LINQ to SQL classes for convenient access in your code.

DataContext Class
All LINQ to SQL queries occur via a **DataContext class**, which controls the flow of data between the program and the database. A specific DataContext derived class, which inherits from the class System.Data.Linq.DataContext, is created when the LINQ to SQL classes representing each row of the table are generated by the IDE. This derived class has properties for each table in the database, which can be used as data sources in LINQ queries. Any changes made to the DataContext can be saved back to the database using the DataContext's **SubmitChanges method**, so with LINQ to SQL you can modify the database's contents.

18.8 (Optional) Querying a Database with LINQ

[*Note:* This section supports Chapters 20–22.] In this section, we demonstrate how to *connect* to a database, *query* it and *display* the results of the query. There is little code in this section—the IDE provides *visual programming* tools and *wizards* that simplify accessing data in applications. These tools establish database connections and create the objects necessary to view and manipulate the data through Windows Forms GUI controls—a technique known as **data binding**.

Our first example performs a simple query on the Books database from Section 18.3. We retrieve the entire Authors table and use data binding to display its data in a **DataGridView**—a control from namespace System.Windows.Forms that can display data from a data source in tabular format. The basic steps we'll perform are:

- Connect to the Books database.
- Create the LINQ to SQL classes required to use the database.
- Add the Authors table as a data source.
- Drag the Authors table data source onto the **Design** view to create a GUI for displaying the table's data.
- Add a few statements to the program to allow it to interact with the database.

The GUI for the program is shown in Fig. 18.26. All of the controls in this GUI are automatically generated when we drag a data source that represents the Authors table onto the Form in **Design** view. The BindingNavigator at the top of the window is a collection of controls that allow you to navigate through the records in the DataGridView that fills the rest of the window. The BindingNavigator controls also allow you to add records, delete records and save your changes to the database. If you add a new record, note that empty values are not allowed in the Books database, so attempting to save a new record without specifying a value for each field will cause an error.

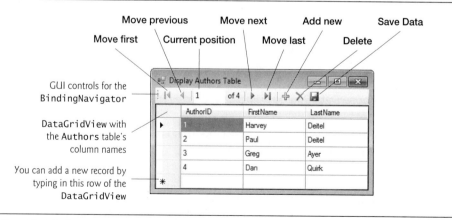

Fig. 18.26 | GUI for the **Display Authors Table** application.

18.8.1 Creating LINQ to SQL Classes

This section presents the steps required to create LINQ to SQL classes for a database.

Step 1: Creating the Project
Create a new **Windows Forms Application** named `DisplayTable`. Change the name of the source file to `DisplayAuthorsTable.cs`. The IDE updates the Form's class name to match the source file. Set the Form's **Text** property to `Display Authors Table`.

Step 2: Adding a Database to the Project and Connecting to the Database
To interact with a database, you must create a **connection** to the database. This will also give you the option of copying the database file to your project.

1. In Visual C# 2010 Express, select **View > Other Windows > Database Explorer** to display the **Database Explorer** window. By default, it appears on the left side of the IDE. If you're using a full version of Visual Studio, select **View > Server Explorer** to display the **Server Explorer**. From this point forward, we'll refer to the **Database Explorer**. If you have a full version of Visual Studio, substitute **Server Explorer** for **Database Explorer** in the steps.

2. Click the **Connect to Database** icon (🐱) at the top of the **Database Explorer**. If the **Choose Data Source** dialog appears (Fig. 18.27), select **Microsoft SQL Server Database File** from the **Data source:** list. If you check the **Always use this selection** CheckBox, the IDE will use this type of database file by default when you connect to databases in the future. Click **Continue** to display the **Add Connection** dialog.

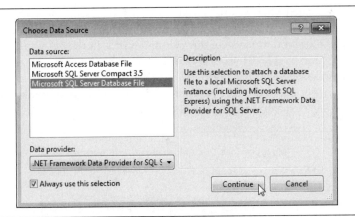

Fig. 18.27 | **Choose Data Source** dialog.

3. In the **Add Connection** dialog (Fig. 18.28), the **Data source:** TextBox reflects your selection from the **Choose Data Source** dialog. You can click the **Change...** Button to select a different type of database. Next, click **Browse...** to locate and select the `Books.mdf` file in the `Databases` directory included with this chapter's examples. You can click **Test Connection** to verify that the IDE can connect to the database through SQL Server Express. Click **OK** to create the connection.

Error-Prevention Tip 18.1
Ensure that no other program is using the database file before you attempt to add it to the project. Connecting to the database requires exclusive access.

Fig. 18.28 | Add Connection dialog.

Step 3: Generating the LINQ to SQL classes

After adding the database, you must select the database tables from which the LINQ to SQL classes will be created. LINQ to SQL uses the database's schema to help define the classes.

1. Right click the project name in the **Solution Explorer** and select **Add > New Item...** to display the **Add New Item** dialog. Select the **LINQ to SQL Classes** template, name the new item Books.dbml and click the **Add** button. The **Object Relational Designer** window will appear (Fig. 18.29). You can also double click the Books.dbml file in the **Solution Explorer** to open the **Object Relational Designer**.

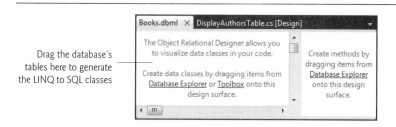

Fig. 18.29 | Object Relational Designer window.

2. Expand the Books.mdf database node in the **Database Explorer**, then expand the **Tables** node. Drag the Authors, Titles and AuthorISBN tables onto the **Object Relational Designer**. The IDE prompts whether you want to copy the database to the project directory. Select **Yes**. The **Object Relational Designer** will display the tables that you dragged from the **Database Explorer** (Fig. 18.30). Notice that the

Fig. 18.30 | **Object Relational Designer** window showing the selected tables from the Books database and their relationships.

Object Relational Designer named the class that represents items from the Authors table as Author, and named the class that represents the Titles table as Title. This is because one object of the Author class represents one author—a single row from the Authors table. Similarly, one object of the Title class represents one book—a single row from the Titles table. Because the class name Title conflicts with one of the column names in the Titles table, the IDE renames that column's property in the Title class as Title1.

3. Save the Books.dbml file.

When you save Books.dbml, the IDE generates the LINQ to SQL classes that you can use to interact with the database. These include a class for each table you selected from the database and a derived class of DataContext named BooksDataContext that enables you to programmatically interact with the database.

Error-Prevention Tip 18.2

Be sure to save the file in the Object Relational Designer before trying to use the LINQ to SQL classes in code. The IDE does not generate the classes until you save the file.

18.8.2 Data Bindings Between Controls and the LINQ to SQL Classes

The IDE's automatic data binding capabilities simplify creating applications that can view and modify the data in a database. You must write a small amount of code to enable the autogenerated data-binding classes to interact with the autogenerated LINQ to SQL classes. You'll now perform the steps to display the contents of the Authors table in a GUI.

*Step 1: Adding the **Author** LINQ to SQL Class as a Data Source*
To use the LINQ to SQL classes for data binding, you must first add them as a data source.

1. Select Data > Add New Data Source... to display the **Data Source Configuration Wizard**.

2. The LINQ to SQL classes are used to create objects representing the tables in the database, so we'll use an **Object** data source. In the dialog, select **Object** and click **Next >**. Expand the tree view as shown in Fig. 18.31 and ensure that **Author** is checked. An object of this class will be used as the data source.

3. Click **Finish**.

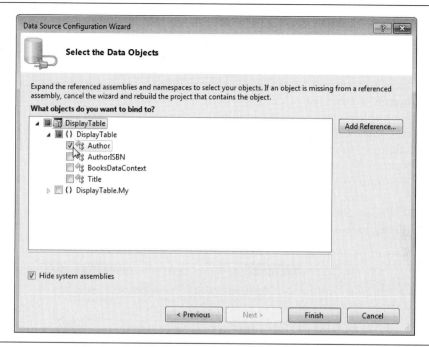

Fig. 18.31 | Selecting the `Author` LINQ to SQL class as the data source.

The `Authors` table in the database is now a data source that can be used by the bindings. Open the **Data Sources window** (Fig. 18.32) by selecting **Data > Show Data Sources**—the window is displayed at the left side of the IDE. You can see the `Author` class that you added in the previous step. The columns of the database's `Authors` table should appear below it, as well as an `AuthorISBNs` entry representing the relationship between the database's `Authors` and `AuthorISBN` tables.

Fig. 18.32 | **Data Sources** window showing the `Author` class as a data source.

Step 2: Creating GUI Elements
Next, you'll use the **Design** view to create a GUI control that can display the `Authors` table's data.

1. Switch to **Design** view for the `DisplayAuthorsTable` class.

2. Click the **Author** node in the **Data Sources** window—it should change to a drop-down list. Open the drop-down by clicking the down arrow and ensure that the

`DataGridView` option is selected—this is the GUI control that will be used to display and interact with the data.

3. Drag the **Author** node from the **Data Sources** window onto the Form in **Design** view.

The IDE creates a `DataGridView` (Fig. 18.33) with the correct column names and a **BindingNavigator** (`authorBindingNavigator`) that contains `Buttons` for moving between entries, adding entries, deleting entries and saving changes to the database. The IDE also generates a **BindingSource** (`authorBindingSource`), which handles the transfer of data between the data source and the data-bound controls on the Form. Nonvisual components such as the `BindingSource` and the non-visual aspects of the `BindingNavigator` appear in the component tray—the gray region below the Form in **Design** view. We use the default names for automatically generated components throughout this chapter to show exactly what the IDE creates. To make the **DataGridView** occupy the entire window, select the `DataGridView`, then use the **Properties** window to set the Dock property to `Fill`.

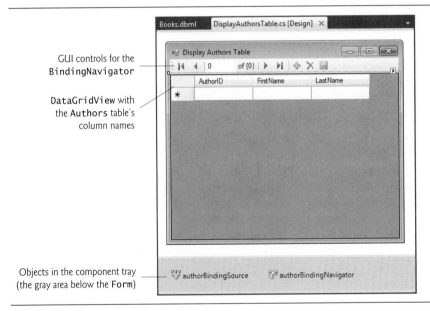

GUI controls for the BindingNavigator

DataGridView with the Authors table's column names

Objects in the component tray (the gray area below the Form)

Fig. 18.33 | Component tray holds nonvisual components in **Design** view.

Step 3: Connecting the *BooksDataContext* to the *authorBindingSource*
The final step is to connect the `BooksDataContext` (created with the LINQ to SQL classes in Section 18.8.1) to the `authorBindingSource` (created earlier in this section), so that the application can interact with the database. Figure 18.34 shows the small amount of code needed to obtain data from the database and to save any changes that the user makes to the data back into the database.

As mentioned in Section 18.7, a `DataContext` object is used to interact with the database. The `BooksDataContext` class was automatically generated by the IDE when you created the LINQ to SQL classes to allow access to the `Books` database. Line 18 creates an object of this class named `database`.

```
1   // Fig. 18.34: DisplayAuthorsTable.cs
2   // Displaying data from a database table in a DataGridView.
3   using System;
4   using System.Linq;
5   using System.Windows.Forms;
6
7   namespace DisplayTable
8   {
9      public partial class DisplayAuthorsTable : Form
10     {
11        // constructor
12        public DisplayAuthorsTable()
13        {
14           InitializeComponent();
15        } // end constructor
16
17        // LINQ to SQL data context
18        private BooksDataContext database = new BooksDataContext();
19
20        // load data from database into DataGridView
21        private void DisplayAuthorsTable_Load( object sender, EventArgs e )
22        {
23           // use LINQ to order the data for display
24           authorBindingSource.DataSource =
25              from author in database.Authors
26              orderby author.AuthorID
27              select author;
28        } // end method DisplayAuthorsTable_Load
29
30        // click event handler for the Save Button in the
31        // BindingNavigator saves the changes made to the data
32        private void authorBindingNavigatorSaveItem_Click(
33           object sender, EventArgs e )
34        {
35           Validate(); // validate input fields
36           authorBindingSource.EndEdit(); // indicate edits are complete
37           database.SubmitChanges(); // write changes to database file
38        } // end method authorBindingNavigatorSaveItem_Click
39     } // end class DisplayAuthorsTable
40  } // end namespace DisplayTable
```

Fig. 18.34 | Displaying data from a database table in a `DataGridView`.

Create the Form's Load handler by double clicking the Form's title bar in **Design** view. We allow data to move between the DataContext and the BindingSource by creating a

LINQ query that extracts data from the BooksDataContext's Authors property (lines 25–27), which corresponds to the Authors table in the database. The authorBindingSource's **DataSource property** (line 24) is set to the results of this query. The authorBindingSource uses the DataSource to extract data from the database and to populate the DataGridView.

Step 4: Saving Modifications Back to the Database

If the user modifies the data in the DataGridView, we'd also like to save the modifications in the database. By default, the BindingNavigator's **Save Data** Button (▥) is disabled. To enable it, right click this Button's icon and select **Enabled**. Then, double click the icon to create its Click event handler.

Saving the data entered into the DataGridView back to the database is a three-step process (lines 35–37). First, all controls on the form are validated (line 35)—if any of the controls have event handlers for the Validating event, those execute. You typically handle this event to determine whether a control's contents are valid. Second, line 36 calls **EndEdit** on the authorBindingSource, which forces it to save any pending changes in the BooksData-Context. Finally, line 37 calls SubmitChanges on the BooksDataContext to store the changes in the database. For efficiency, LINQ to SQL saves only data that has changed.

Step 5: Configuring the Database File to Persist Changes

When you run the program in debug mode, the database file is overwritten with the original database file each time you execute the program. This allows you to test your program with the original content until it works correctly. When you run the program in release mode (*Ctrl + F5*), changes you make to the database persist automatically; however, if you change the code, the next time you run the program, the database will be restored to its original version. To persist changes for all executions, select the database in the **Solution Explorer** and set the **Copy to Output Directory** property in the **Properties** window to **Copy if newer**.

18.9 (Optional) Dynamically Binding LINQ to SQL Query Results

[*Note:* This section supports Chapters 20–22.] Now that you've seen how to display an entire database table in a DataGridView, we show how to perform several different queries and display the results in a DataGridView. The **Display Query Results** application (Fig. 18.35) allows the user to select a query from the ComboBox at the bottom of the window, then displays the results of the query.

18.9.1 Creating the Display Query Results GUI

Perform the following steps to build the **Display Query Results** application's GUI.

Step 1: Creating the Project

First, create a new **Windows Forms Application** named DisplayQueryResult. Rename the source file to TitleQueries.cs. Set the Form's **Text** property to Display Query Results.

Step 2: Creating the LINQ to SQL Classes

Follow the steps in Section 18.8.1 to add the Books database to the project and generate the LINQ to SQL classes.

a) Results of the "All titles" query, which shows the contents of the `Titles` table ordered by the book titles

b) Results of the "Titles with 2008 copyright" query

c) Results of the "Titles ending with 'How to Program'" query

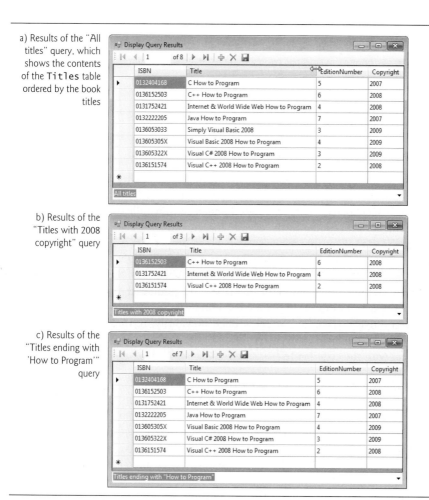

Fig. 18.35 | Sample execution of the **Display Query Results** application.

Step 3: Creating a `DataGridView` to Display the `Titles` Table
Follow *Steps 1* and *2* in Section 18.8.2 to create the data source and the `DataGridView`. In this example, select the `Title` class (rather than the `Author` class) as the data source, and drag the **Title** node from the **Data Sources** window onto the form.

Step 4: Adding a `ComboBox` to the `Form`
In **Design** view, add a `ComboBox` named `queriesComboBox` below the `DataGridView` on the `Form`. Users will select which query to execute from this control. Set the `ComboBox`'s **Dock** property to `Bottom` and the `DataGridView`'s **Dock** property to `Fill`.

Next, you'll add the names of the queries to the `ComboBox`. Open the `ComboBox`'s **String Collection Editor** by right clicking the `ComboBox` and selecting **Edit Items**. You can also access the **String Collection Editor** from the `ComboBox`'s smart tag menu. A **smart tag menu** provides you with quick access to common properties you might set for a control (such as the `Multiline` property of a `TextBox`), so you can set these properties directly in **Design** view, rather than in the **Properties** window. You can open a control's smart tag menu by clicking the small arrowhead (▶) that appears in the control's upper-right corner in **Design** view when the control is selected. In the **String Collection Editor**, add the following three items to queriesComboBox—one for each of the queries we'll create:

1. All titles
2. Titles with 2008 copyright
3. Titles ending with "How to Program"

18.9.2 Coding the Display Query Results Application

Next you must write code that executes the appropriate query each time the user chooses a different item from queriesComboBox. Double click queriesComboBox in **Design** view to generate a queriesComboBox_SelectedIndexChanged event handler (Fig. 18.36, lines 44–78) in the TitleQueries.cs file. In the event handler, add a switch statement (lines 48–75) to change the titleBindingSource's DataSource property to a LINQ query that returns the correct set of data. The data bindings created by the IDE *automatically* update the titleDataGridView *each time* we change its DataSource. The **MoveFirst** method of the BindingSource (line 77) moves to the first row of the result each time a query executes. The results of the queries in lines 53–55, 61–64 and 70–73 are shown in Fig. 18.35(a), (b) and (c), respectively. [*Note:* As we mentioned previously, in the generated LINQ to SQL classes, the IDE renamed the Title column of the Titles table as Title1 to avoid a naming conflict with the class Title.]

Customizing the Form's Load Event Handler
Create the TitleQueries_Load event handler (lines 20–28) by double clicking the title bar in **Design** view. Line 23 sets the Log property of the BooksDataContext to Console.Out. This causes the program to output to the console the SQL query that is sent to the database for each LINQ query. When the Form loads, it should display the complete list of books from the Titles table, sorted by title. Rather than defining the same LINQ query as in lines 53–55, we can programmatically cause the queriesComboBox_SelectedIndexChanged event handler to execute simply by setting the queriesComboBox's SelectedIndex to 0 (line 27).

```
1   // Fig. 18.36: TitleQueries.cs
2   // Displaying the result of a user-selected query in a DataGridView.
3   using System;
4   using System.Linq;
5   using System.Windows.Forms;
6
7   namespace DisplayQueryResult
8   {
9      public partial class TitleQueries : Form
10     {
11        public TitleQueries()
12        {
13           InitializeComponent();
14        } // end constructor
```

Fig. 18.36 | Displaying the result of a user-selected query in a DataGridView. (Part 1 of 3.)

```csharp
15
16        // LINQ to SQL data context
17        private BooksDataContext database = new BooksDataContext();
18
19        // load data from database into DataGridView
20        private void TitleQueries_Load( object sender, EventArgs e )
21        {
22            // write SQL to standard output stream
23            database.Log = Console.Out;
24
25            // set the ComboBox to show the default query that
26            // selects all books from the Titles table
27            queriesComboBox.SelectedIndex = 0;
28        } // end method TitleQueries_Load
29
30        // Click event handler for the Save Button in the
31        // BindingNavigator saves the changes made to the data
32        private void titleBindingNavigatorSaveItem_Click(
33            object sender, EventArgs e )
34        {
35            Validate(); // validate input fields
36            titleBindingSource.EndEdit(); // indicate edits are complete
37            database.SubmitChanges(); // write changes to database file
38
39            // when saving, return to "all titles" query
40            queriesComboBox.SelectedIndex = 0;
41        } // end method titleBindingNavigatorSaveItem_Click
42
43        // loads data into titleBindingSource based on user-selected query
44        private void queriesComboBox_SelectedIndexChanged(
45            object sender, EventArgs e )
46        {
47            // set the data displayed according to what is selected
48            switch ( queriesComboBox.SelectedIndex )
49            {
50                case 0: // all titles
51                    // use LINQ to order the books by title
52                    titleBindingSource.DataSource =
53                        from book in database.Titles
54                        orderby book.Title1
55                        select book;
56                    break;
57                case 1: // titles with 2008 copyright
58                    // use LINQ to get titles with 2008
59                    // copyright and sort them by title
60                    titleBindingSource.DataSource =
61                        from book in database.Titles
62                        where book.Copyright == "2008"
63                        orderby book.Title1
64                        select book;
65                    break;
```

Fig. 18.36 | Displaying the result of a user-selected query in a DataGridView. (Part 2 of 3.)

```
66              case 2: // titles ending with "How to Program"
67                  // use LINQ to get titles ending with
68                  // "How to Program" and sort them by title
69                  titleBindingSource.DataSource =
70                      from book in database.Titles
71                      where book.Title1.EndsWith( "How to Program" )
72                      orderby book.Title1
73                      select book;
74                  break;
75          } // end switch
76
77          titleBindingSource.MoveFirst(); // move to first entry
78      } // end method queriesComboBox_SelectedIndexChanged
79  } // end class TitleQueries
80 } // end namespace DisplayQueryResult
```

Fig. 18.36 | Displaying the result of a user-selected query in a `DataGridView`. (Part 3 of 3.)

Saving Changes

Follow the instructions in the previous example to add a handler for the `BindingNavigator`'s **Save Data** `Button` (lines 32–41). Note that, except for changes to the names, the three lines are identical. The last statement (line 40) displays the results of the `All titles` query in the `DataGridView`.

18.10 Java DB/Apache Derby

The Java SE 6 and 7 Development Kits (JDKs) come bundled with the open source, pure Java database **Java DB** (the Oracle branded version of Apache Derby). Chapters 27–28 use Java DB in data-driven web applications. Similar to MySQL, Java DB has both an embedded version and a network (client/server) version. The tools we use in Chapters 27–28 come with Java DB. For those examples, we use Java DB's network version, and we provide all the information you need to configure each example's database. You can learn more about Apache Derby at db.apache.org/derby. You can learn more about Java DB at www.oracle.com/technetwork/java/javadb/overview/index.html.

Summary

Section 18.1 Introduction

- A database (p. 650) is an integrated collection of data. A database management system (DBMS; p. 650) provides mechanisms for storing, organizing, retrieving and modifying data.
- Today's most popular database management systems are relational database (p. 650) systems.
- SQL (p. 650) is the international standard language used to query (p. 650) and manipulate relational data.

Section 18.2 Relational Databases

- A relational database (p. 650) stores data in tables (p. 650). Tables are composed of rows (p. 651), and rows are composed of columns in which values are stored.

- A table's primary key (p. 651) provides a unique value that cannot be duplicated among rows.

- Each column (p. 651) of a table represents a different attribute.

- The primary key can be composed of more than one column.

- A foreign key (p. 653) is a column in a table that must match the primary-key column in another table. This is known as the Rule of Referential Integrity (p. 653).

- Every column in a primary key must have a value, and the value of the primary key must be unique. This is known as the Rule of Entity Integrity (p. 654).

- A one-to-many relationship (p. 655) between tables indicates that a row in one table can have many related rows in a separate table.

- Foreign keys enable information from multiple tables to be joined together. There's a one-to-many relationship between a primary key and its corresponding foreign key.

Section 18.4.1 Basic **SELECT** Query

- The basic form of a query (p. 656) is

      SELECT * FROM *tableName*

  where the asterisk (*; p. 656) indicates that all columns from *tableName* should be selected, and *tableName* specifies the table in the database from which rows will be retrieved.

- To retrieve specific columns, replace the * with a comma-separated list of column names.

Section 18.4.2 **WHERE** Clause

- The optional **WHERE** clause (p. 656) in a query specifies the selection criteria for the query. The basic form of a query with selection criteria (p. 656) is

      SELECT *columnName1*, *columnName2*, ... **FROM** *tableName* **WHERE** *criteria*

- The **WHERE** clause can contain operators <, >, <=, >=, =, <> and **LIKE**. **LIKE** (p. 657) is used for string pattern matching (p. 657) with wildcard characters percent (%) and underscore (_).

- A percent character (%; p. 657) in a pattern indicates that a string matching the pattern can have zero or more characters at the percent character's location in the pattern.

- An underscore (_ ; p. 657) in the pattern string indicates a single character at that position in the pattern.

Section 18.4.3 **ORDER BY** Clause

- A query's result can be sorted with the **ORDER BY** clause (p. 658). The simplest form of an **ORDER BY** clause is

      SELECT *columnName1*, *columnName2*, ... **FROM** *tableName* **ORDER BY** *column* **ASC**
      SELECT *columnName1*, *columnName2*, ... **FROM** *tableName* **ORDER BY** *column* **DESC**

  where **ASC** specifies ascending order, **DESC** specifies descending order and *column* specifies the column on which the sort is based. The default sorting order is ascending, so **ASC** is optional.

- Multiple columns can be used for ordering purposes with an **ORDER BY** clause of the form

      ORDER BY *column1 sortingOrder*, *column2 sortingOrder*, ...

- The **WHERE** and **ORDER BY** clauses can be combined in one query. If used, **ORDER BY** must be the last clause in the query.

Section 18.4.4 Merging Data from Multiple Tables: INNER JOIN

- An INNER JOIN (p. 660) merges rows from two tables by matching values in columns that are common to the tables. The basic form for the INNER JOIN operator is:

```
SELECT columnName1, columnName2, ...
FROM table1
INNER JOIN table2
    ON table1.columnName = table2.columnName
```

The ON clause (p. 660) specifies the columns from each table that are compared to determine which rows are joined. If a SQL statement uses columns with the same name from multiple tables, the column names must be fully qualified (p. 661) by prefixing them with their table names and a dot (.).

Section 18.4.5 INSERT Statement

- An INSERT statement (p. 661) inserts a new row into a table. The basic form of this statement is

```
INSERT INTO tableName ( columnName1, columnName2, ..., columnNameN )
    VALUES ( value1, value2, ..., valueN )
```

where *tableName* is the table in which to insert the row. The *tableName* is followed by a comma-separated list of column names in parentheses. The list of column names is followed by the SQL keyword VALUES (p. 662) and a comma-separated list of values in parentheses.

- SQL uses single quotes (') to delimit strings. To specify a string containing a single quote in SQL, escape the single quote with another single quote (i.e., ' ').

Section 18.4.6 UPDATE Statement

- An UPDATE statement (p. 663) modifies data in a table. The basic form of an UPDATE statement is

```
UPDATE tableName
    SET columnName1 = value1, columnName2 = value2, ..., columnNameN = valueN
    WHERE criteria
```

where *tableName* is the table to update. Keyword SET (p. 663) is followed by a comma-separated list of *columnName* = *value* pairs. The optional WHERE clause determines which rows to update.

Section 18.4.7 DELETE Statement

- A DELETE statement (p. 663) removes rows from a table. The simplest form for a DELETE statement is

```
DELETE FROM tableName WHERE criteria
```

where *tableName* is the table from which to delete a row (or rows). The optional WHERE *criteria* determines which rows to delete. If this clause is omitted, all the table's rows are deleted.

Section 18.5 MySQL

- MySQL (pronounced "my sequel") is a robust and scalable relational database management system (RDBMS) that was created by the Swedish consulting firm TcX in 1994.
- MySQL is a multiuser, multithreaded RDBMS server that uses SQL to interact with and manipulate data.
- Multithreading capabilities enable MySQL database to perform multiple tasks concurrently, allowing the server to process client requests efficiently.
- Implementations of MySQL are available for Windows, Mac OS X, Linux and UNIX.

Section 18.6 (Optional) Microsoft Language Integrate Query (LINQ)

- .NET's collection classes provide reusable data structures that are reliable, powerful and efficient.
- Lists automatically increase their size to accommodate additional elements.
- Large amounts of data are often stored in a database—an organized collection of data. Today's most popular database systems are relational databases. SQL is the international standard language used almost universally with relational databases to perform queries (i.e., to request information that satisfies given criteria).
- LINQ allows you to write query expressions (similar to SQL queries) that retrieve information from a wide variety of data sources. You can query arrays and Lists, selecting elements that satisfy a set of conditions—this is known as filtering.
- A LINQ provider is a set of classes that implement LINQ operations and enable programs to interact with data sources to perform tasks such as sorting, grouping and filtering elements.

Section 18.6.1 Querying an Array of int Values Using LINQ

- Repetition statements focus on the process of iterating through elements and checking whether they satisfy the desired criteria. LINQ specifies the conditions that selected elements must satisfy, not the steps necessary to get the results.
- The System.Linq namespace contains the classes for LINQ to Objects.
- A from clause specifies a range variable and the data source to query. The range variable represents each item in the data source (one at a time), much like the control variable in a foreach statement.
- If the condition in the where clause evaluates to true for an element, it's included in the results.
- The select clause determines what value appears in the results.
- A C# interface describes a set of methods and properties that can be used to interact with an object.
- The IEnumerable<T> interface describes the functionality of any object that's capable of being iterated over and thus offers methods to access each element in some order.
- A class that implements an interface must define each method in the interface.
- Arrays and collections implement the IEnumerable<T> interface.
- A foreach statement can iterate over any object that implements the IEnumerable<T> interface.
- A LINQ query returns an object that implements the IEnumerable<T> interface.
- The orderby clause sorts query results in ascending order by default. Results can also be sorted in descending order using the descending modifier.
- C# provides implicitly typed local variables, which enable the compiler to infer a local variable's type based on the variable's initializer.
- To distinguish such an initialization from a simple assignment statement, the var keyword is used in place of the variable's type.
- You can use local type inference with control variables in the header of a for or foreach statement.
- Implicitly typed local variables can be used to initialize arrays without explicitly giving their type. To do so, use new[] to specify that the variable is an array.

Section 18.6.2 Querying an Array of Employee Objects Using LINQ

- LINQ can be used with collections of most data types.
- Any boolean expression can be used in a where clause.
- An orderby clause can sort the results according to multiple properties specified in a comma-separated list.
- Method Any returns true if there's at least one element in the result; otherwise, it returns false.

- The First method returns the first element in the query result. You should check that the query result is not empty before calling First.

- The Count method returns the number of elements in the query result.

- The Distinct method removes duplicate values from query results.

- You can select any number of properties in a select clause by specifying them in a comma-separated list in braces after the new keyword. The compiler automatically creates a new class having these properties—called an anonymous type.

Section 18.6.3 Querying a Generic Collection Using LINQ

- LINQ to Objects can query Lists.

- LINQ's let clause creates a new range variable. This is useful if you need to store a temporary result for use later in the LINQ query.

- The StartsWith method of the string class determines whether a string starts with the string passed to it as an argument.

- A LINQ query uses deferred execution—it executes only when you access the results, not when you create the query.

Section 18.7 (Optional) LINQ to SQL

- LINQ to SQL enables you to access data in SQL Server databases using LINQ syntax.

- You interact with LINQ to SQL via classes that are automatically generated by the IDE's LINQ to SQL Designer based on the database schema.

- LINQ to SQL requires every table to have a primary key to support modifying the database data.

- The IDE creates a class for each table. Objects of these classes represent the collections of rows in the corresponding tables.

- The IDE also creates a class for a row of each table with a property for each column in the table. Objects of these classes (row objects) hold the data from individual rows in the database's tables.

- In the class for a row object, an additional property is created for each foreign key. This property returns the row object of the corresponding primary key in another table.

- In the class for a row object, an additional property is created for the collection of row objects with foreign-keys that reference the row object's primary key.

- Once generated, the LINQ to SQL classes have full *IntelliSense* support in the IDE.

Section 18.8 (Optional) Querying a Database with LINQ

- The IDE provides visual programming tools and wizards that simplify accessing data in your projects. These tools establish database connections and create the objects necessary to view and manipulate the data through the GUI—a technique known as data binding.

- A DataGridView (namespace System.Windows.Forms) displays data from a data source in tabular format.

- A BindingNavigator is a collection of controls that allow you to navigate through the records displayed in a GUI. The BindingNavigator controls also allow you to add records, delete records and save your changes to the database.

Section 18.8.1 Creating LINQ to SQL Classes

- To interact with a database, you must create a connection to the database.

- In Visual C# 2010 Express, use the **Database Explorer** window to connect to the database. In full versions of Visual Studio 2010, use the **Server Explorer** window.

- After connecting to the database, you can generate the LINQ to SQL classes by adding a new **LINQ to SQL Classes** item to your project, then dragging the tables you wish to use from the **Database Explorer** onto the **Object Relational Designer**. When you save the .dbml file, the IDE generates the LINQ to SQL classes.

Section 18.8.2 Data Bindings Between Controls and the LINQ to SQL Classes

- To use the LINQ to SQL classes for data binding, you must first add them as a data source.
- Select **Data > Add New Data Source…** to display the **Data Source Configuration Wizard**. Use an **Object** data source. Select the LINQ to SQL object to use as a data source. Drag that data source from the **Data Sources** window onto the Form to create controls that can display the table's data.
- By default, the IDE creates a DataGridView with the correct column names and a BindingNavigator that contains Buttons for moving between entries, adding entries, deleting entries and saving changes to the database.
- The IDE also generates a BindingSource, which handles the transfer of data between the data source and the data-bound controls on the Form.
- The result of a LINQ query on the DataContext can be assigned to the BindingSource's DataSource property. The BindingSource uses the DataSource to extract data from the database and to populate the DataGridView.
- To save the user's changes to the data in the DataGridView, enable the BindingNavigator's **Save Data** Button (🖫). Then, double click the icon to create its Click event handler. In the event handler, you must validate the data, call EndEdit on the BindingSource to save pending changes in the DataContext, and call SubmitChanges on the DataContext to store the changes in the database. For efficiency, LINQ to SQL saves only data that has changed.

Section 18.9 (Optional) Dynamically Binding LINQ to SQL Query Results

- The IDE displays smart tag menus for many GUI controls to provide you with quick access to common properties you might set for a control, so you can set these properties directly in **Design** view. You can open a control's smart tag menu by clicking the small arrowhead (▶) that appears in the control's upper-right corner in **Design** view.
- The MoveFirst method of the BindingSource moves to the first row of the result.

Section 18.10 Java DB/Apache Derby

- The Java SE 6 and 7 Development Kits (JDKs) come bundled with the open source, pure Java database Java DB (the Oracle branded version of Apache Derby).

Self-Review Exercises

18.1 Fill in the blanks in each of the following statements:
   a) The international standard database language is _____.
   b) A table in a database consists of _____ and _____.
   c) The _____ uniquely identifies each row in a table.
   d) SQL keyword _____ is followed by the selection criteria that specify the rows to select in a query.
   e) SQL keywords _____ specify the order in which rows are sorted in a query.
   f) Merging rows from multiple database tables is called _____ the tables.
   g) A(n) _____ is an organized collection of data.
   h) A(n) _____ is a set of columns whose values match the primary key values of another table.
   i) The LINQ _____ clause is used for filtering.

   j) To get only unique results from a LINQ query, use the _____ method.

   k) The _____ clause declares a new temporary variable within a LINQ query.

18.2   State whether each of the following is *true* or *false*. If *false*, explain why.

   a) The orderby clause in a LINQ query can sort only in ascending order.

   b) LINQ queries can be used on both arrays and collections.

   c) The Remove method of the List class removes an element at a specific index.

   d) A BindingNavigator object can extract data from a database.

   e) LINQ to SQL automatically saves changes made back to the database.

Answers to Self-Review Exercises

18.1   a) SQL. b) rows, columns. c) primary key. d) WHERE. e) ORDER BY. f) joining. g) database. h) foreign key. i) where. j) Distinct. k) let.

18.2   a) False. The descending modifier is used to make orderby sort in descending order. b) True. c) False. Remove removes the first element equal to its argument. RemoveAt removes the element at a specific index. d) False. A BindingNavigator allows users to browse and manipulate data displayed by another GUI control. A DataContext can extract data from a database. e) False. You must call the SubmitChanges method of the DataContext to save the changes made back to the database.

Exercises

18.3   Define the following terms:

   a) Qualified name

   b) Rule of Referential Integrity

   c) Rule of Entity Integrity

   d) selection criteria

18.4   State the purpose of the following SQL keywords:

   a) ASC

   b) FROM

   c) DESC

   d) INSERT

   e) LIKE

   f) UPDATE

   g) SET

   h) VALUES

   i) ON

18.5   Write SQL queries for the books database (discussed in Section 18.3) that perform each of the following tasks:

   a) Select all authors from the Authors table with the columns in the order lastName, firstName and authorID.

   b) Select a specific author and list all books for that author. Include the title, year and ISBN number. Order the information alphabetically by title.

   c) Add a new author to the Authors table.

   d) Add a new title for an author (remember that the book must have an entry in the AuthorISBN table).

18.6   Fill in the blanks in each of the following statements:

   a) The _____ states that every column in a primary key must have a value, and the value of the primary key must be unique

b) The _____ states that every foreign-key value must appear as another table's primary-key value.

c) A(n) _____ in a pattern indicates that a string matching the pattern can have zero or more characters at the percent character's location in the pattern.

d) Java DB is the Oracle branded version of _____.

e) A(n) _____ in a LIKE pattern string indicates a single character at that position in the pattern.

f) There's a(n) _____ relationship between a primary key and its corresponding foreign key.

g) SQL uses _____ as the delimiter for strings.

18.7   Correct each of the following SQL statements that refer to the books database.

a) `SELECT firstName FROM author WHERE authorID = 3`

b) `SELECT isbn, title FROM Titles ORDER WITH title DESC`

c) `INSERT INTO Authors ( authorID, firstName, lastName )`
   `VALUES ( "2", "Jane", "Doe" )`

19

PHP

Be careful when reading health books; you may die of a misprint.
—Mark Twain

Reckoners without their host must reckon twice.
—John Heywood

There was a door to which I found no key;
There was the veil through which I might not see.
—Omar Khayyam

Objectives

In this chapter you will:

- Manipulate data of various types.

- Use operators, arrays and control statements.

- Use regular expressions to search for text that matches a patterns.

- Construct programs that process form data.

- Store data on the client using cookies.

- Create programs that interact with MySQL databases.

19.1 Introduction

PHP, or **PHP: Hypertext Preprocessor**, has become the most popular server-side scripting language for creating dynamic web pages. PHP was created by Rasmus Lerdorf to track users at his website. In 1995, Lerdorf released it as a package called the "Personal Home Page Tools." Two years later, PHP 2 featured built-in database support and form handling. In 1997, PHP 3 was released after a substantial rewrite, which resulted in a large increase in performance and led to an explosion of PHP use. The release of PHP 4 featured the new *Zend Engine* from Zend, a PHP software company. This version was considerably faster and more powerful than its predecessor, further increasing PHP's popularity. It's estimated that over 15 million domains now use PHP, accounting for more than 20 percent of web pages.[1] Currently, PHP 5 features the *Zend Engine 2*, which provides further speed increases, exception handling and a new object-oriented programming model.[2] More information about the Zend Engine can be found at `www.zend.com`.

PHP is an open-source technology that's supported by a large community of users and developers. PHP is *platform independent*—implementations exist for all major UNIX, Linux, Mac and Windows operating systems. PHP also supports many databases, including MySQL.

After introducing the basics of the PHP scripting language, we discuss form processing and business logic, which are vital to e-commerce applications. Next, we build a three-tier web application that queries a MySQL database. We also show how PHP can use cookies to store information on the client that can be retrieved during future visits to the website. Finally, we revisit the form-processing example to demonstrate some of PHP's more dynamic capabilities.

Notes Before Proceeding

To run a PHP script, PHP must first be installed on your system. We assume that you've followed the XAMPP installation instructions in Chapter 17. This ensures that the Apache web server, MySQL DBMS and PHP are configured properly so that you can test

---

1. "History of PHP," 30 June 2007, *PHP* `<us.php.net/history>`.
2. Z. Suraski, "The OO Evolution of PHP," 16 March 2004, *Zend* `<devzone.zend.com/node/view/id/1717>`.

PHP web applications on your local computer. For the examples that access a database, this chapter also assumes that you've followed the instructions in Chapter 18 for setting up a MySQL user account and for creating the databases we use in this chapter. All examples and exercises in this chapter have been verified using PHP 5.3.5—the version installed by XAMPP at the time of publication.

Before continuing, take the examples folder for this chapter (ch19) and copy it into the XAMPP installation folder's htdocs subfolder. This is the folder from which XAMPP serves documents, images and scripts.

19.2 Simple PHP Program

The power of the web resides not only in serving content to users, but also in responding to requests from users and generating web pages with dynamic content. Interactivity between the user and the server has become a crucial part of web functionality, making PHP—a language written specifically for handling client requests—a valuable tool.

PHP code is embedded directly into text-based documents, such as HTML, though these script segments are interpreted by the server *before* being delivered to the client. PHP script file names end with .php.

Figure 19.1 presents a simple PHP script that displays a welcome message. PHP code is inserted between the delimiters **<?php** and **?>** and can be placed anywhere in HTML markup. Line 7 declares variable $name and assigns it the string "Paul". All variables are preceded by a **$** and are created the first time they're encountered by the PHP interpreter. PHP statements terminate with a **semicolon (;)**.

Common Programming Error 19.1

Variable names in PHP are case sensitive. Failure to use the proper mixture of cases to refer to a variable will result in a logic error, *since the script will create a new variable for any name it doesn't recognize as a previously used variable.*

Common Programming Error 19.2

Forgetting to terminate a statement with a semicolon (;) is a syntax error.

```
 1   <!DOCTYPE html>
 2
 3   <!-- Fig. 19.1: first.php -->
 4   <!-- Simple PHP program. -->
 5   <html>
 6   <?php
 7      $name = "Paul"; // declaration and initialization
 8   ?><!-- end PHP script -->
 9      <head>
10         <meta charset = "utf-8">
11         <title>Simple PHP document</title>
12      </head>
13      <body>
14         <!-- print variable name's value -->
15         <h1><?php print( "Welcome to PHP, $name!" ); ?></h1>
```

Fig. 19.1 | Simple PHP program. (Part 1 of 2.)

```
16        </body>
17    </html>
```

Fig. 19.1 | Simple PHP program. (Part 2 of 2.)

Line 7 also contains a **single-line comment**, which begins with two slashes (//). Text to the right of the slashes is ignored by the interpreter. Multiline comments begin with delimiter /* on the first line of the comment and end with delimiter */ at the end of the last line of the comment.

Line 15 outputs the value of variable $name by calling function **print**. The value of $name is printed, not the string "$name". When a variable is encountered inside a double-quoted ("") string, PHP **interpolates** the variable. In other words, PHP inserts the variable's value where the variable name appears in the string. Thus, variable $name is replaced by Paul for printing purposes. All operations of this type execute on the server *before* the HTML5 document is sent to the client. You can see by viewing the source of a PHP document that the code sent to the client does not contain any PHP code.

PHP variables are *loosely typed*—they can contain different types of data (e.g., **integers**, **doubles** or **strings**) at different times. Figure 19.2 introduces PHP's data types.

Type	Description
int, integer	Whole numbers (i.e., numbers without a decimal point).
float, double, real	Real numbers (i.e., numbers containing a decimal point).
string	Text enclosed in either single (' ') or double ("") quotes. [*Note:* Using double quotes allows PHP to recognize more escape sequences.]
bool, boolean	true or false.
array	Group of elements.
object	Group of associated data and methods.
resource	An external source—usually information from a database.
NULL	No value.

Fig. 19.2 | PHP types.

19.3 Converting Between Data Types

Converting between different data types may be necessary when performing arithmetic operations with variables. Type conversions can be performed using function **settype**. Figure 19.3 demonstrates type conversion of some types introduced in Fig. 19.2.

```
 1   <!DOCTYPE html>
 2
 3   <!-- Fig. 19.3: data.php -->
 4   <!-- Data type conversion. -->
 5   <html>
 6      <head>
 7         <meta charset = "utf-8">
 8         <title>Data type conversion</title>
 9         <style type = "text/css">
10            p       { margin: 0; }
11            .head   { margin-top: 10px; font-weight: bold; }
12            .space  { margin-top: 10px; }
13         </style>
14      </head>
15      <body>
16         <?php
17            // declare a string, double and integer
18            $testString = "3.5 seconds";
19            $testDouble = 79.2;
20            $testInteger = 12;
21         ?><!-- end PHP script -->
22
23         <!-- print each variable's value and type -->
24         <p class = "head">Original values:</p>
25         <?php
26            print( "<p>$testString is a(n) " . gettype( $testString )
27               . "</p>" );
28            print( "<p>$testDouble is a(n) " . gettype( $testDouble )
29               . "</p>" );
30            print( "<p>$testInteger is a(n) " . gettype( $testInteger )
31               . "</p>" );
32         ?><!-- end PHP script -->
33         <p class = "head">Converting to other data types:</p>
34         <?php
35            // call function settype to convert variable
36            // testString to different data types
37            print( "<p>$testString " );
38            settype( $testString, "double" );
39            print( " as a double is $testString</p>" );
40            print( "<p>$testString " );
41            settype( $testString, "integer" );
42            print( " as an integer is $testString</p>" );
43            settype( $testString, "string" );
44            print( "<p class = 'space'>Converting back to a string results in
45               $testString</p>" );
46
47            // use type casting to cast variables to a different type
48            $data = "98.6 degrees";
49            print( "<p class = 'space'>Before casting: $data is a " .
50               gettype( $data ) . "</p>" );
51            print( "<p class = 'space'>Using type casting instead:</p>
52               <p>as a double: " . (double) $data . "</p>" .
53               "<p>as an integer: " . (integer) $data . "</p>";
```

Fig. 19.3 | Data type conversion. (Part 1 of 2.)

```
54              print( "<p class = 'space'>After casting: $data is a " .
55                  gettype( $data ) . "</p>" );
56          ?><!-- end PHP script -->
57      </body>
58  </html>
```

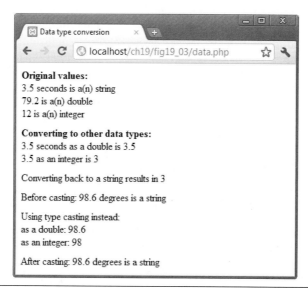

Fig. 19.3 | Data type conversion. (Part 2 of 2.)

Functions *gettype and* settype

Lines 18–20 assign a string to variable $testString, a floating-point number to variable $testDouble and an integer to variable $testInteger. Variables are typed based on the values assigned to them. For example, variable $testString becomes a string when assigned the value "3.5 seconds". Lines 26–31 print the value of each variable and its type using function **gettype**, which returns the current type of its argument. When a variable is in a print statement but not part of a string, enclosing the variable name in double quotes is unnecessary. Lines 38, 41 and 43 call **settype** to modify the type of each variable. Function settype takes two arguments—the variable whose type is to be changed and the variable's new type.

Calling function settype can result in loss of data. For example, doubles are *truncated* when they're converted to integers. When converting from a string to a number, PHP uses the value of the number that appears at the beginning of the string. If no number appears at the beginning, the string evaluates to 0. In line 38, the string "3.5 seconds" is converted to a double, storing 3.5 in variable $testString. In line 41, double 3.5 is converted to integer 3. When we convert this variable to a string (line 43), the variable's value becomes "3"—much of the original content from the variable's declaration in line 14 is lost.

Casting

Another option for conversion between types is **casting** (or **type casting**). Unlike settype, casting does not change a variable's content—it creates a *temporary copy* of a variable's value in memory. Lines 52–53 cast variable $data's value (declared in line 48) from a string to a double and an integer. Casting is useful when a different type is required in a specific operation but you would like to retain the variable's original value and type. Lines 49–55 show that the type and value of $data remain *unchanged* even after it has been cast several times.

String Concatenation

The **concatenation operator** (.) combines multiple strings in the same print statement, as demonstrated in lines 49–55. A print statement may be split over multiple lines—all data that's enclosed in the parentheses and terminated by a semicolon is printed to the XHTML document.

Error-Prevention Tip 19.1

Function print can be used to display the value of a variable at a particular point during a program's execution. This is often helpful in debugging a script.

19.4 Arithmetic Operators

PHP provides several arithmetic operators, which we demonstrate in Fig. 19.4. Line 15 declares variable $a and assigns to it the value 5. Line 19 calls function **define** to create a **named constant**. Function define takes two arguments—the name and value of the constant. An optional third argument accepts a bool value that specifies whether the constant is *case insensitive*—constants are case sensitive by default.

Common Programming Error 19.3

Assigning a value to a constant after it's declared is a syntax error.

Line 22 adds constant VALUE to variable $a. Line 26 uses the **multiplication assignment operator** *= to yield an expression equivalent to $a = $a * 2 (thus assigning $a the value 20). Arithmetic assignment operators—like the ones described in Chapter 6—are syntactical shortcuts. Line 34 adds 40 to the value of variable $a.

Uninitialized variables have undefined values that evaluate differently, depending on the context. For example, when an undefined value is used in a numeric context (e.g., $num in line 51), it evaluates to 0. In contrast, when an undefined value is interpreted in a string context (e.g., $nothing in line 48), it evaluates to the string "undef". When you run a PHP script that uses an undefined variable, the PHP interpreter outputs warning messages in the web page. You can adjust the level of error and warning messages in the PHP configuration files for your platform (e.g., the php.ini file on Windows). For more information, see the online documentation for PHP at php.net.

```
1   <!DOCTYPE html>
2
3   <!-- Fig. 19.4: operators.php -->
4   <!-- Using arithmetic operators. -->
5   <html>
6      <head>
7         <meta charset = "utf-8">
8         <style type = "text/css">
```

Fig. 19.4 | Using arithmetic operators. (Part 1 of 3.)

```
 9              p { margin: 0; }
10           </style>
11           <title>Using arithmetic operators</title>
12        </head>
13        <body>
14           <?php
15              $a = 5;
16              print( "<p>The value of variable a is $a</p>" );
17
18              // define constant VALUE
19              define( "VALUE", 5 );
20
21              // add constant VALUE to variable $a
22              $a = $a + VALUE;
23              print( "<p>Variable a after adding constant VALUE is $a</p>" );
24
25              // multiply variable $a by 2
26              $a *= 2;
27              print( "<p>Multiplying variable a by 2 yields $a</p>" );
28
29              // test if variable $a is less than 50
30              if ( $a < 50 )
31                 print( "<p>Variable a is less than 50</p>" );
32
33              // add 40 to variable $a
34              $a += 40;
35              print( "<p>Variable a after adding 40 is $a</p>" );
36
37              // test if variable $a is 50 or less
38              if ( $a < 51 )
39                 print( "<p>Variable a is still 50 or less</p>" );
40              elseif ( $a < 101 ) // $a >= 51 and <= 100
41                 print( "<p>Variable a is now between 50 and 100,
42                    inclusive</p>" );
43              else // $a > 100
44                 print( "<p>Variable a is now greater than 100</p>" );
45
46              // print an uninitialized variable
47              print( "<p>Using a variable before initializing:
48                 $nothing</p>" ); // nothing evaluates to ""
49
50              // add constant VALUE to an uninitialized variable
51              $test = $num + VALUE; // num evaluates to 0
52              print( "<p>An uninitialized variable plus constant
53                 VALUE yields $test</p>" );
54
55              // add a string to an integer
56              $str = "3 dollars";
57              $a += $str;
58              print( "<p>Adding a string to variable a yields $a</p>" );
59           ?><!-- end PHP script -->
60        </body>
61     </html>
```

Fig. 19.4 | Using arithmetic operators. (Part 2 of 3.)

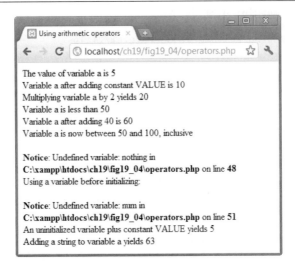

Fig. 19.4 | Using arithmetic operators. (Part 3 of 3.)

Error-Prevention Tip 19.2

Initialize variables before they're used to avoid subtle errors. For example, multiplying a number by an uninitialized variable results in 0.

Strings are converted to integers or doubles when they're used in arithmetic operations. In line 57, a copy of the value of variable `str`, `"3 dollars"`, is converted to the integer 3 for use in the calculation. The type and value of variable `$str` are left unchanged.

Keywords
Keywords (examples from Fig. 19.4 include `if`, `elseif` and `else`) may not be used as function, method, class or namespace names. Figure 19.5 lists the PHP keywords.

PHP keywords				
abstract	and	array	as	break
case	catch	class	clone	const
continue	declare	default	do	else
elseif	enddeclare	endfor	endforeach	endif
endswitch	endwhile	extends	final	for
foreach	function	global	goto	if
implements	interface	instanceof	namespace	new
or	private	protected	public	static
switch	throw	try	use	var
while	xor			

Fig. 19.5 | PHP keywords.

Keywords
Figure 19.6 contains the operator precedence chart for PHP. The operators are shown from top to bottom in decreasing order of precedence.

Operator	Type	Associativity
`new` `clone`	constructor copy an object	none
`[]`	subscript	left to right
`++` `--`	increment decrement	none

`~`
`-`
`@`
`(type)`
	bitwise not
	unary negative
	error control
	cast
		right to left

`instanceof`		none
`!`	not	right to left

`*`
`/`
`%`
	multiplication
	division
	modulus
		left to right

`+`
`-`
`.`
	addition
	subtraction
	concatenation
		left to right

`<<` `>>`	bitwise shift left bitwise shift right	left to right

`<`
`>`
`<=`
`>=`
	less than
	greater than
	less than or equal
	greater than or equal
		none

`==`
`!=`
`===`
`!==`
	equal
	not equal
	identical
	not identical
		none

`&`	bitwise AND	left to right
`^`	bitwise XOR	left to right
`|`	bitwise OR	left to right
`&&`	logical AND	left to right
`||`	logical OR	left to right
`?:`	ternary conditional	left to right

Fig. 19.6 | PHP operator precedence and associativity. (Part 1 of 2.)

Operator	Type	Associativity
=	assignment	right to left
+=	addition assignment	
-=	subtraction assignment	
*=	multiplication assignment	
/=	division assignment	
%=	modulus assignment	
&=	bitwise AND assignment	
|=	bitwise OR assignment	
^=	bitwise exclusive OR assignment	
.=	concatenation assignment	
<<=	bitwise shift left assignment	
>>=	bitwise shift right assignment	
=>	assign value to a named key	
and	logical AND	left to right
xor	exclusive OR	left to right
or	logical OR	left to right
,	list	left to right

Fig. 19.6 | PHP operator precedence and associativity. (Part 2 of 2.)

19.5 Initializing and Manipulating Arrays

PHP provides the capability to store data in arrays. Arrays are divided into elements that behave as individual variables. Array names, like other variables, begin with the $ symbol. Figure 19.7 demonstrates initializing and manipulating arrays. Individual array elements are accessed by following the array's variable name with an index enclosed in square brackets ([]). *If a value is assigned to an array element of an array that does not exist, then the array is created* (line 18). Likewise, assigning a value to an element where the index is omitted *appends* a new element to the end of the array (line 21). The for statement (lines 24–25) prints each element's value. Function **count** returns the total number of elements in the array. In this example, the for statement terminates when the counter ($i) is equal to the number of array elements.

```
1   <!DOCTYPE html>
2
3   <!-- Fig. 19.7: arrays.php -->
4   <!-- Array manipulation. -->
5   <html>
6      <head>
7         <meta charset = "utf-8">
8         <title>Array manipulation</title>
9         <style type = "text/css">
10            p    { margin: 0; }
11            .head { margin-top: 10px; font-weight: bold; }
```

Fig. 19.7 | Array manipulation. (Part 1 of 3.)

```
12          </style>
13       </head>
14       <body>
15          <?php
16             // create array first
17             print( "<p class = 'head'>Creating the first array</p>" );
18             $first[ 0 ] = "zero";
19             $first[ 1 ] = "one";
20             $first[ 2 ] = "two";
21             $first[] = "three";
22
23             // print each element's index and value
24             for ( $i = 0; $i < count( $first ); ++$i )
25                print( "Element $i is $first[$i]</p>" );
26
27             print( "<p class = 'head'>Creating the second array</p>" );
28
29             // call function array to create array second
30             $second = array( "zero", "one", "two", "three" );
31
32             for ( $i = 0; $i < count( $second ); ++$i )
33                print( "Element $i is $second[$i]</p>" );
34
35             print( "<p class = 'head'>Creating the third array</p>" );
36
37             // assign values to entries using nonnumeric indices
38             $third[ "Amy" ] = 21;
39             $third[ "Bob" ] = 18;
40             $third[ "Carol" ] = 23;
41
42             // iterate through the array elements and print each
43             // element's name and value
44             for ( reset( $third ); $element = key( $third ); next( $third ) )
45                print( "<p>$element is $third[$element]</p>" );
46
47             print( "<p class = 'head'>Creating the fourth array</p>" );
48
49             // call function array to create array fourth using
50             // string indices
51             $fourth = array(
52                "January"   => "first",    "February" => "second",
53                "March"     => "third",    "April"    => "fourth",
54                "May"       => "fifth",    "June"     => "sixth",
55                "July"      => "seventh",  "August"   => "eighth",
56                "September" => "ninth",    "October"  => "tenth",
57                "November"  => "eleventh","December" => "twelfth" );
58
59             // print each element's name and value
60             foreach ( $fourth as $element => $value )
61                print( "<p>$element is the $value month</p>" );
62          ?><!-- end PHP script -->
63       </body>
64    </html>
```

Fig. 19.7 | Array manipulation. (Part 2 of 3.)

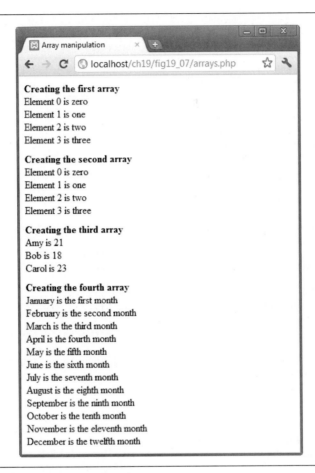

Fig. 19.7 | Array manipulation. (Part 3 of 3.)

Line 30 demonstrates a second method of initializing arrays. Function **array** creates an array that contains the arguments passed to it. The first item in the argument list is stored as the first array element (recall that the first element's index is 0), the second item is stored as the second array element and so on. Lines 32–33 display the array's contents.

In addition to integer indices, arrays can have float or nonnumeric indices (lines 38–40). An array with noninteger indices is called an **associative array**. For example, indices Amy, Bob and Carol are assigned the values 21, 18 and 23, respectively.

PHP provides functions for **iterating** through the elements of an array (line 44). Each array has a built-in **internal pointer**, which points to the array element currently being referenced. Function **reset** sets the internal pointer to the first array element. Function **key** returns the index of the element currently referenced by the internal pointer, and function **next** moves the internal pointer to the next element and returns the element. In our script, the for statement continues to execute as long as function key returns an index. Function next returns false when there are no more elements in the array. When this occurs, function key cannot return an index, $element is set to false and the for statement terminates. Line 45 prints the index and value of each element.

The array $fourth is also associative. To override the automatic numeric indexing performed by function array, you can use operator =>, as demonstrated in lines 51–57. The value to the left of the operator is the array index and the value to the right is the element's value.

The **foreach** control statement (lines 60–61) is specifically designed for iterating through arrays, especially associative arrays, because it does not assume that the array has consecutive integer indices that start at 0. The foreach statement starts with the array to iterate through, followed by the keyword **as**, followed by two variables—the first is assigned the index of the element, and the second is assigned the value of that index. (If there's only one variable listed after as, it's assigned the value of the array element.) We use the foreach statement to print the index and value of each element in array $fourth.

19.6 String Comparisons

Many string-processing tasks can be accomplished by using the **equality** and **comparison** operators, demonstrated in Fig. 19.8. Line 16 declares and initializes array $fruits. Lines 19–38 iterate through each element in the $fruits array.

Lines 23 and 25 call function **strcmp** to compare two strings. The function returns -1 if the first string alphabetically precedes the second string, 0 if the strings are equal, and 1 if the first string alphabetically follows the second. Lines 23–28 compare each element in the $fruits array to the string "banana", printing whether each is greater than, less than or equal to the string.

Relational operators (==, !=, <, <=, > and >=) can also be used to compare strings. Lines 32–37 use relational operators to compare each element of the array to the string "apple".

```
1   <!DOCTYPE html>
2
3   <!-- Fig. 19.8: compare.php -->
4   <!-- Using the string-comparison operators. -->
5   <html>
6      <head>
7         <meta charset = "utf-8">
8         <title>String Comparison</title>
9         <style type = "text/css">
10           p { margin: 0; }
11        </style>
12     </head>
13     <body>
14        <?php
15           // create array fruits
16           $fruits = array( "apple", "orange", "banana" );
17
18           // iterate through each array element
19           for ( $i = 0; $i < count( $fruits ); ++$i )
20           {
21              // call function strcmp to compare the array element
22              // to string "banana"
23              if ( strcmp( $fruits[ $i ], "banana" ) < 0 )
24                 print( "<p>" . $fruits[ $i ] . " is less than banana " );
```

Fig. 19.8 | Using the string-comparison operators. (Part 1 of 2.)

```
25          elseif ( strcmp( $fruits[ $i ], "banana" ) > 0 )
26             print( "<p>" . $fruits[ $i ] . " is greater than banana ");
27          else
28             print( "<p>" . $fruits[ $i ] . " is equal to banana " );
29
30          // use relational operators to compare each element
31          // to string "apple"
32          if ( $fruits[ $i ] < "apple" )
33             print( "and less than apple!</p>" );
34          elseif ( $fruits[ $i ] > "apple" )
35             print( "and greater than apple!</p>" );
36          elseif ( $fruits[ $i ] == "apple" )
37             print( "and equal to apple!</p>" );
38       } // end for
39    ?><!-- end PHP script -->
40    </body>
41 </html>
```

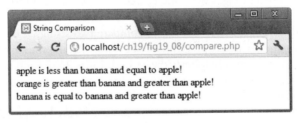

Fig. 19.8 | Using the string-comparison operators. (Part 2 of 2.)

19.7 String Processing with Regular Expressions

PHP can process text easily and efficiently, enabling straightforward searching, substitution, extraction and concatenation of strings. Text manipulation is usually done with **regular expressions**—a series of characters that serve as *pattern-matching* templates (or search criteria) in strings, text files and databases. Function **preg_match** uses regular expressions to search a string for a specified pattern using **Perl-compatible regular expressions** (**PCRE**). Figure 19.9 demonstrates regular expressions.

```
1  <!DOCTYPE html>
2
3  <!-- Fig. 19.9: expression.php -->
4  <!-- Regular expressions. -->
5  <html>
6     <head>
7        <meta charset = "utf-8">
8        <title>Regular expressions</title>
9        <style type = "text/css">
10          p { margin: 0; }
11       </style>
12    </head>
```

Fig. 19.9 | Regular expressions. (Part 1 of 2.)

```
13      <body>
14         <?php
15            $search = "Now is the time";
16            print( "<p>Test string is: '$search'</p>" );
17
18            // call preg_match to search for pattern 'Now' in variable search
19            if ( preg_match( "/Now/", $search ) )
20               print( "<p>'Now' was found.</p>" );
21
22            // search for pattern 'Now' in the beginning of the string
23            if ( preg_match( "/^Now/", $search ) )
24               print( "<p>'Now' found at beginning of the line.</p>" );
25
26            // search for pattern 'Now' at the end of the string
27            if ( !preg_match( "/Now$/", $search ) )
28               print( "<p>'Now' was not found at the end of the line.</p>" );
29
30            // search for any word ending in 'ow'
31            if ( preg_match( "/\b([a-zA-Z]*ow)\b/i", $search, $match ) )
32               print( "<p>Word found ending in 'ow': " .
33                  $match[ 1 ] . "</p>" );
34
35            // search for any words beginning with 't'
36            print( "<p>Words beginning with 't' found: " );
37
38            while ( preg_match( "/\b(t[[:alpha:]]+)\b/", $search, $match ) )
39            {
40               print( $match[ 1 ] . " " );
41
42               // remove the first occurrence of a word beginning
43               // with 't' to find other instances in the string
44               $search = preg_replace("/" . $match[ 1 ] . "/", "", $search);
45            } // end while
46
47            print( "</p>" );
48         ?><!-- end PHP script -->
49      </body>
50   </html>
```

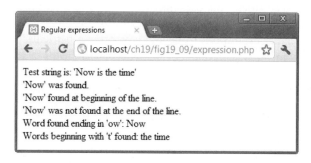

Fig. 19.9 | Regular expressions. (Part 2 of 2.)

19.7.1 Searching for Expressions

Line 15 assigns the string "Now is the time" to variable $search. The condition in line 19 calls function preg_match to search for the **literal characters** "Now" inside variable $search. If the pattern is found, preg_match returns the length of the matched string—which evaluates to true in a boolean context—and line 20 prints a message indicating that the pattern was found. We use single quotes (' ') inside the string in the print statement to emphasize the search pattern. *Anything enclosed in single quotes is not interpolated, unless the single quotes are nested in a double-quoted string literal*, as in line 16). For example, '$name' in a print statement would output $name, not variable $name's value.

Function preg_match takes two arguments—a regular-expression pattern to search for and the string to search. The regular expression must be enclosed in delimiters—typically a forward slash (/) is placed at the beginning and end of the regular-expression pattern. By default, preg_match performs a *case-sensitive pattern matches*. To perform *case-insensitive pattern matches* you simply place the letter i after the regular-expression pattern's closing delimiter, as in "/\b([a-zA-Z]*ow)\b/i" (line 31).

19.7.2 Representing Patterns

In addition to literal characters, regular expressions can include **metacharacters**, such as ^, $ and ., that specify patterns. The **caret** (^) metacharacter matches the beginning of a string (line 23), while the **dollar sign** ($) matches the end of a string (line 27). The **period** (.) metacharacter matches any single character except newlines, but can be made to match newlines with the s modifier. Line 23 searches for the pattern "Now" at the beginning of $search. Line 27 searches for "Now" at the end of $search. Note that Now$ is *not* a variable—it's a *pattern* that uses $ to search for the characters "Now" at the end of a string.

Line 31, which contains a bracket expression, searches (from left to right) for the first word ending with the letters ow. **Bracket expressions** are lists of characters enclosed in square brackets ([]) that match any single character from the list. Ranges can be specified by supplying the beginning and the end of the range separated by a **dash** (-). For instance, the bracket expression [a-z] matches any *lowercase* letter and [A-Z] matches any *uppercase* letter. In this example, we combine the two to create an expression that matches *any* letter. The \b before and after the parentheses indicates the beginning and end of a word, respectively—in other words, we're attempting to match whole words.

The expression [a-zA-Z]*ow inside the parentheses (line 31) represents any word ending in ow. The **quantifier** * matches the preceding pattern zero or more times. Thus, [a-zA-Z]*ow matches any number of letters followed by the literal characters ow. Quantifiers are used in regular expressions to denote how often a particular character or set of characters can appear in a match. Some PHP quantifiers are listed in Fig. 19.10.

Quantifier	Matches
{n}	Exactly n times
{m,n}	Between m and n times, inclusive
{$n,$}	n or more times

Fig. 19.10 | Some regular expression quantifiers. (Part 1 of 2.)

Quantifier	Matches
+	One or more times (same as {1,})
*	Zero or more times (same as {0,})
?	Zero or one time (same as {0,1})

Fig. 19.10 | Some regular expression quantifiers. (Part 2 of 2.)

19.7.3 Finding Matches

The optional third argument to function preg_match is an array that stores matches to the regular expression. When the expression is broken down into parenthetical sub-expressions, preg_match stores the first encountered instance of each expression in this array, starting from the leftmost parenthesis. The first element (i.e., index 0) stores the string matched for the entire pattern. The match to the first parenthetical pattern is stored in the second array element, the second in the third array element and so on. If the parenthetical pattern is not encountered, the value of the array element remains uninitialized. Because the statement in line 31 is the first parenthetical pattern, Now is stored in variable $match[1] (and, because it's the *only* parenthetical statement in this case, it's also stored in $match[0]).

Searching for multiple instances of a single pattern in a string is slightly more complicated, because the preg_match function returns only the first instance it encounters. To find multiple instances of a given pattern, we must make multiple calls to preg_match, and remove any matched instances before calling the function again. Lines 38–45 use a while statement and the **preg_replace** function to find all the words in the string that begin with t. We'll say more about this function momentarily.

19.7.4 Character Classes

The pattern in line 38, /\b(t[[:alpha:]]+)\b/i, matches any word beginning with the character t followed by one or more letters. The pattern uses the **character class** [[:alpha:]] to recognize any letter—this is equivalent to the [a-zA-Z]. Figure 19.11 lists some character classes that can be matched with regular expressions.

Character class	Description
alnum	Alphanumeric characters (i.e., letters [a-zA-Z] or digits [0-9])
alpha	Word characters (i.e., letters [a-zA-Z])
digit	Digits
space	White space
lower	Lowercase letters
upper	Uppercase letters

Fig. 19.11 | Some regular expression character classes.

Character classes are enclosed by the delimiters [: and :]. When this expression is placed in another set of brackets, such as [[:alpha:]] in line 38, it's a regular expression matching a single character that's a member of the class. A bracketed expression containing two or more adjacent character classes in the class delimiters represents those character sets combined. For example, the expression [[:upper:][:lower:]]* represents all strings of uppercase and lowercase letters in any order, while [[:upper:]][[:lower:]]* matches strings with a single uppercase letter followed by any number of lowercase characters. The expression ([[:upper:]][[:lower:]])* represents all strings that alternate between uppercase and lowercase characters (starting with uppercase and ending with lowercase).

19.7.5 Finding Multiple Instances of a Pattern

The quantifier + matches one or more consecutive instances of the preceding expression. The result of the match is stored in $match[1]. Once a match is found, we print it in line 40. We then remove it from the string in line 44, using function **preg_replace**. This function takes three arguments—the pattern to match, a string to replace the matched string and the string to search. The modified string is returned. Here, we search for the word that we matched with the regular expression, replace the word with an empty string, then assign the result back to $search. This allows us to match any other words beginning with the character t in the string and print them to the screen.

19.8 Form Processing and Business Logic

19.8.1 Superglobal Arrays

Knowledge of a client's execution environment is useful to system administrators who want to access client-specific information such as the client's web browser, the server name or the data sent to the server by the client. One way to obtain this data is by using a **superglobal array**. Superglobal arrays are associative arrays predefined by PHP that hold variables acquired from user input, the environment or the web server, and are accessible in any variable scope. Some of PHP's superglobal arrays are listed in Fig. 19.12.

Variable name	Description
$_SERVER	Data about the currently running server.
$_ENV	Data about the client's environment.
$_GET	Data sent to the server by a get request.
$_POST	Data sent to the server by a post request.
$_COOKIE	Data contained in cookies on the client's computer.
$GLOBALS	Array containing all global variables.

Fig. 19.12 | Some useful superglobal arrays.

Superglobal arrays are useful for verifying user input. The arrays $_GET and $_POST retrieve information sent to the server by HTTP get and post requests, respectively, making it possible for a script to have access to this data when it loads another page. For example, if data entered by a user into a form is posted to a script, the $_POST array will contain all of this information in the new script. Thus, any information entered into the form can be accessed easily from a confirmation page, or a page that verifies whether fields have been entered correctly.

19.8.2 Using PHP to Process HTML5 Forms

Forms enable web pages to collect data from users and send it to a web server for processing. Such capabilities allow users to purchase products, request information, send and receive web-based e-mail, create profiles in online networking services and take advantage of various other online services. The HTML5 form in Fig. 19.13 gathers information to add a user to a mailing list.

```
 1   <!DOCTYPE html>
 2
 3   <!-- Fig. 19.13: form.html -->
 4   <!-- HTML form for gathering user input. -->
 5   <html>
 6      <head>
 7         <meta charset = "utf-8">
 8         <title>Sample Form</title>
 9         <style type = "text/css">
10            label  { width: 5em; float: left; }
11         </style>
12      </head>
13      <body>
14         <h1>Registration Form</h1>
15         <p>Please fill in all fields and click Register.</p>
16
17         <!-- post form data to form.php -->
18         <form method = "post" action = "form.php">
19            <h2>User Information</h2>
20
21            <!-- create four text boxes for user input -->
22            <div><label>First name:</label>
23               <input type = "text" name = "fname"></div>
24            <div><label>Last name:</label>
25               <input type = "text" name = "lname"></div>
26            <div><label>Email:</label>
27               <input type = "text" name = "email"></div>
28            <div><label>Phone:</label>
29               <input type = "text" name = "phone"
30                  placeholder = "(555) 555-5555"></div>
31            </div>
32
33            <h2>Publications</h2>
34            <p>Which book would you like information about?</p>
35
36            <!-- create drop-down list containing book names -->
37            <select name = "book">
38               <option>Internet and WWW How to Program</option>
```

Fig. 19.13 | HTML5 form for gathering user input. (Part 1 of 2.)

```
39              <option>C++ How to Program</option>
40              <option>Java How to Program</option>
41              <option>Visual Basic How to Program</option>
42           </select>
43
44           <h2>Operating System</h2>
45           <p>Which operating system do you use?</p>
46
47           <!-- create five radio buttons -->
48           <p><input type = "radio" name = "os" value = "Windows"
49              checked>Windows
50              <input type = "radio" name = "os" value = "Mac OS X">Mac OS X
51              <input type = "radio" name = "os" value = "Linux">Linux
52              <input type = "radio" name = "os" value = "Other">Other</p>
53
54           <!-- create a submit button -->
55           <p><input type = "submit" name = "submit" value = "Register"></p>
56        </form>
57     </body>
58  </html>
```

The form is filled out with an incorrect phone number

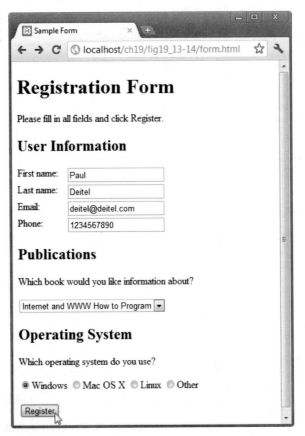

Fig. 19.13 | HTML5 form for gathering user input. (Part 2 of 2.)

The form's `action` attribute (line 18) indicates that when the user clicks the **Register** button, the form data will be posted to `form.php` (Fig. 19.14) for processing. Using `method = "post"` appends form data to the browser request that contains the protocol (i.e., HTTP) and the URL of the requested resource (specified by the `action` attribute). Scripts located on the web server's machine can access the form data sent as part of the request.

We assign a unique `name` (e.g., `email`) to each of the form's controls. When **Register** is clicked, each field's `name` and `value` are sent to the web server. Script `form.php` accesses the value for each field through the superglobal array **$_POST**, which contains key/value pairs corresponding to name–value pairs for variables submitted through the form. [*Note:* The superglobal array **$_GET** would contain these key–value pairs if the form had been submitted using the HTTP *get* method. In general, `get` is not as secure as `post`, because it appends the information directly to the URL, which is visible to the user.] Figure 19.14 processes the data posted by `form.html` and sends HTML5 back to the client.

Good Programming Practice 19.1

Use meaningful HTML5 object names for input fields. This makes PHP scripts that retrieve form data easier to understand.

```
1   <!DOCTYPE html>
2
3   <!-- Fig. 19.14: form.php -->
4   <!-- Process information sent from form.html. -->
5   <html>
6      <head>
7         <meta charset = "utf-8">
8         <title>Form Validation</title>
9         <style type = "text/css">
10           p        { margin: 0px; }
11           .error   { color: red }
12           p.head   { font-weight: bold; margin-top: 10px; }
13        </style>
14     </head>
15     <body>
16        <?php
17           // determine whether phone number is valid and print
18           // an error message if not
19           if (!preg_match( "/^\([0-9]{3}\) [0-9]{3}-[0-9]{4}$/",
20              $_POST["phone"]))
21           {
22              print( "<p class = 'error'>Invalid phone number</p>
23                 <p>A valid phone number must be in the form
24                 (555) 555-5555</p><p>Click the Back button,
25                 enter a valid phone number and resubmit.</p>
26                 <p>Thank You.</p></body></html>" );
27              die(); // terminate script execution
28           }
29        ?><!-- end PHP script -->
30        <p>Hi <?php print( $_POST["fname"] ); ?>. Thank you for
31           completing the survey. You have been added to the
```

Fig. 19.14 | Process information sent from `form.html`. (Part 1 of 2.)

```
32              <?php print( $_POST["book"] ); ?>mailing list.</p>
33         <p class = "head">The following information has been saved
34              in our database:</p>
35         <p>Name: <?php print( $_POST["fname"] );
36              print( $_POST["lname"] ); ?></p>
37         <p>Email: <?php print( "$email" ); ?></p>
38         <p>Phone: <?php print( "$phone" ); ?></p>
39         <p>OS: <?php print( $_POST["os"] ); ?></p>
40         <p class = "head">This is only a sample form.
41              You have not been added to a mailing list.</p>
42     </body>
43  </html>
```

a) Submitting the form in Fig. 19.13 redirects the user to form.php, which gives appropriate instructions if the phone number is in an incorrect format

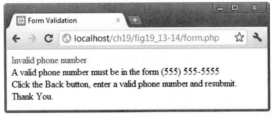

b) The results of form.php after the user submits the form in Fig. 19.13 with a phone number in a valid format

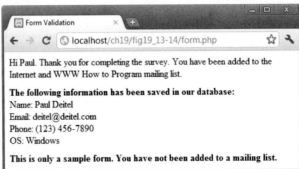

Fig. 19.14 | Process information sent from form.html. (Part 2 of 2.)

Lines 19–20 determine whether the phone number entered by the user is valid. We get the phone number from the $_POST array using the expression $_POST["phone"], where "phone" is the name of the corresponding input field in the form. The validation in this example requires the phone number to begin with an opening parenthesis, followed by an area code, a closing parenthesis, a space, an exchange, a hyphen and a line number. It's crucial to validate information that will be entered into databases or used in mailing lists. For example, validation can be used to ensure that credit card numbers contain the proper number of digits before the numbers are encrypted and sent to a merchant. This script implements the business logic, or business rules, of our application.

Software Engineering Observation 19.1

Use business logic to ensure that invalid information is not stored in databases. Validate important or sensitive form data on the server, since JavaScript may be disabled by the client. Some data, such as passwords, must always be validated on the server side.

In lines 19–20, the expression \(matches the opening parenthesis of the phone number. We want to match the literal character (, so we escape its normal meaning by preceding it with the backslash character (\). This parenthesis in the expression must be followed by three digits ([0-9]{3}), a closing parenthesis, three more digits, a literal hyphen and four additional digits. Note that we use the ^ and $ symbols to ensure that no extra characters appear at either end of the string.

If the regular expression is matched, the phone number has a valid format, and an HTML5 document is sent to the client that thanks the user for completing the form. We extract each input element's value from the $_POST array in lines (30–39). Otherwise, the body of the if statement executes and displays an error message.

Function **die** (line 27) *terminates* script execution. This function is called if the user did not enter a correct telephone number, since we do not want to continue executing the rest of the script. The function's optional argument is a string or an integer. If it's a string, it's printed as the script exits. If it's an integer, it's used as a return status code (typically in command-line PHP shell scripts).

19.9 Reading from a Database

PHP offers built-in support for many databases. Our database examples use MySQL. We assume that you've followed the XAMPP installation instructions in Chapter 17 (XAMPP includes MySQL) and that you've followed the Chapter 18 instructions for setting up a MySQL user account and for creating the databases we use in this chapter.

The example in this section uses a Products database. The user selects the name of a column in the database and submits the form. A PHP script then builds a SQL SELECT query, queries the database to obtain the column's data and outputs the data in an HTML5 document that's displayed in the user's web browser. Chapter 18 discusses how to build SQL queries.

Figure 19.15 is a web page that *posts form data* consisting of a selected database column to the server. The script in Fig. 19.16 *processes the form data*.

HTML5 Document
Line 12 of Fig. 19.15 begins an HTML5 form, specifying that the data submitted from the form will be sent to the script database.php (Fig. 19.16) in a post request. Lines 16–22 add a select box to the form, set the name of the select box to select and set its default selection to *. Submitting * specifies that *all* rows and columns are to be retrieved from the database. Each of the database's column names is set as an option in the select box.

```
1   <!DOCTYPE html>
2
3   <!-- Fig. 19.15: data.html -->
4   <!-- Form to query a MySQL database. -->
5   <html>
6      <head>
7         <meta charset = "utf-8">
8         <title>Sample Database Query</title>
9      </head>
```

Fig. 19.15 | Form to query a MySQL database. (Part 1 of 2.)

```
10        <body>
11          <h1>Querying a MySQL database.</h1>
12          <form method = "post" action = "database.php">
13            <p>Select a field to display:
14              <!-- add a select box containing options -->
15              <!-- for SELECT query -->
16              <select name = "select">
17                <option selected>*</option>
18                <option>ID</option>
19                <option>Title</option>
20                <option>Category</option>
21                <option>ISBN</option>
22              </select></p>
23            <p><input type = "submit" value = "Send Query"></p>
24          </form>
25        </body>
26  </html>
```

Selecting this option results in all columns being displayed

Fig. 19.15 | Form to query a MySQL database. (Part 2 of 2.)

database.php

Script database.php (Fig. 19.16) builds a SQL query with the posted field name then queries the MySQL database. Line 25 concatenates the posted field name to a SELECT query. Lines 28–29 call function **mysql_connect** to connect to the MySQL database. We pass three arguments—the server's hostname, a username and a password. The host name localhost is your computer. The username and password specified here were created in Chapter 18. Function mysql_connect returns a **database handle**—a representation of PHP's connection to the database—which we assign to variable $database. If the connection to MySQL fails, the function returns false and we call die to output an error message and terminate the script. Line 33 calls function **mysql_select_db** to select and open the database to be queried (in this case, products). The function returns true on success or false on failure. We call die if the database cannot be opened.

```
1   <!DOCTYPE html>
2
3   <!-- Fig. 19.16: database.php -->
```

Fig. 19.16 | Querying a database and displaying the results. (Part 1 of 3.)

```
 4    <!-- Querying a database and displaying the results. -->
 5    <html>
 6       <head>
 7          <meta charset = "utf-8">
 8          <title>Search Results</title>
 9       <style type = "text/css">
10            body  { font-family: sans-serif;
11                    background-color: lightyellow; }
12            table { background-color: lightblue;
13                    border-collapse: collapse;
14                    border: 1px solid gray; }
15            td    { padding: 5px; }
16            tr:nth-child(odd) {
17                    background-color: white; }
18       </style>
19       </head>
20       <body>
21          <?php
22             $select = $_POST["select"]; // creates variable $select
23
24             // build SELECT query
25             $query = "SELECT " . $select . " FROM books";
26
27             // Connect to MySQL
28             if ( !( $database = mysql_connect( "localhost",
29                "iw3htp", "password" ) ) )
30                die( "Could not connect to database </body></html>" );
31
32             // open Products database
33             if ( !mysql_select_db( "products", $database ) )
34                die( "Could not open products database </body></html>" );
35
36             // query Products database
37             if ( !( $result = mysql_query( $query, $database ) ) )
38             {
39                print( "<p>Could not execute query!</p>" );
40                die( mysql_error() . "</body></html>" );
41             } // end if
42
43             mysql_close( $database );
44          ?><!-- end PHP script -->
45          <table>
46             <caption>Results of "SELECT <?php print( "$select" ) ?>
47                FROM books"</caption>
48             <?php
49                // fetch each record in result set
50                while ( $row = mysql_fetch_row( $result ) )
51                {
52                   // build table to display results
53                   print( "<tr>" );
54
55                   foreach ( $row as $key => $value )
56                      print( "<td>$value</td>" );
```

Fig. 19.16 | Querying a database and displaying the results. (Part 2 of 3.)

```
57
58                      print( "</tr>" );
59                  } // end while
60              ?><!-- end PHP script -->
61          </table>
62          <p>Your search yielded
63              <?php print( mysql_num_rows( $result ) ) ?> results.</p>
64          <p>Please email comments to <a href = "mailto:deitel@deitel.com">
65              Deitel and Associates, Inc.</a></p>
66      </body>
67  </html>
```

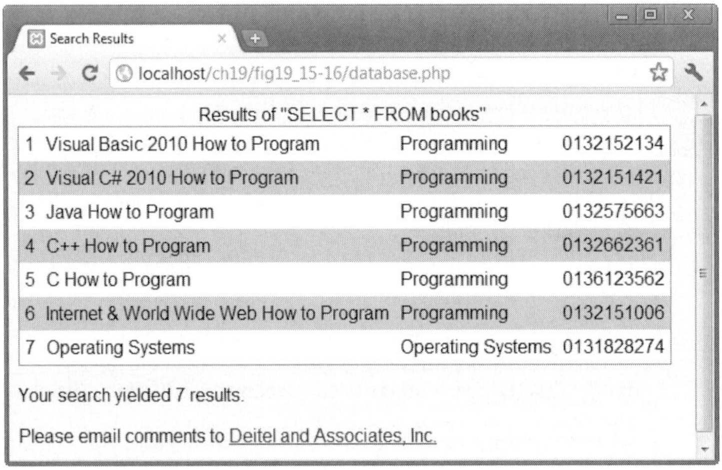

Search Results	×	+		

← → C ⓘ localhost/ch19/fig19_15-16/database.php   ☆ ⚒

Results of "SELECT * FROM books"		
1 Visual Basic 2010 How to Program	Programming	0132152134
2 Visual C# 2010 How to Program	Programming	0132151421
3 Java How to Program	Programming	0132575663
4 C++ How to Program	Programming	0132662361
5 C How to Program	Programming	0136123562
6 Internet & World Wide Web How to Program	Programming	0132151006
7 Operating Systems	Operating Systems	0131828274

Your search yielded 7 results.

Please email comments to <u>Deitel and Associates, Inc.</u>

Fig. 19.16 | Querying a database and displaying the results. (Part 3 of 3.)

To query the database, line 37 calls function **mysql_query**, specifying the query string and the database to query. If the query fails, the function returns false. Function die is then called with a call to function **mysql_error** as an argument. Function mysql_error returns any error strings from the database. If the query succeeds, mysql_query returns a resource containing the query result, which we assign to variable $result. Once we've stored the data in $result, we call **mysql_close** in line 43 to close the connection to the database. Function mysql_query can also execute SQL statements such as INSERT or DELETE that do not return results.

Lines 50–59 iterate through each record in the *result set* and construct an HTML5 table containing the results. The loop's condition calls the **mysql_fetch_row** function to return an array containing the values for each column in the current row of the query result ($result). The array is stored in variable $row. Lines 55–56 construct individual cells for each column in the row. The foreach statement takes the name of the array ($row), iterates through each index value of the array and stores the value in variable $value. Each element of the array is then printed as an individual cell. When the result has no more rows, false is returned by function mysql_fetch_row, which terminates the loop.

After all the rows in the result have been displayed, the table's closing tag is written (line 61). Lines 62–63 display the number of rows in $result by calling **mysql_num_rows** with $result as an argument.

19.10 Using Cookies

A **cookie** is a piece of information that's stored by a server in a text file on a client's computer to maintain information about the client during and between browsing sessions. A website can store a cookie on a client's computer to record user preferences and other information that the website can retrieve during the client's subsequent visits. For example, a website can use cookies to store clients' zip codes, so that it can provide weather reports and news updates tailored to the user's region. Websites also can use cookies to track information about client activity. Analysis of information collected via cookies can reveal the popularity of websites or products. Marketers can use cookies to determine the effectiveness of advertising campaigns.

Websites store cookies on users' hard drives, which raises issues regarding security and privacy. Websites should not store critical information, such as credit card numbers or passwords, in cookies, because cookies are typically stored in text files that any program can read. Several cookie features address security and privacy concerns. *A server can access only the cookies that it has placed on the client.* For example, a web application running on www.deitel.com cannot access cookies that the website www.pearson.com has placed on the client's computer. A cookie also has an *expiration date*, after which the web browser deletes it. Users who are concerned about the privacy and security implications of cookies can disable cookies in their browsers. But, disabling cookies can make it difficult or impossible for the user to interact with websites that rely on cookies to function properly.

The information stored in a cookie is sent back to the web server from which it originated whenever the user requests a web page from that particular server. The web server can send the client HTML5 output that reflects the preferences or information that's stored in the cookie.

HTML5 Document
Figure 19.17 presents an HTML5 document containing a form in which the user specifies a name, height and favorite color. When the user clicks the **Write Cookie** button, the cookies.php script (Fig. 19.18) executes.

Writing Cookies: `cookies.php`
Script cookies.php (Fig. 19.18) calls function **setcookie** (lines 8–10) to set the cookies to the values posted from cookies.html. The cookies defined in function setcookie are sent to the client at the same time as the information in the HTTP header; therefore, setcookie needs to be called *before* any other output. Function setcookie takes the name of the cookie to be set as the first argument, followed by the value to be stored in the cookie. For example, line 8 sets the name of the cookie to "Name" and the value to variable $Name, which is passed to the script from cookies.html. The optional third argument indicates the expiration date of the cookie. In this example, we set the cookies to expire in five days by taking the current time, which is returned by function **time**, and adding the constant FIVE_DAYS—the number of seconds after which the cookie is to expire (60 seconds per minute * 60 minutes per hour * 24 hours per day * 5 = 5 days). *If no expiration date is specified, the cookie lasts only until the end of the current session*—that is, when the user closes the browser. This type of cookie is known as a **session cookie**, while one with an expiration date is a **persistent cookie**. If only the name argument is passed to function setcookie, the cookie is deleted from the client's computer. Lines 13–35 send a web page to the client

```
 1   <!DOCTYPE html>
 2
 3   <!-- Fig. 19.17: cookies.html -->
 4   <!-- Gathering data to be written as a cookie. -->
 5   <html>
 6      <head>
 7         <meta charset = "utf-8">
 8         <title>Writing a cookie to the client computer</title>
 9         <style type = "text/css">
10            label { width: 7em; float: left; }
11         </style>
12      </head>
13      <body>
14         <h2>Click Write Cookie to save your cookie data.</h2>
15         <form method = "post" action = "cookies.php">
16            <div><label>Name:</label>
17               <input type = "text" name = "name"><div>
18            <div><label>Height:</label>
19               <input type = "text" name = "height"></div>
20            <div><label>Favorite Color:</label>
21               <input type = "text" name = "Color"></div>
22            <p><input type = "submit" value = "Write Cookie">
23         </form>
24      </body>
25   </html>
```

Fig. 19.17 | Gathering data to be written as a cookie.

indicating that the cookie has been written and listing the values that are stored in the cookie.

 Software Engineering Observation 19.2

Some clients do not accept cookies. When a client declines a cookie, the browser application normally informs the user that the site may not function correctly without cookies enabled.

 Software Engineering Observation 19.3

Cookies should not be used to store e-mail addresses, passwords or private data on a client's computer.

```
 1   <!-- Fig. 19.18: cookies.php -->
 2   <!-- Writing a cookie to the client. -->
 3   <?php
 4      define( "FIVE_DAYS", 60 * 60 * 24 * 5 ); // define constant
 5
 6      // write each form field's value to a cookie and set the
 7      // cookie's expiration date
 8      setcookie( "name", $_POST["name"], time() + FIVE_DAYS );
 9      setcookie( "height", $_POST["height"], time() + FIVE_DAYS );
10      setcookie( "color", $_POST["color"], time() + FIVE_DAYS );
11   ?><!-- end PHP script -->
12
13   <!DOCTYPE html>
14
15   <html>
16      <head>
17         <meta charset = "utf-8">
18         <title>Cookie Saved</title>
19         <style type = "text/css">
20            p { margin: 0px; }
21         </style>
22      </head>
23      <body>
24         <p>The cookie has been set with the following data:</p>
25
26         <!-- print each form field's value -->
27         <p>Name: <?php print( $Name ) ?></p>
28         <p>Height: <?php print( $Height ) ?></p>
29         <p>Favorite Color:
30            <span style = "color: <?php print( "$Color" ) ?> ">
31            <?php print( "$Color" ) ?></span></p>
32         <p>Click <a href = "readCookies.php">here</a>
33            to read the saved cookie.</p>
34      </body>
35   </html>
```

Fig. 19.18 | Writing a cookie to the client.

Reading an Existing Cookie

Figure 19.19 reads the cookie that was written in Fig. 19.18 and displays the cookie's information in a table. PHP creates the superglobal array **$_COOKIE**, which contains all the cookie values indexed by their names, similar to the values stored in array $_POST when an HTML5 form is posted (see Section 19.8).

Lines 18–19 of Fig. 19.19 iterate through the $_COOKIE array using a foreach statement, printing out the name and value of each cookie in a paragraph. The foreach statement takes the name of the array ($_COOKIE) and iterates through each index value of the array ($key). In this case, the index values are the names of the cookies. Each element is then stored in variable $value, and these values become the individual cells of the table. Try closing your browser and revisiting readCookies.php to confirm that the cookie has persisted.

```
1   <!DOCTYPE html>
2
3   <!-- Fig. 19.19: readCookies.php -->
4   <!-- Displaying the cookie's contents. -->
5   <html>
6      <head>
7         <meta charset = "utf-8">
8         <title>Read Cookies</title>
9         <style type = "text/css">
10           p { margin: 0px; }
11        </style>
12     </head>
13     <body>
14        <p>The following data is saved in a cookie on your computer.</p>
15        <?php
16           // iterate through array $_COOKIE and print
17           // name and value of each cookie
18           foreach ($_COOKIE as $key => $value )
19              print( "<p>$key: $value</p>" );
20        ?><!-- end PHP script -->
21     </body>
22  </html>
```

Fig. 19.19 | Displaying the cookie's contents.

19.11 Dynamic Content

PHP can dynamically change the HTML5 it outputs based on a user's input. We now build on Section 19.8's example by combining the HTML5 form of Fig. 19.13 and the PHP script of Fig. 19.14 into one dynamic document. The form in Fig. 19.20 is created using a series of loops, arrays and conditionals. We add error checking to each of the text input fields and inform the user of invalid entries on the form itself, rather than on an error page. If an error exists, the script maintains the previously submitted values in each form element. Finally, after the form has been successfully completed, we store the input from the user in a MySQL database. Once again, we assume that you've followed the XAMPP installation instructions in Chapter 17 (XAMPP includes MySQL) and that you've followed the Chapter 18 instructions for setting up a MySQL user account and for creating the database MailingList that we use in this example.

Variables
Lines 19–28 create variables that are used throughout the script to fill in form fields and check for errors. Lines 19–24 use the **isset** function to determine whether the $_POST array contains keys representing the various form fields. These keys exist only after the form is submitted. If function isset returns true, then the form has been submitted and we assign the value for each key to a variable. Otherwise, we assign the empty string to each variable.

Arrays
Lines 31–41 create three arrays, $booklist, $systemlist and $inputlist, that are used to dynamically create the form's input fields. We specify that the form created in this document is *self-submitting* (i.e., it posts to itself) by setting the action to the script 'dynamicForm.php' in line 125. [*Note:* We enclose HTML5 attribute values in the string argument of a print statement in single quotes so that they do not interfere with the double quotes that delimit the string. We could alternatively have used the escape sequence \" to print double quotes instead of single quotes.] Line 44 uses function isset to determine whether the **Register** button has been pressed, in which case the $_POST array will contain the key "submit" (the name of the button in the form). If it has, each of the text input fields' values is validated. If an error is detected (e.g., a text field is blank or the phone number is improperly formatted), the corresponding entry in array $formerrors is set to true and variable $iserror is set to true. If the **Register** button has not been pressed, we skip ahead to line 115.

```
1    <!DOCTYPE html>
2
3    <!-- Fig. 19.20: dynamicForm.php -->
4    <!-- Dynamic form. -->
5    <html>
6       <head>
7          <meta charset = "utf-8">
8          <title>Registration Form</title>
9          <style type = "text/css">
10            p        { margin: 0px; }
11            .error   { color: red }
12            p.head   { font-weight: bold; margin-top: 10px; }
13            label    { width: 5em; float: left; }
14         </style>
15      </head>
16      <body>
17         <?php
18            // variables used in script
19            $fname = isset($_POST[ "fname" ]) ? $_POST[ "fname" ] : "";
20            $lname = isset($_POST[ "lname" ]) ? $_POST[ "lname" ] : "";
```

Fig. 19.20 | Dynamic form. (Part 1 of 5.)

```
21      $email = isset($_POST[ "email" ]) ? $_POST[ "email" ] : "";
22      $phone = isset($_POST[ "phone" ]) ? $_POST[ "phone" ] : "";
23      $book = isset($_POST[ "book" ]) ? $_POST[ "book" ] : "";
24      $os = isset($_POST[ "os" ]) ? $_POST[ "os" ] : "";
25      $iserror = false;
26      $formerrors =
27         array( "fnameerror" => false, "lnameerror" => false,
28            "emailerror" => false, "phoneerror" => false );
29
30      // array of book titles
31      $booklist = array( "Internet and WWW How to Program",
32         "C++ How to Program", "Java How to Program",
33         "Visual Basic How to Program" );
34
35      // array of possible operating systems
36      $systemlist = array( "Windows", "Mac OS X", "Linux", "Other" );
37
38      // array of name values for the text input fields
39      $inputlist = array( "fname" => "First Name",
40         "lname" => "Last Name", "email" => "Email",
41         "phone" => "Phone" );
42
43      // ensure that all fields have been filled in correctly
44      if ( isset( $_POST["submit"] ) )
45      {
46         if ( $fname == "" )
47         {
48            $formerrors[ "fnameerror" ] = true;
49            $iserror = true;
50         } // end if
51
52         if ( $lname == "" )
53         {
54            $formerrors[ "lnameerror" ] = true;
55            $iserror = true;
56         } // end if
57
58         if ( $email == "" )
59         {
60            $formerrors[ "emailerror" ] = true;
61            $iserror = true;
62         } // end if
63
64         if ( !preg_match( "/^\([0-9]{3}\) [0-9]{3}-[0-9]{4}$/",
65            $phone ) )
66         {
67            $formerrors[ "phoneerror" ] = true;
68            $iserror = true;
69         } // end if
70
71         if ( !$iserror )
72         {
```

Fig. 19.20 | Dynamic form. (Part 2 of 5.)

```
73                         // build INSERT query
74                         $query = "INSERT INTO contacts " .
75                            "( LastName, FirstName, Email, Phone, Book, OS ) " .
76                            "VALUES ( '$lname', '$fname', '$email', " .
77                            "'" . mysql_real_escape_string( $phone ) .
78                            "', '$book', '$os' )";
79
80                         // Connect to MySQL
81                         if ( !( $database = mysql_connect( "localhost",
82                            "iw3htp", "password" ) ) )
83                            die( "<p>Could not connect to database</p>" );
84
85                         // open MailingList database
86                         if ( !mysql_select_db( "MailingList", $database ) )
87                            die( "<p>Could not open MailingList database</p>" );
88
89                         // execute query in MailingList database
90                         if ( !( $result = mysql_query( $query, $database ) ) )
91                         {
92                            print( "<p>Could not execute query!</p>" );
93                            die( mysql_error() );
94                         } // end if
95
96                         mysql_close( $database );
97
98                         print( "<p>Hi $fname. Thank you for completing the survey.
99                               You have been added to the $book mailing list.</p>
100                              <p class = 'head'>The following information has been
101                                 saved in our database:</p>
102                              <p>Name: $fname $lname</p>
103                              <p>Email: $email</p>
104                              <p>Phone: $phone</p>
105                              <p>OS: $os</p>
106                              <p><a href = 'formDatabase.php'>Click here to view
107                                 entire database.</a></p>
108                              <p class = 'head'>This is only a sample form.
109                                 You have not been added to a mailing list.</p>
110                              </body></html>" );
111                         die(); // finish the page
112                      } // end if
113                   } // end if
114
115                   print( "<h1>Sample Registration Form</h1>
116                         <p>Please fill in all fields and click Register.</p>" );
117
118                   if ( $iserror )
119                   {
120                      print( "<p class = 'error'>Fields with * need to be filled
121                            in properly.</p>" );
122                   } // end if
123
```

Fig. 19.20 | Dynamic form. (Part 3 of 5.)

```
124    print( "<!-- post form data to dynamicForm.php -->
125       <form method = 'post' action = 'dynamicForm.php'>
126       <h2>User Information</h2>
127
128       <!-- create four text boxes for user input -->" );
129    foreach ( $inputlist as $inputname => $inputalt )
130    {
131       print( "<div><label>$inputalt:</label><input type = 'text'
132          name = '$inputname' value = '" . $$inputname . "'>" );
133
134       if ( $formerrors[ ( $inputname ).."error" ] == true )
135          print( "<span class = 'error'>*</span>" );
136
137       print( "</div>" );
138    } // end foreach
139
140    if ( $formerrors[ "phoneerror" ] )
141       print( "<p class = 'error'>Must be in the form
142          (555)555-5555" );
143
144    print( "<h2>Publications</h2>
145       <p>Which book would you like information about?</p>
146
147       <!-- create drop-down list containing book names -->
148       <select name = 'book'>" );
149
150    foreach ( $booklist as $currbook )
151    {
152       print( "<option" .
153          ($currbook == $book ? " selected>" : ">") .
154          $currbook . "</option>" );
155    } // end foreach
156
157    print( "</select>
158       <h2>Operating System</h2>
159       <p>Which operating system do you use?</p>
160
161       <!-- create five radio buttons -->" );
162
163    $counter = 0;
164
165    foreach ( $systemlist as $currsystem )
166    {
167       print( "<input type = 'radio' name = 'os'
168          value = '$currsystem' " );
169
170       if ( ( !$os && $counter == 0 ) || ( $currsystem == $os ) )
171          print( "checked" );
172
173       print( ">$currsystem" );
174       ++$counter;
175    } // end foreach
176
```

Fig. 19.20 | Dynamic form. (Part 4 of 5.)

```
177          print( "<!-- create a submit button -->
178              <p class = 'head'><input type = 'submit' name = 'submit'
179              value = 'Register'></p></form></body></html>" );
180      ?><!-- end PHP script -->
```

a) Registration form after it was submitted with a missing field and an incorrectly formatted phone number

b) Confirmation page displayed after the user properly fills in the form and the information is stored in the database

Fig. 19.20 | Dynamic form. (Part 5 of 5.)

Dynamically Creating the Form
Line 71 determines whether any errors were detected. If $iserror is false (i.e., there were no input errors), lines 74–111 display the page indicating that the form was submitted successfully—we'll say more about these lines later. If $iserror is true, lines 74–111 are skipped, and the code from lines 115–179 executes. These lines include a series of print statements and conditionals to output the form, as seen in Fig. 19.20(a).

Lines 129–138 iterate through each element in the $inputlist array. In line 132 the value of $$inputname is assigned to the text field's value attribute. If the form has not yet been submitted, this will be the empty string "". The notation **$$*variable*** specifies a **variable variable**, which allows the code to reference variables dynamically. You can use this expression to obtain the value of the variable whose name is equal to the value of $*variable*. PHP first determines the value of $*variable*, then appends this value to the leading $ to form the identifier of the variable you wish to reference dynamically. (The expression $$*variable* can also be written as ${$*variable*} to convey this procedure.) For example, in lines 129–138, we use $$inputname to reference the value of each form-field variable. During the iteration of the loop, $inputname contains the name of one of the text input elements, such as "email". PHP replaces $inputname in the expression $$inputname with the string representing that element's name forming the expression ${"email"}. The entire expression then evaluates to the value of the variable $email. Thus, the variable $email, which stores the value of the e-mail text field after the form has been submitted, is dynamically referenced. This dynamic variable reference is added to the string as the value of the input field (using the concatenation operator) to maintain data over multiple submissions of the form.

Lines 134–135 add a red asterisk next to the text input fields that were filled out incorrectly. Lines 140–142 display the phone number format instructions in red if the user entered an invalid phone number.

Lines 150–155 and 165–175 generate options for the book drop-down list and operating-system radio buttons, respectively. In both cases, we ensure that the previously selected or checked element (if one exists) remains selected or checked over multiple attempts to correctly fill out the form. If any book was previously selected, line 153 adds selected to its option tag. Lines 170–171 select an operating system radio button under two conditions. If the form is begin displayed for the first time, the first radio button is selected. Otherwise, if the $currsystem variable's value matches what's stored in the $os variable (i.e., what was submitted as part of the form), that specific radio button is selected.

Inserting Data into the Database
If the form has been filled out correctly, lines 74–95 place the form information in the MySQL database MailingList using an INSERT statement. Line 77 uses the function **mysql_real_escape_string** to insert a backslash (\) before any special characters in the passed string. We must use this function so that MySQL does not interpret the parentheses in the phone number as having a special meaning aside from being part of a value to insert into the database. Lines 98–110 generate the web page indicating a successful form submission, which also provides a link to formDatabase.php (Fig. 19.21).

Displaying the Database's Contents
The script in Fig. 19.21 displays the contents of the MailingList database using the same techniques that we showed in Fig. 19.16.

```
 1    <!DOCTYPE html>
 2
 3    <!-- Fig. 19.21: formDatabase.php -->
 4    <!-- Displaying the MailingList database. -->
 5    <html>
 6       <head>
 7          <meta charset = "utf-8">
 8          <title>Search Results</title>
 9          <style type = "text/css">
10             table   { background-color: lightblue;
11                       border: 1px solid gray;
12                       border-collapse: collapse; }
13             th, td { padding: 5px; border: 1px solid gray; }
14             tr:nth-child(even) { background-color: white; }
15             tr:first-child { background-color: lightgreen; }
16          </style>
17       </head>
18       <body>
19          <?php
20             // build SELECT query
21             $query = "SELECT * FROM contacts";
22
23             // Connect to MySQL
24             if ( !( $database = mysql_connect( "localhost",
25                "iw3htp", "password" ) ) )
26                die( "<p>Could not connect to database</p></body></html>" );
27
28             // open MailingList database
29             if ( !mysql_select_db( "MailingList", $database ) )
30                die( "<p>Could not open MailingList database</p>
31                   </body></html>" );
32
33             // query MailingList database
34             if ( !( $result = mysql_query( $query, $database ) ) )
35             {
36                print( "<p>Could not execute query!</p>" );
37                die( mysql_error() . "</body></html>" );
38             } // end if
39          ?><!-- end PHP script -->
40
41          <h1>Mailing List Contacts</h1>
42          <table>
43             <caption>Contacts stored in the database</caption>
44             <tr>
45                <th>ID</th>
46                <th>Last Name</th>
47                <th>First Name</th>
48                <th>E-mail Address</th>
49                <th>Phone Number</th>
50                <th>Book</th>
51                <th>Operating System</th>
52             </tr>
```

Fig. 19.21 | Displaying the MailingList database. (Part 1 of 2.)

```
53          <?php
54             // fetch each record in result set
55             for ( $counter = 0; $row = mysql_fetch_row( $result );
56                ++$counter )
57             {
58                // build table to display results
59                print( "<tr>" );
60
61                foreach ( $row as $key => $value )
62                   print( "<td>$value</td>" );
63
64                print( "</tr>" );
65             } // end for
66
67             mysql_close( $database );
68          ?><!-- end PHP script -->
69       </table>
70    </body>
71 </html>
```

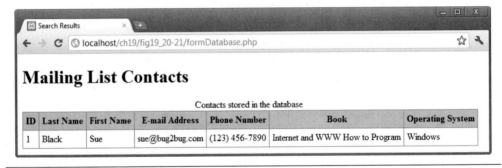

Fig. 19.21 | Displaying the MailingList database. (Part 2 of 2.)

19.12 Web Resources

www.deitel.com/PHP/
The Deitel PHP Resource Center contains links to some of the best PHP information on the web. There you'll find categorized links to PHP tools, code generators, forums, books, libraries, frameworks and more. Also check out the tutorials for all skill levels, from introductory to advanced. Be sure to visit the related Resource Centers on HTML5 (www.deitel.com/html5/) and CSS 3 (www.deitel.com/css3/).

Summary

Section 19.1 Introduction
- PHP (p. 697), or PHP: Hypertext Preprocessor, has become one of the most popular server-side scripting languages for creating dynamic web pages.
- PHP is open source and platform independent—implementations exist for all major UNIX, Linux, Mac and Windows operating systems. PHP also supports a large number of databases.

Section 19.2 Simple PHP Program
- PHP code is embedded directly into HTML5 documents and interpreted on the server.
- PHP script file names end with .php.
- In PHP, code is inserted between the scripting delimiters <?php and ?> (p. 698). PHP code can be placed anywhere in HTML5 markup, as long as the code is enclosed in these delimiters.
- Variables are preceded by a $ (p. 698) and are created the first time they're encountered.
- PHP statements terminate with a semicolon (;, p. 698).
- Single-line comments (p. 699) which begin with two forward slashes (//). Text to the right of the delimiter is ignored by the interpreter. Multiline comments begin with delimiter /* and end with delimiter */.
- When a variable is encountered inside a double-quoted ("") string, PHP interpolates (p. 699) the variable—it inserts the variable's value where the variable name appears in the string.
- All operations requiring PHP interpolation execute on the server before the HTML5 document is sent to the client.

Section 19.3 Converting Between Data Types
- PHP variables are loosely typed—they can contain different types of data at different times.
- Type conversions can be performed using function settype (p. 699). This function takes two arguments—a variable whose type is to be changed and the variable's new type.
- Variables are automatically converted to the type of the value they're assigned.
- Function gettype (p. 701) returns the current type of its argument.
- Calling function settype can result in loss of data. For example, doubles are truncated when they're converted to integers.
- When converting from a string to a number, PHP uses the value of the number that appears at the beginning of the string. If no number appears at the beginning, the string evaluates to 0.
- Another option for conversion between types is casting (or type casting, p. 701). Casting does not change a variable's content—it creates a temporary copy of a variable's value in memory.
- The concatenation operator (., p. 702) combines multiple strings.
- A print statement split over multiple lines prints all the data that's enclosed in its parentheses.

Section 19.4 Arithmetic Operators
- Function define (p. 702) creates a named constant. It takes two arguments—the name and value of the constant. An optional third argument accepts a boolean value that specifies whether the constant is case insensitive—constants are case sensitive by default.
- Uninitialized variables have undefined values. In a numeric context, an undefined value evaluates to 0. In a string context, it evaluates to "undef").
- Keywords may not be used as function, method, class or namespace names.

Section 19.5 Initializing and Manipulating Arrays
- PHP provides the capability to store data in arrays. Arrays are divided into elements that behave as individual variables. Array names, like other variables, begin with the $ symbol.
- Individual array elements are accessed by following the array's variable name with an index enclosed in square brackets ([]).
- If a value is assigned to an array that does not exist, then the array is created. Likewise, assigning a value to an element where the index is omitted appends a new element to the end of the array.

- Function count (p. 706) returns the total number of elements in the array.

- Function array (p. 708) creates an array that contains the arguments passed to it. The first item in the argument list is stored as the first array element (index 0), the second item is stored as the second array element and so on.

- Arrays with nonnumeric indices are called associative arrays (p. 708). You can create an associative array using the operator =>, where the value to the left of the operator is the array index and the value to the right is the element's value.

- PHP provides functions for iterating through the elements of an array. Each array has a built-in internal pointer (p. 708), which points to the array element currently being referenced. Function reset (p. 708) sets the internal pointer to the first array element. Function key (p. 708) returns the index of the element currently referenced by the internal pointer, and function next (p. 708) moves the internal pointer to the next element.

- The foreach statement (p. 709), designed for iterating through arrays, starts with the array to iterate through, followed by the keyword as (p. 709), followed by two variables—the first is assigned the index of the element and the second is assigned the value of that index. (If only one variable is listed after as, it's assigned the value of the array element.)

Section 19.6 String Comparisons
- Many string-processing tasks can be accomplished using the equality and relational operators.

- Function strcmp (p. 709) compares two strings. The function returns -1 if the first string alphabetically precedes the second string, 0 if the strings are equal, and 1 if the first string alphabetically follows the second.

Section 19.7 String Processing with Regular Expressions
- A regular expression (p. 710) is a series of characters used for pattern-matching templates in strings, text files and databases.

- Function preg_match (p. 710) uses regular expressions to search a string for a specified pattern. If a pattern is found, it returns the length of the matched string.

- Anything enclosed in single quotes in a print statement is not interpolated (unless the single quotes are nested in a double-quoted string literal).

- Function preg_match receives a regular expression pattern to search for and the string to search.

- Regular expressions can include metacharacters (p. 712) that specify patterns. For example, the caret (^) metacharacter matches the beginning of a string, while the dollar sign ($) matches the end of a string. The period (.) metacharacter matches any single character except newlines.

- Bracket expressions (p. 712) are lists of characters enclosed in square brackets ([]) that match any single character from the list. Ranges can be specified by supplying the beginning and the end of the range separated by a dash (-).

- Quantifiers (p. 712) are used in regular expressions to denote how often a particular character or set of characters can appear in a match.

- The optional third argument to function preg_match is an array that stores matches to each parenthetical statement of the regular expression. The first element stores the string matched for the entire pattern, and the remaining elements are indexed from left to right.

- To find multiple instances of a pattern, multiple calls to preg_match, and remove matched instances before calling the function again by using a function such as preg_replace (p. 713).

- Character classes (p. 713), or sets of specific characters, are enclosed by the delimiters [: and :]. When this expression is placed in another set of brackets, it's a regular expression matching all of the characters in the class.

- A bracketed expression containing two or more adjacent character classes in the class delimiters represents those character sets combined.

- Function `preg_replace` (p. 713) takes three arguments—the pattern to match, a string to replace the matched string and the string to search. The modified string is returned.

Section 19.8 Form Processing and Business Logic

- Superglobal arrays (p. 714) are associative arrays predefined by PHP that hold variables acquired from user input, the environment or the web server and are accessible in any variable scope.

- The arrays `$_GET` and `$_POST` (p. 714) retrieve information sent to the server by HTTP `get` and `post` requests, respectively.

- A script located on a web server can access the form data posted to the script as part of a request.

- Function `die` (p. 719) terminates script execution. The function's optional argument is a string to display or an integer to return as the script exits.

Section 19.9 Reading from a Database

- Function `mysql_connect` (p. 720) connects to the MySQL database. It takes three arguments— the server's hostname, a username and a password, and returns a database handle (p. 720)—a representation of PHP's connection to the database, or `false` if the connection fails.

- Function `mysql_select_db` (p. 720) specifies the database to be queried, and returns a `bool` indicating whether or not it was successful.

- To query the database, we call function `mysql_query` (p. 722), specifying the query string and the database to query. This returns a resource containing the result of the query, or `false` if the query fails. It can also execute SQL statements such as `INSERT` or `DELETE` that do not return results.

- Function `mysql_error` returns any error strings from the database.

Section 19.10 Using Cookies

- A cookie (p. 723) is a text file that a website stores on a client's computer to maintain information about the client during and between browsing sessions.

- A server can access only the cookies that it has placed on the client.

- Function `setcookie` (p. 723) takes the name of the cookie to be set as the first argument, followed by the value to be stored in the cookie. The optional third argument indicates the expiration date of the cookie. A cookie without a third argument is known as a session cookie, while one with an expiration date is a persistent cookie. If only the name argument is passed to function `setcookie`, the cookie is deleted from the client's computer.

- Cookies defined in function `setcookie` are sent to the client at the same time as the information in the HTTP header; therefore, it needs to be called before any HTML5 is printed.

- The current time is returned by function `time` (p. 723).

- When using Internet Explorer, cookies are stored in a **Cookies** directory on the client's machine. In Firefox, cookies are stored in a file named `cookies.txt`.

- The superglobal array `$_COOKIE` (p. 725) contains all the cookie values indexed by their names.

Section 19.11 Dynamic Content

- Function `isset` (p. 727) allows you to find out if a variable has a value.

- A variable variable (`$$variable`, p. 732) allows the code to reference variables dynamically. You can use this expression to obtain the value of the variable whose name is equal to the value of `$variable`.

- The `mysql_real_escape_string` function (p. 732) inserts a backslash (\) before any special characters in the passed string.

Self-Review Exercises

19.1   State whether each of the following is *true* or *false*. If *false*, explain why.
  a) PHP is open source and platform dependent.
  b) PHP supports only a few databases.
  c) PHP script file names end with .php.
  d) PHP code can be placed anywhere in HTML5 markup, as long as the code is enclosed in the scripting delimiters <? and ?>.
  e) PHP variables are loosely typed.
  f) Function define creates a named variable.
  g) Function preg_replace takes two arguments—the pattern to match and the string to search.
  h) Keywords may be used as identifiers.
  i) Function mysql_connect connects to the MySQL database.
  j) Function strcmp compares two strings.

19.2   Fill in the blanks in each of the following statements:
  a) Type conversions can be performed using function _____
  b) A variable _____ allows the code to reference variables dynamically.
  c) The current time is returned by function _____.
  d) A server can access only the cookies that it has placed on the _____.
  e) Function mysql_error returns any error strings from the _____.
  f) The arrays _____ retrieve information sent to the server by HTTP get requests,
  g) Function preg_replace takes _____ arguments.
  h) The _____ metacharacter matches any single character.
  i) PHP statements terminate with a _____
  j) Function _____ allows you to find out if a variable has a value.

Answers to Self-Review Exercises

19.1   a) False. PHP is open source and platform independent. b) False. PHP supports a large number of databases. c) True. d) False. PHP code can be placed anywhere in HTML5 markup, as long as the code is enclosed in the scripting delimiters <?php and ?>. e) True. f) False. Function define creates a named constant. g) False. Function preg_replace takes three arguments—the pattern to match, a string to replace the matched string and the string to search. h) False. Keywords may not be used as identifiers. i) True. j) True.

19.2   a) settype. b) variable ($$variable). c) time. d) client. e) database. f) $_GET. g) three. h) period (.). i) semicolon. j) isset.

Exercises

19.3   Identify and correct the error in each of the following PHP code examples:
  a)
```php
<?php print( "Hello World" ); >
```
  b)
```php
<?phps
    $name = "Paul";
    print( "$Name" );
?><!-- end PHP script -->
```

19.4   Write a PHP regular expression pattern that matches a string that satisfies the following description: The string must begin with the (uppercase) letter A. Any three alphanumeric characters must follow. After these, the letter B (uppercase or lowercase) must be repeated one or more times, and the string must end with two digits.

19.5   Describe how input from an HTML5 form is retrieved in a PHP program.

19.6   Describe how cookies can be used to store information on a computer and how the information can be retrieved by a PHP script. Assume that cookies are not disabled on the client.

19.7   Write a PHP script named `states.php` that creates a variable `$states` with the value "Mississippi Alabama Texas Massachusetts Kansas". The script should perform the following tasks:

    a) Search for a word in `$states` that ends in `xas`. Store this word in element 0 of an array named `$statesArray`.

    b) Search for a word in `$states` that begins with `k` and ends in `s`. Perform a case-insensitive comparison. Store this word in element 1 of `$statesArray`.

    c) Search for a word in `$states` that begins with `M` and ends in `s`. Store this element in element 2 of the array.

    d) Search for a word in `$states` that ends in `a`. Store this word in element 3 of the array.

    e) Search for a word in `$states` at the beginning of the string that starts with `M`. Store this word in element 4 of the array.

    f) Output the array `$statesArray` to the screen.

19.8   Write a PHP script that tests whether an e-mail address is input correctly. Verify that the input begins with series of characters, followed by the @ character, another series of characters, a period (.) and a final series of characters. Test your program, using both valid and invalid e-mail addresses.

19.9   Write a PHP script that obtains a URL and its description from a user and stores the information into a database using MySQL. Create and run a SQL script with a database named URL and a table named `Urltable`. The first field of the table should contain an actual URL, and the second, which is named `Description`, should contain a description of the URL. Use www.deitel.com as the first URL, and input Cool site! as its description. The second URL should be www.php.net, and the description should be The official PHP site. After each new URL is submitted, print the contents of the database in a table. [*Note:* Follow the instructions in Section 18.5.2 to create the Url database by using the `URLs.sql` script that's provided with this chapter's examples in the `dbscripts` folder.]

20

Web App Development with ASP.NET in C#

... the challenges are for the designers of these applications: to forget what we think we know about the limitations of the Web, and begin to imagine a wider, richer range of possibilities. It's going to be fun.
—Jesse James Garrett

If any man will draw up his case, and put his name at the foot of the first page, I will give him an immediate reply. Where he compels me to turn over the sheet, he must wait my leisure.
—Lord Sandwich

Objectives

In this chapter you'll learn:

- Web application development using ASP.NET.

- To handle the events from a Web Form's controls.

- To use validation controls to ensure that data is in the correct format before it's sent from a client to the server.

- To maintain user-specific information.

- To create a data-driven web application using ASP.NET and LINQ to SQL.

20.1 Introduction

In this chapter, we introduce **web-application development** with Microsoft's **ASP.NET** technology. Web-based applications create web content for web-browser clients.

We present several examples that demonstrate web-application development using **Web Forms, web controls** (also called **ASP.NET server controls**) and Visual C# programming. Web Form files have the file-name extension **.aspx** and contain the web page's GUI. You customize Web Forms by adding web controls including labels, textboxes, images, buttons and other GUI components. The Web Form file represents the web page that is sent to the client browser. We often refer to Web Form files as **ASPX files**.

An ASPX file created in Visual Studio has a corresponding class written in a .NET language—we use Visual C# in this book. This class contains event handlers, initialization code, utility methods and other supporting code. The file that contains this class is called the **code-behind file** and provides the ASPX file's programmatic implementation.

To develop the code and GUIs in this chapter, we used Microsoft's **Visual Web Developer 2010 Express**—a free IDE designed for developing ASP.NET web applications. The full version of Visual Studio 2010 includes the functionality of Visual Web Developer, so the instructions we present for Visual Web Developer also apply to Visual Studio 2010. The database example (Section 20.8) also requires SQL Server 2008 Express. You can download and install these tools from www.microsoft.com/express.

In the next chapter, we present several additional web-application development topics, including:

- master pages to maintain a uniform look-and-feel across the Web Forms in a web application

- creating password-protected websites with registration and login capabilities

- using the **Web Site Administration Tool** to specify which parts of a website are password protected

- using ASP.NET AJAX to quickly and easily improve the user experience for your web applications, giving them responsiveness comparable to that of desktop applications.

20.2 Web Basics

In this section, we discuss what occurs when a user requests a web page in a browser. In its simplest form, a *web page* is nothing more than an *HTML (HyperText Markup Language) document* (with the extension .html or .htm) that describes to a web browser the document's content and how to format it.

HTML documents normally contain *hyperlinks* that link to different pages or to other parts of the same page. When the user clicks a hyperlink, a **web server** locates the requested web page and sends it to the user's web browser. Similarly, the user can type the *address of a web page* into the browser's *address field* and press *Enter* to view the specified page.

Web development tools like Visual Web Developer typically use a "stricter" version of HTML called *XHTML (Extensible HyperText Markup Language)*, which is based on XML. ASP.NET produces web pages as XHTML documents.

URIs and URLs

URIs (Uniform Resource Identifiers) identify resources on the Internet. URIs that start with http:// are called *URLs (Uniform Resource Locators)*. Common URLs refer to files, directories or server-side code that performs tasks such as database lookups, Internet searches and business application processing. If you know the URL of a publicly available resource anywhere on the web, you can enter that URL into a web browser's address field and the browser can access that resource.

Parts of a URL

A URL contains information that directs a browser to the resource that the user wishes to access. Web servers make such resources available to web clients.

Let's examine the components of the URL

```
http://www.deitel.com/books/downloads.html
```

The http:// indicates that the HyperText Transfer Protocol (HTTP) should be used to obtain the resource. HTTP is the web protocol that enables clients and servers to communicate. Next in the URL is the server's fully qualified **hostname** (www.deitel.com)—the name of the web server computer on which the resource resides. This computer is referred to as the **host**, because it houses and maintains resources. The hostname www.deitel.com is translated into an **IP (Internet Protocol) address**—a numerical value that uniquely identifies the server on the Internet. A **Domain Name System (DNS) server** maintains a database of hostnames and their corresponding IP addresses, and performs the translations automatically.

The remainder of the URL (/books/downloads.html) specifies the resource's location (/books) and name (downloads.html) on the web server. The location could represent an actual directory on the web server's file system. For *security* reasons, however, the location is typically a *virtual directory*. The web server translates the virtual directory into a real location on the server, thus hiding the resource's true location.

Making a Request and Receiving a Response

When given a URL, a web browser uses HTTP to retrieve the web page found at that address. Figure 20.1 shows a web browser sending a request to a web server. Figure 20.2 shows the web server responding to that request.

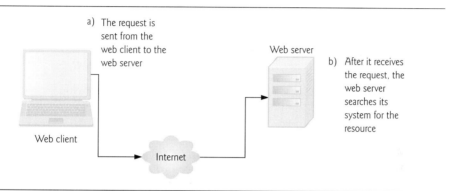

Fig. 20.1 | Client requesting a resource from a web server.

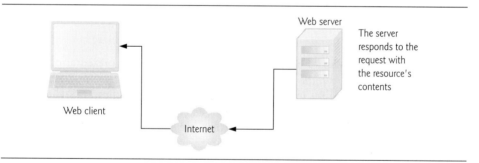

Fig. 20.2 | Client receiving a response from the web server.

20.3 Multitier Application Architecture

Web-based applications are **multitier applications** (sometimes referred to as *n*-**tier applications**). Multitier applications divide functionality into separate **tiers** (that is, logical groupings of functionality). Although tiers can be located on the *same* computer, the tiers of web-based applications commonly reside on *separate* computers for security and scalability. Figure 20.3 presents the basic architecture of a three-tier web-based application.

Information Tier

The **information tier** (also called the **bottom tier**) maintains the application's data. This tier typically stores data in a relational database management system. For example, a retail store might have a database for storing product information, such as descriptions, prices and quantities in stock. The same database also might contain customer information, such as user names, billing addresses and credit card numbers. This tier can contain multiple databases, which together comprise the data needed for an application.

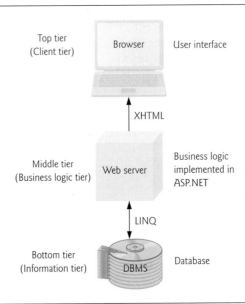

Fig. 20.3 | Three-tier architecture.

Business Logic

The **middle tier** implements **business logic, controller logic** and **presentation logic** to control interactions between the application's clients and its data. The middle tier acts as an intermediary between data in the information tier and the application's clients. The middle-tier controller logic processes client requests (such as requests to view a product catalog) and retrieves data from the database. The middle-tier presentation logic then processes data from the information tier and presents the content to the client. Web applications typically present data to clients as web pages.

Business logic in the middle tier enforces *business rules* and ensures that data is reliable before the server application updates the database or presents the data to users. Business rules dictate how clients can and cannot access application data, and how applications process data. For example, a business rule in the middle tier of a retail store's web-based application might ensure that all product quantities remain positive. A client request to set a negative quantity in the bottom tier's product information database would be rejected by the middle tier's business logic.

Client Tier

The **client tier**, or **top tier**, is the application's user interface, which gathers input and displays output. Users interact directly with the application through the user interface (typically viewed in a web browser), keyboard and mouse. In response to user actions (for example, clicking a hyperlink), the client tier interacts with the middle tier to make requests and to retrieve data from the information tier. The client tier then displays to the user the data retrieved from the middle tier. The client tier never directly interacts with the information tier.

20.4 Your First ASP.NET Application

Our first example displays the web server's time of day in a browser window (Fig. 20.4). When this application executes—that is, a web browser requests the application's web page—the web server executes the application's code, which gets the current time and displays it in a Label. The web server then returns the result to the web browser that made the request, and the web browser renders the web page containing the time. We show this application executing in the Internet Explorer and Firefox web browsers to show you that the web page renders identically across browsers.

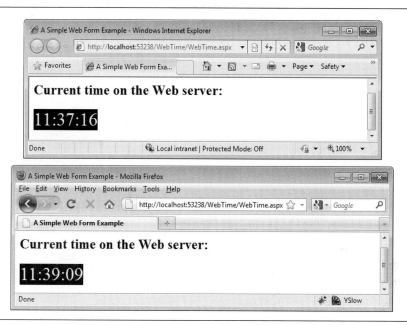

Fig. 20.4 | WebTime web application running in Internet Explorer and Firefox.

Testing the Application in Your Default Web Browser
To test this application in your default web browser, perform the following steps:

1. Open Visual Web Developer.

2. Select **Open Web Site...** from the **File** menu.

3. In the **Open Web Site** dialog (Fig. 20.5), ensure that **File System** is selected, then navigate to this chapter's examples, select the WebTime folder and click the **Open Button**.

4. Select WebTime.aspx in the **Solution Explorer**, then type *Ctrl + F5* to execute the web application.

Testing the Application in a Selected Web Browser
If you wish to execute the application in another web browser, you can copy the web page's address from your default browser's address field and paste it into another browser's address field, or you can perform the following steps:

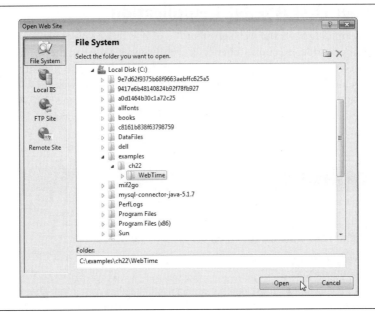

Fig. 20.5 | Open Web Site dialog.

1. In the **Solution Explorer**, right click WebTime.aspx and select **Browse With...** to display the **Browse With** dialog (Fig. 20.6).

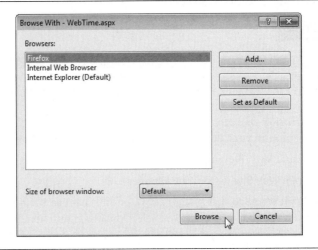

Fig. 20.6 | Selecting another web browser to execute the web application.

2. From the **Browsers** list, select the browser in which you'd like to test the web application and click the **Browse** Button.

If the browser you wish to use is not listed, you can use the **Browse With** dialog to add items to or remove items from the list of web browsers.

20.4.1 Building the WebTime Application

Now that you've tested the application, let's create it in Visual Web Developer.

Step 1: Creating the Web Site Project
Select **File > New Web Site...** to display the **New Web Site** dialog (Fig. 20.7). In the left column of this dialog, ensure that **Visual C#** is selected, then select **ASP.NET** Empty Web Site in the middle column. At the bottom of the dialog you can specify the location and name of the web application.

Fig. 20.7 | Creating an **ASP.NET Web Site** in Visual Web Developer.

The **Web location:** ComboBox provides the following options:

- **File System:** Creates a new website for testing on your local computer. Such websites execute in Visual Web Developer's built-in ASP.NET Development Server and can be accessed only by web browsers running on the same computer. You can later "publish" your website to a production web server for access via a local network or the Internet. Each example in this chapter uses the **File System** option, so select it now.

- **HTTP:** Creates a new website on an IIS web server and uses HTTP to allow you to put your website's files on the server. IIS is Microsoft's software that is used to run production websites. If you own a website and have your own web server, you might use this to build a new website directly on that server computer. You must be an Administrator on the computer running IIS to use this option.

- **FTP:** Uses File Transfer Protocol (FTP) to allow you to put your website's files on the server. The server administrator must first create the website on the server for you. FTP is commonly used by so-called "hosting providers" to allow website owners to share a server computer that runs many websites.

Change the name of the web application from WebSite1 to WebTime, then click **OK** to create the website.

Step 2: Adding a Web Form to the Website and Examining the Solution Explorer
A **Web Form** represents one page in a web application—we'll often use the terms "page" and "Web Form" interchangeably. A Web Form contains a web application's GUI. To create the WebTime.aspx Web Form:

1. Right click the project name in the **Solution Explorer** and select **Add New Item...** to display the **Add New Item** dialog (Fig. 20.8).

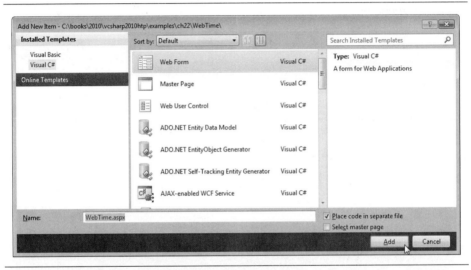

Fig. 20.8 | Adding a new **Web Form** to the website with the **Add New Item** dialog.

2. In the left column, ensure that **Visual C#** is selected, then select **Web Form** in the middle column.

3. In the **Name:** TextBox, change the file name to WebTime.aspx, then click the **Add** Button.

After you add the Web Form, the IDE opens it in **Source** view by default (Fig. 20.9). This view displays the markup for the Web Form. As you become more familiar with ASP.NET and building web sites in general, you might use **Source** view to perform high precision adjustments to your design or to program in the JavaScript language that executes in web browsers. For the purposes of this chapter, we'll keep things simple by working exclusively in **Design** mode. To switch to **Design** mode, you can click the **Design** Button at the bottom of the code editor window.

The Solution Explorer
The **Solution Explorer** (Fig. 20.10) shows the contents of the website. We expanded the node for WebTime.aspx to show you its code-behind file WebTime.aspx.cs. Visual Web Developer's **Solution Explorer** contains several buttons that differ from Visual C# Express. The **Copy Web Site** button opens a dialog that allows you to move the files in this project to another location, such as a remote web server. This is useful if you're developing the application on your local computer but want to make it available to the public from a different location. The **ASP.NET Configuration** button takes you to a web page called the **Web Site Administra-**

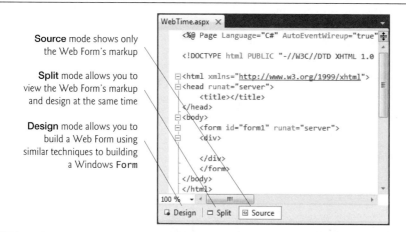

Source mode shows only the Web Form's markup

Split mode allows you to view the Web Form's markup and design at the same time

Design mode allows you to build a Web Form using similar techniques to building a Windows Form

Fig. 20.9 | Web Form in **Source** view.

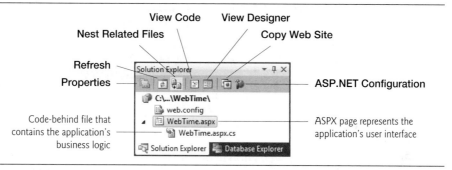

View Code   View Designer

Nest Related Files   Copy Web Site

Refresh

Properties   ASP.NET Configuration

Code-behind file that contains the application's business logic

ASPX page represents the application's user interface

Fig. 20.10 | Solution Explorer window for an **Empty Web Site** project after adding the Web Form WebTime.aspx.

tion Tool, where you can manipulate various settings and security options for your application. The **Nest Related Files** button organizes each Web Form and its code-behind file.

If the ASPX file is not open in the IDE, you can open it in **Design** mode three ways:

- double click it in the **Solution Explorer** then select the **Design** tab
- select it in the **Solution Explorer** and click the **View Designer** (▦) Button
- right click it in the **Solution Explorer** and select **View Designer**

To open the code-behind file in the code editor, you can

- double click it in the **Solution Explorer**
- select the ASPX file in the **Solution Explorer**, then click the **View Code** (▣) Button
- right click the code-behind file in the **Solution Explorer** and select **Open**

The Toolbox
Figure 20.11 shows the **Toolbox** displayed in the IDE when the project loads. Part (a) displays the beginning of the **Standard** list of web controls, and part (b) displays the remain-

ing web controls and the list of other control groups. We discuss specific controls listed in Fig. 20.11 as they're used throughout the chapter. Many of the controls have similar or identical names to the Windows Forms controls used in desktop applications.

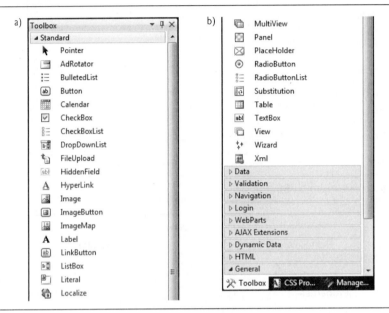

Fig. 20.11 | **Toolbox** in Visual Web Developer.

The Web Forms Designer

Figure 20.12 shows the initial Web Form in **Design** mode. You can drag and drop controls from the **Toolbox** onto the Web Form. You can also type at the current cursor location to add so-called static text to the web page. In response to such actions, the IDE generates the appropriate markup in the ASPX file.

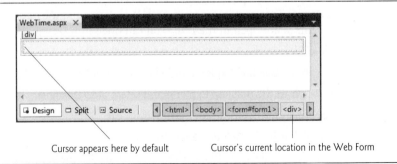

Fig. 20.12 | **Design** mode of the Web Forms Designer.

Step 3: Changing the Title of the Page

Before designing the Web Form's content, you'll change its title to A Simple Web Form Example. This title will be displayed in the web browser's title bar (see Fig. 20.4). It's typically also used by search engines like Google and Bing when they index real websites for searching. Every page should have a title. To change the title:

1. Ensure that the ASPX file is open in **Design** view.

2. View the Web Form's properties by selecting **DOCUMENT**, which represents the Web Form, from the drop-down list in the **Properties** window.

3. Modify the `Title` property in the **Properties** window by setting it to `A Simple Web Form Example`.

Designing a Page

Designing a Web Form is similar to designing a Windows Form. To add controls to the page, drag-and-drop them from the **Toolbox** onto the Web Form in **Design** view. The Web Form and each control are objects that have properties, methods and events. You can set these properties visually using the **Properties** window or programmatically in the code-behind file. You can also type text directly on a Web Form at the cursor location.

Controls and other elements are placed sequentially on a Web Form one after another in the order in which you drag-and-drop them onto the Web Form. The cursor indicates the insertion point in the page. If you want to position a control between existing text or controls, you can drop the control at a specific position between existing page elements. You can also rearrange controls with drag-and-drop actions in **Design** view. The positions of controls and other elements are relative to the Web Form's upper-left corner. This type of layout is known as relative positioning and it allows the browser to move elements and resize them based on the size of the browser window. Relative positioning is the default, and we'll use it throughout this chapter.

For precise control over the location and size of elements, you can use absolute positioning in which controls are located exactly where you drop them on the Web Form. If you wish to use absolute positioning:

1. Select **Tools > Options....**, to display the **Options** dialog.

2. If it isn't checked already, check the **Show all settings** checkbox.

3. Next, expand the **HTML Designer > CSS Styling** node and ensure that the checkbox labeled **Change positioning to absolute for controls added using Toolbox, paste or drag and drop** is selected.

Step 4: Adding Text and a `Label`

You'll now add some text and a `Label` to the Web Form. Perform the following steps to add the text:

1. Ensure that the Web Form is open in **Design** mode.

2. Type the following text at the current cursor location:

   `Current time on the Web server:`

3. Select the text you just typed, then select **Heading 2** from the **Block Format** Combo-Box (Fig. 20.13) to format this text as a heading that will appear in a larger bold font. In more complex pages, headings help you specify the relative importance of parts of that content—like sections in a book chapter.

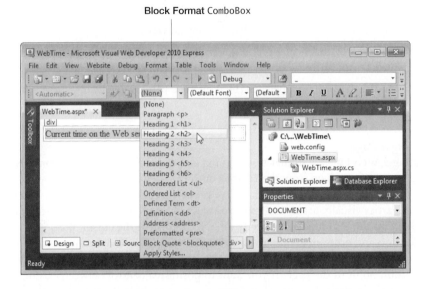

Fig. 20.13 | Changing the text to **Heading 2** heading.

4. Click to the right of the text you just typed and press the *Enter* key to start a new paragraph in the page. The Web Form should now appear as in Fig. 20.14.

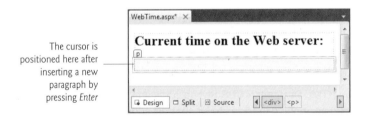

Fig. 20.14 | WebTime.aspx after inserting text and a new paragraph.

5. Next, drag a Label control from the **Toolbox** into the new paragraph or double click the Label control in the **Toolbox** to insert the Label at the current cursor position.

6. Using the **Properties** window, set the Label's (ID) property to timeLabel. This specifies the variable name that will be used to programmatically change the Label's Text.

7. Because, the Label's Text will be set programmatically, delete the current value of the Label's Text property. When a Label does not contain text, its name is displayed in square brackets in **Design** view (Fig. 20.15) as a placeholder for design and layout purposes. This text is not displayed at execution time.

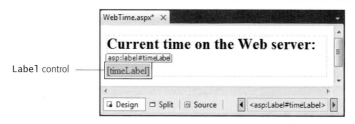

Fig. 20.15 | WebTime.aspx after adding a Label.

Step 5: Formatting the Label

Formatting in a web page is performed with CSS (Cascading Style Sheets). It's easy to use CSS to format text and elements in a Web Form via the tools built into Visual Web Developer. In this example, we'd like to change the Label's background color to black, its foreground color yellow and make its text size larger. To format the Label, perform the following steps:

1. Click the Label in **Design** view to ensure that it's selected.

2. Select **View > Other Windows > CSS Properties** to display the **CSS Properties** window at the left side of the IDE (Fig. 20.16).

Fig. 20.16 | CSS Properties window.

3. Right click in the **Applied Rules** box and select **New Style...** to display the **New Style** dialog (Fig. 20.17).

4. Type the new style's name—.timeStyle—in the **Selector:** ComboBox. Styles that apply to specific elements must be named with a dot (.) preceding the name. Such a style is called a CSS class.

5. Each item you can set in the **New Style** dialog is known as a CSS attribute. To change timeLabel's foreground color, select the **Font** category from the **Category** list, then select the yellow color swatch for the **color** attribute.

6. Next, change the **font-size** attribute to xx-large.

7. To change timeLabel's background color, select the **Background** category, then select the black color swatch for the **background-color** attribute.

New style's name

Font category allows you to
style an element's font

Background category allows
you to specify an element's
background color or
background image

The new style will be
applied to the currently
selected element in the page

Preview of what the
style will look like

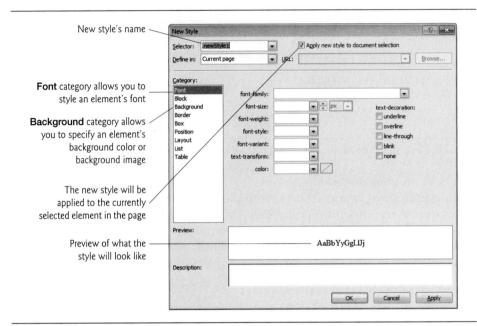

Fig. 20.17 | **New Style** dialog.

The **New Style** dialog should now appear as shown in Fig. 20.18. Click the **OK** Button to apply the style to the timeLabel so that it appears as shown in Fig. 20.19. Also, notice that the Label's CssClass property is now set to timeStyle in the **Properties** window.

Bold category
names indicate the
categories in which
CSS attribute
values have been
changed

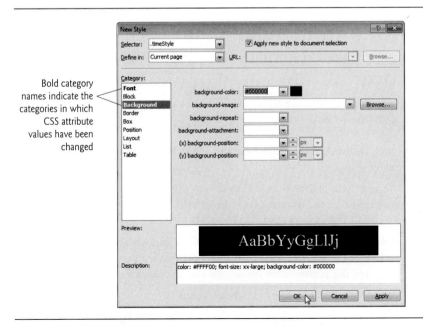

Fig. 20.18 | **New Style** dialog after changing the Label's style.

Fig. 20.19 │ **Design** view after changing the Label's style.

Step 6: Adding Page Logic
Now that you've designed the GUI, you'll write code in the code-behind file to obtain the server's time and display it on the Label. Open WebTime.aspx.cs by double clicking it in the **Solution Explorer**. In this example, you'll add an event handler to the code-behind file to handle the Web Form's **Init event**, which occurs when the page is requested by a web browser. The event handler for this event—named **Page_Init**—initialize the page. The only initialization required for this example is to set the timeLabel's Text property to the time on the web server computer. The code-behind file initally contains a Page_Load event handler. To create the Page_Init event handler, simply rename Page_Load as Page_Init. Then complete the event handler by inserting the following code in its body:

```
// display the server's current time in timeLabel
timeLabel.Text = DateTime.Now.ToString("hh:mm:ss");
```

*Step 7: Setting the **Start Page** and Running the Program*
To ensure that WebTime.aspx loads when you execute this application, right click it in the **Solution Explorer** and select **Set As Start Page**. You can now run the program in one of several ways. At the beginning of Fig. 20.4, you learned how to view the Web Form by typing *Ctrl + F5*. You can also right click an ASPX file in the **Solution Explorer** and select **View in Browser**. Both of these techniques execute the ASP.NET Development Server, open your default web browser and load the page into the browser, thus running the web application. The development server stops when you exit Visual Web Developer.

If problems occur when running your application, you can run it in debug mode by selecting **Debug > Start Debugging**, by clicking the **Start Debugging** Button (▶) or by typing *F5* to view the web page in a web browser with debugging enabled. You cannot debug a web application unless debugging is explicitly enabled in the application's **Web.config** file—a file that is generated when you create an ASP.NET web application. This file stores the application's configuration settings. You'll rarely need to manually modify Web.config. The first time you select **Debug > Start Debugging** in a project, a dialog appears and asks whether you want the IDE to modify the Web.config file to enable debugging. After you click **OK**, the IDE executes the application. You can stop debugging by selecting **Debug > Stop Debugging**.

Regardless of how you execute the web application, the IDE will compile the project before it executes. In fact, ASP.NET compiles your web page whenever it changes between HTTP requests. For example, suppose you browse the page, then modify the ASPX file or add code to the code-behind file. When you reload the page, ASP.NET recompiles the page on the server before returning the response to the browser. This important behavior ensures that clients always see the latest version of the page. You can manually compile an entire website by selecting **Build Web Site** from the **Debug** menu in Visual Web Developer.

20.4.2 Examining WebTime.aspx's Code-Behind File

Figure 20.20 presents the code-behind file WebTime.aspx.cs. Line 5 begins the declaration of class WebTime. In Visual C#, a class declaration can span multiple source-code files—the separate portions of the class declaration in each file are known as **partial classes**. The **partial modifier** indicates that the code-behind file is part of a larger class. Like Windows Forms applications, the rest of the class's code is generated for you based on your visual interactions to create the application's GUI in **Design** mode. That code is stored in other source code files as partial classes with the same name. The compiler assembles all the partial classes that have the same into a single class declaration.

Line 5 indicates that WebTime inherits from class **Page** in namespace **System.Web.UI**. This namespace contains classes and controls for building web-based applications. Class Page represents the default capabilities of each page in a web application—all pages inherit directly or indirectly from this class.

Lines 8–12 define the Page_Init event handler, which initializes the page in response to the page's Init event. The only initialization required for this page is to set the timeLabel's Text property to the time on the web server computer. The statement in line 11 retrieves the current time (DateTime.Now) and formats it as *hh:mm:ss*. For example, 9 AM is formatted as 09:00:00, and 2:30 PM is formatted as 02:30:00. As you'll see, variable timeLabel represents an ASP.NET Label control. The ASP.NET controls are defined in namespace **System.Web.UI.WebControls**.

```
 1   // Fig. 20.20: WebTime.aspx.cs
 2   // Code-behind file for a page that displays the web server's time.
 3   using System;
 4
 5   public partial class WebTime : System.Web.UI.Page
 6   {
 7      // initializes the contents of the page
 8      protected void Page_Init( object sender, EventArgs e )
 9      {
10         // display the server's current time in timeLabel
11         timeLabel.Text = DateTime.Now.ToString( "hh:mm:ss" );
12      } // end method Page_Init
13   } // end class WebTime
```

Fig. 20.20 | Code-behind file for a page that displays the web server's time.

20.5 Standard Web Controls: Designing a Form

This section introduces some of the web controls located in the **Standard** section of the **Toolbox** (Fig. 20.11). Figure 20.21 summarizes the controls used in the next example.

A Form Gathering User Input
Figure 20.22 depicts a form for gathering user input. This example does not perform any tasks—that is, no action occurs when the user clicks **Register**. As an exercise, we ask you

Web control	Description
TextBox	Gathers user input and displays text.
Button	Triggers an event when clicked.
HyperLink	Displays a hyperlink.
DropDownList	Displays a drop-down list of choices from which a user can select an item.
RadioButtonList	Groups radio buttons.
Image	Displays images (for example, PNG, GIF and JPG).

Fig. 20.21 | Commonly used web controls.

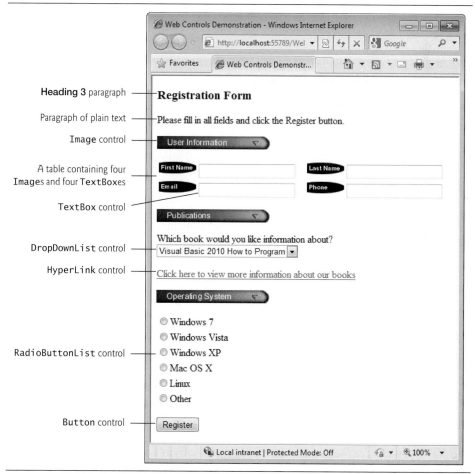

Fig. 20.22 | Web Form that demonstrates web controls.

to provide the functionality. Here we focus on the steps for adding these controls to a Web Form and for setting their properties. Subsequent examples demonstrate how to handle the events of many of these controls. To execute this application:

1. Select **Open Web Site...** from the **File** menu.

2. In the **Open Web Site** dialog, ensure that **File System** is selected, then navigate to this chapter's examples, select the `WebControls` folder and click the **Open Button**.

3. Select `WebControls.aspx` in the **Solution Explorer**, then type *Ctrl* + *F5* to execute the web application in your default web browser.

Creating the Web Site

To begin, follow the steps in Section 20.4.1 to create an **Empty Web Site** named WebControls, then add a Web Form named `WebControls.aspx` to the project. Set the document's `Title` property to "Web Controls Demonstration". To ensure that `WebControls.aspx` loads when you execute this application, right click it in the **Solution Explorer** and select **Set As Start Page**.

Adding the Images to the Project

The images used in this example are located in the `images` folder with this chapter's examples. Before you can display images in the Web Form, they must be added to your project. To add the `images` folder to your project:

1. Open Windows Explorer.

2. Locate and open this chapter's examples folder (ch20).

3. Drag the `images` folder from Windows Explorer into Visual Web Developer's **Solution Explorer** window and drop the folder on the name of your project.

The IDE will automatically copy the folder and its contents into your project.

Adding Text and an Image to the Form

Next, you'll begin creating the page. Perform the following steps:

1. First create the page's heading. At the current cursor position on the page, type the text "Registration Form", then use the **Block Format** ComboBox in the IDE's toolbar to change the text to **Heading 3** format.

2. Press *Enter* to start a new paragraph, then type the text "Please fill in all fields and click the Register button".

3. Press *Enter* to start a new paragraph, then double click the **Image** control in the Toolbox. This control inserts an image into a web page, at the current cursor position. Set the Image's (ID) property to `userInformationImage`. The **ImageUrl** property specifies the location of the image to display. In the **Properties** window, click the ellipsis for the `ImageUrl` property to display the **Select Image** dialog. Select the `images` folder under **Project folders:** to display the list of images. Then select the image `user.png`.

4. Click **OK** to display the image in **Design** view, then click to the right of the Image and press *Enter* to start a new paragraph.

Adding a Table to the Form

Form elements are often placed in tables for layout purposes—like the elements that represent the first name, last name, e-mail and phone information in Fig. 20.22. Next, you'll create a table with two rows and two columns in **Design** mode.

1. Select **Table > Insert Table** to display the **Insert Table** dialog (Fig. 20.23). This dialog allows you to configure the table's options.

2. Under **Size**, ensure that the values of **Rows** and **Columns** are both 2—these are the default values.

3. Click **OK** to close the **Insert Table** dialog and create the table.

By default, the contents of a table cell are aligned vertically in the middle of the cell. We changed the vertical alignment of all cells in the table by setting the valign property to top in the **Properties** window. This causes the content in each table cell to align with the top of the cell. You can set the valign property for each table cell individually or by selecting all the cells in the table at once, then changing the valign property's value.

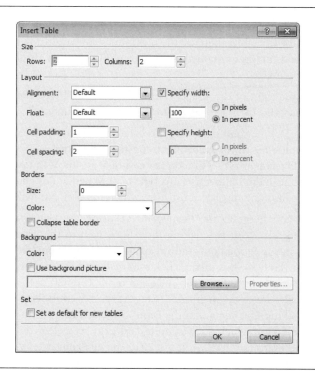

Fig. 20.23 | Insert Table dialog.

After creating the table, controls and text can be added to particular cells to create a neatly organized layout. Next, add Image and TextBox controls to each the four table cells as follows:

1. Click the table cell in the first row and first column of the table, then double click the Image control in the **Toolbox**. Set its (ID) property to firstNameImage and set its ImageUrl property to the image fname.png.

2. Next, double click the TextBox control in the **Toolbox**. Set its (ID) property to firstNameTextBox. As in Windows Forms, a **TextBox** control allows you to obtain text from the user and display text to the user

3. Repeat this process in the first row and second column, but set the Image's (ID) property to lastNameImage and its ImageUrl property to the image lname.png, and set the TextBox's (ID) property to lastNameTextBox.

4. Repeat *Steps 1* and *2* in the second row and first column, but set the Image's (ID) property to emailImage and its ImageUrl property to the image email.png, and set the TextBox's (ID) property to emailTextBox.

5. Repeat *Steps 1* and *2* in the second row and second column, but set the Image's (ID) property to phoneImage and its ImageUrl property to the image phone.png, and set the TextBox's (ID) property to phoneTextBox.

Creating the Publications Section of the Page

This section contains an Image, some text, a DropDownList control and a HyperLink control. Perform the following steps to create this section:

1. Click below the table, then use the techniques you've already learned in this section to add an Image named publicationsImage that displays the publications.png image.

2. Click to the right of the Image, then press *Enter* and type the text "Which book would you like information about?" in the new paragraph.

3. Hold the *Shift* key and press *Enter* to create a new line in the current paragraph, then double click the **DropDownList** control in the **Toolbox**. Set its (ID) property to booksDropDownList. This control is similar to the Windows Forms ComboBox control, but doesn't allow users to type text. When a user clicks the drop-down list, it expands and displays a list from which the user can make a selection.

4. You can add items to the DropDownList using the **ListItem Collection Editor**, which you can access by clicking the ellipsis next to the DropDownList's Items property in the **Properties** window, or by using the **DropDownList Tasks** smart-tag menu. To open this menu, click the small arrowhead that appears in the upper-right corner of the control in **Design** mode (Fig. 20.24). Visual Web Developer displays smart-tag menus for many ASP.NET controls to facilitate common tasks. Clicking **Edit Items...** in the **DropDownList Tasks** menu opens the **ListItem Collection Editor**, which allows you to add ListItem elements to the DropDownList. Add items for "Visual Basic 2010 How to Program", "Visual C# 2010 How to Program", "Java How to Program" and "C++ How to Program" by clicking the **Add** Button four times. For each item, select it, then set its Text property to one of the four book titles.

5. Click to the right of the DropDownList and press *Enter* to start a new paragraph, then double click the **HyperLink** control in the **Toolbox** to add a hyperlink to the

Fig. 20.24 | **DropDownList Tasks** smart-tag menu.

web page. Set its (ID) property to booksHyperLink and its Text property to "Click here to view more information about our books". Set the **NavigateUrl** property to http://www.deitel.com. This specifies the resource or web page that will be requested when the user clicks the HyperLink. Setting the **Target** property to _blank specifies that the requested web page should open in a new browser window. By default, HyperLink controls cause pages to open in the same browser window.

Completing the Page

Next you'll create the **Operating System** section of the page and the **Register** Button. This section contains a **RadioButtonList** control, which provides a series of radio buttons from which the user can select only one. The **RadioButtonList Tasks** smart-tag menu provides an **Edit Items...** link to open the **ListItem Collection Editor** so that you can create the items in the list. Perform the following steps:

1. Click to the right of the HyperLink control and press *Enter* to create a new paragraph, then add an Image named osImage that displays the os.png image.

2. Click to the right of the Image and press *Enter* to create a new paragraph, then add a RadioButtonList. Set its (ID) property to osRadioButtonList. Use the **ListItem Collection Editor** to add the items shown in Fig. 20.22.

3. Finally, click to the right of the RadioButtonList and press *Enter* to create a new paragraph, then add a **Button**. A Button web control represents a button that triggers an action when clicked. Set its (ID) property to registerButton and its Text property to Register. As stated earlier, clicking the **Register** button in this example does not do anything.

You can now execute the application (*Ctrl* + *F5*) to see the Web Form in your browser.

20.6 Validation Controls

This section introduces a different type of web control, called a **validation control** or **validator**, which determines whether the data in another web control is in the proper format. For example, validators can determine whether a user has provided information in a required field or whether a zip-code field contains exactly five digits. Validators provide a mechanism for validating user input on the client. When the page is sent to the client, the validator is converted into JavaScript that performs the validation in the client web browser. JavaScript is a scripting language that enhances the functionality of web pages and is typically executed on the client. Unfortunately, some client browsers might not support scripting or the user might disable it. For this reason, you should always perform validation on the server. ASP.NET validation controls can function on the client, on the server or both.

Validating Input in a Web Form

The Web Form in Fig. 20.25 prompts the user to enter a name, e-mail address and phone number. A website could use a form like this to collect contact information from visitors. After the user enters any data, but before the data is sent to the web server, validators ensure that the user *entered a value in each field* and that the e-mail address and phone-number values are in an acceptable format. In this example, (555) 123-4567, 555-123-4567 and 123-4567 are all considered valid phone numbers. Once the data is submitted, the web server responds by displaying a message that repeats the submitted information. A real business application would typically store the submitted data in a database or in a file on the server. We simply send the data back to the client to demonstrate that the server received the data. To execute this application:

1. Select **Open Web Site...** from the **File** menu.

2. In the **Open Web Site** dialog, ensure that **File System** is selected, then navigate to this chapter's examples, select the Validation folder and click the **Open** Button.

3. Select Validation.aspx in the **Solution Explorer**, then type *Ctrl + F5* to execute the web application in your default web browser.

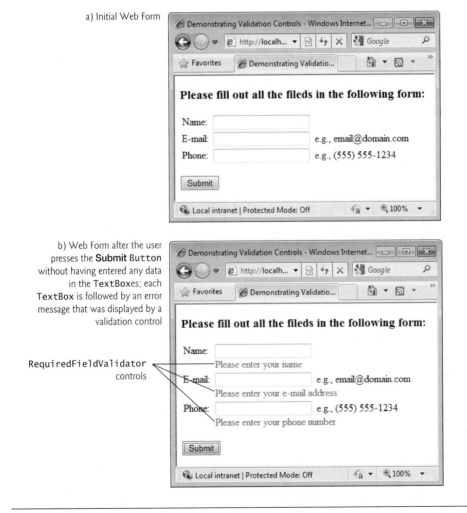

Fig. 20.25 | Validators in a Web Form that retrieves user contact information. (Part 1 of 2.)

c) Web Form after the user enters a name, an invalid e-mail address and an invalid phone number in the TextBoxes, then presses the **Submit** Button; the validation controls display error messages in response to the invalid e-mail and phone number values

RegularExpressionValidator controls

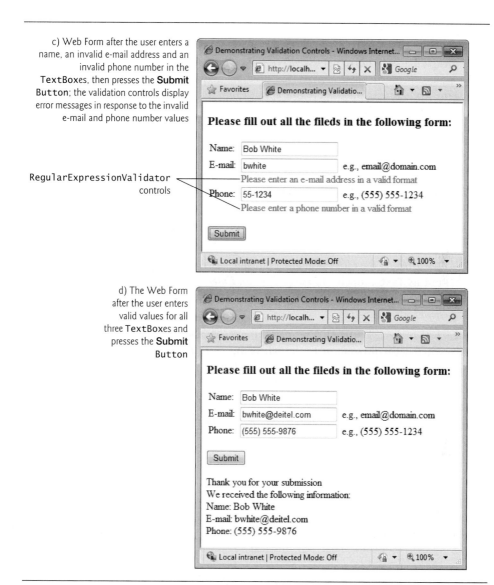

d) The Web Form after the user enters valid values for all three TextBoxes and presses the **Submit** Button

Fig. 20.25 | Validators in a Web Form that retrieves user contact information. (Part 2 of 2.)

In the sample output:

- Fig. 20.25(a) shows the initial Web Form
- Fig. 20.25(b) shows the result of submitting the form before typing any data in the TextBoxes
- Fig. 20.25(c) shows the results after entering data in each TextBox, but specifying an invalid e-mail address and invalid phone number
- Fig. 20.25(d) shows the results after entering valid values for all three TextBoxes and submitting the form.

Creating the Web Site

To begin, follow the steps in Section 20.4.1 to create an **Empty Web Site** named Valida-tion, then add a Web Form named Validation.aspx to the project. Set the document's Title property to "Demonstrating Validation Controls". To ensure that Valida-tion.aspx loads when you execute this application, right click it in the **Solution Explorer** and select **Set As Start Page**.

Creating the GUI

To create the page, perform the following steps:

1. Type "Please fill out all the fields in the following form:", then use the **Block Format** ComboBox in the IDE's toolbar to change the text to **Heading 3** for-mat and press *Enter* to create a new paragraph.

2. Insert a three row and two column table. You'll add elements to the table mo-mentarily.

3. Click below the table and add a Button. Set its (ID) property to submitButton and its Text property to Submit. Press *Enter* to create a new paragraph. By de-fault, a Button control in a Web Form sends the contents of the form back to the server for processing.

4. Add a Label. Set its (ID) property to outputLabel and clear its Text property—you'll set it programmatically when the user clicks the submitButton. Set the outputLabel's **Visible** property to false, so the Label does not appear in the client's browser when the page loads for the first time. You'll programmatically display this Label after the user submits valid data.

Next you'll add text and controls to the table you created in *Step 2* above. Perform the following steps:

1. In the left column, type the text "Name:" in the first row, "E-mail:" in the second row and "Phone:" in the third row.

2. In the right column of the first row, add a TextBox and set its (ID) property to nameTextBox.

3. In the right column of the second row, add a TextBox and set its (ID) property to emailTextBox. Then type the text "e.g., email@domain.com" to the right of the TextBox.

4. In the right column of the third row, add a TextBox and set its (ID) property to phoneTextBox. Then type the text "e.g., (555) 555-1234" to the right of the TextBox.

Using RequiredFieldValidator Controls

We use three **RequiredFieldValidator** controls (found in the **Validation** section of the **Toolbox**) to ensure that the name, e-mail address and phone number TextBoxes are not empty when the form is submitted. A RequiredFieldValidator makes an input control a required field. If such a field is empty, validation fails. Add a RequiredFieldValidator as follows:

1. Click to the right of the nameTextBox in the table and press *Enter* to move to the next line.

2. Add a `RequiredFieldValidator`, set its (`ID`) to `nameRequiredFieldValidator` and set the `ForeColor` property to Red.

3. Set the validator's **`ControlToValidate`** property to `nameTextBox` to indicate that this validator verifies the `nameTextBox`'s contents.

4. Set the validator's **`ErrorMessage`** property to `"Please enter your name"`. This is displayed on the Web Form only if the validation fails.

5. Set the validator's **`Display`** property to `Dynamic`, so the validator occupies space on the Web Form only when validation fails. When this occurs, space is allocated dynamically, causing the controls below the validator to shift downward to accommodate the `ErrorMessage`, as seen in Fig. 20.25(a)–(c).

Repeat these steps to add two more `RequiredFieldValidators` in the second and third rows of the table. Set their (`ID`) properties to `emailRequiredFieldValidator` and `phoneRequiredFieldValidator`, respectively, and set their `ErrorMessage` properties to `"Please enter your email address"` and `"Please enter your phone number"`, respectively.

Using *RegularExpressionValidator* Controls

This example also uses two **`RegularExpressionValidator`** controls to ensure that the e-mail address and phone number entered by the user are in a valid format. Visual Web Developer provides several *predefined* regular expressions that you can simply select to take advantage of this powerful validation control. Add a `RegularExpressionValidator` as follows:

1. Click to the right of the `emailRequiredFieldValidator` in the second row of the table and add a `RegularExpressionValidator`, then set its (`ID`) to `emailRegularExpressionValidator` and its `ForeColor` property to Red.

2. Set the `ControlToValidate` property to `emailTextBox` to indicate that this validator verifies the `emailTextBox`'s contents.

3. Set the validator's `ErrorMessage` property to `"Please enter an e-mail address in a valid format"`.

4. Set the validator's `Display` property to `Dynamic`, so the validator occupies space on the Web Form only when validation fails.

Repeat the preceding steps to add another `RegularExpressionValidator` in the third row of the table. Set its (`ID`) property to `phoneRegularExpressionValidator` and its `ErrorMessage` property to `"Please enter a phone number in a valid format"`, respectively.

A `RegularExpressionValidator`'s **`ValidationExpression`** property specifies the regular expression that validates the `ControlToValidate`'s contents. Clicking the ellipsis next to property `ValidationExpression` in the **Properties** window displays the **Regular Expression Editor** dialog, which contains a list of **Standard expressions** for phone numbers, zip codes and other formatted information. For the `emailRegularExpressionValidator`, we selected the standard expression **Internet e-mail address**. If the user enters text in the `emailTextBox` that does not have the correct format and either clicks in a different text box or attempts to submit the form, the `ErrorMessage` text is displayed in red.

For the `phoneRegularExpressionValidator`, we selected **U.S. phone number** to ensure that a phone number contains an optional three-digit area code either in parentheses and followed by an optional space or without parentheses and followed by a required hyphen. After an optional area code, a phone number must contain three digits, a hyphen and another four digits. For example, (555) 123-4567, 555-123-4567 and 123-4567 are all valid phone numbers.

Submitting the Web Form's Contents to the Server

If all five validators are successful (that is, each TextBox is filled in, and the e-mail address and phone number provided are valid), clicking the **Submit** button sends the form's data to the server. As shown in Fig. 20.25(d), the server then responds by displaying the submitted data in the outputLabel.

Examining the Code-Behind File for a Web Form That Receives User Input

Figure 20.26 shows the code-behind file for this application. Notice that this code-behind file does not contain any implementation related to the validators. We say more about this soon. In this example, we respond to the page's **Load** event to process the data submitted by the user. Like the Init event, the Load event occurs each time the page loads into a web browser—the difference is that on a postback, you cannot access the posted data in the controls. The event handler for this event is **Page_Load** (lines 8–33). The event handler for the Load event is created for you when you add a new Web Form. To complete the event handler, insert the code from Fig. 20.26.

```
1   // Fig. 20.26: Validation.aspx.cs
2   // Code-behind file for the form demonstrating validation controls.
3   using System;
4
5   public partial class Validation : System.Web.UI.Page
6   {
7      // Page_Load event handler executes when the page is loaded
8      protected void Page_Load( object sender, EventArgs e )
9      {
10        // if this is not the first time the page is loading
11        // (i.e., the user has already submitted form data)
12        if ( IsPostBack )
13        {
14           Validate(); // validate the form
15
16           // if the form is valid
17           if ( IsValid )
18           {
19              // retrieve the values submitted by the user
20              string name = nameTextBox.Text;
21              string email = emailTextBox.Text;
22              string phone = phoneTextBox.Text;
23
24              // show the the submitted values
25              outputLabel.Text = "Thank you for your submission<br/>" +
26                 "We received the following information:<br/>";
27              outputLabel.Text +=
28                 String.Format( "Name: {0}{1}E-mail:{2}{1}Phone:{3}",
29                    name, "<br/>", email, phone );
```

Fig. 20.26 | Code-behind file for the form demonstrating validation controls. (Part 1 of 2.)

```
30                      outputLabel.Visible = true; // display the output message
31                   } // end if
32                } // end if
33             } // end method Page_Load
34          } // end class Validation
```

Fig. 20.26 | Code-behind file for the form demonstrating validation controls. (Part 2 of 2.)

Differentiating Between the First Request to a Page and a Postback
Web programmers using ASP.NET often design their web pages so that the current page reloads when the user submits the form; this enables the program to receive input, process it as necessary and display the results in the same page when it's loaded the second time. These pages usually contain a form that, when submitted, sends the values of all the controls to the server and causes the current page to be requested again. This event is known as a **postback**. Line 12 uses the **IsPostBack** property of class Page to determine whether the page is being loaded due to a postback. The first time that the web page is requested, IsPostBack is false, and the page displays only the form for user input. When the postback occurs (from the user clicking **Submit**), IsPostBack is true.

Server-Side Web Form Validation
Server-side Web Form validation must be implemented programmatically. Line 14 calls the current Page's **Validate** method to validate the information in the request. This validates the information as specified by the validation controls in the Web Form. Line 17 uses the **IsValid** property of class Page to check whether the validation succeeded. If this property is set to true (that is, validation succeeded and the Web Form is valid), then we display the Web Form's information. Otherwise, the web page loads without any changes, except any validator that failed now displays its ErrorMessage.

Processing the Data Entered by the User
Lines 20–22 retrieve the values of nameTextBox, emailTextBox and phoneTextBox. When data is posted to the web server, the data that the user entered is accessible to the web application through the web controls' properties. Next, lines 25–29 set outputLabel's Text to display a message that includes the name, e-mail and phone information that was submitted to the server. In lines 25, 26 and 29, notice the use of <br/> rather than \n to start new lines in the outputLabel—
 is the markup for a line break in a web page. Line 30 sets the outputLabel's Visible property to true, so the user can see the thank-you message and submitted data when the page reloads in the client web browser.

20.7 Session Tracking

Originally, critics accused the Internet and e-business of failing to provide the customized service typically experienced in "brick-and-mortar" stores. To address this problem, businesses established mechanisms by which they could *personalize* users' browsing experiences, tailoring content to individual users. Businesses achieve this level of service by tracking each customer's movement through the Internet and combining the collected data with information provided by the consumer, including billing information, personal preferences, interests and hobbies.

Personalization

Personalization makes it possible for businesses to communicate effectively with their customers and also improves users' ability to locate desired products and services. Companies that provide content of particular interest to users can establish relationships with customers and build on those relationships over time. Furthermore, by targeting consumers with personal offers, recommendations, advertisements, promotions and services, businesses create customer loyalty. Websites can use sophisticated technology to allow visitors to customize home pages to suit their individual needs and preferences. Similarly, online shopping sites often store personal information for customers, tailoring notifications and special offers to their interests. Such services encourage customers to visit sites more frequently and make purchases more regularly.

Privacy

A trade-off exists between personalized business service and protection of privacy. Some consumers embrace tailored content, but others fear the possible adverse consequences if the info they provide to businesses is released or collected by tracking technologies. Consumers and privacy advocates ask: What if the business to which we give personal data sells or gives that information to another organization without our knowledge? What if we do not want our actions on the Internet—a supposedly anonymous medium—to be tracked and recorded by unknown parties? What if unauthorized parties gain access to sensitive private data, such as credit-card numbers or medical history? These are questions that must be addressed by programmers, consumers, businesses and lawmakers alike.

Recognizing Clients

To provide personalized services to consumers, businesses must be able to recognize clients when they request information from a site. As we have discussed, the request/response system on which the web operates is facilitated by HTTP. Unfortunately, HTTP is a *stateless protocol*—it *does not* provide information that would enable web servers to maintain state information regarding particular clients. This means that web servers cannot determine whether a request comes from a particular client or whether the same or different clients generate a series of requests.

To circumvent this problem, sites can provide mechanisms by which they identify individual clients. A session represents a unique client on a website. If the client leaves a site and then returns later, the client will still be recognized as the same user. When the user closes the browser, the session typically ends. To help the server distinguish among clients, each client must identify itself to the server. Tracking individual clients is known as **session tracking**. One popular session-tracking technique uses cookies (discussed in Section 20.7.1); another uses ASP.NET's HttpSessionState object (used in Section 20.7.2). Additional session-tracking techniques are beyond this book's scope.

20.7.1 Cookies

Cookies provide you with a tool for personalizing web pages. A cookie is a piece of data stored by web browsers in a small text file on the user's computer. A cookie maintains information about the client during and between browser sessions. The first time a user visits the website, the user's computer might receive a cookie from the server; this cookie is then reactivated each time the user revisits that site. The collected information is intended to be an anonymous record containing data that is used to personalize the user's future visits to the site. For example, cookies in a shopping application might store unique identifiers for users. When a user adds items to an online shopping cart or performs another task resulting in a request to the web server, the server receives a cookie containing the user's unique identifier. The server then uses the unique identifier to locate the shopping cart and perform any necessary processing.

In addition to identifying users, cookies also can indicate users' shopping preferences. When a Web Form receives a request from a client, the Web Form can examine the cookie(s) it sent to the client during previous communications, identify the user's preferences and immediately display products of interest to the client.

Every HTTP-based interaction between a client and a server includes a header containing information either about the request (when the communication is from the client to the server) or about the response (when the communication is from the server to the client). When a Web Form receives a request, the header includes information such as the request type and any cookies that have been sent previously from the server to be stored on the client machine. When the server formulates its response, the header information contains any cookies the server wants to store on the client computer and other information, such as the MIME type of the response.

The **expiration date** of a cookie determines how long the cookie remains on the client's computer. If you do not set an expiration date for a cookie, the web browser maintains the cookie for the duration of the browsing session. Otherwise, the web browser maintains the cookie until the expiration date occurs. Cookies are deleted when they **expire**.

Portability Tip 20.1

Users may disable cookies in their web browsers to help ensure their privacy. Such users will experience difficulty using web applications that depend on cookies to maintain state information.

20.7.2 Session Tracking with HttpSessionState

The next web application demonstrates session tracking using the .NET class **Http-SessionState**. When you execute this application, the Options.aspx page (Fig. 20.27(a)), which is the application's **Start Page**, allows the user to select a programming language from a group of radio buttons. [Note: You might need to right click Options.aspx in the **Solution Explorer** and select **Set As Start Page** before running this application.] When the user clicks **Submit**, the selection is sent to the web server for processing. The web server uses an HttpSessionState object to store the chosen language and the ISBN number for one of our books on that topic. Each user that visits the site has a unique HttpSessionState object, so the selections made by one user are maintained separately from all other users. After storing the selection, the server returns the page to the browser (Fig. 20.27(b)) and displays the user's selection and some information about the user's unique session (which we show just for demonstration purposes). The page also includes links that allow the user to choose between selecting another programming language or viewing the Recommendations.aspx page (Fig. 20.27(e)), which lists recommended books pertaining to the programming language(s) that the user selected previously. If the user clicks the link for book recommendations, the information stored in the user's unique `HttpSessionState` object is read and used to form the list of recommendations. To test this application:

1. Select **Open Web Site...** from the **File** menu.

2. In the **Open Web Site** dialog, ensure that **File System** is selected, then navigate to this chapter's examples, select the `Sessions` folder and click the **Open** Button.

3. Select `Options.aspx` in the **Solution Explorer**, then type *Ctrl + F5* to execute the web application in your default web browser.

Creating the Web Site

To begin, follow the steps in Section 20.4.1 to create an **Empty Web Site** named `Sessions`, then add two Web Forms named `Options.aspx` and `Recommendations.aspx` to the project. Set the `Options.aspx` document's `Title` property to `"Sessions"` and the `Recommendations.aspx` document's `Title` property to `"Book Recommendations"`. To ensure that `Options.aspx` is the first page to load for this application, right click it in the **Solution Explorer** and select **Set As Start Page**.

a) User selects a language from the `Options.aspx` page, then presses **Submit** to send the selection to the server

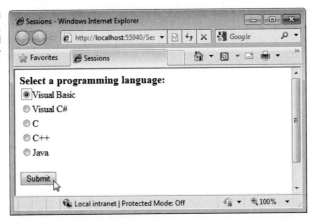

b) `Options.aspx` page is updated to hide the controls for selecting a language and to display the user's selection; the user clicks the hyperlink to return to the list of languages and make another selection

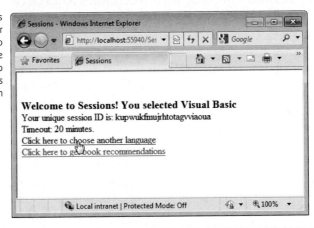

Fig. 20.27 | ASPX file that presents a list of programming languages. (Part 1 of 2.)

c) User selects another language from the Options.aspx page, then presses **Submit** to send the selection to the server

d) Options.aspx page is updated to hide the controls for selecting a language and to display the user's selection; the user clicks the hyperlink to get a list of book recommendations

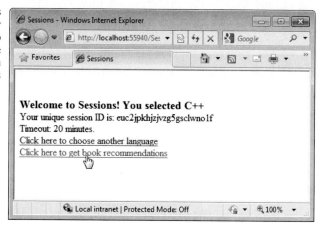

e) Recommendations.aspx displays the list of recommended books based on the user's selections

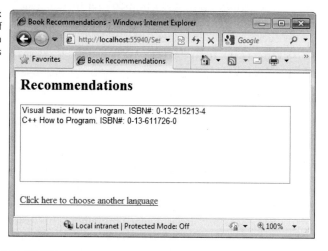

Fig. 20.27 | ASPX file that presents a list of programming languages. (Part 2 of 2.)

20.7.3 Options.aspx: Selecting a Programming Language

The Options.aspx page Fig. 20.27(a) contains the following controls arranged vertically:

1. A Label with its (ID) property set to promptLabel and its Text property set to "Select a programming language:". We used the techniques shown in *Step 5* of Section 20.4.1 to create a CSS style for this label named .labelStyle, and set the style's font-size attribute to large and the font-weight attribute to bold.

2. The user selects a programming language by clicking one of the radio buttons in a RadioButtonList. Each radio button has a Text property and a Value property. The Text property is displayed next to the radio button and the Value property represents a value that is sent to the server when the user selects that radio button and submits the form. In this example, we'll use the Value property to represent the ISBN for the recommended book. Create a RadioButtonList with its (ID) property set to languageList. Use the **ListItem Collection Editor** to add five radio buttons with their Text properties set to Visual Basic, Visual C#, C, C++ and Java, and their Value properties set to 0-13-215213-4, 0-13-605322-X, 0-13-512356-2, 0-13-611726-0 and 0-13-605306-8, respectively

3. A Button with its (ID) property set to submitButton and its Text property set to Submit. In this example, we'll handle this Button's Click event. You can create its event handler by double clicking the Button in **Design** view.

4. A Label with its (ID) property set to responseLabel and its Text property set to "Welcome to Sessions!". This Label should be placed immediately to the right of the Button so that the Label appears at the top of the page when we hide the preceding controls on the page. Reuse the CSS style you created in *Step 1* by setting this Label's CssClass property to labelStyle.

5. Two more Labels with their (ID) properties set to idLabel and timeoutLabel, respectively. Clear the text in each Label's Text property—you'll set these programmatically with information about the current user's session.

6. A HyperLink with its (ID) property set to languageLink and its Text property set to "Click here to choose another language". Set its NavigateUrl property by clicking the ellipsis next to the property in the **Properties** window and selecting Options.aspx from the **Select URL** dialog.

7. A HyperLink with its (ID) property set to recommendationsLink and its Text property set to "Click here to get book recommendations". Set its NavigateUrl property by clicking the ellipsis next to the property in the **Properties** window and selecting Recommendations.aspx from the **Select URL** dialog.

8. Initially, the controls in *Steps 4–7* will not be displayed, so set each control's Visible property to false.

Session Property of a Page

Every Web Form includes a user-specific HttpSessionState object, which is accessible through property **Session** of class Page. Throughout this section, we use this property to manipulate the current user's HttpSessionState object. When a page is first requested, a unique HttpSessionState object is created by ASP.NET and assigned to the Page's Session property.

Code-Behind File for **Options.aspx**
Fig. 20.28 presents the code-behind file for the Options.aspx page. When this page is re-quested, the Page_Load event handler (lines 10–40) executes before the response is sent to the client. Since the first request to a page is not a postback, the code in lines 16–39 *does not* execute the first time the page loads.

```csharp
1   // Fig. 20.28: Options.aspx.cs
2   // Processes user's selection of a programming language by displaying
3   // links and writing information in a Session object.
4   using System;
5
6   public partial class Options : System.Web.UI.Page
7   {
8      // if postback, hide form and display links to make additional
9      // selections or view recommendations
10     protected void Page_Load( object sender, EventArgs e )
11     {
12        if ( IsPostBack )
13        {
14           // user has submitted information, so display message
15           // and appropriate hyperlinks
16           responseLabel.Visible = true;
17           idLabel.Visible = true;
18           timeoutLabel.Visible = true;
19           languageLink.Visible = true;
20           recommendationsLink.Visible = true;
21
22           // hide other controls used to make language selection
23           promptLabel.Visible = false;
24           languageList.Visible = false;
25           submitButton.Visible = false;
26
27           // if the user made a selection, display it in responseLabel
28           if ( languageList.SelectedItem != null )
29              responseLabel.Text += " You selected " +
30                 languageList.SelectedItem.Text;
31           else
32              responseLabel.Text += " You did not select a language.";
33
34           // display session ID
35           idLabel.Text = "Your unique session ID is: " + Session.SessionID;
36
37           // display the timeout
38           timeoutLabel.Text = "Timeout: " + Session.Timeout + " minutes.";
39        } // end if
40     } // end method Page_Load
41
42     // record the user's selection in the Session
43     protected void submitButton_Click( object sender, EventArgs e )
44     {
```

Fig. 20.28 | Process user's selection of a programming language by displaying links and writing information in an HttpSessionState object. (Part 1 of 2.)

```
45        // if the user made a selection
46        if ( languageList.SelectedItem != null )
47           // add name/value pair to Session
48           Session.Add( languageList.SelectedItem.Text,
49              languageList.SelectedItem.Value );
50     } // end method submitButton_Click
51  } // end class Options
```

Fig. 20.28 | Process user's selection of a programming language by displaying links and writing information in an HttpSessionState object. (Part 2 of 2.)

Postback Processing

When the user presses **Submit**, a postback occurs. The form is submitted to the server and Page_Load executes. Lines 16–20 display the controls shown in Fig. 20.27(b) and lines 23–25 hide the controls shown in Fig. 20.27(a). Next, lines 28–32 ensure that the user selected a language and, if so, display a message in the responseLabel indicating the selection. Otherwise, the message "You did not select a language" is displayed.

The ASP.NET application contains information about the HttpSessionState object (property Session of the Page object) for the current client. The object's **SessionID** property (displayed in line 35) contains the **unique session ID**—a sequence of random letters and numbers. The first time a client connects to the web server, a unique session ID is created for that client and a temporary cookie is written to the client so the server can identify the client on subsequent requests. When the client makes additional requests, the client's session ID from that temporary cookie is compared with the session IDs stored in the web server's memory to retrieve the client's HttpSessionState object. HttpSessionState property **Timeout** (displayed in line 38) specifies the maximum amount of time that an HttpSessionState object can be inactive before it's discarded. By default, if the user does not interact with this web application for 20 minutes, the HttpSessionState object is discarded by the server and a new one will be created if the user interacts with the application again. Figure 20.29 lists some common HttpSessionState properties.

Properties	Description
Count	Specifies the number of key/value pairs in the Session object.
IsNewSession	Indicates whether this is a new session (that is, whether the session was created during loading of this page).
Keys	Returns a collection containing the Session object's keys.
SessionID	Returns the session's unique ID.
Timeout	Specifies the maximum number of minutes during which a session can be inactive (that is, no requests are made) before the session expires. By default, this property is set to 20 minutes.

Fig. 20.29 | HttpSessionState properties.

Method submitButton_Click

In this example, we wish to store the user's selection in an HttpSessionState object when the user clicks the **Submit** Button. The submitButton_Click event handler (lines 43–50) adds a key/value pair to the `HttpSessionState` object for the current user, specifying the language chosen and the ISBN number for a book on that language. The `HttpSession-State` object is a dictionary—a data structure that stores **key/value pairs**. A program uses the key to store and retrieve the associated value in the dictionary.

The key/value pairs in an `HttpSessionState` object are often referred to as **session items**. They're placed in an `HttpSessionState` object by calling its **Add** method. If the user made a selection (line 46), lines 48–49 get the selection and its corresponding value from the `languageList` by accessing its `SelectedItem`'s `Text` and `Value` properties, respectively, then call `HttpSessionState` method `Add` to add this name/value pair as a session item in the `HttpSessionState` object (`Session`).

If the application adds a session item that has the same name as an item previously stored in the `HttpSessionState` object, the session item is replaced—session item names *must* be unique. Another common syntax for placing a session item in the `HttpSessionState` object is Session[*Name*] = *Value*. For example, we could have replaced lines 48–49 with

```
Session[ languageList.SelectedItem.Text ] =
    languageList.SelectedItem.Value
```

Software Engineering Observation 20.1

A Web Form should not use instance variables to maintain client state information, because each new request or postback is handled by a new instance of the page. Instead, maintain client state information in `HttpSessionState` objects, because such objects are specific to each client.

Software Engineering Observation 20.2

A benefit of using `HttpSessionState` objects (rather than cookies) is that they can store any type of object (not just `String`s) as attribute values. This provides you with increased flexibility in determining the type of state information to maintain for clients.

20.7.4 Recommendations.aspx: Displaying Recommendations Based on Session Values

After the postback of `Options.aspx`, the user may request book recommendations. The book-recommendations hyperlink forwards the user to the page `Recommendations.aspx` (Fig. 20.27(e)) to display the recommendations based on the user's language selections. The page contains the following controls arranged vertically:

1. A `Label` with its (`ID`) property set to `recommendationsLabel` and its `Text` property set to `"Recommendations"`. We created a CSS style for this label named `.label-Style`, and set the `font-size` attribute to `x-large` and the `font-weight` attribute to `bold`. (See *Step 5* in Section 20.4.1 for information on creating a CSS style.)

2. A `ListBox` with its (`ID`) property set to `booksListBox`. We created a CSS style for this label named `.listBoxStyle`. In the **Position** category, we set the `width` attribute to `450px` and the `height` attribute to `125px`. The `px` indicates that the measurement is in pixels.

3. A `HyperLink` with its (`ID`) property set to `languageLink` and its `Text` property set to `"Click here to choose another language"`. Set its `NavigateUrl` property

by clicking the ellipsis next to the property in the **Properties** window and selecting Options.aspx from the **Select URL** dialog. When the user clicks this link, the Options.aspx page will be reloaded. Requesting the page in this manner *is not* considered a postback, so the original form in Fig. 20.27(a) will be displayed.

Code-Behind File for *Recommendations.aspx*

Figure 20.30 presents the code-behind file for Recommendations.aspx. Event handler Page_Init (lines 8–29) retrieves the session information. If a user has not selected a language in the Options.aspx page, the HttpSessionState object's **Count** property will be 0 (line 11). This property provides the number of session items contained in a HttpSessionState object. If the Count is 0, then we display the text **No Recommendations** (line 22), clear the ListBox and hide it (lines 23–24), and update the Text of the HyperLink back to Options.aspx (line 27).

```
1   // Fig. 20.30: Recommendations.aspx.cs
2   // Creates book recommendations based on a Session object.
3   using System;
4
5   public partial class Recommendations : System.Web.UI.Page
6   {
7      // read Session items and populate ListBox with recommendations
8      protected void Page_Init( object sender, EventArgs e )
9      {
10        // determine whether Session contains any information
11        if ( Session.Count != 0 )
12        {
13           // display Session's name-value pairs
14           foreach ( string keyName in Session.Keys )
15              booksListBox.Items.Add( keyName +
16                 " How to Program. ISBN#: " + Session[ keyName ] );
17        } // end if
18        else
19        {
20           // if there are no session items, no language was chosen, so
21           // display appropriate message and clear and hide booksListBox
22           recommendationsLabel.Text = "No Recommendations";
23           booksListBox.Items.Clear();
24           booksListBox.Visible = false;
25
26           // modify languageLink because no language was selected
27           languageLink.Text = "Click here to choose a language";
28        } // end else
29     } // end method Page_Init
30  } // end class Recommendations
```

Fig. 20.30 | Session data used to provide book recommendations to the user.

If the user chose at least one language, the loop in lines 14–16 iterates through the HttpSessionState object's keys (line 14) by accessing the HttpSessionState's **Keys** property, which returns a collection containing all the keys in the session. Lines 15–16 concatenate the keyName, the String " How to Program. ISBN#: " and the key's corresponding value, which is returned by Session(keyName). This String is the recommendation that is added to the ListBox.

20.8 Case Study: Database-Driven ASP.NET Guestbook

Many websites allow users to provide feedback about the website in a guestbook. Typically, users click a link on the website's home page to request the guestbook page. This page usually consists of a form that contains fields for the user's name, e-mail address, message/feedback and so on. Data submitted on the guestbook form is then stored in a database located on the server.

In this section, we create a guestbook Web Form application. The GUI (Fig. 20.31) contains a **GridView** data control, which displays all the entries in the guestbook in tabular format. This control is located in the **Toolbox**'s **Data** section. We explain how to create and configure this data control shortly. The GridView displays **abc** in **Design** mode to indicate data that will be retrieved from a data source at runtime. You'll learn how to create and configure the GridView shortly.

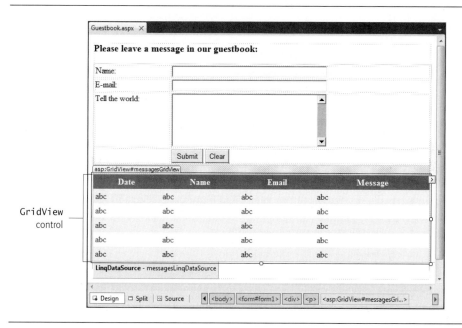

Fig. 20.31 | Guestbook application GUI in **Design** mode.

The Guestbook Database
The application stores the guestbook information in a SQL Server database called Guestbook.mdf located on the web server. (We provide this database in the databases folder with this chapter's examples.) The database contains a single table named Messages.

Testing the Application
To test this application:

1. Select **Open Web Site...** from the **File** menu.

2. In the **Open Web Site** dialog, ensure that **File System** is selected, then navigate to this chapter's examples, select the Guestbook folder and click the **Open** Button.

3. Select Guestbook.aspx in the **Solution Explorer**, then type *Ctrl + F5* to execute the web application in your default web browser.

Figure 20.32(a) shows the user submitting a new entry. Figure 20.32(b) shows the new entry as the last row in the GridView.

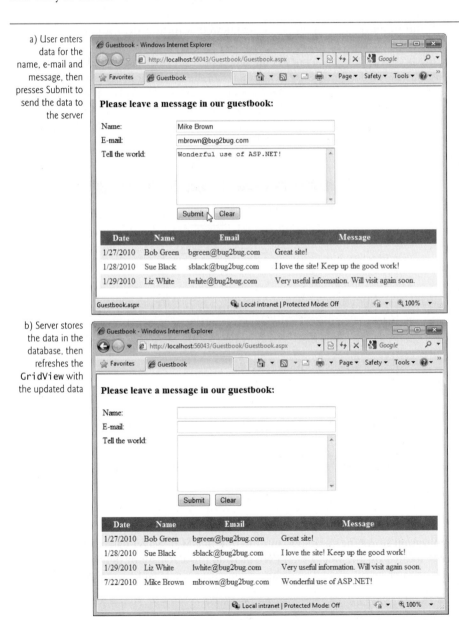

a) User enters data for the name, e-mail and message, then presses Submit to send the data to the server

b) Server stores the data in the database, then refreshes the GridView with the updated data

Fig. 20.32 | Sample execution of the **Guestbook** application.

20.8.1 Building a Web Form that Displays Data from a Database

You'll now build this GUI and set up the data binding between the `GridView` control and the database. We discuss the code-behind file in Section 20.8.2. To build the guestbook application, perform the following steps:

Step 1: Creating the Web Site

To begin, follow the steps in Section 20.4.1 to create an **Empty Web Site** named `Guestbook` then add a Web Form named `Guestbook.aspx` to the project. Set the document's `Title` property to `"Guestbook"`. To ensure that `Guestobook.aspx` loads when you execute this application, right click it in the **Solution Explorer** and select **Set As Start Page**.

Step 2: Creating the Form for User Input

In **Design** mode, add the text `Please leave a message in our guestbook:`, then use the **Block Format** ComboBox in the IDE's toolbar to change the text to **Heading 3** format. Insert a table with four rows and two columns, configured so that the text in each cell aligns with the top of the cell. Place the appropriate text (see Fig. 20.31) in the top three cells in the table's left column. Then place `TextBoxes` named `nameTextBox`, `emailTextBox` and `messageText-Box` in the top three table cells in the right column. Configure the `TextBoxes` as follows:

- Set the `nameTextBox`'s width to 300px.
- Set the `emailTextBox`'s width to 300px.
- Set the `messageTextBox`'s width to 300px and height to 100px. Also set this control's `TextMode` property to `MultiLine` so the user can type a message containing multiple lines of text.

Finally, add `Buttons` named `submitButton` and `clearButton` to the bottom-right table cell. Set the buttons' `Text` properties to `Submit` and `Clear`, respectively. We discuss the buttons' event handlers when we present the code-behind file. You can create these event handlers now by double clicking each `Button` in **Design** view.

Step 3: Adding a `GridView` Control to the Web Form

Add a `GridView` named `messagesGridView` that will display the guestbook entries. This control appears in the **Data** section of the **Toolbox**. The colors for the `GridView` are specified through the **Auto Format...** link in the **GridView Tasks** smart-tag menu that opens when you place the `GridView` on the page. Clicking this link displays an **AutoFormat** dialog with several choices. In this example, we chose **Professional**. We show how to set the `GridView`'s data source (that is, where it gets the data to display in its rows and columns) shortly.

Step 4: Adding a Database to an ASP.NET Web Application

To use a SQL Server Express database file in an ASP.NET web application, you must first add the file to the project's `App_Data` folder. For security reasons, this folder can be accessed only by the web application on the server—clients cannot access this folder over a network. The web application interacts with the database on behalf of the client.

The **Empty Web Site** template does not create the `App_Data` folder. To create it, right click the project's name in the **Solution Explorer**, then select **Add ASP.NET Folder > App_Data**. Next, add the `Guestbook.mdf` file to the `App_Data` folder. You can do this in one of two ways:

- Drag the file from Windows Explorer and drop it on the App_Data folder.

- Right click the App_Data folder in the **Solution Explorer** and select **Add Existing Item...** to display the **Add Existing Item** dialog, then navigate to the databases folder with this chapter's examples, select the Guestbook.mdf file and click **Add**. [*Note:* Ensure that **Data Files** is selected in the ComboBox above or next to the **Add Button** in the dialog; otherwise, the database file will not be displayed in the list of files.]

Step 5: Creating the LINQ to SQL Classes

You'll use LINQ to interact with the database. To create the LINQ to SQL classes for the Guestbook database:

1. Right click the project in the **Solution Explorer** and select **Add New Item...** to display the **Add New Item** dialog.

2. In the dialog, select **LINQ to SQL Classes**, enter Guestbook.dbml as the **Name**, and click **Add**. A dialog appears asking if you would like to put your new LINQ to SQL classes in the App_Code folder; click **Yes**. The IDE will create an App_Code folder and place the LINQ to SQL classes information in that folder.

3. In the **Database Explorer** window, drag the Guestbook database's Messages table from the **Database Explorer** onto the **Object Relational Designer**. Finally, save your project by selecting **File > Save All**.

Step 6: Binding the GridView to the Messages Table of the Guestbook Database

You can now configure the GridView to display the database's data.

1. In the **GridView Tasks** smart-tag menu, select **<New data source...>** from the **Choose Data Source** ComboBox to display the **Data Source Configuration Wizard** dialog.

2. In this example, we use a **LinqDataSource** control that allows the application to interact with the Guestbook.mdf database through LINQ. Select **LINQ**, then set the ID of the data source to messagesLinqDataSource and click **OK** to begin the **Configure Data Source** wizard.

3. In the **Choose a Context Object** screen, ensure that GuestbookDataContext is selected in the ComboBox, then click **Next >**.

4. The **Configure Data Selection** screen (Fig. 20.33) allows you to specify which data the LinqDataSource should retrieve from the data context. Your choices on this page design a Select LINQ query. The **Table** drop-down list identifies a table in the data context. The Guestbook data context contains one table named Messages, which is selected by default. *If you haven't saved your project* since creating your LINQ to SQL classes (*Step 5*), the list of tables *will not appear*. In the **Select** pane, ensure that the checkbox marked with an asterisk (*) is selected to indicate that you want to retrieve all the columns in the Messages table.

5. Click the **Advanced...** button, then select the **Enable the LinqDataSource to perform automatic inserts** CheckBox and click **OK**. This configures the LinqDataSource control to automatically insert new data into the database when new data is inserted in the data context. We discuss inserting new guestbook entries based on users' form submissions shortly.

6. Click **Finish** to complete the wizard.

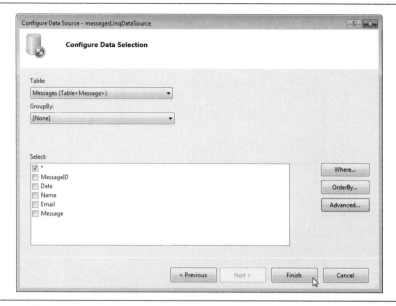

Fig. 20.33 | Configuring the query used by the `LinqDataSource` to retrieve data.

A control named `messagesLinqDataSource` now appears on the Web Form directly below the `GridView` (Fig. 20.34). It's represented in **Design** mode as a gray box containing its type and name. It will *not* appear on the web page—the gray box simply provides a way to manipulate the control visually through **Design** mode—similar to how the objects in the component tray are used in **Design** mode for a Windows Forms application.

The `GridView` now has column headers that correspond to the columns in the `Messages` table. The rows each contain either a number (which signifies an autoincremented column) or **abc** (which indicates string data). The actual data from the `Guestbook.mdf` database file will appear in these rows when you view the ASPX file in a web browser.

Step 7: Modifying the Columns of the Data Source Displayed in the `GridView`
It's not necessary for site visitors to see the `MessageID` column when viewing past guestbook entries—this column is merely a unique primary key required by the `Messages` table within the database. So, let's modify the `GridView` to prevent this column from displaying on the Web Form. We'll also modify the column **Message1** to read **Message**.

1. In the **GridView Tasks** smart tag menu, click **Edit Columns** to display the **Fields** dialog (Fig. 20.35).

2. Select **MessageID** in the **Selected fields** pane, then click the ⊠ Button. This removes the `MessageID` column from the `GridView`.

3. Next select **Message1** in the **Selected fields** pane and change its `HeaderText` property to `Message`. The IDE renamed this field to prevent a naming conflict in the LINQ to SQL classes.

4. Click **OK** to return to the main IDE window, then set the `Width` property of the `GridView` to 650px.

The `GridView` should now appear as shown in Fig. 20.31.

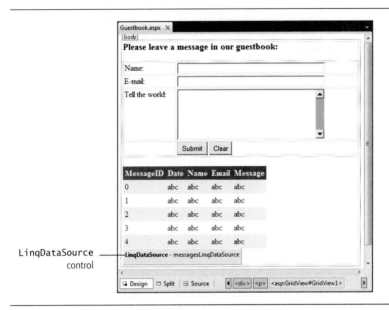

Fig. 20.34 | **Design** mode displaying LinqDataSource control for a GridView.

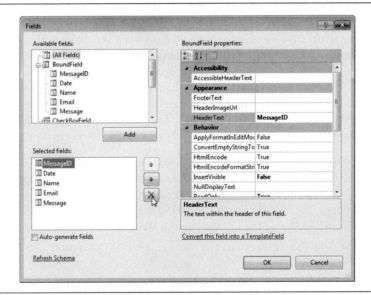

Fig. 20.35 | Removing the MessageID column from the GridView.

20.8.2 Modifying the Code-Behind File for the Guestbook Application

After building the Web Form and configuring the data controls used in this example, double click the **Submit** and **Clear** buttons in **Design** view to create their corresponding Click event handlers in the code-behind file (Fig. 20.36). The IDE generates empty event handlers, so we must add the appropriate code to make these buttons work properly. The event handler for clearButton (lines 37–42) clears each TextBox by setting its Text property to an empty string. This resets the form for a new guestbook submission.

```
1    // Fig. 20.36: Guestbook.aspx.cs
2    // Code-behind file that defines event handlers for the guestbook.
3    using System;
4    using System.Collections.Specialized; // for class ListDictionary
5
6    public partial class Guestbook : System.Web.UI.Page
7    {
8       // Submit Button adds a new guestbook entry to the database,
9       // clears the form and displays the updated list of guestbook entries
10      protected void submitButton_Click( object sender, EventArgs e )
11      {
12         // create dictionary of parameters for inserting
13         ListDictionary insertParameters = new ListDictionary();
14
15         // add current date and the user's name, e-mail address
16         // and message to dictionary of insert parameters
17         insertParameters.Add( "Date", DateTime.Now.ToShortDateString() );
18         insertParameters.Add( "Name", nameTextBox.Text );
19         insertParameters.Add( "Email", emailTextBox.Text );
20         insertParameters.Add( "Message1", messageTextBox.Text );
21
22         // execute an INSERT LINQ statement to add a new entry to the
23         // Messages table in the Guestbook data context that contains the
24         // current date and the user's name, e-mail address and message
25         messagesLinqDataSource.Insert( insertParameters );
26
27         // clear the TextBoxes
28         nameTextBox.Text = String.Empty;
29         emailTextBox.Text = String.Empty;
30         messageTextBox.Text = String.Empty;
31
32         // update the GridView with the new database table contents
33         messagesGridView.DataBind();
34      } // submitButton_Click
35
36      // Clear Button clears the Web Form's TextBoxes
37      protected void clearButton_Click( object sender, EventArgs e )
38      {
39         nameTextBox.Text = String.Empty;
40         emailTextBox.Text = String.Empty;
41         messageTextBox.Text = String.Empty;
42      } // clearButton_Click
43   } // end class Guestbook
```

Fig. 20.36 | Code-behind file for the guestbook application.

Lines 10–34 contain submitButton's event-handling code, which adds the user's information to the Guestbook database's Messages table. To use the values of the TextBoxes on the Web Form as the parameter values inserted into the database, we must create a **ListDictionary** of insert parameters that are key/value pairs.

Line 13 creates a ListDictionary object—a set of key/value pairs that is implemented as a linked list and is intended for dictionaries that store 10 or fewer keys. Lines 17–20 use the ListDictionary's Add method to store key/value pairs that represent each of the four insert parameters—the current date and the user's name, e-mail address, and message. The keys must match the names of the columns of the Messages table in the .dbml file. Invoking the LinqDataSource method Insert (line 25) inserts the data in the data context, adding a row to the Messages table and automatically updating the database. We pass the ListDictionary object as an argument to the Insert method to specify the insert parameters. After the data is inserted into the database, lines 28–30 clear the Text-Boxes, and line 33 invokes messagesGridView's **DataBind method** to refresh the data that the GridView displays. This causes messagesLinqDataSource (the GridView's source) to execute its Select command to obtain the Messages table's newly updated data.

20.9 Case Study Introduction: ASP.NET AJAX

In Chapter 21, you learn the difference between a traditional web application and an **Ajax (Asynchronous JavaScript and XML) web application.** You also learn how to use **ASP.NET AJAX** to quickly and easily improve the user experience for your web applications, giving them responsiveness comparable to that of desktop applications. To demonstrate ASP.NET AJAX capabilities, you enhance the validation example by displaying the submitted form information without reloading the entire page. The only modifications to this web application appear in the Validation.aspx file. You use Ajax-enabled controls to add this feature.

20.10 Case Study Introduction: Password-Protected Books Database Application

In Chapter 21, we include a web application case study in which a user logs into a password-protected website to view a list of publications by a selected author. The application consists of several pages and provides website registration and login capabilities. You'll learn about ASP.NET master pages, which allow you to specify a common look-and-feel for all the pages in your app. We also introduce the **Web Site Administration Tool** and use it to configure the portions of the application that can be accessed only by users who are logged into the website.

Summary

Section 20.1 Introduction
- ASP.NET technology is Microsoft's technology for web-application development.
- Web Form files have the file-name extension .aspx and contain the web page's GUI. A Web Form file represents the web page that is sent to the client browser.
- The file that contains the programming logic of a Web Form is called the code-behind file.

Section 20.2 Web Basics

- URIs (Uniform Resource Identifiers) identify resources on the Internet. URIs that start with http:// are called URLs (Uniform Resource Locators).

- A URL contains information that directs a browser to the resource that the user wishes to access. Computers that run web server software make such resources available.

- In a URL, the hostname is the name of the server on which the resource resides. This computer usually is referred to as the host, because it houses and maintains resources.

- A hostname is translated into a unique IP address that identifies the server. This translation is performed by a domain-name system (DNS) server.

- The remainder of a URL specifies the location and name of a requested resource. For security reasons, the location is normally a virtual directory. The server translates the virtual directory into a real location on the server.

- When given a URL, a web browser uses HTTP to retrieve the web page found at that address.

Section 20.3 Multitier Application Architecture

- Multitier applications divide functionality into separate tiers—logical groupings of functionality—that commonly reside on separate computers for security and scalability.

- The information tier (also called the bottom tier) maintains data pertaining to the application. This tier typically stores data in a relational database management system.

- The middle tier implements business logic, controller logic and presentation logic to control interactions between the application's clients and the application's data. The middle tier acts as an intermediary between data in the information tier and the application's clients.

- Business logic in the middle tier enforces business rules and ensures that data is reliable before the server application updates the database or presents the data to users.

- The client tier, or top tier, is the application's user interface, which gathers input and displays output. Users interact directly with the application through the user interface (typically viewed in a web browser), keyboard and mouse. In response to user actions, the client tier interacts with the middle tier to make requests and to retrieve data from the information tier. The client tier then displays to the user the data retrieved from the middle tier.

Section 20.4.1 Building the WebTime Application

- **File System** websites are created and tested on your local computer. Such websites execute in Visual Web Developer's built-in ASP.NET Development Server and can be accessed only by web browsers running on the same computer. You can later "publish" your website to a production web server for access via a local network or the Internet.

- **HTTP** websites are created and tested on an IIS web server and use HTTP to allow you to put your website's files on the server. If you own a website and have your own web server computer, you might use this to build a new website directly on that server computer.

- **FTP** websites use File Transfer Protocol (FTP) to allow you to put your website's files on the server. The server administrator must first create the website on the server for you. FTP is commonly used by so called "hosting providers" to allow website owners to share a server computer that runs many websites.

- A Web Form represents one page in a web application and contains a web application's GUI.

- You can view the Web Form's properties by selecting DOCUMENT in the **Properties** window. The Title property specifies the title that will be displayed in the web browser's title bar when the page is loaded.

- Controls and other elements are placed sequentially on a Web Form one after another in the order in which you drag-and-drop them onto the Web Form. The cursor indicates the insertion point in the page. This type of layout is known as relative positioning. You can also use absolute positioning in which controls are located exactly where you drop them on the Web Form.

- When a Label does not contain text, its name is displayed in square brackets in **Design** view as a placeholder for design and layout purposes. This text is not displayed at execution time.

- Formatting in a web page is performed with Cascading Style Sheets (CSS).

- A Web Form's Init event occurs when the page is requested by a web browser. The event handler for this event—named Page_Init—initialize the page.

Section 20.4.2 Examining WebTime.aspx's Code-Behind File

- A class declaration can span multiple source-code files—the separate portions of the class declaration in each file are known as partial classes. The partial modifier indicates that the class in a particular file is part of a larger class.

- Every Web Form class inherits from class Page in namespace System.Web.UI. Class Page represents the default capabilities of each page in a web application.

- The ASP.NET controls are defined in namespace System.Web.UI.WebControls.

Section 20.5 Standard Web Controls: Designing a Form

- An Image control's ImageUrl property specifies the location of the image to display.

- By default, the contents of a table cell are aligned vertically in the middle of the cell. You can change this with the cell's valign property.

- A TextBox control allows you to obtain text from the user and display text to the user.

- A DropDownList control is similar to the Windows Forms ComboBox control, but doesn't allow users to type text. You can add items to the DropDownList using the **ListItem Collection Editor**, which you can access by clicking the ellipsis next to the DropDownList's Items property in the **Properties** window, or by using the **DropDownList Tasks** menu.

- A HyperLink control adds a hyperlink to a Web Form. The NavigateUrl property specifies the resource or web page that will be requested when the user clicks the HyperLink.

- A RadioButtonList control provides a series of radio buttons from which the user can select only one. The **RadioButtonList Tasks** smart-tag menu provides an **Edit Items...** link to open the **ListItem Collection Editor** so that you can create the items in the list.

- A Button control triggers an action when clicked.

Section 20.6 Validation Controls

- A validation control determines whether the data in another web control is in the proper format.

- When the page is sent to the client, the validator is converted into JavaScript that performs the validation in the client web browser.

- Some client browsers might not support scripting or the user might disable it. For this reason, you should always perform validation on the server.

- A RequiredFieldValidator control ensures that its ControlToValidate is not empty when the form is submitted. The validator's ErrorMessage property specifies what to display on the Web Form if the validation fails. When the validator's Display property is set to Dynamic, the validator occupies space on the Web Form only when validation fails.

- A RegularExpressionValidator uses a regular expression to ensure data entered by the user is in a valid format. Visual Web Developer provides several predefined regular expressions that you can simply select to validate e-mail addresses, phone numbers and more. A RegularExpressionValidator's ValidationExpression property specifies the regular expression to use for validation.

- A Web Form's Load event occurs each time the page loads into a web browser. The event handler for this event is Page_Load.

- ASP.NET pages are often designed so that the current page reloads when the user submits the form; this enables the program to receive input, process it as necessary and display the results in the same page when it's loaded the second time.

- Submitting a web form is known as a postback. Class Page's IsPostBack property returns true if the page is being loaded due to a postback.

- Server-side Web Form validation must be implemented programmatically. Class Page's Validate method validates the information in the request as specified by the Web Form's validation controls. Class Page's IsValid property returns true if validation succeeded.

Section 20.7 Session Tracking
- Personalization makes it possible for e-businesses to communicate effectively with their customers and also improves users' ability to locate desired products and services.

- To provide personalized services to consumers, e-businesses must be able to recognize clients when they request information from a site.

- HTTP is a stateless protocol—it does not provide information regarding particular clients.

- Tracking individual clients is known as session tracking.

Section 20.7.1 Cookies
- A cookie is a piece of data stored in a small text file on the user's computer. A cookie maintains information about the client during and between browser sessions.

- The expiration date of a cookie determines how long the cookie remains on the client's computer. If you do not set an expiration date for a cookie, the web browser maintains the cookie for the duration of the browsing session.

Section 20.7.2 Session Tracking with HttpSessionState
- Session tracking is implemented with class HttpSessionState.

Section 20.7.3 Options.aspx: Selecting a Programming Language
- Each radio button in a RadioButtonList has a Text property and a Value property. The Text property is displayed next to the radio button and the Value property represents a value that is sent to the server when the user selects that radio button and submits the form.

- Every Web Form includes a user-specific HttpSessionState object, which is accessible through property Session of class Page.

- HttpSessionState property SessionID contains a client's unique session ID. The first time a client connects to the web server, a unique session ID is created for that client and a temporary cookie is written to the client so the server can identify the client on subsequent requests. When the client makes additional requests, the client's session ID from that temporary cookie is compared with the session IDs stored in the web server's memory to retrieve the client's HttpSessionState object.

- HttpSessionState property Timeout specifies the maximum amount of time that an HttpSessionState object can be inactive before it's discarded. Twenty minutes is the default.

- The HttpSessionState object is a dictionary—a data structure that stores key/value pairs. A program uses the key to store and retrieve the associated value in the dictionary.

- The key/value pairs in an `HttpSessionState` object are often referred to as session items. They're placed in an `HttpSessionState` object by calling its `Add` method. Another common syntax for placing a session item in the `HttpSessionState` object is `Session(`*Key*`) =` *Value*.
- If an application adds a session item that has the same name as an item previously stored in the `HttpSessionState` object, the session item is replaced—session items names *must* be unique.

Section 20.7.4 `Recommendations.aspx`*: Displaying Recommendations Based on Session Values*

- The `Count` property returns the number of session items stored in an `HttpSessionState` object.
- `HttpSessionState`'s `Keys` property returns a collection containing all the keys in the session.

Section 20.8 Case Study: Database-Driven ASP.NET Guestbook

- A `GridView` data control displays data in tabular format. This control is located in the **Toolbox**'s **Data** section.

Section 20.8.1 Building a Web Form that Displays Data from a Database

- To use a SQL Server Express database file in an ASP.NET web application, you must first add the file to the project's `App_Data` folder. For security reasons, this folder can be accessed only by the web application on the server—clients cannot access this folder over a network. The web application interacts with the database on behalf of the client.
- A `LinqDataSource` control allows a web application to interact with a database through LINQ.

Section 20.8.2 Modifying the Code-Behind File for the Guestbook Application

- To insert data into a database using a `LinqDataSource`, you must create a `ListDictionary` of insert parameters that are formatted as key/value pairs.
- A `ListDictionary`'s `Add` method stores key/value pairs that represent each insert parameter.
- A `GridView`'s `DataBind` method refreshes the data that the `GridView` displays.

Self-Review Exercises

20.1 State whether each of the following is *true* or *false*. If *false*, explain why.

a) Web Form file names end in `.aspx`.
b) `App.config` is a file that stores configuration settings for an ASP.NET web application.
c) A maximum of one validation control can be placed on a Web Form.
d) A `LinqDataSource` control allows a web application to interact with a database.

20.2 Fill in the blanks in each of the following statements:

a) Web applications contain three basic tiers: ________, ________, and ________.
b) The ________ web control is similar to the `ComboBox` Windows control.
c) A control which ensures that the data in another control is in the correct format is called a(n) ________.
d) A(n) ________ occurs when a page requests itself.
e) Every ASP.NET page inherits from class ________.
f) The ________ file contains the functionality for an ASP.NET page.

Answers to Self-Review Exercises

20.1 a) True. b) False. `Web.config` is the file that stores configuration settings for an ASP.NET web application. c) False. An unlimited number of validation controls can be placed on a Web Form. d) True.

20.2   a) bottom (information), middle (business logic), top (client). b) `DropDownList`. c) validator. d) postback. e) `Page`. f) code-behind.

Exercises

20.3   *(WebTime Modification)* Modify the `WebTime` example to contain drop-down lists that allow the user to modify such `Label` properties as `BackColor`, `ForeColor` and `Font-Size`. Configure these drop-down lists so that a postback occurs whenever the user makes a selection—to do this, set their `AutoPostBack` properties to `true`. When the page reloads, it should reflect the specified changes to the properties of the `Label` displaying the time.

20.4   *(Page Hit Counter)* Create an ASP.NET page that uses session tracking to keep track of how many times the client computer has visited the page. Set the `HttpSessionState` object's `Timeout` property to `1440` (the number of minutes in one day) to keep the session in effect for one day into the future. Display the number of page hits every time the page loads.

20.5   *(Guestbook Application Modification)* Add validation to the guestbook application in Section 20.8. Use validation controls to ensure that the user provides a name, a valid e-mail address and a message.

20.6   *(Project: WebControls Modification)* Modify the example of Section 20.5 to add functionality to the **Register** `Button`. When the user clicks the `Button`, validate all of the input fields to ensure that the user has filled out the form completely, and entered a valid email address and phone number. If any of the fields are not valid, appropriate messages should be displayed by validation controls. If the fields are all valid, direct the user to another page that displays a message indicating that the registration was successful followed by the registration information that was submitted from the form.

20.7   *(Project: Web-Based Address Book)* Using the techniques you learned in Section 20.8, create a web-based Address book. Display the address book's contents in a `GridView`. Allow the user to search for entries with a particular last name.

21

Web App Development with ASP.NET in C#: A Deeper Look

... the challenges are for the designers of these applications: to forget what we think we know about the limitations of the Web, and begin to imagine a wider, richer range of possibilities. It's going to be fun.
—Jesse James Garrett

If any man will draw up his case, and put his name at the foot of the first page, I will give him an immediate reply. Where he compels me to turn over the sheet, he must wait my leisure.
—Lord Sandwich

Objectives

In this chapter you'll learn:

- To use the **Web Site Administration Tool** to modify web application configuration settings.

- To restrict access to pages to authenticated users.

- To create a uniform look-and-feel for a website using master pages.

- To use ASP.NET Ajax to improve the user interactivity of your web applications.

21.1 Introduction

In Chapter 20, we introduced ASP.NET and web application development. In this chapter, we introduce several additional ASP.NET web-application development topics, including:

- master pages to maintain a uniform look-and-feel across the Web Forms in a web application

- creating a password-protected website with registration and login capabilities

- using the **Web Site Administration Tool** to specify which parts of a website are password protected

- using ASP.NET Ajax to quickly and easily improve the user experience for your web applications, giving them responsiveness comparable to that of desktop applications.

21.2 Case Study: Password-Protected Books Database Application

This case study presents a web application in which a user logs into a password-protected website to view a list of publications by a selected author. The application consists of several ASPX files. For this application, we'll use the **ASP.NET Web Site** template, which is a starter kit for a small multi-page website. The template uses Microsoft's recommended practices for organizing a website and separating the website's style (look-and-feel) from its content. The default site has two primary pages (**Home** and **About**) and is pre-configured with login and registration capabilities. The template also specifies a common look-and-feel for all the pages in the website—a concept known as a master page.

We begin by examining the features of the default website that is created with the **ASP.NET Web Site** template. Next, we test drive the completed application to demonstrate the changes we made to the default website. Then, we provide step-by-step instructions to guide you through building the application.

21.2.1 Examining the ASP.NET Web Site Template

To test the default website, begin by creating the website that you'll customize in this case study. Perform the following steps:

1. Select **File > New Web Site...** to display the **New Web Site** dialog.

2. In the left column of the **New Web Site** dialog, ensure that **Visual C#** is selected, then select **ASP.NET Web Site** in the middle column.

3. Choose a location for your website, name it Bug2Bug and click **OK** to create it.

Fig. 21.1 shows the website's contents in the **Solution Explorer**.

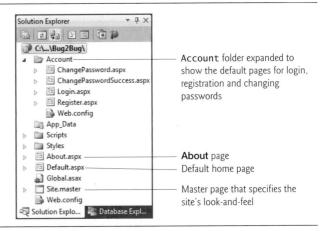

Fig. 21.1 │ The default **ASP.NET Web Site** in the **Solution Explorer**.

Executing the Website
You can now execute the website. Select the Default.aspx page in the **Solution Explorer**, then type *Ctrl + F5* to display the default page shown in Fig. 21.2.

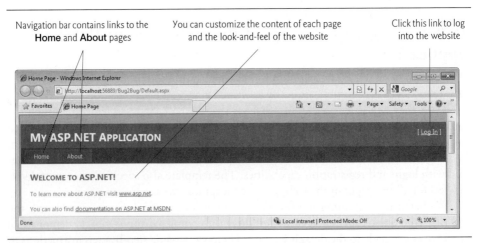

Fig. 21.2 │ Default **Home** page of a website created with the **ASP.NET Web Site** template.

Navigation and Pages

The default **ASP.NET Web Site** contains a home page and an about page—so-called **content pages**—that you'll customize in subsequent sections. The navigation bar near the top of the page allows you to switch between these pages by clicking the link for the appropriate page. In Section 21.2.7, you'll add another link to the navigation bar to allow users to browse book information.

As you navigate between the pages, notice that each page has the same look-and-feel. This is typical of professional websites. The site uses a **master page** and cascading style sheets (CSS) to achieve this. A master page defines common GUI elements that are displayed by each page in a set of content pages. Just as C# classes can inherit instance variables and methods from existing classes, content pages can inherit elements from master pages—this is a form of visual inheritance.

Login and Registration Support

Websites commonly provide "membership capabilities" that allow users to register at a website and log in. Often this gives users access to website customization capabilities or premium content. The default **ASP.NET Web Site** is pre-configured to support registration and login capabilities.

In the upper-right corner of each page is a **Log In** link. Click that link to display the **Login** page (Fig. 21.3). If you are already registered with the site, you can log in with your username and password. Otherwise, you can click the **Register** link to display the **Register** page (Fig. 21.4). For the purpose of this case study, we created an account with the username `testuser1` and the password `testuser1`. You do not need to be registered or logged into the default website to view the home and about pages.

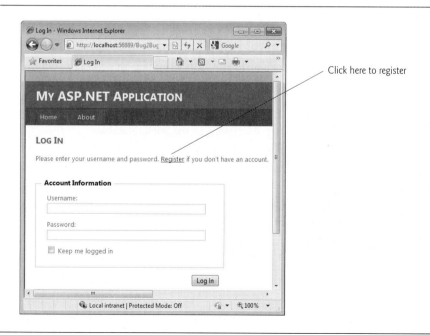

Fig. 21.3 | Login page.

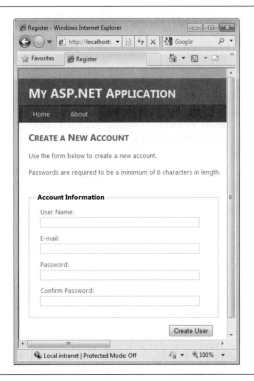

Fig. 21.4 | Register page.

21.2.2 Test-Driving the Completed Application

This example uses a technique known as **forms authentication** to protect a page so that only registered users who are logged into the website can access the page. Such users are known as the site's members. Authentication is a crucial tool for sites that allow only members to enter the site or a portion of the site. In this application, website visitors must log in before they're allowed to view the publications in the Books database.

Let's open the completed Bug2Bug website and execute it so that you can see the authentication functionality in action. Perform the following steps:

1. Close the application you created in Section 21.2.1—you'll reopen this website so that you can customize it in Section 21.2.3.

2. Select **Open Web Site...** from the **File** menu.

3. In the **Open Web Site** dialog, ensure that **File System** is selected, then navigate to this chapter's examples, select the Bug2Bug folder and click the **Open** Button.

4. Select the Default.aspx page then type *Ctrl + F5* to execute the website.

The website appears as shown in Fig. 21.5. Notice that we modified the site's master page so that the top of the page displays an image, the background color of the top of the page is white and the **Log In** link is black. Also, the navigation bar contains a link for the **Books** page that you'll create later in this case study.

Fig. 21.5 | **Home** page for the completed Bug2Bug website.

Try to visit the **Books** page by clicking the **Books** link in the navigation bar. Because this page is password protected in the Bug2Bug website, the website automatically redirects you to the **Login** page instead—you cannot view the **Books** page without logging in first. If you've not yet registered at the completed Bug2Bug website, click the **Register** link to create a new account. If you have registered, log in now.

If you are logging in, when you click the **Log In** Button on the **Log In** page, the website attempts to validate your username and password by comparing them with the usernames and passwords that are stored in a database on the server—this database is created for you with the **ASP.NET Web Site** template. If there is a match, you are **authenticated** (that is, your identity is confirmed) and you're redirected to the **Books** page (Fig. 21.6). If you're registering for the first time, the server ensures that you've filled out the registration form properly and that your password is valid (at least 6 characters), then logs you in and redirects you to the **Books** page.

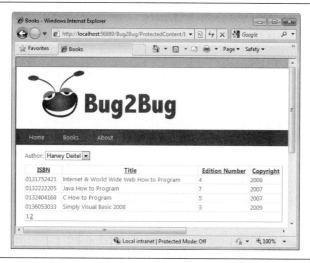

Fig. 21.6 | Books.aspx displaying books by Harvey Deitel (by default).

The **Books** page provides a drop-down list of authors and a table containing the ISBNs, titles, edition numbers and copyright years of books in the database. By default, the page displays all the books by Harvey Deitel. Links appear at the bottom of the table that allow you to access additional pages of data—we configured the table to display only four rows of data at a time. When the user chooses an author, a postback occurs, and the page is updated to display information about books written by the selected author (Fig. 21.7).

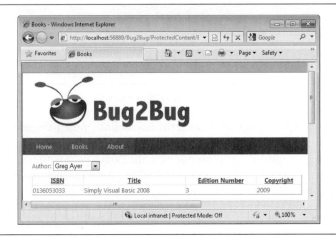

Fig. 21.7 | `Books.aspx` displaying books by Greg Ayer.

Logging Out of the Website
When you're logged in, the **Log In** link is replaced in the upper-right corner of each page (not shown in Figs. 21.6–21.7) with the message "Welcome *username*" where *username* is replaced with your log in name, and a **Log Out** link. When you click **Log Out**, the website redirects you to the home page (Fig. 21.5).

21.2.3 Configuring the Website

Now that you're familiar with how this application behaves, you'll modify the default website you created in Section 21.2.1. Thanks to the rich functionality of the default website, you'll have to write almost no Visual C# code to create this application. The **ASP.NET Web Site** template hides the details of authenticating users against a database of user names and passwords, displaying appropriate success or error messages and redirecting the user to the correct page based on the authentication results. We now discuss the steps you must perform to create the password-protected books database application.

Step 1: Opening the Website
Open the default website that you created in Section 21.2.1.

1. Select **Open Web Site...** from the **File** menu.

2. In the **Open Web Site** dialog, ensure that **File System** is selected, then navigate to the location where you created your version of the Bug2Bug website and click the **Open** Button.

Step 2: Setting Up Website Folders

For this website, you'll create two new folders—one that will contain the image that is used on all the pages and one that will contain the password-protected page. Password-protected parts of your website are typically placed in a separate folder. As you'll see shortly, you can control access to specific folders in a website.

You can choose any name you like for these folders—we chose Images for the folder that will contain the image and ProtectedContent for the folder that will contain the password-protected **Books** page. To create the folders, perform the following steps:

1. Create an Images folder by right clicking the location of the website in the **Solution Explorer**, selecting **New Folder** and typing the name Images.

2. Create a ProtectedContent folder by right clicking the location of the website in the **Solution Explorer**, selecting **New Folder** and typing the name ProtectedContent.

Step 3: Importing the Website Header Image and the Database File

Next, you'll add an image to the Images folder and the database file to the App_Data folder.

1. In Windows Explorer, locate the folder containing this chapter's examples.

2. Drag the image bug2bug.png from the images folder in Windows Explorer into the Images folder in the **Solution Explorer** to copy the image into the website.

3. Drag the Books.mdf database file from the databases folder in Windows Explorer to the project's App_Data folder. We show how to retrieve data from this database later in the section.

Step 4: Opening the Web Site Administration Tool

In this application, we want to ensure that only authenticated users are allowed to access Books.aspx (created in Section 21.2.5) to view the information in the database. Previously, we created all of our ASPX pages in the web application's root directory. By default, any website visitor (regardless of whether the visitor is authenticated) can view pages in the root directory. ASP.NET allows you to restrict access to particular folders of a website. We do not want to restrict access to the root of the website, however, because users won't be able to view any pages of the website except the login and registration pages. To restrict access to the **Books** page, it must reside in a directory other than the root directory.

You'll now configure the website to allow only authenticated users (that is, users who have logged in) to view the pages in the ProtectedContent folder. Perform the following steps:

1. Select **Website > ASP.NET Configuration** to open the **Web Site Administration Tool** in a web browser (Fig. 21.8). This tool allows you to configure various options that determine how your application behaves.

2. Click either the **Security** link or the **Security** tab to open a web page in which you can set security options (Fig. 21.9), such as the type of authentication the application should use. By default, website users are authenticated by entering username and password information in a web form.

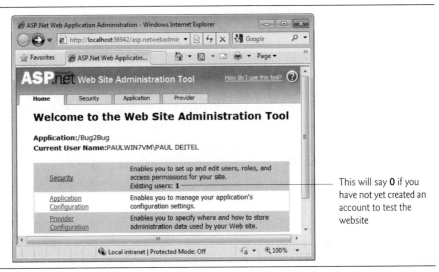

Fig. 21.8 | Web Site Administration Tool for configuring a web application.

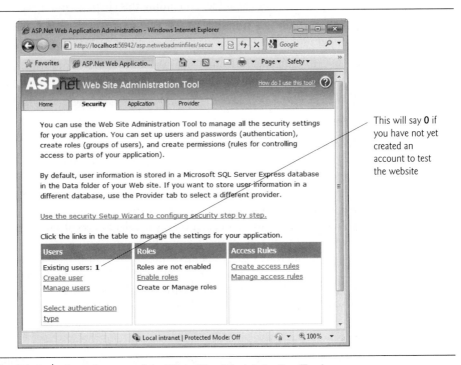

Fig. 21.9 | Security page of the Web Site Administration Tool.

Step 5: Configuring the Website's Security Settings

Next, you'll configure the ProtectedContent folder to grant access only to authenticated users—anyone who attempts to access pages in this folder without first logging in will be redirected to the Login page. Perform the following steps:

1. Click the **Create access rules** link in the **Access Rules** column of the **Web Site Administration Tool** (Fig. 21.9) to view the **Add New Access Rule** page (Fig. 21.10). This page is used to create an **access rule**—a rule that grants or denies access to a particular directory for a specific user or group of users.

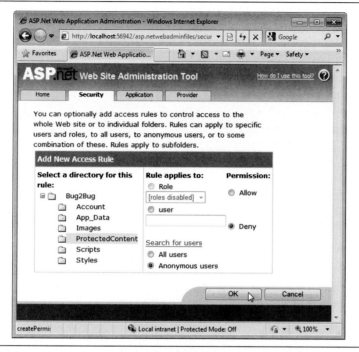

Fig. 21.10 | **Add New Access Rule** page used to configure directory access.

2. Click the `ProtectedContent` directory in the left column of the page to identify the directory to which our access rule applies.

3. In the middle column, select the radio button marked **Anonymous users** to specify that the rule applies to users who have not been authenticated.

4. Finally, select **Deny** in the **Permission** column to prevent unauthenticated users from accessing pages in the `ProtectedContent` directory, then click **OK**.

By default, unauthenticated (anonymous) users who attempt to load a page in the `ProtectedContent` directory are redirected to the `Login.aspx` page so that they can identify themselves. Because we did not set up any access rules for the `Bug2Bug` root directory, anonymous users may still access pages there.

21.2.4 Modifying the `Default.aspx` and `About.aspx` Pages

We modified the content of the home (`Default.aspx`) and about (`About.aspx`) pages to replace the default content. To do so, perform the following steps:

1. Double click `Default.aspx` in the **Solution Explorer** to open it, then switch to **Design** view (Fig. 21.11). As you move the cursor over the page, you'll notice that

sometimes the cursor displays as ⊘ to indicate that you cannot edit the part of the page behind the cursor. Any part of a content page that is defined in a master page can be edited only in the master page.

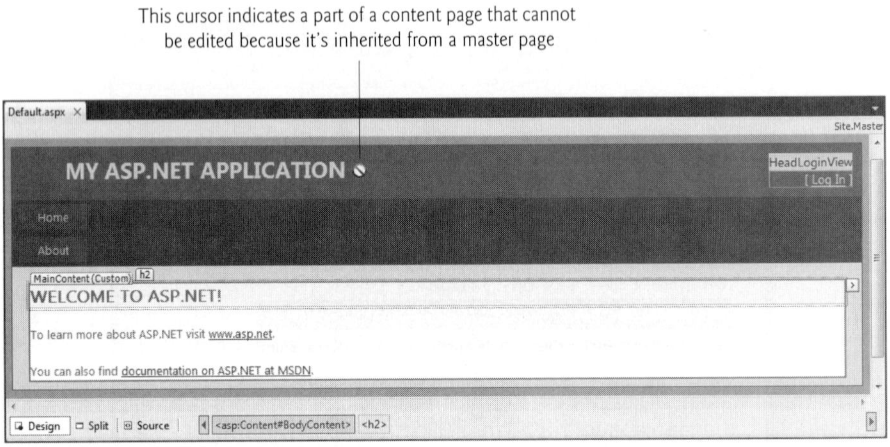

This cursor indicates a part of a content page that cannot be edited because it's inherited from a master page

Fig. 21.11 | `Default.aspx` page in **Design** view.

2. Change the text `"Welcome to ASP.NET!"` to `"Welcome to Our Password-Protected Book Information Site"`. Note that the text in this heading is actually formatted as small caps text when the page is displayed in a web browser—all of the letters are displayed in uppercase, but the letters that would normally be lowercase are smaller than the first letter in each word.

3. Select the text of the two paragraphs that remain in the page and replace them with `"To learn more about our books, click here or click the Books tab in the navigation bar above. You must be logged in to view the Books page."` In a later step, you'll link the words `"click here"` to the **Books** page.

4. Save and close the `Default.aspx` page.

5. Next, open `About.aspx` and switch to **Design** view.

6. Change the text `"Put content here."` to `"This is the Bug2Bug password-protected book information database example."`

7. Save and close the `About.aspx` page.

21.2.5 Creating a Content Page That Only Authenticated Users Can Access

We now create the `Books.aspx` file in the `ProtectedContent` folder—the folder for which we set an access rule denying access to anonymous users. If an unauthenticated user requests this file, the user will be redirected to `Login.aspx`. From there, the user can either log in or create a new account, both of which will authenticate the user, then redirect back to `Books.aspx`. To create the page, perform the following steps:

1. Right click the ProtectedContent folder in the **Solution Explorer** and select **Add New Item....** In the resulting dialog, select **Web Form** and specify the file name Books.aspx. Ensure that the CheckBox **Select master page** is checked to indicate that this Web Form should be created as a content page that references a master page, then click **Add**.

2. In the **Select a Master Page** dialog, select Site.master and click **OK**. The IDE creates the file and opens it.

3. Switch to **Design** view, click in the page to select it, then select **DOCUMENT** from the ComboBox in the **Properties** window.

4. Change the Title property of the page to Books, then save and close the page

You'll customize this page and create its functionality shortly.

21.2.6 Linking from the Default.aspx Page to the Books.aspx Page

Next, you'll add a hyperlink from the text "click here" in the Default.aspx page to the Books.aspx page. To do so, perform the following steps:

1. Open the Default.aspx page and switch to **Design** view.

2. Select the text "click here".

3. Click the **Convert to Hyperlink** (📇) Button on the toolbar at the top of Visual Web Developer to display the **Hyperlink** dialog. You can enter a URL here, or you can link to another page within the website.

4. Click the **Browse...** Button to display the **Select Project Item** dialog, which allows you to select another page in the website.

5. In the left column, select the ProtectedContent directory.

6. In the right column, select Books.aspx, then click **OK** to dismiss the **Select Project Item** dialog and click **OK** again to dismiss the **Hyperlink** dialog.

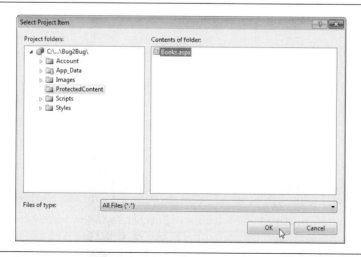

Fig. 21.12 | Selecting the Books.aspx page from the **Select Project Item** dialog.

Users can now click the **click here** link in the `Default.aspx` page to browse to the `Books.aspx` page. If a user is not logged in, clicking this link will redirect the user to the **Login** page.

21.2.7 Modifying the Master Page (`Site.master`)

Next, you'll modify the website's master page, which defines the common elements we want to appear on each page. A master page is like a base class in a visual inheritance hierarchy, and content pages are like derived classes. The master page contains placeholders for custom content created in each content page. The content pages visually inherit the master page's content, then add content in the areas designated by the master page's placeholders.

For example, it's common to include a **navigation bar** (that is, a series of buttons or menus for navigating a website) on every page of a site. If a site encompasses a large number of pages, adding markup to create the navigation bar for each page can be time consuming. Moreover, if you subsequently modify the navigation bar, every page on the site that uses it must be updated. By creating a master page, you can specify the navigation-bar in one file and have it appear on all the content pages. If the navigation bar changes, only the master page changes—any content pages that use it are updated the next time the page is requested.

In the final version of this website, we modified the master page to include the Bug2Bug logo in the header at the top of every page. We also changed the colors of some elements in the header to make them work better with the logo. In particular, we changed the background color from a dark blue to white, and we changed the color of the text for the **Log In** and **Log Out** links to black. The color changes require you to modify the CSS styles for some of the master page's elements. These styles are defined in the file `Site.css`, which is located in the website's `Styles` folder. You will not modify the CSS file directly. Instead, you'll use the tools built into Visual Web Developer to perform these modifications.

*Inserting an **Image** in the Header*

To display the logo, we'll place an `Image` control in the header of the master page. Each content page based on this master page will include the logo. Perform the following steps to add the `Image`:

1. Open `Site.master` and switch to **Design** view.

2. Delete the text `MY ASP.NET APPLICATION` at the top of the page.

3. In the **Toolbox**, double click **Image** to add an `Image` control where the text used to be.

4. Edit the `Image` control's `ImageUrl` property to point to the `bug2bug.png` image in the `Images` folder.

Customizing the CSS Styles for the Master Page

Our logo image was designed to be displayed against a white background. To change the background color in the header at the top of the page, perform the following steps:

1. Just below the **Design** view is a list of `Buttons` that show you where the cursor is currently located in the master page (Fig. 21.13). These `Buttons` also allow you to select specific elements in the page. Click the **<div.header>** `Button` to select the header portion of the page.

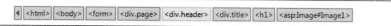

Fig. 21.13 | Buttons for selecting parts of a page in **Design** view.

2. Select **View > Other Windows > CSS Properties** to display the CSS properties (at the left of the IDE) for the currently selected element (the header of the page).

3. At the top of the **CSS Properties** window, click the **Summary** Button to show only the CSS properties that are currently set for the selected element.

4. Change the background property from #4b6c9e (the hexadecimal value for the current dark blue background) to white and press *Enter*.

5. The **Log In** and **Log Out** links use white text in the default website. Now that the background of the header is white, we need to change the color of these links so they'll be visible. In the upper-right corner of the master page click the **HeadLogin-inView** control, which is where the **Log In** and **Log Out** links get displayed.

6. Below the **Design** view, click the `<div.loginDisplay>` Button to display the styles for the **HeadLoginView** in the **CSS Properties** window.

7. Change the color property from white to black and press *Enter*.

8. Click inside the box below **HeadLoginView**. Then, below the **Design** view, click the `<a#HeadingLoginStatus>` Button to display the styles for the **Log In/Log Out** link in the **CSS Properties** window

9. Change the color property from white to black and press *Enter*.

10. We chose to make some style changes directly in the Site.css file. On many websites, when you move the mouse over a hyperlink, the color of the link changes. Similarly, once you click a hyperlink, the hyperlink is often displayed in a different color the next time you visit the page to indicate that you've already clicked that link during a previous visit. The predefined styles in this website set the color of the **Log In** link to white for both of these cases. To change these to black, open the Site.css file from the Styles folder in the **Solution Explorer**, then search for the following two styles:

```
.loginDisplay a:visited
.loginDisplay a:hover
```

Change each style's color property from white to black.

11. Save the Site.master and Site.css files.

Adding a Books Link to the Navigation Bar

Currently the navigation bar has only **Home** and **About** links. Next, you'll add a link to the **Books** page. Perform the following steps:

1. In the master page, position the mouse over the navigation bar links, then open the smart-tag menu and click **Edit Menu Items**.

2. In the **Menu Item Editor** dialog, click the **Add a root item** (⊞) Button.

3. Set the new item's Text property to Books and use the up arrow Button to move the new item up so the order of the navigation bar items is Home, Books and About.

4. Set the new item's NavigateUrl property to the Books.aspx page in the ProtectedContent folder.

5. Click **OK**, then save Site.master to complete the changes to the master page.

21.2.8 Customizing the Password-Protected Books.aspx Page

You are now ready to customize the Books.aspx page to display the book information for a particular author.

Generating LINQ to SQL Classes Based on the Books.mdf Database
The Books.aspx page will provide a DropDownList containing authors' names and a GridView displaying information about books written by the author selected in the DropDownList. A user will select an author from the DropDownList to cause the GridView to display information about only the books written by the selected author.

To work with the Books database through LINQ, we use the same approach as in the **Guestbook** case study (Section 20.8). First you need to generate the LINQ to SQL classes based on the Books database, which is provided in the databases directory of this chapter's examples folder. Name the file Books.dbml. When you drag the tables of the Books database from the **Database Explorer** onto the **Object Relational Designer** of Books.dbml, you'll find that associations (represented by arrows) between the two tables are automatically generated (Fig. 21.14).

Fig. 21.14 | **Object Relational Designer** for the Books database.

To obtain data from this data context, you'll use two LinqDataSource controls. In both cases, the LinqDataSource control's built-in data selection functionality won't be versatile enough, so the implementation will be slightly different than in Section 20.8. So, we'll use a custom Select LINQ statement as the query of a LinqDataSource.

Adding a DropDownList to Display the Authors' First and Last Names
Now that we have created a BooksDataContext class (one of the generated LINQ to SQL classes), we add controls to Books.aspx that will display the data on the web page. We first add the DropDownList from which users can select an author.

1. Open Books.aspx in **Design** mode, then add the text Author: and a DropDownList control named authorsDropDownList in the page's editable content area (which has a white background). The DropDownList initially displays the text Unbound.

2. Next, we'll bind the list to a data source, so the list displays the author information in the Authors table of the Books database. Because the **Configure Data**

Source wizard allows us to create LinqDataSources with only simple Select LINQ statements, we cannot use the wizard here. Instead, add a LinqDataSource object below the DropDownList named authorsLinqDataSource.

3. Open the smart-tag menu for the DropDownList and click **Choose Data Source...** to start the **Data Source Configuration Wizard** (Fig. 21.15). Select authorsLinq-DataSource from the **Select a data source** drop-down list in the first screen of the wizard. Then, type Name as the data field to display in the DropDownList and AuthorID as the data field that will be submitted to the server when the user makes a selection. [*Note:* You must manually type these values in because authorsLinqDataSource does not yet have a defined Select query.] When authorsDropDownList is rendered in a web browser, the list items will display the names of the authors, but the underlying values associated with each item will be the AuthorIDs of the authors. Click **OK** to bind the DropDownList to the specified data.

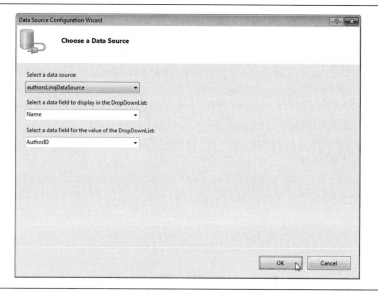

Fig. 21.15 | Choosing a data source for a DropDownList.

4. In the C# code-behind file (Books.aspx.cs), create an instance of BooksData-Context named database as an instance variable.

5. In the **Design** view of Books.aspx, double click authorsLinqDataSource to create an event handler for its **Selecting** event. This event occurs every time the LinqDataSource selects data from its data context, and can be used to implement custom Select queries against the data context. To do so, assign the custom LINQ query to the **Result** property of the event handler's LinqDataSourceSe-lectEventArgs argument. The query results become the data source's data. In this case, we must create a custom anonymous type in the Select clause with properties Name and AuthorID that contain the author's full name and ID. The LINQ query is

```
from author in database.Authors
select new { Name = author.FirstName + " " + author.LastName,
    author.AuthorID };
```

The limitations of the **Configure Data Source** wizard prevent us from using a custom field such as Name (a combination of first name and last name, separated by a space) that isn't one of the database table's existing columns.

6. The last step in configuring the DropDownList on Books.aspx is to set the control's **AutoPostBack** property to True. This property indicates that a postback occurs each time the user selects an item in the DropDownList. As you'll see shortly, this causes the page's GridView (created in the next step) to display new data.

Creating a GridView to Display the Selected Author's Books

We now add a GridView to Books.aspx for displaying the book information by the author selected in the authorsDropDownList.

1. Add a GridView named titlesGridView below the other controls in the page's content area.

2. To bind the GridView to data from the Books database, create a LinqDataSource named titlesLinqDataSource beneath the GridView.

3. Select titlesLinqDataSource from the **Choose Data Source** drop-down list in the **GridView Tasks** smart-tag menu. Because titlesLinqDataSource has no defined Select query, the GridView will not automatically be configured.

4. To configure the columns of the GridView to display the appropriate data, select **Edit Columns...** from the **GridView Tasks** smart-tag menu to display the **Fields** dialog (Fig. 21.16).

5. Uncheck the **Auto-generate fields** box to indicate that you'll manually define the fields to display.

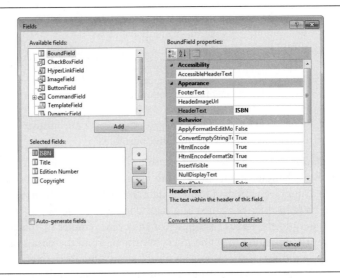

Fig. 21.16 | Creating GridView fields in the **Fields** dialog.

6. Create four BoundFields with the HeaderText ISBN, Title, Edition Number and Copyright, respectively.

7. For the ISBN and Copyright BoundFields, set the SortExpression and Data-Field properties to match the HeaderText. For the Title BoundField, set the SortExpression and DataField properties to Title1 (the IDE renamed the Title column to Title1 to avoid a naming conflict with the table's class—Title). For Edition Number, set the SortExpression and DataField to Edi-tionNumber—the name of the field in the database. The SortExpression speci-fies to sort by the associated data field when the user chooses to sort by the column. Shortly, we'll enable sorting to allow users to sort this GridView. Click **OK** to close the **Fields** dialog.

8. To specify the Select LINQ query for obtaining the data, double click titles-LinqDataSource to create its Selecting event handler. Assign the custom LINQ query to the LinqDataSourceSelectEventArgs argument's Result property. Use the following LINQ query:

```
from book in database.AuthorISBNs
where book.AuthorID ==
   Convert.ToInt32( authorsDropDownList.SelectedValue )
select book.Title
```

9. The GridView needs to update every time the user makes a new author selection. To implement this, double click the DropDownList to create an event handler for its SelectedIndexChanged event. You can make the GridView update by invok-ing its DataBind method.

Code-Behind File for the Books Page

Figure 21.17 shows the code for the completed code-behind file. Line 10 defines the data context object that is used in the LINQ queries. Lines 13–20 and 23–31 define the two LinqDataSource's Selecting events. Lines 34–38 define the authorsDropDownList's SelectedIndexChanged event handler, which updates the GridView.

```
1   // Fig. 21.17: ProtectedContent_Books.aspx.cs
2   // Code-behind file for the password-protected Books page.
3   using System;
4   using System.Linq;
5   using System.Web.UI.WebControls;
6
7   public partial class ProtectedContent_Books : System.Web.UI.Page
8   {
9      // data context queried by data sources
10     BooksDataContext database = new BooksDataContext();
11
12     // specify the Select query that creates a combined first and last name
13     protected void authorsLinqDataSource_Selecting( object sender,
14        LinqDataSourceSelectEventArgs e )
15     {
```

Fig. 21.17 | Code-behind file for the password-protected **Books** page. (Part 1 of 2.)

```
16          e.Result =
17            from author in database.Authors
18            select new { Name = author.FirstName + " " + author.LastName,
19              author.AuthorID };
20      } // end method authorsLinqDataSource_Selecting
21
22      // specify the Select query that gets the specified author's books
23      protected void titlesLinqDataSource_Selecting( object sender,
24        LinqDataSourceSelectEventArgs e )
25      {
26          e.Result =
27            from book in database.AuthorISBNs
28            where book.AuthorID ==
29              Convert.ToInt32( authorsDropDownList.SelectedValue )
30            select book.Title;
31      } // end method titlesLinqDataSource_Selecting
32
33      // refresh the GridView when a different author is selected
34      protected void authorsDropDownList_SelectedIndexChanged(
35        object sender, EventArgs e )
36      {
37          titlesGridView.DataBind(); // update the GridView
38      } // end method authorsDropDownList_SelectedIndexChanged
39  } // end class ProtectedContent_Books
```

Fig. 21.17 | Code-behind file for the password-protected **Books** page. (Part 2 of 2.)

Configuring the GridView to Enable Sorting and Paging

Now that the GridView is tied to a data source, we modify several of the control's properties to adjust its appearance and behavior.

1. In **Design** view, use the GridView's sizing handles to set the width to 580px.

2. Next, in the **GridView Tasks** smart-tag menu, check **Enable Sorting** so that the column headings in the GridView become hyperlinks that allow users to sort the data in the GridView using the sort expressions specified by each column. For example, clicking the Titles heading in the web browser will cause the displayed data to appear sorted in alphabetical order. Clicking this heading a second time will cause the data to be sorted in reverse alphabetical order. ASP.NET hides the details required to achieve this functionality.

3. Finally, in the **GridView Tasks** smart-tag menu, check **Enable Paging**. This causes the GridView to split across multiple pages. The user can click the numbered links at the bottom of the GridView control to display a different page of data. GridView's **PageSize** property determines the number of entries per page. Set the **PageSize** property to 4 using the **Properties** window so that the GridView displays only four books per page. This technique for displaying data makes the site more readable and enables pages to load more quickly (because less data is displayed at one time). As with sorting data in a GridView, you do not need to add any code to achieve paging functionality. Figure 21.18 displays the completed Books.aspx file in **Design** mode.

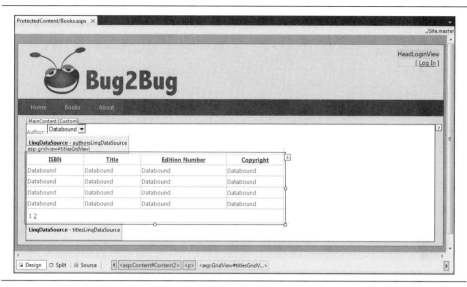

Fig. 21.18 | Completed Books.aspx page in **Design** mode.

21.3 ASP.NET Ajax

In this section, you learn the difference between a traditional web application and an **Ajax (Asynchronous JavaScript and XML) web application**. You also learn how to use ASP.NET Ajax to quickly and easily improve the user experience for your web applications. To demonstrate ASP.NET Ajax capabilities, you enhance the validation example of Section 20.6 by displaying the submitted form information without reloading the entire page. The only modifications to this web application appear in the Validation.aspx file. You use Ajax-enabled controls to add this feature.

21.3.1 Traditional Web Applications

Figure 21.19 presents the typical interactions between the client and the server in a traditional web application, such as one that uses a user registration form. The user first fills in the form's fields, then submits the form (Fig. 21.19, *Step 1*). The browser generates a request to the server, which receives the request and processes it (*Step 2*). The server generates and sends a response containing the exact page that the browser renders (*Step 3*), which causes the browser to load the new page (*Step 4*) and temporarily makes the browser window blank. The client *waits* for the server to respond and *reloads the entire page* with the data from the response (*Step 4*). While such a **synchronous request** is being processed on the server, the user cannot interact with the web page. Frequent long periods of waiting, due perhaps to Internet congestion, have led some users to refer to the World Wide Web as the "World Wide Wait." If the user interacts with and submits another form, the process begins again (*Steps 5–8*).

This model was designed for a web of hypertext documents—what some people call the "brochure web." As the web evolved into a full-scale applications platform, the model shown in Fig. 21.19 yielded "choppy" user experiences. Every full-page refresh required users to reload the full page. Users began to demand a more responsive model.

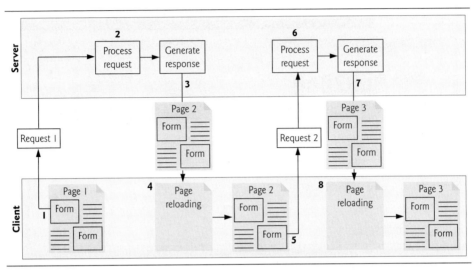

Fig. 21.19 | Traditional web application reloading the page for every user interaction.

21.3.2 Ajax Web Applications

Ajax web applications add a layer between the client and the server to manage communication between the two (Fig. 21.20). When the user interacts with the page, the client requests information from the server (*Step 1*). The request is intercepted by the ASP.NET Ajax controls and sent to the server as an **asynchronous request** (*Step 2*)—the user can continue interacting with the application in the client browser while the server processes the request. Other user interactions could result in additional requests to the server (*Steps 3*

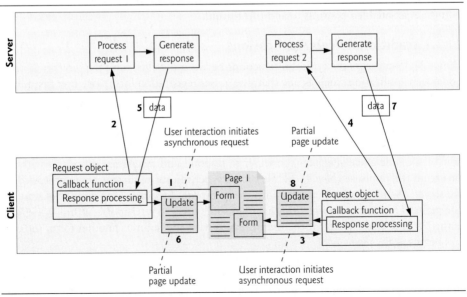

Fig. 21.20 | Ajax-enabled web application interacting with the server asynchronously.

and *4*). Once the server responds to the original request (*Step 5*), the ASP.NET Ajax control that issued the request calls a client-side function to process the data returned by the server. This function—known as a **callback function**—uses **partial-page updates** (*Step 6*) to display the data in the existing web page *without reloading the entire page*. At the same time, the server may be responding to the second request (*Step 7*) and the client browser may be starting another partial-page update (*Step 8*). The callback function updates only a designated part of the page. Such partial-page updates help make web applications more responsive, making them feel more like desktop applications. The web application does not load a new page while the user interacts with it. In the following section, you use ASP.NET Ajax controls to enhance the `Validation.aspx` page.

21.3.3 Testing an ASP.NET Ajax Application

To demonstrate ASP.NET Ajax capabilities we'll enhance the **Validation** application from Section 20.6 by adding ASP.NET Ajax controls. There are no C# code modifications to this application—all of the changes occur in the `.aspx` file.

Testing the Application in Your Default Web Browser

To test this application in your default web browser, perform the following steps:

1. Select **Open Web Site...** from the Visual Web Developer **File** menu.

2. In the **Open Web Site** dialog, select **File System**, then navigate to this chapter's examples, select the `ValidationAjax` folder and click the **Open Button**.

3. Select `Validation.aspx` in the **Solution Explorer**, then type *Ctrl + F5* to execute the web application in your default web browser.

Figure 21.21 shows a sample execution of the enhanced application. In Fig. 21.21(a), we show the contact form split into two tabs via the `TabContainer` Ajax control. You can switch between the tabs by clicking the title of each tab. Fig. 21.21(b) shows a `Validator-CalloutExtender` control, which displays a validation error message in a callout that points to the control in which the validation error occurred, rather than as text in the page. Fig. 21.21(c) shows the updated page with the data the user submitted to the server.

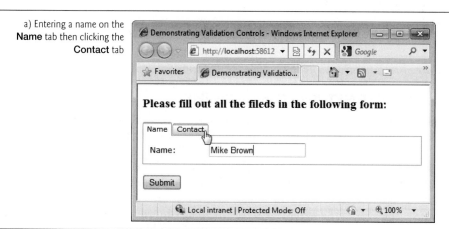

a) Entering a name on the **Name** tab then clicking the **Contact** tab

Fig. 21.21 | Validation application enhanced by ASP.NET Ajax. (Part 1 of 2.)

b) Entering an e-mail address in an incorrect format and pressing the *Tab* key to move to the next input field causes a callout to appear informing the user to enter an e-mail address in a valid format

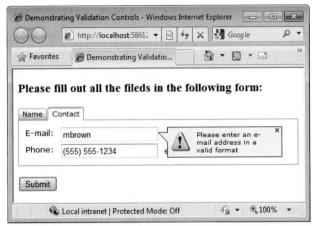

c) After filling out the form properly and clicking the **Submit** button, the submitted data is displayed at the bottom of the page with a partial page update

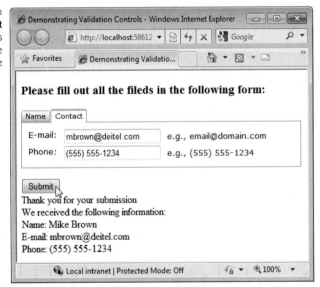

Fig. 21.21 | Validation application enhanced by ASP.NET Ajax. (Part 2 of 2.)

21.3.4 The ASP.NET Ajax Control Toolkit

You'll notice that there is a tab of basic **AJAX Extensions** controls in the **Toolbox**. Microsoft also provides the **ASP.NET Ajax Control Toolkit** as part of the ASP.NET Ajax Library:

```
ajax.codeplex.com
```

The toolkit contains many more Ajax-enabled, rich GUI controls. Click the **Download Button** to begin the download. The toolkit does not come with an installer, so you must extract the contents of the toolkit's ZIP file to your hard drive. Note the location where you extracted the files as you'll need this information to add the ASP.NET Ajax Controls to your **Toolbox**.

Adding the ASP.NET Ajax Controls to the Toolbox

You should add controls from the Ajax Control Toolkit to the **Toolbox** in Visual Web Developer (or in Visual Studio), so you can drag and drop controls onto your Web Forms. To do so, perform the following steps:

1. Open an existing website project or create a new website project.

2. Open an ASPX page from your project in **Design** mode.

3. Right click inside the **Toolbox** and choose **Add Tab**, then type ASP.NET Ajax Library in the new tab.

4. Right click under the new **ASP.NET Ajax Library** tab and select **Choose Items...** to open the **Choose Toolbox Items** dialog.

5. Click the **Browse Button** then locate the folder where you extracted the ASP.NET Ajax Control Toolkit. Select the file AjaxControlToolkit.dll then click **Open**.

6. Click **OK** to close dialog. The controls from the Ajax Control Toolkit now appear in the **Toolbox**'s **ASP.NET Ajax Library** tab.

7. If the control names are not in alphabetical order, you can sort them alphabetically, by right clicking in the list of Ajax Control Toolkit controls and selecting **Sort Items Alphabetically**.

21.3.5 Using Controls from the Ajax Control Toolkit

In this section, you'll enhance the application you created in Section 20.6 by adding ASP.NET Ajax controls. The key control in every ASP.NET Ajax-enabled application is the **ScriptManager** (in the **Toolbox**'s **AJAX Extensions** tab), which manages the JavaScript client-side code (called scripts) that enable asynchronous Ajax functionality. A benefit of using ASP.NET Ajax is that you do not need to know JavaScript to be able to use these scripts. The ScriptManager is meant for use with the controls in the **Toolbox**'s **AJAX Extensions** tab. There can be only one ScriptManager per page.

ToolkitScriptManager

The Ajax Control Toolkit comes with an enhanced ScriptManager called the **ToolkitScriptManager**, which manages the scripts for the ASP. NET Ajax Toolkit controls. This one should be used in any page with controls from the ASP. NET Ajax Toolkit.

Common Programming Error 21.1

Putting more than one ScriptManager and/or ToolkitScriptManager control on a Web Form causes the application to throw an InvalidOperationException when the page is initialized.

Open the Validation website you created in Section 20.6. Then drag a ToolkitScriptManager from the **ASP.NET Ajax Library** tab in the **Toolbox** to the top of the page— a script manager must appear before any controls that use the scripts it manages.

Grouping Information in Tabs Using the TabContainer Control

The **TabContainer control** enables you to group information into tabs that are displayed only if they're selected. The information in an unselected tab won't be displayed until the user selects that tab. To demonstrate a TabContainer control, let's split the form into two tabs—one in which the user can enter the name and one in which the user can enter the e-mail address and phone number. Perform the following steps:

1. Click to the right of the text **Please fill out all the fields in the following form:** and press *Enter* to create a new paragraph.

2. Drag a TabContainer control from the **ASP.NET Ajax Library** tab in the **Toolbox** into the new paragraph. This creates a container for hosting tabs. Set the TabContainer's Width property to 450px.

3. To add a tab, open the **TabContainer Tasks** smart-tag menu and select **Add Tab Panel**. This adds a **TabPanel object**—representing a tab—to the TabContainer. Do this again to add a second tab.

4. You must change each TabPanel's HeaderText property by editing the ASPX page's markup. To do so, click the TabContainer to ensure that it's selected, then switch to **Split** view in the design window. In the highlighted markup that corresponds to the TabContainer, locate HeaderText="TabPanel1" and change "TabPanel1" to "Name", then locate HeaderText="TabPanel2" and change "TabPanel2" to "Contact". Switch back to **Design** view. In **Design** view, you can navigate between tabs by clicking the tab headers. You can drag-and-drop elements into the tab as you would anywhere else.

5. Click in the **Name** tab's body, then insert a one row and two column table. Take the text and controls that are currently in the **Name:** row of the original table and move them to the table in the **Name** tab.

6. Switch to the **Contact** tab, click in its body, then insert a two-row-by-two-column table. Take the text and controls that are currently in the **E-mail:** and **Phone:** rows of the original table and move them to the table in the **Contact** tab.

7. Delete the original table that is currently below the TabContainer.

Partial-Page Updates Using the *UpdatePanel* Control

The **UpdatePanel control** eliminates full-page refreshes by isolating a section of a page for a partial-page update. In this example, we'll use a partial-page update to display the user's information that is submitted to the server.

To implement a partial-page update, perform the following steps:

1. Click to the left of the **Submit** Button and press *Enter* to create a new paragraph above it. Then click in the new paragraph and drag an UpdatePanel control from the **AJAX Extensions** tab in the **Toolbox** to your form.

2. Then, drag into the UpdatePanel the control(s) to update and the control that triggers the update. For this example, drag the outputLabel and the submitButton into the UpdatePanel.

3. To specify when an UpdatePanel should update, you need to define an **UpdatePanel trigger**. Select the UpdatePanel, then click the ellipsis button next to the control's Triggers property in the **Properties** window. In the **UpdatePanelTrigger Collection** dialog that appears (Fig. 21.22), click **Add** to add an **AsyncPostBackTrigger**. Set the ControlID property to submitButton and the

EventName property to Click. Now, when the user clicks the **Submit** button, the UpdatePanel intercepts the request and makes an asynchronous request to the server instead. Then the response is inserted in the outputLabel element, and the UpdatePanel reloads the label to display the new text without refreshing the entire page. Click **OK** to close the dialog.

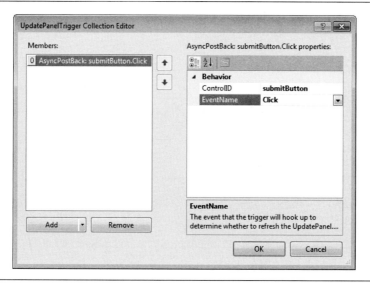

Fig. 21.22 | Creating a trigger for an UpdatePanel.

Adding Ajax Functionality to ASP.NET Validation Controls Using Ajax Extenders

Several controls in the Ajax Control Toolkit are **extenders**—components that enhance the functionality of regular ASP.NET controls. In this example, we use **ValidatorCalloutExtender controls** that enhance the ASP.NET validation controls by displaying error messages in small yellow callouts next to the input fields, rather than as text in the page.

You can create a ValidatorCalloutExtender by opening any validator control's smart-tag menu and clicking **Add Extender...** to display the **Extender Wizard** dialog (Fig. 21.23). Next, choose ValidatorCalloutExtender from the list of available extenders. The extender's ID is chosen based on the ID of the validation control you're extending, but you can rename it if you like. Click **OK** to create the extender. Do this for each of the validation controls in this example.

Changing the Display Property of the Validation Controls

The ValidatorCalloutExtenders display error messages with a nicer look-and-feel, so we no longer need the validator controls to display these messages on their own. For this reason, set each validation control's Display property to None.

Running the Application

When you run this application, the TabContainer will display whichever tab was last displayed in the ASPX page's **Design** view. Ensure that the **Name** tab is displayed, then select Validation.aspx in the **Solution Explorer** and type *Ctrl + F5* to execute the application.

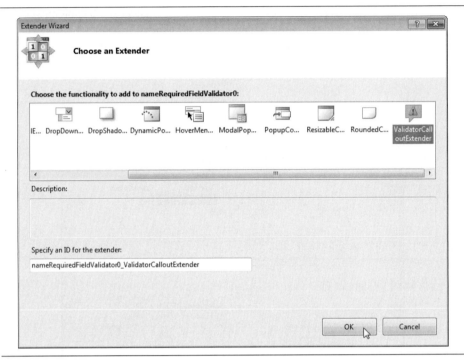

Fig. 21.23 | Creating a control extender using the **Extender Wizard**.

Additional ASP.NET Information
The Ajax Control Toolkit contains many other extenders and independent controls. You can check them out at www.asp.net/ajax/ajaxcontroltoolkit/samples/. For more information on ASP.NET Ajax, check out our ASP.NET Ajax Resource Center at

> www.deitel.com/aspdotnetajax

Summary

Section 21.2 Case Study: Password-Protected Books Database Application
- The **ASP.NET Web Site** template is a starter kit for a small multi-page website. The template uses Microsoft's recommended practices for organizing a website and separating the website's style (look-and-feel) from its content.

Section 21.2.1 Examining the ASP.NET Web Site Template
- The default **ASP.NET Web Site** contains a home page and an about page—so-called content pages. The navigation bar near the top of the page allows you to switch between these pages by clicking the link for the appropriate page.
- A master page defines common elements that are displayed by each page in a set of content pages.
- Content pages can inherit elements from master pages—this is a form of visual inheritance.

- Websites commonly provide "membership capabilities" that allow users to register at a website and log in. The default **ASP.NET Web Site** is pre-configured to support registration and login capabilities.

Section 21.2.2 Test-Driving the Completed Application
- Forms authentication enables only registered users who are logged into the website to access a password-protected page or set of pages. Such users are known as the site's members.
- If you attempt to access a password-protected page without logging in, you're automatically redirected to the login page.
- When you successfully log into the website you're considered to be authenticated.
- When you're logged in, the **Log In** link is replaced in the upper-right corner of each page with the message "Welcome *username*," where *username* is replaced with your log in name, and a **Log Out** link. When you click **Log Out**, the website redirects you to the home page.

Section 21.2.3 Configuring the Website
- To create a folder in a website, right click the location of the website in the **Solution Explorer**, select **New Folder** and type the folder name.
- To restrict access to a page, you typically place it in a directory other than the website's root.
- The **Web Site Administration Tool** allows you to configure various options that determine how your application behaves.
- An access rule grants or denies access to a particular directory for a specific user or group of users.

Section 21.2.4 Modifying the `Default.aspx` and `About.aspx` Pages
- As you move the cursor over a content page, you'll notice that sometimes the cursor displays as ⃠ to indicate that you cannot edit the part of the page behind the cursor. Any part of a content page that is defined in a master page can be edited only in the master page.

Section 21.2.5 Creating a Content Page That Only Authenticated Users Can Access
- When you create a new **Web Form** that should inherit from a specific master page, ensure that the CheckBox **Select master page** is checked. Then, in the **Select a Master Page** dialog, select the appropriate master page and click **OK**.

Section 21.2.6 Linking from the `Default.aspx` Page to the `Books.aspx` Page
- To convert text to a hyperlink, select the text then click the **Convert to Hyperlink** (🐾) Button on the toolbar at the top of Visual Web Developer to display the **Hyperlink** dialog. You can enter a URL here, or you can link to another page within the website.

Section 21.2.7 Modifying the Master Page (`Site.master`)
- A master page is like a base class in a visual inheritance hierarchy, and content pages are like derived classes. The master page contains placeholders for custom content created in each content page. The content pages visually inherit the master page's content, then add content in the areas designated by the master page's placeholders.
- The website's styles are defined in the file `Site.css`, which is located in the site's `Styles` folder.
- Select **View > Other Windows > CSS Properties** to display the CSS properties (at the left of the IDE) for the currently selected element. At the top of the **CSS Properties** window, click the **Summary** Button to show only the CSS properties that are currently set for the selected element.
- To add a link to the navigation bar in the master page, position the mouse over the navigation bar links then open the smart-tag menu and click **Edit Menu Items**. In the **Menu Item Editor** dialog,

click the **Add a root item** (⬚) Button. Set the new item's Text property and use the arrow Buttons to move the new item where it should appear in the navigation bar. Set the new item's Navigate-Url property to the appropriate page.

Section 21.2.8 Customizing the Password-Protected *Books.aspx* Page

- The **Configure Data Source** wizard allows you to create LinqDataSources with only simple Select LINQ statements. Sometimes you must add a LinqDataSource object with a custom query.

- A LinqDataSource's Selecting event occurs every time the LinqDataSource selects data from its data context, and can be used to implement custom Select queries against the data context. To do so, assign the custom LINQ query to the Result property of the event handler's LinqData-SourceSelectEventArgs argument. The query results become the data source's data.

- Setting a DropDownList's AutoPostBack property to True indicates that a postback occurs each time the user selects an item in the DropDownList.

- You can configure the columns of a GridView manually by selecting **Edit Columns...** from the **GridView Tasks** smart-tag menu.

- Checking **Enable Sorting** in the **GridView Tasks** smart-tag menu changes the column headings in the GridView to hyperlinks that allow users to sort the data in the GridView using the sort expressions specified by each column.

- Checking **Enable Paging** in the **GridView Tasks** smart-tag menu causes the GridView to split across multiple pages. The user can click the numbered links at the bottom of the GridView control to display a different page of data. GridView's PageSize property determines the number of entries per page. This technique for displaying data makes the site more readable and enables pages to load more quickly (because less data is displayed at one time).

Section 21.3 ASP.NET Ajax

- A traditional web application must make synchronous requests and must wait for a response, whereas an Ajax (Asynchronous JavaScript and XML) web applications can make asynchronous requests and do not need to wait for a response.

- The key control in every ASP.NET Ajax-enabled application is the ScriptManager (in the **Toolbox's AJAX Extensions** tab), which manages the JavaScript client-side code (called scripts) that enable asynchronous Ajax functionality. A benefit of using ASP.NET Ajax is that you do not need to know JavaScript to be able to use these scripts.

- The ScriptManager is meant for use with the controls in the **Toolbox's AJAX Extensions** tab. There can be only one ScriptManager per page.

- The Ajax Control Toolkit comes with an enhanced version of the ScriptManager called the ToolkitScriptManager, which manages all the scripts for the ASP.NET Ajax Toolkit controls. This one should be used in any ASPX page that contains controls from the ASP.NET Ajax Toolkit.

- The TabContainer control enables you to group information into tabs that are displayed only if they're selected. To add a tab, open the **TabContainer Tasks** smart-tag menu and select **Add Tab Panel**. This adds a TabPanel object—representing a tab—to the TabContainer.

- The UpdatePanel control eliminates full-page refreshes by isolating a section of a page for a partial-page update.

- To specify when an UpdatePanel should update, you need to define an UpdatePanel trigger. Select the UpdatePanel, then click the ellipsis button next to the control's Triggers property in the **Properties** window. In the **UpdatePanelTrigger Collection** dialog that appears, click **Add** to add an AsyncPostBackTrigger. Set the ControlID property to the control that triggers the update and the EventName property to the event that is generated when the user interacts with the control.

- Several controls in the Ajax Control Toolkit are extenders—components that enhance the functionality of regular ASP.NET controls.

- `ValidatorCalloutExtender` controls enhance the ASP.NET validation controls by displaying error messages in small yellow callouts next to the input fields, rather than as text in the page.

- You can create a `ValidatorCalloutExtender` by opening any validator control's smart-tag menu and clicking **Add Extender...** to display the **Extender Wizard** dialog. Next, choose `ValidatorCalloutExtender` from the list of available extenders.

Self-Review Exercises

21.1   State whether each of the following is *true* or *false*. If *false*, explain why.
  a) An access rule grants or denies access to a particular directory for a specific user or group of users.
  b) When using controls from the Ajax Control Toolkit, you must include the `ScriptManager` control at the top of the ASPX page.
  c) A master page is like a base class in a visual inheritance hierarchy, and content pages are like derived classes.
  d) A `GridView` automatically enables sorting and paging of its contents.
  e) Ajax web applications make synchronous requests and wait for responses.

21.2   Fill in the blanks in each of the following statements:
  a) A(n) _____ defines common GUI elements that are inherited by each page in a set of _____.
  b) The main difference between a traditional web application and an Ajax web application is that the latter supports _____ requests.
  c) The _____ template is a starter kit for a small multi-page website that uses Microsoft's recommended practices for organizing a website and separating the website's style (look-and-feel) from its content.
  d) The _____ allows you to configure various options that determine how your application behaves.
  e) A `LinqDataSource`'s _____ event occurs every time the `LinqDataSource` selects data from its data context, and can be used to implement custom `Select` queries against the data context.
  f) Setting a `DropDownList`'s _____ property to `True` indicates that a postback occurs each time the user selects an item in the `DropDownList`.
  g) Several controls in the Ajax Control Toolkit are _____—components that enhance the functionality of regular ASP.NET controls.

Answers to Self-Review Exercises

21.1   a) True. b) False. The `ToolkitScriptManager` control must be used for controls from the Ajax Control Toolkit. The `ScriptManager` control can be used only for the controls in the **Toolbox**'s **AJAX Extensions** tab. c) True. d) False. Checking **Enable Sorting** in the **GridView Tasks** smart-tag menu changes the column headings in the `GridView` to hyperlinks that allow users to sort the data in the `GridView`. Checking **Enable Paging** in the **GridView Tasks** smart-tag menu causes the `GridView` to split across multiple pages. e) False. That is what traditional web applications do. Ajax web applications can make asynchronous requests and do not need to wait for responses.

21.2   a) master page, content pages. b) asynchronous. c) **ASP.NET Web Site**. d) **Web Site Administration Tool**. e) `Selecting`. f) `AutoPostBack`. g) extenders.

Exercises

21.3 *(Guestbook Application Modification)* Add Ajax functionality to the Guestbook application in Exercise 20.5. Use control extenders to display error callouts when one of the user input fields is invalid.

21.4 *(Guestbook Application Modification)* Modify the Guestbook application in Exercise 21.3 to use a UpdatePanel so only the GridView updates when the user submits the form. Because only the UpdatePanel will be updated, you cannot clear the user input fields in the **Submit** button's Click event, so you can remove this functionality.

21.5 *(Session Tracking Modification)* Use the **ASP.NET Web Site** template that you learned about in this chapter to reimplement the session tracking example in Exercise 20.7.

Web Services in C#

A client is to me a mere unit, a factor in a problem.
—Sir Arthur Conan Doyle

...if the simplest things of nature have a message that you understand, rejoice, for your soul is alive.
—Eleonora Duse

Objectives

In this chapter you'll learn:

- How to create WCF web services.

- How XML, JSON, XML-Based Simple Object Access Protocol (SOAP) and Representational State Transfer Architecture (REST) enable WCF web services.

- The elements that comprise WCF web services, such as service references, service endpoints, service contracts and service bindings.

- How to create a client that consumes a WCF web service.

- How to use WCF web services with Windows and web applications.

- How to use session tracking in WCF web services to maintain state information for the client.

- How to pass user-defined types to a WCF web service.

22.1 Introduction

This chapter introduces **Windows Communication Foundation (WCF)** services. WCF is a set of technologies for building distributed systems in which system components communicate with one another over networks. In earlier versions of .NET, the various types of communication used different technologies and programming models. WCF uses a common framework for all communication between systems, so you need to learn only one programming model to use WCF.

This chapter focuses on WCF web services, which promote software reusability in distributed systems that typically execute across the Internet. A **web service** is a class that allows its methods to be called by methods on other machines via common data formats and protocols, such as XML, JSON (Section 22.5) and HTTP. In .NET, the over-the-network method calls are commonly implemented through **Simple Object Access Protocol (SOAP)** or the **Representational State Transfer (REST)** architecture. SOAP is an XML-based protocol describing how to mark up requests and responses so that they can be sent via protocols such as HTTP. SOAP uses a standardized XML-based format to enclose data in a message that can be sent between a client and a server. REST is a network architecture that uses the web's traditional request/response mechanisms such as GET and POST requests. REST-based systems do not require data to be wrapped in a special message format.

We build the WCF web services presented in this chapter in Visual Web Developer 2010 Express, and we create client applications that invoke these services using both Visual C# 2010 Express and Visual Web Developer 2010 Express. Full versions of Visual Studio 2010 include the functionality of both Express editions.

Requests to and responses from web services created with Visual Web Developer are typically transmitted via SOAP or REST, so any client capable of generating and processing SOAP or REST messages can interact with a web service, regardless of the language in which the web service is written. We say more about SOAP and REST in Section 22.3 and Section 22.4, respectively.

22.2 WCF Services Basics

Microsoft's Windows Communication Foundation (WCF) was created as a single platform to encompass many existing communication technologies. WCF increases productivity, because you learn only one straightforward programming model. Each WCF service has three key components—addresses, bindings and contracts (usually called the ABCs of a WCF service):

- An **address** represents the service's location (also known as its **endpoint**), which includes the protocol (for example, HTTP) and network address (for example, www.deitel.com) used to access the service.

- A **binding** specifies how a client communicates with the service (for example, SOAP, REST, and so on). Bindings can also specify other options, such as security constraints.

- A **contract** is an interface representing the service's methods and their return types. The service's contract allows clients to interact with the service.

The machine on which the web service resides is referred to as a **web service host**. The client application that accesses the web service sends a method call over a network to the web service host, which processes the call and returns a response over the network to the application. This kind of distributed computing benefits systems in various ways. For example, an application without direct access to data on another system might be able to retrieve this data via a web service. Similarly, an application lacking the processing power necessary to perform specific computations could use a web service to take advantage of another system's superior resources.

22.3 Simple Object Access Protocol (SOAP)

The Simple Object Access Protocol (SOAP) is a platform-independent protocol that uses XML to make remote procedure calls, typically over HTTP. Each request and response is packaged in a **SOAP message**—an XML message containing the information that a web service requires to process the message. SOAP messages are written in XML so that they're computer readable, human readable and platform independent. Most **firewalls**—security barriers that restrict communication among networks—allow HTTP traffic to pass through, so that clients can browse the Internet by sending requests to and receiving responses from web servers. Thus, SOAP-based services can send and receive SOAP messages over HTTP connections with few limitations.

SOAP supports an extensive set of types. The **wire format** used to transmit requests and responses must support all types passed between the applications. SOAP types include the primitive types (for example, `int`), as well as `DateTime`, `XmlNode` and others. SOAP can also transmit arrays of these types. In Section 22.11, you'll see that you can also transmit user-defined types in SOAP messages.

When a program invokes a method of a SOAP web service, the request and all relevant information are packaged in a SOAP message enclosed in a **SOAP envelope** and sent to the server on which the web service resides. When the web service receives this SOAP message, it parses the XML representing the message, then processes the message's contents. The message specifies the method that the client wishes to execute and the arguments the client passed to that method. Next, the web service calls the method with the specified arguments (if any) and sends the response back to the client in another SOAP message. The client parses the response to retrieve the method's result. In Section 22.6, you'll build and consume a basic SOAP web service.

22.4 Representational State Transfer (REST)

Representational State Transfer (REST) refers to an architectural style for implementing web services. Such web services are often called **RESTful web services**. Though REST itself is not a standard, RESTful web services are implemented using web standards. Each operation in a RESTful web service is identified by a unique URL. Thus, when the server receives a request, it immediately knows what operation to perform. Such web services can be used in a program or directly from a web browser. The results of a particular operation may be cached locally by the browser when the service is invoked with a GET request. This can make subsequent requests for the same operation faster by loading the result directly from the browser's cache. Amazon's web services (`aws.amazon.com`) are RESTful, as are many others.

RESTful web services are alternatives to those implemented with SOAP. Unlike SOAP-based web services, the request and response of REST services are not wrapped in envelopes. REST is also not limited to returning data in XML format. It can use a variety of formats, such as XML, JSON, HTML, plain text and media files. In Sections 22.7–22.8, you'll build and consume basic RESTful web services.

22.5 JavaScript Object Notation (JSON)

JavaScript Object Notation (JSON) is an alternative to XML for representing data. JSON is a text-based data-interchange format used to represent objects in JavaScript as collections of name/value pairs represented as `Strings`. It is commonly used in Ajax applications. JSON is a simple format that makes objects easy to read, create and parse, and allows programs to transmit data efficiently across the Internet because it is much less verbose than XML. Each JSON object is represented as a list of property names and values contained in curly braces, in the following format:

```
{ propertyName1 : value1, propertyName2 : value2 }
```

Arrays are represented in JSON with square brackets in the following format:

```
[ value1, value2, value3 ]
```

Each value in an array can be a string, a number, a JSON object, true, false or null. To appreciate the simplicity of JSON data, examine this representation of an array of address-book entries

```
[ { first: 'Cheryl', last: 'Black' },
  { first: 'James', last: 'Blue' },
  { first: 'Mike', last: 'Brown' },
  { first: 'Meg', last: 'Gold' } ]
```

Many programming languages now support the JSON data format.

22.6 Publishing and Consuming SOAP-Based WCF Web Services

This section presents our first example of **publishing** (enabling for client access) and **consuming** (using) a web service. We begin with a SOAP-based web service.

22.6.1 Creating a WCF Web Service

To build a SOAP-based WCF web service in Visual Web Developer, you first create a project of type **WCF Service**. SOAP is the default protocol for WCF web services, so no special configuration is required to create them. Visual Web Developer then generates files for the WCF service code, an **SVC file** (Service.svc, which provides access to the service), and a **Web.config** file (which specifies the service's binding and behavior).

Visual Web Developer also generates code files for the **WCF service class** and any other code that is part of the WCF service implementation. In the service class, you define the methods that your WCF web service makes available to client applications.

22.6.2 Code for the WelcomeSOAPXMLService

Figures 22.1 and 22.2 present the code-behind files for the WelcomeSOAPXMLService WCF web service that you'll build in Section 22.6.3. When creating services in Visual Web Developer, you work almost exclusively in the code-behind files. The service provides a method that takes a name (represented as a string) as an argument and appends it to the welcome message that is returned to the client. We use a parameter in the method definition to demonstrate that a client can send data to a web service.

Figure 22.1 is the service's interface, which describes the service's contract—the set of methods and properties the client uses to access the service. The **ServiceContract** attribute (line 6) exposes a class that implements this interface as a WCF web service. The **OperationContract** attribute (line 10) exposes the Welcome method to clients for remote calls. Optional parameters can be assigned to these contracts to change the data format and method behavior, as we'll show in later examples.

Figure 22.2 defines the class that implements the interface declared as the ServiceContract. Lines 7–12 define the method Welcome, which returns a string welcoming you to WCF web services. Next, we build the web service from scratch.

```
 I   // Fig. 22.1: IWelcomeSOAPXMLService.cs
 2   // WCF web service interface that returns a welcome message through SOAP
 3   // protocol and XML data format.
 4   using System.ServiceModel;
 5
 6   [ServiceContract]
 7   public interface IWelcomeSOAPXMLService
 8   {
 9      // returns a welcome message
10      [OperationContract]
11      string Welcome( string yourName );
12   } // end interface IWelcomeSOAPXMLService
```

Fig. 22.1 | WCF web-service interface that returns a welcome message through SOAP protocol and XML format.

```
 I   // Fig. 22.2: WelcomeSOAPXMLService.cs
 2   // WCF web service that returns a welcome message using SOAP protocol and
 3   // XML data format.
 4   public class WelcomeSOAPXMLService : IWelcomeSOAPXMLService
 5   {
 6      // returns a welcome message
 7      public string Welcome( string yourName )
 8      {
 9         return string.Format(
10            "Welcome to WCF Web Services with SOAP and XML, {0}!",
11            yourName );
12      } // end method Welcome
13   } // end class WelcomeSOAPXMLService
```

Fig. 22.2 | WCF web service that returns a welcome message through the SOAP protocol and XML format.

22.6.3 Building a SOAP WCF Web Service

In the following steps, you create a **WCF Service** project for the WelcomeSOAPXMLService and test it using the built-in ASP.NET Development Server that comes with Visual Web Developer Express and Visual Studio.

Step 1: Creating the Project
To create a project of type **WCF Service**, select **File > New Web Site...** to display the **New Web Site** dialog (Fig. 22.3). Select the **WCF Service** template. Select **File System** from the **Location** drop-down list to indicate that the files should be placed on your local hard disk. By default, Visual Web Developer places files on the local machine in a directory named WCFService1. Rename this folder to WelcomeSOAPXMLService. We modified the default path as well. Click **OK** to create the project.

Step 2: Examining the Newly Created Project
After you create the project, the code-behind file Service.cs, which contains code for a simple web service, is displayed by default. If the code-behind file is not open, open it by double clicking the file in the **App_Code** directory listed in the **Solution Explorer**. By

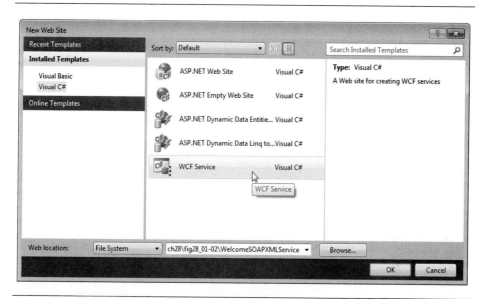

Fig. 22.3 | Creating a **WCF Service** in Visual Web Developer.

default, a new code-behind file implements an interface named IService. This interface (in the file IService.cs) is marked with the ServiceContract and OperationContract attributes. In addition, the IService.cs file defines a class named CompositeType with a DataContract attribute (discussed in Section 22.8). The interface contains two sample service methods named GetData and GetDataUsingContract. The Service.cs contains the code that defines these methods.

Step 3: Modifying and Renaming the Code-Behind File

To create the WelcomeSOAPXMLService service developed in this section, modify IService.cs and Service.cs by replacing the sample code provided by Visual Web Developer with the code from the IWelcomeSOAPXMLService and WelcomeSOAPXMLService files (Figs. 22.1 and 22.2, respectively). Then rename the files to IWelcomeSOAPXMLService.cs and WelcomeSOAPXMLService.cs by right clicking each file in the Solution Explorer and choosing **Rename**.

Step 4: Examining the SVC File

The Service.svc file, when accessed through a web browser, provides information about the web service. However, if you open the SVC file on disk, it contains only

```
<%@ ServiceHost Language="C#" Debug="true" Service="Service"
    CodeBehind="~/App_Code/Service.cs" %>
```

to indicate the programming language in which the web service's code-behind file is written, the Debug attribute (enables a page to be compiled for debugging), the name of the service and the code-behind file's location. When you request the SVC page in a web browser, WCF uses this information to dynamically generate the WSDL document.

Step 5: Modifying the SVC File

If you change the code-behind file name or the class name that defines the web service, you must modify the SVC file accordingly. Thus, after defining class `WelcomeSOAPXMLService` in the code-behind file `WelcomeSOAPXMLService.cs`, modify the SVC file as follows:

```
<%@ ServiceHost Language="C#" Debug="true"
   Service="WelcomeSOAPXMLService"
   CodeBehind="~/App_Code/WelcomeSOAPXMLService.cs" %>
```

22.6.4 Deploying the `WelcomeSOAPXMLService`

You can choose **Build Web Site** from the **Build** menu to ensure that the web service compiles without errors. You can also test the web service directly from Visual Web Developer by selecting **Start Debugging** from the **Debug** menu. The first time you do this, the **Debugging Not Enabled** dialog appears. Click **OK** if you want to enable debugging. Next, a browser window opens and displays information about the service. This information is generated dynamically when the SVC file is requested. Figure 22.4 shows a web browser displaying the `Service.svc` file for the `WelcomeSOAPXMLService` WCF web service.

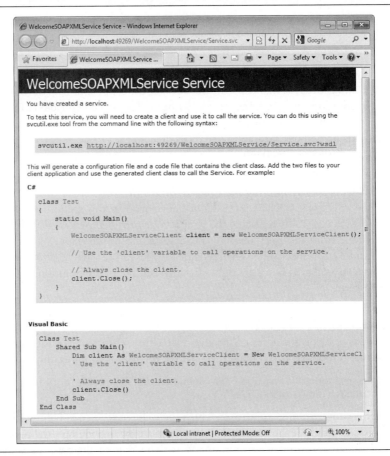

Fig. 22.4 | SVC file rendered in a web browser.

Once the service is running, you can also access the SVC page from your browser by typing a URL of the following form in a web browser:

```
http://localhost:portNumber/virtualPath/Service.svc
```

(See the actual URL in Fig. 22.4.) By default, the ASP.NET Development Server assigns a random port number to each website it hosts. You can change this behavior by going to the **Solution Explorer** and clicking on the project name to view the **Properties** window (Fig. 22.5). Set the **Use dynamic ports** property to **False** and set the **Port number** property to the port number that you want to use, which can be any unused TCP port. Generally, you don't do this for web services that will be deployed to a real web server. You can also change the service's virtual path, perhaps to make the path shorter or more readable.

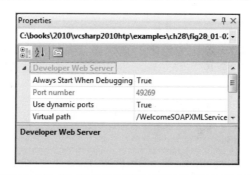

Fig. 22.5 | WCF web service **Properties** window.

Web Services Description Language

To consume a web service, a client must determine the service's functionality and how to use it. For this purpose, web services normally contain a **service description**. This is an XML document that conforms to the **Web Service Description Language (WSDL)**—an XML vocabulary that defines the methods a web service makes available and how clients interact with them. The WSDL document also specifies lower-level information that clients might need, such as the required formats for requests and responses.

WSDL documents help applications determine how to interact with the web services described in the documents. When viewed in a web browser, an SVC file presents a link to the service's WSDL document and information on using the utility **svcutil.exe** to generate test console applications. The svcutil.exe tool is included with Visual Studio 2010 and Visual Web Developer. We do not use svcutil.exe to test our services, opting instead to build our own test applications. When a client requests the SVC file's URL followed by ?wsdl, the server autogenerates the WSDL that describes the web service and returns the WSDL document. Copy the SVC URL (which ends with .svc) from the browser's address field in Fig. 22.4, as you'll need it in the next section to build the client application. Also, leave the web service running so the client can interact with it.

22.6.5 Creating a Client to Consume the WelcomeSOAPXMLService

Now that you've defined and deployed the web service, let's consume it from a client application. A .NET web-service client can be any type of .NET application, such as a Windows application, a console application or a web application. You can enable a client application to consume a web service by **adding a service reference** to the client. Figure 22.6 diagrams the parts of a client for a SOAP-based web service after a service reference has been added. [*Note*: This section discusses building a client application in Visual C# 2010 Express, but the discussion also applies to Visual Web Developer 2010 Express.]

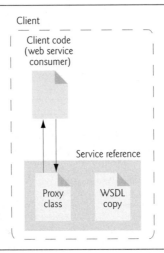

Fig. 22.6 | .NET WCF web-service client after a web-service reference has been added.

An application that consumes a SOAP-based web service actually consists of two parts—a proxy class representing the web service and a client application that accesses the web service via a proxy object (that is, an instance of the proxy class). A **proxy class** handles all the "plumbing" required for service method calls (that is, the networking details and the formation of SOAP messages). Whenever the client application calls a web service's method, the application actually calls a corresponding method in the proxy class. This method has the same name and parameters as the web service's method that is being called, but formats the call to be sent as a request in a SOAP message. The web service receives this request as a SOAP message, executes the method call and sends back the result as another SOAP message. When the client application receives the SOAP message containing the response, the proxy class deserializes it and returns the results as the return value of the web-service method that was called. Figure 22.7 depicts the interactions among the client code, proxy class and web service. The proxy class is not shown in the project unless you click the **Show All Files** button in the **Solution Explorer.**

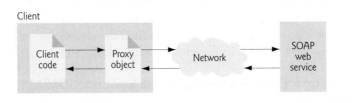

Fig. 22.7 | Interaction between a web-service client and a SOAP web service.

Many aspects of web-service creation and consumption—such as generating WSDL files and proxy classes—are handled by Visual Web Developer, Visual C# 2010 and WCF. Although developers are relieved of the tedious process of creating these files, they can still modify the files if necessary. This is required only when developing advanced web services—none of our examples require modifications to these files.

We now create a client and generate a proxy class that allows the client to access the WelcomeSOAPXMLService web service. First create a Windows application named WelcomeSOAPXMLClient in Visual C# 2010, then perform the following steps.

Step 1: Opening the Add Service Reference *Dialog*
Right click the project name in the **Solution Explorer** and select **Add Service Reference...** to display the **Add Service Reference** dialog.

Step 2: Specifying the Web Service's Location
In the dialog, enter the URL of WelcomeSOAPXMLService's .svc file (that is, the URL you copied from Fig. 22.4) in the **Address** field and click **Go**. When you specify the service you want to consume, the IDE accesses the web service's WSDL information and copies it into a WSDL file that is stored in the client project's Service References folder. This file is visible when you view all of your project's files in the **Solution Explorer**. [*Note:* A copy of the WSDL file provides the client application with local access to the web service's description. To ensure that the WSDL file is up to date, Visual C# 2010 provides an **Update Service Reference** option (available by right clicking the service reference in the **Solution Explorer**), which updates the files in the Service References folder.]

Many companies that provide web services simply distribute the exact URLs at which their web services can be accessed. The **Add Service Reference** dialog also allows you to search for services on your local machine or on the Internet.

Step 3: Renaming the Service Reference's Namespace
In the **Add Service Reference** dialog, rename the service reference's namespace by changing the **Namespace** field to ServiceReference.

Step 4: Adding the Service Reference
Click the **Ok** button to add the service reference.

Step 5: Viewing the Service Reference in the Solution Explorer
The **Solution Explorer** should now contain a **Service References** folder with a node showing the namespace you specified in *Step 3*.

22.6.6 Consuming the WelcomeSOAPXMLService
Figure 22.8 uses the WelcomeSOAPXMLService service to send a welcome message. You are already familiar with Visual C# applications that use Labels, TextBoxes and Buttons, so we focus our discussions on the web-services concepts in this chapter's applications.

Line 11 defines a new ServiceReference.WelcomeSOAPXMLServiceClient proxy object named client. The event handler uses this object to call methods of the WelcomeSOAPXMLService web service. Line 22 invokes the WelcomeSOAPXMLService web service's Welcome method. The call is made via the local proxy object client, which then communicates with the web service on the client's behalf. If you're using the downloaded exam-

```
 1   // Fig. 22.8: WelcomeSOAPXML.cs
 2   // Client that consumes the WelcomeSOAPXMLService.
 3   using System;
 4   using System.Windows.Forms;
 5
 6   namespace WelcomeSOAPXMLClient
 7   {
 8      public partial class WelcomeSOAPXML : Form
 9      {
10         // declare a reference to web service
11         private ServiceReference.WelcomeSOAPXMLServiceClient client;
12
13         public WelcomeSOAPXML()
14         {
15            InitializeComponent();
16            client = new ServiceReference.WelcomeSOAPXMLServiceClient();
17         } // end constructor
18
19         // creates welcome message from text input and web service
20         private void submitButton_Click( object sender, EventArgs e )
21         {
22            MessageBox.Show( client.Welcome( textBox.Text ), "Welcome" );
23         } // end method submitButton_Click
24      } // end class WelcomeSOAPXML
25   } // end namespace WelcomeSOAPXMLClient
```

a) User inputs name and clicks **Submit** to send it to the web service

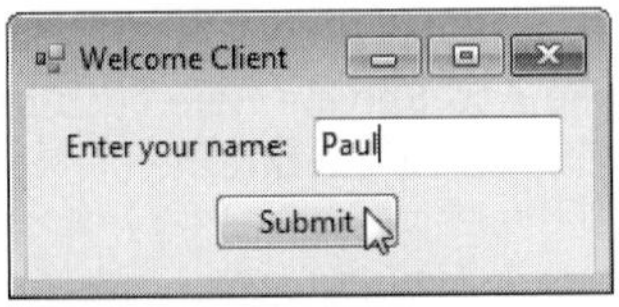

Welcome Client

Enter your name: Paul

Submit

b) Message returned by the web service

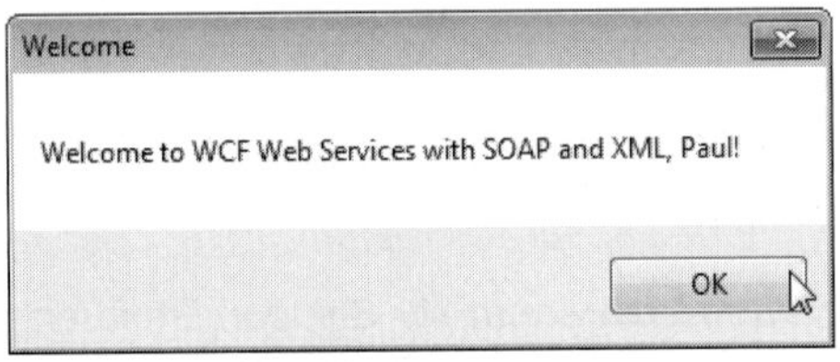

Welcome

Welcome to WCF Web Services with SOAP and XML, Paul!

OK

Fig. 22.8 | Client that consumes the WelcomeSOAPXMLService.

ples from this chapter, you may need to regenerate the proxy by removing the service reference, then adding it again, because ASP.NET Development Server may use a different port number on your computer. To do so, right click ServiceReference in the **Service References** folder in the **Solution Explorer** and select option **Delete**. Then follow the instructions in Section 22.6.5 to add the service reference to the project.

When the application runs, enter your name and click the **Submit** button. The application invokes the Welcome service method to perform the appropriate task and return the result, then displays the result in a MessageBox.

22.7 Publishing and Consuming REST-Based XML Web Services

In the previous section, we used a proxy object to pass data to and from a WCF web service using the SOAP protocol. In this section, we access a WCF web service using the REST architecture. We modify the `IWelcomeSOAPXMLService` example to return data in plain XML format. You can create a **WCF Service** project as you did in Section 22.6 to begin.

22.7.1 HTTP get and post Requests

The two most common **HTTP request types** (also known as **request methods**) are get and post. A **get request** typically gets (or retrieves) information from a server. Common uses of get requests are to retrieve a document or an image, or to fetch search results based on a user-submitted search term. A **post request** typically posts (or sends) data to a server. Common uses of post requests are to send form data or documents to a server.

An HTTP request often posts data to a **server-side form handler** that processes the data. For example, when a user performs a search or participates in a web-based survey, the web server receives the information specified in the XHTML form as part of the request. *Both* types of requests can be used to send form data to a web server, yet each request type sends the information differently.

A get request sends information to the server in the URL. For example, in the following URL

```
www.google.com/search?q=deitel
```

search is the name of Google's server-side form handler, q is the name of a *variable* in Google's search form and deitel is the search term. A ? separates the **query string** from the rest of the URL in a request. A *name/value* pair is passed to the server with the *name* and the *value* separated by an equals sign (=). If more than one *name/value* pair is submitted, each pair is separated by an ampersand (&). The server uses data passed in a query string to retrieve an appropriate resource from the server. The server then sends a **response** to the client. A get request may be initiated by submitting an XHTML form whose method attribute is set to "get", or by typing the URL (possibly containing a query string) directly into the browser's address bar.

A post request sends form data as part of the HTTP message, not as part of the URL. A get request typically limits the query string (that is, everything to the right of the ?) to a specific number of characters. For example, Internet Explorer restricts the entire URL to no more than 2083 characters. Typically, large amounts of information should be sent using the post method. The post method is also sometimes preferred because it *hides* the submitted data from the user by embedding it in an HTTP message. If a form submits hidden input values along with user-submitted data, the post method might generate a URL like www.searchengine.com/search. The form data still reaches the server for processing, but the user does not see the exact information sent.

22.7.2 Creating a REST-Based XML WCF Web Service

Step 1: Adding the WebGet Attribute
IWelcomeRESTXMLService interface (Fig. 22.9) is a modified version of the IWelcome-SOAPXMLService interface. The Welcome method's **WebGet** attribute (line 12) maps a meth-

od to a unique URL that can be accessed via an HTTP get operation programmatically or in a web browser. To use the WebGet attribute, we import the System.ServiceModel.Web namespace (line 5). WebGet's **UriTemplate** property (line 12) specifies the URI format that is used to invoke the method. You can access the Welcome method in a web browser by appending text that matches the UriTemplate definition to the end of the service's location, as in http://localhost:*portNumber*/WelcomeRESTXMLService/Service.svc/welcome/ Paul. WelcomeRESTXMLService (Fig. 22.10) is the class that implements the IWelcomeRESTXMLService interface; it is similar to the WelcomeSOAPXMLService class (Fig. 22.2).

```
 1   // Fig. 22.9: IWelcomeRESTXMLService.cs
 2   // WCF web service interface. A class that implements this interface
 3   // returns a welcome message through REST architecture and XML data format
 4   using System.ServiceModel;
 5   using System.ServiceModel.Web;
 6
 7   [ServiceContract]
 8   public interface IWelcomeRESTXMLService
 9   {
10      // returns a welcome message
11      [OperationContract]
12      [WebGet( UriTemplate = "/welcome/{yourName}" )]
13      string Welcome( string yourName );
14   } // end interface IWelcomeRESTXMLService
```

Fig. 22.9 | WCF web-service interface. A class that implements this interface returns a welcome message through REST architecture and XML data format.

```
 1   // Fig. 22.10: WelcomeRESTXMLService.cs
 2   // WCF web service that returns a welcome message using REST architecture
 3   // and XML data format.
 4   public class WelcomeRESTXMLService : IWelcomeRESTXMLService
 5   {
 6      // returns a welcome message
 7      public string Welcome( string yourName )
 8      {
 9         return string.Format( "Welcome to WCF Web Services"
10            + " with REST and XML, {0}!", yourName );
11      } // end method Welcome
12   } // end class WelcomeRESTXMLService
```

Fig. 22.10 | WCF web service that returns a welcome message using REST architecture and XML data format.

Step 2: Modifying the **Web.config** File

Figure 22.11 shows part of the default Web.config file modified to use REST architecture. The **endpointBehaviors** element (lines 16–20) in the behaviors element indicates that this web service endpoint will be accessed using the web programming model (REST).

The nested **webHttp** element specifies that clients communicate with this service using the standard HTTP request/response mechanism. The **protocolMapping** element (lines 22–24) in the system.serviceModel element, changes the default protocol for communicating with this web service (normally SOAP) to **webHttpBinding**, which is used for REST-based HTTP requests.

```
 1  <system.serviceModel>
 2    <behaviors>
 3      <serviceBehaviors>
 4        <behavior>
 5          <!-- To avoid disclosing metadata information, set the
 6               value below to false and remove the metadata
 7               endpoint above before deployment -->
 8          <serviceMetadata httpGetEnabled="true"/>
 9          <!-- To receive exception details in faults for debugging
10               purposes, set the value below to true.  Set to false
11               before deployment to avoid disclosing exception
12               information -->
13          <serviceDebug includeExceptionDetailInFaults="false"/>
14        </behavior>
15      </serviceBehaviors>
16      <endpointBehaviors>
17        <behavior>
18          <webHttp/>
19        </behavior>
20      </endpointBehaviors>
21    </behaviors>
22    <protocolMapping>
23      <add scheme="http" binding="webHttpBinding"/>
24    </protocolMapping>
25    <serviceHostingEnvironment multipleSiteBindingsEnabled="true"/>
26  </system.serviceModel>
```

Fig. 22.11 | WelcomeRESTXMLService Web.config file.

Figure 22.12 tests the WelcomeRESTXMLService's Welcome method in a web browser. The URL specifies the location of the Service.svc file and uses the URI template to invoke method Welcome with the argument Bruce. The browser displays the XML data response from WelcomeRESTXMLService. Next, you'll learn how to consume this service.

Fig. 22.12 | Response from WelcomeRESTXMLService in XML data format.

22.7.3 Consuming a REST-Based XML WCF Web Service

Class WelcomeRESTXML (Fig. 22.13) uses the System.Net namespace's **WebClient** class (line 13) to invoke the web service and receive its response. In lines 23–25, we register a handler for the WebClient's DownloadStringCompleted event.

```
 1   // Fig. 22.13: WelcomeRESTXML.cs
 2   // Client that consumes the WelcomeRESTXMLService.
 3   using System;
 4   using System.Net;
 5   using System.Windows.Forms;
 6   using System.Xml.Linq;
 7
 8   namespace WelcomeRESTXMLClient
 9   {
10      public partial class WelcomeRESTXML : Form
11      {
12         // object to invoke the WelcomeRESTXMLService
13         private WebClient client = new WebClient();
14
15         private XNamespace xmlNamespace = XNamespace.Get(
16            "http://schemas.microsoft.com/2003/10/Serialization/" );
17
18         public WelcomeRESTXML()
19         {
20            InitializeComponent();
21
22            // add DownloadStringCompleted event handler to WebClient
23            client.DownloadStringCompleted +=
24               new DownloadStringCompletedEventHandler(
25               client_DownloadStringCompleted );
26         } // end constructor
27
28         // get user input and pass it to the web service
29         private void submitButton_Click( object sender, EventArgs e )
30         {
31            // send request to WelcomeRESTXMLService
32            client.DownloadStringAsync( new Uri(
33               "http://localhost:49429/WelcomeRESTXMLService/Service.svc/" +
34               "welcome/" + textBox.Text ) );
35         } // end method submitButton_Click
36
37         // process web service response
38         private void client_DownloadStringCompleted(
39            object sender, DownloadStringCompletedEventArgs e )
40         {
41            // check if any error occurred in retrieving service data
42            if ( e.Error == null )
43            {
44               // parse the returned XML string (e.Result)
45               XDocument xmlResponse = XDocument.Parse( e.Result );
46
```

Fig. 22.13 | Client that consumes the WelcomeRESTXMLService. (Part 1 of 2.)

```
47                    // get the <string> element's value
48                    MessageBox.Show( xmlResponse.Element(
49                       xmlNamespace + "string" ).Value, "Welcome" );
50                 } // end if
51              } // end method client_DownloadStringCompleted
52           } // end class WelcomeRESTXML
53        } // end namespace WelcomeRESTXMLClient
```

a) User inputs name

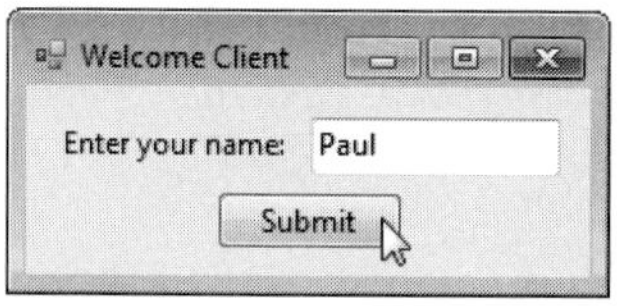

b) Message sent from **WelcomeRESTXMLService**

Welcome Client

Enter your name: Paul

Submit

Welcome

Welcome to WCF Web Services with REST and XML, Paul!

OK

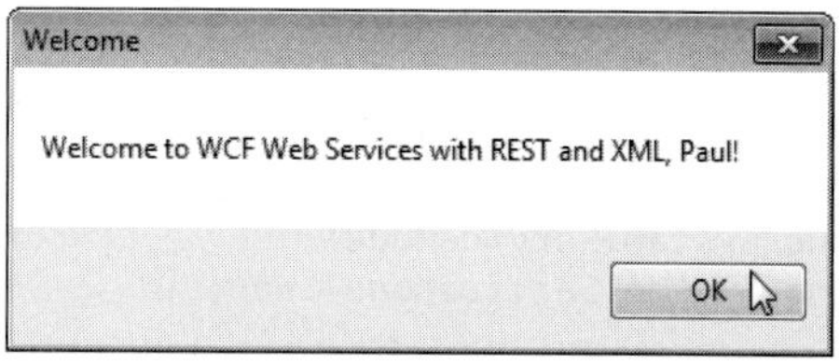

Fig. 22.13 | Client that consumes the `WelcomeRESTXMLService`. (Part 2 of 2.)

In this example, we process the WebClient's **DownloadStringCompleted** event, which occurs when the client receives the completed response from the web service. Lines 32–34 call the client object's **DownloadStringAsync** method to invoke the web service asynchronously. (There's also a synchronous DownloadString method that does not return until it receives the response.) The method's argument (i.e., the URL to invoke the web service) must be specified as an object of class **Uri**. Class Uri's constructor receives a string representing a uniform resource identifier. [*Note:* The URL's port number must match the one issued to the web service by the ASP.NET Development Server.] When the call to the web service completes, the WebClient object raises the DownloadStringCompleted event. Its event handler has a parameter e of type **DownloadStringCompletedEventArgs** which contains the information returned by the web service. We can use this variable's properties to get the returned XML document (**e.Result**) and any errors that may have occurred during the process (**e.Error**). We then parse the XML response using XDocument method Parse (line 45). In lines 15–16, we specify the XML message's namespace (seen in Fig. 22.12), and use it to parse the service's XML response to display our welcome string in a MessageBox (lines 48–49).

22.8 Publishing and Consuming REST-Based JSON Web Services

We now build a RESTful web service that returns data in JSON format.

22.8.1 Creating a REST-Based JSON WCF Web Service

By default, a web-service method with the WebGet attribute returns data in XML format. In Fig. 22.14, we modify the WelcomeRESTXMLService to return data in JSON format by setting WebGet's **ResponseFormat** property to WebMessageFormat.Json (line 13). (WebMessageFormat.XML is the default value.) For JSON serialization to work properly, the objects being converted to JSON must have Public properties. This enables the JSON serialization to create name/value pairs representing each Public property and its corresponding value. The previous examples return String objects containing the responses. Even though Strings are objects, Strings do not have any Public properties that represent their contents. So, lines 19–25 define a TextMessage class that encapsulates a String value and defines a Public property Message to access that value. The **DataContract** attribute (line 19) exposes the TextMessage class to the client access. Similarly, the **DataMember** attribute (line 23) exposes a property of this class to the client. This property will appear in the JSON object as a name/value pair. Only DataMembers of a DataContract are serialized.

```
1   // Fig. 22.14: IWelcomeRESTJSONService.cs
2   // WCF web service interface that returns a welcome message through REST
3   // architecture and JSON format.
4   using System.Runtime.Serialization;
5   using System.ServiceModel;
6   using System.ServiceModel.Web;
7
8   [ServiceContract]
9   public interface IWelcomeRESTJSONService
10  {
11     // returns a welcome message
12     [OperationContract]
13     [WebGet( ResponseFormat = WebMessageFormat.Json,
14        UriTemplate = "/welcome/{yourName}" )]
15     TextMessage Welcome( string yourName );
16  } // end interface IWelcomeRESTJSONService
17
18  // class to encapsulate a string to send in JSON format
19  [DataContract]
20  public class TextMessage
21  {
22     // automatic property message
23     [DataMember]
24     public string Message {get; set; }
25  } // end class TextMessage
```

Fig. 22.14 | WCF web-service interface that returns a welcome message through REST architecture and JSON format.

Figure 22.15 shows the implementation of the interface of Fig. 22.14. The Welcome method (lines 7–15) returns a TextMessage object, reflecting the changes we made to the interface class. This object is automatically serialized in JSON format (as a result of line 13 in Fig. 22.14) and sent to the client.

```
1   // Fig. 22.15: WelcomeRESTJSONService.cs
2   // WCF web service that returns a welcome message through REST
3   // architecture and JSON format.
4   public class WelcomeRESTJSONService : IWelcomeRESTJSONService
5   {
```

Fig. 22.15 | WCF web service that returns a welcome message through REST architecture and JSON format. (Part 1 of 2.)

```
 6      // returns a welcome message
 7      public TextMessage Welcome( string yourName )
 8      {
 9         // add welcome message to field of TextMessage object
10         TextMessage message = new TextMessage();
11         message.Message = string.Format(
12            "Welcome to WCF Web Services with REST and JSON, {0}!",
13            yourName );
14         return message;
15      } // end method Welcome
16   } // end class WelcomeRESTJSONService
```

Fig. 22.15 | WCF web service that returns a welcome message through REST architecture and JSON format. (Part 2 of 2.)

We can once again test the web service using a web browser, by accessing the Service.svc file (http://localhost:49745/WelcomeRESTJSONService/Service.svc) and appending the URI template (welcome/*yourName*) to the address. The response prompts you to download a file called *yourName*, which is a text file. If you save it to disk, the file will have the .json extension. This contains the JSON formatted data. By opening the file in a text editor such as Notepad (Fig. 22.16), you can see the service response as a JSON object. Notice that the property named Message has the welcome message as its value.

Fig. 22.16 | Response from WelcomeRESTJSONService in JSON data format.

22.8.2 Consuming a REST-Based JSON WCF Web Service

We mentioned earlier that all types passed to and from web services can be supported by REST. Custom types that are sent to or from a REST web service are converted to XML or JSON data format. This process is referred to as **XML serialization** or **JSON serialization**, respectively. In Fig. 22.17, we consume the WelcomeRESTJSONService service using an object of the System.Runtime.Serialization.Json library's **DataContractJsonSerializer** class (lines 44–45). The TextMessage class (lines 57–61) maps the JSON response's fields for the DataContractJsonSerializer to deserialize. We add the **Serializable** attribute (line 57) to the TextMessage class to recognize it as a valid serializable object we can convert to and from JSON format. Also, this class on the client must have public data or properties that match the public data or properties in the corresponding class from the web service. Since we want to convert the JSON response into a TextMessage object, we set the DataContractJsonSerializer's type parameter to TextMessage (line 45). In line 48, we use the System.Text namespace's Encoding.Unicode.GetBytes method to convert the JSON response to a Unicode encoded byte array, and encapsulate the byte array in a MemoryStream object so we can read data from the array using stream semantics. The bytes in the MemoryStream object are read by the DataContractJsonSerializer and deserialized into a TextMessage object (lines 47–48).

```
 1   // Fig. 22.17: WelcomeRESTJSONForm.cs
 2   // Client that consumes the WelcomeRESTJSONService.
 3   using System;
 4   using System.IO;
 5   using System.Net;
 6   using System.Runtime.Serialization.Json;
 7   using System.Text;
 8   using System.Windows.Forms;
 9
10   namespace WelcomeRESTJSONClient
11   {
12      public partial class WelcomeRESTJSONForm : Form
13      {
14         // object to invoke the WelcomeRESTJSONService
15         private WebClient client = new WebClient();
16
17         public WelcomeRESTJSONForm()
18         {
19            InitializeComponent();
20
21            // add DownloadStringCompleted event handler to WebClient
22            client.DownloadStringCompleted+=
23               new DownloadStringCompletedEventHandler(
24                  client_DownloadStringCompleted );
25         } // end constructor
26
27         // get user input and pass it to the web service
28         private void submitButton_Click( object sender, EventArgs e )
29         {
30            // send request to WelcomeRESTJSONService
31            client.DownloadStringAsync( new Uri(
32               "http://localhost:49579/WelcomeRESTJSONService/Service.svc/"
33               + "welcome/" + textBox.Text ) );
34         } // end method submitButton_Click
35
36         // process web service response
37         private void client_DownloadStringCompleted(
38            object sender, DownloadStringCompletedEventArgs e )
39         {
40            // check if any error occurred in retrieving service data
41            if ( e.Error == null )
42            {
43               // deserialize response into a TextMessage object
44               DataContractJsonSerializer JSONSerializer =
45                  new DataContractJsonSerializer( typeof( TextMessage ) );
46               TextMessage message =
47                  ( TextMessage ) JSONSerializer.ReadObject( new
48                  MemoryStream( Encoding.Unicode.GetBytes( e.Result ) ) );
49
```

Fig. 22.17 | Client that consumes the WelcomeRESTJSONService. (Part 1 of 2.)

```
50                    // display Message text
51                    MessageBox.Show( message.Message, "Welcome" );
52                } // end if
53             } // end method client_DownloadStringCompleted
54          } // end class WelcomeRESTJSONForm
55
56          // TextMessage class representing a JSON object
57          [Serializable]
58          public class TextMessage
59          {
60             public string Message;
61          } // end class TextMessage
62       } // end namespace WelcomeRESTJSONClient
```

a) User inputs name

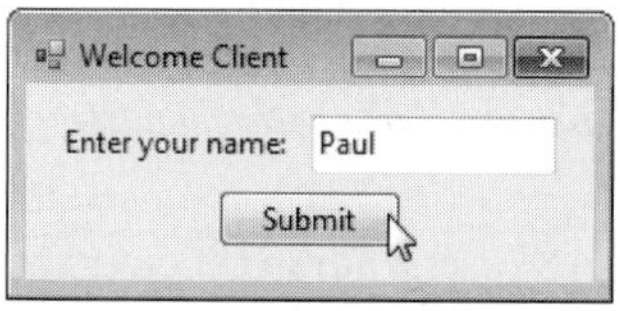

b) Message sent from `WelcomeRESTJSONService`

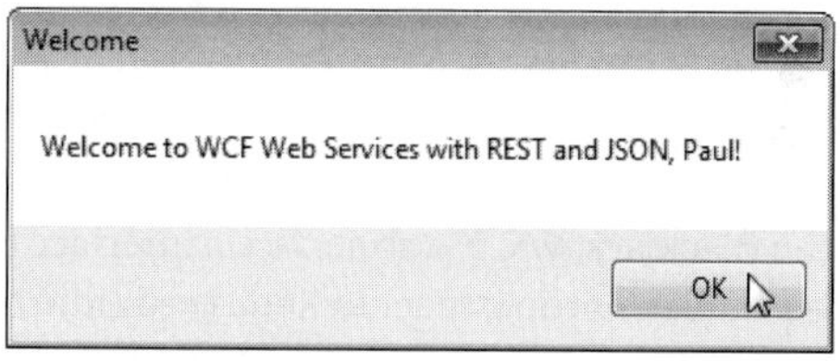

Fig. 22.17 | Client that consumes the `WelcomeRESTJSONService`. (Part 2 of 2.)

22.9 Blackjack Web Service: Using Session Tracking in a SOAP-Based WCF Web Service

In Chapter 20, we described the advantages of maintaining information about users to personalize their experiences. In particular, we discussed session tracking using `HttpSessionState` objects. Next, we incorporate session tracking into a SOAP-based WCF web service.

Suppose a client application needs to call several methods from the same web service, possibly several times each. In such a case, it can be beneficial for the web service to maintain state information for the client. Session tracking eliminates the need for information about the client to be passed between the client and the web service multiple times. For example, a web service providing access to local restaurant reviews would benefit from storing the client user's street address. Once the user's address is stored in a session variable, web service methods can return personalized, localized results without requiring that the address be passed in each method call. This not only improves performance but also requires less effort on your part—less information is passed in each method call.

22.9.1 Creating a Blackjack Web Service

Web services store session information to provide more intuitive functionality. Our next example is a SOAP-based web service that assists programmers in developing a blackjack card game. The web service provides methods to deal a card and to evaluate a hand of cards. After presenting the web service, we use it to serve as the dealer for a game of blackjack. The blackjack web service creates a session variable to maintain a unique deck of cards for each client application. Several clients can use the service at the same time, but method calls made by a specific client use only the deck stored in that client's session. Our example uses a simple subset of casino blackjack rules:

> *Two cards each are dealt to the dealer and the player. The player's cards are dealt face up. Only the dealer's first card is dealt face up. Each card has a value. A card numbered 2 through 10 is worth its face value. Jacks, queens and kings each count as 10. Aces can count as 1 or 11—whichever value is more beneficial to the player (as we'll soon see). If the sum of the player's two initial cards is 21 (that is, the player was dealt a card valued at 10 and an ace, which counts as 11 in this situation), the player has "blackjack" and immediately wins the game. Otherwise, the player can begin taking additional cards one at a time. These cards are dealt face up, and the player decides when to stop taking cards. If the player "busts" (that is, the sum of the player's cards exceeds 21), the game is over, and the player loses. When the player is satisfied with the current set of cards, the player "stays" (that is, stops taking cards), and the dealer's hidden card is revealed. If the dealer's total is 16 or less, the dealer must take another card; otherwise, the dealer must stay. The dealer must continue to take cards until the sum of the dealer's cards is greater than or equal to 17. If the dealer exceeds 21, the player wins. Otherwise, the hand with the higher point total wins. If the dealer and the player have the same point total, the game is a "push" (that is, a tie), and no one wins.*

The Blackjack WCF web service's interface (Fig. 22.18) uses a ServiceContract with the **SessionMode** property set to Required (line 5). This means the service requires sessions to execute correctly. By default, the SessionMode property is set to Allowed. It can also be set to NotAllowed to disable sessions.

```
1   // Fig. 22.18: IBlackjackService.cs
2   // Blackjack game WCF web service interface.
3   using System.ServiceModel;
4
5   [ServiceContract( SessionMode = SessionMode.Required )]
6   public interface IBlackjackService
7   {
8      // deals a card that has not been dealt
9      [OperationContract]
10     string DealCard();
11
12     // creates and shuffle the deck
13     [OperationContract]
14     void Shuffle();
15
16     // calculates value of a hand
17     [OperationContract]
18     int GetHandValue( string dealt );
19  } // end interface IBlackjackService
```

Fig. 22.18 | Blackjack game WCF web-service interface.

The web-service class (Fig. 22.19) provides methods to deal a card, shuffle the deck and determine the point value of a hand. For this example, we want a separate object of the BlackjackService class to handle each client session, so we can maintain a unique deck for each client. To do this, we must specify this behavior in the **ServiceBehavior** attribute (line 7). Setting the ServiceBehavior's **InstanceContextMode** property to

PerSession creates a new instance of the class for each session. The InstanceContextMode property can also be set to PerCall or Single. PerCall uses a new object of the web-service class to handle every method call to the service. Single uses the same object of the web-service class to handle all calls to the service.

```
1   // Fig. 22.19: BlackjackService.cs
2   // Blackjack game WCF web service.
3   using System;
4   using System.Collections.Generic;
5   using System.ServiceModel;
6
7   [ServiceBehavior( InstanceContextMode = InstanceContextMode.PerSession )]
8   public class BlackjackService : IBlackjackService
9   {
10     // create persistent session deck of cards object
11     List< string > deck = new List< string >();
12
13     // deals card that has not yet been dealt
14     public string DealCard()
15     {
16        string card = deck[ 0 ]; // get first card
17        deck.RemoveAt( 0 ); // remove card from deck
18        return card;
19     } // end method DealCard
20
21     // creates and shuffles a deck of cards
22     public void Shuffle()
23     {
24        Random randomObject = new Random(); // generates random numbers
25
26        deck.Clear(); // clears deck for new game
27
28        // generate all possible cards
29        for ( int face = 1; face <= 13; face++ ) // loop through faces
30           for ( int suit = 0; suit <= 3; suit++ ) // loop through suits
31              deck.Add( face + " " + suit ); // add card (string) to deck
32
33        // shuffles deck by swapping each card with another card randomly
34        for ( int i = 0; i < deck.Count; i++ )
35        {
36           // get random index
37           int newIndex = randomObject.Next( deck.Count - 1 );
38
39           // save current card in temporary variable
40           string temporary = deck[ i ];
41           deck[ i ] = deck[ newIndex ]; // copy randomly selected card
42
43           // copy current card back into deck
44           deck[ newIndex ] = temporary;
45        } // end for
46     } // end method Shuffle
47
```

Fig. 22.19 | Blackjack game WCF web service. (Part 1 of 2.)

```
48      // computes value of hand
49      public int GetHandValue( string dealt )
50      {
51          // split string containing all cards
52          string[] cards = dealt.Split( '\t' ); // get array of cards
53          int total = 0; // total value of cards in hand
54          int face; // face of the current card
55          int aceCount = 0; // number of aces in hand
56
57          // loop through the cards in the hand
58          foreach ( var card in cards )
59          {
60              // get face of card
61              face = Convert.ToInt32(
62                  card.Substring( 0, card.IndexOf( ' ' ) ) );
63
64              switch ( face )
65              {
66                  case 1: // if ace, increment aceCount
67                      ++aceCount;
68                      break;
69                  case 11: // if jack add 10
70                  case 12: // if queen add 10
71                  case 13: // if king add 10
72                      total += 10;
73                      break;
74                  default: // otherwise, add value of face
75                      total += face;
76                      break;
77              } // end switch
78          } // end foreach
79
80          // if there are any aces, calculate optimum total
81          if ( aceCount > 0 )
82          {
83              // if it is possible to count one ace as 11, and the rest
84              // as 1 each, do so; otherwise, count all aces as 1 each
85              if ( total + 11 + aceCount - 1 <= 21 )
86                  total += 11 + aceCount - 1;
87              else
88                  total += aceCount;
89          } // end if
90
91          return total;
92      } // end method GetHandValue
93  } // end class BlackjackService
```

Fig. 22.19 | Blackjack game WCF web service. (Part 2 of 2.)

We represent each card as a string consisting of a digit (that is, 1–13) representing the card's face (for example, ace through king), followed by a space and a digit (that is, 0–3) representing the card's suit (for example, clubs, diamonds, hearts or spades). For example, the jack of hearts is represented as "11 2", and the two of clubs as "2 0". After deploying the web service, we create a Windows Forms application that uses the Black-jackService's methods to implement a blackjack game.

Method *DealCard*
Method DealCard (lines 14–19) removes a card from the deck and sends it to the client. Without using session tracking, the deck of cards would need to be passed back and forth with each method call. Using session state makes the method easy to call (it requires no arguments) and avoids the overhead of sending the deck over the network multiple times.

This method manipulates the current user's deck (the List of strings defined at line 11). From the user's deck, DealCard obtains the current top card (line 16), removes the top card from the deck (line 17) and returns the card's value as a string (line 18).

Method *Shuffle*
Method Shuffle (lines 22–46) fills and shuffles the List representing a deck of cards. Lines 29–31 generate strings in the form "*face suit*" to represent each card in a deck. Lines 34–45 shuffle the deck by swapping each card with a randomly selected other card.

Method *GetHandValue*
Method GetHandValue (lines 49–92) determines the total value of cards in a hand by trying to attain the highest score possible without going over 21. Recall that an ace can be counted as either 1 or 11, and all face cards count as 10.

As you'll see in Fig. 22.20, the client application maintains a hand of cards as a string in which each card is separated by a tab character. Line 52 of Fig. 22.19 tokenizes the hand of cards (represented by dealt) into individual cards by calling string method Split and passing to it the tab character. Split uses the delimiter characters to separate tokens in the string. Lines 58–78 count the value of each card. Lines 61–62 retrieve the first integer—the face—and use that value in the switch statement (lines 64–77). If the card is an ace, the method increments variable aceCount (line 67). We discuss how this variable is used shortly. If the card is an 11, 12 or 13 (jack, queen or king), the method adds 10 to the total value of the hand (line 72). If the card is anything else, the method increases the total by that value (line 75).

Because an ace can represent 1 or 11, additional logic is required to process aces. Lines 81–89 process the aces after all the other cards. If a hand contains several aces, only one ace can be counted as 11 (if two aces each are counted as 11, the hand would have a losing value of at least 22). The condition in line 85 determines whether counting one ace as 11 and the rest as 1 results in a total that does not exceed 21. If this is possible, line 86 adjusts the total accordingly. Otherwise, line 88 adjusts the total, counting each ace as 1.

Method GetHandValue maximizes the value of the current cards without exceeding 21. Imagine, for example, that the dealer has a 7 and receives an ace. The new total could be either 8 or 18. However, GetHandValue always maximizes the value of the cards without going over 21, so the new total is 18.

Modifying the *web.config* File
To allow this web service to perform session tracking, you must modify the web.config file to include the following element in the system.serviceModel element:s

```
<protocolMapping>
   <add scheme="http" binding="wsHttpBinding"/>
</protocolMapping>
```

22.9.2 Consuming the Blackjack Web Service

We use our blackjack web service in a Windows application (Fig. 22.20). This application uses an instance of BlackjackServiceClient (declared in line 14 and created in line 48) to represent the dealer. The web service keeps track of the cards dealt to the player and the dealer. As in Section 22.6.5, you must add a service reference to your project so it can access the service. The images for this example are provided with the chapter's examples.

Each player has 11 PictureBoxes—the maximum number of cards that can be dealt without exceeding 21 (that is, four aces, four twos and three threes). These PictureBoxes are placed in a List (lines 51–73), so we can index the List during the game to determine which PictureBox should display a particular card image. The images are located in the blackjack_images directory with this chapter's examples. Drag this directory from Windows Explorer into your project. In the **Solution Explorer**, select all the files in that folder and set their **Copy to Output Directory** property to **Copy if newer**.

GameOver Method

Method GameOver (lines 169–202) shows an appropriate message in the status PictureBox and displays the final point totals of both the dealer and the player. These values are obtained by calling the web service's GetHandValue method in lines 194 and 196. Method GameOver receives as an argument a member of the GameStatus enumeration (defined in lines 31–37). The enumeration represents whether the player tied, lost or won the game; its four members are PUSH, LOSE, WIN and BLACKJACK.

```
1   // Fig. 22.20: Blackjack.cs
2   // Blackjack game that uses the BlackjackService web service.
3   using System;
4   using System.Drawing;
5   using System.Windows.Forms;
6   using System.Collections.Generic;
7   using System.Resources;
8
9   namespace BlackjackClient
10  {
11     public partial class Blackjack : Form
12     {
13        // reference to web service
14        private ServiceReference.BlackjackServiceClient dealer;
15
16        // string representing the dealer's cards
17        private string dealersCards;
18
19        // string representing the player's cards
20        private string playersCards;
21
22        // list of PictureBoxes for card images
23        private List< PictureBox > cardBoxes;
24        private int currentPlayerCard; // player's current card number
25        private int currentDealerCard; // dealer's current card number
26
```

Fig. 22.20 | Blackjack game that uses the BlackjackService web service. (Part 1 of 9.)

```
27        private ResourceManager pictureLibrary =
28           BlackjackClient.Properties.Resources.ResourceManager;
29
30        // enum representing the possible game outcomes
31        public enum GameStatus
32        {
33           PUSH, // game ends in a tie
34           LOSE, // player loses
35           WIN, // player wins
36           BLACKJACK // player has blackjack
37        } // end enum GameStatus
38
39        public Blackjack()
40        {
41           InitializeComponent();
42        } // end constructor
43
44        // sets up the game
45        private void Blackjack_Load( object sender, EventArgs e )
46        {
47           // instantiate object allowing communication with web service
48           dealer = new ServiceReference.BlackjackServiceClient();
49
50           // put PictureBoxes into cardBoxes List
51           cardBoxes = new List<PictureBox>(); // create list
52           cardBoxes.Add( pictureBox1 );
53           cardBoxes.Add( pictureBox2 );
54           cardBoxes.Add( pictureBox3 );
55           cardBoxes.Add( pictureBox4 );
56           cardBoxes.Add( pictureBox5 );
57           cardBoxes.Add( pictureBox6 );
58           cardBoxes.Add( pictureBox7 );
59           cardBoxes.Add( pictureBox8 );
60           cardBoxes.Add( pictureBox9 );
61           cardBoxes.Add( pictureBox10 );
62           cardBoxes.Add( pictureBox11 );
63           cardBoxes.Add( pictureBox12 );
64           cardBoxes.Add( pictureBox13 );
65           cardBoxes.Add( pictureBox14 );
66           cardBoxes.Add( pictureBox15 );
67           cardBoxes.Add( pictureBox16 );
68           cardBoxes.Add( pictureBox17 );
69           cardBoxes.Add( pictureBox18 );
70           cardBoxes.Add( pictureBox19 );
71           cardBoxes.Add( pictureBox20 );
72           cardBoxes.Add( pictureBox21 );
73           cardBoxes.Add( pictureBox22 );
74        } // end method Blackjack_Load
75
76        // deals cards to dealer while dealer's total is less than 17,
77        // then computes value of each hand and determines winner
78        private void DealerPlay()
79        {
```

Fig. 22.20 | Blackjack game that uses the BlackjackService web service. (Part 2 of 9.)

```
80              // reveal dealer's second card
81              string[] cards = dealersCards.Split( '\t' );
82              DisplayCard( 1, cards[1] );
83
84              string nextCard;
85
86              // while value of dealer's hand is below 17,
87              // dealer must take cards
88              while ( dealer.GetHandValue( dealersCards ) < 17 )
89              {
90                 nextCard = dealer.DealCard(); // deal new card
91                 dealersCards += '\t' + nextCard; // add new card to hand
92
93                 // update GUI to show new card
94                 MessageBox.Show( "Dealer takes a card" );
95                 DisplayCard( currentDealerCard, nextCard );
96                 ++currentDealerCard;
97              } // end while
98
99              int dealersTotal = dealer.GetHandValue( dealersCards );
100             int playersTotal = dealer.GetHandValue( playersCards );
101
102             // if dealer busted, player wins
103             if ( dealersTotal > 21 )
104             {
105                GameOver( GameStatus.WIN );
106             } // end if
107             else
108             {
109                // if dealer and player have not exceeded 21,
110                // higher score wins; equal scores is a push.
111                if ( dealersTotal > playersTotal ) // player loses game
112                   GameOver( GameStatus.LOSE );
113                else if ( playersTotal > dealersTotal ) // player wins game
114                   GameOver( GameStatus.WIN );
115                else // player and dealer tie
116                   GameOver( GameStatus.PUSH );
117             } // end else
118          } // end method DealerPlay
119
120          // displays card represented by cardValue in specified PictureBox
121          public void DisplayCard( int card, string cardValue )
122          {
123             // retrieve appropriate PictureBox
124             PictureBox displayBox = cardBoxes[ card ];
125
126             // if string representing card is empty,
127             // set displayBox to display back of card
128             if ( string.IsNullOrEmpty( cardValue ) )
129             {
130                displayBox.Image =
131                   ( Image ) pictureLibrary.GetObject( "cardback" );
```

Fig. 22.20 | Blackjack game that uses the BlackjackService web service. (Part 3 of 9.)

```
132              return;
133          } // end if
134
135          // retrieve face value of card from cardValue
136          string face =
137             cardValue.Substring( 0, cardValue.IndexOf( ' ' ) );
138
139          // retrieve the suit of the card from cardValue
140          string suit =
141             cardValue.Substring( cardValue.IndexOf( ' ' ) + 1 );
142
143          char suitLetter; // suit letter used to form image file name
144
145          // determine the suit letter of the card
146          switch ( Convert.ToInt32( suit ) )
147          {
148             case 0: // clubs
149                suitLetter = 'c';
150                break;
151             case 1: // diamonds
152                suitLetter = 'd';
153                break;
154             case 2: // hearts
155                suitLetter = 'h';
156                break;
157             default: // spades
158                suitLetter = 's';
159                break;
160          } // end switch
161
162          // set displayBox to display appropriate image
163          displayBox.Image = ( Image ) pictureLibrary.GetObject(
164             "_" + face + suitLetter );
165       } // end method DisplayCard
166
167       // displays all player cards and shows
168       // appropriate game status message
169       public void GameOver( GameStatus winner )
170       {
171          string[] cards = dealersCards.Split( '\t' );
172
173          // display all the dealer's cards
174          for ( int i = 0; i < cards.Length; i++ )
175             DisplayCard( i, cards[ i ] );
176
177          // display appropriate status image
178          if ( winner == GameStatus.PUSH ) // push
179             statusPictureBox.Image =
180                ( Image ) pictureLibrary.GetObject( "tie" );
181          else if ( winner == GameStatus.LOSE ) // player loses
182             statusPictureBox.Image =
183                ( Image ) pictureLibrary.GetObject( "lose" );
```

Fig. 22.20 | Blackjack game that uses the BlackjackService web service. (Part 4 of 9.)

```
184         else if ( winner == GameStatus.BLACKJACK )
185             // player has blackjack
186             statusPictureBox.Image =
187                 ( Image ) pictureLibrary.GetObject( "blackjack" );
188         else // player wins
189             statusPictureBox.Image =
190                 ( Image ) pictureLibrary.GetObject( "win" );
191
192         // display final totals for dealer and player
193         dealerTotalLabel.Text =
194             "Dealer: " + dealer.GetHandValue( dealersCards );
195         playerTotalLabel.Text =
196             "Player: " + dealer.GetHandValue( playersCards );
197
198         // reset controls for new game
199         stayButton.Enabled = false;
200         hitButton.Enabled = false;
201         dealButton.Enabled = true;
202     } // end method GameOver
203
204     // deal two cards each to dealer and player
205     private void dealButton_Click( object sender, EventArgs e )
206     {
207         string card; // stores a card temporarily until added to a hand
208
209         // clear card images
210         foreach ( PictureBox cardImage in cardBoxes )
211             cardImage.Image = null;
212
213         statusPictureBox.Image = null; // clear status image
214         dealerTotalLabel.Text = string.Empty; // clear dealer total
215         playerTotalLabel.Text = string.Empty; // clear player total
216
217         // create a new, shuffled deck on the web service host
218         dealer.Shuffle();
219
220         // deal two cards to player
221         playersCards = dealer.DealCard(); // deal first card to player
222         DisplayCard( 11, playersCards ); // display card
223         card = dealer.DealCard(); // deal second card to player
224         DisplayCard( 12, card ); // update GUI to display new card
225         playersCards += '\t' + card; // add second card to player's hand
226
227         // deal two cards to dealer, only display face of first card
228         dealersCards = dealer.DealCard(); // deal first card to dealer
229         DisplayCard( 0, dealersCards ); // display card
230         card = dealer.DealCard(); // deal second card to dealer
231         DisplayCard( 1, string.Empty ); // display card face down
232         dealersCards += '\t' + card; // add second card to dealer's hand
233
234         stayButton.Enabled = true; // allow player to stay
235         hitButton.Enabled = true; // allow player to hit
236         dealButton.Enabled = false; // disable Deal Button
```

Fig. 22.20 | Blackjack game that uses the BlackjackService web service. (Part 5 of 9.)

```
237
238            // determine the value of the two hands
239            int dealersTotal = dealer.GetHandValue( dealersCards );
240            int playersTotal = dealer.GetHandValue( playersCards );
241
242            // if hands equal 21, it is a push
243            if ( dealersTotal == playersTotal && dealersTotal == 21 )
244               GameOver( GameStatus.PUSH );
245            else if ( dealersTotal == 21 ) // if dealer has 21, dealer wins
246               GameOver( GameStatus.LOSE );
247            else if ( playersTotal == 21 ) // player has blackjack
248               GameOver( GameStatus.BLACKJACK );
249
250            // next dealer card has index 2 in cardBoxes
251            currentDealerCard = 2;
252
253            // next player card has index 13 in cardBoxes
254            currentPlayerCard = 13;
255         } // end method dealButton
256
257         // deal another card to player
258         private void hitButton_Click( object sender, EventArgs e )
259         {
260            string card = dealer.DealCard(); // deal new card
261            playersCards += '\t' + card; // add new card to player's hand
262
263            DisplayCard( currentPlayerCard, card ); // display card
264            ++currentPlayerCard;
265
266            // determine the value of the player's hand
267            int total = dealer.GetHandValue( playersCards );
268
269            // if player exceeds 21, house wins
270            if ( total > 21 )
271               GameOver( GameStatus.LOSE );
272            else if ( total == 21 ) // if player has 21, dealer's turn
273            {
274               hitButton.Enabled = false;
275               DealerPlay();
276            } // end if
277         } // end method hitButton_Click
278
279         // play the dealer's hand after the player chooses to stay
280         private void stayButton_Click( object sender, EventArgs e )
281         {
282            stayButton.Enabled = false; // disable Stay Button
283            hitButton.Enabled = false; // disable Hit Button
284            dealButton.Enabled = true; // enable Deal Button
285            DealerPlay(); // player chose to stay, so play the dealer's hand
286         } // end method stayButton_Click
287      } // end class Blackjack
288 } // end namespace BlackjackClient
```

Fig. 22.20 | Blackjack game that uses the BlackjackService web service. (Part 6 of 9.)

a) Initial cards dealt to the player and the dealer when the user presses the **Deal** button.

b) Cards after the player presses the **Hit** button once, then the **Stay** button. In this case, the player wins the game with a higher total than the dealer.

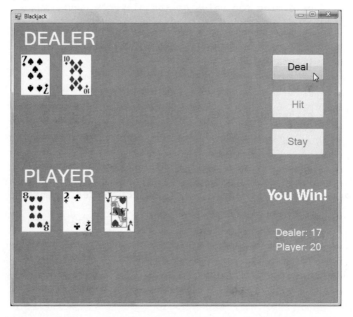

Fig. 22.20 | Blackjack game that uses the BlackjackService web service. (Part 7 of 9.)

c) Cards after the player presses the **Hit** button once, then the **Stay** button. In this case, the player busts (exceeds 21) and the dealer wins the game.

d) Cards after the player presses the **Deal** button. In this case, the player wins with Blackjack because the first two cards are an ace and a card with a value of 10 (a jack in this case).

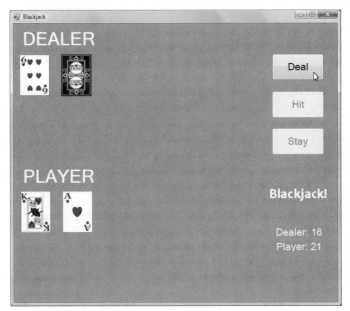

Fig. 22.20 | Blackjack game that uses the BlackjackService web service. (Part 8 of 9.)

e) Cards after the player presses the **Stay** button. In this case, the player and dealer push—they have the same card total.

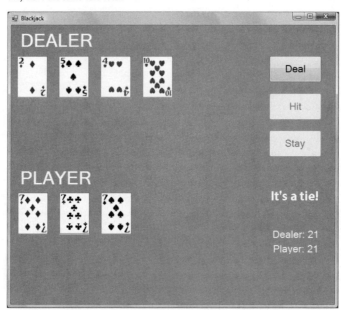

Fig. 22.20 | Blackjack game that uses the `BlackjackService` web service. (Part 9 of 9.)

dealButton_Click *Method*

When the player clicks the **Deal** button, the event handler (lines 205–255) clears the `PictureBox`es and the `Label`s displaying the final point totals. Line 218 shuffles the deck by calling the web service's `Shuffle` method, then the player and dealer receive two cards each (returned by calls to the web service's `DealCard` method in lines 221, 223, 228 and 230). Lines 239–240 evaluate both the dealer's and player's hands by calling the web service's `GetHandValue` method. If the player and the dealer both obtain scores of 21, the program calls method `GameOver`, passing `GameStatus.PUSH`. If only the player has 21 after the first two cards are dealt, the program passes `GameStatus.BLACKJACK` to method `GameOver`. If only the dealer has 21, the program passes `GameStatus.LOSE` to method `GameOver`.

hitButton_Click *Method*

If `dealButton_Click` does not call `GameOver`, the player can take more cards by clicking the **Hit** button. The event handler for this button is in lines 258–277. Each time a player clicks **Hit**, the program deals the player one more card (line 260), displaying it in the GUI. Line 267 evaluates the player's hand. If the player exceeds 21, the game is over, and the player loses. If the player has exactly 21, the player cannot take any more cards, and method `DealerPlay` (lines 78–118) is called, causing the dealer to keep taking cards until the dealer's hand has a value of 17 or more (lines 88–97). If the dealer exceeds 21, the player wins (line 105); otherwise, the values of the hands are compared, and `GameOver` is called with the appropriate argument (lines 111–116).

hitButton_Click *Method*

Clicking the **Stay** button indicates that a player does not want to be dealt another card. The event handler for this button (lines 280–286) disables the **Hit** and **Stay** buttons, then calls method DealerPlay.

DisplayCard *Method*

Method DisplayCard (lines 121–165) updates the GUI to display a newly dealt card. The method takes as arguments an integer representing the index of the PictureBox in the List that must have its image set, and a string representing the card. An empty string indicates that we wish to display the card face down. If method DisplayCard receives a string that's not empty, the program extracts the face and suit from the string and uses this information to find the correct image. The switch statement (lines 146–160) converts the number representing the suit to an int and assigns the appropriate character literal to suitLetter (c for clubs, d for diamonds, h for hearts and s for spades). The character in suitLetter is used to complete the image's file name (lines 163–164).

22.10 Airline Reservation Web Service: Database Access and Invoking a Service from ASP.NET

Our prior examples accessed web services from Windows Forms applications. You can just as easily use web services in ASP.NET web applications. In fact, because web-based businesses are becoming increasingly prevalent, it is common for web applications to consume web services. Figures 22.21 and 22.22 present the interface and class, respectively, for an airline reservation service that receives information regarding the type of seat a customer wishes to reserve, checks a database to see if such a seat is available and, if so, makes a reservation. Later in this section, we present an ASP.NET web application that allows a customer to specify a reservation request, then uses the airline reservation web service to attempt to execute the request. The code and database used in this example are provided with the chapter's examples.

```
 I   // Fig. 22.21: IReservationService.cs
 2   // Airline reservation WCF web service interface.
 3   using System.ServiceModel;
 4
 5   [ServiceContract]
 6   public interface IReservationService
 7   {
 8      // reserves a seat
 9      [OperationContract]
10      bool Reserve( string seatType, string classType );
11   } // end interface IReservationService
```

Fig. 22.21 | Airline reservation WCF web-service interface.

```
 I   // Fig. 22.22: ReservationService.cs
 2   // Airline reservation WCF web service.
 3   using System.Linq;
```

Fig. 22.22 | Airline reservation WCF web service. (Part I of 2.)

```
4
5   public class ReservationService : IReservationService
6   {
7      // create ticketsDB object to access Tickets database
8      private TicketsDataContext ticketsDB = new TicketsDataContext();
9
10     // checks database to determine whether matching seat is available
11     public bool Reserve( string seatType, string classType )
12     {
13        //  LINQ query to find seats matching the parameters
14        var result =
15           from seat in ticketsDB.Seats
16           where ( seat.Taken == false ) && ( seat.Type == seatType ) &&
17              ( seat.Class == classType )
18           select seat;
19
20        // get first available seat
21        Seat firstAvailableSeat = result.FirstOrDefault();
22
23        // if seat is available seats, mark it as taken
24        if ( firstAvailableSeat != null )
25        {
26           firstAvailableSeat.Taken = true; // mark the seat as taken
27           ticketsDB.SubmitChanges(); // update
28           return true; // seat was reserved
29        } // end if
30
31        return false; // no seat was reserved
32     } // end method Reserve
33  } // end class ReservationService
```

Fig. 22.22 | Airline reservation WCF web service. (Part 2 of 2.)

We added the Tickets.mdf database and corresponding LINQ to SQL classes to create a DataContext object (Fig. 22.22, line 8) for our ticket reservation system. Tickets.mdf database contains the Seats table with four columns—the seat number (1–10), the seat type (Window, Middle or Aisle), the class (Economy or First) and a column containing either 1 (true) or 0 (false) to indicate whether the seat is taken.

This web service has a single method—Reserve (lines 11–32)—which searches a seat database (Tickets.mdf) to locate a seat matching a user's request. If it finds an appropriate seat, Reserve updates the database, makes the reservation and returns true; otherwise, no reservation is made, and the method returns false. The statements in lines 14–18 and lines 24–29, which query and update the database, use LINQ to SQL.

Reserve receives two parameters—a string representing the seat type (that is, Window, Middle or Aisle) and a string representing the class type (that is, Economy or First). Lines 15–18 retrieve the seat numbers of any available seats matching the requested seat and class type with the results of a query. Line 21 gets the first matching seat (or null if there is not one). If there is a matching seat (line 24), the web service reserves that seat. Line 26 marks the seat as taken and line 27 submits the changes to the database. Method Reserve returns true (line 28) to indicate that the reservation was successful. If there are no matching seats, Reserve returns false (line 31) to indicate that no seats matched the user's request.

Creating a Web Form to Interact with the Airline Reservation Web Service

Figure 22.23 shows an ASP.NET page through which users can select seat types. This page allows users to reserve a seat on the basis of its class (Economy or First) and location (Aisle, Middle or Window) in a row of seats. The page then uses the airline reservation web service to carry out user requests. If the database request is not successful, the user is instructed to modify the request and try again. When you create this ASP.NET application, remember to add a service reference to the ReservationService.

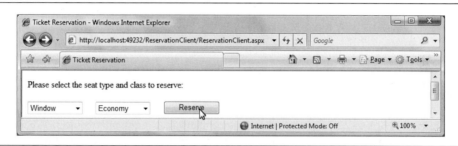

Fig. 22.23 | ASPX file that takes reservation information.

This page defines two DropDownList objects and a Button. One DropDownList displays all the seat types from which users can select (Aisle, Middle, Window). The second provides choices for the class type. Users click the Button named reserveButton to submit requests after making selections from the DropDownLists. The page also defines an initially blank Label named errorLabel, which displays an appropriate message if no seat matching the user's selection is available. The code-behind file is shown in Fig. 22.24.

```
I   // Fig. 22.24: ReservationClient.aspx.cs
2   // ReservationClient code behind file.
3   using System;
4
5   public partial class ReservationClient : System.Web.UI.Page
6   {
7      // object of proxy type used to connect to ReservationService
8      private ServiceReference.ReservationServiceClient ticketAgent =
9         new ServiceReference.ReservationServiceClient();
10
11     // attempt to reserve the selected type of seat
12     protected void reserveButton_Click( object sender, EventArgs e )
13     {
14        // if the ticket is reserved
15        if ( ticketAgent.Reserve( seatList.SelectedItem.Text,
16           classList.SelectedItem.Text ) )
17        {
```

Fig. 22.24 | ReservationClient code-behind file. (Part 1 of 2.)

```
18              // hide other controls
19              instructionsLabel.Visible = false;
20              seatList.Visible = false;
21              classList.Visible = false;
22              reserveButton.Visible = false;
23              errorLabel.Visible = false;
24
25              // display message indicating success
26              Response.Write( "Your reservation has been made. Thank you." );
27          } // end if
28          else // service method returned false, so signal failure
29          {
30              // display message in the initially blank errorLabel
31              errorLabel.Text = "This type of seat is not available. " +
32                  "Please modify your request and try again.";
33          } // end else
34      } // end method reserveButton_Click
35  } // end class ReservationClient
```

Fig. 22.24 | ReservationClient code-behind file. (Part 2 of 2.)

Lines 8–9 of Fig. 22.24 creates a ReservationServiceClient proxy object. When the user clicks **Reserve** (Fig. 22.25(a)), the reserveButton_Click event handler (lines 12–34 of Fig. 22.24) executes, and the page reloads. The event handler calls the web service's Reserve method and passes to it the selected seat and class type as arguments (lines 15–16). If Reserve returns true, the application hides the GUI controls and displays a message thanking the user for making a reservation (line 26); otherwise, the application notifies the user that the type of seat requested is not available and instructs the user to try again (lines

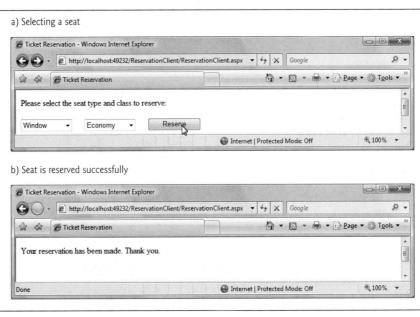

a) Selecting a seat

b) Seat is reserved successfully

Fig. 22.25 | Ticket reservation web-application sample execution. (Part 1 of 2.)

c) Attempting to reserve another seat

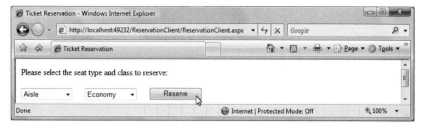

d) No seats match the requested type and class

Fig. 22.25 | Ticket reservation web-application sample execution. (Part 2 of 2.)

31–32). You can use the techniques presented in Chapter 20 to build this ASP.NET Web Form. Figure 22.25 shows several user interactions with this web application.

22.11 Equation Generator: Returning User-Defined Types

With the exception of the `WelcomeRESTJSONService` (Fig. 22.15), the web services we've demonstrated all received and returned primitive-type instances. It is also possible to process instances of complete user-defined types in a web service. These types can be passed to or returned from web-service methods.

This section presents an `EquationGenerator` web service that generates random arithmetic equations of type `Equation`. The client is a math-tutoring application that inputs information about the mathematical question that the user wishes to attempt (addition, subtraction or multiplication) and the skill level of the user (1 specifies equations using numbers from 1 to 10, 2 specifies equations involving numbers from 10 to 100, and 3 specifies equations containing numbers from 100 to 1000). The web service then generates an equation consisting of random numbers in the proper range. The client application receives the `Equation` and displays the sample question to the user.

Defining Class `Equation`
We define class `Equation` in Fig. 22.26. Lines 33–53 define a constructor that takes three arguments—two `int`s representing the left and right operands and a `string` that represents the arithmetic operation to perform. The constructor sets the `Equation`'s properties, then calculates the appropriate result. The parameterless constructor (lines 26–30) calls the three-argument constructor (lines 33–53) and passes default values.

```
1   // Fig. 22.26: Equation.cs
2   // Class Equation that contains information about an equation.
3   using System.Runtime.Serialization;
4
5   [DataContract]
6   public class Equation
7   {
8      // automatic property to access the left operand
9      [DataMember]
10     private int Left { get; set; }
11
12     // automatic property to access the right operand
13     [DataMember]
14     private int Right { get; set; }
15
16     // automatic property to access the result of applying
17     // an operation to the left and right operands
18     [DataMember]
19     private int Result { get; set; }
20
21     // automatic property to access the operation
22     [DataMember]
23     private string Operation { get; set; }
24
25     // required default constructor
26     public Equation()
27        : this( 0, 0, "add" )
28     {
29        // empty body
30     } // end default constructor
31
32     // three-argument constructor for class Equation
33     public Equation( int leftValue, int rightValue, string type )
34     {
35        Left = leftValue;
36        Right = rightValue;
37
38        switch ( type ) // perform appropriate operation
39        {
40           case "add": // addition
41              Result = Left + Right;
42              Operation = "+";
43              break;
44           case "subtract": // subtraction
45              Result = Left - Right;
46              Operation = "-";
47              break;
48           case "multiply": // multiplication
49              Result = Left * Right;
50              Operation = "*";
51              break;
52        } // end switch
53     } // end three-argument constructor
```

Fig. 22.26 | Class Equation that contains information about an equation. (Part 1 of 2.)

```
54
55      // return string representation of the Equation object
56      public override string ToString()
57      {
58         return string.Format( "{0} {1} {2} = {4}", Left, Operation,
59            Right, Result );
60      } // end method ToString
61
62      // property that returns a string representing left-hand side
63      [DataMember]
64      private string LeftHandSide
65      {
66         get
67         {
68            return string.Format( "{0} {1} {2}", Left, Operation, Right );
69         } // end get
70         set
71         {
72            // empty body
73         } // end set
74      } // end property LeftHandSide
75
76      // property that returns a string representing right-hand side
77      [DataMember]
78      private string RightHandSide
79      {
80         get
81         {
82            return Result.ToString();
83         } // end get
84         set
85         {
86            // empty body
87         } // end set
88      } // end property RightHandSide
89   } // end class Equation
```

Fig. 22.26 | Class Equation that contains information about an equation. (Part 2 of 2.)

Class Equation defines properties LeftHandSide (lines 64–74), RightHandSide (lines 78–88), Left (line 10), Right (line 14), Result (line 19) and Operation (line 23). The web service client does not need to modify the values of properties LeftHandSide and RightHandSide. However, a property can be serialized only if it has both a get and a set accessor—even if the set accessor has an empty body. Each property is preceded by the DataMember attribute to indicate that it should be serialized. LeftHandSide (lines 64–74) returns a string representing everything to the left of the equals (=) sign in the equation, and RightHandSide (lines 78–88) returns a string representing everything to the right of the equals (=) sign. Left (line 10) returns the int to the left of the operator (known as the left operand), and Right (lines 14) returns the int to the right of the operator (known as the right operand). Result (line 19) returns the solution to the equation, and Operation (line 23) returns the operator in the equation. The client in this case study does not use the RightHandSide property, but we included it in case future clients choose to use it. Method ToString (lines 56–60) returns a string representation of the equation.

22.11.1 Creating the REST-Based XML EquationGenerator Web Service

Figures 22.27 and 22.28 present the interface and class for the EquationGenerator-Service web service, which creates random, customized Equations. This web service contains only method GenerateEquation (lines 9–26 of Fig. 22.28), which takes two parameters—a string representing the mathematical operation ("add", "subtract" or "multiply") and a string representing the difficulty level. When line 25 of Fig. 22.28 returns the Equation, it is serialized as XML by default and sent to the client. We'll do this with JSON as well in Section 22.11.3. Recall from Section 22.7.2 that you must modify the Web.config file to enable REST support as well.

```
1   // Fig. 22.27: IEquationGeneratorService.cs
2   // WCF REST service interface to create random equations based on a
3   // specified operation and difficulty level.
4   using System.ServiceModel;
5   using System.ServiceModel.Web;
6
7   [ServiceContract]
8   public interface IEquationGeneratorService
9   {
10      // method to generate a math equation
11      [OperationContract]
12      [WebGet( UriTemplate = "equation/{operation}/{level}" )]
13      Equation GenerateEquation( string operation, string level );
14   } // end interface IEquationGeneratorService
```

Fig. 22.27 | WCF REST service interface to create random equations based on a specified operation and difficulty level.

```
1   // Fig. 22.28: EquationGeneratorService.cs
2   // WCF REST service to create random equations based on a
3   // specified operation and difficulty level.
4   using System;
5
6   public class EquationGeneratorService : IEquationGeneratorService
7   {
8      // method to generate a math equation
9      public Equation GenerateEquation( string operation, string level )
10      {
11         // calculate maximum and minimum number to be used
12         int maximum =
13            Convert.ToInt32( Math.Pow( 10, Convert.ToInt32( level ) ) );
14         int minimum =
15            Convert.ToInt32( Math.Pow( 10, Convert.ToInt32( level ) - 1 ) );
16
```

Fig. 22.28 | WCF REST service to create random equations based on a specified operation and difficulty level. (Part 1 of 2.)

```
17        Random randomObject = new Random(); // generate random numbers
18
19        // create Equation consisting of two random
20        // numbers in the range minimum to maximum
21        Equation newEquation = new Equation(
22           randomObject.Next( minimum, maximum ),
23           randomObject.Next( minimum, maximum ), operation );
24
25        return newEquation;
26     } // end method GenerateEquation
27  } // end class EquationGeneratorService
```

Fig. 22.28 | WCF REST service to create random equations based on a specified operation and difficulty level. (Part 2 of 2.)

22.11.2 Consuming the REST-Based XML EquationGenerator Web Service

The MathTutor application (Fig. 22.29) calls the EquationGenerator web service's GenerateEquation method to create an Equation object. The tutor then displays the left-hand side of the Equation and waits for user input.

The default setting for the difficulty level is 1, but the user can change this by choosing a level from the RadioButtons in the GroupBox labeled **Difficulty**. Clicking any of the levels invokes the corresponding RadioButton's CheckedChanged event handler (lines 112–133), which sets integer level to the level selected by the user. Although the default setting for the question type is **Addition**, the user also can change this by selecting one of the RadioButtons in the GroupBox labeled **Operation**. Doing so invokes the corresponding operation's event handlers in lines 88–109, which assigns to string operation the string corresponding to the user's selection.

```
1   // Fig. 22.29: MathTutor.cs
2   // Math tutor using EquationGeneratorServiceXML to create equations.
3   using System;
4   using System.Net;
5   using System.Windows.Forms;
6   using System.Xml.Linq;
7
8   namespace MathTutorXML
9   {
10     public partial class MathTutor : Form
11     {
12        private string operation = "add"; // the default operation
13        private int level = 1; // the default difficulty level
14        private string leftHandSide; // the left side of the equation
15        private int result; // the answer
16        private XNamespace xmlNamespace =
17           XNamespace.Get( "http://schemas.datacontract.org/2004/07/" );
18
```

Fig. 22.29 | Math tutor using EquationGeneratorServiceXML to create equations. (Part 1 of 4.)

```
19      // object used to invoke service
20      private WebClient service = new WebClient();
21
22      public MathTutor()
23      {
24         InitializeComponent();
25
26         // add DownloadStringCompleted event handler to WebClient
27         service.DownloadStringCompleted +=
28            new DownloadStringCompletedEventHandler(
29            service_DownloadStringCompleted );
30      } // end constructor
31
32      // generates new equation when user clicks button
33      private void generateButton_Click( object sender, EventArgs e )
34      {
35         // send request to EquationGeneratorServiceXML
36         service.DownloadStringAsync( new Uri(
37            "http://localhost:49732/EquationGeneratorServiceXML" +
38            "/Service.svc/equation/" + operation + "/" + level ) );
39      } // end method generateButton_Click
40
41      // process web service response
42      private void service_DownloadStringCompleted(
43         object sender, DownloadStringCompletedEventArgs e )
44      {
45         // check if any errors occurred in retrieving service data
46         if ( e.Error == null )
47         {
48            // parse response and get LeftHandSide and Result values
49            XDocument xmlResponse = XDocument.Parse( e.Result );
50            leftHandSide = xmlResponse.Element(
51               xmlNamespace + "Equation" ).Element(
52               xmlNamespace + "LeftHandSide" ).Value;
53            result = Convert.ToInt32( xmlResponse.Element(
54               xmlNamespace + "Equation" ).Element(
55               xmlNamespace + "Result" ).Value );
56
57            // display left side of equation
58            questionLabel.Text = leftHandSide;
59            okButton.Enabled = true; // enable okButton
60            answerTextBox.Enabled = true; // enable answerTextBox
61         } // end if
62      } // end method client_DownloadStringCompleted
63
64      // check user's answer
65      private void okButton_Click( object sender, EventArgs e )
66      {
67         if ( !string.IsNullOrEmpty( answerTextBox.Text ) )
68         {
```

Fig. 22.29 | Math tutor using `EquationGeneratorServiceXML` to create equations. (Part 2 of 4.)

```
69                  // get user's answer
70                  int userAnswer = Convert.ToInt32( answerTextBox.Text );
71
72                  // determine whether user's answer is correct
73                  if ( result == userAnswer )
74                  {
75                     questionLabel.Text = string.Empty; // clear question
76                     answerTextBox.Clear(); // clear answer
77                     okButton.Enabled = false; // disable OK button
78                     MessageBox.Show( "Correct! Good job!", "Result" );
79                  } // end if
80                  else
81                  {
82                     MessageBox.Show( "Incorrect. Try again.", "Result" );
83                  } // end else
84               } // end if
85            } // end method okButton_Click
86
87            // set the operation to addition
88            private void additionRadioButton_CheckedChanged( object sender,
89               EventArgs e )
90            {
91               if ( additionRadioButton.Checked )
92                  operation = "add";
93            } // end method additionRadioButton_CheckedChanged
94
95            // set the operation to subtraction
96            private void subtractionRadioButton_CheckedChanged( object sender,
97               EventArgs e )
98            {
99               if ( subtractionRadioButton.Checked )
100                 operation = "subtract";
101           } // end method subtractionRadioButton_CheckedChanged
102
103           // set the operation to multiplication
104           private void multiplicationRadioButton_CheckedChanged(
105              object sender, EventArgs e )
106           {
107              if ( multiplicationRadioButton.Checked )
108                 operation = "multiply";
109           } // end method multiplicationRadioButton_CheckedChanged
110
111           // set difficulty level to 1
112           private void levelOneRadioButton_CheckedChanged( object sender,
113              EventArgs e )
114           {
115              if ( levelOneRadioButton.Checked )
116                 level = 1;
117           } // end method levelOneRadioButton_CheckedChanged
118
```

Fig. 22.29 | Math tutor using EquationGeneratorServiceXML to create equations. (Part 3 of 4.)

```
119            // set difficulty level to 2
120            private void levelTwoRadioButton_CheckedChanged( object sender,
121               EventArgs e )
122            {
123               if ( levelTwoRadioButton.Checked )
124                  level = 2;
125            } // end method levelTwoRadioButton_CheckedChanged
126
127            // set difficulty level to 3
128            private void levelThreeRadioButton_CheckedChanged( object sender,
129               EventArgs e )
130            {
131               if ( levelThreeRadioButton.Checked )
132                  level = 3;
133            } // end method levelThreeRadioButton_CheckedChanged
134         } // end class MathTutor
135  } // end namespace MathTutorXML
```

a) Generating a level 1 addition equation

b) Answering the question incorrectly

c) Answering the question correctly

Fig. 22.29 | Math tutor using `EquationGeneratorServiceXML` to create equations. (Part 4 of 4.)

Line 20 defines the WebClient that is used to invoke the web service. Event handler generateButton_Click (lines 33–39) invokes EquationGeneratorService method GenerateEquation (line 36–38) asynchronously using the web service's UriTemplate specified at line 12 in Fig. 22.27. When the response arrives, the DownloadStringCompleted event handler (lines 42–62) parses the XML response (line 49), uses XDocument's Element method to obtain the left side of the equation (lines 50–52) and stores the result (lines 53–55). We define the XML response's namespace in lines 16–17 as an XNamespace to parse the XML response. Then, the handler displays the left-hand side of the equation in questionLabel (line 58) and enables okButton so that the user can enter an answer. When the user clicks **OK**, okButton_Click (lines 65–85) checks whether the user provided the correct answer.

22.11.3 Creating the REST-Based JSON WCF EquationGenerator Web Service

You can set the web service to return JSON data instead of XML. Figure 22.30 is a modified IEquationGeneratorService interface for a service that returns an Equation in JSON format. The ResponseFormat property (line 12) is added to the WebGet attribute and set to WebMessageFormat.Json. We don't show the implementation of this interface here, because it is identical to that of Fig. 22.28. This shows how flexible WCF can be.

```
1   // Fig. 22.30: IEquationGeneratorService.cs
2   // WCF REST service interface to create random equations based on a
3   // specified operation and difficulty level.
4   using System.ServiceModel;
5   using System.ServiceModel.Web;
6
7   [ServiceContract]
8   public interface IEquationGeneratorService
9   {
10      // method to generate a math equation
11      [OperationContract]
12      [WebGet( ResponseFormat = WebMessageFormat.Json,
13         UriTemplate = "equation/{operation}/{level}" )]
14      Equation GenerateEquation( string operation, string level );
15   } // end interface IEquationGeneratorService
```

Fig. 22.30 | WCF REST service interface to create random equations based on a specified operation and difficulty level.

22.11.4 Consuming the REST-Based JSON WCF EquationGenerator Web Service

A modified MathTutor application (Fig. 22.31) accesses the URI of the EquationGenerator web service to get the JSON object (lines 35–37). We define a JSON representation of an Equation object for the serializer in Fig. 22.32. The JSON object is deserialized using the System.Runtime.Serialization.Json namespace's DataContractJsonSerializer (lines 48–49) and converted into an Equation object. We use the LeftHandSide field of the deserialized object (line 55) to display the left side of the equation and the Result field (line 67) to obtain the answer.

```
 1    // Fig. 22.31: MathTutorForm.cs
 2    // Math tutor using EquationGeneratorServiceJSON to create equations.
 3    using System;
 4    using System.IO;
 5    using System.Net;
 6    using System.Runtime.Serialization.Json;
 7    using System.Text;
 8    using System.Windows.Forms;
 9
10    namespace MathTutorJSON
11    {
12       public partial class MathTutorForm : Form
13       {
14          private string operation = "add"; // the default operation
15          private int level = 1; // the default difficulty level
16          private Equation currentEquation;  // represents the Equation
17
18          // object used to invoke service
19          private WebClient service = new WebClient();
20
21          public MathTutorForm()
22          {
23             InitializeComponent();
24
25             // add DownloadStringCompleted event handler to WebClient
26             service.DownloadStringCompleted +=
27                new DownloadStringCompletedEventHandler(
28                   service_DownloadStringCompleted );
29          } // end constructor
30
31          // generates new equation when user clicks button
32          private void generateButton_Click( object sender, EventArgs e )
33          {
34             // send request to EquationGeneratorServiceJSON
35             service.DownloadStringAsync( new Uri(
36                "http://localhost:50238/EquationGeneratorServiceJSON" +
37                "/Service.svc/equation/" + operation + "/" + level ) );
38          } // end method generateButton_Click
39
40          // process web service response
41          private void service_DownloadStringCompleted(
42             object sender, DownloadStringCompletedEventArgs e )
43          {
44             // check if any errors occurred in retrieving service data
45             if ( e.Error == null )
46             {
47                // deserialize response into an Equation object
48                DataContractJsonSerializer JSONSerializer =
49                   new DataContractJsonSerializer( typeof( Equation ) );
50                currentEquation =
51                   ( Equation ) JSONSerializer.ReadObject( new
52                   MemoryStream( Encoding.Unicode.GetBytes( e.Result ) ) );
```

Fig. 22.31 | Math tutor using EquationGeneratorServiceJSON. (Part 1 of 4.)

```
53
54                    // display left side of equation
55                    questionLabel.Text = currentEquation.LeftHandSide;
56                    okButton.Enabled = true; // enable okButton
57                    answerTextBox.Enabled = true; // enable answerTextBox
58                } // end if
59            } // end method client_DownloadStringCompleted
60
61            // check user's answer
62            private void okButton_Click( object sender, EventArgs e )
63            {
64                if ( !string.IsNullOrEmpty( answerTextBox.Text ) )
65                {
66                    // determine whether user's answer is correct
67                    if ( currentEquation.Result ==
68                        Convert.ToInt32( answerTextBox.Text ) )
69                    {
70                        questionLabel.Text = string.Empty; // clear question
71                        answerTextBox.Clear(); // clear answer
72                        okButton.Enabled = false; // disable OK button
73                        MessageBox.Show( "Correct! Good job!", "Result" );
74                    } // end if
75                    else
76                    {
77                        MessageBox.Show( "Incorrect. Try again.", "Result" );
78                    } // end else
79                } // end if
80            } // end method okButton_Click
81
82            // set the operation to addition
83            private void additionRadioButton_CheckedChanged( object sender,
84                EventArgs e )
85            {
86                if ( additionRadioButton.Checked )
87                    operation = "add";
88            } // end method additionRadioButton_CheckedChanged
89
90            // set the operation to subtraction
91            private void subtractionRadioButton_CheckedChanged( object sender,
92                EventArgs e )
93            {
94                if ( subtractionRadioButton.Checked )
95                    operation = "subtract";
96            } // end method subtractionRadioButton_CheckedChanged
97
98            // set the operation to multiplication
99            private void multiplicationRadioButton_CheckedChanged(
100               object sender, EventArgs e )
101           {
102               if ( multiplicationRadioButton.Checked )
103                   operation = "multiply";
104           } // end method multiplicationRadioButton_CheckedChanged
```

Fig. 22.31 | Math tutor using EquationGeneratorServiceJSON. (Part 2 of 4.)

```
105
106        // set difficulty level to 1
107        private void levelOneRadioButton_CheckedChanged( object sender,
108           EventArgs e )
109        {
110           if ( levelOneRadioButton.Checked )
111              level = 1;
112        } // end method levelOneRadioButton_CheckedChanged
113
114        // set difficulty level to 2
115        private void levelTwoRadioButton_CheckedChanged( object sender,
116           EventArgs e )
117        {
118           if ( levelTwoRadioButton.Checked )
119              level = 2;
120        } // end method levelTwoRadioButton_CheckedChanged
121
122        // set difficulty level to 3
123        private void levelThreeRadioButton_CheckedChanged( object sender,
124           EventArgs e )
125        {
126           if ( levelThreeRadioButton.Checked )
127              level = 3;
128        } // end method levelThreeRadioButton_CheckedChanged
129     } // end class MathTutorForm
130  } // end namespace MathTutorJSON
```

a) Generating a level 2 multiplication equation

b) Answering the question incorrectly

Fig. 22.31 | Math tutor using EquationGeneratorServiceJSON. (Part 3 of 4.)

c) Answering the question correctly

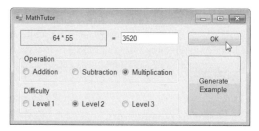

Fig. 22.31 | Math tutor using `EquationGeneratorServiceJSON`. (Part 4 of 4.)

```csharp
 1  // Fig. 22.32: Equation.cs
 2  // Equation class representing a JSON object.
 3  using System;
 4
 5  namespace MathTutorJSON
 6  {
 7     [Serializable]
 8     class Equation
 9     {
10        public int Left = 0;
11        public string LeftHandSide = null;
12        public string Operation = null;
13        public int Result = 0;
14        public int Right = 0;
15        public string RightHandSide = null;
16     } // end class Equation
17  } // end namespace MathTutorJSON
```

Fig. 22.32 | `Equation` class representing a JSON object.

22.12 Web Resources

To learn more about web services, check out our web services Resource Centers at:

    www.deitel.com/WebServices/
    www.deitel.com/RESTWebServices/

You'll find articles, samples chapters and tutorials that discuss XML, web-services specifications, SOAP, WSDL, UDDI, .NET web services, consuming XML web services and web-services architecture. You'll learn how to build your own Yahoo! maps mashups and applications that work with the Yahoo! Music Engine. You'll find information about Amazon's web services including the Amazon E-Commerce Service (ECS), Amazon historical pricing, Amazon Mechanical Turk, Amazon S3 (Simple Storage Service) and the Scalable Simple Queue Service (SQS). You'll learn how to use web services from several other companies including eBay, Google and Microsoft. You'll find REST web services best practices and guidelines. You'll also learn how to use REST web services with other technologies including SOAP, Rails, Windows Communication Foundation (WCF) and more. You can view the complete list of Deitel Resource Centers at www.deitel.com/ResourceCenters.html.

Summary

Section 22.1 Introduction

- WCF is a set of technologies for building distributed systems in which system components communicate with one another over networks. WCF uses a common framework for all communication between systems, so you need to learn only one programming model to use WCF.

- WCF web services promote software reusability in distributed systems that typically execute across the Internet.

- Simple Object Access Protocol (SOAP) is an XML-based protocol describing how to mark up requests and responses so that they can be sent via protocols such as HTTP. SOAP uses a standardized XML-based format to enclose data in a message.

- Representational State Transfer (REST) is a network architecture that uses the web's traditional request/response mechanisms such as GET and POST requests. REST-based systems do not require data to be wrapped in a special message format.

Section 22.2 WCF Services Basics

- WCF service has three key components—addresses, bindings and contracts.

- An address represents the service's location or endpoint, which includes the protocol and network address used to access the service.

- A binding specifies how a client communicates with the service, such as through SOAP protocol or REST architecture. Bindings can also specify other options, such as security constraints.

- A contract is an interface representing the service's methods and their return types. The service's contract allows clients to interact with the service.

- The machine on which the web service resides is referred to as a web service host.

Section 22.3 Simple Object Access Protocol (SOAP)

- The Simple Object Access Protocol (SOAP) is a platform-independent protocol that uses XML to make remote procedure calls, typically over HTTP.

- Each request and response is packaged in a SOAP message—an XML message containing the information that a web service requires to process the message.

- SOAP messages are written in XML so that they're computer readable, human readable and platform independent.

- SOAP supports an extensive set of types—the primitive types, as well as DateTime, XmlNode and others. SOAP can also transmit arrays of these types.

- When a program invokes a method of a SOAP web service, the request and all relevant information are packaged in a SOAP message enclosed in a SOAP envelope and sent to the server on which the web service resides.

- When a web service receives a SOAP message, it parses the XML representing the message, then processes the message's contents. The message specifies the method that the client wishes to execute and the arguments the client passed to that method.

- After a web service parses a SOAP message, it calls the appropriate method with the specified arguments (if any), and sends the response back to the client in another SOAP message. The client parses the response to retrieve the method's result.

Section 22.4 Representational State Transfer (REST)

- Representational State Transfer (REST) refers to an architectural style for implementing web services. Such web services are often called RESTful web services. Though REST itself is not a standard, RESTful web services are implemented using web standards.

- Each operation in a RESTful web service is identified by a unique URL.
- REST can return data in formats such as XML, JSON, HTML, plain text and media files.

Section 22.5 JavaScript Object Notation (JSON)
- JavaScript Object Notation (JSON) is an alternative to XML for representing data.
- JSON is a text-based data-interchange format used to represent objects in JavaScript as collections of name/value pairs represented as strings.
- JSON is a simple format that makes objects easy to read, create and parse, and allows programs to transmit data efficiently across the Internet because it is much less verbose than XML.
- Each value in a JSON array can be a string, a number, a JSON object, true, false or null.

Section 22.6 Publishing and Consuming SOAP-Based WCF Web Services
- Enabling a web service for client usage is also known as publishing the web service.
- Using a web service is also known as consuming the web service.

Section 22.6.1 Creating a WCF Web Service
- To create a SOAP-based WCF web service in Visual Web Developer, you first create a project of type **WCF Service**. SOAP is the default protocol for WCF web services, so no special configuration is required to create SOAP-based services.
- Visual Web Developer automatically generates files for a **WCF Service** project, including an SVC file, which provides access to the service, and a Web.config file, which specifies the service's binding and behavior, and code files for the WCF service class and any other code that is part of the WCF service implementation. In the service class, you define the methods that your WCF web service makes available to client applications.

Section 22.6.2 Code for the WelcomeSOAPXMLService
- The service interface describes the service's contract—the set of methods and properties the client uses to access the service.
- The ServiceContract attribute exposes a class that implements the service interface as a WCF web service.
- The OperationContract attribute exposes a method for remote calls.

Section 22.6.3 Building a SOAP WCF Web Service
- By default, a new code-behind file implements an interface named IService that is marked with the ServiceContract and OperationContract attributes. In addition, the IService.cs file defines a class named CompositeType with a DataContract attribute. The interface contains two sample service methods named GetData and GetDataUsingContract. The Service.cs file contains the code that defines these methods.
- The Service.svc file, when accessed through a web browser, provides access to information about the web service.
- When you display the SVC file in the **Solution Explorer**, you see the programming language in which the web service's code-behind file is written, the Debug attribute, the name of the service and the code-behind file's location.
- If you change the code-behind file name or the class name that defines the web service, you must modify the SVC file accordingly.

Section 22.6.4 Deploying the WelcomeSOAPXMLService
- You can choose **Build Web Site** from the **Build** menu to ensure that the web service compiles without errors. You can also test the web service directly from Visual Web Developer by selecting

Start Without Debugging from the **Debug** menu. This opens a browser window that contains the SVC page. Once the service is running, you can also access the SVC page from your browser by typing the URL in a web browser.

- By default, the ASP.NET Development Server assigns a random port number to each website it hosts. You can change this behavior by going to the **Solution Explorer** and clicking on the project name to view the **Properties** window. Set the **Use dynamic ports** property to **False** and specify the port number you want to use, which can be any unused TCP port. You can also change the service's virtual path, perhaps to make the path shorter or more readable.

- Web services normally contain a service description that conforms to the Web Service Description Language (WSDL)—an XML vocabulary that defines the methods a web service makes available and how clients interact with them. WSDL documents help applications determine how to interact with the web services described in the documents.

- When viewed in a web browser, an SVC file presents a link to the service's WSDL file and information on using the utility svcutil.exe to generate test console applications.

- When a client requests the WSDL URL, the server autogenerates the WSDL that describes the web service and returns the WSDL document.

- Many aspects of web-service creation and consumption—such as generating WSDL files and proxy classes—are handled by Visual Web Developer, Visual C# 2010 and WCF.

Section 22.6.5 Creating a Client to Consume the `WelcomeSOAPXMLService`

- An application that consumes a SOAP-based web service consists of a proxy class representing the web service and a client application that accesses the web service via a proxy object. The proxy object passes arguments from the client application to the web service as part of the web-service method call. When the method completes its task, the proxy object receives the result and parses it for the client application.

- A proxy object communicates with the web service on the client's behalf. The proxy object is part of the client application, making web-service calls appear to interact with local objects.

- To add a proxy class, right click the project name in the **Solution Explorer** and select **Add Service Reference...** to display the **Add Service Reference** dialog. In the dialog, enter the URL of the service's .svc file in the **Address** field. The tools will automatically use that URL to request the web service's WSDL document. You can rename the service reference's namespace by changing the **Namespace** field. Click the **OK** button to add the service reference.

- A proxy object handles the networking details and the formation of SOAP messages. Whenever the client application calls a web method, the application actually calls a corresponding method in the proxy class. This method has the same name and parameters as the web method that is being called, but formats the call to be sent as a request in a SOAP message. The web service receives this request as a SOAP message, executes the method call and sends back the result as another SOAP message. When the client application receives the SOAP message containing the response, the proxy class deserializes it and returns the results as the return value of the web method that was called.

Section 22.7.2 Creating a REST-Based XML WCF Web Service

- WebGet maps a method to a unique URL that can be accessed via an HTTP GET operation.
- WebGet's UriTemplate property specifies the URI format that is used to invoke a method.
- You can test a REST-based service method using a web browser by going to the Service.svc file's network address and appending to the address the URI template with the appropriate arguments.

Section 22.7.3 Consuming a REST-Based XML WCF Web Service

- The WebClient class invokes a web service and receives its response.

- `WebClient`'s `DownloadStringAsync` method invokes a web service asynchronously. The `DownloadStringCompleted` event occurs when the `WebClient` receives the completed response from the web service.

- If a service is invoked asynchronously, the application can continue executing and the user can continue interacting with it while waiting for a response from the web service. `DownloadStringCompletedEventArgs` contains the information returned by the web service. We can use this variable's properties to get the returned XML document and any errors that may have occurred during the process.

Section 22.8.1 Creating a REST-Based JSON WCF Web Service

- By default, a web-service method with the `WebGet` attribute returns data in XML format. To return data in JSON format, set `WebGet`'s `ResponseFormat` property to `WebMessageFormat.Json`.

- Objects being converted to JSON must have `Public` properties. This enables the JSON serialization to create name/value pairs that represent each `Public` property and its corresponding value.

- The `DataContract` attribute exposes a class to the client access.

- The `DataMember` attribute exposes a property of this class to the client.

- When we test the web service using a web browser, the response prompts you to download a text file containing the JSON formatted data. You can see the service response as a JSON object by opening the file in a text editor such as Notepad.

Section 22.8.2 Consuming a REST-Based JSON WCF Web Service

- XML serialization converts a custom type into XML data format.

- JSON serialization converts a custom type into JSON data format.

- The `System.Runtime.Serialization.Json` library's `DataContractJsonSerializer` class serializes custom types as JSON objects. To use the `System.Runtime.Serialization.Json` library, you must include a reference to the `System.ServiceModel.Web` assembly in the project.

- Attribute `Serializable` indicates that a class can be used in serialization.

- A `MemoryStream` object is used to encapsulate the JSON object so we can read data from the byte array using stream semantics. The `MemoryStream` object is read by the `DataContractJsonSerializer` and then converted into a custom type.

Section 22.9 Blackjack Web Service: Using Session Tracking in a SOAP-Based WCF Web Service

- Using session tracking eliminates the need for information about the client to be passed between the client and the web service multiple times.

Section 22.9.1 Creating a Blackjack Web Service

- Web services store session information to provide more intuitive functionality.

- A service's interface uses a `ServiceContract` with the `SessionMode` property set to `Required` to indicate that the service needs a session to run. The `SessionMode` property is `Allowed` by default and can also be set to `NotAllowed` to disable sessions.

- Setting the `ServiceBehavior`'s `InstanceContextMode` property to `PerSession` creates a new instance of the class for each session. The `InstanceContextMode` property can also be set to `PerCall` or `Single`. `PerCall` uses a new object of the web-service class to handle every method call to the service. `Single` uses the same object of the web-service class to handle all calls to the service.

Section 22.10 Airline Reservation Web Service: Database Access and Invoking a Service from ASP.NET
- You can add a database and corresponding LINQ to SQL classes to create a DataContext object to support database operations of your web service.

Section 22.11 Equation Generator: Returning User-Defined Types
- Instances of user-defined types can be passed to or returned from web-service methods.

Self-Review Exercises

22.1 State whether each of the following is *true* or *false*. If *false*, explain why.
- a) The purpose of a web service is to create objects of a class located on a web service host. This class then can be instantiated and used on the local machine.
- b) You must explicitly create the proxy class after you add a service reference for a SOAP-based service to a client application.
- c) A client application can invoke only those methods of a web service that are tagged with the OperationContract attribute.
- d) To enable session tracking in a web-service method, no action is required other than setting the SessionMode property to SessionMode.Required in the ServiceContract attribute.
- e) Operations in a REST web service are defined by their own unique URLs.
- f) A SOAP-based web service can return data in JSON format.
- g) For a client application to deserialize a JSON object, the client must define a Serializable class with public instance variables or properties that match those serialized by the web service.

22.2 Fill in the blanks for each of the following statements:
- a) A key difference between SOAP and REST is that SOAP messages have data wrapped in a(n) _____.
- b) A WCF web service exposes its methods to clients by adding the _____ and _____ attributes to the service interface.
- c) Web-service requests are typically transported over the Internet via the _____ protocol.
- d) To return data in JSON format from a REST-based web service, the _____ property of the WebGet attribute is set to _____.
- e) _____ transforms an object into a format that can be sent between a web service and a client.
- f) To parse a HTTP response in XML data format, the client application must import the response's _____.

Answers to Self-Review Exercises

22.1 a) False. Web services are used to execute methods on web service hosts. The web service receives the arguments it needs to execute a particular method, executes the method and returns the result to the caller. b) False. The proxy class is created by Visual C# or Visual Web Developer when you add a Service Reference to your project. The proxy class itself is hidden from you. c) True. d) True. e) True. f) False. A SOAP web service implicitly returns data in XML format. g) True.

22.2 a) envelope. b) ServiceContract, OperationContract. c) HTTP. d) ResponseFormat, WebMessageFormat.Json. e) Serialization. f) namespace.

Exercises

22.3   *(Phone-Book Web Service)* Create a REST-based web service that stores phone-book entries in a database (PhoneBook.mdf, which is provided in the examples directory for this chapter) and a client application that consumes this service. Give the client user the capability to enter a new contact (service method AddEntry) and to find contacts by last name (service method GetEntries). Pass only primitive types as arguments to the web service. Add a DataContext to the web-service project to enable the web service to interact with the database. The GetEntries method should return an array of strings that contains the matching phone-book entries. Each string in the array should consist of the last name, first name and phone number for one phone-book entry separated by commas. Build an ASP.NET client (Fig. 22.33) to interact with this web service. To use an asynchronous web request from an ASP.NET client, you must set the Async property to true by adding Async="true" to the .aspx page directive. Since the AddEntry method accepts a request and does not return a response to the client, you can use WebClient's OpenRead method to access the service method. You can use the ToArray method on the LINQ query to return an array containing LINQ query results.

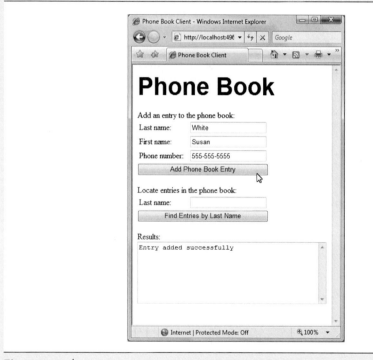

Fig. 22.33 | Template web form for phone book client.

22.4   *(Phone-Book Web Service Modification)* Modify Exercise 22.3 so that it uses a class named PhoneBookEntry to represent a row in the database. The web service should return objects of type PhoneBookEntry in XML format for the GetEntries service method, and the client application should use XML document parsing to interpret the PhoneBookEntry object.

22.5   *(Phone-Book Web Service with JSON)* Modify Exercise 22.4 so that the PhoneBookEntry class is passed to and from the web service as a JSON object. Use serialization to convert the JSON object into an object of type PhoneBookEntry.

22.6 *(Blackjack Modification)* Modify the blackjack web-service example in Section 22.9 to include class Card. Change service method DealCard so that it returns an object of type Card and modify method GetHandValue to receive an array of Cards. Also modify the client application to keep track of what cards have been dealt by using Card objects. Your Card class should include properties for the face and suit of the card. [*Note:* When you create the Card class, be sure to add the Data-Contract attribute to the class and the DataMember attribute to the properties. Also, in a SOAP-based service, you don't need to define your own Card class on the client as well. The Card class will be exposed to the client through the service reference that you add to the client. If the service reference is named ServiceReference, you'll access the card type as ServiceReference.Card.]

22.7 *(Airline Reservation Web-Service Modification)* Modify the airline reservation web service in Section 22.10 so that it contains two separate methods—one that allows users to view all available seats, and another that allows users to reserve a particular seat that is currently available. Use an object of type Ticket to pass information to and from the web service. The web service must be able to handle cases in which two users view available seats, one reserves a seat and the second user tries to reserve the same seat, not knowing that it is now taken. The names of the methods that execute should be Reserve and GetAllAvailableSeats.

Web App Development with ASP.NET in Visual Basic

Objectives

In this chapter you'll learn:

- Web application development using ASP.NET.

- To handle the events from a Web Form's controls.

- To use validation controls to ensure that data is in the correct format before it's sent from a client to the server.

- To maintain user-specific information.

- To create a data-driven web application using ASP.NET and LINQ to SQL.

23.1 Introduction

In this chapter, we introduce **web-application development** with Microsoft's **ASP.NET** technology. Web-based applications create web content for web-browser clients.

We present several examples that demonstrate web-application development using **Web Forms**, **web controls** (also called **ASP.NET server controls**) and Visual Basic programming. Web Form files have the file-name extension **.aspx** and contain the web page's GUI. You customize Web Forms by adding web controls including labels, textboxes, images, buttons and other GUI components. The Web Form file represents the web page that is sent to the client browser. We often refer to Web Form files as **ASPX files**.

An ASPX file created in Visual Studio has a corresponding class written in a .NET language—we use Visual Basic in this book. This class contains event handlers, initialization code, utility methods and other supporting code. The file that contains this class is called the **code-behind file** and provides the ASPX file's programmatic implementation.

To develop the code and GUIs in this chapter, we used Microsoft's **Visual Web Developer 2010 Express**—a free IDE designed for developing ASP.NET web applications. The full version of Visual Studio 2010 includes the functionality of Visual Web Developer, so the instructions we present for Visual Web Developer also apply to Visual Studio 2010. The database example (Section 23.8) also requires SQL Server 2008 Express. See the *Before You Begin* section of the book for additional information on this software.

In Chapter 25 (online), we present several additional web-application development topics, including:

- master pages to maintain a uniform look-and-feel across the Web Forms in a web application

- creating password-protected websites with registration and login capabilities

- using the **Web Site Administration Tool** to specify which parts of a website are password protected

- using ASP.NET AJAX to quickly and easily improve the user experience for your web applications, giving them responsiveness comparable to that of desktop applications.

23.2 Web Basics

In this section, we discuss what occurs when a user requests a web page in a browser. In its simplest form, a *web page* is nothing more than an *HTML (HyperText Markup Language) document* (with the extension .html or .htm) that describes to a web browser the document's content and how to format it.

HTML documents normally contain *hyperlinks* that link to different pages or to other parts of the same page. When the user clicks a hyperlink, a **web server** locates the requested web page and sends it to the user's web browser. Similarly, the user can type the *address of a web page* into the browser's *address field* and press *Enter* to view the specified page.

Web development tools like Visual Web Developer typically use a "stricter" version of HTML called *XHTML (Extensible HyperText Markup Language)*. ASP.NET produces web pages as XHTML documents.

URIs and URLs

URIs (Uniform Resource Identifiers) identify resources on the Internet. URIs that start with http:// are called *URLs (Uniform Resource Locators)*. Common URLs refer to files, directories or server-side code that performs tasks such as database lookups, Internet searches and business application processing. If you know the URL of a publicly available resource anywhere on the web, you can enter that URL into a web browser's address field and the browser can access that resource.

Parts of a URL

A URL contains information that directs a browser to the resource that the user wishes to access. Web servers make such resources available to web clients. Popular web servers include Microsoft's Internet Information Services (IIS) and Apache's HTTP Server.

Let's examine the components of the URL

```
http://www.deitel.com/books/downloads.html
```

The http:// indicates that the HyperText Transfer Protocol (HTTP) should be used to obtain the resource. HTTP is the web protocol that enables clients and servers to communicate. Next in the URL is the server's fully qualified **hostname** (www.deitel.com)—the name of the web server computer on which the resource resides. This computer is referred to as the **host**, because it houses and maintains resources. The hostname www.deitel.com is translated into an **IP (Internet Protocol) address**—a numerical value that uniquely identifies the server on the Internet. A **Domain Name System (DNS) server** maintains a database of hostnames and their corresponding IP addresses, and performs the translations automatically.

The remainder of the URL (/books/downloads.html) specifies the resource's location (/books) and name (downloads.html) on the web server. The location could represent an actual directory on the web server's file system. For *security* reasons, however, the location is typically a *virtual directory*. The web server translates the virtual directory into a real location on the server, thus hiding the resource's true location.

Making a Request and Receiving a Response
When given a URL, a web browser uses HTTP to retrieve and display the web page found at that address. Figure 23.1 shows a web browser sending a request to a web server. Figure 23.2 shows the web server responding to that request.

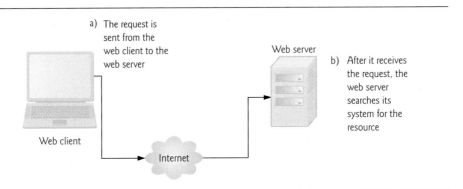

Fig. 23.1 | Client requesting a resource from a web server.

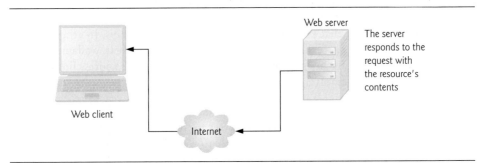

Fig. 23.2 | Client receiving a response from the web server.

23.3 Multitier Application Architecture

Web-based applications are **multitier applications** (sometimes referred to as *n*-tier applications). Multitier applications divide functionality into separate **tiers** (that is, logical groupings of functionality). Although tiers can be located on the *same* computer, the tiers of web-based applications commonly reside on *separate* computers for security and scalability. Figure 23.3 presents the basic architecture of a three-tier web-based application.

Information Tier
The **information tier** (also called the **bottom tier**) maintains the application's data. This tier typically stores data in a relational database management system. For example, a retail store might have a database for storing product information, such as descriptions, prices and quantities in stock. The same database also might contain customer information, such as user names, billing addresses and credit card numbers. This tier can contain multiple databases, which together comprise the data needed for an application.

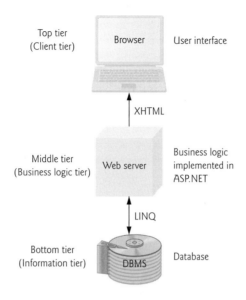

Top tier
(Client tier)

Browser

User interface

XHTML

Middle tier
(Business logic tier)

Web server

Business logic
implemented in
ASP.NET

LINQ

Bottom tier
(Information tier)

DBMS

Database

Fig. 23.3 | Three-tier architecture.

Business Logic

The **middle tier** implements **business logic**, **controller logic** and **presentation logic** to control interactions between the application's clients and its data. The middle tier acts as an intermediary between data in the information tier and the application's clients. The middle-tier controller logic processes client requests (such as requests to view a product catalog) and retrieves data from the database. The middle-tier presentation logic then processes data from the information tier and presents the content to the client. Web applications typically present data to clients as web pages.

Business logic in the middle tier enforces *business rules* and ensures that data is reliable before the server application updates the database or presents the data to users. Business rules dictate how clients can and cannot access application data, and how applications process data. For example, a business rule in the middle tier of a retail store's web-based application might ensure that all product quantities remain positive. A client request to set a negative quantity in the bottom tier's product information database would be rejected by the middle tier's business logic.

Client Tier

The **client tier**, or **top tier**, is the application's user interface, which gathers input and displays output. Users interact directly with the application through the user interface (typically viewed in a web browser), keyboard and mouse. In response to user actions (for example, clicking a hyperlink), the client tier interacts with the middle tier to make requests and to retrieve data from the information tier. The client tier then displays to the user the data retrieved from the middle tier. The client tier never directly interacts with the information tier.

23.4 Your First ASP.NET Application

Our first example displays the web server's time of day in a browser window (Fig. 23.4). When this application executes—that is, a web browser requests the application's web page—the web server executes the application's code, which gets the current time and displays it in a Label. The web server then returns the result to the web browser that made the request, and the web browser renders the web page containing the time. We show this application executing in the Internet Explorer and Firefox web browsers to show you that the web page renders identically in each.

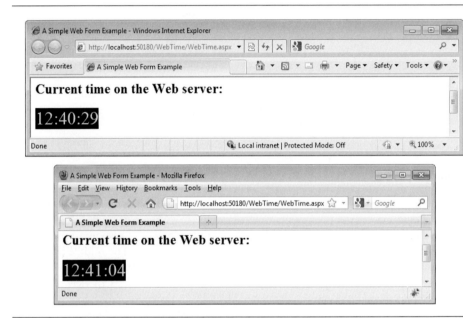

Fig. 23.4 | WebTime web application running in Internet Explorer and Firefox.

Testing the Application in Your Default Web Browser
To test this application in your default web browser, perform the following steps:

1. Open Visual Web Developer.

2. Select **Open Web Site...** from the **File** menu.

3. In the **Open Web Site** dialog (Fig. 23.5), ensure that **File System** is selected, then navigate to this chapter's examples, select the WebTime folder and click the **Open Button.**

4. Select WebTime.aspx in the **Solution Explorer**, then type *Ctrl* + *F5* to execute the web application.

Testing the Application in a Selected Web Browser
If you wish to execute the application in another web browser, you can copy the web page's address from your default browser's address field and paste it into another browser's address field, or you can perform the following steps:

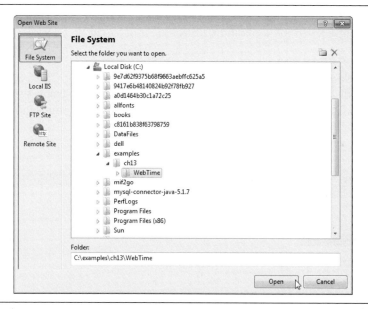

Fig. 23.5 | Open Web Site dialog.

1. In the **Solution Explorer**, right click WebTime.aspx and select **Browse With...** to display the **Browse With** dialog (Fig. 23.6).

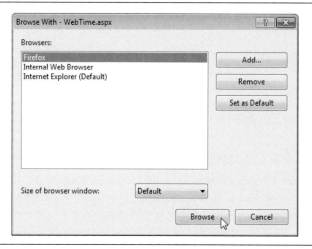

Fig. 23.6 | Selecting another web browser to execute the web application.

2. From the **Browsers** list, select the browser in which you'd like to test the web application and click the **Browse** Button.

If the browser you wish to use is not listed, you can use the **Browse With** dialog to add items to or remove items from the list of web browsers.

23.4.1 Building the WebTime Application

Now that you've tested the application, let's create it in Visual Web Developer.

Step 1: Creating the Web Site Project
Select **File > New Web Site...** to display the **New Web Site** dialog (Fig. 23.7). In the left column of this dialog, ensure that **Visual Basic** is selected, then select **Empty Web Site** in the middle column. At the bottom of the dialog you can specify the location and name of the web application.

Fig. 23.7 | Creating an **ASP.NET Web Site** in Visual Web Developer.

The **Web location:** ComboBox provides the following options:

- **File System:** Creates a new website for testing on your local computer. Such websites execute in Visual Web Developer's built-in ASP.NET Development Server and can be accessed only by web browsers running on the same computer. You can later "publish" your website to a production web server for access via a local network or the Internet. Each example in this chapter uses the **File System** option, so select it now.

- **HTTP:** Creates a new website on an IIS web server and uses HTTP to allow you to put your website's files on the server. IIS is Microsoft's software that is used to run production websites. If you own a website and have your own web server, you might use this to build a new website directly on that server computer. You must be an Administrator on the computer running IIS to use this option.

- **FTP**: Uses File Transfer Protocol (FTP) to allow you to put your website's files on the server. The server administrator must first create the website on the server for you. FTP is commonly used by so-called "hosting providers" to allow website owners to share a server computer that runs many websites.

Change the name of the web application from WebSite1 to WebTime, then click the **OK** Button to create the website.

Step 2: Adding a Web Form to the Website and Examining the Solution Explorer

A **Web Form** represents one page in a web application—we'll often use the terms "page" and "Web Form" interchangeably. A Web Form contains a web application's GUI. To create the WebTime.aspx Web Form:

1. Right click the project name in the **Solution Explorer** and select **Add New Item...** to display the **Add New Item** dialog (Fig. 23.8).

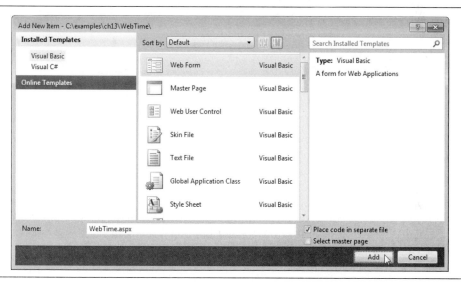

Fig. 23.8 | Adding a new **Web Form** to the website with the **Add New Item** dialog.

2. In the left column, ensure that **Visual Basic** is selected, then select **Web Form** in the middle column.

3. In the **Name:** TextBox, change the file name to WebTime.aspx, then click the **Add** Button.

After you add the Web Form, the IDE opens it in **Source** view by default (Fig. 23.9). This view displays the markup for the Web Form. As you become more familiar with ASP.NET and building web sites in general, you might use **Source** view to perform high precision adjustments to your design or to program in the JavaScript language that executes in web browsers. For the purposes of this chapter, we'll keep things simple by working exclusively in **Design** mode. To switch to **Design** mode, you can click the **Design** Button at the bottom of the code editor window.

Source mode shows only the Web Form's markup

Split mode allows you to view the Web Form's markup and design at the same time

Design mode allows you to build a Web Form using similar techniques to building a Windows Form

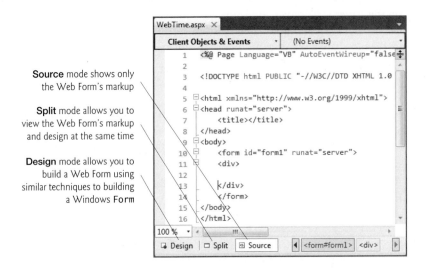

Fig. 23.9 | Web Form in **Source** view.

The Solution Explorer
The **Solution Explorer** (Fig. 23.10) shows the contents of the website. We expanded the node for WebTime.aspx to show you its code-behind file WebTime.aspx.vb. Visual Web Developer's **Solution Explorer** contains several buttons that differ from Visual Basic Express. The **View Designer** button allows you to open the Web Form in **Design** mode. The **Copy Web Site** button opens a dialog that allows you to move the files in this project to another location, such as a remote web server. This is useful if you're developing the application on your local computer but want to make it available to the public from a different location. Finally, the **ASP.NET Configuration** button takes you to a web page called the **Web Site Administration Tool**, where you can manipulate various settings and security options for your application.

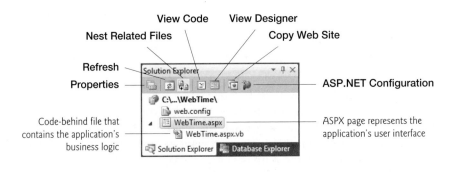

Fig. 23.10 | **Solution Explorer** window for an **Empty Web Site** project.

If the ASPX file is not open in the IDE, you can open it in **Design** mode three ways:

- double click it in the **Solution Explorer**
- select it in the **Solution Explorer** and click the **View Designer** (⊞) Button
- right click it in the **Solution Explorer** and select **View Designer**

To open the code-behind file in the code editor, you can

- double click it in the **Solution Explorer**
- select the ASPX file in the **Solution Explorer**, then click the **View Code** (⊡) Button
- right click the code-behind file in the **Solution Explorer** and select **Open**

The Toolbox

Figure 23.11 shows the **Toolbox** displayed in the IDE when the project loads. Part (a) displays the beginning of the **Standard** list of web controls, and part (b) displays the remaining web controls and the list of other control groups. We discuss specific controls listed in Fig. 23.11 as they're used throughout the chapter. Many of the controls have similar or identical names to Windows Forms controls presented earlier in the book.

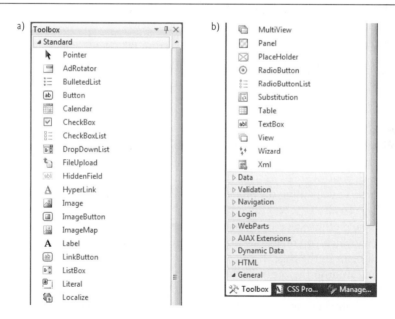

Fig. 23.11 | **Toolbox** in Visual Web Developer.

The Web Forms Designer

Figure 23.12 shows the initial Web Form in **Design** mode. You can drag and drop controls from the **Toolbox** onto the Web Form. You can also type at the current cursor location to add so-called static text to the web page. In response to such actions, the IDE generates the appropriate markup in the ASPX file.

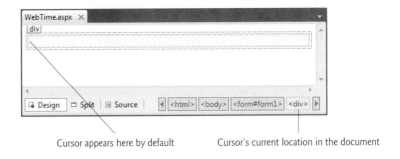

Cursor appears here by default   Cursor's current location in the document

Fig. 23.12 | **Design** mode of the Web Forms Designer.

Step 3: Changing the Title of the Page

Before designing the Web Form's content, you'll change its title to A Simple Web Form Example. This title will be displayed in the web browser's title bar (see Fig. 23.4). It's typically also used by search engines like Google and Bing when they index real websites for searching. Every page should have a title. To change the title:

1. Ensure that the ASPX file is open in **Design** view.

2. View the Web Form's properties by selecting **DOCUMENT**, which represents the Web Form, from the drop-down list in the **Properties** window.

3. Modify the **Title** property in the **Properties** window by setting it to A Simple Web Form Example.

Designing a Page

Designing a Web Form is similar to designing a Windows Form. To add controls to the page, drag-and-drop them from the **Toolbox** onto the Web Form in **Design** view. The Web Form and each control are objects that have properties, methods and events. You can set these properties visually using the **Properties** window or programmatically in the code-behind file. You can also type text directly on a Web Form at the cursor location.

Controls and other elements are placed sequentially on a Web Form one after another in the order in which you drag-and-drop them onto the Web Form. The cursor indicates the insertion point in the page. If you want to position a control between existing text or controls, you can drop the control at a specific position between existing page elements. You can also rearrange controls with drag-and-drop actions in **Design** view. The positions of controls and other elements are relative to the Web Form's upper-left corner. This type of layout is known as relative positioning and it allows the browser to move elements and resize them based on the size of the browser window. Relative positioning is the default, and we'll use it throughout this chapter.

For precise control over the location and size of elements, you can use absolute positioning in which controls are located exactly where you drop them on the Web Form. If you wish to use absolute positioning:

1. Select **Tools > Options....**, to display the **Options** dialog.

2. If it isn't checked already, check the **Show all settings** checkbox.

3. Next, expand the **HTML Designer > CSS Styling** node and ensure that the check-box labeled **Change positioning to absolute for controls added using Toolbox, paste or drag and drop** is selected.

Step 4: Adding Text and a *Label*

You'll now add some text and a Label to the Web Form. Perform the following steps to add the text:

1. Ensure that the Web Form is open in **Design** mode.

2. Type the following text at the current cursor location:

```
Current time on the Web server:
```

3. Select the text you just typed, then select **Heading 2** from the **Block Format** Combo-Box (Fig. 23.13) to format this text as a heading that will appear in a larger bold font. In more complex pages, headings help you specify the relative importance of parts of that content—like sections in a book chapter.

Block Format ComboBox

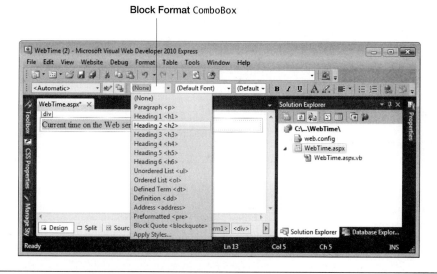

Fig. 23.13 | Changing the text to **Heading 2** heading.

4. Click to the right of the text you just typed and press the *Enter* key to start a new paragraph in the page. The Web Form should now appear as in Fig. 23.14.

5. Next, drag a Label control from the **Toolbox** into the new paragraph or double click the Label control in the **Toolbox** to insert the Label at the current cursor position.

6. Using the **Properties** window, set the Label's (ID) property to timeLabel. This specifies the variable name that will be used to programmatically change the Label's Text.

The cursor is positioned here after inserting a new paragraph by pressing *Enter*

Fig. 23.14 | `WebTime.aspx` after inserting text and a new paragraph.

7. Because the `Label`'s `Text` will be set programmatically, delete the current value of the `Label`'s `Text` property. When a `Label` does not contain text, its name is displayed in square brackets in **Design** view (Fig. 23.15) as a placeholder for design and layout purposes. This text is not displayed at execution time.

`Label` control

Fig. 23.15 | `WebTime.aspx` after adding a `Label`.

Step 5: Formatting the Label

Formatting in a web page is performed with CSS (Cascading Style Sheets). It's easy to use CSS to format text and elements in a Web Form via the tools built into Visual Web Developer. In this example, we'd like to change the `Label`'s background color to black, its foreground color yellow and make its text size larger. To format the `Label`, perform the following steps:

1. Click the `Label` in **Design** view to ensure that it's selected.

2. Select **View > Other Windows > CSS Properties** to display the **CSS Properties** window at the left side of the IDE (Fig. 23.16).

3. Right click in the **Applied Rules** box and select **New Style...** to display the **New Style** dialog (Fig. 23.17).

4. Type the new style's name—`.timeStyle`—in the **Selector:** ComboBox. Styles that apply to specific elements must be named with a dot (.) preceding the name. Such a style is called a CSS class.

5. Each item you can set in the **New Style** dialog is known as a CSS attribute. To change `timeLabel`'s foreground color, select the **Font** category from the **Category** list, then select the yellow color swatch for the **color** attribute.

6. Next, change the **font-size** attribute to `xx-large`.

Fig. 23.16 | CSS Properties window.

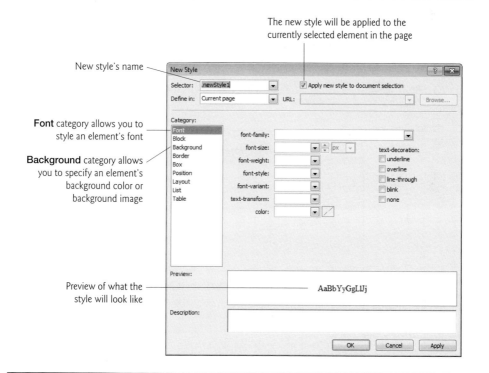

Fig. 23.17 | New Style dialog.

7. To change timeLabel's background color, select the **Background** category, then select the black color swatch for the **background-color** attribute.

The **New Style** dialog should now appear as shown in Fig. 23.18. Click the **OK** Button to apply the style to the timeLabel so that it appears as shown in Fig. 23.19. Also, notice that the Label's CssClass property is now set to timeStyle in the **Properties** window.

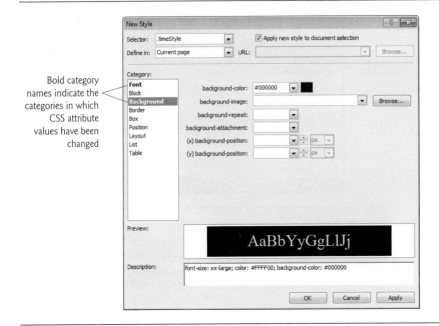

Bold category names indicate the categories in which CSS attribute values have been changed

Fig. 23.18 | **New Style** dialog after changing the Label's font size, foreground color and background color.

Fig. 23.19 | **Design** view after changing the Label's style.

Step 6: Adding Page Logic

Now that you've designed the GUI, you'll write code in the code-behind file to obtain the server's time and display it on the Label. First, open WebTime.aspx.vb by double clicking its node in the **Solution Explorer**. In this example, you'll add an event handler to the code-behind file to handle the Web Form's **Init event**, which occurs when the page is first requested by a web browser. The event handler for this event—named **Page_Init**—initialize the page. The only initialization required for this example is to set the timeLabel's Text property to the time on the web server computer. To create the Page_Init event handler:

1. Select **(Page Events)** from the left ComboBox at the top of the code editor window.

2. Select **Init** from the right ComboBox at the top of the code editor window.

3. Complete the event handler by inserting the following code in the `Page_Init` event handler:

```
' display the server's current time in timeLabel
timeLabel.Text = DateTime.Now.ToString("hh:mm:ss")
```

Step 7: Setting the Start Page and Running the Program

To ensure that `WebTime.aspx` loads when you execute this application, right click it in the **Solution Explorer** and select **Set As Start Page**. You can now run the program in one of several ways. At the beginning of Fig. 23.4, you learned how to view the Web Form by typing *Ctrl + F5* to run the application. You can also right click an ASPX file in the **Solution Explorer** and select **View in Browser**. Both of these techniques execute the ASP.NET Development Server, open your default web browser and load the page into the browser, thus running the web application. The development server stops when you exit Visual Web Developer.

If problems occur when running your application, you can run it in debug mode by selecting **Debug > Start Debugging**, by clicking the **Start Debugging** Button (▶) or by typing *F5* to view the web page in a web browser with debugging enabled. You cannot debug a web application unless debugging is explicitly enabled in the application's `Web.config` file—a file that is generated when you create an ASP.NET web application. This file stores the application's configuration settings. You'll rarely need to manually modify `Web.config`. The first time you select **Debug > Start Debugging** in a project, a dialog appears and asks whether you want the IDE to modify the `Web.config` file to enable debugging. After you click **OK**, the IDE executes the application. You can stop debugging by selecting **Debug > Stop Debugging**.

Regardless of how you execute the web application, the IDE will compile the project before it executes. In fact, ASP.NET compiles your web page whenever it changes between HTTP requests. For example, suppose you browse the page, then modify the ASPX file or add code to the code-behind file. When you reload the page, ASP.NET recompiles the page on the server before returning the response to the browser. This important behavior ensures that clients always see the latest version of the page. You can manually compile an entire website by selecting **Build Web Site** from the **Debug** menu in Visual Web Developer.

23.4.2 Examining `WebTime.aspx`'s Code-Behind File

Figure 23.20 presents the code-behind file `WebTime.aspx.vb`. Line 3 of Fig. 23.20 begins the declaration of class `WebTime`. In Visual Basic, a class declaration can span multiple source-code files—the separate portions of the class declaration in each file are known as **partial classes**. The **Partial modifier** indicates that the code-behind file is part of a larger class. Like Windows `Forms` applications, the rest of the class's code is generated for you based on your visual interactions to create the application's GUI in **Design** mode. That code is stored in other source code files as partial classes with the same name. The compiler assembles all the partial classes that have the same into a single class declaration.

Line 4 indicates that `WebTime` inherits from class **Page** in namespace **System.Web.UI**. This namespace contains classes and controls for building web-based applications. Class `Page` represents the default capabilities of each page in a web application—all pages inherit directly or indirectly from this class.

```
 1    ' Fig. 23.20: WebTime.aspx.vb
 2    ' Code-behind file for a page that displays the current time.
 3    Partial Class WebTime
 4       Inherits System.Web.UI.Page
 5
 6       ' initializes the contents of the page
 7       Protected Sub Page_Init(ByVal sender As Object, _
 8          ByVal e As System.EventArgs) Handles Me.Init
 9
10          ' display the server's current time in timeLabel
11          timeLabel.Text = DateTime.Now.ToString("hh:mm:ss")
12       End Sub ' Page_Init
13    End Class ' WebTime
```

Fig. 23.20 | Code-behind file for a page that displays the web server's time.

Lines 7–12 define the Page_Init event handler, which initializes the page in response to the page's Init event. The only initialization required for this page is to set the time-Label's Text property to the time on the web server computer. The statement in line 11 retrieves the current time (DateTime.Now) and formats it as *hh:mm:ss*. For example, 9 AM is formatted as 09:00:00, and 2:30 PM is formatted as 02:30:00. As you'll see, variable timeLabel represents an ASP.NET Label control. The ASP.NET controls are defined in namespace **System.Web.UI.WebControls**.

23.5 Standard Web Controls: Designing a Form

This section introduces some of the web controls located in the **Standard** section of the **Toolbox** (Fig. 23.11). Figure 23.21 summarizes the controls used in the next example.

Web control	Description
TextBox	Gathers user input and displays text.
Button	Triggers an event when clicked.
HyperLink	Displays a hyperlink.
DropDownList	Displays a drop-down list of choices from which a user can select an item.
RadioButtonList	Groups radio buttons.
Image	Displays images (for example, PNG, GIF and JPG).

Fig. 23.21 | Commonly used web controls.

A Form Gathering User Input

Figure 23.22 depicts a form for gathering user input. This example does not perform any tasks—that is, no action occurs when the user clicks **Register**. As an exercise, we ask you to provide the functionality. Here we focus on the steps for adding these controls to a Web Form and for setting their properties. Subsequent examples demonstrate how to handle the events of many of these controls. To execute this application:

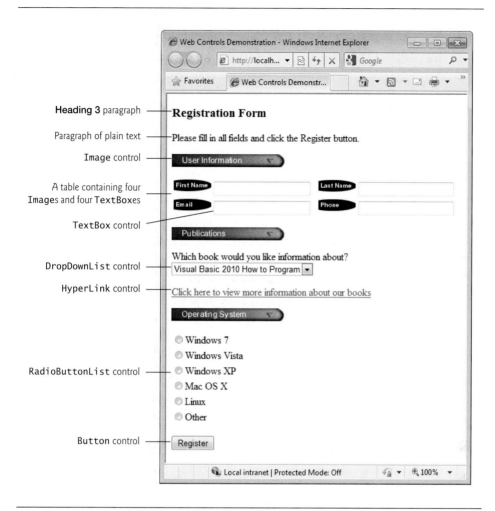

Fig. 23.22 | Web Form that demonstrates web controls.

1. Select **Open Web Site…** from the **File** menu.

2. In the **Open Web Site** dialog, ensure that **File System** is selected, then navigate to this chapter's examples, select the WebControls folder and click the **Open** Button.

3. Select WebControls.aspx in the **Solution Explorer**, then type *Ctrl + F5* to execute the web application in your default web browser.

Create the Web Site

To begin, follow the steps in Section 23.4.1 to create an **Empty Web Site** named WebControls, then add a Web Form named WebControls.aspx to the project. Set the document's Title property to "Web Controls Demonstration". To ensure that WebControls.aspx loads when you execute this application, right click it in the **Solution Explorer** and select **Set As Start Page**.

Adding the Images to the Project

The images used in this example are located in the images folder with this chapter's examples. Before you can display images in the Web Form, they must be added to your project. To add the images folder to your project:

1. Open Windows Explorer.

2. Locate and open this chapter's examples folder (ch23).

3. Drag the images folder from Windows Explorer into Visual Web Developer's **Solution Explorer** window and drop the folder on the name of your project.

The IDE will automatically copy the folder and its contents into your project.

Adding Text and an Image to the Form

Next, you'll begin creating the page. Perform the following steps:

1. First create the page's heading. At the current cursor position on the page, type the text "Registration Form", then use the **Block Format** ComboBox in the IDE's toolbar to change the text to **Heading 3** format.

2. Press *Enter* to start a new paragraph, then type the text "Please fill in all fields and click the Register button".

3. Press *Enter* to start a new paragraph, then double click the **Image** control in the Toolbox. This control inserts an image into a web page, at the current cursor position. Set the Image's (ID) property to userInformationImage. The **ImageUrl** property specifies the location of the image to display. In the **Properties** window, click the ellipsis for the ImageUrl property to display the **Select Image** dialog. Select the images folder under **Project folders:** to display the list of images. Then select the image user.png.

4. Click **OK** to display the image in **Design** view, then click to the right of the Image and press *Enter* to start a new paragraph.

Adding a Table to the Form

Form elements are often placed in tables for layout purposes—like the elements that represent the first name, last name, e-mail and phone information in Fig. 23.22. Next, you'll create a table with two rows and two columns in **Design** mode.

1. Select **Table > Insert Table** to display the **Insert Table** dialog (Fig. 23.23). This dialog allows you to configure the table's options.

2. Under **Size**, ensure that the values of **Rows** and **Columns** are both 2—these are the default values.

3. Click **OK** to close the **Insert Table** dialog and create the table.

By default, the contents of a table cell are aligned vertically in the middle of the cell. We changed the vertical alignment of all cells in the table by setting the valign property to top in the **Properties** window. This causes the content in each table cell to align with the top of the cell. You can set the valign property for each table cell individually or by selecting all the cells in the table at once, then changing the valign property's value.

Fig. 23.23 | Insert Table dialog.

After creating the table, controls and text can be added to particular cells to create a neatly organized layout. Next, add Image and TextBox controls to each the four table cells as follows:

1. Click the table cell in the first row and first column of the table, then double click the Image control in the **Toolbox**. Set its (ID) property to firstNameImage and set its ImageUrl property to the image fname.png.

2. Next, double click the TextBox control in the **Toolbox**. Set its (ID) property to firstNameTextBox. As in Windows Forms, a **TextBox** control allows you to obtain text from the user and display text to the user

3. Repeat this process in the first row and second column, but set the Image's (ID) property to lastNameImage and its ImageUrl property to the image lname.png, and set the TextBox's (ID) property to lastNameTextBox.

4. Repeat *Steps 1* and *2* in the second row and first column, but set the Image's (ID) property to emailImage and its ImageUrl property to the image email.png, and set the TextBox's (ID) property to emailTextBox.

5. Repeat *Steps 1* and *2* in the second row and second column, but set the Image's (ID) property to phoneImage and its ImageUrl property to the image phone.png, and set the TextBox's (ID) property to phoneTextBox.

Creating the Publications Section of the Page

This section contains an Image, some text, a DropDownList control and a HyperLink control. Perform the following steps to create this section:

1. Click below the table, then use the techniques you've already learned in this section to add an Image named publicationsImage that displays the publications.png image.

2. Click to the right of the Image, then press *Enter* and type the text "Which book would you like information about?" in the new paragraph.

3. Hold the *Shift* key and press *Enter* to create a new line in the current paragraph, then double click the **DropDownList** control in the **Toolbox**. Set its (ID) property to booksDropDownList. This control is similar to the Windows Forms ComboBox control, but doesn't allow users to type text. When a user clicks the drop-down list, it expands and displays a list from which the user can make a selection.

4. You can add items to the DropDownList using the **ListItem Collection Editor**, which you can access by clicking the ellipsis next to the DropDownList's Items property in the **Properties** window, or by using the **DropDownList Tasks** smart-tag menu. To open this menu, click the small arrowhead that appears in the upper-right corner of the control in **Design** mode (Fig. 23.24). Visual Web Developer displays smart-tag menus for many ASP.NET controls to facilitate common tasks. Clicking **Edit Items...** in the **DropDownList Tasks** menu opens the **ListItem Collection Editor**, which allows you to add ListItem elements to the DropDownList. Add items for "Visual Basic 2010 How to Program", "Visual C# 2008 How to Program", "Java How to Program" and "C++ How to Program" by clicking the **Add** Button four times. For each item, select it, then set its Text property to one of the four book titles.

Fig. 23.24 | DropDownList Tasks smart-tag menu.

5. Click to the right of the DropDownList and press *Enter* to start a new paragraph, then double click the **HyperLink** control in the **Toolbox** to add a hyperlink to the web page. Set its (ID) property to booksHyperLink and its Text property to "Click here to view more information about our books". Set the **NavigateUrl** property to http://www.deitel.com. This specifies the resource or web page that will be requested when the user clicks the HyperLink. Setting the **Target** property to _blank specifies that the requested web page should open in a new browser window. By default, HyperLink controls cause pages to open in the same browser window.

Completing the Page

Next you'll create the **Operating System** section of the page and the **Register** Button. This section contains a **RadioButtonList** control, which provides a series of radio buttons from which the user can select only one. The **RadioButtonList Tasks** smart-tag menu provides an **Edit Items...** link to open the **ListItem Collection Editor** so that you can create the items in the list. Perform the following steps:

1. Click to the right of the HyperLink control and press *Enter* to create a new paragraph, then add an Image named osImage that displays the os.png image.

2. Click to the right of the Image and press *Enter* to create a new paragraph, then add a RadioButtonList. Set its (ID) property to osRadioButtonList. Use the **ListItem Collection Editor** to add the items shown in Fig. 23.22.

3. Finally, click to the right of the RadioButtonList and press *Enter* to create a new paragraph, then add a **Button**. A Button web control represents a button that triggers an action when clicked. Set its (ID) property to registerButton and its Text property to Register. As stated earlier, clicking the **Register** button in this example does not do anything.

You can now execute the application (*Ctrl + F5*) to see the Web Form in your browser.

23.6 Validation Controls

This section introduces a different type of web control, called a **validation control** or **validator**, which determines whether the data in another web control is in the proper format. For example, validators can determine whether a user has provided information in a required field or whether a zip-code field contains exactly five digits. Validators provide a mechanism for validating user input on the client. When the page is sent to the client, the validator is converted into JavaScript that performs the validation in the client web browser. JavaScript is a scripting language that enhances the functionality of web pages and is typically executed on the client. Unfortunately, some client browsers might not support scripting or the user might disable it. For this reason, you should always perform validation on the server. ASP.NET validation controls can function on the client, on the server or both.

Validating Input in a Web Form
The Web Form in Fig. 23.25 prompts the user to enter a name, e-mail address and phone number. A website could use a form like this to collect contact information from visitors. After the user enters any data, but before the data is sent to the web server, validators ensure that the user *entered a value in each field* and that the e-mail address and phone-number values are in an acceptable format. In this example, (555) 123-4567, 555-123-4567 and 123-4567 are all considered valid phone numbers. Once the data is submitted, the web server responds by displaying a message that repeats the submitted information. A real business application would typically store the submitted data in a database or in a file on the server. We simply send the data back to the client to demonstrate that the server received the data. To execute this application:

1. Select **Open Web Site...** from the **File** menu.

2. In the **Open Web Site** dialog, ensure that **File System** is selected, then navigate to this chapter's examples, select the Validation folder and click the **Open Button**.

3. Select Validation.aspx in the **Solution Explorer**, then type *Ctrl + F5* to execute the web application in your default web browser.

In the sample output:

- Fig. 23.25(a) shows the initial Web Form
- Fig. 23.25(b) shows the result of submitting the form before typing any data in the TextBoxes
- Fig. 23.25(c) shows the results after entering data in each TextBox, but specifying an invalid e-mail address and invalid phone number
- Fig. 23.25(d) shows the results after entering valid values for all three TextBoxes and submitting the form.

a) Initial Web Form

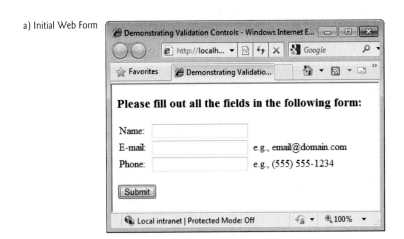

b) Web Form after the user presses the **Submit** Button without having entered any data in the TextBoxes; each TextBox is followed by an error message that was displayed by a validation control

RequiredFieldValidator controls

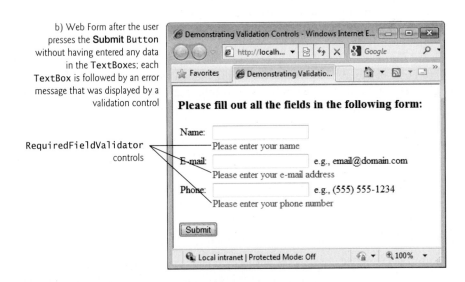

Fig. 23.25 | Validators in a Web Form that retrieves user contact information. (Part 1 of 2.)

c) Web Form after the user enters a name, an invalid e-mail address and an invalid phone number in the TextBoxes, then presses the **Submit** Button; the validation controls display error messages in response to the invalid e-mail and phone number values

RegularExpressionValidator controls

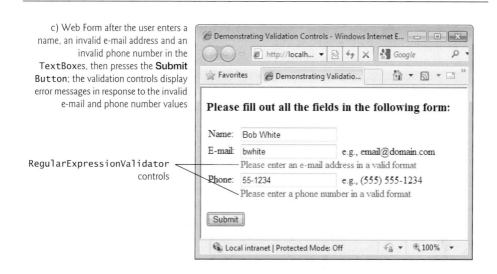

Fig. 23.25 | Validators in a Web Form that retrieves user contact information. (Part 2 of 2.)

Creating the Web Site

To begin, follow the steps in Section 23.4.1 to create an **Empty Web Site** named Validation, then add a Web Form named Validation.aspx to the project. Set the document's Title property to "Demonstrating Validation Controls". To ensure that Validation.aspx loads when you execute this application, right click it in the **Solution Explorer** and select **Set As Start Page**.

Creating the GUI
To create the page, perform the following steps:

1. Type "Please fill out all the fields in the following form:", then use the **Block Format** ComboBox in the IDE's toolbar to change the text to **Heading 3** format and press *Enter* to create a new paragraph.

2. Insert a three row and two column table. You'll add elements to the table momentarily.

3. Click below the table and add a Button. Set its (ID) property to submitButton and its Text property to Submit. Press *Enter* to create a new paragraph. By default, a Button control in a Web Form sends the contents of the form back to the server for processing.

4. Add a Label. Set its (ID) property to outputLabel and clear its Text property—you'll set it programmatically when the user clicks the submitButton. Set the outputLabel's **Visible** property to False, so the Label does not appear in the client's browser when the page loads for the first time. You'll programmatically display this Label after the user submits valid data.

Next you'll add text and controls to the table you created in *Step 2* above. Perform the following steps:

1. In the left column, type the text "Name:" in the first row, "E-mail:" in the second row and "Phone:" in the row column.

2. In the right column of the first row, add a TextBox and set its (ID) property to nameTextBox.

3. In the right column of the second row, add a TextBox and set its (ID) property to emailTextBox. Then type the text "e.g., email@domain.com" to the right of the TextBox.

4. In the right column of the third row, add a TextBox and set its (ID) property to phoneTextBox. Then type the text "e.g., (555) 555-1234" to the right of the TextBox.

Using RequiredFieldValidator Controls
We use three **RequiredFieldValidator** controls (found in the **Validation** section of the **Toolbox**) to ensure that the name, e-mail address and phone number TextBoxes are not empty when the form is submitted. A RequiredFieldValidator makes an input control a required field. If such a field is empty, validation fails. Add a RequiredFieldValidator as follows:

1. Click to the right of the nameTextBox in the table and press *Enter* to move to the next line.

2. Add a RequiredFieldValidator, set its (ID) to nameRequiredFieldValidator and set the ForeColor property to Red.

3. Set the validator's **ControlToValidate** property to nameTextBox to indicate that this validator verifies the nameTextBox's contents.

4. Set the validator's **ErrorMessage** property to "Please enter your name". This is displayed on the Web Form only if the validation fails.

5. Set the validator's **Display** property to Dynamic, so the validator occupies space on the Web Form only when validation fails. When this occurs, space is allocated dynamically, causing the controls below the validator to shift downward to accommodate the ErrorMessage, as seen in Fig. 23.25(a)–(c).

Repeat these steps to add two more RequiredFieldValidators in the second and third rows of the table. Set their (ID) properties to emailRequiredFieldValidator and phone-RequiredFieldValidator, respectively, and set their ErrorMessage properties to "Please enter your email address" and "Please enter your phone number", respectively.

Using *RegularExpressionValidator Controls*

This example also uses two **RegularExpressionValidator** controls to ensure that the e-mail address and phone number entered by the user are in a valid format. Regular expressions are beyond the scope of this book; however, Visual Web Developer provides several *predefined* regular expressions that you can simply select to take advantage of this powerful validation control. Add a RegularExpressionValidator as follows:

1. Click to the right of the emailRequiredFieldValidator in the second row of the table and add a RegularExpressionValidator, then set its (ID) to emailRegularExpressionValidator and its ForeColor property to Red.

2. Set the ControlToValidate property to emailTextBox to indicate that this validator verifies the emailTextBox's contents.

3. Set the validator's ErrorMessage property to "Please enter an e-mail address in a valid format".

4. Set the validator's Display property to Dynamic, so the validator occupies space on the Web Form only when validation fails.

Repeat the preceding steps to add another RegularExpressionValidator in the third row of the table. Set its (ID) property to phoneRequiredFieldValidator and its ErrorMessage property to "Please enter a phone number in a valid format", respectively.

A RegularExpressionValidator's **ValidationExpression** property specifies the regular expression that validates the ControlToValidate's contents. Clicking the ellipsis next to property ValidationExpression in the **Properties** window displays the **Regular Expression Editor** dialog, which contains a list of **Standard expressions** for phone numbers, zip codes and other formatted information. For the emailRegularExpressionValidator, we selected the standard expression **Internet e-mail address**. If the user enters text in the emailTextBox that does not have the correct format and either clicks in a different text box or attempts to submit the form, the ErrorMessage text is displayed in red.

For the phoneRegularExpressionValidator, we selected **U.S. phone number** to ensure that a phone number contains an optional three-digit area code either in parentheses and followed by an optional space or without parentheses and followed by a required hyphen. After an optional area code, a phone number must contain three digits, a hyphen and another four digits. For example, (555) 123-4567, 555-123-4567 and 123-4567 are all valid phone numbers.

Submitting the Web Form's Contents to the Server

If all five validators are successful (that is, each TextBox is filled in, and the e-mail address and phone number provided are valid), clicking the **Submit** button sends the form's data to the server. As shown in Fig. 23.25(d), the server then responds by displaying the submitted data in the outputLabel.

Examining the Code-Behind File for a Web Form That Receives User Input
Figure 23.26 shows the code-behind file for this application. Notice that this code-behind file does not contain any implementation related to the validators. We say more about this soon. In this example, we respond to the page's **Load** event to process the data submitted by the user. This event occurs each time the page loads into a web browser—as opposed to the Init event, which executes only the first time the page is requested by the user. The event handler for this event is **Page_Load** (lines 7–30). To create the event handler, open Validation.aspx.vb in the code editor and perform the following steps:

1. Select **(Page Events)** from the left ComboBox at the top of the code editor window.

2. Select **Load** from the right ComboBox at the top of the code editor window.

3. Complete the event handler by inserting the code from Fig. 23.26.

```vb
 1   ' Fig. 23.26: Validation.aspx.vb
 2   ' Code-behind file for the form demonstrating validation controls.
 3   Partial Class Validation
 4      Inherits System.Web.UI.Page
 5
 6      ' Page_Load event handler executes when the page is loaded
 7      Protected Sub Page_Load(ByVal sender As Object,
 8         ByVal e As System.EventArgs) Handles Me.Load
 9
10         ' if this is not the first time the page is loading
11         ' (i.e., the user has already submitted form data)
12         If IsPostBack Then
13            Validate() ' validate the form
14
15            If IsValid Then
16               ' retrieve the values submitted by the user
17               Dim name As String = nameTextBox.Text
18               Dim email As String = emailTextBox.Text
19               Dim phone As String = phoneTextBox.Text
20
21               ' create a table indicating the submitted values
22               outputLabel.Text = "Thank you for your submission<br/>" &
23                  "We received the following information:<br/>"
24               outputLabel.Text &=
25                  String.Format("Name: {0}{1}E-mail:{2}{1}Phone:{3}",
26                     name, "<br/>", email, phone)
27               outputLabel.Visible = True ' display the output message
28            End If
29         End If
30      End Sub ' Page_Load
31   End Class ' Validation
```

Fig. 23.26 | Code-behind file for a Web Form that obtains a user's contact information.

Differentiating Between the First Request to a Page and a Postback
Web programmers using ASP.NET often design their web pages so that the current page reloads when the user submits the form; this enables the program to receive input, process it as necessary and display the results in the same page when it's loaded the second time. These pages usually contain a form that, when submitted, sends the values of all the controls to the server and causes the current page to be requested again. This event is known as a **postback**. Line 12 uses the **IsPostBack** property of class Page to determine whether the page is being loaded due to a postback. The first time that the web page is requested, IsPostBack is False, and the page displays only the form for user input. When the postback occurs (from the user clicking **Submit**), IsPostBack is True.

Server-Side Web Form Validation
Server-side Web Form validation must be implemented programmatically. Line 13 calls the current Page's **Validate** method to validate the information in the request. This validates the information as specified by the validation controls in the Web Form. Line 15 uses the **IsValid** property of class Page to check whether the validation succeeded. If this property is set to True (that is, validation succeeded and the Web Form is valid), then we display the Web Form's information. Otherwise, the web page loads without any changes, except any validator that failed now displays its ErrorMessage.

Processing the Data Entered by the User
Lines 17–19 retrieve the values of nameTextBox, emailTextBox and phoneTextBox. When data is posted to the web server, the data that the user entered is accessible to the web application through the web controls' properties. Next, lines 22–27 set outputLabel's Text to display a message that includes the name, e-mail and phone information that was submitted to the server. In lines 22, 23 and 26, notice the use of <br/> rather than vbCrLf to start new lines in the outputLabel—
 is the markup for a line break in a web page. Line 27 sets the outputLabel's Visible property to True, so the user can see the thank-you message and submitted data when the page reloads in the client web browser.

23.7 Session Tracking

Originally, critics accused the Internet and business of failing to provide the customized service typically experienced in "brick-and-mortar" stores. To address this problem, businesses established mechanisms by which they could *personalize* users' browsing experiences, tailoring content to individual users. Businesses achieve this level of service by tracking each customer's movement through the Internet and combining the collected data with information provided by the consumer, including billing information, personal preferences, interests and hobbies.

Personalization
Personalization makes it possible for businesses to communicate effectively with their customers and also improves users' ability to locate desired products and services. Companies that provide content of particular interest to users can establish relationships with customers and build on those relationships over time. Furthermore, by targeting consumers with personal offers, recommendations, advertisements, promotions and services, businesses create customer loyalty. Websites can use sophisticated technology to allow visitors to cus-

tomize home pages to suit their individual needs and preferences. Similarly, online shopping sites often store personal information for customers, tailoring notifications and special offers to their interests. Such services encourage customers to visit sites more frequently and make purchases more regularly.

Privacy

A trade-off exists between personalized business service and protection of privacy. Some consumers embrace tailored content, but others fear the possible adverse consequences if the info they provide to businesses is released or collected by tracking technologies. Consumers and privacy advocates ask: What if the business to which we give personal data sells or gives that information to another organization without our knowledge? What if we do not want our actions on the Internet—a supposedly anonymous medium—to be tracked and recorded by unknown parties? What if unauthorized parties gain access to sensitive private data, such as credit-card numbers or medical history? These are questions that must be addressed by programmers, consumers, businesses and lawmakers alike.

Recognizing Clients

To provide personalized services to consumers, businesses must be able to recognize clients when they request information from a site. As we have discussed, the request/response system on which the web operates is facilitated by HTTP. Unfortunately, HTTP is a *stateless protocol*—it *does not* provide information that would enable web servers to maintain state information regarding particular clients. This means that web servers cannot determine whether a request comes from a particular client or whether the same or different clients generate a series of requests.

To circumvent this problem, sites can provide mechanisms by which they identify individual clients. A session represents a unique client on a website. If the client leaves a site and then returns later, the client will still be recognized as the same user. When the user closes the browser, the session ends. To help the server distinguish among clients, each client must identify itself to the server. Tracking individual clients is known as **session tracking**. One popular session-tracking technique uses cookies (discussed in Section 23.7.1); another uses ASP.NET's HttpSessionState object (used in Section 23.7.2). Additional session-tracking techniques are beyond this book's scope.

23.7.1 Cookies

Cookies provide you with a tool for personalizing web pages. A cookie is a piece of data stored by web browsers in a small text file on the user's computer. A cookie maintains information about the client during and between browser sessions. The first time a user visits the website, the user's computer might receive a cookie from the server; this cookie is then reactivated each time the user revisits that site. The collected information is intended to be an anonymous record containing data that is used to personalize the user's future visits to the site. For example, cookies in a shopping application might store unique identifiers for users. When a user adds items to an online shopping cart or performs another task resulting in a request to the web server, the server receives a cookie containing the user's unique identifier. The server then uses the unique identifier to locate the shopping cart and perform any necessary processing.

In addition to identifying users, cookies also can indicate users' shopping preferences. When a Web Form receives a request from a client, the Web Form can examine the cookie(s) it sent to the client during previous communications, identify the user's preferences and immediately display products of interest to the client.

Every HTTP-based interaction between a client and a server includes a header containing information either about the request (when the communication is from the client to the server) or about the response (when the communication is from the server to the client). When a Web Form receives a request, the header includes information such as the request type and any cookies that have been sent previously from the server to be stored on the client machine. When the server formulates its response, the header information contains any cookies the server wants to store on the client computer and other information, such as the MIME type of the response.

The **expiration date** of a cookie determines how long the cookie remains on the client's computer. If you do not set an expiration date for a cookie, the web browser maintains the cookie for the duration of the browsing session. Otherwise, the web browser maintains the cookie until the expiration date occurs. Cookies are deleted when they **expire**.

Portability Tip 23.1

Users may disable cookies in their web browsers to help ensure their privacy. Such users will experience difficulty using web applications that depend on cookies to maintain state information.

23.7.2 Session Tracking with `HttpSessionState`

The next web application demonstrates session tracking using the .NET class **HttpSessionState**. When you execute this application, the `Options.aspx` page (Fig. 23.27(a)), which is the application's **Start Page**, allows the user to select a programming language from a group of radio buttons. When the user clicks **Submit**, the selection is sent to the web server for processing. The web server uses an `HttpSessionState` object to store the chosen language and the ISBN number for one of our books on that topic. Each user that visits the site has a unique `HttpSessionState` object, so the selections made by one user are maintained separately from all other users. After storing the selection, the server returns the page to the browser (Fig. 23.27(b)) and displays the user's selection and some information about the user's unique session (which we show just for demonstration purposes). The page also includes links that allow the user to choose between selecting another programming language or viewing the `Recommendations.aspx` page (Fig. 23.27(e)), which lists recommended books pertaining to the programming language(s) that the user selected previously. If the user clicks the link for book recommendations, the information stored in the user's unique `HttpSessionState` object is read and used to form the list of recommendations. To test this application:

1. Select **Open Web Site...** from the **File** menu.

2. In the **Open Web Site** dialog, ensure that **File System** is selected, then navigate to this chapter's examples, select the `Sessions` folder and click the **Open Button**.

3. Select `Options.aspx` in the **Solution Explorer**, then type *Ctrl + F5* to execute the web application in your default web browser.

a) User selects a language from the Options.aspx page, then presses **Submit** to send the selection to the server

b) Options.aspx page is updated to hide the controls for selecting a language and to display the user's selection; the user clicks the hyperlink to return to the list of languages and make another selection

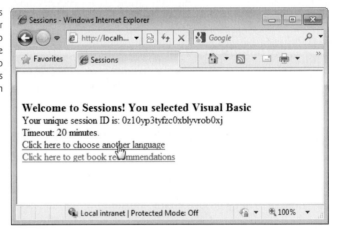

c) User selects another language from the Options.aspx page, then presses **Submit** to send the selection to the server

Fig. 23.27 | ASPX file that presents a list of programming languages. (Part 1 of 2.)

d) `Options.aspx` page is updated to hide the controls for selecting a language and to display the user's selection; the user clicks the hyperlink to get a list of book recommendations

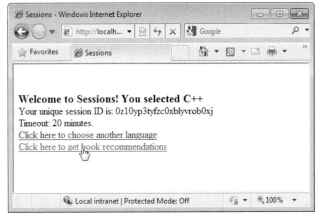

e) `Recommendations.aspx` displays the list of recommended books based on the user's selections

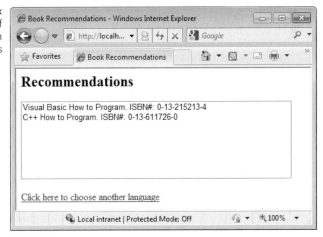

Fig. 23.27 | ASPX file that presents a list of programming languages. (Part 2 of 2.)

Creating the Web Site

To begin, follow the steps in Section 23.4.1 to create an **Empty Web Site** named `Sessions`, then add two Web Forms named `Options.aspx` and `Recommendations.aspx` to the project. Set the `Options.aspx` document's `Title` property to `"Sessions"` and the `Recommendations.aspx` document's `Title` property to `"Book Recommendations"`. To ensure that `Options.aspx` is the first page to load for this application, right click it in the **Solution Explorer** and select **Set As Start Page**.

23.7.3 Options.aspx: Selecting a Programming Language

The `Options.aspx` page Fig. 23.27(a) contains the following controls arranged vertically:

1. A `Label` with its (ID) property set to `promptLabel` and its `Text` property set to `"Select a programming language:"`. We used the techniques shown in *Step 5* of Section 23.4.1 to create a CSS style for this label named `.labelStyle`, and set the style's `font-size` attribute to `large` and the `font-weight` attribute to `bold`.

2. The user selects a programming language by clicking one of the radio buttons in a `RadioButtonList`. Each radio button has a `Text` property and a `Value` property. The `Text` property is displayed next to the radio button and the `Value` property represents a value that is sent to the server when the user selects that radio button and submits the form. In this example, we'll use the `Value` property to represent the ISBN for the recommended book.

    Create a `RadioButtonList` with its (`ID`) property set to `languageList`. Use the **ListItem Collection Editor** to add five radio buttons with their `Text` properties set to `Visual Basic`, `Visual C#`, `C`, `C++` and `Java`, and their `Value` properties set to `0-13-215213-4`, `0-13-605322-X`, `0-13-512356-2`, `0-13-611726-0` and `0-13-605306-8`, respectively

3. A `Button` with its (`ID`) property set to `submitButton` and its `Text` property set to `Submit`. In this example, we'll handle this `Button`'s `Click` event. You can create its event handler by double clicking the `Button` in **Design** view.

4. A `Label` with its (`ID`) property set to `responseLabel` and its `Text` property set to `"Welcome to Sessions!"`. This `Label` should be placed immediately to the right of the `Button` so that the `Label` appears at the top of the page when we hide the preceding controls on the page. Reuse the CSS style you created in *Step 1* by setting this `Label`'s `CssClass` property to `labelStyle`.

5. Two more `Label`s with their (`ID`) properties set to `idLabel` and `timeoutLabel`, respectively. Clear the text in each `Label`'s `Text` property—you'll set these programmatically with information about the current user's session.

6. A `HyperLink` with its (`ID`) property set to `languageLink` and its `Text` property set to `"Click here to choose another language"`. Set its `NavigateUrl` property by clicking the ellipsis next to the property in the **Properties** window and selecting `Options.aspx` from the **Select URL** dialog.

7. A `HyperLink` with its (`ID`) property set to `recommendationsLink` and its `Text` property set to `"Click here to get book recommendations"`. Set its `NavigateUrl` property by clicking the ellipsis next to the property in the **Properties** window and selecting `Recommendations.aspx` from the **Select URL** dialog.

8. Initially, the controls in *Steps 4–7* will not be displayed, so set each control's `Visible` property to `False`.

Session Property of a **Page**
Every Web Form includes a user-specific `HttpSessionState` object, which is accessible through property **Session** of class `Page`. Throughout this section, we use this property to manipulate the current user's `HttpSessionState` object. When a page is first requested, a unique `HttpSessionState` object is created by ASP.NET and assigned to the `Page`'s `Session` property.

Code-Behind File for `Options.aspx`
Fig. 23.28 presents the code-behind file for the `Options.aspx` page. When this page is requested, the `Page_Load` event handler (lines 9–40) executes before the response is sent to the client. Since the first request to a page is not a postback, the code in lines 12–39 *does not* execute the first time the page loads.

Postback Processing

When the user presses **Submit**, a postback occurs. The form is submitted to the server and the `Page_Load` event handler executes. Lines 15–19 display the controls shown in Fig. 23.27(b) and lines 22–24 hide the controls shown in Fig. 23.27(a). Next, lines 27–32 ensure that the user selected a language and, if so, display a message in the `responseLabel` indicating the selection. Otherwise, the message `"You did not select a language"` is displayed.

```vb
 1  ' Fig. 23.28: Options.aspx.vb
 2  ' Process user's selection of a programming language by displaying
 3  ' links and writing information in an HttpSessionState object.
 4  Partial Class Options
 5     Inherits System.Web.UI.Page
 6
 7     ' if postback, hide form and display links to make additional
 8     ' selections or view recommendations
 9     Protected Sub Page_Load(ByVal sender As Object,
10        ByVal e As System.EventArgs) Handles Me.Load
11
12        If IsPostBack Then
13           ' user has submitted information, so display message
14           ' and appropriate hyperlinks
15           responseLabel.Visible = True
16           idLabel.Visible = True
17           timeoutLabel.Visible = True
18           languageLink.Visible = True
19           recommendationsLink.Visible = True
20
21           ' hide other controls used to make language selection
22           promptLabel.Visible = False
23           languageList.Visible = False
24           submitButton.Visible = False
25
26           ' if the user made a selection, display it in responseLabel
27           If languageList.SelectedItem IsNot Nothing Then
28              responseLabel.Text &= " You selected " &
29                 languageList.SelectedItem.Text
30           Else
31              responseLabel.Text &= "You did not select a language."
32           End If
33
34           ' display session ID
35           idLabel.Text = "Your unique session ID is: " & Session.SessionID
36
37           ' display the timeout
38           timeoutLabel.Text = "Timeout: " & Session.Timeout & " minutes."
39        End If
40     End Sub ' Page_Load
41
```

Fig. 23.28 | Process user's selection of a programming language by displaying links and writing information in an `HttpSessionState` object. (Part 1 of 2.)

```
42        ' record the user's selection in the Session
43        Protected Sub submitButton_Click(ByVal sender As Object,
44           ByVal e As System.EventArgs) Handles submitButton.Click
45
46           ' if the user made a selection
47           If languageList.SelectedItem IsNot Nothing Then
48              ' add name/value pair to Session
49              Session.Add(languageList.SelectedItem.Text,
50                 languageList.SelectedItem.Value)
51           End If
52        End Sub ' submitButton_Click
53     End Class ' Options
```

Fig. 23.28 | Process user's selection of a programming language by displaying links and writing information in an `HttpSessionState` object. (Part 2 of 2.)

The ASP.NET application contains information about the `HttpSessionState` object (Session) for the current client. Property **SessionID** (displayed in line 35) contains the **unique session ID**—a sequence of random letters and numbers. The first time a client connects to the web server, a unique session ID is created for that client and a temporary cookie is written to the client so the server can identify the client on subsequent requests. When the client makes additional requests, the client's session ID from that temporary cookie is compared with the session IDs stored in the web server's memory to retrieve the client's `HttpSessionState` object. `HttpSessionState` property **Timeout** (displayed in line 38) specifies the maximum amount of time that an `HttpSessionState` object can be inactive before it's discarded. By default, if the user does not interact with this web application for 20 minutes, the `HttpSessionState` object is discarded by the server and a new one will be created if the user interacts with the application again. Figure 23.29 lists some common `HttpSessionState` properties.

Properties	Description
Count	Specifies the number of key/value pairs in the Session object.
IsNewSession	Indicates whether this is a new session (that is, whether the session was created during loading of this page).
Keys	Returns a collection containing the Session object's keys.
SessionID	Returns the session's unique ID.
Timeout	Specifies the maximum number of minutes during which a session can be inactive (that is, no requests are made) before the session expires. By default, this property is set to 20 minutes.

Fig. 23.29 | `HttpSessionState` properties.

Method submitButton_Click

In this example, we wish to store the user's selection in an `HttpSessionState` object when the user clicks the **Submit** Button. The `submitButton_Click` event handler (lines 43–52) adds a key/value pair to the `HttpSessionState` object for the current user, specifying the language chosen and the ISBN number for a book on that language. The HttpSession-State object is a dictionary—a data structure that stores **key/value pairs**. A program uses the key to store and retrieve the associated value in the dictionary.

The key/value pairs in an HttpSessionState object are often referred to as **session items**. They're placed in an HttpSessionState object by calling its **Add** method. If the user made a selection (line 47), lines 49–50 get the selection and its corresponding value from the languageList by accessing its SelectedItem's Text and Value properties, respectively, then call HttpSessionState method Add to add this name/value pair as a session item in the HttpSessionState object (Session).

If the application adds a session item that has the same name as an item previously stored in the HttpSessionState object, the session item is replaced—the names in session items *must* be unique. Another common syntax for placing a session item in the HttpSessionState object is Session(*Name*) = *Value*. For example, we could have replaced lines 49–50 with

```
Session(languageList.SelectedItem.Text) =
    languageList.SelectedItem.Value
```

Software Engineering Observation 23.1
A Web Form should not use instance variables to maintain client state information, because each new request or postback is handled by a new instance of the page. Instead, maintain client state information in HttpSessionState objects, because such objects are specific to each client.

Software Engineering Observation 23.2
A benefit of using HttpSessionState objects (rather than cookies) is that HttpSessionState objects can store any type of object (not just Strings) as attribute values. This provides you with increased flexibility in determining the type of state information to maintain for clients.

23.7.4 Recommendations.aspx: Displaying Recommendations Based on Session Values

After the postback of Options.aspx, the user may request book recommendations. The book-recommendations hyperlink forwards the user to the page Recommendations.aspx (Fig. 23.27(e)) to display the recommendations based on the user's language selections. The page contains the following controls arranged vertically:

1. A Label with its (ID) property set to recommendationsLabel and its Text property set to "Recommendations:". We created a CSS style for this label named .labelStyle, and set the font-size attribute to x-large and the font-weight attribute to bold. (See *Step 5* in Section 23.4.1 for information on creating a CSS style.)

2. A ListBox with its (ID) property set to booksListBox. We created a CSS style for this label named .listBoxStyle. In the **Position** category, we set the width attribute to 450px and the height attribute to 125px. The px indicates that the measurement is in pixels.

3. A HyperLink with its (ID) property set to languageLink and its Text property set to "Click here to choose another language". Set its NavigateUrl property by clicking the ellipsis next to the property in the **Properties** window and selecting Options.aspx from the **Select URL** dialog. When the user clicks this link, the Options.aspx page will be reloaded. Requesting the page in this manner *is not* considered a postback, so the original form in Fig. 23.27(a) will be displayed.

Code-Behind File for *Recommendations.aspx*

Figure 23.30 presents the code-behind file for Recommendations.aspx. Event handler Page_Init (lines 7–27) retrieves the session information. If a user has not selected a language in the Options.aspx page, the HttpSessionState object's **Count** property will be 0 (line 11). This property provides the number of session items contained in a HttpSessionState object. If the Count is 0, then we display the text **No Recommendations** (line 20), clear the ListBox and hide it (lines 21–22), and update the Text of the HyperLink back to Options.aspx (line 25).

```
1    ' Fig. 23.30: Recommendations.aspx.vb
2    ' Creates book recommendations based on a Session object.
3    Partial Class Recommendations
4       Inherits System.Web.UI.Page
5
6       ' read Session items and populate ListBox with any book recommendations
7       Protected Sub Page_Init(ByVal sender As Object,
8          ByVal e As System.EventArgs) Handles Me.Init
9
10         ' determine whether Session contains any information
11         If Session.Count <> 0 Then
12            For Each keyName In Session.Keys
13               ' use keyName to display one of Session's name/value pairs
14               booksListBox.Items.Add(keyName &
15                  " How to Program. ISBN#: " & Session(keyName))
16            Next
17         Else
18            ' if there are no session items, no language was chosen, so
19            ' display appropriate message and clear and hide booksListBox
20            recommendationsLabel.Text = "No Recommendations"
21            booksListBox.Items.Clear()
22            booksListBox.Visible = False
23
24            ' modify languageLink because no language was selected
25            languageLink.Text = "Click here to choose a language"
26         End If
27      End Sub ' Page_Init
28   End Class ' Recommendations
```

Fig. 23.30 | Session data used to provide book recommendations to the user.

If the user chose at least one language, the loop in lines 12–16 iterates through the HttpSessionState object's keys (line 12) by accessing the HttpSessionState's **Keys** property, which returns a collection containing all the keys in the session. Lines 14–15 concatenate the keyName, the String " How to Program. ISBN#: " and the key's corresponding value, which is returned by Session(keyName). This String is the recommendation that is added to the ListBox.

23.8 Case Study: Database-Driven ASP.NET Guestbook

Many websites allow users to provide feedback about the website in a guestbook. Typically, users click a link on the website's home page to request the guestbook page. This page usually consists of a form that contains fields for the user's name, e-mail address, message/feedback and so on. Data submitted on the guestbook form is then stored in a database located on the server.

In this section, we create a guestbook Web Form application. The GUI (Fig. 23.31) contains a **GridView** data control, which displays all the entries in the guestbook in tabular format. This control is located in the **Toolbox**'s **Data** section. We explain how to create and configure this data control shortly. The GridView displays **abc** in **Design** mode to indicate data that will be retrieved from a data source at runtime. You'll learn how to create and configure the GridView shortly.

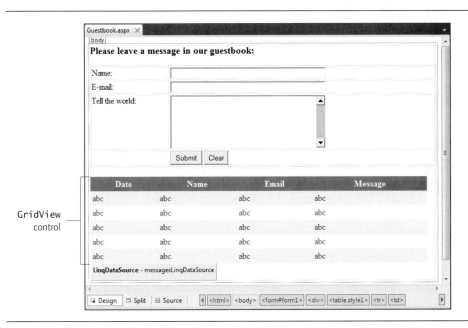

Fig. 23.31 | Guestbook application GUI in **Design** mode.

The Guestbook Database
The application stores the guestbook information in a SQL Server database called Guestbook.mdf located on the web server. (We provide this database in the databases folder with this chapter's examples.) The database contains a single table named Messages.

Testing the Application
To test this application:

1. Select **Open Web Site...** from the **File** menu.

2. In the **Open Web Site** dialog, ensure that **File System** is selected, then navigate to this chapter's examples, select the `Guestbook` folder and click the **Open** Button.

3. Select `Guestbook.aspx` in the **Solution Explorer**, then type *Ctrl + F5* to execute the web application in your default web browser.

Figure 23.32(a) shows the user submitting a new entry. Figure 23.32(b) shows the new entry as the last row in the `GridView`.

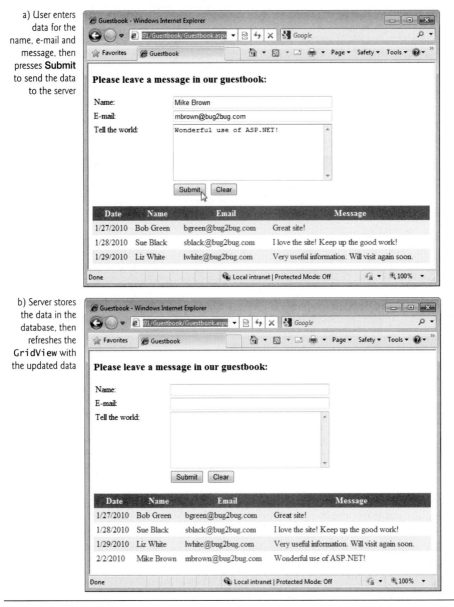

a) User enters data for the name, e-mail and message, then presses **Submit** to send the data to the server

b) Server stores the data in the database, then refreshes the `GridView` with the updated data

Fig. 23.32 | Sample execution of the **Guestbook** application.

23.8.1 Building a Web Form that Displays Data from a Database

We now explain how to build this GUI and set up the data binding between the GridView control and the database. We discuss the code-behind file in Section 23.8.2. To build the guestbook application, perform the following steps:

Step 1: Creating the Web Site
To begin, follow the steps in Section 23.4.1 to create an **Empty Web Site** named Guestbook then add a Web Form named Guestbook.aspx to the project. Set the document's Title property to "Guestbook". To ensure that Guestobook.aspx loads when you execute this application, right click it in the **Solution Explorer** and select **Set As Start Page**.

Step 2: Creating the Form for User Input
In **Design** mode, add the text Please leave a message in our guestbook:, then use the **Block Format** ComboBox in the IDE's toolbar to change the text to **Heading 3** format. Insert a table with four rows and two columns, configured so that the text in each cell aligns with the top of the cell. Place the appropriate text (see Fig. 23.31) in the top three cells in the table's left column. Then place TextBoxes named nameTextBox, emailTextBox and messageTextBox in the top three table cells in the right column. Configure the TextBoxes as follows:

- Set the nameTextBox's width to 300px.

- Set the emailTextBox's width to 300px.

- Set the messageTextBox's width to 300px and height to 100px. Also set this control's TextMode property to MultiLine so the user can type a message containing multiple lines of text.

Finally, add Buttons named submitButton and clearButton to the bottom-right table cell. Set the buttons' Text properties to Submit and Clear, respectively. We discuss the buttons' event handlers when we present the code-behind file. You can create these event handlers now by double clicking each Button in **Design** view.

Step 3: Adding a GridView Control to the Web Form
Add a GridView named messagesGridView that will display the guestbook entries. This control appears in the **Data** section of the **Toolbox**. The colors for the GridView are specified through the **Auto Format...** link in the **GridView Tasks** smart-tag menu that opens when you place the GridView on the page. Clicking this link displays an **AutoFormat** dialog with several choices. In this example, we chose **Professional**. We show how to set the GridView's data source (that is, where it gets the data to display in its rows and columns) shortly.

Step 4: Adding a Database to an ASP.NET Web Application
To use a SQL Server Express database file in an ASP.NET web application, you must first add the file to the project's App_Data folder. For security reasons, this folder can be accessed only by the web application on the server—clients cannot access this folder over a network. The web application interacts with the database on behalf of the client.

The **Empty Web Site** template does not create the App_Data folder. To create it, right click the project's name in the **Solution Explorer**, then select **Add ASP.NET Folder >**

App_Data. Next, add the `Guestbook.mdf` file to the `App_Data` folder. You can do this in one of two ways:

- Drag the file from Windows Explorer and drop it on the `App_Data` folder.

- Right click the `App_Data` folder in the **Solution Explorer** and select **Add Existing Item...** to display the **Add Existing Item** dialog, then navigate to the databases folder with this chapter's examples, select the `Guestbook.mdf` file and click **Add**. [*Note:* Ensure that **Data Files** is selected in the ComboBox above or next to the **Add Button** in the dialog; otherwise, the database file will not be displayed in the list of files.]

Step 5: Creating the LINQ to SQL Classes

You'll use LINQ to interact with the database. To create the LINQ to SQL classes for the `Guestbook` database:

1. Right click the project in the **Solution Explorer** and select **Add New Item...** to display the **Add New Item** dialog.

2. In the dialog, select **LINQ to SQL Classes**, enter `Guestbook.dbml` as the **Name**, and click **Add**. A dialog appears asking if you would like to put your new LINQ to SQL classes in the `App_Code` folder; click **Yes**. The IDE will create an `App_Code` folder and place the LINQ to SQL classes information in that folder.

3. In the **Database Explorer** window, drag the `Guestbook` database's `Messages` table from the **Database Explorer** onto the **Object Relational Designer**. Finally, save your project by selecting **File > Save All**.

Step 6: Binding the GridView to the Messages Table of the Guestbook Database

You can now configure the `GridView` to display the database's data.

1. Open the **GridView Tasks** smart-tag menu, then select **<New data source...>** from the **Choose Data Source** ComboBox to display the **Data Source Configuration Wizard** dialog.

2. In this example, we use a **LinqDataSource** control that allows the application to interact with the `Guestbook.mdf` database through LINQ. Select LINQ, then set the **ID** of the data source to `messagesLinqDataSource` and click **OK** to begin the **Configure Data Source** wizard.

3. In the **Choose a Context Object** screen, ensure that `GuestbookDataContext` is selected in the ComboBox, then click **Next >**.

4. The **Configure Data Selection** screen (Fig. 23.33) allows you to specify which data the `LinqDataSource` should retrieve from the data context. Your choices on this page design a `Select` LINQ query. The **Table** drop-down list identifies a table in the data context. The `Guestbook` data context contains one table named `Messages`, which is selected by default. *If you haven't saved your project* since creating your LINQ to SQL classes (*Step 5*), the list of tables *will not appear*. In the **Select** pane, ensure that the checkbox marked with an asterisk (*) is selected to indicate that you want to retrieve all the columns in the `Messages` table.

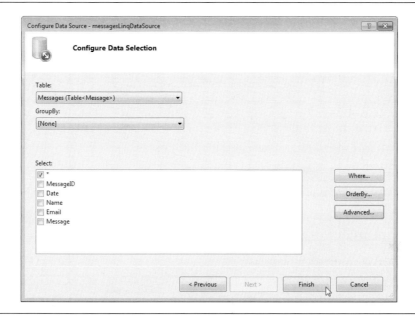

Fig. 23.33 | Configuring the query used by the LinqDataSource to retrieve data.

5. Click the **Advanced...** button, then select the **Enable the LinqDataSource to perform automatic inserts** CheckBox and click **OK**. This configures the LinqData-Source control to automatically insert new data into the database when new data is inserted in the data context. We discuss inserting new guestbook entries based on users' form submissions shortly.

6. Click **Finish** to complete the wizard.

A control named messagesLinqDataSource now appears on the Web Form directly below the GridView (Fig. 23.34). This control is represented in **Design** mode as a gray box containing its type and name. It will *not* appear on the web page—the gray box simply provides a way to manipulate the control visually through **Design** mode—similar to how the objects in the component tray are used in **Design** mode for a Windows Forms application.

The GridView now has column headers that correspond to the columns in the Messages table. The rows each contain either a number (which signifies an autoincremented column) or **abc** (which indicates string data). The actual data from the Guestbook.mdf database file will appear in these rows when you view the ASPX file in a web browser.

Step 7: Modifying the Columns of the Data Source Displayed in the GridView
It's not necessary for site visitors to see the MessageID column when viewing past guestbook entries—this column is merely a unique primary key required by the Messages table within the database. So, let's modify the GridView to prevent this column from displaying on the Web Form.

1. In the **GridView Tasks** smart tag menu, click **Edit Columns** to display the **Fields** dialog (Fig. 23.35).

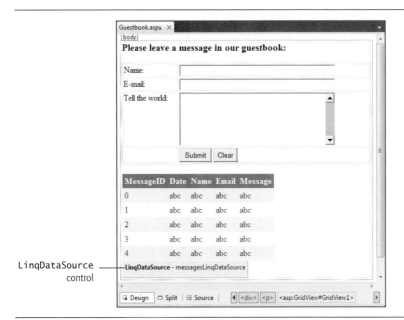

Fig. 23.34 | **Design** mode displaying `LinqDataSource` control for a `GridView`.

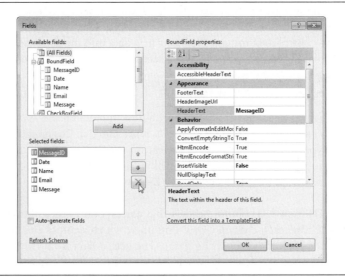

Fig. 23.35 | Removing the `MessageID` column from the `GridView`.

2. Select **MessageID** in the **Selected fields** pane, then click the ☒ Button. This removes the `MessageID` column from the `GridView`.

3. Click **OK** to return to the main IDE window, then set the `Width` property of the `GridView` to 650px.

The `GridView` should now appear as shown in Fig. 23.31.

23.8.2 Modifying the Code-Behind File for the Guestbook Application

After building the Web Form and configuring the data controls used in this example, double click the **Submit** and **Clear** buttons in **Design** view to create their corresponding `Click` event handlers in the code-behind file (Fig. 23.36). The IDE generates empty event handlers, so we must add the appropriate code to make these buttons work properly. The event handler for `clearButton` (lines 36–41) clears each `TextBox` by setting its `Text` property to an empty string. This resets the form for a new guestbook submission.

```vb
 1   ' Fig. 23.36: Guestbook.aspx.vb
 2   ' Code-behind file that defines event handlers for the guestbook.
 3   Partial Class Guestbook
 4      Inherits System.Web.UI.Page
 5
 6      ' Submit Button adds a new guestbook entry to the database,
 7      ' clears the form and displays the updated list of guestbook entries
 8      Protected Sub submitButton_Click(ByVal sender As Object, _
 9         ByVal e As System.EventArgs) Handles submitButton.Click
10
11         ' create dictionary of parameters for inserting
12         Dim insertParameters As New ListDictionary()
13
14         ' add current date and the user's name, e-mail address and message
15         ' to dictionary of insert parameters
16         insertParameters.Add("Date", Date.Now.ToShortDateString())
17         insertParameters.Add("Name", nameTextBox.Text)
18         insertParameters.Add("Email", emailTextBox.Text)
19         insertParameters.Add("Message", messageTextBox.Text)
20
21         ' execute an INSERT LINQ statement to add a new entry to the
22         ' Messages table in the Guestbook data context that contains the
23         ' current date and the user's name, e-mail address and message
24         messagesLinqDataSource.Insert(insertParameters)
25
26         ' clear the TextBoxes
27         nameTextBox.Text = String.Empty
28         emailTextBox.Text = String.Empty
29         messageTextBox.Text = String.Empty
30
31         ' update the GridView with the new database table contents
32         messagesGridView.DataBind()
33      End Sub ' submitButton_Click
34
35      ' Clear Button clears the Web Form's TextBoxes
36      Protected Sub clearButton_Click(ByVal sender As Object, _
37         ByVal e As System.EventArgs) Handles clearButton.Click
38         nameTextBox.Text = String.Empty
39         emailTextBox.Text = String.Empty
40         messageTextBox.Text = String.Empty
41      End Sub ' clearButton_Click
42   End Class ' Guestbook
```

Fig. 23.36 | Code-behind file for the guestbook application.

Lines 8–33 contain submitButton's event-handling code, which adds the user's information to the Guestbook database's Messages table. To use the values of the TextBoxes on the Web Form as the parameter values inserted into the database, we must create a **List-Dictionary** of insert parameters that are key/value pairs.

Line 12 creates a ListDictionary object. Lines 16–19 used the ListDictionary's Add method to store key/value pairs that represent each of the four insert parameters—the current date and the user's name, e-mail address, and message. Invoking the LinqData-Source method Insert (line 24) inserts the data in the data context, adding a row to the Messages table and automatically updating the database. We pass the ListDictionary object as an argument to the Insert method to specify the insert parameters. After the data is inserted into the database, lines 27–29 clear the TextBoxes, and line 32 invokes messagesGridView's **DataBind method** to refresh the data that the GridView displays. This causes messagesLinqDataSource (the GridView's source) to execute its Select command to obtain the Messages table's newly updated data.

23.9 Online Case Study: ASP.NET AJAX

In Chapter 24 (online), you learn the difference between a traditional web application and an **Ajax (Asynchronous JavaScript and XML) web application**. You also learn how to use **ASP.NET AJAX** to quickly and easily improve the user experience for your web applications, giving them responsiveness comparable to that of desktop applications. To demonstrate ASP.NET AJAX capabilities, you enhance the validation example by displaying the submitted form information without reloading the entire page. The only modifications to this web application appear in Validation.aspx file. You use Ajax-enabled controls to add this feature.

23.10 Online Case Study: Password-Protected Books Database Application

In Chapter 24 (online), we include a web application case study in which a user logs into a password-protected website to view a list of publications by a selected author. The application consists of several pages and provides website registration and login capabilities. You'll learn about ASP.NET master pages, which allow you to specify a common look-and-feel for all the pages in your app. We also introduce the **Web Site Administration Tool** and use it to configure the portions of the application that can be accessed only by users who are logged into the website.

Summary

Section 23.1 Introduction
- ASP.NET technology is Microsoft's technology for web-application development.
- Web Form files have the file-name extension .aspx and contain the web page's GUI. A Web Form file represents the web page that is sent to the client browser.
- The file that contains the programming logic of a Web Form is called the code-behind file.

Section 23.2 Web Basics

- URIs (Uniform Resource Identifiers) identify documents on the Internet. URIs that start with `http://` are called URLs (Uniform Resource Locators).

- A URL contains information that directs a browser to the resource that the user wishes to access. Computers that run web server software make such resources available.

- In a URL, the hostname is the name of the server on which the resource resides. This computer usually is referred to as the host, because it houses and maintains resources.

- A hostname is translated into a unique IP address that identifies the server. This translation is performed by a domain-name system (DNS) server.

- The remainder of a URL specifies the location and name of a requested resource. For security reasons, the location is normally a virtual directory. The server translates the virtual directory into a real location on the server.

- When given a URL, a web browser performs uses HTTP to retrieve and display the web page found at that address.

Section 23.3 Multitier Application Architecture

- Multitier applications divide functionality into separate tiers—logical groupings of functionality—that commonly reside on separate computers for security and scalability.

- The information tier (also called the bottom tier) maintains data pertaining to the application. This tier typically stores data in a relational database management system.

- The middle tier implements business logic, controller logic and presentation logic to control interactions between the application's clients and the application's data. The middle tier acts as an intermediary between data in the information tier and the application's clients.

- Business logic in the middle tier enforces business rules and ensures that data is reliable before the server application updates the database or presents the data to users.

- The client tier, or top tier, is the application's user interface, which gathers input and displays output. Users interact directly with the application through the user interface (typically viewed in a web browser), keyboard and mouse. In response to user actions, the client tier interacts with the middle tier to make requests and to retrieve data from the information tier. The client tier then displays to the user the data retrieved from the middle tier.

Section 23.4.1 Building the WebTime Application

- **File System** websites are created and tested on your local computer. Such websites execute in Visual Web Developer's built-in ASP.NET Development Server and can be accessed only by web browsers running on the same computer. You can later "publish" your website to a production web server for access via a local network or the Internet.

- **HTTP** websites are created and tested on an IIS web server and use HTTP to allow you to put your website's files on the server. If you own a website and have your own web server computer, you might use this to build a new website directly on that server computer.

- **FTP** websites use File Transfer Protocol (FTP) to allow you to put your website's files on the server. The server administrator must first create the website on the server for you. FTP is commonly used by so called "hosting providers" to allow website owners to share a server computer that runs many websites.

- A Web Form represents one page in a web application and contains a web application's GUI.

- You can view the Web Form's properties by selecting DOCUMENT in the **Properties** window. The `Title` property specifies the title that will be displayed in the web browser's title bar when the page is loaded.

- Controls and other elements are placed sequentially on a Web Form one after another in the order in which you drag-and-drop them onto the Web Form. The cursor indicates the insertion point in the page. This type of layout is known as relative positioning. You can also use absolute positioning in which controls are located exactly where you drop them on the Web Form.

- When a Label does not contain text, its name is displayed in square brackets in **Design** view as a placeholder for design and layout purposes. This text is not displayed at execution time.

- Formatting in a web page is performed with Cascading Style Sheets (CSS).

- A Web Form's Init event occurs when the page is first requested by a web browser. The event handler for this event—named Page_Init—initialize the page.

Section 23.4.2 Examining **WebTime.aspx**'s *Code-Behind File*
- A class declaration can span multiple source-code files—the separate portions of the class declaration in each file are known as partial classes. The Partial modifier indicates that the class in a particular file is part of a larger class.

- Every Web Form class inherits from class Page in namespace System.Web.UI. Class Page represents the default capabilities of each page in a web application.

- The ASP.NET controls are defined in namespace System.Web.UI.WebControls.

Section 23.5 Standard Web Controls: Designing a Form
- An Image control's ImageUrl property specifies the location of the image to display.

- By default, the contents of a table cell are aligned vertically in the middle of the cell. You can change this with the cell's valign property.

- A TextBox control allows you to obtain text from the user and display text to the user.

- A DropDownList control is similar to the Windows Forms ComboBox control, but doesn't allow users to type text. You can add items to the DropDownList using the **ListItem Collection Editor**, which you can access by clicking the ellipsis next to the DropDownList's Items property in the **Properties** window, or by using the **DropDownList Tasks** menu.

- A HyperLink control adds a hyperlink to a Web Form. The NavigateUrl property specifies the resource or web page that will be requested when the user clicks the HyperLink.

- A RadioButtonList control provides a series of radio buttons from which the user can select only one. The **RadioButtonList Tasks** smart-tag menu provides an **Edit Items...** link to open the **ListItem Collection Editor** so that you can create the items in the list.

- A Button control triggers an action when clicked.

Section 23.6 Validation Controls
- A validation control determines whether the data in another web control is in the proper format.

- When the page is sent to the client, the validator is converted into JavaScript that performs the validation in the client web browser.

- Some client browsers might not support scripting or the user might disable it. For this reason, you should always perform validation on the server.

- A RequiredFieldValidator control ensures that its ControlToValidate is not empty when the form is submitted. The validator's ErrorMessage property specifies what to display on the Web Form if the validation fails. When the validator's Display property is set to Dynamic, the validator occupies space on the Web Form only when validation fails.

- A RegularExpressionValidator uses a regular expression to ensure data entered by the user is in a valid format. Visual Web Developer provides several predefined regular expressions that you can simply select to validate e-mail addresses, phone numbers and more. A RegularExpressionValidator's ValidationExpression property specifies the regular expression to use for validation.

- A Web Form's Load event occurs each time the page loads into a web browser. The event handler for this event is Page_Load.

- ASP.NET pages are often designed so that the current page reloads when the user submits the form; this enables the program to receive input, process it as necessary and display the results in the same page when it's loaded the second time.

- Submitting a web form is known as a postback. Class Page's IsPostBack property returns True if the page is being loaded due to a postback.

- Server-side Web Form validation must be implemented programmatically. Class Page's Validate method validates the information in the request as specified by the Web Form's validation controls. Class Page's IsValid property returns True if validation succeeded.

Section 23.7 Session Tracking
- Personalization makes it possible for e-businesses to communicate effectively with their customers and also improves users' ability to locate desired products and services.

- To provide personalized services to consumers, e-businesses must be able to recognize clients when they request information from a site.

- HTTP is a stateless protocol—it does not provide information regarding particular clients.

- Tracking individual clients is known as session tracking.

Section 23.7.1 Cookies
- A cookie is a piece of data stored in a small text file on the user's computer. A cookie maintains information about the client during and between browser sessions.

- The expiration date of a cookie determines how long the cookie remains on the client's computer. If you do not set an expiration date for a cookie, the web browser maintains the cookie for the duration of the browsing session.

Section 23.7.2 Session Tracking with **HttpSessionState**
- Session tracking is implemented with class HttpSessionState.

Section 23.7.3 **Options.aspx:** *Selecting a Programming Language*
- Each radio button in a RadioButtonList has a Text property and a Value property. The Text property is displayed next to the radio button and the Value property represents a value that is sent to the server when the user selects that radio button and submits the form.

- Every Web Form includes a user-specific HttpSessionState object, which is accessible through property Session of class Page.

- HttpSessionState property SessionID contains a client's unique session ID. The first time a client connects to the web server, a unique session ID is created for that client and a temporary cookie is written to the client so the server can identify the client on subsequent requests. When the client makes additional requests, the client's session ID from that temporary cookie is compared with the session IDs stored in the web server's memory to retrieve the client's HttpSessionState object.

- HttpSessionState property Timeout specifies the maximum amount of time that an HttpSessionState object can be inactive before it's discarded. Twenty minutes is the default.

- The HttpSessionState object is a dictionary—a data structure that stores key/value pairs. A program uses the key to store and retrieve the associated value in the dictionary.

- The key/value pairs in an HttpSessionState object are often referred to as session items. They're placed in an HttpSessionState object by calling its Add method. Another common syntax for placing a session item in the HttpSessionState object is Session(*Name*) = *Value*.

- If an application adds a session item that has the same name as an item previously stored in the HttpSessionState object, the session item is replaced—session items names *must* be unique.

Section 23.7.4 Recommendations.aspx: *Displaying Recommendations Based on Session Values*

- The Count property returns the number of session items stored in an HttpSessionState object.

- HttpSessionState's Keys property returns a collection containing all the keys in the session.

Section 23.8 Case Study: Database-Driven ASP.NET Guestbook

- A GridView data control displays data in tabular format. This control is located in the **Toolbox**'s **Data** section.

Section 23.8.1 Building a Web Form that Displays Data from a Database

- To use a SQL Server Express database file in an ASP.NET web application, you must first add the file to the project's App_Data folder. For security reasons, this folder can be accessed only by the web application on the server—clients cannot access this folder over a network. The web application interacts with the database on behalf of the client.

- A LinqDataSource control allows a web application to interact with a database through LINQ.

Section 23.8.2 Modifying the Code-Behind File for the Guestbook Application

- To insert data into a database using a LinqDataSource, you must create a ListDictionary of insert parameters that are formatted as key/value pairs.

- A ListDictionary's Add method stores key/value pairs that represent each insert parameter.

- A GridView's DataBind method refreshes the data that the GridView displays.

Self-Review Exercises

23.1 State whether each of the following is *true* or *false*. If *false*, explain why.
   a) Web Form file names end in .aspx.
   b) App.config is a file that stores configuration settings for an ASP.NET web application.
   c) A maximum of one validation control can be placed on a Web Form.
   d) A LinqDataSource control allows a web application to interact with a database.

23.2 Fill in the blanks in each of the following statements:
   a) Web applications contain three basic tiers: _____, _____, and _____.
   b) The _____ web control is similar to the ComboBox Windows control.
   c) A control which ensures that the data in another control is in the correct format is called a(n) _____.
   d) A(n) _____ occurs when a page requests itself.
   e) Every ASP.NET page inherits from class _____.
   f) The _____ file contains the functionality for an ASP.NET page.

Answers to Self-Review Exercises

23.1 a) True. b) False. Web.config is the file that stores configuration settings for an ASP.NET web application. c) False. An unlimited number of validation controls can be placed on a Web Form. d) True.

23.2   a) bottom (information), middle (business logic), top (client). b) `DropDownList`. c) validator. d) postback. e) `Page`. f) code-behind.

Exercises

23.3   *(WebTime Modification)* Modify the `WebTime` example in Section 23.4 to contain drop-down lists that allow the user to modify such `Label` properties as `BackColor`, `ForeColor` and `Font-Size`. Configure these drop-down lists so that a postback occurs whenever the user makes a selection. When the page reloads, it should reflect the specified changes to the properties of the `Label` displaying the time.

23.4   *(Page Hit Counter)* Create an ASP.NET page that uses session tracking to keep track of how many times the client computer has visited the page. Set the `HttpSession` object's `Timeout` property to `DateTime.Now.AddDays(1)` to keep the session in effect for one day into the future. Display the number of page hits every time the page loads.

23.5   *(Guestbook Application Modification)* Add validation to the guestbook application in Section 23.8. Use validation controls to ensure that the user provides a name, a valid e-mail address and a message.

23.6   *(WebControls Modification)* Modify the example of Section 23.5 to add functionality to the `Register` `Button`. When the user clicks the `Button`, validate all of the input fields to ensure that the user has filled out the form completely, and entered a valid email address and phone number. If any of the fields are not valid, appropriate messages should be displayed by validation controls. If the fields are all valid, direct the user to another page that displays a message indicating that the registration was successful followed by the registration information that was submitted from the form.

23.7   *(Project: Web-Based Address Book)* Using the techniques you learned in Section 23.8, create a web-based Address book. Display the address book's contents in a `GridView`. Allow the user to search for entries with a particular last name.

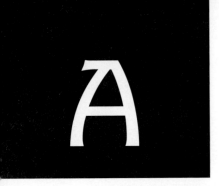

HTML Special Characters

The table of Fig. A.1 shows many commonly used XHTML special characters—called **character entity references** by the World Wide Web Consortium. For a complete list of character entity references, see the site www.w3.org/TR/REC-html40/sgml/entities.html.

Character	XHTML encoding	Character	XHTML encoding
non-breaking space		ê	&#234;
§	&#167;	ì	&#236;
©	&#169;	í	&#237;
®	&#174;	î	&#238;
¼	&#188;	ñ	&#241;
½	&#189;	ò	&#242;
¾	&#190;	ó	&#243;
à	&#224;	ô	&#244;
á	&#225;	õ	&#245;
â	&#226;	÷	&#247;
ã	&#227;	ù	&#249;
å	&#229;	ú	&#250;
ç	&#231;	û	&#251;
è	&#232;	•	&#8226;
é	&#233;	™	&#8482;

Fig. A.1 | XHTML special characters.

HTML Colors

Colors may be specified by using a standard name (such as aqua) or a hexadecimal RGB value (such as #00FFFF for aqua). Of the six hexadecimal digits in an RGB value, the first two represent the amount of red in the color, the middle two represent the amount of green in the color, and the last two represent the amount of blue in the color. For example, black is the absence of color and is defined by #000000, whereas white is the maximum amount of red, green and blue and is defined by #FFFFFF. Pure red is #FF0000, pure green (which the standard calls lime) is #00FF00 and pure blue is #00FFFF. Note that green in the standard is defined as #008000. Figure 4.2 contains the HTML standard color set. Figure B.1 contains the HTML extended color set.

Color name	Value	Color name	Value
aliceblue	#F0F8FF	cyan	#00FFFF
antiquewhite	#FAEBD7	darkblue	#00008B
aquamarine	#7FFFD4	darkcyan	#008B8B
azure	#F0FFFF	darkgoldenrod	#B8860B
beige	#F5F5DC	darkgray	#A9A9A9
bisque	#FFE4C4	darkgreen	#006400
blanchedalmond	#FFEBCD	darkkhaki	#BDB76B
blueviolet	#8A2BE2	darkmagenta	#8B008B
brown	#A52A2A	darkolivegreen	#556B2F
burlywood	#DEB887	darkorange	#FF8C00
cadetblue	#5F9EA0	darkorchid	#9932CC
chartreuse	#7FFF00	darkred	#8B0000
chocolate	#D2691E	darksalmon	#E9967A
coral	#FF7F50	darkseagreen	#8FBC8F
cornflowerblue	#6495ED	darkslateblue	#483D8B
cornsilk	#FFF8DC	darkslategray	#2F4F4F
crimson	#DC143C	darkturquoise	#00CED1

Fig. B.1 | HTML extended colors and hexadecimal RGB values. (Part 1 of 3.)

Color name	Value	Color name	Value
darkviolet	#9400D3	linen	#FAF0E6
deeppink	#FF1493	magenta	#FF00FF
deepskyblue	#00BFFF	mediumaquamarine	#66CDAA
dimgray	#696969	mediumblue	#0000CD
dodgerblue	#1E90FF	mediumorchid	#BA55D3
firebrick	#B22222	mediumpurple	#9370DB
floralwhite	#FFFAF0	mediumseagreen	#3CB371
forestgreen	#228B22	mediumslateblue	#7B68EE
gainsboro	#DCDCDC	mediumspringgreen	#00FA9A
ghostwhite	#F8F8FF	mediumturquoise	#48D1CC
gold	#FFD700	mediumvioletred	#C71585
goldenrod	#DAA520	midnightblue	#191970
greenyellow	#ADFF2F	mintcream	#F5FFFA
honeydew	#F0FFF0	mistyrose	#FFE4E1
hotpink	#FF69B4	moccasin	#FFE4B5
indianred	#CD5C5C	navajowhite	#FFDEAD
indigo	#4B0082	oldlace	#FDF5E6
ivory	#FFFFF0	olivedrab	#6B8E23
khaki	#F0E68C	orange	#FFA500
lavender	#E6E6FA	orangered	#FF4500
lavenderblush	#FFF0F5	orchid	#DA70D6
lawngreen	#7CFC00	palegoldenrod	#EEE8AA
lemonchiffon	#FFFACD	palegreen	#98FB98
lightblue	#ADD8E6	paleturquoise	#AFEEEE
lightcoral	#F08080	palevioletred	#DB7093
lightcyan	#E0FFFF	papayawhip	#FFEFD5
lightgoldenrodyellow	#FAFAD2	peachpuff	#FFDAB9
lightgreen	#90EE90	peru	#CD853F
lightgrey	#D3D3D3	pink	#FFC0CB
lightpink	#FFB6C1	plum	#DDA0DD
lightsalmon	#FFA07A	powderblue	#B0E0E6
lightseagreen	#20B2AA	rosybrown	#BC8F8F
lightskyblue	#87CEFA	royalblue	#4169E1
lightslategray	#778899	saddlebrown	#8B4513
lightsteelblue	#B0C4DE	salmon	#FA8072
lightyellow	#FFFFE0	sandybrown	#F4A460
limegreen	#32CD32	seagreen	#2E8B57

Fig. B.1 | HTML extended colors and hexadecimal RGB values. (Part 2 of 3.)

Color name	Value	Color name	Value
seashell	#FFF5EE	tan	#D2B48C
sienna	#A0522D	thistle	#D8BFD8
skyblue	#87CEEB	tomato	#FF6347
slateblue	#6A5ACD	turquoise	#40E0D0
slategray	#708090	violet	#EE82EE
snow	#FFFAFA	wheat	#F5DEB3
springgreen	#00FF7F	whitesmoke	#F5F5F5
steelblue	#4682B4	yellowgreen	#9ACD32

Fig. B.I | HTML extended colors and hexadecimal RGB values. (Part 3 of 3.)

JavaScript Operator Precedence Chart

This appendix contains the operator precedence chart for JavaScript/ECMAScript (Fig. C.1). The operators are shown in decreasing order of precedence from top to bottom.

Operator	Type	Associativity
.	member access	left to right
[]	array indexing	
()	function calls	
++	increment	right to left
--	decrement	
-	unary minus	
~	bitwise complement	
!	logical NOT	
delete	deletes an array element or object property	
new	creates a new object	
typeof	returns the data type of its argument	
void	prevents an expression from returning a value	
*	multiplication	left to right
/	division	
%	modulus	
+	addition	left to right
-	subtraction	
+	string concatenation	
<<	left shift	left to right
>>	right shift with sign extension	
>>>	right shift with zero extension	
<	less than	left to right
<=	less than or equal	
>	greater than	
>=	greater than or equal	
instanceof	type comparison	

Fig. C.1 | JavaScript/ECMAScript operator precedence and associativity. (Part 1 of 2.)

Operator	Type	Associativity
==	equals	left to right
!=	does not equal	
===	strict equals (no type conversions allowed)	
!==	strict does not equal (no type conversions allowed)	
&	bitwise AND	left to right
^	bitwise XOR	left to right
|	bitwise OR	left to right
&&	logical AND	left to right
||	logical OR	left to right
?:	conditional	right to left
=	assignment	right to left
+=	addition assignment	
-=	subtraction assignment	
*=	multiplication assignment	
/=	division assignment	
%=	modulus assignment	
&=	bitwise AND assignment	
^=	bitwise exclusive OR assignment	
|=	bitwise inclusive OR assignment	
<<=	bitwise left shift assignment	
>>=	bitwise right shift with sign extension assignment	
>>>=	bitwise right shift with zero extension assignment	

Fig. C.1 | JavaScript/ECMAScript operator precedence and associativity. (Part 2 of 2.)

ASCII Character Set

In Fig. D.1, the digits at the left of the table are the left digits of the decimal equivalent (0–127) of the character code, and the digits at the top of the table are the right digits of the character code—e.g., the character code for "F" is 70, and the character code for "&" is 38.

Most users of this book are interested in the ASCII character set used to represent English characters on many computers. The ASCII character set is a subset of the Unicode character set used by scripting languages to represent characters from most of the world's languages. For more information on the Unicode character set, see Appendix F.

ASCII character set

	0	1	2	3	4	5	6	7	8	9
0	nul	soh	stx	etx	eot	enq	ack	bel	bs	ht
1	nl	vt	ff	cr	so	si	dle	dc1	dc2	dc3
2	dc4	nak	syn	etb	can	em	sub	esc	fs	gs
3	rs	us	sp	!	"	#	$	%	&	'
4	(	)	*	+	,	-	.	/	0	1
5	2	3	4	5	6	7	8	9	:	;
6	<	=	>	?	@	A	B	C	D	E
7	F	G	H	I	J	K	L	M	N	O
8	P	Q	R	S	T	U	V	W	X	Y
9	Z	[	\	]	^	_	'	a	b	c
10	d	e	f	g	h	i	j	k	l	m
11	n	o	p	q	r	s	t	u	v	w
12	x	y	z	{			}	~	del		

Fig. D.1 | ASCII character set.

Index